THE SACRED BOOKS OF THE EAST

F. MAX MULLER (ED.)

LIST OF THE 50 VOLUMES

1. Upanishads.
2. Sacred Laws of Aryas.
3. Texts of Confucianism.
4. Zend-Avesta.
5. Pahlavi Texts.
6. Qur'an.
7. Institutes of Vishnu.
8. Bhagavadgita, & c.
9. Qur'an.
10. (i) Dhammapada.
10. (ii) Sutta-Nipata.
11. Buddhist Suttas.
12. Satapatha-Brahmana.
13. Vinaya Texts.
14. Sacred Laws of Aryas.
15. Upanishads.
16. Texts of Confucianism.
17. Vinaya Texts.
18. Pahlavi Texts.
19. Fo-sho-hing-tsanking.
20. Vinaya Texts.
21. Saddharma Pundarika.
22. Gaina-Sutras.
23. Zend-Avesta.
24. Pahlavi Texts.
25. Laws of Manu.
26. Satapatha-Brahmana.
27. Texts of Confucianism (Li Ki).
28. Texts of Confucianism (Li Ki).
29. Grihya-Sutras.
30 Grihya-Sutras.
31. Zend-Avesta.
32. Vedic Hymns.
33. Minor Law-Books.
34. Vedanta-Sutras.
35. Milinda.
36. Milinda.
37. Pahlavi Texts.
38. Vedanta-Sutras.
39. Texts of Taoism
40. Texts of Taoism
41. Satapatha-Brahmana
42. Atharva-veda.
43. Satapatha-Brahmana.
44. Satapatha-Brahmana.
45. Gaina-Sutras.
46. Vedic Hymns.
47. Pahlavi Texts.
48. Vedanta-Sutras.
49. (i) Buddhakarita.
49. (ii) Mahayana Texts.
50. A General Index

The Sacred Books of the East, Vol. 50

A GENERAL INDEX
TO THE
NAMES AND SUBJECT-MATTER
OF THE
SACRED BOOKS OF THE EAST

Edited by

F. MAX MULLER

Compiled by

M. WINTERNITZ
PROFESSOR OF INDIAN PHILOLOGY AND OF
ETHNOLOGY IN THE GERMAN UNIVERSITY OF PRAGUE

with a Preface by

A. A. MACDONELL
BODEN PROFESSOR OF SANSKRIT IN THE
UNIVERSITY OF OXFORD

GYAN

Published by

GYAN

Gyan Publishing House
5, Ansari Road
Daryaganj, New Delhi-110002
Phone: 011-47034999, 9811692060
E-mail: books@gyanbooks.com

Distribution Network
gyanbooks.com
India, USA, Canada, UK, Australia, France

ISBN : 978-81-212-2937-1 (Set)
ISBN : 978-81-212-2659-2 (PB)
First Published, 1910

2nd Impression 2021

Printed at: Gyan Press, Delhi.

The Sacred Books of the East, Vol. 50

A General Index
Edited by: F. Max Muller, Compiled by: M. Winternitz

THE

SACRED BOOKS OF THE EAST

TRANSLATED

BY VARIOUS ORIENTAL SCHOLARS

AND EDITED BY

F. MAX MÜLLER

VOL. L

OXFORD

AT THE CLARENDON PRESS

1910

A GENERAL INDEX

TO THE

NAMES AND SUBJECT-MATTER

OF THE

SACRED BOOKS OF THE EAST

COMPILED BY

M. WINTERNITZ

PROFESSOR OF INDIAN PHILOLOGY AND OF ETHNOLOGY IN THE GERMAN UNIVERSITY OF PRAGUE

WITH A PREFACE BY

A. A. MACDONELL

BODEN PROFESSOR OF SANSKRIT IN THE UNIVERSITY OF OXFORD

OXFORD

AT THE CLARENDON PRESS

1910

CONTENTS

PAGE

Preface vii

Introductory Note xi

List of Religions represented in the S. B. E. . . . xv

List of the Translators xv

Key to Abbreviations xvi

List of the Volumes of the S. B. E. xvi

THE INDEX 1-683

Addenda and Corrigenda; Note on the Editions of Vols. 2, 4, 10 684

PREFACE

BY PROFESSOR MACDONELL

THE period covered by the inception, the publication, and the completion of the *Sacred Books of the East* exactly coincides with the thirty-four years that I have spent in Oxford. When I matriculated, Professor Max Müller, the editor of the series, was about to begin work on the first volume, which appeared while I was still an undergraduate. I lost no time in making his acquaintance, for it was the influence of one of his works that had stimulated me to begin under Professor Benfey the study of Sanskrit at the University of Göttingen, when I left school nearly two years before. During my undergraduate days and later I owed much to Professor Max Müller's advice and encouragement in regard to my studies, which have ever since followed, as far as Sanskrit is concerned, much the same lines as his. I consequently always took a lively interest in the *Sacred Books* edited by him as they successively appeared during the course of a quarter of a century, no fewer than thirty-six volumes having a more or less direct bearing on my own work, and fourteen of the translators being personally known to me. Professor Max Müller lived to see all but one of the forty-nine volumes published under his supervision. Now the fiftieth and concluding volume is at last finished when I myself have already arrived at advanced middle age. Owing to my early relations with the editor and my interest in the series ever since, I am glad to have this opportunity of accompanying with a few words by way of preface the volume that brings the series to an end.

The *Sacred Books of the East* include all the most important works of the seven non-Christian religions that have exercised a profound influence on the civilization of the continent of Asia. Of the Indian religions the Vedic-Brāhmanic system here claims twenty-one volumes, Buddhism ten, and Jainism two. Eight volumes comprise translations of the sacred books of the Persians. Two volumes represent Islām, and six the two main indigenous systems of China, Confucianism and Tāoism. This great undertaking, planned and edited by Professor Max Müller, has been carried out by the collaboration of twenty scholars, all leading authorities in the special departments of Oriental learning to which the works translated by them belong. By thus rendering these religious systems accessible as a whole to the Western world in authoritative translations, Professor Max Müller for the first time placed the historical and comparative study of religions on a solid foundation. But with that large view of the aims and needs of scholarship which distinguished him, he saw that the investigation of the vast material here collected could not become thoroughly effective without the auxiliary aid of a separate index volume presenting that material thoroughly digested and exhaustively classified. This work he entrusted to Dr. Winternitz, who at that time was resident in Oxford and had been assisting him in bringing out his second edition of the *Rigveda* with the commentary of Sāyaṇa. The result, after various unavoidable delays, is the present volume, in which the end in view has been most successfully accomplished by the compiler, now Professor of Indian Philology and of Ethnology in the German University of Prague.

The experience of many years has made me a convinced believer in the great value of full and comprehensive indexes as aids to the scholar, not only because they save his time, but because they tend to render his results more comprehensive. This is especially true at the present time, when the field of research has become so greatly extended in all directions. The view which prevailed among Oriental scholars in my student days was very different. About thirty years ago an eminent Sanskrit scholar began the publication of the *editio princeps* of an important and intricate work, which when completed appeared without an index. The editor declined to yield to the suggestion that he should supply one, declaring that those who wished to consult the book on any point ought to be compelled to read it through. I feel convinced that as a consequence of this attitude, research has been retarded in the branch of learning to which the work in question belongs. Even in recent years I have hardly ever seen an index to Oriental works that has not seemed to me too meagre and consequently inadequate as an instrument of research. Very different is the character of the present substantial volume of 684 pages, which Professor Winternitz has compiled with so much thoroughness and industry. I feel no hesitation in stating that it is the most comprehensive work of the kind that has yet been published. For it is not merely a complete index like vol. xxv of the recently published *Imperial Gazetteer of India*. It also furnishes, in articles of any length, a scientific classification of the subject under various heads. Thus, in the article on Agni, the Indian god of fire, the material relating to that deity is arranged under no fewer than twenty-four subdivisions. Such fullness of treatment saves the book from the inevitable dryness from which it would otherwise suffer. Indeed, its perusal will, I believe, prove interesting not only to the expert, but even to the general reader. The volume, in fact, constitutes a handbook for the study of Oriental religions as far as represented by the *Sacred Books of the East*. By saving the student of these volumes an immense amount of time, it will greatly lighten his labours. The methodical arrangement and the co-ordination of the vast and varied material that they contain are also calculated to stimulate both the historical investigation of each, and the comparative study of all, of the religious systems dealt with in the series. Hence if I were asked to select any one of the fifty volumes of the *Sacred Books of the East* as specially useful, I should certainly choose the last. The Delegates are to be congratulated on rounding off with so valuable an addition a series that reflects so much lustre on the University Press, and has contributed not a little towards establishing its now unrivalled position as a centre of Oriental publication.

A. A. MACDONELL.

OXFORD,
February, 1910.

INTRODUCTORY NOTE
BY THE AUTHOR

Habent sua fata libelli—not only after they have been published, but sometimes even before they are printed. It was in the spring of 1894 that the late Professor Max Müller first suggested to me that I should compile a General Index of the names and subject-matter for the complete series of the *Sacred Books of the East.* Such an Index, he thought, would be a great help to all students of the *Sacred Books of the East,* and of the greatest value for the study of the history of religions. The matter was frequently discussed between us, and we both agreed that if the Index was to be of any use it would have to be, not a bare list of names and important words, with strings of references which no one would have the patience to read through, but an *analytical* Index with *extracts* and even *verbal quotations*, from which the student, with the least possible trouble, might see to which volume and page he had to refer for any information he might want. It was many weeks before the plan took any definite shape: in June, 1894, I laid my proposal of preparing the Index before the Delegates of the University Press, who were from the beginning favourably inclined to it. But as I had to work out a specimen from which the scale and the plan of the Index could be seen more definitely, it was not until March, 1895, that the Delegates could give their final sanction to the work.

Though some of the volumes of the series were still unpublished in 1895—vol. xliv appeared in 1900, and vol. xlviii not until 1904—it was then thought possible to finish the Index volume within two years. When I set to work, and began reading through volume after volume, making notes and extracts for the Index, I certainly hoped that Professor Max Müller would live to see it finished. But, alas, Fate had destined otherwise. Only too soon I found that I had entirely miscalculated the time and labour involved in the compilation of the Index. By the spring of 1898 I had indeed read, and made extracts from, all the volumes that had been published; I had written some 70,000 slips, and these had been sorted and arranged alphabetically. But in 1898 I left Oxford to return to my own country and to a new sphere of work, and the preparation of the Index had to be interrupted for nearly two years. When I took it up again in 1900 I soon found that the huge mass of slips before me represented only the raw material from which the building had to be constructed.

From the beginning it had been clear to me—and this was also Professor Max Müller's view—that this Index volume could not be made like any other Index, but must resemble a Manual of the History of Eastern Religions. For it would have been of little use to collect, under such headings as Ancestor Worship, Animals, Brahman, Buddha, Fire, Funeral Rites, Future Life, God, Gods, Prayer, Sacrifice, Soul, &c., all the passages bearing on these subjects as they occur in the volumes of the *Sacred Books of the East*. It was necessary to make *sub-divisions* in such articles, and to arrange the passages under different *sub-headings*. It was this work of arranging and condensing the raw material that caused so much delay. Many slips had to be rewritten, and the volumes of the *Sacred Books* had constantly to be referred to, and numerous passages to be verified.

These sub-divisions and sub-headings required most careful consideration. It was not possible to make them according to one uniform scheme; they had to be chosen in each case differently as seemed most suitable for practical purposes. Sometimes it was advisable to make them according to the different religions, sometimes according to the subject-matter. Consistency could not be aimed at—the chief aim was practical usefulness. Sometimes it seemed more practical to arrange the passages under several sub-headings, sometimes it seemed preferable to collect them under one heading, indicating subdivision by dashes (—). But it is hardly necessary to enumerate all the devices by which the compiler has tried to make the Index as handy as possible. The reader will easily find them out for himself. There was a time when German scholars scouted the idea of writing or using an Index to learned books. It was thought unworthy of a scholar to look to an Index for reference: he had to read the whole book and all the books on any given subject. But nowadays even German scholars have found out that life is short, and not only art, but in an even greater degree, science is getting very long. It has become impossible to get on without some time-saving machinery. To make this Index supply as far as possible a contrivance of such a kind has been the one and constant aim of the compiler.

Verbal quotations have been given—they are marked as such by the use of *italics*—from passages that seemed especially characteristic and important. That the Index should also include such verbal quotations, was one of the very first suggestions made by Professor Max Müller.

The compiler of an Index to forty-nine volumes of translations from seven different languages, belonging to as many religions, had to grapple with peculiar difficulties. He had not only to make himself acquainted with the terminologies of the different religions represented in the *Sacred Books of the East*, but also to take into account the different translations of the same terms by different translators, sometimes also different spellings of the same names in different volumes. I have tried, as far as was practicable, to collect all things belonging together under one heading, but I must apologize for any inconsistencies that will be found, especially under the letter A. There, e.g. 'Ahura-Mazda' and 'Aûha*r*ma*zd*' are given as two separate articles, while later on in such cases all the passages would have been collected under *one* heading. While apologizing for such and other inconsistencies (which could only have been avoided if the whole manuscript of the Index had been rewritten and its publication delayed still longer), I hope to have given so many *cross-references* that these inconsistencies will not be felt as any serious inconvenience.

When I venture to claim for this volume the title of a sort of Manual of the History of Eastern Religions, I hope I may not be misunderstood. Many books on the History and

Science of Religion have been written during the last twenty years. But most of these books are more concerned with theories on the origin and development of religion than with what, in my humble opinion, should be the foundation of all such theories—a *scientific classification of religious phenomena.* Is it too presumptuous to hope that this Index may prove to be of some help for the fulfilment of this *desideratum* of the Science of Religion? The Index may prove useful, not only for what it contains, but also for what it does *not* contain. The student of religion will look in vain in this Index for such terms as Animism, Fetishism, Tabu, Totemism, and the like. May not this be a useful warning that these terms refer only to the theories and not to the facts of religion? On the other hand, the student will be assured that everything he finds in this Index is a religious fact. Moreover, many things will be found in the Index that, from our point of view, do not refer to religion at all, but to all kinds of matters of importance for the Antiquarian—the student of ancient law, customs, manners, art, and economic life. For there is hardly any phase of human life that is not in some way or other touched upon in the *Sacred Books of the East*—for the simple reason that in ancient religion almost anything and everything has some religious aspect. This is in itself an important lesson to learn. Besides, it shows how useful the Index, and of course still more the *Sacred Books* themselves, must be for all students of the ancient civilizations of India, Persia, China, and Arabia. And if the Index should do nothing else but help to promote the study of the *Sacred Books of the East*, the time and labour devoted to its compilation will not be thrown away.

In conclusion, I have to express my sincere thanks to the Delegates of the University Press for the sacrifices incurred in the publication of this volume, and for the patience they have shown with the many delays that have retarded the completion of the work.

M. WINTERNITZ.

PRAGUE,
January, 1910.

LIST OF RELIGIONS

REPRESENTED IN THE SACRED BOOKS OF THE EAST

I. Vedic-Brâhmanic Religion.
- (*a*) Prayers and Hymns, vols. 32, 42, 46.
- (*b*) Magic, Rites, and Theology, vols. 12, 26, 29, 30, 41, 42, 43, 44.
- (*c*) Philosophy, vols. 1, 8, 15, 34, 38, 48.
- (*d*) Laws, vols. 2, 7, 14, 25, 33.

II. Buddhism, vols. 10, 11, 13, 17, 19, 20, 21, 35, 36, 49.

III. *G*aina Religion, vols. 22, 45.

IV. Confucianism, vols. 3, 16, 27, 28.

V. Tâoism, vols. 39, 40.

VI. Parsi Religion, vols. 4, 5, 18, 23, 24, 31, 37, 47.

VII. Islâm, vols. 6, 9.

LIST OF TRANSLATORS

OF THE SACRED BOOKS OF THE EAST

Beal, Samuel, vol. 19.
Bloomfield, Maurice, vol. 42.
Bühler, Georg, vols. 2, 14, 25.
Cowell, E. B., vol. 49 (i).
Darmesteter, James, vols. 4, 23.
Eggeling, Julius, vols. 12, 26, 41, 43, 44.
Fausböll, V., vol. 10 (ii).
Jacobi, Hermann, vols. 22, 45.
Jolly, Julius, vols. 7, 33.
Kern, H., vol. 21.
Legge, James, vols. 3, 16, 27, 28, 39, 40.
Max Müller, F., vols. 1, 10 (i), 15, 30, 32, 49 (ii).
Mills, L. H., vol. 31.
Oldenberg, Hermann, vols. 13, 17, 20, 29, 30, 46.
Palmer, E. H., vols. 6, 9.
Rhys Davids, T. W., vols. 11, 13, 17, 20, 35, 36.
Takakusu, J., vol. 49 (ii).
Telang, Kâshinâth Trimbak, vol. 8.
Thibaut, George, vols. 34, 38, 48.
West, E. W., vols. 5, 18, 24, 37, 47.

ABBREVIATIONS

Av. = Avesta.

&c. (after a reference) = 'and frequently *in the same volume.*' (For instance, on page 22, col. 1, line 17 the '&c.' means that Agni the Hot*ri* priest occurs frequently in volume 46.)[1]

n. = name.[2]	q. v. = quod vide.
n. d. = name of a deity.	Sk. = Sanskrit.
n. p. = name of a person.	t. c. = title of chapter or part of a work.
n. pl. = name of a place.	t. t. = technical term.
Phl. = Pahlavi.	t. w. = title of a work.
Pr. = Prâkrit.	Zd. = Zend.

References. The large arabic figures denote volumes, the smaller arabic pages, and the smaller roman pages of the Introductions.

[1] Where a very large number of references are given, some references have been italicized to point out the more important passages.

[2] But after a figure, referring to the number of page, = note, and after a Sanskrit term = neuter.

LIST OF THE 49 VOLUMES

OF THE SACRED BOOKS OF THE EAST

VOL.

1 Upanishads.
2 Sacred Laws of Âryas.
3 Texts of Confucianism.
4 Zend-Avesta.
5 Pahlavi Texts.
6 Qur'ân.
7 Institutes of Vish*n*u.
8 Bhagavadgîtâ, &c.
9 Qur'ân.
10 (i) Dhammapada.
10 (ii) Sutta-Nipâta.
11 Buddhist Suttas.
12 *S*atapatha-Brâhma*n*a.
13 Vinaya Texts.
14 Sacred Laws of Âryas.
15 Upanishads.
16 Texts of Confucianism.
17 Vinaya Texts.
18 Pahlavi Texts.
19 Fo-sho-hing-tsan-king.
20 Vinaya Texts.
21 Saddharma-pu*nd*arîka.
22 *G*aina-Sûtras.
23 Zend-Avesta.
24 Pahlavi Texts.
25 Laws of Manu.
26 *S*atapatha-Brâhma*n*a.
27, 28 Texts of Confucianism (Lî *K*î).
29, 30 G*ri*hya-Sûtras.
31 Zend-Avesta.
32 Vedic Hymns.
33 Minor Law-Books.
34 Vedânta-Sûtras.
35, 36 Milinda.
37 Pahlavi Texts.
38 Vedânta-Sûtras.
39, 40 Texts of Tâoism.
41 *S*atapatha-Brâhma*n*a.
42 Atharva-veda.
43, 44 *S*atapatha-Brâhma*n*a.
45 *G*aina-Sûtras.
46 Vedic Hymns.
47 Pahlavi Texts.
48 Vedânta-Sûtras.
49 (i) Buddha*k*arita.
49 (ii) Mahâyâna Texts.

INDEX

Aarâf, the chapter of al A. (Qur'ân) 6, 138–63; *see* Future Life.

Aaron, brother of Moses, a prophet 6, 94, 125; 9, 31; appointed vice-gerent by Moses, 6, 154–6; rebuked by Moses on account of the calf, 9, 41; given to Moses as a minister, 9, 36 sq., 86, 91, 111; and Moses blessed, 9, 172; Moses and A. before Pharaoh, 6, 201–3; 9, 68; they receive a Scripture, 9, 50.

Abâlis, the Zandîk, a heretic, had a disputation with Âtûr-frôbag, 24, xxvii; 47, 119 n.

Âbân, *see* Waters.

'Abbâs, converted to Islâm, 6, xli; negotiations between Abu Sufiyân, 'A., and Mohammed, 6, xli sq.

Abbhâna, Buddhist t.t., when unlawful, 17, 268 sq., 270 sq., 277–80.

Abd allah, father of Mohammed, 6, xviii.

Abdallah ibn Sa'hd ibn Abî Sar'h, amanuensis of Mohammed, pretended to be inspired, 6, lvii, 126, 126 n.

Abdallâh ibn Ubai, strong opponent of Mohammed, 6, lxiii; leader of the Munâfiqûn or 'Hypocrites,' 6, xxxv; 9, 284 n.; spread the calumny against Ayesha, 9, 74 n.; compelled his slave girls to prostitution, 9, 77 n.

Abdallah ibn Umm Maktûm, the poor blind man, at whom Mohammed frowned, 9, 320 n.

'Abd al Muttalib, Mohammed's grandfather, 6, xvii sq.

'Abd ed Dar, as chief of the Kaaba, 6, xvii sq.

'Abd el 'Hareth, n. given to their child by Adam and Eve, 6, 161 n.

Abd er Rahman ibn Auf, converted by Mohammed, 6, xxiii.

'Abd Menâf, chieftain of the Kaabah, 6, xvii sq.

Abduction, *see* Adultery.

Abhaya, a royal prince, who brings up *G*îvaka, the physician, 17, 173 sq., 179; the son of king A. converted by Buddha, 19, 241; a prince of the Li*kkh*avis, on Niga*nth*a doctrines, 45, xv; son of king *S*renika, patron of the *G*ainas, 45, xv n.

Abhayandada, or Giver of Safety, epithet of Avalokite*s*vara, 21, 412.

Abhibhâyatanâni, t.t., eight positions of mastery over delusion, 11, 49–51, 49 sq. n.

Abhidhamma, its position by the side of Vinaya and Sutta, 10 (i), xxxii–xxxiv; taught under the head of Dhamma, 10 (i), xxxiii. *See also* Tipi*t*aka.

Abhidharmakoshavyâkhyâ, quoted, 15, lii n.; quotes Milindapañha, 35, xxvi; 36, xvii.

Abhi*gñ*â*gñ*ânâbhibhû = Mahâbhi*gñ*â*gñ*ânâbhibhû, q.v.

Abhi*gñ*âprâpta, epithet of Sâgarabuddhidhârin, 21, 207.

Abhi*gñ*âs, t.t., magical powers of Arhats, 21, 1 sq. n.

Abhigraha and Graha worshipped by the Snâtaka, 30, 166.

Abhinandana, n. of a Tîrthakara, 22, 280.

Abhinishkrama*n*a-Sûtra, translated into Chinese, 19, xxix.

Abhipratârin *K*aitraratha, *see* *K*aitraratha.

Abhipratârin Kâkshaseni, n. p., 1, 58 sq.; 48, 342.

Âbhîras, became V*ri*shalas, 8, 295.

Abhirati, n. of a world, 21, 177.

Abhi*s*asta, *see* Caste (*e*).

Abhisheka, *see* Anointment, *and* Kings.

Abhishe*k*anîya, *see* Kings (consecration of).

Abhiya*s*asa Kula, of the Mânava Ga*n*a, 22, 292.

Âbhûti Tvâsh*t*ra, n. of a teacher, 15, 119, 187.

Abhyudgatarâga, n. of the epoch

of the Buddha *S*âlendrarâ*g*a, 21, 429.
Ablutions, ceremonial, (pâ*d*îyâ*v*îh), 5, 205, 205 n., 259, 259 n., 272, 278 sq., 298 sq., 299 n., 308, 310, 333, 347–9; 18, 73, 115 sq., 153, 161 sq., 166, 309, 313, 340, 343 n., 360, 363, 365, 383, 433–54, 461; providing a tank for a., 5, 317; prayer when washing the face, 5, 347; three morning and evening a., 19, 260; ceremonial morning ablution, 24, 312 sq., 337 sq., 337 n.; before and after meals, 25, 39–41; perfection not to be reached by a., 45, 294 sq.; *see* Bath, *and* Purification.
Abortion, procuring a., causes loss of caste, 2, 74, 281; 14, 133; laws about destroying embryos, and miscarriage, 4, 177–80; 23, 335; no funeral libations for women who have caused an a., 25, 184; a Bhikkhu who intentionally kills a human being, down to procuring a., is no Sama*n*a, 13, 235; sin of a., 7, 133 sq.; 8, 389; 14, 105 sq., 314 sq.; 23, 280 sq.; 26, 11; 40, 243; the most heinous of crimes, 42, 165, 521, 524, 527; cause of divorce, 33, 183; procured by courtesans, 23, 280 sq. *See also* Homicide, *and* Woman (*c*).
Abraham, Arabian traditions of, 6, liii; chapter of A. (Qur'ân), 6, 238; the faith of A. professed by the Muslims, 9, 65; recognized as a prophet by the Qur'ân, 6, lxxi, 57, 94; 9, 139, 206, 269; sent as an apostle, 6, 183; was a 'Hanîf, not of the idolaters, 6, 19, 54, 58, 90, 124, 137, 263; images of A. and Ishmael in the Kaabah, 6, xiii; the Kaabah rebuilt by A., 6, xvi sq.; 'station of A.' in the Kaabah, 6, lxxiv, 17, 58; made the Kaabah the House of God, 6, 17 sq.; prays that Mecca might be a sanctuary, 6, 242 sq.; established the Kaabah and proclaimed the pilgrimage, 9, 59; monotheism, the ancient faith of A., 6, 1, liv, 18; and the birds, 6, 41; offers wine to God, 24, 225 sq.; worships the stars, the moon, and the sun, until he finds the true God, 6, 124 sq.; destroys the idols, is miraculously saved from the fire, 9, 50 sq., 119 sq., 171, 213, 278; preaches to his idolatrous father, 9, 30, 93 sq.; asked pardon for his idolatrous father, 6, 189; 9, 30, 278; and Nimrod, 6, 40 sq.; commanded to sacrifice Ishmael, 6, lxxiv; 9, 172, 172 n.; entertains the angels, 6, 212 sq., 247 sq.; 9, 120, 246; prays for and is granted a son (Isaac), 9, 171 sq.; God grants him Isaac and Jacob, 9, 30, 120; flees with Lot, 9, 120; the Book and wisdom given to A.'s people, 6, 80; the revelation given in the books of A. and Moses, 9, 329; the pages of Moses and A. who fulfilled his word, 9, 253; the sayings of the A. of the Christians, 18, 107, 107 n.; the people of A. called him liar, 9, 61; and Isaac and Jacob were of the elect, 9, 179 sq.; God has chosen A.'s people, 6, 50.
Abrahat el A*s*ram, invades Mecca with elephants, his army destroyed by birds, 9, 341, 341 n.
Abstinence, with regard to eating, sleeping, sexual intercourse, &c., prescribed for special occasions, 2, 100, 105, 113, 147, 150, 152, 187 sq., 224 sq., 254, 260; 14, 42, 89 sq., 181, 210, 287, 323; 44, 445 sq.; with regard to music, food, sexual intercourse, in mid-summer, 27, 275; on the winter solstice, 27, 304 sq.; to be kept on the fourteenth, fifteenth, and eighth days of the half-month, 10 (ii), 66; the vow of a. from carnal pleasures, on new and full moon days, 12, 1–6; 30, 29, 333 sq.; from certain kinds of food, from sexual intercourse, &c., as penance, 2, 276 sq., 290, 292 sq., 296; 14, 110, 117, 124, 131 sq., 218, 223, 300; of the teacher, before teaching secret doctrines, 29, 77, 81, 141; keeping silence, and standing, after the Godâna rite, 29, 186; before performing a magic rite, 30, 286 sq.; from eating flesh, and from sexual intercourse, enjoined for the officiating priest, 29, 197; enjoined for the Dîkshita, 41, 185 sq.; brahma*k*arya, i.e. a., a means of obtaining a knowledge of Brahman, 1, 131, 131 sq. n.; 38, 307, 315; the world of Brahman found by a. (brahma*k*arya), 1, 130 sq.; sacrifice,

the vow of silence, fasting, and a hermit's life, are really a. (brahma*k*arya), 1, 131; enjoined for the student (brahma*k*ârin), 25, 62 sq.; 29, 192, 309; 30, 67; for students undergoing certain vows, 30, 70 sq., 73, 76 sq., 158 sq.; enjoined for three nights after Upanayana, 29, 402; 30, 274; temporary a. ('three nights') of the newly-married couple, 29, 43, 171, 286, 384; 30, 48, 197, 267; with regard to food at mourning rites, 5, 382, 382 n.; 25, 181; 28, 183-5, 386 sq.; 29, 244, 357; from spirits and flesh after paying a visit of condolence, 27, 163; the eightfold a., proclaimed by Buddha, 10 (ii), 66; enjoined for the Bhikkhu, 11, 190-5; *see* Chastity, Fasting, Uposatha, *and* Vows.

Abstract deities, *see* Gods.

Abu Bekr, converted by Mohammed, 6, xxiii sq., xlvi; buys off converted slaves, 6, xxv; and Ali accompany Mohammed during the flight from Mecca, 6, xxxiii sq.; conducting prayers in the mosque of Medînah, 6, xliv; or Omar, the first to think of editing the Qur'ân, 6, lvii; and Mohammed in the cave, 6, 179; and Mis*t*a'h, 9, 75 n.

Abu *G*ahl, an enemy of Mohammed, 9, 300 n., 336 n.

Abu 'Hâmir, a monk who was opposed to Mohammed, 6, 188 n.

Abu 'l 'Abbâs, reproached for his unbelief, though he gave drink to the pilgrims, 6, 175 n.

Abu Laheb, uncle of Mohammed, 6, xxix; Sûrah A.L. one of the earliest parts of the Qur'ân, 6, lx; 9, 343; will broil in hell, his wife carrying faggots, 9, 343 sq., and n.

Âbûn, *see* Waters.

Abuse, punishments for, a. as a title of law, 2, 167, 238-40; 14, 97; 33, 207, 210 sq., 355-7; 35, 239; is of the quality of passion, 8, 323; penance for abusing a Guru, 7, 176; injunctions against scandalmongers, informers, defamers, spies and backbiters, 9, 74 sq., 239 sq., 341; sin of evil-speaking to others' wives, 37, 130. *See* Backbiting, *and* Defamation.

Abu Sufiyân, leader of the Meccan army in the war against Mohammed, 6, xxxv-xxxvii, 164 n.; negotiates with Mohammed and 'Abbâs, 6, xli sq.

Abu Tâlib, uncle and protector of Mohammed, 6, xxiv sq., xxviii sq.

Accidents, penance performed when a. happen to a king's chariot, &c., 29, 287 sq.

Action, Actions, *see* Good actions, Karman, *and* Works.

Activity, *see* Qualities.

Actors, low social position of, 25, 104, 104 n., 163, 265, 272, 317.

Acts, religious, *see* Works.

'Âd (n. of an ancient Arab tribe), Hûd sent as an apostle to 'Â., 6, 145 sq.; and Thamûd, 6, xlviii, 145 n., 183; 9, 121; the people of 'Â. called their prophet liar, 9, 61, 95, 176, 242; punished for disbelieving in the mission of Hûd, 6, 210 sq., 239; 9, 86, 95, 193, 200, 227, 247, 254, 256, 298, 330.

Adâbhya, t.t., a certain cup of Soma at the Soma service, 44, 105-8.

Adam, the first man, 6, 5; adored by the angels, 6, 5, 138, 246 sq.; 9, 8, 19 sq., 43 sq., 181; Satan (Iblîs) refused to adore A., 6, lxix, 246 sq.; God has chosen A., 6, 50; likeness of A. with God, 6, 54; covenant of God with the posterity of A., 6, 159; and Eve, birth of their first child 'Abd el 'Hareth, 6, 161, 161 n.; story of the two sons of A., 6, 101; A. and Eve worship idols, 6, 161 sq.; broke the covenant with God, 9, 43 sq.; his temptation and fall, 6, 5, 139 sq.; story of A.'s fall criticized, 24, 178-80, 200, 209-12, 217-21; recognized as a prophet by the Qur'ân, 6, lxxi; the Kaabah built by A., 6, xvi.

Âdar, *see* Âtar.

Âdâra, or Pûtîka plants, substitute for Soma plants, are fragrant and blaze up in fire, 44, 451 sq., 451 n.

Âdar-bâ*d*, son of Mahraspand, champion of Zoroastrian orthodoxy, 4, xxxviii, xlvi-xlviii; 24, 256, 256 n.; 31, xli.

Adbhuta Kalpa, Mahâvîra's parents born as gods in, 22, 194.

A*ddh*akâsî, n. of a courtesan who became a Bhikkhunî, 20, 360.

Âdhâkarmika, *G*aina t.t., food specially prepared for a mendicant, 22, 81, 94, 111 sq.
Adharma, Bali-offering to, 2, 107; idols of Dharma and A., 33, 319; Dharma and A., substances, 45, 153, 207 sq.
Adhibhûta, t.t., is all perishable things, 8, 77, 78 n.
Adhidaivata, is the primal being, 8, 77, 78 n.
Adhimâtrakaru*n*ika, n. of a Brahma-angel, 21, 164.
Adhiya*gñ*a is K*r*ish*n*a, 8, 77, 78 n.
Adhrigu, t.t., *see* Prayers (*c*).
Adhvaryu, *see* Priests (*a*, *b*).
Adhyâtma, the manifestation of the Brahman as an individual self, 8, 77, 77 n., 316, 316 n., 338, 342.
Âdi-brahma-*k*ariya*m*, elementary righteousness, 11, 16 n.
Âdi*kk*a (Pâli for Âditya), Buddha, the kinsman of the Â., or the Â. family, x (ii), 8, 69, 93, 174, 210.
Aditi, n. of a goddess.

(*a*) Who she is. Identifications.
(*b*) Relations to other deities.
(*c*) Her appearance, character, and powers.
(*d*) Her cosmic and moral character.
(*e*) Worship of A.

(*a*) Who she is. Identifications.
A. is the earth, 12, 25 sq., 73 sq., 73 n., 85, 307; 26, 47–51, 60, 75, 207, 207 n., 259 sq., 386 sq.; 32, 255, 263; 41, 18, 60, 90, 125, 232, 242, 280, 378; 42, 206; 43, 27, 69; 44, 6, 181, 268, 293; 46, 121; in the lap of A. (the boundless or inviolable earth), 12, 19; 42, 212; a name of the cow, 12, 355; 26, 59, 415 sq.; 29, 276; 30, 174; 44, 474; is speech, 41, 237; the Infinite, 32, 241–3; a name for the distant East, 32, 242 sq.; goddess of freedom, 32, 255; identified with other deities, 32, 254 sq., 261; as a masculine deity, 32, 261–3; Dyaus Aditi, 32, 348, 351; Death is called A., 15, 76; Agni invoked by the name of A., 32, 262; 46, 110, 113, 187, 309; the Sun, the quick A., 46, 326, 329.

(*b*) Relations to other Deities.
A. and the Âdityas, her sons, 32, 242–5, 251 sq., 254, 260; 26, 12 sq., 12 n.; 46, 83; the mother of Mitra, Aryaman, and Varu*n*a, 12, 356; mother of the gods, 41, 238; the mother of noble sons, 29, 33; 42, 181; 46, 237; the birth of her sons, 42, 179, 611; wore an amulet, when she desired a son, 42, 97, 502; the Sun, A.'s offspring, 2, 298; mother of Agni, 12, 131 n.; 41, 232; the wife of the gods, 12, 73 sq., 73 n.; 41, 60; the wife of *R*ita, 32, 261; produced a hymn for Indra, 32, 242; and Daksha, 32, 245–8; and Diti, 32, 255 sq.; 41, 93, 93 n.; fashioned the earthen womb for Agni, 41, 237 sq.

(*c*) Her appearance, character, and powers.
Nature of A., 43, 403; is double-headed, 26, 57; the black antelope skin, the skin of A., 12, 38; A.'s girdle, 41, 236; to her belongs the upper region, 26, 51; the bounty of the Maruts extends far, as the sway of A., 32, 210, 241; brings Rudra's healing, 32, 419 sq.; the ruler of the Fathers, 43, 74.

(*d*) Her cosmic and moral character.
A. is all this whatever there is, 1, 256; is one with all deities, identified with the self, 15, 16; in her cosmic character, 32, 248–51; is made of the deities, is the individual soul, 48, 268; in her moral character, 32, 256–60; Agni invoked to grant Diti and keep off A., 46, 317, 321; Agni invoked to release from sin before A., 46, 354.

(*e*) Worship of A.
The goddess invoked, 46, 110, 115, 127, 186, 647; invoked when sprinkling water round the fire, 29, 378; 30, 19, 142, 253; worshipped at the Vai*s*vadeva sacrifice, 29, 84 sq.; invoked for the protection of a child, 29, 54 sq.; invoked at the *K*aula rite, 29, 184, 301; invoked at the Upanayana, 30, 148; invoked for protection, 32, 258 sq.; invoked with Rudra and the Maruts, 32, 423; invoked at expiatory rite when the Agnihotra cow should lie down whilst being milked, 44, 181; worshipped at the A*s*vamedha, 44, 291 n., 293, 351 n.; informed of

the king's consecration, 41, 90; invoked for long life, 42, 50 sq.; invoked to protect the wife, 42, 181; invoked in Âprî hymn, 46, 237; oblations to A., 12, 304 n., 307 sq.; 44, xlii sq.; opening and concluding (rice-pap) oblations to A., 26, 47–51, 259, 386; 44, 140; rice-pap for A. at the new moon sacrifice, 44, 5 sq.; pap offering to A. at the third seasonal sacrifice, 44, 76, 76 n.; pap offerings to A. at the Sautrâma*n*î, 44, 213 n., 268; her share in the Soma feast, 26, 259 sq.; offering to A. in the Queen's dwelling, 41, 60; offering to A. at the Da*s*apeya, 41, 125; animal sacrifice for A., 41, 125 sq.; the sacrificial ladle, the second hand of A., 42, 183; divinities born from the brahmaudana eaten by A., 42, 629; a rope addressed as A.'s zone, 44, 474.

Âditya, the Sun, a god.

(*a*) His mythological character.
(*b*) Â. and other deities.
(*c*) Â. in philosophical and esoteric teaching.
(*d*) Worship of Â.

(*a*) HIS MYTHOLOGICAL CHARACTER.

Born from the egg, 1, 55; the unborn child, 41, 405; ruler of the sky, 43, 208, 382; the deity in the eastern quarter, 15, 146; why the sun is called Â. (etymology), 15, 310; 44, 130; a being of great merit, 48, 237; the moon is his food, 43, 335; as bowman in the east, 42, 192; Â. Vivasvat, father of Manu, 25, lvii; one of the Vasus, 15, 140 sq.; 44, 116; is the surveyor of food offered to the ancestors, 30, 228; mentioned in the Anugîtâ, 8, 219; the white Yagur-veda revealed by Â., 15, 226; line of battle invented by Â., 29, 234.

(*b*) Â. AND OTHER DEITIES.

A form of Agni, 41, 284; 43, 363; Â. is one-third of Agni or Fire, 15, 75; 43, 402; Agni, Vâyu, Â., and *K*andramas identified with four fires, 44, 127; Â. is heat and light, to him offering is made in Agni at the Agnihotra, 44, 112 sq.; Â. and Indra protected by Trisha*m*dhi, 42, 127 sq.; Indra is Â., yonder sun, 43, 92; Agni, Vâyu, and Â., 15, 48 sq.; 30, 114, 231; 41, 204; 43, 90 sq., 187; 44, 508; Agni, Vâyu, and Â. are the hearts of the gods, 43, 162; Agni, Vâyu, and Â. are all the light, 41, 210, 239; 43, 388 sq.; Agni, Vâyu, Â. are light, might, glory, 44, 173 sq.; Maruts, Â., and Brahma*n*aspati, 42, 126; *S*una and Sîra = Vâyu and Â., 12, 445 n.

(*c*) Â. IN PHILOSOPHICAL AND ESOTERIC TEACHING.

Â. is the highest Brahman, 1, 54 sq.; 15, 302; 34, 216; 38, 342–5; meditations on Â., 34, 216 sq.; 38, 342–5; is one foot of Brahman, 1, 54; 34, 216; secret union of Agni and Â., 15, 46; is the eye, 15, 81; 26, 39; in the pupil of the eye, 15, 106; 48, 417; the blood of the woman is a form of Agni, the seed of the man a form of Â., 1, 232; is the essence squeezed out from heaven, 1, 70; the Sâman verses squeezed out from Â., 1, 70; the Upâ*ms*usavana stone is Â. Vivasvant, 26, 240, 354; the Adhvaryu priest identified with Â., 15, 122; 29, 195; the ideas of Â., &c., are to be superimposed on the members of the sacrificial action, 34, lxxvii; 38, 345–9; worlds of Â., 15, 131; the soul reaches Â. as the fruit of pious works, 38, 347, 385.

(*d*) WORSHIP OF Â.

Who brings to light, invoked by the teacher, 2, 114; invocation of Â., the dweller in heaven, 15, 335; Dyaus with Â. invoked in danger, 29, 232; the student worships Â. as lord of the vow, 30, 156; invoked at the Samâvartana, 30, 163; invoked against the enemies, 42, 128; deity of *G*agatî metre, 43, 330; a new moon offering to Â., 12, 375; leads him who performs the twilight devotions up to heaven, 14, 249; the Â. cup, 26, 408; witnesses watched by Â. and other gods, 33, 245; *see also* Sun, *and* Sûrya.

Âdityâ, the Soma cow is an Â., 26, 59.

Âdityas, a class of deities.

(*a*) Their mythological character.
(*b*) The Â. and other deities.
(*c*) Worship of the Â.

(a) THEIR MYTHOLOGICAL CHARACTER.

The seven or eight sons of Aditi, 32, 242–5, 251–4; twelve Â., the twelve months of the year, 15, 140 sq.; 44, 116; twelve Â. created, 41, 149 sq.; fashioned the sky, 41, 234; their names, 32, 245, 253 sq.; with Varu*n*a at their head, 1, 42; 26, 93; 41, 280; 42, 12; 44, 365; A*ms*a, Bhaga, and Aryaman are three Â., 41, 82 sq., 83 n.; gods of light, 42, 116; rise in the west, 15, 339; the lords of the western region, 43, 101; who dwell in heaven, who dwell in the world, 1, 37; help in battle, 42, 119; called pûtadaksha, 42, 444; are the manes of great-grandfathers, 25, 127; practised penance, 25, 475; the Â. and Aṅgiras sacrificing, 26, 113 sq.; where they wish to lay the Gârhapatya, 43, 118; the honey-lash (of the A*s*vins), mother of the Â., 42, 230; the Kush*th*a plant, thrice begotten by the Â., 42, 6; are noneternal beings, because produced, 34, 202, 216; are the All, 41, 126.

(b) THE Â. AND OTHER DEITIES.

Aditi, the sister of the Â., 29, 275; 30, 174; Sun and Moon, the Â., 42, 57; Indra invoked to combine with the Â., Vasus, &c., 12, 264; Maruts and Â., 32, 412 sq.; 43, 68; the Â. make Soma swell, 30, 179; *G*âtavedas Âditya, 42, 127; Agni is to bring the Â. to the sacrifice, 46, 108; the Â. have made Agni their mouth, or their tongue, 46, 188; Vi*s*vakarman invoked with the Â., 26, 123 sq.; and Aṅgiras worshipped, 42, 191; and Aṅgiras contending for getting first to heaven, 44, 152; Vasus and Aṅgiras, 42, 89; and Vasus invoked for wellbeing, 42, 55; the Â. are united with the Vasus, 42, 135; and Vasus, qualified for meditation on divinities, 48, 335–7; Vasus, Rudras, and Â., three classes of gods, 12, 135, 239; 26, 350, 411; 41, 241, 246, 264; 42, 161; 43, 33, 75; 44, 173, 291 n., 313, 443, 479 sq.; 46, 42; seen within K*ri*sh*n*a, 8, 92; alarmed at the greatness of K*ri*sh*n*a, 8, 94; K*ri*sh*n*a is Vish*n*u among the Â., 8, 88, 88 n.

(c) WORSHIP OF THE Â.

Sâman addressed to them, 1, 37; invited to the sacrifice, 12, 93; 46, 281; invoked at the reception of guests, 29, 198; invoked at the Ash*t*akâ, 29, 207; invoked for protection, 29, 344; 42, 161; invoked at the house-building rite, 29, 347; invoked at the Vâgapeya, 41, 38; invoked to expiate imperfections in the sacrifice, 42, 164; invoked against fever, 42, 443; invoked in an Âprî hymn, 46, 179, 198; invoked to bless the sacrifice, 46, 253; the Yagus belong to the Â., 26, 383, 383 n.; share of the Â., at the laying of the altar-bricks, 43, 68; deities and metres, 43, 53; 'if thou belongest to the Â., I buy thee for the Â.,' 30, 53; worshipped at the Vai*s*vadeva sacrifice, 29, 85; worshipped at the Tarpa*n*a, 30, 243; offering to the Â., 26, 12 sq.; 41, 248 sq.; Soma libations to the Â., 26, 241, 316 n.; the evening libation belongs to the Â., 1, 36 sq., 51; 26, 350–6; arise by the performance of the third Soma pressing, 44, 173, 480 n.; animal sacrifice for the Â., 41, 126; the sacrificial horse to go the way of the Â., 44, 288.

Âdityasambhava, n. of a Tathâgata, 49 (ii), 100.

Adoption, the adopted son, definition, 14, 227; law about a., 14, 74 sq., 87; 18, 184–94, 196; 24, 71, 71 n. 316; 25, 355, 355 n., 359, 361 sq. and n.; 37, 113; adopted sons not to be looked upon as real sons, 9, 139, 139 n., 144, 144 n.; duty of providing an adopted son for a childless man, 24, 279–81; ceremony of a., 14, xlv, 76, 334–6; of illegitimate children, 4, 273; a good work, 24, 74; sin of declining a., 37, 147. *See* Children (sale and gift of, subsidiary sons), *and* Woman (*b*).

Ad*ri*sh*t*a, t.t., *see* Unseen Principle.

Adultery.

(*a*) In religion.
(*b*) In civil law.

(a) IN RELIGION.

One of the five principal sins, 10 (i), 61; a crime in the fourth degree, 7, 136; the sin of a., 10 (ii), 19, 21, 40; 24, 305 sq.,

324–6, 331 sq.; 25, 150, 442, 484; 37, 112, 205; heinousness of a., and atonement for it, 18, 227–232; a priest who has illicit intercourse with another man's wife is a highwayman or a thief, 4, 309; bad reputation, an uncomfortable bed, punishment, and hell, are the four things gained by him who covets his neighbour's wife, 10 (i), 74 sq.; *let the wise man avoid an unchaste life as a burning heap of coals; not being able to live a life of chastity, let him not transgress with another man's wife*, 10 (ii), 65; be an abstainer from the wives of others, 24, 12; penances for a., 2, 286; 7, 174 sq.; 14, 111–13, 232, 235; 25, 465, 467, 467 n.; punishments for a. in future life, 44, 332, 497; the mortal sin of violating a Guru's bed, 7, 133 sq.; 8, 389; 14, 5, 235; 25, 383, 441 sq.; penances for a. with wife of a Guru, 2, 81 sq., 88 sq., 276 sq., 284 sq., 290; 14, 104, 127, 213, 235; 25, 451 sq.; punishments for a. with a Guru's wife in future life, 25, 440, 496; an adulterous wife's guilt falls on the negligent husband, 14, 101; 25, 309; imprecations used by a husband against an adulterer, 15, 218; 29, 289; allusion to a. in the prayer 'Wherein my mother has done amiss,' &c., 30, 227; the wife has to confess any adulterous intercourse at the Varu*n*apraghâsa sacrifice, 12, 396 sq., 397 n.; food given by the paramour of a married woman, or by a husband who allows a paramour to his wife, not to be eaten, 14, 69 sq.; 25, 163; adulterers, husbands who allow a. in their houses, the son of an adulteress, and he who eats food given by persons born through a., excluded from *S*râddha, 2, 145, 257; 25, 104 sq., 108; first committed by Va*d*ak, mother of Dahâk, 18, 217.

(*b*) In civil law.

A. defined, 25, 316; the cause of confusion of castes, 25, 315, 407; law about a., 2, 164–7; 25, 253, 315–21; 33, 177–9, 365–7; punishments for a., 2, 288 sq.; 7, 29; 14, 233, 235; 25, 197, 315, 318–21; 33, 179, 183; 35, 223; 45, 274; punishments for a. with a Guru's wife, 14, 201, 383; witnesses in cases of a., 25, 267; where a man and the wife of another man seize one another by the hair, the man is an adulterer, without witnesses being required, 33, 85; persons addicted to a., inadmissible witnesses, 33, 303; causes loss of caste, 2, 74; a cause of divorce, 33, 183; the adulterer one of the seven kinds of assassins, 7, 41; he who abducts another man's wife may be slain as an assassin, 14, 19; penance for the minor offence of killing adulterous women, 25, 458; women immured for a., 6, 74, 74 n.; women not to be driven away unless they have committed manifest a., 9, 288; son of an adulterer excluded from inheritance, 25, 356. *See also* Incest, Sexual intercourse, *and* Woman (*g*, *h*).

Advaita, t.t., non-duality or monism, taught both by *S*ankara and Râmânuga, 34, xxx, cxxv.

Aêkha, the contagion of, destroyed by Aryan glory, 23, 284 sq.

Aêshm, Aêshma, demon of Wrath, 5, 193, 193 n., 201 sq., 205, 205 n., 215, 217, 220, 223 sq., 227 sq., 366, 366 n.; 18, 93, 96, 113; 24, 17 sq., 17 n., 61; 47, 72, 72 n.; the impersonation of invasion and rapine, 31, xix, xxi n.; of the murderous spear, 4, 126, 140 sq., 224; 23, 33; 31, 280; powers of A., 5, 107–9, 107 sq. n.; the seven evil-instructed ones of A., 47, 8; complains to Aharman of the three things he could not injure in the world, 5, 387–9, 387 n.; assists the Evil Spirit, 23, 297; opposes the departed soul, 24, 17 sq., 17 n.; Sraosha created by Ahura to withstand A., 23, 164; attacked and smitten by Srôsh (Sraosha), 5, 128, 128 n.; 24, 33; 31, 300; spells against A., 4, 126, 140 sq., 140 n., 145–7; 31, 280 (Ahuna-vairya); Mithra invoked against A., 23, 143; flees from Mithra, 23, 144, 154; smiting of A. by propitiation of Spenda*r*ma*d*, 18, 437; Fravashi of Fradhâkh*sh*ti invoked against A., 23,

224; shall bow and flee before the Saoshyan*ts*, 23, 308; Aryan glory destroys A., 23, 284; coming of A. to Kâî-Ûs, 37, 221; set up King Alexander, 47, 83; Kôkharê*d* born from A. and Mânû*s*ak, 47, 143.

Aêta, son of Mâyu, 23, 217.

Aêthrapaiti, the teacher, 31, 318, 323.

Aêthryas, Aêthrapaitis and, 31, 323.

Aêvo-saredha-fyaê*s*ta, n.p., 23, 218.

Aêzemnô, or Ayazem, ancestor of Zoroaster, 37, 261, 261 n.

Afarg, n. of a Zoroastrian teacher and Pahlavi writer, 5, 243, 243 n., 246, 262, 262 n., 264, 264 n., 268, 273, 292; 18, 283, 283 n., 299–304, 299 n., 309, 312–14, 316, 320, 332 sq., 336 n., 361; quoted, 18, 446, 449, 449 n.

Afrâsiyâb, a wicked king, 24, 267.

Afrâsyâb, the Turk, made himself an iron palace under the earth, yet could not escape death, 4, 380 sq.; killed Aghraêratha, 23, 114 n. *See* Frangrasyan.

Âfrînagân, *see* Prayers (*f*), *and* Zend-avesta.

Afrôbag-vindâd, n.p., 5, 146 sq.

A*g*a, lost his son Da*s*aratha, 19, 92; 49 (i), 90.

A*g*â, t.t., that power of the Lord from which the world springs, or the primary causal matter first produced by that power, 34, xxxix, 252–7; the elements beginning with light are meant by A., 34, 254 sq.; denotes the causal matter metaphorically, 34, 256 sq.; the uncreated (Night or Mâyâ), 44, 389, 389 sq. n. *See also* Unborn.

A*g*a Ekapâda, the one-footed goat, the sun, 42, 208, 625, 664; oblation to A. E., 29, 331.

A*g*âima*s*vâk, n.p., 5, 136.

Âgamas, studied by Bhikkhus, 17, 285, 288, 345.

Â*g*âniya ('high-bred'), Buddha's definition of the term, 10 (ii), 92.

Agash, demon of the evil eye, 47, 53, 53 n.

Agastya, a *Ri*shi, son of Mitrâvaru*n*au, author of Vedic hymns, 32, 212, 274, 281, 290, 294; 46, 180, 182; dialogue between Indra, A., and the Maruts, 32, 182, 184, 286–8; employed charms, 42, 23 sq., 319; slew the Rakshas, 42, 33; born without a mother, 14, 180 n.; son of Urva*s*î, and Vâmadeva, seeking Râma, 49 (i), 93, 93 n.; seduced by a heavenly queen, 19, 43 sq.; wooed Rohi*n*î, the wife of Soma, 49 (i), 44; the south, the region of A., 49 (i), 96, 96 n.; went out to hunt to get meat for sacrifices, 14, 71; 25, 173; worshipped at the Tarpa*n*a, 30, 244; the threefold age of A., 29, 55 sq.; Mâna, a name of the Agastyas, 46, 182, 184; Khumbya and A., 23, 224 n.

Âgastya, n. of a teacher, 1, 248.

A*g*âta*s*atru, king of Kâ*s*i, discussion on Brahman between Gârgya Bâlâki and, 1, 300–7; 15, 100–5; 34, cv, 268–74; 48, 378–80, 383; rival of *G*anaka, 12, xliii; Bhadrasena, a son of A., 41, 141, 141 n.

A*g*âta*s*atru (Pâli, A*g*âtasattu), **king of Magadha**, son of Bimbisâra and Vaidehî, 11, 1 sq.; 21, 6; 49 (ii), v; the defeat of A., by Prasena*g*it, 10 (i), 53 n.; prince A. gained over by Devadatta, pays great honour to the latter, 20, 233–8; incited by Devadatta, wants to kill his father, is found out and treated mercifully, 20, 241–3; imprisons his father Bimbisâra, 49 (ii), 161–4; his relations to *G*ainas and Buddhists, 22, xiv sq.; moved by Buddha's conquest over the mad elephant, 19, 248; claims relics of Buddha, and erects a dâgaba over them, 11, 131, 134; the Sâmañña-phala spoken with him, 20, 377.

A*g*aya, a Brâhman, converted by Buddha, 49 (i), 190 sq.

Age, how to inquire about the a. of persons from the king downwards, 27, 115; libations to the a.-grades, 43, 218. *See* Old Age.

Agent, every action requires an a., 34, 337–40.

Ages of the World.

(*a*) Indian Yugas and Kalpas.
(*b*) Zoroastrian millenniums.
(*c*) Chinese world periods.

(*a*) Indian Yugas and Kalpas.

The four Yugas, the Manvantaras and Kalpas, 7, 77–9; 25, xii, lxxxiv–lxxxvii, 20–4; 'conjunctions' (Sandhis), the periods about the close of one and the beginning of another Yuga, 8, 330 n.; an ex-

planation of the Hindu belief in Kalpas, &c., 45, 16 sq. n.; deterioration of the world in the successive a., 33, 3, 3 n.; in the age when men were all virtuous and veracious, there were no lawsuits, 33, 5, 5 n., 277; at the expiration of a Kalpa, all entities enter K*ri*sh*n*a's nature, and at the beginning of a Kalpa he brings them forth again, 8, 82; dissolution of the world at the end of the great world periods, 34, xxvi, 212; there is no measure of the past and the future Kalpas, 34, 361; king resembles the four a., 25, 396; size of mankind in different Kalpas, 36, 133 n.; among all a. the K*ri*ta is the first, 8, 353; the Tretâ age, the age of sacrifices, 15, 30; twelve hundred years of the gods are a Kali Yuga, 7, 77, 77 n.; in the Kali Yuga no *Ri*shis are born, 2, xviii; the sinful Kali Yuga, 2, 175 n.; Niyoga not to be practised in the Kali age, 33, 369; K*ri*ta, Tretâ, Dvâpara as names of dice, 44, 416. *See* Time, *and* World (*c*).

(*b*) ZOROASTRIAN MILLENNIUMS.

Zoroastrian chronology by millenniums, 47, xii sq., xxvii–xxxviii, xli, 15 n., 21–4, 23 sq. n.; four periods of 3,000 years, 18, 198, 198 n.; three millenniums, 24, 345; 37, 254, 254 n.; six millenniums, 37, 405, 405 n.; millennium reigns for each constellation of the zodiac, 5, 149–51, 149 n.; the evil millenniums, 18, 203, 203 n.; signs at the end of millenniums, 37, 33 sq., 279; four periods in the millennium of Zaratû*s*t, 37, 181, 451 sq.; 47, xi sq.; millenniums of Zoroaster, and the three future apostles, 24, 15, 15 n.; 47, 94–118, 94 n.; millenniums before and after Zoroaster, 47, 144; advantages and disadvantages of the period, 37, 21 sq.; evil doings in the ninth and tenth centuries, 37, 257–60, 257 n.; triumph of sacred beings over the demons at four periods, 37, 285; the three periods of the universe: past eternity, present existence, and future eternity, 37, 317, 317 n.; Zoroaster's vision of seven successive ages (tree with seven branches), 47, xxiii sq.; steel age, &c., 47, 87, 126, 126 n.

(*c*) CHINESE WORLD PERIODS.

The period of 'the Grand Course' followed by that of the 'Small Tranquillity,' 27, 364–7, 365 n.; primitive ages, 27, 369; 'the period of great order,' 28, 118; primaeval state of innocence, 3, 255 n.; the primaeval age of perfect virtue when Tâo ruled men, 39, 26–8, 139–41, 277–80, 287–90, 325; 40, 171, 284; the paradisiacal state under the influence of the Tâo, not yet superseded by 'the wisdom of the world,' 39, 60–2; difference between the age of perfect virtue, and the present time, 39, 353 sq.; 'The State of Established Virtue,' where the Tâoist enjoys himself, 40, 30 sq.; the paradisiacal state when men lived like birds, 40, 312; the rulers who disturbed the primaeval paradisiacal state, 39, 295 sq.; how the age of perfect virtue came to an end, 39, 359 sq.; 40, 312 sq., 316 sq. *See also* Paradise.

Aggâ*l*ava, temple of, 10 (ii), 57.

Aggikabhâradvâ*g*a, the Brâhma*n*a, is converted by Buddha, 10 (ii), 20–4.

Aggregates, the five a. (khandhâ), the conditions of individuality and their cause, 11, 148, 148 n.; the dyad of a. assumed by the Bauddhas with its two causes cannot be established, 34, 400–9; the *G*aina doctrine that a. are formed from the atoms, 34, 430 sq.; the seventeenfold aggregate, 38, 65, 65 n. *See also* Skandhas.

Âghâra, *see* Sacrifice (*k*).

Aghora, n. d., the initiated boy given in charge to, 30, 154.

Aghraêratha, a semi-man (half bull, half man), brother of Afrâsyâb, 23, 114 sq. and n., 222, 278, 304. *See* Aghrêra*d*.

Aghrêra*d* (Pahlavi for Aghraêratha), son of Pashang, 5, 117, 135, 135 n.; legend of A., 5, 135 sq.

A*g*îgarta Sauyavasi, king Hari*s*kandra bought *S*una*h*s*e*pa the son of A. S., 14, 87; 44, xxxiv sq.; saved himself from starvation by selling his son, 25, 424, 424 n.

Â*g*îgarti, *see* *S*una*h*s*e*pa.

A*g*ita, a pupil of Bâvarî, his questions answered by Buddha, 10 (ii), 187, 188–91, 210.

Agita, a Bhikkhu who was reciter of the Pâtimokkha at the council of Vesâlî, 20, 408; n. of a Tîrthakara, 22, 280; n. of a Bodhisattva, 49 (ii), 90; conversation between Buddha and the Bodhisattva A., 49 (ii), x, 61–9; applauds the speech of Buddha, 49 (ii), 72. *For* Maitreya Agita, *see* Maitreya.

Agita-Kesakambalî (i.e. A. of the garment of hair), n. of a teacher, 10 (ii), xii, 86 sq.; 11, 106; an Arhat possessed of Iddhi, 20, 79; and Milinda, 35, 8; his materialistic doctrines, 45, xxiii sq.

Agitamâ*n*avapu*kkh*â, t.c., 10 (ii), 190 sq.

Âgîvikas, sect of naked ascetics, 10 (ii), x, xiii; 20, 198 sq.; 21, 263; 36, 308 sq. n.; disputatious Â. do not overcome Buddha, 10 (ii), 63; Niga*nth*as and Â., their views about the soul, 45, xix; Gosâla, leader of the Â., or A*k*elakas, their relation to the *G*ainas, 45, xxix–xxxii.

Ag*ñ*âna, *see* Nescience.

Ag*ñ*ânavâda, i.e. Agnosticism, q. v.

Ag*ñ*ânavidhva*m*sana, the sixty-fourth Tathâgata, 49 (ii), 7.

Âg*ñ*âta-Kau*nd*inya, *see* Kau*nd*inya.

Agni, the God of Fire.

(*a*) His births, his mothers, his parents.
(*b*) Forms and abodes of A.
(*c*) Myth of the hidden A.
(*d*) Names of A.
(*e*) Anthropomorphic conception of A. (his body, his food and drink, his chariot and horses, his wives, children, &c.).
(*f*) Theriomorphic conception of A., and his relations to animals.
(*g*) His relation to the other gods in general.
(*h*) A. as related to individual other gods.
(*i*) A. and the solar deities (Âditya, Sûrya, Ushas, the Asvins).
(*j*) A. as destroyer of demons and all hostile powers.
(*k*) Excellent qualities and transcendent powers of A.
(*l*) A. as a kind and helpful god.
(*m*) A. the god of the house and the clan.
(*n*) A. as connected with women and marriage.
(*o*) A. as the sacrificial fire and the Fire-altar.
(*p*) Men (or demigods) and families who first established A.
(*q*) A. as a priest, and his relations to the priesthood.
(*r*) A. in his relation to the Sacrifice and the Sacrificer.
(*s*) Sacrifices to A.
(*t*) Prayers to A., and A. as related to prayers (and metres).
(*u*) A. as connected with Veda and Veda-study.
(*v*) A. in his moral character.
(*w*) A. as a supreme God of Heaven and Earth.
(*x*) A. in philosophical speculations.

(*a*) HIS BIRTHS, HIS MOTHERS, HIS PARENTS.

Thou, O A., the flaming one, (*art born*) *from out the Heavens, thou* (*art born*) *from out the Waters and the stone* (*the flint*); *thou* (*art born*) *from out the forests and the herbs; thou art born bright, O Lord of men,* (*as belonging*) *to men,* 46, 186, 189; *he has been born in the dwellings as the first, at the bottom of the great* (*air*), *in the womb of this air, footless, headless, hiding both his ends, drawing towards himself* (*his limbs?*), *in the nest of the bull,* 46, 308; puzzles or mysteries concerning the birth, &c. of A., 46, 114 sq.; A. is water-born, cow-born, law-born, is born from the sky, from the breath, 41, 281, 283 sq.; A. born from A., from the pain of the earth, or of the sky, 44, 202; generation of A. (fire-altar), and fashioning the embryonic A., 41, 251–6, 300–3, 309, 310 sq., 319 sq., 344, 351 sq., 354, 358, 362–5, 398 sq.; when the altar is built, A. is born, 41, 332 sq.; the gods wondered at his birth, 46, 219; A. is born at once, 44, 89; his secret birth, 46, 366, 368; when created, sought to burn everything, 12, 342; of double birth, celestial and terrestrial, 46, 52, 141, 176; A. who is born and A. who will be born, twins, 46, 57, 59; grows up within the plants, within the children, and within the sprouting grass, 46, 61; his three births, in the sea, in heaven, and in the waters, 46, 114, 116, 308; his highest and lower birth-places, 46, 215; has three lives, and three births from the Dawn, 46, 275 sq.; produced by the ten young women, i.e. the fingers, by attrition, 46, 75 sq., 114, 116, 147, 150, 160, 256, 287, 292, 294, 302 sq., 306, 341, 391; son of strength, or offspring of vigour, 32, 21 sq.; 41, 255; 46, 16, 45 sq., 92, 103, 119 sq., 129, 147 sq., 157, 209, 211, 220, 261, 268, 273, 277, 289, 291, 297, 300, 316, 352, 371 sq., 375 sq., 382, 385, 391, 403; born living from the dry wood, 46, 64; one blows upon A.

when he is born (i.e. when fire is kindled), 42, 56; born from the deceased, 29, 242 n.; and his mothers, 41, 294 sq.; 46, 114 sq., 117, 141 sq., 144 sq., 147, 217 sq., 343; Dyaus his mother, 41, 272; conceived by the virgin (the wood), 46, 344 sq.; as soon as she had enjoyed love, the well-bearing mother has borne him, 46, 382; his mothers are the plants, 41, 224; 44, 194; is the child of the herbs, trees, and waters, 44, 194; is the child of the waters, of the trees, of that which stands and moves, 46, 70; his births in the waters and in the plants, 41, 294; 46, 114 sq., 117, 188, 219–21; nourished by the waters, 46, 54; is born from the waters, and the waters from A., 46, 117; his seven kind mothers, the waters, 46, 147, 150, 256; is the child of the waters (Apâm napât), 26, 381; 41, 226; 46, 157, 158, 240, 256; 49 (i), 45; creation of A. from the earth, 15, 75; the child of the earth, 15, 221; earth pregnant with A., 29, 45; 30, 199; licks the upper garment of the mother (earth?), 46, 142, 145; no harm can be done to A., when he dwells in his mother's womb, 46, 173; in his mother's lap, 46, 303, 407; the son of I*l*â, 46, 302; the son of the two mothers, 32, 359; 41, 350; 46, 22, 25, 391 sq.; borne by the two Dawns, 46, 363, 416; Heaven and Earth, his parents, 41, 224; 46, 49, 51, 167, 219 sq., 225, 228, 233, 248–50, 291, 336; made his parents new again and again, 46, 241; A., the child of Dyu, 32, 21–3; brought forward from the highest father (Heaven), 46, 147, 150; by his nature he has found his father's udder, 46, 220; the increaser of his father, 46, 141, 144; he bore the germ of the father who begat him, 46, 220, 225 sq.; born from the Asura's belly, 46, 303; the child of the universe, 43, xx, xxiii; created out of Pragâpati, 12, 323; 43, 206; 44, 15; both the father and the son of Pragâpati, 43, xx; being the son of the gods, has become their father, 46, 67; the gods have procreated A. by their thoughts, 46, 228; son of Tvash*tri*, 46, 114, 116, 248, 251.

(*b*) Forms and abodes of A.

Many forms of A., 41, 159–61, 163, 165 sq., 284; three Agnis and the fourth A., 12, 87–9, 108 n., 136; 26, 118; 43, 157; fourfold is A., 12, 47, 47 n.; is threefold, 41, 147, 160, 197 sq., 202, 204 sq., 225 sq., 232, 282, 284, 294, 323, 330, 335–9, 358, 371, 392; 43, 5, 166, 169, 189–91, 204 sq., 236, 251, 304, 364 sq., 402; three forms of A., 46, 147, 149 sq., 229, 231; threefold is his strength, three his abodes, three his tongues, and three his bodies, 46, 281; dwells in three abodes, 46, 376, 391 sq.; Lord of the Earth, Lord of the World, Lord of Beings = the three Agnis, 12, 89; the three-named A., 42, 135, 495; the three older brothers of A., 42, 257; is light and fire, and a god, 34, 217; in the Rig-veda, not only the earthly sacrificial fire, but also an elemental force, 1, xxii; the dead body protected against A. (funeral fire), 29, 241; the flesh-devouring A. (funeral fire), 42, 54, 56; *see also below* A. Vai*s*vânara (p. 13 sq.); A. (funeral pyre) the guide to Yama's seat, 42, 90; the fury of terrible A., 42, 90; as the fire of the lightning, 42, 401; 46, 103, 105, 109, 114–16, 193, 196; the moon a form of A., 41, 229 sq.; in the moon, 46, 116; by his nightly light, the creatures walk, 46, 108; Sun, Vâyu, and fire, three forms of A., 43, xx, 402; *see also* A. and Vâyu *below*, p. 18; Î*s*âna, Mahân Deva*h*, and Pa*s*upati, forms of A., 43, xx; the two Agnis, 42, 216, 627; consists of pairs (males and females), 43, 284 sq.; the Paridhis or 'enclosing-sticks' are Agnis, 12, 87–91; *A.* (*fire*) *is in the earth, in the plants, the waters hold A., A. is in the stones; A. is within men, Agnis* (*fires*) *are within cattle, within horses; A. glows from the sky, to A., the god, belongs the broad air. The mortals kindle A., the bearer of oblations, that loveth ghee. The earth, clothed in A., with dark knees, shall make me brilliant and alert!* 42, 201;

A. in heaven, in the air, in the earth, plants, waters, flints, &c., 41, 43 n., 304; 43, 201-3; 46, 285; seated in all spaces, law-seated, sphere-dwelling, 41, 281; called man-seated, water-seated, barhis-seated, heaven-winning, 43, 183 sq.; brought to many places for the use of the living, 46, 22, 70 sq., 74, 77 sq.; follows the world like a shadow, having filled heaven, earth, and the air, 46, 89; has approached the threefold light, all spaces of the atmosphere, in the abode of the waters, 46, 176; in heaven, in the human dwellings, and in the waters, 46, 266; dwells on the earth, 1, 36; 15, 334; 46, 73; is the essence squeezed out from the earth, 1, 70; the lord of terrestrial beings, 30, 237; the regent of the earth, 43, xx, 208, 381; laid down in the best place of the earth, in the place of I*l*â, 46, 287, 302; dwelt once between the two horns of a wether, 26, 125; moves about within the young sprouting grass, 46, 115, 118; has entered all herbs, 46, 127, 412; in the waters, 12, 22; 30, 226; 41, 293-5, 304 sq.; 42, 14; 44, 193 sq.; 46, 61, 160, 167 sq., 202, 232, 256, 291, 297; A., the lord of the waters, 14, 251; *sitting in the waters he hisses like a swan*, 46, 54; goes to the floods of heaven, to the waters in the ether of the sun, and to those below, 46, 285; the gods made part of A. enter the water, 26, 381; dwelling in the water, worshipped at the consecration of ponds, 29, 135, 135 n.; seated between Heaven and Earth, 46, 244; world of A., a stage on the soul's road to the sun, 1, 275; 38, 385; 48, 746, 748; world of A., attained by a giver of gold, 7, 273; where A. dwells, 30, 218; the Soma asked to enter A.'s dear seat, 44, 108; the highest place of A., 46, 82; part of the hand sacred to A., 14, 25.

(*c*) Myth of the hidden A.

A. hid himself in the waters, and was discovered by the gods, 12, 47, 452; 42, 3, 270-2; the gods search for A., 41, 196-9, 203, 207-9, 214 sq.; the hidden A. sought and discovered by the gods, 46, 54 sq., 61, 64, 66, 82, 84, 127, 173, 175; Pragâpati searches for the hidden A., 41, 161 sq., 360; concealed by the Pa*n*is, 12, 245; hid himself in an A*s*vattha tree, 32, 329; went away from the gods, and entered the mu*ñg*a grass, 42, 249; dwelt in secret, 44, 192; 46, 241, 256; brilliant, though hidden in secret, easily to be found, 46, 343, 385; putting down his feet in secret like a thief, A. has enlightened and freed Atri, 46, 399; searching and digging for A., 41, 200-22, 241 sq.; the hidden A. found by the thoughtful men, 46, 61; the Aṅgiras have discovered the hidden A., 46, 391 sq.

(*d*) Names of A.

Has many names, 46, 281, 372; the newborn A. receives a name, 43, 269, 269 n.; A. for Agri, mystic name, 41, 146; etymology of A., 34, 150; 48, 292; called *Aditi*, 32, 262; 46, 110, 113, 187, 309 sq.; cake offered to A. *Agnimat*, 44, 189; called *Aṅgiras*, 41, 225, 279; 46, 24, 92, 327, 348, 385, 389, 391, 412; the first or best of Aṅgiras, 41, 358; 46, 22, 95, 129; sacrifices to A. *Anîkavat*, 12, 408 sq. and n.; 41, 58 sq.; 44, 76, 76 n.; expiatory cake offering to A. *Apsumat* (abiding in the waters) at the Agnihotra, 44, 193 sq.; is an *Asura*, 46, 399; called *Âyu*, the living one, 46, 142, 170; called *Âyus*, Life, 41, 323; oblations and prayers to A. *Âyushmat*, who rules over vital power, 44, 439; called the *Bharata*, 12, 133; 46, 119, 123; A. *Bhârata* or the god of the Bharata tribe, 12, 114 sq.; 46, 211; called *Bhrigavâna*, 46, 74, 78; A. called *Brihaspati*, 46, 292, 294; a cake for A. *Dât*ri (the giver), 44, xlii sq., 8 sq.; A. *Gârhapatya*, the protector of house, offspring, and cattle, 12, 358 sq.; A. Gârhapatya invoked to free from sin, 42, 165, 167; A. the *Gâtavedas*, 1, 150; 12, 119, 119 n., 136; 26, xxxi sq.; 46, 37, 42, 49, 100, 102, 103, 108, 128, 129, 193 sq., 202, 221, 229, 233, 240, 244, 259, 261, 271, 275, 281, 283, 285, 287, 291, 293 (Agni am I, by birth Gâtavedas), 300, 302, 310, 326, 336, 354, 358, 375 sq.,

377, 387, 413, 418; why called *G*âtavedas, 43, 274; *G*âtavedas, the messenger, 30, 110; *G*âtavedas Vaisvânara invoked for protection, 42, 54; the immortal, life-possessing A. *G*âtavedas grants long life, 42, 57; offering to A. *G*âtavedas, 30, 239; 42, 88; prayer to A. *G*âtavedas, 15, 210; 30, 142 sq., 162; 42, 47 sq., 98, 121, 168, 309, 325 sq.; 44, 382; prayer to A. *G*âtavedas to protect the cows, 30, 185 sq.; prayer to A. *G*âtavedas at offerings to the Manes, 29, 103; 32, 35 sq.; offerings to A. *Grihapati* (the house-lord), 12, 256 n., 259; 26, 215, 320 n.; 29, 352; 41, 69 sq., 71; prayer to A., the householder, 12, 272; A., the house-lord, informed of the king's consecration, 41, 89; offering to A. Grihapati at the unyoking of the king's chariot, 41, 101 sq.; offerings to A. *Indumat*, 12, 319 sq.; oblations to A. *Kâma*, 44, xlii sq.; offering to A. *Kavyavâhana*, 12, 430 sq.; 29, 421; 30, 106; prayer to A. Kavyavâhana at the worship of the fathers, 30, 227 sq., 233, 236; A. called *Mâtarisvan*, 46, 119, 241, 292, 294; offering to A. *Mûrdhanvat*, 44, 34 n., 350 n.; is *Narâsamsa*, 46, 10, 303; *see* Narâsamsa; offering to A. *Pathikrit* (path-maker), 30, 203; 44, xlii sq., 11, 191 sq., 350 n.; offerings to A. *Pavamâna*, and A. *Pâvaka*, 12, 304–8, 304 n., 307 n., 319 sq.; A. *Purîshya* brought from the earth's seat, 41, 201 sq., 201 n.; A. Purîshya, favourable to cattle, 41, 205 sq., 214, 216 sq., 225–7, 257, 305, 310 sq.; the Agnis Purîshyas, 41, 358; A. Purîshya, the fire of the soil, invoked, 44, 189; 46, 285 sq.; invoked as *Rebha*, the divine chanter, 42, 197, 690 sq.; called Ribhu, 46, 240, 243, 382; called *Rudra*, 41, 64; 46, 17, 228, 231, 325, 327, 371, 373; Rudra identified with A., 12, 200–2, 201 n., 206 sq.; 26, 343 n.; 42, 618 sq.; 43, 156 sq., 160, 169 sq., 172, 201 sq.; names of Rudra-Agni, 41, 159–61; called *Sahasvat*, 21, 5 n.; *see* Sahâmpati; expiatory cake offering to A. *Samvarga* (the despoiler), 44, 193; offering to A. *Samvesapati*, 12, 260 n.; called *Sikhin*, 21, 5 n.; expiatory cake offering for A. *Suki* (the bright), 12, 304 n., 305 sq., 307 n., 308; 44, 194; A. *Svishtakrit* (maker of good offerings), established by the gods, 12, 151; offerings and prayers to A. Svishtakrit, 2, 202, 299; 12, 152, 152 n., 158, 199–208, 247, 320 sq., 334, 364, 372, 372 n., 382, 403, 412, 414; 14, 304; 25, 90; 26, 205 n., 207, 209, 316 n., 351 sq., 351 n., 383, 391 n., 395; 29, 43 sq., 84, 163 sq., 175, 192, 204, 208, 222, 272, 279, 290, 337, 352, 387, 391, 420; 30, 22, 35 sq., 40, 100, 102, 145, 158, 191, 196, 222, 227, 236, 240, 242, 254, 264–6, 289 sq., 294; 41, 40 sq., 71–3, 105, 112 sq., 184; 44, 3 n., 11, 18 sq., 36 sq., 41, 54, 65, 189 n., 253 sq., 253 n., 336 n., 337–9, 337 n., 351 n., 356, 358, 483; A. Svishtakrit is Rudra, 44, 338; A. *Tantumat* worshipped, 29, 136; is *Tanûnapât*, 46, 10, 303; *see* Tanûnapât; is the *Usig* of the gods, the good-minded lord of prayers, 46, 52, 233, 261 sq., 297; A. *Vaisvânara; the other Agnis (the other fires) are verily thy branches, O A. In thee all the immortals enjoy themselves. Vaisvânara! Thou art the centre of human settlements; like a supporting column thou holdest men. The head of heaven, the navel of the earth is A.; he has become the steward of both worlds. Thee, a god, the gods have engendered, O Vaisvânara, to be a light for the Ârya*, 46, 49; A. V. blazes sevenfold within the body, 8, 259; A. V. is the fire within man, by which the food is digested, 15, 193, 294, 312 sq.; 34, 143 sq., 146 sq.; 48, 287, 290 sq.; the sun rises as A. V., 15, 272; 41, 391; A. V. has mounted the firmament, the back of heaven, 46, 229; A. V. unites with the sun, 46, 127; A. V. as the funeral fire, 42, 12, 43, 58, 242, 580; what comes into connexion with A. V. becomes cooked, 41, 349, 398; the fiery spirit of A. V., 41, 404; A. V. is the elemental fire, 34, 144, 147; A. V. is the divinity whose body is fire, 34, 144, 147; A. V. cannot be the divinity of fire, or the element of fire, 34, 148 sq.; A. V. is all the fires, 41, 248; A. V., the third of the

elements, a sign of the days, 48, 287 sq.; the earth supports A. V., 42, 200; sand is the seed of A. V., 41, 300, 310 sq., 351; gravel the ashes of A. V., 26, 120; A. V., the king of the kings, a god, 48, 288; discussion on the nature of A. V., 43, 393-8; offerings to A. V., 12, 386 n.; 30, 203; 41, 57 sq., 125, 170, 250 sq.; 43, 207-14; 44, 11, 277, 346; by offerings to A. V., one sanctifies ten ancestors, 14, 117; the Vaisvânara graha for A. V., 26, 298-305; Dîkshâ offering to A. V. at the building of the altar, 41, 247 sq.; A. V. together with Idâ, 41, 334; A. V. is the mouth of the sacrificial horse (Pragâpati), 43, 401; feeding A. V. is the true Agnihotra, 1, 89-91, 89 n.; prayers and hymns to A. V., 26, 44; 42, 196 sq., 494; 43, 274-8; 44, 382; 46, 49 sq., 127, 228-35, 335-7; the Yagñâyagñiya, the praise of A. V., 43, 253, 330; the initiated boy given in charge to A. V., 30, 154; prayer to A. V. Parikshit, 42, 197 sq., 691 sq.; A. V. invoked, 29, 136, 225; 30, 183; 32, 353; 42, 54, 80, 149; 46, 420 sq.; A. V. celebrated by the *R*ishis, 41, 285 n.; invoked against evil-doers and demons of disease, 42, 35, 40; A. V. is the year, 12, 135; 41, 57 sq., 248, 250, 351; 43, 33; A. V. is all these worlds, 43, 208; A. V. has filled the worlds, and heaven and earth, 46, 233; A.V. is the earth, 26, 214; 44, 346; meditations on A. V. as the highest self, and the embodied self, 1, 84-91, 89 n.; 34, 144; 38, 187, 191, 233, 249, 292, 400; 48, 287-95, 629-32, 673, 677-9; A. V. is Purusha (man, person), 34, 146-8; 43, 398; 48, 292; A. V. shaped like a man, abiding within man, 48, 291; A. V. is Brahman, 34, xxxv, 143-53; as A. V. the Lord abides in the creatures, 34, 149 sq.; 48, 248; Mâthava of Videgha carried A. V. in his mouth, 12, 104-6, 104 n.; A. V. is to be meditated upon as a whole, not in his single parts, 34, lxxv; 38, 274-7, 279; the six *R*ishis who wished to obtain a knowledge of A. V., 38, 274-6; A. called *Vasu*, 46, 37, 43, 52, 103, 109 sq. (Vasu of the Vasus), 129, 157 (Vasu together with the Vasus), 211, 215 (the highest V.), 236, 271, 277, 279, 283, 337, 372, 379, 415 sq.; one of the eight Vasus, 1, 41; 15, 140 sq.; 26, 93; 41, 149 n., 150; 42, 116; 44, 116; expiatory cake offering and prayer to A. *Viviki* (the discerning) at the Agnihotra, 44, 192; by offerings to A. *Vratapati* one sanctifies ten ancestors, 14, 117.

(*e*) Anthropomorphic conception of A. (his body, his food and drink, his chariot and horses, his wives, children, &c.).

The bricks of the fire-altar are his limbs, 41, 156; has three heads and seven rays (or reins), 46, 167, 168; with many faces (the fires), 46, 103, 248, 280; whose face is turned everywhere, 46, 125; whose face shines with ghee, 46, 158, 221, 391; his face is bright and beautiful, 46, 157 sq., 302, 340; ghee is his eye, 46, 293; is kindled four-eyed, 46, 23, 29; looks round with a hundred eyes, 46, 137; thousand-eyed, 41, 409; 42, 402; 46, 104; with fiery, golden, strong jaws, 46, 33, 45, 157, 193, 303, 413; eats with his sharp jaws, he chews, he throws down the forests, 46, 157; spreading through the forests, shears the hair of the earth, 46, 54, 61, 129, 173; with sharp teeth, 46, 103, 335, 344, 360; the gold-toothed, 46, 366, 382; the tongues of A., 12, 74; 44, 189, 351; 46, 141, 144; has seven tongues, 43, 205; with the sweet or sharp tongue, 46, 52, 153, 308, 340, 344, 416, 418; with agreeable speech, 46, 352; is yellow-haired, 43, 105; the flames, his golden hair, 46, 42, 129, 148, 268, 275, 296, 385; golden-bearded, 46, 382; his beard shaven by Pûshan, 30, 217; whose back is covered with ghee, 46, 375, 397; called the dark-necked one, 44, 316 sq.; 46, 248; with ruddy limbs, 46, 148, 248; A. is gold-breasted, 32, 416; golden-coloured, 46, 232, 234 sq., 325, 366; gold his seed, 12, 322; 26, 54, 59, 63, 238, 390; 44, 187, 275 n., 462, 467; the milk of the cow is A.'s seed, 12, 326, 330; 26, 54;

feeding A. by kindling sticks, 41, 254–63; plants the food of A., 42, 42; 43, 335; A. is the eater of food, 1, 159; 12, 301, 323; 15, 314; 34, 116 sq.; 44, 63; food offered to A. the eater of food, 12, 303; food-gainer, 12, 127; drinking Soma, 46, 110, 128, 304; adorned with ghee, 46, 137; whose robe is ghee, 46, 275, 296; shoots with arrows, 46, 331; the red horses or flames of A., 32, 16, 19 sq., 24–7, 39; 46, 42, 141, 144, 167 sq., 202, 244 and 246 (seven-tongued), 308, 316, 340 sq., 379 sq.; the stallions of A., 32, 140; harnesses his steeds, 41, 399; the seven reins (or rays) of A., 46, 206–8; has a red or brown horse, 41, 257; 42, 422; *when thou hast yoked to thy chariot the two ruddy, red horses, whom the wind drives forward, and thy roaring is like that of a bull, then thou movest the trees with thy banner of smoke. A.! May we suffer no harm in thy friendship*, 46, 109, 149, 217; comes in a golden chariot, 46, 232, 233, 245, 269, 308, 348; his chariot is light, 46, 141; whose chariot is lightning, 46, 268; compared to a charioteer, 46, 160, 162, 193, 233, 292; is the quick chariot, 46, 261 sq.; wives of A., 46, 59, 141–5, 220, 225 sq.; his wife, the flame, 21, 372 n.; the lover of the dawn, 46, 67; the dawns, his divine consorts, 46, 336; beloved by Night and Dawn, 46, 74, 76; is the mate of the K*ri*ttikâs, 12, 283; is the mate of Vedi, 43, xvii, xvii n.; legend of A. courting the waters, 12, 277 sq., 277 n.; as a father begat the ruddy cows (dawns), 46, 220, 227; the germ of beings, the father of Daksha, 46, 296; produced Ekata, Dvita, and Trita, 42, 521; the kinsman or brother of the rivers, 46, 54.

(*f*) THERIOMORPHIC CONCEPTION OF A., AND HIS RELATIONS TO ANIMALS.

A. (fire-altar) is an animal, 41, 342, 361, 363, 399 sq.; 43, 40, 50, 78; identical with the animal victims, 41, 164–6; Pragâpati wishes to perform sacrifice with A. as the victim, 44, 128; rules over all animals, 42, 50; A. was an animal, and was sacrificed, and he gained that world wherein A. ruleth, 44, 319; the animal living in the water and walking in the forest, 46, 164; the beast, mows off deserts and habitable land like a mower, 46, 382, 387; shakes his horns, like a terrible beast, 46, 142; the buffalo hidden in the depth, 46, 147, 150; the strong bull, v*ri*shan, 32, 144, 146; 46, 137, 142, 147, 167, 244, 271, 308, 312 sq., 326, 335, 366 sq., 370, 393 sq. (red), 423; the bull with a thousand horns, 42, 105, 208 sq., 373; 46, 364; ox sacred to A., 12, 322; 44, 438; Nights and Dawns have been lowing for A., as for the calf, 46, 193; the young calf, which Night and Dawn suckle, 46, 114, 116, 119, 124, 167 sq.; compared to a horse, 12, 102 n., 109, 121; 46, 16, 57, 67, 91, 158, 176, 206 sq., 217, 220, 229, 285, 292, 296 sq., 302, 317, 344, 360, 363 (white racer); shaking his tongue among the plants he waves his tail like a horse, 46, 202; led forward by a great rope (like a horse), 46, 308, 312; is cleaned or groomed like a horse, 46, 360, 364; the horse is A., 41, 204, 212; the white horse, 26, 149; 41, 360; led forward by the horse, 41, 356 sq.; white horse led in front of Agni, 41, 359; a horse (sun) indicates A. at the Agni*k*ayana, 41, 207–12; the roaring snake, 46, 103, 105; the serpent with beautiful splendour, the winged (son?) of P*ri*sni, lights up both gods and men, 46, 193, 196; as a bird, 41, 157; 44, 435; 46, 119, 240, 242, 249; the embryonic A. fashioned into a bird, 41, 273–5; the divine eagle or the lightning, 42, 401; his flames are winged, 46, 331;—the ass sacred to A., 29, 366; rules over cattle, 26, 343, 343 n.; 41, 187; *see also above*, p. 13, A. Purîshya; is the cattle, 41, 196 sq., 198, 392; the gods collected A. from out of the cattle, 41, 230; worshipped at sacrifices for the thriving of cattle, 30, 89, 185 sq.; invoked to protect the footsteps of the cattle, 46, 61–3; implored for nourishment of the cow, 46, 222; accompanied by

three milch cows (oblations or dawns?), 46, 206, 208; has perforated, as it were, the pure udder of the cows, 46, 309; has found the cows (the waters, the sun), 46, 397 sq.

(g) HIS RELATIONS TO THE OTHER GODS IN GENERAL.

Conveys the sacrifice to the gods, 12, 102 sq. n., 113, 116 sq., 127, 322; 33, 255; 41, 398; 43, 124, 268; 46, 32, 42, 61, 83, 100, 135, 179, 222, 256, 283, 300, 302, 348, 397; the carrier (vahni) of oblations, 32, 37 sq.; 46, 37 sq., 52, 138, 228, 241, 259, 261, 296, 303, 346, 375, 379, 391, 416, 418, 423; the gods made him the carrier of offerings, 46, 261, 275, 385 sq.; the approacher of the gods, 43, 194; conveys the oblations addressed to the manes, 7, 84; brings the gods to the sacrifice, 12, 117 sq., 134, 203, 426 sq.; 26, 377; 43, 197 sq.; 46, 1, 6 sq., 8, 24, 37 sq., 42 sq., 92, 100, 108, 153, 179, 236, 241, 244, 249, 268, 279, 291, 316, 346, 364, 375, 377, 418; A. invoked to bring A. to the sacrifice, 12, 426 sq., 427 n.; 46, 38, 41; the helpful carrier of the gods, 46, 137, 240, 307; the messenger of gods and men, 12, 103 n., 110 sq., 121, 129; 26, 115; 30, 10, 110, 145; 42, 64, 113; 46, 6, 31, 37 sq., 52, 74, 83, 92, 179, 209, 215, 217, 232, 240, 244, 257, 261, 275, 308, 316, 343 sq., 346, 348, 372, 380, 385, 391, 412, 418; knows best the ascents to heaven, 46, 344, 346; the steward of the gods, 46, 202, 307; calls the gods to the feast, 12, 91; the best invoker of the gods, the dispenser of a thousand bounties, 44, 66; invoked to announce the song to the gods, 46, 16, 273; promulgates all the races of the gods, 42, 50, 308; knows the gods well, 12, 133; prepares the way that leads to the gods, 42, 184; legend of the gods who deposited their beasts with A., 12, 347; legend of the gods depositing all forms with A., 12, 314 sq., 314 n.; passed over from the gods to men, but not with his whole body, 12, 306; the gods have set him to work at the bottom of the air, 46, 193; the gods have established A. among men, 46, 202; the gods fashioned the opening sacrifice from out of A., 44, 138; is a worshipper of the gods, 46, 67, 232, 318; belongs to all the deities, 41, 375; 46, 173; the gods take food with A. as their mouth, 41, 312; 44, 350, 418; 46, 45, 95, 108, 188; together with all Agnis, with the gods, 46, 289; invoked together with other gods, 42, 80; through A. the gods have won glory and strength, 46, 89, 130; the A.-eyed gods in the east, 41, 48 sq.; leader of the gods in slaying Vritra, 12, 408 sq., 418, 449 sq.; has by fighting gained wide space for the gods, 46, 49; the gods did service to A., 46, 257; reigns among gods and among mortals, 46, 416; encompassed all the gods by his greatness, 46, 64; gods afraid of A. (Rudra), 43, 156 sq., 202; A. going in front of the gods is anointed with the song, 46, 180; *A. is the head, the progenitor of the gods, he is the lord of creatures*, 26, 218; the progenitor of deities, 12, 386; is the first of all gods, 7, 265; 42, 160; is the leader of the divine hosts, 26, 184; is god of the gods, 46, 109; the banner of the gods, 46, 17, 221; *A. is all the deities, since in A. one offers to all deities*, 41, 44; 12, 162 sq., 168; 26, 12, 90, 428; 41, 285; A. (fire-altar) is all beings, all the gods, 43, 388; is the self, the body of all the gods, 41, 369; 43, 256; 44, 505; is the out-breathing of the gods, 43, 295; identified, in turn, with all the gods, 46, 186–92; identified with Varuna, Mitra, the Visvedevâs, Indra, and Aryaman, 46, 371.

(h) A. AS RELATED TO INDIVIDUAL OTHER GODS.

A. and *Âditya*, *see below* A. *Vâyu*, Âditya, *and see* (i) Agni and the solar deities; A. and *Asvin*, *see* (i) A. and the solar deities; A. compared with *Bhaga*, 46, 281, 401; A. could not burn a straw put before him by *Brahman*, 1, 150; runs away from terror of Brahman, 15, 59; Brahman is A., 43, 85; is

the mouth of Brahman, 48, 289; fastened the amulet on, which *Bri̇haspati* tied, 42, 85; identified with the regions (*Disas*), 43, 70, 164 sq., 246, 263, 263 n.; A. incites *Dyaus* to commit incest with his daughter, 46, 74, 78; identified with *Dvita*, 46, 405 sq.; A. is the *Gandharva*, his Apsaras are the herbs, 30, 146 n.; 43, 231; joined with *Idâ*, 46, 375; A. and *Indra*, mutual relation between them, 12, xvi sq. n., 419; is speech, I. breath, 41, 154; I. the nobility, A. the priesthood, 43, 342, 344; the place of A., I., and the Visve Devâs at various sacrifices, 12, xviii sq. and n.; 'For me have A. and I. accomplished my divine aim,' 30, 179; sacrifice to A. and I. every month for one year after the child's birth, 30, 59; offerings to A. and I., as destroyers of demons, 42, 64; A., I., and Sûrya worshipped at the Shodasin, 26, 404-6; A. and I. drink the pressed Soma, 46, 285, 291; brought the Soma-drink to Indra, 42, 116, 241; finds Indra and stays with him, 12, 175 sq.; Dhâtri shaved the head of A. and I., 29, 185; I., Soma, and A., 26, 22; 42, 117, 122, 222; 44, 441; A., I., Sûrya, superior gods, 26, 402-4; kings appear as A., I., Soma, Yama, and the God of Riches, 33, 217 sq.; *see also under* Indra; *Kâma* and A. invoked together, 42, 221 sq., 359, 592; A. is *Ketâ*, 29, 348; invoked in company with the *Maruts*, 32, 53, 68 sq., 82, 94, 337, 339, 352-4, 369, 375, 386, 392 sq., 399; 46, 82, 84, 266, 292 sq.; A. and the Maruts invoked at the restoration of an exiled king, 42, 112, 328; produced the host of the seven *Ri*shis or of the Maruts (?), 46, 75, 80; compared with the Maruts, 46, 130, 138, 341; the Maruts the guardsmen, and A. the chamberlain of king Marutta, 44, 397; and *Mitra* (or 'friend'), 32, 82, 94; is great, and a friend, like Mitra, 46, 38, 46, 100, 158, 193, 202, 333, 341, 371, 389, 401; identified with Mitra, 46, 109, 112, 119, 240 sq.; and Mitra invoked together, 46, 387; A., Mitra, Varu*n*a, and the Maruts sing to A. a pleasant song, 46, 268; Sûrya, A., and *Pragâpati*, the deities of the Agnihotra, 29, 161, 161 n.; sacrifice to A. and Pragâpati, 33, 376; restores Pragâpati who had become relaxed, 41, 151-4, 168; is the right arm of Pragâpati, 43, xx; is the progenitor of the deities, he is Pragâpati, 12, 386; Pragâpati identified with A., 41, xxvii, 144, 148, 151, 153 sq., 165, 167-9, 172 sq., 174, 183, 240 sq., 245, 284, 290, 309, 313, 330, 341, 353, 377, 386; 43, xvii, xix-xxiii, 66; 44, xviii, 275 n.; A. (fire-altar) is Pragâpati, 43, 49, 54, 57, 70 sq., 92, 127, 159 sq., 181, 189 sq., 229, 234, 270, 300, 300 n., 309, 313-15, 321-7, 341, 345-7, 349-52, 362; *Prithivî* (Earth) with A. invoked in danger, 29, 232; oblations to Earth and A., 29, 321; if Apâna is satisfied, the tongue is satisfied, if the tongue is satisfied, A. and the earth are satisfied, 1, 90; terrestrial serpents belonging to A., 29, 328 sq.; is the lotus of this earth, 26, 277; A. is this earth, 41, 154 sq., 169, 183, 347, 364; *Pûshan* has shaven the beard of A., 30, 217; offering to A. and Pûshan, 41, 54 n., 55; *Rudra* and A., see (*d*) Names of A.; *Savit*ri brought A. above the earth, 15, 238; raises his arms like Savit*ri*, 46, 115; like Savit*ri* he has sent his light upward, 46, 340; is truthful like Savit*ri*, 46, 88; is Savit*ri*, 41, 191 sq.; Savit*ri* and A. invoked together, 42, 210; *Skanda*, son of A., 49 (i) 12; A. and *Soma*, offerings to A. and S. conjointly, 2, 299; 12, 43, 159-75, 202, 250, 364; 25, 90; 26, 106-8, 155-62; 29, 161, 390; 30, 254, 336; 41, 45, 54 n., 56, 69, 71; 44, 254, 350 n.; new and full moon offerings to A. and S., 12, 43, 236 sq., 375, 377-80, 377 n.; 29, 17 n., 392; 30, 37; 44, 3 n., 6, 16, 36 sq., 54; animal sacrifices for A. and S., 2, 68; 26, 82 sq., 162, 181-222, 225; 30, 346; 38, 274, 274 n.; 41, 68 sq.; 44, 141, 372 n., 404; 48, 598; A., S., and Vish*n*u are made parts of the thunderbolt, 26, 108, 108 n.; oblations to A.

and Vish*n*u, at the Da*s*apeya, 41, 113 sq., 116 n., 118; A. and S. invoked against sorcerers, 42, 65; for A. and S. the Brahmans beg the sterile cow, 42, 176; relation between A. and S., 26, xviii sq.; offering to A. first, then to S., 26, 386; what is dry relates to A., moist to S., 12, 169, 175; black related to S., white to A., 12, 175; the waters support A. and S., 42, 146 sq.; A. the day, S. the night, 26, 108; from out of A. and S. the gods formed the day of fasting, 44, 139; A. compared with Soma, 46, 360, 362; glory of Indra, A., and S., 26, 22; 42, 117, 122, 222; A. and *Sûrya*, *see* (i) A. and the solar deities; *Trita* blows upon A., 46, 387; A. and *Ushas*, *see* (i) A. and the solar deities; A. and *Vâk* (speech), 26, 365 n., 367 n.; having bestowed a share on A., he bestows lordship on speech, 43, 67; A. worshipped in connexion with *Varuna*, 26, 383; 46, 307; Varu*n*a, Soma, A., 42, 135; A. alone rules over gods like Varu*n*a, 46, 157; Varu*n*a, Mitra, A., 26, 285 sq.; 46, 236; through A., Varu*n*a, Mitra, and Aryaman are glorious, 46, 148; Varu*n*a identified with A., 43, 238 sq.; 46, 240; and the *Vasus*, *see above*, p. 14; A., *Vâyu*, and Indra are above the other gods, 1, 151; A. who sees, Vâyu who hears, Âditya who brings to light, 2, 114; A., Vâyu, and Âditya (or Sûrya), 1, 203; 15, 48 sq., 308; 30, 152 sq.; 43, 187; 44, 265, 291; A. divided himself into A., Vâyu, and Âditya, 15, 75; 41, 284; A. and the earth, Vâyu and the air, Âditya (Sûrya, sun) and the sky or heaven, 12, 325–7; 30, 231; 41, 204; 43, 90 sq.; 44, 27; A., Vâyu, and Âditya are all the light, 1, 54; 41, 210, 239; 43, 388 sq.; 44, 102, 508; A., Vâyu, and Âditya are the hearts of the gods, 43, 162; light is A., might Vâyu, glory Âditya, 44, 173; A., Vâyu, Âditya, and *K*andramas identified with the four fires, 44, 127; A. is Vâyu, 43, 363; A. is *Virâg*, 43, 360; is Virâg, is the regions, is the vital airs, 43, 70, 164 sq.; A. and *Vishnu* are the two halves of the sacrifice, 26, 12; offerings to A. and Vish*n*u, 12, 7; 26, 12 sq.; 29, 18 n.; 41, 44 sq., 54 sq., 54 n., 247 sq.; 44, 140; Vish*n*u and A. identified, 41, 276; A. is *Visvakarman*, 43, 189 sq., 204, 266–8, 266 n.; invoked with Vi*s*vakarman, 44, 202 sq.; A. (the funeral pyre) the guide to *Yama's* seat, 42, 90; A. is death, 12, 324; 38, 267; 43, 365.

(*i*) A. AND THE SOLAR DEITIES (ÂDITYA, SÛRYA, USHAS, THE A*S*VINS).

The Sun appeared when A. had been born, 46, 326, 330; the Red one, the rising sun, 32, 21–3; A. is the sun (Âditya, Sûrya), 15, 46; 41, 216 sq., 222 sq., 226, 231, 271, 273, 275, 304 sq., 308 sq., 309 n., 364, 400, 404; 42, 208–11, 213, 661, 664; 43, 195, 349, 363; 46, 49, 116, 167 sq., 193; *see also above* A. Vai*s*vânara (p. 13); A. is the piece of gold shining between heaven and earth, 46, 119, 124; is placed on the highest skin (the sky?), 46, 164, 166; is like the sun, 46, 67, 173, 176, 194, 213, 230, 268, 350, 418; established in the sun, 43, 239 sq.; 46, 70; is sun-rayed, 43, 105; A.'s breath taken by the sun, whence fire does not blaze, unless fanned, 44, 130; is the light, when the sun goes down, 12, 335; the light of men, 12, 361; 43, 117; is all the light in this world, 41, 384 sq.; by kindling A. men make the sun rise, 46, 379, 381, 403 sq.; discovered the light, 46, 293; has found the sun, 46, 119, 233, 292, 397 sq.; the sun, the day, and the waxing half-moon relate to A., 12, 169; the sight of A. and the sun, i.e. this life, 42, 53; is heat and light, to him offering is made in Âditya, at the Agnihotra, 44, 112 sq.; A. united with A., Savit*ri*, Sûrya, 44, 469 sq.; by means of A. and Âditya the sacrificer ascends to heaven, 44, 473; the eye of Sûrya, the eyeball of A., 26, 77; Sûrya, the eye of Mitra, Varu*n*a, and A., 26, 343; 41, 408; A., Sûrya, the waters, and all

the gods, 42, 205; the brilliancy of A. and Sûrya transferred upon a king, 42, 116; A. and the man in the sun are not equal, 38, 267; one half of the year (when the sun moves northward) belongs to A., 15, 316; A. on this side, and the sun on the other side of the world, 44, 405; hymns addressed to A. in his matutinal character, together with Ushas, the Asvins, and Sûrya, 46, 37–9, 42–4, 281, 356–9; awakens at dawn, 46, 131, 230, 240, 341; reigns by night and at the break of dawn, 46, 103; is the splendour of the dawn, he makes the dawns shine, being kindled in the morning, 46, 108, 194, 244, 271, 363, 423; praised and kindled in the evening and at dawn, 46, 213, 307, 354; deity of the eastern region, 26, 50; 41, 206, 291; 42, 192; 43, 3 sq. and n., 105, 199, 337; the K*ri*ttikâs (in the east) and the month Kârttika sacred to A., 7, 265; 12, 282 sq.

(*j*) A. AS DESTROYER OF DEMONS AND ALL HOSTILE POWERS.

A. is the repeller of the Rakshas, 12, 35 sq., 46, 157 sq., 365; 26, 99, 158, 187, 380 sq.; 41, 52, 371 sq. n.; 42, 64 sq., 402; 44, 464, 497; 46, 49, 102, 346, 367 sq., 397; invoked as Rakshohan, for protection against sorcerers, demons, and evil, 42, 35 sq., 40, 64 sq., 77, 190, 408, 475; spells and wicked men, 46, 32 sq., 96, 103, 109, 125, 138, 170, 181, 233, 271, 273, 277, 289, 326 sq., 331–4, 352, 372, 375, 383; has encompassed the demons, 30, 212; invoked against the demons harassing children, 30, 212; with A. the gods conquered the demons (Asuras), 12, 54 sq., 57; 42, 180; 46, 303; gainer of battles, helps against spells, 42, 78, 180; is removed from the demon of hostility, 42, 51, 365; invoked to drive away fever, 42, 1, 443; takman (fever) comes, as it were, from A., 42, 3; drives away sickness, 46, 6; the destroyer of darkness, 46, 141; removes the poison of snakes, 42, 154; the destroyer of enemies or of V*ri*tra, 46, 49, 51, 92, 102, 281; the conqueror of deceitful foes, 46, 129, 360; the repeller of shafts, 43, 100; devours the hateful enemies, thieves and robbers, 41, 259; invoked against rivals and enemies, 42, 210 sq., 221 sq.; removes sins and their consequences, 42, 163–5, 167, 525; 46, 181; drives away all evils, 12, 345; 41, 229, 360; 43, 84 sq.; burnt up the evil of the gods, 41, 259; is the remedy for cold, 44, 315.

(*k*) EXCELLENT QUALITIES AND TRANSCENDENT POWERS OF A.

A. is a sage, 12, 91; 44, 189, 192, 194; 46, 22 sq., 75, 103, &c.; is skilful, thoughtful, 46, 269, 391; the omniscient, 46, 303, 375; the great seer, the best *Ri*shi, 46, 114 sq., 118, 283; compared to a *Ri*shi, 46, 57; a singer, 46, 271; a good guide, 46, 317; is the guide of Brâhma*n*as, 42, 170; is the eye of gods and men, 43, 199 sq.; knows the birth of gods and men, 46, 70; is immortal, 12, 261; 42, 57; 43, 296; 46, 37 sq., 70, 100, 217, 232, 269, 281, &c.; alone was immortal, when the gods were still mortal, 12, 310; gods laid immortality into A., 43, 156, 177 sq., 256; the gods made him the navel of immortality, 46, 275; the mortals have generated the immortal A., 46, 303; has a knowledge of immortality, 42, 60; reigns over immortality, 46, 423; is busy for the sake of immortality, 46, 291; the drink of immortality is in his mouth, 46, 293; is imperishable and inexhaustible, 30, 231; 41, 284; is long-lived through the trees, 29, 294; never grows old, 46, 131, 167; in whom all life dwells, 46, 138; endowed with hundredfold life, 46, 176; the ancient one, 46, 268 sq., 281; having grown old he has suddenly become young again, 46, 202; the youngest god, 12, 102 n., 108, 108 n., 120, 204; 41, 257 sq., 284, 296, 413; 43, 204; 46, 31, 33, 37, 147 sq., 170, 181, 211, 256, 279, 300, 317, 331 sq., 354, 364, 372, 385, 418, 420; the young child, 1, 141, 142, 145, 164; is like a beautiful youth, 46, 217; is ever-young, a youthful sage, 43, 276;

44, 189; 46, 13, 23, 363; is lord of all powers, 46, 114 sq.; is self-dependent, 46, 281, 350, 354, 371; possesses mysterious power, 46, 389; is the lord and increaser of strength, 46, 164, 259, 380; the baby quail, by the mystic Act of Truth, drives back the great A., 35, 180 n., 185 n.

(*l*) A. AS A KIND AND HELPFUL GOD.

A guardian and a father, 44, 439; 46, 23 sq.; leads one over the paths, 44, 438; is like a beloved wife, 46, 88; the good abode is A., for A. abides with all creatures in this world, 44, 457; is the friend of men, 32, 82, 94; 44, 189; 46, 95; the safest and nearest of the gods, 12, 163; is the lowest god, i.e. nearest to men, 46, 307, 311; looks on all creatures, since he has been born, 46, 137; gives health and wealth, 12, 236; 26, 241; 32, 194; 46, 379; strength, beauty, and wealth dwell in A., 46, 188; winner of horses, giver of wealth, 46, 209; invoked for the treasure of Dyaus or Heaven, 46, 308 sq.; lord of treasures, 44, 192; 46, 49, 52, 70, 82, 215, 375; addressed as food on which everything lives, 46, 37, 40; every nourishment goes towards A., 46, 75; all-enlivener, 46, 281; is all-wealthy, 46, 157, 170; is a bountiful Lord (maghavan), 46, 131, 167, 187; is like the udder of the cows, and the sweetness of food, 46, 67 sq.; called 'the well-harnessed wealth,' 46, 89, 91; gives wealth, long life, offspring, victory, and booty in battle to those who praise him, 46, 22 sq., 31 sq., 37, 45 sq., &c.; a healer, creator of medicine, 30, 143, 145; the god who gives rain, 46, 292, 302.

(*m*) A. THE GOD OF THE HOUSE AND THE CLAN.

The householder or lord of the house (g*ri*hapati), 42, 183; 44, 189; 46, 31, 52, 64, 130, 176, 352, 385, 413; *see also above* A. G*ri*hapati (p. 13); worshipped in the house, 46, 88; the guest of the clans, or of the house, 41, 281, 290, 292; 46, 137, 202, 228, 233, 292, 309 sq., 364, 371, 375, 385, 405; the house-lord of this world, 26, 453 n.; worshipped at the house-building, 29, 347; worshipped on entering a new house, 29, 95 sq.; 42, 141; worshipped on returning home from a journey, 29, 97; protects the house, 12, 358 sq.; invoked to protect the house from fire, 42, 147; prayer to A., at the removal of a house, 42, 194-6, 600; a friend of the house (damûnas), 46, 67, 142, 221, 229 sq., 233, 240, 332, 352, 364, 375, 385; is in every house, 46, 343; the lord of the human clans, 46, 13, 52, 130, 187, 233, 363, 375, 379, 387; is the shepherd of the clans, 46, 108, 119; belongs to many people, dwells among all the clans, 46, 31, 54, 67, 102, 104, 173, 229 sq., 261, 379, 397, 414; the king or leader of the human tribes, 46, 49, 194, 244, 259; protects all settlements, 46, 88.

(*n*) A. AS CONNECTED WITH WOMEN AND MARRIAGE.

Women belong to A., 14, 133; gave women purity of all limbs, 14, 233; the wife-leader, 26, 367, 367 n.; the third husband of the bride, 29, 278 sq.; 30, 190; 42, 254, 323; the lover of maidens, the husband of wives, 46, 57, 59; the girls sacrifice to A., 29, 44, 282; gives the bride to the husband, 29, 283; at the marriage of Soma and Sûryâ, 26, xiv; 29, 283; prayers and offerings to A. at marriage rites, 2, 305; 29, 27, 32, 168 sq.; 30, 49, 187 sq., 190; unites husband and wife, 46, 371; invoked for the protection of the bride, 29, 41, 44, 281 sq., 288; invoked by a maiden for a husband, 42, 94, 323; invoked in a love-charm, 42, 104; invoked to cause the return of a truant woman, 42, 106; the blood of the woman is a form of A., 1, 232; dwells in the menstrual discharge of a maiden, 33, 171 n.; is the causer of sexual union, the progenitor, 26, 98; 29, 27; men worship A., together with their wives, 46, 82; identified with the sacrificer's wife, 46, 348; with the wives of the gods, 26, 365 n.; invoked for off-

spring, 14, 84; 29, 43; 46, 222; protects the offspring, 12, 358 sq.; is both offspring and lord of offspring, 43, 181; invoked for the new-born child, 29, 52, 54, 294; 30, 59, 213, 215 sq.; invoked for a child born under an unlucky star, 42, 109 sq.; 'A man is A.,' Pu*m*savana prayer, 30, 54; invoked to promote virility, 42, 32.

(*o*) A. AS THE SACRIFICIAL FIRE AND THE FIRE-ALTAR.

Is the sacrificial fire, 15, 77; 44, xxi sq., 248; 46, 13, 22, 24, 31–3, 45, &c.; all sacrifices performed in A., 26, 389; 41, 312; material for sacrifice, A.'s body, 12, 26; putting firewood on is regaling A. with food, 43, 189, 191; 44, 268; the eater of oblations, 43, 398; taking his seat in ghr*i*ta, 46, 399; swims in ghr*i*ta, 46, 418; ghee is sacred to A., 43, 189; is the vessel in which offerings are made to the gods, 12, 117; A. seen at the sacrificial place, 41, 207; sits on the Vedi or the sacrificial bed, 46, 141; has always sacrificial straw spread for him, 43, 122; grown strong on the Dhish*n*ya altars, 46, 325, 328; has come to sit down on the sacrificial grass, 46, 348; A. Ukhya (the fire in the pan), 43, 24; in the fire-pan driven about at the Agni*k*ayana, 41, 289–93; the Ukhya Agni as an embryo, 43, 272 sq.; installation and consecration of A., 43, 207–41, 246 sq., 251 sq.; the Vasor dhârâ the Abhisheka of A., 43, 213–15, 213 sq. n., 219 sq., 224 sq.; as the fire-altar, 38, 260–8; 41, 144, &c.; 43, xix–xxiv, 1, &c.; leading forward of A. to the fire-altar, 43, 188–207; the lump of clay representing A., 41, 203–29; the Agni*k*it (builder of fire-altar) becomes A., 43, 296; prayers for prosperity to A. (fire-altar), 43, 108 sq.; doctrines of mystic imports regarding A. (fire-altar), 43, 363–6; A. (fire-altar) identified with Arka (plant and 'light'), 43, 336, 342, 346–9, 398 sq., 404; bricks of the fire-altar, different Agnis, 43, 128, 130, 222, 222 n.; A. (fire-altar) consists of three bricks, viz. *Rik*, Yagus, Sâman, 43, 374; A. (fire-altar), Arkya, and Mahad uktham (great litany), a triad, 44, 172; A. (fire-altar) is the year, 41, 167, 169, 183–5, 198, 206, 220, 232, 244, 250, 254, 260, 269, 271 sq., 293, 295, 307, 330, 333, 335–9, 355, 358, 372, 386; 43, 29 sq., 49, 163, 166 sq., 177, 184, 193, 204 sq., 207, 216, 219–22, 219 n., 240, 253 sq., 271, 281, 294, 320 sq., 323 sq., 349–52, 357–60, 362–4, 386; *see also* A. Vai*s*vânara above, p. 13 sq.; carried about by the sacrificer for a whole year, 43, xix, xxiii; names of the months as manifestations of A. (the year), 43, 219, 219 n.; A. (fire-altar) is all objects of desire, 43, 313. *See also* Fire-altar.

(*p*) MEN (OR DEMI-GODS) AND FAMILIES WHO FIRST ESTABLISHED A.

Established by different families of priests, 46, 52 sq.; and the *Ańgiras*, 26, 113 sq.; 46, 391; sacrificed for Ańgiras, 46, 24; was praised by Ańgiras, 46, 102; kindled by *Apnavâna*, 46, 343; the guest in the clans of *Âyu*, 46, 194, 202; the praise of Âyu, 46, 341, 371; the Âyus have brought him to every house, 46, 52, 343; among the *Bharadvâgas*, 46, 50; placed among men by the *Bhrigus*, 46, 45, 157, 343; the Bhr*i*gus, worshipping him in the abode of the waters, have established him among the clans of Âyu, 46, 202; established by *Manus*, 46, 230, 256, 275, 287 sq., 412; inflamed by Manus in the abode of *Id*, 46, 217; the Purohita of Manus, 46, 232; was born in Manu's firm law, 46, 137; kindled by gods, Manu, *Ri*shis, 12, 116; *being born in the highest heaven A. became visible to Mâtarisvan. By the power of his mind, by his greatness when kindled, his flame filled Heaven and Earth with light,* 46, 157; Mâtari*s*van produced A. by attrition, 46, 74, 147, 173; Mâtari*s*van brought A. to Bhr*i*gu and Manu, 46, 52, 137; became manifest to Mâtari*s*van, 46, 22, 256; the clan-lord of the *Nahusha*, 46, 23; in the homestead of *Purunîtha* Sâtavaneya, 46, 50; whom the *Pûrus* worship, 46, 49; the *Usigs* have set him down

as Hot*ri*, 46, 52 sq., 341, 371; kindled by mortals and by the *Vasus*, 46, 372; the messenger of *Vivasvat*, 46, 22, 45, 47, 391 sq.

(*q*) A. AS A PRIEST, AND HIS RELATIONS TO THE PRIESTHOOD.

A., the priest, 32, 38; 41, 281 (seated on the altar); 42, 50, 109 sq.; 43, 277; 44, xxi sq., 189, 192, 194; 46, 164, 178, 237 (slaughterer), 240, 259 (*ri*tvig), 266, 283, 292, 302, 346; his priestly power, 42, 221; the Hot*ri* priest, 12, 47, 102 sq. n., 108, 111, 129, 138 sq., 203 sq., 250 sq., 427; 15, 122; 26, 114, 118, 377; 29, 194 sq.; 41, 219, 255, 399; 46, 1, 6, 8, 22, 31, &c., 206, 215 (on the Hot*ri*'s seat), 236, 238 (has sat down at heaven's navel), 275 sq., 325 (the Hot*ri* of the two worlds), 340 sq., 363 sq.; legend of the gods choosing A. for their Hot*ri* priest, 12, 87-9; Pravara, choosing A. the Divine Hot*ri*, 12, 114-20, 114 n., 132-5; crosses the sacrificial seat of the worshipper like a Hot*ri*, 46, 88; the god of the seven Hot*ri*s, 46, 303, 343 sq.; Hot*ri* invokes the help of A. for his work, 12, 135; Hot*ri* relates to A., 44, 136, 314; the Purohita of the gods, 42, 79; 46, 1, 38, 41, 45, 137, 228 sq., 261, 391, 401 sq.; the best sacrificer, 12, 111; 46, 100, 119, 129, 137, 176, 194, 215, 236, 259, 266, 268, &c.; A. offers to A., 34, 215; A. is kindled by A., 44, 189; a performer of worship, like Soma, 46, 54; invoked to make the offerings ready, 46, 154, 180; invoked to sacrifice for men to the gods, 46, 95, 96, 100, 108, 198, 209, 215, 221, 228, 236 sq., 259, 268, 275, 279, 291, 303 sq., 395, 412, 418, 423; mixes the honey drink, 46, 218; knows the art of sacrificing and is a separator of sacrificial fires that have become mixed, 46, 385 sq.; offices of the seven priests ascribed to A., 46, 186, 189, 348; the Âgnîdhra is A., 12, 229; 26, 368; knows the duties of every priest, 46, 108 sq.; dismissed at the end of sacrifice, 26, 377; received gold as Dakshi*n*â, 26, 347 sq.; flame of A., his sacrificial ladle, 46, 96, 99; may burn a priest passing between the hearths, 26, 153; the priests make him grow, 46, 395; is the Brahman (priesthood), 12, xvi-xviii, 90, 114 sq., 134; 26, 37 sq.; 41, 89; 43, 342, 344; is both priesthood and nobility, 43, 235; A. is a Brâhma*n*a, 2, 13 n.; 12, 114 sq.; 14, 138; to A. belongs the Brâhma*n*a, 29, 307; 44, 89.

(*r*) A. IN HIS RELATION TO THE SACRIFICE AND THE SACRIFICER.

Protects the offering, 12, 19; 46, 137; the beacon or banner of sacrifice, 46, 52, 119, 130, 232, 259, 261, 302, 391; the first at the sacrifices, 46, 100, 410; the king of sacrifice, 12, 354; 46, 325; the promoter or guide of sacrifice, 44, 351; 46, 137, 164, 266, 287; is achiever and father of sacrifices, 46, 206, 232; friend or kinsman of sacrifices, 46, 244, 308; goes thrice round the sacrifice, 46, 340, 360; produces joy at all sacrifices, 46, 343; comes eagerly to the sacrifice, 46, 92; 48, 331; is the sacrifice, 26, 37 sq.; 41, 45; what is dry in the sacrifice, is of A.'s nature, 26, 49; the fire-wood purified for A. by sprinkling water on it, 12, 84; the Brahman's portion does not injure A., 12, 213; is allowed a share in every offering, 12, 364; anointed with sacrificial gifts, 46, 115; worshipped with hottest kindling-sticks, 46, 129; invoked as personified in each log of fuel put on the sacrificial fire, 46, 236, 238; is to be magnified at the sacrifices, 46, 343; they walk around A., like obedient servants, 46, 131; *to A. belongs this sacrifice. A. is the light, the burner of evil: he burns away the evil of this (sacrificer); and the latter becomes a light of prosperity and glory in this, and a light of bliss in yonder, world*, 12, 315; man maintains A. in this world, A. will maintain him in yonder world, 12, 342 sq.; the sacrificer reaches the world of A., 12, 450; 42, 189; by means of A. (fire-altar), the sacrificer ascends the heavenly world, 43, 198-200; 44, 205, 473; A. is the sacrificer, 43, xxiii, 146 sq., 186, 197, 201, 253, 262, 300, 300 n., 309, 313-15, 321-7, 341; 44, 142;

46, 348; the woof of the Dîkshita's cloth belongs to A., 26, 9; the Dîkshita gives himself up to A. for protection when he lies down to sleep, 26, 44 sq.; solicits from the gods the sacrificer's desire, 12, 253; the sacrificer makes A. his father, brother, son, and friend, 46, 187, 372–4.

(*s*) Sacrifices to A.

Burnt-oblations (cake and butter offerings) to A., 2, 202, 299; 12, 118, 150, 234–6, 386, 401 sq., 406 sq. n., 411, 413, 418; 14, 303, 307; 15, 211; 26, 364 n., 389 sq., 389 n.; 29, 27; 30, 34 sq., 143–5, 336 sq.; 41, 50–2, 250; 44, 29, 36 sq., 41; 48, 144, 155; nourished by offerings of butter or ghee, 46, 3, 199, 386, &c.; Sthâlîpâka offered to A., 14, 306; 30, 264–6; evening oblation for A., 29, 19, 172, 287, 386; 30, 20; morning and evening oblations to A., 30, 196; worshipped at the Vaisvadeva sacrifice, 29, 84; worshipped at the Tarpana, 29, 121, 149; 30, 243; offering to A. at the Sûlagava, 29, 352; Âgya oblation to A. as expiation, 30, 51; oblation to A. at the Sarpabali, 30, 91; the godânakarman sacred to A., 30, 218, 284; oblation to A., to avert an evil omen, 42, 166; worshipped at the new and full moon sacrifices, 12, 375, 377 sq., 377 n., 380; 29, 17 n., 392; 30, 37, 196; 44, 3 n., 54; the Ashtakâ sacred to A., 29, 200; 30, 97; funeral oblations to A., 7, 84; 14, 268; 25, 114; 29, 103, 242; 30, 113; 32, 35 sq.; *see also* A. Kavyavâhana *above*, p. 13; animal sacrifices for A., 26, 218, 221 sq., 312, 428 sq.; 41, 11 sq.; 44, 377, 383 n., 395, 402; the animal slain for the reception of a teacher as a guest is sacred to A., 29, 88; he-goat sacrificed for A., 41, 162; 44, xxv, 299; worshipped by offerings of ghrita, cows and bulls, 46, 211; the first offerings made to A. along with the Seasons, 12, 156 sq.; oblation to A. at the seasonal sacrifices, 44, 74 n., 75; Agnyâdhâna sacrifices for A., 12, 317–22; Agnihotra libation to A., 12, 327, 334–7; 44, 81; deity of a Ritu-graha, 26, 320 n.; Pârtha oblation to A., 41, 82; offering to A., the lord of rites, 41, 112; offering to A. at the Dasapeya, 41, 120–2, 125; invoked at a Soma sacrifice, 42, 179 sq., 182, 184, 188; 44, 142, 208, 443; prayer and oblations to A. at the three savanas, 46, 300 sq.; offerings to A. at the horse sacrifice, 44, 280, 318, 337 n., 350; Agnishtut Agnishtoma is A., 44, 418; rite of consecration for A., 42, 669; one of the gods worshipped at the Mitravindâ sacrifice, 44, 62–6; worshipped at the Sautrâmanî, 44, 233; offerings to A. made by ascetics, 49 (i), 72; better is homage paid to the righteous than worship of A., 10 (i), 32; compared with the Fire (Âtar) worshipped by the Zoroastrians, 4, lii; 31, 80.

(*t*) Prayers to A., and A. as related to prayers (and metres).

Prayers to A., 12, 301, 349–54, 356–60; 14, 216, 251, 318; 26, 21–3, 49, 92, 203, 203 n.; 29, 23; 41, 168 sq.; 43, 141 sq.; prayers and hymns to A., vol. 46; consecratory formula addressed to A., 12, 231 sq.; morning prayer to A., 26, 229 sq. n., 231; 44, 378; praised and invoked, 26, 73, 110, 158 sq., 161, 196, 205, 326 sq. n., 343, 376; 41, 211–13, 219 sq., 256–9, 272 sq., 279, 281 sq., 285 n., 349–51, 358, 398 sq., 404–7; 42, 134; 43, 123 sq., 172 sq., 176 sq., 190, 199, 203 sq., 250 sq., 262, 268, 291; 44, 230, 432; invoked for protection, 12, 261; 29, 247, 280; invoked for long life, 42, 49–53, 60, 552; invoked for lustre, offspring, and life, 42, 231; 44, 238, 267; invoked to release from madness, 42, 32; invoked for success in trade, 30, 178; 42, 148 sq., 353; invoked for the king, 41, 89, 94, 101 sq.; 42, 116; invoked for gain (at gambling), 42, 151; invoked for food, 44, 63; invoked for wealth and affluence, 44, 65; invoked in the hour of death, 1, 313 sq., 313 n.; invoked to unite the deceased with his ancestors, 7, 86 n.; invoked to lead the dead by a good path, 15, 200; invoked at

expiatory rite, 30, 197; 44, 505; invoked at the sprinkling of water, 12, 22; 30, 226; invoked in the Sâmidhenî verses, 12, 102 sq. n., 103–13, 120 sq.; prayers to A. at the setting up of the sacred fire, 30, 201–3; prayer to A., when the fire goes out, 29, 134; invoked at domestic sacrificial rites, 29, 27, 29, 174 sq., 201, 207; invoked at the Vâgapeya, 41, 38; daily worship of A., 42, 149; addressed at the ordeal by fire, 33, 108 n., 109 sq., 255; the priest propitiates A. and the gods, 12, 134 sq.; accomplishes all blessings invoked by the priest on the sacrificer, 26, 184; identified with the front part of the war-chariot in a battle-charm, 42, 120; gazing reverently at A.'s light, 41, 193; worshipped by King *S*uddhodana, 49 (i), 22; lord of prayer (Brahma*n*aspati), 32, 82, 94; accepts the hymn even of the poor sacrificer, 46, 23; carried by prayers as by a vehicle, 46, 130; has been produced or strengthened by prayer, 46, 160, 240, 296, 304, 413; him the pious seek to win by their prayers as the first of the gods, 46, 352; is the voice of praise while heaven and earth listen, 12, 249; deviser of brilliant speech, 46, 215; invoked to make the prayers prosper, 46, 266, 303, 335; wise thoughts for prayers come from A., 46, 352; Gâyatrî, the metre of A., 12, 96, 96 n., 297, 307, 355; 44, 106; the Gâyatrî is A., 26, 87; 43, 178; is of Gâyatra nature, 41, 148, 161, 167, 196, 232, 324, 358, 374; 43, 120, 243, 247, 268, 277, 300, 385; metres in relation to A. (fire-altar), 43, 328–31.

(*u*) A. AS CONNECTED WITH VEDA AND VEDA-STUDY.

The *Rik* verses squeezed out from A., 1, 70; 44, 102; *Rik*as connected with A., 30, 152 sq.; worshipped at the end of the Svâdhyâya, 29, 219; the *Ri*shi of a Kâ*n*da, 30, 242; he who has studied the Veda is like A., 41, 146; has discovered the Sâman for man, 46, 335, 337; invoked at the Upanayana, 29, 189 sq.; 30, 149, 151, 153, 155–61; is the teacher of the initiated student, 29, 188, 306; 30, 151; the Brahma*k*ârin given in charge of A., 29, 64, 79; 30, 154; 44, 86; prayer to A. at the Samâvartana, 29, 313; invoked by the teacher, 2, 114; the Brahma*k*ârin worships A., 29, 66, 75 sq., 83, 307 sq.; offering to A. by the student who broke his vow, 25, 454 sq.; invoked by the student doing penance, 29, 362; the organs, &c., of an unchaste student go to A., 2, 294, 294 n.; is the Lord of Vows, 12, 3; 26, 45, 99, 161; 30, 64, 156, 162; 42, 18; *see also above*, p. 14, A. Vratapati; the vow belonging to A., 29, 229.

(*v*) A. IN HIS MORAL CHARACTER.

A. and *Ri*ta, 46, 103, 160–2, 164, 228, 240, 372, 382, 385, 393 sq.; the guardian of *Ri*ta, 46, 1, 259, 282, 325; kindled on behalf of the *Ri*ta, and born from the *Ri*ta, 46, 32 sq., 54, 161, 181, 220, 281; penetrated by *Ri*ta, 46, 70; the charioteer of *Ri*ta, 46, 158, 229, 350; in the abode of *Ri*ta, 46, 248, 412; is the divine upholder, 43, 194; is the truth, 41, 226, 281; is true and righteous (*Ri*ta-vat), 46, 88, 100, 164, 292, 340, 343, 350, 363; the laws (vrata) of A., 46, 22, 23, 67, 206, 244; administers the law of the gods, 46, 22, 31; immortal A. honours the gods and has never violated the laws, 46, 232; lord of high laws, 46, 42; understands the divine laws and the birth of the human race, 46, 70, 181, 240; has proclaimed his rules to the mortals, 46, 164; his law is not set at naught, 46, 213, 215; the purifier, 46, 6, 8, 52, 115, 211, 228, 241, 257, 259, 261, 275, 296, 335, 341, 343, 375, 382, 414, 418; invoked to purify defiled food, and all sin, 15, 312; invoked to forgive sin, 44, 265; 46, 249, 354; announces the sins of men to the gods, 46, 325 sq.; sins confessed to A., 46, 372; he infringes upon A., who does not give the sterile cow to the Brahmans, 42, 177; leads forward the man who follows crooked ways, 46, 22, 26.

(*w*) A. A SUPREME GOD OF HEAVEN AND EARTH.

The begetter of the two worlds, 46, 119, 244; has procreated the Sky and the Waters, 46, 119; has adorned the sky with stars, 46, 64; has caused the sky to roar, 46, 22; is like the heaven with the stars, 46, 343; the banner and head of heaven, 44, 351; 46, 230; knows the Heaven, 46, 326; has filled with his light all the lights of Heaven, 46, 167; determines the seasons, 46, 114, 116, 281; reigns over heaven and earth, 46, 160 sq., 188, 193 sq., 271; has filled Heaven and Earth and the great Sun, 46, 229, 244; supports earth and sky by his efficacious spells, 46, 61, 241; puts down his feet on the surface of the wide earth, 46, 167; moves in one moment round the terrestrial space, 46, 137, 229; encompasses the earth like heaven, 46, 129; is over-lord of this earth, 41, 385; 43, 228; nothing greater than A. (fire-altar), 43, 163; by his songs fashioned the mountains, 42, 213; through A. everything exists, 43, 4; makes the herbs on the earth ripe and sweet, 1, 211; all food belongs to A., 43, 296; the maker who victoriously stands over all beings, 46, 273; the supporter of everything, 46, 309; has revealed the nights and what stands and moves, 46, 64.

(*x*) A. IN PHILOSOPHICAL SPECULATIONS.

A. as speech, eye, mind, ear, breath, 43, 331–3; identified with speech, 15, 80; 25, 512; 26, 39; 41, 154; 43, 208, 363; having become speech, entered into the mouth, 38, 91 sq.; 48, 417; speech enters into A., at the time of death, 38, 105 sq.; is the deity in the zenith, and abides in speech, 15, 148; is Prâ*n*a, the breath, 15, 275; 43, 274, 349; identified with the vital airs, 43, 246; unites breaths, 42, 51, 366; the Prâ*n*as guided by A. and other divine beings, 48, 576; made up by the *Ri*shis, the vital airs, 43, 122; guardian of the eye, 12, 244, 260; in the dark iris of the eye, 15, 106; identified with Purusha, 25, 512; 44, 259 n.; Highest Person, the inner ruler of A., 48, 155; only a manifestation of the highest Brahman, 15, 302–3; A. explains to Satyakâma one foot of Brahman, 1, 61 sq.; is one foot of Brahman, 1, 54; *there is A.* (*fire*), *the all-seeing, hidden in the two fire-sticks, well guarded like a child* (*in the womb*) *by the mother, day after day to be adored by men when they awake and bring oblations. This is that* (*the Self*), 15, 16; is the highest Self, 34, 150; 41, 270; 48, 292; the emancipated sage is identical with A., 8, 220, 345; is this world, 12, 259; A. (fire-altar) is these three worlds, 43, 169, 171 sq., 187, 235; is sap and substance in this world, 41, 278; that (heavenly) world is A., 48, 289; *see above*, p. 13 sq., A. Vais*v*ânara. *See also* Fire.

Agnibhûti, n. of a *G*aina monk, 22, 286.

Agnidatta, n.p., disciple of Bhadrabâhu, 22, 289. *See also* Kâ*s*yapa.

Agnîdh, Âgnîdhra, *see* Priests (*a*, *b*).

Âgnîdhra (n.), fire-shed. *See* Fire (*e*).

Agnihotra, *see* Fire (*f*).

Agni*k*ayana, t.t., construction of the sacred brick-altar, an important preliminary to the Soma-sacrifice, 44, xiii. *See* Fire-altar.

Agni*k*it, builder of Fire-altar. *See* Fire-altar.

Agni*k*ityâ, t.t., the building of the fire-altar. *See* Fire-altar.

Agnirahasya, t.t., (*a*) 'the mystery of the fire-altars,' a text of the Vâgasaneyins, 34, lxxiv; 38, 214, 216, 260; 48, 641; the *Sând*ilya-vidyâ part of the A., 38, 214, 216; 48, 641. (*b*) 'The mystery of the fire-altar,' in the *S*atapatha, 43, 281–404; 44, xiv.

Agnisava, a certain sacrifice, 43, 298, 298 n.

Agnîshomau, *see* Agni (*b*) A. and Soma.

Agnîshomîya, t.t., animal sacrifices to Agni and Soma. *See* Animal Sacrifices.

Agnish*t*oma, t.t., 'praise of Agni,' a certain Soma-sacrifice, and the chant connected with it. *See* Prayers (*c*), *and* Sacrifices (*j*).

Agnishtoma-sâman, *see* Prayers (*c*).

Agnishvâttas, t.t., the manes of the gods, 25, 112.

Agnivaisyâyana, *see* Agnivesyâyana.

Âgnivesya, n. of a teacher, 15, 118, 118 n., 186, 186 n.

Âgnivesyâyana, n. of a teacher, 1, 267.

Agnivesyâyana (or Agnivaisyâyana); Sudharman of the A. gotra, 22, 286 sq.; 45, xxi; Mahâvîra called an A. by Buddhists, 45, xxi.

Agnividyâ, t.t., the same as the Upakosala-vidyâ, 1, 64 *n*.

Agnîvishnû. *See* Agni (*b*) A. and Vishnu.

Agnosticism, in Buddhism, 11, 293 sq.; 45, xxvi–xxix; doctrine of a. refuted, 45, 241 sq., 315 sq.; of *K*wang-ȝze, 39, 129 sq., 179 n., 194–7; condition of a. exemplified, 39, 176 sq. and n.

Agnyâdhâna, t.t., the laying of the sacrificial fires. *See* Fire (*d*, *e*).

Âgnyâdheya = Agnyâdhâna, q.v.

Âgrahâyanî festival, *see* Sacrifices (*b*), *and* Serpents.

Âgrayana, âgrayaneshti, t.t., offering of first-fruits. *See* Agriculture.

Agriculture.

(*a*) Pursuit of a. recommended or forbidden.
(*b*) Laws relating to a.
(*c*) Religious rites relating to a.
(*d*) Details of agricultural work.

(*a*) Pursuit of a. recommended or forbidden.

The pursuit of a. as a moral duty of the *Zoroastrian*, 4, lxii, lxvii, 21–3, 29–31; 24, 28, 281 sq.; 31, 70, 74, 74 n., 342; 37, 103, 179, 424, 435, 443; *let the good deeds for the furtherance of husbandry be done here*, 31, 357; war opposed to a., 18, 173, 173 sq. n.; the husbandman preferred to the thieving nomad, 31, 38, 45 sq.; the earth pleased by tillage, 5, 376 sq.; 37, 154; wisdom requisite for it, 24, 102; taught to the first man and woman, 47, 6 sq.;—painful toil of sowing and reaping conducts to ease, 3, 201; to pay attention to a., the duty of the people, 3, 471 sq., 472 n.; husbandry dear to the Spirits, 27, 279, 279 n.;—the duty of Vaisyas, 8, 127; 25, 24, 199, 400, 419 sq.; *S*ûdra labourer in a., 25, 168; Brâhmanas as landowners, 2, 228, 228 n.; forbidden to Brâhmanas, 25, 86, 106 sq., 420 sq., 420 n.; not compatible with Veda-study, 14, 176; allowed to Brâhmanas, 14, 13, 176, 236; 25, 129, 325, 427; forbidden to Buddhist monks, 13, 33; 19, 296; Buddha grieved by seeing the pain caused by ploughing, 19, 48; 49 (i), 49 sq.

(*b*) Laws relating to a.

Hindu law relating to a., 2, 168, 240 sq.; 33, 159 sq., 160 n., 339 sq.; boundary disputes, 25, 253, 279, 298–301, 394; damage done by cattle, 25, 296 sq.; negligent cultivator punished for loss of crop, 25, 297; seed more important than soil, 25, 333–5, 418; owner of field and owner of seed share the crops, 25, 336; offences with respect to the seed corn, 25, 394; law about agricultural labourers, 33, 134, 139 sq., 345; a husbandman at the time of harvest must not be put under restraint, 33, 288; tithe, *see* Taxes;—*Persian* law of a., 37, 403; produce of land, law about confiscation, 37, 143;—*Chinese* regulations for husbandmen, 27, 210, 227 sq., 255, 260, 289, 292 sq., 304 sq., 308; private and public fields, 3, 322 n., 369 sq. n., 373, 373 n.; regulations about measuring land, 27, 244–7; instructions given to the officers of husbandry, 3, 320–2; instructions to husbandmen given by government, 27, 270; husbandmen present grain to the emperor, 27, 285; regulations for bad years, 28, 2, 4;—the dues of the fruit, according to *Arabian* law, to be brought on the day of harvest, 6, 133.

(*c*) Religious rites relating to a.

Hindu ceremonies and sacrifices relating to a., 29, 98 sq., 126 sq.; 30, xxviii, 113 sq., 304; 42, 486; sacrifice to Kshetrapati, the lord of the field, 30, 224, 291; ploughing ceremonies, 29, 126 sq., 215, 326 sq.; Buddha attends a ploughing festival, 19, xx; sacrifice to Sîtâ,

29, 333–6; Kârîreshti, a sacrifice offered to bring about rain, 38, 118, 118 n.; the Âgrayana (Âgrayaneshti) or offering of first-fruits, 7, 191 sq.; 12, 369–74; 25, 132 sq., 200; 29, 203 sq., 203 n., 337 sq., 415 sq., 430; 30, 93 sq., 124, 289; 41, 46; 44, 176, 176 n.; harvest offerings, 30, 24 sq.; ploughing, watering, and sowing the ground for the fire-altar, 41, 326–41; ploughing and sowing of the site of the burial ground, 44, 431–3; amulet prepared from a ploughshare, 42, 84 sq., 608 sq.; charm to remove weeds from a field, 42, 465; prayers for success in a., 42, 141 sq., 486, 499, 541;—*Parsi* prayers when sowing corn, 5, 392; rules about sowing, &c., on defiled ground, 4, 67 sq.;—*Chinese* ceremonies relating to a., 27, 254 sq., 255 n.; worship of Hâu-kî, the Father of Husbandry, 3, 319 sq., 341 sq., 371–3, 371 n., 398; 27, 431–4, 432 n.; presentation of first-fruits, 27, 271, 274; spring festivals relating to a., 3, 302; thanksgiving sacrifices for a plentiful year, 3, 323, 331–3, 371–3, 371 n.; agricultural sacrifice at the end of the year, 28, 167; sacrifices to heaven and earth, and spirits of land and grain, 28, 265; ploughing of special fields by rulers, 27, 36; 28, 222, 231, 239; the emperor ploughs his field, 28, 338;—*Arabian* (heathen) customs with regard to tilth, 6, 132 sq.

(*d*) Details of agricultural work:—

People earn a living by gleaning, 17, 117; shape of rice-fields, 17, 207 sq.; list of farming operations, 20, 225 sq.; blight and mildew, 20, 326; simile of the husbandman, 36, 269 sq.; food is threefold: ploughing, rain, seed, 43, 110; implements of husbandmen, 4, 174; buying and selling corn, 18, 174–6, 180–2; irrigation, 24, 338 sq.; *see also* Irrigation; providing in summer for the winter, reaping, 37, 91 sq.; Yâo's care for a. by having a calendar made, 3, 32–4; Shun appoints a Minister of A., 3, 42 sq.; poetical pictures of husbandry, 3, 331–3, 369–72, 444–6; the ordinary man (who does not follow the Tâo) compared to a negligent farmer, 40, 121 sq.

Âgûna, *see* Heaven.

Ahallika, a term of reproach (ghost?), 15, 148.

Ahalyâ, Indra's love affair with, 26, 81, 81 n.; Indra wooed A., 49 (i), 44.

Aham, Sk., 'I.' The Âtman or Self perceived beyond the A. or Ego, 1, xxx; secret name of Brahman, 38, 216 sq., 246. *See also* I.

Ahamkâra, t.t., the principle of egoity, 34, xxiii, 364 n., 376 n., 440, 441; 38, 81. *See* Egoism, *and* I.

Â-hang, n. of Î Yin, 3, 95, 95 n., 118, 118 n. *See* Î Yin.

Ahankâra, *see* Ahamkâra.

Ahar, secret name of Brahman, 38, 216 sq., 246.

Âhâras (food?), pain arises from the Â., 10 (ii), 139 sq.

Aharîsvang, Phl. = Zd., Ashis vanguhi, 'good rectitude,' the angel of perfect rectitude, 37, 227, 229, 244, 292; 47, 85, 85 n. *See* Ard, Arshisang, *and* Ashi Vanguhi.

Aharman, or Ahriman, the Evil Spirit (in Parsi religion).

(*a*) His existence, character, and doings.
(*b*) His relation to Aûharmazd.
(*c*) His antagonism against righteousness and religion, and his love of sin.
(*d*) How to defeat A.
(*e*) Myths and legends of A.

(*a*) His existence, character, and doings.

An older corruption of Angramainyu than Ganrâk-maînôk, 5, 4 n., 112 n.: his existence proved, 24, 150–68; the separate existence of an originator of evil admitted by Christians, 24, 238–42; his is no material existence, 18, 44, 44 n.; different from the evil spirit, 5, 128 n.; 'the co-existent one,' 18, 282; Mânichaean doctrines about A. as the creator, 24, 243–51; and the Christian devil, 5, lxix sq.; the chief of hell, 18, 58, 87; 24, 25, 31; fabricated hell, 4, 376; in darkness, with backward understanding and desire for destruction, was in the abyss, and it is he who will not be, 5, 4; not omniscient, 5, 5, 7; has more predominance in

the dark, 5, 342; called Drûg, the fiend, 5, 14; his body that of a lizard, 5, 16, 105; is all vileness, 5, 158; why he advanced towards the light, though of a different nature, 24, 123 sq.; creatures of A., 5, 6, 17 sq.; 37, 423; death of A.'s creatures does not defile, 4, lxxviii, 60; creates 'falsehood,' 'evil thought,' 5, 9; created the diseases, 4, 228 n.; three tyrants created by A., 4, xlviii; the producer of the demon of wrath, 24, 205, 205 n.; the evil-doing of A., 5, 105 sq., 112 sq.; 24, 101; disturbance by A. and the demons, 5, 214; brought mortality into the world, 18, 198, 198 n.; concealed the results of good and evil, and created false religions, 24, 39 sq.; all misery due to A., 24, 74, 94 sq.; 47, 92; deceives man, 24, 87 sq., 102; wishes men not to understand him, 5, 113, 113 n.; 24, 80; tries most to injure the soul, 24, 88; his miscreations: fiends, idolaters, wolves, 37, 151; the brood of the fiend and the wound-producer of the Evil Spirit, 47, 102.

(*b*) His relation to Aûharmazd.

Relation of A. and Aûharmazd, 5, lxix sq.; origin of Aûharmazd and A., and their difference, 37, 242 sq.; Ormazd and A. created the world, 23, 163, 198; A. as destroyer, and Aûharmazd as creator, 4, 212 n.; 24, 14; Aûharmazd discriminates truly, A. does not, 37, 391 sq.; Ormazd is all perfume, A. all stench, 4, 220 n.; the Zoroastrian rejoices Ormazd and afflicts A., 4, 375; there cannot be any peace and affection between Aûharmazd and A., 24, 36 sq.; is a creature of Aûharmazd, 37, 485; not smitten by Aûharmazd, 24, 66; struggle between Aûharmazd and A., their creation and counter-creation, 4, liv sq., lxi, lxiv; 5, xxiii, 3–10, 14–20, 25–31, 52, 65 sq., 68 sq., 71–4, 99, 105 sq., 113 sq., 116, 155–66, 363, 365; 18, 25 sq., 93–8, 261, 269 sq., 273–5, 282 n., 374, 376 sq., 384 sq.; 23, 22, 296; 24, 32–5, 38, 73 sq., 82 sq., 101, 205–8, 244; 31, xviii sq., 264; 37, 31, 230, 270, 301 sq., 307, 441; vanquished by Ahura Mazda (Ormazd), 4, lxi, lxiv, 100 n., 197 n.; 23, 33, 250; the dog of A. kills creatures of Ormazd, and vice versa, 4, 155–7; refuses to accept the conditions of peace proffered by Aûharmazd, 5, 6 sq.; covenant between Aûharmazd and A., 24, 104, 104 n.; Aûharmazd was aware of A., A. was not aware of Aûharmazd, 5, 155; Aûharmazd will not leave his creatures unto the Evil Spirit, 5, 308; good government produced by Aûharmazd, bad government by A., 24, 43; Ormazd created healing plants, A. the diseases, 4, 228 n.; the primaeval bull created by Ormazd and killed by A., 4, 231 n.; Ahura Mazda requests Mãthra Spe*nt*a and Airyaman to cure the diseases sent by A., 4, 236–40; all good owing to Aûharmazd, all evil to A., 37, 62, 245 sq.; counteracts divine providence, 24, 55. *See also* Dualism.

(*c*) His antagonism against righteousness and religion, and his love of sin.

A. assists the demon-worshippers against the Iranians, 5, li sq., 224–30; the antagonism of A. and the demons brought on by the evil-doers, 5, 207; a liar is a co-operator with A., 24, 322 sq.; the practice of sinners is that of A., 18, 216 sq.; a wrathful man is just like A., 24, 10; a bad ruler equal to A., 24, 45; a false judge is like A., 24, 79; the sinner akin to A., 24, 357; chooses the realm of the wicked, 31, 26, 30 sq.; the wicked, the followers of A. 'the other one,' 37, 388; prevents the worthy from being allotted worldly happiness, 24, 76; the Behrâm fire struggles with the spiritual fiend, 5, 185; opposed to worship of sacred beings, 37, 181, 192, 276 sq.; opposed to creation and to righteousness, 37, 239; pleased by transgression of Zoroastrian law, 5, 109; the sin of unnatural intercourse pleases A. most, 18, 226 sq.; 24, 267 sq.; has appointed the demons Tardy and Afterwards, 24, 346 sq.; injustice produced by A., 37, 73; apostasy produced by A., 37, 328, 346; pre-

dominates over him who works in the dark, 37, 478; will the wicked souls be able to see A.? 18, 44 sq.; and the demons seize the wicked soul in hell, 18, 72; 24, 266 sq.; powerless to inflict harm on the soul of the blessed one, 4, 374.

(*d*) How to defeat A.

He who pleases the seven archangels, his soul never comes into the possession of A., 5, 373; righteous men fight against the fiend, 18, 12, 14; the smiting of A. effected by wisdom, 24, 101; destruction of A. arises from the union of the good, 37, 346; A. and demons defeated by the sacred ceremony, 18, 159 sq., 167; next-of-kin marriage a protection from A. and the demons, 4, 98 n.; 18, 417; contentment good for vanquishing A., 24, 26, 70; who wears the sacred thread-girdle is out of A.'s department, 24, 268; defeated by the spirit of truth, 24, 324; beaten by complete mindfulness, 37, 264; Zoroastrian ceremonial a protection from the annoying spirit, 37, 363 sq.; closing the way of A. into oneself, 37, 433, 439; separation from the destructive Evil Spirit one of the seven perfections of religion, 37, 273; driven back to hell by the Honover, 4, 100 n.; shattered by the Aîrmân supplication, 37, 302 sq.; repelled by recitation of Vâstârem Nask, 37, 446; cries of cock, &c., keep him at a distance, 5, 113, 113 n.; prayer for the destruction of the Evil Spirit, 5, 362; how A. and the demons are confounded, 24, 83 sq.; mountains which are smiters of A. and the demons, 24, 98; a scornful dole for A., 37, 311; the accursed devil becomes cursed, 37, 428, 437.

(*e*) Myths and legends of A.

Adam deluded by A., 24, 179, 179 n.; *Aêshm's* complaint to A. of the three things he could not injure in the world, 5, 387–9, 387 n.; the *Daêvas* his seed and his servants, 31, 54, 58 sq.; the six *demons* from the dark world of A., 5, 10; *Dahâk* begged a favour from A., 5, 80; releases Az-i Dahâk, 5, lii, 233 sq.; Dahâk's descent traced to A., 5, 132; his conflict with the *Earth*, 5, 29 sq.; his conflict with *Gâyômard*, 5, 17–19; Gâyômar*d* delivers his body to A., 24, 58; he appeared a young man of fifteen years to *Geh*, 5, 16; the seven *planets* chieftains of A., 24, 34, 38; his conflict with the *plants*, 5, 30 sq.; his conflict with the *primaeval ox*, 4, 231 n.; 5, 31 sq.; 47, 33; his destruction at the *renovation* of the universe, 5, 128 sq.; 18, 118; 24, 99; 37, 431, 446; 47, xiii; the creatures of A. will perish at the time when the future existence occurs, 5, 5; became confounded and remained in confusion for 3,000 years, 5, 15 sq.; became headstrong and was put out of heaven, 24, 192; his conflict with the *sky*, 5, 25; 18, 261; attacks the sky, the water, the earth, &c., 5, 161–87; sprang like a *snake* out of the sky down to the earth, 5, 17; made impotent by *Sôshyans*, 5, 8, 33; 47, 117 sq.; *stars* assist in the distribution of evil produced by A., 24, 127–38; overturned by *Tâkhmôrup*, 18, 200, 200 n.; kept as a charger by Tâkhmôrup, 24, 59, 60, 60 n.; converted into a horse by Tâkhmôrup, 47, 8; his conflict with the water and with *Tîstar*, 5, 25–9; A. and the demons defeated in the reign of *Vistâsp* and other kings, 5, 198, 201; afflicted through the deeds of Vi*s*tâsp, 24, 65; sends demons to destroy *Zoroaster* before and at his birth, but is dismayed, 37, 227; 47, 140–2; tempts Zaratû*s*t, but is confounded, 24, 103 sq.; A. rushes for the destruction of Zoroaster, but is defeated by him, 37, 164; 47, 58 sq., 123.

Aharûbô-stôtô, son of Mê*d*yômâh, 47, 166.

Ahaspati, n.d., 'lord of days,' 30, 58.

Âhavanîya, *see* Fire (*e*).

Ahi ('the Snake'), slain by Indra, 32, 180, 197.

Ahi Budhnya, oblation to, 29, 331; 41, 96, 96 n.

Ahi*m*sâ, Sk., t.t. (the vow or law of) not injuring (any living being).

(*a*) In Gaina religion.
(*b*) In Buddhism.
(*c*) In Brahmanism.

(*a*) IN *G*AINA RELIGION.

He should not kill, nor cause others to kill, nor consent to the killing of others, 22, 31; *the Arhats and Bhagavats of the past, present, and future, all say thus, speak thus, declare thus, explain thus: all breathing, existing, living, sentient creatures should not be slain, nor treated with violence, nor abused, nor tormented, nor driven away*, 22, 36, 38 sq.; *all beings hate pains; therefore one should not kill them. This is the quintessence of wisdom: not to kill anything. Know this to be the legitimate conclusion from the principle of the reciprocity with regard to non-killing*, 45, 247 sq., 248 n., 311; a wise man should not take the life of living beings, nor cause pain to any creatures, looking upon all living beings as suffering like himself, 22, 30–2, 63 sq.; 45, 25, 33 sq., 251 sq., 254, 259, 271, 295, 311, 351, 404 sq.; the first great vow of the *G*aina not to kill any living being, 22, 202–4; do not kill living beings in the threefold way, 45, 260; giving safety is the best of gifts, 45, 290; a monk should treat all beings as he himself would be treated, 45, 306 sq., 314; towards your fellow creatures be not hostile, 45, 329; wicked men injure plants and animals, 45, 374; abstinence from destroying life destroys Karman, 45, 174; all living beings suffer: hence those who injure living beings will suffer pains in the Sa*m*sâra, while those who practise A. will put an end to all misery, 45, 386 sq.; sins caused by actions injuring the lives in earth, water, fire, plants, animals, wind, 22, 3–14; heretics kill or consent to killing others, 22, 62; those who entertain cruel thoughts against the six classes of living beings are near death, 22, 42; killing living beings causes bondage of the soul, 45, 236; those who kill living beings go to the abode of the Asuras, 45, 259; those who injure living beings go to hell, 45, 21, 279, 286; by hurting any of the living beings (earth, water, fire, and wind bodies, plants, &c.) men do harm to their own souls, and will be born as one of them, 45, 292 sq.; precautions to be taken by *G*aina monks, in order to avoid killing animals, 22, 47, 47 n., 72, 75, 97, 100, 120, 126, 128, 132, 136 sq., 139, 145, 161 sq., 169 sq., 178–83, 304–8; 45, 129, 135 sq., 146 sq.; *he should not scare away (insects), nor keep them off, nor be in the least provoked to passion by them. Tolerate living beings, do not kill them, though they eat your flesh and blood*, 45, 11; mouth-cloth used by *G*ainas to prevent insects entering the mouth, 45, 145, 145 n.; a *G*aina monk should not build a house, nor cook, nor light a fire, because many living beings are killed thereby, 45, 204 sq.; a *G*aina monk should only drink distilled water (without life), 45, 10, 10 n.; a monk must not use cold water, not to injure water-bodies, 45, 255, 255 n.; food is only pure when given with unwashed hands and dishes, on account of the lives contained in water, 22, 103 sq., 117; sin caused by injuring the fire-bodies or lives in fire, 22, 7 sq., 67, 67 n.; 45, 293, 358; certain food forbidden to *G*aina monks on account of dangers to living beings, 22, 88 sq., 104–10; Mahâvîra's abstinence from killing, 22, 81; Buddhist misrepresentation of the *G*aina vow of desisting from doing injury, 45, xvii sq.; living beings injured by sacrificial ceremonies, 22, 12, 18; 45, 55; a bad *S*rama*n*a, through carelessness, hurts living beings, 45, 78 sq.; Arish*t*anêmî, on seeing the animals to be killed for the wedding feast, renounces the world, 45, 114; the Hastitâpasa kill one elephant a year, and live on it, to spare the life of other animals, 45, 418 sq.; *G*aina householders renounce slaughter of animals, as they cannot altogether abstain from injuring the six classes of beings, 45, 421–33, 421 n.; when living beings are killed for the sake of gifts and other meritorious actions, a monk should neither praise nor forbid such acts, 45, 312 sq.; various causes why men injure living beings, 45, 357–60.

(*b*) IN BUDDHISM.

Doctrine of A. in Buddhism and Gainism, 22, xxi–xxviii; *there were formerly three diseases: desire, hunger, and decay, but from the slaying of cattle there came ninety-eight*, 10 (ii), 51; *Ye shall slay no living thing*, 11, 253; *As I am so are these, as these are so am I, identifying himself with others, let him not kill nor cause (any one) to kill*, 10 (ii), 128; *Doing no injury to any one, dwell full of love and kindness in the world*, 35, 254 sq.; *Now wherein, Vâsettha, is his conduct good? Herein, O Vâsettha, that putting away the murder of that which lives, he abstains from destroying life. The cudgel and the sword he lays aside; and, full of modesty and pity, he is compassionate and kind to all creatures that have life!* 11, 189; kindness to all things that live, 10 (i), 36 sq. and n.; 36, 341 sq.; the principal sin of destroying life, 10 (i), 61; the true Brâhmana, the saint, the Bhikkhu, does not kill nor cause slaughter, 10 (i), 92; (ii), 35 sq., 61, 88 sq., 114; a householder must not kill, nor cause to be killed any living being, nor approve of others killing, 10 (ii), 65 sq.; Bhikkhus are to refrain from injuring plants or animals, 11, 190, 192; 13, 4, 33, 46; 17, 22; a Bhikkhu must not intentionally destroy the life of any being down to a worm or ant, 13, 235; a Bhikkhu shall not dig the ground, 13, 33; a Bhikkhu must not sprinkle water, with living creatures in it, on grass or on clay, 13, 35; a Bhikkhu must not drink water with living things in it, 13, 46; the dangers to vegetable and animal life to be prevented by keeping vassa, 13, 298 sq., 300; wooden shoes forbidden, because insects are trod upon and killed, 17, 21; by one case of destruction of life, a man may be re-born in hell, 35, 124; sin of depriving a living being of life unconsciously, 35, 224; a wicked Bhikkhu, who caused a bull to be slain to get its skin, rebuked by Buddha, 17, 29 sq.; already in former births Buddha refrained from hurting living beings, 36, 16; eight classes of men who kill living beings, 36, 17; the Buddhists denounced as eating meat, 45, 416; sacrifices objectionable as connected with slaughter, 10 (ii), 49 sq.; 19, 129, 135; 49 (i), 121; king Suddhodana only offers sacrifices involving no injury to living beings, 49 (i), 24. *See also* Love.

(*c*) IN BRAHMANISM.

A. or harmlessness comes from Krishna, 8, 86; is called knowledge, 8, 103; is his who is born to god-like endowments, 8, 114; is called penance bodily, 8, 119; non-destruction is the highest piety, 8, 348, 378; is an element of the quality of goodness, 8, 325, 373; leads up to final emancipation, 8, 364; some people (sects) are given up to harmlessness, others to destruction, 8, 376; abstention from injuring living beings the duty of all castes, 14, 26 sq.; 25, 416; those are Brâhmanas who can save from evil, who abstain from injuring living beings, 14, 38; he who abstains from injuring living beings obtains heaven, 14, 136; 25, 166 sq.; he is a true Brâhmana who befriends all creatures, 14, 128; 25, 46, 46 n.; the soul is purified by abstention from injuring living beings, 14, 165; who hurts living beings cannot reach the abode of the gods, 14, 176; abstention from injuring living beings is internal purification, 14, 287; abstention from injuring living beings a penance, 14, 312; 25, 476; abstention from injuring living beings the best sacrifice, 14, 139; he who delights in injuring living creatures excluded from Srâddha, 25, 106; remembrance of former births a reward of doing no injury to created beings, 25, 152; sacrifices and the doctrine of A., 19, 129; 38, 130 sq., 310; 48, 598 sq.; *see also* Animal Sacrifices (*a*); the Ocean begs king Arguna to give security to creatures of the sea, 8, 294; the Brahmakârin must not injure animate beings, 2, 188; 25, 62; a Snâtaka shall not hurt any living being, 2, 226; 25, 137; 29, 318;

the ascetic shall avoid the destruction of seeds, and be indifferent towards all creatures, 2, 194; offering safety to all beings, duty of the Sannyâsin, 8, 362; the ascetic promises not to injure any living being, 8, 365; 14, 46, 260, 277, 277 n., 279; 25, 205 sq., 208–10, 212; ascetics must always use strained water, 14, 260, 279; 25, 207, 207 n.; an ascetic who rejects meat at sacrifices and funeral meals goes to hell, 14, 54; hermits should not injure even gadflies or gnats, 14, 293; *see* Compassion, *and* Slaughter.

Ahîna sacrifices, *see* Sacrifices (*j*).

A'hmed = Mohammed, 9, 281 n.

A'hnas ibn Surâiq, n.p., a worldly man of pleasant appearance, but opposed to Mohammed, 6, 29 sq., 29 n.

Ahogaṅga Hill, Sambhûta Sâṇavâsî dwelling there, 20, 394.

A-ho Kan, n.p., disciple of Lăo-lung Ki, 40, 67 sq.

Ahriman, *see* Aharman.

Ahûm-stut, n.p., 23, 203.

Ahunavaiti, title of a Gâtha of the Zend-Avesta, 31, 2–92.

Ahura-Mazda (Ormazd), the supreme God of Mazdeism.

(*a*) The supreme God and Creator.
(*b*) A. in mythology.
(*c*) A. and Zoroaster.
(*d*) A. and morality.
(*e*) Worship of A.

(*a*) THE SUPREME GOD AND CREATOR.

The belief in a supreme God, A., an old element in Zoroastrianism, 4, xiii, lx sq.; parallel with the Asura Varuṇa, 4, xxx, lii; an Aryan god, 4, lxiv; one of the purest conceptions of God, 31, xviii sq.; *Invoke, O Zarathustra! my Fravashi, who am Ahura-Mazda, the greatest, the best, the fairest of all beings, the most solid, the most intelligent, the best shapen, the highest in holiness, and whose soul is the holy Word!* 4, 213; the Creator, 4, 376; 23, 25, 27; 31, 108 sq., 113 sq.; his creations, 4, lxx; 31, 285 sq.; 37, 423; the sixteen perfect lands created by A., 4, 1–10; all good things, made by A., the offspring of the holy principle, 4, 142 sq., 147 sq.; 31, 248, 250; made the aerial way, the earth, and everything, 4, 232–4; made the waters flow and the plants grow, 23, 198 sq.; the maker, the most beneficent of all beings, 4, 204–6; 23, 326; is all-knowing, never asleep, never intoxicated, 4, 215; 23, 25, 27; power and benevolence of A., 31, 93, 95–7, 100–5; his gifts, immortality, righteous order, and kingdom of welfare, 31, 83; victorious strength given by A., 23, 128, 133; the glory made by Mazda, and the victory made by Ahura, 23, 136; a guardian and a friend, 31, 108, 112; the first father of righteous order, 31, 108, 113; bountifulness of A., 31, 145–51; the remedies of A., 31, 347.

(*b*) A. IN MYTHOLOGY.

The sun the eye of A., 31, 199; the stars, his body, 31, 285; the star Jupiter called Ormazd, 31, 199; the waters his wives, 23, 353, 353 n.; 31, 286 sq., 342, 386; how A. purifies the water which he sends down to the Dakhmas, 4, 49, 54 sq.; Garô-nmânem (Garodman), the abode of A., 4, 221; 23, 338; 31, 184 sq. and n.; the helpers of A., 31, 81, 86; higher than all the *Amesha-Spentas*, 4, 283; father and commander of the Amesha-Spentas, 23, 199 sq., 290; has six personified attributes, 31, xviii sq.; court of Ormazd and the archangels, 37, 437; relation of A. (Ormazd) to *Angra Mainyu* (*Aharman*, Ahriman), *see* Aharman (*b*); brought *Ardvi Sûra Anâhita* down to earth, and sacrificed to her, 23, 55–8, 73 sq.; Ardvi Sûra Anâhita, the daughter of A., 31, 321; *Ashi Vanguhi*, daughter of A., 23, 270, 274; *Atar*, son of A., 23, 5, *see* Âtar; assisted by the *Fravashis* in maintaining the world, 23, 180–5, 187, 193 sq.; made Hara Berezaiti the dwelling of *Mithra*, 23, 131 sq.; established Mithra to maintain and look over all the world, 23, 145; brought the healing plants to *Thrita*, 4, 225 sq.; assisted *Tistrya* in his struggle against Drought, 23, 95, 99–101, 103; established Tistrya above all stars, 23, 105; offered sacrifice to *Vayu*, 23, 250; Vayu works the good of A. and the Amesha-Spentas, 23,

259; reigns according as *Vohu Manô* waxeth, 4, 276 n., 277; the creator of Asha, and father of the Good Mind, 31, 37, 44; the father of the Good Mind and of Piety, 31, 123, 126 sq.; the kingdom gained for A. by the Good Mind, 31, 27, 33; the kingdom is for A., 31, 281, 283, 309, 323, 347, 372, 381; calls a meeting of the celestial *Yazatas*, 4, 15; *Yima*, the first mortal who converses with A., 4, 11.

(*c*) A. AND ZOROASTER.

Reveals the law to Zarathustra, 4, lxx–lxxii, 2, 11, 22, &c., 208, 212, 240 n.; 23, 24, 24 n.; 31, 354; invoked by Zarathustra to declare his doctrine, 31, 37, 41; Zoroaster asks A. for his regulations and the path of the Good Mind, 31, 82, 88 sq.; prayer to A. for revelation, 31, 38 sq., 48–50; the twenty-one Nasks formed by A. out of the Ahuna Vairya, 4, xxxvii; conversations between Zarathustra and A., 31, 107–21, 249, 260 sq., 337, 341, 374 sq., 390; taught Zarathustra the sacrifice, 31, 318 sq., 338 sq.; *these are the best words, those which A. spoke to Zarathustra*, 31, 330; directed how the Avesta should be said, 31, 353; established Zarathustra as the master of the material world, 23, 74, 105; colloquy between the soul of the kine, Asha, and A. who appoints Zarathustra, 31, 3–13; Zarathustra obtains stones from A. with which he repels the fiend, 4, 210 sq., 210 n.; confessed the religion of Zoroaster, 23, 142; Zarathustra invokes the holy creation of A., 4, 214.

(*d*) A. AND MORALITY.

He who relieves the poor makes A. king, 4, 101; how close A. is to a man's thoughts, words, and deeds, 4, 289, 288 n.; A. and the other Amesha-Spentas displeased by the bad priest, 23, 156; chooses righteousness and the pious of all ages, 31, 26, 30 sq.; how can the wise man become like A.? 31, 39, 49; the pious are servants of A., 31, 40, 53; the friendship of A. is before the Zarathustrian's mind, 31, 51, 57; doing evil to the wicked, like advising the good, is acting in the love of A., 31, 68, 72; the leading sin of disobedience to A., 31, 69, 73; receives the righteous soul in Paradise, 4, 89; the souls of the righteous pass to the golden seat of A., 4, 220; created good renown and salvation of the soul, 4, 375; helps the soul to pass over the Kinvat Bridge, 31, 261.

(*e*) WORSHIP OF A.

A. worshipped, 23, 32, 162, 332–4, 349–51, 353–7; 31, 195 sq., 199, &c.; prayer to A., 4, xlvii, 100 sq.; 31, 284 sq., 288–90, 320; the fire of A., 4, 115, 281; 31, 284 sq.; offerings and prayers to A. and the Amesha-Spentas, 4, 215, 217, 248; 23, 3, 6, 9 sq., 13, 15, 17 sq., 35, 37, 39, 89, 230, 274; 31, 172, 174 sq.; became sovereign by the Airyama Ishyô prayer, 4, 247; prayer and sacrifice to A. the best of all things, 4, 283, 293; sacrifice to A., 4, 349; Ormazd Yast: the names of A., and their efficacy, 23, 21–31; the memory, the understanding, and the tongue of A. worshipped, 23, 32, 321; who worships the sun benefits A., 23, 86; and the Amesha-Spentas long for the morning service, 23. 142, 142 n.; Mithra and A. invoked together, 23, 148 sq., 158; invoked at the ordeal, 23, 169 sq.; the Fravashi of A. worshipped, 23, 199; 31, 273, 278; Fravashis invoked together with A., 23, 227; the Glory of A. praised, 23, 290; prayer to A. and Asha, 31, 14–24, 62; how is A. to be worshipped? 31, 108, 111 sq.; praise of A., 31, 123 sq., 126–30, 263 sq.; bestows highest good on him who offers sacrifice, 31, 180 sq.; Ahura and Mithra, and all the stars worshipped, 31, 199, 199 n., 205, 210, 216, 220, 225; worshipped by Sraosha, 31, 298; all holy creatures which A. created, worshipped, 31, 328 sq.

Ahurâni, water of Ahura worshipped, 4, 250.

Ahûrvadâspô, ancestor of Zoroaster, 47, 140.

Âi, n.p.; conversation between Duke Âi of Lû and Confucius, 27, 39, 51 sq.; 28, 261–9, 312, 402–10; 39,

229–33; eulogized the deceased Confucius, 27, 159, 159 n.; sends a message of condolence to Khwâi Shang, 27, 187; funeral of his son Tun, 27, 188; wears mourning for his concubine, 27, 189; *K*âu Făng sends a message to Duke Âi, 27, 191; paid a visit of condolence when *K*î-sun's mother died, 27, 197; declines the condolences of Ling, 27, 323; sent Zû Pî to Confucius to learn the proper mourning rites, 28, 166 sq.; Duke Âi and Ȝze-kâo, 28, 169; interview of *K*wang-ȝze with Âi, 40, 49 sq., 49 n.; wishes to employ Confucius in the government, 40, 207 sq.

Aibhâvata, *see* Pratîdar*s*a Ai.

Aibigaya, *see* Aiwisrûthrima.

Aîghâsh, demon of the evil eye, 5, 111, 111 n.

Aikshvâka, n. of a noble family, 45, 321 n., 339; Purukutsa, the Ai. king, 44, 397. *See* B*ri*hadratha.

Ailâpatya, Mahâgiri of the Ai. gotra, 22, 287, 289.

Aîndar, Zd. I*n*dra, the arch-demon, 18, 319, 319 n.

Ainyu, n.p., 23, 217 sq.

Aipivanghu, or Aipivôhu, or Kaî-Apîveh, n. of a king of Iran, 5, 136–9, 136 n.; 23, 222, 222 n., 303.

Air (Sk. antariksha).

(*a*) Air as an element.
(*b*) Air as a deity.

(*a*) AIR AS AN ELEMENT.

The union of earth and heaven is air, 1, 247 sq.; meditation on the person in the air as Brahman, 1, 303; only seen by one who attains to the Adhyâtma, 8, 316; the second entity, its presiding deity lightning, 8, 337, 340; touch is the characteristic of air, 8, 337, 340, 348, 350; sound and touch are its qualities, 8, 384; springs from ether, 34, lii; 38, 18 sq.; is founded on space (ether), 34, 413; the abode of heaven, earth, and so on, 34, 154, 158; when it manifests itself in the form of Parganya, lightning, thunder, rain, and thunderbolts manifest themselves in it, 34, 229; with its five forms, 34, 229; 38, 87; is a product, 38, 3, 18 sq.; fire is produced from air, 38, 20–2; fire is dissolved into air, 38, 26; air is dissolved into ether, 38, 26; in what sense it may be called prâ*n*a, 38, 87; union of Vâyu with the air, 41, 148, 188; heals whatever is injured in the earth, 41, 221; fashioned by the Rudras, 41, 234; is the home of the waters, 41, 416; the sun is the holder of the air, 43, 28; is of Trish*t*ubh nature, 43, 57; is the 'expanse' metre, 43, 88; is the lower abode, 43, 203; three oblations of air or wind on the chariot, 43, 235; is the resting-place in yonder world, as the earth is in this world, 44, 17; steadied by means of the birds and sun-motes, 44, 126; relates to Sarasvatî, 44, 241; is the abode and support of all beings, 44, 407, 477; and Ether, this is the immortal, 48, 535; Buddhist saints walking through the air, 10 (i), 62 sq., & n.

(*b*) AIR AS A DEITY.

Bali-offering to Air, 2, 107 sq.; 29, 320; oblations to Air and Vâyu, 29, 321; deity and brick of fire-altar, 43, 91; is hairless, Vâyu the man, 43, 208; Vai*s*vânara as Air, 43, 395 sq.; one of the eight Vasus, 15, 140 sq.; 44, 116; expiatory oblation to Air, which is a place of abode for all the gods, 44, 505; invoked as a deity, 29, 232; 46, 253. *See also* Vâyu.

Aîrak, n.p., 5, 134.

Airammadîya, a lake in the world of Brahman, 1, 131, 132 n.

Aîrân-vêg, Aîrân vê*g*ô, the most undisturbed land, 24, 86 sq., 86 n., 109 sq.; primaeval home of Mazda-worship, the abode of Yim, 37, 190, 190 n.

Airâva*n*a=Airâvata, q. v.

Airâvata, Indra's elephant, 22, 222, 231; the best of elephants, 45, 290.

Aîri*k*, n.p., son of Frê*d*ûn, 5, 133 sq., 133 n.; 37, 28, 28 n.; 47, 10 sq., 34, 140; reigned twelve years, 5, 150; slain by his brothers, 24, 52, 52 n.; revenged by Mânû*s*-*k*îhar, 24, 61, 61 sq. n.; progenitor of Mânû*s*, 47, 128.

Aîri*z*-râsp Aûspôsinân, n. of a high priest, 5, 115, 115 n.

Airs, vital, *see* Prâ*n*as.

Airya, Sairima, and Tûra, the three sons of Thraêtaona, 4, lix.
Airyak, n.p., 47, 34.
Airyaman, the much-desired, invoked, 23, 4, 13, 35, 37; and Asha-Vahi*s*ta praised together, 23, 41–8; invoked against diseases, sorcerers, and demons, 4, 229, 235, 241; heals diseases, 23, 41, 48; 37, 116 n., 165, 165 n.; the spell of A. most efficacious against diseases, 4, 236–41; the A. Ishyô prayer, 4, 144, 147, 247; 23, 41–7; 31, 293. *See* Airy*e*mâ-ishyô.
Airy*e*mâ-ishyô, *see* Prayers (*f*).
Airyu, son of Thraêtaona, 23, 222, 222 n.
Aishâvîrâ*h*, sons of Eshavîra, a Brahmanical family held in general contempt, 44, 45, 45 n.
Aitareya, n. of a *R*ishi, 1, xcvii n.; worshipped at the Tarpa*n*a, 29, 123, 220; honoured as a teacher, 29, 141. *See* Mahidâsa Ai.
Aitareya-âra*n*yaka, in the beginning a Brâhma*n*a, 1, lxvi sq.; introduction to and translation of Ai., 1, xci–xcviii, 155–268; the first chapter of the Ai. a mere continuation of the Aitareya-brâhma*n*a, 1, xcii; Ai. and Kaushîtaki-upanishad, 1, xcix; Â*s*valâyana or *S*aunaka, author of the fifth book, 29, 153–8; quoted, 8, 87 n., 90 n., 123 n., 180 n.; 38, 421; 48, 773.
Aitareya-brâhma*n*a and Aitareya-âra*n*yaka, 1, xcii sq.; quoted, 8, 20, 222, 265 n., 276 n., 277 n., 280 n.; 38, 421; on the Pravargya ritual, 44, xlvii; takes no account of the horse sacrifice, 44, xvi, xvii n.
Aitareya-upanishad, quoted, 8, 120 n., 123 n., 153 n., 179 n., 187 n., 189 n., 191 n., 251 n., 259 n., 339 n.; 48, 240. *See also* Upanishads.
Âi-thâi Tho, was 'ugly enough to scare the whole world,' but a 'Perfect man' of Tâo, 39, 229–33.
Aiwi*hv*arenah, n.p., 23, 214.
Aiwisrûthrima and Aibigaya (or, Aibigaya 'the life-furtherer,' epithet of Ai.?), worshipped, 31, 197, 201, 204, 209, 215, 219, 224, 384.
A*k*alâ, n. of a giantess, 21, 374.
A*k*alabhrât*ri*, n. of a Sthavira, 22, 286.
Aka-Manah, *see* Akem-manô.
Akampita, n. of a Sthavira, 22, 286.
Akandgar-i Kilisyâkîh, or Alexander the Christian, 5, 200, 200 n.
Akanish*th*as (Akani*tth*a), the last stage before reaching the formless world, 10 (i), 57 n.; heavenly beings, who lull the women of Gautama's seraglio to sleep, 49 (i), 56.
Âkaṅkheyya-Sutta, early Buddhist mysticism in it, 11, x; translated, 11, 205–18.
Akarmabhûmi, one of the parts of the world where men live, 45, 225.
Â*k*ârya, Sk., *see* Teacher.
Âkâ*s*a, Sk., *see* Ether.
Âkâsagotta, n. of a physician, 17, 78 sq.
Âkâ*s*apratish*th*ita, n. of a Tathâgata, 21, 178.
Akatasha (Zd.), Akatâsh (Phl.), n. of a Daêva, 4, 224; spell against the daêva A., 4, 140; fiend of perversion, 5, 109; fiend of inquisitiveness, 37, 182, 182 n.
Akayadha of the Pîdha house, 23, 219.
A*k*elakas, *see* Âgîvikas.
Akem-manô, or Aka-Manah, Zd., evil thought, 5, 10 n.; Zarathu*s*tra unabated by A., 4, 210; assists the Evil Spirit, 23, 297; smitten by Vohu-Manô, 23, 308; opposed to Ahura-Mazda, 31, xviii sq.; the wicked abiding in the actions of A., the Evil Mind, 31, 147, 150. *See* Akôman.
Âkhnangha, n.p., 23, 217.
Âkhrûra, son of Husravah, 23, 223.
Âkhrûrag (?), friend of Keresâsp, 18, 375, 375 n.
Âkh*s*ti, *see* Peace.
Akht, or Akhtô, Phl. = Akhtya, Zd., n. of a wicked wizard, 18, 411, 411 n.; Yôi*s*ta solves the riddles of A. the sorcerer, 23, 72 sq. and n.; enmity of A. the heretic, 37, 297; the wizard, killed, 47, xxx, 166, 166 n.
Akhtya, *see* Akht.
Âkhyâna, *see* Legends.
A*k*iravatî, n. of a river, 11, 167, 167 n., 169, 178–82.
Akôman, Akômanô, Phl. = Zd. Akem-manô, evil thought, one of the six demons of Aharman, 5, 9 sq.,

10 n.; 18, 93, 96; 37, 243, 252 sq., 253 n.; the archfiend, his doings, 5, 106; seized by Vohûman, 5, 128; the stench of A. opposed by Vohûman, 5, 179; the stupefying, 37, 286; thoughts of the wicked due to A., 37, 388; his struggle with Vohûmanô at the birth of Zoroaster, 47, 141 sq. *See* Akem-manô.

Akrê-khira*dô*, or Aghrêra*d* (Zd. Aghraêratha) killed by his brother, 47, 126, 126 n.

Akriyâvâda, Sk., t.t., *see* Philosophy.

Akriyâvâdin, t.t., *see* Nihilists.

Akshamâlâ, a *K*â*nd*âlî, became the wife of Vasish*th*a, 2, 175 n.; 25, 331, 331 n.; 49 (i), 45.

Akshapâda, n. p., the arguments of Buddha, A., and others contradictory, 48, 425, 426.

Akshara, Sk., both 'syllable,' and 'imperishable,' 1, 1 n.; 34, 169; 'syllable,' 41, 158, 203; the Imperishable, the Indestructible, 8, 439; 34, 169–71, 243; 38, 239 sq.; the great Brahman, the one A. (Imperishable One), 43, 343 sq. *See* Imperishable.

Akshâvâpa, Sk., 'the keeper of the dice,' one of the officers of a king, 41, 63, 107 n.

Akshayamati, n. of a Bodhisattva Mahâsattva, 21, 4; Buddha tells A. the wonderful powers of Avalokitesvara, 21, 406–12; informs *K*itradhvaga about the saint Avalokitesvara, 21, 413.

Akshobhya, n. of a Tathâgata, 21, 177; 49 (ii), 99.

Âktâkshya, n.p., quoted, 41, 153.

Âkuli and Kilâta, priests of the Asuras, 12, 29 sq.

Âkûti, invoked in a love-charm, 42, 104, 535.

Âlabhikâ, Mahâvîra at, 22, 264.

A*l*aka, n. of a place, 10 (ii), 184, 188.

Alaka, the two demons A. and Poku fight against each other, 19, 330.

Alakâ, Kuvera, the monarch of, 49 (i), 36.

Â*l*akamandâ, the royal city of the gods, 11, 100, 248; 35, 3.

Âlambâyanîputra, n.p., 15, 225.

Âlambîputra, n. of a teacher, 15, 225.

Â*l*âra Kâlâma, n. of a rival teacher of Buddha, 11, 75–7, 75 n., 79; one of the teachers to whom Gotama attached himself after his pabbaggâ, 13, 89; a teacher of the Bodisat, 36, 43–6.

Alarka, legend of A. who wishes to conquer his mind and senses, 8, 296–300.

Alasanda, Milinda born in the island of A. (Alexandria in Bactria), 35, xxiii, 127.

Alava, the demon, converted by Buddha, 19, 244.

Â*l*avaka, a Yakkha, converted by Buddha, 10 (ii), 29–31.

Â*l*avakasutta translated, 10 (ii), 29–31.

Â*l*avi, the realm of the Yakkha Â*l*avaka, 10 (ii), 29; Buddha dwelt at Â., 10 (ii), 57; 20, 212.

Â*l*avi-Gotama was delivered by faith, 10 (ii), 213.

Albîrûnî, on astrological Sa*m*hitâs called after Manu, 25, xcvii; on the Parsi calendar, 47, xlv sq.

Alborz, Kâûs built seven palaces in A., 4, 262 sq. n. *See* Hara Berezaiti.

Albûrz, *see* Mountains.

Alexander the Great as an Anti-Zoroastrian persecutor, 4, xlviii sq.; mentioned in the Hôm Yast, 4, liv; the Rûman, 5, 151, 151 n., 228; a Roman and a Christian, 5, 200 n.; created immortal by Aharman, 24, 35, 35 n.; devastation of Iran owing to the villain A., 37, xxxi, 9 sq.; 47, 82 sq.; ravages of A. and the Arûmans, 37, 413, 413 n.; calamity of A. burning the scriptures, 37, 423 sq., 430, 435, 437, 446 sq.; carried off a rough draft of the Avesta, and repeatedly burnt it, 37, 437, 441 sq.; the devastator, 47, xi, 126; his conquest of Persia, 47, xv, xxviii; date of his death, 47, xxvii sq.; his accession, invasion, and death, 47, xxxi sq.; 'the two-horned' or DHU 'l Qarnâin, 9, 24 n.

Ali, Abu Tâlib's son, converted by Mohammed, 6, xxiii; Abu Bekr and A., Mohammed's only companions during the flight from Mecca, 6, xxxiii sq.

Âligî and Viligî snake-deities, 42, 28

Âlikhat, n. of a demon harassing infants, 29, 296; 30, 211.

Allâh, chief god of the tribes in Arabia, 6, xii; his supremacy merely nominal, 6, xiv; the unity of A. preached by Mohammed, 6, xxiv; called Ar-Ra'hmân, 'the merciful one,' 6, lxi; angels and deities, daughters of A., 6, lxi; Muslim belief in A., 6, lxvi–lxviii; the ninety-nine attributes or 'good names' of A., 6, lxvii sq.; had 1001 names, 23, 21. *See* God.

Allakappa, n.pl., the Bulis of A., 11, 132; Dâgaba at A., 11, 134.

Allât, chief idol of an Arabian tribe, 6, xii sq.; the divinity of A. recognized and again denied by Mohammed, 6, xxvi sq.; favourite idol of *T*â'if, 6, xliii; feminine form of Allâh, 6, 160 n.; the idol of the *Th*aqîf, 9, 9 n.

Allegory, allegorical sacrifice, sense-organs being the priests, sense-objects the oblations, &c., 8, 261; Brahman (or knowledge of Brahman) described as a forest, 8, 284–8; allegorical explanation of Buddhist stanzas, 10 (i), 70 sqq. n. *See also* Parables.

All-gods, *see* Visve Devâ*h*.

All-Sacrifice, *see* Sarvamedha.

Alms, *see* Begging, Charity, *and* Gifts.

Altar, Sk. Vedi, the altar-ground, or sacrificial ground, its preparation, 12, 47–94, 422–5; 26, 1–3; measuring of it, 12, 62 sq.; 43, 30 sq., 306–11; enclosing the a., 12, 423; construction of two altars (vedi and uttaravedi), 12, 392 sq. and n., 417; 26, 115 sq.; 44, 225, 225 n.; 43, 121, 182 sq.; preparation of the Soma a. with the high a. (uttaravedi), 26, 111–20; Uttaravedi, or northern (or upper) a. not required for Vaisvadeva, 12, 388, 388 n.; plan of sacrificial ground, 26, 475; the Vihâra or sacrificial ground, 30, 331; how to step past it, 44, 57 sq.; Barhis spread on it, 46, 198; speculations on it, 43, xvii, xvii n.; as great as the a. is, so great is this earth, 12, 60; 26, 175; the Vedi is this earth, 41, 345, 349; 43, 171, 235; 44, 248; this a.-ground is the farthest end of the earth, 44, 390; is 'the best place of the earth, the place of I*l*â,' 46, 287 sq.; is a woman, 12, 63, 86; 26, 120; etymology of vedi, 12, 60; the altar-ground, is the world of the gods, 43, 118; is fivefold, sevenfold, 43, 308 sq.; whatever good deed man does that is inside the a., whatever evil deed he does that is outside the a., 44, 45; the Vedi is the Gâyatrî, 44, 56; the high a. (uttaravedi) is the nose of the sacrifice, 26, 113; the sky, 41, 349; the air, 44, 248; the sacrifice, 44, 498. *See also* Fire-altar, *and* Holy places.

Altars, five, *see* Fires, five; to be erected by the king and officers, 28, 206 sq.

Ama, n. of Prâ*n*a, breath, 1, 76.

Âmagandhabrâhma*n*a, n. p., 10 (ii), 40.

Âmagandhasutta, t. c., 10 (ii), 40–2.

Amarâ, the faithful wife of Mahosadha, 35, 294–6.

Amarâvatî, city of the gods on Mount Meru, 12, 110 n.

Ambâ, her son *G*anta, 19, xxvii.

Amba-gâma, n.pl., Buddha at, 11, 66.

Ambala*tth*ikâ, n. pl., Buddha at, 11, 12; the Brahmagâla spoken at the royal rest-house at A., 20, 376.

Ambapâlî = Sk. Âmrapâlî, n. of a famous courtesan, who invites Buddha together with his Bhikkhus to a meal, and presents her mansion to the order of mendicants, 11, 30–3; 17, 105–8; 19, 266; her grove at Vesâlî, 11, 28–34; Vesâlî flourishing through her fame, 17, 171 sq.; sees Buddha and is converted by him, 19, 252–6.

Ambarîsha, verses sung of old by king A., 8, 301–3; having dwelt in the forest, returned to the royal office, 19, 107; 49 (i), 100 sq.

Ambâs, Ambâyavîs, and Ambayâs, in the world of Brahman, 1, 276.

Ambassadors, *see* War.

Ambhi*n*î, teacher of Vâ*k*, 15, 226.

Âmbh*r*i*n*î, the voice of thunder, wife of the Maruts, 32, 275.

Ambikâ, sister of Rudra, 12, 440; is the dispenser of happiness, 12, 441.

Ambrosia, *see* Am*r*ita.

Ameretât, *see* Amerôda*d*.

Amerôdad or Amûrdad, Phl. = Zd. Ameretât, immortality, 5, 10 n.; the archangel, created, 5, 10; protector of plants, 5, 30 sq., 176, 310, 310 n., 359; 31, 207, 207 n., 211, 213 sq., 221 sq., 226–8; has the *k*amba flower, 5, 104; attacks Zâîrîk, 5, 128; propitiated, invoked, and worshipped, 5, 372 sq., 377 sq., 401, 405; 23, 5, 14, 36 sq.; 24, 304; creatures are immortal through A., 37, 291; prescribes the care of plants to Zoroaster, 47, 162; mingles the plants with rain, 24, 112 sq. n.; *see* Immortality; *Horvadad (Haurvatât, Khûrdad) and A.*, two archangels, angels of water and plants, 5, 310, 310 n.; 24, 11, 11 n.; their ritual and worship, 5, 227; 24, 304; 47, 76, 76 n.; are the reward of the holy ones, 23, 31, 31 n.; 37, 388; smite hunger and thirst at the resurrection, 23, 308; their gifts, 23, 312 (food and drink); 37, 286 sq. (cattle), 369 (abundance); 47, 26, 26 n. (water and seeds); unreasonable chatter causes distress to them, 24, 11, 11 n.; 37, 207, 207 n.; are injured by immoderate drinking, 24, 48; are propitiated by grace said before and after eating, 24, 284 sq.; the complete worthiness existing in them, 37, 251; their power produced by Aûharmazd, 37, 264; Zoroaster becomes worthy through them, 37, 268; expounded to Frashôstar, 37, 374.

Amesha-Spentas, or Ameshô-spentas, Zd. = Phl. Ameshôspends (Amshaspands), the archangels.

(*a*) A. in mythology.
(*b*) Worship of A.
(*c*) A. as guardians of Zoroastrian religion and morality.

(*a*) A. IN MYTHOLOGY.

A. belong to later Mazdeism, 4, lxi; parallels to the six A. in Philo's system, 4, lvi sq.; the A. as archangels and God's attributes, 5, lxxii; 31, xviii, xxiv; the seven A., 'immortal benefactors,' or 'archangels,' 5, 10 n.; abstracts, and personified, 31, 71, 77 sq., 176, 179 sq., 180 n.; Indra, Saurva, and Naunghaithya, opposed to the A., 4, lii sq.; Spenta Mainyu and the seven A., 4, 139 n.; 31, 145 sq.; rule over the seven Karshvares of the earth, 4, 213; 23, 163; the Garô-nmânem or paradise of the A., 4, 220 sq.; presiding over the regions of nature, 4, 245, 245 n.; Ahura Mazda and the A., 4, 283; 23, 24; 24, 117; the A. assist Ahura Mazda in smiting the demons of Aharman at the resurrection, 5, 128 sq.; opposed by the demons, 37, 21, 21 n.; Aûharmazd performed the spiritual Yazisn ceremony with them, 5, 14; Vayu works the good of Ahura Mazda and the A., 23, 259; the makers and governors and keepers of Ahura Mazda's creations, 23, 291; compassion of Aûharmazd and the A. with their own creatures, 24, 101; Ahura announces Zarathustra's appointment to the A., 31, 4 sq., 10 sq.; called 'the Ahuras of Mazda,' 31, 34, 34 n., 37, 42; Ahura Mazda will give Universal Weal and Immortality, with Vohumanah, Asha, Khshathra, and Âramaiti, 31, 147 sq.; and Saoshyants, 4, 291, 291 n.; creation of the A., 5, 9 sq.; 24, 32 sq.; the white ermine came into the assembly of the A., 5, 89; every flower is appropriate to an angel (Ameshôspend), 5, 103–5; male and female, 5, 215; 31, 214, 288, 319, 348; enumerated, 23, 49, 142 sq.; stand up, as soon as the moon appears, 23, 90; assist Tistrya, 23, 103; the waters flow and plants grow at the wish of the A., 23, 193 sq.; Ahura Vanguhi, sister of A., 23, 270, 274; Aûharmazd sent A. to Vistâsp, 23, 339; 37, 24; the Drug overcome with the help of the A., 31, 37, 42; how the words Asha, Vohu-manah, &c., are used in the Gâthas, 31, 162 n.; it would not be possible to produce the living existence without the A., 24, 356; spiritual blessings bestowed by the A., 31, 178, 186 sq.; the body of the sun made for the creation of the A., 31, 262; worshipped by Sraosha, 31, 298–300, 298 n.; Sraosha among the A., 31, 300, 300 n.; by Sraosha's might the A. descend upon this earth, 31, 303; dwell together with the good mind, 31, 348, 352; reunion of the A. on the heights of Heaven, 31, 382. *See also* Angels (*b*).

(*b*) WORSHIP OF A.
Offerings and prayers to Ahura Mazda and the A., 4, 213, 215, 217, 248, 349; 5, 191; 23, 3, 6, 9 sq., 13, 15, 17 sq., 35, 37, 39, 89, 230, 274; 31, 172; Aûharmazd and the A. praised by all men on the day of judgement, 5, 126; Ahura Mazda and A. long for the morning service, 23, 142, 142 n.; the Haptân Ya*s*t, invocations of the seven A., 23, 2 sq., 35-40; sacrifice and prayer to the A., the Bountiful Immortals, 23, 22, 31, 166, 350, 352 sq., 355; 31, 14, 17, 17 n., 196, &c.; worship in order to increase the A., 23, 34; who worships the sun benefits the A., 23, 86; the friends of the A. worshipped, 23, 165; Fravashis of the A. worshipped, 23, 199 sq.; 31, 273, 278; the glory of the seven A. praised, 23, 290 sq.; all the A. invoked as personalities and qualities, 31, 71, 77 sq. n.; the Yênhê hâtãm prayer devoted to the A., 31, 269.

(*c*) A. AS GUARDIANS OF ZOROASTRIAN RELIGION AND MORALITY.
A. preside over all good things, 4, 149-54, 149 n.; confess the religion of Zoroaster, 23, 142 sq.; longed for Zarathu*s*tra, 23, 202; when the A. came meeting Zaratu*s*t they wore the sacred thread girdle, 24, 270; the unholy priest displeases the A., 23, 156, 331; do not accept ceremonial from the false-hearted man, 24, 53; a wise and innocent poor man esteemed by the A. more than a foolish king, 24, 105; disturbed by untruth, 37, 73; give brightness, glory, and plenty to the righteous, 23, 337, 340; Vahman introduces the soul to Aurmazd and the A., 4, 374; assist, or come to meet, the righteous soul, 23, 336; 24, 17, 17 n., 20 sq., 30, 81, 266, 279; Âramaiti, Sovereign Power, Good Mind, and Righteous Order bestow a body on the soul, 31, 27, 32 sq. *See also* Gods (*l*).

A*m*hasaspati, n. of a god, lord of trouble, 26, 322.

Amînah, mother of Mohammed, 6, xviii.

Amitâbha, or Amitâyus, n. of a former Buddha, his abode in Sukhâvatî, 21, 178, 389, 417; 49 (ii), xxii sq., 32, 91, 97-101, 166 sq., 169-200; A. and his land Sukhâvatî shown by Buddha *S*âkyamuni, 49 (ii), x, 59-61; worshipped in Sukhâvatî, 49 (ii), 67; one of the Dhyâni-buddhas, 49 (ii), 103, Dharmâkara became A., 49 (ii), x, 28; names of A., 49 (ii), 29 sq.; why he is called A. and Amitâyus, 49 (ii), 97 sq.; those who think of the Tathâgata and of Bodhi will after death see A., 49 (ii), 45 sq.; seen by queen Vaidehî, 49 (ii), 175 sq.; his supernatural powers, 49 (ii), 187; worship of and prayers to A. Buddha, 49 (ii), vi, 1, 28-33; repeating or hearing the name of A. Buddha a means of salvation, 49 (ii), viii sq., 68, 99, 198; glorified by Buddhas, 49 (ii), 45; praised by Bodhisattvas and worshipped by gods and men, 49 (ii), 46-8; meditation on the bodily marks of A., 49 (ii), 179-81.

Amitadhva*g*a, n. of a Tathâgata, 49 (ii), 100.

Amitaprabha, n. of a Tathâgata, 49 (ii), 66.

Amitaskandha, n. of a Tathâgata, 49 (ii), 100.

Amitau*g*as, the couch in the world of Brahman, 1, 276, 277.

Amitâyur-dhyâna-sûtra, t. w., sacred book of the Buddhists in Japan, 49 (ii), v-vii, xx-xxii; translated, 49 (ii), 159-201.

Amitâyus, a name of Amitâbha, 49 (ii), 32. *See* Amitâbha.

Amoghadar*s*in, one of the sixteen virtuous men, 21, 4.

Amoghara*g*a, n. of a Bhikshu, 49 (ii), 2.

'Amr, n.p., joins the Muslim ranks, 6, xli.

Amram, *see* Imrân.

Âmrapâlî, *see* Ambapâlî.

'Amr ibn La'hy, chieftain of Mecca, 6, xvii.

Am*ri*ta, Sk., draught of immortality (cf. 'ambrosia'). *See* Immortality.

Am*ri*tânanda, author of the last four books of the Buddha-*k*arita, 49 (1), x sq., xiv-xvii, 147 n., 200 sq. n.

Am*ri*todana, uncle of Buddha, 19, xxv.

Amru and *K*amru, mythical birds, 23, 210, 210 n.
A*m*sa, n.d., Pârtha oblation to, 41, 82; and Vivasvant invoked with other gods, 42, 160; Agni said to be A., desirous of distributing gods, 46, 186, 190.
A*m*su, a*m*sugraha, t.t., a certain cup of Soma at the Soma sacrifice, 41, 5 sq.; 44, 105 sq.; identified with Pragâpati, 26, 248, 423 sq. *See* Sacrifices (*i*).
Amulets, worn for the sake of prosperity, 30, 93; 42, 541; against diseases and demons, 42, 37–9, 42, 67, 234–6, 258 n., 281, 284, 287, 291, 336 sq., 339 sq., 399 sq., 402 sq., 464, 505–7, 511, 553, 561, 578; life-protecting a., 42, 62 sq., 383 sq., 573, 668 sq.; protection against sorceries or talismans, 42, 79–88, 476, 476 n., 575–8, 605, 608–10; to ensure conception, 42, 96 sq., 501 sq.; for strengthening royal power, 42, 114, 239, 332, 439, 477; to secure love, 42, 275 sq., 276 n.; against curses, 42, 285; a king must wear gems which destroy poison, 25, 251; worn by the Snâtaka, 30, 276; worn by women, 42, 356, 460; consisting of salve, 42, 381; of plants, &c., 42, 693 sq.
Amûrda*d*, *see* Amerôda*d*.
Amusements, *see* Games.
Anâbhibhû = Mahâbhig*ñ*âg*ñ*ânâbhibhû, q. v.
Ânabhimlâta, n. of a teacher, 15, 118.
Anâd*r*ita, n. of a tree deity (?), 45, 48 n.
Anâgâmin, Buddh. t.t., 'one that does not return'; the state of the A. results from the four noble truths, x (ii), 132–44.
Anagha, n.d., offering to A. at rites relating to agriculture, 30, 113 sq.
Anâhe*d*, *see* Ardvî-sûra-Anâhita.
Anâhita, *see* Ardvî-sûra-Anâhita.
Ânanda, n.p., the faithful disciple, attendant, and companion of Buddha, 11, 3, &c.; 13, 202, 206; 17, 36, 41, 43, 68 sq., 87 sq., 101 sq., 118, 191 sq., 240 sq.; 20, 80, 299; 21, 3, 205; 49 (ii), 2, 90, 164 sq.; Â. and five other Sâkyas, with Upâli the barber, become Bhikkhus together, 19, 226; 20, 228–33; 35, 163; 49 (i), 193; dialogues between Buddha and Â., 11, 3, 25–7; 49 (ii), ix sq., 3–60; assembles the Bhikshus in the Service Hall, to be addressed by Buddha, 11, 5 sq.; asks Buddha to leave instructions as to the Order, 11, 36; being possessed by Mâra, does not, until it is too late, ask Buddha to stay longer in this world, 11, 41 sq., 54–8; 20, 379 sq.; weeping at the thought of Buddha's death, 11, 95 sq.; 19, 268–70; comforted by Buddha, 11, 96 sq.; 19, 270–4; his wonderful qualities praised by Buddha, 11, 97–9; and the dying Buddha, 11, 99, 118, 238 sq., 247; 19, 286 sq., 290 sq.; Â. and the crow boys who wish to be ordained, 13, 204 sq.; his superior Bela*tth*asîsa, 17, 48, 226; Roga, the Malla, a friend of Â., 17, 135 sq., 228; Â. and the rules about the robes of Bhikkhus, 17, 208 sq., 213 sq., 233; questions Buddha about schisms, 17, 317; mentioned as one of the principal Thera Bhikkhus, 17, 360; Buddha followed by Kâ*s*yapa, the latter by Â., 19, xi, xiv; remained by Buddha's side when all the other Bhikshus took to flight from the drunken elephant, 19, 247; 35, 297–300, 298 n.; recites the Sûtra Pi*t*aka at the Council of the 500 Arhats, 19, 335; Devadatta tells Â. that he will perform Uposatha for himself, 20, 255; persuades Buddha to admit women into the Order, and intercedes in favour of Bhikkhunîs, 20, 321–8, 380; though not an Arhat, chosen as one of the members of the Council of Râgagaha, 20, 372; obtains Arhatship, 20, 373 sq.; questioned by Mahâ-Kassapa about the Vinaya, 20, 376 sq.; charged with various offences at the council of Râgagaha, confesses them, 20, 379 sq.; imposes the higher penalty on *Kh*anna the Bhikkhu, 20, 381–5; preaches to King Udena's ladies, receives a gift of five hundred robes, and satisfies the king as to how Bhikkhus dispose of property given to them, 20, 382–4; gifts to Â., equal to

those given to Buddha, 20, 402; Buddha's prophecy about Â. who is to be the Buddha Sâgaravaradharabuddhivikrî*d*itâbhi*g*ña, 21, 206-8; remembers the Buddhas of the past, 21, 208 sq.; could remember his previous births, 35, 122; Buddha's prophecy to Â. concerning the duration of the law, 35, 185-7; applauds the speech of Buddha, 49 (ii), 72; Buddha instructs Â. about Sukhâvatî and Amitâyus, 49 (ii), 168, 171 sq., 186, 188, 199-201.

Ânanda, n.p., story of Â. the rich man, 36, 249.

Ânanda, Sk., t.t., *see* Bliss.

Ânandagiri, n.p., mentions Dravi*d*â*k*ârya, 34, xxii.

Ânanda *K*etiya, at Bhoga-nagara, 11, 66.

Ânandamaya, t.t., *see* Bliss.

Anangha*d*, son of Hôshâng, 47, 35.

Ananghas, n. of a family, 47, 140.

Ananta, chief among Nâgas, 8, 89.

Ananta, n. of a Tîrthakara, 22, 280.

Ananta*k*âritra, n. of a chief Bodhisattva, 21, 284.

Anantakâya, attendant on Milinda, 35, 47-9; = Antiochos? 35, xix.

Anantamati, son of a former Buddha *K*andrasûryapradîpa, 21, 19.

Ânantarya sins, *see* Sins.

Anantavikrâmin, a Bodhisattva Mahâsattva, 21, 4.

Anantavîrya, n. of a Tathâgata, 49 (ii), 100.

Anâsava, t.t., free from the four Âsavas, 11, 97 n.

Ana*s*nat Sâṅgamana, a deity identified with the hall fire, 12, 338.

Anâsrava, *G*aina t.t., explained, 22, 37 n.

Anastokh, son of Aîrî*k*, 5, 133.

Anâthapi*nd*ada, or °pi*nd*aka, *see* Anâthapi*nd*ika.

Anâthapi*nd*ika, or °pi*nd*aka, or °pi*nd*ada, n.p., meets with Buddha, receives his teaching, and presents the Vihâra of *G*etavana to the Bhikshus, 19, 201-18, 231; 20, 179-89, 197 sq.; Buddha in A.'s Grove at Sâvatthi, 10 (ii), 17, 20, &c.; 11, 210, 223, 296; 13, 210, 302, 325 sq.; 17, 24, 36, 41, 76, 143, 146 sq., 216, 314 sq., 329, 351, 363, 377, 397; 20, 1, 130, 272, 335, 388; 49 (ii), 89, 111; questions Buddha how lay devotees are 'to behave towards the litigious Bhikkhus,' 17, 318; Buddha addresses him as Sudatta, 20, 182; his daughter *K*ulla Subhaddâ, 36, 308 n.

Anatta*m*, t.t., absence of soul, non-individuality, one of the three parts of Buddhist wisdom, 11, 9 n., 162, 294.

Anavanâmita-vai*g*ayanta, n. of the sphere of Ânanda as Buddha, 21, 206 sq.

Anavanatâ Vai*g*ayanti = Anavanâmita-vai*g*ayanta, q. v.

Anavatapta, n. of a Nâga king, 21, 5.

Ancestors, warriors rewarded and punished before the spirits of the a., 3, 77; the king's a. are the spiritual sovereigns, 3, 109; protect and punish their descendants, 3, 109 sq.; the worshipped a. grant a long line of descendants, 3, 402; calling back the spirit of a deceased, 27, 108, 108 n., 112, 129; the dead treated as spiritual intelligences, 27, 148, 148 n.; discontented ghosts of rulers and princes, 28, 206 sq.; deceased ministers become assessors to Heaven, 3, 207, 207 n.; the date of marriage to be announced to the a., 27, 78; the spirit of the departed should not be a single day without a resting-place, 27, 172; by vigil and purification one seems to see the deceased friends, 28, 211; inscriptions with panegyrics of the a., 28, 251-3. *See* Ancestor Worship, Fathers, Fravashis, Souls, *and* Spirits.

Ancestor Worship.

(*a*) Chinese a. w., general views and rules.
(*b*) Sacrifices to ancestors in China.
(*c*) Representatives of the dead in Chinese a. w.
(*d*) Chinese ancestral temples.
(*e*) A. w. in Parsi religion.
N.B.—On a. w. in India, *see* Fathers, Funeral rites, and *S*râddhas.

(*a*) CHINESE A. W., GENERAL VIEWS AND RULES.

Music and dance at a. w., 3, 61; 28, 32 sq.; in worshipping your ancestors prove your filial piety, 3, 98 sq.; 28, 291, 310 sq.; former kings help the men of later times, 3, 120; Tan rears altars to the kings Thâi, *K*î, and Wăn, and prays for the

life of his brother Wû, 3, 152–4, 152 n.; the a. w. of the common people, according to Confucius, 3, 299 sq.; royal a. w. 3, 300–2; 27, 108; a. w. procures long life, 3, 326; a festival in honour of the ancestors, 3, 374 sq.; Wăn conformed to the example of his ancestors, and their spirits had no occasion for dissatisfaction, 3, 388; when passing by a grave, one should bow forward to the cross-bar, 27, 185; visits to the graves of one's fathers on taking and returning from a journey, 27, 185; nourishment of the living, burial of the dead, and service of the spirits, 27, 388 sq., 391; branches of family and a. w., 28, 43 sq., 43 n.; from a. w. arose the worship of nature gods, 28, 67; worthies to whom a. w. is due, 28, 207–9; ceremonies connected with it, 28, 292 sq.; a. w. under different dynasties, 28, 341 sq.; to reverence the spirits of the departed a duty of rulers, 40, 29; the wicked slight the spirits of ancestors, 40, 243.

(*b*) SACRIFICES TO ANCESTORS IN CHINA.

Sacrificial observances paid to the five Tîs, 3, xxviii sq.; Shun sacrificed a bull to the Cultivated Ancestor, 3, 40, 40 n.; in the twelfth month of the first year Î Yin sacrificed to the former king, and presented the heir-king before the shrine of his grandfather, 3, 92; sacrifices offered by the king to his ancestors, 3, 107, 241 sq. and n., 244, 348; 27, 30 sq.; 28, 42–4, 60 sq.; *Kh*ăng honours Tan by sending him an offering, as if he were a departed spirit, 3, 194, 194 n.; animal sacrifices (red bulls) to the ancestors, 3, 195, 366, 370, 370 n., 387; services for spirits and manes regulated by the Minister of Religion, 3, 228, 228 n.; animal sacrifices at a. w., 3, 300; sacrifices and odes to royal ancestors, 3, 304–36; the ancestors enjoy the sacrifice, and bless the worshipper, 3, 306, 339, 339 n., 343–5, 348, 366–8, 370, 375, 401 sq.; spirits and food offered to the ancestors, 3, 369 sq.; libations poured out to the spirits of the departed, 3, 386 sq. and n.; offerings made to the ancestors during a drought, 3, 420 sq., 420 n., 421 n.; extinction of sacrifices to the ancestors equal to extinction of dynasty, 3, 421; the son's duty to mourn for and sacrifice to his parents, 3, 480, 487 sq.; offerings to the spirits of the ancestors, brought by husband and wife, 16, 182, 184 sq. n.; ancestors associated with God at the sacrifices of ancient kings, 16, 287 sq., 289 n.; sacrifices to the departed, 27, 35 sq., 116 sq., 444–8; 28, 201–6, 221 sq., 231, 233 sq., 238, 240–53; food used at offerings to the deceased, 27, 82; names to be given to relatives when they are sacrificed to, 27, 117 sq.; sacrifices at funeral rites, 27, 133, 137, 139, 141 sq., 151, 153, 156 sq., 157 n., 161, 161 n., 168–71, 175, 177 sq., 189 sq.; 28, 46–8, 48 n., 50, 53–5, 58; sacrifice of Repose, 27, 189 sq.; sacrifices to princes, high ministers, and officers who benefited the people, 27, 274; spoils of the chase sacrificed to all ancestors, 27, 300; sacrifices to deified sovereigns and ministers, 27, 307; united sacrifice in the shrine of the high ancestor, 27, 325; sacrifices by a son of a secondary wife instead of the eldest son, 27, 335–7, 335 n., 336 n.; sacrifices to former masters and sages and to the former aged in the college, 27, 359 sq.; origin and development of offerings to the dead, 27, 369–74, 370 n., 444; sacrifice to an old wife, 27, 404; sacrifice to all ancestors, 28, 167; 'they did not sacrifice to their ancestor,' i.e. they had no religion, 40, 166, 170, 170 n.

(*c*) REPRESENTATIVES OF THE DEAD IN CHINESE A. W.;

Personators or representatives of the dead, 3, 78 n., 82, 409, 409 n.; 27, 87, 87 n., 183, 337 sq., 341, 405 sq., 444, 446; 28, 12, 24 sq., 53, 75, 79 sq., 88, 152, 212, 240–2, 245–9, 291–3; the departed ancestors represented by living relatives, 3, 300 sq.; feast given to the personators of the dead after the sacrifice, 3, 333 sq., 402 sq.;

representatives of the dead at the sacrifice to the ancestors, 3, 365, 365 n., 366 n., 367, 367 n., 369; the personators of the departed spirits respond, blessing the sacrificer, 3, 401 sq.; the impersonators of the deceased should sit with gravity, 27, 62, 62 n.; a son must not act as personator of the dead at a. w., 27, 69, 69 n.; the representative of the dead and the officer of prayer, 39, 170, 352; Kăng-sang *Kh*û worshipped as the representative of the departed, 40, 75.

(*d*) CHINESE ANCESTRAL TEMPLES.

Yâo hands the government over to Shun 'in the temple of the Accomplished Ancestor,' 3, 38, 38 n.; on the first day of the first month of the year after Yâo's death, Shun went to the temple of the Accomplished Ancestor, 3, 41; appointment of an arranger in the Ancestral Temple, 3, 44; new kings appointed in a temple dedicated to the spirits of the ancestors, 3, 51, 51 n.; if the king be not virtuous it will bring the ruin of his ancestral temple, 3, 95; spirits of the a. t. worshipped by the pious, 3, 96; to retain a place in the seven-shrined a. t. is a sufficient witness of virtue, 3, 102, 102 n.; Shâu discontinued the offerings in the a. t., 3, 126, 130; after his successful war Wû sacrifices at the a. t. 3, 133 n., 134; 'guests' of sovereigns assist in the services in the a. t., 3, 162, 162 n.; shrines of sovereigns in the a. t. 3, 303, 311, 313 sq., 322, 326 n., 328 sq.; fish-offering in the a. t. 3, 324 sq.; sacrificial service in the a. t., 3, 365–8, 474 sq. and n.; 27, 112, 115, 218, 220, 223–7, 261, 261 n., 264, 278, 285, 289, 294 sq., 307 sq., 385 sq., 411 sq., 422 sq., 435, 459; 28, 32, 50 sq., 265, 271, 308–11; the officers of Yin assist at the libations in the a. t. of the *K*âu, 3, 379, 379 n.; ancestral temples raised by rulers and officers, 3, 384, 384 n., 424; 16, 341, 342 n.; 28, 204–6; reverence exhibited in the a. t., 3, 388, 485 sq.; 27, 191; feast and archery contest at the close of the sacrifice in the a. t., 3, 399–401; a gift of a libation cup and spirits, to be used for sacrificing in the a. t., 3, 427, 427 n.; 'the ancestral chamber,' 3, 432, 432 n.; to preserve their a. t. the duty of high ministers, 3, 470, 470 n.; King Wan sacrificed to in the Brilliant Hall as the correlate of God, 3, 477; there will be progress and success if a king repairs to the a. t., using great victims, 16, 156 sq., 158 sq. n.; the king goes to his a. t., 16, 194, 196 n., 261; filial piety displayed in the king's worshipping in the a. t., 16, 250 sq.; a sincere worshipper maintains his a. t., 16, 256; ceremony of the banquet following the sacrifice in the a. t. 27, 57 sq.; 28, 446, 454–7; a ruler shall dismount in passing the a. t., 27, 97; the a. t. must be first attended to in the erection of buildings, 27, 103 sq.; ancestral temples of great officers, graves of minor officers, 27, 107; the grand minister of the a. t., one of the six grandees, 27, 109; pulling down part of the wall of the a. t. at the funeral, 27, 144; wailing of the ruler when the shrine of his father burned, 27, 190; duty of the ruler to attend to the observances of the a. t., 27, 217; plan of an a. t., 27, 224 n.; vessels of an a. t. not to be sold, 27, 238; first-fruit offering in the a. t., 27, 271, 274; autumnal sacrifice in the a. t., 27, 293; provisions for worship in the a. t., 27, 308 sq.; offerings in the a. t., on a prince's taking a journey, 27, 314 sq., 326; the new wife presented in the a. t., 27, 322; grand a. t. taking fire, causes interruption of ceremonies, 27, 328–30; proceedings in the a. t., rules of precedence, 27, 354, 357; marriage, capping, deaths, and sacrifices announced in the a. t., 27, 355 sq., 358; emperor lodges in the a. t., when visiting a feudal prince, 27, 375; to die for the a. t., the prerogative of the ruler, 27, 379; number of shrines in a. t., 27, 397; services in the a. t., a natural duty, 27, 397; presentation of a cup at sacrifices in the a. t., 27, 399; in the sacrifices of the a. t. there is the utmost expression of humanity, 27, 413; no

avoiding of names in the a. t., 28, 18; demeanour in the a. t., 28, 25; use of music in the a. t., 28, 101, 127 sq.; prayer-officers of the a. t., 28, 116; placing the spirit-tablets in the a. t., 3, 488; 27, 168, 168n., 171 sq., 192, 313, 313 n.; 28, 48, 50-2, 56 sq., 65-7, 136 sq., 156, 159 sq., 163; two spirit-tablets in one temple shrine, 27, 323 sq.; removal of spirit-tablets from their shrines, 27, 324 sq.; guarding the spirit-tablets in the ruler's absence, 27, 355, 358; from dignity of a. t. arose importance of altars of the land and grain, 28, 67; consecration of an a. t., 28, 169 sq.; emoluments, rank, rewards conferred in the a. t., 28, 233, 247; site for the a. t., 28, 235; ceremonies in the a. t., 28, 258 sq., 262; rulers always lodge in the a. t., 28, 351; capping ceremony performed in the a. t., 28, 427; to secure services in the a. t. one of the ends of marriage, 28, 428; marriage ceremonies in the a. t., 28, 428 sq., 432.

(*e*) A. W. IN PARSI RELIGION.

Sacrifice for the departed soul offered up to Sraosha, 4, 136, 136 n.; 18, 59-63; funeral oblations for the soul of a killed dog, 4, 169; appointed feasts of the ancestors, 5, 208; funeral cakes offered to Rashnû, Âstâd, and Vâê, 5, 383; tenth-day, monthly, and annual ceremonies for the departed, 5, 383; ceremony of the guardian spirits of the righteous in honour of the departed, 18, 173, 173 n.; daily and annual ceremonies for the departed to be performed by the heir, 18, 184, 184 n.; annual worship of the Fravashis as the souls of the dead, 23, 192 sq., 192 n.; offerings to the Fravashis, 23, 197; attending the souls of parents and relatives an indispensable good work, 24, 264; consecration of sacred cakes, 24, 272-4; sacred feast (myazd) in honour of the souls, 24, 273 sq., 283; why ceremonies in honour of the departed souls must be celebrated, 24, 273-5; sacred cakes and ceremonial, sacred feast and benedictions for the departed souls on the ten days of the Fravashis, 24, 298-300; Fravashis *and* souls of departed worshipped, 31, 273, 275, 279; sacrifice to the souls of the dead, 31, 331; Âfrînagân, prayers recited at meals in honour of the deceased, 31, 367-75; adoption for the benefit of departed souls, 37, 147; the departed claim ceremonial, not lamentation, 37, 193; reverencing the spirit of a kinsman, 37, 231. *See also* Fravashis, *and* Funeral rites.

Ancestral Temples, *see* Ancestor Worship (*d*).

Ancient One, the, *see* God.

Andar, or Andra, Zd. I*n*dra, one of the six demons of Aharman, 5, 10, 10 n.; his business, 5, 106 sq.; smitten by Ashavahi*s*t, 5, 128, 128 n.; opposed to the wearing of a sacred girdle, 37, 182, 182 n.; *see also* Îndar, *and* I*n*dra.

Andhaka, n. of a demon slain by *S*iva, 42, 620.

Andhakas, n. of a people, suffered destruction, 49 (i), 116.

Andhakavinda, n.pl., Mahâ Kassapa going from A. to Râ*g*agaha, 13, 254; Buddha at A., 17, 87.

Andhakav*rishn*i, Rathanêmi is an A., 45, 118.

Andhras, in the code of Manu, 7, xxiv.

Andra, *see* Andar.

Aneran, Zd. anaghra, boundless (space), *see* Space.

Aṅga, n.p., converted by Buddha, 19, 241.

Aṅgas, n. of a people, Takman (fever) delivered over to them, 42, 2, 446, 449.

Aṅgas, *see* Vedâṅgas, *and* *G*aina.

Angels.

(*a*) In Mohammedanism.
(*b*) In Parsi religion.
(*c*) In Buddhism.

(*a*) IN MOHAMMEDANISM.

Arabian belief in a., 6, xi, xiii; Muslim belief in a., 6, lxviii sq.; guard the gates of heaven, 6, cvi; 9, 168; God addresses the a. at the creation, 6, 4 sq.; bear witness to what God revealed, 6, 95; adore Adam, 6, 138, 246; 9, 8, 19 sq., 43 sq., 181; Mohammed asked to bring down a., 6, 245; visit

Abraham, 6, 247 sq.; 9, 120; called 'daughters of God' by the Arabs, 6, 256 n.; are not the daughters of God, 9, 5, 212; are not females, 9, 250, 252; if a. were walking on the earth, God would have sent an angel as His apostle, 9, 11; the a. only descend at the bidding of the Lord, 9, 31 sq. and n.; are servants of God, 9, 48, 174; God makes the a. His messengers, endued with wings, 9, 157; oaths by the a. who execute God's behests, 9, 168, 314, 314 n., 318, 318 n.; circling round His throne celebrate the praises of God, 9, 190 sq., 202, 205; obey God in what He bids them, 9, 291; ascend unto God, 9, 300 sq.; the nineteen a. of hell, 9, 309; descend in the 'night of power,' 9, 337; assist the believers in battle, 6, 61 sq., 164, 169, 169 n.; God sends guardian a. to watch over men, 6, 122, 233; sent down to warn men that there is no other God, 6, 251; receive the good in Paradise, the unbelievers in hell, 6, 235, 253; the two numberers or recording a., 9, 72, 243, 243 n.; recording a. note down the secret plots of the infidels, 9, 217; pray for the believers, 9, 191; the lower heaven adorned with guardian a., 9, 200; descend upon the believers, to encourage them, 9, 201 sq.; ask forgiveness for men, 9, 205; the a. (Munkir and Nakîr) take the souls to account, 9, 232; the a. back up him who repents, 9, 291; the spirit and the a. stand in ranks on the last day, 9, 317; guardian a. set over men, writing down what they do, 9, 323; every soul has a guardian angel, 9, 328.

(*b*) In Parsi Religion.

The a. were contending in the world ninety days and nights with the demons of the evil spirit, 5, 19; fire produced under the guidance of the a., 5, 55 sq.; a good king equal to the a., 24, 44; a. and archangels in heaven, 24, 83 sq.; Aûharmazd formed an assembly of a. and archangels, 24, 104; prepared out of fire, 24, 178; four a. round the throne of God, 24, 224; for each man an angel is stationed on the right-hand side, and two a. for the priests, 24, 283; every man of fifteen years must take an angel as his patron spirit, 24, 288 sq.; days named after the a., 37, 34 sq., 35 n.; a. and archangels, *see* Amesha-Spe*n*tas.

(*c*) In Buddhism.

The angel hosts of the guardian a., 11, 48; how many a can stand on the point of a gimlet (needle), 11, 88 n., 315; are the constant attendants of the preachers of the Lotus, 21, 278; *see also* Gods.

Anger, let a man overcome a. by love, 10 (i), 58 sq.; Buddha preaches against lust and a., 19, 263–5; the Bhikshu must be free from a. and hate, 19, 299 sq. *See also* Passion, *and* Wrath.

Aṅghâri, n. of a Gandharva, guardian of Soma, 26, 72.

Anghuyu, n.p., the Fravashi of A. worshipped, 23, 215; 31, 351.

Aṅgir, Atharvan told the knowledge of Brahman to him, 15, 27.

Aṅgiras.

(*a*) A. in the singular, n. of a *R*ishi, and a mythical being.
(*b*) A. in the plural, a family of priests or sorcerers.
(*c*) A. in the plural, a class of divine beings.

(*a*) A. in the singular, n. of a *R*ishi, and a mythical being.

A. meditated on the udgîtha, 1, 6; Bhâradvâ*g*a told the knowledge of Brahman to A., 15, 27; A. told the science of Brahman to *S*aunaka, 15, 42; 48, 284; surpassed by his son *S*ukra, 19, 10; 49 (i), 8; *S*ukra and A. honour Indra in heaven, 19, 95; 49 (i), 93; remodelled the Manusm*ri*ti, 25, xcvi; 33, xii, 274; a sage and a Pra*g*âpati, 25, 14; Kavi, son of A., 25, 58; the sacred texts revealed by Atharvan and A., 25, 436, 436 n.; ceremonies performed A.-like, 41, 154, 201 sq., 205 sq., 214, 227, 233–5, 241–4, 246, 307; Atharvan, A., and Bh*ri*gu as fire-priests, 42, xxiii, xxvii, xxx, xxxii, xxxiv, lvii sq.; oblations to Bh*ri*gu and A., 42, lvii; B*ri*hatsâman, the descendant of A., 42, 171; and Atharvan rule over the heavens, 42, 225; Agni worshipped by A., 46, 42, 102; a name or epithet of

Agni, 12, 102 n., 108; 26, 118; 41, 225, 279; 46, 1, 92, 95, 327, 348, 385, 389, 391, 412; Havishmats (manes), children of A., 25, 112; is the breath, 41, 233–5; the plants descended from A., 42, 43; invoked in an imprecation, 42, 89 sq., 161; the tree *g*aṅgida called A., 42, 38, 280, 673.

(*b*) A. IN THE PLURAL, A FAMILY OF PRIESTS, OR SORCERERS.

The A. kindled (discovered) Agni, 12, 108; 46, 391; Agni, the tutelary god of the A., 49 (i), 22; Agni, the first of the A., 41, 358; 46, 22, 129; the A. as sacrificers, 26, 28 sq.; the Maruts are like the A. with their songs, 32, 416; 'our fathers, the A., have broken even the strong fortresses by their hymns, the rock by their shouting. They have opened to us the path of the great heaven; they have obtained day and sun and the shine of the dawn. They founded the *Ri*ta; they set into motion the thought of it,' 46, 74, 77; B*ri*haspati, descendant of the A., 42, 127 sq.; Agîgarta, an Aṅgiras, 44, xxxvi sq., xxxvii n.; sorceries come from the A., 42, 73, 80, 219, 576, 603, 624; designation of hostile sorcery practices, 42, xviii–xxiv; Saramâ threatens the Pa*n*is with the terrible A., 42, xxiii.

(*c*) A. IN THE PLURAL, A CLASS OF DIVINE BEINGS.

The A. rise above (zenith), 15, 340; sprung from coals (aṅgâra), 26, 388; the court of justice belongs to the A., 29, 362; the A., the children and grandchildren of Brahman, 30, 195; worshipped at the Tarpa*n*a, 30, 243; the A. slay the Dasyus, and destroy their castles, 42, xxxiii, 86; help in battle, 42, 119; the seven *Ri*shis or A., sons of heaven and dawn, break the rock of the cows, 46, 239, 318, 322, 326, 329 sq.;—the *Âdityas* and the A., both sprung from Pragâpati, were contending together for heaven, and sacrificed, 26, 113 sq.; 44, 152; course of Âdityas, and course of A., 26, 383 sq.; Âdityas, Vasus, and A., 42, 89; Âdityas and A. worshipped, 42, 191; the light of the *Bhrigus* and A. is the brightest, 12, 37 sq., 38 n.; Bh*ri*gus, or A., attained the heavenly world, 26, 272; *Yama*, accompanied by the A. and fathers, 12, 364 n.; 30, 226; 44, 481. *See also* Yama Aṅgiras.

Aṅgirasa, Pali for Sk. Aṅgiras, n. of a *Ri*shi, 11, 172.

Âṅgirasa, t.t., Âtharva*n*a='holy,' âṅgirasa='pertaining to sorcery,' 42, 219, 624.

Âṅgirasa, 'a descendant of Aṅgiras'; *Ri*shis led by the old sage Â., 8, 314; an epithet of Buddha, 13, 122; numerous Â., 42, xxxv; Ghora Â., 42, xxi, xxxv; Pra*k*etas Â., 42, 163, 484 sq. *See* Ayâsya Â., Dadhya*ñk* Â., Dharu*n*a Â., Hira*n*yastûpa Â., Kutsa Â.

Âṅgirasa, n. of an author on medicine, 36, 109, 109 n.

Angra-mainyu, Zd., the evil spirit, Aharman and Ganrâk-maînôk in Phl., 5, 3 n., 4 n.; the Daêva of the Daêvas, 4, 224 sq.; A. and the six chief demons, 4, 139 n.; the fiend who is all death, 23, 29; the counter creations of A., 4, 1 sq., 4–10; sends diseases and deformities, 4, 17, 19; noxious animals the creatures of A., 4, 25, 29; creates 99,999 diseases, 4, 236–9; the accursed Khrafstras of A., 23, 310, 310 n.; attacks Zarathu*s*tra and propounds riddles to him, 4, liii, 208, 210, 210 n.; sends the demon Bûiti to kill Zarathu*s*tra, 4, 208–10; Ahura Mazda opposed by A., 31, xviii sq.; not mentioned in Darius's inscriptions, 31, xxx; not mentioned in the first statement of the doctrine of dualism, 31, 25 n.; compare Ahimanyu, 32, 119; flings the Pairikas against the stars that have in them the seed of waters, 23, 104; Takhma Urupa rides A. turned into a horse, 23, 252, 252 n., 292 sq.; drags the souls of the wicked into hell, 23, 340; created Azi Dahâka, 31, 233; spells against A., 4, 126, 138, 141, 146 sq.; 31, 312 sq., 390; conquered by the Airyama Ishyô prayer, 4, 247; 23, 43–7; glorifies the powers of Asha-Vahi*s*ta, 23, 41, 45; religion the

destroyer of A., 4, 370; may A. be destroyed, 23, 22; smitten by Ahura Mazda, 23, 33; 31, 264; flees from Mithra, 23, 144, 151; defeated by prayer to Mithra, 23, 150; gives way to the blows of Spe*n*ta-Mainyu, 23, 183; the Fravashis help against A., 23, 197; Ahura Mazda smites the creation of A., 23, 250; does no harm to the worshipper of Vayu, 23, 262; defeated by Zarathu*s*tra, 23, 274 sq.; Aryan glory destroys A., 23, 284; powerless at the resurrection, 23, 308; sacrifice to smite the wicked A., 31, 280; Sraosha hews down A., 31, 305. *See* Ganrâk-maînôk, *and* Aharman.

Aṅgulimâla, a robber, converted by Buddha, 13, 196; 19, 243; 36, 355.

Aṅguli-mala-parittâ, title of a protecting charm, 35, 213.

Aṅguttara-Nikâya, t.w., and Mahâparinibbâna-Sutta, 11, xxxiv sq.; Dhamma*k*akkappavattana-Sutta belongs to it, 11, 139.

Aṅguttarâpa, n. of a country, 10 (ii), 96 sq.; Buddha at A., 17, 127.

Anidâna, *G*aina t.t., free from sinful acts, 22, 40.

Anikshiptadhura, n. of a Bodhisattva Mahâsattva, 21, 4; 49 (ii), 90,

Anila Vâtâyana, author of a Vedic hymn, 32, 450.

Animals.

(*a*) Origin of a.
(*b*) Classification of a.
(*c*) Zoology.
(*d*) A. as compared with men.
(*e*) Use of flesh, milk, skin, &c., of a.
(*f*) Treatment of a.
(*g*) Laws and regulations about a.
(*h*) Noxious a.
(*i*) A. in mythology.
(*j*) Worship of a.
(*k*) On some special a.

(*a*) ORIGIN OF A.

Creation of a., 5, 10, 31 sq., 46, 179; 15, 86; 25, 15; 37, 150; 41, 402; 43, 74 sq., 403; useful a. created in opposition to noxious creatures, 5, 71–4; creation of noxious creatures, 5, 162 sq.; all a. created by God, 9, 79; Pragâpati fashioned a. from his vital airs, hence a. are vital airs, 41, 402; symbolical creation of a., 43, 36-41; certain a. arise from parts of the body of the bewitched Indra, 44, 214–16; origin of the ape and the bear, 5, 87; 18, 419; origin of the ass and the barren cow, 26, 388; worms, beetles, ants, &c., are the remains of dead Yakkhas, 36, 108 sq.; origin of lion, wolf, and other wild beasts, 41, 131; though being eaten and cooked, a. do not diminish, being established in the womb, 41, 401; rebirth of men in a. as a punishment, 1, 82; 7, 144–7; 8, 105 n., 109 n., 321, 356 n.; 21, 92 sq.; 25, 485, 493, 496–8; 45, 15.

(*b*) CLASSIFICATION OF A.

The five classes of a., 5, 45–52; 23, 182, 182 n., 190 sq.; 47, 160 sq.; five kinds of noxious a. which must be killed, 24, 306 sq.; elephant first of vehicles, lion of forest a., sheep of sacrificial a., snake of dwellers in holes, bull among cattle, 8, 345, 353; behind the men are the beasts, behind the gods are birds, plants, and trees, 12, 140; creatures with teeth on one side only, and with teeth on both sides, 12, 171, 171 n.; small living beings of five kinds, 22, 304; seven domestic and seven wild a., 26, 213; 41, 40 n.; 43, 211, 277; tame a. separate from wild a., 42, 51; there are four kinds of four-footed a., 43, 56; division of a., 5, 179–82; 22, 11; 25, 15 sq.; 36, 101; division of a. into ekendriyas, dvîndriyas, &c., 45, xxx, 219–21.

(*c*) ZOOLOGY.

Three origins of a., from an egg, from a living being, and from a germ, 1, 94; a. born from eggs, from germs, from perspiration, and from wombs, 8, 339; 22, 11; 25, 15 sq.; 36, 101; period of gestation in a., 37, 110 sq.; curious views about the impregnation of some a., 39, 361 sq.; those with nine apertures are born from the womb, those with eight from eggs, 40, 63; are born with bones, though introduced into the womb only as seed, 41, 254; having received the foetus standing, give birth after lying down, 41, 363; of a. the head born first, the tail last, 43, 40; the beast is threefold: father, mother, son; and embryo, amnion, chorion, 43, 110; on the generation of the various kinds of a.,

and how they feed, 45, 394–8; worms and other little a. originate from honey and similar substances, 48, 417 sq.; worms, scorpions, originate from dung, 48, 464; the left side of the belly of a well-filled beast is more raised than the right side, 41, 400; are biggest towards the middle, 43, 40, 50; their right side is the stronger, 43, 40; rise and sit down by their fore and hind parts, 43, 41; fire in men and a., 5, 61; delight in being near the fire, 41, 164, 164 n.; why a. dwell in the air, 43, 45 sq., 50 sq.; draught animals pull with all four limbs, 44, 78; walk on two feet at a time, 44, 78; are of sixteen parts, 44, 252; duration of their life, 45, 220–4.

(*d*) A. AS COMPARED WITH MEN.

Difference between men and a., 10 (ii), 111 sq.; 34, 7 sq.; pretended knowledge of the language of beasts, 11, 196; speech of a. is unintelligible, 26, 268; possess their knowledge by instinct, 24, 39; men acting like cats or herons, i.e. hypocrites, 25, 159 sq.; the *kh*âi (polecats?) sacrifice larger a. and devour the smaller, 27, 292; love among a., 28, 392; envy among a., 37, 92; excluded from the study of the Veda, 34, 197 n.; have reasoning, but no wisdom, 35, 51; cannot attain to insight into the truth, 36, 176; likes and dislikes of different a., 40, 8 sq., 26; man is the two-footed animal, 41, 409; brilliancy of a. (lion, tiger, &c.), transferred upon kings, 42, 116 sq., 477; commit sins, 45, 356; there are individual souls of beasts, birds, creeping a., 48, 198; small creatures (flies, worms, &c.) go to the 'third place' (not to the world of the gods, or of the fathers), 1, 82; reach perfection or heaven by penance, 8, 389; 25, 478, 478 n.; chiefs or kings of a., 5, 88 sq., 88 n., 91; 8, 345; 24, 108, 108 n.; 30, 114; 49 (i), 196 sq.; are communities like men, their fate written in the Book, and they shall be gathered on the judgement day, 6, lxxxv, 119; destroyed for sacrifices, are reborn to higher existences, 25, 175; 48, 599.

(*e*) USE OF FLESH, MILK, SKIN, &C., OF A.

Lawful and forbidden flesh of a., 2, 64 sq., 65 n., 74 sq., 268–70; 7, 162–6; 12, 52; 14, 74 sq., 184 sq.; 25, 171 sq.; selling forbidden meat, 7, 30; not the eating of flesh defiles a man, but a bad mind and wicked deeds, 10 (ii), 40 sq.; boar's flesh eaten by Buddha, 11, 71–3; animal food allowed for hermits, 14, 259; raw flesh, meat broth, and blood allowed as medicaments, 17, 49, 61; flesh of a. which must not be eaten by Bhikkhus, 17, 85 sq.; *G*ainas accuse Buddhists of killing a. to eat meat, 17, 116 sq.; Buddha forbids the meat of a. killed for the purpose, but allows fish, 17, 117; flesh of ass and pig used for sacred feasts, 18, 311, 311 n.; rules about eating meat and killing a., meritoriousness of abstinence from meat, 25, 170, 173–7; a. are food, 43, 46, 56; a. whose milk is forbidden, 2, 268; 7, 167; 25, 170 sq.; skins of a black antelope, a tiger, a he-goat, as garments for students of the three castes, 7, 115; boar's skin for shoes, 41, 102 sq.; tiger's skin, 41, 81, 91–3, 96, 105, 105 n.; 42, 111 sq., 378–80; antelope's skin, *see* Antelope; bull's hide, *see* Bull; the sacrificer at the Vâgapeya steps on the skin of a he-goat, 41, 35; the first layer of the altar appeased on a red ox-skin, 41, 355–7; the sacrificial skin at Soma sacrifices, 42, 180 sq., 612; strainer of goat's hair and sheep's wool a form of goats and sheep, a tail-whisk, a form of kine and horses, 44, 235; dung of a. sacrificed, 30, 125 sq., 128; trade in products of a., 37, 139–42. *See also* Animal sacrifice, Cattle, Horse sacrifice.

(*f*) TREATMENT OF A.

Penance for killing a., 2, 83 sq., 285 sq., 285 n.; 7, 138 sq., 159–61; 14, 113 sq.; 25, 457–9; lawful and unlawful slaughter of a., 5, 319; 7, 169–72; 14, 19, 26 sq. and n.; 25, xxxi, 172–6; 27, 227; 28, 227 sq.; 37, 440, 452; 40, 241; chase of brute beasts lawful, 6, 96 sq.; punishments for injuring or

killing a., 7, 29–31, 35, 40, 173; 14, 202; 25, 304, 306, 444; 'Me he (mâ*m* sa) will eat in the next world, whose flesh (mâ*m*sa) I am tasting here,' 7, 171 sq.; five places where a. are liable to be destroyed, 7, 193; kindness to be shown to draught a., 7, 200; 33, 359; medical treatment of a., 7, 39; 37, 48, 118; antelope, elephant, butterfly, bee, and fish destroyed by the five objects of sense, 8, 155 n.; combats between elephants, horses, buffaloes, bulls, goats, rams, cocks, and quails not to be witnessed by the Bhikkhus, 11, 192; injunctions against annoying a., 17, 24 sq.; the sufferings of a., 19, 158; sin of injuring a., 22, 11–13; 37, 84 sq.; when a *G*aina mendicant perceives hungry a. feeding off offerings thrown on the ground, he should go out of their way, 22, 102 sq.; to be protected, 24, 67; 47, 160 sq.; sins regarding useful a., 24, 96; certain a. must not be killed, and certain parts of killed a. must be consecrated, 24, 295; regard for a., the creatures of heaven, in hunting, 27, 220 sq.; protection of a. in spring, 27, 256, 259; work and food of an injured beast, 37, 67; care of mad a., 37, 105 sq.; ill-treatment of a., 37, 130; the wicked hurt a., 40, 240 sq.; are gelded, 42, 8, 67; punishment for gelding a., 7, 35; spells put into a. by enemies, 42, 76, 457; Zoroaster's kindness to a., 47, 153 sq. *See* Ahi*m*sâ, Animal sacrifices, *and* Cattle.

(*g*) Laws and regulations about a.

False evidence regarding a., 14, 83; 25, 271; owners responsible for offences committed by a., 24, 286; healing a., 7, 31 sq.; 25, 310 sq.; division of property consisting in a., 25, 347–9, 349 n., 351, 357; not to be sold by Brâhma*n*as, 25, 421; as articles of sale, 33, 150; bestial crimes, 7, 29; 33, 180; sequestrator's rights and duties with regard to seized a., 37, 131–4, 136; training of a., 25, 106; to be removed from a king's council, 25, 239, 239 n.; dogs and horses not to be taken to the hall, 27, 96; wealth of an ordinary man described by telling the number of a. he keeps, 27, 116; bulls and stallions sent forth to the females, 27, 266; rules about presenting a., 28, 76; rites performed when mounting an elephant, a horse, &c., 29, 365 sq.; 30, 170, 295; how a. are to be mounted, 41, 361; breeding sheep and dogs, 37, 101; trade in products of a., 37, 139–42; pollution caused by dead a., 5, 260 sq. and n.; pollution of a., 5, 272 sq.; 24, 337; a. not to be looked at by a menstruous woman, 5, 283; bones of five-toed a. defile, 7, 94, 95; impurity caused by a., 7, 100–4, 100 n.; 25, 119; a goat and a horse are pure, as regards their mouths, but not a cow, 7, 102; a *S*râddha is auspicious when performed in sight of a goat, but the sight of a dog, or a tame pig, or a tame cock is to be avoided, 7, 250; Snâtaka not to travel with imperfect or disfigured beasts, 25, 139; inauspicious a., 25, 149; *see also* Omens; which are pure, 25, 192; foxes of evil omen, 40, 76; three unclean a., boar, ram, and dog, 44, 178 sq.

(*h*) Noxious a.

Killing creatures of Ahriman is a pious work, 4, lxxviii, 188; 5, 394; 24, 28, 306 sq.; 37, 86, 149 sq. n., 150 sq.; obnoxious a. created by Ahriman, 4, 4 sq., 25, 29; 5, 17; 18, 96; those a. which are creatures of Ahriman do not defile by their death, 4, 60; the Drug is like Khrafstras or noxious a., 4, 77, 77 n.; Khrafstras produced by hair and nails cut and dropped into holes, 4, 190; red Khrafstras pollute mortals, 31, 85, 87; destruction of noxious creatures by Tî*s*tar, 5, 169 sq.; killing noxious a. as atonement for sin, 4, 207; 5, 281, 300, 300 n., 307; noxious a. may be killed in self-defence, 7, 40; atonement for being bitten by certain a., 25, 471, 471 n.; 30, 128; 'Vermin-killer' for destroying noxious creatures, 37, 162, 162 n.; tigers and snakes, shaft and missile, 43, 107; noxious a. produced by the smiting of Dahâk, 37, 214; charm against poison of

scorpions and insects, 42, 29 sq., 553; charm against wild beasts, 42, 147 sq., 366–9; diseases caused by certain a., 42, 500 n., 501.

(*i*) A. IN MYTHOLOGY.

List of mythical a. described, 5, 67–71, 88 sq., 88 n., 91; the four intelligent creatures (*Kh*ilin, phoenix, tortoise, dragon), 27, 383 sq., 384 n., 393, 410; monsters and dragons in the ocean, 36, 191, 298, 304; men lived in common with the a. in the age of perfect virtue, 39, 140, 278; 40, 171; magic plants discovered by an eagle, or a boar, or an ichneumon, 42, 43 sq., 77, 137, 306, 580 sq.;—the animalcule *Anuddharî* (or Kunthu) which is only seen by monks who have reached the state of perfection, 22, 267, 304; 45, 15, 220, 220 n.; the ox *Barmâyûn*, 37, 218, 220; a boar, called *Emûsha*, raised the earth, and he was her lord Pragâpati, 44, 451; the wolf *Kapûd* and the bird Kamak slain by Keresâsp, 24, 63, 63 n.; dance to *Khwei's* music, 3, 45, 61; the khwei, a one-footed animal, 39, 384, 384 n.; an *ox* decides boundary disputes between Iran and Tûrân, 47, 31–3, 135–8; the *primaeval Bull*, 4, 231, 231 n., 290 sq., 290 n.; 5, 45 sq.; 47, xxix, xli; the seed of the primaeval bull in the moon, 4, 233, 233 n.; 5, 179; 23, 8, 8 sq. n., 16, 88–91, 176, 355; death of the primaeval ox, 5, 20; origin of plants from the primaeval ox, 5, 99 sq., 177–9; the ox Sarsaok, 5, 58, 62, 69 sq.; origin of a. from the primaeval ox, 5, xxiii, 20 n., 179; 37, 150; men going forth on the ox Srûvô (Sarsaok, Srisaok), 5, 186, 186 n.; the immortal ox Hadhayãs or Sarsaok, whose fat yields the elixir of immortality, 18, 111 sq. and n., 118, 171; the dark progeny of the primaeval ox cause the eclipses, 18, 212 sq., 212 n.; the ox Hadhayãs, who causes the perfection of primitive man, 18, 257, 257 n.; primaeval ox attacked by evil spirit, 5, 17 sq., 31 sq., 161 sq., 161 n.; 18, 94, 94 n.; 47, 33, 33 n.; *see also* Gosûrûn; the *Saêna* or Sîmurgh, 23, 241 n., 242; *Sâlaka*, a very tiny animal, 36, 180, 180 n.; the four-eyed bitch, *Saramâ*, 42, 68, 404; the mythical *three-legged ass* in the ocean, 5, 67–9, 67 n.; 24, 111, 111 n.;—with horse, ass, and he-goat, one searches for *Agni*, 41, 198, 204–6, 224–7; *Aharman's* body is that of a lizard, 5, 105; contention between the lizard and the Kar fish, 5, 65 sq.; no brute creation in a *Buddha country*, 49 (ii), 12, 33, 96 sq.; *Krishna* as Lord of beasts, 8, 89 sq.; for *Rudra*, the wild beasts are in the forest and in the waters, 42, 157; the brain of a. the spittle of *Tvash*tri, 26, 202; the four-footed a. protected by *Vasus* and *Rudras*, 43, 68; *Verethraghna* in the shape of a boar, 23, 137, 153, 235; Verethraghna in the shape of a., 23, 231, 233–8; oxen, horses, wolves refuse to kill the child *Zoroaster*, 47, 37–9, 145 sq. *See also* Omens.

(*j*) WORSHIP OF A.

Souls of a. worshipped, 23, 197, 229; 31, 288; food placed on the ground as bali-offering for a., 25, 92; 29, 87; offerings to cats and tigers, 27, 432, 432 n.; sacrifice to all the a., 31, 329; chiefs of a. worshipped, 31, 338; of the earth, and of heaven, invoked as divine beings, 42, 161.

(*k*) ON SOME SPECIAL A.

Simile of the *bat*, 36, 346; sin of killing a *beaver*, 24, 71, 71 n., 350; clouds as *boars*, 32, 72; simile of the boar, 36, 334 sq.; why the king puts on shoes of boar's skin, 41, 102 sq.; vicious boar unclean, 44, 178; earth torn up by boar, 44, 451; the wild *buffalo* and the sarabha assigned to Agni, 41, 411 sq.; the buffaloes, i.e. the priests, quicken the sacrifice, 44, 231; simile of the *cat*, 36, 326 sq.; *deer* sent by the princes as tribute to the king, 27, 433; simile of the deer, 36, 331 sq.; fever allayed by means of a *frog*, 42, 4, 565–8; frogs used at rites for quenching fire, 42, 348–51, 514 sq.; origin of frogs from water, 43, 174–6; *hare* in the moon, 44, 10; *hedgehog* to be preserved, for he kills ants, 5, 331, 331 n., 347; 24, 318; simile of the *jackal*, 36,

329 sq.; jackal produced from the intestine of the dead body filled with foul matter, 44, 203; simile of the *leech*, 36, 347; simile of the *lion*, 36, 338–40; origin of lion, 41, 131; the lion is vigour, 43, 38; *moles* mystically connected with earth and Agni, 12, 278 sq. and n.; mole is Rudra's animal, 12, 440; at mole-hills, a sacrifice to the king of moles, 30, 114; *monkeys* as human monsters, 5, 60 n.; simile of the monkey, 36, 292 sq.; *mules* are good, if tamed, 10 (i), 77; she-mule cannot conceive, 29, 363; 30, 178; 42, 545; she-mule dies when she foals, 35, 236, 236 n.; simile of the *mungoose*, 36, 329; *otters* sacrifice fish in spring, 27, 221, 251, 251 n.; similes of the *panther*, 36, 285–7; *porcupine* used in charms against snake-poison, 42, 428; simile of the *rat*, 36, 328; let him wander alone like a *rhinoceros*, 10 (ii), 6–11; simile of the *scorpion*, 36, 328 sq.; simile of the road *spider*, 36, 351; simile of the *squirrel*, 36, 284; 'treading on the tail of a *tiger*,' expression for what is hazardous, 16, 78 sq., 80 n.; tiger's skin used at the coronation, 41, 81, 91–3, 96, 105, 105 n.; 42, 111 sq., 378–80; tiger typifies danger to life, 42, 110, 518; tiger is vigour, 43, 38; origin of tiger, 44, 203, 215; man-tiger, similar to werewolf, 44, 414; *Will o' the wisp*, 42, 411; *wolves*, four-legged and two-legged, 37, 86; ceremony on a place attacked by *worms*, 30, 128 sq.; charms against worms, 42, 22–5, 313–20, 452–5; exorcism of vermin infesting grain, 42, 142. Other animals, *see separately, and also* Parables (*c*).

Animal sacrifices.

(*a*) History of a. s.; different views about them.
(*b*) Different kinds of a. s.
(*c*) The victim.
(*d*) The Yûpa, or sacrificial post to which the victim is bound.

(*a*) HISTORY OF A. S.; DIFFERENT VIEWS ABOUT THEM.

'It is for sacrifices that beasts have been created by the Self-existent (Brahman) himself. Sacrificing causes the whole universe to prosper; therefore is the slaughter (of beasts) for a sacrifice no slaughter. The sin of him who kills deer for the sake of gain, is not so great (and visited less heavily) in the world to come, than the sin of him who eats meat which has not been offered to the gods. Plants, cattle, trees, amphibious animals, and birds, which have been destroyed for the purposes of sacrifice, obtain exaltation in another existence (in which they are born as Gandharvas, or other beings of a high rank),' 7, 169; flesh of animals slain for sacrifices may be eaten, 2, 270, 270 n.; slaughter of animals for a. s. permitted, 8, 289 sq.; 14, 26 sq. and n., 54, 71; 25, 172–6; occasions on which a. s. should be offered, 29, 87–9, 88 n.; 30, 256 sq.; though implying injury to living beings, a. s. offered in accordance with the Veda, is a sacred duty and leads to heaven, 25, 175 sq.; 38, 130 sq., 310; 48, 598 sq.; not alluded to in the *R*iksa*m*hitâ, 44, xvii; the Âprî hymns destined for the Prayâga offerings of the a. s., 46, 9; a hymn used at the ritual of the a. s., 46, 283 sq.; he who offers living victims will reside high in heaven, 46, 24; the sacrificial fires long for the sacrificer's flesh, he offers to them an animal to redeem himself, 44, 118 sq.; he who performs a. s. eats food every six months in yonder world, 43, 299; by a. s. the sacrificer confers upon himself immortal life, 44, 118 sq.; by sacrificing he-goats, ewes, and cows, he gains these animals, 44, 218; in pressing Soma, they slay it, the animal victim is slain, the haviryag*ñ*a is slain with mortar and pestle, and the two mill-stones, 12, 308; 26, 65, 340; 44, 2; substituting lower for higher animals, and vegetable for a. s., 44, xxxvii; when they spread the sacrifice, they kill it, 44, 2 sq.; origin and development of a. s., 12, 50–2; 26, 178 sq.; rice and barley the sacrificial essence of all animals, 26, 199, 199 n.; the cake a symbol of a. s., 12, 49–52 and n.; animals constitute a sacrifice, 44, 155; ascetic censuring an

Adhvaryu priest for destruction of life at a. s., 8, 289–93; the ancient Brâhma*n*as offered sacrifices without killing cows, 10 (ii), 49 sq.; no religious merit nor final rescue to be gained by a. s., 19, 129, 135; the sin of slaying animals for sacrificial purposes, 22, 12, 18; all kinds of a. s. offered by king Okkâka, 10 (ii), 50 sq.; to gain great riches, the Brâhma*n*as cause the king to offer a. s., 10 (ii), 50 sq.; king *S*uddhodana abstains from a. s., 49 (i), 24; bloody and bloodless s. in Zoroastrianism, 4, lxii; camels may be sacrificed and eaten, 9, 60; use and naming of animals for sacrificial purposes, 27, 116 sq.; animals only to be killed for rites, 40, 241.

(*b*) DIFFERENT KINDS OF A. S.

Agni worshipped by sacrifices of ghr*i*ta, heifers, bulls, and cows with calf, 46, 211; the *Agnîshomîya* or a. s. to Agni and Soma, 26, 162–222, 225; 30, 346; 43, 245, 260 sq.; 44, 119 n.; 48, 598; twenty-one Agnîshomîya a. s. at A*s*vamedha, 44, 372, 375; eleven Agnîshomîya a. s. at Purushamedha, 44, 404; meat-offering to *Ahura*, 31, 80, 84; meat-offerings for various *angels* and guardian spirits, 5, 335–8; a. s. at *Ashtakâ* and Anvash*t*akya festivals, 29, 105, 206 sq., 344, 417–21; 30, 97–102, 112 sq., 294; tame and wild animals offered at the *A*s*vamedha* 44, 296 n., 298 sq. and n., 306–8, 310 sq., 331, 338, 338 sq. n., 382–4, 382 sq. n., 388; *on the* A*s*vamedha *itself see under* Horse-sacrifice; a. s. at the *building* of the fire-altar, 41, 155–7, 161–86, 197–9, 204, 236, 400–13; 43, 2 n., 3, 358, 392; at the house-building, 29, 429; 30, 122; at the building of a city, 3, 183; blood-consecration of new buildings, 28, 169 sq.; a. s. offered at the conclusion of *covenants*, 27, 112; 40, 164, 164 n.; ritual and general rules for the a. s. at *domestic ceremonies*, 29, 30, 176–8, 360 sq., 418 sq.; 30, 98–101, 234–6, 360 sq.; *expiatory* a. s. to Fire and Waters, 4, 206 sq., 207 n. slaughter of a dun cow in expiation of murder, 6, 9, 9 n.; sacrifice of a cow, a penance, 7, 138; animal sacrifice at the reception of *guests*, 26, 85; 29, 200, 275 sq.; 30, 131, 256, 278 sq.; animal sacrifice at the *'Hagg*, 6, lxxiv; a. s. at the *king's consecration*, 41, 68 sq., 125 sq., 129–35, 136 n., 137; the flesh of animals to be offered to the *manes*, 7, 249; 25, 124 sq.; 29, 359; 30, 231, 256; sacrifice of a cow to the Fathers, 30, 234–6; the animal to cover the dead body, 29, 238, 241 sq.; at *marriage*, 30, 256; to the god *Nârâyana* they formerly offered animals, 8, 280; sacrifice to *Nirriti* of an ass by a student who has broken his vow of chastity, 2, 85, 289; 14, 117 sq., 215 sq.; 25, 454 sq.; 29, 361 sq.; the *Pasubandha* or a. s. as part of Soma sacrifice, 7, 191; 12, 378 sq., 378 n.; 26, xi; 41, xii–xiv, xvi–xviii, xxiv, 11–17, 418; 43, 260, 298 sq.; 44, xiv, 118–30, 118 n., 119 n.; a. s. to be offered once in each half-year at the solstices, 7, 191; 25, 133; by the victim he puts flavour into the Soma feast, 26, 314; to be performed at least once a year, 44, 119; victims for different gods at the different Soma sacrifices, 26, 312 sq., 397 sq. n., 428 sq.; at the end of every Soma sacrifice a sterile cow (anubandhyâ) sacrificed to Mitra and Varu*n*a, 26, 215 n., 217, 387 sq., 391–7; 41, 87; 43, 263–6; 44, xxii; the a. s. is a great Soma sacrifice, 44, 120; some perform the a. s. without Soma, others with Soma, 44, 122 sq.; the animal sacrifice uninterrupted by the Sattra, 44, 176; *Pasu-purodâsa*, or 'animal cake' offering belonging to every a. s., 26, 199 sq.; 41, 136 sq. and n., 173, 175; 43, 245, 247 sq., 247 n., 265; 44, 221, 555; consists of omentum, animal cake, and the chief oblation, 41, 180; to *Pragâpati*, 26, 429, 429 n., 441, 443 sq.; to Vâyu and Pragâpati, 41, 171–5; to Pragâpati, Sûrya, Indra, and Agni, 44, 127 sq.; the animal victim once belonged to Savit*ri*, now to Pragâpati, 44, 174; at the *Purushamedha*, 44, 404, 411; victims at the Purushamedha set free, 44, 411;

Rudra, lord of a. s., 32, 419 sq.; at the *Sarvamedha*, 44, 419 sq.; at the *Sautrâmanî*, 44, 213 sq. n., 216–22, 221 n., 229, 245, 251, 261, 271–3; hairs of wild beasts put into the Surâ cups at the Sautrâmanî, 44, 218 sq., 229 sq., 261; at the *Seasonal* sacrifices, 44, 309 n., 383, 402; slaughtering of animals and other preparations for a. s. at season-festivals, 37, 15 sq.; lawful and unlawful animals for season-festivals, 37, 429, 434; a. s. to the *spirits* of the land, of the path, and of the four quarters, 3, 371, 371 n., 373, 399, 399 n.; 27, 295; the *Sûlagava* sacrifice to Rudra, 29, 255–8, 351–3, 355; 30, 220–4; a bull sacrificed at a *thanksgiving service*, 3, 333, 333 sq. n.; the animal victim for *Tvashtri* set free, 26, 177 sq.; at the *Vâgapeya* rite, 41, 11–17; animals slain by Lomasa Kassapa at the Vâkapeya sacrifice, 36, 16–19, 16 sq. n.

(*c*) The victim.

Inspection and selection of animals for victims, 3, 343, 343 n.; 27, 266, 288; 28, 222 sq.; 39, 220; at a. s. the blood of the victim is the share of the Rakshas, 12, 265 sq.; game caught in hunting used for a. s., 14, 71; 16, 192 n.; 27, 295; a pregnant animal not used as a victim in sacrificing to God, 27, 417, 417 n.; lowest victims offered in bad years, 28, 166; gifts of mares and camels for a. s., 31, 111, 120; pigs fed for a. s., 40, 18; the shamman, wild buffalo, and sarabha unfit for sacrifice, 41, 410–12; sterile cow sacrificed to remove the blemish of sterility from the house, 42, 299; white cow sacrificed to remove leprosy, 42, 711; only male victims used at great a. s., 27, 256, 256 n.; by male victims the (male) Sacrificer ransomes himself, 44, 119; symbolical victims, a ram and a ewe made of barley porridge, 12, 395 sq., 402 sq.; images of a. eaten instead of meat, 25, 174, 174 sq. n.; images of a. made at the *Kaitra* festival, 29, 132; fivefold is the victim, 26, 24; 44, 154; five victims at the building of the fire-altar, 41, 156, 164, 166, 171, 400; man, horse, ox, sheep, goat, as victims, 12, 50; 41, 162, 166; 43, 299 sq.; the Ekâdasinî or set of eleven victims, 26, 173, 173 n., 217–22; the killing of the victim, 26, 178–84, 189; skinning and cutting open of the victim, 26, 193 sq.; cutting up of it, 26, 200 sq.; offering of the portions, 26, 204 sq.; touching of the victim's remains, 26, 209, 209 n.; cutting out and offering of the omentum (*vapâhoma*), 26, 194 sq., 198, 392; 29, 177, 207, 256, 360, 418 sq.; 30, 99 sq., 113, 235, 360 sq.; 44, 125, 388, 392 sq., 420; the anguish of the victim, in being slaughtered, becomes concentrated in the heart, which must be cooked separately, 44, 125; collection of fodder for the sacrificial victims, 27, 278; to 'quiet' a victim is to kill it, 44, 321; sacredness of the victims slain at sacrifices, 14, 193; the animal killed at the a. s. assumes a divine body and goes up to heaven, 25, 175; 48, 599; the victim rests in immortal life, 26, 198; honour to be rendered to a sacrificial victim, 27, 97; victims must not be sold, 27, 238; the sacrificial ox, in spite of his ornaments and food, would wish to be a solitary calf when led into the ancestral temple, 40, 212; Pragâpati is all the sacrificial animals, 43, 299 sq.; the victim, as Pragâpati, represents all deities, 43, 404.

(*d*) The Yûpa or sacrificial post to which the victim is bound.

The sacrificial stake is the crest-lock of sacrifice personified, 12, 126; the stake belongs to Vishnu, 12, 162, 164; etymological legend concerning the Yûpa, 12, 160 sq. and n.; 26, 21, 36, 39, 46, 101, 174; impurity caused by touching a sacrificial post, 7, 94; 14, 30, 30 sq. n., 171, 183; 29, 224 sq.; 30, 181 sq.; 'a white horse at a post' means Agni at the sacrificial stake, 26, 149; setting up the sacrificial stake, 26, 162–78; 44, 123 sq.; being about to cut the stake, he offers the *yûpâhuti* or 'stake-offering,' 26, 162 sq.; set of eleven stakes, 26, 173, 176 sq., 221;

twenty-one stakes, 44, 373, 383; the yûpa is a means of ascending to the 'Blessed,' 26, 173 sq.; is a thunderbolt, 26, 174–6; material, form, and size of yûpa, 41, 31; 44, 123 sq.; is eight-cornered, 26, 174; 41, 31; a wife-stake set up for the wives, 26, 177; the mounting of the sacrificial post, 41, 31–5; 44, 254; the 'tree,' i.e. the sacrificial post invoked in the Âprî hymns, 46, 12, 154, 199, 237, 239, 377 sq.; liturgical verses addressed to it, 46, 252–5; upright stands the post, like a new-born foal, 46, 340.

Animisha, n. of a demon harassing infants, 29, 296; 30, 211.

Animosity, *see* Hatred.

Anîrân, n.d., has the Hôm, 5, 105; invoked, 5, 404, 404 n., 406.

Aniruddha, n.d., and philosophical t.t.; the sun-god as a unity of Vasudeva, Saṅkarsha*n*a, Pradyumna, and A., 11, 267 n.; a manifestation of the highest being, 34, xxiii, 441 sq.; a form of Vâsudeva, denotes the principle of egoity, 34, 440; 48, 524–6; cannot spring from Pradyumna, 34, 441, 442.

Aniruddha, n.p., an eminent Arhat, 21, 2; 49 (ii), 2, 90; one of the five hundred Arhats who are to become future Buddhas, 21, 198; *see* Anuruddha.

Aniyata sins, *see* Sins.

A*n*kasa, n.p., 23, 218.

An-kwo, *see* Khung A.

Anna, Sk., food, means earth, and all that is heavy, firm, dark in colour, 1, 94 n. *See* Food.

Anna-homas, t.t., food-oblations, 41, 37 n.; 44, 296, 297 n., 314 n., 377.

Annapati, n.d.; prayer to A., the lord of food, 29, 338.

Annaprâ*s*ana, *see* Child (*b*).

Aññâtako*nd*añña, *see* Ko*nd*añña.

Annihilation, *see* Samaya.

A*n*o*gg*â, or Priyadar*s*anâ, daughter of Mahâvîra, 22, 193 sq., 256.

Anointment of Dîkshita with fresh butter, 26, 13 sq.; of the sacrificial stake, 26, 170; of the victim, 26, 183; of sacrificer at Râ*g*asûya, 41, 80 sq.; of sacrificer at Agni*k*ayana, 43, 226 sq., 251; of the sacrificing king with fat gravy at Sautrâma*n*î, 44, 250–2. *See also* Kings.

Anoma-dassî, n. of a saint afflicted with disease, 36, 10.

Anotatta lake, Buddha at the, 13, 124 sq.

An Phing-*k*ung, was niggardly in sacrifices, 27, 402, 402 n.; 28, 165, 165 n.

Ansârs, and Muhâ*g*erîn who fled with Mohammed, 6, 172 n., 187, 262; three of the A. who refused to accompany Mohammed were forgiven, 6, 190, 190 n.

Antaka, the Ender, n.d.; the initiated boy given in charge to A. 30, 154; expiatory formula to A., 44, 337 n.

Antara*ñg*ikâ *S*âkhâ, of the Ve*s*avâ*t*ika ga*n*a, 22, 291.

Antariksha, *see* Air.

Antaryâmi-brâhma*n*a, t.c. (B*ri*hadâra*n*yaka-upanishad 3, 7), 34, xxviii; 48, 214, 319, 356, 422, 457, 537, 544, 627.

Antaryâmin, t.t., 'the ruler within,' the internal ruler, is the self, the Brahman, or the Lord, 15, 132 sq.; 34, xxviii, xxxv, xlii sq., lxii–lxiv, xcviii, c, cxiii, 130–5; 48, 226; is not the pradhâna, 34, 132 sq.; cannot mean the embodied soul, 34, 133–5.

Antelope, one of five animals, 8, 155 n.; the skin of the black a. (k*ri*sh*n*â*g*ina) used at sacrifices, 12, 23–5, 23 n., 38, 265; 26, 25–8, 32, 75, 77; 41, 185 sq.; 44, 132, 249–51, 254, 290 n., 447, 461 n., 467 n., 499; soma placed on black a. skin, 26, 160; two black a. skins represent heaven and earth, 26, 25; black a. skin represents sacrifice, 41, 215–17, 215 n., 219, 222, 266; 43, 226 sq.; 44, 249, 447; is the earth, 44, 216; its hairs are the metres, 41, 266; 44, 249, 448; the dead body laid on a black a. skin, 44, 200, 203; gift of a black a., 14, 135; the horn of an a. used for magic cures, 42 15, 336–8; gom*ri*ga, a bovine a. one of the three chief victims at the A*s*vamedha, 44, 298, 338, 338 sq. n., 388.

Antideva, n. of a king, reverenced the priest Vasish*th*a, 19, 12; 49 (i) 10, 10 n.; a king who reached final

bliss, 49 (i), 94 sq.; Sâ*m*kr*i*ti A., 49 (i), 101.

Antinomies, each suggesting the existence of its corresponding opposite, 39, 47 sq.; the usefulness of being of no use, 39, 132, 217–22; a cluster of a., 39, 188; startling antithetic statements, 39, 239, 239 n.

Antioch, people of, destroyed for disbelief in Jesus' disciples, 6, cv; 9, 163 sq.

Ântrîmukha, n. of a demon harassing children, 30, 211.

Ants, Solomon and the, 9, 101; a.-hills inauspicious, 29, 140; simile of the white a., 36, 326; a. an antidote against poison, 42, 27, 30, 268, 511 sq., 552 sq., 553 n., 555; produce healing-water, 42, 9, 278; earth from an a.-mound used in medical charms, 42, 234, 287, 511; a. gnaw the bowstring of Vish*n*u, 44, 442 sq., 450.

Anuddharî, *see* Animals (*i*).

Anugîtâ, t.w., an episode of the Mahâbhârata, 8, 197–206; its relation to the Upanishads, 8, 197, 200, 207–12, 215, 224, 226 sq.; relation between A. and Bhagavadgîtâ, 8, 197 sq., 207–10, 215, 218 sq., 222, 227; Brâhma*n*a Gîtâ, and Guru*s*ishyasa*m*vâda, 8, 198–204; work of one author, 8, 204–6; its date and position in Sanskrit literature, 8, 206–27; its relation to the Dharma*s*âstras, 8, 208, 210, 215–19; its relation to Buddhism, 8, 212–15; its language, 8, 227; its metre, 8, 227; translation, 8, 227–394; ends with the fourth chapter, 8, 256 n.

Anugopâ restored to sight by Buddha, 49 (i), 197.

Anumati, n.d., goddess of conception, 42, 98, 461; is this earth, 41, 44; Sinîvâlî and A., phases of the moon, 42, 461; offering to A., 25, 90; 29, 84, 319, 321; 41, 42, 44, 54 n.; 43, 264, 264 n.; 44, xlii, xliv; worshipped at the Upâkara*n*a, 29, 221; funeral oblation to A., 29, 242; sacrifice to A. at the ploughing rite, 29, 326; invoked when sprinkling water round the fire, 29, 378; 30, 19, 142, 253; sacrifice of the newly married couple to Agni, Pragâpati, Vi*s*ve devâs, and A., 30, 49; invoked in a love charm, 42, 104, 535; invoked to drive out evil bodily marks from a woman, 42, 109; invoked in a cattle charm, 42, 143, 304; Sarasvatî, A., and Bhaga invoked, 42, 173.

Anumlo*k*antî, n. of a nymph, 43, 107.

Anupâdisesa, t.t., 'none of the five attributes remaining,' is the principal thing, 10 (ii), 167.

Anupalipta, n. of the eighth Tathâgata, 49 (ii), 6.

Anupamamati, one of the sixteen virtuous men, 21, 4.

Anupiyâ, a town of the Mallas, Buddha residing there, 20, 224–33.

Anuprava*k*anîya, *see* Sacrifices (*b*).

Anurâdhapura, the chronicles preserved in the Mahâvihâra of, 10 (i), xvi sq., xx, xxii sq.

Anuruddha, n.p., in Pali, Aniruddha in Sk., 21, 2 n.; 49 (ii), 2 n.; the *S*âkya, converted, 19, 226; 20, 224–33; 35, 163; what he said when Buddha died, 11, 118, 119, 121; 19, 305 sq.; praises the departed Buddha, 19, 310–20; A., Nandiya, and Kimbila, Bhikkhus who live in perfect harmony, Buddha visiting them, 17, 309–12; questions Buddha about schisms, 17, 317; mentioned among the principal Thera Bhikkhus, 17, 360; sayings of A. the elder, 36, 296, 347, 351. *See also* Aniruddha.

Anu*s*âsana, 'precepts' (the Vedâṅgas?), to be studied, 44, 98.

Anu*s*aya, *see* Karman.

Anush*t*ubh, *see* Metres.

Anuvâda, Sk., t.t., a statement referring to something already known, explanatory comment, 34, 221; 38, 55, 66, 138, 216, 221, 308 sq., 322, 322 n.; 48, 14, 45, 678, 694, 696 sq.

Anuvidita, t.t., Buddha's definition of the term, 10 (ii), 91.

Anvâdhyas, Âpyas, Sâdhyas, and Maruts, the divine guardians of the sacrificial horse, 44, 359.

Anvâkhyâna, old tale, not true, 44, 14.

Anvârambha*n*îya, *see* Sacrifices.

Anvash*t*akya, *see* Animal Sacrifices (*b*), *and* Sacrifices (*i*).

Anyata*h*plakshâ, n. of a lotus-lake in Kurukshetra, 44, 70.

An-zre, n.p., knew well the rules of propriety, 27, 174 sq.
Aoighimatastîra, n.p., 23, 218.
Aôshânar, is full of wisdom, 18, 90, 90 n. *See* Aôshnar.
Aôshnar (Aoshnara, Aôshnôr), grandson of Pâûrvâgîryâ, 18, 171, 171 n.; son of Pouru-gîra, 23, 221, 221 n.; chancellor of Kaî-Ûs, 47, x, 13 sq.
Apadesa, *see* Mahâpadesâ.
Apa*k*ara, = Pari*k*ara, 35, 287 n.
Apâlâ, n.p., identified with Sûrya's daughter, 26, xiv n.; was free from widowhood, 29, 33.
Apalâla, a Nâga, converted by Buddha, 19, 246.
Apãm Napâ*t* (Napâ*d*), the great sovereign, 4, 250; swift-horsed, with many wives, 23, 6 n., 14, 20, 36, 38, 71; 31, 319; the son of the Waters, Lightning, invoked and worshipped, 23, 6, 6 n., 12, 14, 20, 36, 38, 299; through Ti*s*trya the waters come from the high A.N., 23, 94, 94 n.; divides the waters amongst the countries, 23, 102, 249 n.; increases the excellencies of countries, 23, 202; seizes the priestly glory, 23, 299; the Ahura Napâ*t*-apãm worshipped, 31, 197, 204, 209, 215, 219, 224, 326, 331, 346, 351, 362, 381, 383 sq., 392.
Apâm Napât, the lightning, 42, 589; the Child of the Waters, 46, 157, 158; Agni identified with A.N., the 'quick inciter,' 46, 187, 191.
Âpa*n*a, a town in Aṅguttarâpa, 10 (ii), 96-9; 17, 129-34.
Apâna, *see* Prâ*n*as.
Apântaratamas, born on this earth as K*ri*sh*n*a Dvaipâyana, and entrusted with the office of promulgating the Vedas, 38, 235-8; 48, 529; reborn, though he had reached intuition of the highest truth, 48, 650 sq.
Apâôsh, Phl., Apaosha, Zd., the demon of drought, his struggle with Tî*s*tar (Ti*s*trya), 5, 27 sq., 112, 170 sq.; 18, 266 sq., 267 n.; 23, 92, 99-101; fiend of death, 23, 284 sq.
Apapalika, n. of the courtesan Ambapâli in the Burmese legend, 11, 33 n.
Apapâtra, *see* Caste (*e*, *f*).
Aparâ*g*itâ (Aparâ*g*ita), n. of the city or palace of Brahman in the Brahman world, 1, 131, 132 n., 275, 277; n. of the Vimâna from which Arish*t*anemi descended, 22, 276.
Aparânta(ra)tamas, *see* Apântaratamas.
Aparisrava, *G*aina t.t., explained, 22, 37 n.
Âpas (Water), etymology of the word, 15, 310.
Âpastamba, teachers quoted by, 2, xxvii sq.; quotes the *S*atapatha Brâhma*n*a as Vâ*g*asaneyaka, 12, xxxix sq., xl n.; his date, 12, xl sq.; relation between Â. and Baudhâyana, 14, xxxv-xxxix; satiated at the Tarpa*n*a, 14, 253 n., 255; a half-divine being in the Mahâbhârata, 25, lxiii; — history of the Â. school, 2, xv-xlvi; the Taittirîya-Brâhma*n*a and Sa*m*hitâ called Â.-Brâhma*n*a, and Â.-sa*m*hitâ, 2, xvii sq.; the Â. school belongs to Southern India, 2, xxxii-xl.
Âpastamba-sûtras, something very like an Upanishad occurs in them, 1, lxvii; language of the Â., 2, xliii-xlvi; the Â. G*ri*hya-, *S*rauta-, and Dharma-sûtras, 2, xiii-xv; 30, xxix, xxxii n., xxxiii; the Â. G*ri*hya-sûtra translated, 30, 248-97; the Â. Ya*gñ*a-Paribhâshâ-sûtras translated, 30, 309-71; the Â. on the Purushamedha, 44, xxxiii n., xxxix n., xl n.
Âpastambha, older name of Âpastamba, 14, xlii n.
Âpastambîya-Dharma-sûtra, aphorisms on the sacred law, part of the Kalpa-sûtra, 2, xi sqq.; the Â. and its commentary, 2, xlvi-xlviii; translated, 2, 1-171; doctrines of Bhagavadgîtâ compared with Â., 8, 20-4; mentions Upanishads as part of Vedic literature, 8, 212; its relation to the Anugîtâ, 8, 215-19, 226; on sale and gift of children, and Kshetraga sons, 25, xciii sq.; quoted, 8, 397; 38, 421; 48, 187, 410, 773.
Apâsya, meditated on the udgîtha, 1, 6.
Âpayâ, n. of a river, 46, 287 sq.
***A*pîvêh**, Kaî-A. or Kavi Aipivanghu, 37, 224, 224 n.

Apnavâna, and the Bh*ri*gus kindled Agni, 12, 350, 350 n.; 46, 343.

Apologues, *see* Parables, *and* Tales.

Apostasy, apostates, *see* Heresy.

Apostles, or prophets,

(*a*) In Islâm.
(*b*) In Zoroastrianism.

(*a*) IN ISLÂM.

Chief a. recognized by the Qur'ân, 6, lxxi; Abraham, Ishmael, Isaac, Jacob, Moses, and Jesus were a., 6, 19; belief in the a., a dogma of Islâm, 6, 24; God sent them with good tidings and with warnings, 6, 30 sq., 141; 9, 20, 210; no difference between God's a., 6, 46, 56 sq., 57 n.; were Jesus' helpers, 6, 53; God's covenant with them, 6, 57, 57 n.; 9, 139; called liars, or mocked at, 6, 62 sq., 69, 116, 119, 245; 9, 49, 66-8, 157, 159, 211; Mohammed but one of many a. who were sent before and have passed away, 6, 63, 94, 125; 9, 129, 198; sincere believers make no distinction between God and His apostles, 6, 92 sq.; rejected by the Jews, 6, 107; ask God for a miracle, 6, 114; people punished for not listening to the a. sent by God, 6, 144-54, 183, 194, 201, 208-18, 236, 239 sq.; 9, 46 sq., 61, 86 sq., 163 sq., 175 sq., 185, 190, 192-5, 242, 286, 294; every nation has its a., 6, 198, 254; no a. sent save with the language of his people, 6 238; a., sent before Mohammed, had wives and children, 6, 237; no a. could bring a sign save by God's permission, 6, 237; God fails not in promise to His apostles, 6, 244; God does not punish without sending an a. first, 9, 3, 114; some of the a. preferred to others, 9, 7; all sent with the message of God's unity, 9, 47; an a. has only his plain message to preach, 9, 119; were sent with manifest signs, 9, 269.

(*b*) IN ZOROASTRIANISM.

The three future a., 18, 13 n., 14 n., 92 sq., 93 n., 112 n., 170, 299 n.; 24, 15, 15 n.; 47, x; the decree of a., 18, 131, 336, 336 n.; Zaratûst the true a., 18, 386; a. and prophets appointed by the creator, 24, 180, 180 n.; a. would be better than God, if God were the cause of evil, 24, 201; prophets and a. slain, 24, 205. *See also* Saoshyãs, *and* Sôshâns.

Appamaññas, *see* Meditations.

Apramâda, Sk., t.t., *see* Earnestness.

Âprî-hymns, *see* Prayers (*c*).

Apsarâ, the A. who makes the winnings in the game of dice, 42, 149 sq., 414.

Apsaras (plur. Apsarasas), nymphs; five hundred A. go towards the knower of Brahman, to adorn him, whereupon he moves towards Brahman, 1, 276; achieved their great beauty by living as Brahma*k*ârins, 8, 178; among women who are a source of happiness, the A. are chief, 8, 347; the Gandharvas their husbands or companions, 12, 269 n.; 42, 33 sq.; 44, 69 n.; fair maidens with their chariots and musical instruments, in Yama's heaven, 15, 6; the beauty of A. even is unreal, 19, 254; five hundred A. attend on the mother of Buddha, 19, 351, 353 sq.; created, 25, 15; world of the A., 25, 157; produced by activity, 25, 494; worshipped at the Tarpa*n*a, 29, 121, 219; Indra has created glory for the A., 29, 316; Agni's A. are the herbs, 30, 146 n.; the insight that dwells with the A., 30, 159; the scent that dwells with the A., 30, 166; like bright red ornaments, 32, 308; invoked in a charm against mania, 42, 32, 520 sq.; their amusements, 42, 33; rivers and trees their dwellings, 42, 33, 409; a talisman against the A., 42, 80; invoked as goddesses of love, 42, 104, 534 sq.; the dog-like A., 42, 125; as evil demons, 42, 205, 425; the Germanic elfs, 42, 409; the wives of Kâma, the Gandharva, 42, 536; as mates for protection of the worlds, 43, 105-8; are sun-motes, mates of Sûrya, 43, 231; are plants, mates of Agni, 43, 231; are stars, the mates of the Moon, 43, 232; are the waters, mates of Vâta (wind), 43, 232; are offering-gifts, the mates of sacrifice, 43, 232 sq.; are hymn-verses and hymn-tunes, 43, 233; serve the divine person under the name of 'fragrance,' 43, 373; story of the A. Urvas*î* and

King Purûravas, 44, 68-74; swim about in the shape of swans, 44, 70; are the people of Soma Vaishṇava, 44, 366; the A. Sakuntalâ conceived Bharata, 44, 399; divine chariots thronged with them, 49 (i), 29; in the palace of Kuvera, 49 (i), 36; the gods charmed by them, 49 (i), 38; the sun surrounded by A. in his royal garden, 49 (i), 40; wait upon Kuvera, 49 (i), 56; in Indra's world, 49 (i), 88; the A. in heaven praise Buddha, 49 (i), 180; in Sukhâvatî, 49 (ii), 42, 44; A. and Gandharvas, *see* Gandharvas.

Âptoryâma, *see* Sacrifices.

Âptyas, legend of the Â., i.e. the gods Trita, Dvita, and Ekata, 12, 47-9.

Apûrva, Sk., t.t., supersensuous principle, 34, lxv; 38, 109, 110 n., 181, 182, 183, 347 n. *See* Karman, *and* Works.

Apvâ, goddess of impurity, invoked against the enemies, 42, 122, 325, 327.

Âpyas, Sâdhyas, Anvâdhyas, and Maruts, the divine guardians of the sacrificial horse, 44, 359.

Ara, or Âra, a lake in the world of Brahman, 1, 131, 132 n., 275 sq.

Ara, n.p., 23, 211.

Ara, n. of a Tîrthakara, 22, 280; a king who became a Gaina monk, 45, 86, 86 n.

Arabian Nights, story of the island-whale, 23, 295 n.

Arabs, rulers of Persia, 5, 151; their pre-Mohammedan religion, 6, xi-xvi; manners and customs of the pagan A., 6, ix-xi, 89, 89 n., 132-4; A. of the desert denounced as the worst hypocrites, 6, 186 sq.; some are good Muslim, 6, 187; clans of A. contending as to who is the more numerous, 9, 340, 340 n.; descended from Tâz, 37, 27 sq.; destroyed by Pêshyôtanô, 47, xii; creatures of the evil spirit, 47, xviii, 104.

Araḍâ, n.d., offering to, at rites relating to agriculture, 30, 113 sq., 113 n.

Ârâḍa Kâlâma, or Ârâla, or Arâḍa, n. of a famous teacher, 19, xxi, 80 sq.; Buddha's meeting and conversation with Â., 19, 95, 130-41; 49 (i), 92, 121; dead, when Buddha began to preach, 19, 167 sq.; 49 (i), 169; has gained insight into absolute bliss, 49 (i), 77.

Arahat, *see* Arhat.

Arahat-Buddha, *see* Buddha.

Ârâla, *see* Ârâḍa.

Âramaiti, or Piety (personified), invoked with Ahura and other Ameshôspends, 31, 14-24, 77 sq., 152, 155 sq., 156 n., 176, 179; clothed the souls with bodies, 31, 27, 32 sq.; daughter of Ahura-Mazda, 31, 37 sq., 44, 123, 126 sq., 126 n.; good and bountiful Piety, 31, 58; associated with the earth, 31, 58 n., 149 n., 152, 156 n., 159 n.; departs from the evil-doers, 31, 81, 87; creatrix of righteous beings, 31, 87; increased Universal Weal and Immortality, 31, 88; the instructor of men in Ahura's regulations, 31, 95, 101; prayer with Â. (Piety), 31, 96, 102; prayer for Piety, 31, 98, 106; who fashioned Â. together with Sovereign Power? 31, 109, 114; influence of Â. on men's actions, 31, 109, 116; increases sacred orderliness, 31, 109, 114; the Yasnas of Â., 31, 124, 129; where Piety joins hand in hand with the Righteous Order, 31, 143; the two hands of Â., 31, 146, 148; the joyful meadows of her peace, 31, 146, 149, 149 n.; appears with holy Khshathra, 31, 152, 158 sq.; Vohumanah, Â., and Khshathra, 31, 167; the Bountiful, worshipped, 31, 196, 256 sq., 325, 339, 360 sq., 387; chosen by the Zoroastrian, 31, 248; Ahura-Mazda approached by the kinship of Â., 31, 252; the holy woman who is as the bounteous Â., 31, 342; the ideal wife, 31, 386. *See* Ârmaiti Speṇta, *and* Ârmat.

Ârâmas, *see* Vihâras.

Ârambhas, t.t., exertions, pain arises from them, 10 (ii), 139.

Araṅg, mother of Îsaḍvâstar, 47, 106, 111, 115.

Araṅg-i Birâḍân, epithet of Ururviga, 5, 143 sq.

Âraṇi, bewitched Bhadrasena Âgâtasatrava, 41, 140 sq.

Araṇis, t.t., the churning-sticks used for producing fire, 12, 275, 294 sq. n.; 44, 74; penance and sacred learn-

ing are the two A. by which the fire of knowledge is produced, 8, 308.
Âranyakas, or forest-books, the Upanishads occur in them, 1, lxvi sq., xci; are liturgical, 1, xci; Sâṅkhya-yoga, Vedas, and Â. are members of one another, and together are called Pañkarâtra, 48, 530; teach that all the subordinate principles have their true Self in Brahman, 48, 530 sq. *See* Aitareya-âranyaka.
Aranye-nûkya, t.t., 'to be recited in the forest,' certain oblations so called, 44, 336 sq. and n.
Araru, n. of a demon, 12, 57, 57 n., 64 n.; a name of evil dreams, 42, 167, 485.
Arask, 'malice,' a fiend, 5, 107 sq.
Ârâst, demon of falsehood, 5, 111.
Ârâstâî, or Ârâsti (Ârâstîh), n.p., father of Maidhyômaungha, 5, 141, 141 n., 145; 23, 203, 203 n.; 47, 163; brother of Pôrûshaspô, 47, 155.
Ârâsti, Ârâstîh, *see* Ârâstâî.
Arati, daughter of Mâra, 10 (ii), 159.
Arâti, the demon of grudge, 42, 15, 57, 82, 109, 172 sq., 187, 261, 423–5; as nightmare, a naked woman, 42, 173, 424 sq.; A. and Ârâtis in doubtful connexion with Agni, 46, 366, 370.
Aravaostra, son of Erezvat-danghu, 23, 218.
Arawisanasp, n.p., 5, 136.
Arâyas, demons of grudge, 42, 162, 205.
Arbuda, a demon-serpent, slain by Indra, 42, 633 sq.; King A. Kâdraveya, whose people are the snakes, 44, 367.
Arbudi, prayer to A. and Nyarbudi for help in battle, 42, 123–7, 631–5, 637.
Archangels, *see* Amesha-Spentas.
Archdevils, *see* Demons.
Archery, as a discipline of virtue, 3, 59, 59 n.; drinking and a. contests at festivals in honour of the ancestors, 3, 374 sq. and n., 400 sq.; the game of pitch-pot, 27, 50 sq.; 28, 397–401; ceremonies connected with a. competitions, 27, 56 sq., 59; 28, 446–53, 462; instruction in a., 27, 233, 478; 36, 253 sq.; and music, 27, 424, 424 n.; *see also* Music; practised at the birth ceremonies for a boy, 27, 472; introduced by King Wû, 28, 124; in a. something like the way of the superior man, 28, 307; similes of a., 36, 71, 253 sq., 369–72.
Architecture, how a city is built, 35, 53; 36, 208 sq. *See* Houses, *and* Vihâras.
Ard, all kinds of wild flowers belong to, 5, 104; Vohûman in the thoughts, Srôsh in the words, A. in the actions, 18, 18 sq., 18 n.; i. e. the angel Ashi Vanguhi, opposed by Varenô, 18, 270, 270 n. *See* Arshisang, *and* Ashi Vanguhi.
Ardâî-fravard, meat-offering to, 5, 337, 337 n.; protects Zoroaster, 47, 145.
Ardakhshîr, the Kayân king, 5, 193; arranger and restorer of the world, 5, 199, 199 n.
Ardashîr, *see* Artakhshatar.
Ardavahist, Ardavahistô, *see* Ashavahist.
Ardâ-Vîrâf, age of the book of, 18, 397; allusions to next-of-kin marriage in the A., 18, 397 sq.
Ardhaka, Rudra the slayer of, 42, 155, 619 sq.
Ardibahist, *see* Ashavahist.
Ardibehest, *see* Ashavahist.
Ardisvang, Phl. for Ashi Vanguhi, 23, 270 n. *See* Ard, Ashi Vanguhi.
Ârdraka, n. of a prince, his disputes with various heretical teachers, 45, 409–19; turned monk, an elephant pays reverence to him, 45, 409 n.
Ârdrakakkha, *see* Ullagakkha.
Ardvî Sûra Anâhita, Phl. Arêdvî-sûr, Arekdvîksûr, Arekdvisûr, Anâhid, angel or goddess of the waters, 4, 80, 80 n., 230; 5, 67 n.; 37, 227, 227 n., 229; the undefiled water of A., 5, 90; 18, 117, 117 n.; Hôm grown at the source of A., 5, 100; the course and benefit of the water of A., 18, 262 sq.; the heavenly spring from which all waters flow, 23, 8, 16, 52 54 sq., 57, 84, 181 sq., 356 sq. her descent from heaven, 23, 52, 55–8, 73 sq.; runs from mount Hukairya into the sea Vouru-Kasha, 23, 174, 181 sq.; — protects lying-in women, 4, 230; watches

over procreation, 23, 54 sq., 74, 181 sq.; 31, 317; — the 'Αναῖτις of the Greeks, 23, 52 sq.; described, 23, 77 sq., 82 sq.; hates the Daêvas, is holy and beneficent, 23, 181; the Ahurian One, the daughter of Ahura-Mazda, 31, 320 n., 321 sq.; protects Zoroaster, 47, 145; guards the seed of Zaratûst, 5, 144, 144 n.; 23, 195 n.;—temple of A., 4, xli sq.; sacrifices to A., 5, 336, 336 n.; 23, 54–84; praised and worshipped, 23, 30; 31, 336, 340; the Âbân Yast devoted to her, 23, 52–84; prayers to A., and the Waters, 31, 316 sq., 320–4, 320 n.

Arêdvîsûr, *see* Ardvî Sûra Anâhita.

Aregadarsi, or Aregadharsn, n.p., ancestor of Zoroaster, 47, 34, 140.

Aregangha*nt*, the Turanian, 23, 212.

Aregaona, n.p., 23, 214.

Aregat-aspa, conquered by Vîstâspa, 23, 79–81, 79 n., 117, 280, 306. *See* Argâsp.

Arekdvisûr (Arekdvîksûr), *see* Ardvî Sûra Anâhita.

Aresh, falsehood of the demon A., 37, 241 sq.; colloquy of the demon A. and Zaratûst, 37, 246 sq. and n.

Arezahis, the, worshipped, 31, 349.

Arezô-shamana, slain by Keresâsp, 18, 370; 23, 296.

Arezrâspâh, Arezrâspô, son of Spânsnâyôs, 37, 218 sq. and n.; came to Frashôstar for religious inquiry, 37, 413, 413 n.; 47, 81, 81 n. *See* Erezrâspa.

Arezûra, 'the neck of A.,' a mount at the gate of hell, 4, 24, 24 n., 225; 5, 15 n.; 24, 58 n. *See* Hell (*b*).

Arezva, Arezvâk, Av. Erezvau, high-priest, 23, 213; 47, 83–5, 83 n.

Argâsp, Av. Aregat-aspa, king of the Khyôns, defeated by Vistâsp, 5, 40, 218; 37, 24 sq. and n., 369, 412; 47, xi, xxx, 68–70, 68 n., 72 sq., 75, 126. *See* Aregat-aspa.

Arghya, *see* Guests.

Arguna, conversations between Krishna and A., 8, 3 sq., 40–131, 197 sq., 229 sq., 310–12, 393 sq.; also called Gudâkesa, a great hero in battle, 8, 37–9; Krishna is A. among the Pândavas, 8, 91; Krishna shows himself in his divine form to A., 8, 92–9; a mystic name of Indra, 12, 285; 41, 99; appointed to guard the sacrificial horse, 44, xxvii–xxix.

Arguna Kârtavîrya, a king, dialogue between him and the Ocean, 8, 293 sq.

Arhaddatta, n.p., disciple of Susthita and Supratibuddha, 22, 293.

Arhaddatta, n.p., disciple of Simhagiri Gâtismara, 22, 293.

Arhat, Pali Arahat, a holy man, a saint; Arhats, saints.

(*a*) Use of the term A., becoming an A.
(*b*) Attainments of A.
(*c*) Worship of A.

(*a*) Use of the term A., becoming an A.

Few men become A., 10 (i), 24; are the true Brâhmanas, 10 (i), 89–95; the term explained, 10 (ii), x; he who, without being an A., pretends to be an A., is the lowest outcast, 10 (ii), 23; called Tevigga, 11, 162; relation between A. and Bodhisattvas in the Saddharmapundarîka, 21, xxxvi sq.; epithets of A., 21, 1 sq.; A. and Bhagavats of the past, present, and future, 22, 36; title of Mahâvîra, the founder of Gainism, 22, 201; 34, 430, 434; 48, 517, 520; disciples of Buddha who became A., 10 (ii), 15, 80, 95, 105; 11, 110; when the five Bhikkhus were converted, there were six A. in the world, 13, 102; Buddha's prophecy about the five hundred A. who are to become future Buddhas of the name of Samanta-prabhâsa, 21, xxx, 198–204; list of names of A., accompanying Buddha, 21, 2 sq.; are never born in low families, 22, 225; the mothers of A. wake up after seeing the fourteen auspicious dreams, 22, 246 sq.; Buddhist nuns become Arhats, 49 (i), 200.

(*b*) Attainments of A.

The blessedness of the Arhat, 10 (i), 27–30; the Arhat cannot commit a serious sin, 10 (i), 70, 71 n.; the Arhat knows his former abodes, sees heaven and hell, has reached the end of births, and is perfect, 10 (i), 95; mystical knowledge of A., 11, 209; the six things attained by A., 17, 10–13; 'make known their

Insight' by delivering a discourse in the presence of Buddha, 17, 10–13; compared to middle-sized plants, 21, 126 sq.; go to heaven to see Sakka, 35, 11 sq.; read the thoughts of others, 35, 18, 23; suffer no mental pain, do not carry favour nor bear malice, 35, 69 sq.; cannot be angry or offended, 35, 152 sq.; pure and free from stain, 35, 200; are not afraid of death, 35, 206–10; are without fear, 35, 297–300; the Arhat (called Brâhma*n*a) described, 36, 26–8, 28 n.; suffers bodily pain, but not mental, 36, 75–8; cannot offend against moral law, but against the Rules of the Order, 36, 98–101; every A. knows about emancipation &c., 36, 100; dwell in Nirvâ*n*a, 36, 191, 193; the sevenfold wisdom of A., 36, 207 sq., 218, 220, 229, 231 sq., 233; morality of Bhikkhus and A., 36, 221, 221 n.; Bhikkhus and A. of different degrees, officers in the 'city of Righteousness,' 36, 231–9; having conquered all evil, they enter Nirvâ*n*a, 49 (i), 177, 179.

(*c*) Worship of A.

The foolish man scorns the rule of the A., 10 (i), 46, 46 n.; so long as the Vaggians support the A., so long they will prosper, 11, 4; a true hearer of the Tathâgata is worthy of a dâgaba, 11, 94 sq.; the world would not be bereft of A., if brethren were to live the perfect life, 11, 107 sq., 107 n.; 35, 186–9; an A. not to be addressed by his private name, 19, 173; must always be saluted, 20, 196; are not to be acknowledged as such, if they do not firmly believe in the law of Buddha, 21, 42 sq.; obeisance to the A., &c., the principal benediction, 22, 217; the Bodisat as an elephant honoured the A., 36, 20–2; miracles at the graves of A., 36, 174–6; the Bhikshu shall associate with A. and other saints, 36, 358; the commandments well proclaimed by the A., 45, 251. *See also* Arhatship, Holy persons, Saints, *and* Saintship.

Arhatship, or saintship, the noble eightfold path which ends in, 11, ix; attained by Sâl*k*a, *Kh*anna, *S*âriputra, 11, 25; 20, 385; 21, 61; the Bhikkhus who are lamps unto themselves shall reach the very topmost height, i.e. A. or Nirvâ*n*a, 11, 39, 39 n.; *and ere long he attained to that supreme goal of the higher life for the sake of which noble youths go out from all and every household gain and comfort to become houseless wanderers—yea, that supreme goal did he, by himself, and while yet in this visible world, bring himself to the knowledge of, and continue to realize, and to see face to face! And he became conscious that rebirth was at an end, that the higher life had been fulfilled, that all that should be done had been accomplished, and that after this present life there would be no beyond!* 11, 110; 17, 9; 20, 384 sq.; is the uprooting of the upâdâna, 11, 148 n.; three qualities required for A., 11, 210 sq. n.; how a Bhikkhu may obtain A., emancipation of heart and of mind, 11, 218; A. and the Ten Fetters, 11, 222; more important than Nirvâ*n*a, 11, 243 sq.; the Âsavas, and the theory of A., 11, 293 sq.; the supreme goal, after which there is no rebirth, 17, 9 sq.; So*n*a attained to A., 17, 10; Dabba realized A., when seven years old, 20, 4 sq.; real A. obtained by Buddha-knowledge, 21, 115; it is an artifice of Buddha that he teaches Nirvâ*n*a at the stage of A., 21, 189; the merit of establishing a man in A., 21, 330 sq., 334; stages leading up to A., 21, 330 sq.; 35, 25–9, 25 sq. n., 55 sq.; the seven conditions of A., 35, 52, 58; 36, 137 n.; a layman, who has attained to A., must either die, or become a Bhikkhu, 35, 233; 36, 96–8; discussions about A., 36, xxiii, xxvi sq.; supreme attainment, the only condition of A., 36, 56–8; what is the use of becoming a recluse, if laymen can attain to A., 36, 56–8; the fruits of the various stages of A., 36, 215 sq.; A., 'the jewel of emancipation,' 36, 224 sq.; previous keeping of the vows, a condition of A., 36, 254 sq.; similes showing what qualities a Bhikkhu must have to realize A., 36, 275–373; four paths of A., 36, 338. *See also* Nirvâ*n*a.

Arig, ancestor of Zoroaster, 47, 140.

Aris, *see* Erekhsha.

Arishtanemi, chieftain of the sacrifice, is an autumn month, 43, 107.

Arishtanemi, the Arhat, life of, 22, 276–9; was a Gautama, and his skin was black, 45, 112; was to marry, but on seeing the animals doomed to death for the wedding feast, turned monk and became a great saint, 45, 112–15.

Arithmetic, young men get a living by learning, 13, 201; with and without the help of fingers, 35, 91 sq., and n.; a means of remembering, 35, 123.

Arittha, a Bhikkhu, who holds a sinful doctrine, 17, 377–82.

Ariyas, 'the elect,' 'the noble,' 10 (ii), x; their knowledge, 10 (i), 9, 9 n.; the law as preached by the A., 10 (i), 23; the rule of the A., 10 (i), 46, 46 n.; the sight of the A. is good, to live with them is happiness, 10 (i), 55; the heavenly world of the A., 10 (i), 60; a man is called Ariya, who has pity on all living creatures, 10 (i), 66, 66 n.; defined by Buddha as one who is not reborn, 10 (ii), 92. *See also* Ârya.

Arka, is the sun, 8, 219 sq., 346, 346 n.; 43, 349; a name of the Self, 15, 311; mystery of A., the flame, the sacred fire, fire-altar, 43, 334–6, 342, 346–9, 398 sq., 402, 404; 44, xviii.

Arka, a plant, Calotropis gigantea, its mystery, 43, 157 sq., 166, 334–6, 342, 346–9.

Arkanânas Âtreya, n. of a priest, 32, 359.

Arkya, 'what relates to the Arka,' is the fire (Agni), 43, 342 sq., 402; 44, 172.

Ârmaiti Spenta, invoked against the Drug, 4, 101, 230; invoked against the demons, 4, 241; mother of Ashi Vanguhi, 23, 274.

Ârmat (Av. Ârmaiti), opposed by Târôkmat (Av. Tarômaiti), 37, 263 sq., 263 n.

Arrogance, deluded by ignorance sacrificers indulge in, 8, 116; abandoned by lovers of Krishna, 8, 128; is the cause of ruin, 41, 1; 44, 22. *See also* Pride.

Arrow, one a.'s range is as much as Pragâpati crosswise, 41, 25; three a. handed to the king at the Râgasûya, 41, 88; a. means strength, 41, 236; in parables and similes, 35, 159; 36, 169; 45, 362.

Arshan, n. of a king of Iran, 23, 222, 222 n., 303.

Ârsheya-brâhmana, t.w., quoted, 38, 421.

Arshisang, the rich in wealth, Av. ashis vanguhi, 5, 86, 86 n., 403, 405. *See* Ard, *and* Ashi Vanguhi.

Ârshtishenas, make five Avadâna cuttings, 12, 192 n.

Arshya, n.p., 23, 209.

Arstât, n.d., Truth, who makes the world grow, worshipped, 23, 6, 9 sq., 11, 15, 17, 19, 36, 38, 40, 164, 166, 168, 178, 184; the unholy priest displeases A., 23, 156; Âstâd Yast devoted to A. and Hvarenô, 23, 283–5; who advances the settlements, worshipped, 31, 198, 205, 209 sq., 215, 220, 224, 256, 345, 388. *See also* Âstâd.

Arsti, the Ascendancy of A. praised, 31, 306.

Arsvant, n.p., 23, 210.

Ârtabhâga, *see* Gâratkârava Â.

Ârtabhâgîputra, n.p., 15, 225.

Artakhshatar, or Ardashîr Pâpakân, a king of Iran, son of Pâpak, summoned Tôsar (Tansar) to expound the Avesta, 4, xxxviii sq., xli–xlvi, xlviii, lv; 37, 414; called Vohûman, the same as Artaxerxes, 5, 137 sq., 150 n., 151, 198 sq., 198 n.; restored the monarchy of Iran, 37, xxxi; founder of the Sâsânian dynasty, 47, xii, 85, 85 n.; an organizer of religion, 47, 127, 127 n.

Arteries, or veins, Sk. Nâdîs; connexion between the a. of the heart and the rays of the sun, 1, 132–4; 15, 328 sq.; 38, 143 sq., 378 sq.; in deep dreamless sleep, the soul enters into the a. of the heart, 1, 133; 15, 167; 34, 191; 38, 141–6; there are 101 a. of the heart, one of them penetrating the crown of the head, 1, 134; 15, 23, 277, 320 sq.; 38, 378; called Hita, 15,

159 sq., 167; by means of them the soul departs from the body, 34, lxxix, lxxxii; the junction of the a. and rays is the way of the departing soul, 38, 382.

Artha, 'Wealth' (personified), worshipped at the Tarpa*n*a, 30, 244.

Artha*s*âstra, Sk., knowledge of *S*ûdras and women, 2, xxxii, 171, 171 n.

Arthavâdas, Sk., 'glorifying passages' in Scripture, as means of knowledge, 34, lxxv, 198, 217–22, 225 n., 304, 318, 318 n., 348, 355; 38, 212 n., 213 n., 227, 235, 246, 246 n., 251, 254 sq., 261, 264, 286, 290, 299 n., 310–12, 418 sq.

Artisan, an ascetic should not live by the occupation of an a., 8, 208, 365. *See* Professions, *and* Society (four classes of).

Arts; dancers, singers, bards disreputable, 25, 104 sq., 317, 381, 443; bards may speak to married women, 25, 316; sin of dancing and singing, 25, 443; music and other a. despised, 39, 139 sq., 269, 278–80, 286, 292 sq., 328 sq., 328 n., 342; seventy-two a., 45, 108. *See* Actors, *and* Music.

Arûm, Zoroastrianism spread to, 24, 171, 171 n.

Arûmans, n. of a people, 24, 52, 52 n.; termed untruthful, 24, 172, 172 n.

Aru*n*a Aupave*s*i, grandfather of *S*vetaketu Âru*n*eya, 12, xli; his teaching, 12, 313, 452; 26, 249 n.; 43, 393 sq.; teacher of Uddâlaka, 15, 226.

Arundhatî, or Akshamâlâ, wife of Vasish*th*a, 25, 331 n.; 30, 244.

Arundhatî, a plant, protects cattle, 42, 144, 490 sq.

Âru*n*eya, *see* *S*vetaketu Â.

Âru*n*i, *see* Uddâlaka Â.

Âru*n*is, meditate on the heart as Brahman, 1, 206.

Arunmukhas, Indra delivered the A., the devotees, to the wolves, 1, 293.

Arûpadhâtu, *see* Heaven (*b*).

Arusha, n. of a solar deity, the morning sun, 32, 20–3.

Arvâvasu, a Hot*ri* of the gods, 12, 137, 137 n.

Ârya, title prefixed to the names of Sthaviras, 22, 286–94; *S*ûdra and Â. created, ruled by day and night, 43, 74 sq.; *S*ûdra woman the Â.'s mistress, 44, 326; the gods have engendered Agni, to be a light for the Â., 46, 49. *See* Ariya.

Âryadatta, *see* Datta.

Aryag, n.p., 47, 140.

Ârya*g*ayanti *S*âkhâ, founded by *G*ayanta, 22, 288; founded by Ârya Ratha, 22, 293.

Âryaghosha, a Ga*n*adhara of Pâr*s*va, 22, 274.

Ârya*k*etaka Kula, of the *K*âra*n*a Ga*n*a, 22, 292.

Âryakuberâ *S*âkhâ, founded by Ârya Kubera, 22, 293.

Aryaman.

(*a*) A. in mythology.
(*b*) Worship of A.

(*a*) A. IN MYTHOLOGY.

'A.'s road,' the path of the deceased, 2, 158; 41, 59, 122; chief among the manes, 8, 89; Pûrve Phalgunî (constellation) assigned to A., 12, 285 n.; gives the bride to the husband, 29, 282; 30, 189; finds out the infamous enemies, 32, 273, 278; Maruts compared with A., Mitra and Varu*n*a, 32, 326, 330; the grandfather of the plant silâ*k*î, 42, 20; Varu*n*a, Mitra, A. kindle Agni, 46, 31; A., Mitra, and Varu*n*a fill the cloud, 46, 103; is glorious through Agni, 46, 148; Agni is A., the lord of beings, 46, 186; Agni invoked to bring A. to the sacrifice, 46, 316; Agni announces man's sins to A., 46, 325; Agni is A. when bearing the secret name of the maidens, 46, 371.

(*b*) WORSHIP OF A.

Prayer to Mitra, A., and Varu*n*a, sons of Aditi, 12, 356; invoked in an Upanishad, 15, 45, 53; worshipped at marriage, 29, 44, 168 sq., 282; 30, 45; invoked in the prayer at the initiation, 29, 64; invoked with the Maruts, 32, 386; invited to the Soma, 32, 408; invoked at sacrifices, 41, 38, 83; 46, 13, 38; invoked in charms to obtain a husband, 42, 94 sq., 323, 491; invoked in a charm for easy parturition, 42, 99, 243; invoked to remove evil

bodily marks from a woman, 42, 109; invoked in a cattle charm, 42, 143; invoked with other gods, 42, 160; 44, 385.
Aryam*n*a, a demon harassing children, 30, 211.
Aryan, the glory of the A. regions, 4, 223, 223 n.; Anaryan, i. e. hostile countries, 4, 347; *Hv*arenô, or the glory of the A., worshipped, 23, 7, 7 n., 11, 15, 18, 283–5, 358; the A. clans, longing for the gods, praise Agni, 46, 100, 119; Aryans and Dasyus, the pious and impious, the two kinds of men, 46, 182, 183. *See also* Âryas.
Âryanâgilâ *S*âkhâ, founded by Nâgila, 22, 288; founded by Vagrasena, 22, 293.
Aryans, *see* Âryas, *and* Caste (*d*, *f*).
Âryapadmâ *S*âkhâ, founded by Ârya Padma, 22, 293.
Âryapadmilâ *S*âkhâ, founded by Padmila, 22, 288.
Ârya*ri*shipâlitâ *S*âkhâ, founded by Ârya *Ri*shipâlita, 22, 293.
Âryas, definition of Âryâvarta, 'the country of the Â.,' 14, 2–4, 147 sq.; countries which it is sinful to visit for Â., 14, 148; a righteous man shall dwell in a village where Â. form the majority, 14, 243 sq.; Mlê*kkh*as do not understand the language of Â., 45, 241; some men born as Â., some as non-Â., 45, 339. *See* Ariyas, Ârya, Aryan, Caste (*d*, *f*).
Âryasenikâ *S*âkhâ, founded by Ârya Senika, 22, 293.
Âryatâpasî *S*âkhâ, founded by Tâpasa, 22, 288, 293.
Âryava*g*râ *S*âkhâ, founded by Ârya Vagra, 22, 293.
Âryâvalokite*s*vara, instructs *S*âriputra in the Pra*gñ*âpâramitâ, 49 (ii), 147–9, 153 sq.
Âryâvarta, n. of India, defined, 14, 2–4. *See* Geography (of India).
Ârzûr, slain by Gâyômar*d*, 24, 58.
Â*s*â, 'Region,' offerings to, 30, 113 sq.; 42, 486.
Asabana, Kara A., and Vara A., Turanians, 23, 71, 71 n.
Asabani, wife of Pourudhâkh*s*ti, 23, 225.
Asamaratha, is a rainy month, 43, 106.
Asâm-i Yamâhu*s*t, chief in the River Nâîvtâk, 5, 118, 118 n.; 18, 256 n.
Asa*m*v*ri*ta, *see* Hell (*a*).
Âsandîvat, *G*anamegaya in, 44, 396.
Asan*h*vanva*nt*, n.p., 23, 203.
A*s*ani, offering to A. at the *S*ûlagava, 29, 352; at rites relating to agriculture, 30, 113 sq.; = the lightning, 41, 160; n. of Rudra (Agni), 41, 160.
Â*s*âpati, 'Lord of the regions,' offerings to, 42, 486.
Asat, Sk., t.t., that which is not, τὸ μὴ ὄν, non-being, non-entity, non-existent; in the beginning there was A. only, 1, 54, 93; the origin &c. of the world cannot proceed from it, 34, 17 sq.; not absolute non-existence, 34, 266–8; denotes 'Being' previous to the differentiation of names and forms, 34, 267; denotes another quality only, 34, 332–4; compared with 'the son of a barren woman,' 34, 338 sq.; the cause of the world, 34, 341; entity does not spring from it, 34, 415–18; Brahman cannot spring from it, 38, 20; arose from the earth, 42, 71, 398.
Asat Pâ*m*sava, deity of the place where they throw the ashes from the sacred fires, 12, 338 sq.
Âsava (Pali) or Â*s*rava (Sk.), the Âsavas, Buddhist t.t., imperfections of the mind, bad influences, 10 (i), 13 sq. n., 25 sq. n.; 11, 293–5; 20, 263, 263 n.; the four streams of sensuality, individuality, delusion, and ignorance, 11, 97 n., 218, 218 n.; 35, 274, 274 n.; Buddha teaches the destruction of Â., 11, 296–307; the *G*inas have reached extinction of Â., 13, 91; the five Bhikkhus were released from the Â., 13, 102; a man becomes a Sama*n*a by the destruction of the Â., 35, 251 sq.; twenty-five qualities preventing the destruction of the Â., 36, 141–3. *See* Âsravas.
Asceticism, badly-practised, leads to hell, 10 (i), 75; Buddha's attitude towards a., 10 (ii), xv n., 67; 11, 146 sq.; 13, 92–4; 17, 111, 113 sq.; 19, 74–6, 79, 143–5, 174 sq., 235, 260 sq.; 36, 60–2; 49 (i), 72–4, 132–4, 174; different kinds of a.,

19, 72–4, 80; 49 (i), 71 sq.; Devadatta causes a schism in the Saṃgha by demanding stricter rules of a. which Buddha rejects, 20, 252 sq.; never extolled in the Saddharmapuṇḍarîka, 21, xxxvii; pârivrâgya, the state of the wandering mendicant, enjoined by sacred law, 34, lxxv; 38, 295–303; enjoined by the side of learning and childlike state, 34, lxxvi; 38, 322–7. *See also* Ascetics, *and* Austerity.

Ascetics (Sannyâsins, Bhikshus, Pârivrâgakas, Munis, wandering mendicants).

(*a*) Rules for a.
(*b*) Laws concerning a.
(*c*) Different kinds of a.
(*d*) Life and state of a.

(*a*) RULES FOR A.

Rules for Sannyâsins or a., 2, 153 sq., 193 sq.; 7, 279–91; 8, 212, 362–8; 14, 46–9, 259 sq., 279–84; 25, 205–16; he who has no aversion and no desire is an ascetic, 8, 63; must not earn anything, 8, 363; eight observances of a., 8, 364; the outward signs of a. do not purify a mortal who has not overcome desires, 10 (i), 38 sq.; (ii), 41 sq.; the Paribbâgakas of different sects had assemblies on the 14th, 15th, and 8th day of each half-month, 13, 239 sq.; the a. of different sects retire in the rainy season, in order not to destroy life, 13, 298; an ascetic who rejects meat at sacrifices or funeral meals goes to hell, 14, 54; an ascetic who slides back into civil life cannot reach heaven, 14, 237, 237 n.; hermits may become a., 14, 273 sq.; ceremonies on entering the order of a., 14, 273–9; before becoming an a., a man must first perform the duties of the other âsramas, 15, 300; he who does not touch the objects of the senses is an a., 15, 315; garments of bark, phalaka cloth, hair, skins, feathers worn by a., 17, 246 sq.; meditations of a., 25, lxix, 209–13, 211 n.; receive food at Srâddhas, 25, 120; food fit for a., 25, 177; not to follow worldly pursuits, 25, 208, 208 n.; three staves worn by a., 25, 395, 485, 485 n.; meditation only is prescribed for a., not action, 34, lxxv; 38, 295–303, 306; a. who have broken their vows of chastity, 34, lxxvi; 38, 317–20; Muniship enjoined for a. as a means of knowledge, 38, 322–4; the a. is to live not manifesting himself, 38, 325–7.

(*b*) LAWS CONCERNING A.

Food of those who have become a. without the rules of the law, forbidden, 2, 69; law regarding female a., 7, xxiv, 135; 25, 317, 317 n.; offence of entertaining a. at sacrifices, 7, 34; exempt from fare or toll, 7, 36; 49 (i), 170; debts of a. to be discharged by sons or grandsons, 7, 45; an apostate from asceticism becomes the king's slave, 7, 37; 33, 135 n., 136 sq.; cannot be witnesses, 7, 48; alms to be given to a., 7, 192–4; 25, 92, 92 n.; 29, 320; must not be offended, 25, 154; eldest brother deprived of his share in estate by becoming an a., 25, 376 n.; 33, 195; sexual intercourse with female a., a kind of incest, 33, xvii, 179, 180 n.; ordeals should not be administered to a., 33, 101, 260; when the husband has become an ascetic, the wife may marry another man, 33, 185; punishment for a. who violate the duties of their order, 33, 265; judicial proceedings for a., 33, 281.

(*c*) DIFFERENT KINDS OF A.

Naked a., 2, 154; 10 (i), 38 sq. n.; 11, 126 sq.; 17, 217 sq., 220, 245 sq.; 36, 308 sq. n.; some a. go with matted hair and skins, others are clean-shaven and without covering, 8, 375; discontented are some pabbagitas, 10 (ii), 7; different kinds of a., 13, 41 n.; Gaṭilas, Brahmanical a. wearing matted hair, 13, 118–35, 118 n., 136, 141, 190 sq.; 17, 130, 132, 134 n.; Sramaṇas and Tâpasas, 15, 169; four kinds of a., 15, 266 sq. n.; false a. condemned, 15, 341; a. who live on the remains of offered food, 17, 71; a. who live like deer, 19, 72 sq.; 49 (i), 70, 70 n., 72; certain a. wear nothing except what they can procure from dust heaps or cemeteries, 20, 89; the vows of Brahmanic, Buddhist, and

*G*aina a. compared, 22, xxii–xxxii; backsliding and apostate a., 22, 58–60; some a. subsist by gleaning ears of corn, 25, 93; *G*aina a. die by voluntary starvation, 25, 204 n.; orders of a., 25, 210; Ârdraka and the Hastitâpasa (a. who kill one elephant a year and live on it to spare the life of other animals), 45, 418 sq.

(*d*) LIFE AND STATE OF A.

A. reach the world of Brahman, 1, 144; 8, 66; 15, 301; Lakshmî resides in a., 7, 299; their entire freedom from worldliness, 8, 159, 159 n.; dialogue between an Adhvaryu and an a., 8, 289–93; true a., 10 (i), 39, 50; are the true Brâhma*n*as, 10 (i), 90 sq.; Buddha an ascetic, 10 (ii), xv; old a., and the young Sama*n*a Gotama, 10 (ii), 87; when Brâhma*n*as know the Self, and have risen above the desire of sons, wealth, and new worlds, they wander about as mendicants, 15, 129, 179 sq.; the noble life of the religious mendicant, 22, 22 sq.; parents lament when their sons wish to become a., 22, 54 sq.; a. and Brâhma*n*as, 38, 27; not afflicted by pain, 38, 64; the state of being grounded in Brahman belongs to a., 38, 300–3; enjoy immortality, 38, 301; childlike state, which is enjoined for a., means absence of strong sensual passions, absence of guile, pride, and the like, 38, 325–7; Buddha (Gautama) meets with an ascetic, 49 (i), 51 sq. *See also* Asceticism, Â*s*ramas, Austerity, Bhikkhus, *G*aina monks, Holy persons, Meditation, Monks, Muni, Niga*nth*as, Pabba*gg*â, Paribba*g*akas, Pârivrâ*g*akas, Sama*n*as, Sannyâsin, *and S*rama*n*as.

Asha, Zd., Righteous Order (compare Sk. *Ri*ta).

(*a*) More or less personified.
(*b*) Worshipped as a divine being.
(*c*) Asha Vahi*s*ta, one of the Ameshaspe*n*tas.
(*d*) Worship of Asha Vahi*s*ta.

(*a*) MORE OR LESS PERSONIFIED.

A. and Vohu-manô, 4, 191; waxes by pious acts, 4, 285; obtains all things, 4, 294 n., 295; he who gives to the ungodly harms A., 4, 297; Righteous Order of Ahura-Mazda, 31, xxi; colloquy between A., Ahura, and the Soul of the Kine, 31, 3–11; Ahura, the Creator of A., 31, 37, 44; Gr*e*hma opposed to A., 31, 55, 63 sq.; in order to maintain A., welfare of soul and body is sought for, 31, 94, 98; the realm of Ahura furthered in A., 31, 109, 116; where Piety and A. join hand in hand, 31, 143; Ahura-Mazda, the father of A., 31, 146, 148; prayer for A., 31, 185; Haoma, the springs of A., 31, 240; Ahura-Mazda approached by the kinship of A., 31, 252; the glorious works of A., in which the souls of the dead find delight, 31, 256; Ahura approached with his Righteousness, 31, 285; Ashi Vanguhi closely knit with A., 31, 296 sq.; may A. conquer the Demon of the Lie, 31, 311; Âramaiti, whose are the laws of A., 31, 361.

(*b*) WORSHIPPED AS A DIVINE BEING.

Zarathu*s*tra, the first praiser of A. (Ashem Vohû), 23, 201 sq.; invoked by Zarathu*s*tra, 31, 5, 12 sq.; invoked with Ahura, 31, 14–24, 62, 70, 75, 182, 307; the Drû*g* delivered into the hands of A., 31, 27, 33; prayers and sacrifice to Ahura-Mazda, A., and Vohu-manô, 31, 174 sq.; the wicked pollute A.'s path, 31, 184; invoked to appear in the village, 31, 310.

(*c*) ASHA VAHI*S*TA, ONE OF THE AMESHASPE*N*TAS.

'Perfect Righteousness,' 4, liii, 213; 5, 10 n.; gives a good passage to him who has a spiritual Master, 4, 291; the righteous will see A. V., 4, 294 n., 295; a name of Ahura-Mazda, 23, 25, 25 n.; creature of Ahura-Mazda, 23, 31, 33; is Divine Order and Fire, 23, 41; the crushing Ascendant of A. V., 23, 128, 133; assists the Good Spirit, 23, 297; earliest mention of A. V., 31, 15, 22, 22 n.; the thirty-three gods, lords of A. V., 31, 199, 205, 210, 216, 220, 225; gods worshipped because of A. V., 31, 212, 218, 227, 274, 322, 329, 339; a praiser of Haoma better than A. V., 31, 241; the soul passes over the *K*inva*t* bridge to Heaven

and A. V., 31, 261; the Kingdom is for Ahura and A. V., 31, 283; the longing blessing of A. V., 31, 345; Mazdayasnian doctrines have their growth from A. V., 31, 354.

(*d*) Worship of Asha Vahista.

A. V., Vohu Manô, and Khshathra Vairya invoked, 4, 245; A. V. invoked and worshipped, 23, 4 sq., 5 n., 13 sq., 30, 35–8, 285, 351, 353; 31, 196 sq., &c.; the Ardibehist Yast in praise of A. V. and Airyaman, 23, 41–8; a blessing is A. V., or Righteousness (called) the Best, 31, 228 sq., 247, 253, 266, 297, 309, 359, 371, 379, 381, 383 sq.; praised by the Ashem Vohû prayer, 31, 266–8. *See also* Ashavahist.

Ashâdha, a king who reached final bliss, 49 (i), 94.

Âshâdha Sâvayasa, his opinions quoted, 12, 4.

Ashâdhi Sausromateya, n.p, 41, 171.

Ashâhura, son of Gîsti, 23, 212.

Asha-nemah, n.p., 23, 219.

Asha-sairyãk, n.p., 23, 213.

Ashasaredha, son of Asha-sairyãk, 23, 213; son of Zairyãk, 23, 213.

Asha-savah, n.p, 23, 214.

Ashâshagahad, -ê *Hvandkãn*, a high-priest, 5, 115, 115 n.

Ashaskyaothna, son of Gayadhâsti, 23, 212.

Ashastu, son of Maidhyô-maungha, 23, 209.

Ashavahist, or Ashavahisto, or Ardavahist (Ardibahist, Ardibehest), Phl., the archangel Asha Vahista, Zd., created, 5, 10 sq.; has the mouse-ear (flower), 5, 104; smites Andar, 5, 128; protects fire, 24, 271; connected with the healing of the sick, 37, 116, 116 n.; world in the guardianship of A., 37, 244; replies to Gôs-aûrvan, 37, 393; the Airyaman of A., 37, 405; the original creature A., 37, 411 sq.; interferes to diminish slaughter of cattle, 47, xii, 109; Pâtakhsrôbô, king of the Arabs, through A., 47, xxv, 12 sq.; Vohu-manô and A. descend with a stem of Hôm to cause the birth of Zaratûst, 47, xxix, 22–8; assists Zoroaster in converting Vistâsp, 47, 67–9, 164; gives Vistâsp the Hôm to drink, 47, 70 sq.; prescribes the care of the sacred fire, 47, 161, 161 n.;—worshipped, 5, 139, 401, 405; meat-offering to A., 5, 336; protector of fire, how to be propitiated, 5, 359, 372 sq, 375; ceremonial of A., 37, 184; invoked, 37, 296. *See* Asha (*c*, *d*).

Ashâvanghu, son of Bivandangha, 23, 210, 210 n.

Ashavazang, son of Pôrûdakhstôîh, one of the seven immortal rulers, 18, 256, 256 n., 258 n.

Ashavazd, or Ashavazdah, son of Pourudhâkhst, one of the immortals, 5, 118, 118 n.; 23, 70 sq., 71 n., 212, 212 n.; 37, 203, 203 n.

Ashavazdah, son of Sâyuzdri, 23, 70 sq., 212.

Ashemaogha, Zd., t.t., heretics; the ungodly fasting heretic, 4, 48, 48 n.; denounced as the type of wickedness, 4, 60 sq., 195 sq.; no defilement caused by the death of an A., 4, 60 sq., 154 sq.; the false cleanser, an A., 4, 135 sq.; the ungodly A. kills the bull, 4, 231; the malice of the two-legged A., 23, 26, 26 n.; 31, 257; smitten by Airyaman, 23, 44–6; confounded by Mãthravâka, 23, 208, 208 n.; Zarathustra invoked against the unholy A., 23, 261; the Waters worshipped to contradict the A., 31, 322. *See also* Heretics.

Ashem-yahmâi-ustâ, n.p., 18, 256 n.; 23, 216, 216 n. *See* Yakhmayûsad.

Ashem-yêNhê-raokau, n.p., 23, 215.

Ashem-yêNhê-vereza, n.p., 23, 215.

Ashes, the foul part of Agni's food, 41, 261; taking down the a. from the fire-pan to the water, and bringing back part of it whereby Agni is reproduced from the waters, 41, 293–5.

Ashi, *see* Ashi Vanguhi.

Ashisang, *see* Ard, Arshisang, Ashi Vanguhi.

Ashi Vanguhi, the good Blessedness or Sanctity, invoked and worshipped, 4, 222; 23, 11, 18, 162, 164, 166, 330, 332; 31, 200, 206, 211, 217, 226, 296 sq., 298, 324,

343 sq., 345, 348, 351, 353, 358; imparts riches to the righteous, 4, 222 n.; follows behind Tistrya, 23, 104; proceeds with Mithra, 23, 136; Mithra's chariot embraced by A. V., 23, 136; bestows all the good and riches ('Ashi's remedies'), 23, 188, 188 n., 270–3, 270 n.; in the shape of a fair maiden, 23, 209; the Fravashis bless the house with the presence of the kind A. V., 23, 230; is Piety personified, 23, 270; daughter of Ahura-Mazda, sister of Amesha-Spentas, 23, 270, 274; the Ashi Yast devoted to her, 23, 270–82; praises and loves Zarathustra, 23, 274 sq.; rejects offerings of all sterile people (old men, courtesans, and children), 23, 280 sq.; legend of A. V. hiding herself, 23, 280 sq., and n.; her healing virtues, 31, 347. *See* Aharîsvang, Ard, *and* Arshisang.

Ashôpaoirya, n.p., 23, 214.

Ashôraokah, son of Frânya, 23, 204.

Ashô-urvatha, n.p., 23, 214.

Ashôvahist, n.p., 5, 148.

Ashô-zust, *see* Birds (*b*).

Ashtâd, the victorious, comes to meet the departed soul, 4, 373.

Ashtakâ, as a deity, 29, 102, 104; A. festivals, *see* Animal Sacrifices (*b*), *and* Sacrifices (*i*).

Ashtâpada, Rishabha died on the summit of Mount A., 22, 285.

Âs ibn Wail, threatened with childlessness, 9, 343 n.

Asidaka, demon, converted by Buddha, 19, 244.

Asiknî river, medicines on the, 32, 402.

Âsila, n. of a great ascetic, 45, 268, 269 n.

Asita, the Rishi, calls Krishna the first god, 8, 87, 87 n.; the Isi A. descends from heaven to see Buddha, who has just been born, and prophesies about the child, 10 (ii), 124–8; 19, xix, 12–18, 93, 355–60, 363 sq.; 49 (i), 10–14, 20, 91; curative plant from A.'s dwelling, 42, 31; incantation of A., 42, 107, 255; A. Devala, for Âsila? 45, 269 n.

Asita Dhânva, a king, whose people are the Asuras, 44, 368, 368 n.

Asita Vârshagana, n. of a teacher, 15, 226.

Askânian kings, 5, 151, 199 sq. and n.

Âsmân, his flower, 5, 104; invoked, 5, 403, 405. *See also* Heaven (*g*).

Âsmarathya, n. of a teacher, 34, xix, xcix, 150 sq., 276 sq., 279 sq.; 48, 293, 391.

Asmô-hvanvant, one of the first followers of Zarathustra, 23, 33 n., 203; Fravashi of A. worshipped, 23, 321.

Asmôk-khanvatô, Zd. Asmô-hvanvatô, n.p., 47, xxx, 165.

Asnya, the day-lords of the ritual order, worshipped, 31, 196, 204, 209, 215, 219, 223, 368, 379.

Asoka, Sk., Âsoka, Pali, the king, inscriptions of, 8, 223; A. and Indian chronology, 10 (i), xxxv–xlv; his edict of Bhabra, 13, xxvi sq.; schism settled by A., 19, xii sq.; A. and the Buddhist Church, 19, xiv; raises eighty-four thousand Stûpas, 19, xxix, 336 sq., 336 n.; Asvaghosha on A., 19, xxxvii; obtained the first holy fruit (Srotâpanna), 19, 337; his reference to the Buddhist Scriptures, 35, xxxvii sq.; outdone by the courtesan Bindumatî, 35, 182; Kathâ Vatthu, a controversial work of the period of A., 36, xx. *See* Kâlâsoka.

Aspengargâk, a demon, 5, 28, 28 n.; in contest with the rain, 5, 112, 112 n.

Âspigâns, family name of Frêdûn, 47, 34; ten Â., 47, 140.

Aspôpadhô-makhsti, n.p., 23, 214.

Âsramapada, n. of a park in Benares, 22, 273.

Âsramas, Sk., t.t., the four orders or stages of life, viz. student, householder, hermit, and ascetic, 1, 35 n.; 7, 14; 8, 216 sq.; 14, 41, 258–62; 25, 205; he who performs the duties of the Â., reaches the world of Brahman, 1, 144; 8, 315 sq.; 15, 300 sq.; duties common to all the four Â., 2, 153; some Smritis allow only the Â. of the householder, 2, 153 n.; the order of the householder is the best, for the other Â. derive their existence from that of the householder, 2, 158–61, 193;

7, 194; 8, 354, 358; 14, 44; 25, lxvii sq., 89, 89 n., 214 sq., 214 n.; the order of householder is the best, because the others do not beget offspring, 14, 260–2; householder and ascetic, 48, 708–12; 49 (i), 94 sq.; after having studied the Veda one may make his choice between the four Â., 2, 192, 192 n.; different purifications and allowances of food for householders, students, hermits, and ascetics, 7, 196; 14, 37; the duties of the four Â. are not for the emancipated, 8, 307; breaking through the law of the Â., the chief complaint of Brâhma*n*as against Buddhists, 15, li; the three Vehicles (yânas), imitations of the Â., 21, xxxiv n., xxxvi; the system of the four Â. older than Buddhism and *G*ainism, 22, xxix; Â. and castes, 22, xxxi sq.; three Â. obligatory, 25, 71, 71 n.; 48, 693–6; *when he has paid, according to the law, his debts to the great sages, to the manes, and to the gods, let him make over everything to his son and dwell (in his house), not caring for any worldly concerns*, 25, 169, 205; legal decisions about Â., 25, 321 sq. and n.; four Â. known by the Veda, 25, 505, 507; 38, 297–303; three men of the first three Â. must be in a legal assembly, 25, 510, 510 n.; the law protects the four Â., 33, 8; the duties connected with them are obligatory on him also who does not strive after mukti, 34, lxxv; 38, 312–15; persons who do not belong to any one of them have also claims to knowledge, 34, lxxvi; 38, 315–17; but it is better to belong to one of them, 38, 316 sq.; Â. requiring chastity are open to men whether they have reached householdership or not, 38, 295; *G*aimini's opinion on these Â., 38, 295–7; four, not three, 38, 300 sq.; those belonging to the three former Â. obtain the world of the blessed, while the mendicant enjoys immortality, 38, 301; all works enjoined on them must be had regard to with a view to the springing up of knowledge, 38, 309; of him who has entered on a higher one there is no descending to a lower one, 38, 317 sq.; the duties of the other Â. are incumbent on the householder, as well as those of his own stage, 38, 324 sq.; as all the four Â. are equally taught by Scripture, they are to be gone through equally, 38, 325; the stages of studentship and householdership must precede the hermit's stage of life, 45, 62 sq.; he who possesses knowledge, may give up the state of a householder, 48, 693; members of all Â. have a claim to knowledge of Brahman, 48, 702–4; even those who stand outside the Â. are qualified for knowledge of Brahman, 48, 704 sq.; *better than to be outside the Â. is the condition of standing within an Â. The latter state may be due to misfortune; but he who can should be within an Â., which state is the more holy and beneficial one*, 48, 705. *See also* Ascetics, Brahma*k*ârin, Hermits, *and* Householders.

Âsrava, *see* Âsava.

Âsravas, *G*aina t.t., explained, 22, 37 n.; there are as many Â. as there are parisravas, 22, 37; influx of Â. through all bad channels, 45, 99; stopped by expiation of sins and self-denial, 45, 163 sq.; how the soul becomes free from Â., 45, 174; monks free from Â., 45, 313, 377; the six Â., sources of Karman, 45, 316 n.; *G*ainas should believe in the existence of Â., 45, 407.

Ass, offering of an, penance for inchastity, 2, 85, 289; 14, 118, 215; putting on the skin of an a., part of a penance, 2, 89 sq.; 7, 120; riding naked on an a., punishment for unchaste women, 14, 109 sq.; 25, 318; shaving with the urine of an a. in punishments for unchastity, 25, 319, 321; parading on an a., a punishment for Brâhma*n*as, 33, 204; parading on an a., punishment for violating an unwilling woman, 33, 366;—mythical three-legged a. in the sea Varkash, 5, 67–9, 67 n.; 24, 111, 111 n.;—he-a. is a *S*ûdra and belongs to Agni, 29, 366; with twofold sperm, 29, 366; 41, 197; simile of the a., 36, 279; how the a. was created, 41, 147; the a. a substitute for cow and sheep, 41,

197; the a., searching for Agni, addressed, 41, 204 sq., 224 sq.; imbued with sorrow, 41, 225; represents Vaisya and Sûdra, 41, 227.

Assagi, one of the first converts of Buddha, 11, 155 n.; receives the ordination from Buddha, 13, 100; Sâriputta converted by A., 13, 144–7; followers of A. and Punabbasu, wicked Bhikkhus, 17, 347–57; animosity of the followers of A. and Punabbasu against Sâriputta and Moggallâna, 20, 211 sq.

Assagutta, n. of a great Arhat, teacher of Nâgasena, 35, xxv, xxvii n., 11–14, 23–6; mentioned by Ñânakitti and Mahânâma, 36, xviii sq.

Assaka, n.p., 10 (ii), 184.

Assassins, assassination, *see* Homicide.

Assault, law about, 2, 238 sq.; 4, lxxxii, 34, 39–45; 25, 253, 267, 303–6; 33, 86, 207–12, 355, 357–9; 35, 269 sq.; 37, 36–55, 68, 72, 403, 472 sq.; against a Brâhmana causes loss of heaven, &c., 2, 282 sq. and n.; 25, 155; different kinds of a., 5, 239–42 n., 379 sq.; beating an innocent man, 5, 322; to be punished by the king, 14, 97; penance for a., 14, 212; sinful bodily action, 25, 484; about use of weapons, 37, 40, 43, 47, 49.

Assemblies, nobles, Brâhmanas, householders, Samanas, angels, gods, Mâra, and Brahma, are the eight kinds of a., 11, 48 sq. *See also* Corporations.

Assembly (of monks), *see* Samgha.

Associations, transgression of a compact settled among all kinds of, 33, 153–5. *See also* Corporations.

Asta-aurvant, conquered by Vîstâspa, 23, 117, 279.

Âstâd, n.d., has the white Hôm, 5, 104; the victorious, 5, 228; funeral cakes to Â., 5, 383; 24, 351; stationed at the *Kinvat* bridge, 5, 383 n.; invoked, 5, 403, 405; cake offering to Â., 18, 61 sq.; ceremonial of Â., 37, 183, 183 n.; the good promoter of the world, 37, 210. *See* Arstât.

Asterisms, *see* Nakshatras, *and* Stars.

Asthikagrâma, Mahâvîra stayed at, 22, 264, 264 n.

Astivihâd, *see* Astô-vîdhôtu.

Astô-vîdâd, Phl., *see* Astô-vîdhôtu.

Astô-vîdhôtu, Zd., or Astivihâd, or Astô-vîdâd, Phl., the demon of death, 4, 47, 47 n., 52, 52 n., 377, 379–81; 5, 19, 19 n.; 18, 93, 95 sq., 105 sq., 111, 113; 24, 17 sq., 17 n., 21; 37, 193, 200, 200 n.; drags the wicked soul to hell, 4, 89 n.; 'the evil flyer,' 5, 111 sq., 111 n.; sent with diseases by Aharman, 5, 164 sq.; casts a noose around the neck of the dead, 18, 52, 52 n.; Vâê identified with A., 18, 62 n.

Astrologers, to be listened to by a king, 2, 236; 7, 21; unfit to be witnesses, 33, 88.

Astrology, and the interpretation of dreams, 3, 350 n.; duty of the grand recorder to observe the motions of the heavenly bodies, 27, 254; the business of the Brâhmanas, 35, 247; that men by a. know the future is a proof of the reality of the world, 45, 317;—ascetics and Buddhist monks should not practise a., 10 (ii), 176; 11, 197 sq.; 14, 48; 19, 296; 25, 208; a sinful or impure occupation, 14, 220; 25, 106; 42, l. *See also* Divination, Nakshatras, *and* Stars.

Astronomy, astronomical data and Chinese chronology, 3, 13, 15, 20–30; Yâo's care for the regulation of the calendar, to determine the seasons of agriculture, 3, 24–8, 32–4; the Chinese zodiac, 3, 25; chart representing the principal zodiacal stars in China about B.C. 2300, with note and table, 3, 26–30; Shun reduced the system of the Seven Directors (Great Bear), 3, 38 sq., 39 n.; two ministers of the Board of A. punished for negligence, esp. in overlooking an eclipse of the sun, 3, 81–3; 'the five dividers of time' and the calendar, 3, 142; the superior man regulates his astronomical calculations, and makes clear the seasons and times, 16, 328, 329 n.; Bhikkhus dwelling in the woods must learn the stations of the constellations and the direc-

tions of the sky, 20, 292–4; definitions of new and full moon days, 30, 25–7; a king must show honour to astronomers before entering the court, 33, 280; astronomical tables, 37, xlvi sq. (correction to 18, 333 sq.); knowledge of a. one of the principal accomplishments of a priest, 45, 137, 137 n. *See also* Nakshatras, Stars, *and* Time.

Astvat-ereta, i.e. Saoshyant, 23, 211, 215, 220, 307 sq.

Ast-vidâd, *see* Astô-vîdhôtu.

Asu, expiatory oblation to A. (breath of life) at a Soma-sacrifice, 44, 210.

Asura, Varuna the A., 42, 11, 241; the king or Indra, the manly A., 42, 111, 380; Rudra the A. of the highest heaven, 46, 187, 191; Agni born from the A.'s belly, 46, 303; as the A.'s germ, Agni is called Tanûnapât, 46, 303; Agni, the A., 46, 399; a liberal giver called A., 46, 420.

Âsura, an unbeliever is called so, 1, 137.

Asura-Rakshas, Pûru was an A., 41, 292; the Asuras are often called A., 44, 95, *see* Asuras; are the niggards and scorners of the gods, 44, 430.

Asuras or Demons.

(*a*) Their nature, character, and abodes.
(*b*) Stories about the A.
(*c*) Gods and A.
(*d*) Worship of A.

(*a*) Their nature, character, and abodes.

The A. are the cause of evil breath, evil speech, &c., 1, 4 sq.; are created, 7, 4; 8, 387; 25, 15; Pragâpati the father of gods and A., 12, 54, 54 n., 59, 110, 144, 153, 198, 265, 279, 286 sq., 310, 370; 15, 189; 26, 30, 105, 135, 142, 301; 41, 1, 254, 256, 289, 387; 43, xvii, 193, 257; 44, 22, 423, 429; created by the downward breathing of Pragâpati, 44, 13;—delusive nature of A. and Râkshasas, 8, 83; dwell beneath Meru, 12, 110 n.; part of the belly relating to the A., 12, 172; to them Pragâpati gave darkness and illusion, 12, 362; try to tamper with the food offered to the fathers, 12, 365; 14, 53, 269; 25, 117; carried by a runner, 15, 74; 43, 401; are liable to destruction, 15, 289; suffer for their deeds and are subject to transmigration, 45, 250, 318; mentioned along with other superhuman beings, 19, 348; 36, 130; 45, 225 sq., 382; 49 (ii), 30, 70; dwell in the ocean, 20, 302, 305; 35, 175; marriage rite of the A., 25, 79–82; wealth of those who perform no sacrifices is called property of the A., 25, 434; speak barbarous language, 36, 31 sq.; voice of the A. in the cart wheels, 26, 132; among the pañkaganâh, 34, 262; metres of the A., i.e. metres of less than ten syllables, 38, 228, 228 n.; sacrifice into their own mouths, 41, 1; 44, 22; the wile of the A., 42, 67, 341; sorceries coming from the A., 42, 80; know wisdom, 42, 268; in the Atharvaveda, 42, 268 sq.; magic art the Veda of the A., 44, 368; relinquish truth, 43, 257 sq.; serve the Purusha as mâyâ, 43, 373; burial rites of people of A. nature (Easterns and others), 44, 423, 430; the weapons of A. are real, 48, 125; souls of A., 48, 198; have bodies and sense-organs, 48, 330;—those who have not arrived at the highest knowledge, go after death to the worlds of the A. covered with blind darkness, 1, 311; heretics and sinners are reborn in the world of the A., the dark place, 19, 304; 45, 15, 28, 34, 231, 246, 259, 363, 367, 430; no A. in a Buddha country, 49 (ii), 12, 33; Asuraloka, realm of evil spirits, 49 (ii), 97 n.

(*b*) Stories about the A.

The A. worshipped breath as Abhûti or not-being, and thus they were defeated, 1, 213; the A. cried out against the injustice of killing animals for sacrificing, 10 (ii), 51; Manu's bull with the A.-killing voice, 12, 29 sq.; Araru was an Asura and Rakshas, 12, 57; Parâvasu, Hotri of the A., 12, 137; the A. have perished, but there are creatures living like them still, 12, 362; the A. pierced speech, breath, eye, ear, and mind with evils, but were finally conquered by the

breath in the mouth (mukhya), 15, 78 sq.; Suras and A. carry Mahâvîra's throne, 22, 198; disputes occurring in the assemblies of gods, men, and A., 22, 268; how the A. offered an animal sacrifice, 26, 207; the Asura Namu*k*i, 41, 92, 135; *see* Namu*k*i; the Asura Svarbhânu, 41, 406, 406 n.; dig remedies into the ground, 42, 9, 21, 268, 279, 516; the kâlakâñga A. piled up a fire-altar, to ascend to heaven, 42, 13, 500; the ant the daughter of the A., 42, 27, 268; *K*andramas conquered the golden cities of the A. and Dânavas, 42, 85; B*ri*haspati and the seers destroy the A., 42, 127 sq.; the people of King Asita Dhânva, 44, 368; the A., appearing in the air with hideous shapes, beat the people who insult the monk Harikê*s*a 45, 53.

(*c*) GODS AND A.

Struggle between Devas (gods) and A., 1, 4 sq.; 12, 54, 59, 64, 110 sq., 113 sq., 125 sq., 144 sq., 150, 153–8, 171, 198 sq., 265 sq., 269 sq., 279 sq., 286 sq., 297, 310 sq., 409 n.; 15, 78 sq.; 19, 262, 307; 26, 14, 30–2, 74 sq., 82 n., 93, 98 sq., 105 sq., 115, 131, 135, 142, 147, 175 sq., 240, 249, 252, 279, 291, 301, 303, 433; 41, 1, 254, 256 sq., 289, 387 sq.; 42, 82, 86; 43, 193, 195, 198, 200, 257–61; 44, 22, 105, 270 sq., 337, 423, 429; Devas and A., trying to search out the Self, 1, 134–42; 15, 343; practise the life of Brahma*k*ârins for freedom from death, 8, 151 sq., 152 n.; Devas and A. approach Pra*g*âpati as pupils, 8, 282 sq.; 48, 328; the A. defeated by the gods, 10 (ii), 125; 30, 107; 42, 71, 199, 268; 44, 42 sq.; A. and Rakshas disturb the sacrifice of the gods, 12, 8 sq., 12, 34 sq., 69, 113 sq., 125 sq., 150 sq., 297, 370–3; 43, 192 sq.; Kapila, an Âsura, striving with the gods, 14, 260 sq.; the Devas were the younger, the A. the elder ones, 15, 78; the gods cast the remedies up again, which the A. dug into the ground, 42, 21 sq.; gods succeed with the sacrifice, A. come to nought, 43, 78; not true are the legends of the fight between gods and Asuras, 44, 14; when the gods were passing upwards to heaven, the A. enveloped them in darkness, 44, 91 sq., 95;—conquered by Indra, after he had obtained the knowledge of the Self, 1, 307; struggle between Indra and the A., 15, 342; 26, 399; Indra, destroyer of the A., 29, 342; 42, 79, 83, 137, 215, 222 sq.; 43, 193.

(*d*) WORSHIP OF A.

Prayer to the A. on touching water, 12, 3 n.; after repeating a text sacred to the A., one must touch water, 29, 31; Brahma*k*ârin given in charge to A., 30, 153 sq.; Asura (Ahura) worship in India and Iran, 31, xxxii; expiatory oblation to the A., in case of certain mishaps at the Soma-sacrifice, 44, 207. *See also* Demons, *and* Râkshasas.

Asuravidyâ or magic, 44, 368 n.

Âsurâya*n*a, n. of a teacher, 15, 118 n., 119, 186 n., 187, 226.

Âsuri, n. of a teacher, his opinion quoted, 12, 169, 300, 329, 357, 431 n., 432, 448; 26, 349 n., 417; 44, 447; in a list of teachers, 15, 119, 187, 226; Kapila and Â, 15, xl; 34, 291 n.

Âsurî, allured Indra away from the gods, 42, 103, 268, 547; found the remedy for leprosy, 42, 268 sq.

Asûrîk, n.p., 5, 135.

Âsurivâsin, Prâ*s*nîputra Â., n.p., 15, 226.

Asurya, or Asûrya worlds, in the Î*s*â-upanishad, 1, ci.

A*s*va, son of Samudra, a *Ri*shi, saw the Âprî-verses of the horse, 44, 302.

A*s*vaghosha, 'The Sermons of A.' in Chinese, 19, xxx, xxxv; author of the Buddha-*k*arita, 19, xxx–xxxiii, xxxvi sq.; 49 (i), ix sq.; three authors of that name, 19, xxxi; a musician, 19, xxxvi; quotes Manu, 25, xcvii.

A*s*va*g*it, one of the first five disciples of Buddha, 19, 172; A. and Vâshpa convert *S*âriputra, 19, 193; a distinguished Arhat, 21, 2; n. of a Bhikshu, 49 (ii), 2.

A*s*vala, a priest of *G*anaka Vaideha, questions Yâ*gñ*avalkya, 15, 121–5.

Â*s*valâyana, Aitareya-âra*n*yaka and Sûtras of, 1, xciii, xcv sq.; satiated at the Tarpa*n*a, 14, 255 (Â. *S*aunaka); 29, 123, 220; on birth ceremonies treated in Upanishads, 15, 222 n.; honoured as teacher, 29, 141; works of Â. and his teacher *S*aunaka, 29, 153–8. *See* Kausalya Â.

Â*s*valâyana-G*ri*hya-Sûtra, notes on, 29, 153–8; 30, xiii sq., xxii, xxvii, xxxi sq., xxxvii; translated, 29, 159–259.

Â*s*valâyana-Sm*ri*ti, based on the G*ri*hya-sûtra, 25, xxii.

A*s*vamedha, Sk., t.t., the horse-sacrifice; *he who offers a horse-sacrifice, conquers all sin, he destroys the guilt of the murder of a Brâhmana*, 2, 275; bathing with the priest at the end of A. frees from sin, 2, 81, 284; 14, 122, 127; truth is more than a thousand A., 7, 51 sq.; A., the king of sacrifices, removes all sin, 7, 133, 135, 181; 25, 445, 447, 482; 44, 298, 396; meritoriousness of A., 7, 171, 260; 25, 177; 33, 285; 44, 129; King Okkâka, instructed by the Brâhma*n*as, brought about assamedha, i.e. A., and other sacrifices, 10 (ii), 50; speculations on the A., 15, 73–7, 122–5; where those go who have performed an A., 15, 127 sq.; Mantras used at the A., 32, 30; 42, 662, 666; pâriplava, recitation of certain stories at stated intervals during the year occupied by the A., 38, 305 sq., 305 n.; 44, 361 sq.; 48, 697 sq.; an obsolete or disused sacrifice, 41, xxvi; 44, 334, 334 n.; a supernumerary rite, 41, 246; the A. is yonder sun, 43, 239, 404; A. included in the building of the fire-altar, 43, 298; the sacrificial horse, Pragâpati, the universe, 43, 401, 401 n.; etymology of the word A., 43, 403; Arka and A. become death, 43, 404; history and significance of A., 44, xv–xxxiii; A. a Kshatriya's sacrifice, 44, xvii, 347; Varu*n*a, the deity of A., 44, xx; offering to Gumbaka at the purificatory bath at the end of the A., 44, xxxix; offered by Pragâpati, 44, xlii, 289; Purushamedha performed like the A., 44, xlii sq., xliv; the new and full moon sacrifice represented as an A., 44, 33–5; performance of the A., 44, 274–403; is the bull among sacrifices, 44, 276; all the gods are concerned in it, 44, 278 sq., 336; the A. means royal sway, 44, 288 sq., 303; worldly blessings (sons, rains, &c.), acquired by it, 44, 294 sq.; Pragâpati reserves the A. for himself, assigning the other sacrifices to the gods, 44, 295; the A. is the sacrificer, 44, 327; *verily he who performs the A. makes Pragâpati complete, and he (himself) becomes complete; and this, indeed, is the atonement for everything, the remedy for everything. Thereby the gods redeem all sin, yea, even the slaying of a Brahman they thereby redeem; and he who performs the A. redeems all sin, he redeems the slaying of a Brahman*, 44, 328; advantages to be gained by the A., 44, 344 sq., 347; right season for it, 44, 347 sq.; is everything, 44, 348–50, 354, 360, 378, 384, 395 sq.; the keepers of the horse at the A. will all become kings, 44, 359 sq.; sovereign rule gained by the A., 44, 370; domestic and wild animals sacrificed at the A., 44, 382 sq.; is successful when the horse sniffs or turns away, 44, 384; in the A. all objects of desire are contained, 44, 387, 391; forms part of the Sarvamedha, 44, 419.

A*s*vamedha Bhârata, n.p., given as author of a Vedic hymn, 46, 420 sq.

A*s*vapati Kaikeya, king, knows the Self, and instructs five Brâhma*n*as, 1, 85–91; 34, 227 n.; 38, 276; 43, 393–8; 48, 288, 290, 677 sq., 688.

Asvapna, or the sage Sleepless, 42, 54, 60, 571.

A*s*vasena, king of Benares, father of Pâr*s*va, 22, 271.

A*s*vastomîya, t.t., a set of oblations at the horse-sacrifice, 44, 337 n., 341 sq.

Â*s*vatarâ*s*vi, *see* Bu*d*ila Â.

A*s*vattha (tree), *see* Trees.

A*s*vatthâman, a Kaurava, 8, 38.

A*s*vayug, the two, and the full moon of Â*s*vayuga worshipped, 29, 130.

Â*s*vayu*g*a, *see* Sacrifices (*b*).

Asvins, the two, Asvinau.

(*a*) The A. in mythology.
(*b*) Worship of the A.

(*a*) THE A. IN MYTHOLOGY.

The Nâsatya or A., and the Naunghaithya, 4, liii; seen within Krishna, 8, 92; alarmed at the greatness of Krishna, 8, 94; are the Adhvaryus of the gods, 12, 16, 53; 26, 239, 276; 43, 23-30, 33; 44, 245; 'with the arms of the A.,' 12, 16, 42, 53, 213; 26, 136, 141, 167, 181, 239; 29, 63; 30, 151, 232; 41, 39, 53, 201, 214; 43, 228; 44, 253 n., 449, 474; the sacrifice-tortoise did not stand still for the A., 12, 161; the two A. have declared that fame is gained by the procreation of sons, 14, 271; Dadhyañk teaches the A. the doctrine called 'honey,' 15, 116 sq., 119, 187; 26, 277; 44, 471; Buddha mistaken for one of the two A., 19, 72; 49 (i), 71; world of the A., 25, 165; the two A. at the marriage of Soma and Sûryâ, 26, xiv; 42, 95, 503; the heavenly physicians, 26, 274 sq.; 42, 48, 52, 85, 310, 310 n., 329, 389; 43, 23; 44, 216 sq., 243, 243 n.; legend of the A. restoring Kyavana's youth, 26, 274 sq.; are heaven and earth, 26, 276 sq. and n.; 'lotus-crowned,' 26, 277; performed cures with parched grains, 26, 315 n., 316 n.; the chariot of the A., 29, 365; 30, 170; produce the embryo with their golden kindling-sticks, 30, 199; red birds of the A., 32, 26, 321; called mada-kyut, 32, 134-6; by two syllables gained two-footed men, 41, 40 n.; are of the same womb, 41, 62; cured Indra, 41, 131 sq.; 44, 216 sq., 249, 252; help Indra in slaying Namuki, 41, 135; 44, 222 sq., 232; connected with agriculture, 41, 329; 42, 512; their wonderful deeds, 41, 334; unite lovers, 42, 100 sq., 312; bring back an exiled king, 42, 112; call the king to the throne, 42, 113; have measured the earth, 42, 200; took the part of Pragâpati below waist and above feet, 43, 28; became everything here, 43, 30; 44, 253; Pragâpati produces creatures by union with the A., 43, 32 sq.; Dadhyañk, fitted by the A. with a horse's head, 44, xlviii, 444 sq.; the A. are the eyesight, 44, 217 sq.; the earth relates to the A., 44, 241, 247; the healing medicine of the A., 44, 253 n.; the two A. are the ears, 44, 263; all the gods except the two A. performing a sacrifice, 44, 441; restored the head of the sacrifice, 44, 471, 475, 477, 482-4, 490; lovers of honey, 44, 471; 46, 358 sq.; Agni united with the two A., 46, 37-9; Agni is like the bright one on the path of the A., 46, 302, 305; drive on chariots and horses, 46, 358. *See also* Nâsatyas.

(*b*) WORSHIP OF THE A.

Gifts bestowed on Brâhmanas in the month Âsvina, please the two A., and procure beauty, 7, 269; invoked for offspring, 15, 221; 29, 43, 287; 30, 199; morning prayer to the A., 26, 229 sq. n.; 46, 356-9; Soma libations to the two A., 26, 266 n., 272-8, 312, 312 n., 320 n., 409 sq.; 32, 408; 42, 231; 46, 44; worshipped at the Âsvayuga sacrifice, 29, 130, 332; invoked to give intelligence to the new-born child, 29, 182; invoked at the Upanayana, 29, 188; 30, 66; invoked by the guest when accepting the Madhuparka, 29, 198; invoked by the student to bestow insight, 29, 308; 30, 153, 159; prayer to the A. at the Samâvartana, 29, 313; sacrifice to the A. at ploughing, 29, 326; invoked by the Snâtaka, 30, 169; invoked to protect the cows, 30, 184; invoked to protect the bride, 30, 188; asked to sprinkle the sacrifice with their whip, i.e. rain, 32, 187 sq.; offering to the A. in the charioteer's house, 41, 61 sq.; animal sacrifice and other Sautrâmanî offerings for the A., 41, 129-37, 136 n.; 44, 213 sq. n., 216-18, 221 n., 222, 224, 233, 241, 243-7, 253, 261-3, 273 n.; invoked to establish harmony, 42, 136; invoked to slay vermin infesting grain, 42, 142; invoked with the rest of the pantheon, 42, 160; hymn to the honey-lash of the A., 42, 229-32, 587-91; offering to the A., 42, 486, 486 n.; the milk when

being milked or ladled out at the Agnihotra belongs to the A., 44, 81; two goats sacrificed to them at the Asvamedha, 44, 300; worshipped at the Pravargya, 44, 468, 475, 477, 482-4; invoked together with Agni, 46, 281, 316, 356-9; invoked to grant long life, 46, 360; invited to sit down on the sacrificial grass, 46, 418.

Âtalî, mother of Upâli, 19, 227.

Âtânâtiya-parittâ, a protecting charm, 35, 213.

Âtar, or Âtarô, or Fire, Zoroastrian god; worship of Â. and Agni, 4, lii; struggle between Â. and Azi, Indra and Ahi, 4, lii; Â. and Vohu-manô protect against demons, 4, 101, 101 n., 230, 241; worship of Â., the son of Ahura-Mazda, 4, 184, 198 sq.; 23, 5, 5 n., 7 sq., 14-16, 36, 38, 316, 322 n., 339, 344; watches over pregnant bitches and women, 4, 184, 184 n.; blesses him who brings him dry wood, 4, 199; the day Â., 5, 95; has the marigold flower, 5, 104; invoked, 5, 402, 405; Âtar, with all (sorts of) Âtars or Fires, 23, 8, 16, 358; a source of healing, 23, 8, 16, 358; drives behind Mithra, 23, 153; Vohu-manô and Â. help Ahura against Angra Mainyu, 23, 198; Â., the son of Ahura-Mazda, fights against Azi Dahâka, 23, 297 sq.; blesses the man who worships him, 23, 338; Âtas Nyâyis, prayer to Â., 23, 349, 357-61. *See also* Fire (*b*, *g*).

Âtare-danghu, n.p., 23, 207.

Âtaredâta, n.p., 23, 206.

Âtare-hvarenah, n.p., 23, 207.

Âtarekithra, n.p., 23, 206.

Âtarepâta, n.p., 23, 206.

Âtare-savah, n.p., 23, 207.

Âtarevakhsha, *see* Priests (*e*).

Âtarevanu, n.p., 23, 206.

Âtare-zantu, n.p., 23, 207.

Âtarô, *see* Âtar.

Âtarô-Aûharmazd, a Zoroastrian teacher, 5, 243, 243 n.

Âtarôbôndak, n.p., 5, 145.

Âtarô-dâd, n.p., 5, 145.

Âtarô-frôbâg, n.p., 5, 194, 194 n. *See* Âtûr-frôbag.

Âtarô-frôbâg Nôsâî, n. of a Zoroastrian teacher, 5, 243, 243 n.

Âtarô-Mitrô, n.p., 5, 194.

Âtarô-pâd, or Âtûr-pâd, son of Zaratûst, 5, 159 n., 304, 304 n.; 37, 6 n.; 47, xxxvi sq.

Âtarô-pâd, or Âtûro-pâd, or Âtûr-pâd, son of Màraspend, 4, 286 sq., 286 n.; 5, 145, 147, 148 n., 308, 333; 24, 256, 256 n.; 37, xxxiv, xl, xlii, 10, 30, 30 n.; 47, 87, 87 n., 127, 127 n.; restorer of the true religion, 5, 199, 199 n.; underwent the ordeal of melted metal, 5, 376, 376 n.; 24, 171, 171 n.; 47, 74 sq.; born in the steel age, 37, 181; Â. and the Nasks, 37, 415; his son Avarethrabau, 47, xii; his date and work, 47, xxxv-xxxvii.

Âtarô-pâd, or Âtûr-pâd, son of Hâmîd (Hêmîd), 5, 148, 148 n.; 18, xxvii, 150 n.; a compiler of the Dînkard, 18, 399 n.; 24, xxvii, 139 n.; 37, xxxii-xxxiv, xxxviii.

Âtarô-pâd, son of Dâd-farakh, 5, 244 n.

Âtarô-pâd, n.p., 5, 194, 194 n.

Âtarô-pâtakân, n.p., 5, 194.

Âtaro-tarsah, n.p., 5, 137.

Âthabbana-veda, Pali for Âtharvana-veda. *See* Atharva-veda.

Atharvan, the eldest son of Brahmâ, 15, 27; 48, 284; the sacred texts, revealed by A. and Aṅgiras, 25, 436, 436 n.; was the first that kindled Agni, 41, 217; is the breath, 41, 217; auspicious rites called A. rites, 42, xviii-xxiv; Sânti, wife of A., 42, xxi n.; A., Aṅgiras, and Bhrigu, fire-priests, 42, xxiii, xxvii, xxx, xxxii-xxxiv, lvii sq.; a charm against wild beasts called 'A.'s crusher of tigers', 42, 148; Aṅgiras and A. rule over the heavens, 42, 225; author of a hymn, 42, 362; Dadhyañk, son of A., 44, xlviii, *see* Dadhyañk Âtharvana; expiatory oblation to A. at the Soma-sacrifice, 44, 208; a woman who has miscarried sacrificed to A. at the Purushamedha, 44, 415.

Âtharvana, *see* Bhishag Â., Dadhyañk Â., *and* Kabandha Â.

Âtharvanas, *see* Âtharvanikas.

Âtharvana-Upanishads, *see* Upanishads.

Atharvan Daiva, teacher of Dadhyañk, 15, 120, 187; 42, xxxiv sq.

Atharvâṅgiras, Prâ*n*a the true work of the, 15, 275; as a name of the Atharva-veda, 42, xvii–xxv; 44, xv, 97; plants âtharva*n*a and âṅgirasa, holy and magic, 42, 219, 624.

Âtharva*n*ikas, their rite of carrying fire on the head before the study of the Veda, 15, 42; 38, 186, 189 sq.; 48, 629, 631; the seven libations (from the saurya libation up to the *s*ataudana l.) are limited to the Â, 38, 189, 190.

Atharvans worshipped at the Tarpa*n*a, 30, 243; slayers of Rakshas and Dasyus, 42, xxxiii, 33; the A. tied the amulet on, 42, 86; the divine A. in heaven invoked, 42, 161.

Atharva*s*iras, an Upanishad, quoted by Gautama and Baudhâyana, 1, lxvii, 52 n.

Atharva-veda, Upanishads of the, 1, lxvii; quoted by Âpastamba, 2, xxvii, 119, 119 n.; Artha*s*âstra (knowledge which *S*ûdras and women possess) a supplement of the A., 2, xxxii, 171, 171 n.; for its study a second initiation is necessary, 2, 2 n.; mentioned after the other Vedas in the Vish*n*u-sm*ri*ti, 7, xxxi; deadly incantations in the A., 7, 41; not mentioned in the Bhagavadgîtâ, 8, 18 sq.; mentioned in Sanatsugâtîya, 8, 145, 180; the Bhikkhu must not apply himself to practising the hymns of the Âthabba*n*a-veda, 10 (ii), 176; A. and the Aṅgiras, 12, 38 n.; 44, xxxvii n.; charms of the A., the weapon of the Brâhma*n*a, 25, 436, 436 n.; charms against disease in the A., 36, 109 n.; names of the A., 42, xvii–xxviii, xxxi–xxxiii, xxxviii, xlvii, liii; *S*âkhâs of the A., 42, xxii sq., xxiii n., lxi sq.; the Veda of the Kshatriyas, 42, xxv sq., xxxvii; position of the A. in Hindu literature, 42, xxviii–lvi; theosophic hymns in the A., 42, xxix, xl, lxvi; A. and Rig-veda, 42, xxx sq.; the A. in the hymns of the *S*aunakîya-Sa*m*hitâ, 42, xxxi–xxxiii; A. in the Yagus Sa*m*hitâs and Brâhma*n*as, 42, xxxiii–xl; its inferiority, 42, xlix; in the view of its ritualistic literature, 42, lvii–lxxi; exaltation of the A., 42, lviii sq.; and *S*rauta ritual, 42, lxx sq.; selected hymns of the A. translated and explained, *vol.* 42; Vaitâna-sûtra and Gopatha-brâhma*n*a of A., 44, xvi sq.; Atharvans and Aṅgiras, two different collections of A. texts, 44, xxxii; the Atharvans are the Veda, 44, 365.

Atheism, a crime in the fourth degree, 7, 137; penance for a., 7, 176; to be avoided, 25, 154; a minor offence, 14, 5; 25, 444; is of the quality of Darkness, 25, 491.

Atheists defile the company at a *S*râddha, 2, 256; 25, 103, 103 n.; become outcasts, 2, 280; the ordeal by sacred libation must not be administered to a., 7, 55; 33, 116 sq., 116 n.; penances for a., and for receiving gifts from a., 14, 114 sq.; Digambaras referred to as a., 24, 146 n.; assertions of a. denounced, 24, 146–50; deny revelation (Veda), 25, 31, 31 n.; a country infested by a. soon perishes, 25, 256; a. kings, 25, 308; cannot be witnesses, 33, 87; gifts not to be accepted from a., 33, 220.

Athrat, n.p., 5, 137, 137 n.

Âthravan, Parsi fire-priests. *See* Priests (*e*).

Âthwya, Thraêtaona, son of Â., 4, 246; 23, 61; 31, 233, 233 n.

Âthwyas are rich in cattle, 23, 326, 326 n., 328.

Âthwyôza, n.p., 23, 211.

Atidhanvan *S*aunaka, n.p., 1, 17.

Atigrahas, t.t., eight grahas (organs of sense) and A. (objects of sense), 15, 125 sq.

Ati*kkh*andas, *see* Metres.

Atirâtra, *see* Sacrifice (*j*).

Âtithya, Sk., t.t., ceremony of reception of guests. *See* Guests.

Ativâdin, Sk., t.t., one who makes a final supreme declaration, 1, 120 n.; he who understands that spirit (prâ*n*a) is all this becomes an a., 1, 120 sq.; in reality he is an a. who declares the Highest Being to be the True, 1, 121; 34, 163–7; 48, 301–5.

Âtmabodha-Upanishad, *see* Upanishads.

Âtman, Sk., t.t., the Self, meanings and translations of the word, 1,

xxviii-xxxii; to know the Â. was to be the Â., 1, xxx; identified with the Brahman and with the Sat, 1, xxx sq.; Buddha's doctrine of Nirvâ*n*a, and the Brahmanic theory of the Â., 22, xxxiii; meaning 'body,' 26, xxix; means the internal organ, 38, 81; translated by 'vital breath,' 46, 88; Â. or Brahman given as author of a Vedic verse, 46, 293. *See* Self, *and* Soul.

Âtmavidyâ, i.e. the Upakosala-vidyâ, 1, 64 n.

Â*t*nâra, *see* Para Â.

Atoms, refutation of the Vaiseshika tenet that the world originates from a. set in motion by the ad*r*ish*t*a, 34, xlviii, 1 sq., 16, 289, 317 sq., 354, 381–400; 48, 495–500; conjunction of a. the material cause of the world, 34, 46, 382, 382 n., 387 n.; 48, 426; possess the qualities of colour, &c., according as they are a. of earth, water, fire, or air, 34, 382, 382 n., 386, 402; are of spherical form, 34, 382, 382 n.; subsist during a certain period without producing any effect, 34, 382; during the period of each pralaya they are isolated and motionless, 34, 382 n.; the form of extension of an effect depends on the number of a., not on their form of extension, 34, 382 sq., 383 n.; cannot be divided themselves, 34, 386 sq.; Ka*n*âda's reasons for the permanence of a., 34, 392 sq.; relation of the a. and the four elements, 34, 393 sq.; atomic theory not accepted by any authoritative persons, 34, 394–400; may be decomposed by their passing back into the indifferenced condition of the highest cause, 34, 400; external things can neither be a. nor aggregates of a., 34, 419; Bauddha and *G*aina theories of aggregate of a. as the cause of the world refuted, 34, 403, 430 sq.; 48, 501, 516–20; Karman consists of a., 45, 194 sq.; one of the four kinds of inanimate things possessing form, 45, 208, 208 n.; being without parts they cannot be the cause of the world, 48, 475; consist of parts, 48, 482; the smallness of a., 49 (ii), 142.

Atonement, *see* Penances, *and* Sins.

Atraya*h*, the poets of the fifth Ma*nd*ala of the Rig-veda, 1, 216.

Âtreya, n. of a teacher, quoted by Baudhâyana, 14, xl n.; in a list of teachers, 15, 118 n., 119, 187; author on medicine, 19, 11; Dakshi*n*â given to an Â. who is not an officiating priest, 26, 346, 346 n.; quoted by Hira*n*yakesin, 30, 200; worshipped at the Tarpa*n*a, 30, 245; quoted in the Vedânta-sûtras, 34, xix; 38, 320; 48, 707.

Âtreyas, family n., authors of Vedic hymns, 46, 364–97, 401–24.

Âtreyî, t.t., a woman who has bathed after her courses, 7, 133 n.; 14, 107.

Âtreyîputra, n.p., 15, 224 n., 225.

Atri, and other sages ask Brahman about final emancipation, 8, 314; the germ miscarried by Speech developed into A., 12, 131; one of the seven *R*ishis, 15, 106; surpassed by Âtreya as an author on medicine, 19, 11; 49 (i), 9, 9 n.; quoted in Manu-sm*r*iti, 25, xxvi sq., 78; a sage and Pragâpati, 25, 14; Barhishads, manes born of A., 25, 112; dispels the darkness of the Asuras, 26, 346; satiated at the Tarpa*n*a, 29, 122, 220; 30, 244; thrown into the fiery pit and saved by the Asvins, 32, 218; restored light to the sun, 41, 66 n.; the *R*ishi A. employed charms, 42, 23 sq., 319; the sun freed by Indra and A., 42, 294; A. and the Atris, connected with the Ka*n*vas, 46, 42 sq.; Agni identified with the *R*ishi A.? 46, 214; his spells may loose Agni's bonds, 46, 366; Agni worshipped by A., 46, 376, 382, 413; the *R*ishi Isha Âtreya called A., 46, 383; Agni has freed A., 46, 399; author of Vedic hymns, 46, 421.

Atrin, an ogre, devouring demon, 32, 154, 158; 42, 37, 62, 65.

Attada*nd*asutta, t.c., 10 (ii), 177–80.

Attainments, the three, Buddhist t.t. (tisso sampattiyo), viz. life as man, life as god, and Arhatship, 35, 146 n.; 36, 356.

A*tth*aka, n. of a *R*ishi, 11, 172.

A*tth*akavagga, part of the Suttanipâta, 10 (ii), 146–83.

Atthasâlinî, mentions Assagutta, 36, xviii.

Attha Vimokkhâ, Pali t.t. *See* Deliverance (eight stages of).

Atthissara, Devadatta will become a Pakkeka-Buddha under the name of A., 35, 167.

Atula, n.p., a pupil of Buddha, 10 (i), 58, 59 n.

Atula, n. of an author on medicine, 36, 109.

Âtumâ, Buddha at, 11, 77 sq.; 17, 140–2.

Âtûr-farnbag, son of Farukhŏ-zâd, first compiler of the Dînkard, 37, xxxi–xxxiv, 411, 411 n.; sayings of A. as to the Gyêmarâ (Gemara) of the Jews, 47, xiii sq., 119 sq. and n. *See* Âtûr-frôbag.

Âtûr-frôbag, son of Farukhûzâd, 18, xxvii, 252, 252 n.; quoted by Mardân-farukh, 24, xxvi; Rôshan, son of Â., 24, xxvi sq.; Dînkard of Â., 24, 120 n., 139, 139 n., 146, 162, 169 sq.; = Hêr-Frôvag, 18, 289 n.

Âtûrŏ-bûgêd, n. of a high-priest, 18, 318.

Âtûrŏ-Frôbag-vindâd, name of a high-priest, 18, 318.

Âtûrŏ-mahân, n.p., 18, xxii, 3, 3 n.

Âtûrŏ-pâd, n.p., 18, 346, 357. *See also* Âtarô-pâd.

Âtûr-pâd, *see* Âtarô-pâd.

Âtûr-pâdîyâvand, Pahlavi writer, quoted, 24, xxvi, 121, 138, 138 sq. n., 162, 169.

Atyagnishtoma, *see* Sacrifice (*j*).

Aûdak, or the demon Uda, and Yim, 37, 212 sq. and n.; *see also* Uda.

Audanya, *see* Mundibha Au.

Audavâhi, n. of a teacher, 15, 118 n.; worshipped at the Tarpana, 29, 123, 220.

Audbhâri, see Khandika Au.

Auddâlaki, *see* Uddâlaka Âruni.

Audgâhamâni, quoted by Gobhila, 30, 97 sq.

Audgrabhana, t.t., elevatory oblations at Soma-sacrifice, 44, 289 sq. n., 291, 292 n.

Audulomi, n. of a teacher, his opinions quoted, 34, xix, lxxxiv, xcix, 277 sq., 278 n., 279, 280; 38, 321, 409 sq.; 48, 392, 394, 708, 760 sq.

Auguries, *see* Divination, Fate, *and* Omens.

Aûharmazd, or Ormazd, the supreme god of Parsi religion, Phl., the same as Zd. Ahura-Mazda.

(*a*) A. as the supreme God and Creator.
(*b*) A. in mythology.
(*c*) A. and Zoroaster.
(*d*) A. and morality.
(*e*) Worship of A.

(*a*) A. AS THE SUPREME GOD AND CREATOR.

The creator, 5, *3–20*, *53 sq.*, 57, *62*, *65 sq.*, 69, 76, *90 sq.*, 105 sq., *121–3*, 127, 155, *159 sq.*, *183 sq.*, 195, &c.; 18, 3, 12, 14–20, *25 sq.*, 33, &c., 80–3, *86–94*, 116 sq., 120, *197 sq.*, 200, 200 n., *225*, 267, 279, 307 sq., 324, *386*, *412*; 24, *3–5*, *7 sq.*, *32 sq.*, 40, 43, 53, 59 sq., 65, *70*, *73 sq.*, *82*, *85*, *92*, *98 sq.*, *117 sq.*, 128, 132, *133–6*, *257*, 271, 274, 276, 279, 299, *323*, 328 sq., 343, 345; 37, 22, 26, 35, 102, 116, *150*, 152 sq., 165, 168, 172, 190, 217, 229–31, 239, *248 sq.*, 270, 282, 289, 296, 303 sq., 306, 311, 322, *334 sq.*, 344, 369 sq., 438–40, 443, 445, 453 sq., 456 sq.; 47, 3–6, 9, 15, 21, 26, 47, 49 sq., 53, 70 sq., 77, 79, 119; complete sovereignty of the creatures of A. in the future existence, 5, 5 sq.; life of the creatures of A., 18, 42; created the bird Vâresha, 5, 52; *A. created nothing useless whatever*, 5, 74; completes his work on resurrection day, 5, 126; created Iran, 5, 216 sq., 219, 224, 229 sq.; the verdure which A. has given abundantly, 5, 339; assisted by the spirit of wisdom in the creation, 24, 98 sq.; *the conclusion is this, that the creator is the healer and perfect ruler, the maintainer and nourisher, protecting and preserving the creatures; not a producer of the disease, a causer of the pain, and an inflicter of the punishment of his own creatures*, 24, 133, 138; compared to an orchard-owner, 24, 134–6; the will of the creator is all good, he cannot be the causer of evil, 24, 155–60, 166–8, 173–202, 205–8; his sagacious creativeness, 37, 362; origin and effect produced for A., 37, 383; produces the renovation, 47, 118;—is supreme in omniscience and good-

ness and unrivalled in splendour, 5, 3 sq.; his place 'endless light,' 5, 4; the good spirit, is independent of unlimited time, 5, 4; is omniscient, 5, 5, 7, 14, 76, 196; 18, 33, 80 sq., 103, 220, 225; 37, 22, 168; 47, 15; his triumph in the end, 5, 8; is all goodness, 5, 158, 305, 307; is an intangible spirit, 5, 372; sovereignty of the far-seeing spirit A., 18, 12; is not visible except through wisdom, 18, 44; is a spirit amongst spirits, 18, 64 sq., 65 n., 82; all-watchful and all-knowing, 18, 93; *A., the good creator, granting forgiveness and full of goodness, would not abandon any creature to the fiend*, 18, 223, 223 n.; heaven the seat of A., 18, 275; 24, 30, 83 sq.; wisdom of A., 24, xvi; 37, 240, 317, 356 sq., 363; is most forgiving, 24, 66; allots happiness alike among the good and the bad, 24, 76; compassion of A. and the angels with their own creatures, 24, 101; the four elements pertaining to A., 24, 129, 129 n.; is sagacious and all-knowing, 24, 157 sq.; omniscient and omnipotent, good and merciful, 24, 173 sq.; no one should despair of the mercy of A., 24, 260–2; the highest abjudicator, 37, 178; happiness produced by A., 37, 211; dominion given to A., 37, 307; seeing the throne of A., 37, 314; eternity of A., 37, 325; miraculousness of A., 37, 329; work of A. in the Gâthic lore, 37, 342 sq.; guardianship of A., 37, 352 sq.; invoked as 'greatly wise lord,' 37, 352; gratification comes from A., 37, 359; expounding the spirit of A., 37, 359; above the archangels, 47, 22 n.

(*b*) A. IN MYTHOLOGY.

A. sends his angels to assist Pêshyôtanû against the demons, 5, li, 224–30; relation between Aharman and A., 5, lxix sq.; proposed peace to the evil spirit, 5, 6; deliberates with the Fravashis as to the means for overcoming Aharman, 5, 14; throws the evil spirit into hell, 5, 128 sq.; was aware of Aharman, Aharman was not aware of A., 5, 155; is more predominant than the evil spirit, 18, 25 sq.; tokens of the final victory of A. over Aharman, 18, 99–113; finally conquers Aharman, 24, 34 sq.; why he did not use his omnipotence to repel Aharman, 24, 124–7; recited the Ahunavar to confound Aharman, 37, 11, 11 n.; colloquy of three deceitful demons with A., 37, 252–4; his opposition to the demons, 37, 264; discriminates truly, Aharman does not, 37, 391 sq.; Aharman a creature of A., 37, 485;—the spirit of prosperity (Spênâk-maînôk) represented by A., 5, 3 n.; in his angelic capacity, one of the seven Ameshaspends, 5, 10 n.; performed the spiritual Yazisn ceremony with the archangels, 5, 14; ground up the healing fruit, bînâk, 5, 18; assists Tîstar, 5, 27; the fire which shoots up before A., 5, 61; the Albûrz of A., 5, 74 sq., 75 n.; has myrtle and jasmine, 5, 104; stars and moon and sun and fire of A., 18, 11; married with his daughter Spendarmad, 18, 392 sq. and n., 396, 401, 415 sq.; 37, 273 n., 274, 365 sq.; fire the son of A., 18, 371, 374, 376 sq.; the fire of A., 24, 96; stars assist in the distribution of good produced by A., 24, 127–38; sends archangels to Vistâsp, 37, 24; spiritual chieftainships through A., 37, 167; resists the wish of fire to leave the world, 37, 188–90; father of Vohûman, 37, 273 n., 274, 333; four marvels produced by A. in yonder world, 37, 281; giving Spendarmad to A., 37, 334, 341; gratified by love of Vohûman, 37, 341 sq.; the bodily form of A., 37, 351; the progeny of A., 37, 356; teaches Masyê how to sow corn, 47, xxv, 6; speaks to Hadish, 47, xxv, 7.

(*c*) A. AND ZOROASTER.

A. gives Zaratûst a prophecy about the future of the Iranian nation and religion, 5, l sq.; exhibits the Fravashi of Zaratûst to Gôsûrvan, 5, 20 sq., 21 n.; created Zaratûst to preach carefulness, 5, 84; conversations between A. and Zoroaster, 5, 121, 192–235, 310, 314, 352, 372–9, 382, 385 sq.; 18, 25 sq., 44, 307, 381, 415–17, 419–23,

431-53, 455; 24, 261, 288, 322, 329, 331, 343, 345, 349, 360; 37, 164, 193 sq., 206, 210 sq., 210 n., 233-6, 260, 267-72, 367, 375 sq., 379, 384-90, 453-64, 469, 474 sq.; 47, 54, 56, 60-2, 86, 99-105; exhibits to Zoroaster the torments of hell, 5, 350; confers omniscience on Zoroaster, 18, 92, 92 n.; shows to Zaratûst the state of the soul of Keresâsp, 18, 371-82; 37, 198; revealed his religion to Zoroaster, 24, 40, 104, 170; 37, 181, 261; 47, 3, 14 sq.; chants taught by A. to Zoroaster, 37, 23; conferences of Zoroaster with A., 37, 29, 31 sq.; 47, x sq., xv, 14-16, 35, 46-50, 47 n., 64, 123, 135, 138, 157-60, 163; has given all prosperity to Zoroaster, 37, 68; produced Zoroaster with a goodness like his own, 37, 196; appoints Zoroaster as priest, 37, 227; 47, 142 sq.; advises Zoroaster, 37, 229 sq.; admonishes Zoroaster to maintain his religion, 37, 230 sq.; praises Zoroaster, 37, 267-9; exhibits to Zoroaster the future existence, 37, 267; assists Zoroaster, 37, 291; conference of A. with Yim, 47, 9; argues with the archangels about the birth of Zaratûst, 47, 22 sq.; sends the archangels to assist Zoroaster in converting Vistâsp, 47, 67 sq.; informs Nêryôsang, 47, 129, 129 n.; Zoroaster's connexion with A. through Yim and Nêryôsang, 47, 139; religion manifested through Spendarmad and A., 47, 134; sends Vohu-manô to defeat Akômanô at the birth of Zoroaster, 47, 142; sends archangels to protect the infant Zoroaster, 47, 145.

(*d*) A. AND MORALITY.

A. receives the righteous soul in heaven, 4, 374; 18, 63-6; 24, 21, 25, 30 sq., 274, 299; 37, 164 sq.; what is within A.'s will, is good: what is against his will is sin, 5, 157 sq.; will not leave his own creatures unto the evil spirit, 5, 308; A. and the righteous man, 5, 359; protector of the righteous man, how to be propitiated, 5, 372-4; the splendour of A. becomes their own in heaven, when men propitiate the archangels, 5, 375-9; through next-of-kin marriage one will not become parted from the possession of A. and the archangels, 5, 389; created the creatures for progress, and we are to promote whatever is his wish, 18, 15 sq.; takes account of the thoughts, words, and deeds of the creatures, 18, 33; will the righteous souls be able to see A.? 18, 44 sq.; when a righteous man dies, A. provides a teacher to take his place, 18, 50 sq.; the good creatures are, as it were, defiled unto A., 18, 341, 341 n.; a just judge is like A., 24, 79; *that one wish which A., the lord, contemplates as regards men is this, that 'ye shall fully understand me: for every one who fully understands me, comes after me and strives for my satisfaction,'* 24, 80 (cf. 5, 113 n.); leaves no good creature captive in the hands of enemies, 24, 138, 206; forgives sins for the high-priest, 24, 289; distressed, when priests or parents are offended, 24, 302; blesses a liberal man, 24, 342; gives to a person who confers a benefit upon any one, ten times as much, 24, 357; his helpfulness in good works, 37, 20; lodgement of A. upon a good ruler, 37, 70; righteousness is the production of true awe of A., 37, 233; is aware of all you do, 37, 266; glorified by virtue, 37, 323; making A. the ruler over one's own person, 37, 334, 336 sq., 339 sq.; all excellence for A., 37, 351 sq.; he whose rule is for A., 37, 372, 375 sq.; the guardian of a true servant, 37, 374; he who is like him is he who is his own creature, 37, 458.

(*e*) WORSHIP OF A.

All men praise A. and the archangels at the resurrection, 5, 126; A. and the archangels invoked and worshipped, 5, 191, 214 sq., 362, 364 sq., 367; 18, 159 sq., 159 n., 167; 37, 232-4, 298, 303, 309 sq., 438, 444 sq.; meat-offering to A., 'the supreme chief,' 5, 336, 336 n.; invoked and worshipped, 5, 401, 404; 18, 3, 384-7; 37, 34, 349, 395-7, 463; praised in a peroration,

18, 276; invoked and praised in a benediction, 18, 279, 324, 357, 366; 24, 3 sq., 255, 255 n.; 37, 3; priests of A., 18, 296 sq.; heterodoxy a contest with A. and Zaratû*s*t, 18, 330; Keresâsp prays to A. for heaven, 18, 371, 374, 376–8; worship of A. one of the best four things, 18, 417; prayer to A., 18, 442–4; to remember A. as creator, and Aharman as destroyer, is good, 24, 14; gratified by Vi*s*tâsp, 24, 65; by wearing the sacred thread-girdle one is established in A.'s department, 24, 268 sq.; propitiated by prayers said before and after meals, 24, 284; thanksgiving due to A., 24, 328 sq.; keeps watch with regard to pollution by dead matter, 24, 353; sin of scorning A., 37, 206; the priest a friend of A., 37, 261; benefit of worship of A., 37, 267; praise, obeisance, and ceremonial for the creator A., 37, 274 sq.; giving joy to A., 37, 311; priests the habitation of A., 37, 328; daughterly reverence to A., 37, 373; gratification of A., 37, 381; ceremonial of A., 37, 346 sq.; 47, 168; one whose spirit is connected with A., 37, 354; priestly authority of A., 37, 393; about knowing the Lord, 37, 435; advantage through possession of A., 37, 394; comes near the reciter of the Vâstârem Nask, 37, 446; his bountifulness extolled by Masyê and Masyâôî, 47, 6. *See also* Ahura-Mazda, Dualism, *and* Zoroastrianism.

Aûha*r*ma*zd*, n. of a king, father of Shâhpûr, 24, 171, 171 n.

Aûha*r*ma*zd*-dâ*d*, n.p., Mar*d*ânfarukh, his son, 24, 120.

Au*k*athya, *see* Dîrghatamas Au.

Aukshagandhi, n. of an Apsaras, 42, 33.

Aupa*g*andhani, *see* Aupagañghani.

Aupa*g*añghani, or Aupagandhani, n. of a teacher, quoted by Baudhâyana as opposed to the practice of Niyoga, 2, xx, 132 n.; 14, xl, 229, 229 n.; in a list of teachers, 15, 119, 186 n., 187.

Aupamanyava, *see* Prâ*k*îna*s*âla Au.

Aupanishadas, or Vedântins, denoted by *S*añkara with the term asmadîyâ*h* 'ours,' 34, xx sq.

Aupasvatîputra, n. of a teacher, 15, 225.

Aupatasvini, *see* Râma Au.

Aupave*s*i, *see* Aru*n*a Au.

Aupâvi *G*âna*s*ruteya, descended from the upper regions, 41, 2 sq.

Aupoditeya, i.e. Tumi*ñg*a Au. Vaiyâghrapadya, quoted, 12, 271, 271 n.

Aur*n*avâbha, n. of teachers, 15, 186 n.

Aurva, miraculously born from the thigh, 19, 2; 49 (i), 6.

Aurvadasp, n.p., 5, 140.

Aûrva*d*âsp, or Khrûtâsp, father of Dahâk, 18, 228, 228 n.

Aûrvâitâ-dang, the Tûr, ruler of the Kîgs and Karaps, 47, x sq., xxv sq.; Zoroaster preaches to him, 47, xxx; protects Zoroaster, but refuses to be converted, 47, 51–5, 51 n.

Aûrvakhsh, n.p., 5, 137, 137 n.

Aurvasâra, worships Vayu and escapes from Husravah, 23, 256 sq.; killed by Husravah, 23, 304, 304 n.

Aurva*s*eya, i.e. Agastya, q. v.

Aûrvata*d*-nar, son of Zoroaster, 5, 142, 142 n.

Aurva*t*-aspa, Kavi Vî*s*tâspa, son of, 23, 78; other sons of Au., 23, 205 n.

Aûshbâm, n.p., 5, 139, 139 n.

Aûshdâ*s*târ, *see* Mountains.

Aûshe*d*ar, or Hûshê*d*ar (Ukhshya*d*-ereta in the Avesta), son of Zaratû*s*t, the future apostle, his coming, 5, lii, lv sq., lviii sq., 144, 355; 18, 13, 13 n., 170; 37, xxxii, 33, 33 n., 285; 47, xii, 15 sq., 15 n., 94, 101, 105–7, 156; his millennium, 5, li sq. n., 219 n., 220, 220 n., 228 n., 230–3, 230 sq. n.; 24, 15, 15 n.; 47, xxxi, xxxiv–xxxviii, 107–12, 125, 127; when he comes, the river Nâhvtâk will flow suitable for horses, 5, 85, 85 n.; his miraculous birth, 5, 231 n., 233 n.; is liturgical, 18, 91, 91 n.; a producer of the renovation, 37, 437.

Aûshê*d*ar-mâh, or Hûshê*d*ar-mâh, the same as Zd. Ukhshya*d*-nemangh, the future apostle, 5, lii, 355; 18, 13, 13 n., 170; 37, 34, 34 n., 285; 47, 15–17, 15 n., 107, 111 sq., 111 n., 156; millennium of the

apostle Aû., who destroys Dahâk, 5, lii, 121, 233-5; 24, 15, 15 n.; 47, xii sq., xxxi, 112-14, 116, 125, 127; son of Zoroaster, 5, 144, 144 n.; 37, 285; is legal, 18, 91, 91 n.

Aûsikhshes, opponents of Zoroaster, descended from the demon of Wrath, 47, xiv, 143, 143 n.

Aûsindôm, *see* Us-hindu.

Auspicious marks, au. objects, *see* Omens.

Auspicious rites, belong to the quality of passion, 8, 324; performed for procuring success or prosperity, 14, xxxiii, 25, 76, 76 sq. n., 159, 159 sq. n., 297, 299, 306 sq., 322 sq., 329-33; 29, 226; performed by the interpreters of dreams, 22, 245; performed at the birth ceremonies of Mahâvîra, 22, 255; teaching au. r., a disreputable occupation, 25, 387, 387 n.; 33, 223; performed on mounting a chariot, an elephant, &c., 29, 209-11, 363-6; for averting disease, misfortune, evil omens, and other dangers, 29, 224-6, 432 sq.; 30, 124-9; for the obtainment of special wishes, 29, 425-8, 430-3; 30, xxviii sq., 24 sq., 114-20, 124-9, 175-9, 267, 295 sq., 306 sq.; performed before an ordeal, 33, 104; *see also* Ceremonies, Omens, Sacrifices, *and* Witchcraft.

Auspicious sights, *see* Omens.

Auspicious times, *see* Time.

Austerity, austerities, a branch of the law, 1, 35; one of the feet of the Brâhmî Upanishad, 1, 153; for the sake of penance, 2, 275, 277, 283 sq.; 14, 109, 116, 125, 129, 311 sq., 323-8; 25, 451, 470, 476-9; a means of purification, 7, 96, 97; 25, 187 sq.; 48, 700; one purified by au. sanctifies a company, 7, 254; practising au. in sacred places confers eternal bliss, 7, 256; enjoined for hermits and mendicants, 7, 277 sq.; 14, 259, 293 sq.; 25, 202-4, 203 n.; 38, 300 sq.; 48, 695; not required for devotion, 8, 69; K*ri*sh*n*a cannot be seen by au., 8, 98 sq.; good and bad forms of au., 8, 118-21; if not practised with a view to the fruit, a means of sanctification, 8, 122; preliminary to acquisition of true knowledge, 8, 147, 258, 369; 15, 64, 66, 179; 48, 704; immortality, or final release, union with Brahman, supreme bliss attained by au., 8, 164-6, 164 n., 178, 247, 247 n., 300, 339; 15, 301; 25, 212, 501, 508; 45, 152; one of the twelve great observances of a Brâhma*n*a, 8, 182; leads to heaven (not to final emancipation), 8, 184, 184 n., 367; 43, 362; forms part of the conduct of the good, 8, 242, 376; a preliminary of concentration of mind, 8, 248; renunciation is the best au., 8, 312, 369; au. is the truth, 8, 315; au. and other pious works end in destruction, 8, 355; the sages attained the godhead by au., 8, 388; benefits and powers resulting from au., 8, 388 sq.; 25, 477-9, 477 sq. n.; does not purify a mortal who has not conquered his doubt, 10 (ii), 41 sq.; Pragâpati practises au. for the purpose of creation, 12, 384; 41, 145, 147, 157; 43, 375-80, 375 n., 403; prescribed for Bhikkhus, 13, 14; good conduct more important than au., 14, 34; 19, 260 sq.; practising au. makes Brâhma*n*as worthy receptacles of gifts, 14, 38 sq.; sacred learning and au. joined together are powerful, 14, 129; staying constantly in water, 14, 136; practising au. frees from sin, 14, 176; at rites securing success, 14, 323; giving food, speaking the truth, and compassion on all living beings, better than au., 14, 328; the highest au.: pain in sickness, carrying a dead person into the forest, placing a dead person on the fire, 15, 194; one should mortify one's flesh to give up connexion with the world, 22, 39 sq.; au. the chief virtue in the K*ri*ta age, 25, 24; study of the Veda is the highest au., 25, 60 sq.; prescribed for Snâtakas, 25, 134; by practising au. one obtains the faculty of remembering former births, 25, 152; lost by self-complacency, 25, 166; higher births obtained by au., 25, 412; has the quality of goodness, 25, 491; practised by a childless wife, 33, 369; the path of the gods cannot be attained by faith

and au., unaided by knowledge, 38, 234; the stage of life, in which au. is the chief thing, 38, 298; there is no perpetuity in au., 44, 418; a means for obtaining the end of sacrifice, 44, 441; enjoined for *G*aina monks, 22, 57 sq., 68; on the religious postures of *G*aina monks and nuns, 22, 178 sq.; the twenty-two troubles (parîsaha) which a *G*aina monk must cheerfully bear, 45, 8–15; kâyotsarga (particular positions of the body) and other kinds of au., 45, 159–61, 164, 166–8, 171, 229 sq.; au. are twofold, external and internal, and each of them is sixfold, 45, 157, 174–80; purity produced by peculiar au., 45, 157, 157 n.; of no good when performed for the sake of fame, 45, 300; practised by King *S*uddhodana, 49 (i), 24 sq. *See* Abstinence, Asceticism, Ascetics, *and* Mauna.

Autathya, husband of Mamatâ, 49 (i), 44, 44 n.

Authorities (four great), *see* Mahâpadesa.

Auttami, a Manu, 25, 19.

Autumn, *see* Seasons.

Aûzâv, n.p., 5, 137.

Aûzôbô, the Tûhmâspian, son of Tûmâsp, monarch of Iran, 5, 136, 136 n.; 37, 28, 28 n.; 47, xxix, 11.

Avabhâsa, n. of a Buddha field, 21, 142.

Avabhâsaprabha, n. of a god, 21, 4.

Avabh*ri*tha, t.t., bath at the end of a Soma sacrifice. *See* Bath.

Avadhi, t.t., a kind of transcendent knowledge, 22, 223, 268, 274, 278, 284; 45, 120, 120 n.

Avahya, son of Spe*n*ta, 23, 217.

Avakâ plants (lotuses), used at the building of the fire-altar, 41, 392 sq.; 43, 48 sq.; mean water, 41, 393; 43, 48 sq.; etymology of A., 43, 175; burial-ground covered with them, 44, 436.

Avakâ*s*a, t.t., certain verses so called, 44, 469 sq., 469 n., 492.

Ava*kkh*edavâda, the doctrine that the soul is the highest self in so far as limited by its adjuncts, 34, lviii, xcviii.

Avalokite*s*vara, worshipped as a god, 19, 207 n.; as a Saviour, 19, 292 n.; a Bodhisattva Mahâsattva, 21, 4; the Bodhisattva A., if implored or his name pronounced, affords safety in all anxiety and protection from all dangers, 21, 406–16; implored by women to secure the birth of beautiful offspring, 21, 409; is capable of assuming any shape whatever, 21, 410–12, 415; pious gift to A., 21, 412; hymn of adoration to A., 21, 415–18; will become a Buddha by the side of Amitâbha, 21, 417; the Buddha-son, 49 (ii), x, xxii sq., 48, 52; Mahâsthâma and A. attend the Buddha Amitâyus, 49 (ii), 176, 178; meditation on A., 49 (ii), 181–7, 200; A. and Mahâsthâma preach to the sinner, 49 (ii), 197.

Â*v*ân, n.d., the water-lily is Â.'s flower, 5, 104; invoked, 5, 402, 405.

Avântaratamas, *see* Apântaratamas.

Avanti, n.pl., Mahâ Ka*kk*âyana in, 17, 32; there are but few Bhikkhus in A. and the southern country, 17, 33 sq., 38 sq.; special rules for the Bhikkhus in A. and the southern country, 17, 33–40.

Âvara*n*â, 'veils,' Pali t.t., 11, 182 n. *See* Hindrances.

Avârao*s*tri, n.p., 23, 208.

Avare-g*a*u, son of Aoighimatastîra, 23, 218.

Avarethrabah, son of Râstare-vagha*nt*, 23, 209.

Avarethrab*a*u, surname of Zaratû*s*t, son of Âtû*r*-pâ*d*, 37, 30, 30 n.; 47, xii, 87 sq. and n.

Avarice, injunction against it, 6, 27; produced from passion, 8, 108 sq.; freedom from a., 8, 114, 284, 332, 344; lust, anger, and a., the threefold way to hell, 8, 117, 378; the self joined to a. is death, 8, 155; one of twelve qualities to be avoided, 8, 166, 181; the chief vice, 8, 302 sq., 302 n.; is of the quality of darkness, 8, 320; senses caused by the production of a., 8, 335; the wheel of life rendered unsteady by a. and desire, 8, 357, 357 n.; the Brahma*k*ârin must be free from a., 8, 361.

Avarnak, n.p., 5, 139.
Avarôstar, his son Vohûnêm, 47, 165.
Avasânas and **Avasânapatis** (i.e. Residences and Lords of Residences), worshipped as deities, 2, 107 n.
Avatâras (incarnations), the highest person in his A. does not consist of Prakriti, 48, 241.
Avâush, demon of drought, 24, 133, 133 n.
Avênak, to be corrected to Hindûk, 37, xlvi sq.
Aveshti, t.t., 38, 266. *See* Sacrifices (*j*).
Avesta, 'Zend-A.,' 'A. and Zand,' 5, x, 327; Bundahis, a translation from an A. original? 5, xxiv; A. in the sense of prayers, 5, 312, 318, 323, 371; 'it is revealed by the A.,' 5, 385; 'A. and Zand' known to the priests, 5, 385; 18, 201 sq., 201 n., 296; whether a priest who knows the A., or one who knows the commentary, be entitled to a higher rank, 18, 155–9; the Zand teaching of the A., 18, 357; A. and Zand revealed to Zoroaster by Aûharmazd, 24, 346; 37, 258; decision of judges to be made from A. and Zand, 37, 63; preservation of A. and Zand by Dârâî and Valkhas, 37, 413, 413 n.; collection of A. and Zand after the destruction by Alexander, 37, 437, 447; Zoroaster produces A. and Zand, 47, xxii. *See also* Zend-Avesta.
Avidyâ, Sk., Aviggâ, Pali, t.t., Nescience, Ignorance. *See* Nescience.
Avidyândhakâravidhvamsana-kara, the 35th Tathâgata, 49 (ii), 6.
Aviggâ, Pali, the same as Sk. Avidyâ. *See* Nescience.
Avîki, *see* Hell (*a*).
Avikshit, Kârandhama A., a Gina king, 19, 328, 328 n.
Âvikshita, *see* Marutta Â.
Avrak, constellation, together with Tîstar, 5, 25 sq., 168.
Avyâkrita, Sk., t.t., the Undeveloped, 34, cxix. *See* Avyakta.
Avyakta, Sk., t.t., the Undeveloped, the Unevolved. *See* Undeveloped.
Ayanghad (Ayanghas), n.p., 47, 35, 140.
Ayara, lords of the days in their length, worshipped, 31, 379.
Âyasthûna, *see* Gânaki Â.
Ayâsya Ângirasa, a name of Breath (mukhya prâna), 15, 80, 82, 83; n. of a teacher, 15, 119, 187.
Ayâthrima, the advancer, worshipped, 31, 198, 205, 210, 216, 220, 224, 335, 338, 368, 370, 372.
Ayavas, Yavas and, lords of creatures, 43, 69, 69 n., 76.
Ayazem, son of Ragan, ancestor of Zoroaster, 5, 141; 47, 34 n., 140.
Ayêhi, sterility, a demon, 4, 234.
'Âyeshah, wife of Mohammed, 6, xxix; 9, 290 n., 307 n., 344 n.; vindication of her character and denunciation of her accusers, 6, xcix; 9, 74 sq., 74 n., 78 n.
Ayôasti, son of Pouru-dhâkhsti, 23, 211.
Âyogava, Marutta Âvikshita, the Â. king, 44, 397.
Âyu, or Âyus, son of Urvasî and Purûravas, 12, 389 n.; 26, 91; 46, 318, 323 sq.; n. of Agni, 26, 118; 41, 323; 46, 142; prayer to Â. and other gods, 44, 385; a mythical ancestor of mankind, 46, 119, 122 sq., 317, 321; Agni is the guest of Â., 46, 194; the Bhrigus established Agni among the clans of Â., 46, 202; Agni, the praise of Â., 46, 341, 371; Agni the homestead for the Â., 46, 382. *See also* Âyus.
Âyupâla, n. of a Buddhist teacher, 35, xxv; confuted by Milinda, 35, 30–33.
Âyus, men who brighten and enliven everything, 32, 353, 355; name of a clan of ancient worshippers of Agni, 46, 45, 52, 171, 343.
Âyushya rite, *see* Child (*b*).
Âyûta, n.p., 23, 215.
Âz, or Âzŏ, Phl., the same as Zd. Âzî, or Âzi, demon of Greed, 5, 110 sq.; 18, 95; 24, 33, 33 n., 50; 37, 253, 253 n.; 47, 101; extinguishes the fire, 4, 198, 198 n.; defeated, 5, 128 sq.
Âzar, father of Abraham, 6, 124, 124 n.
Âzâta, son of Karesna, 23, 209.
Azhi Dahâka, *see* Dahâk.

Âzî, or Âzi, *see* Âz.
Az-i Dahâk, *see* Dahâk.
Azi Sruvar, one of the seven heinous sinners, 18, 217, 217 n.
Azŏ, *see* Âz.
Azrâ'îl, the angel of death, 6, lxix.

B

Baal, Elias protested against the worship of, 9, 173.
Babel, overthrow of the tower of, 6, 253 n.
Bâbhrava, *see* Vatsanapât B.
Bâbhravya, a teacher, worshipped at the Tarpa*n*a, 29, 122, 141, 220.
Babhru, a teacher, worshipped at the Tarpa*n*a, 29, 122, 141, 244.
Babhru, the brown one, a demon of disease, 42, 30, 466.
Babhrukar*n*a, the brown-eared one, a demon of disease, 42, 30, 466.
Babylon, Azi Dahâka in Bawri or B., 23, 60, 60 n.
Backbiting, freedom from the habit of, 8, 114, 326, 364; one of the defects of self-restraint, 8, 168; one of the defects of frenzy, 8, 183; is of the quality of passion, 8, 323; punishments in hell for b., 10 (ii), 121 sq. *See also* Abuse, Defamation, *and* Slander.
Bâ*d*, *see* Wind.
Bâdarâya*n*a, his Vedânta-sûtras posterior to Bhagavadgîtâ, 8, 30–3; 34, cxxvi; quoted by Hira*n*yake*s*in, 30, 200; the author of the Vedânta-sûtras, 34, xi; and the chief distinguishing doctrines of *S*aṅkara and Râmânuga, 34, lxxxvii–ci; the system of B. had greater affinities with that of the Bhâgavatas and Râmânuga than with that of *S*aṅkara, 34, c; quoted in the Vedânta-sûtras, 34, 198, 218; 38, 182 sq., 285, 290, 297 sq., 318, 360, 402 sq., 410, 412 sq.; 48, 326 sq., 336, 626, 694; the foremost among those who understand the Veda, 48, 529; his views opposed to *G*aimini's, 48, 686, 689; his view on Brahman as the soul's aim, 48, 752; his view on the released soul, 48, 761, 763. *See also* Vedânta-sûtras.
Bâdari, quoted by Baudhâyana, 14, xl n.; quoted in the Vedânta-sûtras, 34, xix, lxxxii sq., xc sq., 151; 38, 121; 48, 293, 592, 748, 750, 763; thinks that the souls are led to the lower Brahman, 38, 389–92, 393–402; asserts the absence of a body and sense-organs on the part of the released, 38, 411 sq.
Bâdeyîputra, n. of a teacher, 15, 224 n.
Bâdhva, n. of a teacher, 1, 259 sq., 259 n.
Baêshatastîra, n.p., 23, 218.
Ba*g*âbo*g*â, a demon harassing children, 30, 211.
Bahak, n.p., 5, 145–7, 145 n.
Bâhak, n.p., 5, 145.
Bâhavi, a teacher, satiated at the Tarpa*n*a, 29, 220.
Bâhîkas, n. of a people, call Rudra Bhava, 12, 201.
Bahman, *see* Vohûman.
Bahman Pûngyah, his account of the Nasks, 37, 418, 418 n.; his Rivâyat, 37, 451.
Bahman Ya*s*t, account of its contents, 5, l–lii; and Vohûman Ya*s*t, 5, lii sq.; its age, 5, liii–lvi; MSS. and Pâzand and Persian versions of it, 5, lvi–lix; 47, xxiv; B. or Zand-i Vohûman Yasno, translated, 5, 189–235; refers to next-of-kin marriage, 18, 399.
Bahrâm, or Verethraghna, 4, 221 n. *See* Verethraghna.
Bahrâm fire, *see* Fire.
Bâhuka, n. of a great ascetic, 45, 268.
Bahuputta *K*etiya at Vesâli, 11, 40, 58.
Bâhva, when questioned about Brahman by Vâshkalin, explained it to him by silence, 38, 157.
Bahv*r*i*k*as, i.e. the theologians of the Rigveda, 44, 72, 72 n.
Bahv*r*i*k*a-Upanishad, *see* Upanishads (*a*).
Bakht-âfrî*d*, n.p., 5, 194; quoted, 5, 395.
Bakkula, superior to Buddha in bodily health, 36, 8–12, 11 n.
Bala (plur. balâni), Sk. and Pali t.t. *See* Power.
Balaam, alluded to, 6, 159 n.
Balabhadra, king of Sugrîva, father of M*r*igâputra, 45, 88.

Balâbhigña, n. of a Tathâgata, 49 (ii), 67.

Baladevas are never born in low families, 22, 225; the mothers of B. wake up after seeing four auspicious dreams, 22, 246.

Bâlakalonakâra-gâma, Buddha at, 17, 308.

Bâlâki, discussion on Brahman between Gârgya B. and Agâtasatru, 1, 300-7; 15, 100-5; 34, cv, 268-74; 48, 378-80, 383; addressed, 44, 165. *See also* Gârgya.

Balakôshtha, chief of a *Kândâla* tribe, 45, 50 n.

Bâlamukhyâ, the Bhikshu Manthâlagautama seduced by her, 49 (i), 38 sq.

Balance, the right edge of the Vedi a b., in which the Sacrificer is weighed, 44, 45. *See also* Ordeals.

Balasri, or Mrigâputra, q.v.

Balhika Prâtipîya, the Kauravya king, 44, 269, 272.

Balhikas, n. of a people, 42, 2, 446, 448 sq.

Bali, a chief of demons, 21, 6; Namuki represents B. in the Gaina version of the myth of the three strides of Vishnu, 45, 86 n.; a younger brother of Dhruva, 49 (i), 94; Indra, B., and Nahusha, 49 (i), 113; world of the dead, the domain of B., 49 (i), 197.

Bali, Sk., t.t., certain offerings. *See* Sacrifices (*i*).

Balissaha, disciple of Mahâgiri, 22, 289.

Bambhâri, guardian of Soma, 26, 72.

Bâmdâd, Mazdîk son of, 5, 194, 201.

Bâna, his date, 8, 28 sq.; refers to the Nârada-smriti, 33, xviii.

Bandhu, a Gaupâyana, 46, 415.

Banishment, *see* Samgha.

Banners, *see* War.

Barashnûm, *see* Purification.

Barâzak, the causer of strife, 37, 203, 203 n.

Barâzd = Ibairaz, one of the immortals, 18, 258 sq. n.

Barbarians (Mlekkhas), a Snâtaka must not speak to, 2, 220; 7, 228; talking to b. defiles, 7, 95; after having bathed, one must not converse with b., 7, 205; the term 'barbarian countries' explained, 7, 255; country of b. to be avoided by the wandering Gaina mendicant, 22, 137 sq.; Asuras speak like b., 26, 31 sq.; do not understand the language of Âryas, 45, 241.

Barber, legend of the old b. who became a Bhikkhu, 17, 140-2.

Baremna, n.p., 23, 216.

Bareshnûm, *see* Purification.

Baresma (Baresôm, Barsom), t.t., bundle of sacred twigs, held by the Parsi priest when reciting prayers, 4, 22 sq., 22 n., 50, 61 sq.; 5, lxxii, 212, 227, 229; 18, 142, 142 n., 164 sq. and n.; 24, 103, 103 n.; 37, 96, 162 sq. and n.; consecration of B. for sacrifices, 4, 207; 5, 283 sq., 284 sq. n., 307, 333, 338, 370; the trees that yield up B. worshipped, 4, 214 sq. and n.; 23, 158; the sacrificer must keep his eyes on the B., 4, 215, 215 n.; the plucking of the B. twigs, 4, 289 n.; the preparation of the B., 4, 357 n., 359, 361, 363, 365; 5, 205; to be kept free from pollution, 5, 251; 18, 432 sq.; defiled by the look of a menstruous woman, 5, 278 sq., 281, 283 sq., 285; 24, 334, 334 n.; spread in three, five, seven, and nine bundles, 31, 299, 299 n.

Baresôm, *see* Baresma.

Barhis, Sk., t.t., the sacrificial grass (spread for the gods at Hindu sacrifices), offerings made to it, 12, 147-50, 153, 157, 233, 235, 319, 321, 400 n.; offered up at the end of sacrifice, 12, 264; B. means offspring, 12, 428, 436; sacred kusa grass trimmed and spread out for the gods, 32, 81, 84 sq.; the simplest form of an altar, 32, 380; the forest plants its essence, 44, 21; spread out at sacrifices, the gods invited to sit on it, 46, 6, 8, 13, 38, 43, 153, 198, 209, 228 sq., 236, 257, 266, 340, 348, 367, 414, 418; sprinkled with butter, 46, 8; they have spread the eastward-turned sacrificial grass, 46, 179; the divine B. invoked in Âprî hymns, 46, 198, 377.

Barku Vârshna, his opinion as to fast-day food, 12, 5; says that sight is Brahman, 15, 155.

Barmâyûn, n.p., and Katâyûn were with Frêdûn, 5, 133.

Barmâyûn, the ox, *see* Animals (*i*).
Barrenness, five kinds of spiritual b. (pañ*k*a *k*etokhilâ), and the means to be freed from them, 11, 221–5, 228 sq., 232.
Barsom, *see* Baresma.
Bartarûsh prophesies the future of Zoroaster, 47, xxi.
Barzînkarûs, Zoroaster confided to his care, 47, xxi.
Barzû Qiyâmu-d-dîn, Dastûr, his account of the Nasks, 37, 433, 433 n.
Bâshkala, teacher, worshipped at the Tarpa*n*a, 29, 123.
Ba*s*i, n. of a Daêva, 23, 49 sq., 49 n.
Bastavairi, n.p., 23, 207, 207 n.
Bat, *see* Animals (*k*).
Bath, Bathing.

(*a*) Occasions for which it is enjoined.
(*b*) Persons for whom it is enjoined.

(*a*) OCCASIONS FOR WHICH IT IS ENJOINED.

As a penance or part of a penance, 2, 81, 85–7, 89, 277, 279 sq., 284, 292, 295, 297; 7, 88 sq., 91, 93–5, 121, 149, 151, 157, 165, 167, 174, 176, 181; 14, 30, 110 sq., 114, 121 sq., 124, 127 sq., 183, 212, 218, 223, 241, 295 sq., 312, 318 sq., 322; 25, 453, 457, 466, 469, 472, 474–6, 482; the student's solemn b. which terminates his period of studentship, 2, 92 sq., 192, 216, 216 n.; 7, 120, 120 n; 14, 156, 158; 29, 91 sq., 227, 230, 312 sq., 315, 379 sq., 407 sq.; 30, 82 sq., 161 sq., 165 sq., 275–7; 44, 49 sq. (like the concluding offering of a sacrifice); before sacrificing, 2, 156; after the funeral ceremony, 2, 278; 14, 90; 29, 243, 246; 44, 438; *distress and misfortune, bad dreams and evil thoughts are taken from him even who only sprinkles himself with water: that is the law. He who regularly takes the prescribed bath (every morning), does not experience the tortures of Yama's hell. By the regular bath criminals even obtain their absolution*, 7, 208; after an eclipse of sun or moon, 7, 218; before eating, he must sprinkle his feet, hands, and face, 7, 220; merely b. in sacred places or Tîrthas confers eternal bliss, 7, 256; b. in the month Kârttika removes every sin, 7, 265; b. in Mâgha and Phâlguna procures the advantages attending an eclipse of the sun or mcon, 7, 270; he who bathes in a river and worships King Dharma on the 14th day of both halves of every month is purified from sin, 7, 270; purity of self attained by b., 8, 64 n.; performed with a view of deliverance from Varu*n*a's power, 12, 406 sq. and n.; b. of a readmitted outcast, 14, 78; a rite of purification, 14, 171, 182 sq.; 25, 178 sq., 181, 183, 187, 194; before the twilight devotions, 14, 246; expiatory rites connected with b., 14, 249–52; 29, 247; ceremony of b., on entering the order of ascetics, 14, 278; at rites securing success, 14, 323; at the Dîkshâ, 26, 8 sq.; avabh*ri*tha, or expiatory b. at the end of the Soma sacrifice, 26, 378–85, 422 sq.; 41, 87, 185; 44, 96, 121 sq. and n., 138, 211, 264–9, 343 sq. (a*s*vamedha), 438; the avabh*ri*tha identified with death, 1, 52; 38, 221; purificatory b. (*s*ûlâvabh*ri*tha) after the animal sacrifice, 26, 215–17; suspended during mourning, 27, 181; b. before the Tarpa*n*a rite, 29, 120; at the end of the Godâna rite, 29, 186; before auspicious or magic rites, 29, 291; before the Upanayana, 30, 271; before undergoing an ordeal, 33, 105, 110, 116, 118; of the judge before administering an ordeal, 33, 250.

(*b*) PERSONS FOR WHOM IT IS ENJOINED.

Rules about b. for Snâtakas, 2, 97; 25, 142, 149, 160; 29, 124, 126; enjoined for the Brahma*k*ârin, 2, 186 sq.; 14, 42; 25, 62; a Snâtaka shall bathe frequently, 2, 219; a Snâtaka must not bathe naked, 2, 225; 29, 317; the student must plunge into the waters like a stick, 7, 116, 116 sq. n.; rules about b. for householders, 7, 204–8; 14, 238; a hermit must bathe at morning, noon, and evening, 7, 277; 8, 361; 14, 45, 259; 25, 199, 202 sq.; enjoined for the ascetic, 8, 364; 14, 281 sq.; some

sects are for b., others for the omission of b., 8, 375; rules about b. for Buddhist Bhikkhus, 13, 44 sq.; 17, 35, 39; 20, 66-8, 110; the pupil should attend to his upagg*h*âya when he is going to the *g*antâghara (hot sitting bath), 13, 157 sq.; rules about b. for Buddhist nuns, 20, 367-9; prescribed for the ascetic as a penance for unintentional injury to living beings, 25, 210; definition of Snâna or b., 29, 375; *G*aina monks should abstain from b., 45, 296 sq. *See also* Ablutions, *and* Purification.

Bath-houses, a king overthrown by the Magi for having built, 4, lxxvii, lxxvii n.

Bathing-places, holy, *see* Holy places.

Battle, battle charms, battle songs, *see* War.

Bauddha doctrines, *see* Buddhism.

Baudhâyana, relation between the schools of B. and Âpastamba, 2, xvi, xix-xxiv, xxiv n.; 25, xciii; wrote a commentary on the Vedânta-sûtras, 8, 32; deplorable state of the MSS. of the Sûtras of B., 14, xxix-xxxv; *S*rautasûtra, G*ri*hyasûtra, and Dharmasûtra, their relation to one another, 14, xxx sq., 150 sq. n.; the G*ri*hyasûtra of B. and its Pari*s*ish*t*as, 14, xxxii sq.; his position among the teachers of the Taittirîya-veda, 14, xxxv-xxxix; teachers on Dharma quoted by B., 14, xl sq., xl n.; belongs to Southern India, 14, xli-xliii; his date, 14, xliii; mentioned in the Baudhâyana-Dharmasûtra, 14, 160, 160 n., 163 sq., 297, 297 n., 299, 336; Ka*n*va B. satiated at the Tarpa*n*a, 14, 255. *See also* Bodhâyana.

Baudhâyana-Dharmasûtra, its relation to the Gautama-Dharmasûtra, 2, liii-lvii, lix sq.; to the Vish*n*u-sm*ri*ti, 7, xix sq.; relation between the B. and Vâsish*th*a Dharma*s*âstra, 14, xvii, xxi; belongs to the Black Yagur-veda, 14, xxix; interpolations in B., 14, xxxiii-xxxv; Vedic texts quoted in the B., 14, xxxix sq.; text and translation of the B., 14, xliii-xlv, 141-333.

Baudhîputra, n. of a teacher, 15, 224 n.

B*a*ungha, son of S*a*ungha, 23, 218.

Bâvarî, n. of a teacher, 10 (ii), xii; disciples of B., 10 (ii), xii sq.; his accomplishments, and the three marks on his limbs, 10 (ii), 189; the Brâhma*n*a B. cursed by another Brâhma*n*a, is comforted by a deity, and shown by Buddha 'the way to the other shore,' 10 (ii), 184-213.

Bawri = Babylon, 23, 60, 60 n.

Bayak, n. of a demon, 5, 132, 132 n.

Beasts, *see* Animals.

Beatitude, highest. *See* Bliss, Highest good, Nirvâ*n*a, *and* Release.

Beauty, goddess of, *see* Lakshmî, *and* S*r*î.

Beaver, *see* Animals (*k*).

Bedr, allusions to the battle of, 6, xxxvi sq., 47 n., 61-6, 66 n., 86 n., 165 n., 171 n.; 9, 20 n., 62 n., 70 n., 257 n., 274 n., 276 n.

Bees, simile of the b. collecting honey, 1, 101; 8, 188, 309, 309 n.; the b. inspired by the Lord to build hives, 6, 257; antelope, elephant, butterfly, b., and fish, 8, 155 n.; omen of b. making honey in the house, 29, 139.

Begging, for him who knows breath as Brahman there is the secret vow 'Beg not,' 1, 280, 281; rules about b. for the Brahma*k*ârin, his duty of b., 2, 11-14, 190 sq.; 7, 115, 117, 120; 8, 360; 14, 57 sq., 151 sq., 157; 25, 39, 63 sq.; 29, 68, 73, 191, 308 sq., 402; 30, 67, 157; 33, 132; 44, 49 sq.; part of a penance, 2, 89 sq., 283, 289; 14, 124, 211, 300, 309, 327; 25, 445, 455, 467, 481; when b. is lawful, 2, 123 sq., 203 sq.; 14, 240; 25, 424-7, 430 sq. and n.; rules about b. for the ascetic, 2, 154, 194; 7, 279; 8, 362-4; 14, 47, 260, 279-81, 283; 25, 208 sq.; a means of livelihood for Brâhma*n*as, 2, 227; 14, 288 sq.; 25, 128 sq.; to subsist on alms is better than fasting, 14, 46; rules about b. for the Snâtaka, 14, 159; 25, 134; 29, 124; food which a student obtains by b. is always pure, 14, 170; 25, 192; a sin for one who has finished stu-

dentship, 14, 220; 29, 317; rules about b. for Buddhist monks, 19, 298; 20, 250 sq., 289–92; 36, 33–7, 286–8, 319 sq., 326, 339 sq., 346; the hermit in the forest to live by alms, 25, 203; enjoined for the Dîkshita, 26, 45 n.; rites performed when going out for b., 30, 294 sq.; about b. and beneficence, 37, 39.

Behaviour, *see* Etiquette.

Being, *see* Sat.

Beings, three origins of b., from an egg, from living being, from a germ, 1, 94; 48, 595 sq.; penance for selling living b., 7, 177; the world and its b. (gods, Mâras, Brahman, b. comprising gods, men, Sama*n*as, and Brâhma*n*as, &c.), 10 (ii), 30, 45, 96, 142 sq.; 11, 72, 187, 288; 21, 21, 64 sq., 115, 163, 363; 36, 28, 221; 49 (ii), 24, 72, 102; classes of b., Sama*n*as, Brâhma*n*as, devas, Mâra, Brahman, 13, 97, 136 sq.; sounds of the different b. in this world, 21, 338–40; list of b. in the world, 36, 101 sq.; 43, 373; 49 (ii), 60, 113, 130; the b. and the lord of b., 41, 158; 43, 73; all living b. freed from death by means of certain hymns, 43, 70; Pragâpati, the lord (the body) of living b., 43, 76, 350, 354; the Brahma*k*ârin, at the initiation, is committed to all b. for security from injury, 44, 87; classes of beings (sattâ, pâ*n*â, bhûtâ, *g*îvâ), 45, xxvi, xxvi n., xxx, 42 sq.; the six kinds of living b., viz. earth-bodies, water-bodies, fire-bodies, wind-bodies, plants, and animals, 45, 146, 213–18; classification and description of all living b. and things without life, 45, 206–29; the six classes of living b. which a *G*aina monk should be careful not to hurt, 45, 292, 302, 311, 350 sq., 400–5, 421; denizens of hell, brute animals, gods, men, and suchlike b. commit sins, 45, 356; on the generation of the various classes of animate and inanimate b., through the efficacy of Karman, 45, 388–98; six orders of b., 49 (i), 200, 200 n.; denial of the idea of b., 49 (ii), 117–44; the b. in the five paths of existence, 49 (ii), 182, 182 n. *See also* Bhûtas, Souls, *and* Superhuman Beings.

Bekkah = Mecca, q.v.

Bela*tth*a Ka*kk*âna, converted by Buddha, 17, 93–7.

Bela*tth*asîsa, superior of Ânanda, had a disease of thick scabs, 17, 48, 226.

Bela*tth*iputta, *see* Sañgaya Bela*tth*iputta.

Belief, perception based on b., b. on the attention of a tutor, 1, 122; necessary for being convinced, 37, 289; b. that the gods exist, 42, 158, 622; B. and Unbelief represented as two women, 44, 110–12; b. in Amitâbha Buddha, 49 (ii), ix sq., 62 sq. *See also* Dogma, *and* Faith.

Bells and organ as musical instruments, 3, 61; a network of b. hung round the Palace of Righteousness, 11, 267 sq.; b. with wooden tongues sounded for making announcements, 27, 260; 28, 34; peal of b. of Sui, 28, 37; a wonderful b.-stand, 40, 22 sq., 22 n.; taxes collected to be employed in making b., 40, 31 sq.

Beluva, n.pl., Buddha at, 11, 34 sq.

Benares, a great city, 11, 99, 247; Buddha at B., 11, 146; 13, 90–116; 16, 80; 17, 21, 214; 49 (i), 170–3; Buddha begins to turn the wheel of the law at B., 11, 153 sq.; 19, 168–72; 21, xxix, 56, 70; Pâr*s*va born at B., 22, 271; Buddha goes to B. (Vârâ*n*asî), 49 (i), 164–70; converts made by Buddha at B., 49 (i), 190–2.

Be*n*dva, a chief, hostile to Zoroastrianism, 31, 160, 162 sq.

Benedictions, *see* Prayers.

Benevolence in man and in nature, 16, 356, 357 n.; b., righteousness, propriety, and understanding: four constituents of human nature, 27, 10; is the heart of man, 27, 383 n.; b. is man, 28, 269 n., 312, 312 n.; cannot be a substitute for the Tâo, 39, 346–8; when the Tâo was lost, b. came, 40, 312;—*b. and righteousness*, 16, 423 sq.; 27, 44; 28, 332 sq., 344; are the instruments of a ruler, 28, 257; government based on them, 28, 312 sq.; people would become

filial and kindly if b. and r. were discarded, 39, 61 sq.; are detrimental to goodness, 39, 80 sq., 281–7, 293, 357; are mere excrescences on human nature, called in to distort and vex the world, 39, 139, 268–80, 295 sq.; Confucius and Lâo-ȝze discourse on them, 39, 145, 399 sq.; the place of b. and r. and virtue in Tâoism, 39, 305 sq.; 40, 43 sq., 79, 95, 285 sq.; in the age of perfect virtue people were upright without knowing that to be so was righteousness; loved one another without knowing that to do so was b., &c., 39, 325; the perfect man of Tâo pushes back b. and r., 39, 342; are no good, except for a short time, 39, 355 sq.; are opposed to the Tâo, 40, 58 sq., 284; what is the greatest b., righteousness, and good faith, 40, 87; the dangers of b. and r., 40, 108 sq.; Confucius manifests b. and r., 40, 193; as regarded by the Superior Man, 40, 215.

Beni *Gh*anm, built a mosque in opposition to Mohammed, 6, 188 sq., 188 n.

Bere*g*ya, n.d., worshipped, 31, 197, 205, 209, 215, 220, 224, 387.

Berezi*s*nu, son of Ara, 23, 211.

Berezva*nt*, n.p., 23, 218.

Berezyar*s*ti, n.p., 23, 206.

Betrothal, *see* Marriage.

Betting, *see* Gambling.

Bêvarâsp = Dahâk, q. v.

Bhadda, became an inheritor of the highest heavens, 11, 26.

Bhaddasâla, officer of the Nanda kings, waged war against *K*andagutta, 36, 147.

Bhaddavatikâ, n. of an elephant, 17, 118.

Bhaddiya, n. of town, 17, 22, 124–7; Me*nd*aka of Bh., 17, 121–7.

Bhaddiya, converted by Buddha, 11, 155 n.; 13, 99; 35, 163.

Bhaddiya, the Sâkya Râ*g*a, renounces the world persuaded by Anuruddha, and reaches supreme happiness, 20, 227–33.

Bhadra, one of the five first disciples of Buddha, 19, 172.

Bhadra, of the Gautama gotra, a Sthavira, 22, 294.

Bhadra, of the Kâ*s*yapa gotra, a Sthavira, 22, 294.

Bhadra, n. of the world in which Ya*s*odharâ is to be a Buddha, 21, 257.

Bhadrâ, King Kausalika's daughter, insults the monk Harikê*s*a, is compelled to marry him, but he refuses her, 45, 50 n., 53.

Bhadrabâhu, n. of a Sthavira, 22, 287 sq.; the head of the *G*aina church, when the Aṅgas were collected, 22, xliii.

Bhadra*g*it, n. of a Bhikshu, 49 (ii), 2.

Bhadraguptika Kula, of the U*d*uvâ*t*ika Ga*n*a, 22, 291.

Bhadrakâlî, n.d., Bali offering to, 25, 91; 29, 86.

Bhadrapâla, one of the sixteen virtuous men, 21, 4; heading 500 Bodhisattvas, 21, 360.

Bhadrasena, son of Agâta*s*atru, bewitched by Âra*n*i, 41, 141, 141 n.

Bhadravargîyas, five, the first disciples of Buddha, 21, 2 n.

Bhadrâvudha, n. of a Brâhma*n*a, 10 (ii), 187, 205, 210, 213.

Bhadrâvudhamâ*n*avapu*kkh*â, t.c., 10 (ii), 205.

Bhadraya*s*as, disciple of Suhastin, 22, 291.

Bhadrayaska Kula, of the U*d*uvâ*t*ika Ga*n*a, 22, 291.

Bhadrika, a distinguished Arhat, 21, 2.

Bhadrikâ, n.pl., Mahâvîra at, 22, 264.

Bhadrikâ, a goddess, who was a cow in her former birth, 49 (i), 166 sq.

Bhadrîyikâ *S***âkhâ**, of the U*d*uvâ*t*ika Ga*n*a, 22, 291.

Bhaga, a Vedic god, the speed of, 1, 76; why he is blind, 12, 210; Uttare Phalgunî assigned to Bh., 12, 285 n.; oblation to Bh. at the wedding, 29, 32, 283; invoked in the prayer at the initiation, 29, 64; gives the bride to the husband, 29, 282; 30, 189; invoked for agricultural success, 30, 113 sq.; 42, 140; Pârtha oblation to Bh., 41, 82; invoked in a charm against mania, 42, 33; grants life, 42, 53; Bh. or Fortune, invoked by maidens wishing to obtain a husband, 42, 94 sq.,

324; connected with marriage, 42, 95; as a love-god, 42, 101; B*ri*haspati and Bh. join (husband and wife?) together, 42, 135; Vish*n*u and Bh. in a list of gods, 42, 160; Sarasvatî, Anumati, and Bh. invoked, 42, 173; invoked for help, 42, 204; invoked in the morning, 46, 38; Agni, as Bh., rules over wealth, 46, 187; invited to the sacrifice together with Agni, 46, 281; Agni compared with Bh., 46, 281; Agni announces man's sins to Bh., 46, 325; the bestower or dispenser of riches, 46, 401 sq.

Bhâgadugha, title, carver or tax-gatherer of a king, 41, 63, 63 n.

Bhagavadgîtâ, no historical data about it, 8, 1 sq.; its titles, 8, 2, 28; how quoted by *S*a*n*karâ*k*ârya, 8, 2; called an Upanishad, 8, 2, 200; a genuine portion of the Mahâbhârata? 8, 2–6; is a dialogue between K*r*ish*n*a and Ar*g*una, 8, 3 sq., 40–131; its style and language, 8, 4, 11, 13–15; no sectarian or Brahmanizing spirit in it, 8, 6; relation between Bh. and Upanishads, 8, 2, 5, 7 sq., 13, 15–19, 23, 26 sq., 34, 34 n., 36, 210, and notes to 45 sq., 50–4, 57 sq., 61 sq., 64–8, 71, 74, 76, 78 sq., 80 sq., 84 sq., 88–91, 93, 100, 102–6, 108, 111–14, 119, 123 sq., 129, 146; its author, 8, 6 sq.; anterior to the systems of Sanskrit philosophy, 8, 7–13; its date and position in Sanskrit literature, 8, 7–34; inconsistencies in its teaching, 8, 11–13; its versification, 8, 15 sq.; its attitude towards the Vedas, 8, 16–20, 25; its relation to Buddhism, 8, 24–7, 36, and notes to 45–52, 56, 59 sq., 62–6, 68–71, 79, 84, 88 sq., 101, 103, 105, 108 sq., 111 sq., 114, 118, 123; and Sâ*n*khya and Yoga philosophy, 8, 27; referred to by Bâ*n*a, 8, 28; allusions to it in Kâlidâsa's works, 8, 29 sq.; its priority to the Vedânta-sûtras, 8, 30–3; its text, 8, 34 sq.; its number of stanzas, 8, 35; translation, 8, 35–131; teaching and study of the Bh., 8, 129 sq.; its relation to the Sanatsugâtîya, 8, 135, 137, 142, 144–8, and notes to, 150–6, 158–61, 163–5, 167 sq., 170–3, 175–7, 179 sq., 184–6, 188 sq., 193 sq.; relation between Bh. and Anugîtâ, 8, 197 sq., 207–10, 215, 218 sq., 222, 227, 230 n.; the teaching of the Bh., and the Saddharmapu*nd*arîka, 21, xxvi–xxviii, xxix n., xxxi n., xxxiv n., xxxvi; the doctrine of the Bh. a fusion of the Brahman theory of the Upanishads with the belief in a personal highest being, 34, cxxvi; as an authority for Bâdarâya*n*a, 34, cxxvi; quoted, 38, 421; 48, 773–5. *See also* Î*s*varagîtâ.

Bhagavat, *S*vetadîpa, 'the white island,' the abode of Bh. or Vish*n*u, 7, 156; title of Buddha, 10 (ii), x.

Bhâgavatas, Vish*n*uitic sect of, 7, xxviii; or Pa*ñk*arâtras, forerunners of Râmânu*g*as, 34, xxii sq.; their views refuted according to *S*a*n*kara, approved of according to Râmânu*g*a, 34, li sq., 439–43; their system nearer to Bâdarâya*n*a than that of *S*a*n*kara, 34, c; their theory of the origin of the world, 34, cxvii; 48, 524–31; system of Bh., and Bhagavadgîtâ, 34, cxxvi; and Mahâbhârata, 34, cxxvii; contradictions in their system, 34, 442 sq.; doctrine of Bh. stated, 34, 440.

Bhâgavitti, *see K*ûla Bh.

Bhagav*r*itti, Sk., t.t., one living by prostitution of his wife, 33, 88 n.

Bhaggâ, Buddha at, 20, 125.

Bhagu (Pali for Bh*r*igu, q.v.), n of a *R*ishi, 11, 172.

Bhagu, one of the first converts made by Buddha, 20, 228–33; 35, 163; a Thera, 17, 238; Buddha's visit to him, 17, 308 sq.

Bhaisha*g*yarâ*g*a, n. of a Bodhisattva Mahâsattva, 21, 4, 213–23, 394, 404; the Bodhisattvas Bh., and Mahâpratibhâna, with their retinue promise to divulge the Saddharmapu*nd*arîka after Buddha's Nirvâ*n*a, 21, 255; pronounces talismanic words, for those who keep the Lotus of the True Law, 21, 370–2; is identical with Sarvasattvapriyadar*s*ana in a former birth, 21, 376, 385, 389, 392; was in a former birth the prince Vimalagarbha, 21, 430.

Bhaisha*g*yarâ*g*asamudgata, n. of a prominent Bodhisattva, 21, 394;

was in a former birth the prince Vimalanetra, 21, 430.

Bhaksha (Drink personified), expiatory oblation to Bh. at a mishap in the Soma-sacrifice, 44, 210.

Bhakti or Faith, in the Bhagavadgîtâ, 8, 441; *but see* Faith; Bh. in the *S*vetâ*s*vatara-Upanishad, and the *S*â*nd*ilya-sûtras, 15, xxxiv.

Bhala, the sun worshipped with the formula 'To Bh. svâhâ,' 30, 120.

Bhâllabeya, or Bhâllaveya, his opinions quoted, 12, 206, 293; 44, 354, 393.

Bhâllavins, the Nidâna (a Vedic work) of the, 14, 3; quoted, 14, 147; a mantra of the Bh., 38, 227 sq.

Bhallika, a merchant, one of the two first lay-disciples of Buddha, 13, 81–4; 49 (i), 166 sq.

Bhâlukîputra, n.p., 15, 225 sq., 226 n.

Bhâmanî, a name of the Lord or the highest Self, 34, 125; 48, 272.

Bhanabhadra, converted by Buddha, 19, 243.

Bha*nd*a-gâma, Buddha at, 11, 64–6.

Bharadvâ*g*a, knew most, lived longest, and performed the greatest austerities among the *R*ishis, 1, 169; the *R*ishi of the sixth Ma*nd*ala of the Rig-veda, 1, 216; taught by Indra, 1, 220; committed adultery, 2, 175 n.; Bh. and other sages ask Brahman about final emancipation, 8, 314; became equal to Brahman, 14, 329; one of the seven *R*ishis, 15, 106; the family name of former Buddhas, 21, 19; accepted cows from B*r*ibu, 25, 424; worshipped at the Tarpa*n*a, 29, 122, 220; 30, 244; author of the Agnish*t*oma, 41, xiv; author of an imprecation, 42, 89, 295 sq.; is the mind, 43, 7; Agni praised by the Bharadvâgas, 46, 50; son of B*r*ihaspati by Mamatâ, 49 (i), 44, 44 n.:—Bh. Dhanvantari worshipped at the Vai*s*vadeva sacrifice, 29, 84; Bh. Bârhaspatya, author of Vedic hymns, 32, 370, 435.

Bharadvâ*g*a, a disciple of Buddha, 49 (ii), 90.

Bhâradvâ*g*a, dispute between Bh. and Vâse*tth*a as to whether a man is a Brâhma*n*a by birth, or by deeds, and their conversion by Buddha, 10 (ii), 108–17; Vâse*tth*a and Bh., two young Brâhma*n*as, go to Buddha to ask him about the true path to union with Brahman; Buddha instructs them, and they are finally converted, 11, 168–203; n. of a *R*ishi, 11, 172; n. of teachers, 15, 118, 118 n., 119, 186 n., 187; n. of an eminent Arhat, 21, 2; Sthaviras of the Bh. gotra, 22, 286, 291; worshipped at the Tarpa*n*a, 29, 123; a tree talking to Bh., 35, 241; quoted, 43, 352. *See* Aggika Bh., Gardabhîvibhîta Bh., Kasi Bh., Pi*nd*ola Bh., Satyavâha Bh., Suke*s*as Bh., Sundarika Bh.

Bhâradvâ*g*a, relation between the schools of Bh. and Âpastamba, 2, xvi, xxiii sq., xxiv n.

Bhâradvâ*g*îputra, n. of a teacher, 15, 225, 224 n.

Bharata, Agni called the Bh., 12, 133; 41, 292; 46, 119, 123; killed, 19, 83; King Bh. and the *R*ishi Vasish*th*a, 19, 95; the Maruts give to Bh. a strong horse, 32, 327, 332; seized the sacrificial horse of the Satvats, 44, xxx, 401; Bh. Dau*h*shanti, son of Du*h*shanta and *S*akuntalâ, performed a horse-sacrifice, 44, 399; a king who became a *G*aina monk, 45, 85, 85 n.

Bhârata, epithet of Agni (the god of the Bh. tribe), 12, 114 sq.; 46, 211; the throne-seat of the Bhâratas, 41, 105. *See also* A*s*vamedha Bh.

Bhârata, t.w., the Bh. and the Mahâbhârata satiated at the Tarpa*n*a, 29, 220.

Bharatas, wide sway belongs to them, 44, 399; the greatness of the Bh. not attained by men before them nor by those after them, 44, 399, 401; the two Bh., Deva*s*ravas and Devavâta, 46, 287 sq.; Agni shines for the Bh., 46, 391.

Bhârata-sa*m*hitâ, i.e. the Mahâbhârata, 48, 528.

Bhâratî, or Hotrâ Bhâratî, a goddess, 46, 154, 156; Mahî is independent of Bh., 46, 11 sq.; invoked in Âprî hymns, 46, 179, 199; in concord with the Bhâratîs, 46, 237;

offerings to Sarasvatî, I*d*â, and Bh., 12, 400 n.
Bhâravi, mentions Manu, 25, cxiii.
Bhargas, identified with deities, explanation of the word, 15, 310.
Bhârgava, and other sages ask Brahman about final emancipation, 8, 314; numerous Bh., 42, xxxv; = Bhr*i*gu's son; *see* Bhr*i*gu. *See also* Vaidarbhi Bh., *and* Somâhuti Bh.
Bharhut Thûpa, the birth of Buddha on the bas-reliefs of, 11, 47 n.
Bharu*k*i, quoted by Râmânuga, 34, xxi.
Bhâru*n*da, *see* Birds (*b*).
Bhâsa, one of the princes of mountains, 8, 346.
Bhâshika-sûtra, for the accentuation of the *S*atapatha-brâhma*n*a, 34, 258 n.
Bhâshyakâra, Drami*d*a referred to as, 34, xxii; quoted, 48, 17, 100. *See* Drami*d*a.
Bhâshyas, works, satiated at the Tarpa*n*a, 29, 220.
Bhâskara, quoted 48, 459.
Bhaumeyikas, *see* Bhavanavâsins.
Bhauvana, *see* Vi*s*vakarman.
Bhava, a name of Rudra, 12, 201; 29, 256; 41, 160; a name of the Self, 15, 311; offering to Bh. at the *S*ûlagava, 29, 352; 30, 221 sq.; invoked for protection of cattle, 30, 87; is Parganya, 41, 160; as a ruler of sky and earth, 42, 157 sq.; the enemies slain by the club of Bh., 42, 118, 585; reverence to Bh.'s weapon, 43, 151; Bh. and Rudra worshipped, 43, 152; Bhavas (plur.) in sea and air, 43, 155; Bh., i.e. *S*iva, pleased at the birth of his son Kârttikeya, 49 (i), 16;—*Bh. and Sarva* invoked together, 42, 56, 75, 119, 155–9, 161, 406 sq., 618–22; their arms are mottled, 42, 119, 586; are lords of cattle, 42, 155–9; are the thousand-eyed slayers of Vr*i*tra, 42, 158; they punish him who denies the sterile cow to the Brahmans, 42, 175.
Bhâvanâs, *G*aina t.t., meditations conducive to purity of soul, 45, 69, 69 n.
Bhavanavâsins, or Bhaumêyikas, one of the four kinds of gods, 45, 225.
Bhavânî, n.d., offering to, 29, 352.
Bhavishya(t)-purâ*n*a, quoted, 2, xxix sqq., 160; on penances, 25, 445 n., 446 n., 447 n., 449 n., 460 n.
Bhaya-bherava Sutta, t.w., 11, 168 n.
Bheda, Sk., t.t., individual existences, 34, xxv.
Bheda, n.p., perished because he did not present the sterile cow, 42, 179.
Bhedâbheda, t.t., relation of being neither absolutely different nor absolutely non-different, of the soul to Brahman, 34, xix, 277 n.; 48, 42 sq., 134 sq., 189–93, 195, 518.
Bhesha*g*a, or 'medicine,' a work of the Âtharva*n*ikas, 44, 365 n.
Bhikkhunîs, or Buddhist nuns, obtained salvation, 11, 25 sq.; a Bhikkhu shall not have his robe washed, or dyed, or beaten, or given him by a Bh. who is not related to him, 13, 20; nor shall he get his goat's wool (for his rug or mat) attended to by her, 13, 26; offences committed by Bhikkhus in their relation to the Bh., 13, 35–7, 56; 20, 335 sq.; a novice who has sexual intercourse with Bh. should be expelled, 13, 214 sq.; boundaries of the Bhikkhunî-sa*m*ghas, 13, 256 n.; must not be present at the Pâtimokkha recitation of Bhikkhus, 13, 295 sq.; Bhikkhus may visit sick Bh. even in vassa, 13, 308; rules about disciplinary proceedings against Bh., 13, 308 sq.; 20, 324, 332–4, 358 sq., 365 sq.; Pavâra*n*â should not be held in an assembly of Bhikkhus before Bh., 13, 337; rules about the robes of Bh., 17, 212 sq. n.; 20, 340 sq., 343; bathe together with courtesans in the river A*k*iravatî, 17, 222 sq.; dresses for Bh. to bathe in, 17, 222 sq.; on division of robes between the Samghas of Bhikkhus and Bh., 17, 253 sq.; present at a Sa*m*gha of Bhikkhus, 17, 269; cannot raise a protest in a Sa*m*gha of Bhikkhus, 17, 271; their dependence on the Bhikkhu-sa*m*gha, 17, 318; 20, 322–6; the office of giving exhortation to the Bh., 17, 338, 340, 372; superintend new buildings, 17, 359 n.; disputes of

Bh. and Bhikkhus, 20, 34; are not to be saluted by Bhikkhus, 20, 195, 328; cannot create a schism, 20, 266; 35, 163; a Bh. cannot make one of the requisite number to cause a schism, 20, 266; on the duties of Bh., 20, 320–69; cut off their hair and put on orange-coloured robes, 20, 321; eight chief rules for the conduct of Bh. towards Bhikkhus, 20, 322–5; receive exhortation from Bhikkhus, but cannot exhort Bhikkhus, 20, 323, 324; rules about the Pâtimokkha ceremony for Bh., 20, 330 sq.; rules about confession for Bh., 20, 331 sq.; may be taught the Vinaya by Bhikkhus, 20, 334; misbehaviour of Bhikkhus towards Bh. punished by their not having to be saluted by the Bhikkhunî-sa*m*gha, 20, 335 sq.; rules about the exhortation for Bh., 20, 336–40; not allowed back-scratchers, ointments, making tattoo marks, and similar things, 20, 341–3; the Bhikkhunî-sa*m*gha inherits from Bh., 20, 343 sq.; occupations forbidden to Bh., 20, 343; rules of conduct for Bh. towards Bhikkhus, 20, 344 sq.; a Bh. carrying away a foetus in her bowl, 20, 345 sq.; food stored up allowed to be handed over to the Bh. by the Bhikkhus, 20, 346 sq.; rules for Bh. in their courses, 20, 347 sq.; rules about the upasampadâ ordination of Bh., 20, 349–55; appointment of instructors to Bh. to be made by a formal act of the Bhikkhunî-sa*m*gha, 20, 352; rules for Bh. at meals, 20, 355 sq.; rules for Bh. about holding the Pavâra*n*â, 20, 356–8; cannot perform any official acts towards a Bhikkhu, but a Bhikkhu can do so towards a Bh., 20, 358 sq.; vehicles allowed to them, 20, 359 sq.; not allowed to adopt the forest life, 20, 362 sq.; dwellings for Bh., 20, 363 sq.; rules for Bh. with child who are unconscious of the fact of their conception, 20, 364 sq.; companion appointed for a Bh. under Mânatta penance, 20, 365 sq.; who have thrown off the robes, or joined a sect of Titthiyas, cannot be received into the Order again, 20, 366; rules for Bh. about bathing, 20, 367–9; will become preachers of the law, Bodhisattvas, and attain perfect enlightenment, 21, xxx, 256–8; a Bodhisattva must shun Bh. who are fond of banter and chatter, 21, 265; Bh. in the classical dramas, 33, xvii; mentioned before Bhikkhus, 36, 3; he who has outraged a Bh. cannot be converted, 36, 78 n., 177; the first Bh., 49 (i), 192. *See also* Bhikkhus (*c*), *and* Woman (*e*).

Bhikkhus, or Buddhist monks (Pali bhikkhu = Sk. bhikshu, a mendicant).

(*a*) Advantages of monastic life, exalted position of Bh., duties towards them.
(*b*) Moral precepts for Bh.
(*c*) The Bh. as members of the Order (Sa*m*gha).
(*d*) Daily life of Bh. (costume, food, medicine, dwelling, utensils, &c.).
(*e*) Buddha and the Bh.

(*a*) ADVANTAGES OF MONASTIC LIFE, EXALTED POSITION OF BH., DUTIES TOWARDS THEM.

The wise man should follow the bright state of the Bh., 10 (i), 25 sq., 25 n.; *the Bhikshu, full of delight, who is calm in the doctrine of Buddha will reach the quiet place* (*Nirvâna*), *cessation of natural desires, and happiness. He who, even as a young Bhikshu, applies himself to the doctrine of Buddha, brightens up this world, like the moon when free from clouds*, 10 (i), 88; the true Brâhma*n*a (Arhat) keeps aloof both from laymen and from Bh., 10 (i), 92; the life of the Bh. praised, as compared with family life, 10 (ii), 6–11, 33–6, 65; 11, 187 sq.; gifts of food, drink, garments to be made to them, 10 (ii), 66, 79, 81–4; 35, 41, 49; characteristics of Bh., worthy of offerings, 10 (ii), 82–4; are independent, 10 (ii), 154–6; the Bh. is a great man; he has overcome desire in this world, 10 (ii), 191 sq.; how to translate the word Bhikkhu, 11, 5 n.; a union between a Bh. and Brahmâ is possible, 11, 202 sq.; Buddhist Bh. and Sannyâsins the same, 15, li sq.; invited to *S*râddhas, 29, 106 n.; their position in the classical dramas, 33, xvii; if laymen

can attain to Nirvâna, what is the use of becoming a Bh.? 35, 31; 36, 250-61; possessed of the power of Iddhi, 35, 126, 129 sq.; why Bh. must be reverenced even by converted laymen, 35, 229-33; their exalted position, 35, 267; evil deeds cannot be kept secret from Bh., 35, 295; Bhikkhus who are free from evil Karma can become Arhats in a moment, others have to trouble themselves about recitations, buildings, and gifts, 36, 92-6; worshipped by Nâgas, Yakshas, men, and Mâras, 36, 120; ten individuals worthy of becoming Bh., 36, 253; a worthy Bh. is like a king, 36, 265-7; bow to no one, 36, 338 sq., 339 n.; those who feed two thousand Bh. acquire great merit, and become gods, 45, 415 sq.

(*b*) Moral precepts for Bh.

A Bh. who delights in earnestness is close upon Nirvâna, 10 (i), 10 sq.; are to strive after separation from the world, 10 (i), 22; fools wish for precedence among the Bh., 10 (i), 22; Buddha's description of a true Bh., 10 (i), 39; (ii), 88; must not be envious, 10 (i), 62, 62 n., 85 sq.; not he who only begs, but he who adopts the whole law, is a Bh., 10 (i), 65; not by outward signs can the Bh. attain the extinction of desires, 10 (i), 66, 74; moral precepts for the Bh., 10 (i), 85-8; (ii), 174-7, 180-3, 191; 11, 187-200; 19, 296-305; 36, 59; the Bh. who discards all passions compared to a snake that casts his skin, 10 (ii), 1-3; admonished to be pure and live together with the pure, 10 (ii), 46 sq.; the right path for Bh. explained by Buddha, 10 (ii), 60-2, 64 sq.; the Bh. undergoes no censure, for he is calm and independent, having shaken off the dogmas of philosophy, 10 (ii), 148-50; the Muni, though near Nibbâna, should not think himself the best, 10 (ii), 157; should keep aloof from philosophical disputes, 10 (ii), 159, 161 sq., 167; how they cross the stream of birth and old age, 10 (ii), 191-5; conditions under which the Bh. will prosper, 11, 6-11; should be mindful and thoughtful, 11, 28 sq.; *be ye lamps unto yourselves. Be ye a refuge to yourselves. Betake yourselves to no external refuge. Hold fast to the truth as a lamp. Hold fast as a refuge to the truth. Look not for refuge to any one besides yourselves*, 11, 38; by leading a life of uprightness, by quietude of heart, contemplation, spiritual insight, and solitude, Bh. obtain what they desire, 11, 210-18; want of concord with the Bh., spiritual barrenness, 11, 224 sq., 229; Buddha rebukes quarrelsome Bh., 17, 291-306; an example of Bh. living in love and concord, 17, 309-12; shall not commit suicide, 35, 273-5; twenty-eight good qualities in the vows of Bh., 36, 251 sq.; eighteen good qualities of those who carry out the vows of Bh., 36, 252 sq.; the thirteen extra vows of Bh., 36, 268, 268 sq. n.; are unmoved either by ill-will or love, 36, 309.

(*c*) The Bh. as members of the Order (Samgha).

Rules about the reception into the order of Bh., 10 (ii), 94 sq.; 11, 109 sq.; how Bh. are to address each other, 11, 112; rules for Bh. in the Samgha, *vols.* 13, 17, 20; their relations to the Bhikkhunîs, 13, 20, 26, 35-7, 56, 308, 337; 17, 253 sq., 269, 271; 20, 34, 195, 322-6, 328, 334-6, 344-7, 358 sq.; 36, 3; how they must not behave towards one another, 13, 33 sq., 44, 46, 50-2; must not give food to ascetics of other sects, 13, 40 sq.; on Bh. going to the army, 13, 43; a Bh. must not conceal a serious offence of another Bh., 13, 46; procedure against Bh. who bring false accusations against Buddha, 13, 47-9; instruction in good manners for Bh. in their intercourse with the laity, 13, 59-67; different forms of ordination of Bh., 13, 73 sq. n.; the four Interdictions for Bh., 13, 234-6; temporary expulsion of Bh. for refusal to see or to atone for an offence, 13, 236-8; how to maintain peace among the Bh., 13, 263-5; regulations about reproving a Bh. for an offence, 13, 264 sq.; cases of Bh. risking a

schism, 13, 289 sq.;—*disciplinary proceedings against Bh.* guilty of or suspected of an offence, 13, 14, 340–9, 351 sq., 354 sq.; 17, 276–84, 329–439, 395 n.; the Tagganiya-Kamma or Act of Rebuke, 17, 329–42; the Nissaya-Kamma or Act of Subordination, 17, 343–6; the Pabbâganiya-Kamma or Act of Banishment, 17, 347–58; the Patisâraniya-Kamma or Act of Reconciliation, 17, 359–69; Ukkhepaniya-Kammas or Acts of Suspension for not acknowledging, and for not atoning for, an offence, 17, 370–6; for not renouncing a sinful doctrine, 17, 377–83; rules for Bh. placed on probation, 17, 384–93; thrown back to the commencement of probation, 17, 393 sq., 404 sq., 406 sq., 420 sq., 428;—contempt for Bh. who have entered the Order in their old age, 17, 140 n.; qualifications for Bh. to be appointed to an official post, 17, 200, 201; 20, 25, 25 n., 202; disqualifications of Bh., 17, 248–51; lawful and unlawful restoration of an expelled Bh., 17, 273, 283 sq., 291, 319 sq.; expulsion of an erudite Bh. should be avoided for fear of bringing about a schism, 17, 285–9; superintend the erecting of buildings for the Samgha, 17, 359, 359 n.; 20, 189–91, 215 sq.; different classes or grades of Bh., 20, 6 sq., 193; no official act is to be carried out against Bh. who have not confessed themselves guilty, 20, 22–4; description of a Bh. qualified to be chosen on a jury, and entitled to warn another Bh., 20, 50 sq., 315–17; proceedings against obstinate Bh., 20, 57–61, 259 sq.; salutation and apportionment of the best seat, water, and food shall be according to seniority, 20, 191–9, 206 sq.; Bh. who are not to be saluted, 20, 195 sq.; the Sattarasa-vaggiya Bh. turned out of a Vihâra by the *Kh*abbaggiya Bh., 20, 200 sq.; rules of conduct for incoming Bh., 20, 272–80; duties of Bh. towards one another, 20, 272–98; rules of conduct for resident Bh. towards incoming Bh., 20, 280–2; rules of conduct for Bh. about to leave the Vihâra, 20, 282–4; rules of conduct for Bh. in their lodging-places, in the bath-rooms, in the privies, 20, 294–8; rules about one Bh. warning another in respect of any sin he has committed, 20, 315–19; how conscientiously they make general use of everything given to them, 20, 383 sq.; initiation of Bh., 29, 58 sq. n.; only a Bh., under no disability, can create a schism, 35, 163; recitation of Scriptures, looking after buildings, and seeing to gifts, enjoined for Bh., 36, 92–6; punishments of those who, being unworthy, take the vows, 36, 261–4. *See also* Ordination *and* Samgha.

(*d*) Daily life of Bh. (costume, food, medicine, dwelling, utensils, &c.).

Have their hair and beard cut off, and put on yellow robes, 10 (i), 5 sq. and n.; (ii), 10; 11, 187 sq.; 13, 110, 115, 132 sq., 187, 209, 216; 17, 5 sq., 32; 35, 18 sq., 30, 231 sq.; 36, 20 sq.; contempt for dress impressed on Bh., 11, xliv; costume of Bh., 11, 101 n.; rules regarding the robes of the Bh., 13, 18–24, 28–30, 36, 45, 54 sq., 59 sq., 151–8, 160, 162, 164, 254–7; 17, 35, 39 sq., 193–240, 245–55, 386; 20, 73, 90–8, 142–6, 253; should wear robes made of rags taken from a dust-heap, 13, 173; called Mu*nd*aka or 'shavelings,' 15, xxvii; rules for their foot-clothing, 17, 13–24, 31, 34 sq., 39; the distribution of robes of Bh. at the Ka*th*ina ceremony, 17, 146–70 and n., 203 sq., 234–40, 248–55;—rules about food allowed to Bh., 13, 37–40; 17, 67–97, 117 sq., 128 sq., 130–3, 138 sq., 143–5, 220–5; rules concerning invitations to meals, 13, 41–3, 56 sq.; rules about begging and eating meals, 13, 62–5, 73–5; 20, 135, 153 sq., 250 sq., 253; how Bh. should behave when going on their rounds and in the dining-halls, 13, 151–4; 20, 289–92; are to live on morsels of food given in alms, 13, 173; one Bh. alone is not to pass through a town begging, 19, 194 n.; rules about their alms-bowls, 20, 81–90; rules of conduct for Bh. at meals, 20, 284–9; laxer

rules of the Vaggian Bhikkhus about eating, discussed at the council of Vesâlî, 20, 386, 397 sqq., 409–12;—decomposing urine is the medicine allowed to Bh., 13, 174; sick Bh. may be visited by other Bh. even during vassa, 13, 305 sq.; on medicaments to be used by Bh., 17, 41–61, 65–8, 76 sq., 78–80, 89, 97, 144 sq., 221–5; 20, 154; must wait one upon the other in sickness, 17, 240–5; proceedings for the case of a Bh. being insane, 20, 18–22, 57 sq.; allowed to let blood, 20, 77; rules concerning sick Bh., 20, 199 sq.; —the itinerant mendicant is beset with pain, therefore let no man be an itinerant mendicant, 10 (i), 72; homeless state of Bh., 11, 188; 36, 313; rules about dwellings for Bh., 13, 35, 57; 20, 157–63, 170–9, 189–91, 208–16, 253; should dwell at the foot of a tree, Vihâras, &c., being extra allowances, 13, 173; Vihâras and other edifices built by laymen for Bh., 13, 302–5; rules of conduct for Bh. dwelling in the woods, 20, 292–4; why should houses (Vihâras) be built for the houseless Bh.? 36, 1–4; *see also* Vihâras;—utensils allowed to Bh., 13, 24–30, 53 sq.; 17, 20, 45, 49, 51–9, 205 sq., 226–30; 20, 68, 86 sq., 90–102, 117, 130–5, 137–42, 146–8 (tooth-sticks), 155 sq., 222; are not allowed to acquire gold or silver, or engage in any kind of buying or selling, 13, 26 sq.; 17, 66 sq., 128 sq.; 20, 386–92, 399, 413; 36, 122 n.; luxuries to be avoided by Bh., 13, 44 sq., 52–5; 20, 68–71; the four Resources of religious life (begging food, rags as robes, dwelling at the foot of a tree, urine as medicine), 13, 173 sq., 234; must abstain from all sexual intercourse, 13, 234 sq.; vehicles allowed to Bh., 17, 25–7; rules about mats, seats, &c., for Bh., 17, 27–31, 35, 39; 20, 197, 386, 399, 413; rules for the Bh. about sleeping, 17, 226; 20, 115–17, 163 sq., 166–9; on the daily life of the Bh., 20, 66–156; rules for Bh. about bathing, 20, 66–8, 110; not allowed to castrate themselves, 20, 77 sq.; rules about nail-cutting, hair-dressing, &c., for Bh., 20, 136–41. *See also* Vows.

(*e*) BUDDHA AND THE BH.

Buddha exhorts the Bh. to spread the truths of his religion, 11, 60 sq.; how they behaved at Buddha's death, 11, 119; the five Bh. whom Buddha chooses as his disciples, 11, 146; 13, 90–102; a Deva in the shape of a Bh. appears before the Bodhisattva, 19, 49 sq.; Bh. and Bodhisattvas, 21, xxxv, 12 sq.; Buddha's prophecy about the 2,000 disciples who are to become the future Buddhas Ratnaketurâ*g*as, 21, 210–12; Bh. are not to worship Buddha, 35, 246–8; description of Bh. in the train of Buddha, 49 (ii), 2. *See also* Holy persons, Novices, Preaching, *and* Sekha.

Bhikshus, *see* Bhikkhus.

Bhikshu-sûtra, by Pârâ*s*arya, 8, 32 sq.

Bhîma, hero of the Mahâbhârata, 8, 37 sq.

Bhîma, n. of Rudra, 29, 256; 30, 221 sq.

Bhîmasena, a Pârikshita, who offered horse-sacrifice, 44, 396.

Bhisha*g* Âtharva*n*a, a *R*ishi, 42, xxi, xxxv.

Bhîshma, his death, 8, 3; the oldest of the Kauravas, 8, 38; and Dro*n*a, 8, 39 sq., 42, 95 sq.; chooses the time of his death, 38, 380; 48, 741 sq.; though outside the â*s*ramas, was yet well grounded in knowledge of Brahman, 48, 704; son of Gaṅgâ, 49 (i), 95; killed Ugrâyudha, 49 (i), 113 sq.

Bhîshmagar*g*itasvararâ*g*a, n. of numerous Tathâgatas, 21, 354 sq., 357, 360.

Bhîshmasvara = Bhîshmagargitasvararâ*g*a, q.v.

Bhôga, Râ*g*îmatî, daughter of the Bh. or Bhoga king, 45, 118, 118 n.

Bhoga-nagara, n.pl., Buddha at, 11, 66–70.

Bhogas, a class of Kshatriyas, 45, 71, 71 n., 339.

Bhrâ*g*a, guardian of Soma, 26, 72.

Bh*r*igu, chief among great sages, 8, 89; Râma, a descendant of Bh., 8, 294; chapter of Bh. Vâru*n*i, 15,

64–9; 34, 199; his son B*r*ihaspati more accomplished than he, 19, 10; 49 (i), 8; the Manu-sm*r*iti the Sa*m*hitâ of Bh., 25, xi–xiii, xvii, xcii, xcv sq., cvi, cvi n., cx, 19; 33, xii–xiv, 2 sq. n., 3, 272, 274, 334; quoted in Manu-sm*r*iti, 25, xxvi sq., 78; a sage and a Pragâpati, 25, 14; Somapas (manes), sons of Bh., 25, 112; the offspring of fire, son of Manu, 25, 169 sq., 169 n.; cursed the fire, 25, 398 n.; sprung from Manu, proclaims the law, 25, 483; Sumati, son of Bh., 33, xi, xiii sq., 3, 3 n.; Bh. and other sons of Brahman's mind were again born at the sacrifice of Varu*n*a, 38, 235; connected with the Atharva-veda, 42, xxiii, xxvi sq. (Bh*r*igvaṅgirasa*h*); connected with the production of fire, 42, xxvii, xxx; Atharvan, Aṅgiras, and Bh., 42, xxxii sq., xxxiv, lvii sq.; oblations to Bh. and Aṅgiras, 42, lvii; when they infringed upon Bh., the S*r*iñ*g*aya Vaitahavyas perished, 42, 171, 433; Bh.-Aṅgiras, authors of hymns of the Atharva-veda, 42, 416, 444; myth of Bh., son of Varu*n*a, instructed by his father, 44, xiv, 108–12; Mâtari*s*van brought Agni to Bh., 46, 52; Agni called Bh*r*igavâ*n*a or Bh.-like, 46, 74, 78; Râma, son of Bh., 49 (i), 95.

Bh*r*igu, Buddha in the hermitage of Bhârgava, i. e. Bh.'s son, 19, 59; 49 (i), 62, 92.

Bh*r*igu, a Purohita, converted by his sons, became a monk and reached perfection, 45, 61–9.

Bh*r*igus, i. e. descendants of Bh*r*igu, n. of an ancient family; the light of the Bh. and Aṅgiras is the brightest, 12, 37 sq., 38 n.; kindled or established Agni among men, 12, 350; 46, 45, 130, 157, 202, 228, 343; Bh. or Aṅgiras, attained the heavenly world, 26, 272; peculiar sacrificial rites of the Bh., 29, 390 sq., 416; 30, 34 sq., 93; worshipped at the Tarpa*n*a, 30, 243; Bh., Atharvans, and Aṅgiras, 42, 433; sacrificing together with the Bh., 43, 200; sacrifice offered up by the Bh., 43, 262; Mâtari*s*van kindled Agni for the Bh., 46, 241.

Bh*r*igu-valli, i. e. the third Adhyâya of the Taittirîyaka-Upanishad, 15, xxviii.

Bhrû*n*ahatyâ, Sk., the killing of an embryo, 44, 341 n. *See also* Abortion.

Bhu*g*yu Lâhyâyani, questions Yâ*g*ñavalkya, 15, 127 sq.; 34, cv.

Bhûman, Sk., t.t., the Infinite, 1, 123 n.; where one sees nothing else, hears nothing else, understands nothing else, that is the Bh., 1, 123; is bliss, 1, 123; 34, 163; is immortal, or immortality, 1, 123; 34, 163, 168; rests in its own greatness, 1, 123; explained as the Infinite, 1, 123 sq.; is all this, 1, 123; explained as the Self, 1, 124; 48, 678 sq.; is Brahman, 34, xxxv, 162–9; 48, 299–308; in it the ordinary activities of seeing, &c., are absent, 34, 168 sq.; knowledge of Bh., 38, 412.

Bhumma*g*aka, one of the *Kh*abbag-giya Bhikkhus, 20, 9–17, 118.

Bhûtâ, female disciple of Sambhûta-vigaya, 22, 289.

Bhûtadattâ, female disciple of Sambhûtavigaya, 22, 289.

Bhûtas, 'Beings,' or goblins, daily offerings to them, one of the 'five great sacrifices,' 2, 47 sq., 109, 109 n., 195, 201; 7, 214; 14, 256; 25, 87 n., 88–92, 88 n., 95, 132; 29, 199, 217; 44, 95; food eaten at a *S*râddha by persons related to the giver, reaches not the Manes nor the gods, but the Bh., 2, 143 sq.; those who worship the Bh. go to the Bh., 8, 85; worship of Bh., of the quality of darkness, 8, 118; actions for gods, Pit*r*is, Bh., and guests, 8, 306; the bands of Bh. extol the emancipated saint, 8, 345; Î*s*vara, the lord of gods, Bh., Pi*s*â*k*as, &c., 8, 354; are liable to destruction, 15, 289; space the resort of Bh., 36, 316, 316 n.; gods, demons, Bh., &c., assemble to see Kê*s*i and Gautama, 45, 121 sq.; injury done to living beings for the sake of Bh., 45, 357. *See also* Beings.

Bhûtas, t.t., entities, or elements. *See* Elements.

Bhûtâtman, Sk., the elemental Self in the bodies, 15, 295–7, 295 n., 299 sq.

Bhûtavat, i. e. Rudra, punishes Pragâpati for his incest, 12, 209 n., 284 n.

Bhûtavîras, n. of a family of priests, 43, 345 n.
Bhûti, the goddess of welfare, worshipped, 29, 334; 41, 324.
Bible (Old and New Testaments); Zend-Avesta and B., 4, lxix, lxxii n.; B. and other Sacred Books of the East, 15, xx; references to the O.T., 24, 176 n., 179 n., 180 n.; criticism of the O.T., 24, 178 sq., 200, 208–29; references to N.T., 24, 189 n.; criticism of N.T., 24, 225, 225 n., 229–43.
Bilâl, an Abyssinian slave, the first who called to prayer in Islâm, 6, xxiii sq., xxxiv, lxxii.
Bimbisâra (also called *S*re*n*ya or Seniya), king of Magadha, tries to tempt Buddha with wealth, 10 (ii), 67 sq.; has a large body of troops, 10 (ii), 99; King Seniya B. and myriads of Magadha Brâhma*n*as and householders converted by Buddha, 13, 136–40; his five wishes fulfilled, 13, 140; Buddha as his guest in Râgagaha, 13, 140–3; presents the pleasure garden Ve*l*uvana to Buddha and the fraternity of Bhikkhus, 13, 143 sq.; his physician *G*îvaka, 13, 191 sq.; 17, 179 sq.; persuades Buddha not to admit persons in royal service into the order, 13, 194 sq.; issues a decree for the protection of the Sakyaputtiya Sama*n*as, 13, 197; suggests to Buddha the institution of Uposatha, 13, 239 sq.; asks the Bhikkhus to postpone Vassa, 13, 301; King B. and So*n*a Ko*l*ivisa, 17, 1 sqq.; eighty thousand overseers of townships of King B. are converted by Buddha, 17, 2–5; presents Pilindavakkha with park-keepers, 17, 61 sqq.; sends his minister to see Me*n*daka, 17, 122–4; installs Sâlavatî as courtesan in Râgagaha, 17, 172; King B. and Paggota, 17, 186 sq. n.; Buddha's meeting with B., 19, xxi, 113–31; 49 (i), 105–22; offers to divide his empire with Buddha, 19, 117–19; becomes a disciple of Buddha, 19, 187–93; 49 (i), 192 sq.; invites the Bhikkhus to eat the mangoes in his park, 20, 73 sq.; wants to build a residence for the Sa*m*gha, 20, 178 sq.; his son Agâtasattu wants to kill him, 20, 241–3; 49 (ii), 161–4; related to Mahâvîra, 22, xiii–xvi; dialogue between King *S*re*n*ika, i.e. B., and a *G*aina monk, 45, 100–7, 100 n.; abolished the ferry-fee for ascetics, 49 (i), 170; his consort Vaidehî, 49 (ii), v; B. becomes an Anâgâmin, 49 (ii), 167.
Bindu, n. of a Vedic poet, 32, 410.
Bindumatî, the courtesan, makes the Ganges flow backwards, 35, 182–4.
Birds.

(*a*) B. in religious belief and worship.
(*b*) Some special, real, and mythical b.

(*a*) B. IN RELIGIOUS BELIEF AND WORSHIP.

B. which take away impurity, 5, 246, 246 sq. n.; re-birth of the wicked in b., 8, 109 n., 321; simile of b. abandoning their nests, 8, 142 n., 164; the selfs of devotees as b. flying away happily, 8, 189, 189 n.; extol the emancipated saint, 8, 345; the two b. which are unchanging and unintelligent (understanding and egoism, or the great and the individual self), 8, 371, 371 n.; reach perfection by penance, 8, 389; Solomon knows the speech of b., 9, 100 sq.; origin of the hazelcock, the sparrow, and the partridge, 12, 164 sq.; 41, 130; b. two-footed like men, 12, 384; the manes roam about as b., 14, 268; wise b., 23, 203 n.; b. deities yield enjoyments from fear of punishment, 25, 219; worshipped at the Tarpa*n*a, 29, 121, 219; evil omens from b., 29, 136; 30, 182 sq.; 42, 82, 124, 127, 129, 155, 157, 166 sq., 186, 205, 474, 555; invited to lick the grass anointed with sacrificial food, 29, 391; 30, 37; how created, 41, 148; jaundice transferred to yellow b., 42, 8, 263–6, 566; fire made of b.'s nests at magic rite, 42, 458; bird-shape of the fire-altar, 43, xxi sq., xxvi sq., 1 n., 4 n., 19–21, 22 n., 112 n., 114–16, 120 sq., 135–7, 140, 148 sq., 168, 168 n., 177, 179 sq., 180 n., 201, 250 sq. and n., 272, 274, 285–9, 296, 300–6, 311, 363, 391, 402; 44, 434 sq.; of b. the body is produced first, then the right wing, then the tail, then the

left wing, 43, 136, 139; flesh of b. not to be eaten by one who has built a fire-altar, 43, 296; contract and expand their wings and tail, 43, 300, 301 sq.; are the people of King Târkshya, 44, 369; mythic b. on the Hôm tree, 47, 24 sq.; praise Buddha, the Law, and the Church, 49 (ii), 96 sq., 174.

(*b*) SOME SPECIAL, REAL, AND MYTHICAL B.

The little bird which bustles with the sound 'ahalak' represents the people, 44, 325; the b. *Amritavâkâ* produces the Kshiprasyena, 43, 370, 370 n.; the holy b. *Ashô-zust* that eats nail-parings, 4, 192, 192 n.; 5, 71; 24, 275 sq., 275 n.; the *Bhârunda* b. with two necks and three legs, 22, 261; 45, 19; the holiness of the *cock*, the bird of Sraosha, 4, 196–200, 197 n.; the b. Parôdars or Kahrkatâs (Karetô-dãsu), i.e. the cock, that awakes the worshipper in the morning, 4, 197, 197 n., 199; 23, 322, 322 sq. n.; cocks and fowls crow, driving away wizards and demons, 5, 330 sq., 331 n.; 24, 293 sq.; similes of the cock, 36, 280–283; value of the domestic cock, 37, 163; how a fighting-cock is trained, 40, 20, 20 n.; the female *crane* conceives without a male, 34, 348; 38, 126; simile of the Indian crane, 36, 345, 345 n.; the *crow*, the *Kândâla* among birds, 2, 266 n.; simile of the crow, 36, 291 sq.; dogs and black b. (crows) classed with women and *S*ûdras, 44, 446; 'a crow at a tîrtha,' i.e. a person in a wrong place, 49 (ii), 94 n.; the eyeball of the divine *eagle*, 42, 68, 401; the talon-slaying eagle, king of birds, created from Indra's courage, 44, 215; courage, the sway of birds, secured by the two feathers of an eagle, 44, 221, 230; the *falcon* (syena) is first, strongest among b., 8, 353; 26, 80; a falcon formed of the Gâyatrî, an eagle from the Trish*t*ubh, 44, 173; the b. *Garuda*, *Garutmat*, *see separately*; the *griffon* b. on the tree of all seeds, 5, 71, 176; 23, 173 n., 210 n.; 24, 112, 112 n.; the griffon b. and the bat different from all other b., 5, 182; talking *Hamsas* (flamingoes), 1, 56, 62 sq.; the miraculous power of Ha*m*sas, of going through the ether, 10 (i), 47 sq. and n.; Ha*m*sa, a name of the Self, 15, 311; flamingo is able to distinguish and separate milk and water when mixed, 38, 149; the ha*m*sa b. (the soul? the sun?) does not rest at night, 42, 28, 462; *hawks* sacrifice b., 27, 283 sq.; simile of the *house-pigeon*, 36, 344; simile of the *Kakravâka* b., 36, 340 sq.; the gigantic b. *Kamak* slain by Keresâsp, 18, 378 n., 381; 24, 63, 63 n.; mythical b. Kãmrôs, 5, 70, 100, 100 n.; 23, 173 n., 210 n.; the b. *Karshipta* brings the religion of Mazda into the Vara of Yama, 4, 20; the b. Karsipt knew how to speak words, 5, 70, 70 sq. n.; the mythic b. Kînâmrôs, 24, 112, 112 n.; simile of the *owl*, 36, 344 sq.; simile of the *Penâhikâ* b., 36, 342 sq.; fabulous gigantic b. *Phăng*, 39, 164 sq., 164 n., 165 n., 167; the voices of the *phoenixes*, as a token of prosperity, 3, 209, 209 n.; the phoenix a b. of good omen, 3, 406, 406 n.; the *raven* of Verethraghna, and the raven's feather, 23, 241–3; Saêna or *Sîmurgh* on the tree of all seeds, 23, 173 n., 210 n.; the *swallow* instrumental in the birth of Hsieh, 3, 307, 307 n.; there is no b. wiser than the swallow, 40, 38 sq., 39 n.; Apsaras in the shape of *swans*, 44, 70; the eyesight of the *vulture*, 23, 240, 267. *See also* Animals, Omens, *and* Parables (*c*).

Birth; conception is first b.; when the child is born, that is the second b.; when departing from hence he is born again, that is his third b., 1, 243 sq.; miraculous b., 3, 423 sq. and n.; 19, 2 sq.; 49 (i), 6; the rite of initiation a second b., 7, 119, 127; 8, 176; to one that dies, b. is certain, 8, 45; K*r*ish*n*a has passed through many b., 8, 58 sq.; all beings are deluded at the time of b., 8, 76, 116; men of sinful b., 8, 85, 255; b. and death are from God, 8, 86; the self the source of God's b., 8, 194; Kâsyapa knew the truth about b. and death, 8, 232; the soul coming to the b., 8,

239; mode of b. is fourfold, viz. from eggs, from germs, from perspiration, and from wombs, 8, 339; the true b. should be reckoned from conception, 13, 229; existence by apparitional b. in Sukhâvatî, 21, 417; what b. means when applied to the sprout, 34, 340; the terms 'b.' and 'death,' if applied to the soul, have a metaphorical meaning, 38, 28 sq.; may take place without the 'five oblations,' i.e. not in the ordinary way, 38, 125 sq.; a woman, a cow, or a mare brings forth within the space of a year, 44, 12; man is born thrice, first from his parents, a second time by sacrifice, a third time when his dead body is placed on the fire, 44, 23–5. *See also* Child, Generation, Impurity, Life, Man, *and* Transmigration.

Bishkalâ, deity (?) of parturition, 42, 99, 245.

Bîtak, n.p., 5, 134; 47, 34, 140.

Biva*n*dangha, n.p., 23, 210, 210 n.

Blessedness, *see* Ashi Vanguhi.

Blessing, *see* Bliss, *and* Prayers.

Blind, the b. ones did not damage Agni by looking at him (?), 46, 173, 175. *See also* Parables (*f*).

Blindness is the equality of darkness, 8, 320, 322.

Bliss (Sk. ânanda), when one obtains b., then one performs sacred duties, 1, 122; the Infinite is b., 1, 123; the b. of Brahman, 15, 54–63; 34, 67; 38, 201–4; various degrees of b. described, 15, 59–62, 171 sq.; is Brahman, 15, 66; 34, 65, 75; what is the nature of b.? 15, 157; Brahman is the cause of b., 34, 67; absolute b. the result of higher knowledge, 34, 138; (Brahman as) the bhûman is b., 34, 163, 168; attaches to the state of deep sleep, 34, 163, 164, 168; the Self consisting of b. (ânandamaya) is the highest Self, 34, xxxiii sq., 64–77; 48, 209–37; constitutes the nature of the self, 34, 168; highest b., *see* Highest Good, *and* Nirvâ*n*a.

Blood, how food turns into b., 8, 252; semen and b. produced by Samâna and Vyâna, 8, 275; the b. of the victim at animal sacrifices is the share of the Rakshas, 12, 265 sq.; charms against the flow of b., 42, 22, 45, 174, 234, 257, 385, 483, 531; oblations of b., 44, 394.

Blood-money, *see* Homicide.

Bloodshed, *see* Homicide.

Boar, *see* Animals (*k*).

Boat, *see* Parables (*f*).

Bodha and Pratibodha, the alert and the watchful divinities, 42, 54, 60, 571.

Bodhâyana, n. of Baudhâyana, given in MSS., 14, xliii n.; composed a *vri*tti on the Vedânta-sûtras, 34, xxi; 48, 3; quoted by Râmânu*g*a, 34, xxi; author of the Kalpa-sûtra, 34, xxi.

Bodhi, a king's son, shows hospitality to Buddha and the Bhikkhus, 20, 125–9.

Bodhi, Sk. and Pali, t.t., enlightenment, or highest perfect knowledge, *see* Knowledge (*c*).

Bodhi tree, *see* Trees.

Bodhiru*k*i, translated the Va*g*ra*kkh*edikâ into Chinese, 49 (ii), xiii.

Bodhisatta (Pali), or Bodhisattva (Sk.), a Bodisat, 'one whose essence is enlightenment,' i.e. one destined to become a Buddha, a Buddha Elect, or a future Buddha; the infant Buddha called B., 10 (ii), 125; when a B. is born or dies there is an earthquake, 11, 46 sq.; King Sudassana a B., 11, 239, 241, 285–8; by Buddha's power the earth bursts open and innumerable B. arise from within the clefts, who pay homage to Buddha, whose disciples they all have been, 21, xxx, 281–97, 442; different meanings of the term B., 21, xxxiv–xxxvii; epithets of B., 21, 3; list of names of B., 21, 3 sq.; become visible in the Buddha-fields, 21, 7 sq., 66 sq.; 49 (ii), 17 sq.; grand feats of charitableness, and a great variety of good actions performed by B., 21, 11–15; the six perfections and perfect enlightenment preached to them, 21, 18; will in future be Buddhas, 21, 60; the vehicle of the B., 21, 78–80, 88 sq.; compared to trees, 21, 126 sq.; compared to great *Ri*shis with transcendent faculties, 21, 134;

moving on aerial cars, 21, 199; rules of conduct for B. who are to preach the law, 21, 262–73; rewards of the B. who are wise preachers of the law, 21, 274–80; the different grades of B., 21, 311 sq., 314 sq.; hospitality towards Pratyekabuddhas and B., 21, 318, 318 n.; the term B. used in the sense of religious preachers, 21, 338, 338 n., 340–51; their body is pure and clear, and the world with all beings is mirrored in it, 21, 349 sqq.; Buddha deposits and entrusts his perfect enlightenment into the hands of the B., 21, 440 sq.; the B. Vessantara, 35, 178; 36, 114–32; for each B. everything is settled beforehand when and where he is to be born and to become enlightened, 35, 270–2; the B. as a god in Tusita heaven, 35, 271, 292; 49 (i), 4; how Devadatta, in former births, could be equal or superior to the B., 35, 283–93, 293 n.; the B. always meets with certain persons, such as Devadatta or Sâriputta, in different births, 35, 291 sq.; the conduct of the B. Lomasa Kassapa defended, 36, 16–19; the B. as an elephant, and as the Brahman Gotipâla, 36, 20–2; teachers of the B., 36, 43–6; ten qualities of B., 36, 116; differences between B., 36, 132 sq. and n.; why did the B. Gotama undergo penance? 36, 132–44; the B. Gotama becomes disgusted with the world, seeing the women in his harem, 36, 135 sq., 135 n.; all B. pursue sexual pleasures, until a son is born to them, 49 (i), 26; Buddha addresses the Nirmitâ B., 49 (i), 155 sq., 155 n.; pay homage to Buddha, 49 (i), 156–8; come to worship Amitâyus, 49 (ii), 46–8; will be born in Sukhâvatî, 49 (ii), 66 sq.; instructed by the Buddha, 49 (ii), 111–13; there will always be B. even in the periods of corruption, 49 (ii), 115–17, 115 sq. n. *See also* Buddha (*c*), *and* Holy Persons.

Bodhisattvâvadâna - kalpalatâ, t.w., by Kshemendra, 36, xvii.

Bodisat, *see* Bodhisatta.

Body, anything separated from the b. (like *cuttings of hair, nail-parings*) considered as dead matter, and hence impure, 4, lxxviii sq., 190, 190 n.; 5, 205, 246, 246 n., 254; nail-paring seized by the demons, 5, 71; precautions in cutting hair and nails, 5, 207, 207 n.; 24, 275 sq.; 37, 162; nail-paring prayed over lest it turn into weapons of demons, 5, 342; Snâtakas and hermits to wear hair and nails unclipped, 25, 139 sq., 140 n., 199; Snâtaka not to step on bodily refuse, 25, 141, 150; *see also* Hair;—*lucky and unlucky marks* of the b., 7, 230 sq.; 10 (ii), 189; 11, 196 sq.; 14, 35, 35 n., 53; 25, 153, 228; 43, 81, 81 n., 95; 45, 113, 366 sq.; unlucky marks of the b. due to crimes committed in former births, 14, 108 sq.; 25, 440 sq.; auspicious and inauspicious bodily marks of a bride, 25, 75–7; 29, 21, 165; 30, 42, 257; bodily marks foreshadowing the greatness of a man, 35, 17;—the *worthlessness*, impurity, fragility, and transitoriness of the human b., 7, 281–3; 8, 44 sq., 245, 343; 10 (i), 14, 17, 41 sq., 54, 54 n.; (ii), xvi, 32 sq., 147; 15, 288, 298 sq.; 22, 24, 44; 25, 212; 45, 8, 89 sq.; meditations on the b., 7, 281–6; 8, 252; the bonds of the b., 8, 107; this b., void of enlightenment, seems a hell, 8, 155; the transient b. abandoned by the devotee, 8, 250, 253; b. tied down by action, 8, 307; freed from the b., the devotee is released, 8, 331; passions and sins proceed from the b., 10 (ii), 46; leave the b. behind, that thou mayest never come to exist again, 10 (ii), 209; how a Bhikkhu is to regard the b., 11, 38; passion for a b., spiritual bondage, 11, 225 sq., 230; twelve impurities of the human b., 25, 193; the product of nescience, 34, 244; the b. compared to a wound, 35, 115; ten qualities inherent in the b., 36, 75 sq.;—*b. and soul*, the b. explained as the Kshetra, or 'field,' the soul being the 'knower of the field,' 7, 286 sq.; 8, 102–6; acquisition of the b. by the self, 8, 44; purity of self attained

with the b., i.e. by bathing, 8, 64, 64 n., 362; God dwells as fire in the b. of creatures, 8, 113, 118; the wicked torment the organs in their b., 8, 118; actions performed by the b., 8, 123, 123 n.; the wise remove even here the self out of the b., 8, 176; the self tranquillized by the exhaustion of the primary elements of the b., 8, 246; the self within the self, i.e. the b., 8, 248, 344, 392; as the soft fibres are extended from the Muñga grass, so does a devotee see his self extracted from the b., 8, 249; the mind is within the b. the upholder of the frame, 8, 262; the unconscious b. compared to fuel, 8, 290; how did the b. become intelligent? 15, 291 sqq.; etymology of sarîra, or 'body,' 25, 9, 9 n.; the Undeveloped, 34, 246; is the b. the sufferer, or the soul? 34, 379; the Sâṅkhya cannot admit a real connexion of the soul and the b., 34, 379; Brahman's secret names with reference to the Devas and to the b., 38, 216 sq.; embodied soul and b. viewed as non-different, 38, 374; founded on the mind, food being the connecting-link, 41, 270; the b., if boneless, is immortal, 43, 178 sq.; fire-altar and certain hymns are the Sacrificer's divine, immortal b., 43, 279; definitions of the term b., 48, 420–4;—the gross b. and the *subtle b.*, 8, 160 n., 187, 187 n., 190, 333 n.; 34, 244 sq.; 38, 65 n., 372; subtle b. due to the soul's higher knowledge, not due to Karman or works, 34, lxxi; subtle b. is beyond the soul, 34, 244; subtle b. meant by the term avyakta, 34, 241 sq., 244; the warmth which we perceive in the living b. belongs to the subtle b., 38, 372;—*anatomy* of the human b., 7, 281–6; consists of the five elements, 7, 283; 8, 342 sq.; 49 (i), 177; the b. a city with nine portals, 8, 65, 65 n., 108, 317, 343; how the b. perishes, and how it is produced, 8, 235–45; how bodies are formed by food digested, 8, 252; made up of the sixteen (eleven organs and five great elements), 8, 391, 391 n.; the b. is a town with eleven gates, belonging to Brahman, 15, 18; there is a fiend and a fire in the human b., when the fire conquers the fiend, there is a sneeze, 24, 265 sq.; parts of the b. identified with the elements, 25, 512; thirty-two kinds of organic matter in the human b., 35, 42, 42 n., 44; seventy-six members of the b., 37, 42; consists of three elements, fire, water, and earth, 38, 104; water (liquid matter) preponderates in the b., 38, 104 sq.; is there a ruler among the parts of the b.? 39, 180; six members of the b., 39, 226; consists of twenty-five parts, 41, 353, 353 n.; 43, 168, 168 n., 222; this b. (trunk) is the best, the largest, the most vigorous of limbs, 43, 20, 20 n.; the b. is warm, being kindled by the sun, 43, 135; the b. of birds produced before wings and tails, 43, 136; the b. consists of thirty limbs, 43, 167, 167 n., 222, 383, 383 n., 387; the b. consists of pairs, 43, 284; consists of five mortal parts (hair, skin, flesh, bone, marrow) and five immortal parts (mind, voice, breath, eye, ear), 43, 290, 292; hair, skin, flesh, bone, and marrow, the five parts of the b. 43, 309; hundred and one parts of the b., 43, 325 sq.; there is vital air in each limb of the b., 43, 326; the parts of Pragâpati's b., 43, 347; the fire-altar identified with the b. of man, 43, 387; parts of the b. of the Sacrifice as Man, 44, 19 sq.; how Pragâpati fashions for himself a b. (arms, fingers, &c.), 44, 74–8; the Year represented as a man, parts of his b. (fingers, &c.), 44, 160-5; the parts of the sacrificer's b. formed by parts of the sacrifice, 44, 259–64; the b. of man consists of three parts, 44, 261; sacrificial implements at Pravargya arranged to form parts of a human b., 44 498–500;—*parts of the b.:* strength is exerted by the *arm*, 41, 200; the arms are fifteenfold, 43, 79; from the armpit (of the bird-shaped fire-altar) water springs forth, 43, 169, 169 sq. n.; the wings are the bird's arms, and by means

of the arms food is eaten, 43, 306; the *belly* gets all food, 43, 115; 44, 37; the *fingers* and toes and their joints, 41, 417; 43, 325; 44, 75, 161; what is *knee*-high is below, 43, 158; knee-high is this world, 44, 249; the sacrificer lifted up knee-high, 44, 254; *limbs* of the b. dependent on the vital airs, 41, 151; 43, 19; *male organ* of three parts, and one joint, 44, 19; man sports with the male organ, 44, 76; the testicles, 44, 500; reaching up to the *mouth*, means above, 43, 159; 44, 254; the Samâna (intestinal breath) is at the *navel*, 8, 258, 266 n., 271 n.; 43, 17 sq.; cavities above the navel pure, below impure, 25, 192; 41, 267; the navel goes all round, 41, 86; navel of the earth, 41, 258, 267; below the navel is seed, 41, 267; food above the navel is immortal, below mortal, 43, 285; what is navel-high is middle, 43, 158 sq.; 44, 254; the *ribs* are the middle, 43, 20, 31 sq.; lie against the chest, 43, 114; thirteen ribs on each side, 44, 164; why there are two *thighs*, 41, 306; the thigh-bone the largest, 43, 137; rules about cleaning the *teeth*, 7, 196–8; the mystery of man's teeth, 44, 52, 54 sq.; the *tongue* is Sarasvatî, by the tongue one distinguishes the taste of food, 44, 263; the great Brahman (nature) a *womb* in which God casts his seed, 8, 107; the Brahma*k*ârin enters, as it were, the womb of the preceptor, 8, 175; how a man enters the womb, 8, 241; the womb lies close to the belly, 43, 115; the womb does not enlarge along with the child that has been born, 43, 309; the womb is the bearer, because Pragâpati by it bore creatures, 44, 114. *See also* Bones, Ear, Eye, Hand, Head, Heart, *and* Organs.

Bo*gg*ha*n*gâ (satta), Pali t.t. *See* Wisdom (seven kinds of).

Bondage, five kinds of spiritual, (pa*ñk*a *k*etaso vinibandhâ), and the means to be freed from them, 11, 221 sq., 225–32.

Bonds, the five, or the five things leading to lust, 11, 181; salvation by destruction of the three B., 11, 213; how a Bhikkhu may become an inheritor of the highest heavens by destruction of the five B., 11, 213 sq.

Bones, bricks are Agni's b., 43, 20; the b. in the body run both lengthwise and crosswise, 43, 135; no transverse b. in wings and tail of birds, 43, 135; man's wellbeing (safety, strength) is the b., 43, 327; the b. of a fat and a lean person are alike, 44, 20; the b. of the dead man collected, arranged, burnt, buried, 44, 117, 117 n., 200, 433 sq., 433 n.; there are three hundred and sixty b. in man, 43, 387; 44, 169.

Bonzes, Bodhisattvas = Vandyas = B., 21, 318 n.

Books, or manuscripts, purified by sprinkling water over them, 7, xxii sq., 105, 105 n. *See* Sacred Books.

Boons, *see* Wishes.

Bôr-tôrâ, ancestor of Frê*d*ûn, 5, 132; the Âspîgân, 47, 34.

Boundary disputes, a title of law, 33, 155–64, 274, 351–5.

Bow, strung at the Râ*g*asûya, 41, 87; is the nobleman's strength, 41, 89; a b. with three arrows given as sacrificial fee, 44, 11; Vish*n*u with a b. and three arrows, 44, 442.

Brâ*d*ar-vakhsh, *see* Tûr-î B.

Brâ*d*-rêsh, *see* Tûr-î Brâ*d*ar-vakhsh.

Brâ*d*rôk-rêsh, *see* Tûr-î Brâ*d*ar-vakhsh.

Brâ*d*rô-rêsh, *see* Tûr-î Brâ*d*ar-vakhsh.

Brâ*d*-rôyi*m*, a Karap, 47, 143.

Brâ*d*-rûkhsh, a Karap, enemy of Zoroaster, 47, 143, 148.

Brahmâ, *see* Brahman (masc.).

Brahmadatta, king of Benares, King Dîghîti of Kosala, and young Dîghâvu, 17, 293–305; the Brahmagâla spoken concerning Suppiya and B., 20, 376; Devadatta as King B., 35, 290; Sambhûta born as B. king of the Pa*ñk*âlas, 45, 57–61.

Brahmadatta *K*aikitâneya, n.p., 15, 83.

Brahmadhva*g*a, n. of a Tathâgata, 21, 178.

Brahmadvîpikâ-Sâkhâ, founded by Ârya Samita, 22, 293.

Brahmagâla Suttanta, where and when spoken, 20, 376; on the sixty-two heresies, 36, xxiii–xxv.

Brahmaghosha, n. of a Tathâgata, 49 (ii), 6 sq., 100.

Brahma-gîtâ, subtitle of part of Anugîtâ, 8, 310 n.

Brahma Gyotishprabha, n. of a Brahmakâyika god, 21, 5.

Brahmahatyâ (Brahman-slaying personified), expiatory oblation and formula to, 44, 337 n., 340 sq.

Brahma Kalpa, the Lankântika Vimânas are eightfold in, 22, 195.

Brahmakârin, religious student, student of the Veda: to dwell as a B. in the house of a tutor, a branch of the law, 1, 35; approaches his teacher, carrying fuel in his hands, 1, 85, 135, 137, 139 sq., 273, 306; duties and restrictions imposed on B., 2, xxii sq., 7–29, 182–5, 186–92; 7, 116–21, 123–31; 8, 216 sq., 360 sq.; 14, 40–2, 149–58; 25, 37–44, 50–74; 29, 66, 68, 73–6, 80, 83 sq., 191–3, 223, 306, 308–10, 402; 30, 66 sq., 151, 157, 160 sq., 274; 33, 132 sq.; 44, 48–50, 90; 48, 695; the Naishthika or perpetual B. who always lives with his teacher, 2, 18, 18 n., 153, 192 n., 193; 7, 120; 8, 377 n.; 14, 40 sq., 258; 25, 73 sq.; 38, 318 sq.; rules for the B. who has returned home from his teacher, 2, 27–32, 37, 48–54, 66 sq.; 8, 358 n.; 25, 73–5; *see also* Samâvartana; penances for a B. who breaks his vows, esp. that of chastity, 2, 85 sq., 288–90, 294 sq.; 14, 117–19, 214–16, 294 sq., 318 sq.; 25, 63 sq., 70, 454 sq., 462 sq.; 29, 361 sq.; 30, 317; 38, 318–20; 48, 706; eats much, 2, 123; 14, 265 sq., 281; sin of the B. who breaks the vow of chastity, 2, 281 sq.; is exempt from fare or toll, 7, 36; 25, 325; laws of impurity (on death, &c.) for a B., 7, 96; 14, 177; 25, 179 sq., 183–5, 192 sq.; his initiation, 7, 114 sq.; 44, 86 sq.; *see also* Upanayana; the Yogin should adhere to the rules of a B., 8, 69, 79; life as a B. is a good penance, 8, 119; gods and demons practise the life of B., 8, 146, 151 sq., 152 n.; practising the life of a B. is immortality, 8, 153; life as a B., part of the conduct of the good, 8, 169, 242, 326; knowledge of Brahman acquired by living the life of a B., 8, 175–9; he who adheres to the Brahman, identifying himself with the Brahman, becomes a true B., 8, 283 sq.; a pupil described as a self-restrained ascetic and a B., 8, 312; life of B., the first of the four Âsramas, 8, 316, 354 n.; 38, 298, 300; must be engaged in sacred study, 8, 360 sq.; the ascetic must live as a B., 8, 364; the sacrifice taught by the father to his son when he is a B., 12, 162; rules for B. in sickness, 14, 214 sq.; costume of B., 25, 37 sq.; 32, 232–4; entertained at Srâddhas, 25, 64 sq., 110; duration of studentship, 25, 74 sq.; 29, 309; must receive food at the Vaisvadeva, 25, 92; 29, 86; one who has broken his vow of studentship excluded from Srâddha and from the company of honourable men, 25, 104, 107; 38, 320; offence of personating a B., 25, 160; shall not perform obsequies except for parents and teacher, 25, 183 sq. n.; cannot be made a witness, 25, 265; 33, 88; must not eat Srâddha food, 25, 462 sq. and n.; ceremony on his setting out on a journey, 29, 90, 230 sq.; shall not be a charioteer, 29, 364; duties of B. undergoing special vows, 30, 70–7; law regarding the property of a B., 33, 243 sq.; B. = 'pure in conduct,' said of Buddha, 35, 117 sq.; glorification of the sun as a B., 42, 214–17, 626–8; initiates the Unnetri for the sacrificial session, 44, 137. *See also* Holy persons, Teacher, Veda (*c*), *and* Women (*d*).

Brahmakârin, n. of a Ganadhara of Pârsva, 22, 274.

Brahmakariyam (Pali), 'noble life,' different meaning from Sk. brahmakarya, 11, 285 n.

Brahmakarya, Sk., t.t., religious studentship, 44, 86, 86 n.; life as a Brahmakârin, *see* Brahmakârin; the vow of abstinence, esp. chastity, *see* Abstinence *and* Chastity.

Brahmakâyas, or Brahmakâyikas,

a class of gods, 7, 293; Buddha mistaken for one of the B., 19, 72; the 12,000 followers of Brahma Sahâmpati, 21, 5.

Brahmaketu, the 77th Tathâgata, 49 (i), 7.

Brahmaliptaka Kula, of the Kau*t*ika Ga*n*a, 22, 292.

Brahmaloka, the world of Brahman (masc.), how can one obtain it? 10 (ii), 84 sq.; what B. means, 34, 180 sq.; long life of the gods in B., 45, 84, 84 n.; *see also* Brahma-world.

Brahman (neut., Nom. Brahma, masc., Nom. Brahmâ).

(*a*) The B. (neuter) in the sense of holy word or priesthood.
(*b*) Nature and qualities of the B. (neut.) as the divine principle.
(*c*) Names, forms, and symbols under which the B. (neut.) is meditated upon.
(*d*) Oneness of the B. (neut.).
(*e*) The B. (neut.) and the world.
(*f*) The B. (neut.) and the individual soul.
(*g*) Devotion to and absorption in the B. (neut.).
(*h*) Knowledge of the B. (neut.).
(*i*) The higher and the lower B.
(*j*) Passages in which B. may be either masc. or neuter.
(*k*) The god B. (masc.), also called Sahampati, Svayambhû, Hira*n*yagarbha.

(*a*) THE B. (NEUTER) IN THE SENSE OF HOLY WORD OR PRIESTHOOD.

Vasukra, the author of a hymn, identified with the B., 1, 169; the Brahman priest is full of B. (Veda), 1, 259; is the self seen in the great hymn, 1, 260; identified with the Vedas, 1, 279; 'slayers of the B.' i.e. of the Veda, are called those whose father and grandfather have not been initiated, 2, 5; Vish*n*u fond of B. (Veda), 7, 293; those who are first in the Vedas are forms of the B., 8, 161; Agni or fire is the B., 12, 90, 114 sq., 134, 341; 26, 37 sq.; 43, 85; Palâ*s*a tree is B., 12, 90, 90 n.; identified with speech, truth, and the three Vyâh*ri*tis, 12, 296 sq.; the B. and the threefold science, 12, 449 sq.; 25, 483; delivered the creatures over to Death, except the Brahma*k*ârin, 14, 156; 44, 48; placed its majesty in the Brâhma*n*as, 14, 199; invoked to purify from sin, 14, 251; offerings to B. (priesthood) and Kshatra, 15, 211; is B*ri*haspati, or the Lord of prayer, 26, 23, 59, 59 n., 180; 29, 280; 43, 192; 44, 258, 314, 402, 411; B. is sacrifice, 26, 23, 35; by the Dîkshâ the sacrificer is born of the B., 26, 35; means worship, Vedic religion or priests, 26, 78, 219 sq.; 42, lxiii; as the sacerdotium or sacred writ, is the truth, 26, 272; Tutha is the B., 26, 344; the Brahmodya or discussion on the B. at the end of a Sattra, 26, 452 sq. and n.; B. which is long-lived through the Brâhma*n*as, invoked to give long life to the new-born child, 29, 294; the teacher places the student to be initiated in the B., 30, 152; is the source of the Veda, 34, xxxii, 19–22; king and priest address each other as B., 41, 108–10; first created from the egg, 41, 146; Pragâpati is the whole B., 41, 353; 44, 409, 409 n.; meaning charm, spell, 42, lxvi; 46, 194; spiritual exaltation, supports the earth, 42, 199, 202; begotten by the Brahma*k*ârin (the sun), 42, 215; begotten from Time, 42, 224 sq., 686; U*kkh*ish*t*a is B., 42, 226–9, 629 sq.; B.'s layer (of the fire-altar), 43, 81; the *Ri*shis are the first-born B., 43, 100; the B. (mystic science) has nothing before it and nothing after it, 43, 338; the B.'s fore-portion, 44, 36; kindling-verse identified with the B., 44, 39; the Brahma*k*ârin makes himself over to B., 44, 86 sq.; daily sacrifice to the B., consisting in Veda-study, one of the 'five great sacrifices,' 44, 95–9, *see also* Veda (*c*); by the B. (holy writ, holiness, priesthood) he gains the heavenly world, 44, 221; the seven-syllabled B. (holy writ), 43, 314 sq.; expiatory formula addressed to the B., 44, 337 n.

(*b*) NATURE AND QUALITIES OF THE B. (NEUT.) AS THE DIVINE PRINCIPLE.

B. is the True (Sat, τὸ ὄντως ὄν), pure Being, 1, 98 n., 130, 201, 278 sq.; 8, 315; 12, 296 sq.; 15, 18, 36, 58, 108, 190 sq., 306; 26, 272; 34, lii, 167, 266 sq., 332; 38, 19 sq., 160, 216 sq., 234; 48, 45, 71, 193, 302–5, 432, 616, 652; as

conceived by the true philosopher, and by ordinary people, 1, 125 sq. n.; *this is the immortal, the fearless, this is B.*, 1, 130, 135, 136, 138, 140; 48, 313, 320, 352; names and forms are contained in the B., the Immortal, the Self, 1, 143; 44, 27 sq.; its relation to the senses, 1, 147 sq.; 8, 104, 104 n., 386; its relation to the Devas or gods, 1, 149–51; 8, 153; 15, 68, 302, 324; 34, xiv; 38, 219; is of the nature of intelligence, or pure knowledge, 1, 246, 246 n.; 15, 150 sq.; 34, xxiv sq., 25, 68, 264; 38, 156 sq., 160, 168; 48, 23, 81, 84, 103–5, 111–13, 115, 126, 131 sq., 143, 176, 193, 240, 561, 618, 660; various meanings of B. in Bhagavadgîtâ, 8, 11; free from all imperfections, and endowed with all auspicious qualities, 8, 65, 104, 180, 257; 34, xxviii, 107, 328; 38, 101, 201–4; 48, 78 sq., 81 sq., 88, 94, 96, 124, 127, 143, 156, 182, 200, 208 sq., 215, 218, 229, 240, 259, 271, 323 sq., 327, 354, 375, 394, 402 sq., 406–8, 413 sq., 422, 429, 444 sq., 460, 469, 476, 584, 607–21, 689 sq.; has no beginning nor end, is unborn and immortal (imperishable, indestructible), 8, 77, 103, 180, 192, 248; 15, 28, 36, 235, 255, 302, 335 sq.; 34, 83, 169–71, 349; 48, 308–11, 535, 652 sq., 660; is neither existent nor non-existent, 8, 103, 103 n.; devoid of qualities, 8, 104; 34, xxv, xxviii; 38, 239, 394 sq.; 48, 26–9; it is of no colour, 8, 179; smaller than small, larger than the largest, 8, 180, 285; 15, 28, 36, 39, 338; 34, 113 sq.; 48, 264 sq., 367; B. is glory, 8, 180; 38, 393; produced and developed from the pure principle, 8, 186; the highest B. is very far off, 8, 369; three syllables, viz. na mama, 'not mine,' are the eternal B., 8, 391; there is nothing greater than B., 8, 392; 48, 621–5; is the Great, 15, 18; 48, 4; from terror of B., the wind blows, the sun rises, Agni, Indra, and Death run away, 15, 21, 59; 34, 130, 230 sq.; is eternal, pure and changeless, 15, 28; 34, 25, 34, 327; 38, 397; 48, 393, 400; is omnipresent, 15, 18, 28, 335; 34, 89, 91 sq., 120, 125, 172; 38, 180, 390–4, 396; 48, 624 sq.; spoken of as in heaven and beyond heaven, 34, 96 sq.; is the bridge of the Immortal, 15, 36; 34, 154, 156, 622 sq.; is the best, 15, 37; is devoid of parts, 15, 39; 34, 135–9, 349–52; 38, 396; 48, 192 sq., 473; the bliss of B., B. is bliss, 15, 56, 61 sqq., 61 sq. n., 66, 150 sq.; 34, 25, 65–8, 72 sq., 75–7, 169; 48, 84, 113, 193, 198, 200, 208–37, 240, 254, 276 sq., 307, 376, 389, 402, 413 sq., 442, 550, 618, 653; in the beginning B. knew its Self only, 15, 88; *this is the B., without cause and without effect, without anything inside or outside; this Self is B., omnipresent and omniscient*, 15, 117; is Svayambhu, self-existent, 15, 120, 188, 227; 43, 404; 44, 417 sq.; *see also under* (*k*); is the safe support, 15, 235; in it is the triad (subject, object, and the mover or ruler), 15, 235 sq.; the only universal being, of an absolutely homogeneous nature, 34, xxiv, xxvii sq., xxx; 48, 113; is associated with Nescience (Mâyâ, Avidyâ), 34, xxv, xxx, 362; 48, 212, 215 sq., 494; compared with a magician, 34, xxv; according to *S*ankara impersonal, with Râmânuga a personal God, 34, xxviii, xxx, cxxiii, cxxiv n.; cannot have originated from anything else, 34, lii, 266 sq., 332; 38, 19 sq.; is devoid of form, 34, lxiii, lxiv, 306 sq.; 38, 154–75; 48, 610 sq.; discussions on the nature of B., 34, lxiv sq., xcv sq.; 38, 101, 133–83; later definitions of B., e.g. as sa*kk*idânanda, 34, xcii; etymology of the word, 34, 14; 48, 158; *B., which is all-knowing and endowed with all powers, whose essential nature is eternal purity, intelligence, and freedom, exists. . . . The existence of B. is known on the ground of its being the Self of every one. . . . And this Self* (*of whose existence all are conscious*) *is B.*, 34, 14; is all-knowing, 34, 19–22, 25, 47, 49, 362; 48, 156, 215, 234, 259, 316, 354, 375, 394, 413 sq., 460; can it be designated by a masculine noun? 34, 76; is a place of rest, 34, 83; is the internal ruler over the devas and so on, 34, 130–2; is different from

name and form, 34, 232 sq.; 38, 97; there is nothing either beneficial to be done by it or non-beneficial to be avoided by it, 34, 344; is endowed with powers, omnipotent, 34, 354–6, 362; 48, 156, 215, 259, 316, 354, 413 sq., 460; is free from all difference, and twofold characteristics cannot belong to him, 38, 152–4, 156 sq.; its limiting adjuncts are presented by Nescience merely, 38, 153; is inside of the limiting adjuncts, 38, 158 sq., 178 sq.; 48, 192 sq.; is the highest of gods, 43, 59; is the firstborn from afore, 44, 459 sq.; not devoid of all difference, 48, 78–102; *the True, Knowledge, the Infinite is B.*, 48, 79 sq., 143, 158, 159 sq., 180, 184, 210, 212, 233, 240, 254, 303, 375, 402, 404, 445, 453, 550, 611 sq., 623, 638, 652, 656; B. defined, 48, 80; what constitutes the body of the B., 48, 88, 254; Nescience contradictory to B., 48, 126; appears in manifold modes, 48, 143; is self-luminous, 48, 208, 348 sq., 393, 445; has no connexion with Prak*ri*ti, nor with Karman, 48, 240, 256, 607; why it is not subject to pleasure and pain, 48, 265 sq.; is invisible, unseizable, higher than the Imperishable, 48, 282–7; of boundless love towards his devotees, 48, 316; *numberless powers, lying beyond the sphere of all ordinary thought, belong to B., and qualify it for creation, and so on, just as heat belongs to fire*, 48, 474, 476; differs in nature from all other things, 48, 28, 475 sq., 584; in all meditations on B. the essential qualities of B. are to be included, 48, 637–43. *See also* God, Lord, *and* Self (*d*); world of the B., *see* Brahma-world.

(*c*) Names, forms, and symbols under which the B. (neut.) is meditated upon.

Meditation on B. under symbols (pratîkopâsana), 1, 201; 48, 718–20; not comprehended by symbols, 8, 367; only those who have not worshipped B. under a symbol are led to B., 34, lxxxii; 38, 402–4; B.'s name a mere outward symbol, 34, 92; two secret names of B., *aham* and *ahar*, 38, 216–18; 48, 642; the Great B. is the one *Akshara* into which all beings pass, 43, 343 sq.; why it is called a *bank*, 38, 176 sq.; *Bhûman*, that which is much, is B., 34, 162–9; 48, 302; meditation on *breath* (Prâ*n*a) as B., 1, 65 sq., 213, 280 sqq.; 15, 36, 56, 64 sq., 142, 153 sq., 194 sq.; 34, 84–7, 97–106, 229–31, 272; 42, 622 sq.; 48, 246, 256, 276 sq.; B. as represented by Vâyu and Prâ*n*a, 1, 59 n.; hidden in breath, 1, 233 sq.; meditation on the absorption of the gods into breath or B., 1, 288–90; the vital airs are the effects of B., 38, 76; Indra and Prâ*n*a is B., 48, 250–4; *Buddha* is, esoterically, the Highest B., 21, xxvii sq.; the great *chariot* which is pervaded by the B., 8, 386; the *city of B.*, the body, and in it the small lotus of the heart, and in it the small ether, 1, 125–7, 126 n.; 15, 37, 54; 34, 174 sq., 178; 38, 219; 48, 314–25, 660, 666 sq.; the city of B. called Aparâgitâ, 1, 131, 132 n.; meditation on *consideration* or thought as B., 1, 114; 38, 160; *Earth*, a form of B., 1, 65 sq.; meditation on B. as *ether* (Kha), 1, xxv sq., xxvi n., 46 sq., 53, 65 sq., 118, 126 n., 143, 143 n.; 34, 81–4, 110, 114, 126 sq., 144, 174–92, 232 sq.; 38, 6–8, 12, 17 sq., 248; 48, 242–6, 256, 273, 276 sq.; before ether was produced, B. existed without ether, 38, 17; ether is an effect of B., 38, 18; ether is dissolved into B., 38, 26; the person in the *eye* is B., 1, 67, 135; 15, 64, 335; four *feet* or sixteen parts of B., 1, 53 sq., 60 n., 60–4; 15, 345; 34, 90, 95; 38, 219; 48, 622 sq.; meditation on *fire* as B., 1, 65, 118; 15, 335; 34, 92; the Adhvaryus consider B. the self in the sacrificial fire, 1, 260; the source of fire, 38, 20–2; the highest B. in the form of intestinal heat, 48, 248; meditation on *food* as B., 1, 65, 117; 15, 55, 64, 194 sq.; the B. as a *forest*, 8, 284–6, 288, 288 n., 372, 386 sq.; meditated upon as the *Gâyatrî* verse, 1, 44–6, 158, 162, 194; 34, 93–6;

'having joy for its *head*,' a figurative representation of B., 48, 637–9; *hearing* is B., 15, 156; as seated in the cave of the *heart*, 1, 47, 47 n.; 8, 252 n.; 15, 36, 39, 318; 34, 113 sq., 350; 38, 410; 48, 367, 642 sq.; the heart is the highest B., 15, 158; *heaven*, a form of B., 1, 66; the sound *Him* is B., and serves to obtain B., 1, 176; meditation on *hope* as B., 1, 119; the abode of *Lakshmî*, 48, 3; *light* is B., 15, 306, 335 sq.; 34, 87–93, 96 sq., 185, 191, 194, 231 sq.; 48, 247–9, 256, 611 sq., 618; is the light of lights, 15, 37; 48, 335 sq., 366, 373; as shining in the sun, in the moon, in the fire, in the lightning, 15, 318, 322; as abiding within the sun, and within the eye, 34, lxx, 123–8; 38, 216–18; 48, 642; is the *lightning*, 1, 66, 151 sq., 152 n.; 15, 192; relation between the *Lord* and the Highest B., 15, xxxvi–xxxviii, 245; 34, xxv, xxvii, xxx, cxxiii, cxxiv n.; 48, 4; the *Mahâvrata* day is B., 1, 162, 169, 260; the Mahâvrata ceremony is for attainment of B., 1, 162; *man*, the abode of B., B. in the shape of man, 1, 205 sq.; meditation on *memory* as B., 1, 119; meditation on *mind* as B., 1, 53 sq., 65, 112, 152, 152 n.; 15, 36, 64, 157; 34, 107–12; 38, 391; meditation on the *name* as B., 1, 110 sq.; means '*Nature*,' 8, 11; is an intelligent principle, and cannot be identified with the non-intelligent pradhâna of the Sâṅkhyas, 34, xxxii, 47–64, 300; 48, 256; *Om* identical with B., 7, 183; 8, 79, 282 sq.; 14, 278, 316; 25, 45; Om is the bow, the Self is the arrow, B. is the aim, 15, 36; Om, Tad, Sat, the threefold designation of the B., 8, 120 sq.; Ka (*pleasure*) is B., 1, 65; 34, 126 sq.; 48, 273, 276 sq.; meditation on *power* as B., 1, 116; *Pragâpati* is B., 15, 190; 43, xxiv; the self-existent B., teacher of Pragâpati, 43, 404; the *Purusha* or Highest Person is B., 15, 19; 25, 6, 6 n., 513; 34, 174; 48, 4, 207 sq.; the highest oneness reached by seeing the lord of the world as the Person who has his source in B., 15, 38; the word B. denotes the Highest Person (Purusha), the highest Self, and the Lord, 48, 4, &c.; meditation on *reflection* as B., 1, 115; *sight* is B., 15, 155; S*iva*, Hara, Rudra, &c., as names of B., 15, xxxiii sq.; 48, 667; the essence of Rudra, 15, 324; superior to *S*iva, 34, xiv; meditation on *speech* as B., 1, 111; 12, 296 sq.; 15, 36, 64, 152 sq.; '*as far as B. reaches, so far reaches speech;'—wherever there is B., there is a word; and wherever there is a word, there is B.*, 1, 186; meditation on B. as word and non-word, 15, 321 sq.; meditation on the *sun* as B., 1, 54 sq., 65 sq.; 15, 306, 317 sq., 335 sq.; 41, 366; 43, 94; 44, 459 sq.; compared to reflected images of the sun and the like, 38, 157–9; 48, 613–15; is the light equal to the sun, 44, 388; is called *Tadvana*, 1, 152, 152 n.; *time* and non-time, two forms of B., 15, 317; compared to a fig-*tree*, whose roots grow upward and whose branches grow downward, 15, 21; the great tree of B., 8, 370, 370 n., 372; meditation on *understanding* as B., 1, 115 sq.; 8, 338 sq.; 15, 57, 65; *Vâyu* invoked as the visible B., 15, 45, 53; worship of *Vishnu* (Nârâya*n*a, K*r*ish*n*a) as the supreme B., 7, 156; 8, 87, 110, 110 n.; 25, 5, 5 n.; 34, xxxi n.; the lord B. seated on his lotus seat within K*r*ish*n*a, 8, 93; K*r*ish*n*a greater than B., 8, 96; the great B. is a womb in which K*r*ish*n*a casts the seed, 8, 107; Vish*n*u full of the B., 8, 347, 354; the highest place of Vish*n*u, 15, 324; B. superior to Vish*n*u, 34, xiv; the highest B., i.e. Vish*n*u, possesses two forms, 48, 89; B. or Vishnu the Self of the world, 48, 92 sq.; called Vâsudeva by the Bhâgavatas, 48, 524 sq.; meditation on *water* as B., 1, 117; water, the quarters, the stars, the moon, are forms of B., 1, 66; meditation on *will* as B., 1, 112 sq., 113 n.

(*d*) ONENESS OF THE B. (NEUT.).

All this is B. Let a man meditate on that (visible world) as beginning, ending, and breathing in it (the B.)

. . . *He from whom all works, all desires, all sweet odours and tastes proceed, who embraces all this, who never speaks and who is never surprised, he, my self within the heart, is that B.*, 1, 48; 48, 133; is the Self seen in earth, heaven, air, &c., within all, 1, 260; 15, 128 sq.; 34, 154-62, 230; 48, 259, 318 sq., 371-4; all worlds are contained in B., 15, 21; 48, 768; pervades everything, 8, 104; 48, 92 sq.; is all things perceptible, B. alone is all this, B. is the Self of the world, 8, 180, 192; 15, 37, 307; 34, xxviii, xxx, 23, 94, 107, 109-11, 156, 267, 357; 38, 138, 165, 208, 341; 48, 20 sq., 85, 88, 91, 93-5, 133, 257, 260 sq., 290, 306, 394 sq., 399, 408, 458, 659, 662, 687; both unity and diversity or manifoldness are true of B., as there are elements of plurality in it, 8, 374 sq., 374 n.; 34, xxviii, 321 sqq., 345 sq.; 48, 89; everything is centred in it, 15, 36; the bright, immortal Person in everything, the Self, the Immortal, B., and the All are the same, 15, 113-17; being one only, rules over all germs, over all forms, over all and everything, 15, 255 sq.; one only without a second, and undivided, nothing apart from B. exists, 34, xxviii sq., l, 286, 321, 349-54, 395 sq.; 38, 12, 13, 158, 160, 168-71, 175-80, 202, 327-9, 410; 48, 28 sq., 39, 73, 80, 91, 105, 126 sq., 176, 566; some metaphorical expressions, seemingly implying that there is something different from B., explained, 34, lxv; 38, 175-80; all things are effects of B., or are B. itself, 34, cxix sq.; is the real giver of the gifts bestowed by princes on poets and singers, 34, 80 n.; Indra declares that he is one with B., 34, 101 sq.; the ten objects and the ten subjects cannot rest on anything but Brahman, 34, 104; subsists apart from its effects, 34, 350; *the fishermen are B., the slaves are B., B. are these gamblers; man and woman are born from B.; women are B. and so are men*, 38, 61 sq.; 48, 191, 559 sq.; although one only, it is, owing to the plurality of its powers, meditated upon in more than one way, 38, 220; the uniform B. viewed as manifold through Nescience, 48, 127, 180, 344; is Heaven and Earth, 48, 191; *all sentient and non-sentient beings spring from B., are merged in him, breathe through him, are ruled by him, constitute his body; so that he is the Self of all of them*, 48, 717.

(*e*) THE B. (NEUT.) AND THE WORLD.

The B. as the cause or creator of the world, 1, 64; 15, 231-7; 34, xxix sq., xl, xlvii sq., l, lii, 50, 60 sq., 202, 233, 267-74, 299-317, 344, 352 sq., 361 sq., 381-6; 38, 3-73, 391 sq.; 44, 27 sq., 409; 48, 28, 200, 215 sq., 234, 240, 242, 254-6, 271, 285, 354-408, 413-79, 532-40, 584, 608, 643, 767; the source of all beings, the womb of the world, 15, 28; 34, 83, 85, 135-9, 288; 48, 140; is the support of the universe, 8, 104, 180, 180 n., 192; *is that from which the origin, subsistence, and dissolution of this world proceed*, 8, 180, 192; 34, xxxii, xcii sq., 15-19, 107, 109, 117, 283; 48, 3, 94, 156-61, 174, 255, 258-61, 266; is the seed of the tree of worldly life, 8, 313; in the beginning B. was all this, 15, xviii, 318; 44, 27 sq.; 48, 391; *that from whence these beings are born, that by which, when born, they live, that into which they enter at their death, try to know that. That is B.*, 15, 64; 48, 91, 156; covered himself, like a spider, with threads drawn from the first cause (pradhâna), 15, 263; not only the operative but also the material cause of the world, 34, xl, xciv sq., 49, 60 sq., 264 sq., 283-8, 317, 320-30, 346 sq., 361 sq.; 48, 142; creates the world without instruments, 34, xlix sq., xcv, 346-9, 354-6; creation and reabsorption of the world a mere sport of B., 34, l, 356 sq.; 48, 405 sq., 476 sq., 610; as a creator and dispenser, acts with a view to the merit and demerit of the individual souls, and has so acted from all eternity, 34, l, 357-61; relation of the non-sentient matter to B., 34, lxv; 48, 242; called Non-being, previously

to the origination of the world, 34, 267; is different from the world, 34, 284; 48, 188 sq., 413 sq., 417; the order in which the elements are retracted into B. is the reverse of that in which they are created, 38, 25 sq.; 48, 402–6; by offering up his own self in the creatures, and the creatures in his own self, B. compassed lordship over all creatures, 44, 417 sq.; the world (Pradhâna, Prak*ri*ti) constitutes its body, 48, 93, 135, 406, 419–24, 518 sq., 542, 544; was the wood, the tree from which they shaped heaven and earth, 48, 401; the maker, the Lord, the Person, the womb, 48, 407; the non-difference of the world from B., the highest cause, proved, 48, 430–67; the entire world springs from Nescience attached to B., which in itself is absolutely unlimited, 48, 445; where B. abides during pralaya and creation, 48, 460; effects by its mere will and wish the creation of the world, 48, 471 sq.; divides itself into ether, air, &c., 48, 473; devoid of parts, yet creates, 48, 473 sq.; B. and the world related, as the snake and its coils, 48, 618–21; the power of creating and ruling the world belongs to B. only, not to the released soul, 48, 766–71. *See also* Cause.

(*f*) THE B. (NEUT.) AND THE INDIVIDUAL SOUL.

The recognition of the self in man as identical with the highest Self or B. is the highest object of the Upanishads, 1, xxv; 15, xxvi; 34, xxxii, civ sq., 22–47, 265 sq.; 48, 174–200, 255 sq.; Âtman or Self is one with the B., 1, xxx; 15, 36, 178–81, 237, 290 sq.; 34, 14, 30 sq., 36, 45, 79, 105, 241, 264 sq.; 38, 209, 288; 48, 23 sq., 184, 191, 205, 258, 560, 564, 658; relation of the individual soul to B., 1, 84; 34, xix, xxx sqq., lvii sqq., xcvii–c, 64–289; 38, 61–73, 396 sq.; 48, 195 sq., 257–353, 393, 459, 559, 561; *thou art that* (tat tvam asi), 1, 101–9; 34, xxvii, xlix, 23, 31, 54–6, 104, 113, 115 sq., 122, 125, 185, 197, 250 sq., 266, 279, 321–3, 326, 343, 345; 38, 32, 46, 65 sq., 138, 140, 173, 197, 209 sq., 238, 243, 291, 333–7, 339, 370, 397, 408; 48, 126, *129–38*, 184, 191, 203 sq., 209, 214–18, 228 sq., 344, 458, 467, 541, 560, 564, 659, 759; colloquy of the departed and B., 1, 278 sq.; it dwells not on earth, nor in the sky, &c., but only in the self of the devoted man, 8, 179 sq.; man, being abandoned by the B. (i.e. the mind), is said to be dead, 8, 238; individual soul and B. are absolutely one, 8, 241; 14, 278, 278 n.; 34, xx, xxv, xxvii, xxx, 104, 114–16, 322, 343 sq.; 38, 30, 31, 33 sq., 42 sqq., 138, 146, 149; 48, 21, 102, 269, 467; the B. and the released soul, the released soul united with the B., 8, 248, 250; 34, xxx, 157, 178, 180 sq., 191; 38, 392–402, 408 sq.; 48, 160, 192, 296–8, 354; *I am B.*, 15, 88; 34, 31, 44, 104, 115, 185, 326; 38, 32, 46, 66, 173, 339, 355, 408; is the principle from which a mortal springs again after death, 15, 150 sq.; he only who is alone, i.e. knows his self to be one with B., is satisfied, 15, 236; 'My soul (âtman) dwells in the B. that it may be immortal,' 30, 228; the soul is a part of B., 34, xxv; 48, 558–67; both matter and the individual souls are real constituents of B.'s nature, 34, xxviii; in it the individual soul is merged in the state of deep sleep, 34, lxi sq., 180, 273; 38, 144–9, 152–66, 176; 48, 604 sq.; individual soul different from B., 34, 114–16, 344 sq.; 48, 209, 242, 256, 427 sq., 468 sq., 658; soul and B. both different and non-different, 34, 277 n., 345; 48, 191; is superior to the individual soul, 34, 345; is 'that,' the inward Self is 'thou,' 38, 335; has individual souls for its body, 48, 130, 132, 141 sq., 254, 392, 394, 406, 435–7, 469 sq.; is the internal ruler of the individual souls, 48, 132–4, 607–11; the soul has its Self in B., 48, 133 sq., 141; B., soul, and matter, in their relation, 48, 138–45, 227; imparts to the released souls infinite bliss, 48, 198 sq.; the Person of the size of a thumb is B., 48, 325–7, 347–9; all beings are effects of B., and hence have B. for their inner Self, 48,

353; soul saved by meditation on B., 48, 394; cannot be fully understood by the individual soul, 48, 396; the imperfections of the soul are not B.'s, 48, 563 sq., 607–11; the term B. applied to the individual soul, 48, 655 sq.; to be meditated upon as the Self of the devotee, 48, 716–18.

(*g*) DEVOTION TO AND ABSORPTION IN THE B. (NEUT.).

The path of the gods leading to B., 1, 68, 80, 276–8; 15, 327 sq.; 34, xxix sq.; 38, 383 sq.; 48, 648–51, 747 sq.; union with the B. reached by good conduct, by performing religious rites, and the like, 2, 218; 7, 183; 8, 106, 162, 235, 313, 336, 339 sq., 342, 370; 14, 249, 266, 309; 15, 176 sq., 336; 25, 25, 34, 34 n., 45, 45 n., 212 sq., 212 n., 419, 419 n.; sacrifice of B. with B., in B. by B. for B., 8, 61, 61 n.; the sage possessed of devotion attains to unity with B., 8, 64, 64 n., 70, 234 n., 245, 245 n., 398, 413; happiness in union with B. that is free from defects and equable, 8, 65 sq., 66 n.; 48, 327; the devotee of K*r*ish*n*a fit for union with B., 8, 110; the true Brâhma*n*a he who is attached to the B., 8, 147; the devotee attains to that B. after perceiving which he understands the Pradhâna, 8, 253; final release is assimilation with B., 8, 253, 253 n., 255; 34, 28 sq., 34; 38, 329; 45, 413; 49 (i), 130; the seat of the B. (brahmayoni) in the self, 8, 257, 326, 326 n.; Mind and Speech go to B., the self of all beings, to ask which of them is superior, 8, 263 sq. and n.; speaking of the B., Speech always produces eternal emancipation, 8, 265; tranquillity is the eternal B., 8, 277; he who adheres to the B., identifies himself with the B., becomes a Brahma*k*ârin, 8, 283 sq.; *there is nothing else more delightful than that, when there is no distinction from it . . . Entering it, the twiceborn do not grieve, and do not exult. They are not afraid of anybody, and nobody is afraid of them*, 8, 285; those whose wishes are fixed on good vows, and whose sins are burnt up by penance, devote themselves to B., 8, 288; assimilation with the B. obtained by going the path of the four Âsramas, 8, 316; 14, 275; the mode of conduct which is full of the B., 8, 341; various Brâhmans teach various paths leading to union with B., 11, 168, 168 n., 170 sq.; the Brahmanic teaching as to union with B. criticized by Buddha, 11, 171–85; meditating on the syllable Om, the ascetic becomes one with B., 14, 283 sq.; 'the vessel of B.,' the body of the ascetic, 14, 284, 284 n.; 25, 214; by worshipping B. he becomes B., 15, 67 sq.; let us love the old B., 15, 241; by knowledge, penance, and meditation one goes beyond B. (m.) to union with B. (n.), 15, 301; having broken through the four spheres of the Sun, the Moon, the Fire, and Goodness, the worshipper beholds B., 15, 338; Veda-knowledge and Veda-study procure union with B., 25, 165, 507; 44, 99; he who knows the Self enters B., the highest state, 25, 513; union with B. is the reason for the absence of all contact with evil, 38, 144; on the attainment of B. there take place the non-clinging and the destruction of sins, 38, 353–6; having destroyed by fruition all good and evil works, he becomes one with B., 38, 362 sq.; 48, 726 sq.; there is absolute non-division from B. of the parts merged in it, 38, 376 sq.; six doors to the B., viz. fire, wind, waters, moon, lightning, sun, 44, 66 sq.; inquiry into the mode of the going to B. of him who knows, 48, 728–43. *See also* Brahma-nirvâ*n*a.

(*h*) KNOWLEDGE OF THE B. (NEUT.).

B. is the flower, the secret doctrines are the bees, 1, 40; *a father may . . . tell that doctrine of B. to his eldest son, or to a worthy pupil. But no one should tell it to anybody else, even if he gave him the whole sea-girt earth, full of treasure, for this doctrine is worth more than that*, 1, 44; is perceived by the warmth of the body, is seen and heard, 1, 47; meditation on B. with reference to the body and with reference to the

gods, 1, 53 sq., 58, 151 sq., 152 n.; 15, 67 sq.; shining of the face of one who knows B., 1, 64, 67; meditations on B. and their results, 1, 66 sq.; 34, lxv–lxxv, 25, 31, 94, 105–11, 174; 38, 19 n., 177 sq., 184–284, 333–7, 342–5, 402; 43, xxiv, 400; 48, 26, 82 sq., 99 sq., 155 sq., 185–9, 255, 294, 651 sq., 715 sq.; we know B., and yet do not know it, 1, 148 sq., 149 n.; by knowledge of B. we obtain immortality or final release, 1, 149; 8, 77, 103; 15, 245, 258 sq., 322; 34, 41–3, 283; 38, 285, 290–306, 355; 48, 83, 198, 274 sq., 624; *he who knows that highest B. becomes even B.*, 1, 276 sq.; 8, 81; 15, 41, 54, 256 sq.; 34, 25, 29, 31, 186; 38, 375–7; 48, 16, 18, 23, 100, 183, 188, 192, 209 sq., 214, 233 sq., 392, 681, 686; discussion on B. between Bâlâki and Agâtasatru, 1, 300–7; texts giving instruction about the B., 8, 102; is the sole, the highest object of meditation or knowledge, 8, 104, 127 sq., 310, 369; 48, 87, 311–14, 395, 637–85, 689 sq.; meditation leads to union with B., 8, 128, 128 n.; 15, 301; understanding of the B. by means of the Vedas, 8, 147, 171–4, 369; 34, 10, 23 sqq.; knowledge of the B. the highest achievement of a Brâhma*n*a, 8, 160, 182; 25, 25, 25 n.; the gods inferior to those who know the B., 8, 161, 161 n.; 15, 49; Brahma-vidyâ, the eternal mystery, 8, 166, 166 n.; knowledge of B. acquired by living the life of a Brahma*k*ârin, 8, 175–9; not to be seen in the four Vedas, 8, 179 sq.; attained by means of knowledge, not by works, 8, 180, 185; 15, 39; knowledge of the B. will not lead to littleness, 8, 191; K*r*ish*n*a declared to Arguna the Supreme B., the seat of the B., 8, 230 sq.; is not to be apprehended by the senses, but only by the mind, 8, 257 sq.; 15, 22, 39; *G*anaka turns the wheel, the nave of which is the B., 8, 306; knowledge of B. obtained by penance and sacred learning, 8, 308; *as in a mirror, so* (*B. may be seen clearly*) *here in this body; as in a dream, in the world of the Fathers; as in the water, he is seen about in the world of the Gandharvas; as in light and shade, in the world of Brahmâ*, 15, 22; can only be apprehended by the words 'He is,' 15, 23; knowledge of B. the foundation of all knowledge, told by Brahmâ, 15, 27 sq.; only pious Brâhma*n*as worthy of receiving the science of B., 15, 41 sq.; *he who knows the B. as non-existing becomes himself non-existing; he who knows the B. as existing, him we know himself as existing*, 15, 57; he who knows that he is B. becomes all this, 15, 88; teaching of B. by No, no, 15, 108, 185; 34, lxiv; 38, 166–75; 48, 611 sq., 615–18, 661; is a deity about which we are not to ask too much, 15, 131; in B. knowledge and ignorance are hidden, 15, 255; no sins ever approach him who knows B., 15, 319; means of the worship and knowledge of B., 15, 343 sq.; teaching the B., 25, 51; knowledge of B. purifies, 25, 187 sq.; knowledge of B. increased by Brâhmanic rites and Veda-study, 25, 204; 48, 147; ascetics recite texts and meditate on B., 25, 205 sq.; knowledge of B. the subject of the *G*ñânakâ*n*da, 34, x, lxx, lxxviii sq., 9–15, 19, 31, 73, 138, 157, 159, 324; 38, 8, 162 sqq., 378, 393; on the qualification of gods for brahma-vidyâ or knowledge of B., 34, xxxvii, 216–23; 48, 326–35; Sûdras not qualified for brahma-vidyâ, 34, xxxvii, 223–9; 48, 337–47; Scripture does not contradict itself on the all-important point of B., 34, xl, 263–8; is to be known only from Scripture (Vedânta texts, Upanishads), 34, lxiv sq., 22–47, 307, 350–2, 355; 48, 3, 74 sq., 155, 161–74, 255, 617 sq.; different modes or forms of meditation on B., 34, lxvii sq., lxxiv, lxxvi, 107–9; 38, 201–4, 337–40; 48, 629–43; knowledge of B. is not subordinate to action, but independent, 34, lxxv, 10–12, 29; 38, 285–95; fruit or result of knowledge of B., 34, 11, 14, 18, 24 sq., 26–9, 231, 266, 300, 327; 38, 117 n., 229 sq., 236, 353–63, 372–5, 419; 48, 5, 7; conditions for engag-

ing in the inquiry into B., 34, 12; 48, 10 sq., 305; the body is an abode for the perception of B., 34, 178; texts exhorting us to strive to see B., 34, 349; Bâhva explained B. by silence, 38, 157; is not apprehended because it is unevolved, 38, 171; in the state of perfect conciliation the Yogins apprehend it, 38, 171 sq.; not the subject of injunctions, 38, 185, 162–6, 359; some persons, although knowing B., yet obtained new bodies, 38, 235; the state of being grounded in B. belongs to the wandering mendicant, 38, 300–3; Atharva-veda correlated with knowledge of B., 42, lix; inquiry into B., 48, 3–156; to be known after the knowledge of works has taken place, 48, 5; knowledge of B. puts an end to Nescience, 48, 9, 11; meditation on B. and knowledge of B. the same, 48, 82 sq.; release not due to knowledge of non-qualified B., 48, 129–38; Nescience not terminated by cognizing B. as the Universal Self, 48, 145–7; meditation on non-dual B. enjoined by all Vedânta texts, 48, 193, 197–9, 252, 260, 316, 715 sq.; even men knowing B. must avoid what is forbidden and do what is prescribed, 48, 288; meditation on B. is the means of attaining intuition, 48, 305, 681, 732; knowledge of B. to be understood as knowledge of the Veda in general, 48, 631; Brâhma*n*as discourse on the supreme B., 49 (i), 127. *See also* Knowledge, *and* Meditation.

(*i*) THE HIGHER AND THE LOWER B.

B. (m.) who is full of the B. (n.) is lord of all entities, and identical with Vish*n*u, 8, 347; higher and lower B., 'the two entered into the cave (of the heart),' 15, 12 n.; two forms of B., the material and the immaterial, the mortal and the immortal, 15, 107 sq., 306; B. (m.) a personal god, only a manifestation of the Brahman (n.), 15, 302 sq.; the syllable Om is the high and the low B., 15, 308; highest and lower B. distinguished, 34, xix sq., xxxii sq., xxxvi (masc. and neut.), 61–4, 171–4; 38, 7, 166, 202 sq., 401 sq.; 48, 313 sq.; lower B. associated with Mâyâ, 34, xxv; lower B. called Î*s*vara, the Lord, 34, xxv, xxvii; in its causal and its effected state, 34, xxix; 48, 336, 422, 459, 542; higher and lower B. not distinguished by Upanishads, nor by Bâdarâya*n*a, nor by Râmânuga, 34, xxxi, c, cxiii, cxv sq.; the B. to which the departed soul is led by the path of the gods is not the highest B., but the lower B., 34, lxxxii, xc sq.; 38, 389–402; 48, 748–52; *S*a*n*kara's distinction between a lower and a higher B. not valid, 34, xci–xciv; the lower B. is the vital principle in all creatures, 34, 172 n.; the world of the lower B. is called Satyaloka, 34, 181; lower B. is for the purpose of worship or meditation, 34, 330; 38, 155 sq., 161 sq., 391; the qualified B. is the object of the discussion on the difference or non-difference of the cognitions of B., 38, 185; results of meditations on the qualified B., 38, 161 sq., 185, 402–4; the qualified B. is fundamentally one with the unqualified B., 38, 248; worlds of B. can only refer to the lower B., 38, 390; on account of its proximity to the higher B., the lower B. can be designated by the word 'B.,' 38, 391; immortality is possible only in the highest B., not in the effected one, 38, 392; the qualified B. also may be spoken of as being the Self of all, 38, 394; B. having for its body all beings in their gross state, is the effect of B. having for its body all beings in their subtle state, 48, 132–4; Prak*ri*ti denotes B. in its causal phase when names and forms are not yet distinguished, 48, 399; used in a double sense, 48, 533 sq.; differentiation of names and forms is the work of B., not of Hira*n*yagarbha, 48, 578–83; the effected or the highest B. is the soul's aim, according as the meditation is, 48, 752–4.

(*j*) PASSAGES IN WHICH B. MAY BE EITHER MASC. OR NEUTER.

B. at the head of the Sâdhyas, 1, 43; obtained the victory for the Devas, 1, 149 sq.; worshipped by

prayers and offerings, 2, 108, 203, 299; 11, 180; 25, 91; 29, 85, 121, 141, 150, 161, 189, 207, 210, 219, 221 sq., 232, 290, 294, 319–21, 323, 344, 347, 368; 30, 124, 148 sq., 169, 175, 183, 194 sq., 243; 36, 41; 42, 94, 323; 43, 25, 291; a part of the house called 'seat of B.,' 2, 108; marriage rite of B., 7, 108; 25, 79; 29, 166; Vish*n*u is B. personified, 7, 293; 8, 347; appealed to as umpire, by the quarrelling Prâ*n*as, 8, 271, 273 sq.; 15, 202; teaching and studying the Veda a sacrifice to B., 14, 256 sq.; 25, 49, 87 sq.; 29, 217 sq.; 44, 95–9; funeral oblations offered in the mouth of B., 14, 268; the night of B., the muhûrta sacred to B., 14, 276, 309; 25, 143, 143 n.; worshipped by ascetics, 14, 280; the teacher is the image of B., 25, 71; punishment, formed of B.'s glory, 25, 218.

(*k*) THE GOD B. (MASC.), ALSO CALLED SAHAMPATI, SVAYAMBHÛ, OR HIRA*N*YAGARBHA.

Branches of knowledge traced back to B., 1, 44, 144; 8, 312, 314–93; 14, 163 sq.; 15, xxxix, 27, 227, 256; 43, xviii; 48, 284; the Self is B., 1, 245; is the essence of the Veda, Veda belongs to him, 1, 259; 29, 368; men who perform sacrifices dwell after death with the gods and B. in heaven, 2, 140; the age of one B., a day and a night of B., 7, 1, 1 n., 78; 8, 79 sq., 80 n.; 25, 20 sq.; acquired his present exalted position in consequence of good deeds (Karman) in former existences, 7, 153; 11, 163 sq.; 48, 259; part of the hand sacred to B., 7, 198; 14, 21, 166; 25, 40; four-faced (*K*aturmukha), 8, 83, 90, 93, 103, 345; 25, 254; 48, 90, 312 sq.; in the list of gods of the Anugîtâ, 8, 219; B. Svayambhû, the first of the Devas, the maker (creator) and preserver of the world, 8, 244; 15, 27–9, 315; 25, 3–18, 21 sq., 24 sq.; 35, 37; 45, 244 sq.; 48, 236, 238; is the first among all the patriarchs (Pragâpatis), 8, 354; the Plaksha, the ever holy field of B., 8, 354; the virtuous praised by B. even, 10 (i), 59; no one in the world of Brahmans equal to Buddha, 10 (ii), 14, 30, 45; 'B. is my witness,' 10 (ii), 78; Buddha compared with B., 10 (ii), 84; 19, 220; 49 (i), 104; the divine, and the human, and B.'s region, B.'s treasure, 10 (ii), 90; he who is endowed with the threefold knowledge, is calm, and has destroyed regeneration, he is B. and Sakka, 10 (ii), 117; 'who, be he a god, or B., or Inda,' 10 (ii), 189; union with B., only to be attained by Right Conduct, 11, x, 159–64, 183–5, 201–3; assemblies of B. one of the eight kinds of assemblies, 11, 48; the wheel of the empire of Truth set rolling by Buddha, cannot be turned back by B., 11, 154; the idea of B. in Buddhism, 11, 162–5; of modern Hindu theism, 11, 163; in each of the infinite world systems there is a B., 11, 164; a friend and follower of Buddha, 10 (ii), 119 sq.; 11, 116 sq., 117 n., 164; 13, 124; 19, 347 sq., 350, 352; 21, 69 sq., 349; 35, 118, 118 n., 301 sq.; 36, 24, 343, 373; 49 (i), 198, 200; (ii), 91, 165; beseeches Buddha to proclaim the truth, 11, 164; 13, 84–8; 19, 165–7; 21, 55; 36, 41 sq.; 49 (i), 168, 173; Buddha knows B., the world of B., and the path which leads to it, 11, 185 sq.; worship of B. denounced, 11, 199; 36, 21; a king surrounded by trusty servants is superior even to B., 14, 82; sacrificers are equal to B., 14, 102; 25, 185; through penances Bharadvâ*g*a and others became equal to B., 14, 329; that part of the Self which belongs to ra*g*as is B., 15, 304; Sanatkumâra, the son of B., 19, 24; unmoved in the midst of the kalpa-fire, 19, 184; Indra humbly approaches B., 19, 188; 49 (i), 107; established by Buddha, 19, 193; the swan his vehicle, 19, 309 n.; B. Sahâmpati and his 12,000 followers, 21, 5; men may be reborn as Brahmans, 21, 125; seats of B. gained by hearing the Dharmaparyâya preached, 21, 332, 335; is the king of all Brahmakâyika gods and father of the Brahma-world, 21, 387; saints

preach under the shape of B., 21, 401, 411; Manu the son of self-existent B., 25, xii, lvii, lxi, lxiv, 19, 19 n., 26; laws (of Manu) revealed by B., 25, xv, xvii, xcviii, 19, 354; 33, 35, 35 n.; born in the mundane egg, 25, 5, 5 n.; 48, 312, 580; creates and destroys the world over and over again, 25, 17 sq., 21 sq.; created animals for sacrifices, 25, 175; 'the court of (four-faced) B.,' 25, 254; true testimony is revered by B. himself, 25, 268; created the castes, 25, 326, 413; in the highest order of beings produced by Goodness, 25, 495, 495 n.; messenger of B. invoked against the demons, 30, 212; ordeals ordained and watched by B., 33, 115, 119, 253, 315; Mahâ-B. is mighty, and he is only one, 36, 50; Brahmans (pl.), the highest gods, also long for the righteous man, 36, 221; sons of B.'s mind, 38, 235; compact of B*ri*haspati with Indra and B., 42, 127; the spotless B. is the moon, 44, 317; with Soma for his leader, 44, 318; B. *K*aturmukha, Sanaka, and similar mighty beings dwelling in this world, 48, 90; beings from B. down to a blade of grass, 48, 156, 259, 445, 473; Nârâya*n*a alone existed, not B., nor *S*iva, 48, 240, 461, 522; represents the souls in their collective aspect, 48, 312 sq.; the Devas from B. downward possess a body and sense-organs, 48, 328–30; is created and the Vedas delivered to him, 48, 334 sq.; B. and the other gods originated from the Self, 48, 367; eight hundred millions of Brahmans (inhabitants of the B. worlds) purified by the eye of wisdom, 49 (i), 180; a preacher of the Law attains the supreme throne of B., 49 (i), 185; B., Vish*n*u, and *S*iva, 49 (i), 196–8, 200; precedence of the great B., 49 (ii), 57; the palace of Lord B., 49 (ii), 172. *See also* Hira*n*yagarbha, Sahampati, *and* Svayambhû; B.'s heaven, world of B., *see* Brahma-world.

Brahman, m., t.t., a certain priest. *See under* Priests (*a*, *b*).

Brâhma*n*a (masc.), **Brâhma*n*as**, members of the priestly caste.

(*a*) B. as priests at religious rites.
(*b*) B. reverenced as holy and divine beings.
(*c*) Duties of B. and restrictions for them.
(*d*) Exceptional laws regarding B.
(*e*) B. and kings or nobles (Kshatriyas).
(*f*) B. in Buddhist and *G*aina texts.

(*a*) B. AS PRIESTS AT RELIGIOUS RITES.

Speaking to B. is auspicious and purifying, 2, 34, 221; 30, 184, 199, 208; to be fed at all rites for gods or manes, 2, 138, 151; 7, 156, 262; 14, 256 sq.; 25, 93, 98; 29, 320; 30, 119; take the place of sacred fire at *S*râddhas, 2, 140; 25, 114; to be fed at *S*râddhas, 2, 143, 148, 150 sq., 255; 7, 76 sq., 83–7, 253–5; 14, 267, 270; 25, 98–111, 113 sq., 116–24; 30, 225, 234–6, 292 sq.; B. who are unfit to be invited to a *S*râddha, 2, 145; 7, 252 sq.; 14, 51 sq.; 25, 103, 107, 109, 111; B. who sanctify a company at the *S*râddha, 2, 146, 259; 7, 253–5; 14, 52 sq.; 25, 110 sq., 110 n.; represent the deceased ancestors at the *S*râddha, 7, 85 n., 232–8, 232 n., 250 sq.; 29, 105–8, 111, 250–5; offerings to the manes offered in the mouth of B., 14, 268; 30, 228; are the ancient deities of the funeral sacrifice, 25, 114; an enemy of B. excluded from *S*râddha feasts, 25, 104; the hand of a B. is the mouth of the Fathers, 29, 254;—distribution of food to B. at the end of religious rites, 2, 299; 12, 309 n.; 29, 15 sq., 32, 101, 130, 135, 171, 176, 192, 205, 208, 215, 250, 272, 288, 293, 300, 327, 331–3, 336, 338, 349 sq., 354, 374; 30, 14, 38, 84, 93, 158, 160, 175, 184, 203, 241, 246, 265, 286, 288; offence of neglecting to invite and feed a B. or of insulting him by offering him uneatable food, 7, 33; gifts bestowed on B., 7, 159–61, 181, 263–70, 274–6; 14, 135–9; 30, 218, 284; 42, 141, 145, 360; 49 (i), 15, 22; pronounce auspicious words, benedictions, 7, 215, 237; 29, 172, 205, 215, 250; 30, 95, 137, 158, 160, 162, 184, 203, 204, 241, 269, 271, 279, 283; sacrifices without gifts of food to B. condemned, 8, 119; 25, 93; B. only can be priests, 12, 25, 25 n.; 30, 321;

worship of Agni and the eastward migration of the B. from the Sarasvatî to the Sadânîra, 12, 104 n., 105 sq.; '*The B. (priests) are the guardians of this sacrifice;' for guardians of the sacrifice, indeed, are those B. who are versed in the sacred writ, because they spread it, they originate it*, 12, 134, 225; what is agreeable to the B. is auspicious, 12, 135; fulfilment of wishes obtained by B. staying in one's house, 12, 292; no one but a B. is allowed to drink of the residue of the Agnihotra, 12, 338, 338 n.; the word of a B. purifies, 14, 72, 171; 25, 191; offerings made into the mouths of B. are the best, 14, 138 sq.; the hand of a B. is his mouth, 14, 209; 29, 118; legends repeated in the assembly of B., 15, 14; food given to B. reaches the gods, 29, 16; the place of the B. at a sacrifice, 29, 24; prâ*s*ita, a sacrifice deposited in a B., 29, 31; gifts made to B. at a wedding, 29, 38 sq.; 30, 196; a name pleasing to the B. to be given to a child, 29, 50; Veda-study to be interrupted in the presence of B. who have not had their meal, 29, 118; the bride's shift to be given to a B., 29, 171; 30, 270; shave the child's hair, 29, 185; 30, 217; fees to be given to B. at the end of studentship, 29, 227; *but see also* Teacher; five B. breathe upon the new-born child, 29, 295; fed at the beginning of ceremonies, 29, 301, 304, 428; 30, 137, 162, 204, 269, 271, 279, 283; of all food a due portion must be given to B., 29, 388; 30, 24; only a B. may make the Bali-offerings for the householder, 30, 23; B. women pronounce blessings at the Sîmantonnayana, 30, 55; do not eat an uncompleted sacrifice, 42, 142; sterile cows must be given to the B., 42, 174–9, 656–61; a cow presented to an offended B., 44, 195; the metal vessels of a deceased sacrificer to be given to a B., 44, 205, 205 n.; the Sautrâma*n*î is a B.'s sacrifice, 44, 260; a B. lute-player sings of the king's sacrifices and gifts, 44, 356 sq., 359; are the fields on which gifts sown grow up as merit, 45, 52; congratulate King *S*uddhodana on Buddha's birth, and receive gifts, 49 (i), 8–10.

(*b*) B. REVERENCED AS HOLY AND DIVINE BEINGS.

Do not speak evil of the B., 1, 32; 8, 320; 14, 298; 25, 166; one should not curse a B., and not say to him anything except what is auspicious, 1, 251; 7, 155; 25, 436; purification prescribed on touching a B., 2, 59; classed as sacred with gods, idols, cows, and the like, 2, 94 sq., 220; 7, 228; 14, 36, 245, 323; 25, 135–8; 33, 222; to be honoured and revered, 2, 128; 7, xxix, 13, 194; 8, 119; 25, 86, 399, 588; *a B. who has studied the Vedas and a he-goat evince the strongest sexual desires*, 2, 136; witnesses to be sworn in the presence of the gods, the king, and B., 2, 247; 25, 269; death in a fight for the sake of B. purifies, procures heaven, &c., 2, 250; 7, 18, 67; 14, 106; 25, 185, 416, 447; remains always pure, 2, 254; 14, 132 sq.; 25, 424; gods and B. must be present at ordeals, 7, 55; 33, 260, 262; *the gods are invisible deities, the B. are visible deities. The B. sustain the world. It is by the favour of the B. that the gods reside in heaven; a speech uttered by B. (whether a curse or a benediction) never fails to come true. . . . When the visible gods are pleased, the invisible gods are surely pleased as well*, 7, 77; have the power to purify from sin and defilement, 7, 103; 25, 447 sq.; when a B. has met with an accident, Vedic study must be interrupted, 7, 125; he must not step on the shade of a B., 7, 203; superhuman power of a pious B., 7, 243, 245; 25, 398; the B., the Veda, and the sacrifices created by the Brahman, 8, 120; denounced as impostors by unbelievers, 8, 214; the Anugîtâ told to K*r*ish*n*a by a B. who came from the heavenly world and the world of Brahman, 8, 231; B*r*ihaspati is the lord of B., 8, 346; these B., the creators of the world, 8, 387; 25, 436; the B. is the repeller of the Rakshas, 12, 36; the B. are the human gods, 12, 309 sq., 374; 25, 398 sq., 447; 26, 341;

42, 164, 329, 529; a learned B. resembles a sacred fire, 14, 18, 18 n., 51; 25, 93; a Snâtaka should not pass between a fire and a B., nor between two B., 14, 61; learned B. incur no guilt, for a learned B. resembles a fire and the sun, 14, 130 sq.; a B. is a fire, for Agni is a B., 14, 138 sq.; *what B. riding in the chariot of the law (and) wielding the sword of the Veda, propound even in jest, that is declared to be the highest law*, 14, 145; have two names, two mouths, two kinds of virile energy, and two births, 14, 209 sq.; way must be made for a B., 14, 243; a place where B. sit, sacred, 14, 249; the eternal greatness of the B. is neither increased nor diminished by works, 14, 261, 274; duties towards B., 15, 52; 25, 588; 44, 100; power of their curse, charms and incantations their weapons, 15, 218; 25, 436, 436 n.; 42, 170 sq., 430–2; encomium of the B., 25, xii, 24–6; Somapas, &c., the manes of B., 25, 112; not to be touched by one who is impure, 25, 151; a fort must be supplied with B., 25, 228; to be honoured after a victory, 25, 248, 248 n.; to protect B. arms may be taken up, 25, 315; a learned Brâhmana is lord of the whole world, 25, 385; is superior to all castes, 25, 402; doing good to and worshipping B., a penance, 25, 446, 476; produced by Goodness, 25, 494; Bali offerings to Brahman and the B. at the Vaisvadeva sacrifice, 29, 85; worshipped at the Tarpana, 29, 122; to Agni belongs the B., 29, 307; 44, 89; food and the B. protect the house, 29, 348; before reaching B., one should dismount from a carriage, 29, 364; Râvana or another demon, the B. with ten heads, the first to be born, 42, 25, 374 sq.; charms found by B., Rishis, gods, 42, 29; have found medicinal plants, 42, 34, 292; imprecations against the oppressors of B., 42, 169–72, 184, 430–6; *he that injureth a B., whose kin are the gods, does not reach Heaven by the road of the Fathers*, 42, 170; descendants of the Rishis, 42, 183 sq.; as weather-prophets, 42, 532 sq.; *all beings, indeed, pass into the B., and from the B. they are again produced*, 44, 85; suffering and evil fastened on a B. (as scapegoat), 44, 181, 181 n., 183; a B. descended from a Rishi represents all the deities, 44, 195 sq.; born with spiritual lustre, 44, 294; whosoever sacrifices, sacrifices after becoming a B., 44, 348; the B. is everything, 44, 412.

(*c*) DUTIES OF B. AND RESTRICTIONS FOR THEM.

In the solitude of the forest a B. should be searched for, 1, 57; a B. by birth only, i.e. a B. who has not studied the Veda, 1, 92; 14, 144; 25, 59; qualities of a B. deeply versed in the Vedas, i.e. a Sishta, 2, 215–18; 14, 38–40; 25, 509; Lakshmî resides in a B. who studies the Veda, 7, 299; only a Brâhmana learned in the Veda has a right to the prerogatives of his caste, 14, 16–18; *see also* Veda (*c*; knowledge of);—unworthy B. whose food must not be eaten, 2, 69; 14, 71; lawful and unlawful occupations for B., 2, 72 sq., 212 sq., 215, 227 sq.; 7, 179; 8, 217 sq.; 14, 146, 146 n., 221; 25, lxviii, 86, 100, 109, 128–31, 272, 399, 587 sq.; 33, 221, 347; shall never take up arms, 2, 90; 42, 262; to protect himself or other B., a B. may take up arms, 2, 214; 14, 236; sixfold mode of life of B., 2, 215; 8, 359 sq., 359 n.; 25, 419; their merit in carrying out the corpse of a deceased B. who has no relatives, 7, 75; are purified by abandoning the world, 7, 97; 25, 188; one who is benevolent towards all creatures is justly called a B., 7, 184; 14, 128; 25, 46, 46 n.; worthy and unworthy B., 7, 274–6; 25, 51; duties of B., 8, 21 sq., 217 sq.; 14, 224; 25, 587 sq.; 33, 221; the true B. he who is attached to the Brahman, 8, 147, 182; pious B. who know the Brahman, 8, 158–61, 165, 165 n.; he is the true B. who swerves not from the truth, 8, 171; twelve great observances of a B., 8, 182; all companies of B. extol him who has become emancipated, 8, 345; shall not speak barbarous language, 14, 40; 26, 32; B. who do not perform

the twilight devotions are equal to Sûdras, 14, 248; the three debts of a B., 14, 261 sq., 271; let a B. become a Muni, and then he is a B., 15, 129 sq.; humility required of them, 25, lxvii, 59 sq.; unworthy B. who are like cats and herons (hypocrites), 25, 159, 159 n.; 45, 417; B. who renounce the world, but continue to live as householders, 25, 214–16, 214 n.; must not recover property by sacrificing or teaching, 25, 313; a B. fined for not inviting his neighbour to festivals, 25, 322, 322 n.; in distress may live by alms, 25, 424; may teach and sacrifice for despicable men in times of distress, 25, 424 sq.; penances for B. who acquire property by reprehensible methods, 25, 470, 470 n.; should be taught the Sâvitrî at once, 44, 89; four duties of B.: Brâhmanical descent, befitting deportment, fame, and the perfecting of the people, 44, 100; must not consume spirituous liquors, 44, 233, 260; those B. who know nought of the Asvamedha, may be despoiled by the keepers of the sacrificial horse, 44, 360; discourse on the supreme Brahman, 49 (i), 127.

(*d*) Exceptional laws regarding B.

The most heinous crime of slaying a B., 1, 84; 2, 71, 90, 266, 278, 280, 283 sq., 292 sq.; 7, 132, 134; 14, 101, 122, 175; 25, 161, 270, 309, 382 sq.; 42, 522; 44, 328, 340 sq., 396; *no greater crime is known on earth than slaying a B.; a king, therefore, must not even conceive in his mind the thought of killing a B.*, 25, 320, 451 n.; a murder other than the slaying of a B. is no murder, 44, 340; 45, 363 n.; *see also* Brahmahatyâ;—are exempt from opprobrious, capital, and corporal punishments and servitude, 2, 125, 125 n., 216, 245; 14, 201, 233; 25, 320; 33, 203 sq., 229, 362; foes declaring themselves to be cows or B. must not be slain, 2, 229, 229 n.; the sin of accusing a B. of a crime, 2, 282; their privileges, 7, 19; 33, 219–22; how to be punished, 7, 25; 33, 58, 388; crime of committing B. to slavery, 7, 37; a learned B. cannot be a witness, 7, 48; not subject to certain ordeals, 7, 54 sq.; 33, 248; forms of marriage legitimate for a B., 7, 108; 14, 206; 25, 79, 82; crime of stealing the gold or cattle of B., 2, 280; 7, 133 sq.; 14, 5, 108, 132, 201, 213, 218, 293, 296, 299; 25, 311, 383; 33, 228, 363; penances and punishments for offending or hurting B., 7, 138, 177, 180; 25, 154, 444, 472 sq., 588; 33, 348; the three lower castes shall live according to the teaching of the B., 14, 7 sq.; perjury, and speaking untruth, permitted for the sake of a B., 14, 83; 25, 273; 33, 303; fighting with B. forbidden, 14, 200; a B. shall have two names, 14, 209 sq.; 30, 215; non-Brâhmanical teachers in times of distress, 25, 73; threatening a B., a crime, 25, 155; receive part or whole of a found treasure, 25, 259; property of a learned B. not lost by limitation or adverse possession, 25, 279; 33, 61, 311 sq.; enrich themselves through others, 25, 284; may appropriate property for sacrificial purposes, 25, 313, 432 sq.; property taken from mortal sinners to be given to B., 25, 385; doubtful points of law settled by B. who are Sishtas, 25, 509 sq.; debts due to deceased B. must be paid to relatives or B., 33, 69; household property and alms of B. are free of duty, 33, 127; property found by B. does not go to the king, 33, 146; superior value of property belonging to B., 33, 205; what has been given to B. can never be taken back, 33, 221; a B. is the root of the tree of justice, 33, 282; as witnesses, 33, 301; oaths by B., 33, 315; a B. cannot be forced to do work for debts, 33, 330; inherit in default of relatives, 33, 379; property of B. not to be given as sacrificial gift, 44, 402, 412, 420.

(*e*) B. and kings or nobles (Kshatriyas).

A king who is slain in attempting to recover the property of B. performs the most meritorious sacrifice, 2, 163; a king gains endless worlds by giving land and money to B.,

2, 163; a king must not levy any tax upon B., 2, 164; 7, 16; 14, 8, 98 sq. and n.; kings and B. versed in the Vedas uphold the moral order in the world, 2, 214 sq. and n.; *the king is master of all, with the exception of B.*, 2, 234 sq.; assist the king as judges, 2, 237 sq.; 25, 253-6, 255 sq. n., 264, 322; 33, 250, 288, 388, 390; kings or B. examine witnesses, 2, 248; property of B. who die without heirs goes to other B., not to the king, 2, 309, 309 n.; 7, 68; 14, 93 sq.; 25, 368; 33, 202; as officers and advisers of a king, 7, 20, 41; 25, 225; king's duty towards learned B., 7, 21-3; 25, 221, 229 sq., 237, 239, 323, 397-9, 431, 434 sq.; 33, 218 sq., 346 sq.; owing to the disappearance of B. the Kshatriyas became V*ri*shalas, 8, 295; Kshatriyas procreated by B. on Kshatriya women, 8, 295, 295 n.; are the bridges of piety; whence they must be protected by the kings, 8, 348; follow in the train of a king, 12, 47; the king must never take property of B., 14, 179 sq., 201; 25, 369; 33, 338; King *G*anaka Vaideha testing the knowledge of the B., 15, 121-49; B. and Kshatriyas are nothing but the Self, 15, 182; 34, 275 sq.; to be worshipped by the king, 25, 221; 33, 280; king must be lenient towards B., 25, 221; Kshatriyas degraded by not consulting B., 25, 412, 412 n.; power of B. greater than that of the king, 25, 436; 41, 110; *two persons, a B. and a king, are declared to be exempt from censure and corporal punishment in this world; for these two sustain the visible world*, 33, 210, 216; there is no difference between kings and B., 33, 220; he to whom the B. and the Kshatriyas are but food is the highest Self, 34, xxxv, 116-18; are not qualified for the râgasûya-sacrifice, 34, 218; are not the food of kings, their king being Soma, 41, 72, 95; 43, 249; the B. is an object of respect after the king, 41, 96; do not engage in disputation with Râganyas, 44, 114; king can oppress B., but fares the worse for it, 44, 286. *See also* Caste (*b*).

(*f*) B. IN BUDDHIST AND *G*AINA TEXTS.

Buddhaghosa a learned B., 10 (i), xxi; etymology of Bâhma*n*o, Pali for B., 10 (i), liv, liv n., 89, 89 sq. n.; the Buddhist saint, the Arhat, as the true Brâhma*n*a, 10 (i), 39, 89-95; (ii), 89, 113-17, 151 sq., 171-4, 179, 195, 207 sq.; 13, 78-80; 36, 26-8, 28 n., 314; a true B. goes scatheless, though he have killed father and mother, 10 (i), 70, 70 sqq. n.; pleasant is the state of a B., 10 (i), 79; no one should attack a B., but no B. should let himself fly at his aggressor, 10 (i), 90; *a man does not become a B. by his platted hair, by his family, or by birth; in whom there is truth and righteousness, he is blessed, he is a B.*, 10 (i), 90 sq.; three kinds of B., Titthiyas, Âgîvikas, and Niga*nth*as, 10 (ii), xiii; as described in the Sutta-Nipâta, 10 (ii), xiii sq.; there are B., born in the family of preceptors, friends of the hymns, who commit sins; their birth does not save them from hell nor from blame, 10 (ii), 23; converted by Buddha, 10 (ii), 40-2, 52, 79 sq., 103-6, 186-213; Buddha's description of the pious customs of the B. of old, and their gradual degeneration, 10 (ii), 48-52; a Thera called a B., 10 (ii), 57; Buddha the best of the five B., 10 (ii), 59; disputatious B., contrasted with Buddha, 10 (ii), 63; B. together with B. ask truly, Art thou a B.? 10 (ii), 75; to whom a B. should offer, 10 (ii), 82-4; Buddha warns Ke*n*iya not to invite him, because Ke*n*iya is intimate with the B., 10 (ii), 97; is a man a B. by birth or by deeds? 10 (ii), 108-17; a B. may, by intense meditation, cause an earthquake, 11, 45 sq.; will honour the remains of the Tathâgata, 11, 91, 99, 247; Sama*n*a-brâhma*n*a, B. by saintliness of life, 11, 105 sq., 105 n.; compared to the Scribes and Pharisees of the New Testament, 11, 160; their phraseology assumed a different meaning when used by Buddha, 11, 161-5; Buddha's criticism of the teaching of the B. as to

union with Brahman, 11, 171–85; various B. teach various paths, such as the Addhariya B., the Tittiriya B., the *Kh*andoka B., the *Kh*andava B., the Brahma*k*ariya B., 11, 171, 171 n.; how they recite the Vedas, 11, 172 sq.; B. and laymen (brâhma*n*a-gahapatikâ), 11, 258 n., 261; behave badly at dinners given to them, 13, 152; the Lokâyata system of the B. not allowed to the Bhikkhus, 20, 151 sq.; an honorific title used by Buddhists and *G*ainas, 22, xxx; among those who are not attached to the world, there is real Brahmanhood, 22, 45; B. a title of Mahâvîra, 22, 63, 66, 82 sqq., &c.; 45, 301, 301 n., 310; Buddha calls himself a B., i.e. an Arahat, 36, 8, 8 n., 10; think themselves the highest among men and revile the Bhikkhus, 36, 21 sq.; B. only worthy of gifts, 36, 120 sq. n.; B. and Buddhists, both reformers, 36, 127 sq. n.; the superiority of monks to B., 45, 50–6; a true monk who is exempt from all Karman is a true B., 45, 138–41; called 'holy cats' by Ârdraka, 45, 417; B. and Sama*n*as, *see* Holy persons, Castes, Priests, *and* *S*rotriyas.

Brâhma*n*a (neuter), title of texts, 'sayings of Brahmans,' applicable to all old prose traditions, 1, lxvi; several Upanishads occur in B., 1, lxvi sq.; B. and Âra*n*yakas, both liturgical, 1, xci sq.; in the sense of Upanishad or secret doctrine, 1, 264, 264 n.; the B. literature, 12, ix, xxii–xxv, xlvii; B. means a dictum on ceremonial, 12, xxii sq.; B. and Mantrasa*m*hitâ to be studied, 25, 144; G*ri*hya ceremonies mentioned in B., 30, xiv–xxii; interpretation of Mantras in the B., 32, 29, 56, 359 sq.; mystic sense, dogmatic explanation of an oblation, 43, 240; B., Mantras, and arthavâdas, 48, 330; *see also* Aitareya-B., Kaushîtaki-B., Pa*ñk*avi*ms*a-B., *and* *S*atapatha-B.

Brâhma*n*adhammikasutta, t.c., 10 (ii), 47–52.

Brâhma*n*agîtâ, title of a chapter of the Anugîtâ, 8, 256 n., 310 n.

Brahmânanda-vallî, the second Adhyâya of the Taittirîyaka-Upanishad, 15, xxvii sq.

Brahma*n*aspati, invoked to purify from sin, 14, 251; the lord of Brahman or speech, 15, 82; the Lord of prayer, a name of the Creator, 43, xiv; lord of the priesthood, 43, 73; is the sun, 44, 453; invoked at the Pravargya, 44, 453, 476 n., 478; Agni identified with B., the Brahman priest among the gods, 46, 186, 190; the same as B*ri*haspati, q.v.

Brahman-egg, created, 48, 127, 334, 731.

Brahma-nirvâ*n*a, t.t., Brahmic bliss, 8, 27 n., 52, 52 n., 176, 176 n.

Brahmanism, germs of Buddhism and *G*ainism in it, 22, xxxii.

Brahman-slaying, *see* Brahmahatyâ, *and* Brâhma*n*a (*d*).

Brahmapura, city of Brahman, 34, 178. *See* Brahman (*c*).

Brahma*ri*shi, worshipped, 29, 141.

Brahmasa*m*stha, i.e. he who is firmly grounded in Brahman, obtains immortality, 1, 35.

Brahmasattra, *see* Veda (*c*).

Brahma *S*ikhin, n. of a Brahmakâyika god, 21, 5.

Brahmasûkta, in the Sa*m*hitopanishad of the Âtharva*n*as, 38, 62; 48, 191.

Brahma-sûtras, 'texts about the Brahman,' not the Vedânta-sûtras, 8, 31, 102; another name for Vedânta-sûtras, 34, xiv n.; *see* Vedânta-sûtras.

Brahmasvaranâdâbhinandita, n. of the 42nd Tathâgata, 49 (ii), 6.

Brahma-upanishad, or the secret doctrine of the Veda, its teaching, and its result, 1, 44; 34, 94; 48, 336, 525.

Brahmavar*k*asa, Sk., t.t., 1, 29 n.

Brahma-veda = Atharva-veda, 42, xxvii sq., xxviii n., xxx, xliii, lix, lxii–lxvii.

Brahmavidyâ, knowledge of the Brahman, *see* Brahman (*b*).

Brahmavidyâbhara*n*a, on Bauddha sects, 34, 401 n., 404 sq. n.

Brahma-vihâras, *see* Meditations.

Brahma-world (world of the Brahman, neut., or of Brahman, masc.), all creatures day after day go into the B., and yet do not discover it, 1, 129; 48, 317 sq.; deep sleep is

absorption in the B., 1, 129; 15, 171; 48, 317 sq.; is free from all evil, and lighted up once for all, 1, 130; belongs to those who find it by abstinence (brahma*k*arya), 1, 130 sq.; 38, 384; details about it, its lakes, &c., 1, 131, 132 n., 275 sq.; the sun is the door of it, 1, 134; the Devas are in the B., and meditate on the Self as taught by Pragâpati, 1, 142; *having shaken off the body, I obtain self made and satisfied the uncreated world of Brahman*, 1, 143; obtained by him who performs the duties of studentship, householdership, and of the mendicant, 1, 144; is water, 1, 279; by lifelong service to a teacher the professed student gains the B., 2, 193; 7, 120, 129; 25, 72 sq., 157; a well-conducted Snâtaka will never fall from it, 2, 226; obtained through the Brâhma marriage rite, 7, 108; attained by a giver of a hundred milch cows, 7, 272; even the B. only temporary, 8, 79 sq., 80 n.; a wise Brâhma*n*a came from B., 8, 231; the imperceptible seat of the Brahman, the highest world, 8, 234; Satyaloka or B., 8, 234 n.; the highest goal of Brâhma*n*as and Kshatriyas, 8, 255; Mâtaṅga, the *K*â*nd*âla, went to the B., 10 (ii), 23; he who pretends to be an Arhat, without being one, is a thief even in the B., 10 (ii), 23; Buddha teaches the beings in B., 10 (ii), 96, 142 sq.; is void like other worlds, 10 (ii), 208; no one in it can digest what Buddha digested, 11, 72; the turning of the wheel of the empire of Truth heard in B., 11, 155; Buddha understands the B. as all other worlds, 11, 185–7; the Iddhi of reaching in the body up to the B., 11, 214; Sudassana entered it, 11, 285; Buddha will not lay aside his body in any place of B., 11, 288; he who fulfils the duties of a householder never falls from it, 14, 44 sq., 49; gained by self-immolation, 14, 136; the reward of a Brâhma*n*a who follows the rules of the law, 14, 224; by teaching the rule of Pragâpati one becomes exalted in it, 14, 332; Brahman (neut.) seen in it, as in light and shade, 15, 22; worlds of Pragâpati woven into the worlds of Brahman, 15, 131; bliss in the B., 15, 172 sq., 176; 25, 169, 204, 204 n.; he who knows the Self obtains the B., 15, 180; from the worlds of Brahman there is no return, 15, 208; blissful state in the B. obtained by meditation on God, 15, 236; this B. in the moon belongs to those who beget children, but that pure B. belongs to those who practise penance, abstinence, and truth, 15, 273 sq.; as a reward for meditation on Om, 15, 282; 34, 174; he is led up to the B. by the Sâman, 15, 282; 34, 173; 48, 311 sq.; Hira*n*yagarbha dwells in the B., 15, 282; 34, 173; rebirth in the B., 19, 138; the Akanish*th*as and Âbhâsvaras in the B., 21, 340, 346; a pious Brâhma*n*a goes to the highest dwelling-place, 25, 92, 92 n.; is the small ether, 34, 180; not 'the world of Brahman,' but 'the world which is Brahman,' 34, 180 sq.; 48, 751 sq.; how far is the B.? 35, 126 sq.; one of the four great continents, 35, 130; Arahatship or birth in the B. the two highest rewards of universal love, 35, 279; the Bodisat reborn in the B., 36, 19, 22; one of the fourteen worlds, 48, 328, 429; on the passing away of the effected B., at the pralaya the souls go to the highest Brahman, 48, 749 sq.; reached by mendicants, 49 (i), 128. *See also* Worlds.

Brahmayag*ñ*a, *see* Veda (*c*).

Brahmîsundarî, n.p., at the head of the nuns in *R*ishabha's time, 22, 284.

Brâhmî-upanishad, not a title of the Kena-upanishad, 1, lxxxiii, lxxxix; penance, restraint, sacrifice are its feet, the Vedas its limbs, the True its abode, 1, 152 sq.

Brahmodya, t.t., riddles from the Veda, given at *S*râddha feasts, 25, 118, 118 n.; theological discussions between the priests as part of ceremony, 44, 79, 79 n., 314–16, 388–91; is the complete attainment of speech, 44, 391.

Brahmopanishad, *see* Brahma-upanishad.

Brahmopâsana, t.t., meditation on Brahman, and pratîkopâsana, 1, 201. *See* Brahman (*c*, *b*).

Brahmo Samâj, 1, lxiv.

Breath (Sk. prâ*n*a).

(*a*) Regulation of breathing.
(*b*) The b. of life, the vital principle, the soul.
(*c*) The chief vital air and the organs of the soul.
(*d*) B. as a divine principle or being.

(*a*) Regulation of breathing.

Stopping the b., as part of a penance or of a ceremony, 2, 86, 129, 183, 185, 290, 293, 293 n.; 12, 367; 14, 46 (highest form of austerity), 120 sq., 125–7, 162, 162 n., 247, 251, 251 sq. n., 278, 295, 308, 313–18; 25, 44 sq., 459, 461, 471 sq., 479; 29, 118; 30, 115, 243; stopping of the b. removes all sin, 7, 181–3; stopping of the b. enjoined for ascetics, 7, 281; 8, 372 sq.; 25, 210 sq.; 35, 130 sq.; the sacrificer, by drawing in his b., establishes the fire in his soul, 12, 311; the observance of breathing up and down (prâ*n*a-vrata), 15, 98; management of b. to bring about Tâoistic perfection, 39, 24, 51, 53 sq.; manipulating the b. to secure longevity, 39, 95 sq., 146, 364; 40, 139 n.;—the going b. is unclean, defiles the fire, 4, lxxvi, lxxvi n., lxxviii, 172 sq. n.; 25, 137; the Paitidâna or mouth-veil to prevent defilement by b., 4, 172, 172 sq. n., 273; 5, 333 sq. and n.

(*b*) The b. of life, the vital principle, the soul.

Prâ*n*a, meaning b., spirit, and life, is the conscious self (pragñâtman), 1, xxv, 120 n., 236, 290 sq., 294–300, 307; 34, 105; Om a name of it, 1, xxv; called ana, the breather, 1, 74, 74 n.; everything is food for b., 1, 74; 15, 203 sq.; 38, 211, 213, 309 sq.; 43, 398 sq.; water is the dress of b., 1, 74; 15, 203 sq.; 38, 211–14; 48, 640 sq.; called Ama, 1, 76; 15, 82; the subtlest portion of water becomes b., 1, 96–8; 38, 366; comes from water, and will not be cut off, if you drink water, 1, 97; mind in deep sleep and at death is merged in b., and b. in fire, 1, 99, 101, 108, 307; 38, 366–8; 48, 729 sq.; prâ*n*a springs from the Self, 1, 124; 34, 167; is attached to the body, as a horse is attached to a cart, 1, 142, 142 n.; is life and death and immortality, 1, 213 sq., 294; 15, 56; 34, 164; 48, 250–4; simile of the chariot mounted by Prâ*n*a or b., mind being the driver, 1, 234; is the beam on which the house of the body rests, 1, 252, 257; marrow is b. and seed, 1, 258; the dying person says, 'B. to air and to the immortal,' 1, 313; 15, 200; soul dwells in the seat of the b., the heart, 8, 242; is food, 12, 223, 304; 26, 212, 348; 41, 379, 394 sq.; 44, 269; is fire, 12, 311–13; 43, 327; by its departure man departs, by its staying he lives, 15, 283 sq.; 48, 572; the Sun as the outer Self, and B. as the inner Self, 15, 305–12; the heart is b., and the animal is b., 26, 204, 211; the Ukthya graha is his undefined b., and as such the self of his, 26, 292 sq.; there is no soul in the b., 35, 48 sq.; is most beneficial for man, 34, 98; strength is b., 34, 99; denotes either the individual soul or the chief vital air, or both, 34, 102 sq.; is the abode of the power of action, 34, 105; remains awake in the state of deep sleep, 34, 162–8; may be called 'higher' with reference to the body, 34, 172; spoken of as a 'person,' 34, 261; the causal substance of mind, 38, 366; is merged in the individual soul, on the departure of the soul, 38, 367 sq.; the soul, with the b., goes to the elements, 38, 368; knowledge depends on b., 40, 139, 139 n.; it is by its b. that we control whatever creature we grasp, 40, 262; the body is the house of the b., 40, 270; the spirit is the child of the b., 40, 272; fashioned from fire, 43, 4; is the wind, 43, 33, 66, 333; why b. is warm, 43, 135; the immortal element of man, 43, 327; identified with the Yagus, 43, 337, 340; the man in the eye is b., 43, 371; rite of breathing over a new-born child, 44, 129 sq.; etymology of prâ*n*a, b., 44, 263; food eaten by means of b., 44, 263 sq.; is the transformer of seeds, 44, 345; is the individual soul, 48, 300–4, 379,

383; is different from air, it is an instrument of the soul, 48, 573, 575.

(*c*) THE CHIEF VITAL AIR AND THE ORGANS OF THE SOUL.

The *mukhya prâna, b. in the mouth, or chief vital air*, is free from evil, 1, 5; its importance for the other vital breaths or senses, 1, 5 sq.; 38, 89, 95; by it the Devas conquered the Asuras, 1, 5; 15, 79 sq.; there is one unmoving life-wind, 8, 274; a hymn addressed to the chief Prâ*n*a, who is identified with all the gods, 15, 275 sq.; is produced from Brahman, is distinct from air in general and from the other vital airs, and is minute, 34, lix; 38, 84–91, 93–6; 48, 575; according to the Sâṅkhyas, the combined function of all organs, 38, 86; various powers ascribed to it, 38, 87; is independent in the body, like the individual soul, 38, 87; is subordinate to the soul, 38, 88; has five functions like mind, 38, 89 sq.; acts under the guidance of Vâyu, 38, 91 sq.; is not a sense-organ, 38, 93 sq.; accompanies the soul when leaving its body, 38, 102; glorified in the Udgîtha-vidyâ, 38, 192–5; esoteric knowledge about it, 44, 83 sq.; created, 48, 572 sq.;—Vâyu among the Devas, b. (prâ*n*a) among the Prâ*n*as, the end of all, 1, 58; 34, lxxiv; 38, 256–9; swallows during sleep and at death all senses, but produces them again at the time of waking, 1, 59, 59 n., 295 sq.; 43, 332; is the best among the senses or organs, 1, 73 sq., 207, 290 sq., 294 sq.; 15, 97 sq., 201–4, 274 sq.; 38, 256; when b. departs, the other senses depart with it, 1, 223; the union of speech and mind, 1, 248; b. and speech swallow each other; speech is the mother, b. is the son, 1, 256; the inner Agnihotra, or the offering of b. in speech, and of speech in b., 1, 266, 283; 48, 294 sq.; *see also* Prâ*n*âgnihotra; is the beginning of all words, 8, 353; the triad of mind, speech, b., 15, 93–7; is one of the pa*ñk*aganâ*h*, or 'five-people,' 34, 260–2; speech, b., and mind presuppose fire, water, and earth, 38, 78 sq.; b. and speech, male and female, 43, 285; speech created B., B. the Eye, 43, 377 sq. *See also* Prâ*n*as.

(*d*) B. AS A DIVINE PRINCIPLE OR BEING.

Identified with the sun, 1, 7, 214; all these beings merge into b., and from b. they arise, 1, 20; 34, 85 sq.; 48, 569; prâ*n*a, spirit or b., is all whatever exists here, 1, 49, 120; 34, 64; 44, 15; prâ*n*a or b. is the highest Brahman, 1, 55–8, 55 n., 58 sq. n., 65, 65 n., 233 sq., 280 sqq.; 15, 65, 142, 154, 194; 34, xxxiv, 84–7, 97–106, 272; 38, 143; 48, 246, 250–4, 256, 276 sq.; is the oldest and the best, 1, 72, 76; 38, 84 sq., 186 sq.; 48, 636 sq.; is sattya, the true, 1, 209; all things are supported by b., 1, 210; 15, 275; 43, 47 sq.; *Indra said: 'I am Prâna (b.), O Rishi, thou art Prâna, all things are Prâna. For it is Prâna who shines as the sun, and I here pervade all regions under that form,'* 1, 219, 236, 294; 48, 250–4; is Hira*n*yagarbha, 1, 236; 15, 16; is the couch of Brahman, 1, 277; meditation on the absorption of the gods into b. or Brahman, 1, 288–90; is blessed, imperishable, immortal, independent of good and bad actions, the guardian of the world, the king of the world, the lord of the universe, and Indra's self, 1, 299 sq.; Aditi arises with Prâ*n*a, 15, 16; b. in which everything trembles is Brahman, 15, 21, 21 n.; 34, xxxvii, 229–31; the Person (purusha) is the b., 15, 38; 25, 513; is the one god, 15, 142; 34, 200, 269; 44, 117; is the Self, 15, 287, 290, 311–13; 34, 231; 48, 569; Time (Kâla) is b., and only a manifestation of Brahman, 15, 302; invoked for protection, 29, 232, 348; is the bhûman b. or the highest Self? 34, 162–8; through knowledge of the b. as Brahman immortality arises, 34, 229–31; is the maker of all the persons, the person in the sun, the person in the moon, &c., 34, 269; by means of b. the gods aroused the sun, 42, 51; Prâ*n*a, life or b., exalted as the supreme spirit, 42, 218–20, 622–6; Prâ*n*a as a rain-god, 42, 218 sq., 623 sq.; is the Vi*s*vagyotis, 43, 131; 'he who waketh in

the worlds and sustaineth all beings,' the b., identified with the Agnihotra, 44, 47 sq.; food and b. are the two gods, 44, 117; a term referring to the Highest Reality, 48, 522; meditation on prâ*n*a, 48, 679.

Breathings, *see* Prâ*n*as.

B*ri*bu, Bharadavâ*g*a accepted cows from the carpenter B., 25, 424, 424 n.

Brick Hall, the, at Nâdika, 11, 24, 25 n., 27.

B*ri*hadâra*n*yaka - upanishad quoted, 8, 401; 38, 421-3; 48, 773-5; King *G*anaka in the B., 12, xliii; portion of the *S*atapatha-brâhma*n*a, 15, xxx; 44, xiii, xlix sq.; editions of it, 15, xxx; in the Kâ*n*va and Mâdhyandina texts, 15, xxx; 34, lxxxix, 134, 260 n., 262 sq.; 38, 214, 308; 48, 403, 422 sq., 544, 735; translated, 15, 71-227; germs of Mâyâ doctrine in the B., 34, cxvii, cxx sq.

B*ri*hadratha, n.p., 46, 33, 36.

B*ri*hadratha Aikshvâka, n. of a king, taught by *S*âkâyanya, 15, xlvii, 287-90, 326-9.

B*ri*haduktha Vâmadevya, worshipped at the Tarpa*n*a, 30, 244; a *Ri*shi, saw the Âprî verses of the horse, 44, 302; had a golden ornament at his neck, 46, 407.

B*ri*haspati, or Brahma*n*aspati, the Lord of Prayer.

(*a*) B. in mythology.
(*b*) Worship of B.

(*a*) B. IN MYTHOLOGY.

B., the lord of B*ri*hatî or speech, 1, 6; 15, 82; meditated on the udgîtha, 1, 6; chief among domestic priests, 8, 89; is the lord of Brâhma*n*as, 8, 346; a form of Agni, 12, xvi sq. n.; 14, 216; 32, 82, 94; 42, 52, 110, 541, 552; 46, 292, 294; is the Brahman priest of the gods, 12, 6 sq., 215; 26, 435; 41, 122 sq.; 46, 190; B. Âṅgirasa ordains the sacrifice to men, 12, 66 sq.; the portion of the sacrifice taken out of Pra*g*âpati was appeased by B., 12, 211, 211 n., 213; the world of B., 14, 309; the bliss of B., 15, 60, 61 sq. n.; having become *S*ukra, he brought forth the false knowledge, to protect Indra against the Asuras, 15, li, 342; the gods pay worship to B., 19, 78; is the Brahman (priesthood), 26, 23, 59, 59 n., 180, 219 sq.; 41, 3, 23-6, 67, 70, 82; 43, 192; 44, 64, 258, 314, 402, 411; accompanied by the All-gods, 26, 93; 44, 480 sq.; oppressed by Soma, 26, 258 sq.; the wise, 26, 286; Soma begotten by B., 26, 366; Dhât*ri* shaved the head of B., 29, 56, 185; put the garment of immortality on Indra, 29, 304; Pûshan has shaven B.'s head or beard, 30, 61, 217; knows the demons, 30, 212; where B. dwells, 30, 218; the Purohita of the gods, 30, 240; 41, 59; 42, 79; 44, 258; drawn by red horses, 32, 17; blew the gods together, 32, 246 sq.; represents Agni and Indra, 32, 246 sq. n.; 43, 134; offered the Vâ*g*apeya, 41, 2 sq., 5; the upper region belongs to B., 41, 2, 59, 122; 42, 193; the highest heaven of B., 41, 23; afraid of the Earth, and the Earth afraid of B., 41, 34; plants urged forward by B., 41, 341 n.; 42, 44; is Âṅgirasa, representative of witchcraft performances, 42, xxiii sq., 127 sq.; frees from death, 42, 50, 52, 552; knows the life-bestowing gold, 42, 63; the amulet which B. tied, 42, 85-7, 610; the hostile army repulsed by B., 42, 119; Maruts, Âditya, and B., 42, 126; compact of B. with Indra and Brahman, 42, 127; with the Vasus, 42, 135; Indra, B., and Sûrya in a list of gods, 42, 160; Indra Brahma*n*aspati, 42, 163, 213; B. punishes him who withholds the sterile cow from the Brâhma*n*as, 42, 178, 660; undid Vala, 42, 193, 596; deity of B*ri*hatî metre, 43, 53, 330; share of Savit*ri* and lordship of B., 43, 69; lord of animals, 43, 74; the repeller of shafts, 43, 103; Indra's ally against the Asuras, 43, 192; B. and Indra, priesthood and nobility, 43, 228 sq.; the lord of the Brahman, bestows holy lustre, 44, 64; made over-lord for warding off of the fiends, 44, 465; the wind worshipped as identical with B., 44, 480 sq.

(*b*) WORSHIP OF B.

Offerings to B., 2, 108; 26, 23 sq.; 348; 29, 85, 85 n.; 41, 82, 113, 116, 120-3, 125; worshipped at the

Upanayana and else in connexion with studentship, 2, 294, 294 n.; 25, 454 sq.; 29, 65, 65 n., 190, 315 sq., 362; 30, 147, 151 sq.; Mantras in praise of B., 7, 266; the Hot*ri* invokes the help of B. for his work, 12, 135; prayers and invocations to B., 12, 355; 14, 216, 318; 15, 45, 53; 26, 23 sq., 59, 59 n.; 41, 383; 43, 291; invoked to cleanse from sin, 14, 250; animal victim (barren cow) for B., 26, 219 sq., 388 sq., 389 n.; 44, 411, 411 n.; worshipped at the wedding, 29, 32, 286; 30, 188; the animal slain for the hospitable reception of a priest is sacred to B., 29, 88; (lord) of the Brahman, invoked for protection, 29, 280; invoked at the house-building rite, 29, 347; 42, 140; invoked for success in trade, 30, 178; invoked to protect cattle, 30, 184; 42, 143; worshipped at the Tarpa*n*a, 30, 243; the B*ri*haspatisava, or B. Soma feast, 41, xxiv sq., 34 sq., 34 n.; offering to B. at the Vâ*g*apeya, 41, 21 sq., 28, 36, 38 sq.; offering to B. at the house of the Purohita, 41, 59; sacrifice to Mitra and B., 41, 66–8; offering to B. Vâ*k*, 41, 70 sq.; invoked in medical charms, 42, 29, 554; invoked to promote virility, 42, 32; invoked for long life, 42, 47, 49; invoked against sorcerers, 42, 65; Brahma*n*aspati *G*âtavedas invoked to render the inauspicious auspicious, 42, 110, 541; B. and Bhaga join (husband and wife?) together, 42, 135; invoked against rivals, 42, 211; one of the gods worshipped at the Mitravindâ sacrifice, 44, 62–6; his share of the Agnihotra, 44, 81; worshipped at the A*s*vamedha, 44, 281, 402; invited to the sacrifice together with Agni, 46, 281.

B*ri*haspati, n. of a sage; B. and other sages ask Brahman about final emancipation, 8, 314; *S*ukra and B., sons of Bh*ri*gu and Aṅgiras, 19, 10; 49 (i), 8; the great ascetic B., deluded by a woman, begot Bharadvâ*g*a, 19, 44; 49 (i), 44, 44 n.; addressed Indra's son *G*ayanta, 19, 96; 49 (i), 93; the Moon begat Budha on the spouse of B., 49 (i), 45; a holy sage, 49 (i), 76.

B*ri*haspati, n. of an author of heretical doctrines, 15, li; disregards the Karma-Kâ*nd*a, 48, 409; the author of a materialistic and atheistic Sm*ri*ti, 48, 412.

B*ri*haspati, n. of the author of a law-book; conversation between Manu and B., 25, lxxix; on Manu's attitude towards Niyoga, 25, xciv, 339 n.; remodelled the Manu-sm*ri*ti, 25, xcvi, cix; 33, xii, 274; mentioned in the B.-sm*ri*ti, 33, 284.

B*ri*haspati-sm*ri*ti, on the Manu-sm*ri*ti, 25, xiv, xvi sq.; a Vârttika on the Manu-sm*ri*ti, 25, cviii–cx; its date, 25, cix sq.; 33, xvi, 275 sq.; its relation to the code of Manu, 33, 271–5; relation between Nârada-sm*ri*ti and B., 33, 274 sq.

B*ri*hatî, *see* Metres.

B*ri*hatsâman, the descendant of Aṅgiras, 42, 171.

B*ri*hat-Saṅkha-Dharma*s*âstra, in prose and verse, 25, xxi sq.

Brothers, *see* Family.

Bû*d*, n. of a demon, 47, 58.

Buddha.

(*a*) Names and titles of a B.
(*b*) Appearance of a B. in the world.
(*c*) Life of Gotama B. Sakyamuni.
(*d*) Bodily and mental characteristics of a B.
(*e*) Transcendent knowledge and miraculous powers of a B.
(*f*) Gotama B. as a preacher and teacher.
(*g*) The Dhamma or Doctrine of B.
(*h*) B. and his Order.
(*i*) Deification and worship of B.
(*j*) Plurality of Buddhas.

(*a*) NAMES AND TITLES OF A B.

Names or religious titles of B., 10 (i), 49–52; (ii), x, xv n., 89; 19, 170 sq.; 49 (i), 155 sq., 181–4; called Nâga or Mahânâga, 'the great elephant,' 10 (i), 77 n.; Sugata, title of B., 10 (i), 69, 94, 94 n.; (ii), x; 48, 514, 520, 531, 544; his title Tathâgata, 10 (i), 94 sq. n.; (ii), 14, 37, 39, 76–8; 11, 147 n.; 13, 82 sq. n.; 19, 167, 167 n.; 49 (ii), 133; *G*ina, name of a B., 10 (ii), x, 127, 186; 13, 91; 19, 275; 21, 8, &c.; 49 (i), 173; Sakyamuni, the Sakya sage, 10 (ii), x, 186; is a Sama*n*a, 10 (ii), xiv; is an ascetic or Muni, 10 (ii), xiv sq., 42; addressed as Sakka, 10 (ii), 58, 196, 202, 207 sq.; is the King of the Law (dharmarâ*g*an), 10 (ii), 102;

21, 58, 91, 122, 166, 244 sq., 275–7, 388; 35, 253 sq., 253 n.; called Tevigga, 'wise in the Vedas,' 11, 159; the good physician, 19, 170, 266, 276, 305, 315, 353; 21, 158, 277 sq., 310; 36, 8, 8 n., 10, 40; 49 (i), 145, 182; a saviour of mankind, 19, 291, 292 n., 350; the god over all gods (devâtideva), 19, 348; 21, xxv–xxviii, 301 n.; 35, 167, 300; 36, 12, 56, 83, 125, 215, 219, 274, 279, 281, 283, 285, 290 sq., 295, 298, 300–2, 305 sq., *305 n.*, 310, 312–5, 317, 319, 323–5, 327, 331, 337, 340 sq., 344–6, 352–4, 358, 363–365, 368; the term B. as used by Gainas and Buddhists, 22, xx, 264; 45, 45, 45 n.; calls himself a Brahman, and a king, 36, 8, 8 n., 10, 25–30.

(*b*) Appearance of a B. in the world.

Enjoyed the pleasures of heaven before he was born the last time, 10 (i), 35 n.; difficult is the birth of a B., 10 (i), 49, 52; 19, 369 sq.; 49 (ii), 69; his seven re-births before his last, 11, 288; is not subject to Nirvâ*n*a, but only produces a semblance of it, and he repeatedly appears in this world, 21, xxv sq.; has existed since time immemorial, is the Âdibuddha, 21, xxv sq., 154 sq., 154 n., 224 sq.; is unlimited in the duration of his life, he is ever lasting, 21, xxx, 298–310, 300 n.; appears in the world for the one object only, to open the eyes of creatures for the Tathâgata-knowledge, 21, 40; the self-born One, 21, 45–7, 114, 217 sq., 309 sq., 362, 440; the son of B. who has completed his course shall once be a Gina, 21, 48; he who knows the law of the Buddhas becomes a B., 21, 53; when one becomes B., then one will be completely extinct, 21, 63; has preached the law in thousands of worlds, 21, 242; beautiful visions of the preacher of the Lotus of the True Law, he sees himself as a future B., 21, 278–80; B. and the Bodhisattvas, 21, 294 sq., 297; his complete extinction a mere device, 21, 303–8; 'He will spread the bundle of grass on the terrace of enlightenment,' i. e. he will become a B., 21, 391 sq., 392 n.; how do you know that B. existed? 35, 109; 36, 206–43; why must there be only one B. at a time? 36, 47–51; *there is one being, O brethren, who is born into the world for the good and for the weal of the great multitudes, out of mercy to the world, for the advantage and the good and the weal of gods and men. And what is that being? A Tathâgata, an Arahat B. supreme*, 36, 56; a preacher of the Law becomes a B., 49 (i), 185, 187. *See also below* (*i*).

(*c*) Life of Gotama B. Sakyamuni.

Legends of B. and Zoroaster, 4, liii; the oldest version of the history of his life, 13, 73 sq. n.; lives of B. in Chinese translations, 19, xvi–xxx; B. and Mahâvîra contemporaries, 22, xvi; life of B. and life of Mahâvîra compared, 22, xvii sq.; B. gives Bimbisâra an account of his family, 10 (ii), 68 sq.; the Sama*n*a Gotama of the Sakya clan, 11, 169; *see also* Sakya; *S*âkyamuni, one of the sixteen sons of the B. Mahâbhi*g*ñâ*g*ñânâbhibhû, 21, 179; his connexion with the feudal aristocracy, a cause of his success, 22, xiii;—story of his conception and birth, 19, xix, 1–20; 49 (i), 1–16; thirty-two miraculous signs on the eve of B.'s birth, 19, 344 64; Asita's prophecy about the child, 10 (ii), 125–7; 19, 7–12; rejoicing of the gods at the birth of B., 10 (ii), 125; state of happiness in the country, after the birth of B., 19, 20–3;—the child B. consecrated king by water coming down from heaven, 19, 4; childhood of B., 19, 23; 49 (i), 17–20; the baby Gotama meditates in his cradle, 36, 143, 143 sq. n.; not hurt by falling from the roof of a pavilion, 49 (i), 22;—living as prince Gautama in the palace, 19, xx, 24–9; 49 (i), 20–6; palaces built and dancing women procured for the youth Bodhisattva, 19, 360 sq.; the prince not deluded by women, 19, 38–46; 49 (i), 36–48; seeing the women of his seraglio asleep, 36, 135 sq.; 49 (i), 56–9;—his excursion, and visions of old age, sickness, and death, 19, xx, 29–37;

49 (i), 27–35, 43; his vision of an ascetic, 19, xx, 49 sq.; 49 (i), 51 sq.; on seeing a piece of ploughed land he meditates on birth and death, 49 (i), 49–51; asks his father's permission to become a hermit, 19, 51–3; 49 (i), 53–5; his flight from home, 19, xx sq., 56–8; 49 (i), 59–62; after dismissing Kandaka with a message to his father, becomes a wandering mendicant, 19, 59–70; 36, 135 sq., 139; 49 (i), 62–9; cuts off his knot of hair, 19, 68; 49 (i), 68; obtains the hermit's dress, 19, 68 sq.; 49 (i), 68 sq.; takes rags from a dustheap, to make himself a dress, and god Sakka helps him to wash them, 13, 125; his meeting and discussions with the hermits in the Bhârgava hermitage, 19, 70–81; 49 (i), 70–8; lamentations in the palace on the news of his having become an ascetic, 19, 82–92; 49 (i), 79–91; Purohita and prime minister try to bring the prince back to his father, 19, 93–110; 49 (i), 91–103;—the people of Râ*g*agr*i*ha pay homage to B. going about as a mendicant, 19, 111–14; his meeting and conversations with King Bimbisâra at Râ*g*agr*i*ha, 10 (ii), 67–9; 13, 136–44; 19, 113–31; 49 (i), 104–22; his meeting and conversations with Ârâma or Arâ*d*a, and Udraka, 19, 131–42; 49 (i), 123–32; practises austerities for six years at the Nairañ*g*anâ, 19, xxi sq., 143–5; 49 (i), 132–4;—his words on the attainment of Buddhahood, 10 (i), 43 sq. n.; account of the events after his attaining Buddhahood, 13, 73–151; under the Bodhi-tree, 13, 73–8; 19, 146–65; 36, 27; 49 (i), 135–47, 159 sq.; under the A*g*apâla-tree, 13, 79 sq.; his conquest of Mâra, the tempter, 10 (i), 44 n.; (ii), 69–72; 13, 113 sq., 116; 19, xxii sq., 147–56; 35, 222 sq.; 36, 27, 211 sq.; 49 (i), 137–47; infinitely more powerful than Mâra, 35, 219–23; the food-offering of the shepherd girls to B. before reaching Bodhi, 19, 366 sq.; 35, 243, 245; reached full enlightenment, 21, 293 sq., 296, 298 sq., 301; 49 (i), 155 sq.; the attainment of Buddhahood was his ordination, 35, 118; though he had reached Buddhahood, B. devoted himself to meditation for three months, 35, 196–8; under the Mu*k*alinda-tree, protected by the Nâga king, 13, 80 sq.; 49 (i), 164 sq.; under the Râ*g*âyatana-tree, 13, 81–4; at the request of Brahmâ, the gods and former Buddhas, he resolves to preach the law ('turn the wheel of the law'), 13, 84–8; 19, 165–7; 21, 54–6; 49 (i), 168–73; why B., after attaining to omniscience, hesitated whether he should preach the Truth or not, 36, 38–42;—converts made by B., 10 (ii), 5, 14 sq., 23 sq., 29, 31, 42, 52, 79 sq., 85, 94 sq., 103–6, 117; 11, 79 sq., 108–10, 153, 155, 155 n., 203; 13, 84, 102–12, 116–34, 139 sq.; 17, 2–5, 96 sq., 108–17, 124–8, 135–9; 19, 168–201, 218, 226 sq., 240–6, 248; 35, 282 n.; 36, 247–50; 49 (i), 190–200; his disciples Sâriputta and Moggallâna, 10 (ii), 119 sq.; 13, 144–51; 35, 257 sq. and n., 301 sq.; dialogue between B. and Mâgandiya whose daughter he refuses, 10 (ii), 159–62; 36, 183; shed a golden light, when seeing the maturity of the minds of Pi*ṅ*giya and Bâvarî, 10 (ii), 212 sq. n.; his love for Ânanda, 11, 96 sq.; meets Upaka of the Â*g*îvika sect and declares himself to be the *G*ina, 13, 90 sq.; the five Bhikshus, who became his first disciples, 13, 90–102; 19, 142, 145, 168, 172–8, 180; 21, 56; 49 (i), 132 sq., 169, 171–3, 180; sends his disciples out to preach the Truth, 13, 112 sq.; 19, 183; the people of Magadha annoyed at B. on account of his making converts, reviled the Bhikkhus, 13, 150 sq.; visited by So*n*a Ku*t*ika*nn*a, 17, 33–40; at Ko*t*igâma, 17, 104–8; cured by *G*îvaka Komârabha*kk*a, 17, 191 sqq.; waits upon a sick Bhikkhu, 17, 240 sq.; wearied by the quarrelsome Bhikkhus of Kosambî, retires into solitude, 17, 312 sqq.; turns the 'Wheel of the Law,' 19, 168–79; B. and Anâthapi*nd*ika, 19, 201–18; 20, 183 sq.; and the courtesan Âmrapâlî, 19, 252–6, 266; his prophecies about his chief

disciples who are to become future Buddhas, 21, xxix, 142–52; dialogue between B. and Ânanda, 49 (ii), ix sq., 3–60; B. *S*âkyamuni shows to Ânanda the Buddha Amitâbha and Sukhâvatî, 49 (ii), x, 59–61; conversation between B. and Agita, 49 (ii), x, 61–9; at Râ*g*agr*i*ha, 49 (ii), 1 sq.; conversation between B. and *S*âriputra, 49 (ii), 91–102;—admonishes his son Râhula, 10 (ii), 55 sq.; ordination of his son Râhula, 13, 208–10; his meeting with his father and kinsmen, 19, 218–30; visits his home and parents, 49 (i), 195–200; ascends to heaven, to preach to his mother, 19, 240 sq. and n.; 49 (i), 200; (ii), vi; how he escapes the attacks of his wicked cousin Devadatta, 19, 246–9; 20, 238–50, 260 sq.; 35, 290; the splinter of rock hurting his foot, 35, 248–51; attacked by an elephant at Râ*g*agaha, 35, 297–300, 298 n.; Queen Vaidehî's vision of B., 49 (ii), 165;—at Pâ*t*aligâma or Pâ*t*aliputra, 17, 97–104; 19, 249–52; his prophecy about Pâ*t*aliputta, 17, 101 sq.;—the date of his death, 10 (i), xxxv–xlv; 11, xlv–xlviii; a dire sickness fell upon him during the rainy season, at Beluva, but by a strong will he keeps his hold on life so as not to depart, without taking leave from his disciples, 11, 35 sq.; eighty years of age, 11, 37; will not die, until the order of the brethren and sisters is established, and his religion fully proclaimed among men, 11, 43, 53; announces the time of his death, 11, 44, 54, 59, 61, 81 sq.; 19, 267–9, 274 sq.; 35, 199; his last illness caused by the meal of boar's flesh offered by *K*unda, the smith, 11, 72 sq.; 35, 242–6, 244 n.; his death, 11, 85–116, 238 sq.; 19, 307 sq.; before his death, addresses the brethren to utter any doubt they may have, but they are all silent, 11, 113 sq.; his last days, 19, 277–307, 365–71; comforts the Mallas who are grieved about his departure, 19, 288–90; his last words, 11, 114; 19, 306 sq.;—has completely left birth and death behind him and dispelled sin, 10 (ii), 58; how the remains of the Tathâgata are to be treated, 11, 91–3, 125 sq.; how the news of his death was received by gods and men, 11, 116–22; by the knowledge of the four noble truths, B. became free from rebirth, 11, 152 sq.; how the news of B.'s death was received by the Bhikkhus, 20, 370 sq.; his dead body saluted by women first, 20, 379; has passed away, but exists in his doctrine and discipline, 35, 113 sq., 149 sq. *See also* Bodhisattva.

(*d*) Bodily and mental characteristics of a B.

B. is bright with splendour day and night, 10 (i), 89; thirty-two signs of a great man possessed by B., 10 (ii), 67, 99–102, 187 sq.; 11, 64 n.; 19, 8 sq., 14, 95, 112 sq. and n., 229, 355–7, 359 sq.; 21, 47, 50, 189 sq., 194, 246 sq., 252 sq., 282, 364, 427, 436; 35, 116, 237; 36, 44; 49 (i), 11, 67, 77 sq., 87, 106, 191; (ii), 27, 36, 52, 74, 125, 140, 174, 174 n., 178, 180, 183; the colour of his skin becomes bright on the night of his attaining to perfect enlightenment, and on the night in which he passes away, 11, 81 sq., 82 n.; darts a flash of light from the circle of hair between his eyebrows, 21, 7, 393; 49 (ii), 166; is short of stature, 21, 395; bodily appearance of a B., 49 (ii), 3 sq.; not to be seen by the shape of his visible body, nor by signs, 49 (ii), 115, 137, 140; rays issue forth from his mouth, 49 (ii), 166 sq.; sixteen cubits high, 49 (ii), 186 sq., 187 n.;—the excellent qualities of B., 10 (ii), 25–7, 76–8; 11, 27; 17, 34; *Gotama . . . is said to be 'a fully enlightened one, blessed and worthy, abounding in wisdom and goodness, happy, with knowledge of the world, unsurpassed as a guide to erring mortals, a teacher of gods and men, a blessed B.,'* 11, 169, 187; leader and guide of gods and men, 19, 350, 362; 35, 167; 36, 55 sq., 83, 120; B. a wise father, his disciples are like sons to him, 21, xxix, 72–90, 108; is impartial, just as sun and moon shine over all beings alike, 21, 128, 136; his abode is kindness to all beings, his robe is

sublime forbearance, his pulpit is complete abstraction, 21, 222, 224; as a king, bestowing immense alms, 21, 243 sq.; compared to a physician, 21, 304–6, 309; 35, 116, 165, 168 sq., 240 sq.; is incomparable, 35, 109 sq.; how can B. be kind and pitiful and omniscient, and yet have admitted Devadatta to the Order, who created a schism, and had to suffer torments in hell for it? 35, 162–70; how B. could be free from all sins, and yet suffer bodily pain, 35, 190–5; the best of all the best in the world of gods and men, 35, 221; 36, 10–12, 12 n., 50; is free of all self-regard, he does not seek after a following, but the followers seek after him: in this sense he is a leader, 35, 225 sq.; the Bhikkhus who vomited blood on hearing B.'s discourse suffered harm by their own deeds, not by B., 35, 234–7; is perfect in courtesy of speech, 35, 237–41; did B. boast? 35, 253 sq.; cannot be angry, 35, 257–60; unmoved by temporary inconvenience, 36, 24; the eighteen characteristics of a B., 36, 135, 135 n.; loved his enemies as his only son, 36, 355; the B. only knows the virtues of a B., 49 (ii), 70; the sun-like B., 49 (ii), 166.

(*e*) TRANSCENDENT KNOWLEDGE AND MIRACULOUS POWERS OF A B.

B.-knowledge, B.-eye, 10 (ii), 63, 207 sq.; 11, 187; 13, 87 sq.; 49 (ii), 129 sq., 135; his power of prophecy, 11, 18 n.; 35, 5 sq.; knows Brahmâ, the world of Brahmâ, and the path which leads to it, 11, 185 sq.; possessed of ten Noble States, ten Powers (Balas), and ten attributes of Arhatship, and understands the ten Paths of Kamma, 13, 141 sq.; 36, 134 sq. and n.; 49 (i), 157, 157 n., 159 sq., 172; (ii), 22; knows the thoughts of others, 13, 248; 17, 7, 192; has no master, and his wisdom is self-taught, 19, 169 sq. and n.; 36, 43–6; his wonderful power of remembering the past, 21, xxix, 153 sqq.; his omniscience, 21, 118 sq., 120 sq.; 35, 116, 154–62, 270–3, 301 sq.; 36, 100, 109–11; 49 (i), 183; the sixfold and fourteen-fold knowledge of a B., 36, 134 sq., 135 n.; the four bases of confidence of a B., 36, 134, 134 n.; remembers his former births, 49 (i), 148;—food which can only be digested by B. or a disciple of B., 10 (ii), 14; no harm can be done to a B., 10 (ii), 30, 45 sq.; 35, 222; crosses the river Ganges miraculously, 11, 21; 17, 104; 19, 251 sq.; by his great and clear vision, sees fairies, 11, 18; 17, 101 sq.; might remain in this world throughout the Kalpa, 11, 41 sq., 54–8; 35, 198–201; an earthquake caused by the great events in the life of the B., 11, 47 sq.; his 'transfiguration,' 11, 82 n.; works miracles, 13, 119–34; 21, xxxi, 364–8; his miraculous power of transferring himself from one place to another, 13, 248 sq.; 17, 7, 9; heals the wound of Suppiyâ, who has cut her own flesh, 17, 83 sq.; Bela*tth*a's sugar, thrown into the water at B.'s order, hisses and bubbles and sends forth smoke, 17, 95; during the rainy season, B. with his Bhikkhus vanishes from *G*etavana and appears at the house of Visâkhâ, not a single Bhikkhu being wet from rain, 17, 219; his transcendental powers, 19, 318 sq.; 21, 30–7; his mystic trance, 21, 6 sq.; miracles allowed by B., 21, 421; the earth became smooth, when B. walked along it, 35, 248 sq.; why B. prefers not to work miracles, 36, 24 sq.; flies through the sky, 49 (i), 170.

(*f*) GOTAMA B. AS A PREACHER AND TEACHER.

His manner of teaching, 10 (ii), xiv–xvi; 13, 104 sq.; 17, 4, 96, 137, 330 sq.; 20, 183; 21, 18, 71 sq., 181–3, 187–9, 303 sq.; 35, 234–7; reproached by Bhâradvâga with idleness, explains his work as a kind of ploughing, 10 (ii), 12 sq.; rejects what is acquired by reciting stanzas, 10 (ii), 13, 78; preached to the eight kinds of assemblies and then vanished away, 11, 48 sq.; his teaching open to all, 11, 187; sends his earliest disciples out to preach his doctrine to all the world, 13, 112 sq.; his relations to other sects,

esp. the *G*ainas, 17, 108–17, 125; his tolerance, 17, 114–17; sermons of Buddha, 19, 186 sq., 190–2, 202–5, 222–4, 233–40, 253–6, 258–65, 270–4, 283–5, 296–305; allows the Bhikkhus to learn the word of the Buddhas each in his own dialect, 20, 150 sq.; the difference between B. and other teachers, 20, 235 sq.; his preaching is for the benefit of all creatures, as the rain pours down on all plants, 21, xxix, 119–27; creatures like blind-born men led to Nirvâ*n*a by B., 21, xxix, 129–41; preaches only after being asked thrice by *S*âriputra, 21, 36–8; means of his teaching: Sûtras, stanzas, *G*âtakas, parables, &c., 21, 44 sq.; whatever B. has spoken is true, 21, 301 sq., 309; deposits and entrusts his perfect enlightenment into the hands of the Bodhisattvas, 21, 440 sq.; his words many-sided, and apparently contradictory, 35, 137; why he did not answer certain questions, 35, 204–6; was in constant receipt of alms, 35, 219; sets rolling his royal chariot-wheel of righteousness, 35, 253, 253 n.; is lord of the Scriptures, 35, 302; pleased by parables, preached by himself, 35, 302; rules as to restraint with regard to food do not apply to a B. who has attained to perfection, 36, 6 sq., 7 n.; 'discovered a way that was unknown,' for the teaching of former Buddhas had been lost, 36, 13–16; begins his discourses by preaching the virtue of almsgiving, 36, 31–3.

(*g*) THE DHAMMA OR DOCTRINE OF B.

Nirvâ*n*a has been shown by B., 10 (i), 69; (ii), 39; against philosophy (di*tth*i, dar*s*ana), 10 (ii), xii; *see also* Philosophy; dialogue between the rich herdsman Dhaniya and B., the one rejoicing in worldly security, the other in his religious belief, 10 (ii), 3–5; a dialogue between a deity and B. on the things by which a man loses and those by which he gains in this world, 10 (ii), 17–19; his description of the Brâhma*n*as of old, 10 (ii), 48–52; explains the fate of Nigrodhakappa who had attained Nirvâ*n*a, 10 (ii), 57–60; explains the duties of Bhikkhus and householders, 10 (ii), 62–6; authorities for the true teaching of B., 11, 67–70; he alone discovered the four noble truths, 11, 150–2; states the characteristics of a true Brâhma*n*a, 13, 79 sq.; his sermon on 'The Burning,' 13, 134 sq.; 35, 234; gives an exposition of his moral teaching to the *G*aina Sîha, 17, 110–16; refuses to discuss questions of being and not-being, 19, 108 sq.; on the vanity of worldly life and pleasures, 19, 121–30; B. will perish, but the law is one and constant, 19, 274; his doctrine has only one flavour, the flavour of emancipation, 20, 304; 21, 120 sq., 124; 35, 131 sq.; his law is not to be found by reasoning, but must be learnt from the Tathâgata, 21, 39 sq.; announces final extinction for the education of creatures, though himself he does not become finally extinct, 21, 303 sq.; variety of Bauddha doctrines due either to the difference of the views maintained by B., or else to the difference of capacity on the part of the disciples of B., 34, 401; though he propounded the doctrine of the reality of the external world, was himself an Idealist, 34, 418; teaches three mutually contradictory systems, 34, 428; sayings of B. quoted, 35, 80, 102 sq., 115, 150, 170, 185–90, 194 sq., 198–201, 202, 204, 206, 224 sq., 229, 246, 251, 253 sq., 257 sq., 261, 264, 268 sq., 270 sq., 273 sq., 279, 294; 36, xxvi, 1–3, 4, 8, 10, 13, 16, 23, 25, 31, 43, 51, 54, 56, 60, 83 sq., 92, 125, 274, 279, 281, 283, 285, 290 sq., 295, 298, 300–2, 305 sq., 310, 312–15, 317, 319, 323–5, 327, 331, 337, 340 sq., 344–6, 352–4, 358, 363–5, 368; looks upon future life as dung, 35, 200 sq.; how could B. teach kindness towards all beings, and yet enjoin punishment for him who deserves it? 35, 254–7; did not teach for the sake of gifts, yet he recommends first of all almsgiving, 36, 31–8; his attitude towards asceticism, 36, 60–2; fools cannot realize the religion of B., 36, 71 sq.; sub-

jects for meditation taught by B., 36, 212 sq.; the ninefold word of the B., 36, 230, 236, 238, 246, 274, 290 sq., 306; taught the Akriyâvâda, Mahâvîra the Kriyâvâda, 45, xvi; the arguments of B. and others contradictory, 48, 425 sq.; four classes of followers of B., viz. Vaibhâshikas, &c., 48, 500, 510, 514; theory of nothingness his real view, 48, 515; on the soul, 48, 544; B.'s desire is, that there may be no fresh birth, 49 (i), 73, 76 sq.; Klesas, Mâras, ignorance, and Âsravas conquered by B., 49 (i), 160; describes the wheel of the law, 49 (i), 180 sq.; B. instructs Subhûti on the path of Bodhisattvas, 49 (ii), 112–44; no-origin the highest goal of B., 49 (ii), 133. *See also* Buddhism, Dhamma, *and* Morality.

(*b*) B. AND HIS ORDER.

Explains his relation to the order of mendicants, after his death each Bhikkhu should be a leader to himself, 11, 36–9, 112; gives up holding the Uposatha and reciting the Pâtimokkha himself, 20, 306; his strong reluctance to admit women into the order, 20, 320–6; the Sûtra must not be taught to fools, 21, 91 sq., 95–7; *it may be, Ânanda, that in some of you the thought may arise: 'The word of the Master is ended. We have no teacher more!' But it is not thus, Ânanda, that you should regard it. The Truth which I have preached to you, the Rules which I have laid down for the Order, let them, when I am gone, be the Teacher to you*, 35, 150; B. and the Order, as parents and children, or as a king and his servants, 36, 52–4. *See also* Sa*m*gha.

(*i*) DEIFICATION AND WORSHIP OF B.

The law of the well-awakened B. to be worshipped, 10 (i), 90; whosoever reviles B. or his disciple is an outcast, 10 (ii), 22; worship of B., 10 (ii), 28 sq.; 11, xviii; 19, 337 sq.; 35, 151; 49 (i), 166 sq.; worship of B. and Dhamma, 10 (ii), 29, 31; 19, xxvii; worship of B., Dhamma, and Sa*m*gha, *see* Jewels (the three); the eight persons praised by the righteous, they are worthy of offerings, being Sugata's disciples, 10 (ii), 38; deserves the oblation, 10 (ii), 76–8; B. praised, 10 (ii), 93 sq., 96, 99, 101 sq., 106, 110, 180, 186, 195, 204 sq., 207, 209–11; 13, 136; 17, 124 sq., 129 sq.; 21, 116 sq.; 36, 239–42; 49 (ii), 3–5; the reference to worship of relics in the Mahâ-parinibbâna-sutta, as a possible basis for chronological argument, 11, xv, xvii sq.; the places of his birth, &c., are places of pilgrimage, 11, 90 sq.; a Tathâgata or Arahat-Buddha is worthy of a dâgaba, 11, 93 sq.; relics of B. claimed by kings and peoples, 11, 131–6; 19, 325–35; praised as the Saviour of mankind by gods and Nâgas, 19, 153–5; to meditate on B., a moral precept, 19, 235; to one who follows the teaching of B., B. is ever near, 19, 289 sq.; hymns of praise in honour of the departed B., 19, 310–22; the bones of B.'s body preserved as relics, 19, 324 sq.; relics of B. placed on the head as a token of reverence, 19, 334; when in the world, B. brought deliverance to all, and so do his relics after his Nirvâ*n*a, 19, 337; worship of relics of B., 19, 337; 21, 50–2, 96, 403; 35, 144–54, 246–8; *see also* Stûpas; his counterpart, Nârâya*n*a, as the Highest Brahman, 21, xxvii sq.; is an ideal, a personification, and not a person, 21, xxviii; heavenly flowers fall, and the Buddha-fields tremble when he meditates, 21, 6 sq.; as a father of the world, 21, 76 sq., 76 n., 88–90, 309; punishments in hell and transmigration of those who scorn his doctrine, 21, 92–5; as a creator, 21, 238 sq., 238 n., 300 n.; the master of the world, worshipped by men and gods, 21, 258; is the one and everlasting Brahma, 21, 301 n., 310 n.; if B. has passed away entirely, how can he accept gifts and worship of his relics? 35, 144–54; the footprint of B., 19, 244; 36, 241, 241 n.; immense merit acquired by those who believe in, and read, preach, copy, keep, and worship the Sûtra setting forth the duration of life of B., 21, xxx, 311–27; making images

of B., a great merit, 21, 50 sq.; Buddhists live as under the eye of the B., 35, 110; a wicked man who thinks of B. in the hour of death will be reborn among the gods, 35, 123 sq.; he who gives to B. a handful of lotuses, will not enter purgatory for 91 Kalpas, 35, 129; does not accept gifts, yet gifts made to him bear fruit, 35, 146 sq., 150 sq.; worship paid to the bowl of Buddha, 35, 248 n.; the gods infused the Sap of Life into his dish, 36, 37 sq., 37 n.; he who has wounded a B. cannot be converted, 36, 78 n.; how gifts to B. were rewarded, 36, 147; the Arhat B. surpasses the Creator, and sun and moon, 49 (i), 1; praised by all kinds of superhuman beings, 49 (i), 145 sq., 157–9; relics of B., and *K*aityas, 49 (i), 166 sq.; *S*âkyamuni seen by the beings in Sukhâvatî, 49 (ii), 61; beings born in Sukhâvatî through hearing B.'s name, 49 (ii), 65; *S*âkyamuni glorified by other Buddhas, 49 (ii), 102; prayers addressed to B., 49 (ii), 162, 164; how to perceive B. with one's mind, 49 (ii), 178.

(*j*) Plurality of Buddhas.

The moral teaching of all the B., 10 (i), 50; B. are worshipped, 10 (i), 52; 21, 409 sq.; 49 (i), 188 sq.; (ii), 16 sq., 53 sq.; are free from vanity and are never shaken, 10 (i), 63; *you yourself must make an effort, the Tathâgatas are only preachers*, 10 (i), 67; B. reject what is acquired by stanzas, 10 (ii), 13, 78; the Tathâgatas act with a purpose, 10 (ii), 58; appear seldom in the world, 10 (ii), 103; 11, 104, 186 sq.; 21, 423 sq.; speak nothing untrue, 11, 2; Buddha termed the successor of the B. of old, 21, 86 sq.; B. of the past, present, and future, 11, 13 sq., 97; 35, 138; 49 (ii), 148, 154, 168; their word enduring for ever, 11, 233; they sometimes ask questions about what they know, in order to preach or institute a rule, 13, 176, 327; 17, 69, 141 sq.; the Bodhisattva remembers former B., 19, 50; 49 (i), 162; miracles at the birth of former B., 19, 146; 49 (i), 7; all B. or *G*inas of past ages have 'gone out as a lamp,' 19, 275; *K*aityas in honour of former B., 19, 323; the seven supreme B. worshipped in a snake-charm, 20, 77, 77 n.; cannot be deprived of life by violence, their death is natural, 20, 247; Bodhisattvas who had propitiated hundred thousands of B., 21, 3; B. who had reached final Nirvâ*n*a, became visible in the Buddha-fields, 21, 8, 10; how they preach in numerous Buddha-fields, 21, 10 sq.; miracles always appear when B. are about to preach, 21, 16–29; appearing like golden columns, &c., 21, 24 sq.; disciples of Buddha shall become B. in the future, 21, 45 sq., 59, 89, 112–15, 128, 189 sq.; all former B., many thousands in number, taught only one vehicle, 21, 49, 53; the former B. encourage Buddha to preach the law, 21, 55 sq.; the B. have spoken in many mysteries, 21, 59; Bodhisattvas will in future be B., 21, 60; their thirty-two characteristics, 21, 62 sq.; men who think of becoming B. themselves, compared to the highest plants, 21, 126; a thousand less four B. have to appear in the Bhadrakalpa, 21, 193; the seven Tathâgatas, the seventh being Buddha himself, 21, 193; by the power of Buddha there appear the Tathâgata-frames in thousands of Buddha-fields, all preaching the law, 21, 231 sqq.; all the Buddha-frames are Buddha's own proper bodies, 21, 238, 300 n.; the wise preacher must always think 'How can I and these beings become B.?' 21, 270; the preacher must always feel towards B. as if they were his fathers, 21, 271, 273; the apparition of the B. tends to the welfare of men, 21, 303 sq.; future and past B. will be seen by him who promulgates the Lotus of the True Law, 21, 369; Buddhist theory of former B., and *G*aina theory of Tîrthakaras, 22, xxxiv sq.; B. or Tathâgatas used in the sense of Tîrthakaras, 22, 32; 45, 314 sq., 314 n., 320, 320 n., 332; the relics of B. are worshipped not

for the benefit of the B., but of the worshippers, 35, 144–54; the thinking powers of B. and Pa*kk*eka-Buddhas, 35, 158–60; it was their custom to keep the Pâtimokkha secret, 35, 265 sq.; they are above the law, 36, 7, 7 n.; Buddha supreme, compared with the Pa*k*-*k*eka-Buddhas, 36, 13 n.; the teaching of the former B. was entirely lost when Buddha rediscovered it, 36, 13–16; always proclaim the Truth at the request of Brahmâ, 36, 41 sq.; Buddhas, Pa*kk*eka-Buddhas, and disciples of Buddha, 36, 101; there are B. and Pa*kk*eka-Buddhas in the world, 36, 101; all B. are alike in all the Buddha-qualities, 36, 133–5; preaching enjoined for them, 36, 357; throwing open the door for the immortals and B., 40, 283; Tathâgatas cannot be born again, 45, 332; list of Tathâgatas, 49 (ii), 66 sq., 99–101; three former B., 49 (i), 172; multitudes of sons of the *G*inas and Suras, 49 (i), 173; eighty-one Tathâgatas beginning with Dîpaṅkara and ending with Loke*s*vara-râ*g*a, 49 (ii), ix, 6 sq.; requested to turn the wheel of the law, 49 (ii), 26; proceed from rays sent out by lotus-flowers, 49 (ii), 36; glorify Amitâbha, 49 (ii), 45; of the ten quarters, 49 (ii), 181, 184, 189; the former Buddha Dîpaṅkara prophesies that *S*âkyamuni will become a B., 49 (ii), 133, 133 n.; the Buddha Kassapa, *see under* Kassapa. *See also* Holy persons, Pa*kk*eka-Buddhas, *and* Pratyeka-Buddhas.

Buddhabhadra, translator of the Kwo-hu-yin-ko-king, 19, xxv.

Buddha-countries, *see* Buddha-fields.

Buddhadâsa, the Buddhist Suttas translated from Pali into Singhalese, in his reign, 10 (i), xiv.

Buddha-fields, or Buddha-countries (Sk., Buddhakshetra), tremble when Buddha enters on his meditation, 21, 6 sq., 9, 20, 24; become illuminated by the light proceeding from Buddha's eyebrow, 21, 7–9, 20 sq., 24; description of B., 21, 66–9, 142–51, 194 sq., 197, 206 sq., 232–5, 238 sq., 308, 321, 429; Buddhas appearing in myriads of B., 21, 232; Loke*s*vararâ*g*a teaches the excellences of B., 49 (ii), ix sq., 10; Dharmâkara describes his B., 49 (ii), ix sq., 10–22; in the six or ten quarters, 49 (ii), 99–101, 173; Buddha shows them to Queen Vaidehî, 49 (ii), 166. *See also* Saha-world, *and* Sukhâvatî.

Buddhaghosa, commentator of the Tipi*t*aka, 10 (i), xii; consulted old Pali MSS., 10 (i), xiii sq.; his age, 10 (i), xiv–xxvi, xxxix; account of B. given in the Mahâva*m*sa, 10 (i), xxi sqq.; his Sumaṅgala-Vilâsinî, commentary on the Mahâparinibbâna-Sutta, 11, xxxi sq.; his references to the Milindapa*ñ*ha, 35, xiv–xvi.

Buddha*g*îva translated the Vinaya into Chinese, 19, xxvi.

Buddha-*k*arita, Chinese translation by Dharmaraksha, 19, ix; titles of chapters in the Sanskrit B., and in the Chinese translation, 19, 340–3; translated, *vol.* 49 (i); A*s*vaghosha, the author of it, 49 (i), ix sq.; Sanskrit text of it, 49 (i), ix, xii; Chinese and Tibetan translation of the B., 49 (i), x sq.; its influence on the classical Sanskrit poetry, 49 (i), xi sq.

Buddhakshetra, *see* Buddha-fields.

Buddhava*m*sa, t.w., the preaching of it at Kapila-vatthu, 36, 249.

Buddhi, Sk., t.t., intellect, intelligence, various meanings of the term, 8, 11, 440 sq.; 34, lv sqq.; 38, 436; 48, 786; difference between manas and b., 15, xiv, xiv n. *See* Intelligence.

Buddhism.

(*a*) Its doctrines.
(*b*) Its history.

(*a*) ITS DOCTRINES.

Buddhist technical terms, 10 (i), liii–lv; 49 (ii), 39 sq., 96, 96 n., 171, 174; the four noble truths and the eightfold path, 10 (ii), 44; 19, 175–7, 200, 224, 305; 21, 18, 90 sq., 172 sq., 185, 354 sq.; 36, 6, 245 n.; 49 (i), 175 sq.; (ii), 148, 154, 193; the original doctrine of B., as contained in Pali Suttas, 11, xx–xxii; summary of B., its chief

doctrines, 11, 60–3, 65, 116 sq., 117 n.; 13, 146; 19, 202–5, 292–5; 20, 305, 329 sq.; 35, 66 sq.; 36, 6, 47, 137, 207 sq., 218, 232 sq., 264 sq., 267, 303 sq., 304 n., 321 sq., 365; 49 (i), 13 sq.; (ii), 171, 174, 193; a system of earnest self-culture and self-control, 11, 62 n.; central doctrine of B., 11, 143 sq.; B. not monotheistic, 11, 164 sq.; declared in one stanza, 13, 146; 19, 194, 194 n.; to escape old age, disease, and death, the chief aim of B., 19, 16–18, 32–7, 41 sq., 44–9, 51 sq., 58, 94, 99, 103, 121, 128 sq., 133 sq., 136 sq., 143, 160–2, 176 sq., 203–5, 224, 236, 265, 280 sq., 337 sq., 371; 35, 273, 275, 278; 49 (i), 27–35, 43, 46 sq., 51, 54, 96 sq., 120, 124; the principal tenets of B. as conceived by Buddha under the Bodhi-tree, 19, 160–3; *the light of a lamp in a dark room lights up equally objects of all colours, so it is with those who devote themselves to religion—there is no distinction between the professed disciple and the unlearned*, 19, 239; three principal doctrines of B., 34, 401; teaches the eternal flux of everything that exists, 34, 403 n.; denies authoritativeness of Scripture, 34, 412; summary of B. as learnt by Nâgasena, 35, 21 sq.; psychology of B., 35, 86–99, 132–4; worshippers of Buddha like trees with the trunk of contemplation, &c., 35, 151; a Buddhist confession of faith, 36, 55, 55 sq. n.; the religion of the Conquerors is not put to shame by backsliding, 36, 63–75; a tank full of the waters of emancipation, 36, 63 sq., 66 sq.; five good qualities of the religion of the Conquerors, 36, 69–72; its doctrines illustrated by the parable of the city of Righteousness, 36, 208–43; sorrow, and the path that leads to cessation of sorrow, 36, 345; the stages of the Excellent Way and the six modes of Insight, 36, 360; philosophical doctrines of B., 36, 361 sq., 362 sq. n.; on the Self and new sense-organs in a new body, 38, 103 sq.; denies the existence of a separate Âtman, 45, 399 n.; doctrine of B. that sins are only committed by conscious acts, refuted, 45, 414–17; the theory of a universal Nothing is the real purport of B., 48, 514; the chain of causation, 49 (i), 177–9; the rewards of teaching and spreading the Law, 49 (i), 184–9; the ideal of B. as represented by the beings in Sukhâvatî, 49 (ii), 55–9. *See also* Buddha (*g*), Dhamma, Jewels (the three), *and* Philosophy.

(*b*) ITS HISTORY.

Introduction of B. into China, 3, xiii, xiii n.; influence of B. on Tâoism, 3, xxii; 39, xi sq., 1–3, 23, 33, 42–4, 129, 131, 155, 197 n., 313 n.; 40, 139 n., 238 n., 266; legends of B. applied to Lâo-ȝze, 39, 35 n.; the 'three jewels' of B. and of Tâoism, 39, 111; transrotation of births in Tâoism and B., 39, 150; 40, 10 n.; the 'Extinction' of the Buddhists and the Doing Nothing of the Tâoists, 40, 288; by mastering the mysteries of the Tâo, the Mahâyâna will be understood, 40, 293;—Zoroastrianism and B., 4, liii sq., 209 n.; B. in Iran, 4, liv;—date of B. and Yogasûtras, 8, 9 n.; relation between Bhagavadgîtâ and B., 8, 23–7, 36, and notes to pp. 45–52, 56, 59 sq., 62–6, 68–71, 79, 84, 88 sq., 101, 103, 105, 108 sq., 111 sq., 114, 118, 123; Sanatsugâtîya prior to B., 8, 147; relation of Anugîtâ to B., 8, 212–15, 225 sq., 306 n., 376 n.; Buddhist sects, 8, 213; 19, xi–xvi; 34, 15 n.; *see also* Yogâkâras; Buddhist councils, 10 (i), xii–xlv; 13, xxi–xxiii; 19, 335; 35, 204, 204 n.; the First Council not mentioned in the Mahâparinibbâna-Sutta, 11, xi–xv; the date of the Council of Vesâli, 11, xix n.; Council of Pâtaliputra, 19, xii sq., xvi, xxxvii; the first Council under the presidency of Ânanda, 19, 335 sq., 335 n.; 'The Recitation,' i.e. the Council of Râgagaha, 35, 242, 242 n.; the Council of Kanishka did not establish a new canon, 36, xvi sq.;—Southern and Northern Church, their difference with regard to mystical powers, 11, 207–9; the germs of B. in the Upanishads, 15, xxvii, li sq.; Mahâ-

yâna, Hînayâna, Vaipulya, 19, x sq.; 49 (ii), ix; periods of development of Northern B., 19, x–xvi; how far the Saddharmapu*nd*arîka represents orthodox B., 21, xxviii sq.; political reasons for its success, 22, xiii sq.; relation between B. and *G*ainism, 22, xviii–xxxv; its doctrines refuted, 34, xxvi, li, 340, 400–28; prophecies as to the duration of B., 35, 185–90; 49 (i), 13 sq.; there is no esoteric B., 35, 264–8, 264 sq. n., 267 sq. n.; the Pâtimokkha kept secret, in order that the Dhamma may not be treated shamefully, 35, 266 sq.; corrupt B. of Nepal and Tibet, 36, 7 n.; ceremonies in Mahâyâna B., 49 (i), 199; doctrines of B. (Bauddhas and *G*â*n*ayas) refuted, 45, ix, 238, 242 sq.; Buddhist views on the origination of the world refuted, 48, 500–16; to be rejected by the Vedântin, 48, 520, 531. *See also* Buddhists.

Buddhist canon, *see* Tipi*t*aka.

Buddhist Church, *see* Sa*m*gha.

Buddhist Laymen dedicate Vihâras and other edifices to the Bhikkhus, 13, 302–5; proceedings against a Bhikkhu who gives offence to a layman, 17, 359–69; proceedings of the Sa*m*gha against them, 'turning the bowl down,' 20, 119–25; are given to lucky phrases (maṅgalikâ), 20, 153; judges between Bhikkhus, 20, 388–93; a Pâ*t*aliputta merchant studies the Abhidhamma, 35, 27 sq.; B. l. attain to comprehension of the truth without having renounced the world, 35, 31 sq.; different classes of B. l., 35, 229; superiority of Bhikkhus to laymen, 35, 229–33; become Arahats, 36, 56–8, 96–8; a layman who has committed a Pârâgika offence cannot comprehend the truth nor aspire to Arahatship, 36, 78–81, 78 n.; attain to Nirvâ*n*a, 36, 244–50, 253–5.

Buddhist mendicants or monks, *see* Bhikkhus, *and* Sama*n*as.

Buddhist nuns, *see* Bhikkhunîs.

Buddhist Order, *see* Sa*m*gha.

Buddhists mentioned in the Yâ*gñ*avalkya-sm*ri*ti, 7, xxi; perhaps mentioned in the Vish*n*u-sm*ri*ti, 7, xxix sq., 202, 202 n.; in China and Japan, 11, 245 sq.; 49 (ii), v; persecuted by Pushyamitra, 19, xv; different classes of B., 21, 125 sq.; controversies with Gaotema, the heretic, i.e. with B., 23, 184, 184 n.; are atheists, 25, 31 n.; B. and Brâhma*n*as, both reformers, 36, 127 sq. n.; their accounts of *G*ainas and A*k*elakas, 45, xvii–xxxii; doctrines which they owe to the 'heretics,' 45, xxvii–xxix; perhaps meant by Pa*ñk*aku*s*îla, 45, 80 n.; say 'pleasant things (môksha) are produced from pleasant things (comfortable life),' 45, 269, 269 n.; as Akriyâvâdins, refuted, 45, 316, 316 n.; Crypto-B. who take shelter under a pretended Vedic theory, 48, 513.

Buddhist Sacred Books, Chinese translations of, 3, xiii, xiii n.; 49 (ii), vi sq., xiii, xxi sq., xxiv sq., 73 sq.; Buddha not the author of the Pali Suttas, 11, xx; in the Vinaya also, as in the Sutta Pi*t*aka, Buddha himself is the actor and speaker, 13, xvii sqq.; the council of Vesâlî, and the date of the Vinaya Pi*t*aka, 13, xxi–xxiii; Sûtra Pi*t*aka settled in the first Council by Ânanda, 19, 335; example of the style of the expanded Sûtras, as translated into Chinese, 19, 344–64; the same title given to different works in Chinese translations, 19, 364; which was the oldest language of the B. S. B.? 21, xiv–xviii; their vocabulary and that of the *S*atapatha-Brâhma*n*a, 21, xvi sq.; the nine divisions in them, 21, 44 sq., 45 n.; their relation to Mahâbhârata and Manu-sm*ri*ti, 25, xci n.; at the council held for the fixing of the Scriptures, elders were in doubt about the minor and lesser regulations, 35, 204, 204 n.; the Atharva-veda in the B. S. B., 42, lvi; information about *G*ainas in B. S. B., 45, xv–xxiii; works ascribed to Buddha by Buddhists in Japan, 49 (ii), vi; date of Mahâyâna-sûtras, 49 (ii), xxi–xxiii; list of B. S. B., 49 (ii), xxiv–xxvi; Mahâyâna-sûtras, and Vaipulya-sûtras, 49 (ii), 102 sq., 188, 190, 195; meritoriousness of studying, hearing, and teaching Mahâyâna-sûtras, 49 (ii),

126–32, 168, 188, 190, 195; twelve divisions of Mahâyâna books, 49 (ii), 186, 195 sq. *See also* Tipi*t*aka.

Budha, Purûravas, son of, 44, 69 n.; begotten by the Moon, 49 (i), 45.

Budha Âtreya, author of Vedic hymns, 46, 364.

Bu*d*ila Â*s*vatara*s*vi, n. of a teacher, 1, 84, 87; 15, 199; 26, 425; 43, 393, 395.

Bû*g*i, n. of a Daêva, 23, 49 sq., 49 n.

Bû*g*isravah, n.p., 23, 205, 205 n.

Bû*g*ra, son of Dâzgarâspa, 23, 209.

Bûidhi, n. of a demon, 4, 145 sq.

Buildings, *see* Architecture, House, *and* Vihâras.

Bûiti, the Daêva, sent to kill Zarathu*s*tra, 4, liii, 208–10; a personification of Buddhism, 4, 209 n.; in a list of Daêvas, 4, 224. *See also* Bût.

Bûkht-Narsîh, i.e. Nebuchadnezzar, q.v.

Bulis of Allakappa claim relics of Buddha, and erect a dâgaba, 11, 132.

Bull declares the Brahman to Satyakâma, 1, 61; the storm-floods of the heavenly b. as urine, 4, lxxv; glorification of the b. (primaeval b., or species of the b.), 4, 231, 231 n., 249; 23, 93, 350; the primaeval b., *see under* Animals (*i*); the ceremony of setting a b. at liberty (*vri*shotsarga), 7, 260–3; 29, 100 sq., 353–5; 33, 162, 162 n.; priests of Asuras kill Manu's b., 12, 29; represents Indra, 12, 416; Fravashi of the b. worshipped, 23, 200; leading round a b., 29, 249; consecrated hairs of the tail of a white b. used at sacrifices, 31, 349; b. among the cows (storm among the clouds), 32, 63, 73; simile of the b., 36, 333 sq.; a b. set at liberty as sacrificial fee, 41, 45 sq., 56, 61; a b. is the Pragâpati among the cows, 41, 58; is Indra's own animal, 41, 60; one of the five sacrificial animals, 41, 162, 165 sq.; is eight-hoofed, 41, 177; the b. is vigour, 43, 38 sq.; origin of the b., 44, 215; has an excrescence or hump, 44, 276; *see also* Ox;—'a bull's hide' as a measure, 7, 272, 272 n.; b.'s hide used for auspicious rites, esp. at weddings, 29, 41, 171, 181, 247 sq., 285, 383; 30, 47, 50, 193 sq., 263; 42, 185, 645;—*bull's urine* (*gômêz*) as a means of purification, 4, lxxiii, lxxv, lxxv n., lxxix, 63 sq., 63 n., 79, 81 n., 91 sq., 93, 98 sq., 106, 107 n., 120 sq., 124 n., 125 n., 126–31, 188, 216 sq. and n., 278 n., 279; 5, lxxiii, 262, 269 sq., 270 n., 272 sq., 279, 281 sq., 333, 348 sq., 348 n.; 18, 162 n., 171, 171 n., 284 n., 305, 307–13, 309 n., 310 n., 317, 331, 339 sq., 358, 360, 365, 433–7, 433 n., 445, 447, 449, 451–5, 457; 23, 336; 24, 60 n., 297 n., 337 n., 340 n.; 37, 126, 480 sq. *See also* Nîrang.

Bundahi*s*, its title and contents, 5, xxii–xxiv, xxxv–xxxvii, xliv sq.; called Zand-âkâs, 5, xxiii, 3, 3 n.; a translation or epitome of the Dâmdâ*d* Nask, 5, xxiv, 177 sq. n., 181 n.; 37, 14 n., 465, 465 n.; MSS. and recensions of the B., 5, xxiv–xliii, 2; translations of the B., 5, xxv–xxvii, xliii–xlv; its date, 5, xli–xliii, xlvii; 18, xxvii; translated, 5, 1–151; paraphrased by Zâ*d*-sparam, 5, 153; written after Alexander, 37, 437, 447; chronology of the B., 47, xxvii–xxxv, xxxviii.

Bûr*g*, the angel, co-operator with Tî*s*tar, 5, 26, 169; rouses the bird *K*âmrô*s*, 5, 70.

Burial-ground, *see* Cemetery.

Burial-mounds, *see* Stûpas.

Burma, the Dhammathats or lawbooks of, 33, 275 sq.

Bûshâsp, demon of slothfulness, 5, 110, 366, 366 n.; 18, 93, 95.

Bûshyâsta, spell against the long-handed gaunt B., 4, 145 sq.; demon of sleep and laziness, 4, 197, 197 n., 199; 23, 323; 31, 346 n.; flees from Mithra, 23, 144, 155; the yellow B. destroyed by Aryan Glory, 23, 284.

Bût, Zd. Bûiti, the demon (Bhûta) 'whom they worship among the Hindûs,' 5, 111, 111 n. *See* Bûiti.

Bûtâsp, the Bodhisattva, 4, liii.

Byârshan, king of Iran, 23, 222, 222 n., 303.

C

Calamities (such as drought, &c.) brought about by the defilement of water or fire, 4, 82, 82 n.

Calendar, *see* Time.

Calf, first-born, as priest's fee, 12, 373, 390; c. of eighteen months, 43, 39; white c. of black cow, 43, 200.

Calumny, and false accusation against a Guru, are mortal sins, 2, 281; the sin of accusing a Brâhma*n*a, 2, 282; 14, 122; guilt incurred by false accusation, 17, 135; 14, 107; penance for falsely accusing a Guru, 14, 114; punishments for calumniating a bride or a suitor, 33, 172.

Capital punishment, *see* Punishments.

Carpenter, simile of the, 35, 96; the house of a c. the resting-place of the sacrificial horse, 44, 360.

Carriage, *see* Chariot.

Cart, *see* Chariot.

Caste, castes.

(*a*) Mutual relation of the c., their duties and occupations.
(*b*) Brâhma*n*as and Kshatriyas.
(*c*) Kshatriyas and Vai*s*yas.
(*d*) The twice-born c. or Âryans.
(*e*) Low c. and outcasts.
(*f*) Mixture of c., mixed c.
(*g*) Religious view of c.
(*h*) Religious rites different according to c.
(*i*) The c. and the law.
(*j*) C. disregarded.

(*a*) MUTUAL RELATION OF THE C., THEIR DUTIES AND OCCUPATIONS.

The Brâhma*n*a is one of Soma's mouths, with which he eats the Kshatriyas; the Kshatriya is one of Soma's mouths, with which he eats the Vai*s*yas, 1, 287; initiation, study of the Veda, and kindling the sacred fire ordained for the three higher c., to serve the other c. the duty of the *S*ûdra, 2, 1 sq.; occupations of c. in times of distress, 2, lvi sq., 211–14; 14, 20, 235 sq.; 25, 420–30; respect due to members of different c., 2, 48; 25, 53, 53 n., 55, 58; difference of c. with regard to the rules about saluting, 2, 53, 209 sq., 209 n.; 25, 52 sq.; lawful and unlawful occupations for members of the four c., 2, 123 sq., 211–14, 227–34, 234 n.; 7, 13, 136 sq., 189; 10 (ii), 112, 116 sq.; 14, 11–18, 20, 175 sq.; 25, lxxii, 325–7, 419, 499; 29, 124; 33, 54–8, 68 n.; 35, 247 sq.; precedence among the various c., 2, 125 sq., 125 n.; a king shall choose his officers from the three higher c., 2, 163; *all men must serve those who belong to higher c.*, 2, 234; the c. of Kâyasthas or scribes, 7, xxiv, xxx, 46; duties of the four c., and law regarding the relation between them, 7, 12 sq., 27–9; 8, 126 sq.; 14, 199; 25, xii, 1, 24 sq., 27, 32 sq., 400–2, 416, 478; 25, cvn.; *a Brâhmana, though only ten years old, and a member of the kingly c., though a hundred years old, must be considered as father and son; and of these two, the Brâhmana is the father. The seniority of Brâhmanas is founded upon sacred knowledge; of Kshatriyas, upon valour in arms; of Vaisyas, upon grain and* (*other*) *wealth; of Sûdras, upon* (*priority of*) *birth*, 7, 131; a rich man surrounded and waited upon by a crowd of Brâhmans, Kshatriyas, Vai*s*yas, and *S*ûdras, 21, 101; king the protector of the system of c., 7, 14; 25, 221; the peculiar laws of c. to be observed in the absence of special rules of revealed texts, 14, 4, 4 n.; *a Kshatriya shall pass through misfortunes which have befallen him by the strength of his arms, a Vaisya and a Sûdra by their wealth, the chief of the twice-born by muttered prayers and burnt-oblations*, 14, 129; 25, 436; *S*ûdras created to serve the Brâhma*n*as, 25, 326; Brâhma*n*as may appropriate property from Vai*s*yas and *S*ûdras for sacred purposes, 25, 432 sq.; the law protects the four c., 33, 8; usury allowed for Vai*s*yas, but not for Brâhma*n*as, 33, 68; a Kulika, head of a caste, 33, 89 n.; Sâgala crowded with Brâhmans, nobles, artificers, and servants, 35, 3; Vai*s*ya and *S*ûdra surrounded by Kshatriya and Brâhma*n*a, 41, 227; *S*ûdra, Râga, Brâhman, 42, 72; people, as compared with nobles and Brâhma*n*as, are like iron, as compared with gold and silver, 44, 339, 339 n.; minstrels, harlots, gamblers, eunuchs are to be neither *S*ûdras nor Brâhma*n*as, 44, 417; Brâhma*n*as, Kshatriyas, Vai*s*yas, *K*â*nd*âlas, Vukkasas, hunters, merchants, *S*ûdras, 45, 301.

(*b*) BRÂHMA*N*AS AND KSHATRIYAS.

Agâta*s*atru, the Kshatriya, teaches the Brâhma*n*a Gârgya Bâlâki, 1, 306; 15, 100 n., 103; a Brâhma*n*a of ten

years to be considered as the father of a Kshatriya of a hundred years, 2, 53; Kshatriyas, when assisted by Brâhma*n*as, do not fall into distress, 2, 236; *Brâhmanas, united with Kshatriyas, uphold gods, manes, and men*, 2, 238; Brâhma*n*as are lords over all other c., 7, 215; Gâyatrî = Brâhma*n*as, Trish*t*ubh = Kshatriyas, 12, 96; Kshatriyas and Brâhma*n*as represented by Indra and Agni, 12, 419; 26, 362; 44, xxii; etiquette between Brâhma*n*a and king, 15, 162 sq.; a Kshatriya sage teaches a Brâhma*n*a, 15, 204 sqq.; Kshatriyas and Brâhmans are fixed in Prâ*n*a, 15, 275; the monastical order of *G*ainas and Buddhists chiefly intended for Kshatriyas, not for Brâhma*n*as, 22, xxx sq.; the embryo of Mahâvîra removed from the southern Brâhmanical part to the northern Kshatriya part of Ku*nd*apura, 22, 190 sq., 219, 223, 226–8; a Kshatriya and a learned Brâhma*n*a must never be despised, 25, 150; mutual relation of Kshatriyas and Brâhma*n*as, rivalry between them, 25, 399, 399 n.; 43, 345 n.; 44, 131–4; from out of the priesthood (Brahman) the nobility (Kshatra) is produced, 25, 399, 399 n.; 44, 226 sq.; Brâhma*n*a the root, Kshatriya the top of the sacred law, 25, 447; by the Dîkshâ the sacrificer, of whatever c. he be, becomes a Brâhma*n*a, 26, 35; Brahman and Kshatra, two vital forces, 26, 124; prayer for the priesthood and nobility, 26, 144; 43, 231–5; 44, 294, 485 sq.; a Brâhma*n*a can be without a Kshatriya, but a Kshatriya not without a Brâhma*n*a, 26, 270 sq.; Kshatriyas learn their duties from Brâhma*n*as, 35, 233; the Bodhisattva reflects whether he should take birth as a Kshatriya or a Brâhma*n*a, 35, 272; Brâhma*n*as superior to Kshatriyas, 35, 290; was Buddha a Brâhma*n*a or a Kshatriya? 36, 25–30; Buddhist phrase 'Khattiyas and Brahmans,' 36, 127 n.; Buddhas always born as Brâhma*n*as or Kshatriyas, 36, 132 n.; Vâgapeya for Brâhma*n*as and Kshatriyas, Râgasûya for Kshatriyas, 41, xxiv sq., 3 sq., 23–5; kindling-sticks for Kshatriyas and priests, both are Agni, 41, 259 sq.; the Kshatriya must give a sterile cow to the Brahmans, 42, 177; Brâhma*n*as and Râganyas contend with one another in the theological disputations, 44, 112–15; why a Brâhma*n*a and a Râganya must perform the lute-playing at the horse-sacrifice, 44, 286 sq. *See also* Brâhma*n*as (*e*), *and* Kshatriyas.

(*c*) Kshatriyas and Vai*s*yas.

The Vai*s*yas serve, store up for the Kshatriyas, 12, 82, 94; Kshatra and Vi*s*, represented by Prastara and Barhis, 12, 92 sq.; the Pravara in the case of Kshatriyas and Vai*s*yas, 12, 115 n.; Kshatriyas represented by Indra (and Agni), Vai*s*yas by the Vi*s*ve Devâ*h*, 12, 371; 26, 220 sq.; Indra (or Varu*n*a) the nobility, Maruts the people, and the nobility are the controllers of the people, 12, 387, 393, 399, 401 sq.; 26, 334 sq., 338, 395 sq. n., 396 sq.; the people are the nobleman's food, 26, 65 sq.; 41, 13, 153; 43, 125, 129, 132 sq., 132 n.; the nobility surrounded by the people, 26, 146; 44, 466; peasantry obedient to the nobility, 26, 227 sq.; 44, 227, 303; Vai*s*ya or Râganya at the Vâgapeya chariot race, 41, 29; king sprinkled with consecration water by a Râganya and Vai*s*ya, 41, 83 sq.; milk is the nobility, Surâ-liquor the peasantry, the nobility is produced from out of the peasantry, 44, 225, 228.

(*d*) The twice-born c. or Âryans.

Three c. mentioned by the names of Brâhma*n*a, Râgan, and Vi*s*, 1, 143, 143 n.; what wise men of the three twice-born c. approve, is virtue, 2, 72; pure men of the first three c. shall be cooks, or *S*ûdras under certain restrictions, 2, 104 sq.; a Snâtaka shall live in a place chiefly inhabited by Âryans, 2, 225; a Snâtaka shall always behave as becomes an Âryan, 2, 226; the three first c. called twice-born, 7, 12, 119; *those countries are called barbarous (mlekkha) where the system of the four c. does not exist; the others are denoted Âryâvarta (the abode of the Âryans)*; 7, 255; the twice-born

are the first among men, 8, 353; Sa*m*skâras and Veda-study for the three higher c., 8, 358; the twice-born c. and the *S*ûdras, 14, 9 sq.; 25, 402; twice-born men shall reside in pure countries, *S*ûdras anywhere, 25, 33; Âryan has three births, 25, 61; *S*ûdras personating twice-born men to be punished, 25, 381, 380 sq. n., 388; non-Âryan origin cannot be concealed, 25, 415; different duties of Âryans and non-Âryans, 25, 418; how far *S*ûdras may imitate Âryans, 25, 428–30; falsely attributing to oneself high birth, a mortal sin, 25, 441; the gods (and hence also the sacrificer who is consecrated) only commune with the three higher c. who alone are able to sacrifice, 26, 4; nobility and priesthood and the people are this all, 26, 291 sq.; cruel punishments of *S*ûdras proffering a false accusation against twice-born men, 33, 33; men only of the three higher c. entitled to the study of the Veda, 34, 197; 'the *S*ûdra and the Ârya' = all men, 42, 68, 402; Brahman (priesthood), Kshatra (nobility), and peasantry, 43, 67 sq.; Kshatra (nobility), *S*ûdras and Âryas created, 43, 74 sq.; prayer to be delivered from sins committed against *S*ûdra or Ârya, 44, 265; it is a rare chance to be born as an Ârya, for many are the Dasyus and Mle*kkh*as, 45, 43. *See also* Society, Vai*s*ya, *and* *S*ûdra.

(*e*) Low c. and outcasts.

Gifts which may be accepted even from an Ugra, or a *S*ûdra, 2, 27, 27 n., 65 sq., 65 n.; near a *S*ûdra, a *K*â*nd*âla and an outcast, as near a burial-ground, the study of the Veda must be interrupted, 2, 34, 261; 7, 124; 14, 121 sq., 210; 29, 81, 324; he shall not study the Veda in a village where *K*â*nd*âlas live, 2, 34; 14, 64; 29, 324; food brought or looked at by an Apapâtra, *S*ûdra, Ugra, outcast, or Nishâda is impure, 2, 60, 60 sq. n.; 7, 163; 14, 69; 25, 162–4; intercourse with outcasts and with Apapâtras forbidden, 2, 74; 7, 133, 187 sq.; 14, 5, 109, 230; 25, 497; penance for a Brâhma*n*a who has served a man of 'the black race,' 2, 87, 87 sq. n.; how one should behave towards teachers and relations who have lost their c., 2 88; it is sinful and defiling to touch or speak to, or look at a *K*â*nd*âla, outcast, or Mle*kkh*a, 2, 103 7, 94 sq.; 14, 121, 171, 183; 25, 119, 183; dogs, outcasts, and *K*â*n*-*d*âlas receive a share at meals, 2, 122; 14, 50; 25, 92; outcasts do not inherit, 2, 133; 14, 89; 25, 372 sq. and n.; 33, 194; a funeral meal looked at by dogs, Apapâtras, *S*ûdras, *K*â*nd*âlas, or outcasts, is defiled, 2, 145, 259; 7, 250; alms may be accepted from all c. except Abhi*s*astas and outcasts, 2, 190; garments of the mourners to be given to men of the lowest c., 2, 254; the crow, the *K*â*nd*âla among birds, 2, 266 n.; those who associate with outcasts, become outcasts, 2, 278, 280; 14, 222; 25, 467 sq. and note; definition of the term outcast, 2, 280; women become outcasts by intercourse with men of lower c., 2, 281; the seven lowest c., 7, 29 n.; funeral ceremonies for outcasts, 7, 93; mire and water defiled by being touched by low-caste people, 7, 102; during penance one must not speak to *S*ûdras and outcasts, 7, 151; 25, 476; sin of living as a Vrâtya or outcast, 7, 176 sq.; 25, 442, 442 n.; after having bathed, he must not converse with low-caste persons, or outcasts, 7, 205; a Snâtaka must not speak to low-caste persons, 7, 228; *S*vapâka, the lowest of c., 8, 65; 10 (ii), 23; 45, 50, 55, 59; Kshatriyas became V*ri*shalas, 8, 295; Buddha's definition of an outcast, 10 (ii), 21–3; law about outcasts, 14, 67 sq.; penance for intercourse with low-caste and outcast females, 14, 104; cohabitation with Apapâtra women and female outcasts, an Upapâtaka sin, 14, 219; outcasts shall live together, sacrificing for each other, teaching each other, marrying amongst each other, 14, 220; no V*ri*shala or V*ri*shalî should touch a woman in her courses, 15, 219; is intercourse with the sons of outcasts permitted? 14, 220 sq.; associating with outcast teachers or

pupils is sinful, 14, 239; a Snâtaka shall not travel with outcasts, Vrishalas, or Sûdras, 14, 243; 30, 87; Vrâtyas or outcasts, excluded from initiation, 25, 37, 405–7, 406 n.; he who neglects the twilight devotions becomes an outcast, 25, 49; outcasts excluded from Srâddha feasts, 25, 103; alliance with outcasts through Veda or marriage, 25, 105; a Snâtaka shall not dwell in a country swarming with men of low c., 25, 138, 141; flesh of animals slain by *K*ân*d*âlas is pure, 25, 192; *K*ân*d*âlas and Svapa*k*as, their mode of life and occupation, 25, 414 sq. and n.; penance for sacrificing for Vrâtyas, 25, 471; outcasts unfit to be witnesses, 33, 89; *K*ân*d*âlas used for searching after a thief, 33, 206; gifts not to be accepted from outcasts, 33, 220; occult sciences described as the arts of *K*ân*d*âlas, *S*abaras, Dravi*d*as, &c., 45, 366. *See also* Initiation (Vrâtyas), Sins (Abhi*s*astas), *and* *S*ûdras.

(*f*) Mixture of c., mixed c.

Low mixed c. of *K*ân*d*âlas, from union of *S*ûdra with a Brâhma*n*a woman, 1, 82, 91; 2, 103, 103 n.; 15, 169; 25, 343, 404 sq., 411; definition of, and law regarding mixed c., 2, lx sq.; 7, 66 sq.; 14, xxv, 94, 94 n., 196–8; 25, lxxi sq., lxxxi, 402–18; 33, 186–8; union of a twice-born man with a *S*ûdra wife is sinful and degrading, 2, 69; 7, 112; 10 (ii), 49; 14, 70, 228, 228 n., 244; 25, 466 sq. and n.; cohabitation of Âryan women with *S*ûdras, and Âryan men with Apapâtra women causes impurity, 2, 74 sq.; low mixed c., Paulkasas, Vainas, 2, 103, 103 n.; 15, 169; mixed c. of Nishâdas, 2, 103 n.; 7, 163; 14, 228; 25, 163; 30, 317; intermarriage between different c. sinful, 2, 130 sq.; 25, 184, 184 n.; the son of a Brâhma*n*a who follows the profession of a Kshatriya, and the son of a *S*ûdra born from a Brâhma*n*a woman defile the company at a *S*râddha, 2, 145; those who have been killed in trying to prevent mixture of c. go to heaven, 7, 18; crimes degrading to a mixed c., 7, 138; 25, 444, 455; intermingling of c. results from neglect of rites, 8, 41, 55; in order to prevent a confusion of c., Brâhma*n*as and Vai*s*yas may take up arms, 14, 20, 236; a Brâhma*n*a who has intercourse with a *K*â*nd*âla female becomes an outcast, or a *K*â*nd*âla, 14, 235; a teacher's wives of equal or of different c., 25, 68 sq., 68 n.; learning and an excellent wife may be acquired even from men of low c., 25, 72 sq., 72 n.; intermarriage between different c., 25, 75, 77–9, 83, 86; great offence of a Brâhma*n*a, who, being invited to a *S*râddha, dallies with a *S*ûdra woman, 25, 111; intercourse with a *S*ûdra female after having partaken of a *S*râddha dinner injures the manes, 25, 121; by intercourse with inferior people a Brâhma*n*a becomes a *S*ûdra, 25, 167; if there were no punishments, a confusion of c. would arise, 25, 219; 33, 216; king's consort must be of equal c., 25, 228; intermixture of c. to be prevented by the king, 25, 285; arms may be taken up when the twice-born c. are threatened with destruction, 25, 314, 314 n.; mixture of c. caused by adultery, 25, 315, 315 n.; seduction of maidens by men of lower c., 25, 317 sq.; females of low birth attained the qualities of high-born husbands, 25, 331 sq.; confusion of c. caused by Vena, 25, 339; standing of wives of different c., 25, 342 sq.; offspring of Âryan father and non-Âryan mother preferable to offspring of non-Âryan father and Âryan mother, 25, 417 sq.; those who have intercourse with women of the lowest c. are reborn as Pretas, 25, 497; mixed assemblages (of members of different c.) are illegal, 33, 154; intercourse with unchaste women, but not of higher c., permitted, 33, 180 sq.; pa*ñk*aganâ*h* = the four c. and the Nishâdas, 34, 262; a man of a mixed c. shall kill the dog at the horse-sacrifice, 44, 279 n.; the *S*ûdra woman is the Ârya's mistress, 44, 326; the son of a Vai*s*ya woman not initiated, 44, 326.

(*g*) RELIGIOUS VIEW OF C.

Men are reborn in higher or lower c., according to their actions, 1, 82; 2, 102 sq., 103 n., 126; 7, 144; 8, 322; 25, 485, 496 sq.; 45, 15; a Brâhma*n*a should be chosen as a teacher, Kshatriyas or Vai*s*yas only in times of distress, 2, 111; 14, 154; origin or creation of c., 8, 59; 12, 296; 14, 25; 15, 89 sq.; 25, 14, 14 n., 24 sq., 26 n., 326, 413; 43, 74 sq.; c. and Â*s*ramas, 8, 315 sq.; 22, xxxi sq.; the three qualities in the three c., darkness in the *S*ûdra, goodness in the Brâhma*n*a, 8, 329; a Bhikkhu's power of remembering to what c. he belonged in a previous birth, 11, 216; the c. system, and the Brâhma*n*as, 12, xii sq.; Indra, Agni, Vi*s*ve-devâs represent nobility, priesthood, and peasantry, 12, xvi–xviii; 43, 342, 344; ceremonies of excommunication and readmission of a sinner, 14, 77 sq., 216; 25, 468–70; a Snâtaka shall beg from Brâhma*n*as, Kshatriyas, Vai*s*yas, and Carpenters, 14, 159, 159 n.; manes of the four c., 25, 112; four c. known by the Veda, 25, 505; three metres corresponding to the three c., 29, 59 n.; Snâtaka prays to become beloved among Brahman (i.e. Brâhma*n*as), Vai*s*yas, *S*ûdras, and kings, 30, 167; the sacrifice is for the three c., 30, 315–17; all the four c. are fit for the knowledge of the Itihâsas and Purâ*n*as, 34, 229; there are four c., but none of them vomits Soma, 41, 131; sacrificial offerings mystically identified with Brahman (priesthood), Kshatra (nobility), and Vi*s* (people), 44, 41; men of all the four c. seized at the Purushamedha, 44, 409 sq., 413, 417; protection invoked for Kshatra, Brahman, and Vi*s*, 44, 496; if there were only one Soul, there could not be Brâhma*n*as, Kshatriyas, Vai*s*yas, and *S*ûdras, 45, 418; difference of c. results from the soul's connexion with a body, though all souls are parts of Brahman and equal, 48, 564 sq.

(*h*) RELIGIOUS RITES DIFFERENT ACCORDING TO C.

Difference of c. with regard to initiation, 2, 3 sq., 175–7; 7, 114 sq.; 14, 56–8, 150–2; 25, 36–9; 29, 58–60, 66, 70 n., 187 sq., 303 sq., 307, 309–11, 399 sq.; 30, 63 sq., 64 n., 137, 139, 148 sq., 270 sq., 274; difference of c. with regard to the rules for Brahma*k*ârins, 2, 9 sq., 12, 21; 8, 217; 29, 308; 32, 232–4; a Brahma*k*ârin should not beg from low-caste people, 2, 11, 11 n.; difference of c. with regard to sipping water, 2, 58 n.; 7, 199; a Brahma*k*ârin shall not eat in the house of Kshatriyas, Vai*s*yas, or *S*ûdras, 2, 66 sq.; penances for murder of members of the four c., 2, 78–80, 83, 284 sq.; 14, 107 sq., 212; penances different for different c., 2, 84; 7, 168 sq., 175; 14, 162, 301; difference of c., and reception of guests, 2, 110, 110 n., 207; 7, 216; 14, 239; 29, 198, 274; 30, 172, 277; gifts produce different merit according to the c. of the receiver, 2, 203; rules regarding impurity for the different c., 2, 249, 252 sq.; 7, 87, 89, 93–6; 14, 21, 29, 167; gifts which a Brâhma*n*a may accept from members of all c., 2, 265; difference of c. with regard to forbidden food, 7, 39; difference of c. and funeral ceremonies, 7, 75; certain intoxicating drinks unclean for a Brâhma*n*a, but not for a Kshatriya and a Vai*s*ya, 7, 95 sq.; 44, 233; wives of different c., their participation in religious duties performed by the husband, 7, 111 sq.; different names to be given to children of the four c., 7, 113, 113 sq. n.; 25, 35; 29, 297 sq.; different forms of calls for the four c., 12, 28, 28 n., 452; Havishk*ri*t formulas for members of the four c., 12, 28, 28 n.; difference of c. with regard to constructing the sacred fires, 12, 207 n.; different seasons suitable for the Agnyâdheya for the three c., 12, 290 sq.; different marriage rites for different c., 14, 206 sq.; 25, 79–82; bathing before sandhyâ prescribed for all c., 14, 246; an ascetic may beg alms from men of all c., 14, 281; difference in ceremonies

according to c., 25, 41 sq., 65, 95, 182, 184 sq. and n., 186; *S*ûdras from whom a Brâhma*n*a may accept food, 25, 168; a dead Brâhma*n*a shall not be carried out by a *S*ûdra, 25, 187; a Brâhma*n*a shall never beg from a *S*ûdra property for a sacrifice, 25, 435; different gifts at marriage to be given by the four c., 29, 39, 285; different rules for the *K*û*d*âkarman for the three c., 29, 55; different site for building a house for the different c., 29, 212, 428; 30, 120; difference of c. with regard to salving after bath, 29, 228; sacrificial fees for the Godâna different for the three c., 29, 403; 30, 70; the sacred fire to be taken from members of the three c., 30, 15; the Rathakâra c. admitted to the Agnyâdhâna, 30, 316; Nishâda chieftains admitted to the Gavedhuka sacrifice, 30, 317; difference of c. in sacrificial details, 30, 337; Mahâvrata ceremonies for Brâhma*n*as, Agni*k*ayana rites also for other c., 43, xxv sq. and n.; different size of sepulchral mound for the four c., 44, 435.

(*i*) THE C. AND THE LAW.

Offences causing loss of c., 2, 7, 74 sq., 89, 92, 280–2; 7, 138; 14, 5, 217–19, 235; 25, 444, 482; difference of c., and law of adultery, 2, 166 sq.; 14, 112 sq., 232 sq.; 25, 316, 316 n., 319–21; 33, 179, 366 sq.; different punishments for different c., 2, 167, 238–40, 245; 7, 33 sq.; 25, 275 sq., 302–4, 382, 384, 386; 33, 203 sq., 228–31; marriage laws (number of wives, wives of different c.) and c., 2, 196; 7, 106; 11, 175; 14, 5 sq., 92 sq., 196; 29, 277; 33, 165 sq. and n., 185; rights of children according to c. of the mothers, 2, 198–200 and n.; 25, 350 sq. and n., 356–8, 365 n., 371, 371 n.; difference of c., and law about giving evidence, 2, 246 sq.; 7, 50–2; 14, 82; 25, 264–6, 266 n., 269 sq., 272, 274; 33, 81, 81 n., 88, 91, 100, 245; difference of c. (sons of wives of different c.) and law of inheritance, 2, 308 sq.; 7, 64 sq., 70–3; 14, 89, 225 sq., 225 n.; 25, 357–9, 364, 367 n.; 33, 192, 201, 371 sq., 374–6; difference of c. with regard to a treasure found, 7, 19; offences and punishments, with regard to the relation of c., 7, 33 sq.; law of debt (interests) different for different c., 7, 42; 14, 15, 15 n.; 25, 278, 285 sq.; 33, 66, 66 n.; difference of c. and the law of ordeals, 7, 53 sq.; 33, 115, 117; the crime of homicide, and the four c., 2, 78–80, 83, 284 sq.; 7, 132, 133 sq., 136, 157 sq.; 14, 107 sq., 212; 25, 448, 455 sq. and n.; difference of c., and illicit sexual intercourse, 7, 174 sq.; 14, 109 sq.; 33, 179; legal procedure to be in accordance with the sum of the science of the first two c., 14, 79, 79 n.; women become outcasts only by murder of a husband, or of a learned Brâhma*n*a, or of a foetus, 14, 133; difference of c. in criminal law, 14, 201 sq.; even a despicable Brâhma*n*a may be a judge, but never a *S*ûdra, 25, 255 sq. and n.; suitors at a trial examined in the order of the c., 25, 256; 33, 290, 290 n.; peculiar laws and customs of c., 14, 96; 25, 260, 260 n., 262, 294; stolen property must be restored to men of all c., 25, 260; difference of law of theft according to c., 25, 313; law of abuse and defamation between different c., 25, 301–3; 33, 355 sq.; taxes to be levied from the four c., 25, 427 sq. and n.; difference of c. and law about slavery, 33, 137 sq. and n.; the wife of one expelled from caste may marry another man, 33, 185; law about assault, and difference of c., 33, 209–11, 357, 359; Karâlaganaka lost his caste by carrying off a Brâhman's daughter, 49 (i), 45.

(*j*) C. DISREGARDED.

View of c. in the Bhagavadgîtâ, 8, 21–5, 208–10; view of c. in Buddhism, 8, 25; Brâhma*n*a and *S*vapâka alike (manifestations of Brahman), 8, 65, 65 n.; even Vai*s*yas and *S*ûdras attain the supreme goal, how much more Brâhma*n*as and royal saints, 8, 85 sq., 85 n., 255; Buddha's definition of an outcast, illustrated by the

story of a *Kând*âla who was reborn in the Brahma world, 10 (ii), 20–3; *not by birth does one become an outcast, not by birth does one become a Brâhmana; by deeds one becomes an outcast, by deeds one becomes a Brâhmana*, 10 (ii), 23; 45, 140; disagreement of c. on the Dhamma being lost, 10 (ii), 52; Buddha is neither a Brâhma*n*a, nor a king's son, nor a Vessa (Vai*s*ya), but a wandering mendicant, 10 (ii), 74 sq.; *do not ask about descent, but ask about conduct; from wood, it is true, fire is born; (likewise) a firm Muni, although belonging to a low family, may become noble, when restrained (from sinning) by humility*, 10 (ii), 76; who has seen Buddha, is appeased, even if he be of black origin, 10 (ii), 103; the truth proclaimed by Buddha is open to all, 11, 187; Bhikkhus belonging to different c. before entering the Order, 20, 192 sq., 193 n.; the four c. renounce their names and lineage when they become Buddhist monks, 20, 304; the monk Harikê*s*a-Bala, born in a family of *S*vapâkas, converts a Brâhma*n*a, 45, 50, 54 sq.; a Brâhma*n*a or Kshatriya, an Ugra or a Li*kkh*avi, when entering the order, is not stuck up on account of his Gotra, 45, 321 sq.; men of different c. may become Brâhma*n*as, according to *S*aivas, 48, 521.

Castration not allowed to Bhikkhus, 20, 77 sq.

Categories, twenty-five, of the Sâṅkhya system, 34, 257–60; difficulties with regard to the six c. of the Vai*s*eshikas, 34, 394 sqq.; seven, two, five c. of the *G*ainas, 34, 428 sq., 430; five c. of the *S*aivas, 34, 435; nine c. or developments, 45, 153, 154.

Caterpillar, soul compared to a, 38, 103, 352.

Cattle, law relating to, 2, 168 sq., 241; 7, 36 sq.; 25, 253, 295–8, 336 sq.; 33, 67, 141–3, 160–4, 160 n., 346; 37, 119 sq., 403; the Earth feels most happy where flocks and herds thrive, 4, 23 sq.; creation of c., 5, 18; 26, 406–9; 37, 237; Aharman's contest with the c., 5, 177–82; duties towards c., 5, 374; 31, 69, 73; 37, 237–40; prayers for c., 5, 392; 12, 185; 26, 449; Arabian customs with regard to c., 6, 89, 89 n., 112, 112 n., 115 n., 132–4, 134 n.; punishment for depriving c. of their virility, 7, 35; tending c. duty of Vai*s*yas, 8, 127; 25, 325, 400, 419; created for men, 9, 167, 198; 37, 283; rites and prayers auspicious resp. inauspicious for c., 12, 64, 64 n., 71 n., 104, 172, 206 sq., 212, 342, 347, 353–5, 358; are fivefold, 12, 219, 228; c. means home, 12, 234; the asterism Rohi*n*î connected with c., 12, 283 sq.; about selling c. to foreigners, 18, 182 sq.; Drvâspa keeps the flocks in health, 23, 111; three times a day take care of the beneficent c., 23, 339; rearing of c. meritorious, 24, 28; Brâhma*n*as must not tend c., 25, 272; c. rearing one of the ten modes of subsistence, 25, 427; wealth means c., 26, 180; 44, 126; foul smell of c. not to be shunned, 26, 266 sq.; at first did not submit to being given away, 26, 344; are related to the Âdityas, 26, 353, 353 n., 356; Vâyu leader of c., 26, 362; c. are food, 26, 446 sq.; 41, 33; 43, 52, 56 sq., 87, 110, 115, 218 sq., 335; ceremonies and sacrifices relating to c., 29, 99–101, 130, 215 sq., 255–9, 353–5, 410 sq.; 30, xxviii, 37, 87–9, 116–18, 127–9, 184–6, 304; 44, 10, 12, 119, 123, 127 sq.; P*ri*shâtaka or Â*s*vayuga festival for the sake of c., 29, 130, 203, 332 sq., 415; 30, 92 sq.; *S*ûlagava sacrifice for averting plague in c., 29, 255–8; 30, 220–4, 291; Rudra invoked to protect the c., 30, 37; Rudra dwells among c., 30, 181; brandmarks on c., 35, 122; duties of shepherds, 37, 81–4; religious duty of tending and care of c., 37, 126 sq., 179, 248, 286 sq., 312, 318 sq., 370; 47, 168; on c. breeding, 37, 129, 139; remedies for c., 37, 129; mutual service of man, c., and sacred beings, 37, 265; wisdom produced by care of c., 37, 334; benefit for a husbandman through c., 37, 344; repletion unnecessary for c., 37, 381; salt

means c., 41, 33; Agni is c., 41, 196-8; both gods and men subsist on c., 41, 229; Dhûrvâ-brick, representing c., put on the fire-altar, 41, 379-81; charm against worms in c., 42, 23, 317-20; charms for the prosperity of c., 42, 143-5, 150, 303 sq., 351 sq., 359-61, 412-14, 490, 493; a shepherd's charm against wild beasts and robbers, 42, 147 sq., 366-9; Bhavâ and *S*arva, the lords of c., 42, 155; marked, 42, 174, 658; charm against sterility in c., 42, 299; charm to bring stray c. home, 42, 496; Rudra invoked not to hurt c., 43, 154, 162; two-footed man established among four-footed c., 44, 26; in winter c. waste away, 44, 45; gratified at the Agnihotra, 44, 82; the sacrifice is c., 44, 116; even whilst seeing clearly they do not know anything, 44, 130; offspring, c., and heaven as reward of the pious, 44, 165, 170, 309 sq.; milk, the light of c., 44, 215; the cups of milk (at the Sautrâma*n*î) are c., 44, 229; recurring death of c., 44, 271; won by the sacrificer, by means of the *G*agatî metre, 44, 284; consist of sixteen parts, 44, 342; secured by the B*ri*hatî metre, 44, 371; metres are c., 44, 376 n.; are neither domestic nor wild, 44, 376 n.; when the c. overflow with milk, all the gods subsist thereon, 44, 508; Ashavahi*s*tô interferes to diminish slaughter of c., 47, xii; pleased by the conversion of Vi*s*tâsp, 47, 74; kindness towards c. enjoined, 47, 107 sq. *See also* Bull, Calf, Cow, Goat, Ox, *and* Sheep.

Causation, chain of, *see* Nidânas.

Cause, causes: K*ri*sh*n*a greater than Brahman and first c., 8, 96; pradhâna, nature or material c., 8, 106 n., 191, 191 n., 244; the end of the great c. can never be reached, 8, 192; the self having no c., 8, 247, 309; where there are c. there is inconstancy and delusion, 8, 335; all beings have been created by nature, not by a c., 8, 387, 387 n.; discussions on the c. of the world, 15, 231-7; 19, 206-12; whatever is originated, the Sâṅkhyas say, is originated from inherent c., non-inherent c., and operative c., 34, 5 sq.; causal matter is metaphorically represented as a she-goat, 34, 256 sq.; only the one highest c. is true, 34, 322; four kinds of c. admitted by the Bauddha, 34, 409, 409 n.; things exist either through Karma, or a c., or the seasons, 36, 103, 107 sq.; a Bodhisattva should not believe in the idea of a c., 49 (ii), 114 sq.;—seed and product, c. and effect, 8, 383 n.; relation of c. and effect, 34, xxix, xlix, 300-6, 309, 311, 320-43, 350, 367, 396 sq., 396 n., 399, 436, 442; 38, 9, 20, 451; 48, 415-19, 430-4, 445 sq., 453-5, 459, 463-6, 471, 482 sq., 541. *See also* Nidânas, Pradhâna, Upâdâna, *and* World (*b*).

Cave (of the heart), *see* Heart.

Cave dwellings, in which Buddha stayed, 11, 56 sq.

Celibacy, *see* Monks.

Cemetery (burial-ground), Veda study must be interrupted in a, 2, 33; 14, 64; 25, 147; 29, 116, 324; rags for pa*m*sukûla robes got from a c., 17, 197 sqq.; impurity caused by touching a pyre or c., 14, 30; ascetics making a vow to wear nothing except what they can procure from dustheaps or c., 20, 89; a Snâtaka shall not go to a c., 29, 126; selection and preparation of the place for a c., 29, 236 sq., 237 n.; Rudra invoked on a c., 29, 366; bridal procession passing a c., 30, 262; preparing of burial-place and tomb, 44, 421-40. *See also* Dakhmas.

Ceremonies.

(*a*) In Indian religions.
(*b*) In Parsi religion.
(*c*) In Chinese religions.

(*a*) IN INDIAN RELIGIONS.

The Pu*n*yâhava*k*ana ceremony, 2, 49 n.; the ceremony of sipping water, 2, 54-9, 57 sq. and n.; *see also* Purification; costume of the Brâhma*n*a when performing c., 2, 54; one should not invite a sinner to dinners given at religious c., 2, 75; even with a fallen mother there shall be no communion in religious c., 2, 88; to prevent the interruption of c. begging is permitted, 2, 123; rules about the fire for domestic c.,

2, 201, 201 n.; money may be taken from rich men who neglect their religious duties to defray the expenses of c., 2, 273; to be performed by the husband together with the eldest wife, 7, 111 sq.; penance for omitting the daily rites, 7, 179; 25, 472, 472 n.; the eternal rites of families destroyed by destruction of a family, 8, 41 sq.; Vedic c. not a true means of emancipation, 8, 146; gifts made at c., 8, 169; through ignorance of the truth c. become amplified, 8, 171; rites and c. condemned, 11, 10, 10 n., 199, 300 n., 301; the ascetic shall discontinue the performance of c., 14, 46; families perish by neglect of sacred rites, 25, 86; daily c. of a householder, 25, 87–97; the rites prescribed in the Veda, a means of obtaining union with Brahman, 25, 212, 212 n.; rites without knowledge of the soul not sufficient, 25, 213, 213 n.; Kshatriyas degraded by omission of c., 25, 412; domestic rites and c., *vols.* 29 and 30; c. at the emancipation of a slave, 33, 138 sq.; religious c. performed by several persons jointly, 33, 338; c. in Mahâyâna Buddhism, 49 (i), 199. *See also* Auspicious rites, Hair, Marriage, Sacraments, Sacrifices, *and* Works.

(*b*) IN PARSI RELIGION.

C. restored by Pêshyôtanû, 5, li sq., 227, 229; Aûharmazd performs the Yazisn ceremony with the archangels, 5, 14; the Gêtô-kharîd rite and other c., 5, 127, 127 n., 292, 292 n., 351; 18, 234, 234 n., 237; 24, 262 sq. and n.; Mazdayasnian c., 5, 205 sq., 211 sq.; five c. which when performed are good works, and when neglected sins, 5, 351 sq., 351 n.; ceremonial worship and sacred feast, 5, 362; the merits of different c., 5, 380 sq., 381 n.; about the cost of religious c., 18, 201–9, 242 sq., 250–5; to order religious rites, an atonement for sin, 18, 232; celebrating c. a good work, 24, 27 sq., 27 n.; how the c. of the sacred beings ought to be considered, 24, 94 sq.; annual Rapithwin ceremony, 24, 264; duty of performing Gâdangôî, 24, 285 sq., 285 n.; Navazûd ceremony, 24 262 sq. and n., 316 sq.; explanation of c. and ritual, 37, 23; assault against one about to celebrate a sacred c., 37, 49, 49 n.; a thief liberated to celebrate a religious c., 37, 59 sq.; on the day of battle, 37, 89; at the five periods of the day and night, 37, 167; three grades of c., 37, 192; great ordinance of the ceremonial of Aûharmazd, 37, 346 sq.; religion of Aûharmazd made progressive by c., 37, 363; why c. are performed, 37, 381 sq.; worship of the sacred beings, 37, 395 sq.; the c. which go to the bridge of sin, 37, 477; the wizard Mahrkûs destroyed by the Dâhmân Âfrîn ritual, 47, xii, 108. *See also* Sacrifices (*o*).

(*c*) IN CHINESE RELIGIONS.

A minister appointed to direct 'the three c.,' 3, 44, 44 n.; in c. it is better to be sparing than extravagant, 16, 105 n.; 'the ornamental observances of society,' 16, 231, 232 n.; arise when things are subjected to restraint, 16, 434, 440 n.; their supposed prevalence in Chinese religion, 27, 12 sq.; valueless without truth and reverence, 27, 25 sq., 394 sq., 403, 403 n., 408 sq., 411–14, 415 n., 416 sq., 439, 445 sq.; their importance for government and morality, 27, 39, 367, 375–9, 386, 388–93; 28, 261–6; discourse of Confucius on c., 27, 40; 28, 270–7; rules of c. presented under the figure of dykes, 27, 41 sq.; 28, 284–99; are suggested by the course of nature, and conformed to the feelings of man, 27, 59; 28, 465 sq.; how to practise c. in a foreign country, 27, 101 sq.; the six ceremonial observances, 27, 230, 248; their origin and development, 27, 364–72, 385–90; enumerated, 27, 367, 388; 28, 430; on the things to be used for c., and details about time, number, &c., 27, 395–448, 448 n.; regulation of expenditure for c., 27, 396; number of rules of c., 27, 404, 404 n.; are not the expression of feelings, 27, 406 sq.; promote righteousness and humility, 27, 413 sq.; 28, 219 sq.; different c.

under different dynasties, 27, 438, 466–8; 28, 35–9, 324, 341 sq.; c. and music as moral forces, 28, 95–116, 125–9; music employed at c., 28, 101; how they were framed, 28, 101 sq.; the object of c. and music, 28, 224–6; five kinds of c., 28, 236, 236 n.; their instructive and moralizing power, 28, 257–60; a ruler must know the principles of c. and music, 28, 278; c. that have no embodiment, 28, 279 sq.; 300 usages of c. and 3,000 modes of demeanour, 28, 323; only to be discussed by the emperor, 28, 324; are necessary, 28, 331 sq.; the demonstration of humanity, 28, 409; how the Tâoist looks upon c., 39, 140, 271, 278–80, 293, 305 sq., 342, 369; by c. men impose on one another, they are but the flowers of the Tâo, and the commencement of disorder, 40, 58 sq.; cultivated by Confucius, 40, 193; attacked by Mo-ʒze, 40, 218; unguent of the Chrismal rite sprinkled on the head (of children, idols, &c.), 40, 270 sq.; began to be practised when the Tâo was laid aside, 40, 284 sq.; c. and music in the age of perfect virtue, 40, 312.

Cessation, two kinds of it assumed by the Bauddhas, 34, 410 sq., 413.

Chain, *see* Bonds, the five.

Chamberlain, *see* Kshatt*ri*.

Changer (Vikart*ri*), n.d., invoked at the house-building rite, 29, 347.

Chaos: the gods of the southern and northern seas brought Ch. to an end by boring holes in him, 39, 138, 266 sq., 267 n.

Chariot (cart, carriage), ceremonies connected with cart containing rice for sacrifice, 12, 12–19; pole of ch. bound with thongs, 12, 452; Soma-carts and cart-shed, 26, 127–34; cart-wheels described, 26, 132 n.; ceremonies on mounting a ch., 29, 209–11, 363–5; 30, 295; gods drive on ch., 32, 14, 29, 63, 82, 97, 107, 126, 159, 169, 210, 272, 296, 313, 319 sq., 326, 333 sq., 337 sq., 340, 343, 352, 357, 363, 366, 368, 370, 391 sq., 400 sq., 408, 413, 444, 449; 41, 289 sq.; 42, 120; 46, 245; gods invoked for wealth of horses, ch., ch.-horses, &c., 32, 296, 341; racing ch., 32, 352; 46, 173, 193, 213; bounteous like lords of ch., 32, 416; spokes of ch.-wheels, 32, 416; ch.-race at the vâgapeya, 41, xxiv, 17–29; ch., is a thunderbolt, is a winner of wealth, 41, 18, 98; carriage and pair, the priest's fee, 41, 50; oblations relating to the ch. at the râgasûya, 41, 101 sq.; yoke-pin's throw, and yoke as measures of distance, 41, 123, 349; driving the sacrificial fire on a ch., 41, 289–91; first the right, then the left ox yoked, 41, 291, 327; consecration of war-ch., 42, 120, 587; offering made on head of ch., 43, 233 sq.; ch. is yonder sun, 43, 234 sq.; by oblations of air the gods yoked the ch. for the obtainment of wishes, 43, 236; if two smashed ch. were to unite, there would be one fit for driving, 44, 198; is completed, i.e. held together with cords, 44, 318, 318 n.; a victorious ch., 46, 271. *See also* Parables (*f*).

Charioteer, night like a, 32, 357; Maruts called ch., 32, 364, 375; three horses, the warrior and the ch., 41, 50, 102; not to get down from chariot along with the king, 41, 104; king and ch. stepping on the war-chariot, 42, 587; Agni compared to a ch., 46, 37, 100, 221, 229, 233, 292, 350, 360. *See also* Parables (*f*).

Charity, sacrifice, and Veda study, the three kinds of good works, 1, 35; 8, 98 sq., 340; 15, 179; 25, 307; 48, 695, 699; rewards of ch. in next life, 1, 80; 4, 200, 383; 19, 213–16; 24, 184 sq., 342 sq.; 37, 204, 313; 38, 124; portions of the harvest to be left for the benefit of the widow, 3, 373, 373 n.; 28, 296; the Earth is pleased by him who makes gifts to the faithful, 4, 31; contract of ch. to co-religionists, 4, 34, 45 sq.; *he who relieves the poor makes Ahura king*, 4, 101, 210, 251; he who refuses gifts to the faithful, makes the Drug pregnant with fiends, 4, 201; Zoroastrian virtue and duty of ch., 4, 218, 266, 285–7, 286 n.; 5, 209; 18, 174 sq.; 23, 316, 320 n., 336–8, 344; 24, 19, 24, 282, 329; 37, 180, 307, 319–21; *see also* Râta (Genius of Ch.); mutual ch. between brethren

in the Faith, 4, 292 n., 293; ch. one of the three best things, 4, 293; gifts to the righteous, the best sacrifice, 4, 357; the soul clothed with garments given in ch., 5, 127, 341, 341 n., 383 n.; mutual assistance of the creatures is the will of Aûharmazd, 5, 158; game to be preserved for the poor, 5, 301, 301 n.; advantage of excessive almsgiving, 5, 325, 345; meat-offering to (personified) Compassion and sustenance of the poor, 5, 337; forsaking a righteous man in affliction, a discomfort to the earth, 5, 361; almsgiving a duty of the Moslim, 6, lxxi, lxxiii, 2, 6, 11, 15, *24*, *58*, 60, 62, 77, 105, 149, 156, 163, 173–5, 183 sq., *186 sq.*, 235, 242; 9, 4, 31, 60 sq., 65, 78, 80, 99, 113, 131, 143, 160, *165*, 199, 209, *266–8*, *272*, *285*, *287*, 301, *308*, 332, *334 sq.*, 338, 342; feeding a poor man, a substitute for a fast, 6, 26; *expend in alms in God's way and be not cast by your own hands into perdition; but do good, for God loves those who do good*, 6, 28; to whom alms should be given, 6, 31, 181; 9, 128; duty towards orphans, 6, 32, 71 sq., 77, 90, 135; 27, 259; 'the surplus' to be expended in alms, 6, 32; *O ye who believe! expend in alms of what we have bestowed upon you, before the day comes in which is no barter, and no friendship, and no intercession; and the misbelievers, they are the unjust*, 6, 39 sq.; of almsgiving in God's way, 6, 41–4; alms not to be given for appearance sake, 6, 78; part of blood-money remitted as alms, 6, 85; share of the spoils to be given to the poor, 6, 168; alms not to be accepted from misbelievers, 6, 180 sq.; God rewards those who give alms, 6, 191; 9, 155; leads to final emancipation, 8, 114; duty of Kshatriyas, 8, 127; one of the twelve great observances, 8, 167, 182; giving away of sons and wealth to deserving men, 8, 169; how ch. should be exercised, 8, 183 sq.; want of ch. a mark of the quality of darkness, 8, 320; the various acts of public ch., belong to the quality of passion, 8, 324; the duty of the good, 8, 326; 25 164 sq.; the hermit should always give alms of whatever he has for food, 8, 361; be not niggardly in God's cause, 9, 232 sq.; food given to the poor and the orphan and the captive 'for God's sake,' 9, 312 sq.; the wealthy denounced who do not care for the poor and the orphan, 9, 331; the duty of all castes, 14, 26; 25, 24, 401, 420; cannot save him whose conduct is vile, 14, 34; the Pâramitâ of ch., 19, 366–8; grand feats of charitableness of Bodhisattvas, 21, 11 sq., 14, 243; accumulation of merits acquired by acts of ch. compared with that acquired by occupation with sacred books, 21, 320–7; keeping the Lotus of the True Law is a greater merit than bestowing the whole world full of jewels on Buddhas, &c., 21, 386; prayers, sacrifices, and ch. offered to Mithra, 23, 121; provision of lodgings for the sick and poor, a good work, 24, 75; liberality of thought, of word, and of deed, 24, 121 sq.; gifts to the poor for the benefit of one's soul, 24, 184 sq.; nothing is to be given to a sinner, 24, 354; the chief virtue in the Kali age, 25, 24; duty of giving alms to ascetics and students, 25, 92 sq., 92 n.; the hermit to give alms of water, roots, and fruit, 25, 199 sq.; given up by the ascetic, 25, 205; property destined for ch., is indivisible, 25, 379, 379 n.; provision made for orphans, widowers, widows, and cripples, 27, 243 sq.; acts of ch. enjoined on the Emperor for the third month of spring, 27, 264; compassion to be shown to orphans and widows, 27, 298; to relieve suffering, and shelter the poor, the first care of Zoroastrianism, 31, xxii, 80 sq., 85, 85 n.; houses for the poor built, 31, 300; *render ye the needy rich*, 31, 357; charitable associations, 33, 348, 349 sq.; alms less meritorious than sacrifices, 34, 27; duty of almsgiving, especially in the days of the Fravashis, 37, 18; about begging and beneficence, 37, 39; squandering alms, 37, 70; praise of liberality, 37, 91; reducing liber-

ality, limit of a wife's liberality, 37, 99; illiberal opulence, 37, 176 sq.; what you give to a disciple of Zoroaster is as if given to Zoroaster, 37, 196, 196 n.; reward of liberality towards the worthy, 37, 249 sq.; liberality for the Mazda-worshipper is for the archangels, 37, 280; he who gives to the needy gives himself up to Zaratûst, 37, 324; practising ch. benefits the sun, 37, 326; liberal giving is repaying a debt, 37, 336; giving to the wise is a foundation of learning, 37, 371; development of the world through liberality to the poor, 37, 372; ministration of the poor through Aûharmazd, 37, 458; *the sage does not accumulate (for himself). The more that he expends for others, the more does he possess of his own; the more that he gives to others, the more does he have himself*, 39, 123 sq.; 40, 55; better is he who controls himself, than he who gives, every month, thousands of cows, 45, 39; Zoroaster's charitableness, 47, 152–4; ch. is helpful to knowledge, 48, 704. *See also* Begging, Gifts, Priests (*c*, *d*), *and* Teacher (fee).

Charms: a Brahmakârin learns poison ch. and such things from his teacher, 2, 19 n.; ch. cannot save a man who is in the bonds of death, 7, 81 sq.; battle-ch., 23, 243; 42, 98, 117–33, 233–5, 262 sq., 325–7, 404 sq., 436–40, 510 sq., 545, 582–7, 631–9; love-ch., 30, 269 sq.; 42, 99–105, 274–7, 311–13, 356–9, 459 sq., 512 sq., 534–6, 539 sq., 546 sq.; by means of ch. Siddhas make rain, extinguish fire, and ward off poison, 35, 181, 181 n.; snakes compelled by ch. (Pirit) to suck the poison back again or prevented from biting, 35, 212, 213 n., 215 sq.; Kshatriyas have secret formulas handed down in families, 35, 265; protecting ch. against death, 42, 55–60; against curses, 42, 91, 285; a sleeping-ch. at an assignation, 42, 105 sq., 372 sq.; to allay discord and appease anger, 42, 134–7, 361–4, 479–81, 492, 494 sq., 550 sq.; to gain victory in debate, or influence in the assembly, 42, 137–9, 275, 304–6, 508 sq., 543 sq.; to avert sin, evil omens, and the like, 42, 163–8, 473–5, 483–5, 521–9, 555 sq., 564 sq.; for easy delivery in child-bed, 42, 247; to cure diseases, *see under* Diseases; pertaining to women, *see* Women (*b*). *See also* Prayers, *and* Witchcraft.

Chase, *see* Animals (*f*), *and* Hunting.

Chastity enjoined for the Brahmakârin or Vedic student, 2, 8, 186, 188; 7, 120 sq.; 25, 62 sq.; 29, 309; 30, 70 sq., 76, 160; 33, 132; 48, 695; Brahmakârin who breaks the vow of ch., 2, 85, 257, 281 sq., 289, 294 sq.; 14, 117 sq., 215 sq., 294 sq.; 29, 361 sq.; 38, 318–20; 48, 706 sq.; enjoined for the ascetic, 2, 153, 193; enjoined for the hermit, 2, 155; 7, 277; 14, 45; 25, 203; those who keep the vow of ch. reach immortality, 2, 158; enjoined for mourners during the period of impurity, 2, 254; to be observed on the day of a Srâddha, 2, 258; as a penance, 2, 283, 286; 25, 447, 476; enjoined for believers, 9, 65, 76 sq.; the Bhikkhu should live a life of ch., 10 (ii), 18 sq.; 11, 189; 13, 7 sq., 32, 42; of the ancient Brâhmanas, 10 (ii), 49; *let the wise man avoid an unchaste life as a burning heap of coals*, 10 (ii), 65 sq.; *ye shall not act wrongly touching the bodily desires*, 11, 253; offences against ch., 13, 16 sq.; restrictions as to a Bhikkhu's preaching to women, 13, 32 sq.; Buddhist monk threatened by dangers of offending against ch., 13, 261, 315, 340; 20, 312; certain Bhikkhus followed evil practices offending against ch., 17, 347–54; enjoined for Snâtakas at certain periods, 25, 149, 149 n.; chaste Brâhmanas reach heaven, 25, 196 sq.; to be observed by the youth after the first shaving, 29, 303, 403; to be observed during a ceremony for procuring wealth, 29, 428; 30, 120; to be observed before performing a magic rite, 30, 269 sq.; knowledge belongs to those who are bound to ch., 38, 295 sq.; the stages of life for which ch. is obligatory, 38, 297–303, 317 sqq.; the ten conditions of perfect ch., for Gaina monks, 45, 73–7; enjoined for Gaina monks, 45, 74, 91 sq., 162,

185 sq., 296, 302 sq., 307, 308, 324, 330, 333, 350, 380, 411; he who does not carnally love divine, human, or animal beings, is a true Brâhma*n*a, 45, 139; heretics do not lead a life of ch., 45, 245; is the highest of austerities, 45, 291; observed by those who abandon works and possess knowledge of Brahman, 48, 693; not recommended by Gaimini, 48, 694. *See also* Abstinence, *and* Sexual intercourse.

Chatter, sin of unseasonable, 5, lxi, 287 sq., 288 n., 290–3; 24, 11, 11 n.; 37, 152.

Chest, the imperishable, which has the sky for its circumference and the earth for its bottom, &c., 1, 49 sq.

Child, Children.

(*a*) Religious beliefs about ch.
(*b*) Religious ceremonies connected with ch.
(*c*) Ch. in physiology, law, and custom.

(*a*) Religious beliefs about ch.

The quality of the ch. depends on the marriage rite of the parents, 2, 128; 14, 207 sq. and n.; 25, 82 sq.; 29, 166; *in thy offspring thou art born again, that, mortal, is thy immortality*, 2, 159; the heavenly bliss of the ancestors depends on the procreation of ch., 2, 159 sq.; the sins of their ch. do not hurt the ancestors, 2, 160; no religious rites or restrictions enjoined for ch. before their initiation, 2, 185 sq. and n.; 14, 10, 150; dreams of bears forbode sons, dreams of snakes daughters, 3, 350; the duty and religious merit of begetting ch. (sons), 4, lxii, 46 sq., 47 n.; 5, 325, 345; 14, 26, 44, 56, 260–2, 271–3; 18, 225 sq., 429, 429 n.; 25, 205; 37, 109; used as assistant priests, 4, 308 n., 309–11, 365; 37, 95; Mâshya and Mâshyôî eat their ch., 5, 57, 57 n.; there is no begetting of ch. after the resurrection, 5, 127; unseasonable chatter no sin for ch., 5, 290 sq.; father responsible for sins of ch., 5, 291, 291 n., 305 n.; 37, 129 sq.; when his wife becomes pregnant by him, a man is freed from mortal sin, 5, 307; new-born ch. not to be shown to a sinful person, 5, 322; good works of ch. shared by parents, 5, 325, 345; 24, 313; 37, 470; he who has no kinsmen, no ch., is released, 8, 246; Mohammed's enemies shall be childless, 9, 343; begetting ch. a debt to the ancestors, 12, 190 sq., 190 n.; 49 (i), 100; offspring produced by sacrifice, 12, 257; men's offspring their death, 12, 361; birth of ch. causes interruption of Veda-study, 14, 211; 29, 115, 142; a wife, childless for three years, becomes at last a mother: a good omen, 16, 179, 181 n.; a wife who is pregnant, and will not nourish her ch.—inauspicious, 16, 179, 181 n.; the wife's duty to nourish her ch., 16, 333; succession of life through ch. commendable, 18, 92, 92 sq. n.; results of good deeds manifested in ch., 18, 141; 'to remove the burden of offspring' by assisting in their support, an atonement for sins, 18, 232, 236; sterility hateful to Ashi Vanguhi, 23, 280 sq.; a virtuous ch. is a good supporter of fame, 24, 41; the worst child, 24, 69; the tie of ch. is the most pleasant, 24, 82; for the welfare of the soul after death it is necessary to leave a ch., 24, 278–81; the fiend Sêg threatens infants, 24, 294; Veda-study, sacrifices, and procreation of sons fit the body for union with Brahman, 25, 34; sins of the father fall on ch. and grandchildren, 25, 156; importance of preserving the purity of offspring, 25, 328 sq. and n.; are the cause of happiness in this world and after death, 25, 332; conception without sexual intercourse, 35, 185, 306; ch. under seven years cannot attain to Nirvâ*n*a, 36, 177–81; condemned for wizard's spells, 37, 65; sins of ch., 37, 77; sin of giving weapons to ch., 37, 78; fit for judgeship, if acquainted with the law, 37, 80; spiritual perception of ch., 37, 111; the excellence of virtuous offspring, 37, 179; childlessness a punishment in hell, 37, 211; tokens at the time of childbirth, 37, 427; the guilt which remains unpunished at the death of a man falls upon his posterity, 39, 39; 40, 244 sq., 244 n.; the Tâoist sage like a little ch., 40,

80-2; progeny is all the light, 41, 239; 43, 129; symbolism of generation of ch., 41, 239 sq.; 43, 128, 130; by giving sterile cows to Brahmans, one obtains ch., 42, 174; continue the life of the parents, 42, 185, 646; he alone is ruler who propagates ch., 43, 230. *See also* Birth, *and* Embryo.

(*b*) Religious ceremonies connected with ch.

Secret name given to ch. at birth, 1, 178 sq., 178 n.; 29, 395; 30, 55, 215, 281; 41, 159; sacrifices and rites connected with conception, pregnancy, and birth of ch., 1, 244 n.; 5, 322; 7, 112-14; 11, 1 n.; 12, 85; 15, 215-21 (conception), 221-4, 222 n.; 19, 7, 19 sq.; 22, 254 sq.; 23, 341; 24, 277, 286 sq., 319; 25, 33-6, 34 n.; 27, 27, 471-6; 29, 46-57, 179, 182 sq., 293-8, 393-9; 30, xxi, 55, 58 sq., 62, 208-18, 253, 280, 282, 301 sq.; 37, 100 sq.; 42, 97-9, 109 sq., 242-5, 247, 284, 356 sq., 460 sq., 467, 517 sq., 540 sq., 545 sq., 574 sq.; 47, 30; 49 (i), 15, 22; prayers and rites of a father setting out on a journey or returning from it for the welfare of his ch., 1, 288; 12, 357-9; 29, 183, 298, 397; 30, 59, 215 sq., 283; impurity caused by the birth of ch., 2, 59, 250 sq.; 4, lxxix sq. and n.; 5, 272, 280-2, 280 n.; 7, 87-91; 14, 177 sq., 180, 298; 24, 339 sq.; 25, 146, 162, 177-81; 29, 355; *see also* Impurity; impurity of women after miscarriage, 4, 62-5, 91 sq.; 5, 280-2, 280 n.; 24, 340 sq.; 25, 179, 179 sq. n.; 37, 159; fire to be kept for the protection of the unborn and new-born ch. from demons, 4, 184 n.; 5, 342-4; 18, 59, 59 n.; 24, 277; 37, 480; prayers for the protection of the lying-in woman, 4, 230, 232-4, 232 n.; ceremony of tying the sacred thread-girdle, 5, 320 sq.; 18, xxviii; 24, 309 sq., 347, 349; 37, 471, 474-6; *see also* Costume; pregnancy becomes scarcer, and fewer male ch. are born, where the fire is not maintained properly, 5, 339; 24, 271; 37, 191 sq.; rite of circumcision not mentioned in the Qur'ân, 6, lii; funeral rites for ch., 7, 90; 14, 177; 24, 310; 25, 120, 180; 27, 340 sq.; 29, 245, 355; Nishekakarman, ceremony of impregnation, 7, 112 sq., 113 n.; Pu*m*savana, or ceremony to cause the birth of a male, 7, 113, 113 n.; 29, 42 sq., 45 sq., 179 sq., 291 sq., 393 sq.; 30, 52-4, 209 sq., 280 sq.; 37, 110; 42, 97, 357 sq., 460 sq.; Sîmantonnayana, or ceremony of parting the hair of the pregnant woman, 7, 113, 113 n.; 29, 47-9, 137 sq., 180, 181 sq., 276, 292 sq., 394 sq.; 30, 54 sq., 208 sq., 253, 279 sq.; 42, 545; *G*âtakarman, or birth-ceremony, 7, 113; 25, 34; 29, 49-51, 137 sq., 182 sq., 395; 30, 55 sq., 210-14, 281-3; 37, 100; 38, 28 sq.; 42, 293; the Nâmadheya (nâmakara*n*a) or name-giving rite, 7, 113; 11, 1 n.; 15, 223; 22, 192, 255; 25, 35, 35 n., 180; 27, 78 sq., 144, 473-5; 29, 50, 182 sq., 297 sq., 395-7; 30, 57 sq., 215, 282 sq.; 37, 101; 42, 573; Âdityadar*s*ana, or ceremony of taking the child out to see the sun, 7, 114; Annaprâ*s*ana, or ceremony of first feeding, 7, 114; 11, 1 n.; 29, 54 sq., 183 sq., 299 sq.; 30, 216, 283; the *K*û*d*âkara*n*a (*K*au*d*a, or *K*aula-karman) or tonsure rite, 2, 253, 253 n.; 7, 114; 25, 34, 36, 177, 180; 29, 55-7, 184-6, 276, 301-3, 380, 397-9; 30, 41, 60-3, 216-18, 253, 283 sq.; 37, 124; 42, 309; prayer for the son, that he may continue the sacrifice, 12, 273, 273 n., 357; prayers for offspring, 12, 369 n.; 23, 360 sq.; 25, 123; 26, 124; 42, 18; ceremonies to secure the birth of ch. with certain qualities wished for, 15, 219 sq.; 29, 171; 30, xxi; portion of deceased ch. at funeral meals, 25, 120; by eating a cake sacred to the manes, a wife will bring forth an excellent son, 25, 124; 29, 424; special rites for the sake of offspring, 26, 98, 173, 177, 213-15, 382; on the ceremonies of capping, 27, 26, 54 sq., 79, 144, 316 sq., 317 n., 355, 358, 437 sq., 437 n., 451, 478; 28, 9, 52 sq., 162, 425-7; shaving ceremony of a ch., 27, 473; 37, 124; girls take the hairpin on

reaching maturity, 27, 451, 479; 28, 52 sq., 172; archery performances at the birth of a son, 28, 452; the Garbharakshana, 29, 47; the mother's getting up from childbed, 29, 51 sq.; how to procure male or female offspring, 29, 167 sq.; prayers and rites of a wife who desires to conceive, 29, 287, 291; Balis offered by a wife for the protection of offspring, 29, 290 sq.; Medhâganana and Âyushya rites for the new-born ch., 29, 293 sq.; charms against diseases of ch., caused by demons, 29, 296 sq.; 30, 213 sq., 219 sq., 286 sq.; 42, 283, 341–3; placing a boy on the bride's lap, 30, 50, 263; Soshyantîhoma, sacrifice for the woman in labour, 30, 55; monthly sacrifice in commemoration of the ch.'s birth, 30, 58 sq.; Kshipraprasavana, or ceremony for accelerating the confinement, 30, 210, 281; ceremony at a miscarriage, 30, 210; fumigation of new-born ch. to keep evil demons away, 30, 211 sq.; charms to prevent miscarriage, 42, xxxviii, 298 sq., 302; charm against worms in ch., 42, 23–5, 452–5; prayer for long life pronounced over a boy, 42, 50 sq., 306 sq.; five Brâhmanas breathe over the new-born son, 44, 129 sq., 129 n. *See also* Woman (*b*).

(*c*) CH. IN PHYSIOLOGY, LAW, AND CUSTOM.

Gift and sale of ch., 2, 132, 132 n.; 8, 169; 14, 75, 228, 335; 25, xciii, 442; games of ch., 3, 350, 350 n.; illegitimate ch., 4, 178–80; 24, 325; must be supported for seven years, 4, 183, 183 n.; on the nature of conception and generation, procreation of male or female ch., 5, 60 sq.; 25, 84; 37, 109–11; discrimination in accepting the child of a handmaid, 5, 323 sq., 323 n., 344 sq.; about suckling ch., 6, 35; 9, 132; birth and weaning of ch., 9, 226; when the ch. is born, there is breath, as long as it is not born, it breathes in accord with the mother's breath, 12, 305; whether generation of ch. depends more on father or on mother, 14, 180; 25, 417 sq.; family in which no male ch. are born to be avoided in choosing a bride, 25, 76; whether ch. belong to the begetter or to the owner of the soil, 25, 333–7; 33, 176 sq.; crime of killing ch., 25, 382; 40, 243; how punished, 25, 382; how ch. style themselves in speaking to their parents, 27, 113; law about ch., 27, 66; name of a posthumous heir announced to the spirits and in the ancestral temple, 27, 311–14; nurses chosen for the ch., 27, 472 sq., 476; dependence of ch., 33, 51; law about minority, 33, 51, 51 n.; the property of ch. not lost by adverse possession, 33, 61; are incompetent witnesses, 33, 89 sq.; 37, 38; not to be subjected to the ordeal by water, 33, 113; crimes committed by ch., 37, 41, 46 sq., 76; guardianship of a child, 37, 101, 162; born with head first, 41, 233; why they try to speak and stand up at the end of a year, 41, 388; 44, 12 sq.; are born after being fashioned for a year, 43, 274; 44, 87 sq.; 'child,' favourite name of the horse, 44, 288. *See also* Abortion, Adoption, Family, Parables (*f*), Parents, Son, *and* Woman (*g*).

China: Sovereigns of Ch. and their titles, 3, xxvi–xxix; early historical documents in Ch., 3, 4–6; chronology of Ch., and principal eras, 3, 13, 15, 20–30; the three religions of Ch., 3, xiii–xxii; 39, 1 sq.; 40, 311 n., 315, 320 n.; sacred books of Ch., 3, xiii–xxii; 49 (ii), xxvi; *see also* Confucianism; geography of Ch., 3, 64–76; how the King of Ch. charms the great ocean, 35, 182.

Chiromancy, treatises on, 42, 260.

Christianity, and Zoroastrianism, 5, lxix sq.; established in Arabia, 6, xiv; its relation to Islâm, 6, xlvii–lii; Trinity and sonship of Jesus denounced, 6, 95, 108; Buddhism and Ch., 11, 165 sq., 208, 222; alleged Christian influences in the Upanishads, 15, xxxi; falsehood about the Messiah, 18, 107 sq.; criticisms of Christian doctrines, 24, xxv, xxvii sq., 225, 225 n., 229–43.

Christians, fiends with red banners (Ch.?) in Iran, 5, li, 215 sq.; referred to as infidels, 5, lxi, 297,

297 n.; treated as infidels by Mohammed, 6, xlvii; Jews, Ch., or Sabaeans, whosoever believe in God, will have their reward, 6, 8; disputes between Jews and Ch., 6, 15; Paradise not exclusively for Jews and Ch., 6, 15; Jews and Ch. opposed to Islâm, 6, 16; Mohammed warned against the Ch., 6, 99; Jews and Ch. not the 'Sons of God,' 6, 100; to be judged by what God has revealed, 6, 104; Jews and Ch. not to be taken for patrons, 6, 105 sq.; Jews and Ch. appealed to and reproved, 6, 106 sq.; nearest in love to the Muslims, 6, 109; say that the Messiah is the Son of God, 6, 177; God will decide between Jews, Sabaeans, Ch., and other faiths, 9, 58; rebuked for introducing monkery, 9, 269; rebuked for not believing in Mohammed's mission, 9, 337 sq.

Church, Buddhist. *See* Samgha.

Circumambulation, honouring a person by going round him towards the right (generally three times), 2, 25; 7, 236 sq.; 10 (ii), 119 sq., 188; 11, 15, 17, 30, 33, 42, 71, 80; 13, 108, 140, 193, 240; 17, 6, 36, 62, 83, 92, 98, 101, 192, 194, 228, 259, 360 sq.; 19, 81; 20, 103, 184, 235, 253, 257, 320, 327, 382; 21, 158, 162, 283, 397, 425; 22, 196; 30, 292; 35, 28; 45, 41, 101, 107, 134; 49 (i), 157, 166; (ii), 10, 112; seven times, 21, 381, 398, 431;—c. of temples, 2, 276 sq. n.; 29, 125; of the holy shrines at the 'Hagg ceremonies, 6, xi; Kaabah seven times circumambulated, 6, xlii, lxxiv, 17; 9, 59; Pradakshi*n*a, the sun-wise c., 12, 37 n. (comp. Gaelic deasil), 272, 272 n.; 44, 323, 323 n., 468; the Adhvaryu walks round the Hot*ri* from left to right, 12, 132 n.; of the altar, 12, 264–6, 425, 432, 432 n., 435, 441 sq.; 26, 283; 43, 170; of the fire, 12, 339, 344, 345 n.; 25, 38 sq.; 29, 37 sq., 68, 177, 360, 384; 30, 20, 29, 222; 44, xxvi; at the wedding, 29, 168 sq., 279, 283, 382; 30, 46, 191, 198, 260 sq.; at the Upanayana, 29, 306; 30, 150; —of the funeral pile three times, 17, 299 sq.; 19, 323; the Devas turn round the Buddha babe to the right, 19, 364; worship of a Stûpa by c., 21, 247; of the animal victim, 26, 186 sq., 187 n.; of the grave, 27, 193; of water at a wedding, 29, 36; of the ground where a house is built, 29, 213, 214; of the burial place, 29, 238, 245 sq.; of the unlucky fire turning the left side towards it, 29, 247; of the house, to protect it from serpents, 29, 330; 30, 238, 288; c. and 'circummingere' of a run-away servant, 29, 350; 30, 176, 296; of the house at the Âgrahâya*n*î ceremony, 30, 95; c. and sprinkling water round the new house, 30, 286; sacred objects to be worshipped by turning the right side towards them, 33, 222; at holy rites, 42, 323; priest walks about the patient to be cured from snake-poison, towards the left, 42, 425 sq.; of a sacrifice, 42, 475; 46, 360; the king's wives walk round the dead horse, in sun-wise fashion, 44, 322 sq., 323 n.; carrying fire round (paryagnikara*n*a), *see* Fire (*d*).

Circumcision, *see* Child (*b*).

Civil law, *see* Law.

Civilization, sketch of the progress of, 16, 382–5, 386 sq. n.

Clothes, clothing, *see* Costume, *and* Garments.

Cloud, Sudassana's Horse Treasure called 'Thunder-c.,' 11, 255, 255 n.; springs from smoke, 41, 85; is the udder whence the shower of wealth flows, 43, 221; called the black bull, and the leather bag, 46, 103, 105; musical c., 49 (ii), 19. *See also* Parganya.

Cloud-spirits, *see* Gods (*j*).

Cook, *see* Birds (*b*).

Cognition (vidyâ), unity of the, 34, 152; 38, 214–16; the self whose nature is unchangeable, eternal c., 34, 185 sq.; internal c. cannot be the abode of mental impressions, 34, 426 sq.; discussion on the separateness or non-separateness of the cs. (vidyâs) of Brahman, which form the subject of the different Vedânta-texts, 38, 101, 184–279; cs. connected with members of sacrificial acts, 38, 252–6, 274; compared with sacrifices, 38, 280;

should there be cumulation of the different cs. or option between them? 38, 280–4; the fruit of all cs. is the intuition of the object meditated upon, 38, 281; cs. which have the qualified Brahman for their object, 38, 330. *See also* Knowledge, *and* Meditation.

Cohabitation, *see* Sexual intercourse.

Coins, dirham (δραχμή), silver c., 18, 180, 180 sq. n.; Dînâras mentioned, 25, xvii, cvii, cx; 33, 232, 275, 317; explanation of value of different c., 33, 231 sq., 316 sq., 391; gold c., 44, 51, 53. *See also* Money.

Cold, effect of it on the body, 8, 238.

Colours, the three, red, white, black, the only thing that is true in the elements, 1, 95 sq.; five c., 3, 59; 27, 382; 28, 111; 39, 55, 269, 274, 279, 286, 328; white the sacred colour of the Shang, red that of the *K*âu dynasty, 3, 327, 333 n.; of victims at sacrifices, 3, 333 sq. n., 343, 343 n., 373, 373 n., 387; twelve forms of c., 8, 384; c. of the veins, and c. on the path to heaven, 15, 167, 177; yellow one of the five 'correct' c., 16, 103 n., 121, 122 n., 128, 129 n., 145, 146 n., 167, 171, 173 n., 304, 305 n., 421; 28, 11, 11 n.; white the colour of mourning, 27, 69; c. used for war and for mourning, 27, 125 sq.; correct and illegitimate c., 27, 238, 238 n.; regulations about dyeing, 27, 278; c. of the different quarters, 27, 328, 328 n.; choice of c. in ceremonies, 27, 405; yellow the c. of the earth, 27, 436; names of c., 32, 17–19, 24; all c. contained in the ruddy, 41, 355; blue and red are magic c., 42, 69, 120, 395, 564, 564 n., 566 sq., 583, 587; c. or outward appearance is everything, 44, 354; the word 'c.' used in a general sense for everything that is perceived by the eye, 45, 187 n.

Comet, *see* Omens.

Commotions, *see* Iñgitas.

Compassion, to all beings, part of the conduct of the good, 8, 114, 243, 326; the ascetic should walk with circumspection over the earth out of c. to all beings, 8, 364; thoughts of pity, the second of the 'infinite feelings,' 9, 201 sq., 273. *See also* Ahimsâ, *and* Charity.

Concentration (of mind on the Brahman), *see* Yoga.

Conception, *see* Child.

Concubines, *see* Marriage, *and* Woman (*f*).

Conduct, *see* Morality, *and* Sîlas.

Confections, *see* Samkhârâs.

Confession of sins accepted, 6, 187 sq.; *when confessed the sin becomes less, since it becomes truth*, 12, 397; the ceremony of c. on the Uposatha, 13, 1 sq., 56 sqq., 242 sq., 245, 282–6; 20, 23 sq.; c. of sin accepted by Buddha, 17, 259–61; 20, 122 sq.; *for this, O Bhikkhus, is called progress in the discipline of the noble one, if one sees his sin in its sinfulness, and duly makes amends for it, and refrains from it in future*, 17, 261; the regular form of c. and acceptance of it, 17, 261; 20, 122, 244; c. and atonement of sins, 17, 274 sq.; proceeding against a Bhikkhu on c. of guilt, 20, 61–4; rules about c. for Bhikkhunîs, 20, 331 sq.; c. of sin in an assembly of Brâhmanas and Kshatriyas, 25, 447; in religion of the Parsis, 31, 285, 288; 37, 46, 145; purifies from sin, 33, 230; in *G*aina religion, 45, 158 sq., 162–4, 179, 384. *See also* Sins.

Confucianism, the religion of China par excellence, 3, xiv; sacred books of C., 3, xiv–xx; destruction of literature of C. by the tyrant of *Kh*in, 3, xvii sq., 6–8; the ritual books of C., 3, xviii sq.; relation between C. and Tâoism, 3, xxii; 39, xii, xv sq., 1–3, 132, 139, 141, 144 sq., 147, 152, 242 n.; 40, 192–201, 288; ceremonies and theology in C., 27, 12–14; the different teaching of the different *K*ings, 27, 38; 28, 255–60; its philosophy and morals exhibited in the *K*ung Yung, 27, 43 sq.; 28, 300–29, 301 n.; Confucian teaching presented in the book Tâ Hsio, 27, 53 sq.; 28, 411–24; triumphed over Tâoism, 39, 33; the Confucian classics recommended as teaching the Tâo, 40, 216, 216 n.

Confucianists, the Literati and the

Mohists or followers of Mo Tî, 39, 182, 182 n., 296, 360; 40, 73, 99 sq., 105, 276, 312; some Literati, students of the Odes and ceremonies, open a grave, to take a pearl from the mouth of the dead, 40, 134 sq., 134 n.; the Literati make hypocritical speeches, 40, 178; Hwan the Confucian scholar makes his brother study the principles of Mo, 40, 204 sq.; Literati and Mohists think how to remedy the world, 40, 286. *See also* Mohism, *and* Mohists.

Confucius.

(*a*) His life and personality.
(*b*) His works and teachings.

(*a*) HIS LIFE AND PERSONALITY.

Interviews between Lâo-ʒze and C., 3, xxi; 39, 2 sq., 34 sq., 317 sq.; 40, 46–9, 47 n.; C. and Lâo-ʒze assist together at a burial, 27, 339; C. and Lâo-ʒze discourse on benevolence and righteousness, 39, 145, 339 sq.; instructed by Lâo-ʒze about the Tâo, 39, 152, 354–7, 354 n., 360–2; 40, 63–6, 292; 'The Old Fisherman' gives C. a lesson in Tâoism, 39, 159; 40, 192–201; being under a condemning sentence of Heaven, C. has not got the Tâo, 39, 252 sq., 252 n.; defeated by Lâo-ʒze, 39, 357 sq.; converted to Tâoism, 40, 32–6, 32 n.; Lâo Lâi-ʒze lectures C., 40, 135 sq., 135 n., 291; how he attained to enjoyment in the Tâo, 40, 289; Hsüan Nî, i.e. C., sighed over 'the Dragon' Lâo-ʒze, 40, 314;—the Duke of *K*âu appears to C. in dreams, 3, 152; his marriage-name *K*ung-nî, 3, 465 n.; 27, 40; 39, 203 n.; historical or legendary accounts of C. in the book Than Kung, 27, 17 sq.; presided at an archery competition, 27, 57; 28, 449 sq.; did he divorce his wife? 27, 122 n., 131 sq. n.; mourns for ʒze-lû, 27, 123 sq., 124 n.; buried his mother in the same grave with his father, 27, 123–5; C. and the mourning rites for Po-kâo, 27, 134 sq.; his death, and mourning for him, 27, 138 sq., 141, 156, 159, 159 n.; as minister of Crime in Lû, 27, 150, 150 n.; has his dog buried, 27, 196 sq., 197 n.; on the spies in Sung, 27, 198; his friendship for Yüan Zang, 27, 198 sq., 199 n.; the guest of Shâo-shih, 28, 171; name of his mother, 27, 190; his visits to *Kh*î and Sung, 27, 368, 368 n.; wore pendant balls of ivory, 28, 19; at meals, 28, 21; called 'the Master,' 28, 227, 229; 39, 309 n., 317; called *Kh*iû, 28, 305, 305 n.; eulogized as the ideal sage, 28, 326 sq., 327 n.; his favourite disciple Yen Hui, 39, 132, 203–10; 40, 158 sq.; and *Kh*ieh-yû, the madman of *Kh*û, 39, 132, 221 sq. and n.; though reduced to extreme distress, plays and sings and is happy, 39, 148, 385–7; 40, 160 sq.; his sorrow at Hui's going to *Kh*î, 39, 149; 40, 7 sq.; when in his sixtieth year, C. changed his views, 39, 156; 40, 144 sq., 144 n.; interview between C. and the robber *K*ih, 39, 157 sq.; 40, 166–76; on terms of friendship with Liû-hsiâ Hui, 39, 157 sq.; 40, 166 sq., 166 n., 175 sq.; C. and Shû-shan the Toeless, 39, 228 sq.; conversation between the Duke Âi of Lû and C. about Âi-thâi Tho, 39, 229–33; wishes to deposit his books in the library of *K*âu, 39, 338 sq. and n.; his misfortunes, 40, 32, 34, 34 n., 37, 160, 172, 197; C. and Wăn-po Hsüeh-ʒze, 40, 44; described by Yen Yüan as a mental thaumaturgist, 40, 44–6, 45 n.; reproaches Yen Yüan for criticizing King Wăn, 40, 53; *K*ü Po-yü, his friend, 40, 124 n.; C. about Duke Ling of Wei, 40, 124–26; C. and ʒăng-ʒze, 40, 145; his costume, 40, 168, 172; a truly noble scholar, 40, 177; received presents from Thien *Kh*ang, 40, 177, 177 n.; did not see his mother, 40, 180, 180 n.; how he devotes himself to benefiting the kingdom, 40, 193; treated with reverence by great rulers, 40, 200; Yen Ho describes C. to Âi of Lû as unfit to be entrusted with the government, 40, 207–9; the scholar of Lû, favourable judgement passed on him, 40, 216, 216 n.; C. and ʒze-sang Hû, 40, 289 sq.; and Yen-ʒze, 40, 293; and Zăn *Kh*iû, 40, 293; *K*wang-ʒze's relation to C., 40, 321 sq.

(*b*) HIS WORKS AND TEACHINGS.

He was a transmitter and not a maker, 3, xiv, 3; author of *Kh*un

*Kh*iû or 'Spring and Autumn,' 3, xix sq.; the Hsiâo King, conversations between C. and his disciple Ȝăng-ȝze, 3, xx, 449–51, 461 sq., 465–88; quotes the Shû King, he did not compile it, 3, 2–4; on the old historical documents, 3, 5; Preface to the Shih ascribed to him, 3, 276, 296; what he did for the Shih King, 3, 280–4, 337; reformed the music, 3, 284; on ancestor worship, 3, 299 sq., 302; Appendixes of the Yî King ascribed to him, 16, xiii sq., xvii–xix, 1–3, 7 sq., 26, 28–31, 46 sq., 53 sq., 360 n., 364 sq. n., 371 n.; on the study of the Yî King, 16, 1; the best teacher of the Chinese nation, 16, 31; how he spoke of the Lî *K*î, 27, 1; replies to the questions of Ȝăng-ȝze, 27, 21 sq., 311–42; C. and Ȝâi Wo, on the constitution of man, 27, 36; 28, 220-2; on the teaching of the *K*ings, 27, 38; 28, 255 sq., 258; conversation between Duke Âi and C., 27, 39; 28, 261–9; discourses to his three disciples on ceremonies and government, 27, 40; 28, 270–7; discourse of C. with Ȝze-hsiâ on the sovereign as 'the parent of the people,' 27, 41; 28, 278–83; 'Words of the Master,' not really those of C., 27, 44–6; 28, 330–64; on the conduct of the scholar, 27, 51 sq.; 28, 402–10; on the jade symbol, 27, 59; 28, 463 sq.; on the law of inheritance, 27, 120; on funeral rites and mourning, 27, 122–5, 127, 129–31, 134, 136–8, 146, 148–50, 153, 155 sq., 160, 170, 172 sq., 175 sq., 175 n., 182, 184 sq., 192 sq., 202; 28, 152 sq., 160, 163, 164, 168, 394; on revenge for bloodshed, 27, 140; on oppressive government, 27, 190 sq.; on education of princes, 27, 351; on ceremonies, 27, 364–72, 401, 403, 414 sq., 423 sq., 437; on music, 27, 419; 28, 121–4; on court-robes, 28, 11; on sacrifices, 28, 166 sq., 213; on filial piety, 28, 217; on the state of equilibrium and harmony, 28, 301–29; does not search for what is mysterious, 28, 303 sq.; handed down the views of Yâo and Shun, Wăn, and Wû, 28, 326; on festivities in the country districts, 28, 440–2, 442 n.; on archery, 28, 452 sq.; his Tâo or Path of duty different from Lâo-ȝze's Tâo, 39, 29; did not accept the doctrine of returning good for evil, 39, 31; advises Ȝze-kâo, the duke of Sheh, 39, 132, 210–14; expounds and extols Tâoism, 39, 136, 250–7, 253 n., 255 n., 257 n.; C. and the swimmer in the cataract, 39, 150; 40, 20 sq., 20 n.; a description of Tâoism ascribed to him? 39, 192 sq. n.; difference between Tâoists and C. as to pursuit of knowledge, 39, 198 n.; on the virtues of a Tâoist sage, 39, 223–6, 322; 40, 72 sq.; conversations and parables intended to ridicule his views, 39, 351–4; said to have studied six books, 39, 360; the knowledge of C. made little of, 39, 375 sq.; tells the story of the hunchback who, by his concentration of mind, is clever in catching cicadas, 40, 14 sq. and n.; about the ferryman who handled the boat like a spirit, 40, 15 sq.; warns men against injuring the life by indulging in sensual desires, 40, 17 sq.; instructs Yen Hui about the Human and the Heavenly, 40, 37–9; describes the True men of old, 40, 55; instructs his disciple Zăn *Kh*iû, 40, 71 sq.; makes 'a speech without words,' 40, 104 sq., 104 n.; on the duties of a master, 40, 117 sq.; on the difficulty of knowing the mind of man, and nine methods of testing it, 40, 209; about putting aside subjects concerning which doubts are entertained, 40, 296, 296 n.

Congregation Day, prayers to be said on, 9, 283, 283 n.

Conjugal intercourse, *see* Sexual intercourse.

Conjunction (sa*m*yoga): the distinction of the Vai*s*eshikas between c. and inherence, 34, 390, 396 sq.; the connexion between the Lord and the souls and pradhâna cannot be c., 34, 436.

Conjurers, *see* Sorcerers.

Connubial intercourse, *see* Sexual intercourse.

Consanguinity, *see* Family.

Conscience, the righteous souls met by their own c. in the shape of a beautiful maiden, the wicked souls by their own c. in the shape of an old woman, 23, 315–17, 319 sq. n., 343 sq. *See also* Works (*c*).

Consciousness, pain arises from, 10 (ii), 135 sq.; the cessation of c. stops name and form, 10 (ii), 191; *the non-existence of external things cannot be maintained, on account of our c. of them*, 34, 418–24; being and c. are one, 48, 33; is self-proved, 48, 33–5, 47–50; is eternal and incapable of change, 48, 35 sq.; there is no real difference between c. and conscious subject, 48, 36–8; being and c. are not one, 48, 47; is not eternal, 48, 50–2; there is no c. without object, 48, 52–4; is capable of change, 48, 54 sq.; the attribute of a permanent conscious self, 48, 56 sqq.; the view that the conscious subject is unreal, owing to the aha*m*kâra, refuted, 48, 61–7; the conscious subject persists in deep sleep, 48, 67–9; c. of the 'I' persists in the state of release, 48, 69–72.

Consecration of ponds, wells, tanks, gardens, 29, 134–6; c. of the sacrificer for a sacrifice, *see* Dîkshâ.

Consideration (*k*itta), meditation on it as Brahman, 1, 114.

Constellation, *see* Stars.

Contamination, *see* Impurity, *and* Nasu.

Contemplation, *see* Meditation.

Contentment, the devotee is always contented, 8, 60, 101; c. is from K*r*ish*n*a, 8, 86; virtue of c., 8, 325 sq.; better than fame or wealth or life, 39, 87 sq.; ambition the greatest guilt, discontent the greatest calamity, 39, 89.

Contracts, law about, 4, lxxxii, 34–9, 45 sq., 255; breaking c., a sin against Mithra, 23, 120, 120 n., 149 sq.; c. breakers amongst the creatures of Angra Mainyu, 31, 313; breach of c. of service, a title of law, 33, 131–44; inscribed on slips of wood or bamboo, 39, 121, 133; the Tâoist regards the conditions of a c., 39, 121 sq.; bloody sacrifices offered at the conclusion of c., 40, 164, 164 n.

Convents, *see* Monasteries, *and* Vihâras.

Converts, *see* Buddha (*c*).

Corporations, violation of agreements between members of, 25, 253, 293 sq., 293 n.; 33, 346–50; legal assemblies of cultivators, artisans, &c., forming c., 33, 281 sq.; documents to be read before assemblies of c., 33, 308. *See also* Assemblies.

Corpse(s): the earth grieved by c. buried in it or lying on Dakhmas, 4, 24 sq. and n.; he who digs out most c. of dogs and men, and pulls down most Dakhmas, pleases the earth, 4, 26; eating of a c. an abomination, 4, 81, 81 n.; in towns where a c. lies, Veda-study must be interrupted, 14, 64; water, fire, earth contaminated by a c., 18, 229, 229 sq. n.; the ocean will not brook association with c., but throws them out, 20, 301, 303; headless c. dance over the battlefield, 36, 147; pollution through a c., 37, 153 sq., 256 sq.; hideousness of the c., and misery of its consciousness, 37, 200 sq.; fire distressed by carrying a c., 47, 101. *See also* Death (*c*), Drug, *and* Impurity.

Cosmogony, *see* Creation, *and* World (*b*).

Cosmology, *see* World (*d*).

Costume of a Brâhma*n*a householder, esp. during religious ceremonies, the sacrificial cord (yag*ñ*opavîta, prâ*k*înavîta), 1, 285, 285 n.; 2, 54, 108, 110, 180 sq., 278; 7, 114 sq., 117, 119; 8, 359; 12, 228 n., 361, 361 n., 364 n., 365 n., 421, 424, 424 n., 426, 428, 433 sq., 436; 14, 44, 49, 49 n., 165 sq., 181, 186–8, 224, 255, 269, 269 sq. n.; 18, 132 n.; 25, 38, 41, 127; 29, 86, 122, 162, 217, 220, 252, 252 n., 255, 356, 374; 30, 13, 16–18, 16 n., 44 n., 107, 146, 219, 226, 244, 251, 299, 331 sq.; 38, 298; of the Brahma*k*ârin, 2, 9 sq., 23, 176 sq.; 8, 360; 14, 56 sq., 150, 152; 25, 37 sq., 41; 29, 59–62, 67 sq., 82–4, 187 sq., 191, 304 sq., 309 sq., 401 sq., 404; 30, 63 sq., 67, 70 sq., 73, 138 sq., 147 sq., 157, 160, 272, 274 sq.; 32, 232–4; of a Snâtaka, 2, 29, 93, 219, 223; 7, 225, 227; 14, 60, 62, 159, 242; 25, 134, 139; 29, 91 sq., 104, 315 sq., 318,

408 sq.; 30, 84, 86, 163, 166–9, 276 sq.; during the performance of magic rites, 2, 150, 150 n.; of the ascetic, 2, 154, 194; 14, 47, 260, 274, 277–9, 291; 49 (i), 68 sq., 75, 77; of the hermit, 2, 155, 195, 195 n.; 8, 361; 14, 45, 259, 293 sq.; 25, 199, 199 n.; of *S*ûdras, 2, 233; some sects wear skins, others go without covering, 8, 375; upper garment to be worn on certain occasions, 14, 245; worn at a fast, 14, 307; of Buddhist monks, 19, 181 sq., 197; 35, 18 sq., 30; 36, 57; Mau*ñg*îbandhana, tying the sacred girdle, 25, 34, 37 sq. and n., 61; of the Dîkshita, 26, 28 sq., 32–4; of teacher and pupil, 29, 226–8; of the king in battle, 29, 233 sq.; of the bride, 30, 44; of umpire fixing boundary, 33, 352; insignia of religious orders, 33, 361; local c. and c. of castes to be preserved, 33, 390; —sacred thread-girdle and sacred shirt to be worn by Zoroastrians, 4, 193–5, 193 n., 195 n., 198, 204, 204 n., 279, 325, 357, 359; 5, lxi, 106 sq., 128 sq., 129 n., 205, 208, 212, 285–9, 286 n., 314 sq., 320 sq.; 18, xxviii, 122 n., 130, 133 sq., 133 n.; 23, 29, 349; 24, 11, 11 n.; 37, 96, 125, 163, 182, 182 n., 289; 47, 50, 134, 151; reasons for wearing the sacred thread-girdle, 18, 122–34, 122 n.; 24, 268–70; *see also* Child (*b*); the sacred shirt, the garment of Vohûman, 18, 129, 129 n., 133, 133 n., 162; the Nîrang-i Kustî, or girdle formula, 18, 383–8; sin of being improperly dressed or shod, 5, lxi, 287–9, 287 n., 288 sq. n., 320, 320 n.; 18, 123, 123 n., 133 sq.; 24, 11, 11 n., 307; 37, 182, 182 n.; —at state ceremonies in Chinese courts, 3, 240 sq.; of the wild tribes in China, 3, 249, 249 n.; at sacrifices, 3, 334, 334 n.; 27, 104, 115, 227, 242 sq., 278, 467; 28, 141, 186–8; different according to rank, 3, 469, 469 n.; 28, 9–20, 14 n.; kings wear red, nobles scarlet knee-covers, 16, 162, 164 n.,; at various ceremonies, 27, 27 sq., 242 sq., 432 sq., 437 sq.; 28, 1–3, 9–20, 14 n., 23; men wear the cap, women the hairpin, 27, 40; *see also* Child (*b*); Shăn Î, the long dress in one piece, 27, 50; 28, 395 sq.; of mourning, 27, 69, 69 n.; fashion of clothes regulated by the emperor, 27, 217; crime of using strange garments, 27, 237 sq.; regulations for dresses, 27, 288; of rulers and others at ancestor-worship, 27, 374, 374 n.; c. and ornaments as marks of distinction, 27, 400; of the king at border sacrifices, 27, 429 sq.; dark-coloured robes worn during vigil and purification, 27, 448; of boys and girls, 27, 449–51; of the learned, 40, 49 sq., 49 n.; of Confucius, 40, 168, 172; of Mohists, 40, 220, 222, 222 n. *See also* Garments.

Councils: Zoroastrianism settled by a disputation under Shâhpûhr II, 4, xxxviii, xlvii; council convoked by Emperor Hsüan to discuss the text of the Chinese classics, 27, 6; Buddhist c., *see* Buddhism (*b*).

Countries, *see* Geography.

Courage, the virtue of, 8, 90, 114, 124, 167 sq., 182, 325, 373; one of the changes of the Kshetra, 8, 102 n., 103; three kinds of c., 8, 125 sq.; duty of Kshatriyas, 8, 126; a term signifying the great Self, 8, 332; Manly C., a genius, 23, 10, 18, 136 sq., 295; prayer as powerful as Manly C., 23, 160.

Courtesan, *see* Prostitution.

Courts of Justice, *see* Judicial procedure.

Covetousness: *whosoever is saved from his own c. these are the prosperous*, 9, 275, 287. *See also* Avarice.

Cow, cows.

(*a*) Sacredness of the c. and its products.
(*b*) C. in mythology and mysticism.
(*c*) Miscellaneous.

(*a*) Sacredness of the c. and its products.

The father makes a lowing sound over his son's head, saying: 'I low over thee with the lowing sound of c.,' 1, 288; tending c., a penance, 2, 80, 81 n.; 7, 162; 25, 459, 481; taking the c. of Brâhma*n*as from robbers, end of a penance, 2, 81; are sacred, 2, 94 sq., 220; 7, xxix; 14, 36; 25, 135–7, 151; 31, 249; 33, 222; duties towards c., 2, 221; 7, 228; 14, 242 sq.; foes declaring

themselves to be c. or Brâhma*n*as must not be slain, 2, 229, 229 n.; men slain for the sake of c., 2, 250; 7, 67; 25, 185; food smelt at by a c. forbidden, 2, 266; the sin or crime of killing c., penances and punishments for it, 2, 281; 7, 136, 158 sq.; 14, 202; 25, 442, 453; the cleanser delights the c., 4, 133; dying for c. secures beatitude, 7, 18; 25, 416; feeding of c. an expiatory rite for *S*ûdra, 7, 50; *c. are auspicious purifiers, upon c. depend the worlds, c. alone make sacrificial oblations possible (by producing sacrificial butter), c. take away every sin.... Scratching the back of a c. destroys all guilt, and giving her to eat procures exaltation in heaven. In the urine of c. dwells the Ganges, prosperity (dwells) in the dust (rising from their couch), good fortune in cow-dung, and virtue in saluting them. Therefore should they be constantly saluted*, 7, 105 sq.; when c. have met with an accident, or have not eaten, Veda-study must be interrupted, 7, 125; 29, 118; food given to a c., equal to alms given to ascetics, 7, 193; when a c. or a Brâhma*n*a has met with a calamity, one must not eat on that day, 7, 218; the first among quadrupeds, 8, 353; *like unto a mother, a father, a brother, and other relatives, the c. are our best friends, in which medicines are produced. They give food, and they give strength, they likewise give (a good) complexion and happiness; knowing the real state of this, they did not kill c.*, 10 (ii), 50 sq.; land is purified by being trodden on by c., 14, 24, 188; 25, 190; a Brâhma*n*a who protects c. is worthy to receive gifts, 14, 39; bestowing gifts for the use of c. meritorious, 14, 136; to protect c., a Brâhma*n*a or Vai*s*ya may take up arms, 14, 236; way must be made for a c., 14, 243; he shall raise his arm in the midst of a herd of c., 14, 245; a performer of rites securing success should worship c., Brâhma*n*as, manes, and gods, 14, 323; suckling c. not to be interrupted, 25, 138; must not be offended, 25, 154; touching a c. purifies, 25, 183, 472; for the sake of fodder for a c. one may swear falsely, 25, 273; damage done by c. and cattle sacred to the gods, 25, 297, 297 n.; taking grass for feeding c. is no theft, 25, 313; doing good to or dying for c. a penance, 25, 446 sq.; worshipping and serving c. in atonement for slaying a c., 25, 453 sq.; scattering grass to a c., a kind of oracle, 25, 470; the sacrificer must not be naked in the presence of a c., 26, 9; *the gods spake, 'Verily, the c. and the ox support everything here: come, let us bestow on the c. and the ox whatever vigour belongs to other species!'* 26, 9, 11; the Dîkshita shall not eat the flesh of a c. or an ox, 26, 11; called 'the great ones,' 26, 14; the c. for which the Soma is bought, 26, 54-63, 69-71, 74, 156; different-coloured c. sacred to Soma, Indra, and the Fathers, 26, 62 sq.; worshipped at the Tarpa*n*a, 29, 122, 219; the hi*m*kâra of the c., 29, 298; a Snâtaka should not point out a c. suckling her calf, 29, 318; at the Â*s*vayuga sacrifice they let the calves join their mothers, 29, 332 sq.; when driving towards c. in a chariot, one should dismount in the middle of them, 29, 364; he who expels the evil world-destroyer benefits the c., 31, 131 sq., 136, 136 sq. n.; men toil for the c., and Ahura created the plants for her, 31, 152, 155 sq.; he who spreads Zoroastrianism furthers the kine, 31, 169 sq., 171 sq.; curse of the c. and horse, when they are stinted, 31, 244 sq.; the Zoroastrian deprecates all violence against the c., who is Ahura-Mazda's, 31, 248; the Fravashi of the kine worshipped, 31, 252; the herd-owner is the father of the kine and the typical saint, 31, 306 n., 307 sq.; the farm-house with its pastures which give pasture to the kine and the holy cattle-breeding man worshipped, 31, 337 sq., 341; *harm not the inexhaustible wide-ruling c.*, 41, 406, 406 n.; the c. of a Brâhma*n*a inviolable, 42, 169-72, 430 sq.; he who kicks a c. will be bereft of his shadow, 42, 214; tainted is the milk of a c. suckling an adopted calf, 44, 198;—drinking the Pañ*k*agavya (the five productions of a c., viz. milk, sour milk, butter, urine, and dung) as a purification, 2,

276 n.; 7, 89, 89 n., 95–7, 103, 150 sq., 168, 175; 14, 131, 168–72, 174, 183, 187 n., 188, 190 sq., 324–8; 25, 449, 453, 464, 474; cow-dung a means of purifying, 7, 97, 105, 260; 14, 24, 64; 25, 187, 190; hair of c. a means of purifying, 7, 100; drops of water falling from the horns of a c. produce religious merit and expiate sins, 7, 105; six products of the c. (urine, dung, &c., and Goro*k*anâ), propitious, 7, 105 sq., 105 n.; swallowing barley-corns dissolved in the excrements of a c., an expiatory rite, 7, 154; altar smeared with cow-dung, 14, 262, 307; 29, 22, 162, 269, 276, 334, 376 sq.; 30, 14, 27, 43, 64, 89; 44, 191; great merit of drinking gruel made of barley-grains which have passed through a cow, 14, 299; c.'s urine used for purification, 25, 190; a witness shall hold gold, cow-dung, or blades of sacred grass in his hand, 33, 302; horn of a c. used for medical charms, 42, 481 sq.; dried cow-dung used for burning dead body, 44, 202;—cow-pens, sacred places, 2, 276; 14, 117, 249, 311; 25, 136, 138; Veda not to be studied in a cow-pen, 25, 147; penance of living in a cow-pen, 25, 446, 453, 470; Samâvartana ceremony performed in a cow-shed, 30, 165, 275.

(*b*) C. IN MYTHOLOGY AND MYSTICISM.

The wish-granting c., 8, 89; 42, 183; 49 (i), 157; the rays of the sun as heavenly c., 12, 271, 271 n.; the earth is a c., 12, 308; 44, 268; the c. is food and sacrifice, 12, 325 sq.; the milk of the c. is Agni's seed, 12, 326, 330; *see also* Milk; I*d*â, Aditi, Sarasvatî, divine names of c., 12, 355; 26, 415 sq.; 41, 406 n.; 44, 474; the c. are children of the Sun, 14, 134 sq.; speech meditated on as a c., 15, 193; the body and soul of the c. (Drvâspa, Go*s*ûrûn, Gô*s*), 23, 9, 17, 110; Mithra delivers the c. (like Indra), 23, 141, 141 n.; man's skin was put on the cow, 26, 9, 13 sq.; 41, 31 n.; the c. is food and hence breath, 26, 348; the c. with the five names, the five seasons, 29, 342; Ushas, the c., 29, 343; the kine's soul, the emblem of the pious, 31, xix–xxi; the Soul of the Kine (Geu*s* Urvan) complains to Ahura and Asha, 31, 3–11; Ahura, the Creator of the Kine, 31, 38, 44 sq., 146, 148, 181; eating kine's flesh introduced by Yima, 31, 55, 61; the sacred kine blasphemed by Daêva-worshippers, 31, 55, 62, 62 n.; evil are those who have slain the kine's life by a blessing, 31, 55, 63; they who work in the toil of the mother-kine further the highest wisdom, 31, 82, 90; for whom has Ahura made the mother-kine, 31, 109, 114; the Karpan and the Usig gave the kine to rapine, 31, 121; striving to gain the sacred kine, 31, 177, 180; the Karpans grant no pastures to the kine, 31, 184; the kine, the body of the kine, and the kine's soul worshipped, 31, 196, 244, 256, 278, 287 sq., 324 sq., 348, 362, 385, 391; the moon, which contains the seed of the kine, 31, 199, 210, 216, 225, 256; the c. (days, clouds) released by Indra, 32, 14, 37, 44; clouds as c., 32, 295 sq., 299; is of Varu*n*a's, of Rudra's nature, 41, 51 sq.; a c. means these worlds, 41, 156; the fire-pan is a c., 41, 237; created from Pra*g*âpati's breath, 41, 402; the c. is wide-ruling and is food, 41, 406; the milch-c. is vigour, 43, 39; the bricks of the fire-altar as milch-c., 43, 171–4; a black c. with a white calf symbolical of night and sun, 43, 200; the thousand-streamed c. milked by Ka*n*va, 43, 203; man's form (wealth) is kine, 44, 261; *the c. lowed at the sight of the sun*, 46, 57; Dyaus approached the speckled c., 46, 74, 79; Mitra and Varu*n*a watch over the beloved ambrosia in the c., 46, 75; *Saramâ found the strong stable of the c. from which human clans receive their nourishment*, 46, 83; the lowing milch-c. of *R*ita, 46, 88; Agni, the father of the ruddy c. (dawns), 46, 220, 227; waters or dawns represented as c., 46, 248, 250, 313; Agni has perforated, as it were, the pure udder of the c., 46, 309; the c. (dawns) imprisoned in the rock

delivered by the seven *Ri*shis or Aṅgiras, 46, 309, 313, 318, 322, 326, 329 sq.; the secret name of the c., 46, 371; Agni has found the c., 46, 397. *See also* Bull, Cattle, Gô*s*, Gô*s*ûrvan, *and* I*d*â.

(*c*) MISCELLANEOUS.

C. slain or let loose at the reception of guests, 2, 120, 120 n.; 29, 199 sq., 275 sq., 433 sq.; 30, 129, 131, 174; the offering of the barren (anubandhyâ) c., 26, 215 n., 217, 387–9, 391–7; 41, 87; 43, 263–5; 44, 402, 411; two Madhuparka c., sacrificed at a wedding, 29, 34; sacrificed at the Ash*t*akâ, 29, 344; killed in honour of a deceased person, 29, 359; a sterile c. offered with the dead body, 44, 205 n.; a c. wont to cast her calf, victim at horse sacrifice, 44, 300; bovine victims, as the highest kind of animals represent all animals, 44, 332, 332 n.;—purification of c. from contamination, 4, 93 sq., 144; sacrifice to Pûshan in a fire kindled among the c., at the ceremony of setting a bull at liberty, 7, 261; milking the c. at sacrifices, 12, 183–9, 409 sq., 412, 415; the Agnihotra c., 12, 353, 353 n.; 44, 46, 48, 181–3; Â*s*vayuga sacrifice, besprinkling the c., 29, 415; ceremonies when the c. are sick, 29, 432 sq.; prayer for the c., 31, 283, 332, 363; sham fight for c. at the Râgasûya, 41, 98–101, 100 n.; the samrâ*g*-c. which supplies the milk for the pravargya, 44, 131–4, 474, 503; tail of barren c. tied to the left arm of a dead man, 44, 438 n.;—religious merit of giving c., c. as fees for priests and teachers, 7, 264 sq., 272; 14, 135, 137; 15, 1; 41, 46, 51 sq., 60; 44, 46, 113, 115, 503; offered as a prize for him who best knows Brahman, 15, 121 sq., 132, 152–8; sterile c. must be given to the Brahmans, 42, 174–9, 656–61; a c. longing for the bull presented to an offended Brâhma*n*a, 44, 195;—bestial crimes with c., 2, 287 sq.; 14, 118; the c. that are like goats, 10 (ii), 51; punishment for stealing c., 33, 228, 362; readily take to a boar, 41, 103; most fit to yield livelihood, 41, 237; have four nipples, 41, 237; a milked-out c. worn out, 41, 257; the redness of the c., 42, 7, 265; milked by sitting person, 43, 172; woman, mare, and c. bring forth within a year, 44, 12; born as one yielding milk 44, 294; have proper names, 44, 474, 474 n.

Cow-dung, *see* Cow (*a*).

Cow-pen, *see* Cow (*a*).

Craftsmen, *see* Labourers.

Crane, *see* Birds (*b*).

Craving, *see* Desire, *and* Ta*n*hâ.

Creation.

(*a*) In Indian religions and philosophies.
(*b*) In Zoroastrianism.
(*c*) In Islâm.
(*d*) In Confucianism and Tâoism.

(*a*) IN INDIAN RELIGIONS AND PHILOSOPHIES.

All c. springs from the Sat, 1, xxxi, 93; 48, 399, 453, 456 sq., 472 sq., 478; from the egg, 1, 54 sq.; 15, 337; 44, xiv, xviii sq., 12–18; 48, 578–83; from the non-existent what exists was born, 1, 93; 15, 58; 41, 143; 48, 465; according to the *Kh*ândogya-upanishad, 1, 93–7, 100, 100 n.; 38, 4; the Person, by his speech, breath, &c., created earth (with fire), sky (with air), &c., 1, 210–12; from the Âtman, 1, 237–41; 2, 77; 34, 69; 48, 391; use of the word tap for 'to create,' 'to brood over,' 1, 238 n.; of the senses, &c., and their presiding deities, 1, 238–40; is the work of Pragâpati and of the sages, 2, 160; 25, lxv; by Vish*n*u, 7, 1, 3–5; 8, 354; K*r*ish*n*a created the four castes, 8, 59; from Brahman, 8, 104; 15, 28 sq., 58; 34, 117; 38, 183; 44, 27 sq.; 48, 473, 475, 532–40, 561; by K*r*ish*n*a (the father) and Brahman (the womb), 8, 107; from the Brahman the waters are produced, from the waters the gross body, 8, 187; transmigration begins with the c. of beings, 8, 234; of the Pradhâna, and the three worlds, by Brahman, 8, 244; from what were the movable and immovable entities born? 8, 311; the eternal c., consisting of the great self, of egoism, of the ten senses, and the mind, and the elements, 8, 317; the c. of

the qualities is eternal, 8, 331; the great self the first c. from the unperceived (Prak*ri*ti), 8, 332 sq.; the Mahat or Egoism the second c., 8, 333 sq.; from egoism the five great elements were born, 8, 335; of gods, men, &c., by nature, not by actions, 8, 387; by Pra*g*âpati, 8, 388; 12, 296, 322–7; 38, 206; 44, xix, 12–18, 62; of the earth, 12, 280 n.; 41, 232; Pra*g*âpati created three generations which passed away, the fourth remained, 12, 384–91; c. and creator have a phenomenal character only, 15, xxxvi; 34, 357; the world arises from Brahman, as the spider sends forth and draws in its thread, as plants grow on the earth, as hairs spring forth on the head, 15, 28; everything comes from the heavenly Person, 15, 34 sq.; order of c., 15, 54 sq.; 38, 3–24, 26–8; everything produced from Death or Hunger, 15, 74 sqq.; 43, 402 sq.; of men and beasts, by the Self, 15, 85 sq.; of the gods, Brahman's highest c., 15, 86–90; in the beginning this world was water, 15, 191; 32, 2, 10; 44, xix, 12–18; Pra*g*âpati produced matter and spirit, that they might produce creatures, 15, 272; of lifeless creatures, afterwards animated, by Pra*g*âpati, 15, 292 sq.; the world uttered by Pra*g*âpati, 15, 308; Manu's and Bh*r*igu's accounts of the c., 25, xii, lxvi, lxxxi–lxxxiii, lxxxvii–xc, xcv, 2–18, 21 sq., 24 sq., 27; 48, 410; Pra*g*âpati created the eaters and those who are eaten, 25, 173 sq.; the Creators of the universe, 25, 495, 495 n.; 42, 226; this all results from the sacrifice, 26, 155; 43, xiv; the gods caused the seed to spring, from it coals sprung, from them the Aṅgiras, then the animals, 26, 387 sq. and n.; cattle created from Pra*g*âpati, the sacrifice, 26, 406–9; Hira*n*yagarbha established heaven and earth, 32, 1 sq.; owing to an act of volition on the Lord's part, 34, xxix; 48, 471 sq.; according to Râmânu*g*a, 34, l, liii sq.; 48, 790; according to the Upanishads, 34, cv sq., cxviii, 140–2, 263–6; 38, 3, 22, 374–7; preceded by intention on the part of the Creator, 34, 47 sq.; 38, 206; 48, 119, 201; Brahman and ether before and after c., 34, 50, 286; 38, 8; is preceded by the word, 34, 203 sq.; each new c. is the result of the religious merit and demerit of the animated beings of the preceding c., 34, 214; the relation of senses and sense-objects is the same in different creations, 34, 214 sq.; the world was evolved at the beginning of the c. in the same way as it is at present seen to develop itself by names and forms, viz. under the rulership of an intelligent creator, 34, 268; no separate c. of the individual soul, 34, 279; 38, 31; a multiform c. exists in the individual Self, and in gods, &c., 34, 352 sq.; the c. of this world is mere play to the Lord, 34, 357; 48, 405 sq., 476 sq.; in consequence of the Lord's conjunction with Mâyâ, the c. is unavoidable, 34, 357 n.; neither c. nor pralaya could take place, if the atomic theory were adopted, 34, 386–9, 391; c. according to the Vai*s*eshika system, 34, 387; is the c. taking place in dreams a real one, or does it consist of illusion? 38, 133–41; the so-called real c. is not absolutely real, 38, 138; accomplished by some inferior Lord different from and superintended by the highest Self, 38, 206; of the elements, different from the c. of the worlds, 38, 206–8; of the universe, 41, 143–61; 48, 242–6, 460 sq., 465 sq.; of animals, 41, 199, 402; heaven and earth were together at first, 41, 318; the four Vedas in accounts of the c., 42, lii; the earth was formerly water upon the ocean of space, 42, 200; everything created by Rohita (the sun), 42, 213 sq.; the sun as the primaeval principle of the universe represented as a Brahman disciple, 42, 214–17, 626 sq.; everything created by Time, 42, 224 sq.; creative principles, 42, 629; the sacrifice a microcosmic representation of the destruction and c. of the universe, 43, xv, xvii, xix; symbolized in the building of the fire-altar, 43, 30–6, 47, 147 sq.;

Pragâpati and the vital airs produce the universe by praises and sacrifices, 43, 71–6; mind as the ultimate cause of the universe, 43, 374–80; Pragâpati created the three worlds, the three lights, and the three Vedas, 44, 102 sq.; observance of Pravargya is the same as c., 44, 458, 458 n., 468, 472, 478, 493, 504, 510; refutation of the different views of c., 45, 244 sq.; all texts referring to c. teach that the Supreme Lord is the cause of c., 48, 206; c. by Brahman entering into all non-intelligent beings with the living soul, 48, 217 sq., 226; effected by Brahmâ and other divine beings in each Kalpa, 48, 238; four classes of creatures evolved according to their Karman, 48, 328; Pragâpati evolved names and forms by means of the Veda, 48, 332; c. and pralaya, 48, 333 sq., 368, 603; the Lord of Mâyâ creates all this, 48, 368; what was the wood, what was the tree from which they shaped heaven and earth? 48, 401, 475; Brahman in all Kalpas again and again creates the same world, 48, 405; by Nârâyana, 48, 472, 522; God is the operative cause in c., Karman the material cause, 48, 478 sq.; the flow of c. goes on from all eternity, 48, 479; results from connexion of Prakriti and soul, 48, 490, 492; the Prânas created, 48, 568–70; oneness of all previous to c., 48, 572; the differentiation of names and forms belongs, not to Hiranyagarbha (i.e. Brahmâ), but to Brahman, 48, 578–83; creative fervour, *see* Tapas.

(*b*) In Zoroastrianism.

Accounts of c. in Avesta and Pentateuch, 4, lviii; of Aûharmazd and counter-c. and attacks of the Evil Spirit, 4, lxx, 1–10; 5, 5 sq., 9–14, 17–20, 33, 52, 54 sq., 65 sq., 71–4, 105 sq., 113 sq., 159 sq.; 18, 93–8; 24, 32 sq.; 31, xix, 25 sq., 30, 292 sq.; the Good Spirit, and the Amesha-Spentas made the c., 4, 212; by Ahura-Mazda, 4, 221; 5, 3, 121–3, 360; 18, 307 sq.; 24, 117 sq.; 31, 285 sq.; 37, 229–31, 248 sq., 270, 439 sq., 456; account of it in the Bundahis, 5, xxiii, 5–114; of prototypes, 5, xxiii, 5, 5 n., 156; of demons, 5, 6, 9 sq.; Pahlavi and Avesta words meaning 'to create,' 5, 9 n.; of the archangels, 5, 9 sq.; order of c., 5, 10; of seas and rivers, 5, 28 sq.; of mountains, 5, 29 sq.; of plants, 5, 30 sq.; of animals, 5, 31 sq.; 37, 150; of man, 5, 52–4; 18, 25 sq., 88, 197–9, 224 sq.; 24, 117 sq.; completed in 365 days, 5, 91; of Time, 5, 160; each of the archangels has produced his own c., 5, 373; the purpose of c., 18, 15–19, 25 sq.; 24, 181 sq.; 37, 443; c. and resurrection, 18, 82, 82 n.; 37, 431; the sky and the creatures provided in it by Aûharmazd, 18, 86–93; Ahura-Mazda assisted by the Fravashis in the work of c., 23, 187; Gâhambârs celebrated in commemoration of the c., 24, 27 n.; due to the innate wisdom of Aûharmazd, 24, 98 sq., 99 n.; proofs of the existence of a creator derived from the evident design in the c., 24, 139–51, 164–7; criticism of the Old Testament account of c., 24, 208 sq., 212–17; Mânîchaean account of c. criticized, 24, 243 sq.; that which exists, that which is in the course of emerging into existence, and that which shall be, 31, 262; Ahura and one of the Ameshôspentas created all things, 31, 298, 298 n.; the ancient institutions created before the sky, the water, &c., 31, 346; account of it in the Dâmdâd Nask, 37, 13 sq., 14 n.; of corn, 37, 102 sq.; of man and cattle, 37, 238 sq.; for the benefit of the creatures, 37, 296; Ahunavair prayer the first of c., 37, 303 sq., 303 n.; goodness of the c. by Aûharmazd, 37, 420 sq.; the best c., *see under* Highest Good.

(*c*) In Islâm.

God created men and the world, 6, 3, 127 sq., 232, 245 sq., 251 sq.; of man from clay, Adam and Eve, 6, 4 sq., 138 sq., 161, 246 sq., 251; 9, 56, 65 sq., 126, 136, 158 sq., 167 sq., 181 sq., 196 sq., 242 sq., 248, 253 sq., 258, 264, 312, 320, 323, 328, 332, 336; God created heavens and earth, 6, 69, 115, 144, 242; 9, 122 sq., 125 sq., 132, 134,

157, 164 sq., 177, 182, 186, 188, 196 sq., 205 sq., 208, 211, 222, 224, 242, 247, 286, *303*, 316, 319; God created the world in six days, 6, 144, 192, 205; 9, 88, 135 sq., 199 sq., 244, 244 n., 266; is a sign of God's power, 6, 193; 9, 47 sq.; of the ginns, 6, 245 sq.; 9, 248, 258; God produces the c. and turns it back again, 9, 119; is a proof of resurrection, 9, 167; no flaw to be seen in God's c., 9, 292 sq.; the marvels of c., 9, 330.

(*d*) In Confucianism and Tâoism. Origin of all things from heaven and earth, 27, 380–4; heaven and earth separated from the Grand Unity, 27, 386 sq. and n.; music appeared at the Grand Beginning of all things, 28, 104; rites promote the return to the beginning, 28, 219; no c. in Tâoism, 39, 19–21, 129, 185, 187; evolution not c. of material forms, 39, 51 sq.

See also World (*a*).

Creator, created men together with the sacrifice, 8, 53; K*ri*sh*n*a (Vish*n*u) is the father and c. of the world, 8, 53, 59, 83, 90, 97, 347; K*ri*sh*n*a is the C. whose faces are in all directions, 8, 90; truth prescribed by the C., 8, 170; Brahman (m.), the C., 8, 231 n., 354 n.; the Mahat is the C. of the three worlds, 8, 334; the emancipated sage is the supporter and the C., 8, 345; God as the c., 15, 260 sqq.; the letters invented by the C., 33, 304; Vedânta-texts differ with regard to the order of creation, but not with regard to the C., 34, 264; described as all-knowing, the Lord of all, the Self of all, without a second, 34, 264 sq.; is non-different from the created effects, 34, 265; belief in the existence of a c., 37, 289; lordship bestowed on the C., 43, 68; the lord of the seven *Ri*shis, 43, 73; there must be a c., as the world is an effected thing, 48, 162–6, 169; God the C. not liable to the charge of mercilessness, 48, 486 sq.; Buddha surpasses the C., 49 (i), 1. *See also* Ahura-Mazda (*a*), Brahman (*b*, *k*), Creation, Dhât*ri*, God, Hira*n*yagarbha, Ka, Nârâya*n*a, Pragâpati, *and* Tâo.

Crimes, classification and lists of c., 7, xxx; 13, xxiv sqq.; 25, lxxii; 37, 44 sq.; capital c. and their punishments, 7, 26 sq.; different c. and their punishments, 7, 26–41, 132–40; unnatural c., 7, 29; c. in the case of which ordeals are permitted, 7, 53; in the fourth degree, 7, 135–8; list of c. and their punishments in hell and transmigration, 7, 141 sq., 144–9; the Bhikkhu refrains from all kinds of c., 11, 191; those who attack preachers shall go the way of parricides, matricides, oil-millers, sesamum-pounders, and of those who use false weights and measures, 21, 374 sq.; c. for which witnesses are unnecessary, 33, 85 sq.; heinous c. a title of law, 33, 202–6; list of ten principal c., 33, 234 sq. *See also* Sins.

Criminal Law, *see* Law.

Cripples, *see* Deformities.

Cross-roads, to be passed with one's right turned towards them, 2, 226; 7, 200; 25, 135; offering an ass to Nir*ri*ti on a c., 2, 289; 29, 361; one must not stop at a c., 7, 200; 25, 150; Dâgabas erected at c., 11, 93, 125 sq.; Rudra worshipped on c., 12, 408 n., 439; 29, 366; certain (Kâmya) sacrifices on c., 14, 117 sq.; 29, 431; 30, 119 sq., 124 sq., 127; looking on a c. at a pot filled with water and reciting a prayer, a penance, 14, 330; a monk or nun should not ease nature on c., 22, 182; the unlucky fire thrown down on a c., 29, 247; the bridal procession on c., 30, 49; Rudra dwells on c., 30, 180 sq.; as omens, 30, 262; worshipped, 31, 291; balance for an ordeal erected in a c., 33, 104; obstructions of c. forbidden, 33, 158; magic rites performed on a c., 42, 292, 292 n., 473, 473 n., 519, 519 n.

Crow, *see* Birds (*b*).

Cruelty, of kings in warfare, 17, 298 sq., 304.

Curds, *see* Milk.

Curse, causes impurity, or even loss of caste, 2, 92; pronouncing a c. a kind of murder, 7, 41; Bâvarî cursed

by another Brâhma*n*a, because he cannot give him 500 pieces of money, 10 (ii), 185; consequences of cursing a priest, 12, 122–4; how the sacrificer should avert a c., 12, 298 sq.; 26, 28; the gods cannot be cursed, 26, 96; fear of c., 26, 396; men deprived of virility by the c. of a spiritual guide, 33, 167; horse treads down c., 41, 205; calamity consequent on c., 42, 44, 509; disease consequent on deceiving or cursing, 42, 59; charm against c., 42, 72, 91, 93, 285; shall recoil on him who sends them, 42, 77 sq. *See also* Imprecations.

Cushions, wrought of gold threads, for the priests to sit on, 44, 360 sq.

Customs, peculiar to the south, and to the north of India, 2, liii sq., 145, 146 n.; 14, 146 sq. and n.; to be learnt from women, 2, 171; 30, 255; a Brâhma*n*a should know the c. of the world, 2, 215, 215 n.; as sources of the law, 2, 237; 14, 2, 4, 146 sq., 181, 230; 25, liv, 30–3, 30 n., 253, 253 n., 260 sq. and n.; 33, 7 n.; not only c. ordained in revealed and traditional texts, but established c. also must be observed by a Snâtaka, 7, 230, 230 n.; family and local c. to be observed, 25, 36, 36 n., 38; 29, 132, 167, 184, 186, 186 n., 285, 301, 303 sq., 336, 399, 408; 30, 62, 218, 224, 284, 291; 33, 67, 76, 242, 282, 339, 357; auspicious c. to be followed, 25, 151 sq.; in discharging a mission to another state, its c. are to be observed, 27, 63; when entering a country one should ask about its c., 27, 93; to study the c. of the people, the poems are collected by the grand music-master for the emperor, 27, 216; c. in different countries differ according to the soil, 27, 228–30; superior to written law, 33, 15, 15 n.; customary modes of recovering debts, 33, 72, 72 n.; the king must maintain the c. settled among corporations, 33, 153–55; judgement based on c., 33, 285 sqq.; some local c. quoted, 33, 287; *the time-honoured institutions of each country, caste, and family should be preserved intact; otherwise the people would rise in rebellion; the subjects would become disaffected towards their rulers; and the army and treasure would be destroyed*, 33, 287; forbidden local c., 33, 389 sq.; the law of the rulers is custom, 37, 412.

D

Dabba, the Mallian, an Arhat, 20, 4–18; 118–25.

Dâ*d*ar*d*â, n.p., 5, 145.

Dâ*d*-Aûha*r*ma*zd*, n. of a priest, 5, 194, 221, 221 n.

Dadhi, Sk., *see* Milk.

Dadhikrâ or Dadhikrâvan, a mythical horse, 41, 27; praises of D. sung, 44, 326; worshipped at the horse-sacrifice, 44, 387; invoked together with Agni, 46, 281 sq.

Dadhya*k* Âtharva*n*a, teaches the A*s*vins, 15, 116 sq., 120, 187; 26, 277; 44, 471; the A*s*vins fixed a horse's head on him, 15, 116; 44, xlviii, 444 sq.; kindles Agni, 32, 153; 41, 218; is speech, 41, 218; Âtharva*n*a or Âṅgirasa, 42, xxvii n.; chaplain of the gods, 42, xxxv.

Dâ*a*îrâ*d*, n.p., 5, 145.

Dâ*d*istân-î-Dînîk, t.w., its author, 5, xlii, xlvi–xlix; 18, xiii sq., xxii, 3, 3 n.; its date, 18, xxii; subjects treated in it, 18, xxiii sq.; translated, 18, 1–276; quoted in the Dînkar*d*, 18, 269 n.

Dâ*d*-sparam, *read and see* Zâd-sparam (5, 434).

Daêna, Zd., Dîn, Dînô, Phl., Faith, religion, revelation, religious rites, 5, xxiii sq., lxxiii, 4 n.; the hundred-petalled rose is D.'s, 5, 104; D. or Zoroastrian Religion personified as an angel, 5, 403, 405; 18, 270 sq. and n.; 23, 10, 18, 264; Dîn Ya*s*t dedicated to D. and *K*ista, 23, 264–9; he who defends the holy D. is as meat and drink to the people, 31, 161, 164; Zarathu*s*tra prays for right discernment how to propagate the Faith, 31, 161, 164 sq. *See also* Dîn-pavan-Âtarô, Dîn-pavan-Dînô, Dîn-pavan-Mitrô, Revelation, *and* Zoroastrianism.

Daênô-vazah, n.p., 23, 214.

Daêvas, Daêvayasna, a worshipper of the D., or false gods, 4, li, 85 sq.,

85 n.; D. of Zoroastrians, and Vedic Devas, 4, li–liii; 31, xix; winter, a work of the D., 4, 4, 10; grieved by the growing of corn, 4, 30 sq.; Dakhmas haunted by them, 4, 89 sq.; wicked men are D. and worshippers of D., 4, 104; the fire kills D., the brood of darkness, 4, 115; spells against the D., 4, 139–41, 197; 23, 44 sq.; 31, 390 sq.; abnormal issues of women, the work of D., 4, 187; an offence to religion is an offering to the D., 4, 190, 190 n.; 31, 58; uncleanness of hair and nails produce D., 4, 190–2; Âzi, made by the D., 4, 198; take hold of the Zoroastrian who goes without the sacred girdle, 4, 204; Angra Mainyu, the Daêva of the D., 4, 209; dismayed by the birth of Zarathustra, D. rush back into hell, 4, 209, 224 sq.; Zarathustra, the foe of the D., 4, 211; 23, 201 sq., 305; 31, 235; Vohu-manô defiled by the D., 4, 216; when the man is dead, the D. cut off his eyesight, 4, 218; tremble at the perfume of the soul of the righteous, 4, 220, 374 sq.; 23, 335; 37, 165; sacrifices not properly offered or offered after sunset go to the D., 4, 347; 23, 76; annihilation of the D., 23, 22; smitten by the name of Ahura-Mazda, 23, 24, 26, 33; Yâtus (sorcerers) are either men or D., 23, 38, 38 n.; smitten by invoking Haurvatât, 23, 49 sq.; D., Yâtus, and Pairikas, 23, 57–9, 65 sq., 128, 134, 161–3, 252; of Mâzana, 23, 59, 59 n., 111, 276; should not the sun rise up, the D. would destroy everything, 23, 86; defeated by Haoshyangha, 23, 111, 275 sq.; struck by Mithra, 23, 126, 136, 144, 153–5; Fravashis kill thousands of D., 23, 191; the heavenly lights oppressed by the D., and helped by the Fravashis, 23, 194; Mâzainya and Varenya D., 23, 224, 251, 292 sq.; 31, 280; Verethraghna destroys D., 23, 232, 247; the sacrifices of the D., 23, 245; Vayu works against the D., 23, 261 sq.; overcome by Yima, 23, 293; the D. and their worshippers chose the Worst Mind, 31, 26, 30 sq.; are a seed from the Evil Mind, 31, 54, 58; men seduced by the D., led astray from Ahura, 31, 54, 58 sq.; D. and Khrafstra-polluted mortals, 31, 81, 85, 85 n., 260; Daêva-worshippers have never been good kings, 31, 121; despised by Ahura-Mazda, 31, 129; imprecations against the D. and their worshippers, 31, 160 sq., 163 sq.; the revelation given against the D., 31, 199, 206, 211, 217, 221, 225, 259, 272, 277, 328; Haoma invoked against D., 31, 236; pressing, tasting, praising Haoma avails to the smiting of the D., 31, 241; abjured by the Zoroastrian, 31, 247–9; Sraosha battles with the D., 31, 301 sq., 305; protection from D. by worship, 31, 306; Ardvi Sûra Anâhita efficacious against the D., 31, 317; the sacrificial words hold the D. subject, 31, 361. *See also* Demons (*a*), *and* Heretics.

Daêva-worshippers, *see* Heretics.

Daêvô*t*bi*s*, son of Takhma, 23, 204.

Dâgabas, *see* Stûpas.

Dahâka, or Dahâk, or Azi Dahâka, or Az-î Dahâk, or Zohâk, or Bêvarâsp: Babylon his residence, 4, xlix sq.; the serpent D. fettered, smitten, by Thraêtaona, or Frê*d*ûn, 4, 9, 9 n., 226, 245 sq.; 5, 234, 397; 18, 110 sq. and n., 201; 23, 61 sq., 61 n., 113, 242, 254 sq., 277, 294, 307; 31, 233; 37, 28, 177, 214–18; 47, 10, 10 n., 116; Vadhaghna or D., a great ruler of nations, 4, 211, 211 sq. n.; however powerful he was, D. could not escape death, 4, 381, 385; released by Aharman, but killed by Sâm or Keresâsp, 5, lii, 233–5; 18, 78, 110 sq. and n., 372, 378; 23, 195 n.; 24, 110 n.; 37, 198 sq., 198 n.; 47, xiii, 114, 114 n.; bound on the Dimâvand mountain, 5, 40; 23, 59 n., 61 sq., 61 n.; the fire Frôbak saved from the hand of D., 5, 63; begged a favour from Aharman, 5, 80; origin of the negro-race in his reign, 5, 87; legends of D., 5, 119; punished in hell, 5, 125; Spîtûr, with D., cut up Yim, 5, 131; his genealogy, 5, 131 sq., 131 n.; his evil reign, 5, 133, 213; 37, 27, 27 n., 212–18; ruled a thousand years, 5,

150; dark forms with the face and curls of D., 5, 163; witchcraft and idolatry of D., 5, 228; 37, 185; 47, xxvi, 66 sq.; there is no D. after the renovation, 18, 118; one of the seven heinous sinners, 18, 217, 228; demons and witches of the assembly of D., 18, 418; the three-mouthed, sacrificed to Anâhita, 23, 60 sq., 60 n.; ravished the two daughters of Yima, 23, 62, 62 n.; wished to empty the earth of men, and sacrificed to Vayu, 23, 253 sq. and n.; struggle between Âtar and D., 23, 297 sq.; with a thousand senses, 23, 326; created immortal by Aharman, 24, 35, 35 n.; advantage from Az-î D., the Bêvarâsp, 24, 60 sq.; received a thousand years' dominion from Aharman, 24, 103; his wickedness, 24, 267; 37, 111; revolt of Gâvah of Ispahân against D., 24, 323 sq., 323 n.; Dahâkas and Mûrakas, 31, 245; five defects of D., 37, 177; Bêvarâsp, a title of D., 37, 214, 214 n.; his accession, 47, xxix; a devastator, 47, 126; impenitence of D. destroyed, 47, 163, 163 n. *See also* Serpents.

Dahara-vidyâ, knowledge of Brahman within the heart, 1, 133 n.; 34, lxxv; 38, 219, 233, 393 n., 410.

Da*hv*yuma, worshipped, 31, 197, 204, 209, 215, 219, 224, 251, 259, 278, 337, 383 sq.

Dâît, *see* Rivers.

Daityas: hundred thousands of princes of the D. have been destroyed by Kâla, 7, 79; their manes, 25, 112; caused by goodness, 25, 494.

Dâityô-gâtu, *see* Fire (*g*).

Daiva, or the science of portents, 1, 109, 110, 111, 115.

Daivâpa, *see* Indrota D.

Daiva Parimara, a meditation on the absorption of the gods into prâ*n*a or Brahman, 1, 288–90.

Daiva Smara, a ceremony performed by one who desires to become dear to any man or woman, 1, 282 sq.

Daivodâsi, *see* Paru*kkh*epa D.

Daiwi, Lying, a Daêva, 4, 224.

Daiyâmpâti, n.p., 43, 273.

Dakhma(s): the dead taken to a D., 4, 54, 95, 95 n., 96 n., 98; 5, 205 n., 247, 247 sq. n., 249 n.; pulling down D. a pious act, and an atonement for sin, 4, 88–90, 269; haunted by Daêvas and murderers, 4, 89 sq., 90 n.; Phl. dakhmak, 'depository for the dead,' 5, lxxiii, 265, 265 n., 361; description of D., 5, 247 sq. n. *See also* Funeral rites (*c*).

Dakkhi*n*âgiri, town in Magadha, 10 (ii), 11; Buddha at D., 13, 206; 17, 207 sq.

Dakkhi*n*âpatha, the South (of India), 10 (ii), 184.

Daksha, recites for Âru*n*i, 12, 335 n.; Pragâpati was D., hence the Dâkshâya*n*a sacrifice, 12, 375 sq.; father of the gods (senses), 14, 299; how he married his daughters, 25, 352, 352 n.; cursed the moon, 25, 398 n.; Aditi and D., 32, 245–8; assumed a new body, 38, 235; one of the Âdityas, 42, 444; Agni, his father, 46, 296; Agni has been laid down with the nourishment of D., 46, 297; is the personified intelligence, 46, 298; Agni in the arms of D., 46, 401.

Daksha-sm*ri*ti, quoted, 48, 411.

Dâkshâya*n*as, the Dâkshâya*n*a sacrifice performed in the royal family of the, 12, 374 sq., 377.

Dakshi*n*â(s), sacrificial gift(s), priests' fee(s), Sk., t.t.: penance, liberality, righteousness, kindness, truthfulness are D., 1, 51; given to the officiating priests, 1, 85; 7, 262, 266, 275, 279; 12, 7, 266, 275, 292, 303 sq. and n., *308–10*, 322, 373 sq., 390; 15, 1, 146; 25, 205; 26, 56 sq., 114–16, 148, 333 sq., 340–9, 388–90, 422, 425 sq.; 29, 49, 68, 74, 131, 135–7, 176, 182, 186, *196 sq.*, 220, 250, 288, 303, 353, 361, 384, 392, 399, 403, 405, 420; 30, 38 sq., 49, 58, 63, 68, 70, 75, 265; 41, 44–6, 50–2, 55–66, 99, 101, 112, 119, 121 sq., 124 sq., 137 sq., 141 sq., 186, 252, 331; 42, 87, 89, 174–98, 380, 494, 595–600, 610, 645, 656, 688–92; 43, 148, 237, 237 n., 271; 44, 217, 218 n., 222, 268, 412 sq., 420 sq.; 46, 24, 363, 365; sacrifices without D. condemned, 8, 119, 119 n.; 44, 7; highest knowledge is the D. at allegorical sacrifice of the

sense-organs, 8, 261, 261 n.; final emancipation is the D. at the allegorical sacrifice of concentration of mind, 8, 280; law about D., 25, 291 sq. and n.; 33, 125 sq.; arms may be taken up in defence of D., 25, 315; importance of giving proper D., 25, 438, 438 n.; the far-seeing D., 26, 61; Dakshi*n*â-Homas or oblations at the giving of the D., 26, 340–9; of a thousand cows, 26, 414–18, 414 n., 426; 41, 140; are Apsaras, 43, 232 sq.; sacrifice praised for the D., 43, 233; let there be no bargaining as to D., 43, 280; the D. wins food, 43, 285; giving away all his property as D., 43, 321, 321 n.; cows of D. stand south of altar, 44, 17; imperishable world gained by giving away as D. this earth, replete with wealth, 44, 96; *G*anaka of Videha performs sacrifices with numerous D., 44, 115; the right time for bringing up the D., 44, 120 sq.; are healing medicine, 44, 217; the D. at the horse sacrifice, 44, 274 sq., 306, 343 sq., 348, 350, 353, 357, 357 n., 397 sq., 400, 402; gold (of a hundred grains) as D., 44, 275, 275 n., 352, 356, 358; Brâhma*n*as sing about the D. of the sacrificer at the A*s*vamedha, 44, 286 sq.; given at the burial rite, 44, 439; at the Pravargya, 44, 446, 490 sq., 490 n., 503 sq.; are glory, 44, 446; must not be given away by the priest, 44, 446; Agni protects him who gives D., 46, 24. *See also* Gifts *and* Priests (*c*).

Damnak, n.p., 5, 139 sq.

Damsels, *see* Woman.

Dânavas: Î*s*vara, the lord of gods, D., Bhûtas, &c., 8, 354; V*ri*tra called a D., 12, 166; sprang from the manes, 25, 112; their manes, 25, 112; give enjoyments due from them through fear of punishment, 25, 219; story of a certain D. who swallowed his wife, to guard her, 35, 216 sq., 217 n.; *K*andramas conquered the golden cities of the Asuras and D., 42, 85; the Asuras so called, 44, 95; gods, D., Gandharvas, &c., 45, 121 sq. *See also* Dânus.

Danâyû, mother of V*ri*tra, 12, 166.

Dancing, at the rites of ancestor worship, 3, 305, 305 n., 328, 343, 375; in honour of King Wû, 3, 334–6; devotion to d., belongs to the quality of passion, 8, 325; at ceremonies, 27, 435; 28, 274; instruction in d., 27, 478, 478 n.; at the worship of the duke of *K*âu, 28, 33; with shield and axes, 28, 102, 102 n.; music and d., 28, 112 sq.; at sacrifices, 28, 241, 253 sq.; names of metres derived from choregic movements, 32, xcv–xcvii, cxii.

Da*nd*akas, suffered destruction, 49 (i), 116.

Dangers: ten cases of d., when the Pâtimokkha must be interrupted, 13, 261, 294 sq.; 20, 312.

Danghu-frâdhah, n.p., 23, 214.

Danghu-srûta, n.p., 23, 214.

Dantavakra, the best of Kshatriyas, 45, 290, 290 n.

Danu, father of V*ri*tra, 12, 166.

Dânus, a Turanian tribe, conquered by Ashavazdah, 23, 71; the Turanian D. destroyed by the Fravashis, 23, 189.

Dânus and Dânavas, demons, 32, 114 sq.; Ku*n*âru lurking with the D., 43, 275.

Dârâî, Kâ*d* his great preceptor, 5, 145, 145 n.; son of Kîhar-âzâ*d*, and D. son of D., 5, 150 sq. n., 151; D. son of D., ordered the preservation of Avesta and Zand, 37, 413, 413 n.; reign of D., 47, xxviii, xxxi.

Dârâ Shukoh, the Upanishads translated into Persian by or for him, 1, lvii sq., lx sq., lxvi, lxviii, lxxxviii, xci, xcvii.

Dâraya*t*-ratha, n.p., 23, 210.

Darbha-grass, seven bunches of, made at the beginning of the sacrifice, 12, 84; bunch of D. placed on the altar, 41, 332; 43, 182; is both water and plants, 41, 332; grew from waters loathing V*ri*tra, 41, 332; as an 'appeaser of wrath,' 42, 137, 480; D. and lotus-leaf in the centre of the fire-altar, 43, xx, 1 n., 44 sq. and n., 118 sq. and n., 358, 365 sq., 365 n., 368, 368 n., 374, 388, 393; a means of purification, 44, 195, 274; covered over the burial-ground, 44, 436.

Dârbhya, *see* Rathavîti.

Darius, proclaims Ahura-Mazda, 4, lxi; a Mazda-worshipper, but not a Zarathustrian, 31, xxx-xxxii.
Darkness, *see* Qualities.
Darsapûrnamâsa, *see* Sacrifices (*l*).
Darsinika, defeated by Vîstâspa, 23, 117, 280.
Darûn, *see* Sacrifices (*b*).
Darvihomas, *see* Sacrifices (*i*).
Dasabalakâsyapa, one of the five first disciples of Buddha, 19, 172; Vâshpa so called, 19, 193 n.
Dasagvas, carried on the sacrifice first, 32, 296, 306 sq.
Dasapeya, t.t., *see* Sacrifices (*j*).
Dasaratha, laments the loss of his son Râma, 19, 92; 49 (i), 90; Râma, the *Ri*shi, fought against D., 19, 330; horse sacrifice of D., 44, xxix; the chariot of D.'s son coming back, 49 (i), 80.
Dasârhas, a clan descended from Yadu, 45, 113, 113 n., 115.
Dasârna, n. of a country and people, 45, 57, 87.
Dasârnabhadra, the king of Dasârna, turned *G*aina monk, 45, 87, 87 n.
Dâsas, strongholds of which they were the lords, 46, 263.
Dâsîkharbatîkâ Sâkhâ, of the Godâsa Gana, 22, 289.
Dâstâghni, n.p., 23, 218.
Dastân, n.p., 5, 139 sq., 139 n.
Dâstânîk, Veskö progeny, descendants of Nîvîk and, 37, 198, 198 n.
Dâstayana, or Dâstayâni, his brood killed by Keresâspa, 18, 370, 372; 23, 296.
Dasyu, Dasyus: V*ri*tra called a D., 12, 166; race or caste, 25, 192, 265, 410, 410 n., 413, 434, 499; cannot be witnesses, 25, 265, 266 n.; demons originated from them, 42, 67; defeated by Indra, 42, 83, 118, 222 sq; the earth destroys the blasphemous D., 42, 203; there are many D. and Mlekkhas, 45, 43; Agni invoked against the D. (sing. or plur.), 46, 33, 49, 102, 375, 383, 397; Aryans and D., the pious and impious, 46, 182, 183; the gods have overpowered them, 46, 303.
Datta: Ârya D. (Dinna), n. of a Sthavira, 22, 274, 288; Ârya D. of the Gautama gotra had two disciples, 22, 293.
Dattaka, author of a Kâmasâstra, 45, 274 n.
Daughters, offered as presents, 1, 57 sq.; inherit, 2, 134; 25, 348, 352, 370 sq.; Yâo, to test Shun, gives him his two d. in marriage, to see his behaviour towards them, 3, 14, 36; do neither wrong nor good, only about the spirits and the food they will have to think, and to cause no sorrow to their parents, 3, 350 sq., 350 n.; preference of sons to d., 5, 323 sq., 344 sq.; the appointed d. in place of a son, 7, 62, 65; 14, 85 sq. and n., 226; 25, cix, 77, 352–5; 33, 375 sq.; sale of d., 14, 221; 25, 84 sq., 291, 345; how to secure the birth of a learned d., 15, 219; daughter's son to be entertained at a Srâddha, 25, 102, 118 sq.; not to quarrel with d., 25, 157; the highest object of tenderness, 25, 158; guardianship over d., 37, 146 sq.; reverence and duties of a d., 37, 382. *See also* Family, *and* Marriage.
Dauhshanti, *see* Bharata D.
Daungha, son of Zairita, 23, 204.
Daurgaha, n. of a horse, 44, 397; patronymic of Purukutsa, 44, 397 n.
Davâns, who did only one good work in his life, 5, 350 sq., 350 n.; 37, 469.
David, and Goliath, 6, 39; Psalms given to D., 6, 94; 9, 7; disbelieving Jews cursed by D., 6, 108; a prophet, 6, 125; makes coats of mail, 9, 52, 151; mountains and birds made subject to D., 9, 52, 52 n.; D. and Solomon gave judgement about a field, 9, 52, 52 n.; endowed with knowledge, 9, 100; mountains and birds sing praises with D., of D., 9, 151, 177; was endowed with might, 9, 176; the parable of the ewe lambs proposed to D., 9, 177; warned not to follow lust, 9, 177.
Dawn, the Woman Treasure of the King of Glory, 11, 257, 310; Pragâpati's daughter, 12, 209; wedded to Indra, 12, 337; sacrifice to the D., 31, 387; 44, 297 n., 298; Arushî, the red D., 32, 23 sq.; red cows of the D., 32, 23, 26; Aditi beyond the D., 'the face of

Aditi,' 32, 243; brings horses, 32, 329; Dyu, the bull of the D., 32, 343, 346; the dew-lighted Ds. come striving together, 32, 348, 351; Savitri flasheth forth after the D., 41, 273; Agni and the Ds., 41, 280; 46, 108, 145, 194, 240, 275, 336, 363; has ruddy cows, 41, 334; is night, heaven, day, 44, 298; Agni, the two Asvins, and the D., 46, 37–9; the sun, the lover of the D., 46, 67 sq.; 'the reddish white one,' 46, 142, 145; the red Ds. invoked for food, 46, 143; the two Ds. invoked in Âprî hymns, 46, 179 sq., 236 sq., 239; the shine of the goddess D. rose up, 46, 309; the mother of the cows, 46, 309, 314; the mother of the seven *Ri*shis, 46, 314, 318, 322; red cows or Ds., 46, 326, 329 sq.; approaches like a milch-cow, 46, 363; Night and D., *see* Night. *See also* Sacred times, Sûryâ, *and* Ushas.

Dawrâmaêshi, n.p., 23, 217.

Day: seven days of the week, 7, xxix, 242; D. (personified) wedded to Indra, 42, 337; invoked for protection, 29, 348; a sacrifice to D. after having seen an evil dream, 30, 184; the d. after the d. is the whole year, 44, 155;—a d. and night of Brahman, 8, 79 sq.; d. and night are a pair, 8, 277; d. is threefold, and night is threefold, 8, 330; d. was first, and then night, 8, 352; ends with the setting of the sun, night with the sun's rising, 8, 354; Day(s) and Night(s), goddesses, 41, 243; 42, 161; 44, 141, 296, 298; the sun is encompassed by d. and night, 41, 271; d. and night nourish Agni, 41, 271, 273; universe encompassed by d. and night, 41, 287; days and nights are endless, 41, 352; d. and night the rulers of Ârya and *S*ûdra, 43, 75; the separating metre is the d., 43, 89; days and nights are Pragâpati's joints, 43, 281; how d. and night were created, 44, 14; d. a form of priestly dignity, night a form of nobility, 44, 286; d. and night are the two tawny ones, 44, 316. *See also* Sacred times, *and* Time.

Dâzgara-gau, n.p., 23, 219.

Dâzgarâspa, n.p., 23, 209.

Dead, the, *see* Ancestor worship; dead matter, *see* Death (*c*).

Death.

(*a*) D. personified, a deity.
(*b*) D. in religious belief and philosophy.
(*c*) D. in religious ceremonies.

(*a*) D. PERSONIFIED, A DEITY.

D. asked to settle a difficult law-question, 2, 98, 98 sq. n.; expiatory formula addressed to D., 2, 293; 44, 337 n.; the power of D. brought in by heresy, 4, 194; the deceiving, unseen D., 4, 224; exorcism against D. and sickness, 4, 228 sq.; Ast(ô)-vîdâ*d*, demon of D., 5, 19 n.; 37, 193; K*ri*sh*n*a is D. who seizes all, 8, 90, 95 sq.; his form cannot be perceived, 8, 153; different from Yama, 8, 153, 153 n.; the king of D., 10 (i), 17; (ii), 208; Age and D. drive the life of men, 10 (i), 37; does not see him who despises the world, 10 (i), 47; the messengers of D. have come near to thee, 10 (i), 60; the means of deliverance from the snares of D., 10 (ii), 27; be fools the indolent, 10 (ii), 55; the strong net of deceitful D., 10 (ii), 59; Agni as D., 12, 324; 38, 267; 43, 365; the Sun (the man in the sun) is D., 12, 343 sq.; 38, 267; 43, 366 sq., 371 sq., 374; 44, 26; 48, 672; self-sacrifice offered to D. as a penance, 14, 106; Brahman made the created beings over to D., all except the Brahma*k*ârin, 14, 156; one quarter of the Vedic student belongs to D., 14, 157; Rudra and D. invoked, 14, 264; Na*k*iketas in the house of D. (M*ri*tyu, Yama), 15, xxii, 2–24; 48, 361; runs away from terror of Brahman, 15, 21, 59; everything produced from D. or Hunger, 15, 75; 43, 402–4; is the devatâ of the person in the shadow, 15, 144; a robber with drawn sword, follows us all, 19, 128 sq.; why D. has power over Brâhma*n*as, 25, 169 sq.; man is born as a debt owing to D., 26, 152; homage to D., 42, 53, 56, 570; the lord of cattle, 42, 58; the powerful king, 42, 111, 380; D. and Sleep, 42, 167; as a teacher, 42, 216; Pragâpati identified with D., 43, xxiii, 356–8; confounded by

Pragâpati, 43, 77; searched for Pragâpati, 43, 290; created by Pragâpati, 43, 290; Pragâpati overpowered by D., 43, 361; does not die, but is within the immortal, 43, 366; man in the right eye is D., 43, 371 sq., 374; is both near and far away, 43, 372; one or many, 43, 372; the Brahman delivered the creatures over to D., 44, 48; oblations to the Deaths at the horse-sacrifice, 44, 339–41; there is only one D. in yonder world, even Hunger, 44, 340; invoked at funeral rite to go another way, 44, 434; D. leads off a man in his last hour, only Karman following him, 45, 59 sq.; mankind is harassed by D., 45, 64 sq.; the Imperishable who moves within D., of whom D. is the body, whom D. does not know, 48, 242, 469. *See also* Kâla, Mâra, M*ri*tyu, *and* Yama.

(*b*) D. IN RELIGIOUS BELIEF AND PHILOSOPHY.

D. and the breath in the mouth, 1, 5 sq.; fate of the soul after d., how it departs from here, and where it goes, 1, 76, 82 n., 107 sq. n.; 15, 18 sq., 23, 126 sq., 173–7, 204, 208; 34, lx, lxxviii sq.; 38, 121–6, 364–419; 45, 372, 377; 48, 728–43; *when a man departs from hence, his speech is merged in his mind, his mind in his breath, his breath in heat (fire), heat in the Highest Being*, 1, 100 sq., 100 n., 107 sq.; 48, 728–31; when a man departs, he goes upwards by the rays of the sun, 1, 133 sq.; 12, 269, 269 n.; absorption of the other senses into prâ*n*a or breath, at the time of d., 1, 295 sq.; when a man dies, gods and fiends struggle for the possession of his soul, 4, 88 sq., 89 n.; the Aogemaidê, a treatise on d., and life after d., 4, 372–86; is inevitable, 4, 377–85; 8, 355; 10 (i), 69; (ii), 106–8; 11, 58 sq., 89 sq., 96, 116 sq., 119, 121, 127 sq., 240, 289; 19, 270–6; 20, 371; 35, 213 sq.; 36, 102; 37, 176; 45, 18, 249 sq., 256, 259; 49 (i), 66 sq.; there is a remedy for everything but d., 5, 396; *wheresoe'er ye be d. will overtake you, though ye were in lofty towers*, 6, 83; an ascetic must neither wish for d., nor for life, 7, 280; 8, 246; 35, 70; no occasion to grieve about d., 8, 45 sq. and n.; 10 (ii), 106–8; 11, 59, 89 sq., 96; d. in performing duty is preferable, 8, 56; release from old age and d., 8, 77, 249; is from K*r*ish*n*a, 8, 86; exists not, 8, 149, 151 sq., 191, 191 n.; freedom from d. by ceremonies, 8, 152; delusion and heedlessness called d., 8, 152–5, 152 n.; sensuality, desire, wrath lead children to d., 8, 154, 154 n.; destroyed by knowledge, 8, 155; 43, 404; vanquished, i.e. final emancipation attained, 8, 178 sq., 178 n.; Kâ*s*yapa knew about birth and d., 8, 232; devoid of warmth, breath, beauty, and consciousness, man is said to be dead, 8, 238; all life ends in d., 8, 355; 10 (i), 41 sq.; 11, 153, 153 n.; two syllables, viz. mama 'mine,' are d., 8, 391, 391 n.; every soul shall taste of d., 9, 48, 123; a return to God, led by the angel of d., 9, 136, 186 sq.; dying agony of an infidel, 9, 311 sq.; *d. carries off a man who is gathering flowers and whose mind is distracted, as a flood carries off a sleeping village . . . before he is satiated in his pleasures*, 10 (i), 17, 16 sq. n.; existence is the stream of d., 10 (ii), xv; *sad is the d. of him who longs, unworthy is the d. of him who longs. . . . Cast away desire for these (cities, &c.)! long not after life!* 11, 280–4; life after d. only for him who offers the Agnihotra, 12, 324; after d. man is reproduced from out of the fire, 12, 343; *a mortal ripens like corn, like corn he springs up again*, 15, 2 sq.; Na*k*iketas asks Yama about the mystery of d., 15, 5–7; is but a condiment, swallowed up by the Self, 15, 11; 34, 116 sq.; is unreal, immortality is real, 15, 84; everything is the food of d., 15, 126; fire is d., and that is the food of water, d. is conquered again, 15, 126; the sage knows from the Yi what can be said about d. and life, 16, 353; are the spirits distressed at the d. of a righteous man? 18, 50 sq.; how the life departs from the body, 18, 51–53; introduced by the evil spirit, 18, 95, 105 sq. and

n.; 'Buddha-knowledge,' 'seeing Nirvâna,' euphemistic terms for d., 21, 52 sq. n., 118 n.; there is nothing inaccessible for d., 22, 19; the sage desires d. as the dissolution of the body, 22, 61; why people disregard d., 24, 50; not a complete dissolution of existence, 24, 136, 208; the cause of d., 24, 161; old age, disease, and d., 25, 209, 212; falsehood allowed to prevent the d. of a person, 25, 272; premature d., 28, 52 sq.; 36, 162–74; spoken of as dissolution, 28, 203; the round of birth, action, d., 34, xxvii; not necessary for the condition of being free from the body, 34, 41, 43; the highest Self different from the individual soul in the state of d., 34, 233-6; release from the jaws of d. by knowledge of the highest Self, 34, 247; what it means when applied to the sprout, 34, 340; all men are afraid of d., 35, 206–13; the terms 'birth' and 'd.' if applied to the soul, have a metaphorical meaning, 38, 28 sq.; has the power of manifesting those works whose fruit has not yet begun, 38, 113, 117–19; the state of swoon is the door of d., 38, 152; 48, 606 sq.; identification of the Avabh*ri*tha-ceremony with d., 38, 221; the d. of the body is the term of the attainment of final release, 38, 357 sq., 363; certain times favourable for dying, 38, 379–81; 48, 740 sq.; ideas about d. and life in Tâoism, 39, 21–3; 40, 55, 146, 281 sq.; the Tâo as an antidote against d., 39, 92 sq.; 40, 32; firmness and strength the concomitants of d., 39, 118; birth and d. merely changes of the same kind in the process of evolution, 39, 149; 40, 4–6, 4 n., 10, 47 sq., 47 n., 65; story of Mr. Deformed and Mr. One-foot who are not afraid of d., 39, 149; 40, 5 sq.; *how do I know that the love of life is not a delusion? and that the dislike of d. is not like a young person's losing his way, and not knowing that he is (really) going home?* 39, 194; loosing the cord by which the life is suspended, 39, 201 sq., 248; unity of life and d., 39, 229; d. and life are ordained from Heaven, 39, 241; a mere change for the sage, 39, 332, 365; d. and life are not far apart, but why they have taken place cannot be seen, 40, 130; one hundred and one kinds of d., 42, 49 sq., 58, 162, 307, 565; he that will live is warm, he that will die is cold, 43, 135 sq.; ceases through immortality, 43, 327; why people say 'he has been cut off,' 43, 371; retribution after d., 44, xiv; 45, 372, 377; the fool's 'd. against one's will,' and the sage's 'd. with one's will,' 45, 20–4; a monk should learn the method of dying a religious d., 45, 299; antagonistic to the origination of knowledge, 48, 18; the term 'd.' denotes Nescience, 48, 23; the word 'd.' denotes darkness, i.e. non-intelligent matter in its subtle state, 48, 140; the departing soul is held embraced by the highest Self, 48, 352; when he has departed, there is no more knowledge, 48, 395; he who moves within d., of whom d. is the body, whom d. does not know, he is the inner Self of all, the one god Nârâya*n*a, 48, 403 sq.; soul in deep sleep and in d. unconscious, 48, 765 sq.; when men die, they pass into dissolution as far as regards this world, 49 (i), 108. *See also* Future Life, Immortality, Life, Nirvâ*n*a, *and* Suicide.

(*c*) D. IN RELIGIOUS CEREMONIES.

Hymns and prayers recited when d. approaches, 1, 261, 313 sq., 313 n.; 23, 312 sq.; 24, 344; signs and premonitory symptoms of approaching d., 1, 261 sq.; causes interruption of Veda-study, 2, 36 sq.; 14, 208 sq., 209 n., 211; 29, 115 sq., 324, 414; 30, 80; impurity caused by d. or dead matter, 2, 59, 249–54; 4, lxxi–lxxxi, 49–51, 58–85, 87 sq., 92–102, 105–15, 119–55, 190; 5, lx, 245–76, 310, 319 sq., 332; 7, 87–94; 14, 177 sq., 180–2, 298; 18, 35, 39–43, 52 n., 161, 161 n., 283, 292 sq. and n., 431, 455–8; 24, 111, 335–7, 339–41, 353–5; 25, 146, 163, 177–87; 29, 355, 357–9; 37, 153–60; for three days after the d. of a man there is danger lest somebody else should die in that

house, 4, lxxiii; useful animals which destroy dead matter, 5, 72 sq.; seven (eight) kinds of d. which delay the arrival of the Nasûs, 5, 331 sq., 331 n.; the folly of bewailing the dead, 10 (ii), 107 sq.; by what means can the sacrificer overcome d.? 15, 122; renunciation of sins at the time of d., 24, 309; sin of eating dead matter, 24, 336, 353, 356; terms to be used in speaking of the d. of men and animals, 27, 112, 117 sq.; three kinds of d. on which no condolence should be offered, 27, 131; how to speak of d. of different persons, 27, 132 sq.; 28, 133 sq.; ceremony to be performed after the d. of a Guru, to prevent the d. of other members of the family, 29, 246–50; prayers to ward off d., 29, 248 sq.; prayer to avert involuntary d., 29, 427; 30, 118; ceremonies to avert occurrence of d. in family, 30, 296 sq.; striking a dead person, 37, 48; lamenting over the dead prohibited, 37, 193; rites by which the consecrated king is freed from violent d., 41, 90 sq., 94; prayers for exemption from the dangers of d., 42, 53–60, 569 sq.; he conquers recurring d. (i.e. the round of birth and d.) by the Mitravindâ sacrifice, 44, 66; he is freed from recurring d. who studies his daily Veda-lesson, 44, 99; a possessor of esoteric knowledge conquers recurrent d., and attains the full measure of life, 44, 174; expiatory rite in case of d. of sacrificer when the Agnihotra-milk has been put on the fire, 44, 184 sq.; recurring d. warded off from cattle of sacrificer, 44, 271; recurring d. of the fathers warded off, 44, 272; fear (at funeral rites) of other members of the family following the deceased in d., 44, 424, 426, 440. *See also* Impurity.

Debts: law about d. and interests, 2, 69, 69 n., 244; 4, 35 n.; 6, 44 sq.; 7, 39 sq., 42–6, 74; 14, 82; 18, 184; 25, xxix sq., 253, 262–4, 272 sq., 277–86; 33, 41–120, 263 sq., 273, 299, 308 sq., 319–32, 320–4, 328, 331 sq., 339, 388–90; 37, 65, 138 sq., 141–3; imprisonment of debtors, 13, 199; to be paid before partition of property, or by the heir, 25, 379, 379 n.; 33, 197; sacrifice for one who cannot pay d., 30, 113; sureties and pledges, 33, 61, 70–5, 77; one enslaved for d., 33, 135 n., 136 sq.; contract of d., bond, 33, 305; law about pledge, 33, 322–6; a cause why some people become monks, 35, 50; a father may deposit his son as a pledge, 36, 122; discharge of d. on the death of creditor, 42, 528;—the three d. to the gods, *R*ishis, and Manes, 7, 137; 12, 190 sq., 190 n.; 14, 56, 271 sq.; 25, 169, 205, 215, 346, 443, 443 n.; 38, 295; 49 (i), 100.

Decay, *see* Death (*b*).

Deeds, *see* Good Works, Karman, Thought, *and* Works.

Deer, *see* Animals, *and* Hunting.

Defamation, a title of the law, 2, 84 sq., 281 sq., 290 sq., 295; 14, 122, 222; 25, 253, 267, 301–3, 484; fine for d. of a maiden, 25, 294. *See also* Abuse, *and* Backbiting.

Defilement, Defiling, *see* Impurity.

Deformities: deformed persons excluded from *S*râddha feasts, 2, 258; 14, 52; 25, 103 sq., 107 sq., 119 sq.; d. considered as sins, 14, 4, 103; 42, 521; due to crimes committed in former births, 14, 109; 25, 440 sq.; deformed people excluded from sacrifices, 28, 76; food not to be accepted from hermaphrodites, 25, 162; crippled and deformed people to be removed from councils of a king, 25, 239; deformed and crippled people cannot be witnesses, 25, 266; 33, 88 sq.; cripples not to pay taxes, 25, 322; cripples, idiots, madmen, &c., cannot inherit, but must be supported, 25, 372 sq.; cripples, idiots, &c., may marry, 25, 373, 373 n.

Deities, *see* Gods.

Deliverance: what sort of d. is there for the Muni who is free from desire? 10 (ii), 202 sq.; eight stages of d. (vimokkhâ), 11, 49 n., 51 sq., 212 sq. *See also* Emancipation.

Deluge, when the waters of it spread abroad, Yü arranged and divided the regions of the land, 3,

309; legend of the d. in Avesta and Pentateuch, 4, lviii sq.; Zoroastrian legend of Yima and the d., 4, 10 sq., 15–21, 251 n.; Tahmuras and the d., 4, 384 n.; caused by Tîstar, 5, 26, 26 n.; Noah and the d., 6, 209 sq.; 9, 66 sq., 119, 255 sq.; at the end of the world, 8, 97 n., 106 n., 260; the punishment of the d., 9, 298 sq.; legend of Manu and the d., 12, 216–19 and notes; 25, lviii; 26, xxx sq.; 42, 679 sq.; the deluging rain of Malkôs, 18, 109, 109 n.; 24, 59, 59 n.

Delusion, attachment to objects of desire is the great, 8, 322; the contact of objects of sense with senses is the source of d., 8, 335; human body characterized by d., 8, 343; the wheel of life is enveloped in the waters of d., 8, 356 sq.; the whole world under a d., 39, 326 sq. *See also* Illusion, Mâyâ, *and* Papañ*k*a.

Demons.

(*a*) In Iran.
(*b*) In India.
(*c*) In China.

(*a*) In Iran.

Impurity is being possessed of d., 4, lxxii–lxxxi; 18, 342, 342 n.; threaten the new-born child, 4, lxxix sq. and n., 184 n.; 24, 319; concourse of the d. at the gate of hell, 4, 24, 24 n.; 5, 15 sq., 36; 24, 28 sq. and n.; improper ceremonies appropriated by them, 4, 26 n.; 5, 369, 369 sq. n.; 37, 23, 194; the six chief d. and Angra Mainyu, 4, 139 n.; repelled and destroyed by fire, 4, 184 n., 272; 5, 317, 342–4; 24, 277, 355 sq.; 37, 122; cock and dog drive away the d., 4, 197, 197 n.; 5, 73, 331 n.; 24, 293 sq.; Aharman formed many d., 5, 6; discomfited, and destroyed, 5, 8, 25, 198 sq., 230, 364, 367; 18, 85; 24, 83 sq., 101; 37, 227 sq.; 47, 125; names and accounts of d., 5, 9 sq., 18 sq., 27 sq., 105–14, 128 sq., 215 sq.; the assistants or confederates of Aharman, 5, 15–17; 18, 93–113; their incursion upon the world, 5, 17–19, 28; 37, 254 sq.; the Mâzînîkân d. (Mâzainya daêva), 5, 18; 18, 105, 105 n.; 37, 221, 221 n.; abide in hell, 5, 19; 18, 58, 75; 24, 9; struggle between angels and d., 5, 19; 18, 270 sq., 319, 319 n.; 37, 21, 21 n., 263 sq.; introduce disaster, 5, 24; 18, 24; 24, 101; 37, 23, sin of worship of d., 5, 54, 57, 224, 302, 369, 369 sq. n.; 24, 15, 23, 72; 37, 23, 148, 151 sq., 181 sq., 206, 207 n., 254, 326; 47, 6, 69, 86, 93, 95, 98, 102, 120; men led astray by the d., 5, 55–7; 18, 271; become powerful by men's misdeeds, 5, 56 sq.; use nail-paring as weapons, 5, 71, 342; apes, bears, and negroes originated from intercourse with d., 5, 87; seized on by the angels at the resurrection, 5, 128 sq.; drag the sinner to hell, 5, 161; 24, 12, 81; figures of d. demolished, 5, 193, 198; the d. with dishevelled hair (i.e. hostile races) rush into Iran, 5, 201–3, 202 n., 215, 217, 220, 223 sq., 227 sq.; antagonism of Aharman and the d. to man, 5, 207, 214; 18, 402; 37, 255 sq., 263 sq.; the leathern-belted d., 5, 223; idol temples their abodes, 5, 227, 229; attack him who eats in the dark, 5, 310; all worship reaches either angels or d., 5, 310; attack Zaratûst, oppose his birth, 5, 317, 343; 37, 469; 47, xiv, xxi, 19 sq., 27–31, 140 sq.; are in the north, 5, 318, 318 n., 346, 370 n.; fifteen fiends, 5, 358; soul threatened by d., 5, 373; 24, 17, 17 n., 21; soul saved by Srôsh from d., 5, 382; he whose begetting is owing to the d. has no part in the resurrection, 5, 384 sq.; resurrection a fear and vexation to the d., 18, 38; assault of the d. on the corpse, 18, 38, 42; no d. after the renovation of the universe, 18, 74, 118; five kinds of d. of life (evil passions), 18, 87 sq., 88 n.; of Mâzendarân, 18, 93, 93 n.; 24, 244 sq., 244 n.; unable to injure their enemies, the d. destroy their friends, 18, 113, 113 sq. n.; sacred girdle a means of contesting the d., 18, 129–32; torment the apostate in hell, 18, 138; defeated by the sacred ceremony, 18, 159 sq., 163, 163 n., 168–70, 172; seize upon the heinous sinners, 18, 219, 219 n.; cause heinous sin, 18, 220 sq.; exorcism

against evil d., 18, 384, 384 n., 437, 444; 31, 240; hostile to next-of-kin marriage, 18, 402, 410–13, 417–20, 422, 424; sins and evil passions personified as fiends, 24, 9, 50, 82, 126, 126 n.; mock the wicked soul in hell, 24, 25, 31, 52; slain by Hôshâng, 24, 58; 47, xxv, 8; smitten by Frêdûn, 24, 61; destroyed by Vistâsp, 24, 65; wicked man called 'demi-demon,' 24, 82 sq.; kept back from disturbing the passage of the stars, 24, 91 sq.; mountains which are smiters of the d., 24, 98; deceive men, 24, 102; confounded by religious ceremonies, 24, 103 sq.; Fravashis protect the body of Keresâsp against the d., 24, 110; opposed to the sacred beings, 24, 164; a fiend in every human body, 24, 265 sq.; make use of water poured away at night, 24, 292 n.; Zarathustra urges the overthrow of the demon of Rapine, 31, 152, 156; imprecations against the demon of Rapine, and her devotees, 31, 161, 163 sq.; Dahâkas and Mûrakas are born in the house where Haoma is not worshipped, 31, 245; Sraosha invoked against Wrath and other d., 31, 303 sq.; vexed by just judgement, 37, 102; destruction of d. through the growth of corn, 37, 154; Vendîdâd or 'law opposed to the d.,' 37, 156, 402, 446; frightened by the birth of Zaratûst, 37, 165; prayers powerful against the d., 37, 165 sq. and n.; inward talk of the d., 37, 167; Ahunavair recited for smiting the d., 37, 173 sq.; 47, 7, 58–60, 62 sq.; the rich who gives nothing is produced by the d., 37, 176 sq.; serpents produced by the d., 37, 196; repelled by the spirit of the consecrated cake, 37, 197; the seven arch-d., 37, 213, 213 n.; repulsed by Zoroaster, 37, 227 sq.; 47, xi, 33, 58–60, 62 sq., 123 sq.; non-possession of rulers and high-priests, their law, 37, 232; the patron spirits of mankind sickened by d., 37, 243, 243 n.; three deceitful d. and their colloquy with Aûharmazd, 37, 252–4, 253 n.; Hôm-water not for demon-worshippers, 47, 57; Mazda-worship opposed to the d., 18, 126; 37, 168, 271, 410; 47, 51, 58; the d. denounced, 37, 272, 275; the d. and the wicked deny the renovation, 37, 284; four triumphs of the sacred beings over the d., 37, 285; gratified by the wicked, 37, 301; demon-worship antecedent to Zoroastrianism, 47, xxvi, 43 sq. and n.; Zoroaster opposed the worship of the d., 47, xxvi sq., 47, 51, 154; smiting the fiend, the duty of man, 47, 5; how the d. tempt men, 47, 60–2; shattered by revelation from the Avesta, 47, 64; d. in hell disabled by the conversion of Vistâsp, 47, 72; wizards, demon-worshippers, demon-consulters, 47, 124; duty of the priest to struggle with his own fiend, 47, 169; duty of severing the fiend from one's reason, 47, 170. *See also* Akem-manô, Daêvas, *and* Drûg.

(*b*) In India.

One should use for Srâddhas such materials, by which the d. are kept aloof, 7, 247; demoniac state of mind of evil-doers, 8, 75; neither gods nor d. understand the manifestation of Krishna, 8, 87; Pralhâda, chief among d., 8, 89, 89 n.; alarmed at the greatness of Krishna, 8, 94, 96; beings divided into godlike and demoniac, 8, 114 sq., 118; gods and d. practise the life of Brahmakârins for freedom from death, 8, 151 sq., 152 n.; were vanquished through heedlessness, 8, 152, 152 n.; the paths of action are destroyed by d., 8, 257; their natural inclination towards ostentatiousness, 8, 282; evil-doers reborn as d., 8, 321; all d. extol the emancipated sage, 8, 345; Vishnu is the ruler of gods, d., Nâgas, &c., 8, 347; the demon causing madness, 12, 123; danger from d., 13, 261, 313, 340; 20, 312; Kâka, a slave begotten by a d., able to travel sixty yoganas in one day, 17, 188 sq.; feasts at festivals of d., 22, 92; the winds invoked to protect the cattle from slaughtering hosts, 29, 99; imprecations against d. harassing children, 29, 296 sq.; 30, 211 sq., 214, 219 sq.,

286 sq.; the Cleaver, a d. causing headache, 29, 350; Rakshas and Pi*s*â*k*as driven away by the staff of the Snâtaka, 30, 169; the Tongueless One invoked at a rite to gain victory in disputes, 30, 178; Vâyu protects from powerful d., 32, 445; one possessed by a demon cannot be a witness, 33, 88; Agni invoked against the hating d., 41, 229; d. of disease, 42, 1–48, 67, 273, 280–3, 290 sq., 302 sq., 407, 442, 445, 449, 466, 475, 519, 562; Kush*th*a invoked against female spooks, 42, 5 sq.; d. that seek to devour, 42, 58; imprecations against d., 42, 64–71, 237 sq., 285, 298, 393–404, 458; charm against female d. hostile to men, cattle and home, 42, 66 sq., 298–302; eat raw meat, 42, 69, 395; Indra drives away the d. of grudge, 42, 148; invoked with gods, 42, 162; exorcised, 42, 187; Earth invoked to drive away d., 42, 205; goblins and d., shaft and missile, 43, 106; prayer to be preserved from the fiercely-howling d., 44, 266; human sacrifices to d. at the Purushamedha, 44, 413 sq.; Agni invoked against ghouls and sorcerers, 46, 32 sq., 109; Yâtu, a bad demon, 46, 393; evil d. possessing men's bodies, driven out, 48, 168; description of d., the hosts of Mâra, 49 (i), 139–44. *See also* Asuras, Atrin, Bhûtas, Dânavas, Dasyus, Goblins, Kinnaras, Pi*s*â*k*as, Râkshasas, *and* Superhuman beings.

(*c*) In China.

'The demon regions,' 3, 412, 412 n.; the demon of drought, 3, 421, 421 n.

Departed, the, *see* Ancestors, Ancestor-worship, Death, Fathers, Pretas, Souls, *and* Spirits.

Deposits, *see* Property.

Desh*tri*, n.d., invoked at the marriage, 29, 278.

Desh*trî*, n.d., Prâ*n*a is, 42, 219.

De*s*iga*n*in, *see* Kshamâ*s*rama*n*a D.

Desire(s): giving up all d. the highest happiness, 8, 49, &c., 405; 10 (i), 43, 43 sq. n., 51, 66, 73; 14, 139 sq.; *see also* Nirvâ*n*a, *and* Tranquillity; produced from attachment, and anger produced from d., 8, 50; the foe in this world, 8, 57 sq.; sin is d., 10 (ii), xv sq.; the Tâo requires being without d., 39, 47, 49, 79; 40, 251 sq. *See also* Pleasures, *and* Ta*n*hâ.

Destiny or fate, and actions, 4, 267 sq.; is predominant over everything, 5, 396 sq.; 24, 57, 89; d. and divine providence, 5, 397; 24, 55; everybody's augury fastened on his neck, 9, 2 sq.; the infidels predestined not to believe, 9, 162 sq.; what things happen through d., and what through exertion, 18, 214–16; why worldly goods are not allotted so truly as spiritual, 24, 37 sq.; impossibility to contend with d., 24, 54 sq.; it is by d. that a bad man succeeds, and a good one fails, 24, 93 sq.; stars preside over d. of man, 24, 227 sq.; 37, 445; all undertakings depend on fate and human exertion, 25, 249, 249 n.; controlled by self, 37, 342; its influence on men, 40, 268.

Determination is fifteenfold, 11, 233, 233 n.

Deva, in the sense of God, in the Upanishads, 15, xxiv, xxxvi.

Devabhâga *S*rautarsha, Purohita of the Kurus and S*riñ*gayas, 12, 377.

Devadatta, recited the Pâtimokkha before laymen, 13, 266; Buddha restores to life an elephant killed by D., 19, xx; hurls a rock against Buddha, 19, 246, 246 n.; lets loose a drunken elephant, to kill Buddha, 19, 246–9; 35, 282 n.; Bhaddiya, Anuruddha, Ânanda, Bhagu, Kimbila, D., and Upâli the barber, become Bhikkhus, 20, 228–33; not honoured with the epithet 'venerable,' 20, 231 n.; possessed of the powers of Iddhi, 20, 233 sq.; 35, 290; gains over prince Agâtasattu and is greatly honoured by him, 20, 233–8; his ambition to become leader of the Sa*m*gha, 20, 234, 238–41; incites Agâtasattu to murder his father, 20, 241 sq.; 49 (ii), 161; his futile attempts to kill Buddha, 20, 243–50; 35, 193, 249, 251; 36, 355; causes a schism in the Sa*m*gha, 20, 251–65; 35, 227, 292; Buddha learnt the Lotus of the True Law from D., who is to

be the future Buddha Devarâ*g*a, 21, xxx, 244–8; D. the seer who taught Buddha, identical with Prabhûtaratna (?), 21, 246 n., 247; swallowed up by the earth, 35, 153, 292; why was D. admitted to the Order, if Buddha knew that a schism would be created by D., and that D. would suffer torments of hell for it? 35, 162–70; at the moment of his death D. took refuge in Buddha, 35, 167; will become a Pa*kk*eka-Buddha, 35, 167 sq.; why D. in former births was equal or superior to the Bodhisattva, 35, 283–93, 293 n.; D. and Buddha, in the Sâkya clan, 35, 290; as a god, was the Unrighteous, and was then burnt in purgatory, 35, 292; in the *G*âtakas, 35, 303 sq.; being immoderate in food, heaped up evil Karman for a Kalpa, 36, 5; whence his affinity with Buddha? 49 (ii), 165.

Deva*g*anavidyâ, or 'demonology,' is the Veda, 44, 368, 368 n.

Devakî, mother of K*r*ish*n*a, 1, 52; 8, 229; wife of King Vasudêva, 45, 112, 113 n.

Devala calls K*r*ish*n*a the first god, 8, 87, 87 n.; author of a Dharma-sûtra, 34, 289; n. of a great ascetic, 45, 268, 269 n.

Devamantiya, Demetrios? 35, xix; an attendant of King Milinda, 35, 36–9, 47 sq.

Devamata, dialogue between Nârada and, 8, 274 sq.

Devânandâ, Brâhma*n*î mother of Mahâvîra, 22, 190 sq., 218–21, 223, 226–30.

Devapatha, t.t., or path of the gods, 1, 72 n. *See also* Path.

Devarâ*g*a: Devadatta shall become the Buddha D., 21, 247.

Devarâta, the name given to *S*una*h*-*s*epa by Vi*s*vâmitra, 44, xxxv.

Devarddhi, president of the *G*aina council of Valabhi, 22, xxxvii–xl; Kshamâ*s*rama*n*a D., 22, 295.

Devas (gods), how they become immortal, 1, 11, 33; are dependent on the sun, 1, 27; 15, 16; the sun is their honey, 1, 38; *true, the D. do not eat or drink, but they enjoy by seeing the nectar*, 1, 41–3; meditations on Brahman with reference to the D., 1, 53 sq., 58; 38, 216 sq.; the god Vâyu is the Self of the D., 1, 59; offer on the five altars, viz. the other world, Par*g*anya, this world, man, woman, 1, 78 sq.; 15, 207 sq.; the departed in the moon are loved (or eaten) by the D., and rejoice with them, 1, 80, 80 sq. n.; are in the world of Brahman, and meditate on the Self, 1, 142; Brahman's relation to the D., 1, 149–51; 38, 219; the seed of Pra*g*âpati are the D., the seed of the D. is rain, 1, 205; all the D. worship Brahman, 15, 18; sacrifices lead to where the one Lord of the D. dwells, 15, 31; begotten from the highest Person, 15, 35; when the sage dies, his D. (senses) enter into their corresponding D., 15, 41; all D. bring offerings to him who knows Brahman, 15, 49; like men and cattle, D. breathe after breath, 15, 56; the bliss of the D. born in the Â*g*âna heaven of the sacrificial D., and of the thirty-three D., 15, 60, 61 sq. n.; absorption of the D. in Brahman, 15, 68; carried by a racer, 15, 74; do not like that men should know Brahman, 15, 88; Indra, Varu*n*a, &c., the Kshatras among the D., 15, 89; world of the D. obtained by sacrifices, 15, 90; D., fathers, and men, are speech, mind, and breath, 15, 94; evil does not approach the D., 15, 97; classes of D.: Vasus, Rudras, Âdityas, Vi*s*ve Devas, Maruts, 15, 89; worlds of the D., 15, 131; D. by birth and D. by merit, 15, 172; 48, 238; bliss in the world of D., 15, 172, 176; produced by Pra*g*âpati, are the true, 15, 191; the eternal ruler over the D. is Brahman, 34, 130–2; the powers of the D. constitute the Self of the organs of the body, 38, 257; the prâ*n*as so called, 48, 585; 'he is like a beast for the D.,' 48, 589;—D. and Asuras, trying to search out the Self, 1, 134–42; 15, 343; 48, 328; performing sacrifice, disturbed by Asuras, 12, 34 sq., 69, 113 sq., 125 sq., 150 sq., 297, 370–3; struggle between D. and Asuras, 15, 78–98; have conquered the Asuras through

Indra, 29, 342; Brahma*k*ârin given in charge to D. and Asuras, 30, 153 sq.; metres of the D. and of the Asuras, 38, 228, 228 n.; succeed with the sacrifice, Asuras come to nought, 43, 78; path of the D., *see* Path. *See also* Asuras, *and* Gods (*a-k*).
Devasopâna, the world of the Tathâgata Devarâ*g*a, 21, 247.
Deva*s*ravas Bhârata, produced Agni by attrition, 46, 287 sq.
Devasû, divine quickeners, offerings to, 41, 69, 72; 43, 246.
Devatâ, Sk., 'deity,' t.t. used for the elements, 1, xxiii n., 95 sq., 100; the Sat is parâ d., 'the highest being,' 1, xxxiv, 94, 94 n., 101, 108; in Pali, fairy, god, genius, or angel, 11, 45 n. *See also* Gods (*a-k*).
Devavâta Bhârata, produced Agni by attrition, 46, 287 sq.; S*riñg*aya, the son of D., 46, 361.
Devayâna, Sk., t.t., path of the gods. *See* Path.
Devayânî, altercation between *S*armish*th*â and, 14, xli.
Devî, the son of Agni seated on her side, 49 (i), 12.
Devil, is to you a foe, so take him as a foe, 9, 157; privy talk is only from the d., 9, 272; god invoked against the d., 9, 345; charmed by an exorcist, 35, 38.
Devils, pelted with shooting-stars, 6, 245; 9, 168, 293, 322; sent to tempt misbelievers, 9, 33 sq.; could not have brought the Qur'ân, 9, 98; descend upon the poets, 9, 99; mates of the unbelievers, 9, 201, 201 n., 213 sq.; when d. incite you, seek refuge with God, 9, 202. *See also* Demons.
Devil-worshippers, live in the hollows of trees, 13, 318; use skulls for bowls, 20, 89; wear the hair in their nostrils long, 20, 139.
Devotee, *see* Yogin.
Devotion or Tapas, everything supported by it, 7, 278; d. or Yoga, *see* Yoga.
Dewy Season, *see* Seasons.
Dha*g*a, one of the eight Brahmans who took note of the marks on Buddha's body, 36, 44.
Dha*g*agga-parittâ, a protecting charm, 35, 213.
Dhamma (Pali), Dharma (Sk.), Buddhist t.t., Truth, the True Law, teaching of Buddha, 10 (i), xxiii; (ii), 47, 63–6, 76–80, 175, 177, 186, 201 sq., 209; 11, 62, 64, 117 sq.; 49 (i), 52; different meanings of Dh., 10 (i), xlv, 3 sq. n., 68 n.; (ii), x; 13, xxviii–xxx, 3 n.; difficult is the hearing of the Dh., 10 (i), 49; happy is the teaching of the Dh., 10 (i), 52; the gift of the Dh. (dhammadâna) exceeds all gifts, 10 (i), 83, 83 n.; worship the law (Dh.) of Buddha, as the Brâhma*n*a worships the sacrificial fire, 10 (i), 90; he who expounds and explains the Dh., is a Maggade*s*in Sama*n*a, 10 (ii), 16; he who loves Dh. is the winner, he who hates Dh. is the loser in this world, 10 (ii), 17; he who approves of the Dh. of the wicked is a loser in this world, 10 (ii), 17; worship of Buddha and Dh., 10 (ii), 29, 31; Dh., well observed, conveys happiness, 10 (ii), 30; four dhammas or virtues, truth, justice, firmness, and liberality, 10 (ii), 31; the Dh. as to the acquisition of Nibbâna, 10 (ii), 31, 39; standing firm in the Dh., 10 (ii), 42; the sweetness of the Dh., 10 (ii), 43; the blessing of the hearing of the Dh. at due seasons, 10 (ii), 44; Buddha on the Dh. of the old and new Brâhma*n*as, 10 (ii), 48–52; one should choose a good teacher of the Dh., and worship him, 10 (ii), 52 sq.; those who delight in Dh. obtain the highest good, 10 (ii), 54 sq.; understanding the Dh. thoroughly is the chief duty of the Bhikkhu, 10 (ii), 60–2; he to whom all Dhammas are destroyed, Tathâgata, 10 (ii), 78; a supernatural insight in all Dhammas, 10 (ii), 78; Buddha teaches the Dh., that is good in the beginning, in the middle, and in the end, 10 (ii), 96; turning the wheel of Dh. (Dhamma*k*akkappavattana), i.e. the setting in motion onwards of the royal chariot-wheel of the supreme dominion of the Dh., or the Foundation of the Kingdom of Righteousness, 10 (ii), 102 sq., 125, 127; 11, 140 sq.; 13, 91, 97 sq.; the Dhs., or the four noble truths, 10 (ii), 132; *for those that are enveloped there is gloom, for those that do not see*

there is darkness, and for the good it is manifest, for those that see there is light; (even being) near, those that are ignorant of the way and the Dh., do not discern (anything), 10 (ii), 144 sq.; Dhammas or doctrines, 10 (ii), 149 sq., 151, 153 sq., 164 sq., 172 sq., 183, 191; let the Bhikkhu learn every Dh. inwardly or outwardly, 10 (ii), 175; Bâvarî is perfect in his own Dh., 10 (ii), 189; having learnt the best Dh. one crosses the stream, 10 (ii), 196 sq.; the Dhs. lead to the other shore, 10 (ii), 209 sq.; Buddha's Dh., the instantaneous, the immediate, the destruction of desire, freedom from distress, whose likeness is nowhere, 10 (ii), 211 sq.; leads to salvation, 11, 27; he who has doubts in the Dh. is not free from spiritual barrenness, 11, 224, 228; eighteen things by which one may conclude that a Bhikkhu is wrong according to the Dh., 17, 315 sqq.; by knowing Dh. we know Buddha, 35, 110; he who weeps for the death of his mother, and he who weeps out of love for the Dh., 35, 119; no wisdom of any use without investigation of the Dh., 35, 128; is the most minute thing, 35, 132; a lay disciple must always stand by Dh., 35, 143 sq.; is the best in the world, 35, 229, 229 n.; kindness towards all beings, the characteristic of Dh., 35, 255; cannot be perceived without practising the vows of a recluse, 36, 255; one has to find out Dh. by oneself, 49 (i), 101 sq.; the eye of Dh. (dhamma*k*akkhu), 11, 82, 96, 119, 127, 153, 153 n.; 49 (i), 180; Dh. and Sa*mg*ñâ, in Mahâyâna metaphysics, 49 (ii), xiv sq., 117. *See also* Buddha (*g*), Buddhism, Dharma, Jewels (the three), *and* Preaching.

Dhamma - *k*akka - ppavattana - Sutta, t.c., 'the Foundation of the Kingdom of Righteousness,' 11, ix, 137–55; belongs to the Aṅguttara Nikâya, and occurs in the Lalita Vistara, and Vinaya Pi*t*aka, 11, 139 sq.; its historical value, 11, 140–5.

Dhamma*k*akkhu, Pali, t.t., the eye of Truth. *See* Dhamma.

Dhamma*k*ariyasutta, t.c., 10 (ii), 46 sq.

Dhammantari, n. of an author on medicine, 36, 109, 109 n.

Dhammapada, t.w., quoted, 8, 36, 50 n., 51 n., 52 n., 69 n., 71 n., 84 n., 101 n., 102 n., 108 n., 123 n., 241 n.; 35, 284 n.; 36, 4 n., 353; translated, 10 (i); a canonical book of Buddhism, 10 (i), ix sq.; a commentary to it, by Buddhaghosa, 10 (i), x; its date, 10 (i), x–xxvi; the title of Dh., its meaning, 10 (i), xlv–xlix; translations of the Dh., 10 (i), xlix–lii; he who lives in the way that has so well been taught in the Dh., is called a Magga*g*îvin Sama*n*a, 10 (ii), 16.

Dhamma-pâla: the Bodisat as prince Dh., 35, 290.

Dhammarakkhita, n. of teacher of Nâgasena, 35, xxv, 26–9.

Dhammasenâpati or Upatissa, 11, 1 n.

Dhamma-vinaye, how to be explained, 11, 223 n.

Dhammika, Buddha explains to him the duties of Bhikkhus and householders, 10 (ii), 62–6.

Dhammikasutta, t.c., 10 (ii), 62–6.

Dhanagiri, disciple of Si*m*hagiri *G*âtismara, 22, 293; of the Vâsish*th*a gotra, a Sthavira, 22, 294.

Dhana*ñg*aya, n. of Ar*g*una, 8, 38, 48 sq., 63, 74, 93, 100, 125, 130, 230, 310, 394; worshipped at the Tarpa*n*a, 30, 244.

Dhanapâla(ka), n. of the elephant who rushed upon Buddha at Râ*g*a*g*aha, 35, 297, 298 n., 300; 36, 248.

Dhanapati, Bali offering to him at the Vai*s*vadeva, 29, 86.

Dhanarddhi, disciple of Mahâgiri, 22, 290.

Dhaniya, the rich herdsman, his dialogue with Buddha, 10 (ii), 3–5; he and his wife take refuge in Buddha, 10 (ii), 5.

Dhaniya, the potter's son, subject of the second Pârâgika, 20, 375.

Dhaniyasutta, t.c., Sutta of the cowherd Dhaniya, 10 (ii), 3–5; 36, 285.

Dhânyâyana, a Brahman, converted by Buddha, 49 (i), 193.

Dhânva, *see* Asita Dh.

Dhânvana, Asita Dh., king of Asuras, 44, 368 n.

Dhanvantari, offerings to, 2, 202; 25, 90; 29, 161, 163, 179; the

physician of the gods, 36, 109 n. *See* Bharadvâga Dh.

Dharaṇendra, the best of Nâgas, 45, 290.

Dharaṇîdhara, n. of a Bodhisattva Mahâsattva, 21, 4; one of the sixteen virtuous men, 21, 4.

Dharaṇindhara, n. of Bodhisattva, 21, 418.

Dhâraṇîs, Sk., i.e. talismanic words, spells. *See* Spells.

Dharma, Sk., t.t., religious duty, merit, 34, 26, 299 sq., 429; qualifying particulars, 38, 186; Dh. and Adharma, as substances, 45, 153, 207 sq. *See* Dhamma, *and* Piety.

Dharma, Justice, n. of a god: Bali-offering to Dh. and Adharma, 2, 107; worship of King Dh. (dharmarâga) on the fourteenth of both halves of every month, 7, 270; in the Anugîtâ, 8, 219; appears before Ganaka disguised as a Brâhmaṇa, 8, 224, 306; Duty, Law, or Justice personified, 25, 22, 255, 352, 495; daughters of Daksha married to Dh., 25, 352; worshipped at the Tarpaṇa, 30, 244; the favourite abodes of Dh., 33, 104 n.; the balance a symbol of Dh., 33, 253; the ordeal by Dh., 33, 315 sq., 316 n., 319.

Dharma, n. of a Tîrthakara, 22, 280; n. of different Sthaviras, 22, 294 sq., 294 n.

Dharma, n. of a Tathâgata, 49 (ii), 100.

Dharmadhara, n. of a Kinnara king, 21, 5.

Dharmadhara, n. of a Tathâgata, 49 (ii), 100.

Dharma-dhâtu, mystic world of the Northern Buddhists, 19, 324, 324 n.

Dharmadhvaga, n. of a Tathâgata, 49 (ii), 100.

Dharmagahanâbhyudgatarâga, n. of a former Buddha, 21, 208.

Dharmagupta, Chinese translation of the Saddharma-puṇḍarîka, by Gñânagupta and Dh., 21, xix–xxi, xxiii; translated the Vagrakkhedikâ, 49 (ii), xiii.

Dharma Indra, the king whose people are the gods, 44, 370.

Dharmakakra, chief of the sons of the Ginas, 49 (i), 173.

Dharmâkara, a pupil of the Tathâgata Lokesvararâga, 49 (ii), ix sq., 7–10; describes his own Buddha-country, 49 (ii), 11–22; becomes Buddha Amitâbha, 49 (ii), 28; his prayers, 49 (ii), 177, 194.

Dharmaketu, the 70th Tathâgata, 49 (ii), 7.

Dharmamati, son of a former Buddha Kandrasûryapradîpa, 21, 19; the 78th Tathâgata, 49 (ii), 7.

Dharmamativinanditarâga, the 39th Tathâgata, 49 (ii), 6.

Dharmapâlin, father of Sâriputra, 49 (i), 193.

Darmaphala, a life of Buddha brought to China by, 19, xviii; translated the Kung-pen-k'i-king, 19, xxiv.

Dharmaprabhâsa, a future Buddha, 21, 194–8.

Dharmaprahrâda: story of Dh., Kumâlana, and Death, 2, 98, 98 sq. n.

Dharmarâga, *see* Dharma.

Dharmaraksha, translator of the Phû-yau-king, 19, xxv; translated the Buddhakarita into Chinese, 49 (i), x.

Dharmaraksha, translated the Buddhakarita into Chinese, 19, ix, xxx, xxxii, xxxiv sq.; translated the Mahâparinirvâṇa-sûtra into Chinese, 19, 365; Chinese translation of the Saddharmapuṇḍarîka, by Dh., 21, xx, xxiii.

Dharmaruki, divinity of a tree, 49 (i), 169.

Dharmasâstras, or (Hindu) Law-books, as authorities on law, 2, 237, 237 n.; Anugîtâ and Dh., 8, 208, 210, 215–19; only to be taught to son or pupil, 14, 124, 322; teach penances, 14, 312, 317; mentioned in the Mânava-smriti, 25, xxv sq., 31, 118, 510; free from sectarian influence, 25, liv sq.; their character as school-books, 25, liv–lvi; metrical Smritis and floating mass of Slokas, 30, xxxvii; the king should listen to the exposition of the Purâṇas and law-books, 33, 280; the Atharva-veda in the Dh., 42, xlv–li; founded on Brâhmaṇas, Mantras, and Arthavâdas, 48, 330. *See also* Smriti.

Dharma-sûtras, the basis of the

metrical Smritis (Dharmasâstras), 2, ix–xi and n.; 25, xviii–xxiii, liii sq.; their sources, 25, xi; the works of ordinary mortals, 25, xi; their purpose, 25, xi sq.; their antiquity, 25, xix; Mânava-smriti later than Dh., 25, xxvi; referred to by Patañgali, 25, li sq.; quoted by Medhâtithi, 25, cxix, cxix n.; relation between Srauta-sûtras, Grihya-sûtras, and Dh., 30, xxix–xxxv.

Dharmavyâdha, *see* Religious hunter.

Dhartri, worshipped at the Tarpana, 30, 244.

Dharuna Âṅgirasa, author of Vedic hymns, 46, 400.

Dhâtri, the Creator, 15, xxiv; Manu and Dh. perform the punarâdheya, 12, 314 n.; a name of the Self, 15, 311; invoked and worshipped, 26, 376; 29, 86, 207, 320, 344, 347; 30, 151, 244; 41, 54 n.; 42, 20, 54, 126, 160, 389; has ordained procreation, 29, 45; invoked and worshipped at the Sîmantonnayana, 29, 47 sq., 181; 30, 208; has shaven the head of Brihaspati and Indra, 29, 56, 56 n., 185; invoked at the marriage, 29, 278; invoked for conception, 30, 199; oblations to Dh. for the new-born child, 30, 214; protects from all evils, 42, 81; shaped the being, 42, 86; invoked in charms to obtain a husband, 42, 94 sq., 324; supports earth, heavens, and sun, 42, 95; made overlord for warding-off of the fiends, 44, 464 sq. *See* Creator, *and* Pragâpati.

Dhâtusena, nephew of Mahânâma, 10 (i), xv–xviii.

Dhîra or Viriyavat (firm), definition of the term, 10 (ii), 91.

Dhîra Sâtaparneya, n. of a teacher, 43, 331.

Dhishanâ, n. of a goddess, 46, 12, 119–22, 228; a goddess of the earth, and of wealth, 46, 120 sq.;—Dhishanâs, goddesses, 41, 242 sq., 243 n.; are speech, 41, 243.

Dhishnya hearths, *see* Fire (*e*).

Dhotaka, n. of a Brâhmana, 10 (ii), 187, 196 sq., 210.

Dhotakamânavapukkhâ, t.c., 10 (ii), 196 sq.

Dhrishtadyumna, n. of a hero, 8, 39; not born in the ordinary way, 38, 125, 126; 48, 595.

Dhrishtaketu, n. of a warrior, 8, 37.

Dhritarâshtra, n. of a king, informed about the battle of Kurukshetra, 8, 3, 37–43; his sons, the Kauravas, 8, 41–3, 95; Sanatsugâtîya, a dialogue between Sanatsugâta and Dh., 8, 135 sq., 149–94; his character, 8, 141; Dh. Vaikitravîrya, mentioned in the Kâthaka, 12, xliii n.; his sacrificial horse seized by Satânîka, 44, xxx, 401; head of the four Mahârâgas, 49 (i), 196 sq.;—n. of a god, 21, 4.

Dhriti, an ascetic, converted by Buddha, 49 (i), 191.

Dhritiparipûrna, the Bodhisattva, will be the Buddha Padmavrishabhavikrâmin, 21, 67.

Dhritis, t.t., oblations for the safe keeping of the horse at the Asvamedha, 44, 285, 285 n., 364, 364 n.

Dhruva, his brothers Bali and Vagrabâhu, 49 (i), 94.

Dhruvasena, king of Ânandapura, 22, 270 n.

DHu'l Kifl, was patient and entered into the mercy of God, 9, 53, 53 n.; was of the righteous, 9, 180.

DHu'l Qarnâin, travels to the ocean of the setting sun, and builds a rampart to keep in Gog and Magog, 9, 24 sq. and n.

DHu'nnûn, *see* Jonah.

Dhutaṅgas, *see* Vows.

Dhvasan Dvaitavana, king of the Matsyas, offered a horse-sacrifice, 44, 398.

Dhvasra, n.p., 32, 360 sq.

Dhyânas, Sk., t.t., *see* Ghânas, *and* Meditation.

Dialectics, *see* Philosophy.

Dialogues, *see* Parables.

Dibba-kakkhu, t.t., 'the heavenly eye,' superhuman knowledge of present Births, 11, 209, 218. *See also* Eye.

Dice, Krita among, 44, 330.

Difference, does not admit of logical definition, 48, 31–3; of substance can be proved, 48, 39–46.

Digestion, explained, 8, 113, 252, 273 n., 275 n.; juicy food causes indigestion, 8, 236 n.

Dîgha Nikâya, t.w., Tevigga Sutta from, 11, 159; Mahâ-sudassana Sutta, 11, 237; Mahâparinibbâna Sutta from the D., quoted, 36, 352. *See also* Tipi*t*aka.

Dîgha-pingalo: Â*l*âra was D., 11, 75 n.

Dîghâvu: the story of D., the son of King Dîghîti of Kosala, 17, 296–305.

Dîghîti, king of Kosala, 17, 293–305.

Dîkshâ, Sk., t.t., consecration or initiation as the preparatory rite for the upâsana of those who live in the forest, 1, 75 sq., 75 n.; rite of initiation for a Soma sacrifice, 12, 24, 25 n., 447 n.; 26, xxxii, 1–47, 161 sq.; 29, 319; personified, 14, 196; 26, 150; the Avântaradîkshâ or intermediary consecration, 26, 97–104; the sacrificer consecrates himself for the sake of this All, 26, 155; the D. offering, 26, 12 sq., 161; 41, 44; 43, 258; repeated, when substitutes of the Soma-plant had to be used, 26, 422 sq.; for the Sattra or sacrificial session, 26, 440–6; 44, 135–8; repeated for each Soma-sacrifice, 41, 4 n.; at the Vâgapeya, 41, 17; as part of the king's Abhishe*k*anîya ceremony, 41, 68 sq., 68 n.; Pragâpati and the beings consecrated themselves for a year, 41, 158; for the building of the fire-altar, 41, 180 sq. and n., 185 sq., 246–97, 247 n.; supports the earth, 42, 199; is Speech, 43, 67; at the animal sacrifice, 44, 121 sq.; from out of faith the gods fashioned the D., 44, 138; is the body of the sacrifice, 44, 240; no D. at the Sautrâma*n*î, 44, 240, 240 n.; for the horse-sacrifice, 44, 289–95, 371 sq.; there are twelve days, 44, 371; for the Purushamedha there are twenty-three Dîkshâs, 44, 403. *See also* Anointment.

Dîkshita, the Consecrated, rules for, 26, 4–11, 19 sq., 33 sq., 38–47; draws nigh to the gods, 26, 4, 20, 38, 42, 44; becomes an embryo, 26, 19 sq., 29, 33 sq., 73; begging enjoined for him, 26, 45 n.; abstinence enjoined for him, 41, 185 sq.

Dîn, *see* Daêna.

Dînâ-î Maînôg-î Khira*d*, or 'Opinions of the Spirit of Wisdom,' title and contents, 24, xv sq., 3 n.; its date and author, 24, xvi sq.; MSS. and versions of it, 24, xviii–xxv; translated, 24, 1–113.

Dînârâs, mentioned in the Kalpa-sûtra, 22, 233, 233 n.; in the Nârada-smr*i*ti, 33, xvii sq., 32.

Dînkar*d*, t.w., compilers and editors of the, 5, 148 n.; 24, xxvii, 139 n.: its date, 18, xxvii; 24, 139 n.; 37, xxxiii, 488; quoted, 18, xxix, 370–2, 370 sq. n.; 24, xxvi, 120 n., 139, 146, 162, 162 n., 169 sq., 202 sq. and n.; quotes the Dâ*d*istân-î Dînîk, 18, 269 n.; allusions to next-of-kin marriage in the D., 18, 394–7, 399–415; its importance, 24, 139 n.; its account of the Nasks, 37, xxix sq., xxxviii–xlvi; its early history, 37, xxx–xxxiii; transmission of the text down to the present MSS., 37, xxxiii–xxxviii; translation of books viii and ix, Contents of the Nasks, 37, 1–397; from Books iii and iv of the D., 37, 406–18; quotes from an older 'Exposition of the Good Religion,' 47, ix, 3 sq., 3 n.; legendary history of Zoroaster in the D., 47, ix–xvi, 3–130.

Dinna = Sabbadinna, q.v.

Dînô, *see* Daêna.

Dîn-pa(van)-Âtarô, or Dînô, has the orange-scented mint, 5, 104; invoked, 5, 402, 405.

Dîn-pa(van)-Dînô, Trigonella the flower of, 5, 104; invoked, 5, 403, 405.

Dîn-pa(van)-Mitrô, or Dînô, the flower of, 5, 104; invoked, 5, 402, 405.

Dîn-vi*g*irgard, account of the Nasks from the, 37, 438, 438 n.

Dîpankara, nomination of Buddha by, 19, xviii; n. of a Tathâgata, 21, 22, 28, 300; 49 (ii), ix, 6, 71; a former Buddha, 49 (ii), 122, 131–3.

Dîpava*m*sa, founded on the Sinhalese A*tth*akathâs, 10 (i), xiii, xvi sq.; its date, 10 (i), xiii; 11, xxii; the dates of Buddhist Patriarchs, according to the D., 10 (i), xlii–xlv; lists of Kings and Theras in the D., 11, xlvi sq.

Dîrghabhadra, disciple of Sambhûta-vigaya, 22, 289.

Dîrghâgama, a canonical work of Buddhism, 19, xxiv.

Dîrghânakha, uncle of *S*âriputra, converted by Buddha, 49 (i), 193.

Dîrghatamas Au*k*athya, author of Vedic hymns, 46, 143, 149, 154, 158, 161, 164, 167, 170, 174, 176, 178; the blind son of Mamatâ, 46, 170, 171; 49 (i), 44 n.

Discussions, of scholars and kings respectively, 35, 46.

Diseases, treated as cases of impurity, 4, lxxx; and deformities, the work of Angra Mainyu, 4, 17, 19, 227–9; lists of d., 4, 227–9, 235, 241; spells against Death and Sickness, 4, 229; rain invoked to cure d., 4, 231; caused by demons, 5, 112; 24, 265; causes of d. and death, 8, 236 sq.; caused by offences committed in a former life, 8, 321; 14, 109; 22, 53 sq.; 25, lxxii, 92, 105, 108, 341, 440 sq.; 35, 152; caused by sorcery, 17, 60; four classes of d., 21, 130; sixteen d., 22, 53 sq.; charms and magic rites to cure d. and possession by demons of d., 22, 187 sq.; 42, 1–48, 57–60, 67, 233–7, 241 sq., 246–52, 257–60, 263–74, 277–84, 286–94, 302 sq., 308–11, 313–22, 336–9, 341–3, 369–71, 373–8, 384–9, 406–11, 414–23, 425–8, 441–56, 463–6, 468–73, 475, 481–3, 488–90, 500 sq., 503–7, 509–14, 516–21, 530–2, 536 sq., 552–5, 557–69, 578–82, 600–2, 669–81, 697; the god that caused a d. shall cure it, 42, 34; driven away by the Airyaman prayer, 23, 41, 44; to avert d. the Fravashi of Thraêtaona is worshipped, 23, 221; old age, death, d., 25, 209, 212; how to cure d. at a sacrifice, 26, 40 sq. and n.; Rudra invoked against d., 29, 137; ceremony for averting d., 29, 224, 236, 432 sq.; the initiated boy given in charge to D., 30, 154; Karman and other causes of d., 35, 191–5; cured by Pirit (charms) and medicines, 35, 213–19, 213 n.; caused by evil eye, 37, 101 sq.; healed by sacrificial rites, 41, 50; healed by Vedic verses, 41, 141; transmission of d., 42, 47 sq., 309 sq.; salve (âñgana) protecting from d., 42, 61 sq.; amulet warding off d., 42, 82;—persons afflicted with leprosy and similar d. excluded from *S*râddhas, 2, 258; 14, 52; 25, 103, 105 sq., 108; lepers, &c., excluded from sacrifices, 23, 75; insane and suffering persons cannot be witnesses, 25, 265, 265 n.; 33, 303; dropsy, the punishment of Varu*n*a, 25, 269 n.; sufferers from pestilence slain, 27, 178; ceremonies against pestilence, 27, 266, 288, 307, 423; a cure for headache, 29, 350; dog-demon or epilepsy, 30, 219 sq.; sons afflicted with chronic d. disinherited, 33, 194; regulations about contagious d., 37, 98;—prayer against Yakshman (consumption), 41, 341 n.; charm against takman (fever) and related d., 42, 1–7, 246–52, 270–4, 414–19, 441–52, 468–70, 565–9, 676–81; charms against dropsy and similar d., 42, 11–13, 241 sq., 471, 562–4; charms against kshetriya, hereditary d., 42, 13–16, 286–90, 292–4, 336–9; charms against leprosy, 42, 16, 266–70; charms against poison, 42, 25–30, 373–8, 425–8, 461–3, 511 sq., 552–5; charm against mania, 42, 32 sq., 518–21; fever and cough, the missiles of Rudra, 42, 157; fever connected with lightning, 42, 271 sq.; leprosy cured by the sacrifice of a white cow, 42, 711; children's d., *see* Children (*b*).

Disputations, on spiritual matters, 44, 50–6.

Diti, n.d., and Aditi, 32, 243, 255 sq.; 41, 93, 93 n.; Agni invoked to grant and keep off Aditi, 46, 317, 321; sons of D., 49 (i), 196.

Di*tth*igatika, Pali t.t., a philosopher, 10 (ii), 158.

Divâkara, translated the Lalitavistara into Chinese, 19, xxviii.

Divination.

(*a*) In China.
(*b*) In India.

(*a*) IN CHINA.

Yî King, a book of d., d. by it, 3, xvii; 16, xv, 2, 4 sq., 10 sq., 22, 31, 40–3, 54, 170, 172 n., &c.; with the tortoise-shell and divining stalks, 3, 50 sq., 104, 112, 120, 140 n., 145–7, 145 n., 152–4, 154 n., 156–61, 207, 349, 358, 381 n., 383, 437 sq., 438 n.;

16, 20 sq., 40 sq., 150, 318 n., 364 n., 365–74, 368 sq. n., 371 n., 374 sqq. n., 380 sq., 381 sq. n., 404 sq.; 27, 92, 94, 103, 128, 181, 384 sq.; 28, 4, 74, 77, 289, 295, 320, 320 n.; 40, 52, 80, 136 sq., 137 n.; d. and dreams, 3, 128; by the tortoise-shell, about the founding of a city, 3, 183, 188–90, 395, 395 n., 437, 437 n.; with a handful of grain, 3, 359, 359 n.; about (the time for) sacrifices, 3, 399, 399 n.; 27, 428 sq.; 28, 53 sq., 349–51; about the site for burying and funeral, 3, 487; 28, 51, 135 sq., 156, 180; 40, 125; object of d., 16, 40–2; doubts in the use of d., 16, 41, 41 n.; formation of the lineal figures by the divining stalks, 16, 42 sq.; about marriage, 16, 65; 28, 298, 428; sincerity in having recourse to d., 16, 65, 217; diviners and exorcists employed, 16, 190, 192 n.; alluded to, 16, 221; hexagrams of the Yî derived from the manipulating with divining stalks, 16, 241 n.; good fortune and bad indicated by the emblems of the Yî King, 16, 350 sq., 351 n.; is a 'help extended to man from Heaven,' 16, 351; with hexagrams and stalks, 16, 356 sq., 358 n.; the Yî King arose from the manipulation of the divining stalks, 16, 422, 422 sq. n.; by tortoise-shell, in buying a concubine, 27, 78; about the proper time for undertakings, 27, 94; the Grand-diviner, one of the six grandees, 27, 109; when it should not be resorted to, 27, 119; false reports about consultings of tortoise-shell and stalks punished with death, 27, 238; smearing tortoise-shells and divining stalks with blood, 27, 298; one of the minor arts, 27, 348; by tortoise-shell at birth ceremonies, 27, 472; rules about d., 28, 71; about ceremonies, 28, 223; is making Heaven the Decider, 28, 233, 233 n.; a man without constancy cannot be a diviner, 28, 363; at the capping ceremony, 28, 426; by physiognomy, 40, 106. *See also* Yî King.

(*b*) In India.

Low arts, and lying practices, as d. from marks on the body, auguries, dreams, &c., forbidden to Buddhist and Gaina monks, 11, 194, 196 sq., 199; 19, 296; 36, 287; 45, 34, 70 sq., 70 n., 105, 366 sq.; fortune-telling a disreputable occupation, 11, 194; 25, 387; 42, 1; 45, 80; an ascetic shall not subsist by d., astrology, palmistry, 14, 48; 25, 208; from the direction taken by the Sâhasrî cow, when let loose, 26, 416; relating to future marriage, 29, 165; 42, 323, 491; prognostications from dreams, comets, meteors, &c., the business of Brahmans, 35, 247 sq.; from marks of the body, 36, 158 sq.; regarding the new-born child, 42, 242 sq.; the fact that men by arts of d. know the future proves the reality of the world, 45, 317. *See also* Omens, *and* Oracles.

Divine Doors, invoked in Âprî hymns, 46, 8, 153, 179, 198, 236, 377.

Divinities: in meditations connected with constitutives of sacrificial works the idea of the d. is to be transferred to the sacrificial items, not *vice versa*, 34, lxxvii; 38, 345–9; intelligent presiding d. are connected with everything, 34, 304; the vital airs act under the guidance of d., 38, 91 sq.; d. who act as the guides of the vital airs and co-operate with them stop their co-operation at the time of death, 38, 106; even priests who do not know the d. of sacrifices, perform them, 38, 254; the organs of the body and the d. are non-different, 38, 257. *See also* Gods.

Divinity, the highest, is endowed with all powers, 34, 354 sq. *See also* Brahman.

Divodâsa, king of Benares, 49 (i), 192.

Divorce, *see* Marriage.

Documents: proof by written d. in legal procedure, 7, xxiv; 14, xxvi, 80 sq.; 25, xcix–ci; 33, xiii, 5, 7 sq., 7 n., 21, 23, 30, 35, 198; boundaries recorded in writing, 25, 299, 299 n.; various kinds of d., as a means of proof, 33, 58–60, 64 sq., 70, 75–9, 242 sq., 248, 294, 297, 302, 304–9, 311–14, 325, 331, 334, 339, 348; recording the victory of a litigant party, 33, 235, 295, 297 sq.;

written plaint and answer, 33, 236 sq., 292–4, 296; written grants, 33, 347.

Dog, dogs, in the Avesta, 4, lxxi, 155–69; 37, 161, 161 n.; the Corpse-Drug expelled by 'the look of the d.' (Sag-dîd), 4, lxxii, lxxiv sq., lxxiv n., lxxxi, 77, 77 n., 83, 83 n., 99, 99 n., 106, 106 n., 120; 5, 245 sq. and n., 259 sq., 259 n., 261 n., 262 sq., 267, 319 sq., 332; 18, 42, 42 n.; 24, 335 sq.; 37, 153; *see also* Sag-dîd; punishments for killing d., 4, lxxxiv sq., 155–9, 185, 272; happy the house where the d. thrives, 4, 23; d. and men, mentioned together, 4, 24, 26, 32, 67, 69, 73, 78 sq., 81, 93 sq., 95, 106; impurity caused by the death of the different kinds of d., 4, 59, 78; hatefulness of the tortoise, or the d. of Ahriman, 4, 155, 157; holiness of the hedgehog, the d. of Ormazd, 4, 155–7, 156 n.; usefulness of the d., 4, 159 sq., 164 sq., 168; the food due to the d., 4, 160–2; 37, 114; treatment of mad d., 4, 163 sq.; d. and wolves, 4, 165 sq.; virtues and vices of d., 4, 166 sq.; 5, 72–4; the holy water-d., 4, 168; penalties for killing a water-dog, 4, 168–76; cleansing d., one of the good works, 4, 175; sins committed by ill-treatment of d., 4, 176 sq.; duties towards bitch and whelps, 4, 180–4; on breeding d., 4, 184 sq.; keep the *K*inva*d* bridge, 4, 219, 219 n.; classes of d., 5, 48 sq.; reward of the d. for protecting the sheep, 5, 51 sq.; use of the d. at the Bareshnûm ceremony (to destroy Nasu*s*), 18, 450–2, 450 n.; d. punished for wilful murder, 23, 340; must be fed and well treated, 24, 292 sq.; assist the soul at the *K*inva*d* bridge, 24, 293; demons frightened away by the bark of d., 24, 293; burial of d. and horses, 27, 196 sq.; shepherd-d., their rights and duties, 37, 81–4; protection of d., 37, 162;—boiled at drinking festivals, 28, 443, 443 n., 457 n.; how Hsü Wû-kwei judges of d., 40, 92 sq.;—penance of a Brâhma*n*a who is bitten by a d., 14, 121; used at the cure of palsy, 42, 501; moon the heavenly d., 44, 10–12; an unclean animal, 44, 178; a 'four-eyed' d. killed at the horse-sacrifice, 44, 279, 279 n.; d., crows, women and *S*ûdras are untruth, 44, 446.

Dogmas, of Islâm, viz. belief in God, the last day, the angels, the Book, and the prophets, 6, 24, 46, 91; belief in Zoroastrian d., a good work, 24, 73–5; disbelief of the wicked, 37, 193.

Dôgundaga (Sk. dvikundaka), n. of a god or class of gods, 45, 88, 88 n., 108.

Do*n*a, the Brâhman, divides the relics of Buddha, 11, 133 sq.; erected a dâgaba over the vessel in which Buddha's body had been burnt, 11, 135.

Donkey, *see* Ass.

Doors, *see* Divine Doors.

Dowry, *see* Woman (*a*).

Dragon, *see* Animals (i), Dahâka, *and* Snake.

Drâhyâya*n*a, *S*rauta-sûtra of, 29, 371.

Drama, origin of the, 32, 287.

Drami*d*a, quoted by Râmânu*g*a, 34, xxi sq., xlix; 48, 487; preceded *S*aṅkara, 34, xxii; D. or Dravi*d*a, 34, xxii n.

Drami*d*a-bhâshya, of Drami*d*a, quoted 34, xxii, xlix; 48, 99, 428 sq.

Drami*d*â*k*ârya, *see* Drami*d*a.

Draôna, Drôn, t.t., *see* Sacrifices (*b*).

Drâtha, n.p., 23, 210.

Draupadî, the sons of, 8, 38 sq.; not born in the ordinary way, 38, 125; 48, 595.

Dravi*d*a, Dravi*d*â*k*ârya, *see* Drami*d*a.

Dravi*d*as, a mixed caste, 7, xxiv; 25, 406, 407 n., 412; became V*ri*shalas, 8, 295; the art of D., an occult science, 45, 366.

Dravi*n*odas, deities of *Ri*tu-grahas, 26, 320 n.

Dreams: seeing a woman in d. is a sign that one's sacrifice has succeeded, 1, 76; d. are false and unreal, relatively only, 1, 132 sq. n.; 34, 325; the Self in the state of d., 1, 138 sq.; 38, 56; d. foreboding death, and propitiatory ceremony to ward off their evil consequences, 1, 262 sq.; prognostication by and

interpretation of d., 3, 128, 350 sq., 350 n.; 27, 344; 36, 157–61; 48, 604; diviners of d. derided, 3, 354; belief in d., 6, xxi; in the story of Joseph, 6, 219, 223 sq., 230; impurity caused by bad d., 7, 94; indulging in d., 8, 269; gods, &c., seen in d., 8, 387 n.; *the nature of tranquillity is as when one sees a d.*, 8, 392, 392 n.; in d. the person of the sleeper (purusha) moves about freely, 15, 104; the soul in d., 15, 163–73; 34, lx; 38, 133–41; 48, 764; explanation of d., 15, 280; in the early history of Buddha's life, 19, xix, xxi sq.; fourteen auspicious d. seen by the mother of Mahâvîra, 22, 219 sqq., 231–40, 244–7; of Marudevî, the mother of the Arhat *R*ishabha, 22, 281 sq.; Fravashis invoked against evil d., 23, 208; the sun worshipped by one who sees bad d., 29, 224; expiatory rites and sacrifices on seeing bad d., 30, 81, 183 sq.; are the work, not of the individual soul, but of the highest Lord, 34, lx sq.; some d. are auspicious omens, others the reverse, 34, 325; 38, 136 sq.; variety of d. while the dreaming person remains one, 34, 346; the idealist's example of the ideas in d., 34, 420; the ideas of the waking state are not like those of a d., 34, 424 sq.; d. and the idea of a soul, 36, xxii; a discussion on d., 36, 157–62, 162 n.; place of d., the intermediate place, 38, 133; the Self is the shaper of lovely things in d., 38, 133 sq., 137 sq.; the world of d. is mere illusion, 38, 134–6, 140 sq.; moving about in d., 38, 135; are outside the body, 38, 135; experts in the science of d., 38, 136; their purpose and cause, 38, 137 n.; in d. we have perceptions while the body lies motionless, 38, 272; salve, a protection from evil d., 42, 61; charms and rites against evil d., 42, 69, 167, 221, 483 sq., 592; amulet against evil d., 42, 82, 605; evil d. and misfortunes wiped off on him who passes between the sun and a person, 42, 214; birth of Zoroaster announced by d., 47, xxi; are unreal, and yet the cause of the knowledge of real things (good or ill fortune), 48, 75; things seen in d. are Mâyâ, 48, 86; things created in d., 48, 120 sq.; the veins (hita) the abode of d., 48, 379, 384; cognitions of the waking state are different from d., 48, 513 sq.; the things appearing in d. are the creation of the Lord, not of the soul, 48, 601–4; are the reward or punishment for deeds of minor importance, 48, 603. *See also* Divination, Mâyâ, *and* Omens.

Drinking, *see* Spirituous Liquors.

Dri*sh*advatî, n. of a river, 46, 287 sq.

Driwi, Malice, a Daêva, 4, 224.

Drôn, *see* Draôna.

Dro*n*a, Bhîshma and, 8, 39 sq., 42, 95 sq.; the Brahman D. restores peace among the kings fighting for the relics of Buddha, 19, 327–33; not born in the ordinary way, 38, 125, 126.

Dro*n*âsa, n. of a demon harassing infants, 29, 296.

Drought, produces a lawless condition, 44, 18.

Dru*g*, Phl. Drûg, 'fiend,' 5, lxxiii, 14; —the D. Nasu, or Corpse-D., fiend of corruption, 4, lxxii sq., lxxv, lxxxi, 26 sq. and n., 50 sq., 58 sq., 71–4, 76–9, 81–4, 93 sq., 99–101, 99 n., 106–13, 107 n., 120, 213; 37, 157, 160; D. Nasu takes the shape of a fly, 4, 77 sq., 99 sq., 112, 128 sq.; the D. Nasu rushes upon those who refuse to reward the cleanser, 4, 132 sq.; the D. Nasu, a creature of the Daêva, 4, 211;—hell, the mansion of the D., 4, 24, 24 n., 122, 122 n., 176, 223; 31, 141; is with the wicked man while he is alive, with the righteous man when he is dead, 4, 60 sq.; comes from Hell in the north, 4, 67 n., 76, 76 n.; expelled by spells and purification, 4, 125 n., 126–30, 133 sq., 136–48, 230, 235, 241; 23, 47, 50 sq.; 31, 392 sq.; the wicked, embodiments of the D., 4, 189, 192; sins that make the D. pregnant with a brood of fiends, 4, 200–4; 37, 164, 207; weakened by pious deeds, 4, 285; tremble at the perfume of the blessed soul, 4, 375; becomes pregnant by food thrown towards the north at night, 5, 318,

318 n., 346; the names of Ahura-Mazda protect from the D., 23, 29; destroyed by invocations of the Amesha-Spentas, 23, 38; Sraosha, the best smiter of the D., 23, 160, 162 sq.; Fravashis assist Ahura-Mazda against the D., 23, 183; Fravashis protect from the D., 23, 197; creation will grow deathless, and the D. shall perish, 23, 290–2, 307; driven away by Vîstâspa, 23, 306, 308; prayer against the D., 23, 334; personified deceit, the Lie-demon, 31, xix, 55, 64, 141; conquered by Asha, 31, 27, 33 sq., 311; Zarathustra prays for the defeat of the D., 31, 42; banished to hell, 31, 110, 117; delivered to Asha, put to death by Mãthras, 31, 110, 118; smitten by the saint, 31, 153; the power of the D. (Lie-demon) as opposed to Asha, 31, 160, 163; the wicked a son of the Lie's creation, 31, 177, 182; warning against the D., 31, 192; the Dragon Dahâka, the worst D., 31, 233; the most loathsome of beings, 31, 249; how shall we drive the D. from hence, 31, 313. *See also* Demons.

Drûgâskân, n. of a demon, son of the evil spirit, 5, 132.

Drugs, *see* Medicine.

Druh, the snares of, 32, 386; demon of guile, 42, 14 sq.

Druma, n. of a Kinnara king, 21, 5.

Drumâksha, the king, and his son returned from the forest to the kingdom, 19, 108; king of the Sâlvas, 49 (i), 101.

Drumasiddha, king of Yogins, 49, (i), 197.

Drums, *see* Music.

Drunkenness, *see* Spirituous Liquors.

Drupada, n. of a warrior, 8, 37, 39.

Drvâspa, meat-offering to, 5, 336; epithet of Gôs, the Cow genius, 23, 9, 17, 110.

Drvê Zênîgâk, Av. Drvau Zainigâus, smitten by Frangrâsîyâk, 47, 116, 116 sq. n.

Dualism: in what sense Zoroastrianism is d., 4, xiii, lxvii; 5, lxviii–lxx; 31, xviii sq.; principle of d. in Zoroastrianism is pre-Alexandrian, 4, lxi; purely Iranian, 4, lxiv; covenant of the two spirits, 5, 5; Mohammedan monotheism a protest against Persian d., 6, lii, 115, 115 n.; Mazda-worship not more dualistic than Christianity, 18, xxiv; the beneficent spirit and the evil spirit, the authors of all the good and evil, 18, 14, 14 n.; contest of the good and evil spirits from the creation to the resurrection, 18, 81–117, 82 n.; good and evil not from the same source, 24, xxv; accounts for the origin of evil, 24, 124–38, 152–68, 173–202; the two chief doctrines about the origin of good and evil, 24, 168; two evolutions said to be in Christianity, 24, 238–42; the doctrine of d., struggle between good and evil, 31, 25–36, 40 sq.; 37, 250 sq., 384–6; the pious mind questions both the good and the evil Spirits, 31, 38, 46 sq.; is the first and best Mãthra, 31, 122 sq., 125 sq.; the dualistic moral law, 31, 132, 138; the world made by the two Spirits, 31, 302; good and evil, angels and demons, 37, 21, 21 n.; predominance of good over evil in the end, 37, 243; Aûharmazd demonstrates the duality of original evolutions to Zoroaster, 47, 157 sq. *See also* Evil, Morality, Yin and Yang, *and* Zoroastrianism.

Duality, *see* Unity.

Dughdâ, *see* Dûkdâûb.

Dûghdâvŏ, *see* Dûkdâûb.

Dughdhava, *see* Dûkdâûb.

Dûkdak, *see* Dûkdâûb.

Dûkdâûb, or Dughdâ, or Dûghdâvŏ, or Dughdhava, or Dûkdak, or Dûkdâv, mother of Zoroaster, 4, 371; 5, 144, 317, 317 n., 343; 37, 444, 469; 47, 26–8, 35, 122, 138 sq.; glory descends from heaven at her birth, 47, xxix.

Dûkdâv, *see* Dûkdâûb.

Dukkata, *see* Sins.

Dulâ, mother of the dog-demons harassing children, 30, 220.

Dundubhisvaranirghosha, n. of a Tathâgata, 49 (ii), 100.

Dundubhisvararâga, n. of numerous Tathâgatas, 21, 358.

Dûr, n. of Breath (mukhya prâna) as a deity, 15, 80.

Dûraêkaêta, a Turanian, 23, 71.

Dûrânsarûn, magician, tries to kill the infant Zaratust, 47, xxi.
Dûrâsrôb(ô), or Dûrêsrôbô, son of Mânûskihar, 5, 134, 134 n., 138, 141, 146; 47, 34, 147; a Karap, renowned for witchcraft, 47, xxvi, 20 n., 35–40, 43–6; ancestor of Zoroaster, 47, 140; the Karap, destroyed by Zoroaster, 47, 150 sq.
Durgâ, her epithets or names as spells, 21, 371 n., 372 n., 373 n., 435 n.
Durgaya Krishna, n. of a Sthavira, 22, 294 n.
Dûrnâmîk, n.p., 5, 146.
Dûrôshasp, n.p., 5, 135, 137.
Dûrvâ grass, *see* Plants.
Duryodhana, hero of the Mahâbhârata, 8, 37 sq.
Dushpradharsha, n. of a Tathâgata, 49 (ii), 100.
Dushprasaha, n. of a Tathâgata, 49 (ii), 66.
Dushtarîtu Paumsâyana, expelled from his kingdom, 44, 269–72.
Dutthatthakasutta, t.c., 10 (ii), 148–50.
Duty, duties, should not be fulfilled merely to gain worldly advantages, 2, 71 sq.; five cardinal d., 3, 38, 49; the courses of d. are from Heaven, 3, 129; every one who performs a great d. has much value, 5, 90 sq.; one's natural d., though defective, is better than another's d. well performed, 8, 56, 127; d. of the householder, 8, 358–60; common to all castes, 14, 26; the d. of creatures is to understand and perform the will of the Creator, 24, 166 sq.; two classes of d., 25, 160 sq.; the different d. in the ten or five relationships of man, 27, 37; 28, 245–9, 313; the divisions of the day, monitors and guides of d., 31, 109, 114. *See also* Good Works, Morality, *and* Taxes.
Duwâr, a favourite idol with young (Arabian) women, 6, xiii.
Duzyâirya, the Pairika or demon, 'Bad year,' 23, 107 sq., 107 n.
Dvaipâyana, *see* Vyâsa.
Dvaitavana, *see* Dhvasan D.
Dvaitavana, n. of a lake, 44, 398.
Dvâpara age, *see* Ages of the world (*a*).
Dvârakâ (or Dvârâvatî), town of Krishna, 8, 230; 45, 113; Arishtanêmi in D., 22, 277; 45, 115.
Dvârâvatî, *see* Dvârakâ.
Dvayatânupassanâsutta, t.c., 10 (ii), 131–45.
Dvâzdah-hômast, ceremony of, 24, 330 sq., 330 n.
Dvimukha, king of Pañkâla, became a Gaina monk, 45, 87, 87 n.
Dvipadâs, t.t., certain offerings at the Asvamedha, 44, 342 sq. *See also* Metres.
Dvîpâyana, n. of a great ascetic, 45, 268, 269 n.
Dvipitaka, an impossible term, 10 (i), xxxii, xxxii n.
Dvita, an Âptya deity, 12, 47, 48 n., 49; Ekata, D., and Trita, 42, 521 sq.; Âtreya, author of a Vedic hymn, 46, 405 sq.
Dvivedaganga, his commentary on the Brihadâranyaka-upanishad, 15, xxx.
Dwelling, *see* House.
Dyaus, *see* Dyu.
Dyu (Heaven), Nom. Dyaus, one of the Vasus, 15, 140 sq.; Indra, the child of D., 15, 221; with Âditya invoked in danger, 29, 232; Agni, the child of D., 32, 21–3; 41, 272; Maruts, the tall bulls of D., boys, sons, servants, men of D., 32, 106, 110 sq., 154 sq., 326, 347, 401, 405 sq., 412; called aditi, 'the unbounded sky,' 32, 261, 348, 351; the bull of the Dawn, 32, 343, 346; Maruts roar like D., 32, 392; mother of the Maruts, 32, 444, 448; Ushas, or D., 42, 661; let D., the sky, roar down, 46, 25; the treasure created by D., the father, the begetter, 46, 308, 309; Agni announces man's sin to D., 46, 325. *See also* Heaven (*e*), *and* Sky.
Dyumna Visvakarshani Âtreya, author of a Vedic hymn, 46, 414.
Dyutâna, the son of the Maruts, is the wind, 26, 144.

E

Eagle, *see* Birds (*b*).
Ear, one of the organs of the head, 41, 402; 43, 190; is the quarters,

43, 10, 333; introduced from the left side, made one only, 43, 11, 15; the eye created the e., the e. created work, 43, 378 sq.; the two ears connected by a channel, 44, 36; the two Asvins are the ears, 44, 263; what he speaks, that one hears with the e., 44, 263.

Earnestness (apramâda), the virtue of, 10 (i), 9–11; frees from the arrow of pain, 10 (ii), 55.

Earth.

(*a*) Cosmological ideas about it.
(*b*) E. as an element, its sacredness, &c.
(*c*) E. as a deity.

(*a*) COSMOLOGICAL IDEAS ABOUT IT.

E. produced from water, 1, 94, 100; 34, lii; 38, 23 sq.; 48, 536; the seven Karsvaras or regions of the e., 4, 222, 222 n., 377; 5, 32 sq., 67, 69, 175, 232; 18, 79, 79 n., 263; 23, 86, 96, 102, 104, 123, 123 n., 135, 141 sq., 163, 171 sq., 181 n., 182, 202, 254, 292 sq.; 24, 35 sq. n., 36, 100, 269, 269 n., 271, 301; 31, 58, 58 n., 303, 313, 317; 37, 26 sq., 189, 212, 214 sq., 220, 271; 47, 15, 34 sq., 41, 80, 108, 111, 148; creation of the e., 5, 10; 12, 280 n.; the regions of the e., and their chieftains, 5, 115–20; seven heavens and seven earths, 9, 290; represented as a great cube, 16, 61 n.; divided in three parts, 23, 181, 181 n.; one of the worlds, 25, 157; three earths, 26, 118; 41, 27; 42, 30, 68, 400 sq., 471; the womb from which everything has sprung, 26, 260; seven spaces of the e., 29, 341; 48, 477; rests on air and water, 35, 175 sq., 176 n.; there is only one e., 36, 50; is dissolved into water, 38, 26; is four-cornered, 41, 155; is threefold, 41, 239; the truth is this e., for this e. is the most certain of these worlds, 41, 364; nine earths, oceans, heavens, 42, 228, 631; was of the size of a span in the beginning, 44, 451; was raised by the boar Emûsha, 44, 451; is higher than the water, 44, 502; a place of abode for all the gods, 44, 505. *See also* World (*d*).

(*b*) E. AS AN ELEMENT, ITS SACREDNESS, ETC.

Black the colour of e., 1, 95, 96; 38, 23 sq.; e. or food, 1, 96–8, 100; 38, 23 sq.; its subtilest portion becomes mind, 1, 96–8; sacredness of the e., how to keep it from defilement by dead matter, 4, lxii, lxiv, lxxv–lxxvii, 67–70, 87 sq., 133, 142–4, 185 sq.; 5, 248 n.; 18, 229; 26, 43; a means of purifying, 4, 79, 93, 130; 7, 96, 97, 98, 102; a Snâtaka must not scratch the ground, nor crush clods of e., 7, 227; a cow in the act of bringing forth a young one, compared to the e., 7, 264; one of the ten fires at the allegorical sacrifice of the sense-organs, 8, 261; is the source of smells, 8, 337, 340, 348 sq., 352; sound, touch, colour, taste, and smell are the five qualities of e., 8, 383 sq.; the disciple of Buddha will overcome this e., 10 (i), 16; sins caused by actions injuring the souls of e., 22, 3–5; yellow the colour of the e., which occupies the central place, 27, 436, 436 n.; as everything depends on the e., so all good qualities depend on virtue, 35, 52 sq.; seeds are planted without the consent of the e., 35, 150; called 'night,' 38, 23 sq.; is the *Rik*, 38, 345–9; is the resting-place in this world, 44, 17; is the source of prosperity, 44, 18; touching the e., in an expiatory rite, 44, 30; 'from the e. I take thy body,' 44, 133 sq.; is a womb, and milk is seed, 44, 180; is foul matter, 44, 203; is a good abode, 44, 457; white is this e., 44, 463; the Mahâvîra pot made of clay (e.) and water (sky), 44, 492; origin and feeding of the e.-bodies, 45, 397 sq., 397 n.; e.-bodies commit sins, 45, 403 sq.

(*c*) E. AS A DEITY.

E., the deity, invoked in a curse, 1, 251; sacrifices to E., 2, 108; 3, 302; 27, 218, 220, 222, 385 sq., 425; 28, 203; 29, 320 sq., 388; 30, 22; 44, 505; invoked and worshipped, prayers to E., 3, 126 sq.; 4, 221; 23, 11, 19, 229; 28, 60; 29, 207, 219, 340; 30, 96, 241; 31, 251, 286 sq.; 32, 423; 41, 34, 253, 346 sq.; 42, 161; 46, 110, 115, 127, 253; filial piety is the righteousness of E., 3, 473; spoken of as Spenta

Ârmaiti, 4, lxvii; 18, 393 n., 401; what comforts and discomforts most the E., 4, lxxi, 21–31; 5, 360 sq.; 37, 153; the cleanser delights E., 4, 133; made by Ahura, 4, 221; attacked by the evil spirit, 5, 29 sq., 173–5; pleased by agriculture, cattle rearing, and virtuous conduct, 5, 376 sq., 377 n.; 37, 154; colloquy of Vish*n*u and the E., 7, 5–12, 41, 77, 291–7; sustained by those who follow the lâw, 7, 8; colloquy of E. and Lakshmî, 7, 297–301; supports all things, 8, 113; Mother E. and Father Heaven, 12, 229; 42, 166; 44, 238, 287, 325; is a spotted cow, 12, 242 sq., 308; the queen of serpents, 12, 301 n., 302; 26, 451; Sky and E. as husband and wife ('Heaven I, E. thou'), 15, 205, 220; 29, 168, 282; bears Agni in her womb, 15, 221; a manifestation of Brahman, 15, 303; the unlimited capacity of the E., emblematic of the course of the superior man, 16, 214 sq., 215 n.; overthrows the full and replenishes the humble, 16, 226, 226 sq. n.; the symbol of the E. and the sun entering into its midst, 16, 241, 242 n.; all things receive their nourishment from the E., 16, 426, 427 n.; Mother E., 21, 371 n.; 41, 34, 60; purified by the Sun, 23, 86; Fravashi of the E. worshipped, 23, 200; Zamyâd Ya*s*t inscribed to the Genius of the E., 23, 286–309; the mother the image of the e., 25, 71; as the E. supports everything, so does a king, 25, 396 sq.; produces the sources of wealth, 27, 378; the firm one, the son of the E., 29, 328; 'Heaven am I, and I am E.,' 29, 363; the initiated boy given in charge to the E., 30, 154; 'I know thy heart, O E., that dwells in heaven, in the moon,' 30, 212; staggering, yet rejoicing under the onslaught of the Maruts, 32, 337, 339, 347; rules the world, 35, 9; if there were two Buddhas, the E. would tremble, not being able to bear the goodness, 36, 49; Bhikkhus should be like the E., 36, 307–9; the 'notes' of the E., i.e. sounds heard in nature, 39, 177 sq. and n.; all things are produced from the E. and return to the E., 39, 300; friendly relation between B*ri*haspati and the E., 41, 34; is a milch-cow, yielding all desires, 41, 60; prayer of the king to Mother E., 41, 103; Varu*n*a and the E., 41, 103; injured by digging in her, 41, 220 sq.; mother of Agni Purîshya, 41, 311; bears what is desirable, 41, 387 sq.; bears healing plants, the remedy against poison, 42, 27, 31; hymn to Mother E., 42, 199–207, 639–44; identified with a brick of the fire-altar, 43, 91; plants the hair of its beard, Agni the man, 43, 208; Vai*s*vânara as E., 43, 394; no mortal must give her away, else she will sink into the midst of the water, 44, 421; invoked at the burial, 44, 433; the first-born of this world, 44, 450, 450 n.; 'on the E.'s place of divine worship,' 44, 450–2, 456; is afraid of the Pravargya, blessings invoked on her, 44, 462–4; having become a mare, the E. carried Manu, and he is her lord Pra*g*âpati, 44, 451 n., 466; Agni, when spreading through the forests, shears the hair of the E., 46, 54; has spread herself far and wide, 46, 83; Dhisha*n*â as the E., 46, 120 sq.; Agni licks the face of Mother E., 46, 145; Agni announces man's sins to E., 46, 325; care and propitiation of the E., 47, 162. *See also* Heaven (*c*, *f*), P*ri*thivî, *and* Zamyâ*d*.

Earth-demon, the firm one, oblation to, 29, 201, 213, 345.

Earthquake, caused by the chief events in Buddha's life, 11, 44, 116, 155; 19, 146, 163, 268 sq., 307, 345, 350; 49 (i), 7, 141; causes of an e., 11, 45–8; 35, 171 sq.; caused by Vessantara's generosity, 35, 170–8; the earth shook six times in honour of Nâgasena, 36, 373; expiatory rite on the occasion of an e., 42, 640.

Easing nature, rules about, 2, 93 sq., 220, 222 sq.; 4, 201 sq., 202 n.; 5, 317 sq.; 7, 194–6; 14, 36 sq., 60, 164, 173 sq., 245; 24, 12, 12 n., 317; 25, 136 sq., 143, 146, 152 sq., 192 sq., 472; 29, 318 sq.; 37, 207 sq.; singing of Gâthas must be interrupted when e. n., 4, 325;

prayer for making water, 5, 318; 24, 317; rules of purification, 6, 78, 98; rules about it for the Dîkshita, 26, 43 sq.; micturition towards the sun sinful, 42, 214, 668. *See also* Impurity.

East, *see* Quarters.

Eater, the, is the highest Self, 34, xxxv, xlii, 116–18.

Eating, rules relating to it, 2, 59–71, 96, 99 sq., 122 sq., 204, 265–70; 5, 310; 7, 216–21; 10 (ii), 66; 14, 25, 36–9, 146; 15, 312 sqq.; 25, 39 sq., 96; 27, 2–4, 7, 20 sq., 79–83, 83 n.; 29, 86 sq., 191, 320 sq.; 37, 180, 182 sq.; rules of e., for the hermit, 2, 195; 7, 277 sq.; 8, 361 sq.; 14, 45, 259, 292–4; 25, 199–204; for Snâtakas, 2, 223–5; 14, 60–2; 25, 138–41; 29, 123 sq., 409 sq.; 30, 85; for ascetics, 7, 279, 362–4; 14, 46–8, 280–3; 25, 199–201; for Buddhist Bhikkhus, 11, 190 sq., 253, 253 n.; 13, 37–40, 62–5; 17, 67–97, 117 sq., 128 sq., 130–3, 138 sq., 143–5, 220–5; 19, 296, 298; 20, 73–5, 135, 153 sq., 253, 284–9; 35, 272; 36, 9 sq., 98–100, 98 n., 99 n., 281 sq., 330 sq., 339 sq., 349 sq.; for Gaina monks, 22, 71, 88 sq., 103–10, 114 sq., 117 sq.; 45, 5 sq.;—rinsing the mouth before and after e., is dressing the breath with water, 1, 74, 74 n.; 15, 204, 312; 38, 211–14; about e. at night, 5, 346 sq.; the Tathâgatas do not accept food with their hands, 13, 82; e. represented as a sacrifice offered by the Self to the Self, 15, 312 sqq.; prayers before and after e., and cleansing the mouth, 18, 133–6; 23, 312; 24, 282–5; moderate e. good for the body, 24, 14; ablution before e., 25, 193; e. together of the newly-married couple, 30, 48 sq.; sin of e. on the road, 37, 129. *See also* Food, *and* Meals.

Echo: meditation on the person in the e. as Brahman, 1, 304.

Eclipses of the sun and moon, evil omens, ceremonies to avert them, 3, 82, 82 n., 355; 28, 434; 42, 533; the time of an e. auspicious for a *S*râddha, 7, 241; advantages attending an e. of the sun or moon, 7, 270; ceremonies interrupted on account of an e. of the sun, 27, 328–30, 338 sq.

Economy: Ahura-Mazda does not allow us to waste anything of value, 4, 66, 80 sq.; *waste not wastefully, for the wasteful were ever the devil's brothers*, 9, 4; Muslims should be neither extravagant nor miserly, 9, 89; in his expenditure the superior man exceeds in e., 16, 344.

Ecstasy, *see* Meditation.

Eden, the Garden of, 6, 183, 235, 253; 9, 180, 191.

Education, *see* Instruction, *and* Teacher.

Eggidatta, *see* Kâ*s*yapa.

Ego, *see* I.

Egoism, egoity (aha*m*kâra): the ascetic free from e., emancipated, 8, 52, 313, 326, 332 sq., 366, 368, 370 sq., 389 sq.; deluded by e. a man thinks himself the doer of actions, 8, 55; one of the eight divisions of man, 8, 73 sq.; as part of the creation, 8, 317; a development of the Mahat is e., 8, 333 sq., 382; is of three descriptions, 8, 334 n.; from e. the five great elements were born, 8, 335; eleven organs produced from e., 8, 336; the cause of the whole course of worldly life, and self-consciousness, with Rudra as the presiding deity, 8, 338; the wheel of life is lit up by the great e., 8, 356, 356 n.; the great e., the boughs of the tree of worldly life, 8, 371; understanding and e., the two birds, 8, 371 n.; is of the nature of seed and a product, 8, 383; is above space, the highest element, 8, 385; those who perform actions, full of e., go near Pragâpati, 8, 389; Aniruddha identical with the principle of e., 34, xxiii, 440; accomplishes all actions and enjoys their results, 34, 34. *See also* Aham, Aha*m*kâra, *and* I.

Eka, a teacher quoted by Âpastamba, 2, xxvii, 70.

Ekâda*s*inî, t.t., set of eleven stakes, 26, 173, 176 sq., 218 sq., 221; 44, 301 n., 309 sq. and n., 335, 335 n., 404 sq. *See also* Animal sacrifice (*d*).

Ekadhanâ, *see* Water (*b*).

Ekâgratâ, t.t., 'one-pointedness,'

i.e. concentration of thought, 1, xxiii sq.
Ekana*l*â, n. of a Brâhma*n*a village, 10 (ii), 11.
Ekapadâ, *see* Metres.
Ekarshi, n. of a teacher, 15, 120, 187.
Eka*s*â*m*gî, daughter of Mahâkautuka, converted by Buddha, 49 (i), 198 sq.
Eka-sâ*t*aka, a Brahman and a devout Buddhist, 35, 172; 36, 147.
Ekâsh*t*akâ, personified as a goddess, and mother of Indra, 29, 338 n., 342; sacrifice and prayer to E., 29, 424; 30, 114, 114 n.; the consort of the year, 30, 233, 236. *See also* Ash*t*akâ, *and* Festivals.
Ekata, an Âptya deity, 12, 47, 48 n., 49; E., Dvita, and Trita, 42, 521 sq.
Ekavrâtya, n. of a dog-demon harassing children, 30, 219.
Ekoddi*st*a, *see* *S*râddha.
Ekuttara Nikâya, *see* Tipi*t*aka.
Elapatra, a Nâga, worships Buddha, 49 (i), 191.
Elders, *see* Old Age, *and* Theras.
Elements (entities, Bhûtas): creation of the three e., viz. fire, water, earth, 1, xxxiii sq., 94; 38, 4, 26–8; tripartition of the three e., 1, 95–7, 100; 38, 98–100, 104; 48, 119 sq., 369 sq., 578–83, 586; e. and sense-organs, 1, 96–8; 8, 337, 340–3, 348, 352, 383–5; 34, 281; 38, 26–8; the five e., viz. earth, air, ether, water, and fire, 1, 221; the five e. in the body of man, 1, 223; 8, 238; 38, 242; five hsing or e. (?), 3, 139–41, 140 sq. n.; Purusha separate from the twenty-four e., 7, 287, 287 sq. n.; twenty-four or twenty-five e., 7, 290; 8, 317, 373, 373 n.; the five e. supported by Vish*n*u, 7, 291; included in the Kshetra, 8, 102; the enjoyer of the qualities devoid of the qualities of the five e., 8, 247; subtle e., 8, 247 n., 318 n.; five great e. (Mahâbhûtas), 8, 258 n., 317; 15, 296; 38, 4, 4 n.; the great e. are the branches of the tree of worldly life, 8, 313, 313 n., 371; dissolution of the world into the five great e., 8, 335, 387 sq.; from egoism the five great e. were born, 8, 335, 382; three seats for all e., viz. land, water, space, 8, 339; he who has vanquished the five e. obtains the highest seat in heaven, 8, 344; fire is the lord of the e., 8, 346; the five great e. the outer rim of the wheel of life, 8, 355; life made up of the entities beginning with the Mahat and ending with the gross e., 8, 357; the truth about the five great e. must be known by the Sannyâsin, 8, 368; the five great e. are of the nature of seed and products, 8, 383; mind the ruler of the five e., 8, 385 sq.; no reference to the five e. in the Yî King, 16, 33; the four e. pertaining to Aûha*r*ma*zd*, 24, 129, 129 n.; all existence derived from the four e., 24, 136, 143; the minute perishable particles of the five e., 25, 13, 13 n.; identified with the parts of the body, 25, 512; the five e. in man and nature, 27, 380–4; the origin, the subsistence, and the retraction of the e. all depend on Brahman, 34, lii; 38, 24–6; the re-absorption of the e. into Brahman takes place in the inverse order of their emission, 34, lii; 38, 25 sq.; the subtle e. completely merged in Brahman when final emancipation is reached, 34, lxxix sq.; 38, 371 sq.; the three e. denoted by the three colours, red, white, black, 34, 254 sq.; the product of Nescience, 34, 281; the atoms and their respective e., 34, 393 sq., 402; endowed with intelligence, 38, 24 sq.; in obtaining a different body the soul goes enveloped by subtle parts of the e., 38, 101–4, 371 sq.; breath and soul unite themselves with all e., 38, 368 sq.; 48, 730 sq.; the aggregate of the e. continues to exist up to the final union with Brahman, 38, 371, 376 sq.; materialists explain everything by the five e., 45, 342 sq. *See* Earth, Fire, Skandhas, Tanmâtras, Upadhis, Vi*s*eshas, *and* Water.
Elephants, Airâvata, chief among, 8, 89, 89 n.; use of e. as vehicles, 8, 208; the e. as the emblem of endurance and self-restraint, 10 (i), 77 sq., 77 n.; Buddha descends from heaven as a white e., and

enters his mother's side, 11, 47 n.; 19, xix; curious belief as to e. look, 11, 64, 64 n.; the E. Treasure of King Sudassana, 11, 254 sq., 274, 279, 281, 286 sq.; the lord of e. a good rebirth, 14, 136; the hermit's life and the life of the e., 17, 308, 312 sqq.; Devadatta's maddened e. tamed by Buddha through the power of love, 19, 247 sq.; 20, 247–50; young e. imitate the old ones, 20, 260 sq.; Samantabhadra mounts a white e. for the protection of preachers, 21, 433 sq.; the e. fashioned from the flesh of Mârtâ*nd*a, 26, 13; one should not accept an e. as a gift, 26, 13; Maruts compared with wild e., 32, 107, 117; the wonderful e. Uposatha of *K*akkavatti, 36, 128 sq.; simile of the e., 36, 335–7; Padma, the e. supporting the world, 49 (i), 17, 17 n. *See* Erâva*n*a, *and* Airâvata.

El'Huzzâ, *see* Huzzâ.

Elias, made to die for a hundred years, 6, 41 n.; a prophet, 6, 125; = DHu 'l Kifl, 9, 53 n.; protested against the worship of Baal, 9, 173, 173 n.

Elisha, a prophet, 6, 125; was of the righteous, 9, 180.

Elixir, *see* Life.

Emancipation, or final release, or liberation (moksha, mukti, Sk.).

(*a*) How to reach it.
(*b*) Its nature and character.

(*a*) How to reach it.

Highest knowledge leads to it, 1, 235; 7, 287; 8, 179; 15, 236, 243, 264–6; 34, xxvii, xxix, lxxvii sq., 29, 63, 71, 92, 282, 291, 300, 316, 327 sq., 380 n., 423; 38, 55, 101, 101 n., 165 sq., 235–8, 357, 370 sq., 397–400, 414 sq.; 48, 83, 274, 387, 482; asceticism and similar means of obtaining it, 2, 78; 7, 184; 8, 69, 114 sq., 117, 127, 127 n., 231, 235, 245–53, 362–8; 14, 137 sq.; 22, 51 sq.; 25, 205–16; 34, lxxiii; 45, 152–7, 184–92, 308, 313; 48, 145; reached through meditation on the self, 8, 17, 78–83; 25, 169; 38, 52 n., 53; 48, 98, 100, 556; devotion (Yoga) alone leads to e., 8, 72 sq., 242; 15, 320; 48, 413, 625–8; sacrifice and penance performed for final e., 8, 120; Veda-study and Vedic rites not the true means of e., 8, 146, 309; 34, 27 sqq.; 48, 58, 181; attained by living as a Brahma*k*ârin, 8, 178, 178 n.; obtained by him who knows Rudra as the creator, 15, 252 sq.; reached by cutting off the consequences of Karman, 19, 293; 38, 355 sq.; 'the reward conferred by the Vedânta,' 25, 59, 59 n.; through hermit's life and voluntary death, 25, 204 n.; by degrees, 34, lxxxix sq., 174, 223; 38, 162, 185, 391; taught of him who takes his stand on the Sat, 34, 55–7; 48, 203 sq.; results from the highest Lord, 38, 58 sq., 139; the existence of a remainder of works does not stand in its way, 38, 119; cannot be dependent on locality, time, and special causes, as the fruit of works is, 38, 356; results from knowledge with works added, 38, 359; 48, 9; to be reached by cutting off love and hatred, 45, 45 sq.; depends on faith, 45, 156, 156 n.; seventy-three articles necessary in order to reach it, 45, 158–73; noble birth is no use for him who desires e., 45, 322 sq.; those whom women do not seduce value e. most, 45, 330; not due to knowledge of a non-qualified Brahman, 48, 129–38; destruction of body not necessary for e., 48, 184; e. in this life (*g*îvan-mukti) impossible, 48, 186 sq.; for the souls of men who are intent on their duties, 48, 411; the time of final e., as resulting from good works, not fixed, 48, 713 sq.; *we know from Scripture that this Supreme Lord, when pleased by the faithful worship of his Devotees ... frees them from the influence of Nescience; ... allows them to attain to that supreme bliss which consists in the direct intuition of His own true nature: and after that does* not *turn them back into the miseries of Samsâra*, 48, 770.

(*b*) Its nature and character.

Having become united with Purusha, a man obtains e., 7, 290; is assimilation with the Lord, 8, 69; is the highest goal, 8, 50, 54 n., 67, 125 n., 255; 48, 255; a means of escaping death and rebirth, 8, 152-5;

22, 211–13; the devotee who is released is esteemed higher than he whose conduct is good, 8, 243; one of the four Hot*ri*s, by whom this universe is enveloped, 8, 278; the seven organs, causes of e., 8, 278; is the Dakshi*n*â at the allegorical sacrifice of concentration of mind, 8, 280; the fruit of the tree intelligence in the forest Brahman, 8, 286; the nature of e., 8, 292 sq.; 48, 270 sq., 755–71; he who has achieved e., being beyond all actions and Â*s*ramas, is one with God and the Universe, 8, 306–8, 306 sq. n.; dialogue between a preceptor and a pupil on the subject of final e., 8, 310–17, 332 sq., 336, 339–45, 349, 351 sq., 355, 358, 362–74, 385, 388–94; some people extol e., others all kinds of enjoyment, 8, 376; freedom from desires and worldly bonds is e., 15, 332 sqq.; Ârâ*d*a's theory of e., 19, 137–41; as the great ocean has only one flavour, so Buddha's doctrine has only one flavour, the flavour of e., 20, 304; eight degrees of e., 21, 79; 49 (ii), 2, 193; the only scope of Buddha's teaching is e. and rest, 21, 120 sq., 124; is an eternally and essentially disembodied state, 34, 28 sq., 283, 328; 48, 181 sq., 210, 238; is Brahman, or oneness with Brahman, 34, 28 sq., 33 sq., 283 n., 322; 38, 329; 48, 180, 192, 203 sq., 270 sq., 392; 49 (i), 130; is of the nature of the eternally free Self, 34, 32 sq.; is something to be ceremonially purified, 34, 33; cause of desire of e., 34, 198; 48, 4; a being desirous of it becomes a deva, 34, 223 n.; depends on the true nature of the cause of the world, 34, 316; impossible on the Sâṅkhya view of the soul and Prak*ri*ti, 34, 372–4, 380 sq.; 48, 491, 494; is impossible, if the world and the souls constitute one Self, 34, 378; the Sâṅkhya doctrine of e., 34, 380 n.; 38, 69 sq.; no being desirous of e. could be assumed, on the Bauddha doctrine, 34, 406 sq.; nor on the *G*aina doctrine, 34, 430, 432; one of the *G*aina categories, 34, 428; 45, 154; 48, 517; Buddha's teaching a tank full of the waters of e., 36, 64; Buddha's 'jewel of e.,' 36, 224 sq.; consists, according to the Vai*s*eshikas, in the absolute non-origination of the nine qualities of the Selfs, 38, 69; the Self freed of the aggregate of eight in e., 38, 83, 83 n.; state of e. and of sleep, 38, 148 sq., 414 sq.; dissolution of the world means e., 38, 162; 48, 178 sq.; is cessation of 162; Nescience, 38, 174; 48, 9, 11, 270 sq., 438; springs up in this life or in the next, 38, 329 sq., 357 sq.; is something not to be effected at all, 38, 359; is a fruit like other fruits, 38, 405 sq.; the state of e. is analogous either to the waking state or to that of a dream, 38, 413; *G*ainas should maintain the doctrine of the soul's bondage and e., 45, 408; one of the four chief ends of human action, 48, 6; consciousness of the I persists in the state of e., 48, 69–72; false doctrine that e. is the annihilation of the Self, 48, 70; individual Self cannot become the highest Self by means of final e., 48, 98; obstacles in the way of e. removed by Scripture, 48, 183; is the pure existence of the highest Self consequent on the passing away of the limiting adjuncts, 48, 271; called 'heaven-world,' 48, 361; in state of e. the soul has no specific cognitions, 48, 395, 545, 551; means passing over into Non-being (with Buddhist), 48, 514; consists in attaining to the Highest Person, from that Highest Person only, 48, 625–8; different views about e., 49 (i), 99 sq. *See also* Deliverance, Immortality, Perfection, *and* Salvation.

Embryo, hate of the, 8, 240–2; 26, 19 sq., 27–9; Ahura-Mazda, with the help of the Fravashis, watches over the e., 23, 182 sq., 185, 187; treatment of the e. found in the animal victim, 26, 391–7; consecrated king represented as an e., 41, 78, 125 sq.; garments representing vestures of the e., 41, 86 sq., 86 n.; how the e. is born, Agni as e., 41, 251 sq., 256; 43, 272; freed from death through a Stoma, 43, 69; e.-killing (bhrû*n*ahatyâ) and slaying of a Brâhma*n*a, 43, 272; 44, 341 n.; offering to the fire for the

welfare of the e., 47, 30. *See also* Child.
Emperor, *see* Ruler.
Emptiness, *see* Nihilism.
Emûsha, n. of the boar who raised the earth, 44, 451.
E*n*â, *see* Senâ.
Enlightenment (Bodhi), *see* Knowledge.
Enoch, and Seth, the prophets of Sabaeanism, 6, xi; Idrîs identified with E., 9, 31.
Entanglements, *see* Hindrances.
Entity, does not spring from nonentity, 34, 415–18; entities, *see* Elements.
Ephesus, story of the Seven Sleepers of, 9, 14–16, 14 n.
Equanimity, one of the four 'infinite' feelings, 11, 201 sq., 273. *See also* Tranquillity.
Equinox, *see* Sacred Times.
***Ê*rân-shâh**, son of Yazad-yâr, son of Ti*s*tar-yâr, 24, 255 sq. and n.
Eras, *see* Time.
Erâva*n*a, the king of elephants, came to listen to Buddha, 10 (ii), 63.
Erâvatî, n. of a river near Ku*n*âlâ, 22, 297.
Ereda*t*-fedhri, the maiden, becomes the mother of the Saviour Saoshya*nt*, 23, 195 n., 226, 226 n.
Eredhwa, n.p., 23, 215.
Erekhsha (Phl. Ari*s*), the swift archer, 23, 95, 95 n., 103.
Erenavâ*k*, and Savanghavâ*k* delivered by Thraêtaona, 23, 62, 62 n., 113, 255, 277.
Erethe, thought, genius, 23, 11, 282; worshipped, 31, 200, 211, 217, 226.
Erezrâspa, son of Uspâsnu, a high-priest, 23, 216, 216 n.; 37, 219 n. *See also* Arezrâs*p*âh.
Erezva*t*-danghu, n.p., 23, 218.
Êri*k*ô, son of Dûrêsrôbô, 47, 34 n., 147.
Er-raqîm, story of the Fellows of the Cave and, 9, 14–16, 14 n.
Esdras, made to die for a hundred years, 6, 41 n.
Eshavîra, a Brâhmanical family held in contempt, 44, 45 n.
Esoteric doctrine, *see* Secret doctrines.
Essence, the subtile, is the root of everything, 1, 101–9.
Eternal, the, Eternal happiness, Eternity, *see* Immortality, *and* Nirvâ*n*a.
Ether (âkâ*s*a): Om means e., and e. is the origin of all things, 1, xxv, 17; as a name of Brahman, 1, xxv sq., xxvi n., 46, 53, 118, 126 n., 143, 143 n., 303; 21, xxvii; 34, xxxiv, xxxviii, 81–4, 114, 182, 232 sq., 273, 287; 38, 6–8, 12, 248; 48, 242–6, 256, 276 sq., 349–53, 661; e. within the heart, and the e. around us, are the same, 1, 46, 126; 48, 643, 661; the e. in the heart is Brahman, 1, 65, 65 n., 126 n.; 34, xxxvi, 174–92; 38, 144; 48, 314–25; the departed sacrificers, &c., go from the world of the fathers to the e., from there. to the moon, 1, 80; *e. (or space) is better than fire. For in the e. exist both sun and moon, the lightning, stars, and fire (agni). Through the e. we call, through the e. we hear, through the e. we answer. In the e. or space we rejoice (when we are together), and rejoice not (when we are separated). In the e. everything is born, and towards the e. everything tends when it is born. Meditate on e.*, 1, 118; the small e. in the lotus of the heart, 1, 125 sq., 129; 48, 384, 631 sq.; the small e. within the heart is not affected by old age, nor by the death of the body, 1, 126 sq.; is the revealer of all forms and names, 1, 143; the union of earth and heaven, 1, 247 sq.; Bali-offering to the E., 2, 203; 29, 290, 388; 30, 22; is the body, which Brahman created for himself, 8, 244 n.; has no support, 15, lii n.; in the e. within the heart it is the Person, consisting of mind, immortal, golden, 15, 49; everything is woven in the e., 15, 137; the e. is woven in the Akshara (the Imperishable), 15, 137–9; 34, 243; the Self, the e. within the heart, 15, 179; the Lotus of the heart is the same as e., 15, 306; the supreme light of the e. within the heart, 15, 343; the two elementary principles are really one e., 16, 357 n.; offering and prayer to the E., 26, 23; is not coeternal with Brahman, but springs from it as its first effect, 34, lii; 38, 3–18; is the Udgîtha, 34, 83; although all-pervading, is spoken of

as limited and minute, 34, 114; distinction between the outer and the inner e., 34, 175, 176 sq.; the highest Lord is greater than e., 34, 177; the small e. cannot mean the individual soul, 34, 177; origination of e., 38, 3–18; is divided, therefore must be an effect, 38, 14, 15; is non-eternal, because it is the substratum of a non-eternal quality, viz. sound, 38, 17; is the abode of air, 38, 18; is dissolved into Brahman, 38, 26; air is dissolved into e., 38, 26; the body, consisting of water, which the soul assumes in the moon, becomes subtle like e., but not identical with e., 38, 127; the e. within the heart spoken of as the place of sleep, 38, 144; the one e. is made manifold, as it were, by its connexion with different places, 38, 179; origin of the world from the Thâi *K*î or Primal Ether, 39, 243 sq. and n.; 40, 311 sq.; influence of e. and of destiny on men, 40, 268; Vai*s*vânara as E., 43, 395; e. and the five senses, 48, 371–4; a term referring to the Highest Reality, 48, 522; a mere irrational non-entity (Buddhist view), 48, 506 sq.; created by Brahman, 48, 532–5. *See also* Brahman (*c*), Space, *and* Yin and Yang.

Ethics, *see* Morality.

Etiquette: rules about saluting and honouring teachers, Gurus, &c., 2, 20 sq., 24 sq., 28, 30 sq., 38, 50–4, 207–11; 8, 62, 140; 14, 67–9, 152–5; 25, 51–6, 67–9; 29, 125; persons with whom one should not sit at dinner, 2, 61, 61 n., 67–71; how a householder should behave towards guests according to their caste, 2, 110; how the householder should receive teachers, 2, 112 sq.; precedence among the various castes, 2, 125 sq.; how the Brahma*k*ârin should behave in the presence of Gurus, 2, 187 sqq.; â*k*âryâ*h* = 'my teacher,' e. forbidding to mention the name of one's teacher, 2, 196, 196 n., 199, 199 n.; to whom way must be made, 2, 211; 14, 67–9, 243; 33, 219, 219 n.; rules of e. to be observed by Snâtakas, 2, 220 sq., 223 sq.; 14, 61 sq.; rules about e., salutation, &c., 6, 84; 9, 81 sq.; the ascetic is free from the ceremony of salutation, 8, 324, 351, 366, 370; smaller rules of demeanour, 27, 31 sq., 115 sq.; 28, 68–81; rules of e. when visiting, 27, 70 sq., 76 sq.; mention of certain names to be avoided, 27, 93, 100 sq.; e. in relations to superiors, 27, 99 sq. *See also* Titles.

Etymologies, fanciful, and puns, 1, 6, 8, 11, 13 sq., 21 n., 24 n., 26–8, 27 n., 44 sq., 49 n., 50 sq., 68, 99, 99 n., 129–31, 132 n., 157, 162, 170, 172, 205–9, 213 n., 215 sq., 242, 278 sq.; 12, 144, 147, 153, 160 sq. and n., 162, 166, 176 sq., 191, 234, 277, 288, 308, 323–5, 440; 15, 55, 75–7, 80, 82, 85, 89, 99, 106 sq., 140 sq., 191 sq., 194–7, 310, 323; 26, 21–3, 36, 39, 46 sq., 71 sq., 101, 142, 168, 174, 202 sq., 246, 258, 260, 266, 281, 327 sq., 340, 379, 388, 399, 432 sq.; 41, 13, 21, 28, 33, 143, 146–9, 152 sq., 156, 158 sq., 162, 250, 268–70, 318, 326, 332, 332 n., 365, 367, 369 sq., 374, 378, 380, 390 sq., 395, 414 sq.; 42, 703; 43, 5, 7, 9 sq., 54 sq., 65, 69, 69 n., 92, 92 n., 156 sq., 156 n., 175, 179, 230, 230 n., 261, 265, 265 n., 336 sq., 341–4, 341 n., 346–8, 352, 371–3, 390, 399, 402 sq.; 44, 27, 152, 162 sq. and n., 421, 423; e. of puttra, 'son,' 7, 65; 15, 96; 25, 354; of mâ*m*sa, 'flesh,' 7, 171 sq.; 25, 177; of atithi, 7, 215; of Purusha, 7, 290; of Bâhma*n*a, Sama*n*a, Muni, &c., 10 (i), 65 sq., 89 sq. and n.; 36, 26, 26 n.; of Brahma*k*ârin, 35, 117 sq., 117 n.; of Samudda, 35, 131 sq., 131 n.; etymological stories (Bak-kula), 36, 11 n.; of words for 'river,' 42, 146, 348 sq.

Eunuchs, food of, not to be eaten, 2, 68, 71; 14, 69, 71; cannot inherit, 2, 133, 309; 14, 89; 25, 372 sq. and n., 376 n.; excluded from *S*râddha feasts, 2, 256; 25, 103, 106; penance for killing e., 2, 286; 25, 457; should not receive ordination, 13, 215; to be maintained by the king who takes their property, 14, 100; women of the seraglio punished by e., 19, 55; look of e. contaminating, 25, 119;

are unfit to sacrifice, 25, 161; not to be struck in battle, 25, 231; may marry, 25, 341, 373, 373 n.; 33, 166 n.; shall not be witnesses, 33, 87; the ordeal by sacred libation unfit for e., 33, 117; cannot keep a secret, 35, 141; cannot be converted, 36, 177; a long-haired man, i.e. a e., 41, 9, 90 sq.; costume of e., 42, 108, 538 sq.; the e. is neither woman nor man, 44, 219 sq.; sacrificed at the Purushamedha, 44, 413, 417. *See also* Castration.

Evayâmarut, 'the quick Marut,' n. of Vish*n*u (?), 32, 363–5; E. Âtreya, author of a Vedic hymn, 32, 365.

Eve, *see* Adam.

Evidence, *see* Witnesses.

Evil, caused by the Asuras or demons, 1, 4 sq.; ten e. ways, 3, 94, 94 n.; whether e. may be done for the sake of good, 5, 385 sq.; Muslim to ward off e. with good, 6, 235; e. of birth, death, &c., 8, 103; action as being full of e. to be abandoned, 8, 121; the cause of e., 8, 156 n.; good and e. are a pair, 8, 277; let a man overcome e. by good, 10 (i), 58; Buddha on the origin of all kinds of e., 10 (ii), 164–7; how the temporal e. is to be regarded, 18, 22 sq.; the e. in the world is definite and terminable, 18, 91; if there were a God, there could be no e., 19, 206–8; origin of e., 24, xxv; 31, 3 sq., 26; *see also* Dualism; those who do e. to the wicked act in love of Ahura-Mazda, 31, 68, 72; eight defects of man, and four e. in the conduct of affairs, 40, 196 sq.

Evil Eye, cast by the Daêvas, 4, 225; medicine against it, 4, 227–9; by it Ahriman corrupts the good creatures of Ormazd, 4, 236 n.; Agash, demon of the e. e., 5, 111 sq., 111 n.; 47, 53 n.; mischief caused by the e. e., 10 (i), 29 n.; 37, 101 sq.; 47, 45; good eye, and e. e., 23, 4 sq. n.; created by Ahriman, smitten by the Airyaman prayer, 23, 44–6; spells against it, 23, 161; of the bride, 29, 278; 30, 189; charm against e. e., 42, 39, 91, 285 sq.; salve protecting from it, 42, 61; Zoroaster killed by the e. e., 47, 77.

Evil mind, *see* Akem-Manô.

Evil spirit, *see* Aharman, *and* Mâra.

Evil spirits, spells against, 21, 372, 374, 407, 414, 433; exorcism of, 29, 147 sq.; slain by the full moon sacrifice, 44, 6. *See also* Demons, *and* Râkshasas.

Evil thought, *see* Akem-Manô.

Evil works, *see* Karman.

Evolution, versus Illusion, 15, xxxvii.

Ewe, *see* Sheep.

Excommunication, *see* Caste (*e*, *i*).

Excrements, voiding of, *see* Easing nature.

Existence, six states of it, viz. hell, brute creation, world of ghosts, demons, men, gods, 21, 7, 10, 329, 352; 49, (ii), 182, 182 n., 184; worldly and spiritual e., 24, 153 sq., 185 sq.; 37, 14, 18, 31, 231, 233, 249, 274, 288, 317, 408, 416 sq., 439; 47, 3 sq., 43; what is, and what is not in the world, 36, 101–3.

Exorcisms, against enemies, during sacrifices, 43, 171; 44, 271, 279 sq., 337. *See also* Witchcraft.

Expiatory rites, on seeing bad dreams, 1, 262 sq.; for a false witness, 7, 50; addressed to Vish*n*u, 7, 155 sq., 156 n.; connected with bathing, 7, 204; 14, 249–52; are of the quality of passion, 8, 324; to be performed after the death of a Guru, and when afflicted by other misfortune, 29, 246–50; e. r. and the results of works, 38, 117 n., 353, 354; not possible in the case of one who has lapsed from the condition of a Naish*th*ika, 38, 318 sq.; 48, 706 sq. *See also* Omens, Penances. Pratikrama*n*a, Sacrifices (*b*), *and* Sin (*c*).

Eye: the person who is seen in the e. is Brahman, 1, 14 sq., 67, 135; 34, xxxiv sq., 77–81, 123–30; 48, 272–6; person in the right e. and person in the sun, 1, 15; 15, 191; 38, 217 sq., 244–7; person in the e. called Sa*m*yadvâma, Vâmanî, and Bhâmanî, 1, 68; person in the e. is not affected by anything, 1, 68 n.; person within the e. is the real agent of seeing, 1, 135 n.; person

of the e. is there where the sight has entered into the void, 1, 142; persons in the right e. and in the left e., 1, 305 sq.; 43, xxii, 368–74; the e. material, the person in the right e. the immaterial, 15, 107; Indra is in the right e., his wife in the left e., 15, 159, 344 sq.; secret name of person in the right e., Aham, 15, 192; the e. is truth, for the person in the e. proceeds to all things, 15, 309; person within the e. is not a deity of the sun, 34, 124, 130; how different beings serve the divine person in the e., 43, 373; the person within the e. different from the soul, viz. the highest Self, 48, 237–42;—Arka, deity presiding over the e., 8, 219; enters the sun at death, 8, 290; e. of knowledge, 8, 239; Buddha 'the e. in the world,' 11, 89 n.; the divine e. and the e. of flesh, 35, 179–85; 36, xxv; fashioned from the sun, 43, 8; is yonder sun, 43, 332; is motion, in accordance with the e. the body moves, 43, 337 sq.; Breath created the E., the E. the Ear, 43, 377 sq.; twinkling of the e., 44, 169; the e. is threefold, the white, the black, and the pupil, 44, 246; two men in the eyes, 44, 263; optical delusions, 48, 121 sq., 123; the e. of truth, *see* Dhamma.

Ezekiel, his vision of the dry bones, 6, 37 n.

Ezra, is the son of God, 6, 177, 177 n.

Ez Zaqqum, tree of hell, *see* Zaqqum.

F

Fâ, n. of King Wû, q. v.

Fables: the hen and the crow, and the chicken, 17, 362; of the partridge, the monkey, and the elephant, who want to find out who is the eldest of the three, 20, 193 sq.; how it was found out that the ewe excelled other animals in maternal love, 45, 270 n.

Fa-hien, translated the Vinaya into Chinese, 19, xi, xiii, xxvi sq.

Fairies, haunting the sites of buildings, 11, 18, 19 n.; 17, 101 sq.

Faith, required without signs, 6, 136; those who are full of f. are released from actions, 8, 56; he who has f. obtains knowledge, 8, 63; who is devoid of f. is ruined, 8, 63; he who is full of f. is the most devoted of all devotees, 8, 72 sq., 99, 102; worship with f., 8, 76, 358; those who have no f., return to this life, 8, 82; those who worship other divinities with f., worship God, 8, 84; f. is of three kinds, 8, 117 sq.; penance practised with f. is good, 8, 119, 121; belief in a future world the duty of Brâhma*n*as, 8, 126; he who studies the Bhagavadgîtâ with f., will be freed from sin, 8, 130; those who, full of f., cast aside worldliness, reach the highest goal, 8, 255; piety has f. for its characteristic, 8, 316; f. is of the nature of goodness, want of f. belongs to the quality of darkness or of passion, 8, 319–21, 324 sq.; full of f. the householder shall perform the five sacrifices, 8, 358; one should eat what is consecrated by f., 8, 365; perform actions with f., 8, 378; man alone of all creation undertook the responsibility of f., 9, 149; is the best property for a man, 10 (ii), 30; f., **reason**, and works, 11, 11 n.; meditation in Buddhism corresponds to f. in Christianity, 11, 145; *want of f. is the greatest sin; for f. is the highest austerity. Therefore the gods do not eat offerings given without f.*, 14, 173; f., the right, the true, absorption (yoga), and the great (intellect?) constitute the body of the inner self, 15, 56 sq.; *S*raddhâ, f., abides in the heart, 15, 146; Samâdhi or right f., 19, 303, 303 n.; unwavering f. in the religion of Zaratû*s*t, the first good work, 24, 257 sq.; the characteristic marks of f., tranquillization and aspiration, 35, 54–6; the man full of f. is worthy to become a Bhikkhu, 36, 253; the path of the gods cannot be attained by f. and austerities, unaided by knowledge, 38, 234; *S*raddhâ or f. is 'religious zeal' that makes the sacrificer liberal to the priest, 42, 424; the I*d*â is f., 44, 41 sq.; fire is f.,

truth sacrificed in f., 44, 46; out of f. the gods fashioned the initiation (dîkshâ), 44, 139, 240; the daughter of Sûrya, 44, 226; a means of obtaining the end of sacrifice, 44, 441; a monk must not give way to scepticism about future life, the Ginas, &c., 45, 14; one of the four requisites to reach beatitude, 45, 16, 152; the characteristics of f. and how it is produced, 45, 154–7; necessary to reach perfection, 45, 160 sq., 170 sq.; nine kinds of obstruction to right f., 45, 172, 172 n., 193; in Brahman, and its preliminary means, 48, 305; *whatever he does with knowledge, with f., with the Upanishads, that is more vigorous,* 48, 682–4, 688; difference, in Sukhâvatî, between beings who doubt, and those who believe in Buddha, 49 (ii), 62–5. *See also* Bhakti, Daêna, *and* Islâm.

Fa-kheu-king, t.w., 10 (i), l sq.

Fa Kheu Pi Hu, t.w., 10 (i) lii; quoted, 11, 117 n.

Fă-khin, translated a life of Buddha into Chinese, 19, xxx.

Falcon, *see* Birds (*b*).

Family.

(*a*) F. law and f. life.
(*b*) Parents and children, brothers.

(*a*) F. LAW AND F. LIFE.

Ceremony of casting off a member of the f. who has committed a mortal sin, 2, 277–9; f. reunions on the occasion of ancestor worship, 3, 300; the f. and the next of kin answerable for fulfilment of contract, 4, lxxxii, 34, 36–8, 36 n.; evils flowing from extinction of a f., 8, 41 sq.; f. life and intercourse with others should be avoided, 10 (ii), 6–11; to save the life of wife and f., presents may be accepted from anybody, 14, 70; retribution of good and evil takes place in the f., 16, 47 sq., 419 sq.; regulation of the f., importance of f. ties, 16, 136–8, 138 n., 312 sq., 313 n.; 28, 62–7, 62 n., 258 sq., 411, 416–19; the normal state of a f., 16, 242, 243 n.; law about guardianship of a f., 18, 188–94, 196; 37, 113, 478; Buddhist monks must give up all f. ties, 19, 302; how families perish, 25, 86; division of f. estate, divided and undivided, 25, 105 n., 283 sq. and n., 347, 373–9; 33, 370 sq., 383 sq.; charity must not be exercised while one's f. lives in distress, 25, 432; a priest should be a Brâhma*n*a of a renowned f., 26, 345; duty of avenging the death of father, brother, and friend, 27, 92; duties between members of a f., 27, 379 sq.; when a f. is in good condition, 27, 390 sq.; there are no two masters in a f., 28, 285; wife and children and brothers—the charm of life, 28, 307; the householder only is independent, 33, 50 sq.; a householder neglecting his f., 37, 45; benefit of wife and children, 37, 71; precedence of father to son, senior to junior, male to female, 39, 335; the whole f. responsible for a man's evil deeds, 40, 245.

(*b*) PARENTS AND CHILDREN, BROTHERS.

Precedence of elder brothers in marriage, and religious ceremonies, 2, 130; 14, 329; 25, 103 sq., 107 sq., 442; 42, 164 sq., 521, 523–8; sons who have enforced a division of the f. estate against the father's will, not to be invited to a *S*râddha, 2, 258; filial piety and fraternal duty, 3, 169; 28, 440; filial piety, chief moral duty, 3, 175, 212, 212 n., 394, 480 sq.; 19, 96 sq.; 27, 14, 467; 28, 226–9, 268 sq., 269 n., 290 sq.; 39, 212, 347; cousins called 'brothers,' 3, 211; filial piety, and ancestor worship, 3, 300 sq.; 28, 211 sq., 294 sq., 310 sq.; love rendered to the mother, reverence to the ruler, both to the father, 3, 470; rules for a son in remonstrating with his parents, 3, 483 sq.; 27, 114; *there is awe for the father, and also for the elder brother. Wife and children, servants and concubines are like the common people, serfs, and underlings,* 3, 488; kindness towards parents and kindred, 6, 11, 77, 135; 9, 3 sq., 118, 132, 225 sq.; child to obey father and mother, 8, 243; 24, 78; a son dealing with the troubles caused by his father or mother, 16, 95 sq., 97 n., 290 sq.; parents must not be distressed, 24, 301 sq.;

parents or teacher, who is more venerable, 25, xxiv, 56 sq. and n., 157; reverence due to father, mother, elder brother, and teacher, 25, lxvii, 71 sq., 154; a girl without a brother not to be married, 25, 77, 77 n.; forsaking mother or father, 25, 104; position of the eldest brother in f., 25, 157 sq., 346–8, 376 sq. and n.; impurity of parents on death and birth of children, 25, 178 sq.; fine for defaming mother, father, wife, brother, son, teacher, 25, 302; a son or a younger brother may be beaten as punishment, 25, 306; mother, father, wife, son not to be cast off, 25, 321, 442; son's duty to protect the mother, 25, 328; begging for parents allowed, 25, 430; rules for children in serving their parents and parents-in-law, 27, 27, 449–58; filial piety, and respect to be paid by juniors to elders, 27, 37; 28, 217, 226–32; mourning a manifestation of filial piety, 27, 48; 28, 377, 379, 392; duty to parents, 27, 67–9, 75, 83, 114; 28, 24, 267, 269; the filial piety of Shăn-shăng, 'the Reverential Heir-son,' 27, 126 sq.; a son must not give away f. property, 27, 160; how the poor discharge duties of filial piety, 27, 182; mourning for a foster-mother, 27, 326 sq. and n.; rights of the eldest son by the proper wife, 27, 335–7, 335 n., 336 n.; parents and children, 27, 456 sq., 476; a son on the death of parents, 28, 24; filial piety in sacrifice, 28, 236–8, 244 sq.; affection shown by the mother, honour by the father, 28, 340 sq.; father higher than mother, but love the same for both, 28, 467; reverence to parents connected with reverence to the Creator, 37, 343 sq.; father, mother, or priest not to be distressed, 37, 483; 'when a younger brother comes, the elder weeps,' 39, 362, 362 n.; fathers should instruct their sons, and elder their younger brothers, 40, 166 sq.; opposing a father or elder brother, a crime, 40, 241 sq. *See also* Daughters, Father, Inheritance, Marriage, Mother, Sons, *and* Wife.

Fan, minister of instruction of Yû, 3, 355 sq.; maternal uncle of *Kh*ung-*r*, 27, 166; 'Uncle F.,' his virtue not commended by Wăn-ȝze, 27, 199; uncle of Duke Wăn of Ȝin, 28, 421.

Fan, conversation between the king of *Kh*û and the ruler of, 40, 55 sq., 55 n.

Făng, or Khang Shû, appointed to be marquis of Wei, 3, 164–71; announcement about drunkenness made to F., 3, 171–9; instructed about government, 3, 179.

Fang-hsün, a name of Yâo, 3, 32, 32 n.

Fang-hwang, sprites haunting wilds, 40, 19.

Făng-î, got the Tâo, and became lord of the Great River, 39, 244, 244 n.

Fang-*kh*î, minister of Yâo, 3, 34.

Fang-kwang-tai-*k*wang-yan-king, Chinese translation of the Lalita-vistara, 19, xxviii.

Fang Ming, charioteer to Hwang-Tî, 40, 96.

Fares, *see* Taxes.

Farhank, mother of Kaî-Apîvêh, 5, 138 sq.; daughter of Vidhirisâ, 18, 171, 171 n.

Farîdûn, = Thraêtaona, 4, 245.

Farukhûzâ*d*, n.p., 18, 289.

Fasting.

(*a*) In India.
(*b*) In China.
(*c*) In Zoroastrianism.
(*d*) In Islâm.

(*a*) In India.

*S*vetaketu, after f. for fifteen days, cannot remember the Vedas, 1, 97 sq.; f. is really abstinence, 1, 131; as a penance, or part of penance, 2, 80, 82–4, 86 sq., 121, 129, 184 sq., 275, 277, 290 sq., 296, 299, 301 sq.; 7, 88, 95, 130, 149–81; 14, 30, 58, 109, 113, 116 sq., 119–23, 131 sq., 185, 211, 217, 222 sq., 248, 266, 306, 308 sq., 311, 318 sq., 323–8, 330; 25, 164, 172, 465, 472–5, 478, 482; 29, 120, 140, 172; 30, 181; 43, 255 sq.; on new and full moon days, 2, 100; 10 (ii), 25; 12, 1 sq., 4 sq., 172 sq., 180, 340; 29, 16, 172, 389, 393; 30, 25, 27–9, 265, 333; 44, 1 sq., 7–10, 20–2, 31; in connexion with special vows, 2, 105, 152; 29, 80; 30, 74; after the

funeral, 2, 137; 14, 28; no f. allowed to women apart from their husbands, 7, 111; 25, 196; taking a single meal consisting of food fit for oblations, each day of the month Kârttika, purifies from sin, 7, 265; at a worship of Vishnu, 7, 268 sq.; enjoined for hermits, 7, 278; 14, 293; recommended by some sects, forbidden by others, 8, 375; the fool who fasts is not worth the sixteenth particle of those who have well weighed the law, 10 (i), 21; does not purify a man, 10 (ii), 41; a Muni should take little food, 10 (ii), 129 sq.; Upavasatha or f.-day before the Agnyâdheya, 12, 291; to subsist on alms is better than f., 14, 46; 25, 64; forbidden (except as penance) for householders and students, 14, 266; on entering the order of ascetics, 14, 274, 276; Brâhma*n*as seek to know the Self by f., 15, 179; various modes of f., 22, 298–300; 45, 175 sq., 175 n., 230; mental derangement in consequence of f., 22, 300 n.; at the debtor's door, a mode of recovering debts, 25, 262 n.; 33, 72 n., 330, 330 n.; milk as fast-food for the sacrificer during his Dîkshâ, 26, 6, 28, 37–43, 37 n., 110 sq., 156; 41, 262; 43, 255 sq., 342 n.; 44, 119, 119 n.; the Brahma*k*ârin shall fast at the end of the daily Veda recitation, 29, 73; when on a journey one should not fast, 29, 90; to avert evil omens, 29, 139; previous to an auspicious rite, 29, 180, 291; at ceremonies for the obtainment of special wishes, 29, 425, 428, 430 sq.; 30, 115–17, 119, 125, 127; general rules about f., 29, 425; during the time of an omitted sacrifice, 30, 40; husband and wife fast, when the nuptial fire goes out, 30, 193, 261; before ordeals, 33, 105, 116, 118, 250, 260; when a single man has to determine a boundary, he must first fast, 33, 352; of a wife, 33, 369; disuse of food does not conduce to attainment of insight, 36, 61 sq.; when the sacrificer enters on the fast, he gives himself up to the gods, 44, 22; at the Sautrâma*n*î, 44, 240, 240 n.; the fast is the head of the sacrifice, and the initiation its body, 44, 240; kept by *G*aina laymen, 45, 384; *see also* Pôsaha; the vow of f. called ahoratra, 49 (i), 199; observed by Mahâyâna Buddhists, 49 (ii), 192 sq. *See also* Abstinence, *and* Uposatha.

(*b*) IN CHINA.

F. in preparation to ancestor worship, 3, 300, 304 n.; 39, 352; as a preliminary to marriage ceremonies, 27, 78, 441; in preparation to a sacrifice, 27, 87, 87 n.; 28, 331; in midsummer, 27, 275; on the winter solstice, 27, 304; of the father at the birth of a child, 27, 471; before going to the ruler, 28, 6; rules about it, 28, 19; seven days of f., 28, 292; 'the f. of the mind,' 39, 208 sq.; a mechanic fasts in order to become of concentrated mind, 40, 22. *See also* Abstinence.

(*c*) IN ZOROASTRIANISM.

He who fasts commits a sin, 4, 47 sq., 47 n.; for three nights, when one passes away, 5, 341, 341 n.; proper f. consists in not committing sin, 24, 348.

(*d*) IN ISLÂM.

The fast of Rama*dh*ân, 6, xxxv, lxxi–lxxiii, 25 sq.; f. as a penance, 6, 28, 85, 110 sq.; 9, 271; glad tidings to the believers who fast, 6, 189.

Fatalism, *see* Predestination.

Fatalists, their views refuted, 45, 239, 345–7.

Fate, *see* Destiny.

Father, may teach his eldest son, 1, 44; 'the f.'s tradition to the son,' a ceremony performed by the f., when going to depart, 1, 291 sq.; 15, 96; dispute between f. and son, 7, 34 sq.; 25, 105, 105 n.; f. not to pay the debt of his son, 7, 45; pleasant in the world is the state of a f., 10 (i), 79; f., mother, and child, 15, 94; duties of a son to his f., 27, 121, 343–5, 343 n., 349, 352–4, 361–3; courses for f. and son, 27, 397; who has made the son revering the f.? 31, 109, 114; responsibility of f. for crimes of children, 37, 41, 187; disputing the debts of a f., 37, 65; gentle and kind to his son, 43, 25, 60, 206; in early life the sons subsist on the resources of their f., in later

life the f. subsists on the sons' resources, 44, 157; the f. is the same as the son, and the son is the same as the f., 44, 187; sons lovingly touch their f. when he comes home, 44, 204; f. and son part company, 44, 308. *See also* Family, Inheritance, Marriage, *and* Sons.

Father-in-law, *see* Relatives.

Father of Husbandry, *see* Gods (*n.*).

Father of War, *see* Gods (*n.*).

Fathers (Pit*ris*, Manes).

(*a*) The F. in Mythology.
(*b*) The F. and Morality.
(*c*) Worship of F.

(*a*) The F. in Mythology.

They are dependent on the setting sun, 1, 27;—*world of the f.*, why does it never become full? 1, 77, 82; obtained by sacrifices, offspring, &c., bliss in it, 1, 80, 127; 15, 90, 172, 176; 42, 166; 44, 236 sq.; Brahman seen in it as in a dream, 15, 22; in the south-east is the door to it, 44, 424; the mourners return from it to the world of the living, 44, 438 sq.; it is destitute of all light, 49 (i), 151;—the f. go to the moon, 1, 81 sq., 81 n., 273; moon the light of the f., 12, 361; the moon regulates time for the f., 25, 20, 20 n.; Soma (the moon) and the f., 26, xiii, 50, 363, 363 n.; 42, 89 sq.;—they appear sitting on the altar, 2, 148; live in heaven until the destruction of the world, 2, 160; night and day of the f., 7, 78; innumerable f. have passed away, 7, 78 sq.; part of the hand sacred to the f., 7, 198; 14, 25, 166; 25, 40 sq.; Lakshmî praised as the food of the f., 7, 298; Aryaman, chief among f., 8, 89, 89 n.; Yama, king in the world of the f., 8, 153, 346; 41, 299; 42, 161; 44, 236 sq., 365, 481 sq.; Râma is requested by his f. to desist from killing the Kshatriyas, 8, 295 sq., 300; the south is the region of the f., 12, 63; 14, 28; 26, 1–4, 165; 29, 122; 41, 330 n.; 43, 226; 44, 82, 82 n., 198–200, 199 n., 225, 236 sq., 424, 485; 45, 372, 377; offered food to V*ri*tra in the afternoon, 12, 166; the intermediate quarters represent the f., 12, 228, 228 n.; the gods are immortal, the f. are mortal, 12, 290, 295; gods, f., and men, 12, 367 n.; 25, 504; 26, 155; 42, 87, 126, 223, 229; are the guardians of houses, 12, 368, 368 sq. n., 436; are the seasons, 12, 421; 43, 243 sq., 244 n.; classification of the f., 12, 421, 421 n., 427, 429 sq., 429 n.; 25, lxvii, 15, 111 sq., 112 n., 127; 41, 136; abide in the third world from here, 12, 425 n.; roam about as birds, 14, 268; the bliss of the f., 15, 60, 61 sq. n.; created, 25, 15; 43, 74; are primaeval deities, 25, 111; sprang from the sages, from the f. the gods and Dânavas, 25, 112; penances adopted by gods, sages, and f., 25, 473; in the second order of existences caused by goodness, 25, 495; all-gods include the f., 26, 359 n., 360; dwell on the earth, in the air, in heaven, 30, 108, 229; dwell on the hearth, 32, 218; f. and mortals read the abridged code of Manu, 33, 3; among the pa*ñk*agana*h*, 34, 262; create many things by their mere intention, 34, 347 sq.; rise owing to their mere will, 38, 410 sq.; stars are the lights of righteous men gone to heaven, 41, 244; a remedy, arisen from the foundation of the f., 42, 10; conduct men afar, 42, 54; dying = following the f., 42, 59; Rakshas, serpents, pious men, f., 42, 162; road that leads to the f. in the heavens, 42, 183 sq.; follow the Brahma*k*ârin (the sun), 42, 214; serve the Person in the eye under the name of 'svadhâ,' 43, 373; recurring death of the f., 44, 272; the uneven years and single Nakshatras belong to the f., 44, 423; in that respect the f. share in the world of men that they have offspring, 44, 424, 427; are the world of the plants, 44, 429; are in secret, 44, 433, 435; are three in number, 44, 465, 465 n., 467, 481 sq., 487; *once for all the F. have passed away*, 44, 482, 488; path of the f., *see* Future Life (*b*).

(*b*) The F. and Morality.

The departed in the moon, after their good works are consumed, return again to new births, 1, 81 sq., 81 n.; the f. of a man who spurns food given by a sinner, do not eat his oblations for fifteen years, 2, 71;

do not teach what is virtue and what is sin, 2, 72; he who decides wrongly, destroys his f., 2, 98; procreation of sons, a debt to the f., 2, 159 sq.; 14, 261 sq., 271 sq.; 25, 82; 49 (i), 100; *see also* Debts (the three); a Snâtaka, by his good conduct, will liberate his parents, ancestors, and descendants from evil, 2, 226; gods, f., and men upheld by Brâhma*n*as, united with Kshatriyas, 2, 238; by lying to a Guru one destroys seven ancestors and seven descendants, 2, 291; he who plants trees, gladdens the f., 7, 271; extol the emancipated saint, 8, 345; reach perfection by penance, 8, 389; cried out against the injustice of killing cows for sacrifices, 10 (ii), 51; by what means the Bhikkhu can procure blessings for departed friends, 11, 211, 211 n.; the fate of the f. depends on the true or false evidence of witnesses, 14, 82 sq., 203; 25, 271; 33, 92–4, 92 n.; sins whereby the f. suffer, 14, 46, 46 n., 315; 42, 171; sins of the f., 14, 321; 42, 73, 604; heavenly bliss of oneself and of f. depends on wife and children, 25, 332; the Snâtaka shall be careful about his duties towards f. and gods, 29, 124; saved by a lawful marriage, 29, 166; on their way to Brahman, shake off their good and evil deeds, 38, 229–31; rivers of ghee and honey flow for the f. of him who studies his daily Veda lesson, 44, 97 sq.; prayer to be delivered from sins against men and f., 44, 265.

(*c*) Worship of F.

Oblations and libations for the f., 1, 33, 66 n.; 25, 203; 26, 154, 154 n., 357 n.; 29, 243 sq., 253 sq., 315, 325; 30, xxviii, 146; 42, 60; 44, 76 n., 211; daily offerings to the f., one of the 'five great sacrifices,' 2, 48, 108, 108 n., 195, 201; 7, 193 sq.; 8, 306; 14, 50, 256; 25, 62, 132; 29, 217, 321; 30, 23; 44, 95 sq., 96 n., 176, 176 n.; are the deities at a Srâddha, 2, 140; any gifts may be accepted when required for the worship of the f., 2, 265; 7, 188; ancestors and descendants sanctified by certain rites, 2, 302; 14, 117, 309, 331; satisfied by reciting the Vedas and other sacred texts, 7, 126; 29, 219; animal sacrifices for the f., 7, 170 sq.; 14, 26 sq. and n.; 25, 174–6; 26, 62, 190; 29, 89; 30, 112 sq., 256; depend on householders for support, 7, 194; oblation of water to the f. before crossing a river, 7, 203; offerings to gods and f. after having bathed, 7, 206 sq.; to be worshipped at the Vai*s*vadeva sacrifice, 7, 214; 29, 86, 162, 320, 388; the f. drink from a pool, from which the bull set at liberty has drunk, and the earth dug up by such a bull, is delicious food for the f., 7, 262 sq.; fall down to hell, when the offerings of food and water are neglected, 8, 41 sq.; those who worship the f. go to the f., 8, 85; satiated at the Tarpa*n*a rite, 8, 325; 14, 253, 255 sq.; 25, 87–91, 93; 29, 115, 123, 149 sq., 220, 223; 30, 246; prayer to the f., 12, 3 n.; 26, 24 n.; he who does not eat becomes a sacrificer for the f., 12, 5; the Adhvaryu propitiates gods and f. at the beginning of sacrifice, 12, 127 sq.; the adorable the f., the worshipful the gods, 12, 139; the Pi*nd*apit*ri*yag*ñ*a or oblation of obsequial cakes to the f., 12, 184 n., 361–9; 26, xxx; 29, 424; 30, 111 sq., 338; times suitable for the worship of the f., 12, 289 sq.; gratified at the Agnihotra, 12, 333; 44, 82, 82 n.; rites for the f. different (with regard to sacred cord, &c.) from those for the gods, 12, 362–6, 421–3, 425–36; 14, 165; 26, 29; 29, 22, 24 sq., 31, 111, 162, 209, 252, 390; 30, 17, 27, 31, 99, 111, 146, 251, 253, 331 sq.; 44, 198–200, 429–34, 467 sq.; presenting the f. with food, water, collyrium, oil, garments, 12, 368, 368 sq. n.; 30, 107–12, 229 sq.; the Mahâpit*ri*yag*ñ*a, or great sacrifice to the f., 12, 408 n., 415, 417 n., 420–37, 420 n.; meals in honour of the f., 14, 25; food refused by the f., 14, 71; the water-pot not to be used for worship of the f., 14, 164; the sacred fires at offerings to the f., 14, 192; ablution after offerings to the f., 14, 193; 30, 330; libation to the f. offered after the gods have been

satisfied, 14, 238; food given to the f. before eating, 14, 265; *the offering to the manes secures long life and heaven, is worthy of praise and a rite ensuring prosperity*, 14, 266; libations to the f. offered by the ascetic, 14, 278; a performer of rites securing success shall worship cows, Brâhma*n*as, f., and gods, 14, 323; Prâ*n*a is the first offering to the f., 15, 275; consume the offerings through the mouths of Brâhma*n*as, who represent the f., 25, 25, 90, 111, 114, 119; wife assists at offerings to the f., 25, 78 sq.; rite in honour of the f. more important than that in honour of the gods, 25, 113; offerings to the f. accompanied by the Svadhâ call, 25, 117, 122; 42, 177; 44, 234, 423; sacrificial food pleasing to the f., 25, 124 sq.; worshipped at the Ash*t*akâ festivals, 25, 152; 29, 103 sq., 206–9, 344, 417, 420–4; 30, 97, 104–11, 232–6, 293 sq., 341, 341 n.; do not accept the food of one who disdains a freely-offered gift, 25, 167; fish used for offerings to the f., 25, 172; the thrum of the Dîkshita's cloth belongs to the f., 26, 9; Yama invoked with the f., 26, 122 sq., 123 n.; a pit that is dug is sacred to the f., 26, 143, 168 sq.; ceremonies for f. not to be changed by one going to a foreign country, 29, 102; the Nândîmukha f. worshipped, 29, 111; monthly offerings to the f., 29, 209; the vow belonging to Agni together with the f., 29, 229; 'sprinkled butter' used for the f., 29, 237; invoked for protection, 29, 280 sq.; invoked to give long life to the new-born child, 29, 294; when driving towards f. (?) he should dismount, when he has reached them, 29, 364; invoked for offspring, 30, 110; offering to the f. at the house-building ceremony, 30, 123; prayer to Agni at offerings to the f., 32, 35 sq.; worship of the f., gods, and Brâhma*n*as to be performed separately after a partition, 33, 370 sq.; who profits by offerings to the dead? 36, 151 sq.; the hollow in the sacrificial post sacred to the f., 41, 31; worshipped at the Sautrâma*n*î, 41, 136; 44, 233 sq., 236–8, 272; strangers do harm by offering to one's f., 42, 73, 603; invoked to help in battle, 42, 119, 585; invoked for success in an assembly, 42, 138, 544; shares of gods, f., and men (priests), of the sacrifice, 42, 180, 612; offerings to father, grandfather, and great-grandfather, 43, 15 n.; if he does not eat (on a fast), he becomes consecrated to the f., 44, 21; by bathing the student drives off hunger from his kinsmen and his f., 44, 50; the f. gratified by the sacrifice, the world of the f. gained by the sacrificer, 44, 272; the eaters (*s*ma*s*â*h*) amongst the f. destroy in yonder world the good deeds of him who has no sepulchre prepared for him, 44, 422; what is good for the living is also good for the f., 44, 425; the clod deposited between the grave and the village, as a boundary between f. and the living, 44, 440; worshipped at the Pravargya, 44, 481 sq., 485, 487 sq., 487 n.; seated upon the Barhis, 44, 487, 487 n. *See also* Ancestor worship, Ancestors, *and S*râddhas.

Fear, the sage or devotee is devoid of, 8, 50, 67, 69, 86, 101, 114, 126, 151, 246, 250, 287, 292, 344; death produced by delusion and f., 8, 155, 357; the hermit fears nobody, and nobody is afraid of him, 8, 285; is of the quality of darkness, 8, 320; absence of f. has the quality of goodness, 8, 325; f. and falsehood worse than death, 24, 50, 67.

Female, female ascetics, females, *see* Women.

Ferîdûn = Thraêtaona, q. v.

Festivals: Ash*t*akâ (Anvash*t*aka, Ekâsh*t*akâ) f., 2, 36; 13, 130; 14, 270; 17, 211; 25, 148, 148 n., 152; 29, 102–5, 205–9, 223, 341–5, 414, 417–24; 30, 80, 97–113, 232–6, 293 sq., 304 sq.; 36, 331; during certain f. recitation of the Veda is forbidden, 2, 36, 42, 42 n., 263 sq.; 14, 65, 65 n.; 29, 115, 142, 414; 30, 80; to be kept by a king, 2, 236, 236 n.; observance of the seasons, 10 (ii), 41 sq.; *see also* Seasons; f. of the Gaṅgâ and the Mahî, 17, 25; 20, 359; a f. celebrated by children, with their

ornaments on, and decked with garlands, 17, 63; f. on the mountain-top at Râgagaha, 20, 71, 168; white cloth spread out for ceremonial purposes, 20, 127–9; in honour of gods or sacred places, 22, 92; Gaina monks or nuns should not accept food at f., 22, 92–7; duty of Brâhma*n*as to invite neighbours to f., 25, 322; the Âgraya*n*a, or partaking of the first-fruits, 29, 98 sq.; a f. in the autumn month of Â*s*vayuga, 29, 130, 203, 332 sq., 415; 30, 92 sq.; the *K*aitra f., 29, 132; 42, 666; a f. on the Mâgha day, after the Praush*th*apada full moon, 29, 209, 331 sq.; ceremonies at different times of the year, 30, 304 sq.; the Indramaha-f., 42, 353, 510; the spring-f. during the Âgrahâya*n*a full moon, 42, 365, 551; f. of Indra's banner, 49 (i), 11 n., 89; Mârga*s*îrsha and *S*râva*n*a f., *see* Serpents; monthly f., *see* Sacred times;—celebration of the season f., Gâhânbârs, a good work, 4, 301 sq., 315, 315 n., 327–43; 5, 91–7, 208, 351, 351 n., 363, 387–9, 388 sq. n., 391; 18, 157, 157 sq. n., 161, 161 n.; 24, 27, 27 n., 100, 264; 31, 367; 37, 15–17, 15 n., 84, 95, 167, 173, 422, 429, 434, 440 sq., 477, 483; 47, 154 sq., 154 n.; celebration of the Rapîtvîn, 5, 95 sq., 352; 37, 477; in honour of the Fravashis, 5, 315, 315 n.; the Hamaspathmaêdha (All Souls) f., 23, 192 sq., 192 n.; sacred cake to be consecrated every year on the day Khurdâ*d* of the month Fravardîn, 24, 314 sq., 314 n.; monthly (mâhya) and yearly (yâirya) f., 31, 198, 205, 210 sq., 216, 220, 335, 338; *see also* Mâhya; the five Gâtha-days, and the Ardibahi*s*t, 31, 367;—drinking f. in the districts, 27, 56; 28, 435–46; public banquets, 27, 57 sq.; 28, 446, 454–7.

Fetters, the ten, or Sanyoganas, to be broken before entering on the Noble Path, 11, 222; removed by thorough penetration, 11, 307.

Fiend, *see* Mâra.

Fiends, *see* Demons.

Filial piety, *see* Family (*b*).

Final beatitude, liberation, release. *See* Emancipation.

Fines, *see* Punishment.

Firdausi, *see* Shâh Nâmah.

Fire.

(*a*) The element f.
(*b*) The god F.
(*c*) Purity, resp. defilement, of f.
(*d*) F. worship in India: the sacred f.
(*e*) F. worship in India: the three or more sacred fires.
(*f*) F. worship in India: the Agnihotra or f.-offerings.
(*g*) F. worship in Iran.

(*a*) THE ELEMENT F.

F. produced from the Sat, or the Brahman, 1, 93, 100; 38, 20–2; 48, 532–4; produces water, 1, 94, 100, 117 sq.; 38, 22 sq.; red the colour of f., 1, 95, 96; its subtlest portion becomes speech, 1, 96–8; breath is merged in f., at death, 1, 101, 108; is merged in the Highest Being, at the death of the body, 1, 101, 108; united with air, warms the ether, 1, 117; meditation on f. as Brahman, 1, 118, 304; worldly uses of the f., 4, 115–19; first production of f., 5, 55 sq.; 42, xxvii, xxx; diffused through the six substances, 5, 159; Aharman mixed darkness and smoke with the f., 5, 163; 'the Good Diffuser' in men and animals, 5, 184 sq.; in plants, waters, and heaven, 5, 185; 42, 54, 191 sq., 571; 43, 184; the nature of wisdom is just like f., 5, 394; ordeal by f., 7, 59; 31, 39, 51; 37, 59; the internal f. of digestion (Vai*s*vânara), 7, 59; 8, 113; 11, 260, 260 n.; 34, 89 sq., 92, 143 sq., 146 sq.; 35, 244, 244 n.; 36, 97; 48, 287, 290–4; the f. of knowledge, 8, 279, 279 n., 308; is the first of the elements, 8, 353, 353 n.; God speaks to Moses from the f., 9, 35, 35 n., 100, 111; resides in the right ear of a goat, in the right hand of a Brâhma*n*a, in water, and in Ku*s*a grass, 14, 160; takes up water, 14, 162, 162 n.; the seven tongues or flames of the f., 15, 31; 33, 14, 14 n.; 49 (i), 197; the simile of the sparks and the f. (individual souls and Brahman), 15, 34; 34, 277 n., 279; 38, 29, 30, 61, 62, 139; the Self compared to the f. produced by the two ara*n*is, 15, 236 sq.; God is like the f. that has set in the ocean, 15, 265; the

symbol of f., tending upwards, 16, 243; the vital f. in the life of creatures, 18, 42, 42 n., 172, 172 n.; 24, 265 sq.; churning the f., 19, 161, 174, 302; 26, 90–2; 42, 460 sq.; 44, 188; 46, 302–6; the f. of lust, malice, and delusion, 19, 186; 36, 197, 257, 257 n., 260, 366; means of producing f., 20, 292, 292 n.; 27, 449 sq.; 35, 85, 85 n.; the f.-bodies live only three days, 22, 7 n.; sins caused by actions injuring the souls in f., 22, 7 sq., 67, 67 n.; 45, 293, 358; nature of f. and water, 24, 123 sq.; sprang from water, 25, 399, 399 n.; 33, 114; false oath permitted for the sake of fuel, 27, 273; springs from air, 34, lii, 20–2; 48, 535 sq.; the Lord constitutes the Self of the intestinal f., 34, 92, 147, 149; 48, 248; f.-extinguishing apparatus, 35, 67 sq.; all on f. is this endless becoming, 36, 200; water is dissolved into f., and f. into air, 38, 26; is Sâman, 38, 345–9; is sun, wind, earth, 41, 317; as vital air, 41, 317; is immortality, 41, 366; the different kinds of f., 42, 54; fever and f., 42, 565; breath fashioned from f., 43, 4; is kindled by the breath, 43, 399; one of the six doors to the Brahman, 44, 66 sq.; gold made a type of f., 44, 125; why it does not blaze unless fanned or kindled, 44, 130; ordinary f. is a promiscuous eater, an eater of raw flesh, 44, 201; origin and feeding of f.-bodies, 45, 397, 397 n.; the infant Zoroaster rescued from f., 47, 36 sq.; f. of torment, *see* Hell (*a*, *c*). *See also* Parables (*f*), *and* Vaisvânara.

(*b*) The god F.

F. carries the offerings to the gods, 2, 71; 12, 230 sq.; 25, 167; worship of Agni and Âtar, 4, lii; F. (the son) of Ahura-Mazda, 4, 101; 23, 120; 31, 37, 41, 80, 84, 96, 102, 260, 284 sq., 313–16, 319; 37, 453 sq.; 47, 67; 'f.-creature' and other names wherein is the word f., 4, 203; 203 n.; sacrifices to the F., 4, 206 sq., 217, 223; 5, 337; Aharman's conflict with the F., 5, 17, 19, 184–6; Bûrzîn F., 5, 38, 41, 173, 229; the F. Vâzist opposes the demon Apâôsh, 5, 171; the F. Frôbâ, 5, 229; K*ri*sh*n*a is F. among the Vasus, 8, 88, 97; the moon together with the f., upholding all beings, 8, 257; is all the deities, 8, 276; the presiding deity of speech, 8, 338; is the lord of the elements, 8, 346; f. is male, water is female, 12, 9 sq.; 18, 410; gold is the firstborn of F., 14, 134; the protector of vows, 14, 305; Fravashi of F. worshipped, 23, 200; morning service of the F., 23, 322 n.; prayer to the F., son of Ahura-Mazda, 23, 334; 31, 307 sq.; Bh*ri*gu, offspring of F., 25, 169, 169 n.; a guardian of the world, 25, 185, 216 sq.; the spy of the world, 25, 274; the King in the character of F., 25, 396 sq., 397 n.; made to consume all things by Bh*ri*gu, 25, 398, 398 n.; is the mouth of the gods, 29, 254; 33, 109; Ahura and his F. and mind protect Zarathustra, 31, 132, 138; Ahura-Mazda will give his gifts in connexion with the F., 31, 147, 150; Ahura invoked for a sign from the holy F., 31, 177, 182, 182 n.; Ahura-Mazda's son, worshipped, 31, 196 sq., 196 n., 199, 204, 205 sq., 208–10, 212, 214–16, 218 sq., 220, 222–5, 227, 251, 256, 258, 270–2, 274–7, 320, 323, 325, 331, 346, 348, 351, 353, 358, 374, 381–4; 37, 184; the herds which have the f. and its blessings, 31, 360; enmity of F. to Keresâsp, 37, 198 sq., 199 n.; assisted by truth, 37, 355; deity and metre, 43, 53; created, 43, 380, 402; the glory of Zoroaster descends from endless light to f., and from f. to the mother of Zoroaster, 47, 18 sq., 139; assists Zoroaster in converting Vistâsp, 47, 67–9, 164. *See also* Agni, *and* Âtar.

(*c*) Purity, respectively defilement, of f.

Do not rinse the mouth or spit before the f., 1, 29; rules about the treatment of f., 2, 56, 56 n., 128 sq.; a means of purifying, 2, 66 sq.; 7, 96, 98, 101, 103; 14, 60, 121, 160 sq., 188, 190, 241; 25, 187; 33, 109; sin of defiling, extinguishing f., precautions that it may not be contaminated, 4, lxxvi, lxxvi n., lxxviii, 50, 50 n., 82, 121 sq., 186, 285; 5,

lxi, 248 n., 255 sq. and n., 258, 281–3, 285, 300, 307, 334 n., 396; 7, 227; 14, 36; 18, 229, 310 sq., 371–4, 376–80, 432 sq.; 24, 67, 71, 311, 336 sq.; 25, 137, 151; 31, 284; 37, 90 sq., 103, 108, 122 sq., 149, 155, 162, 162 n., 186–90; 47, 101; 48, 565; does not kill, 4, 49, 52, 52 n.; purification of the f., defiled by the dead, 4, 113–15, 142 sq.; 37, 160; the cleanser delights the f., 4, 133; trembles in front of boiling water, 4, 283, 283 n.; 24, 311; is always pure, 14, 132; 25, 398; 33, 216; purified by Ka, 14, 331; the purity of the sacred f., 18, 258; must be cold before the ashes are removed, 24, 311 sq.; contaminated by a menstruous woman, 24, 332; if the sun shines on f., it is a sin, 24, 334 sq.; a symbol of divine power and purity, 31, xix; water and f. disturbed by untruth, 37, 73; wounded by being poked, 41, 49 sq.

(*d*) F.-WORSHIP IN INDIA: THE SACRED F.

The pupil comes to the teacher with f.-wood in his hand, 1, 60, 85, 135, 139 sq., 306; 15, 33, 271; 44, 53 sq.; the departed is carried to the f. (of the funeral pile) from whence he sprang, 1, 79; rules about the sacred f., 2, 1 sq., 201, 201 sq. n.; 25, 104, 108; 29, 385 sq.; 30, xxvi, 138; 38, 306; daily worship of the f., 2, 16 sq.; 25, 151 sq., 239; 29, 286 sq.; at night one should not study in a wood where there is no f. nor gold, 2, 44; before placing fuel on the f. it must be sprinkled with water, 2, 55; the sin of abandoning one's sacred f., 2, 69, 256 sq. and n.; 7, 135, 176; 25, 103; is a sacred object, 2, 94; 14, 36; 33, 222; a Brahma*k*ârin, when on a journey, shall throw part of the alms into the f. (instead of offering it to the teacher), 2, 135 sq.; the ascetic lives without a f., 2, 154; 14, 283; kindling of one f. enjoined for the hermit, 2, 155, 155 n., 157, 195; 14, 45, 259; 25, 199; money may be taken, to defray the expenses of religious rites, from a rich man who does not kindle the sacred f., 2, 273; oblations in the f. part of penances, 7, 151; the sacred f. kindled at the wedding, 7, 191; 14, 42, 236; 25, 87; 29, 170 sq.; 30, 193, 261; on entering the place where sacred f. is kept, let him raise his arm, 7, 228; 14, 245; 25, 138; the student's daily worship of the sacred f., by bringing a log to it, 8, 360; 14, 156 sq.; 25, 42, 50, 62, 64; 29, 75 sq., 191, 307–9, 313; 30, 66 sq., 155 sq., 159 sq., 271 sq., 274; 44, 48 sq.; the ascetic keeps a f., 8, 362; worshipped by Brâhma*n*as, 10 (i), 90; (ii), 74; worshipping of the f. does not purify, 10 (ii), 41; feeding the sacrificial f., recommended by Mâra, 10 (ii), 69; the principal thing in sacrifice is the sacred f., 10 (ii), 105; origin of the f.-ritual of the Vâ*g*asaneyins, 12, xxxi sq., xxxv; the raw flesh-eating, corpse-eating, and the sacrificial f., 12, 33 sq.; Paryagnikara*n*a, carrying the f. round a sacred object, 12, 45 sq., 45 n.; 26, 187 n.; 44, xli, 307; is the womb of the sacrifice, 12, 141 sq.; 26, 19 sq.; 44, 3; the f. in the sacrificer's innermost soul, 12, 311 sq.; he who speaks the truth worships the f., 12, 312 sq.; Brâhma*n*as who keep no sacred f. are like *S*ûdras, 14, 33 sq. and n.; teacher compared with the sacred f., 14, 40 sq.; a Snâtaka should not pass between a f. and a Brâhma*n*a or between two fires, 14, 61; sin of extinguishing the sacred f., 14, 104, 114; the Snâtaka must keep a sacred f., 14, 159; touching f. after dinner, 14, 263; younger brother must not kindle the sacred f. before the elder, 14, 329; the rite of the Âtharva*n*as of carrying f. on the head, 15, 42; 38, 186, 189 sq.; 48, 629, 631; Kâ*s*yapa gave up f.-worship, 19, 188 sq.; *S*râddha offerings made in the sacred f. or in the hand of a Brâhma*n*a, 25, 114; stealing a sacred f., 25, 312; taking fuel for the sacred f. no theft, 25, 313; sacrificial food offered only in f., 26, 59 sq., 178 sq.; 44, 283; what he offers in the f., thereby the gods exist, 26, 154; the sacrifice is f., 26, 171; carrying the

f. round the animal victim, 26, 177 sq., 186 sq.; 29, 176 sq.; 30, 234 sq.; 44, xxvi, 307, 307 n., 410 sq.; Agnyâdheya or the setting up of the sacred domestic f., 29, 12–14, 12 n., 20, 270–2, 276 sq.; 30, 14 sq., 201–3; Agnipra*n*ayana, the carrying forward of the f., 29, 23, 162; a man setting out on a journey makes the f. enter himself or the two kindling-sticks, 29, 133 sq.; 30, 203; expiatory rite, if the sacred f. goes out, 29, 134; 41, 263–5; preparing the place for the sacrificial f., 29, 162; the domestic f. to be kept and worshipped, 29, 172, 269; 30, 261, 267; a f.-brand thrown into the direction whence danger is expected, 29, 231 sq.; renewal of the sacred f. after a death or other calamity, 29, 246–8, 246 sq. n.; the two kindling-sticks handed over to the sacrificer, 29, 265–8; sprinkling water round the sacrificial f., 29, 378; 30, 141 sq.; the Sûtikâgni or f. used at the confinement, 30, 211, 214; placing the f. in the new-built house, 30, 285 sq.; one who has forsaken his f. cannot be a witness, 33, 87; the king must worship those who keep a sacred f., 33, 346; a wife deceased before her husband takes away his sacred f., 33, 377; charm to ward off danger from f., 42, 147, 514–16; is the immortal element of sacrifice, 43, 326 sq.; the sacrificial horse coupled with the sacred f. (Arka), as the representative of Agni-Pragâpati, 44, xviii; the f. is faith, the ghee is truth, 44, 46; by sacrificing with f. produced by two Ara*n*is of A*s*vattha tree, Purûravas becomes a Gandharva, 44, 73 sq.; churned out at the seasonal sacrifices, 44, 77; these worlds have light on both sides, through f. on this side, and through the sun on yonder side, 44, 149; by means of the circumambient f. enemies are shut out from sacrifice, 44, 271; tending the f., cannot be a means of reaching perfection, 45, 294 sq.; the rubbing of f. by two firesticks represented as an act of generation, 46, 302, 304 sq.; circumambulated, *see* Circumambulation. *See also* Agni (*o*).

(*e*) F.-WORSHIP IN INDIA: THE THREE OR MORE SACRED FIRES.

Pupils attend the teacher's s. f., 1, 64; the s. f. teach Upako*s*ala, 1, 64–7; libations in the Gârhapatya, Dakshi*n*a, and Âhavanîya f. as penances, 1, 70; the doctrine of the five f., heaven, rain (Parganya), earth, man, woman, and our being born in them, 1, 78–80, 80 n., 84; 15, 207 sq.; 34, lxxxiii, cviii; 38, 101–32, 186–9, 233–5, 298, 383, 400, 403; 48, 273–7, 585, 595, 652, 753; as members of the Vai*s*vânara Self, 1, 89; the teacher holds, with regard to alms, the place which the Âhavanîya f. holds with regard to a sacrifice, 2, 14; the three f. at a sacrifice, 2, 117, 117 n.; 14, 56, 192–5; 25, 71 sq.; 30, 321–3, 353, 363 sq.; 48, 291; the hermit with wife and children and his sacred f., 2, 156; 7, 276; to be kept by a king, 2, 161; sin of extinguishing or neglecting the s. f., 2, 287; 14, 4 sq.; 25, 438, 442 sq.; 44, 82–5, 187–96; he must not eat in a house where the s. f. are preserved, 7, 221; one who keeps five f. sanctifies a company, 7, 254; 14, 19; 25, 110, 110 n.; the ascetic repositing the s. f. in himself, 7, 279; 14, 275 sq., 280, 291; 25, 203, 205; to be regardless of fruits of action, not discarding the s. f., is renunciation, 8, 67; one of the ten f. at the allegorical sacrifice of the sense-organs, 8, 261; Âhavanîya and Gârhapatya f., 8, 262; 12, 207 sq.; 44, 516, 535; 46, 236, 238; the sacrificer sleeps in one of the chief f.-houses, 12, 1, 6; preparation of the sacrificial f., 12, 1 sq., 87–92, 95–114, 230–2; only oblations offered in blazing f. are successful, 12, 146, 174; they strew grass round the f., for the sacrifice dreads nakedness, 12, 208; the Gârhapatya f. is a house, 12, 272; the Agnyâdhâna (Agnyâdheya) or establishment of the s. f., 12, 274–322; 25, 438; 43, 296, 296 n.; 44, 1 n., 2; producing (churning) the s. f., 12, 275, 292–5, 293 n., 294 sq. n., 311 sq., 389, 389 n.; the Punarâdheya or re-establishment of the s. f., 12, 285, 285 n., 313–22, 313

n.; 46, 368; so long as he has not set up the s. f., the sacrificer is a mere man, 12, 292, 294; Sabhya or hall f. kept up by Kshatriyas, 12, 302 n.; Agnyupasthâna, or worship of the s. f., 12, 338–60; the householder worships the s. f. when setting out on a journey, and returning home, 12, 357–60; Samidhs (kindling-sticks), 12, 400 n.; 44, 567; the Prâ*n*as, Apâna, &c., identified with the s. f., 15, 279 sq.; 44, 190; the three s. f. form the mouth-endowed body of the Self, 15, 308; meditation on the s. f., 15, 331 sq., 334; the s. f. injure him who neglects sacrifices, 25, 133; made to blaze when portents interrupt the Veda-study, 25, 145; kindled again after cremation of the wife, 25, 198; the dhish*n*yas or hearths, 26, 147–55, 148 n., 441–6; 41, 317 sq., 317 n.; 43, 241–5, 358, 360; if weakness comes upon the sacrificer, he is led to the Âhavanîya f., 26, 148, 148 n.; kindling the sacrificer, 26, 385 sq., 386 n.; the sacrificial f. at Sattras, 26, 441–6; where the wife and the f. are, this is the home, 29, 89; restore a sick person to health, 29, 236; are fond of the village, 29, 236; the s. f. at the funeral, 29, 238 sq., 242 sq., 356; 44, 175; the fiction concerning the three s. f., 34, 146; as the Gârhapatya the highest Self may be represented because it is the Self of all, 34, 150; a sixth f. mentioned by the Vâgasaneyins, 38, 187–9; the making of the fire-pan (ukhâ), 41, 229–46; 44, 579 sq.; building of the Gârhapatya hearth, 41, 298–319; 43, 117–21; spells put into the s. f., 42, 76; Ukhya f. carried in a pan for a year, 43, 191 n., 198, 198 n., 272 sq., 272 n., 308, 324; Agnisava, 43, 298, 298 n.; the f.-pan a womb, 43, 341; f.-pan represents the universe, 43, 353 sq., 354 n.; thirty-six thousand Arka-f. produced by Mind, Speech, &c., 43, 375–80, 375 n.; the sacrificial f. to be laid down at new moon, not under an asterism, 44, 1 sq.; the offerer of the Agnihotra kept up by his f., 44, 47; Anvâhârya-pa*k*ana f., 44, 83, 178, 183; whilst he is offering the Agnihotra, the Sacrificer's f. become worn out, and he renews them again by the animal sacrifice: with the f. the Sacrificer and his house and cattle are worn out and renewed, 44, 118 sq.; the s. f. long for flesh, 44, 119; worshipped to avoid being driven from one's home, 44, 126; symbolism of the four sacrificial f. at the animal sacrifice, 44, 127; animal sacrifice in the s. f. thrown together, 44, 174; the three f. are the three worlds, 44, 178; he who lays down his two f. spreads himself all over these worlds, 44, 178; how the sacred f. are to be treated when the Agnihotrin dies, 44, 197–200; by burning the Sacrificer they unite him with his f., 44, 200–2; the f. by which the dead Sacrificer is burnt, lovingly touch him even as sons their father, 44, 204; sacrificial f. not kept up by the Kâ*s*is, 44, 401; the sacrificer of a Purushamedha takes up the two f. within his own self, 44, 412; Âgnîdhra (n.) or f.-shed, 44, 515; the three sacrificial f. the heads of Agni, 46, 168; establishment of s. f. not obligatory for those whose condition of life involves chastity, 48, 698.

(*f*) F. WORSHIP IN INDIA: THE AGNIHOTRA OR F.-OFFERINGS.

Five A. oblations offered to the Prâ*n*as, 1, 89–91; 15, 279 sq.; 38, 249–52; 48, 294 sq.; as hungry children sit round their mother, so do all beings sit round the A., 1, 91; he who offers the A. with a full knowledge of its purport, offers it in all worlds, in all beings, in all Selfs, all his sins are burnt, 1, 91; the inner A. is better than the ordinary A., 1, 283; 8, 191; 38, 263; reception of a guest during an A., 2, 118 sq.; meal time regulated by A., 7, 218; the A. as the first among sacrifices, 8, 353; 15, 30 sq., 51 sq.; 17, 134; 25, 130, 130 n., 132; 44, 502; 45, 138; the A. or Morning and Evening Libations, and the worship of the fires, 12, 173, 186, 322–60, 374 sq., 374 n., 407, 415, 443 sq.; 26, 37, 37 n., 390; 43, 274, 297, 297 n., 299, 356; 44, xiv,

118 sq.; if the A. were not offered, the sun would not rise, 12, 328; the A. as a domestic sacrifice, obligatory for every householder, morning and evening offerings in the domestic fire, 2, 51; 7, 191; 12, 333 sq.; 14, 265; 29, 14, 18 sq., 89, 136, 172, 286 sq., 386, 392; 30, 15 sq., 19–21, 39, 196 sq., 265 sq.; 42, 84, 145; the A. is the ship that sails heavenwards, 12, 345 sq.; 44, 185, 190; the *Gat*ilas, who were converted by Buddha, flung their hair, their braids, and their things for the A. into the river, 13, 132 sq.; good conduct more important than the A., 14, 34; the hermit offers the A., 14, 45, 292, 294; 49 (i), 74; an Agnihotrin may perform secret penances, 14, 125; gifts to Brâhma*n*as better than A., 14, 138 sq.; 25, 229; the Nâ*k*iketa rite a kind of f.-sacrifice, which leads to heaven, 15, xxi sqq., 4 sq., 9, 12; 34, 247–52; 48, 269; the merit of offering sacrifices, especially the A., 15, 51 sqq., 334, 336–8; times for the A., 25, 32, 32 n., 122; 48, 527; A. not interrupted by impurity after death, 25, 182, 183 n.; wife burnt with the A. fires, 25, 198; the A. with three sacred fires, 25, 200; persons unfit to offer the A., 25, 437, 437 n.; the permanent obligation of the A., 34, lxxviii; 38, 191, 296 sq., 296 n., 313, 358–61; 48, 177, 693 sq., 702 sq., 725 sq.; offered during a whole month at the ayana of the Ku*nd*apâyins, 38, 250 n., 251, 314; transference of the fire from the Gârhapatya fire to the two other fires, at the A., 38, 251; a text relating to the A. which forms part of the mahâpit*ri*yag*ñ*a, 38, 299 sq.; A. offered on the eve of battle, 42, 122, 510; to be offered by the sacrificer himself in new and full moon nights, 44, 21 sq., 34 sq.; esoteric doctrines about the A., 44, 46–8; Uddâlaka Âru*n*i's teaching on the A., 44, 79–85; worlds conquered by the A., 44, 111 sq.; *G*anaka of Videha on the A., 44, 112–15; after performing the A., one approaches the fires saying 'Wealth,' and becomes firmly established by offspring and cattle, 44, 126; the A. of one who performs a sattra, 44, 175; expiatory ceremonies in connexion with the A., 44, 178–96; the A. is a sacrificial session ensuring death in old age, 44, 178; sacred to Pra*g*âpati, 44, 183; is a long sacrificial session, 44, 197, 200; how it is performed when the Agnihotrin dies, 44, 197–200; tainted is the A. of one who is dead, 44, 198; prayers for the morning and evening service, 46, 37 sq., 39, 42 sq., 317; speaking of truth incumbent on the Agnihotrin, 48, 303.

(*g*) F. WORSHIP IN IRAN.

Sacredness and worship of f. in Zoroastrianism, 1, xxii; 4, xiii, lxii, lxiv, lxxv–lxxvii, lxxix sq.; 5, lxi, 298–300, 298 n., 299 n., 375, 375 n., 393–6; 18, 163 sq., 164 n., 171 sq., 290 sq.; 31, 258; 37, 231, 266 sq., 350 sq., 358, 368, 470; 47, 91, 154, 161, 161 n.; Ardashîr blamed for destroying the sacred f. of the Muleîk ut-tavâif, 4, xliv sq.; keeps away or kills the fiends, 4, lxxvi, lxxix sq., 115, 184 n.; 5, 229, 317, 342–4; 37, 122; 47, 141; the sacred Bahrâm (Vâhrâm) f., 4, lxxvi, 115 n., 272; 5, 185, 202, 206; 24, 96; 47, 161, 161 n.; meritoriousness of bringing f.-brands to the Dâityô-gâtu, or Bahrâm f., 4, 115–19, 115 sq. n.; kept to watch over a pregnant woman and a new-born child, 4, 184 n.; 5, 316 sq., 322; 18, 59, 59 n.; 24, 277; 37, 480; 47, 30; how often the f. of Ahura-Mazda must be fed, 4, 256, 256 n.; they who treat not friendly his f., offend Ahura-Mazda, 4, 281; worship of the f. one of the three (four) best things in the world, 4, 293; 18, 417; offerings not to be made, without looking at the f., 4, 347; worship of the f. re-established by Pêshyô-tanû, 5, li, 227, 230; on the nature of the five kinds of f., 5, 61–4, 61 n.; the sacred f. Gu*s*asp (Gû*s*n-asp), 5, 173, 229; 24, 271, 271 n.; 37, 190; opposed to witchcraft, 5, 185; the f. Vi*s*nâsp, 5, 218; consecration of f. and water, 5, 224–7; prayer on presenting anything to the f., 5, 333, 333 n.; advantage of keeping a f. in

the house, 5, 339 sq.; holy-water presented to the f., 5, 341 sq., 375, 375 n.; 18, 232, 251; holy f., 5, 362; 47, 76, 82; prayer for the f. when seeing the f., 5, 371; kept burning at the three nights' ceremony, 18, 59; formula addressed to the f. (tava âthrô), 18, 141, 143, 143 n.; priests protectors of the sacred f., 18, 353; duty of maintaining the s. f., 24, 270–2, 301, 355 sq.; 37, 96, 163 sq., 188, 190–2; salutation of the f., 24, 358; the altar f. an aid of grace, 31, 95, 100; about f.-wood, 37, 48, 126; atonement for injuring the f. of Varahrân, 37, 86; about the f. in the house, 37, 122; care of the f. when travelling, 37, 125; neglect of f. causes want of offspring, 37, 191 sq.; the f. pleased by the conversion of Vistâsp, 47, 74; abode of the s. f., *see* Fire-temple.

Fire-altar: the altar is female, the f. is male, 12, 63; after having built the f., one must not approach a Sûdra wife, 14, 96; leading forward of the fire to the f., 26, 121–6; 43, 188–207; penance for pushing against a f., 29, 224; f. made of mind, &c., do not constitute part of the sacrificial action, 34, lxxiv; 38, 259–68; the Agni*k*ayana (Agni*k*ityâ), or building of the f., 38, 261 n., 264; 41, xxvi sq., 143–419; 43, xiii, xxi, 1–280; layers and bricks of the f., 41, 186–90, 355 sq., 362; 44, 542 (ish*t*akâ), 544 (*k*iti), 546 (lokamp*rin*â), 552 (nâkasad), 554 (pañ*k*a-*k*û*d*â), 560 (punas*k*iti), 564 (*ri*tavyâ), 566 (sâdana), 573 (sp*rit*), 574 (s*r*ish*t*i), 576 (svayamât*rinn*â), 582 (vâlakhilyâ), 586 (visvagyotis); the ashes from the fire-pan at the Agni*k*ayana thrown into the water, 41, 293–7; preparation of the site of the great Âhavanîya f., 41, 325–417; the fire-pan on the f., 41, 396–401; plan of f., 41, 419; ceremony of building the householder's f., 42, 354; the mystery of the f., 43, xiii–xxvi, 281–404; ritual of the f. later than the rest of the sacrificial system, 43, xiii, xviii; takes a full year to complete, 43, xix, xxiii; represented as the Universe, 43, xix sq., 381–90; lotus-leaf in its centre, 43, xx, 1 n., 44 sq. and n.; has the shape of a large bird, 43, xxi sq., 1 n., 4 n., 19–21, 22 n., 112 n., 114–16, 120 sq., 135–40, 148 sq., 168, 168 n., 177, 179 sq., 180 n., 201, 250 sq. and n., 272, 274, 285–9, 296, 300–6, 311, 363, 391, 402; 44, 588 (wing of altar); bricks of the f. representing parts of the universe, 43, 2 n., 23–9, 41–57, 47 n., 80, 82, 90–103, 109, 121–4, 127–34, 138, 140–8, 271, 364; diagram showing the central parts of the layers, 43, 17, 24, 48, 71, 98; represents Purusha-Pragâpati and the divine body of the sacrificer, 43, 30, 226 sq., 252, 256; 44, xiv, 428; the Agni*k*ayana higher than an ordinary sacrifice, 43, 121, 214 n.; sprinkling the f., 43, 169 sq.; is speech, 43, 173; drawing of frog, lotus-flower, and bamboo-shoot across it, 43, 174–7; is an island, 43, 187; mounting the f., 43, 198–200; its different bricks are so many Agnis, 43, 222, 222 n.; Agniyogana, or Yoking of the f., 43, 249–55; the Agni*k*ayana includes all sacrificial rites, 43, 266, 296–9; rules for repeated Agni*k*ayana, 43, 271–4; propitiatory hymn to make good deficiencies in the building of the f., 43, 274–8; the building of the f. must not be performed for another person, 43, 278–80; the triad F., Mahad uktham, and Mahâvrata, 43, 281–9; how to measure its dimensions, 43, 305–12; sevenfold, hundredfold, and hundred and one-fold, 43, 312–15; time for building the f., 43, 316–20; number of bricks, 43, 357–61; identified with the metres, 43, 384–6; built so as to look in all directions, 43, 390–3; the Agni*k*ayana a preliminary to the Soma-sacrifice, 44, xiii; human sacrifice at the building of the f., 44, xxxvii–xxxix; is twenty-one-fold, 44, 334 sq., 334 n.; the greatest possible f. built at the Sarvamedha, 44, 418; the tomb of a builder of a f. to be made in the shape of the f., 44, 428; the bones of the deceased arranged like the bird-shaped f., 44, 434 sq.; burial rite for one who has built, and one who has

not built, a f., 44, 439 sq.; Agni*k*it or builder of a f., 44, 516; Mantras for the construction of the f., 46, 285 sq. *See also* Agni (*o*), *and* Altar.

Fire-bodies, *see* Fire (*a*).

Fire-places, in India and Ceylon, 36, 86 sq. n.

Fire-priest, *see* Priests (*a*, *e*).

Fire-temple (abode of the sacred fires), ceremonial worship in it, 5, 310, 310 n.; 18, 162, 162 n., 173, 242, 242 n.; 24, 28; 37, 119; three times every day the archangels form an assembly in the f., 5, 393; ceremony for the living soul celebrated in it, 18, 242.

Fire-worshippers, hold the doctrine of deeds having their reward, 13, 190 sq.

Firmament, *see* Sky.

Fish: the Kara f., chief of the creatures living in water, 4, 223, 224 n.; sexual intercourse of f., 5, 61; the Kar f. protects the Hôm, 5, 65 sq.; 24, 111, 111 n.; the f. Vâs of Pan*k*âsa*d*varân, 5, 66; the ox-f. exists in all seas, 5, 71; Makara, chief among f., 8, 90, 90 n.; eating the flesh of f., a kind of penance, 10 (ii), 41; Buddha allows the Bhikkhus to eat f., 20, 252 sq.; mighty f. hundreds of leagues long, 20, 302; 35, 130, 186; 36, 90; the eyesight of the Kara f., 23, 239, 266; stories of the island-whale, 23, 295, 295 n.; f. offerings, 28, 78, 78 n.; the f. of fifty fins, and the sacred beast that stands in Vouru-kasha, worshipped, 31, 291; the fabulous f. Khwăn, 39, 164 sq., 167.

Fishing, regulations for, 27, 260, 263 sq., 264 n., 277, 307.

Five-people (pa*ñk*a ga*n*â*h*), rest in the Self, 15, 178, 178 n.; what is meant by them, 34, xl, 257–63; beyond the f., i.e. far away, 42, 92; the fivefold dwellings of the f., 46, 194.

Flamingoes (Ha*m*sas), *see* Birds (*b*).

Flesh, *see* Animals (*e*).

Flood: expiatory oblation to the F., if the Soma meets with any mishap at the purifying bath concluding the Soma-sacrifice, 44, 211; Wind worshipped under the name of F., 44, 479. *See also* Deluge.

Flowers, as offerings, 8, 85; celestial f. worn by K*r*ish*n*a, 8, 93; similes of f., 8, 285 sq., 313, 371; 10 (i), 16–19; rain of heavenly (Ma*nd*ârava, Mañ*g*ûshaka) f. in honour of Buddha, 11, 86 sq.; 20, 370, 370 n.; 21, 6, 9, 20, 24, 69, 156 sq., 162–71, 183 sq., 232, 234, 308, 313, 315, 378; the Bodhisattva smells heavenly f., 21, 345; vision of Mandâra f., 22, 233 sq.; rain of f. in Sukhâvatî, 49 (ii), 95. *See also* Lotus.

Foetus, *see* Embryo.

Folklore, *see* Fables, *and* Tales.

Food.

(*a*) F. in mythology and philosophy.
(*b*) F. in law and ritual.
(*c*) Lawful and forbidden f.

(*a*) F. IN MYTHOLOGY AND PHILOSOPHY.

F., the deity of the pratihâra hymns, for all beings live when they partake of f., 1, 20 sq.; produced from water, 1, 94; 43, 232; the word 'f.' (anna) denotes 'earth,' 1, 94 n.; 38, 23 sq.; 48, 536; *see also* Earth; is the root of the body, 1, 99, 99 sq. n.; depends on rain, 1, 117; 8, 54; meditation on f. as Brahman 1, 117; 15, 64–9, 194, 302 sq., 312–16; by means of f. he obtains everything, 1, 203 sq.; the creation of f., 1, 240 sq.; 41, 402; no one who does not eat, has strength to do holy works, 4, 31; all creatures produced by f., 8, 54; 15, 55, 64–9; three kinds of f. (according to the three Gu*n*as), 8, 118; how f. is digested and bodies are formed in the womb, 8, 252; is the highest of all things to be swallowed, 8, 353; f. and breath identified, 12, 304; 15, 194; 38, 211, 213; milk the first f., and f. means progeny, 12, 385 sq., 388, 394; goddess of f., 14, 240; creatures depend on f., f. is life, hence gifts of f. must be made, 14, 245; everything rests on f., 15, 66 sq.; seven kinds of f. produced, 15, 91–3; f. and breath are the two gods, 15, 142; *from f. are born all creatures that live on earth; afterwards they live on f., and in the end (when they die) they return to it*, 15, 315; f. of the souls in heaven

and in hell, 18, 66 sq. and n., 72; 24, 21 sq., 21 n., 25; is threefold, 26, 28; 43, 93, 110; 46, 141, 143; means cattle, 26, 172; prayer to the Lord of F., 29, 54, 348; the support of all beings, 36, 369; satisfies if proportionate to the body, 41, 260, 330; the body linked to f. by means of vital airs, 41, 270; 43, 139; mortar and pestle represent f., 41, 393-7; is taken from the front (of the mouth) towards the back, 41, 402; is the resort of the waters, 41, 416; all f. is water, for one eats by moistening the f., 43, 35; 44, 443; is seventeenfold, 43, 79; evil driven away by means of f., 43, 87; a sick man, when he gets better, asks for f., 43, 87; the essence of f. is invisible, 43, 95; how f. benefits the body, 43, 135, 139; the arrows of the terrestrial Rudras, 43, 165; represented by sour curds, honey, and ghee, 43, 184 sq.; is variegated, 43, 196; immortal and mortal parts of f., 43, 285; by means of the arms f. is eaten, 43, 306; when enclosed in the body, f. becomes the body itself, 43, 341; f. consumed by man in this world, consumes him in the other, 44, 260; f. of mankind in the future ages, 47, 112-14, 117.

(*b*) F. IN LAW AND RITUAL.

Robbery permitted to sustain life, after having not eaten at the time of six meals, 2, 273; the ceremony of 'honouring one's f.' before a meal, 7, 220, 220 n.; f. given for reciting stanzas, rejected by Buddha, 10 (ii), 13; fast-day f., 12, 2, 5 sq.; 42, 534; f. of king must be hallowed by Mantras and mixed with antidotes against poison, 25, 251; special f. for penances, 25, 449, 452 sq., 455, 459-61, 463-5, 470 sq., 474 sq., 478; first f. of the child (annaprâ*s*ana), 29, 50, 182, 183 sq., 299 sq.; 30, 216, 283; 37, 122; *see also* Child (*b*); used for ancestor-worship, 29, 251 sq.; a wife who always eats before her husband may be divorced, 33, 184; moderation in f., a condition of moral conduct and a holy life, 35, 4-7; three right views regarding f., 36, 252, 252 n.; giving no f., a mode of engaging in conflict, 37, 40, 44, 67; proportion of f. for mankind and cattle, 37, 91 sq.; daily f. of men, women, children, and dogs, 37, 114; sin of deprival of f., 37, 115 sq., 123, 130, 141; all f. must be consecrated, 37, 192; prayer for f., 37, 332; 41, 262 sq.; merit of providing f. for the good, 37, 333 sq.; kinds of f. given to sacrificer, 41, 36 f.; put on the bricks used for building the fire-altar, 41, 155; 43, 91; is served from the right side, 43, 226; accepted from a Brâhma*n*a, not from a low person, 48, 565. *See also* Abstinence, Eating, *and* Meals.

(*c*) LAWFUL AND FORBIDDEN F.

Remains of f. impure, 1, 18; 44, 446; restrictions as to f., for the Brahma*k*ârin, 2, 8, 12 n., 12-16, 191; 8, 360; 14, 118 sq., 119 n.; rules about lawful and forbidden f., 2, 59-71, 74 sq., 265-70, 274; 6, 23 sq., 58, 94, 97, 106, 109-11, 134 sq., 262 sq.; 7, 33, 39, 136, 187; 8, 279; 10 (ii), 40 sq.; 14, 33 sq. and n., 44, 69-75, 104 sq., 115, 121, 130 sq., 154, 171-3, 184 sq., 222, 224, 237, 239, 250 sq., 263, 287, 298, 310, 313, 317, 319, 329; 25, lxviii sq., xciv, 161-4, 168, 170-7, 441, 441 n., 443, 443 n., 497; 27, 462 sq.; 33, 287; 38, 311 sq.; penances for eating impure or forbidden f., 2, 85-7, 287 sq., 290, 295; 7, 153 sq., 162-9; 14, 131; 25, 460-3, 481 sq.; 29, 224; fit for sacrifices, 2, 138 sq., 296, 300 sq. and n.; 14, 70; 25, 123-5; 30, 267; *but see also* Sacrifices (*b*); f. to be avoided for a special vow, 2, 147; forbidden f. must be avoided even in times of distress, 2, 213; of *S*ûdras, 2, 233; 14, 49; fit for *S*râddhas, 2, 256; 14, 54 sq.; forbidden f. becomes pure by scattering earth on it, 2, 292, 292 n.; polluted by a menstruous woman, 5, 279, 283, 340 sq. n.; not to be thrown away to the north at night, 5, 318; f. over which God's name has been pronounced, not to be rejected, 6, 130; fruit and cattle created by God, therefore lawful f., 6, 133 sq.; reproval of those who prohibit lawful f., 6, 199; honey

lawful f., 6, 257; great religious merit of him who does not eat meat, 7, 171; when illicit f. may be eaten, 7, 187–9; 34, lxxv; 38, 309–12; 48, 701 sq.; cattle are lawful f., 9, 59; persons in whose house it is lawful to eat f., 9, 81 sq., 82 n.; of a Brâhma*n*a slayer forbidden, 14, 101; 25, 309; Ka*s*mîrians eat meat, 14, 147 n.; f. defiled by various causes, 15, 312; Brâhma*n*as are abstainers from f. at night and at the wrong time, 17, 130; milk of goats, the best f., 24, 45; defiled and purified, 25, 190 sq.; 48, 17; common people eat raw flesh, 26, 395 n., 396 n.; list of dishes, rules about f., 27, 459–64; honey forbidden to the Brahma*k*ârin, 44, 90; flesh is the best kind of f., 44, 119; abstinence from acids and salt does not lead to perfection (as some think), 45, 294; purity in matters of f. enjoined for those who know Brahman, 48, 702. *See also* Abstinence, *and* Animals (*e*).

Fools, who do not know the true law, 10 (i), 20–2; company of f. and wise men, 10 (i), 55.

Foot-clothing, of Buddhist Bhikkhus, 17, 13–24, 31, 34 sq., 39.

Fo Pan-ni-pan-king, Chinese translation of a Buddha-Parinibbâna-Sutta, 11, xxxvi; 19, 365.

Fo-pen-hing-king, a life of Buddha, 19, xvi sq., xxviii.

Fo-pen-hing-tsih-king, a life of Buddha, 19, xxix.

Forefathers, *see* Fathers.

Foreigners, law regarding, 37, 46 sq., 51, 57 sq., 113; sin of delivering an Irânian to f., 37, 72; worthiness of destroying f., 37, 89; family alliance with f., 37, 99; about f. seeking wives, 37, 100; as physicians, 37, 118.

Forest, meditation in the, 8, 251. *See* Hermits.

Foresters, *see* Hermits.

Forgiveness, *see* Morality.

Form, the reality or non-reality of the idea of, 11, 49–51; deliverance from the hindrance to thought arising from the sensations and ideas due to external f., 11, 51 sq.; passion for a f., spiritual bondage, 11, 226, 230 sq. *See also* Colours, *and* Names (and forms).

Fornication, *see* Sexual intercourse.

Fortune, *see* Bhaga.

Fortune-telling, *see* Divination.

Fo-sho-hing-tsan-king, t.w., Chinese translation of A*s*vaghosha's Buddha-*k*arita, 19, ix sq.; translated *vol.* 19.

Fo-shwo-*k*ung-hu-mo-ho-ti-king t.w., a life of Buddha, 19, xxx.

Four Noble Truths, *see* Truths.

Frabaretar, *see* Priests (*d*).

Frâda*d*-gadman, Phl., Av. Frâda*t*-*h*varenô, n.p., one of the producers of the renovation, 18, 78 sq. and n.; 23, 219, 220 n.

Fradadhafshu, *see* Frâda*t*fshu.

Frâ*d*akhshtô, *see* Fradhakh*s*tô.

Frâda*t*fshu, worshipped, 31, 197, 204, 209, 215, 219, 223, 349, 373, 381 sq.

Frâda*t*-*h*varenah, *see* Frâda*d*-gadman.

Frâda*t*-nara, son of Gravâratu, 23, 217.

Frâda*t*-vanghu, son of Stiva*nt*, 23, 216.

Frâda*t*-vîra, worshipped, 31, 197, 204, 209, 215, 219, 224, 383.

Frâda*t*-vîspãm-hu*g*âiti, worshipped, 31, 204, 209, 215, 219, 224, 384 sq.

Fradhakh*s*tô, son of the Khumbîks, one of the seven immortals, 18, 256, 256 n., 258 n.; 23, 224, 224 n.; 37, 203, 203 n.

Fradhidaya, n.p., 23, 203.

Fragûzag, n.p., 5, 134; 47, 34, 140.

Frahimravâ, or Frâhîmrava*n*ã-zôi*s*, n.p., Zoroaster's maternal grandfather, 5, 144; 47, 18, 18 n.

Frâh-vakhsh-vindâ*d*, n.p., 5, 145.

Frâ*k*îh, a demon-worshipper, 47, 13.

Frâ*k*ithra, son of Berezva*nt*, 23, 218.

Frâ*k*ya, son of Taurvâti, 23, 213.

Franghâdh, the holy maid, 23, 225.

Franghrasyan, *see* Frangrasyan.

Frangrâsîyâk, *see* Frangrasyan.

Frangrasyan (or Frâsîyâ*v*, or Frangrâsîyâk), of Tûr, the Turanian, 4, 1 sq.; 5, 38, 134 sq. and n., 150; 37, 28, 28 n., 225; 47, 116, 116 sq. n.; his irrigation works, 5, 79, 82, 84; 18, 214, 214 n.; 47, xxix, 134;

punished in hell, 5, 125; his struggle with Mânûsk̂ihar, 5, 135 sq.; 24, 62, 62 n.; his evil reign, 5, 213, 228; offered to Anâhita in his cave under the earth, 23, 64 sq., 64 n.; killed by Husravah or Khûsrôî, 23, 114 sq., 278, 304, 307, 307 n.; 24, 64, 64 n.; 47, 14, 116; tries in vain to seize the priestly glory of the Aryans, 23, 300–2, 305; created immortal by Aharman, 24, 35, 35 n.; his exploits, 24, 61; bound by Haoma, 31, 246; defeated by Aûzôbô, 47, 11, 11 sq. n.; sought the glory of Zaratûst, 47, 33 sq., 33 n. *See also* Afrâsyâb.

Frânya, n.p., 23, 204.

Fraora-ostra, n.p., 23, 217.

Frârâzi, son of Tûra, 23, 217.

Frashâîtar, n.p., 5, 145 sq., 146 n.

Fras-hãmvareta, n.p., 23, 206, 206 n.

Frashaostra (Frashôstar), son of Hvôva, father-in-law of Zarathustra, 23, 207 sq., 207 n.; 37, 397; Zarathustra preached to him, 23, 331; 31, 133, 142 sq.; Zarathustra prays for him, 31, 15, 22; *G*âmâspa and F., the two leaders, 31, 76, 76 n.; 37, 130, 130 n.; a protector of the Zarathustrian Faith, 31, 161, 165 sq., 250; presented a blest form, 31, 185; offers propitiation to Ahura-Mazda, 31, 190 sq.; questions Zarathustra as to the rites, 31, 327; priests come to F. for religious inquiry, 37, 219, 219 n., 413, 413 n.; 47, 80 sq. and n., 165 n.; disciple of Zoroaster, 37, 230; praise of F., 37, 236, 290, 297, 299; joyfulness in righteousness taught to F., 37, 374; utterance of F., 37, 406; his death, 47, xxx, 165, 165 n.; converted, 47, 125.

Frashâvakhsha, n.p., 23, 210.

Frashôkareta, n.p., 23, 206.

Frashôstar, *see* Frashaostra.

Frâsîyâv, *see* Frangrasyan.

Frasp-i *K*ûr, n.p., 5, 135.

Frasrûtâra, n.p., 23, 216.

Frast, n.p., 5, 146.

Frâta, n.p., 23, 203.

Fratîra, n.p., 23, 218.

Fraud, *see* Theft.

Frava, n.p., 23, 214.

Fravâhar, Phl., 'guardian spirit 5, lxxiii, 14.

Fravâk, and Fravâkaîn, one of the first seven pairs of men, 5, 58 sq.; Hôshyang, son of F., 5, 131; 47, 35; son of Sîyâ(k)mak, 5, 132; 47, 128, 128 n., 140; great-grandson of Gâyômar*d*, 18, 89, 89 n.

Fravâkaîn, one of the first women, 5, 58.

Fravarâne, *see* Zoroastrianism.

Fravar*d*în, the cockscomb, the flower of, 5, 104; invoked, 5, 403, 405. *See also* Fravashis.

Fravashis (prototypes, guardian angels): F. of Ahura-Mazda and other gods, 4, 213; 23, 199 sq.; 31, 273, 278; the mighty F. of the righteous invoked and worshipped, 4, 221, 245; 5, 313, 313 n., 392; 18, 167, 173, 240 sq., 357; 23, 6, 10, 13 sq., 17, 20, 33 n., 36, 38, 179–230, 321, 350–3; 31, 278 sq.; the Fravashi of Thraêtaona worshipped, 4, 246; 31, 389 sq.; the Fravashi of the holy Yima, 4, 262; of the holy men of Turanian nations, 4, 266; sacrifice to the souls and F., 4, 349; 31, 309, 331; come to meet and bring aliments, &c., to the departed soul, 4, 373 sq.; their creation, 5, 5 n.; 18, 89; 47, xxviii, xli; engaged in the defeat of fiends, 18, 104; not rendered wicked by the sin of the soul, 18, 104, 104 n.; angels, souls, and F. attend to the wishes of the creator, 18, 120; pleased by ceremonial, 18, 159 sq.; 37, 174, 184; are free from disturbance through the glory of the creator, 18, 261, 261 sq. n.; heaven their seat, 18, 275; Keresâspa's body watched over by 99,999 F., 18, 369; the soul and Fravashi of the bull, 23, 16; come for help and joy, 23, 26; the Fravashi of Zarathustra worshipped, 23, 93; 31, 208, 212, 218, 222 sq., 227, 244, 252 sq., 255, 273, 275, 278, 324, 327, 351, 358, 380; 47, 4 sq., 16, 73, 139; give virtuous offspring to the truthful, 23, 120; in the train of Mithra, 23, 136, 145; the Fravar*d*in Yast dedicated to them, 23, 179–230; what they are, 23, 179; of next-of-kin, 23, 180, 228, 230; different classes of F. worshipped, 23, 180, 184 sq., 230; 31,

201, 212, 218, 227, 272 sq., 275, 279, 331, 351, 358, 373; assist Ahura-Mazda in maintaining the world, 23, 180–5, 187, 193 sq.; watch over procreation, 23, 183, 185, 187; 31, 273; help in battle, 23, 184, 186–91, 196 sq., 222 sq.; invoked in danger, 23, 185; their numbers, 23, 194–6; send water to their kindred, 23, 196; souls and F. different, 23, 197, 228, 230; 31, 279, 279 n., 294; of the first man, of Zarathustra, of his pupils, and his followers, worshipped, 23, 200–11; of holy men and heroes worshipped, 23, 211–24, 226–8; assist Aûharmazd against Aharman, 5, 14, 14 n.; 23, 198 sq.; of warriors and the righteous assist the Sky against the Evil Spirit, 5, 25; co-operators with Tîstar, 5, 26, 169; 23, 92, 102, 102 n.; a myriad F. of the righteous protect Sâm, 5, 119; 24, 110; guard the seed of Zaratûst against the demons, 5, 144; arrayed as warriors by Aûharmazd, 5, 167; diligence of F., 5, 170; use of cakes at ceremonies for the F., 5, 315, 315 n.; meat-offerings to F., 5, 336 sq., 337 n.; duty of celebrating the days of the F., 5, 352; 24, 100, 100 n., 264, 298–300; 37, 17–19, 17 n., 422, 429, 441, 477; funeral offerings to the F., 5, 383 sq.; 24, 351; justice, wisdom, and the desire of the Creator are in the spirit which is the pure guardian angel, 18, 12, 12 n.; soul, animating life, preserving guardian spirit, acquiring intellect, &c., 18, 17; ceremony of the F. on the fourth day after death, 18, 60; invoked against fiends, 23, 223 sq.; of holy women worshipped, 23, 224–88; how they manifest themselves, 23, 322; angels and F. are with the righteous soul, 24, 81, 81 n.; Haptôk-ring, with 99,999 guardian spirits of the righteous keeps back the demons, 24, 91 sq.; the stars are the F., created by Aûharmazd, 24, 92; protect the Hôm, 24, 111; the Fravashi one of the appliances of the soul, 24, 145; every object has a Fravashi as co-operator, 24, 156, 156 n.; the departed souls bring with them 9,999 F. of the righteous, 24, 274; do not appear in the Gâthas, 31, 27, 32 n.; of the saints, and of women having many sons worshipped, 31, 197, 204, 209, 215, 219, 224; of the saints invoked and worshipped, 31, 199, 205, 207, 210, 214–16, 220, 222, 225, 256, 259, 273, 275, 278 sq., 286, 296, 311, 319, 327 sq., 345, 351 sq., 358, 362, 374, 380, 382, 385 sq., 389; the F. of the Kine, and of the holy Gaya Maretan, worshipped, 31, 252; have power over nature, 31, 272 sq.; prayers for the approach of the F., 31, 272 sq.; invoked in connexion with the waters, 31, 317 sq.; the Fravashi and soul of Zaratûst, 37, 31; ceremony for the F. for the sake of male offspring, 37, 110; claim ceremonial, not lamentation, 37, 193; the Fravashi of Khûsrôî, 37, 222 sq., 222 n.; the Fravashi of Zarathustra placed into his body by the archangels, 47, 21–9; Zarathustra's Fravashi in the Hôm, 47, 136 sq., 139. *See also* Ancestor worship (*e*), *and* Soul (*c*).

Frâyaodha, son of Karesna, 23, 209.

Frâyat-ratha, n.p., 23, 210.

Frâyazanta, n.p., 23, 212, 225.

Frazîstô, demon, opposes the departed soul, 24, 17.

Frazûsak, n.p., 5, 134; 47, 34, 140.

Frêdûn, Av. Thraêtaona, introduced talismans, 4, 385; fettered and smote Azi Dahâka, 4, 385; 5, 119, 234, 397; 18, 110, 110 n., 201; 37, 177, 214–18; 47, 10, 116, 163 n.; drove the negroes from Iran, 5, 87; genealogy of F. the Âspiyân, descendant of Yim, 5, 132 sq., 132 n.; 37, 27–9, 27 n.; 47, 140; exacted vengeance for Yim, 5, 133; his descendants, 5, 133–5, 137, 145; 24, 52 n.; 47, 10 sq.; the glory of F. settled on the root of a reed, 5, 138; reigned five hundred years, 5, 150; primaeval sovereign, 18, 13, 13 n.; 47, 121, 128; is full of healing, 18, 90; the Fravashi of F. kept away fiends, 18, 104, 104 n.; created immortal, misled by Aharman, 24, 35, 35 n.; his exploits, 24, 61, 61 n.; neglected religion, 24, 102; his war with the Mâzendarân, 37, 216–18; Zoroaster descended

from F., 47, xxi; his accession, 47, xxix; report about Zaratû*s*t explained by Yim and F., 47, 31; monarch of Khvanîras, 47, 34. *See also* Thraêtaona.

Free Will, *see* Will.

Frêh-khûr*d*, n.p., 5, 135.

Freh-mâh, n.p., 5, 146, 146 n.

Freh-Srôsh, n.p., 5, 148.

Frên (Fr*e*ni, Frênô), daughter of Zoroaster, 5, 142; 23, 204 n., 224; 47, 166.

Fr*e*nah, son of Frâyaza*n*ta, 23, 212.

Fr*e*ni, n. of the wives of several heroes, 23, 225. *See also* Frên.

Frênô, mother of Zaratû*s*t's mother, 47, 138, 138 sq. n. *See also* Frên.

Friars, *see* Bhikkhus.

Friend, sin of treachery to, 8, 41; 25, 270; a man's own self is his f., 8, 68; the devotee is alike to f. and foe, 8, 101, 110; he who is a f. of all is released, 8, 246; who is a f., 10 (ii), 42 sq.; etiquette among f., 25, 54 sq.; betrayer of f. excluded from *S*râddha, 25, 105; impurity on the death of f., 25, 182.

Friendship, ode on the value of, 3, 347; six characteristics of f., 8, 183; the highest of all associations, 37, 115, 115 n.

Frîftâr, demon of deceit, 5, 111.

Frînâspa, son of Kaêva, 23, 217.

Frî*s*, n.p., ancestor of Zoroaster, 5, 134; 47, 140.

Frog, *see* Animals (*k*).

Frôhakafra, son of Merezîshmya, 23, 219.

Fruits, three varieties of badara or jujube, 44, 214 sq., 219. *See also* Parables (*b*, *e*, *f*).

Frya, n.p., 23, 211, 215.

Fryân, n.p., 5, 146; sons of F., 18, 256.

Fryâna, n. of a family, 23, 216; a tribe, converted to Zoroastrianism, 31, 133, 141, 141 n.

Fryânaks, praise of the Tûrânian family of the, 37, 280, 280 n.

Fryânô, n.p., 5, 145.

Fshûshô-mãthra, worshipped, 31, 337, 341.

Fû, preserved tablets of the Shû from destruction, 3, 7 sq., 11.

Fû-hsî, or Pâo-hsî, devised the eight trigrams, 3, xvi sq.; 16, 11–14, 22, 27, 32, 48 sq., 382 sq., 385 sq. n., 422 sq. n.; his diagrams, 16, 376 n.; invented nets for hunting and fishing, 16, 383, 386 n.; deified as Thâi Hâo, 27, 250 n.; got the Tâo, and by it wrought wonders, 39, 135, 210, 210 n., 244; a primaeval sovereign, 39, 287; broke up the Primal Unity, 39, 370, 370 n.; F. and Hwang-Tî, 40, 55.

Fû-hsiâ, mourning rites for him, 27, 141.

Fû *Kh*âi, king of Wû, his incursion into *Kh*ăn, 27, 178, 178 n.

Fumigation, of sacrificial vessels, 41, 240; 44, 455 sq.

Fû-mo, his son taught the Tâo, 39, 246 sq. and n.

Funeral rites (mourning, funeral sacrifices, funeral meals).

(*a*) In China.
(*b*) In India.
(*c*) In Iran.

(*a*) In China.

Mourning and f. r. for kings, 3, 41, 113, 113 n., 237–42; 27, 108; periods of mourning, 3, 97, 113, 113 n., 202; 16, 385, 387 n.; 27, 49 sq., 121, 124, 127, 129–34, 132 n., 133 n., 146, 151, 157 sq., 160, 172, 179, 200, 205 sq., 243, 316–21, 330 sq., 341 sq.; 28, 45 sq., 50, 53, 58 sq., 137–40, 150, 154 sq., 157 sq., 160–4, 184, 192, 295, 372 sq., 377, 380–3, 385 sq., 389–94, 467–9; sacrifices by a king for a deceased father, 3, 118 sq.; a king must give attention to the mourning rites, 3, 137; mourning costume, 3, 243, 245; 27, 30, 47 sq., 59 sq., 103, 120, 125 sq., 133, 136, 139, 141–4, 146 sq., 153, 156–60, 158 n., 164 sq., 169, 169 n., 174, 189, 198, 202–8 and Tables, 1–6; 28, 9 sq., 13, 19 sq., 40–59, 64, 75, 262, 272, 378–91, 379 n., 465–70; 39, 335; burying living persons with the dead, 3, 443 sq.; 27, 181–4; rules about mourning and f. r., 3, 487 sq.; 27, 30, 34 sq., 47 sq., 84, 87–9, 93, 102 sq., 223; 28, 26, 40–59, 63 sq., 66, 68–71, 75, 77, 81, 97, 116, 132–68, 173–200, 293–5, 375–94; 40, 30, 219; the superior man in mourning exceeds in sorrow, 16, 344; the introduction of proper burial rites,

16, 385, 387 n.; prominence of mourning rites in the Lî Kî, 27, 14; sending presents for the use of the dead, 27, 34; 28, 140 sq., 144–7, 156 sq., 164, 194 sq.; mourning rites in case of absence from home, 27, 46 sq.; 28, 365–74; dressing and coffining the corpse, 27, 47, 138–42, 144 sq., 149 sq., 152–9, 167 sq., 172 sq., 176 sq., 186 sq., 222 sq.; 28, 375, 377 sq.; (*the proper method of mourning*) *does not come down from heaven, it does not come forth from the earth; it is simply the expression of the human feelings*, 27, 48; 28, 379; white the colour of mourning, 27, 69 n.; mourning and visits of condolence, 27, 87–9, 93, 105, 122–7, 129–208, and Tables 1–6, 331–5, 332 n., 341; interment and accompanying the funeral, 27, 89, 222 sq., 369; the carriage of a deceased ruler following at his interment, 27, 96, 96 sq. n.; rules about burying and raising graves, 27, 121–3, 125 sq., 131 sq., 141, 144 sq., 154–7, 163, 170, 175, 177, 184, 188, 189 n., 192 sq., 202, 369; mourning for a divorced mother, 27, 122; things placed in the grave with the coffin, 27, 124, 124 n., 154; anniversary of death of a parent, 27, 124; 28, 211 sq.; sacrifice at the end of the period of mourning, 27, 129 sq., 160, 160 n.; washing the corpse, 27, 132, 144; sacrifices at f. r., 27, 133, 137, 139, 141 sq., 151, 153, 156 sq., 157 n., 161, 161 n., 168–71, 175, 177 sq., 189 sq., 312 sq., 315–20, 332 sq., 333 n.; 28, 138 sq., 141 sq., 150–3, 150 n., 155 sq., 158–61, 163 sq., 178, 184, 192, 194, 271, 293, 373, 376 sq., 381 sq., 387–9, 467, 469; expense of mourning rites, 27, 145, 222; 28, 348; utensils used for f. r., 27, 148; calling the dead back, 27, 153 n., 157, 167, 340, 369; 28, 49, 132, 136, 143, 174 sq.; 39, 251, 251 n.; filling the mouth of the corpse, 27, 157, 168, 193, 369; 28, 145, 156, 164, 293; origin of f. r., 27, 176–8, 368 sq., 369 n.; dogs and horses buried, 27, 196 sq.; ground set apart for graves, 27, 228; the aged exempt from them, 27, 241 sq., 466; preparations for f. r. made during old age, 27, 241, 465; exemption from military and official duties on account of mourning, 27, 243, 341 sq., 374; 28, 466, 466 n.; mourning and f. r. regulated in winter, 27, 299, 302; mourning for a ruler to whom an heir is born immediately after his death, 27, 311–14; funerals of both parents taking place together, 27, 315 sq.; wife presiding at f. r., 27, 316; mourning in case of death occurring during arrangements for the capping of a son or for marriage, 27, 316 sq., 320–3; two playing the part of an orphan son at f. r., 27, 323 sq.; mourning for a foster-mother, 27, 326 sq. and n.; f. r. for king and queen cause interruption of rites of audience and of sacrifices, 27, 328–31; pronouncing the eulogy, 27, 333 sq., 334 n.; for a ruler dying abroad, 27, 334; sacrifices to one who has died prematurely, 27, 337 sq.; burials stopped by an eclipse of the sun, 27, 338 sq.; for children, 27, 340 sq.; of rulers, 27, 354–9; nourishment of the living, burial of the dead, and service of the spirits, 27, 388 sq., 391; use of f. r. and sacrifices, 27, 397; burials different for different persons, 27, 398; filial piety shown in mourning, 27, 413; 28, 237 sq.; mourning interrupted at border sacrifices, 27, 429; 28, 217; ornaments and wrapping used at f. r., 28, 39; terminal sacrifices and sacrifice of repose, 28, 46–8, 48 n., 50, 53–5, 58; inscription on the coffin, 28, 49; reverence the most important thing in f. r., 28, 153; importance of f. r., 28, 258 sq.; offerings of pork and dried meats, 28, 262; mourning without garb, 28, 279–81; for great officers, and officers, 28, 310; who is to act as presiding mourner, 28, 373, 383; mourning worn for king and queen, 28, 434; when a man dies in battle, they do not employ the usual appendages of plumes, 39, 230 sq.; how a Tâoist performed f. r. for his mother, 39, 253 sq.; statues of men on graves, 40, 101, 101 n.; abstinences and privations in mourning, 40, 140 sq., 141 n.; *K*wang-ʒze on

his burial, 40, 212; Mo-ȝze would have no wearing of mourning and only the simplest burial, 40, 218 sq.

(*b*) In India.

He who knows goes the path of the gods, whether people perform f. r. for him or no, 1, 68; carrying out and burning the dead person, 1, 79; 7, 75; 12, 343; 29, 237–43, 355 sq.; 42, 90, 185, 297; 45, 60; unbelievers deck out the body of the dead with perfumes, flowers, &c., 1, 137, 137 n.; mourners shave their hair and beard, 2, 36; bathing for twelve days after the death of a Guru, 2, 36 sq., 36 n.; performed for a sinner who has done penance, 2, 81, 279; details about f. r., 2, 137 sq.; 7, 75–83; 14, 177 sq., 180–2; 29, 236–46, 355–9; 30, xxviii, 305; 38, 109 n.; 42, 253 sq.; 44, xiv sq., 197–205; performed for those who have performed sacrifices, 2, 159; may be performed by children before initiation, 2, 186 n.; 14, 10; water libations to the dead offered by the relatives, 2, 253 sq.; 7, 75 sq.; 11, xlii sq.; 14, 27–30, 177 sq., 180–2; 25, 179 sq., 183 sq.; 29, 324, 355–7; 33, 373; 49 (i), 90; performed for a (living) relative who is cast off, 2, 278; funeral oblations offered by the heir, 7, 65; 14, 177 sq., 180–2, 226 sq.; 25, 352–5, 364, 364 n., 365 n., 366, 368 n.; 33, 193–5; f. oblation must be offered by a son, even though he inherit no property, 7, 65; plunging into water, after the funeral, and return of the mourners, 7, 75 sq.; 29, 243 sq., 246, 357; walking round the pile from left to right, 7, 75; 11, 129; 17, 299 sq.; rules about impurity, abstinence from certain kinds of food, &c., 7, 76; 14, 27–30, 177 sq., 180–2; 25, 179, 181, 186 sq.; 33, 373; collecting the bones, 7, 76; 25, 178; 29, 245 sq.; 44, 117 n.; consolatory speeches addressed to the mourners, 7, 77–9; the relatives should not weep, but perform the obsequies to the best of their power, 7, 79 sq.; *give rice and a jar with water to the man who has passed into the abode of disembodied spirits*, 7, 80; how outcasts receive offerings of water, 7, 93; suicides do not receive offerings of water, 7, 93; 14, 119; a student breaks his vow by performing f. r. except for parents or teachers, 7, 96; 14, 118, 214; penance for performing f. r. for a stranger, 7, 178 sq.; their effect on the departed, 7, 189; cremation and burial ceremonies among Buddhists, 11, xxxix–xlv, 122–33; 19, 322–4; mourning women, 11, xli; 42, 55, 124 sq., 127, 156, 620, 634 sq., 638; the coffin carried round the grave three times, 11, xlii; treatment of the body of a universal king, and of a Buddha, 11, 92 sq., 125 sq.; funeral feasts, 11, 131–5; enumerated among the public spectacles which the Bhikkhu avoids, 11, 192; to be performed by a widow, 14, 89 sq.; on touching a funeral pile, a Brâhma*n*a must bathe, 14, 171; the dead are taken to the fire, in that fire the Devas offer man, and from that oblation man rises, brilliant in colour, 15, 208; dance and music at Buddha's funeral, and at the erection of *K*aityas over relics, 19, 322 sq., 322 n., 335; Vedic texts required for f.r. may be recited by an uninitiated and a *S*ûdra, 25, 61; children buried, 25, 120, 180; 29, 355; smoke from a burning corpse to be avoided by a Snâtaka, 25, 139; for those fallen in battle, 25, 186, 186 n.; cremation called a burnt-offering, 25, 187, 187 n.; for a faithful wife, 25, 198; sacrificial utensils burnt with the dead body, 29, 241 sq.; 30, 323; first offerings to the deceased, 29, 357–9; f. r. as sorcery practices, 42, 77, 253 sq., 297, 435 sq.; spells put into the funeral fire by enemies, 42, 77; the Kûdî-plant fastened to the dead, 42, 172, 436; the dead body washed, 42, 172, 436; preparation of the burial-ground and tomb, depositing of the charred bones in the sepulchral mound, purification and bath, 44, xlvi, xlix, 421–40; burning a sacrificer in his sacrificial fires, 44, 175; peculiar f. r. of the Eastern and other ungodly people, 44, 423, 430; in non-sunwise direction, 44, 429, 431 n. *See also* Ancestor worship, Fathers (*c*), *and S*râddhas.

(*c*) In Iran.

Disposal of the dead, carrying the corpse to the Dakhma, its exposure to dogs and birds, 4, lxiv, lxxvii sq., lxxvii n., 74 sq., 75 n., 97–9; 5, 247–50, 247 sq. n.; 18, 34–44, 34 n., 35 n., 44 n., 161, 161 n.; 24, 16, 16 n., 329, 335 sq.; 37, 108, 157, 159; mortal sin of burning (cooking) or burying the corpse, 4, lxxv–lxxvii, lxxvii n., lxxxvi sq., 7, 9, 9 n., 103, 113, 113 n., 189, 189 n., 265, 271; 5, 204; 23, 80; 24, 29; 31, 318; 37, 154, 159 sq., 256; tears and wailing for the dead sinful, 4, 6; 24, 29, 29 n., 358 sq.; the Harôyu leave the house where a man died for nine days or a month, 4, 6, 6 n.; tears shed for the dead make the river which prevents the crossing of the *K*inva*t* bridge, 4, 6 n.; let no man by himself carry a corpse, 4, 26 sq., 268; to carry a corpse, before thé Sag-dîd has been performed, is a mortal sin, 4, 27, 27 n.; 37, 153 sq.; punishments for burying the corpse of a dog or of a man, 4, 32 sq.; disposal of the dead during winter when it is not possible to take them to the Dakhma, 4, 49, 53 sq., 96 sq., 96 n.; he who has not, within a year, laid the dead on the Dakhma, incurs the same penalty as for murder, 4, 54; no clothing must be wasted on the dead, 4, 66, 66 n., 81, 102 sq., 102 n.; 5, 340 sq., 341 n.; 24, 272 sq.; 37, 108, 157; the three nights' celebration for the departed, offerings of cakes and clothing, and ceremonial of Srôsh, 4, 89 n.; 5, 315, 315 n., 352, 382–4, 383–5 n.; 18, 58–63, 173, 173 n., 237–42, 237 n., 238 n.; 24, 351 sq.; 37, 183, 183 n., 205, 471, 477; purification of the house, where a man has died, 4, 95 sq. and n.; purification, by the Sag-dîd, of the ways along which the corpse has been carried, 4, 99–102; how long the Upaman (impurity after death) lasts for different relatives, 4, 148–54; sacrifice to the fire, and libations to the good waters for the dead, 4, 149–54, 149 n.; dog made to gaze at the corpse, Sag-dîd, 4, 160 n., 161 n.; 5, 245 sq., 259 sq., 259 n., 261 n., 262 sq., 267, 319, 332; 18, 42, 42 n.; 24, 335 sq.; washing and clothing the dead forbidden, 5, 204; consecrating the sacred cakes in the corpse chamber, 5, 205, 205 n.; ceremonies necessary for the welfare of the departed soul, 5, 294 sq., 295 n.; 18, 237, 237 n., 421, 421 n.; due ceremonies to be performed for the sinner who has been executed, 5, 307 sq., 308 n.; presentation of holy-water to the nearest fire after death, 5, 341 sq.; burying the dead a discomfort to the earth, 5, 361, 361 n.; whose duty it is to order the ceremonies after a death, 18, 184, 184 n., 187; not to be performed for heinous sinners, 18, 219; the Sîrôzah recited in honour of the dead, 23, 2; sacred cake consecrated for the benefit of the soul, 24, 272 sq.; walking after the bier a good work, 24, 273; search must be made where a corpse is supposed to be buried, 24, 294 sq.; to be performed for a child of seven, 24, 310; why meat should not be eaten for three days after a death in the house, 24, 341 sq.; the Avesta must be recited and ceremonial performed for the dead, 24, 358 sq.; burial and cremation of the dead not forbidden in the Mazdaism of Darius, 31, xxxi sq., xxxi n., xxxiii sq.; sheep slaughtered after the 'three nights,' 37, 99, 99 n.; announcing the name of the deceased, 37, 487. *See also* Death (*c*), *and* Impurity.

Future Life.

(*a*) In Zoroastrianism.
(*b*) In Brahmanism.
(*c*) In Buddhism.
(*d*) In Islâm.
(*e*) In Chinese religions.

(*a*) In Zoroastrianism.

Zoroastrian belief in resurrection, f. l., and future rewards and punishments, 4, lxi, lxiv, lxvii; 31, xx; 37, 193; the soul of the wicked driven away from paradise, 4, 51, 51 n.; retribution of sins and good works in hell and heaven, 4, 61 n., 115–19, 133, 209, 218–20, 270 sq.; 18, 23–5, 23 n., 30–8, 44–9, 53–8, 63–74, 76, 121, 137–41, 150 sq.,

274 sq., 421 sq., 426; 24, 29–32, 146, 149, 258–62, 265–7, 327 sq. and n.; 31, 27 sq., 34 sq., 39, 52, 95, 100, 161, 167; 37, 85 sq., 121, 204 sq., 287 sq., 290–2, 294, 296, 300 sq., 308 sq., 316 sq., 349, 391–3, 424, 430, 435, 440, 443, 452, 473 sq.; how the soul of the faithful is received in Paradise, 4, 89, 285, 287, 291, 293, 297; no soul comes to meet the departing soul of the wicked, 4, 158; world of the holy ones, and world of the wicked, 4, 208; 23, 177, 327, 329, 360; spiritual world to be preferred to this world, 4, 294 n., 295; 24, 77, 329; 37, 8 sq.; future existence, or tanû-î pasînŏ, 5, 3; is unlimited and for ever lasting, 5, 5; creatures of Aûharmazd and Aharman in f. l., 5, 5; in it men will be unpersecuted by Aharman, perfect, and immortal, 5, 14; the soul hovers about the body for three days and nights after death, 5, 108 sq., 109 n., 302 sq. and n., 306, 382 n.; 18, 37, 46, 46 n., 232 n.; 24, 16 sq. and n., 22; the rich man in hell, and the poor man in paradise, 5, 197 sq.; hope of f. l., 5, 211; sins and good works of the soul weighed in the scales of Rashnû, 5, 241 sq. n.; 18, 232 n.; 23, 168; 24, 54, 54 n.; recompense of good and bad works in heaven, hell, and among the ever-stationary, 5, 293–5, 294 n.; 24, 38; 37, 22, 32 sq.; retribution of good works in f. l., 5, 310; 24, 313 sq.; 31, 133 sq., 144, 227; 37, 164 sq.; passage of the soul to fire, stars, moon, sun, 5, 341 sq., 342 n.; 24, 352; 37, 465 sq.; how far good works done by others benefit the soul of the departed, 18, 26–9; judgement on the soul after the third night, 18, 27, 27 n., 30 sq., 30 n., 33 sq., 33 n., 54, 61 sq. and n., 66, 71; 47, 56 sq. and n.; angels take account of sin and good works, 18, 32 sq., 33 n.; fate of the soul of the wicked after death, 18, 33 sq., 34 n., 70–4, 76; 23, 318–21, 340–5; 24, 22–5, 51–3, 289; the places to which the righteous and the wicked go, 18, 46 sq., 47 n.; the soul received by its good works in the shape of a maiden, 18, 47 n., 49, 49 n., 54, 117 n., 150, 150 n.; 24, 19 sq., 19 n.; fate of the righteous and wicked souls for the first three nights, 18, 53–6; 37, 251; fate of the soul of the righteous after death, 18, 63–70, 76; 23, 314–18; 24, 16–22; account to be rendered by the soul of good and bad works, 18, 66; 24, 137, 137 n., 258; 24, 279 sq., 297, 299, 319, 326, 352, 361; 37, 33; purification and end of punishment of the wicked souls, 18, 73 sq., 73 n.; Aûharmazd promotes the prosperity of the two existences, 24, 4; angels assisting the departed soul, 24, 17, 17 n., 81; 37, 292; angels and archangels come to meet the righteous soul, 24, 20 sq., 30, 266, 279; the wicked soul received by his wicked deeds in shape of a hideous maiden, 24, 23 sq.; who does not provide for the spiritual existence is the most unforeseeing man, 24, 67; the way to heaven, and the danger of hell, 24, 68; belief in heaven and hell a good work, 24, 75, 83; what is the end of worldly and the end of spiritual existence, 24, 79–81; story of the poor man who is offered one foot of the throne appointed for him in heaven, 24, 226–8; the man who did only one good work, suffering torments in all limbs, but one foot being outside, 24, 261; 37, 469; fate of the souls of children, 24, 310; treasury of good works kept by the angels in the other world, 24, 327, 327 n.; grades of heaven and hell, 24, 344; prayer to Ahura for spiritual rewards, 31, 152, 157 sq., 289 sq.; that better path that leads to the Best World, 31, 345; reward of warriors in f. l., 37, 88; the ever-stationary existence, 37, 199, 199 n.; those who accept Zoroastrianism worthy of supreme heaven, 37, 232, 234; three nights' punishment in hell, 37, 272; four marvels produced by Aûharmazd in yonder world, 37, 281; evidence as to f. l., 37, 284; man prepared for f. l. by fire, 37, 296; a throne in yonder world procured by supporting the good, 37, 321; priests indicate the way to yonder world, 37,

335; arrival of the wicked in the fiend's abode, 37, 375; what every one shall do in the f. l., 37, 393–7; acting for the sake of the other existence, 37, 394; souls go up to the best existence, 47, 147 sq. *See also* Garô-nmânem, Heaven (*g*), *K*invat bridge, Paradise, Resurrection, *and* World (*b*).

(*b*) IN BRAHMANISM.

The path of the Devas or gods that leads to Brahman, and its stations, 1, 68, 72 n., 77, 80, 82 n., 272 n., 274 n., 275; 15, 39, 208; 34, xxix, lxxxii, cvii, 128; 38, 297, 381–9, 233–5, 364–404; 44, 319 sq.; 48, 745 sq.; *this is the path of the Devas, the path that leads to Brahman. Those who proceed on that path, do not return to the life of man*, 1, 68, 80; the two paths, of the gods and of the fathers, to Brahman and to the moon, 1, 77, 82 n.; 8, 80 sq. and n., 314, 314 n.; 12, 267, 267 n., 268 n.; 15, 205, 208 sq.; 44, 237 sq. and n., 434, 434 n.; 48, 742–4, 746 sq., 749, 751, 753, 756; path of the fathers that leads to the moon and rebirth, and its stations, 1, 80 sqq., 272 n., 274 n.; 38, 108, 124, 234, 381, 384; 42, 170; 48, 589, 594; who is admitted to the path of the gods, 1, 80, 82 n.; 34, lxxi sq., cvii, cix; 38, 124, 231–5, 391, 418 sq.; 48, 594, 650–2; a third path or place for small creatures, worms, &c., 1, 82, 272 n.; 15, 209; 38, 123–5; plants and animals destroyed for the purposes of sacrifice, obtain exaltation in f. l., 7, 169, 170; meritorious acts, even without devotion, lead to happy future births, but devotion leads to final emancipation, 8, 72 sq.; as wives attain the worlds of their husbands, a Brâhma*n*a is asked by his wife what goal she will reach, 8, 256, 306–8; what paths are happy? 8, 311; kings who protect good men attain the infinite seat after death, 8, 348; the dutiful Brahma*k*ârin conquers heaven, and reaching the highest seat, does not return to birth, 8, 361; the released Sannyâsin attains to the highest seat, 8, 368; body in f. l., 12, 268 n.; Agni maintains the man who maintained him in this world, in yonder world, 12, 342 sq.; men die again and again in yonder world, 12, 343 sq.; four paths lead to the world of the gods, 14, 258, 261; those who know Brahman, go on the path where there is white, blue, yellow, green, red, 15, 177; results after death of good and bad actions, 25, 29, 31, 33, 40, 57, 72–4, 100–2, 107 sq., 131, 155, 159 sq., 165–7, 174–7, 196 sq., 209 sq., 224, 230, 268, 270–3, 276, 285, 307–9, 327, 332, 386 sq., 416, 429, 431 sq., 435 sq., 437, 477 sq., 487–9; the deathless state or final liberation, 25, 29 sq., 29 n.; bliss in heaven, 25, 79, 89; gross body created for the torments in hell, 25, 487 sq. and n.; Aditi, the life to come, 32, 255 sq.; *man is born into the world made by him*, 41, 181, 181 n.; the Agni*k*it born in yonder world as one made of gold, 43, 295; how the organs of the departed sage pass into the elements, whence he becomes a deity, 43, 333; the highest state attained by knowledge, not by sacrifices, 43, 389 sq.; fate in yonder world according to knowledge, 43, 400; *when he dies, and they place him on the fire, and when he thereupon comes into existence again, he is born a third time*, 44, 23 sq.; by the sacrifice the sacrificer after death receives a new body, 44, 23–7, 24 n., 33, 259, 428, 458 n.; they place him on the balance in yonder world; and whichever of the two will rise that he will follow, 44, 45, 45 n.; punishments awaiting the guilty in f. l. (?), 44, 108–12, 108 n.; the other world gained by imparting sacred knowledge, 44, 132 sq.; whatever food a man consumes in this world, that consumes him in yonder world, 44, 260; there is only one death in yonder world, even hunger, 44, 340; the 'eaters' among the fathers in yonder world destroy the good deeds of him who has no sepulchre prepared for him, 44, 422; undefined is yonder world, 44, 430, 432; the righteous one is yonder world, 44, 457; when yonder world overflows, all the gods

and all the beings subsist thereon, 44, 508. *See also* Emancipation, *and* Heaven (*d*).

(*c*) IN BUDDHISM.

The evil-doer suffers, the virtuous man delights, in f. l, 10 (i), 6 sq., 47 sq.; Upasîva's question and Buddha's answer as to f. l., 10 (ii), 197–9; what sort of deliverance is there for him who is free from desires? 10 (ii), 202 sq.; longing for f. l. blamed, 11, 10, 10 n., 27, 142; 35, 174; 36, 66; Buddha describes to Ânanda the fate after death of several of his followers, 11, 25–7; different views of a f. l., 19, 105; f. l. looked upon as dung by Buddha, 35, 200 sq.; question as to a Tathâgata's life after death not answered by Buddha, 35, 206; Nirvâ*n*a allays the craving after f. l., 36, 190; the Bhikkhu shall resolve never to enter upon any f. l., 36, 285; *seek not rebirths afar in future states. Pray, what could heaven itself advantage you! Now, in this present world, and in the state in which you find yourselves, be conquerors!* 36, 328; uncertainty regarding f. l., 49 (i), 99; reception of the Buddhist devotee after death in the land of bliss, 49 (ii), 189–99.

(*d*) IN ISLÂM.

Bridge over hell, Es Sirâ*t*, and partition wall, El Aarâf, 4, 219 n.; 6, lxix, 143; 9, 32 n.; Arabian belief in f. l., 6, xiv; happiness in paradise for the believers and righteous, everlasting torments in hell fire for the unbelievers and wicked, 6, xxv, lxi, 4, 11, 33, 47 sq., 50, 62, 69–71, 74, 89, 109, 115, 141–4, 196; 9, 17 sq., 26, 31 sq., 39 sq., *57 sq.*, 62 sq., 84 sq., 94, *118 sq.*, 123, 126, 132, *136 sq.*, 157 sq., *160 sq.*, *166*, *169 sq.*, *180*, 183–5, 191, 194, 201 sq., 205, 207, *216 sq.*, *220*, 228, *229 sq.*, 233 sq., *249*, *260–9*, 273, 276 sq., *287*, 297, 309 sq., *312–17*, 319, *324 sq.*, 327, 334, 338; paradise promised to those fallen in war, 6, xxxvi, xlii, 82 sq.; 9, 282; eschatology, 6, lxix–lxxi; *fear the day wherein ye shall return to God; then shall each soul be paid what it has earned, and they shall not be wronged*, 6, 44; those who are killed in God's way, are assembled to God, 6, 65, 70; paradise and pure wives for believers, 6, 80; tortures of hell described, 6, 80; lasting woe in the fire for disbelievers, 6, 102; the next world preferable to this world, 6, 118 sq., 178, 235, 253; 9, 3, 124, 207, 209, 213, 329; return to God, 6, 137; promise of paradise for the believer, 6, 183, 185, 187, *192 sq.*, 196, 207, 217, *235*, 237, 241, *247*, *253*, 261; 9, 290 sq.; misbelievers love this world's life better than the next, 6, 238, 262; disbelief in f. l. rebuked, punishment for it, 6, 252, 256; 9, 2, 99 sq., 126, 150 sq., 252 sq.; all souls pass through hell, but the good will not be harmed, 9, 32, 32 n.; *verily, the life of this world is but a provision, but, verily, the hereafter, that is the abode of stability*, 9, 194. *See also* Paradise, *and* Resurrection.

(*e*) IN CHINESE RELIGIONS.

King 'went on high and died,' 3, 45, 45 n.; 27, 108, 108 n.; 'his recently ascended majesty' = the deceased king, 3, 244; ancestor worship and belief in f. l., 3, 301; King Wăn is on high and ascends and descends on the left and the right of God, 3, 377 sq., 378 n.; the three sovereigns Thâi, *K*î, Wăn were in heaven, when Wû became their successor, 3, 393; a lady comforts her lover that when dead they will share the same grave, 3, 440; no reference to f. l. in a widow's expression of grief at the death of her husband, 3, 441; man when dead is in the ghostly state, 28, 203 sq.; descriptions of purgatory in modern manifestoes of Tâoism, 39, xii, 43 sq.; retribution in this life, not in f. l., 39, 39; 40, 235 sq., 244, 244 n.; the happiness of the state after death, 39, 149; 40, 6 sq.

See also Death (*b*), Hell, Immortality, Moon (*d*), Nirvâ*n*a, *and* Soul (*e*).

Fû Yüeh, *see* Yüeh.

G

***G*âbâla**, *see* Satyakâma *G.*, *and* Mahâ*s*âla *G.*

*G*abâlâ, mother of Satyakâma, 1, 60.
*G*âbâlas, how they speak of the highest Lord, 34, 152 sq.; 38, 338; their text on the fourth stage of life, 38, 295, 297, 302 sq.
*G*âbâla-upanishad, quoted, 38, 423; 48, 696; *see* *G*âbâlas.
*G*âbâlâyana, n. of a teacher, 15, 186.
Gabriel, the archangel, 6, lxix; people of Antioch destroyed by a shout from G., 6, cv; 9, 164, 164 n.; 'the Holy Spirit,' the instrument of the revelation, 6, cxiv n., 261; 9, 10 n., 32 n., 98, 210, 308 n.; Mohammed's vision of G. on Mount Hirâ, 6, cxv; 9, 322; revealed the Qur'ân, 6, 13, 13 n.; causes Pharaoh to be a sign to the Israelites, 6, 203 n.; warns Joseph, 6, 221 n.; taught Mohammed, 9, 251 n.; backs him up who repents, 9, 291; announces the birth of Jesus from the Holy Spirit, 24, 229 sq.
Gada, and Nadi, brothers of Kâ*s*yapa, converted by Buddha, 19, 185–7.
Gadgadasvara: visit of the remarkable Bodhisattva G. to the Saha-world, 21, xxxi, 393–405; pays homage to a Buddha by making music, 21, 399 sq.; can assume any shape whatever in order to preach the Lotus of the True Law just as wanted, 21, 400–3.
Gâdhi, Vi*s*vâmitra, son of, 25, 222, 222 n.
Gadhwithw, n. of a demon, 5, 132.
Gadûg, a term used for evil beings, 24, 128, 128 n.
Gaêvani, son of Vohu-nemah, 23, 213.
Ga*g*asa, i. e. Hastinâpura, the capital of the Pâ*nd*avas, 8, 394, 394 n.
*G*agatî, *see* Metres.
Gagga, a mad Bhikkhu, 13, 279; 20, 18 sqq.
*G*aghrûdh, the holy maid, 23, 225.
*G*âg*r*ivi, the sage Vigilant, a deity or a *R*ishi, 42, 54, 60, 571.
Gâhânbârs, *see* Festivals.
Gahapati, *see* G*r*ihapati.
Gaha*tth*a, Pali, t. t., Sk. G*r*ihastha, a householder, 10 (ii), x.
*G*ahi: the courtesan an incarnation of the demon *G*., 4, 205, 205 n.; kills the holy bull, 4, 231, 231 n.; the evil done by *G*., the demon, 4, 234; 23, 226; makes one pine, 23, 44–7. *See also* *G*aîni.
Gâhs, the five periods of the day, 5, 13 sq. and n., 94, 94 n., 127 n., 297 sq. n., 371, 371 n.; explanation of the G., as places in heaven, 24, 263, 263 n.; prayers recited at the G., translated, 31, 377–88.
*G*aigîshavya, a *R*ishi, obtained deliverance, 19, 139; 49 (i), 130.
*G*aimini maintains that work is indispensable to knowledge, 1, 315; worshipped at the Tarpa*n*a, 29, 122, 149, 220; quoted by Nârada, 33, 265; the author of the Pûrva-Mîmâ*m*sâ-sûtras, quoted in the Vedânta-sûtras, 34, xi, xix, lxv, lxxxii–lxxxiv, xc sq., 149–52, 216 sq., 272–4; 38, 180–2, 285–8, 295–7, 317 sq., 360, 392–402, 408 sq., 412; 48, 292, 294, 335, 382 sq., 626, 705 sq., 750, 752, 759 sq., 763; the *S*ârîraka-doctrine connected with *G*.'s doctrine, 48, 5; his views opposed to Bâdarâya*n*a's, 48, 686 sq., 694.
*G*aimini-G*r*ihyasûtra quoted, 2, 190 n.
*G*aimini - pûrvamîmâ*m*sâ - sûtra, its subject is dharma, 34, 26; quoted, 38, 423 sq.; 48, 778. *See also* Pûrva-Mîmâ*m*sâ-sûtra.
*G*aina church, its extent at the time of Mahâvîra's death, 22, 267 sq.; dates relating to its history, 22, 270; councils and their dates, 22, 270 n.; its extent under the *G*ina Pâr*s*va, 22, 274; its extent under Arish*t*anemi, 22, 278; its extent in the period of the Arhat *R*ishabha, 22, 284; called the 'Gotra where the Vow of Silence is practised,' 45, 321.
*G*aina monks (Nirgrantha *S*rama*n*as, Niga*nth*a Sama*n*as), must walk carefully so as not to kill living beings, 8, 364 n.; their conduct contrasted with that of Buddha, 17, 108–17, 125; *G*. m. or Nirgranthas, 21, 263; follow the precepts of the Arhat (*G*ina), 21, 265, 265 n.; the ideal of the good monk who has given up all attachments, 22, 44, 55–8, 60 sq., 66 sq., 211–13; 45,

318 sq., 377–81; rules of conduct for them, 22, 47–9; 45, 31–5, 69–73, 109–11, 123, 129–36, 203–6, 246–8, 296 sq., 306–15, 333 sq., 351–5, 364 sq., 404 sq., 411; how they should behave towards women, 22, 48; 45, 271–8; their nakedness, 22, 56, 57 n., 68, 69, 73, 79, 259 sq.; 45, xxii, 9, 11, 13, 22, 106, 296, 304, 380; how they should behave towards heretics and faithless householders, 22, 62–5; their dwelling-places, 22, 64, 82; 45, 12; rules with regard to their clothing and outfit, 22, 67 sq., 67 n., 69, 71, 73, 79; it is better for a monk to commit suicide than breaking the vow, 22, 68 sq., 70, 70 n.; rules for G. m. in sickness, 22, 69 sq., 71 sq.; 45, 266–8; rules about eating for G. m., 22, 71, 204; 45, 5 sq., 75 sq., 79 sq., 91, 185 sq., 204 sq., 243 sq., 246 sq., 255, 258, 296, 303 sq., 306 sqq., 312, 353 sq., 379, 416; suicide by starvation recommended to them, 22, 72 sq.; rules for G. m. following the model life of Mahâvîra, 22, 79–87; grades of G. m.: teacher, sub-teacher, &c., 22, 113; abstain from bathing, 22, 124; 45, 295 sq.; the vow of a monk: *I shall become a Sramana who owns no house, no property, no sons, no cattle, who eats what others give him; I shall commit no sinful action; Master, I renounce to accept anything that has not been given*, 22, 171; the five great vows of G. m., 22, 202–10; 45, 89; regulation of their possessions, 22, 205–7; are spiritual descendants of Sudharman, 22, 287; disciplinary rules for G. m., especially pupils, 45, 1–8; rules about begging food, for G. m., 45, 5 sq., 13, 25 sqq., 34, 71 sq., 131–4 and n., 146 sq., 205; twenty-two troubles (parîsaha) which they must know and vanquish, 45, 8–15; outward tokens will not save a sinful monk, 45, 22 sq., 25 sq., 104–6, 123; should not live by fortune-telling, &c., 45, 34, 70 sq., 70 n., 80; Nami contrasts the happiness of m. who have retired from the world, with the anxieties of household life, 45, 37–40; on the virtues and superiority of a very learned monk, 45, 46–9; the superiority of G. m. to Brâhma*n*as demonstrated, 45, 50–6; *you may as well dig rocks with your nails, or eat iron with your teeth, or kick fire with your feet, as treat contemptuously a monk... for in his wrath he might reduce the world to ashes*, 45, 53 sq.; the 'sacrifice' of a monk described, 45, 55 sq.; should abstain from practising medical art, 45, 71; ten conditions for the realization of celibacy, 45, 73–7; what they should avoid, 45, 77–80, 301–6; G. m. might by the power of his wrath reduce millions of men to ashes, 45, 81; their duties and vows, 45, 91 sq., 106; pluck out their hair, 45, 92, 115, 262; imitate the life of wild animals, getting food anywhere and not caring about medicine in sickness, 45, 97 sq.; by becoming a true monk, one becomes a protector of one's self and of others, 45, 100–7; their use of clothes according to Pâr*s*va and Mahâvîra, 45, xxx, 121, 123; rules for easing nature, 45, 134 sq.; regulations for the every day life of monks during every part of the day and night, 45, 142–9; by six kinds of abstinence they destroy Karman, 45, 174; different kinds of collecting alms, 45, 177 sq. and n.; duties of upâsakas and bhikshus, 45, 182; should not mix with heretics, 45, 246; the holy life of a monk the only road to destruction of Karman, 45, 249–61; relations try to tempt the monk back to household life, 45, 252, 263 sq.; troubles, temptations, and difficulties with which a monk has to battle, 45, 261–71; some are unable to preserve chastity, 45, 262; how they should exert themselves for the annihilation of Karman and for liberation, 45, 298–301; the conceited monk will not obtain liberation, but only the monk who is free from all pride, 45, 320–3; duties of teachers and pupils, 45, 324–8; *S*rama*n*as who are materialists, 45, 341 sq.; meditations on life and the true law which lead men to turn monks, 45, 347–51; story of a monk who, by magic arts,

carries off all women, and is killed by the king, 45, 383 n.; a true monk is always alone, even when preaching in a crowd of thousands, 45, 410; called Kumâraputras, 45, 421; should not eat with householders, 45, 428. *See also* Preaching, *and* Women (*d*).

*G*aina **monks and nuns,** rules for them about the begging of food, clothes, &c., 22, 88–119, 157–70, 297–303; how they should rub themselves clean, 22, 100; rules about lodging-places, 22, 120–35, 171–7, 309 sq.; rules for them about wandering from village to village, 22, 136–48; how they should behave on board of a boat, 22, 139–42; modes of speech enjoined for them, 22, 149–56; regulations as to their taking possession of anything, 22, 171–7; rules for them when going to perform religious postures or choosing a place for study, 22, 178–80; rules for them about easing nature, 22, 180–3, 308; they should not go to hear music or to witness any entertainment, 22, 183–6; should neither be pleased with nor prohibit householders who rub or wipe the mendicant's feet or do anything for the sake of their health, 22, 186–8; rules for them to be followed during the Pa*gg*usan, 22, 296–311; rules for them in sickness, 22, 297 sq., 306 sq.; rules about eating, 22, 297–303; rules about clothes, 22, 302; how the monks and nuns should wear their hair, 22, 308.

*G*aina **nuns,** thirty-six thousand, with *K*andanâ at their head, 22, 267; Queen Kamalâvatî determines to become a nun, 45, 67; cut off their hair, 45, 116, 116 n.; women pretend to become nuns or lay-disciples in order to tempt monks, 45, 274.

*G*aina **religion** (*G*aina doctrines, *G*ainism), relation of Anugîtâ to it, 8, 224 sq.; doctrines taken from Brahmanism, 8, 225; political reasons for its success, 22, xiii sq.; information about it collected from Buddhist writings, 22, xvi sq.; 45, xv–xxiii; its origin independent of Buddhism, 22, xviii–xxxv; refutation of its doctrines, 34, li, 428–34; recent literature on it, 45, xiii sq.; the Saptabhaṅgînaya as a weapon against Agnosticism, 45, xxvii sq.; the six Lê*s*yâs (subtile bodies), and Gosâla's division of mankind into six classes, 45, xxx, 56 n.; marks of its antiquity, 45, xxxiii sq., xxxvi sq.; its relation to Vedânta, Sâṅkhya, and Vai*s*eshika, 45, xxxiii–xxxviii; the Samitis, and Guptis, and Sa*m*varas, 45, 50, 52, 55, 55 n., 73 sq., 73 n., 98, 104 sq., 105 n., 107, 129–36, 174, 200, 248, 325, 355 n., 377; doctrines expounded and illustrated by parables, 45, 123–9; the vows called yamas, 45, 136, 136 n.; its fundamental principles expounded, 45, 152–7; Samitis, Guptis, and religious exercise generally produce faith, 45, 156; list of articles of *G*. faith following the number of their subdivisions, 45, 180–4; its true Kriyâvâda doctrine, 45, 318 sq., 319 n.; the syâdvâda argumentation, 45, 327, 327 n., 405 sq. n.; lay devotees well grounded in the knowledge of the Âsravas, Sa*m*vara, realization and annihilation of Karman, bondage and final liberation, 45, 382; what a *G*aina should maintain and what he should not maintain, if he is to avoid error in points of doctrine, 45, 405–9; doctrines which a monk should teach, 45, 410. *See also* Morality (*b*), *and* Philosophy.

*G*ainas, their chronology, and the death of Buddha, 10 (i), xli sq.; the two sects of the *G*., *S*vetambaras and Digambaras, 10 (i), 39 n.; 45, xxi sq., xxxii n., 119 n.; their relation to the Âgîvikas (A*k*elakas), 13, 90 sq.; 45, xxix–xxxii; trustworthiness of their traditions, 22, xxxv–xlvii; seven sects of the *S*vetâmbaras, 22, xxxvi; Digambaras stigmatized as heretics by the *S*vetâmbaras, 22, xxxvi; their crude system of astronomy, 22, xl; the Aṅgas collected by the Saṅgha of Pâ*t*aliputra formed the canon of the *S*vetâmbaras only, 22, xliii; the three vows of the *G*., 22, 63 n.; believe in the co-existence of con-

trary qualities in one and the same thing, 22, 63 n.; their five great vows, 22, 202–10; 45, 98, 109, 355 n.; Digambaras referred to as atheists, 24, 146 n.; acknowledge seven, two, or five categories, 34, 428 sq., 430; their belief in souls in water, 36, 85, 85 n.; their views about the soul, 38, 104; 45, xix; Buddhist doctrines misrepresented by *G*., 45, xviii; existed before Mahâvîra, and were an important sect at the time when Buddhism rose, 45, xxii sq.; doctrines which they owe to the 'heretics,' 45, xxvii–xxix; their strange hagiology, 45, xxxii; the Trairâ*s*ikas, or *G*aina followers of the Vai*s*eshikas, their views refuted, 45, 245, 245 n.; 'mixed state,' i.e. the life of laymen who are followers of the *G*. without abstaining from all sins, 45, 381–4; vows and fasts kept by *G*. laymen, 45, 383 sq.; by undertaking particular vows *G*. householders gradually conform to the rules of monastic state, 45, 423–32; some householders do not strictly observe the Pôsaha fast, but keep other monastic vows, 45, 429, 431; their theory about the origin of the world, and refutation of it, 48, 516–20.

*G*aina **Sûtras**, age of the extant literature, redaction of the Siddhânta, 22, xxxv, xxxvii–xlvii; 45, xl; their language, 22, xl sq.; 45, 1 n., 2 n., 6 n., 22 n., 114 n., 249 n.; first book of the Â*k*ârâṅga Sûtra and that of the Sûtrak*ri*tâṅga Sûtra, among the most ancient parts of the canon, 22, xli; metres employed in them, 22, xli sq.; the Pûrvas incorporated in the 12th Aṅga, the D*ri*sh*t*ivâda, 22, xliv sqq.; tradition about the fourteen Pûrvas existing besides the Aṅgas, 22, xliv sqq.; the Â*k*ârâṅga Sûtra, its two books different in style and manner, and of different date, 22, xlvii sq.; the Â*k*ârâṅga Sûtra, its translation, 22, xlviii–li, 1–213; commentaries on the Â*k*ârâṅga Sûtra, 22, li; the Kalpa Sûtra, its different parts, its translation, 22, li–liii, 215–311; the four Vedas and esp. Atharva-veda in *G*. S., 42, lvi; the Sûtrak*ri*tâṅga Sûtra, 45, xxxviii–xli, 233–435; the Uttarâdhyayana Sûtra, 45, xxxviii–xli, 1–232; Sudharman knew the twelve Aṅgas, 45, 120; the *G*. creed set forth in the twelve Aṅgas, 45, 130; faith created by study of Sûtras, the eleven Aṅgas, Prakîr*n*as, and D*ri*sh*t*ivâda, 45, 155; sixteen Gâthâs to be studied, 45, 182, 182 n.; a monk is to study the twenty-three lectures of the Sûtrak*ri*tâṅga, 45, 183; twenty-six chapters of the Da*s*â*s*rutaskandha, B*ri*hat Kalpa, and Vyavahâra Sûtras, and twenty-eight lectures of the Â*k*ârâṅga Sûtra, 45, 183, 183 n.; Uttarâdhyayana Sûtra, its title, 45, 232 n.; the Ga*n*adharas of Mahâvîra knew the twelve Aṅgas, the fourteen Pûrvas, and the whole Siddhânta of the Ga*n*ins, 22, 287; heretics declare the twelve Aṅgas, &c., to be wrong, 45, 345. *See also* Sacred Books.

*G*aîni (*G*ainis), the same as the female demon *G*ahi, 4, 90 n.; 31, 192 n.; make diseases grow stronger, 4, 90, 90 n.; spell against them, 4, 229, 229 n., 235, 241; 31, 242 sq.; defeated by Zarathu*s*tra, 23, 305. *See also G*ahi.

*G*ainism, *see G*aina religion.

*G*aivali, *see* Pravâha*n*a *G*.

*G*aivantâyana, n. of a teacher, 15, 186 n.

Gâk, n.p., 5, 146.

Ga*kk*ha, *G*aina t.t. = Ga*n*a, 22, 288 n.

*G*aladharagar*g*itaghoshasusvaranakshatrarâ*g*asaṅkusumitâbhi*gñ*a, n. of a Tathâgata, 21, 419–28.

*G*âlandharâya*n*a, the gotra of Devânandâ, 22, 190 sq., 218 sq., 223, 226.

Gâlava, n. of a teacher, 1, 267; 15, 119, 187.

*G*aleniprabha, n. of a Tathâgata, 49 (ii), 100.

*G*âli, son of Vessantara, 35, 174; 36, 115, 131.

*G*amadagni, father of Râma, 8, 294 sq., 300; special rites of the descendants of *G*., 12, 192 n.; 29, 168, 175 n., 390; one of the seven *Ri*shis, 15, 106; his threefold age, 29, 55; 30, 62, 162; worshipped at the Tarpa*n*a, 29, 122; 30, 244;

flowers brought by G. for Faith, 29, 316; 30, 168; employed charms, 42, 23 sq., 319; dug up a plant, to promote the growth of his daughter's hair, 42, 31, 537; the *Ri*shi G. is the eye, 43, 9; *Ri*shi of âprî-verses, 44, 302; is Pragâpati, 44, 302.

Gâmadagnyas, descendants of Gamadagni, *see* Gamadagni.

Gâmâspa, Gâmâsp, one of the first converts of Zoroaster, 4, 359; 23, 331; 31, 250; 37, 230; 47, 125; meat-offering to the Fravashi of G., 5, 336, 336 n.; of the Hvôvas, the high-priest, 18, 149, 149 n.; 23, 207 sq., 208 n.; his care for the sacred fire, 18, 380; sacrifices to Anâhita, 23, 70, 70 n.; the younger, 23, 219; prime minister of Vîstâspa, 23, 324–6, 329; champion of Zoroastrianism, 31, 76, 76 n., 166, 166 n.; the Hvôgva, gained the kingdom of Ahura, 31, 185 sq.; habits of Frashôstar and G., 37, 130, 130 n.; praise of G., 37, 290, 297; Pôrûkâst his wife, 37, 299 sq., 299 n.; the learned, 37, 397; words of G. in the Mãthra, 37, 406; made omniscient, 47, xxiii; had the Avesta written on ox-hides, 47, xxx, 127; passes away, 47, xxx; priest of priests after Zoroaster, 47, 165.

Gambha, n. of an Asura, 42, 572.

Gambling, and betting, law about, 2, 162; 25, lxx sq., lxxx, cix, 254, 282, 380 sq.; 33, 45, 212–14, 271, 329, 385 sq.; forbidden for Brahmakârins and Snâtakas, 2, 188; 7, 227; 25, 140; house to be built so that it should be free from g., 2, 212; gambler and keeper of g.-house excluded from *S*râddhas, 2, 258; 25, 103, 105, 105 n.; forbidden, 6, 32, 32 n., 110; success in g., acquired by a *S*râddha, 7, 245; of cheats K*ri*sh*n*a is the game of dice, 8, 91; belongs to the quality of passion, 8, 324; a cause of loss, 10 (ii), 18; a game of dice played by the priests at the laying down of the Sabhya fire, 12, 302 n.; a sin, 14, 220; a vice of kings, 25, 223; gamblers are 'open rogues,' 'thorns' to be removed by the king, 25, 387, 494; 33, 223, 360 sq.; ceremony against the dog-demon performed in the g.-hall, 30, 219, 287; allowed by Nârada, 33, xv; property acquired by g. is 'black wealth,' 33, 54; gamblers not to be witnesses, 33, 83, 87, 303; game of dice and ceremonies on the gaming-ground at the king's consecration, 41, 63 sq., 106–8, 106 sq. n., 109 n., 111 sq.; the gaming-board is fire, and the dice its coals, 41, 64, 112; prayers and rites for success in g., 42, 69, 149–51, 412 sq., 548 sq.; the brilliancy of the dice, 42, 116; meat, liquor, and dice, 42, 144, 493; dice used for magic cures, 42, 470; a gambler sacrificed to dice at the Purushamedha, 44, 414, 416. *See also* Parables (*f*).

Gambû, disciple of Sambhûtavigaya, 22, 289; of the Gautama gotra, a Sthavira, 22, 295, 295 n.

Gambudîpa, or India, so called after the Gambu tree, 13, 127.

Gambu-gâma, Buddha at, 11, 66.

Gambuka, the naked ascetic, 36, 249.

Gâmbûnada-prabhâsa: Mahâ-Kâtyâyana is to be the future Buddha G., 21, 148 sq.

Gambûnâman, n. of a Sthavira, 22, 287.

Gambûsvâmin, disciple of Sudharman, 22, 1.

Games: list of g. and amusements forbidden to Bhikkhus, 11, 193; 17, 348 sq.; the game of pitch-pot, 27, 50 sq.; 28, 397–401; monks should not play ash*t*âpada (chess?), 45, 303, 303 n. *See also* Hunting.

Gâmi, the goddess of maternity, 42, 323, 323 n.

Gamshê*d*, i.e. Yima, 4, 10.

Ga*n*a: meaning of the terms G., Kula, and *S*âkhâ, 22, 288 n.; the head or founder of a G., one of the superiors of Gaina monks, 22, 306.

Gâna, *see* Vri*s*a G.

Ganadatta, disciple of Bhadrabâhu, 22, 289.

Ga*n*adhara, Gaina t.t. = chief disciple, 22, 1 n., 306; Ga*n*as and G. of Pâr*s*va, 22, 273 sq.; Arish*t*anemi had eighteen G., 22, 278; *Ri*shabha had eighty-four G., 22, 284; Mahâvîra had nine Ga*n*as and eleven G., 22, 286 sq.; the G. and their dis-

ciples do as Mahâvîra did, 22, 296; Garga was a Sthavira and G., 45, 149, 149 n.

*G*anaka, king of Videha, and Yâg*ñ*avalkya, 1, lxxiv sq., 300; 8, 304 n.; 12, xxxi, xlii sq.; 15, 152–77, 161 n.; 44, 46, 112–15; by action alone did *G.* work perfection, 8, 54; 'turned the wheel,' 8, 215; Dharma appears before *G.* disguised as a Brâhma*n*a, 8, 224; wants to banish a Brâhma*n*a from 'his dominions,' but finds that he must call all or nothing his own, 8, 303–6, 304 sq. n.; father of Sîtâ, wife of Râma, 12, xliii; *G.* and Aupagandhani, 14, 229, 229 n.; a wise and liberal king, 15, 100, 100 n.; patron of learned Brâhma*n*as, 15, 121; on the knowledge of the Gâyatrî, 15, 199; without a teacher acquired power of abstraction, 19, 11; reached final bliss, 19, 139; 49 (i), 95, 130; Sulabhâ entered into his body to carry on discussion with him, 38, 237; the Mitravindâ sacrifice went away to *G.*, 44, 66; became a Brahman, 44, 115; performed many sacrifices with numerous gifts to the priests, 44, 115; 48, 688; instructed the twice-born in the rules of Yoga, 49 (i), 9.

*G*ânaki **Ayasthû*n*a**, pupil of *K*ûla Bhâgavitti, 15, 214; teaches the priest *S*aulvâyana, 44, 61.

Ganâ Mainyô = Zanâ Mainyô = Ahriman, 4, 373.

*G*anameg*a*ya, son of Parikshit, Mahâbhârata related to him, 8, 229; Tura Kâvasheya, his high priest, 12, xxxii; they pour out cups full of fiery liquor in the palace of *G.*, 44, 95; Indrota performed the horse-sacrifice for him, 44, 396.

*G*ânanti, satiated at the Tarpa*n*a, 29, 220.

*G*anârdana, n. of K*r*ish*n*a or Vish*n*u, 7, 5; 8, 41 sq., 52, 88, 99, 233, 393. *See* Vish*n*u.

Ga*n*as (troops of gods), the Maruts the princes among, 8, 346; are liable to destruction, 15, 289.

Ga*n*as and Ga*n*adharas of *G*ainas, 22, 273 sq., 278, 284, 286 sq.

*G*ana **Sârkarâkshya**, n.p., 1, 84, 87; 43, 393, 396.

*G*âna*s*ruti **Pautrâya*n*a**, the pious giver, called a *S*ûdra by Raikva, 1, 55–8; 34, 223–7; 38, 305 sq.; 48, 338–42.

Ga*n*d*a*mba tree, 36, 247.

Gandarep(ô), *see* Ga*n*darewa.

Ga*n*darewa (Gandarep), the golden-heeled, slain by Keresâsp, 18, 370 sq., 374–6, 381; 23, 63, 63 n., 295; 24, 63; 37, 198, 198 n.; 47, 12; born from Yim with a witch, 18, 419; Parsha*n*ta, son of G., 23, 217; lives beneath the waters, is the son of Ahura, 23, 255 sq., 256 n.; 24, 63.

Gandha, a Yaksha, who worships Buddha, 49 (i), 170.

Gandhabbas, *see* Gandharvas.

Gandhahastin, n. of a Bodhisattva, 49 (ii), 90.

Gandhaprabhâsa, n. of a Tathâgata, 49 (ii), 100.

Gandhâra(s), n. of a country and people, 1, 105 sq., 105 n.; 11, 135; a king of G., converted by Buddha, 19, 242.

Gândhâras, the art of, an occult science, 45, 366.

Gandhâris, takman (fever) delivered over to the G., 42, 2, 446.

Gandharva (sing.): the G. Vi*s*vâvasu, 12, 90, 90 n.; 26, 52; 43, xiv; women belong to him, 14, 133; 33, 171 n.; gave women their melodious voice, 14, 233; the G. Vi*s*vâvasu presides over procreation, 15, 220; 29, 45; Avalokite*s*vara assumes the shape of a G., 21, 411; Vena, a G. representing the rainbow, 26, 281 n.; worshipped and invoked at the wedding, 29, 32, 289; 30, 84; Soma gave the bride to G., 29, 278 sq.; 30, 44, 190; 42, 254, 323; Agni is the G., his Apsaras are the herbs, 30, 146 n.; the concord of which the G. is possessed, 30, 199; colloquy of the G. possessing a woman, and Yâg*ñ*avalkya, 15, 127, 132; 34, cv, 219; the heavenly, thought-cleansing G., 41, 5; the heavenly G. is yonder sun, 41, 195; a plant for promoting virility dug up by the G. for Varu*n*a, 42, 31, 370.

Gandharvas (plur.): gods, G., or Manes do not teach what is virtue and what is sin, 2, 72; created,

7, 4; 8, 387; 25, 15; world or worlds of G., 7, 109, 271; 15, 130 sq., 172, 176; marriage rites of the G., 7, 109; 25, 79–82; 29, 166; *K*itraratha, chief among G., 8, 89; alarmed at the greatness of K*ri*sh*n*a, 8, 94; achieved their beauty by living as Brahma*k*ârins, 8, 178; Vish*n*u is the lord of G., snakes, Rakshas, &c., 8, 347; do not know the path of the gods, 10 (i), 95; gods and Gandhabbas (Pali for G.), 10 (ii), 115; the husbands of the Apsaras, 12, 269 n.; 42, 33 sq.; Brahman seen in the world of G., as in the water, 15, 22; the bliss of the human and the divine G., 15, 59 sq., 61 sq. n.; carried by a stallion, 15, 74; worshipped at the Tarpa*n*a, 29, 121, 219; are fond of women, females possessed by them, 15, 127, 132; 26, 53, 233 sq.; 34, cv; 42, 34; heavenly musicians, 19, 25, 54; 22, 237; Gandhabbas dwell in the ocean, 20, 302, 305; four Gandharvakâyikas with many hundred thousand G. in their suite, 21, 5; names of G., 25, 112; compelled by fear to yield enjoyments, 25, 219; produced by activity, 25, 494; seized the bull (Soma?), 26, xiv; stole the Soma, 26, 52–4, 58; are Soma-wardens, 26, 71 n., 72, 72 n., 150–2, 233 sq., 364 sq.; water oblation to the G., 29, 325; the mind, the splendour that dwells with the G., 30, 159, 166; gods and G. read the original code of Manu, 33, 3; among the pa*ñk*aganâ*h*, 34, 262; seven and twenty G., 41, 19 sq. and note; snatch away oblations, 42, 33 sq., 410 sq.; know healing plants, 42, 43; a talisman against the G., 42, 80; the G. and Ka*s*yapas lead forth, 42, 210; live on the shores of waters, 42, 410; Agni, Sûrya, Moon, Wind, Sacrifice, Mind, as G., 43, 231–3; serve the Person in the eye under the name of 'form,' 43, 373; the racer (Vâgin) carries the G., 43, 401; find fault with the sacrifice of the *Ri*shis, 44, 29 sq.; Yavamân, the winnowing-basket, Uddâlavân, husbandry, and Antarvân, grain, being names of G., 44, 30; carry off the lambs of Urva*s*î, 44, 69; produce a flash of lightning, 44, 70; make Purûravas one of themselves, 44, 73 sq.; are the people of King Varu*n*a, 44, 365; the pious monk will be honoured by gods, G., and men, 45, 8; souls of G., 48, 198; beings born as G. on account of religious merit, 48, 238; Fata Morgana, a town of the G., 48, 449; gods and G., 49 (i), 197; the perfumes of the Gandharvarâ*g*a, 49 (ii), 41;—*G. and Apsaras*, 29, 229; 42, 160, 370, 534; charms to drive out Apsaras and G., 42, 33, 408 sq.; G. and Apsaras invoked against enemies in battle, 42, 119; G. and Apsaras, serpents, and other evil spirits, 42, 125 sq.; G. and Apsaras have partaken of the fragrance of the earth, 42, 202; G. and Apsaras, as evil demons, 42, 205; G. and Apsaras, founded upon time, 42, 225; gods, fathers, men, G. and A., 42, 229; G. and Apsaras cause madness, 42, 520 sq.; Apsaras, the wives of Kâma, the Gandharva, 42, 536; offerings to G. and Apsaras, 43, 229–233; G. and Apsaras gratified at the Agnihotra, 44, 82; to G. and Apsaras, an outcast sacrificed at Purushamedha, 44, 414. *See also* Superhuman beings.

Gandharvî, the woman of the waters, 42, 520 sq.

Gandhottama, n. of a Tathâgata, 49 (ii), 100.

Ga*n*esa, worshipped, 7, xxi; 25, 106 n.; 29, 140 n.

Gaṅgâ, *see* Ganges.

Ganges, the bones of the cremated corpse, to be thrown into it, 7, xxx, 76; its water the purest of all, 7, 205; the first or the best of rivers, 8, 90, 354; 45, 290; Buddha crosses the overflowing river G., 11, 21; 17, 104; 19, 251 sq.; feast of the G. and the Mahî, 17, 25; 20, 359; bathing in the G. as a religious rite, 19, 26; descent of the G., 23, 52; the Brâhma*n*a tribes on the banks of the G., 30, 208; Bharata offered horse-sacrifice near the G., 44, 399; the heavenly G., 45, 92; mother of Bhîshma, 49 (i), 95.

*Gañ***gabha**, worshipped by the Snâtaka, 30, 166.

Ga*n*ika Kula, of the Ve*s*avâ*t*ika Ga*n*a, 22, 291.
Ganrâk-maînôk, Phl., the evil spirit, 5, 3 n., 4 n. *See* Aharman, Angra-mainyu, *and* Evil spirit.
*G***anta**, son of Ambâ, 19, xxvii.
*G***ânusso*n*i**, n. of a Brâhma*n*a, 10 (ii), 109; 11, 167, 168 n.
Gaokerena, *see* Haoma.
Gaoma*nt*, son of Zavan, 23, 218.
Gaopivanghu, n.p., 23, 211.
Gaotema, i.e. Gotama Buddha, Zoroastrian controversies against him, 4, liii; 23, 184, 184 n.
*G***arâbodha**, n.p., 46, 17, 19.
Garahadinna, story of, 36, 249.
*G***arâsutta**, t.c., 10 (ii), 154–6.
*G***âratkârava** Ârtabhâga questions Yâ*g*ñavalkya, 15, 125–7; 34, lxxxi, cxii; 38, 373 sq.; 48, 734.
Garbhâdhâna, *see* Sexual intercourse.
Garbharaksha*n*a, t.t., *see* Child (*b*).
Garbha-upanishad, quoted, 48, 364.
Gardabhâli, a monk, converted King Sa*ñ*gaya, 45, 82 sq.
Gardabhîvibhîta Bhâradvâ*g*a, quoted, 15, 155 sq.
Garga, the learned sage, compares bad pupils to bad bullocks, 45, 149–52.
Gârgî Vâ*k*aknavî (daughter of Va*k*aknu), questions Yâ*g*ñavalkya, 15, 130 sq., 136–9; 48, 308–10; worshipped at the Tarpa*n*a, 29, 122 sq., 220; possessed the knowledge of Brahman, 38, 315.
Gârgîputra, n. of teachers, 15, 224 n.
Gârgya in list of teachers, 15, 186; worshipped at the Tarpa*n*a, 29, 122 sq., 220. *See also* Bâlâki, *and* Sauryâya*n*in.
Gârgyâya*n*a, n. of a teacher, 15, 186.
Garments: sin of clothing the dead, 5, 340 sq., 341 n.; offered to the departed spirit, 5, 383, 383 n.; legend explaining why men wear g., 12, 9 sq.; gifts of g. to the priests and the poor, for the departed soul, 18, 150, 150 n.; 24, 351 sq.; dress of silk is good for the body, of cotton for the soul, 24, 49, 49 n.; g. of hair or bark or hide when doing penance, 25, 449, 451–3, 455; sin of burning leathern and woollen g., 37, 85; mode of wearing g., 37, 91; made to float away at the final bath after sacrifice, 44, 267; a hundred g. the priests' fee, 44, 353; are man's outward appearance, 44, 353. *See also* Costumes.
*G***arôdanghu**, son of Pairi*s*tîra, 23, 210, 210 n.
Garô-nmânem (Garôthmân, Garô*d*man), 'the abode of song,' the Paradise of the Parsis, 4, 220 sq., 220 n., 221 n., 232–4, 375, 386; 5, 294 sq., 294 n.; 23, 200, 291, 335; G., the place of eternal weal, and the *K*invat bridge, 23, 12, 20; Mithra invoked to gather the libations and lay them in the G., 23, 127, 133; Mithra drives forth from G., 23, 152; abode of the Good Spirit, 23, 296; G. of Ahura-Mazda, 23, 357; praised, 31, 170, 172; the pious soul received by Ahura-Mazda into his G., 31, 184 sq. and note. *See also* Heaven (*g*), *and* Paradise.
*G***arôvanghu**, son of Frâyaza*n*ta, 23, 212.
Garshâsp, *see* Keresâspa.
Gar*s*ta, son of Kavi, 23, 218.
Garu*d*a, son of Vinatâ, chief among birds, 8, 90, 90 n.; 49 (i), 144; (ii), 57; G. and Nâga chiefs carry Mahâvîra's throne, 22, 198; the enemies of serpents, 35, 38; Venudeva, the best of birds, 45, 290, 290 n. *See also* Superhuman beings.
Garutmat, the winged one, whose head is the Triv*r*it, &c., 29, 49; not hurt by poison, 42, 25, 375.
*G***asabhadda**, *see* Ya*s*obhadra.
*G***asa*m*sa**, n. of Siddhârtha, Mahâvîra's father, 22, 193, 256.
Gâsânbâr, Phl. 'season-festival,' 5, lxxiii.
*G***âtakarman**, t.t., birth ceremony, *see* Child (*b*).
*G***âtakas** (tales of former births of the Buddha): life of Buddha prefixed to the *G*., 11, 208 sq.; Buddha teaches by means of Sûtras, stanzas, *G*., and parables, 21, 44 sq.; quoted in the Milindapañha, 35, xli sq., 180 n., 183 n., 185 n., 216, 280 sq., 283 n., 294–6, 294 n.; 36, 6, 6 n., 16–19, 16 n., 18 n., 20–2, 20 n.,

81 n., 146 n., 291, 306, 310, 341, 342 n., 344, 344 n., 349; Vessantara *G.*, 35, 170–8; 36, 114–32; the Sivi *G.*, 35, 179–85; talking trees in the *G.*, 35, 241; in which Devadatta occurs as the Bodisat's enemy, 35, 283–93 and notes, 303 sq. *See also* Tales.

***G*âtavedas**, *see* Agni (*d*).

Gâthas of the Zend-Avesta are post-Alexandrian, 4, lxv sq.; Philo, and the writers of the G., 4, lvi sq.; invoked and worshipped, 4, 222, 222 n.; 31, 293–5, 329 sq., 336 sq., 339 sq., 356 sq., 356 n., 373, 382; quoted, 5, 167 sq. and note, 350; not to be recited over the dead, 5, 318; mystic signification of the G., 5, 352–69; difficulties and methods of interpretation, 31, x–xv, xvii sq., xxxvii–xlvi; their antiquity, 31, xxv sq.; relative age of the G., 31, xxvi sq., 91 sq.; their importance, 31, 1 sq.; translated, 31, 3–194; mentioned in the Haoma and Srôsh Ya*s*ts, 31, 243 sq., 243 n., 299, 299 n.; duty of knowing the G., 37, 73 sq.; purport of the G., 37, 169 sq.; unforgetfulness and power of the spirit of the G., 37, 178 sq.; work of Aûhar*mazd* in the Gâthic lore, 37, 342 sq.

Gâthâs (songs, strophes), good and bad, 10 (i), 31; singing G. at the Sîmantonnayana rite, 29, 48 sq.; quoted, 44, 98, 101, 326 sq., 396–401.

Gâthin: Indra becomes Ku*s*ika's son G., 26, 82 n.; G. Kau*s*ika, author of Vedic hymns, 46, 279, 281, 283, 285. *See also* Kau*s*ika, *and* Ku*s*ika.

Gâthina, *see* Vi*s*vâmitra G.

***G*a*t*ilas,** *see* Ascetics (*c*).

***G*âtismara,** *see* Si*m*hagiri *G*.

***G*atuka*n*nin,** n. of a Brâhma*n*a, 10 (ii), 187, 204, 210.

***G*atuka*nn*imâ*n*avapu*kkh*â,** t.c., 10 (ii), 204 sq.

***G*âtukar*n*ya,** n. of a teacher, 1, 267; 15, 118 n., 119, 186 n., 187.

***G*âtûkar*n*ya,** worshipped at the Tarpa*n*a, 29, 123; 30, 244.

Gau*d*apâda-Kârikâ, quoted, 34, xcix, cxxvii; 38, 424; 48, 775.

Gau*d*as, the art of, an occult science, 45, 366.

Gaupavana, n. of a teacher, 15, 118, 185 sq.

Gaupâyanas or Laupâyanas, authors of Vedic hymns, 46, 415.

Gâuri, n.p., 23, 215.

Gaurî, wife of Balakôsh*th*a, 45, 50 n.

Gaurîviti *S*âktya quoted, 44, 250.

Gautama, father of *S*vetaketu, 1, 77–9; 15, 205–8; Auddâlaka (Uddâlaka) Âru*n*i, addressed as G., 1, 88, 271, 273; 44, 52 sq., 79; asked Brahman about final emancipation, 8, 314; one of the seven *Ri*shis, 15, 106; n. of teachers, 15, 118, 118 n., 119, 186, 186 n., 187; *Ri*shi G. seduced by an Apsaras, 19, 39; 49 (i), 39; Indra in love with the wife of the *Ri*shi G., 19, 43; 26, 81 n.; 49 (i), 44; an appellation of disrespect in addressing Buddha, 19, 172 sq., 173 n.; Tîrthakaras of the G. gotra, 22, 218; Sthaviras of the G. gotra, 22, 286 sqq., 289, 293 sqq.; Indra calls himself G., 26, 82, 82 n.; satiated at the Tarpa*n*a, 29, 220; 30, 244; Kêsi and G., leaders of the two branches of the *G*aina church, 45, xxii. *See also* Gotama, Hâridrumata, Indrabhûti, Nodhas, Sudharman, *and* Uddâlaka.

Gautama, son of Utathya, quoted in Manu-sm*ri*ti, 25, xxvi sq., 78.

Gautama-Dharma-sûtra is the manual of a G.-*K*ara*n*a of the Sâmaveda, 2, xlix–liii; 14, xiii; 25, 613; its priority to the other Dharma-sûtras, 2, liii–lx; its language, 2, lix; its date, 2, lx sq.; its text and commentary 2, lxii; translated, 2, 174–310; G. and Vish*n*u-sm*ri*ti, 7, xx; quoted, 8, 208, 213 n., 218 n., 225 n., 236 n., 353 n., 354 n., 359 n., 362 n., 363 n., 365 n.; 14, xvii, xxi, xxxiv, xl, 30, 147, 236; 25, xxvii, xxx; 30, 97; 33, 376; 48, 590; quotes Manu, 25, xxxiv sq.

Gautami, worshipped at the Tarpa*n*a, 29, 123.

Gautamî, a name of Gotama Buddha's wife, 49 (i), 82, 86.

Gautamî, Pra*g*âpatî, aunt of the Buddha, 19, 23, 64, 84–6; 21, xxx, 256 sq.; restored to sight by Buddha, 49 (i), 197; becomes a Buddhist nun, 49 (i), 199 sq.

Gautamîputra, n.p., 15, 224 n., 225.

Gautamîyâ Sâkhâ of the Mânava Ga*n*a, 22, 292.
Gâvah of Ispahân stood by truth, against Dahâk, 24, 323 sq., 323 n.
Gavâmpati, disciple of Buddha, an eminent Arhat, 13, 110 sq.; 21, 2; 49 (ii), 90.
Gavayan, n.p., 23, 203.
Gavedhukâ Sâkha of the *Kâra*n*a* Ga*n*a, 22, 291.
Gavish*th*ira Âtreya, author of Vedic hymns, 46, 364.
Gaya, incantation of, 42, 107, 255; G. Âtreya, author of Vedic hymns, 46, 387, 390; Buddha visits the royal sage G., 49 (i), 132.
Gayâ, Buddha at, 10 (ii), 45; 21, 293 sq., 298 sq.; 49 (i), 192; *S*râddhas offered at G., 14, 55.
*G***aya**, a king who became a *G*aina monk, 45, 86 sq., 86 n.
Gayadhâsti, son of Pouru-dhâkh*s*ti, 23, 212, 225.
*G***ayadratha**, a warrior, 8, 96.
*G***ayaghôsha**, a *G*aina monk, formerly a Brâhma*n*a, 45, 136–41.
Gayâ-Kâ*s*yapa, *see* Kâ*s*yapa.
Gaya Maretan, *see* Gâyômar*d*.
*G***ayanta**, a Brâhman, met death for his son's sake, 19, 92, 92 n.
*G***ayanta**, disciple of Vagrasena, 22, 288.
*G***ayanta**, son of Indra, 19, 94; 30, 290 n.; 49 (i), 93; spoken to by B*ri*haspati, 19, 96; Buddha, the prince, compared with G., 49 (i), 92.
*G***âyantîputra**, n.p., 15, 225.
Gayâsîsa, Buddha at, 13, 134 sq.; Devadatta with his followers at the hill G., 20, 256–9.
Gâyatrî (metre and verse), called prâ*n*a or breath, 1, 29 n.; 12, 100; meditated upon as Brahman, 1, 44–6, 158, 162, 194; 34, 93–6; 44, 409; 48, 248 sq.; is the first of all metres, 1, 187; 8, 90, 90 n., 353; identified with the earth, 12, 110 sq., 195 n.; 41, 148; as a falcon carried off the Soma, 12, 183 sq., 183 n., 233; 26, 52, 78, 88, 150, 241; 42, 401; 44, 122; speculations on the G., 15, 196–9; 41, 158, 160 sq.; is everything whatsoever exists, 34, 90, 93–5; consists of three feet, these worlds being three in number, 44, 26; the golden, brilliant-winged G. who bears the sacrificer to the heavenly world, 44, 53, 56; a Gâyatra hymn, 46, 7. *See also* Metres.
Gayô-Maratan, *see* Gâyômar*d*.
Gâyômar*d* (Gaya Maretan, Gayô-Maratan), the first man, 4, 254; 5, 19, 20 n., 52 sq., 59, 88; 18, 60, 60 n., 401 sq., 411; 23, 227; 24, 58; 31, 260 n.; 37, 26, 26 n.; 47, x, xxix, xli, 4–6, 121; promises not to resort to suicide, 4, 372 n.; king of the mountain, overcome by death, 4, 383 sq.; representing mankind, 5, xxiii; the righteous man, 5, 15 n.; 37, 454, 456, 460; Aharman's conflict with G., 5, 17 sqq., 161 sq., 161 n., 164–6, 168, 182–4; when he passed away he fell to the left hand, 5, 20; Gô*s*ûrvan and G., 5, 20, 163; his bones first roused up, 5, 123; Mâshya, son of G., 5, 130; first ancestor of Zoroaster, 5, 141 n.; 47, 35, 140; his reign for three thousand years, 5, 149; 24, 345; first ruler of the world, 18, 13 sq., 13 n.; 23, 33 n.; his greatness, 18, 21; among the preparers of the renovation of the universe, 18, 77; made mortal by the evil spirit, 18, 94; destroyed by the demon of death, from his seed sprang Marhayâ and Marhîyôih, 18, 105, 105 n.; origin of G. and of mankind, 18, 197–9, 198 n.; son of Aûharma*zd*, 18, 393 n., 401; called Vohûman, 18, 393 n.; his Fravashi worshipped, 23, 200 sq.; 31, 252, 273, 278 sq.; invoked and worshipped, 23, 350; 31, 324, 362; advantage of his actions, 24, 57 sq., 57 n.; shared heaven through wisdom, 24, 102; afflicted by the demons, 37, 254; predominance of those of the nature of G., 37, 332.
Gêfar-tôrâ, ancestor of Frê*d*ûn, 5, 132; 47, 34.
*G***êh**, the fiend of menstruation, 5, 15 sq., 15 n., 283 n. *See* Woman (*e*).
*G***ehila**, of the Vâsish*th*a gotra, a Sthavira, 22, 294.
Gemara, of the Jews, 47, xiii sq., 119 sq. and n., 129.
Gems: wish-conferring gem, 8, 179; 36, 58 sq., 74, 119, 193, 256, 256 n., 258, 264, 267; 49 (i), 157; (ii) 50,

174; g. to be found in the ocean, 20, 302; 36, 303, 303 n.; a wonderful gem presented to Buddha by a Nâga, 21, 252 sq.; magic gem which clears muddy water, 35, 55, 55 n.; list of g., 35, 177; the mystic g. of sovranty, 36, 14, 14 n., 128. *See also* Amulets, Jewels, *and* Parables (*f*).

*G*emshîd, *see* Yima Khshaêta.

Gem-Treasure, *see* Jewels.

Gem-trees, *see* Jewels.

Generation: semen and blood produced by the Prâ*n*as, 8, 275; generative power is immortal, 41, 354; is only on this side of sky and sun, 43, 128, 130. *See also* Birth, Child (*c*), *and* Sexual intercourse.

Genii, *see* Sâdhyas.

Genital organ, one of the (ten, eleven) organs of the body, 8, 261, 336; connected with the self, 8, 338; by means of it he sheds the essence of food as seed, 44, 264.

Geography: the sixteen perfect lands created by Ahura-Mazda, 4, 1–10; mythical g., 24, 85–7. *See also* India, Iran, Khvanîras, Mountains, *and* Rivers.

*G*eta, a prince from whom Anâthapi*nd*ada obtained the *G*etavana, 19, 216 sq. and n.; 20, 187 sqq.; 49 (i), 193 sq.

*G*etavana, garden and monastery, founded at Sâvatthi by Anâthapi*nd*ada, 10 (ii), 17, 20, &c.; 11, 167 n., 238, 238 n., 296; 19, 213–18, 230 sq.

Geurva, Haoi*s*t, son of, 37, 224, 224 n.

G*eus*urvâ, Av., = Phl. Gôsûrvan (q.v.), 5, 20 n.

*G*hâna, Pali t.t., four kinds of meditation, 11, 115 n., 212, 271 sq., 272 n. *See* Meditation.

Gharma, *see* Pravargya.

Gha*t*îkâra, a potter, invited *G*otipâla to visit the Buddha, 36, 21; no rain fell upon his hut, 36, 23 sq.

Ghaura, *see* Ka*n*va G.

Ghee (ghr*i*ta), or clarified butter, is the sap of heaven and earth, of the universe, 12, 372 sq.; 41, 333, 390; is a purifier, 26, 8; belongs to the gods, 26, 14; is a thunderbolt, 26, 106, 169 sq.; is consecration water, 41, 79; is seed, 41, 211 sq.; offered on the fire-altar, 43, 182 sq.; is sacred to Agni, 43, 189; is fiery mettle, 44, 274, 296, 312, 410 sq.; is the resource of the gods, 44, 296, 410.

Ghora, a work of the Atharvans, 44, 366 n.

Ghora, *see* Ka*n*va.

Ghora Âṅgirasa, communicates his view of the sacrifice to Kr*i*sh*n*a, the son of Devakî, 1, 52.

Ghosel, *see* Purification.

Ghoshamati, son of a former Buddha, 21, 19.

Ghosts, 'a carriage full of ghosts,' an impossible thing, 16, 140, 142 n. *See also* Pretas, Spirits, *and* Superhuman beings.

Ghouls, *see* Demons.

Ghr*i*takau*s*ika, n. of a teacher, 15, 119, 186.

Ghr*i*tâ*k*î, a nymph, 43, 107; 49 (i), 39.

Giantesses, *see* Superhuman beings.

*G*ibt, idols of ancient Arabs, 6, 79.

Gideon and Saul confused, 6, 38 sq., 38 n.

Gifts, rules about making and accepting g., 2, 65 sq., 203 sq., 265 sq.; 7, 87; 14, 68, 70 sq.; 25, lxviii, 133 sq., 158 sq., 167 sq., 592; 27, 78, 84–6, 89, 423; 28, 76 sq.; 33, 220 sq.; making of g. purifies a sinner, 2, 70; 25, 188, 477; making of g. accompanied by a water-libation, 2, 122, 203; 13, 143; 14, 277 n.; 17, 250 sq., 251 n.; 19, 231; meritoriousness of g. to learned Brâhma*n*as, 2, 163; 7, 21 sq.; 10 (ii), 50 sq.; 14, 134–9, 240; 25, 93, 99–102, 133, 229 sq., 430 sq., 434 sq.; giving g., a penance, 2, 275, 277, 279, 285 sq.; 4, 172–5; 6, 28, 110 sq., 188; 9, 271; 14, 109, 113 sq., 116, 118, 125, 134 sq., 137, 222, 295, 302, 305 sq., 311 sq., 328, 330 sq.; 25, 445 sq., 454, 456–9, 477; 29, 120; g. of honour, made by a king to his chief minister, 3, 194, 267, 267 n.; g. to a woman from her male relatives, 7, 69; 25, 374; illicit g., 2, 292, 292 n.; 7, 136, 136 n., 187–9; 14, 115, 130, 239, 310, 317; 25, 109, 142 sq., 167 sq., 424–6, 435, 438, 444, 481; g. for purposes of sacrifices must

not be employed for any other purposes, 7, 192; the householder's duty of making g., 7, 192–4, 215–17, 8, 358 sq.; 14, 237, 262; 25, 92, 164 sq.; the merit of different kinds of pious g., and their corresponding rewards, 7, 263–76; 25, 165–7, 165 n., 229 sq.; certain times auspicious for certain kinds of g., 7, 263, 265–70; the skin of a black antelope, adorned and covered with all sorts of jewels, given to a Brâhma*n*a, 7, 263 sq.; fit and unfit persons to receive g., 7, 274–6; 10 (ii), 80–4; 14, 38 sq.; 24, 53, 82, 291 sq.; 25, 59, 107, 158 sq., 430 sq. and n., 444, 444 n.; protection is more meritorious than any g., 7, 271; fruit of g. obtained by devotion, 8, 81; good and bad kinds of g., 8, 120 sq., 242, 324 sq., 330; g. made without respect to fruit, a means of sanctification, 8, 121 sq.; g. made at ceremonies, 8, 169; sacrifice, g., and other pious works end in destruction, 8, 355; giving and accepting of g. the duty of Brâhma*n*as, 8, 359; 25, 24, 158 sq., 419, 426; some Brâhma*n*as are for meditation, others for sacrifice, others for g., 8, 376; the gift of the law exceeds all g., 10 (i), 83, 83 n.; meritoriousness of g., 10 (i), 84; 11, 20, 20 sq. n.; 17, 223 sqq.; 30, 31–8, 145–8, 150, 155; made to Bhikkhus and to the church of the Buddha, 11, 27, 33; 35, 134 sq.; the meritoriousness of g. to Buddha, 11, 80, 84; 35, 242–6; 36, 24, 31–8; 49 (ii), 119, 123, 136, 139, 141, 143; perpetual grant made by Sudassana, 11, 263 sq.; at sacrifices and funeral oblations g. must be given to learned Brâhma*n*as only, 14, 17 sq.; rules about g. of robes to Bhikkhus or the Sa*m*gha, 17, 194 sq., 219–25, 251–5; to the priests and the poor, 18, 150 sq., 150 n., 154 sq.; made at the birth of a prince, 19, 19 sq.; wishing g., for which the donor expects a particular result in a future birth, 20, 9, 9 n.; the great merit of giving Vihâras to the Sa*m*gha, 20, 160; 36, 3; resumption of g., a title of the law, 25, ciii, 253, 282–4, 292, 292 n.; 33, xiii, 128–30, 341–3; of a thousand cows, 25, 110; a hermit not to receive g., 25, 200; once only does a man say, 'I will give,' 25, 335; 33, 171; offered to the Dîkshita, 26, 45; for the dead, 27, 34; 28, 140 sq., 144–7, 156 sq., 164, 194 sq.; about g. of introduction, 27, 119; g. of condolence, mourning g., 27, 134, 136 sq., 154 sq., 155 n., 183, 356; 28, 69 sq.; interchange of g. between ruler and ministers, 28, 21–3, 69 sq.; given to Brâhma*n*as at a wedding, 29, 38 sq.; made at the end of ceremonies, 29, 57; distribution of g. to be avoided for some days after the funeral, 29, 244 sq.; what is given away at a *S*râddha brings prosperity, 29, 254; prayers recited when receiving g., 29, 367 sq.; one about to give alms must not be arrested, 33, 19; deeds of g., 33, 305 sq.; great meritoriousness of g. of land, 33, 306; inalienable g., 33, 314; duty of king to bestow g. on Brâhma*n*as, 33, 347; invalid g., 33, 354; Buddhas do neither accept nor refuse g., 35, 145; to be given to the Order rather than to the Buddha, 36, 51–5; a Sama*n*a purifies g. made to him, 36, 82–4; why do Bhikkhus trouble about g.? 36, 92–6; the meritoriousness of g. illustrated by the story of Vessantara, 36, 114–32; ten g. that are disapproved, 36, 120 sq.; a Bhikkhu should always share g. he has received with others, 36, 292; law about righteous g., 37, 68, 106 sq., 441; g. of the righteous, 37, 72; g. to righteous teachers, 37, 95 sq.; damaged g., 37, 137; the soul desires giving of g., 37, 193; righteous g. at the season-festivals, 37, 483; sacrifices, g. and austerities are purifying, 48, 700. *See also* Charity, Priests (fees), Teacher (fees).

G*iggh*akû*t*a, 'Vulture's Peak,' n. of a mountain, 10 (ii), 80.

Gihin, Pali t.t. = Gaha*tth*a, householder, 10 (ii), x.

*G*ihvâvat Vâdhyoga, n. of a teacher, 15, 226.

*G*im, *see* Yima.

*G*ina, title used by Buddhists and *G*ainas, 22, xix sq.; title of Ma-

hâvîra, 22, 201; or Tîrthakara, 34, 429; 'there is now no *G*., but there is a highly esteemed guide to show the way,' 45, 45; the arguments of Buddha, *G*., and others contradictory, 48, 425, 426; teaching of *G*. to be rejected by the Vedântin, 48, 531. *See also* Buddha (*a*), *and* *G*inas.

***G*inakalpika**, a, who wears no clothes, 22, 57 n.

***G*inas**, whatever they have declared, is truth, 22, 49 sq.; are born as gods in their former existence, 22, 189, 217 sq., 271, 276, 281; lives of the *G*., 22, 217–85; adoration of twenty-four *G*., 45, 159, 163. *See also* Buddha (*j*), Saints, *and* Tîrthakaras.

***G*inns**, created out of smokeless fire, 6, xiii, 246; 9, 258; subject to birth and death, 6, xiii; the daughters of Allâh, 6, xiii; Mohammed an apostle both for men and *g*., 6, xiv, 131; 9, 304 sq., 304 n.; hysterical symptoms explained as possession by *g*., 6, xxi; Mohammed's vision of *g*. crowding around him, 6, xxx; Muslim belief in the *g*., 6, lxix sq.; those who made the *g*. partners with God rebuked, 6, 127 sq. and n.; 9, 174; hell filled with *g*. and men, 6, 160, 218; 9, 136; mankind and *g*. together could not produce the like of the Qur'ân, 9, 10; Iblîs was of the *g*., 9, 20; Mohammed said to be possessed by a *g*., 9, 69; work for Solomon, 9, 101 sq., 151, 151 sq. and n.; misbelievers believe in *g*., 9, 155; misbelievers among *g*. and men, 9, 226; listened to the Qur'ân, 9, 228; *g*. and mankind worship God, 9, 248, 259 sq.; lonely places haunted by *g*., 9, 305 n.

Giribba*g*a, in Magadha, 10 (ii), 67.

Girirâ*g*aghosha, the 12th Tathâgata, 49 (ii), 6.

Girirâ*g*aghoshe*s*vara, the 49th Tathâgata, 49 (ii), 6.

Girls, *see* Woman.

Girnâr, mount, on its summit Arish*t*anemi reached Kevala, and died, 22, 277, 279; Mount G. or Raivataka, sacred to *G*ainas and Hindus, 45, 115 n.

***G*ish*n*u**, a god, a name of the great self, 8, 219, 332.

***G*i*s*ti**, n.p., 23, 212.

Gîtâ, i.e. Bhagavadgîtâ, q.v.

***G*itvan *S*ailini**, said that speech is Brahman, 15, 152.

***G*îva**, Sk. t.t., individual or personal soul, 34, xxv. *See* Self, *and* Soul.

***G*îva**, n.p., *see* *G*îvaka.

***G*îvaka** Komârabha*kk*a, physician of King Bimbisâra and one of the chief partisans of Buddha, 13, 191–3; 17, 180 sq., 193–6; 19, 241, 241 n.; 49 (ii), 163 sq.; son of the courtesan Sâlavatî, performs wonderful cures, 17, 172–94; recommends to Buddha the construction of cloisters and bath-rooms, 20, 102 sq.

***G*îvala *K*ailaki**, quoted, 12, 336.

***G*îvanmukti**, t.t., release of one while still living. *See* Emancipation, *and* Nirvâ*n*a.

Gîw, son of Gû*d*arz, 5, 118.

Gladness, goddess, worshipped at the Pravargya, 44, 453.

Glâva Maitreya, other name of Vaka Dâlbhya, 1, 21.

Glory, kingly G. and unconsumed G. worshipped, 31, 200, 206, 211, 217, 221, 226.

Glow-worm, seen disappear here and there in darkness, 8, 239.

***G*ñâna**, Sk., knowledge, pure intelligence or thought, 34, xxv.

***G*ñânagupta**, or *G*ñânakûta, translated the Fo-pen-hing-tsih-king, 19, xxix; Chinese translation of the Saddharma-pu*nd*arîka, by *G*. and Dharmagupta, 21, xix–xxi, xxiii.

***G*ñâna-kâ*nd*a**, Sk. t.t., the portion (of the Veda) which relates to knowledge, and Karma-kâ*nd*a, 1, lxiii, lxxx; systematized by the Uttara Mîmâ*m*sâ, 34, x, xii; includes Âra*n*yakas and Upanishads, 34, x; its subject is the knowledge of Brahman, 34, x; not limited to the higher castes only, 34, xi; in need of systematic defence, 34, xi; two different parts of it, 34, xxvii; final escape from the sa*m*sâra to be obtained by the *G*. only, 34, xxix. *See also* Knowledge, Philosophy, *and* Veda (*f*).

***G*ñânâkara**, n. of a son of a Buddha, 21, 157.

***G*ñât*r*iputra**, *see* Mahâvîra.

***G*ñât*r*is**, Mahâvîra of the clan of the,

22, 191, 194, 248, 254–6; a noble family, followers of a king, 45, 339.
Gñâtri **Sha*nd*a**, n. of a park, Mahâvîra proceeds to it, 22, 199, 259.
Goat, a red, offered to the Manes, 2, 148, 148 n.; cleaned grain held up before a g., 7, 101; is the first among sacrificial animals, 8, 353; symbolical sacrifice of a he-g., 12, 275, 292, 292 n.; milk of g. the best food, 24, 45; belongs to Pragâpati, 26, 71 sq., 74; 41, 35, 171; g.'s skin, 41, 35; easier to cook than other victims, 41, 130; how created, 41, 147, 173, 245, 401; 43, 38; 44, 214, 452; he-g. sacrificial animal, 41, 162, 165 sq., 204 sq.; 44, 298; is sacred to Agni, 41, 225; corresponds to the Brâhma*n*a, 41, 227; g.'s hair, 41, 229 sq.; contains all forms of cattle, 41, 230; eats all kinds of herbs, 41, 245; g.'s milk, 41, 245; 44, 452, 457, 477; supports the earth, 46, 61 sq.; Agâ, g. and 'unborn' principle, 48, 367, 370. *See also* Agâ, *and* Animals (*e*, *g*).
Gôbâk-abû, maiden mother of the apostle Sôshâns, 47, 115, 115 n.
Gobhara*n*a, or *K*u-fa-lan, translator of Fo-pen-hing-king, 19, xvi sq.
Gobhila-G*ri*hya-sûtra, and Khâdira G*ri*hya-sûtra, 29, 371–3; and the Mantra-Brâhma*n*a, 30, 3–11; translated, 30, 13–132.
Goblins (pi*s*a*k*illikâs) reside in hollow trees, 13, 318; g. or Bhûtas, *see* Bhûtas, Demons, Pi*s*â*k*as, Râkshasas, *and* Superhuman beings.
God.

(*a*) G. or Allâh in the Qur'ân.
(*b*) G. (Heaven, Thien, Tî) in Chinese Sacred Books.
(*c*) G. (Yazdân) in Zoroastrian Sacred Books.
(*d*) G. (Î*s*vara, the Lord) in Sacred Books of India.

(*a*) GOD OR ALLÂH IN THE QUR'ÂN. Unity of G., 6, lii, liv, lxi, lxxi, 22 sq., 95, 127 sq., 137, 177, 205, 235–7, 244, 251 sq., 255; 9, 26, 168; wherever you turn there is G.'s face, 6, 16; did not beget a son, 6, 16, 95, 128; 9, 13 sq., 29, 34, 47, 71, 83, 182, 217; unity, self-subsistence and omnipotence of G., 6, 40, 40 n., 46–50, 54, 84, 117, 127 sq.; Arabs call angels 'daughters of G.,' 6, 256, 256 n.; *there is no G. but He*, 9, 35, 42, 47 sq., 55, 59 sq., 66 sq., 71–3, 80, 89, 101, 104 sq., 115, 117, 119, 157, 168 sq., 176, 181 sq., 188, 190–2, 196 sq., 199, 218, 224, 231, 247, 287, 305 sq.; unity of G. preached by Abraham, 9, 50 sq.; has no daughters, and is not akin to the ginns, 9, 174, 212, 250, 252; the doctrine of the unity of G. terrifies the idolators, 9, 187; *say, 'He is G. alone! G. the Eternal! He begets not and is not begotten! Nor is there like unto Him any one!'* 9, 344; — ruler of the day of judgement, 6, 1; His is the kingdom of the heavens and the earth, 6, 15 sq., 59, 62, 68 sq., 90, 95, 100, 102 sq., 115 sq., 123, 157, 190, 196, 199 sq., 218, 234, 238, 258; 9, 32, 34 sq., 47, 63, 82 sq., 91, 134 sq., 150, 161, 181, 187, 205, 210, 217 sq., 223 sq., 235, 253, 266, 286, 292, 327; is mighty and wise, 6, 30, 32, 37, 41, 45 sq.; is omniscient, 6, 35, 45, 47, 50, 111, 121 sq., 184, 205, 233; 9, 55, 64 sq., 71, 82, 101, 105 sq., 115, 123, 133, 135, 145, 150, 158, 161, 167, 183, 192, 203, 206, 237, 241, 266, *271*, 286–8, 293, 328; is Lord of grace over the worlds, 6, 39; is mighty and avenging, 6, 46; alone is powerful, 6, 144, 204, 241 sq.; not the weight of an atom can escape G., 6, 200; lightning and thunder celebrate His praise, 6, 233; the signs of G., night and day, &c., 6, 257–9, 261 sq.; 9, 2, 126–30, 134, 164 sq., 182, 184, 186–8, 198, 202, 208 sq., 220 sq.; the birds in the vault of the sky, none holds them in but G., 6, 259; if the sea were ink and the trees pens they would not suffice to write the words of G., 9, 26, 134; His are the best of names, 9, 13, 13 n.; a day with G. is a thousand years (and more) with men, 9, 61, 135, 301; His omnipotence, 9, 70 sq.; is the light of the heavens and the earth, 9, 78; His power over nature 9, 79, 87–9, 104 sq., 158, 164 sq., 293 sq.; quickens the earth with rain, sends winds, &c., 9, 123 sq., 129 sq., 158; makes the angels His messengers, 9, 157; respites men for a time, 9, 162; attributes and names of G., 9, 277; — belief in G.

inculcated, 6, 2–4, 8, &c.; 9, 3, &c.; serve ye none but G., 6, 11; 9, 3, 5; the curse of G. is on the misbeliever, 6, 22, 165, 170, 261 sq.; he who disbelieves in idols and believes in G. has got hold of religion, 6, 40; obey G. and the Apostle, 6, 50, 68, 74, 80–3, 163, 165, 183; 9, 79 sq., 143 sq., 148 sq., 232, 241, 287; it is not G. who wrongs the misbelievers, but it is themselves they wrong, 6, 61, 198, 216; 9, 121, 125; misbelievers do not hurt G., but themselves, 6, 67; pardons anything short of idolatry, 6, 79, 88 sq.; belief in G. and fear of G. inculcated, 6, 90 sq.; could send a sign, if He pleased, 6, 119; trust in G. alone, 6, 129; the Meccans would not have believed, even if G. had sent signs, 6, 129; belief depends on G.'s grace, 6, 130 sq., 203 sq.; 9, 314, 322; who disbelieve on G., their works are as ashes blown by the wind, 6, 240; all creation adores G., 6, 255; 9, 5 sq., 47, 58, 79, 266, 273, 280, 282, 286; will defend believers, but loves not the misbelieving traitor, 9, 60; cares not for the rejection of His message by the infidels, 9, 90; honour belongs to G. alone, 9, 158; rebuke to those who say they serve false gods as a means to approach G., 9, 182; — the Creator, 6, 3–5, 52, 54, 71, 100, 115, 117, 123, 127 sq., 144, 192 sq., 205, 232, 234, 239 sq., 242, 245 sq., 249, 251; 9, 11 sq., 34, 37 sq., 83, 88, 104 sq., 122 sq., &c.; *the Originator of the heavens and the earth, when He decrees a matter He doth but say unto it, 'BE,' and it is*, 6, 16; manifested in His creation, 6, 69; has not created heaven and earth in sport, 9, 47 sq., 219; the best of creators, 9, 66; created every beast, 9, 79; produces the creation and then turns it back, 9, 119, 126 sq.; created ginn and mankind to worship Him, 9, 248; — He is forgiving and merciful, 6, 1, 24 sq., 27, 29, 32 sq., 36, 50, 62, 65, 75 sq., 86–8, 90, 93, 102, 108, 111, 134, 137, 144, 166, 171, 173, 176, 186–8, 204, 209, 229 sq., 252, 262 sq.; 9, 6, 21, 55, 63, 73, 75, 77, 82 sq., 100, 109, 139, 142, 146, 149 sq., 161, 190, 205, 208, 235, 239–41, 270, 272, 280, 287, 290, 308; *sends down of His grace on whomsoever of His servants He will*, 6, 12, 14; the G. of Abraham, Ishmael, Isaac, and Jacob, 6, 18 sq.; is with the patient in all calamities, 6, 21 sq.; He created men, and to Him do they return, 6, 22, 192, 197, 205, 257; 9, 70, 119, 123, 132 sq., 183, 244, 272, 294, 336; *whatsoever good ye do, verily, of it G. knows*, 6, 31; guides whom He will unto the right path, 6, 31; will redouble a good loan many a double, 6, 37; dispute between Abraham and Nimrod about G., 6, 40 sq.; revives the dead, 6, 41; 9, 56 sq., 205; fashions you in the womb as He pleases, 6, 46 sq.; victory is but from G., 6, 62; it is not for any soul to die, but for G.'s permission, 6, 63; 9, 285; He quickens and He kills, 6, 65, 157, 190, 199, 246; 9, 63 sq., 70, 128 sq., 197, 218, 244, 253, 266, 312, 320; only can help, in dangers of land and sea, 6, 65 sq., 122; 9, 8 sq., 17, 124, 164 sq.; made a covenant with the Muslim, as with the children of Israel, 6, 98 sq.; G. and the Apostle to be taken as patrons, 6, 105; takes men to Himself in sleep, 6, 122; obliges no soul more than it can bear, 6, 135, 142; 9, 289; bids only justice, 6, 140; *whoso fears G. and does what is right, there is no fear for them, nor shall they grieve*, 6, 141; the earth is His, He gives it for an inheritance to whom He pleases, 6, 152; appears to Moses on the mountain, 6, 154; the good names of G. not to be perverted, 6, 160; mentioning of G.'s name protects from the devil, 6, 162; *nought shall befall us save what G. has written down for us*, 6, 180; good-will from G. is the mighty happiness, 6, 183; does not forgive the hypocrites, 6, 184; when in distress men turn to G., but forget Him after deliverance, 6, 193–5, 255; guides unto truth, 6, 197; *He it is who made for you the night, that ye might rest therein, and the day to see therein; verily, in that are signs unto a people who can hear*, 6, 200; is the best of judges, 6, 204; *there is no beast that walks*,

but He taketh it by its forelock, 6, 211; knows what each female bears, 6, 233; ordered all things for the benefit of mankind, 6, 242, 251 sq.; 9, 63, 66, 164 sq., 206, 211, 293–5, 319, 321; His decree will come to pass, 6, 250; thankfulness for G.'s favours enjoined, 6, 258 sq.; is with those who fear Him, and with those who do well, 6, 264; never say, 'I am going to do that to-morrow,' except 'if G. please,' 9, 16; is best at rewarding, and best at bringing to an issue, 9, 19; men dispute about G. and follow devils, 9, 56 sq.; the name of G. to be mentioned over cattle when slaughtered, 9, 60; judges between the religions of the different nations, 9, 64; Abraham praises and prays to G., 9, 93 sq.; appears to Moses in the fire, 9, 100, 111; has subjected nature to man, 9, 133, 211, 221; the ship rides on the sea by the favour of G., 9, 134, 208, 221; sends water to the sterile land and brings forth corn for men, 9, 138, 159 sq., 184, 242, 246, 264 sq.; man's ingratitude to G., 9, 183, 187, 204; when the devil incites you, seek refuge with G., 9, 202; speaks to man only by inspiration, 9, 210; nigher to man than his jugular vein, 9, 243; hymn in praise of G.'s bounties, 9, 258–62; the Lord of ascents, His judgement cannot be repelled, 9, 300 sq. *See also* Allâh.

(*b*) G. (Heaven, Thien, Tî) in Chinese Sacred Books.

Chinese words for G., 3, xxiii–xxix; 16, xix sq., 51 sq.; 'G.' and 'Heaven' used without distinction, 3, 196–8, 477 sq. n.; 27, 386–8 n.; 39, 16–18; lamentation and appeal to Heaven, the great G., 3, 354; the 'seat of Tî' or 'the G. given position,' 16, 223, 223 n.; — dynasties founded, kings appointed and favoured by G., are the correlates of G., 3, 58, 114, 144, 153, 159–61, 163, 184, 196–8, 245, 266, 309 sq., 319, 378 sq., 379 n., 389–92, 477; 16, 287 sq., 289 n.; employs Thang to punish the wicked *K*ieh, 3, 87; King Thang will examine good and bad in himself and his people with the mind of G., 3, 91; a virtuous king called the fellow of G., 3, 99, 99 n.; secures the good order of the kingdom, 3, 111; Heaven made instructors (kings) for the inferior people that they might be able to be aiding to G., 3, 126; curses the wicked King Shâu, 3, 130, 222; Wăn's fame ascended up to the high G., and G. approved, 3, 166, 208; the king the great son and vice-gerent of G., 3, 185; Thang brightly administered the bright ordinances of G., 3, 221; appointed Thang to regulate the boundaries of the kingdom, 3, 307; King Wăn in heaven ascends and descends on the left and the right of G., 3, 378, 378 n.; when G. gave the command, Shang became subject to *K*âu, 3, 379; King Wăn served G., and so secured the great blessing, 3, 381, 392; speaks to King Wăn, 3, 391 sq., 391 n.; worshipped by King Wû after his victory, 28, 60; — sacrifices (offered by kings) to G., 3, 39, 126, 163, 302, 321, 343, 343 n., 392, 392 n., 397, 422, 422 n.; 16, 150, 255, 255 n., 287 sq., 289 n., 341, 342 n.; 27, 25, 218, 220, 293, 385, 407, 410, 413 sq., 417, 430 sq., 430 n.; 28, 32, 167, 212, 212 n., 311, 338 sq., 349; requires the punishment of the enemy, 3, 85, 135; has conferred a moral sense even on inferior people, 3, 89 sq.; 'the Spiritual Sovereign in the high heavens,' 3, 90, 90 n.; sends down blessings on the good, miseries on the evil-doer, 3, 95, 208, 214 sq., 259 sq.; Shâu serves neither G. nor the spirits of heaven and earth, 3, 126; roused to anger by Khwăn's disturbing the five elements, did not give him the Great Plan, 3, 139; leads men to tranquil security, 3, 197; man cannot dare to rest in the favour of G., 3, 206; Thâi-wû's virtue was made to affect G., 3, 207; able ministers honour G. in the discharge of their duties, 3, 221 sq.; displeased with cruel punishments, 3, 256; appointed wheat and barley for the nourishment of all, 3, 320; encouragement by saying, 'G. is with you,' 3, 342, 382; foreseeing providence of G., 3,

390 n.; Kiang Yüan trod on a toe-print of G., and conceived, 3, 397; pleased with the smell of sacrifices, 3, 399; the people's misery ascribed to G.'s having reversed His usual course of procedure, 3, 408, 408 n.; how vast is G., the ruler of men below, how arrayed in terrors, 3, 410; not G. has caused the evil time, but it arises from not following the old ways, 3, 412; King Hsüan expostulates with G. and all the spirits whose help in a terrible drought might be expected, 3, 419–23; the work of G. in nature, 16, 48, 50–3, 425–7, 426 n.; an unfathomable spiritual power working in all operations, 16, 357, 358 n.; prayer to G. for a good year in spring, and ploughing the field of G., 27, 254 sq., 255 n.; summer sacrifice for rain to G., 27, 273 sq., 274 n.; worship of G. who dwells in the great heaven, 27, 278, 309; accepts victims which are complete and entire, 27, 288; produce gathered from 'the acres of G.,' 27, 293; origin of the worship of G., 27, 370, 370 n.; the Tâo before G., 39, 50, 60, 68 sq., 84, 243; Tâoism denies the existence of a personal G., 39, 134; 'the divinity in man,' is the name for the spirit trained according to the Tâo, 39, 146 sq., 367; the Tâoist sage ascends among the immortals and arrives at the place of G., 39, 313 n., 314; a power to which the Tâo requires submission, coming near our idea of G., 40, 38 n. *See also* Heaven (*a*), Tâo, Thien, *and* Tî.

(*c*) G. (YAZDÂN) IN ZOROASTRIAN SACRED BOOKS.

The will of G. is the law of righteousness, 4, 100, 210; 23, 23; religion of G., 5, 64, 194; perversion of G.'s work, is of the Evil spirit, 5, 112; in undertaking anything one should say, 'in the name of G.,' 5, 112; prayer to G., 5, 136; praise of G., 5, 185; invoked in a benediction, 5, 235, 239, 369, 379, 399, 404; worship of G., 5, 308, 316 sq., 392; horses of G., 5, 404, 404 n.; G. or ya*z*dânŏ, plur., 18, 4, 4 n.; created male and female, 18, 401; mystical power of names of G., 23, 21; conversation with G. on the Holy Word, 23, 128, 133; proofs of the existence of a Creator, 24, 139–51, 164 sq.; knowledge of G. the beginning of all knowledge, 24, 140; necessity of understanding the sacred being, 24, 166–8; inconsistency of those who ascribe both good and evil to G., 24, 173–202; four requisites of divinity, 24, 174; inconsistencies in the assertions of various sects regarding G., 24, 202–51; surrounded by angels, 24, 224; casts worshippers into hell, 24, 224 sq.; comes to Abraham who offers Him wine, 24, 225 sq.; criticism of the Godship of Christ, and of the Trinity, 24, 231–5; nothing happens without the will of G., 24, 235 sq.; the kindness and generosity of the sacred being, 24, 256 sq.; existence, unity, purity, and matchlessness of the sacred being, 24, 270; cannot be responsible for permanent evil, 31, 26.

(*d*) G. (ÎSVARA, THE LORD) IN SACRED BOOKS OF INDIA.

One God—who is he?—swallowed the four great ones, he, the guardian of the world, 1, 58; fire (heat) is merged in G., at the death of the body, 1, 101, 108; G. is the True, 1, 121; causes men to do good and evil actions, 1, 299; 38, 59; 48, 558; pervades everything, the whole world a manifestation of Him, 1, 311, 314; 8, 127; 15, 243; 34, xxviii, cxix, 111, 442; 48, 86 sq., 101 sq., 396, 700; is the origin and the dissolution of the whole Universe, Higher than Him there is none else, all this is strung on Him as pearls on a thread, 8, 74; 34, xxvi sq.; 48, 359; is the Creator, the cause and origin of all, 8, 86 sq., 190, 192; 15, 260–7; 19, 195; 34, xxviii, 16 sq., 46, 48 sq., 61, 135–42, 243, 254, 263–6, 270 sq., 328; 38, 24 sq., 183, 416; 43, xiv; 48, 206 sq., 209, 558; creates the universe by means of changes, 8, 157; His difference from the universe, 8, 164, 164 n.; He is the Lord of all, the master of all, the ruler of all, &c., 15, 179, 232; 19,

106; 48, 352; rules the Pradhâna, 15, 235 sq.; 34, 434 sq., 437 sq.; 48, 396 sq., 522 sq.; is the creator of the illusory world, 15, 251 sq.; the cause of the bondage, existence, and liberation of the world, 15, 265; 38, 58 sq.; creates Brahman and delivers the Vedas to him, 15, 265 sq.; is not the cause of the world, 19, 161, 206–8, 294; 49 (i), 176; created the king, 25, 216; created Punishment, His own son, 25, 218 sq.; not a mere operative cause, 34, li, 284, 434–40; 48, 413, 522 sq.; has a shape consisting of the threefold world, 34, 145 sq.; the supporting of all things up to ether can be the work of G. only, 34, 170; Lords, such as Hira*n*yagarbha, &c., are able to continue their previous forms of existence in each new creation, 34, 213, 215; dependency of the world on Him, 34, 242–5, 290, 370; 38, 415 sq.; is the evolver of names and forms, 34, 328 sq.; 38, 96–8; 48, 350; the creation of this world is mere play to Him, 34, 357; may, although Himself unmoving, move the universe, 34, 369; creates things in dreams, 48, 120 sq., 764; is not an agent, because He has no body, 48, 172; is not touched by the evils of creation, 48, 429, 477 sq.; He only possesses the power of ruling the world, 48, 769 sq.;—meditation on G., 8, 78; 15, 232–4; 34, 441; abides alike in all entities, and is not destroyed if they are destroyed, 8, 106; *worshipping Him with the proper works man attains to perfection*, 8, 127; 48, 700; *dwells in the heart of all creatures, whirling, by His mysterious power, all creatures as if mounted on a machine*, 8, 129; 48, 557; is eternal, 8, 157, 186–94; 38, 416; the relation between G. and the individual soul, 8, 187, 187 n., 192–4, 192 n.; 15, 325; 34, xxix, xxxix, xlix, 279, 329, 343–6, 434 sq.; 38, 59–61, 65 sq., 138–40, 244 sq., 291, 338–40, 416–18; 48, 128, 209, 396; is unborn, moving about day and night, without sloth, 8, 192, 194; *should one fly, even after furnishing oneself with thousands upon thousands of wings, and even though one should have the velocity of thought, one would never reach the end of the (great) cause*, 8, 192; *He is without symbols, and also without qualities, nothing exists that is a cause of Him*, 8, 309; not affected by pleasure and pain, 8, 352; 38, 63–5; 48, 427; Buddhism antagonistic to the belief in G., 11, 142; 19, 161, 206–8, 294; 34, 403; mythological deities, the Lord (Pra*g*âpati), and the Highest Self, 15, xxxiii sq.; the personality of G. in the *S*vetâ*s*vatara-Up., 15, xxxvi; relation between G. and the Highest Brahman, 15, xxxvi–xxxviii, 38; 34, xxv, xxvii, xxx, lxii–lxiv, xcviii, 70, 81, 159 sq., 187, 234; 38, 290 sq., 418; by knowing G., final emancipation is obtained, by meditating on Him, the blissful state in the Brahma-world is reached, 15, 236; *He sees without eyes, He hears without ears, without hands and feet He hastens and grasps*, 15, 248; 48, 476; spreads out one net (sa*m*sâra) after another and draws it together again, 15, 255; full description of G., 15, 260–7; by His light all this is lightened, 15, 265; the highest bridge to immortality, 15, 266; a hymn in praise of the Lord of the Universe in whom all gods are, 15, 303; the Undiscernible One, 25, 495, 495 n.; hymn to the Unknown G., 32, xxvii, 1–13; manifests itself in a fourfold form, 34, xxiii; as a retributor and dispenser, 34, xxvi; G. or the lower Brahman, 34, xxvii, xci, xcii; is all-powerful, all-knowing, all merciful, His nature is fundamentally antagonistic to all evil, 34, xxviii, 15, 79, 125, 136 sq., 329, 357; matter and souls constitute the body of G., 34, xxviii; *S*a*n*kara's personal G., is something unreal, 34, xxx; Râmânuga's Brahman is a personal G., 34, xxx, cxxiii sq., cxxiv n.; cannot be reproached with cruelty, on account of His regarding merit and demerit, 34, xlix, 343–6, 357–60; 38, 180–3; 48, 488; the intelligent Self is G., 34, 15, 234, 290; 38, 337–40; is without a body, 34, 50 sq., 438; 48, 421; the one within the sun and the eye is G.,

34, 77–81, 124 sq.; 38, 416 sq.; has no special abode, but abides in His own glory, 34, 78; the sole topic of all worldly songs and of Scripture, 34, 80, 160; His nature is Mâyâ, He is the ruler of Mâyâ, 34, 80, 357 n., 370 sq.; 48, 367; although present everywhere, He is pleased when meditated upon as dwelling in the heart, 34, 114, 196; immortality and fearlessness ascribed to Him, 34, 125; the lordly power of the gods is based on Him, 34, 130; 'measured by a span,' 34, 144, 150–3, 192, 195 sq.; the perception of G. in the gastric fire, 34, 147, 149; has the heaven for His head, &c., and is based on the earth, 34, 148; forms the head, &c., and is based on the chin of the devout worshipper, 34, 148; worshipped as Vaisvânara, 34, 149 sq.; is greater than ether, 34, 177; is a limitary support, 34, 181 sq.; *there is only one highest Lord ever unchanging, whose substance is cognition, and who, by means of Nescience, manifests Himself in various ways, just as a thaumaturg appears in different shapes by means of his magical power*, 34, 190; is the absolute ruler of the past and the future, 34, 196; His position analogous to that of Parganya, 34, 358; His essential goodness affirmed by Sruti and Smriti, 34, 358; the Lord Pasupati, Siva, 34, 435; Scripture the production of the omniscient G. and the omniscience of G. based on Scripture, 34, 437; soul, gods, and G., 36, xxii sq.; meant by the term 'he who renders tripartite,' 38, 97; is everlastingly free from Nescience, 38, 149; is free from all qualities, 38, 340; there is also a form of G. not abiding in effected things, 38, 417 sq.; is all-knowing, 42, 88, 389; 48, 444, 523; Breath is the one G., 44, 117; there must be no questioning beyond the deity, 44, 117, 117 n.; understood by Person (Purusha), or Highest Self, or Brahman, 48, 4, &c., 352; *intelligence pure, free from stain, free from grief, free from all contact with desire and other affections, everlastingly one is the highest Lord—Vasudeva apart from whom nothing exists*, 48, 23; specific power of the knowledge of G., 48, 116; His essential nature is knowledge, 48, 128; Nârâyana, and other names of the one G., 48, 133, 667; existence of G., how to be proved apart from Scripture, 48, 162–9, 497; dwells in the hearts of all creatures, 48, 356 sq.; the Ancient who is difficult to be seen, 48, 361; Hara, the one G., 48, 364; is the enjoyer of all sacrifices, 48, 411 sq., 627; good and evil works please or displease G., 48, 487; Gainas hold that there is no G., 48, 516; *offerings and pious works, all this He bears who is the nave of the Universe, He is Agni and Vâyu, He is Sun and Moon*, 48, 627; called 'That which is,' 48, 658 sq.; purity of mind and heart, due to the grace of G., leads to knowledge, 48, 710; knowledge of G. propitiates G., and thus destroys the displeasure of G. due to previous sins, 48, 723; the continuance of the body's life due to G.'s pleasure or displeasure caused by good or evil deeds, 48, 725; the released soul experiences different worlds created by G. engaged in playful sport, 48, 764; *we know from Scripture that there is a Supreme Person whose nature is absolute bliss and goodness; who is fundamentally antagonistic to all evil; who is the cause of the origination, sustentation, and dissolution of the world; who differs in nature from all other beings, who is all-knowing, who by His mere thought and will accomplishes all His purposes; who is an ocean of kindness as it were for all who depend on Him; who is all-merciful; who is immeasurably raised above all possibility of any one being equal or superior to Him; whose name is the highest Brahman*, 48, 770. *See also* Brahman, Creator, Great One, Îs, Îsvara, Ka, Krishna, Nârâyana, Person (Purusha), Pragâpati, *and* Self (highest).

Godâna, Godânakarman, *see* Hair.

Godâsa, founder of the G. Gana, 22, 288.

Goddesses: the powers of the gods represented by their wives, 1, 151 n.; Hsüan Kiang appears like a goddess, 3, 436, 436 n.; fame, fortune, speech, &c., 8, 90; offerings to the wives of the gods, 12, 75 sq., 75 n., 256 n.,

258; 29, 352; 44, 174 sq.; g. of learning, 14, 299; the pious received in paradise by nymphs, 21, 345, 436; the three g. Sarasvatî, I*d*â, and Bhâratî, 26, 186 n.; 42, 512; Tvash*tri*, and the wives of the gods, 26, 320 n.; spin the bride's and the Brahma*k*ârin's garment, 29, 277 sq.; 30, 147; forenoon, afternoon, noon, evening, midnight and dawn invoked as g., 29, 347; oblations to the g., 30, 143; 43, 263–5; the golden-armed goddess, seated in the midst of the gods, 30, 179; divine women (wives of the gods, Dhisha*n*âs, days and nights, metres, stars), 41, 242–4; the goddess of the field, 42, 89; wives of the gods and other g. invoked, 42, 162; 46, 245; evil qualities as female divinities, 42, 423.

Godhâvarî, n. of a river, 10 (ii), 184.

Gods.

(*a*) Names, classes, and numbers of Hindu g.
(*b*) Origin of g. (India).
(*c*) Characteristics, food of the g. (India).
(*d*) Abodes of g. (India).
(*e*) G. and men in India.
(*f*) All the g. and individual g. (India).
(*g*) Myths and legends of Hindu g.
(*h*) Worship of g. in India.
(*i*) Hindu g. in philosophy.
(*j*) G. in Buddhism.
(*k*) G. in *G*aina religion.
(*l*) Angels and archangels in Zoroastrianism.
(*m*) G. or sacred beings (Yazatas, Yazdân) in Zoroastrianism.
(*n*) Chinese spirits or spiritual beings (Kwei-shăn).
(*o*) False g. in Islâm.

(*a*) Names, classes, and numbers of Hindu g.

Lists of g., 1, 238–40, 245, 288–90; 7, 212–14; 8, 219–21; 14, 252–5; 29, 120–2, 280; 30, 243; 41, 40 n.; 42, 80; 44, 281; 46, 186–92; sacrifices to g., like Kumâra, who formerly were men, 2, 40, 40 n., 263 n.; the eight Lokapâlas or guardians of the world, Indra, &c., 7, 4, 4 n.; 25, 185 sq., 186 n., 216 sq., 256; 33, 104, 107, 109; father, mother, and teacher, compared to the three g., 7, 128; are threefold (of the three Gu*n*as), 8, 331; men are more numerous than g., 12, 342; as many g. as there were of old, so many g. there are now, 12, 351; the Ga*n*as, the lord of the g., the goddess of learning, and the lord of learning, 14, 299; faith, right knowledge, wisdom, and other abstract ideas deified, 14, 308; 26, 21 sq.; 29, 121 sq., 221, 321; 30, 145; 41, 250; number and classes of g., their spheres and abodes, 15, 139–49; the 3,306 g. are only the various powers of them, 15, 140; the g. of the different quarters, all enter into the sun, 15, 338–40; Agnishvâttas, the manes of the g., 25, 111 sq.; Vaimânika g. produced by goodness, 25, 494, 495 n.; g. and demi-gods in the scale of creatures, 25, 494 sq.; eleven g. in heaven, eleven on earth, eleven in the waters, 26, 290; three kinds of g., Vasus, Rudras, and Âdityas, 26, 350; 46, 42 sq.; thirty-three g. (8 Vasus, 11 Rudras, 12 Âdityas, 2 Heaven and Earth), and Pra*g*âpati, 26, 411; 30, 240; 41, 9, 79; 42, 187; 44, 115, 151, 206–11, 252, 257 sq.; 46, 42, 245; list of the Nakshatras with their presiding deities, 29, 53 sq.; domestic g., 29, 319 sq.; earth, air, heavens, quarters, waters, rays, ocean, invoked for protection, 29, 343 sq.; all kinds of g. invoked at the house-building, 29, 347 sq.; the thirty-three g., the Brahman's children, 30, 194 sq.; their number, 34, 200; all g. comprised in the Vasus, Rudras, Âdityas, Vi*s*vedevas, and Maruts, 34, 202 n.; among the pa*ñk*aganâ*h*, 34, 262; the devasû or Divine Quickeners, 41, 69–72; 43, 246–9, 246 n.; six deities who became the universe, 41, 187–9; are threefold (of sky, air, earth), 41, 239, 239 n.; are sevenfold, 41, 241; all kinds of divine beings invoked in a battle-charm, 42, 119 sq.; prayer for deliverance from calamity, addressed to the entire pantheon, 42, 160–2, 628 sq.; deities of metres, 43, 53, 330 sq.; the divine host, 43, 373; 46, 42 sq.; number of g. stationary, 43, 128; Food and Breath are the two g., 44, 117; the three g. are the three worlds, for therein all the g. are contained, 44, 117; are of three orders, 44, 291, 291 n.; as many as there are g. of the Seasonal offerings, so many are all

the g., 44, 383, 393; in the air, and in the heavenly light, 46, 245; three hundred and three thousand g. and thirty and nine did service to Agni, 46, 257; the secret names of the g., 46, 378; Kshattras among the g., 48, 461; wives of the g., *see* Goddesses. *See also* Devas, Superhuman beings, Suras, *and also below* (*j*, *k*).

(*b*) Origin of G. (India).

The Devas worshipped breath as Bhûti or being, and thus became great beings, 1, 213; anywhere at the birthplace of a deity, *S*râddhas should be performed, 7, 260; obtained their divinity by living as Brahma*k*ârins, 8, 178; the devotee creates for himself even the divinity of the g., 8, 250; created, 8, 387; 25, 12, 12 n.; 43, 289; 48, 461; the sons of Heaven and Earth, 12, 225; the highest creation of Brahman, when he created the g., 15, 86–90; sprang from the manes, 25, 112; the state of g. reached by the quality of goodness, 25, 493; obtained their authority by means of the sacrifice, 26, 21, 36, 39, 46, 101, 174, 445; born of the mind, 26, 42; a kind of theogony, 32, 246 sq.; belief in the existence of the g., 42, 158, 622; were born of the u*k*-*kh*ish*t*a, 42, 229; the birth of the g. is the year, 43, 144; the Brahman (neut.) created the g., 44, 27; after the procreation of the g. offspring is produced, 44, 44; are the offspring of Manu, 46, 42 sq.; originated from the Self, 48, 367.

(*c*) Characteristics, food of the G. (India).

Their exalted character denied, 8, 16 sq., 76, 76 n.; worship the pure great light, 8, 186; become deluded, wishing for pleasure, 8, 322; enlightenment is the characteristic of g., 8, 348; the path-finding g., 12, 263 sq.; are immortal, imperishable, 12, 290, 295, 444; 38, 388; 43, 148; 44, 174; how they became immortal, 12, 310 sq., 343; 26, 147 sq., 346; 41, 157; 43, 220, 256, 356 sq.; 44, 5, 28; are the rays of the sun, 12, 328; 26, 254; are trebly true, 14, 277, 319; are mortal, 15, 289; age of the g., 25, 20–2; are invisible, 26, 19; 34, 201; do not sleep, 26, 44; 32, 8; are hidden to men, 26, 76; always speak the truth, 26, 95 sq.; 43, 257 sq.; 44, 447; the threefold age of the g., 29, 56; 30, 162; are long-lived through ambrosia (am*ri*ta), 29, 294; *the so-called deathlessness of the g. only means their comparatively long existence. And their lordly power also is based on the highest Lord and does not naturally belong to them*, 34, 130; 38, 17; having several bodies at the same time, they come to many sacrifices, 34, 198–201, 217; 48, 330 sq.; naturally possess all supernatural powers, 34, 200, 219; have certain characteristic shapes without which the sacrificer could not represent them to his mind, 34, 221 sq.; possess a body and sense-organs, 34, 355; 48, 328–30; exist in the state of highest power and glory and cannot enter, in this wretched body, into the condition of enjoyers, 38, 93; may be called light and so on, because they represent light and so on, 38, 388; are free from decrepitude, 42, 51, 365; immortality and truth in the g., 42, 84; the g. love the mystic, 43, 156, 158, 175, 179, 372, 398; 44, 443; made themselves boneless and immortal, 43, 178; are of joyful soul, 43, 339 sq.; have no loathing for anything, 44, 184, 186; 'the patient g. who give no reply,' 48, 68; souls of g., 48, 198; are liable to suffering, 48, 327; are qualified for meditation on divinities, 48, 335–7;—Vâyu, the eater, and his food, viz. Agni, Âditya, *K*andramas, Ap, 1, 59, 59 n.; subsist on sacrifices, 7, 194; 12, 66 sq., 176; 26, 154; 41, 1; 44, 22, 508 sq.; sacrificial food for the g. is am*ri*ta (ambrosia), 12, 40 sq.; 26, 191; the moon is Soma, the food of the g., 12, 176, 181, 362, 380; 26, xiii; 44, 6, 9 sq., 34; the sacrifice their food, immortality their sap, the sun their light, 12, 361; living food of the immortal g., 26, 201; the souls are the food of the g., 38, 110–12; the circle of the never-ending food of the g., 43, 221; how the g. eat

food, 43, 295; the hymn of praise is food for the g., 44, 232; ghee is their favourite resource, 44, 296, 342, 410; all the g. subsist on rain, 44, 507; subsist on the milk of cattle, 44, 508; when Soma overflows, all the g. avail themselves thereof, 44, 510; sun made into honey (nectar) for the enjoyment of the g., 48, 368 sq., 370; *the g. in truth do not eat nor do they drink; by the mere sight of that amrita they are satisfied*, 38, 111; 48, 589.

(*d*) Abodes of G. (India).

East, the quarter of the g., 1, 176; 12, 63, 422; 26, 1–4; 44, 448; formerly men and g. lived together, then the g. went to heaven in reward of their sacrifices, 2, 140; 12, 160, 199 sq., 207 sq.; 26, 307; 44, 43; the sacrificer ascends to the g., 2, 140; 12, 294; 14, 302, 331 sq.; 26, 1, 4; 43, 267 sq.; 44, 372; world of the g., obtained by good and pious actions, 7, 109, 129; 8, 84, 233, 254 sq., 316, 322, 327, 389; 14, 258, 261; what deity one worships to that he goes after death, 8, 76, 78; abide in the house of the sacrificer, 12, 4 sq.; dwell in heaven, 12, 109; 26, 260; 43, 97, 103, 109, 113, 116 sq., 148; dwell on the top of Mount Meru, 12, 110 n.; 'the ladder of the g.' whereby the g. and *Ri*shis reached their high station, 14, 309; priests rule over the world of the g., 25, 157; the place of worship a high spot as being nearer to the g., 26, 1 sq., 1 n.; by the metres the g. attained heaven, 26, 230, 328; 44, 156, 172; paths between heaven and earth, trodden by the g., 29, 337; 42, 51, 365; the soul goes from the world of the g. to Vâyu, 38, 386; who vie with the sun, who are in rivers, or mountains, 42, 35, 408; a tree as the seat of the g., 42, 416; established themselves in this world by means of animals, 43, 56 sq.; seven worlds of the g., 43, 277, 314; all the g. abide here on the new moon day, 44, 2; worlds of the g. (in the north) and the fathers, 44, 225; did not know the Pavamâna to be the heavenly world, 44, 304; the g. who are in this world and who are in the heavenly world, 44, 328; North-east the region of both g. and men, 44, 359; the earth, the air, and the sky, regions, Nakshatras and waters, places of abode for all the g., 44, 505 sq.; may the divine doors open themselves, that the g. may come forth, 46, 153; to the g. go the worshippers of the g., those devoted to Vish*n*u go to Vish*n*u, 48, 627; path of the g., *see* Future Life (*b*). *See also* Heaven.

(*e*) G. and men in India.

'*I know myself reaching as far as the g., and I know the g. reaching as far as me. For these g. receive their gifts from hence, and are supported from hence*,' 1, 212 sq.; do not teach what is virtue and what is sin, 2, 72; Brâhma*n*as are the human g., 7, 77; 12, 309 sq., 374; 26, 341; 42, 164, 529; beings divided into godlike and demoniac, 8, 114 sq.; are inferior to the men of true knowledge, 8, 146, 161, 161 n.; are engaged in gifts, 8, 282; reach perfection by penance, 8, 389; g. are the truth, man is the untruth, 12, 4, 16; 26, 63, 238, 344; 33, 93; in the beginning g. and men were together, 12, 347 sq.; give the enjoyments through fear of punishment, 25, 219, 219 n.; desert a country ruled by a wicked king, 25, 220; *the wicked, indeed, say in their hearts, 'Nobody sees us'; but the g. distinctly see them*, 25, 269; 'speech of the g.,' false evidence with a pious intention, 25, 272; the king shall emulate the g., 25, 396 sq.; Brâhma*n*as have power over the g., 25, 398, 398 n., 447; penances adopted by g., sages, and manes, 25, 473, 475; the Veda the eternal eye of the manes, g., and men, 25, 504; know the mind of man, 26, 94; blamed for not being liberal enough, 32, 81, 87; the laws (vrata) of the g., 32, 237–9; 46, 367, 370; read the original code of Manu, 33, 3; men deprived of virility by the wrath of a deity, 33, 167; a king is a deity, 33, 221; cannot perform sacrifices, hence not

entitled to the study of the Veda, 34, 197 n.; Vyâsa and others conversed with the g. face to face, 34, 222 sq.; the vital airs, at the time of death, enter into them, 38, 105 sq.; the souls of sacrificers enjoy themselves with the g., 38, 112; g. were first, then men, 41, 262; 43, 228, 252, 257; longer is the life of the g., shorter the life of men, 41, 344; have given the remedy against poison, 42, 27; charms found by Brahmans, *Ri*shis, and g., 42, 29; sins committed by the g. cause madness, 42, 32, 520; disease sent by the g., 42, 41; rescue men from death, 42, 53–5; this world is most dear to the g., 42, 60; the g. who have brought on trouble, again remove it, 42, 67; spells prepared by g., 42, 78; slain enemies join the g., pious men, and departed Fathers, 42, 126; all the g. follow the Brahma*k*ârin (the sun), 42, 214 sq.; men do (at sacrifices) what the g. did, 43, 83 sq.; a Brâhma*n*a descended from a *Ri*shi represents all g., 44, 195 sq.; followed the laws of *Ri*ta, 46, 54, 64.

(*f*) ALL THE G. AND INDIVIDUAL G. (INDIA).

Pragâpati brooded over the three g., Agni, Vâyu, Âditya, and squeezed out the three Vedas, 1, 70; instructed by Pragâpati, 8, 282 sq.; 25, 164; 43, 175; 44, 103; g., men, and Asuras, the threefold descendants of Pragâpati, 15, 189; 41, 194 sq.; 43, 220; created by Pragâpati, 25, 14, 14 n.; 41, 157; 43, 350; 44, 13, 15; heal Pragâpati by oblations, offered in Agni, 41, 152–4; in union with the life-sustaining g. Pragâpati creates, 43, 32; Pragâpati and the g. converse like father and sons, 43, 59 sq.; Pragâpati bestows shares and lordship on the g., 43, 67–70; offer Pragâpati up in sacrifice, 43, 304 sq.; afraid of Pragâpati, the Death, 43, 356; the sacrificial horse fettered for the g., for Pragâpati, 44, 277 sq.; Pragâpati assigned the sacrifices to the g., 44, 295 sq.; Pragâpati desired to gain the world of the g. and that of men, 44, 306; by the A*s*vamedha the g. restored the eye of Pragâpati, 44, 328; the horse of the A*s*vamedha belongs to all g., not only to Pragâpati, 44, 336; behind Pragâpati are all the g., 44, 393; the g. perish and are created again by Pragâpati, by means of the Veda, 48, 331 sq.;—Indra is above the other g., 1, 151, 307; 8, 88; Agni, Vâyu, and Indra are above the other g., 1, 151; Agni, Soma, and Indra represent all the g., 12, 168 sq.; from terror of Brahman fire and sun burn, Indra, and Vâyu, and Death run away, 15, 21; Agni, Indra, and Sûrya, superior to the other g., 26, 402–4; to Indra belongs the first chariot, to the g. the second, 42, 152; draw together round Indra, 43, 127; Indra and Agni are all the g., 43, 278; are the people of King Dharma Indra, 44, 370;—Agni brings the offerings to the g. or the g. to the sacrifice, 2, 71; 12, 117 sq.; 14, 71; 43, 197 sq., 268; 46, 1, 6–8, 24, 92, 100, 108, 135, 153, 198, 261; chose Agni for their Hot*ri*, 12, 87–9; kindled Agni, 12, 116; 46, 31, 49; the vow belonging to Agni together with g. and men, 29, 229; bestowed immortality on Agni, 43, 156, 177; possessed of a good Agni, 46, 13; Agni and the other g., 46, 16 sq., 22, 31, 37, 49 sq., 64, 67, 70, 83, 89, 119, 173, 275, 303, 418; he is called a friend of the g., to whose sacrifice Agni comes, 46, 92; Agni invoked against hostile powers of g. and mortals, 46, 211; *see also* Agni (*c*, *g*);—the three g., Brahman, Vish*n*u, and *S*iva, 7, xxii, 128; 15, 304, 308; have been destroyed by Kâla, 7, 79; Lakshmî in g., 7, 299; even those who worship other g. with faith, worship only K*ri*sh*n*a, 8, 84; 48, 411; K*ri*sh*n*a the source of g. and sages, 8, 86; do not understand K*ri*sh*n*a, 8, 86 sq.; all g. seen within K*ri*sh*n*a, 8, 92–4; are desiring to see the divine form of K*ri*sh*n*a, 8, 99; Vish*n*u is the ruler of g., demons, and Nâgas, &c., 8, 347; of all g., Dânavas, Bhûtas, &c., Î*s*vara is the lord, 8, 354; Daksha, the father of the g. who are born from

the internal organ, 14, 299; Agni and the other chief g. are only the chief manifestations of the highest Brahman, 15, 302, 303; the Self identified with *S*ambhu, Bhava, Rudra, Pra*g*âpati, Hira*n*yagarbha, Vish*n*u, Nârâya*n*a, 15, 340 sq.; all the g. are Aditi, 32, 255, 261; the king as the God of Riches, 33, 217 sq.; the thousand-eyed god, 42, 68, 402; the armies of the g., having the sun as their ensign, 42, 133; neither g. nor men can escape Bhava and *S*arva, 42, 159; Trita, the scapegoat of the g., 42, 521–3; Agni, Vâyu, and Rudra are the hearts of the g., 43, 162; the many g. and the one God, 44, 115–17; Âhavanîya fire, the womb of the g., 44, 271; subsist on the sun, 44, 470, 508; guarded by the sun, 44, 471; the matutinal g., Agni, the two A*s*vins, the Dawn, the rising Sun, 46, 39; the rain-giving god, 46, 43.

(*g*) MYTHS AND LEGENDS OF HINDU G.

Day and night of the g., 7, 77; 25, 20; 'ponds dug by the g.,' natural lakes, 7, 205, 205 n.; 33, 112, 112 n.; perform sacrifices, 12, 8 sq., 12; 26, 47–9, 52, 74 sq., 89, 93–9, 131, 147, 149–52, 174 sq., 178 sq., 194, 202, 240, 249, 252, 275 sq., 279, 291, 301, 303, 386, 433, 446; 41, 1; 44, 7, 15–19, 22, 317, 441–4; the sacrifice escaped the g., 12, 23, 140; 26, 89, 235; the sacrifice that became a tortoise, the g., and the *Ri*shis, 12, 160–2; deposited their beasts with Agni, 12, 347; formerly g., men, and fathers drank visibly together, now invisibly, 12, 367 n.; 26, 155; ran a race, 12, 370 sq.; 26, 327 n.; 41, 1 sq.; slew V*ri*tra by means of sacrifice, 12, 408–10, 417–20, 437, 444 sq., 449; 41, 48; sins committed by the g., 14, 321; 42, 73, 604; the whole world sprang from the g., 25, 112; the g. even swore oaths, 25, 273, 273 n.; 33, 98 sq.; accidents caused by the will of the g., 25, 325; proclaimed the power of austerity, 25, 479; the celestial hosts approached the g., 26, 179 sq.; procured holy and medical plants, 42, 4 sq., 38 sq., 280; release the sun and the *ri*tam from darkness and sin, 42, 15; sorceries performed by the g., 42, 39; conquered all the world in battle, 42, 86; pour love into the waters, 42, 105, 535; quarrels among the g., 42, 134, 363; human sacrificer imitates the rites performed by the g., 43, 22 sq., 30, 33, 41, 58 sq., 82, 117, 145, 156, 169, 188, 190–5, 198, 200, 202, 215 sq., 217 sq., 223–5, 236–9, 255 sq., 270, 275 sq., 303, 316; afraid of the Rakshas, 43, 104 sq.; 44, 453, 462, 467, 478; how they recovered the nectar of immortality, 43, 255; the Haya (steed) carries the g., 43, 401; fashioned the initiation and other parts of the sacrifices, 44, 138; performed a sacrificial session of a thousand years, 44, 170 sq.; gold is a form of the g., 44, 236; come on chariots, 46, 38, 237, 245; struggle of g. (Devas) and Asuras, *see* Asuras (*c*).

(*h*) WORSHIP OF G. IN INDIA.

A Sâman interwoven in the g., 1, 32; offerings to all the g. (Vai*s*vadeva, Devaya*gñ*a), 2, 48, 48 n., 195, 201 sq., 299; 14, 49 sq., 304, 308; 25, 91, 132; 29, 84–7, 89 sq., 161 sq., 321; 44, 95 sq.; as long as he is impure, he shall avoid pronouncing the names of the g., 2, 94; Snâtaka shall not speak evil of the g., and must be careful about his duties towards them, 2, 95, 225; 29, 124; Bali offerings to the servants of the g., the g. inside the house, and the g. of the points of the horizon, 2, 107, 107 n., 202, 202 n.; 29, 290; Brâhma*n*as and Kshatriyas uphold g., manes, and men, 2, 238; witnesses to be sworn in the presence of the g., the king, and Brâhma*n*as, 2, 247; the strength, &c., of a student who breaks the vow of chastity goes to the g., 2, 294, 294 n.; he who performs penances becomes known to all the g., 2, 299; 14, 297; reverence towards g. and Brâhma*n*as enjoined for all castes, 7, 13; *S*râddhas begin and end with rites in honour of the g., 7, 85, 238; 12, 363 sq., 433 sq.; 14, 53 sq., 238; 25, 98, 98 n.,

113 sq., 113 n., 121; the householder's duty of worshipping the g., 7, 194; 8, 118, 243, 306; part of the hand called 'Tîrtha sacred to the g.,' 7, 198; 14, 25, 166; 25, 40 sq.; he who sacrifices pleases the g., and the g. reward the sacrificer, 8, 53, 61; 12, 248; 48, 626 sq., 720; those who worship the g. go to the world of g., 8, 84; 12, 450 sq., 451 n.; 44, 259, 272; paying reverence to g., a good penance, 8, 119; contempt of the g. is a sin, 8, 320; 25, 154; the good householder eats what remains after offerings to g. and guests, 8, 358; the hermit should eat after the g. and guests are satisfied, he should eat little, depending on the g., 8, 361 sq.; invoked by Brâhmans, 11, 180; he who enters the vow before sacrifice, approaches the g., 12, 6; the offerings announced or pointed out to the g., 12, 17, 32; 30, 343 sq.; the oblation shall gladden the g., 12, 27; the sacrifice is performed for the g., the seasons, and the metres, 12, 79–81; sit round the altar, 12, 86; the Barhis, or the Prastara, the seat of the g., 12, 87, 93; the priests propitiate g., 12, 127 sq., 134 sq.; man owes the debt of sacrifice to the g., 12, 190 sq., 190 n.; 14, 46, 56, 271; 25, 169; 49 (i), 100; the power of the g. is the sacrifice, 12, 251; are dismissed at the end of the sacrifice, 12, 263 sq.; 26, 377 sq.; 41, 185; times suitable for the worship of the g., 12, 289 sq.; go to the house of him who sets up the sacred fire, and performs the Agnihotra, 12, 291, 328 sq.; new-moon libation to the horses of the g., 12, 375, 382 sq. and n.; are desirous of purity and themselves pure, and love a pure sacrifice, 14, 186; worshipped during penances, 14, 303–6; 25, 476; a performer of rites securing success, must worship cows, Brâhma*n*as, and g., 14, 323; Ka purifies by a certain rite Sahasrâksha, Fire, Wind, Sun, Soma, Yama, and other lords of the g., 14, 331; feasts in honour of the g., 25, 64 sq.; marriage rite of the g. (daiva), 25, 79–82; 29, 166; ordain the consumption of meat for sacrifices, 25, 174; to be worshipped after a victory, 25, 248, 248 n.; husband receives his wife from the g., 25, 344, 344 n.; wealth of those who offer sacrifices is called property of the g., 25, 434 sq.; cooked offerings for the g., 26, 201; all g. draw nigh to the victim, thinking that it is immolated for them, 26, 203; food given to Brâhma*n*as, reaches the g., 29, 16; Yama and all g. contained in the Ash*t*akâ, 29, 102; adoration to g., *R*ishis, Manes, and men, 29, 150; Agni, Indra, Pra*g*âpati, Vi*s*ve Devâs, Brahman are regularly worshipped where there is no special rule with regard to the deity of a sacrifice, 29, 163; satisfied by reciting the Vedas and other sacred texts, 29, 218; 44, 96 sq., 101; satiated at the Tarpa*n*a, 29, 219; invoked to give long life to the new-born child, 29, 294; water oblations to the g. at the Utsarga, 29, 325; Bali offering to the protecting deities of the furrow, 29, 335 sq.; the pupil at the Upanayana given in charge of the g., 29, 401; 30, 272; there can be no substitute for the deity of a sacrifice, 30, 353; delight in prayers, 32, 86; sacrifices enjoined by them, 32, 238 sq.; ordeal to be performed in the presence of the guardians of the world, 33, 104; high value of property belonging to g., 33, 205; look on with divine eyes when a witness gives evidence, 33, 245; the judge worships the g. before performing an ordeal, 33, 250 sq.; oaths by g., 33, 315; fine for stealing property of a deity or Brâhma*n*a, 33, 363; invoked for long life, 42, 50 sq.; an amulet for g., fathers, and men, 42, 87; all the g. call the king to the throne, 42, 113; Brâhma*n*as strike those who revile the g., 42, 169–71; the sterile cow belongs to the g., therefore must be given to the Brahmans, 42, 175–9, 656; bricks of the fire-altar identified with g., 43, 90 sq.; the sacrifice is the self of the g., 43, 103; 44, 504; from left to right is the way with the g., 43, 136, 139, 147; only that is a deity to whom oblations

are offered, 43, 240, 245 sq.; if he eats on new and full moon nights, he eats whilst passing over the g., 44, 21; the sacrificer gives himself up to the g. (by the fasts) and redeems himself by the (new and full moon) sacrifice, 44, 22 sq.; theory regarding the full and new moon in respect of the g. (sun and moon, earth and sky, night and day), 44, 31; he who offers to the g. is inferior to the self-offerer, 44, 38; offerings to the g. compared to tribute brought to a king, 44, 38; fill gold cups for him who having offered ghee, offers sacrificial portions, 44, 61; *S*rî dismembered by the g., and restored by a sacrifice, 44, 62–5; P*ri*sh*th*ya and Abhiplava are the two wheels of the g. crushing the Sacrificer's evil, 44, 149; how the Mahâvrata yielded itself to the g., 44, 159; rites for the g. and rites for the Fathers, how distinguished, 44, 198–200, 430–4; *may the g. protect me through the g.*, 44, 258; prayer to be delivered from sins against the g., 44, 265 sq.; all the g. are concerned in the horse-sacrifice, 44, 278 sq., 311, 352; went in quest of the A*s*vamedha, 44, 284; depart from those who speak impure speech at the sacrifice, 44, 387; the Udgât*ri* called 'friend of the g.,' 44, 388; all the g. made guardians of the Pravargya sacrifice, 44, 453; what is baked, belongs to the g., 44, 456; sacrifice a feast of the g., 46, 6, 283; spirits or deified objects connected with the sacrifice, 46, 8–12; the Aryan clans long for the g., 46, 100. *See also* Debts (the three), Idols, *and* Sacrifices (*e*).

(*i*) HINDU G. IN PHILOSOPHY.

Teaching of Brahman with regard to the g., 1, 151 sq., 152 n.; the elements and the five senses or Prâ*n*as represented as g., 1, 185; 8, 123, 123 n., 337–40, 349 sq.; 15, 98, 274; 34, 303–5; 41, 273, 395; 43, 32, 185 sq., 304; 48, 417, 576, 586 sq.; union of the g., as entered into the body, 1, 208, 233, 238–40; all the g. are produced by knowledge of the Self, 1, 245; the human body represented as a lute made by the g., 1, 264; the absorption of the two classes of g. (viz. fire, sun, moon, lightning, and the senses, &c.) into Brahman or breath, 1, 288–90; never reached the Self, 1, 311; 8, 367, 391; through freedom from heedlessness the g. attained to the Brahman, 8, 152 n., 153; are not pleased with a cessation of mortal form, 8, 254 sq.; the science of final emancipation is a great mystery even among the g., 8, 254; speech relates to all the g., 8, 338; the sage who is assimilated with the Brahman, is identical with the g., and extolled by g. and demons, 8, 345; Hara, Rudra, *S*iva, &c., as names of the Highest Self, 15, xxxiii sq., 16; have doubted as to death, 15, 5 sq.; Brahman is all g., the g. being but his manifestation, 15, 86; Prâ*n*a identified with the g., 15, 274–6; 34, 200, 269; the g. identified with the Atman, 25, 512; whether g. are capable of the knowledge of Brahman, 34, xxxvii, 198 sq., 216–23; 48, 326–35; create many things by their mere intention, 34, xciv, 347 sq.; possess unobstructed knowledge, 34, 99; are qualified for the study and practice of the Veda, 34, 198 sq.; may have the desire of final release, 34, 198; to them the Veda is manifest of itself (without study), 34, 199; undergo discipleship, 34, 199; multiform creations exist in them, 34, 353; the performers of sacrifices are objects of enjoyment for the g., 38, 111; 48, 588 sq.; g. worship Prâ*n*a, 42, 219; serve the Person in the eye under the name of 'strengthening food,' 43, 373; by naming the g. everything here is named, 43, 390; as the Year the Sacrificer goes to the g., 44, 140, 155; Highest Person, the inner ruler of Agni and other g., 48, 155; the g. create each in his own world what they require, God creates the entire world, by mere volition, 48, 472.

(*j*) G. IN BUDDHISM.

Dialogue between a deity and Buddha, g. taught by Buddha, 10 (ii), 17–19, 43 sq.; 11, 142; 13,

122 sq.; the g. rejoice at the birth of Buddha, 10 (ii), 94, 125 sq.; 19, 4-6, 13, 344 sq., 347-56; how they felt about Buddha's death, 11, 88-90, 119-21, 127; 19, 308, 318; pay homage to the remains of Buddha, 11, 124, 128 sq.; rejoice and pay homage to Buddha when he reaches Bodhi and founds the Kingdom of Truth, 11, 153-5; 13, 97 sq.; 19, 58, 163 sq., 178 sq.; 21, 160-71, 184; 35, 243; 49 (i), 68 sq., 136, 155 sq., 165-7; instrumental in making Buddha (Yasa) resign the world, 13, 83, 89, 103; 19, 32-4, 36, 49, 54, 56-8, 68 sq., 88, 144, 152-5; 21, 55; 35, 220 sq.; 36, 45, 45 sq. n.; 49 (i), 30, 32, 34, 52, 68, 168, 173; scatter scents and flowers and raise heavenly music at Buddha's funeral, 19, 323; pay homage to the newborn Buddha, 19, 361-4; 49 (i), 7; Indra, Brahma Sahâmpati with all the other g. strew garments and heavenly flowers on Buddha, 21, 69 sq., 313, 315, 366; the four classes of the audience of a Buddha, monks, &c., g. and other superhuman beings, 21, 69, 162, 213, 222 sq., 225, 253, 376, 383, 412, 431, 442; pay homage to Buddhas, 21, 156 sq., 162-71, 183 sq., 308; Indras, Brahmas, and Brahmakâyikas show honour to the preacher, 21, 347, 349; worship relics of Buddhas, 35, 148 sq., 151, 247; when Buddha was eating the g. infused the sap of life into his dish, 36, 37 sq., 37 n.; g. and men adopted the Dhamma, after Brahmâ had adopted it, 36, 41 sq.;—the disciple of Buddha will overcome the world of the g., 10 (i), 16; envy the Arhat, 10 (i), 28, 49; 20, 233; not even g. could change into defeat the victory of a man who has vanquished himself, 10 (i), 31 sq.; the Buddhist view of the g., 10 (i), 31 sq. n.; 11, 162-5; the uncharitable do not attain the world of the g., 10 (i), 48; we shall be like the bright g., feeding on happiness, 10 (i), 53, 53 n.; the virtuous praised by the g., 10 (i), 59, 86; the true Brâhma*n*a is he who has risen above all bondage both to men and to g., 10 (i), 93 sq.; do not know the path of the Arhat, 10 (i), 95; (ii), 115; world of g., Mâras, and Brahmans, 10 (ii), 14, 30, 45, 96, 142 sq., 208; 11, 187, 288; vehicles of the g., 10 (ii), 23; 21, 345, 350; 36, 117; cried out against the injustice of killing cows for sacrifices, 10 (ii), 51; the g. worship Indra, 10 (ii), 52; g. and men depend on desire, 10 (ii), 55; the g. hear the well-spoken words of Vâsava, 10 (ii), 64; the pious householder goes to the g. by name Sayampabhas, 10 (ii), 66; g. as adepts of Buddha and friends of Buddhists, 10 (ii), 85 sq., 185 sq.; 13, 81 sq.; 20, 401; are subject to time, 10 (ii), 90; a Muni is to be worshipped by g. and men, 10 (ii), 91; Buddha, the enlightened of g. and men, 10 (ii), 96; the thirty-three (Tidasa, Tâvati*m*sa) g., 10 (ii), 125; 11, 18, 32, 32 n., 48; 17, 101, 107; 35, 11, 13; a god, or Brahman, or Inda, the husband of Sugâ, 10 (ii), 189; Buddha has penetrated all things concerning the g., 10 (ii), 213; good men called g., 11, 20 sq. and n.; Buddha, the teacher of g. and men, 11, 27, 41, 54, &c.; 19, 331; 21, 119 sq.; 35 167, 237; can, by intense meditation, cause an earthquake, 11, 45 sq.; their royal city Â*l*akamandâ, 11, 100, 248; 35, 3; their existence depends on Karma, 11, 119 sq. n.; world of Brâhma*n*as and Sama*n*as, g. and men, 11, 152 sq., 187, &c.; the wheel of the empire of Truth set rolling by Buddha, cannot be turned back by any god, 11, 153 sq.; seven kinds of g., 11, 154, 154 n.; an immeasurable bright light beyond even the power of the g., appeared in the universe, when Buddha founded his kingdom of righteousness, 11, 155; converted by Buddha, 11, 155 n.; 19, 240 sq.; 36, 248-50; 49 (i), 180; the higher g. are opapâtika, there being no sex or birth in the heavens, 11, 214 n.; aspiration to belong to one or other of the angel hosts (deva-nikâya), is a spiritual bondage, 11, 227, 231 sq.; cloud-spirits of cold, heat, air, wind, and rain, 11, 255 n.; deities residing in trees, 13, 126; 35, 242; they

who honour the g. by offerings, will be honoured by the g. in return, 17, 103; are liable to old age, decay, and death, 19, 18, 18 n., 159 sq., 275, 275 n., 371; pay worship to B*ri*haspati, 19, 78; subject to transmigration, 19, 160, 224; 35, 12 sq., 38; established by Buddha, 19, 193; if Î*s*vara be the maker of the world, people ought not to adore more g. than one, 19, 207; the site of Pâ*t*aliputra protected by g., 19, 250; Buddha god over all g., 19, 262 n., 348; 35, 167; 36, 12, 56, 83, 125, 215, 219, 274, 279, 281, 283, 285, 290 sq., 295, 298, 300–2, 305 sq., *305 n.*, 310, 312–15, 317, 319, 323–5, 327, 331, 337, 340 sq., 344–6, 352–4, 358, 363–5, 368; immortal, but not self-existent, 19, 271 n.; are filled with fear, 19, 287, 337; general grief in heaven when a Deva's day of merit comes to an end, 19, 287, 287 n.; names, different classes, and numbers of g., 19, 308; 21, 4 sq.; 49 (i), 129, 141, 157 sq., 180, 196 sq.; (ii), 26, 30; praise Nirvâ*n*a, 19, 309 sq.; worship Buddha, 19, 337; 49 (ii), 165, 201; Buddha as a god, 21, xxiv–xxviii; after hearing Buddha's law, beings may come to be g. or men, Indras, Brahmas, or rulers of the universe, 21, 125; g. and men will behold each other in Buddha-fields, 21, 194; protect the Bodhisattva, 21, 274; voices of g. and Nâgas, heard by the preacher, 21, 339; the Akanish*th*as and Âbhâsvaras in the Brahma-world, 21, 340; girls, wives, youths and maidens amongst the g., 21, 342; Devanikâyas, Brahmakâyikas, and Mahâbrahmas, 21, 342, 345; odours exhaled by the g., 21, 342, 345; the preacher discerns g. and demons by his smell, 21, 344 sq.; rebirth among the g., 21, 436; 35, 124; shout their approval, when Nâgasena preaches and attains to insight, 35, 22, 26, 29; considered as Buddhist laymen, 35, 31 sq., 31 n.; 36, 248–50; Nâgasena is capable of discussing things with the g., 35, 37; men who, even in their human body, mounted up to the abode of the Thirty-Three, 35, 172; mystic cults of certain g., 35, 266; different from the spirits called 'not men' (amanussâ), 35, 279, 279 n.; evil deeds cannot be concealed from the g. who can read the hearts of men, 35, 295; Buddha is above the god of g., 35, 300; soul and g., 36, xxii sq.; the parrot who caused the heaven of the Thirty-Three to shake, 36, 6; Buddha, chief of g. and men, 36, 55 sq., 120; exalt Vessantara on account of his gift, 36, 116; change of precedence among the g., 36, 127 n.; Akani*tth*a, the highest of all g., 36, 130; men who in this life already attained to glory in Tidasapura (city of the g.), 36, 145 sq.; dreams caused by a god, 36, 157, 160 sq.; miracles caused by g. out of pity for men, 36, 175; miracles worked out of pity for g. and men, 36, 175; certain g. called 'The Formless Ones,' 36, 187 sq.; Buddha's religion for g. and men, 36, 214, 217–21, 221 n., 229, 240, 242, 321, 327; preachers of the Law become g., 49 (i), 185, 187; where Buddhism is preached, there shall be no fear of g., Nâgas, Yakshas, &c., 49 (i), 188; no difference between g. and men in a Buddha country, 49 (ii), 12, 42, 62; where the Trâyastri*ms*a and other g. live in Sukhâvatî, 49 (ii), 37; the pleasures of Paranirmitava*s*avartin g., 49 (ii), 40; in the train of Buddha, 49 (ii), 70, 90 sq.; Buddhas, Bodhisattvas, Bhikshus, and g., 49 (ii), 189; obtain Bodhi, 49 (ii), 199. *See also* Angels (*c*), *and* Fairies.

(*k*) G. IN *G*AINA RELIGION.

On g. in *G*aina religion, 10 (i), 32 n.; worship of prophets as g. by *G*ainas and Buddhists, 22, xxi; a *G*aina should not trust in the delusive power of the g., 22, 77; a *G*aina should not say 'the god rains' but 'the air rains,' nor speak of the god of thunder, god of lightning, 22, 152; Mahâvîra's existence among the g., 22, 190, 218 sq.; the four orders of g., Bhavanapatis, Vyantaras, *G*yotishkas, and Vimânavâsins, 22, 191, 195, 202, 252; bustle among the g. and goddesses at the birth and death of Mahâvîra, 22,

191 sq., 251 sq., 256, 265; the name Venerable Ascetic Mahâvîra was given by the g., 22, 193, 256; Mahâvîra's parents, after living as ascetics, were born as g., 22, 194, 256; the Ku*nd*aladharas, the Laukântika and Maharddhika g., 22, 195; miracles performed by the g. when Mahâvîra retired from the world, and reached the highest knowledge, 22, 195–202; orders and numbers of g., 22, 222 sq.; 45, 183, 183 n.; disputes occurring in the assemblies of g., men, and Asuras, 22, 268; sages who though no g. have obtained the powers of g., 22, 268; state of the g., one of the happy existences, 22, 268 n.; saints born among the g. in their former existence, 22, 271, 281; 45, 35; the body of monks who fast longer than four days is inhabited by a deity, 22, 300 n.; Mahâvîra surrounded by g. and goddesses, 22, 311; the pious monk will be honoured by g., Gandharvas, and men, 45, 8; pious monks reborn as g. of great power and small imperfections, 45, 8; men born as g. according to their actions, 45, 15, 30 sq., 57, 61, 84, 259, 384, 415, 417; *to the highest regions, in due order, to those where there is no delusion, and to those which are full of light, where the glorious (g. dwell)—who have long life, great power, great lustre, who can change their shape at will, who are beautiful as on their first day, and have the brilliancy of many suns—to such places go those who are trained in self-control and penance, monks or householders, who have obtained liberation by absence of passion*, 45, 23; the life and pleasures of the g. surpass human pleasures a thousand times and more, 45, 29 sq.; the state of the Kevalin higher than that of the g., 45, 30 n.; shower down a rain of perfumed flowers and water, and heavenly treasure, at the conversion of a Brâhma*n*a, 45, 54; a monk should not be frightened by voices of g., 45, 72; pay homage to a chaste monk, 45, 77; long life of the g., 45, 84, 84 n.; calamities produced by g., animals, and men, 45, 110, 181, 255; descend from heaven to celebrate the renunciation of a saint, 45, 114 sq.; attend the meeting of Kesi and Gautama, 45, 121; conjuring a god, a means of extorting alms, employed by bad monks, 45, 133 n.; carnal love towards divine beings, 45, 139; from desire of pleasure arises the misery of the world, the g. included, 45, 187; duration of Lê*s*yâs of g., 45, 202; classification and description of g., and duration of their life, 45, 225–9, 381; why people are born as Abhiyôgidêvas, Kilvishadêvas and Asuras, 45, 231 n.; the world created by the g., 45, 244; even g. must suffer for their deeds, 45, 250; the Supar*n*a g. reside in the *S*âlmalî tree, 45, 290; the Lavasaptamas, the highest of those g. who live very long, 45, 291; do not reach final beatitude, 45, 331; some pious men become liberated saints, others g., 45, 331 sq., 352; commit sins, 45, 356; *G*ainas should believe that g. and goddesses exist, 45, 408. *See also* Vimânas.

(*l*) ANGELS AND ARCHANGELS IN ZOROASTRIANISM.

A. assist the Mazdayasnians against demons and demon-worshippers, 5, li sq., 224–30; how each of the archa. can best be propitiated, 5, lxii, 372–9; thirty a. and archa., 5, 103–5, 103 sq. n.; no a. come to the body of him who does not perform ablution, 5, 299; all worship reaches either the a. or the demons, 5, 310; a. and archa. invoked, praised, worshipped, 5, 312–14; 18, 324, 357; 37, 34 sq., 168, 232–4, 277, 293 sq., 298, 303, 315 sq., 438, 444 sq., 463; 47, 51, 95; the activity of the seven archa., 5, 357, 357 n.; archa. are intangible spirits, but must be worshipped, 5, 372 sq. n.; the thirty a. and archa. presiding over the days of the month, 5, 401–6, 406 n.; 23, 3; heavenly and earthly a. invoked, 18, 3; spiritual life and glory for the soul owing to the a., 18, 22 sq.; they dwell in heaven, 18, 57, 275; Srôsh to be reverenced separately from all the other a., 18, 61, 61 n.; archa. assemble in the middle of the sky, 18, 87; a. vanquish wizards

and witches, 18, 88 sq.; a. attend to the wishes of the Creator, 18, 120; seven archa. in the propitiatory dedication of the sacred cake, 18, 143 sq.; archa. pleased by the ceremonial, 18, 159 sq., 159 n.; 37, 173 sq.; a. not attacked by the stench of unnatural sin, 18, 220 sq.; archa. are immortal, undistressed, and omniscient, 18, 221; archa. assist Tîstar against Apâôsh, 18, 267; a. opposed by the fiends, 18, 270 sq., 319, 319 n.; a. are distressed by an imperfect purification rite, 18, 294; a. intercede for the soul of Keresâsp, 18, 378–80; archa. sit around Aûharmazd, 18, 415 sq.; archa. and a. of the spiritual and worldly creations propitiated, 24, 3 sq., 4 n., 8; a., archa., and spirits gratified by Vistâsp, 24, 65; goodness of the archa. the cause of prosperity of the world, 37, 196; Kâî-Ûs attempts to reach the heavenly region of the archa., 37, 221; he who provides for the Mazda-worshipper provides for the archa., 37, 280; assistance by the archa., 37, 291 sq.; wisdom of archa., 37, 305; increasing the strength of the archa., 37, 341; obeisance to the archa., 37, 360 sq., 378; exploits of the archa., 37, 364; contentment of the archa., 37, 370; archa. lodge in him who loves Vohûman, 37, 382; Zoroaster's conference with the archa., 47, xv, xxi, xxiv, xxvii, xxx, 156–62; Zoroaster's spiritual body with the archa., 47, xxviii sq.; archa. protect agriculture, 47, 7; Zoroaster's guardian spirit and body united by the archa., 47, 21–9; archa. opposed to harm, 47, 55; archa. assist Zoroaster in converting Vistâsp, 47, 67–70, 81, 124, 164; archa. send forth the soul of Srîtô from heaven, 47, 79; archa. report the birth of Zoroaster, 47, 87; apostles confer with the archa., 47, 106, 112; archa. sent by Aûharmazd to protect the infant Zoroaster, 47, 145; glory of the seven archa., 47, 148; reverence of the emanations of the six archa., 47, 168. *See also* Ameshaspentas, *and* Angels (*b*).

(*m*) G. OR SACRED BEINGS (YAZATAS, YAZDÂN) IN ZOROASTRIANISM.

Abstract deities worshipped by the adherents of Zoroastrianism, 4, lxi, lxv; 23, 30; natural deities in early Zoroastrianism, 4, lxi, lxv; prayers and sacrifices to all the g. offered by Zoroastrians, 4, 221–4, 245, 248; the holy g. and the great Ratu, 4, 250; Aûharmazd and the angels who are the whole of the heavenly and earthly sacred beings (yazdân), 5, 155; spirits of the sky, water, earth, plants, animals, mankind, and fire, 5, 156; g. or sacred beings invoked and worshipped by the devout, 5, 312; 18, 123–5, 134–6, 166–73, 279–81, 325 sq.; 24, 10, 12 sq., 26, 43 sq., 78; 37, 34 sq., 344 sq., 377, 428 sq., 431, 436, 466 sq.; meat-offerings apportioned to g., 5, 335–8; resurrection the happiness and hope of the good spirits, 18, 38; are the spirits distressed when a righteous man dies? 18, 50 sq.; man, a servant of the g., 18, 122 sq., 125; good spirits co-operate in the preparation of the sky, 18, 261; one Yast for every Amshaspand and every Ized, 23, 1–3; thirty g. and numerous abstract deities invoked, 23, 2–20; glory of the gods in the heavens and in the material world, 23, 291 sq., 352; the sacred being is the best protection, 24, 41; divine providence overrules destiny, 24, 55; belief in the s. b. a good work, 24, 75; fear of s. b., 24, 78; ceremonies are a thanksgiving to the s. b., 24, 94 sq.; demons the opponents of the s. b., 24, 164; the pantheon of Zoroastrianism, 31, 195–203; thirty-three lords of the ritual order, 31, 198 sq., 198 n., 205, 210, 216, 220, 225; all the Yazads, heavenly and earthly, worshipped, 31, 202, 207, 212, 218, 222 sq., 227, 254 sq., 257, 259, 272, 274, 277, 319, 328, 374, 382, 389, 391; Fravashis of the Yazads worshipped, 31, 273; sacrifices to the lords of spiritual and of earthly creatures, of aquatic animals, beasts, and birds, 31, 335; triumphs of the s. b. over the demons, 37, 23, 285; 47, 123; bringing of the word from

the s. b., 37, 31; gratified by justice, 37, 102; spirits of fire, water, and plants hurt by the destruction of a righteous man, 37, 149; ceremonials of the various s. b., 37, 183 sq. and n.; 47, 168 sq.; assembly of the s. b., 37, 189; mutual service of man, cattle, and s. b., 37, 265; worship of s. b. not to be neglected under any circumstances, 37, 276 sq.; who is liberal to the s. b. is free from destruction, 37, 282; reverence for s. b. a good work, 37, 311–13; s. b. gratified by proper care of cattle, 37, 318 sq.; s. b. gratified by virtuousness, 37, 323–7; power of s. b. increased by love of their affairs, 37, 335; body and life given to the s. b., 37, 352 sq.; discrimination in the affairs of the s. b., 37, 373 sq.; the s. b. instruct Masyê and Masyâôî in arts and manufacture, 47, xxv, 7 sq.; friendship of Zaratûst for the s. b., 47, 47; s. b. are beneficent and righteous, 47, 69.

(*n*) CHINESE SPIRITS OR SPIRITUAL BEINGS (KWEI-SHĂN).

Shun sacrificed to the Six Honoured Ones, to hills and rivers, and to the host of sp., 3, 39, 39 n.; thanksgiving sacrifices to the sp. of the land and of the four quarters, 3, 371, 371 n., 373, 373 n.; people suffering injury protest to the sp. of heaven and earth, 3, 90; Thang fears to offend 'the Powers above and below,' 3, 91; sp. of hills and rivers were all in tranquillity, as long as kings were virtuous, 3, 93; sp. of heaven and earth worshipped, 3, 96, 126; 27, 307; worship of the sp. of the land and grain, 3, 96, 126; 16, 256; 27, 107, 115, 183, 191, 218, 222, 225 sq., 278, 300, 309, 313–15, 329 sq., 373, 397, 416; 28, 33, 67, 101, 222, 235, 253, 265; accept only the sacrifices of those who are sincere, 3, 99; victims devoted to the sp. of heaven and earth, 3, 123; invoked for help in war, 3, 135; pious rulers behave gravely and respectfully to sp. and men, 3, 163; the spirit of the land sacrificed to in a new city, 3, 183; the king should sacrifice to the sp. above and beneath, 3, 186; services to sp. and to Heaven, 3, 217; the Minister of Religion regulates the services for sp. and manes, 3, 228, 228 n.; perfect government and bright virtue have a piercing fragrance for the spiritual intelligences, 3, 232; the descents of sp. ceased when *Kh*ung and Lî made an end of the communications between earth and heaven, 3, 257, 257 sq. n.; ancestors become tutelary sp., 3, 301; 'all spiritual beings' or 'the hundred sp.' presiding over all nature, 3, 318, 318 n.; hearken to him who seeks a friend, 3, 347, 347 n.; hearken to the officers who quietly fulfil their duties, 3, 365; great altar to the sp. of the land raised by Than-fû, 3, 384, 385 n.; unseen by men, one is still under the observation of sp., 3, 388, 388 n., 415; sacrifice to the spirit of the path, 3, 399, 399 n., 425 sq., 425 n.; 27, 314 sq.; 'host of all the sp.,' one of the titles of the sovereigns of China, 3, 405, 405 n.; King Hsüan expostulates with God and all the sp. whom he expects to allay a terrible drought, 3, 419–23; sacrifices to the sp. of the four quarters and of the land, 3, 422; Kwei-shăn or sp., what they are, 16, 32, 34, 45, 355 sq. n.; inflict calamity on the full and bless the humble, 16, 226, 226 sq. n.; men of worth employed to do service to sp., 16, 324, 325 n.; sacrifices to sp. or phenomena of nature, 27, 36; 28, 203, 209, 218, 218 n.; 39, 300 n.; sacrifices to sp. of hills and rivers, and of the quarters, 27, 116, 216 sq., 273, 278, 307, 313–15, 376, 385 sq., 397; 28, 101; sacrifice to the Father of War, 27, 220; those who gave false reports about appearances of sp. put to death, 27, 238; sacrifices to the sp. of the ground, 27, 259, 259 n.; sacrifice to the 'first match-maker,' 27, 259; husbandry dear to the sp., 27, 279, 279 n.; prayer to 'the Honoured ones of Heaven,' 27, 300, 300 n.; the ruler's intercourse with sp., 27, 375, 377; the sp. of nature as associates for men, 27, 383 sq.; enjoy the virtue of the superior man, 27, 394;

things used for rites shall be in accordance with the requirements of the sp., 27, 395, 395 n.; distinction between g. and manes, 27, 430, 430 n.; the Father of Husbandry, 27, 431; communion with the sp. by sacrifices, 27, 434–6; marriage a service of the sp., 27, 441 sq.; do not take liberties with or weary sp., 28, 73; music and ceremonies bring down the sp. from above, 28, 114; the honouring of sp., 28, 219, 341 sq.; the Spiritual Intelligences served with reverence, 28, 239; communion with the Spiritual Intelligences attained by purification, 28, 240, 245; sacrifices give expression to the loving feeling towards the sp., 28, 271; the powers of sp., 28, 307 sq. and n.; the superior man presents himself before them, 28, 325; the Spiritual Intelligences of heaven and earth, 28, 349; eight sp. worshipped by the founder of the *Kh*in dynasty, 39, 41, 41 n.; the power of the sp. or manes, 39, 82, 104; sp. of the land worshipped under an oak-tree, 39, 217–19; from the Tâo came the mysterious existences of the sp., 39, 243, 243 n.; the Tâoist sage suffers not from ghosts and is not scared by the sp. of the dead, 39, 333; the Tâoist sage suffers no reproof from the sp. of the dead, 39, 365; tutelary sp. of the land do not bestow their blessings selfishly, 39, 382; altars raised to the spirit of the grain, 40, 75; man's relation to men and sp., 40, 83, 83 n.; sp. in heaven and earth take account of men's actions and curtail their lives according to the gravity of their transgressions, 40, 235 sq., 244; bad men revile the sp., 40, 242; the Divine Ruler of the eastern Hwa, the Divine Ruler of the Golden Gate, and the Royal-mother of the West, 40, 248 sq. *See also* Ancestor Worship (*a*, *b*).

(*c*) FALSE G. IN ISLÂM.

Nature-g. (Ginns) worshipped by the Arabs, 6, xi sq.; patron deities of Arabian tribes, 6, xii; false g. can neither harm nor profit people, 6, 194, 204; are lifeless, cannot create anything, 6, 252; 9, 64, 83, 161; if there were other g., they would rebel against God, 9, 5; themselves have recourse to God, 9, 7, 7 n.; deny their worshippers on judgement day, 9, 32; cannot defend the idolators against God, 9, 49; are helpless and cannot help, 9, 153, 167; are punished in hell, as well as the idolators, 9, 169; worship of false g., in order to be brought nearer to God, 9, 182; desert their worshippers on the last day, 9, 204. *See also* Ginns.

Gog and Magog, 9, 25, 25 n., 54.

Gôgôsasp, or Gôsasp, n. of a Zoroastrian teacher, 5, 243, 243 n., 265 sq., 275.

Gôkar*d* (or Gôkerânô, or Gôkerenô), *see* Haoma, *and* Trees.

Gô*k*îhar, 'the great one of the middle of the sky,' 5, 21 sq. and n.; leader of planets, 5, 113 sq., 113 n.; falls from a moonbeam on to the earth, 5, 125; burns the serpent in the melted metal, 5, 129, 129 n.

Gôk-patŏ, *see* Gôpatshah.

Gold, man consists of, 1, 205; at night one should not study in a wood where there is no fire nor g., 2, 44; is, like fire, a means of purification, 2, 66 sq.; 7, 101; 44, 235 n., 236, 239, 239 n.; eating g., a penance, 2, 276, 276 n.; 14, 117, 311; its origin, 5, 183; 18, 199; Asvattha tree of golden leaves, 8, 189; the first among precious things, 8, 209, 353; one should not wish for g., 8, 365; used at auspicious rites, 12, 276 sq. n., 277 sq.; 26, 63, 74, 100 n., 224, 238; 29, 22, 36, 50 sq., 143, 182, 214, 294; 30, 56, 166 sq., 210, 213, 258 sq., 276, 281 sq.; 42, 94, 322, 348 sq.; 44, 537 sq.; Agni's seed became g., 12, 277 sq., 322; 26, 54, 59, 63, 238, 390; 41, 45, 59, 121; 44, 187, 275, 462, 467; born from fire, 14, 134; 25, 189, 189 n.; 42, 63; gift of g. meritorious, 14, 135; Gâmbûnada g., 19, 23; 49 (ii), 173, 176, 178, 180, 182; new-born child fed with g., honey, and butter, 25, 34, 34 sq. n.; Snâtaka wears golden ear-rings, 25, 134; the offering with g. before the buying of Soma, 26, 52–60; is immortal,

immortality, immortal life, 26, 70, 198, 206, 394, 425; 41, 29, 35, 84, 92 sq., 203, 265, 366, 382; 43, 251, 291, 343; 44, 203, 239, 348–50; used at sacred rites, 26, 130, 145, 197 sq., 203, 205 sq., 256 n., 401 n.; 41, 35, 84, 92 sq., 112; 44, 537 sq.; as Dakshi*n*â, 26, 342 sq., 345–8; is light, 26, 346; 41, 366; 44, 203, 303, 348 sq.; is life, 26, 347; he breathes over g. after the offering of Soma cups, 26, 425; 44, 108; is sacred, 33, 222; g. and fire necessary in a court of justice, 33, 277–9; a witness shall take g. in his hands, 33, 302; elixir of g., 40, 254; g. plate representing the sun, and g. man, at the building of the fire-altar, 41, 155, 166, 265–7, 271, 313, 323, 364–79, 375 sq. n., 382; 43, xxii, 1 sq. n., 18, 146, 147 n., 295, 342 sq. and n., 355 n., 358, 366–74, 388 sq., 391–3; is fire, 41, 366; 44, 348 sq.; g. chips thrown into the heads of the animals on the fire-altar, 41, 402 sq., 409; pearl shell born of g., 42, 62, 383 sq.; as an amulet for long life, 42, 63, 668 sq.; the immortal light, 42, 183, 192, 654; 43, 343; strewing chips of g. on the fire-altar, 43, 96, 146 sq., 182 sq., 201, 291, 294; a g. coin as prize at a disputation, 44, 51, 53; a chip of g. made a type of the fire, resp. of the sun, 44, 125; sacrifice offered on g. when the sacred fire goes out, 44, 187; a piece of g. representing the sun, 44, 195; seven chips of g. placed on the seven seats of vital airs of the corpse, 44, 203; from the seed of Indra, 44, 215; is a form of the gods, 44, 236; a g. and a silver plate as symbols of lightning and hail, 44, 251; a g. plate of a hundred grains' weight used at the Sautrâma*n*î, 44, 261; is a form (symbol) of the nobility, 44, 303 sq.; priests and sacrificer seated on g. stools at the horse-sacrifice, 44, 360 sq.; serves for repelling the fiends, 44, 462, 467; a plate of white g. (i.e. silver) placed below the Pravargya pot, 44, 462; a g. plate put on the top of the Mahâvîra pot, 44, 467 sq.; warlike accoutrements must not be of g., 47, 161. *See also* Metals, Money, *and* Theft.

Golden germ, *see* Hira*n*yagarbha.

Golden person, *see* Person.

Goliath (*G*âlût), story of David and, 6, 39.

Gômêz, Zd. and Phl. t.t. 'bull's urine,' as a means of purification. *See under* Bull.

Gom*r*iga, 'bovine antelope,' 44, 298, 299 n., 338, 338 n., 382, 388.

Gonaddha, n. of a town, 10 (ii), 188.

Good, good and evil, *see* Dualism, *and* Morality.

Good conduct, *see* Morality.

Good mind, *see* Vohu-manô.

Goodness, forgiveness, courage, harmlessness, &c., constitute the quality of, 8, 373 sq.; wisdom without g. is useless, 24, 37; the origin of ceremonial is in g. and truth, 24, 94 sq.; threefold g., ten moral precepts of Buddha, 49 (ii), 167 sq.; quality (gu*n*a) of g., *see* Qualities.

Good works, prayer, and sacrifice, 4, 281–3; no g. w. reach him who is not ceremonially pure, 5, 299; how one should perform g. w., 8, 314, 325–8; finding fault with g. w., a mark of the quality of darkness, 8, 320; the Brahman to be attained by g. w., viz. sacrifice, gifts, sacred study, 8, 339 sq.; g. w. ordered in his lifetime benefit the departed soul, 18, 27–9, 28 n.; on the growth of g. w., 18, 29 sq.; balance of sins and g. w. at the judgement on the soul, 18, 30–3; effect of doing more g. w. than are necessary for attaining heaven, 18, 120 sq., 121 n.; g. w. and sins done unwittingly, 24, 5 sq.; nine chief g. w., divided into seven classes, 24, 26 sq.; thirty-three g. w., 24, 73–5; which is the best g. w., 24, 113; the causes of g. w. and sins, 24, 133; all sects teach to perform g. w. and abstain from crime, 24, 193; heaven cannot be obtained through any g. w., except by certain ceremonies, 24, 263; the six indispensable g. w., 24, 264 sq.; are of no use unless performed with the authority of the priests, 24, 266 sq., 267 n.; share of g. w. imputed to

others, 24, 269, 269 n.; g. w. measured according to the scale of sins which they counterbalance, 24, 273, 273 n., 303, 306 sq., 311–13, 317, 330–2, 334 sq., 343 sq., 347, 349, 358, 361; cases where one person shares in the results of g. w. of another, 24, 278, 280–2; in case of any doubt as to sins and g. w. a high-priest must be consulted, 24, 290; 37, 479; shall not be postponed for the morrow, 24, 344–7; 37, 378 sq.; lead to heaven, evil works to hell, 35, 283, 291; the merit of g. w. can be transferred to others without diminishing, 36, 155 sq. and n.; mutual relation of sin and g. w., 37, 54 sq.; merit of certain g. w., 37, 204 sq.; efficiency of g. w., 37, 234–6; praise of g. w., 37, 283; g. w. and wealth, 37, 295; zealousness for g. w., ethics of labour, 37, 316 sq.; practising g. w. is welcoming Aûha*r*maz*d* in oneself, 37, 334, 336 sq., 339 sq.; sin mingled with g. w., 37, 335 sq.; immortality produced by g. w., 37, 338 sq.; are an assistance of the renovation of the universe, 37, 343, 345; mankind improved by g. w. done publicly, 37, 362, 370 sq.; diligence in g. w., 37, 367, 382; soul expanded by a g. w., 47, 149; valued higher than sacrifice, 49 (i), 23; three kinds of g. w. according to Buddha, 49 (ii), v sq. *See also* Karman, Morality, Retribution, *and* Works.

Gôpaîtŏ, the spiritual chief of Aîrân-vêgô, 24, 87, 87 n.

Gôpaîtôshah, half ox, half man, frees the sea from noxious creatures, 24, 111 sq. *See also* Gôpatshah.

Gopaka, n. of a Thera, 17, 238.

Gopâla's mother, the fame of her good deeds reached even to the gods, 35, 172; on giving a meal to some Elders, she became the chief queen of King Udena, 36, 146.

Gopâlatâpanî-upanishad, modern, 1, 52 n.

Gopatha-brâhma*n*a, Vaitâna-sûtra older than, 44, xvi sq.

Gôpatshah, or Gôk-patŏ, title of Aghrêra*d*, 5, 117, 117 n.; son of Aghrêra*d*, 5, 135 sq., 135 n.; one of the seven immortals, 5, 195; 18, 257, 257 n., 258 n.; 37, 202 sq. and n.; half bull, half man, 23, 114 sq. n. *See also* Gôpaîtôshah.

Gopî, or Ku-i, wife of Buddha, 19, xx sq.

Gopikâ, daughter of Maitra, converted by Buddha, 49 (i), 198–200.

Gô*s*, genius of cattle, 5, 21 n., 104, 213 n., 336 n.; connected with the Moon, 23, 88, 88 n.; Gô*s* Ya*s*t devoted to G., 23, 110–18; the Soul of the Bull worshipped, 23, 245. *See also* Cattle, Cow, *and* Gô*s*-aûrvan.

Go*s*âla Makkhaliputra (Pali, Gosâla), *see* Makkhali-Gosâla.

Gô*s*asp, *see* Gôgô*s*asp.

Gô*s*-aûrvan (Gô*s*ûrvan, Gô*s*ûrûn), soul of the primaeval ox, 4, 294 n., 295; 5, 20 sq., 20 n., 21 n., 163; 18, 380, 380 n.; 37, 407; the wailing and complaint of G., 5, 20 sq., 163; 37, 237–40, 318, 390, 393; the same as Gô*s*, 5, 402, 405; 23, 110; protects Keresâsp from hell, 18, 380; 37, 199, 199 n. *See also* Animals (*i*).

Goshira, converted by Buddha, 19, 245.

Go*s*ruti Vaiyâghrapadya, n.p., 1, 75.

Gô*s*t-i Fryân, one of the immortals, 5, 195, 195 n.

Gôsûbar, its origin, 18, 419.

Gô*s*ûrûn, *see* Gô*s*-aûrvan.

Gô*s*ûrvan, *see* Gô*s*-aûrvan.

Gotama (Buddha), his disciples are always well awake, 10 (i), 71 sq.; G.'s gate and G.'s ferry at Pâ*t*aliputta, called after Buddha, 11, 21; 17, 103 sq. *See* Buddha.

Gotamaka *K*etiya, at Vesâli, 11, 40, 58.

Gotama Râhûga*n*a, Purohita of Videgha Mâthava, 12, xli, 104–6; Indra passed himself off as G., 26, 82 n.; author of Vedic hymns, 32, 127 sq., 155, 160, 169 sq., 176; 46, 93, 95, 97, 100, 102, 104; discovered the Mitravindâ sacrifice, 44, 66; Vâmadeva appeals to his father G. for kinship with Agni, 46, 332; G.'s Stoma (form of chanting), 44, 375.

Gotamas, family of *R*ishis, 32, 109, 125; 46, 52, 100, 102; worship the Maruts, 32, 169, 176.

Gotamî, *see* Mahâpagâpati G.

Gotamîputra, n. of a teacher, 15, 225.

*G*otipâla, the Bodisat as the young Brahman, 36, 20–2.

Government, principles and methods of, 3, 38–41, 46–8, 53–6, 79 sq., 115 sq., 179–81, 219–25; 28, 263–8, 312–18; 39, 96 sq., 100–5, 108 sq., 117 sq., 122 sq., 136, 144, 259–62, 267 n., 333–8; 40, 96 sq., 121–4, 215; five orders of the nobles, 3, 136 sq. and n.; 'the Great Plan' for the g. of the nation, 3, 138–49; eight objects of g., 3, 141 sq. and n.; 27, 230, 248; the threefold business of g., 3, 231, 231 n.; filial piety in g., 3, 473–80, 483, 486; to be entrusted to good and able feudal princes, 16, 62, 63 n.; how to promote union among the different members and classes of a state, 16, 75 n.; lessons of good g. to be learned from a well, 16, 164–6, 166 sq. n., 253; ornament and beauty help the course of g., but are not sufficient in great matters of judgement, 16, 294 sq., 295 n.; characteristics of good and bad g., 24, 43–5; science of g. to be learnt by the king, 25, 222; proceedings of g. in the different months, 27, 20 sq., 249–310; interchange of missions between different courts, 27, 58; 28, 458–64; oppressive g. more terrible than tigers, 27, 190 sq.; of state expenditure, 27, 221 sq., 239; exemption from g. service, 27, 243; importance of ceremonies for g., 27, 375–9; an ideal state, 27, 391–3; notice taken of very old people by g., 27, 466; ceremonies, music, punishments, and laws as instruments of g., 28, 93, 97–9, 105–7, 107 n., 272, 276 sq., 352 sq., 356 sq.; brought in harmony with the laws of heaven and earth, 28, 106; five things by which ancient kings secured good g., 28, 216; nine standard rules of g., 28, 314–16; g. under different dynasties, 28, 341–3; good g. depends on the regulation of the family, 28, 411, 417–19; twenty-one chieftainships, 37, 167; five chieftainships, 37, 308; let men be, and there will be no necessity for governing them, try to govern it, and the world will be full of trouble, 39, 142 sq., 291–8, 302 sq.; 40, 285–8; ideal g. without rewards and punishments, 39, 315; the g. of sages, of virtuous men, and of spirit-like men explained, 39, 323 sq.; governing the world is like taming horses, 40, 284. *See also* King, Parables (*d*), *and* Taxes.

Go-vikartana, one of the king's 'jewels,' 41, 63.

Govinata, a form of the A*s*vamedha, 44, 400 sq.

Govinda, n. of K*r*ish*n*a, 8, 40, 43. *See* K*r*ish*n*a.

Govindarâ*g*a, author of Manu*t*îkâ, 25, cxxvi–cxxviii, cxxxi.

Graha, meanings of the word, 26, 432 sq. *See also* Sacrifices (*k*).

Graha and Abhigraha worshipped by the Snâtaka, 30, 166.

Grahas, and Atigrahas, eight organs and objects of sense, 15, 125 sq. *See also* Senses.

Grâhi, 'seizure,' the demon of fits, 42, 15, 34, 49, 57, 187; the fetter of G. (attack of disease), 42, 165, 525.

Grain offered, are a form of day and night, parched g. a form of Nakshatras, 44, 296.

Grâma*n*î, Sk., t.t., headman, one of the king's 'jewels,' 41, 60 sq., 111.

Grammar, grammatical terms in Bhagavadgîtâ, 8, 90.

Grammarians quoted, 48, 60, 79.

Grandsire, *see* Brahman (masc.), *and* Pragâpati.

Grants, royal, 7, xxi n., 21 sq. *See also* Gifts.

Grasping, *see* Upâdâna.

Grass-stalks, sacrificial, 43, 185. *See also* Plants (Darbha, Dûrvâ g.).

Gratitude, duty of, 24, 328–30, 357.

Gravâratu, n.p., 23, 217.

Graves, *see* Ancestor worship.

Great Complex, King Sudassana's chamber of the, 11, 267 sq., 271, 274, 277, 278, 281, 285, 287.

Great One, the, Mahat, is the second creation, 8, 333 sq., 333 n.; first manifests itself as Vish*n*u, then as Brahman or *S*iva, 8, 333 n.; comprehended in the form of knowledge, 8, 350, 350 n.; the wheel of life made up of the entities beginning with the G. and ending with the gross elements, 8, 357; is a development of the Unperceived (Pradhâna), 8,

382; beyond the G. there is the Undeveloped, 15, 13, 22; 34, 237 sq.; is Buddhi or power of intellect, 15, 313; 34, 238 n.; is the individual soul, 25, 486; 34, 244; is one of the three entities of the Sâmkhyas, 25, 486, 486 n., 490, 495; 34, 238, 296; 48, 282, 287; originates from the Undeveloped, if it be the intellect of Hiranyagarbha, 34, 244; has a different meaning as a Sâmkhya term, and in Vedic use, 34, 252; of the Yoga-smriti, 34, 296; the subtle elements of material things proceed from it, 34, 376; creation from the G. down to the Brahman-egg and Hiranyagarbha, 48, 334.

Greed, *see* Avarice, Âz, *and* Sins.

Greeks, their astronomy alluded to in the Yâgñavalkya-smriti, 7, xxi; the week of the G., in the Vishnu-smriti, 7, xxix, xxxii, xxxii n.; overcome by the Persians, their triumph prophesied, 9, 124 sq. and n.

Grehma, opposed to Righteousness, 31, 55, 63 sq., 64 n.; an opponent of Zarathustra, 31, 55, 64.

Gridhrakûta, or 'Vulture's Peak,' where Buddha stays at Râgagaha, n. of a hill, 11, 1 sq., 11, 55; 21, xxvi, xxxii, 1, 235, 248 sq., 307 sq., 321, 396, 398, 431.

Griffon bird, *see* Birds (*b*).

Grihapati, Sk. (Pâli, Gahapati), 'house-lord,' meanings of the word, 11, 257 sq. n.; title of the principal sacrificer at a sacrificial session, 41, 158 n.; 44, 131, 131 n., 135.

Grihasthas, or householders, go the path of the gods, 1, 80.

Grihya-sûtras, birth ceremonies in, 15, 222 n.; translated, *Vols.* 29 and 30; based on Smriti, 29, xvii sq.; relation between Sâṅkhâyana and Pâraskara G., 29, 17 n., 20 n., 28 n., 34 n., 37 n., 39 n., 88 sq. n., 105 n.; 30, xxxviii sq.; their place in Vedic literature, 30, ix–xxiii, xxix–xxxvii; metrical texts on Grihya ritual, 30, xix, xxxv–xxxvii; contents and arrangement of the G., 30, xxiv–xxix, 299–307; their relation to the Srauta and Dharma-sûtras, 30, xxix–xxxv; their relation to one another, 30, xxxvii–xxxix; domestic ceremonies derived from practice, not from Sruti, 30, 251; the Atharva-veda in the G., 42, xliii–xlv.

Grimbhaka, demons in Vaisramana's service, 22, 248 n.

Grimbhikagrâma, town in which Mahâvîra reached Nirvâna, 22, 201, 263.

Gritsamada, the Rishi of the second Mandala of the Rig-veda, 1, 215; 32, 298, 429; 46, 188, 195, 200, 213, 216, 218; satiated at the Tarpana, 29, 122, 219 sq.; an ancient Vedic family, 46, 203.

Grudge, demon of, *see* Demons.

Guardian angels, *see* Angels.

Guardian spirits, *see* Fravashis.

Gudâkesa, n. of Arguna, 8, 43, 88, 92.

Gûdarz, Gîw, son of, 5, 118.

Guests, daily gift of food to men, one of the five 'great sacrifices,' 2, 48; 7, 193, 215 sq.; 8, 306, 358; 12, 190 sq.; 14, 239 sq.; 25, 88 sq., 92–7; 44, 95; duties towards g., 2, 109 sq., 112, 138, 161 sq.; 7, 207; 8, 243, 361; 14, 69, 265; 15, 3 sq., 51 sq.; 25, 133; 27, 155, 397; 37, 91; 48, 270; rules for the reception of g., its importance and meritoriousness, 2, 114–22, 204–7; 7, 217; 8, 216; 14, 43–5, 49–51; 27, 407; 28, 20, 171; 29, 87–90, 92; reception of g. represented as a sacrifice offered to Pragâpati, 2, 117 sq.; g. who are worthy of a cow and the honey mixture, 2, 120 sq.; 14, 49, 244 sq.; hermit and ascetic must honour g., 2, 195; 8, 361, 364; 14, 259, 292, 294; observances to be paid to g., one of the eight objects of government, 3, 142; animals slain for the honouring of g., 7, 170; 14, 26 sq.; 25, 175; 27, 227; 30, 256, 266; 45, 27 sq.; depend upon householders for support, 7, 194; *let him not suffer a guest to stay at his house unfed. . . . By honouring a guest he obtains heaven*, 7, 215; hospitality of the Arabs, 9, 147 n.; the fathers at the Pindapitriyagña presented with water like g., 12, 365, 368, 433, 435; definition of the term 'guest,' 14, 43; presents for the purpose of honouring g. may be accepted from anybody, 14, 70; *let him never turn away a*

stranger from his house, 15, 67; ceremonies at the reception of g., 19, 172; 25, 79; 29, 197–200, 273–6, 384, 433–5; 30, 129–32, 171–5, 277–9, 305 sq.; 49 (i), 10, 171 sq.; permission to study the Veda must be obtained from one's g., 25, 148; g. rules over the world of Indra, 25, 157; quarrels with g. to be avoided, 25, 157; presents received with the honey-mixture, 25, 374, 374 sq. n.; penances for slaying or casting off suppliants for protection, 25, 469, 471; Âtithya, or g.-offering given to King Soma, 26, 85–92, 100; 41, 355; 43, 259; 44, 491; entertained with the game of pitch-pot, 27, 50 sq.; 28, 397–401; feasting of g. at the Hsiang meeting, 27, 56; 28, 435–46; rules of etiquette for host and g., 27, 71 sq., 74–6, 79–81, 96, 105; the aged exempt from duties towards g., 27, 241; gifts and offerings between host and g., 27, 414; no rules of hospitality between ruler and minister, 27, 421; 28, 295; minister received as g. by the ruler, 28, 7 sq.; humility the principal thing for visitors and g., 28, 77 sq.; sacrifice at hospitable receptions, 28, 292; bridegroom received as g., 29, 34; 30, 48, 256; the householder should eat before his g., 29, 321; Snâtaka received as g., 29, 409; 30, 84 sq., 171–5.

Guggulû, n. of an Apsaras, 42, 33.

Guhadeva, quoted by Râmânuga, 34, xxi.

Guhagupta, one of the sixteen virtuous men, 21, 4.

Guha*tth*akasutta, t.c., 10 (ii), 147 sq.

Guhya: a *G*aina should not say 'god of the sky! god of the thunderstorm!' &c., but 'the air; the follower of G.,' &c., 22, 152.

Guhyakas, produced by Activity, 25, 494, 494 n.

***G*umbaka**, i.e. Varu*n*a, offering to, 44, xxxix, 336 n., 340 n., 343.

Gu*n*abhadra, translator of a life of Buddha into Chinese, 19, xxv sq.

Gu*n*âkhya, *S*âṅkhâyana, mentioned in the Kaushîtaki-Âra*n*yaka, probably not the author of the *S*âṅkhâyana-G*ri*hya-sûtra, 29, 4 sq.

Gu*n*aprabha, Vasubandhu's pupil and *S*rî-Harsha's teacher, 21, xxii.

Gu*n*as, Sk., t.t., three constituent elements or qualities of pradhâna, *see* Qualities.

Gu*n*a*s*ilaka, a *K*aitya at Râ*g*ag*ri*ha, 22, 311.

Guru, Sk., t.t., 'venerable person,' i.e. certain relatives and the teacher: definitions, 2, 51, 51 n.; 7, 128; 33, 265; how they should be saluted, 2, 51 sq., 51 n.; 7, 129;—violating a G.'s bed, a mortal sin, penances and punishments for it, 1, 84; 2, 89; 7, 133; 8, 389; 14, 5, 104, 127, 132, 201, 296, 299; 25, 338, 383, 451 sq., 452 n., 480, 496; 33, 229 sq.;—obedience towards G., 7, 13, 13 n.; fine for defaming G., 7, 28; he who offends a G. commits a minor offence, 14, 5; self-possessed men are corrected by their G., 33, 230; the king must show honour to G. before entering the court, 33, 280. *See also* Teacher (*a*).

Guruskandha, one of the princes of mountains, 8, 346.

Gustahm, *see* Vistauru.

Gû*s*tâsp (pers. for Vî*s*tâsp), *see* Vî*s*tâspa.

***G*utika**, converted by Buddha, 19, 241.

Guttila, the musician, went up to heaven even in his human body, 35, 172; 36, 146.

Gû*z*ak, wife of Hôshyang, 5, 58; daughter of Aîrî*k*, 5, 133 sq., 133 n.; 47, 34, 140.

***G*valanâdhipati**, n. of a Tathâgata, 49 (ii), 67.

***G*vara**, worshipped at the Tarpa*n*a, 30, 244.

Gymnosophists, *see G*ainas.

***G*yotishprabha**, n. of a Tathâgata, 49 (ii), 6, 66. *See* Brahma *G*.

***G*yotish*t*oma**, *see* Sacrifices (*j*).

H

Habâspa, n.p., 23, 206.

'***H*abbâb**, story of 'Hâsîy ibn Wâîl and, 9, 33 n.

'Hab'hab, a stone worshipped by the Arabs, 6, xiii.

'Habîb en Na*gg*ar, stoned to death

for believing the disciples of Jesus, 6, cv; 9, 163 sq., 164 n.

Hadhaokhdha, worshipped, 31, 337, 337 n., 341.

Hadhayâs, *see* Animals (*i*).

'Hadîgah, a rich widow, becomes the wife of Mohammed, 6, xix, xxi, xxiii; her death, 6, xxix; converted by Mohammed, 6, xlix.

Hadish, a sacred being, 47, x, xxv, 7.

Hâê*k*a*d*âsp(ô), n.p., ancestor of Zoroaster, 5, 140; 47, 34, 140.

Haê*k*a*t*-aspid, daughter of Zarathustra, 31, 191.

Hagar, the well Zemzem near Mecca discovered by, 6, xvii.

'Hagg, pilgrimage to Mecca, duty and rites of, 6, xi, xiii, xvii, xxviii, xxxix–xli, liii, lxxi, lxxiii–lxxv, 22, 27–9, 58, 173; 9, 59, 59 n., 236 sq. and n.; is burdensome and useless nowadays, 6, lxxvi; chase and game forbidden during 'H., 6, 96 sq., 110 sq.

'Hagr: the fellows of El '*H*. (Thamûd) punished, 6, 249, 249 n.

Hail, a terrible form of rain, 44, 251.

Hair, how the Vedic student should wear his, 2, 8, 37; 8, 360; 14, 41; 25, 69 sq.; 29, 400; 30, 63, 160; customs about the h., and beard, 2, 178, 178 n., 219, 219 sq. n.; 14, 11 sq. n., 77, 159, 344; 29, 169, 323; arrangement of h. of the ascetic and hermit, 2, 194 sq.; 8, 362; 10 (i), 38, 41, 90; (ii), 74, 96, 98, 126, 188; 14, 45, 47, 259, 274, 285, 287; 25, 199; 49 (i), 75; the kinsmen untie their locks at the ceremony of overturning the water-vessel of a sinner, 2, 278; shaving the h. or wearing it in braids, a penance, 2, 300; 14, 104, 108, 124, 223; 25, 446, 449, 453, 456; cuttings or shavings of h. defile, 4, lxxviii, 190–2; untimely white h. produced by the Daêvas, 4, 90, 90 n.; considered as plants, 4, 191, 191 n.; bathing ordained after tonsure of the head, 7, 94; some sects wear matted h., others are clean-shaven, 8, 375; tonsure of Sama*n*as, 10 (i), 65; (ii), 41, 74; 11, 187 sq.; 35, 19, 19 n.; 36, 83; 45, 140; the sacrificer's h. and beard shaven, 12, 1, 407, 443, 448–50, 448 n.; 26, 5–7; gifts of h. (as garments) to the Fathers, 12, 369 n.; 30, 230; shaving the hair of women as punishment, 14, 109 sq.; 33, 183; cutting the hair at the beginning of rites, vows, and fasts, 14, 300, 303, 323; 29, 247; having the head shaven, a sin, 18, 408, 408 n.; modes of h.-dressing forbidden to Bhikkhus, 20, 69 sq., 138 sq.; ceremony of shaving the beard (Godâna, Ke*s*ânta), 25, 42, 42 n.; 29, 56 sq., 186 sq., 227, 276, 301–3, 380, 402–4; 30, 41, 69 sq., 218, 253, 284 sq.; 42, 306 sq., 665; clipping nails or h., 25, 139, 140 n.; do not wear false h., 27, 76, 76 n.; about women's h.-dress in mourning, 27, 129; shaving ceremony for a child, 27, 473; cut or shaved before the student's initiation, 29, 61, 187, 193, 304; 30, 138, 271; the student has his h. cut at the Samâvartana, 29, 91, 314, 408; 30, 163–5, 275; h. and beard of the dead body cut, 29, 237; family customs regarding the arrangement of the h., 29, 301, 303, 399, 408; 30, 62, 218, 284; Snâtaka has his h. cut, 30, 84; razors known before the Aryan separation, 32, 235; shaving the head, a punishment for Brâhma*n*as, 33, 204; about shaving the h., 37, 124; a king does not shave his h., 41, 126, 128; the Ke*s*avapanîya or h.-cutting sacrifice at the king's consecration, 41, 126–8; h. of lion, wolf, tiger at Sautrâma*n*î, 41, 132; 44, 218, 229; charms to promote the growth of h., 42, 30 sq., 470 sq., 536 sq.; prayer on shearing h. and beard, 42, 57; modes of dressing the h., 42, 108, 538 sq.; nothing injures one at the h., 43, 158; h. and form, 43, 295; how it grows and gets grey, 44, 52 sq., 55; the mystery of man's h., and the sacrificial grass, 44, 52 sq., 55 sq.; as many h.-pits as sweat-pores and as twinklings of the eye, 44, 169; the hair of victim, when wetted, comes off, 44, 313; *K*û*d*â-kara*n*a or tonsure of the child's hair, *see* Child (*b*); parting the h. at the Sîmantonnayana, *see* Child (*b*). *See also* Body.

Haira*n*yanâbha, A*t*nâra's son, the Kausalya Para, 44, 397.

'Hâlid, commander of the Meccan cavalry, 6, xxxviii; joins the Muslim ranks, 6, xli.

Hâli*gg*a, *see* Hâridraka.

Hâlingava, quoted, 43, 363.

Hâmân, the prime minister of Pharaoh, 9, 108, 108 n., 112; punished, 9, 121, 193; Moses sent to H., 9, 192; told to build a tower for Pharaoh to mount up to Heaven, 9, 194.

Hamaspathmaêdhaya, worshipped, 31, 198, 205, 210, 216, 220, 225, 335, 338, 368, 370, 372.

Hãm-baretar vanghvãm, n.p., 23, 211, 211 n.

Hâmî*d*, n.p., 5, 148.

Ha*m*sa birds, *see* Birds (*b*).

'Hamzah, Mohammed's uncle, slain in battle, 6, xxxviii, 264 n.

Han: systematic chronology in China began with the H. period, 3, 20 sq.; investiture of the marquis of H., 3, 426; recovery of the Ritual Books under the H. dynasty, 27, 2–5.

Hand: tîrthas or parts of the h. sacred to different deities, 7, 198; 12, 365 n., 366 n.; 14, 21, 25, 166, 238, 255; 25, 40 sq.; 29, 252, 252 n.; 30, 18; organs of action, 8, 53 n., 261, 359; laid down, palm upwards, for protection, 44, 465.

Hăng, *see* Thien *Kh*ăng-ȝze.

Hangâûrûsh, son of *G*âmâsp, 47, xxx, 165.

Hanghaurv*a*ungh, son of *G*âmâspa, 23, 208.

'Hanîfs, a sect of Arabian thinkers, 6, xv sq.; Islâm, the faith of the 'H., 6, 204; 9, 127 sq.; exhortation to become 'H., 9, 59; Jews and Christians bidden to become 'H., 9, 338.

Hantrîmukha, n. of a demon harassing infants, 29, 296.

Han Ying, his text of the Shih King, 3, 287.

Hâo, Duke, as a mourner, 27, 318.

Haoi*s*t, son of Geurva, 37, 224, 224 n.

Haoma (Phl. Hôm), overthrew the Keresâni (Alexander), 4, xlviii; 31, 237 sq., 237 n.; Vedic Soma, Avestic H., 4, lii; 26, xii, xvi; 31, 230 sq.; worship of H. Aryan, 4, lxiv; purification of the H., 4, 73 sq.; the dead become immortal by tasting of the white H., 4, 74 n.; the plant of life, king of healing plants, 4, 74 n., 226; 5, 90; 31, 241; 37, 165; preparation of H. for sacrifices, 4, 207, 351–3; the white or Gaokerena H., round which the healing plants grow, 4, 227, 227 sq. n.; approached Zarathu*s*tra, 4, 258; 31, 231; use of H. at sacrifices, 4, 288 n., 289; 18, 160 n., 163–5 and n., 169 sq., 170 n.; the angel, co-operator with Tî*s*tar, 5, 26, 169; 37, 292, 292 n.; lizard created to injure the H., 5, 65; the white H., the healing and undefiled, 5, 100; the white H. belongs to Â*s*tâ*d*, 5, 104; the H. of the angel H., of three kinds 5, 105; Hûsh, the drink of immortality, prepared from H., 5, 126; white H., the counteractor of decrepitude and death, 5, 176 sq.; H.-juice given to a new-born infant, 5, 322; 24, 286 sq.; 37, 122; meat-offering to the angel H., 5, 336, 336 n., 338, 338 n.; the white H., an ingredient of the elixir of immortality, 18, 112, 112 n.; washing of polluted H. twigs, 18, 363; Gaokerena, the white H., invoked and worshipped, 23, 5, 5 n., 12, 14, 20, 32, 36 sq., 271; golden, tall, enlivening, 23, 20; the increaser of the world, 23, 102, 102 n.; worships Drvâspa, 23, 114, 114 n.; offered a sacrifice to Mithra, 23, 141 sq.; established as a priest by Ahura-Mazda, 23, 142; the Fravashis watch the H., 23, 194 n.; drinking of H. is attended with Asha and Ashi Vanguhi, 23, 271; worshipped Ashi Vanguhi, 23, 277 sq.; prayer recited when drinking H., 23, 312; H. and sacred twigs, 24, 103, 103 n.; where the H. is grown, 24, 111, 111 n.; H. and Parahaoma, and the (offered) Haomas worshipped, 31, 208, 212, 214, 221 sq., 227 sq., 230, 246, 270 sq., 276, 291, 348; among the offerings to the gods, 31, 213 sq., 223, 227 sq., 270 sq., 274 sq., 280, 349 sq., 353 sq., 374 sq.; the H.-ya*s*t, worship and praise of H., 31, 230–44; drives

death afar, 31, 231–7, 244–6, 291; invoked against demons and all evil creatures, 31, 236, 238–40; grants knowledge and wisdom to students, 31, 237; grants offspring to women, husbands to maidens, 31, 237; grants speed to racers, 31, 237; grows on the mountains, 31, 238, 240–3, 291; pressings of H., 31, 240; the pressing, tasting, or praising of H. avails to the smiting of the Daêvas, 31, 241; curses the man who holds him from full outpouring, 31, 244 sq.; praised, 31, 246; bound the Turanian Frangrasyan, 31, 246; the reviver and healer, worshipped Sraosha, 31, 302; curing with H.-water, 47, xi, xxv, 57 sq.; H.-water used by Zoroaster, 47, xxvi; guardian spirit of Zaratûst passed, through H., to his parents, 47, xxix, 21–9, 21 n.; milk mixed with H., 47, 27 sq., 28 n.; Zoroaster bringing H.-water from the river meets Vohûmanô, 47, 47 sq., 155 sq.; Vistâsp drinks H., the fountain of life, 47, 70 sq., 71 n.; Zoroaster's guardian spirit is in the H., 47, 136 sq., 139; pouring H.-juice into water, 47, 154. *See also* Plants (*b*), Sacrifices (*b*, *k*), *and* Soma.

Haomô-hvarenah, n.p., 23, 214.

Hâôshâng, *see* Hôshâng.

Haoshyangha, *see* Hôshâng.

Happiness, five sources of, 3, 149; three sorts of h., 8, 126; what is true h., 10 (i), 53–5; 13, 81; a life in h. and mindfulness with a wise friend, or in solitude, 17, 307 sq.; perfect peace is sublime h., 20, 231–3. *See also* Bliss, *and* Highest Good.

Haptanghâiti, *see* Yasna.

Haptôiringa, *see* Haptôk-rîng.

Haptôk-rîng (Av. Haptôiringa), the star Ursa Major, chieftain of the north, 5, 12, 12 sq. n., 21; 24, 131; seas under his protection, 5, 44; meat-offering to H., 5, 337, 337 n.; keeps off demons, witches, and wizards, 24, 91 sq.

Hara, used in the sense of God, 15, 235; identified with strength, 25, 512; n. of Rudra, 29, 256; is immortal and imperishable, 48, 139, 364.

Hara Berezaiti, or Haraiti Bareza (Mount Albûrz, or Alborz), both the waters and the light come from it and return there, 4, 230, 232–4, 232 n.; 18, 263, 263 n.; seven palaces in it, 4, 262 sq. n.; 37, 220 sq.; revolution of the sun round it, 5, 22–4; the first of mountains, 5, 29 sq., 34–6, 41 sq., 91, *174 sq.*; rivers flow forth from it, 5, 74–7, 75 n., 172; 24, 98; Albûrz and the Dâîtih peak, 18, 46–8, 48 n.; the mountain where Mithra dwells, 23, 131 sq., 141; the sun rises above it, 23, 150; stars move round it, 23, 174; 24, 91 sq.; the abode of the clouds is on it, 24, 86, 86 n.; star Vanand protects its passes and gates, 24, 91, 91 n.; arranged around the world, 24, 100, 100 n.; below it is the Kinvat Bridge, 31, 19, 19 n.; 37, 210.

Haradatta, quoted by Nandapandita, 7, xxxiii.

Haraiti Bareza, *see* Hara Berezaiti.

Hardâr, n.p. 5, 141.

Hardarsn, n.p., 5, 141.

Hardhar, n.p., 47, 34.

Hare, in the moon, 44, 10; 'horn of a h.,' 48, 433, 453, 508 sq.

Haredhaspa, n.p., 23, 214.

Harem, *see* Woman (*a*, *f*).

Hareth, n. of Satan, 6, 161 n.

Hari, epithet of Rudra, 2, 298; n. of Vishnu or Krishna, 7, 7; 8, 92, 131, 219, 347; 48, 93; is contemplated in the sacred stone called Sâlagrâm, 34, 114; the Creator, 48, 87; all beings a play of H., 48, 406; all this is the body of H., 48, 423; the Lord H. condensed the Vedânta-texts in an easy form, 48, 527; Buddha compared with H., 49 (i), 171. *See also* Vishnu.

Hari, a noble family of Gainas, 22, 92, 218, 225.

Hâridraka (Pr. Hâligga) Kula of the Kârana Gana, 22, 292.

Hâridrumata, Gautama, teacher of Satyakâma, 1, 60; 34, 228; 48, 343.

Hârikarnîputra, n. of a teacher, 15, 224 n.

Harikesa, epithet of Indra, 2, 298.

Harikêsa-Bala, a Kândâla who had become a monk, 45, 50 n.

Hari*n*egamesi, the divine commander of the foot troops, ordered by *S*akra to exchange the embryos of Devânandâ and Tri*s*alâ, 22, 227 sqq.
Harishê*n*a, a king who became a *G*aina monk, 45, 86, 86 n.
Hari*sk*andra, King, bought the son of Agîgarta Sauyavasi, 14, 87; vows to sacrifice his son to Varu*n*a, 44, xxxiv.
Hârîta, quoted in law-books, 2, xxviii, 49, 65, 66 n., 70, 88 sq., 91 sq.; 14, xvii, xx sq., xxvii, xl, 10, 220.
Hâritagotra, *S*rîgupta of the, 22, 291.
Harita Ka*s*yapa, n. of a teacher, 15, 226.
Hâritamâlâkârî, *S*âkhâ of the *K*âra*n*a Ga*n*a, 22, 291.
Hâritâyana, gotra, 22, 286.
Hârîtî, n. of a giantess, 21, 374.
Harlot, *see* Prostitution.
Harmlessness, *see* Ahi*m*sâ.
Harmya, *see* Hell (*a*).
Hârût, and Mârût, two fallen angels, 6, xiv, 14, 14 n.
Harya*g*vâyana, worshipped at the Tarpa*n*a, 30, 244.
Haryaksha, n. of a demon harassing nfants, 29, 296.
Hâsar, measure of time, 5, 308, 308 sq. n.
Hâshim, Mohammed's grandfather, 6, xvi, xviii.
Ha*s*i, n. of a Daêva, 23, 49 sq., 49 n.
'Hâsîy ibn Wâil said he should have wealth and children on the judgement day, 9, 33, 33 n.
Hasta, of the Kâ*s*yapa gotra, a Sthavira, 22, 294 n.
Hasta, guardian of Soma, 26, 72.
Hastilipta (Pr. Hatthili*gg*a), a Kula of the Uddeha Ga*n*a, 22, 290.
Hastin, of the Kâ*s*yapagotra, a Sthavira, 22, 294.
Hastinâpura, Sambhûta took the resolution to become there a universal monarch in some later birth, 45, 56 sq., 60; residence of Mahâpadma, 45, 86 n.
Hastipâla: Mahâvîra died at Pâpâ in King H.'s office of the writers, 22, 264, 269.
Hastiyâma, n. of a park at Nâlandâ, 45, 420.
Hate, *see* Hatred.
Ha*th*a-yoga, always occasions death, 8, 297 n.
Hatred, the devotee free from, 8, 51, 63, 101; self-restraint is freedom from h. and other defects, 8, 168; desire and h. are born from nature, 8, 288. *See also* Love, *and* Passion.
Hatthi-gâma, Buddha at, 11, 66.
Hâu, title of Chinese sovereigns, 3, xxvi.
Hâu-*k*î, his wonderful conception and birth, perils of his infancy, 3, 396 sq. and n.; what he did for agriculture, 3, 398; as the founder of certain sacrifices, 3, 398 sq., 398 n.; 28, 350; invoked against a drought 3, 420; associated with God at sacrifices, 3, 422 n.; 28, 32; sacrifices to H. as the correlate of Heaven, 3, 477, 477 n.; his meritorious services, 28, 340. *See also Kh*î.
Hâu Mû, about the rites of mourning, 27, 152.
Haurvatâ*t*, *see* Ho*r*vada*d*.
Hâu-thû, attending spirit of Hwang Tî, 27, 280; sacrificed to as the spirit of the ground, 28, 208.
Hâu 3*h*ang, disciple of Hsiâ-hâu Shih-*kh*ang, 3, 287; a Lî scholar, 27, 7; his treatise *Kh*ü Thâi *K*î, 27, 17.
Hâvanan, *see* Priests (*d*).
Hâvani, lord of the ritual order, worshipped, 31, 196, 201 sq., 204, 207, 209, 215, 219, 223, 254, 379 sq.; thirty-three gods round about H., 31, 198.
Hazân, a Karap, 47, 143.
Head, placing the life-breath in the, 8, 79; the self is without a h., 8, 367; etymology of Sk. *s*iras or h., 41, 144 sq., 401; h. of a child or young animal born first, 41, 233; 43, 40, 287; human h. placed on ukhâ, 41, 311, 404; is the birthplace of the breaths, 41, 396; 43, 57; measures a span, is four-cornered, contracted in the middle, 41, 396; 44, 454; is threefold, 43, 78, 114; 44, 163, 335, 499; consists of two bones, 43, 78, 387; fivefold vital air in h., 43, 190.
Healing plants, *see* Plants (*b*).

Heart, the small ether in the lotus of the, 1, 125 sq.; 34, xxxvi, 174–92; 38, 144; 48, 314–17, 660 sq.; the self abides in it, 1, 129; the dying devotee confines the mind within the h., 8, 79, 239; the Lord is seated in the lotus-like h. of all beings, 8, 88, 104, 113, 129, 187 n., 194, 281 sq., 283 n., 332; the being of the size of a thumb in the h., 8, 192; is the breath or seat of the breath, 8, 242 n.; 26, 204; the h. and the seat of the h., 8, 252; perceiving all entities in one's own h., 8, 342; the great self, the h. of all beings, 8, 345; supporter of consciousness in the h., 8, 350; the two entered into the cave (of the h.) are Brahman and the individual soul, 15, 12; 34, xxxv, xlii, 118–23; 38, 240; 48, 98, 267 sq.; one thinks with the h., with the mind, 43, 95; Agni, Vâyu, Âditya are the hs. of the gods, 43, 162; is smooth, round, and near the right arm-pit, 43, 180 sq.; this h. is, as it were, in secret, 44, 36. *See also* Arteries.

Hearth: harmya, fire-pit, h., house, 23, 216–18; spirit of the h., 40, 236; striding over the h. a crime, 40, 243; offences committed in the treatment of the fire and the h., 40, 244. *See also* Fire (*e*).

Heat, or tegas, 1, 93 n.; effects of h. on the body, 8, 237; cold and h., *see* Pairs of opposites.

Heathen, *see* Heretics.

Heaven (Sky, Heavenly world).

(*a*) H. (Thien), a supreme and moral power in China.
(*b*) H. and Rulers in China.
(*c*) H. and Earth in China.
(*d*) H. or Svarga world in India.
(*e*) H. (Dyaus) as a deity in India.
(*f*) H. and Earth in India.
(*g*) H. (Âsmân, Garô*d*mân) in Zoroastrianism.
(*h*) Plurality of Heavens.

(*a*) H. (Thien) a supreme and moral power in China.

The term Thien or H. interchanged with Tî and Shang Tî (God) to denote the Supreme Power, 3, xxiv sq., 196–8, 477 sq. n., 354; 39, 15–18; sacrifices offered to H., 3, 39, 134, 302, 317 sq.; 27, 36, 427, 437; 28, 202, 217 sq.; sends down calamities (on the offender), 3, 51 sq., 108, 120–2, 157 sq., 160 sq., 170, 177 sq., 236, 266, 408–10, 417–19; 27, 256, 279; 40, 107; virtue moves H., 3, 52; appeal to (azure) H. in sorrow, 3, 52, 184, 360 sq., 364, 418, 428 sq., 434 sq., 434 n., 435 n., 439, 439 n., 441, 444; the source of moral laws, 3, 55 sq., 129, 169; punishments appointed by H., 3, 77, 83, 85–7, 90, 126, 130, 132, 135, 219; warnings of H. conveyed by eclipses and the like, 3, 81, 81 n.; sends down misery or happiness and length of years on men according to their conduct, 3, 89, 99, 101, 109, 119, 174, 207; 16, 299 sq. n.; 40, 246; the way of H. is to bless the good, and make the bad miserable, 3, 90; 16, 285, 286 n.; makes no mistakes, 3, 90, 417; 16, 230, 230 n.; the bright requirements of H., i. e. the worship of the gods and ancestors, 3, 96; 28, 415; calamities sent by H. may be avoided, but from those brought on by one's self there is no escape, 3, 98; 28, 359; secures the tranquillity of the people, aiding them to be in harmony with their condition, 3, 139, 139 n.; fulfilling to the end the will of H., one of the five sources of happiness, 3, 149; decree of H. is not to be changed, 3, 157, 161, 236; the will of H. intimated by divination, 3, 159, 189 sq.; awful though H. be, it yet helps the sincere, 3, 167; H.'s appointments are not unchanging, 3, 171, 379 sq.; 28, 420 sq.; approves, if spirits are used only at sacrifices, 3, 176; the bright principles of H., 3, 176, 197; sacrifices ascend to H., 3, 177; the aged have matured their counsels in the sight of H., 3, 185; the favour of H. is not easily preserved, not to be depended on, 3, 206; the virtue of great H., 3, 206, 209, 259; the dread majesty of H., 3, 208, 210, 241, 262, 264, 380, 380 n.; *Great H. has no partial affections; it helps only the virtuous*, 3, 212; services to spirits and to H., 3, 217; 'the way of H.,' or virtuous conduct, 3, 248; 16, 229, 372; 27, 39 sq., 367, 389; 28, 268; 39, 121 sq., 210; 40, 257–9; the oppressed declare their innocence to H., 3,

256, 354, 357 sq.; those who preside over criminal cases are the shepherds of H., 3, 259; accordance with the will of H., 3, 260, 379; 16, 261; allows us to make use of punishment, 3, 260; is impartial, but men ruin themselves, 3, 264; prosperity sent down from H., 3, 306; 16, 286, 318, 322, 323 n.; the ordinances of H. are deep and unintermitting, 3, 314, 357; 16, 251, 251 n.; 28, 322; made the lofty hill, 3, 316; its appointment is not easily preserved, 3, 329 sq., 330 n.; inspects all our doings, 3, 330; does not weary in its favour, 3, 335; sends inflictions, is charged with injustice and cruelty, 3, 351–3, 353 n.; the calamities of the lower people do not come down from H., 3, 357; the angry terrors of compassionate H. extend through this lower world, 3, 358; bad officers do not stand in awe of H., 3, 358; what H. confers, when once lost, is not regained, 3, 359; who art called our parent, 3, 361; azure H. invoked against slanderers, 3, 361; offerings made to the ancestors, that their descendants may receive the blessings of H., 3, 370, 370 n.; the way of H. is hard and difficult, 3, 376; the doings of high H. have neither sound nor smell, 3, 379 sq., 380 n.; model of action afforded by H. to men, 3, 380 n.; 16, 414, 415 n.; 39, 146, 161, 365–7; 40, 208; enlightens the people, 3, 409, 409 n.; gave birth to the multitudes of the people, 3, 410, 425; great H. is intelligent and clear-seeing, 3, 410, 416; it is not H. that flushes your face with spirits, so that you follow what is evil, 3, 411; those whom H. does not approve of sink down in ruin, 3, 414; is letting down its net of crime in which are many calamities, 3, 428 sq.; mysteriously great H. is able to strengthen anything, 3, 429, 429 n.; filial piety is the method of H., 3, 473, 479; 'H. in the midst of a mountain,' symbolical of great accumulation, 16, 37, 300, 300 n.; will set its seal to the virtue of him who restrains himself, 16, 155, 157 n.; symbolic meaning of H., 16, 213 sq., 214 n.; 'the Heavenly or H.-given seat,' 16, 218, 218 n., 223 n.; diminishes the full and augments the humble, 16, 226, 226 sq. n.; 'the procedure of H.,' characterized by change, 16, 229, 229 n.; progress proceeding from correctness is the appointment of H., 16, 234, 234 n.; sincerity is the response of man to H., 16, 263, 264 n.; in its motion, is a symbol of strength, and of untiring activity, 16, 267, 268 n.; divination is 'help extended to man from H.,' 16, 351; the sage rejoices in H. and knows its ordinations, 16, 354; produced the spirit-like things, and the sages took advantage of them, 16, 374, 374 n.; he whom H. assists is observant of what is right, 16, 375 sq.; 'the great man,' the equal of H., 16, 417, 418 n.; 28, 327; sends down rain, 27, 201; decision in law courts 'according to the judgement of H.,' 27, 236; the most forlorn of H.'s people, 27, 244; the blessing of H. secured by ceremonies, 27, 371, 376, 376 sq. n.; the author of all things, 27, 377 n., 430; produces the seasons, 27, 378; rules of ceremony have their origin in H., 27, 388; the border sacrifice an illustration of the way of H., 27, 430; harmony of H. and man, 28, 210; 39, 144, 332 sq.; 40, 257–64; by ceremonies and music man becomes H.-like, 28, 224; the supreme Decider, 28, 233, 233 n.; a filial son serves his parents as he serves H., 28, 269; commands of superiors taken as if from H., 28, 288; accordance with the nature of H. is the path of duty, 28, 300, 301 n.; the superior man does not murmur against H., 28, 306 sq., 338; 40, 242; perfection of nature characteristic of H., 28, 317; the superior man knows H., 28, 325; the Tâoistic idea of Thien or H., 39, 15–18, 154, 196, 196 n.; 40, 112 sq., 112 n.; a great sage called 'H.,' 39, 17 sq., 299, 299 n., 301–3; the full possessor of Tâo is like H., 39, 60; the work of the Tâoist like that of H., 39, 111 sq.; is lenient, but does not allow offenders to escape, 39, 116; though H. hates the ill-doer, yet its

judgements do not always prove that he who suffers is an ill-doer, 39, 116 sq.; presides over the infliction of death, 39, 117; the Tâo or way of H. is unselfish, that of man selfish, 39, 119; there is no other H. but what belongs to man's own mind, 39, 129, 182; unity with H. obtained by renouncing worldly life, 39, 150; 40, 12; *Kh*ing completed his bell-stand, when his H.-given faculty and the H.-given qualities of the wood were concentrated on the work, 39, 150; 40, 22 sq.; the Southern Ocean is the 'Pool of H.,' 39, 164, 167; the notes or sounds of H., 39, 177 sq., 178 n.; as a synonym of Tâo, 39, 178 n., 182, 182 n., 185, 185 n., 229 n., 234 n., 278 n., 306; 40, 61, 61 n.; that the Master of the Left has but one foot, is from H., not from man, 39, 200; death and life ordained from H., 39, 241; to be regarded like a father, but the Tâo to be loved more, 39, 241 sq. and n.; creatures cannot overcome H., 39, 248 sq.; *the small man of H. is the superior man among men; the superior man among men is the small man of H.*, 39, 253, 253 n.; what disturbs the regular method of H. causes disorder in the world, 39, 302; spirit-like, and yet requiring to be exercised, 39, 305; those who do not understand H. are not pure in their virtue, 39, 306; he who has forgotten himself has become identified with H., 39, 318; the ancients sought first to apprehend H., the Tâo came next, 39, 336; six extreme points and five elements belong to H., 39, 346; the music of H., 39, 348–51; 'the gate of H.,' 39, 357; union (between father and child) by H.'s appointment, 40, 35; 'a man in appearance, but having the mind of Heaven,' description of a master of the Tâo, 40, 42, 42 n.; Tâoist teacher called H., 40, 51, 68; the harmony of H. will come to him who looks only at the Tâo, 40, 61; the people of H. are those whom their human element has left, 40, 82; those who cannot stop where they cannot arrive by means of knowledge, will be destroyed on the lathe of H., 40, 83; the door of H. is non-existence, 40, 85; the sage is skilful H.wards, but stupid manwards, 40, 88 sq.; the true men of old did not by their human efforts try to take the place of H., 40, 110; the sage follows the direction of H., 40, 116, 199; if the breath of creatures be not abundant it is not the fault of H., 40, 139; the mind of man more difficult to know than H., 40, 209; regarded as the primal source by the sagely man, 40, 215; protects the good man, 40, 237; the bad man slights H.'s people, 40, 239; to H. belong the five mutual foes (elements), and the same five foes are in the mind of man, 40, 258 sq.; has no feeling of kindness, but the greatest kindness comes from it, 40, 261 sq.; when H. seems most wrapt up in itself, H.'s operation is universal in its character, 40, 262; the title 'H.-honoured,' 40, 265 sq.; 'H.-endowed men,' 40, 265–8; ether and destiny depend on H., 40, 268. *See also* God (*b*).

(*b*) H. AND RULERS IN CHINA.

'Son of H.,' designation of Chinese sovereigns, 3, xxv, xxv n., 83, 113, 120, *144*, 220, 244, 325, 352, 406, 425, 428, 467 sq., *468 n.*, 472, 483, 485; 16, 88, 285; 27, 82, 99, *107 sq.*, &c.; 28, 31, &c., *347*; 39, 307 n., 308 n., 331; 40, 158, 170, 181, 189–91, 195; appoints the kings, 3, 45, 47, 50, 58, 62, 99, 119, 121, 128, 134 sq., 154, 157, 167, 181, 196–9, 207 sq., 210, *217*, 236, 244, 308, 312, 316, 335, 378, 381, 389, 394, 402, *404*; 16, 276 sq. n.; 27, 108 sq.; 28, 347; 39, 338, 338 n.; the work of government is H.'s, men must act for it, 3, 55; protects and establishes the king, and makes him virtuous so as to enjoy every happiness, 3, 91, 93, 96, 98, 101, 104, 162, 347 sq.; virtuous kings give heed to the commands of H., 3, 104; intelligent kings act in accordance with the ways of H., 3, 115; King Thang became equal to great H., 3, 118; wicked King Shâu does not reverence H., 3, 125; made rulers for the help of the

people, 3, 126, 264; loves the people, and punishes wicked sovereigns who do not carry out the mind of H., 3, 126–8; the oppressed people cry to H., 3, 127; gave the Great Plan to Yü, 3, 140; sends a thunderstorm to reveal the virtue of Tan, 3, 155 sq.; the king, the servant of H., which has assigned to him a great task, 3, 159; overthrow of a dynasty no usurpation, but the will of H., 3, 166, 184, 196–9, 213–17; guides and protects kings who are obedient to H., 3, 185 sq.; the king shall be the mate of great H. and reverently sacrifice, 3, 186; king prays to H. for a long-abiding decree in his favour, 3, 187 sq.; the king responds to the favouring decree of H., 3, 192; favours those who obey the king, 3, 200, 218; the inflictions of H. carried out by the king, 3, 200; indulgence in ease is not the way to secure the favour of H. for a king, 3, 203; deceased ministers associated with H. in sacrifices to it, 3, 207, 207 n.; that kings have good ministers is a favour of H., 3, 208, 210; the princes of Yin kept reckoning on some decree of H., 3, 214, 216; approved of the ways of Wăn and Wû, and gave them the four quarters of the land, 3, 245; commissioned the swallow to give birth to Shang (Hsieh), 3, 307; Thang received the blessing of H., 3, 310; sent Î Yin down as a minister to Thang, 3, 311; by its will is inspecting the kingdom, 3, 312; sacrifice to H. associated with King Wăn, 3, 317; the correlate of H., 3, 319 sq.; 476 sq., 476 n.; 16, 46 sq.; 28, 201 sq.; a great sovereign gives rest even to great H., 3, 325, 325 n., the purpose of H. carried out by Wû in the plain of Mû, 3, 342; grants blessing to the prince (Hsî), 3, 345; blessing of H. invoked by the king for his lords, 3, 373 sq., 374 n.; the posterity of Wû will receive the blessing of H., 3, 394; robbers and oppressors have no fear of the clear will of H., 3, 407, 407 n.; a king invokes H. to allay a drought, 3, 422 sq.; Thang overcame Hsiâ, and Wû Shang, in accordance with the will of H., 16, 254; a general in whom the king has reposed entire confidence has 'received the favour of H.,' 16, 276, 276 n.; the ancient sovereigns were helped by H., 16, 383; the ruler on his tour of inspection announces his arrival to H., 27, 216; emperor's sacrifice to H., 27, 222; gives the eulogy for a deceased emperor, 27, 333 sq., 334 n.; whatever good the son of H. possessed, he humbly ascribed its merit to H., 28, 233; is with the virtuous ruler, 28, 308 sq.; desiring to know men, the wise ruler should know H., 28, 313; the purposeless and yet powerful spontaneity of H., a pattern for rulers of the world, 39, 143 sq., 307–14, 307 n., 318, 318 n., 330–38, 346; a son of H., and a co-worker with H., 39, 207; the sons of H. are those whom H. helps, 40, 82. *See also* Rulers.

(*c*) H. AND EARTH IN CHINA.

Are the parents of all creatures and things, 3, 125, 476; 16, 238 sq., 356, 357 sq. n., 429 sq.; 40, 12, 94; worshipped, sacrifices to them, 3, 129, 405 n.; 27, 116, 116 n., 225, 227, 323, 329, 373, 397, 410, 425; 28, 253, 265, 271 sq.; addressed by King Wû when going into battle, 3, 135; worshipped during a drought, 3, 420, 420 n.; are a pattern for the conduct of men, 3, 473; 16, 39 sq., 238 sq., 281, 282 n., 359 sq., 360 n.; 27, 380–4, 387 sq.; 28, 305, 326 sq., 393; 39, 52, 66, 334–8, 364; 40, 60 sq.; are served with intelligence by showing filial piety to fathers and mothers, 3, 484 sq. and n.; their marriage, and their sons and daughters, 16, 49 sq.; symbolism of their reciprocal influence, 16, 223 sq., 224 n., 418–21; harmony between them symbolical of harmony in the state, 16, 227, 227 sq. n.; 28, 100, 104, 106; 'the mind of H. and E.' the love of life and of all goodness, 16, 233, 233 n.; nourish all things, 16, 235; correctness and greatness seen in the character of H. and E., 16, 240, 241 n.; their union emblematic of marriage, 16, 242, 243 n., 257, 258 n.; 27, 55; are separate, but the work which they

do is the same, 16, 243; H. dispensing and E. producing, 16, 247, 248 n.; by their union (marriage) all things spring up, 16, 250; 27, 439 sq.; 28, 265; undergo their changes, and the four seasons complete their functions, 16, 254, 262; their interaction symbolical of men's operations, 16, 259, 259 n.; H. is lofty and honourable, E. is low, hence their symbols *Kh*ien and Khwăn (male and female), 16, 348 sq.; H., E., and man (ruler), the 'three Powers,' 16, 351, 351 sq. n., 402, 402 sq. n., 423 sq., 424 n.; 27, 377 sq.; 28, 115, 115 n., 256 sq., 300 sq., 301 n., 319, 319 n.; 40, 258-60; the Yî King made on a principle of accordance with H. and E., 16, 353 sq.; their great attribute is the giving and maintaining life, 16, 381; all things were produced after H. and E., 16, 433, 435; are in harmonious co-operation in spring, 27, 255; begin to be severe in autumn, 27, 285; no intercommunion of H. and E. in winter, 27, 298; the rules of propriety are rooted in H. and have their correspondencies in E., 27, 367; separated from the Grand Unity, 27, 386 sq.; harmony and graduation in them, 28, 99; music has its origin from H., ceremonies from E., 28, 100-5, 114 sq.; a pattern for the relation of ruler and minister, 28, 103 sq.; represented by musical notes, 28, 111; music the lesson of H. and E., 28, 128, 130; worshipped at the ruler's ploughing of the field, 28, 222; virtue of ancient rulers equal to that of H. and E., 28, 281 sq.; 40, 48 sq.; great as they are, men are dissatisfied with some of their actions, 28, 304; their characteristics, 28, 322; evolved from the Tâo, 39, 67 sq.; 40, 290 sq., 293; unite and send down the sweet dew, 39, 74; the Great Powers whose influences extend to all below and upon them, 39, 143, 307 sq.; do nothing, and yet there is nothing that they do not do, 39, 149; 40, 3 sq.; there is nothing which H. does not cover, and nothing which E. does not sustain, 39, 228, 258; clearly understanding their virtue is what is called 'The Great Root,' and 'The Great Origin,' 39, 332; regarded by Tîs and kings as their author, 39, 333; H. has a more honourable, E. a lower position, 39, 335 sq.; the principles of H. and E. to be followed, 39, 381; cause inflictions, such as hunger, thirst, &c., 40, 37 sq., 38 n.; under the control of the Tâo, 40, 47, 47 n.; body, life, his nature, and his offspring are only entrusted to men by H. and E., 40, 62 sq.; how it was before H. and E., 40, 71 sq.; to respond to the feeling of H. and E., the right thing for a Tâoist ruler, 40, 95; the sage embraces them both in his regard, 40, 105; are grandly complete by doing nothing, 40, 106; happiness only in the pursuit of the perfect virtue of H. and E., 40, 107; are the greatest of all things that have form, 40, 128; Tâoists of later ages no longer saw the undivided purity of H. and E., 40, 217; the bad man appeals to them to witness to the mean thoughts of his mind, 40, 242; H. is pure, E. is turbid, H. moves, E. is at rest, 40, 250; their method proceeds gently and gradually, 40, 263; the Tâo is in H. and E., but they are not conscious of it, 40, 267. *See also* Nature.

(*d*) H. or Svarga world in India.

The five men of Brahman, the doorkeepers of h., 1, 47; is the altar on which the Devas sacrifice the *S*raddhâ libation, 1, 78; obtained by esoteric knowledge, 1, 129 sq., 153, 233; 8, 368; 15, 177; 44, 177, 264; the world of the gods, the reward of the sacrificer, 2, 140, 159; 12, 157 sq., 252, 254 sq., 260 sq., 266, 310, 345 sq., 450 sq., 451 n.; 26, 173, 307, 424, 449 sq.; 41, 7, 32 sq. and n., 286 sq., 322, 344 sq.; 42, 183-5, 187, 189-91; 43, 198-200, 217 sq., 267 sq., 279 sq., 391; 44, 38, 42 sq., 53, 56, 61, 68, 79, 81, 143, 151, 185, 190, 204 sq., 239, 280 sq., 297, 309 sq., 328, 473, 482 sq.; 46, 24; 48, 681; 49 (i), 110; rewards in h., 2, 169 sq.; the reward of true witnesses, 2, 246 sq.; 33, 93; assault against a Brâhma*n*a

causes loss of h., 2, 282 sq. and n.; fallen warriors go to h., 7, 18; 8, 46 sq.; 25, 230; the reward of good conduct and pious actions, 7, 108; 8, 158 sq., 159 n., 322, 327, 344, 360 sq.; 10 (i), 35, 35 n.; 11, 17, 91, 94 sq.; 17, 100; 35, 283, 283 n.; 36, 230; 45, 83; faithful wives will gain h., 7, 111; 14, 232; attained by worship of Vishnu, 7, 156; is a merely temporary good, sorrowful and not worth having, 8, 48 sq. and n., 240; 19, 74 sq., 80, 121, 159 sq., 203 sq., 206; 48, 177, 181; 49 (i), 72 sq., 76 sq.; the gods pass upwards to the world of h. by penance, 8, 389; 44, 91 sq., 505; a few only go to h., 10 (i), 47; better than going to h. is the reward of the first step in holiness, 10 (i), 48; the Arhat sees both h. and hell, 10 (ii), 116; one tooth of Buddha is honoured in h., 11, 135; living in the forest as a hermit is the road to h., 14, 291, 294; there is no death in h., 15, 4; reached by the road of the Fathers, 15, 177; 42, 170; birth in h., the aim of ascetics, 19, 74 sq., 79 sq.; 49 (i), 72 sq., 76 sq.; Buddha ascends to h. to preach to his mother, 19, 240 sq. and n.; he who makes peace in the Samgha will be happy in h. for a kalpa, 20, 254, 268; the gods convey the sacrificer to h., 26, 190; '*may there be a place for me in the world of the gods!' With this hope he offers whoever offers: that same sacrifice of his goes to the world of the gods; and behind it goes the gift he gives to the priests, and holding on to the gift follows the sacrificer*, 26, 342 sq., 345, 348 sq.; the dead go to h., 29, 242 sq.; that within which the h., the earth, &c., are woven, is Brahman, 34, xxxv, 154–62; if the Gaina maintains that h. exists, or does not exist, and is eternal or non-eternal, nobody will act for the purpose of gaining it, 34, 430; the Abhidhamma preached in h., 36, 248; the consecrated king supposed to have ascended to h., 41, 104, 104 n.; north-east the gate of h., 41, 252; prayer for h. after remission of sins, 42, 165 sq.; the firmament is the world of h., 43, 250, 304; 'the life of a hundred years makes for h.,' 43, 323 sq.; begging alms from pious women makes for h., 44, 50; the gate of h. opened by sprinkling water in the northerly direction, 44, 82; the conclusion of the 'sacrifice to the Brahman' (Veda-study), 44, 96; out of the world of h. the gods formed the Udayanîya Atirâtra, 44, 140; Âdityas and Angiras contend together who shall be first to reach h., 44, 152; the h. of the living, 44, 212; by the Brahman (the priesthood) he gains h., 44, 221; fathers led to the world of h., 44, 238; by means of the golden light the Sacrificer goes to h., 44, 303; the horse knows the world of h. and leads the Sacrificer to it, 44, 304–6; sacrificial horse led to h. where the pious dwell, 44, 319; the way to h. not known to the gods, but to the sacrificial horse, 44, 320; that is h. where they immolate the victim, 44, 323; by preparing the knife-paths, the Sacrificer makes for himself a bridge for the attainment of h., 44, 326; established upon the Brihatî, 44, 402 sq.; Sûrya is the heavenly world, 44, 502; the palace Saudharman in h., 45, 291; ridge of h., 46, 45; carrying Agni, they opened the doors of h., 46, 68. *See also* Brahman-world, Future Life, Sky, Transmigration, *and* Worlds.

(*e*) H. (Dyaus) as a deity in India.
Used in a curse, 1, 251; invoked and worshipped, 2, 108; 29, 207, 242, 321; 32, 423; 44, 297 sq., 297 n., 505; 46, 110, 115, 127; 'If thou like, rain, O Sky,' 10 (ii), 3–5; Sky or Dawn, the daughter of Pragâpati, 12, 209; invoked to protect the bride, 30, 188; Father H., 41, 390; 46, 150; starry H., the bull with a thousand horns, 42, 105, 373; Vaisvânara as H., 43, 396; one of the eight Vasus, 44, 116; H. is day, dawn is night, 44, 298; Father H. committed incest with his daughter, 46, 74 sq., 78, 80; the two eyes of H., sun and moon, 46, 83, 86; Agni imparts strength to the Father H.,

46, 144; the Aṅgiras, sons of H., 46, 318; the red young child of H., probably Soma, 46, 360, 362.

(*f*) H. AND EARTH IN INDIA.

Their sons are the gods, 12, 225; Mother E. and Father H., 12, 229; 42, 50, 166, 207; 44, 238, 287, 325; 46, 144; when H. and E. are in harmony, it rains, 12, 241, 241 n.; invoked and worshipped together, 12, 248 sq., 253 sq., 369–73, 388; 25, 90; 26, 23, 104, 330 sq. and n., 396 n., 397; 29, 98 n., 126 sq., 161, 203 sq., 219, 290, 315, 337, 337 n., 367 sq.; 30, 59, 213; 32, 249 sq., 347; 42, 3, 14, 23, 48, 50, 89, 113, 115, 139, 296, 453; 44, 75, 75 n., 81, 337, 337 n., 342 n., 347, 449 sq., 484 sq., 488; 46, 23, 143, 253; salt, the savour of h. and e., 12, 278; were once close together, 12, 278 n.; dangerous are the paths between h. and e., 12, 356; as husband and wife, 15, 205, 220; the universe rests on them, 26, 19, 104, 292; 44, 87; endowed with strength and sap by the sacrificer, 26, 145, 194; beings enclosed between them, 26, 213 sq.; 46, 291; nothing is beyond them, 26, 396 n.; are the thirty-second and thirty-third gods, 26, 411; 'H. I, E. thou,' 29, 36, 168, 282; 30, 190; Vedic student given in charge of them, 29, 306; 30, 154; 44, 87; 'H. am I, and I am E.,' 29, 363; Pragâpati is H. and E., 41, 28; informed of the king's consecration, 41, 90; the parents or mothers of Agni, 41, 224, 350; 46, 168, 233, 249 sq., 291, 293, 336; Agni shines between them, 41, 273; the two worlds, are reta*h*si*k*, 41, 383 sq.; the bestowers of happiness, 42, 57; parents of demons, 42, 67, 340; are the two sides of the war-chariot, 42, 120; hate him who slays a Brâhma*n*a, 42, 169; produced by Rohita (the sun), 42, 208; father and mother of plants, 42, 419; upheld by the Brahman, 43, 59; separated, 43, 75; fit into one another, 43, 126; deities of B*ri*hat and Rathantara, 43, 330; are out- and up-breathing, 44, 488; the two worlds turned towards each other, 46, 67; filled by Agni, 46, 157, 229; the two variegated, great goddesses, 46, 161, 163, 291; Agni invoked to make them inclined, 46, 194, 271; establish Agni as Hot*ri* priest, 46, 244; the two wives, the two milch-cows of Agni, 46, 244, 246; the two well-established goddesses, turned to the East, 46, 245.

(*g*) H. (ÂSMÂN, GARÔ*D*MÂN) IN ZOROASTRIANISM.

Invoked and worshipped, 4, 213 sq., 221, 221 n.; 31, 363; four grades of h. (star station, moon station, sun station, and endless light), 5, 4, 34, 34 n., 294 n.; 24, 20, 29 sq., 100 sq.; 37, 351, 351 n.; the reward of the righteous, 5, 124, 127; 18, 56 sq., 63–70, 70 n., 76; 31, 390; the one place which is good, 5, 335; 18, 4, 4 n.; *thou shouldst not consider even any one hopeless of h.*, 5, 349 sq.; 37, 73; splendour of Aûha*r*maz*d* in h. for those who propitiate the archangels, 5, 375–9; is in the uppermost part of the sky, 18, 87; attained by ceremonies, 18, 237, 237 n.; 24, 262 sq. and n.; the seat of Aûha*r*maz*d*, angels, archangels, and guardian spirits, 18, 275; Keresâsp prays to Aûha*r*maz*d* for h. or better existence, 18, 371, 374, 376–8; by which good works people arrive most at h., 24, 73, 83 sq.; attained through wisdom, 24, 99, 102; if there is no discrimination of good from evil, there is misery even in h., 24, 198; obtained by steadfastness in religion and good works, 24, 321 sq.; treasury of good works in the 'endless light' h., 24, 327 n.; thirty-three ways to h., 24, 343; as the 'best mental state,' 31, 25, 30; the righteous saints go to the happy abode of the Good Mind and of Ahura, 31, 34 sq.; is Good Mind, 31, 66, 66 n.; H. and E. worshipped, 31, 256, 291; the best world of the saints, 31, 257, 322 sq., 345, 363, 372; the shining h., the first-made earthly object, 31, 346; Kâî-Ûs attempts to reach the h. of the archangels, 37, 221; the way to supreme h., 37, 313; souls and archangels in the light of supreme h., 47, 79. *See also* Garô-nmânem, *and* Sky.

(*b*) PLURALITY OF HEAVENS.

The world of Brahman in the third h. from hence, 1, 131; the h. of Tusita (Tushita), 10 (ii), 126; 49 (i), 4; Bhikkhus become inheritors of the highest h., there to pass entirely away, thence never to return, 11, 25 sq., 213 sq.; gods born in the Âgâna h., 15, 60, 61 n.; thirty-three hs., 19, 122; Brahma and other hs., 19, 138 sq.; three stars around the Trayastrimsa h., 19, 201; three hs., 32, 50 sq.; 42, 68, 400; 46, 198; Maruts in the highest, in the middle, in the lowest h., 32, 352; Asvattha tree in the third h., 42, 4, 6, 416; invoked, 42, 161; nine earths, oceans, hs., 42, 228, 631; the Mahâprâna h., 45, 84; rebirth in h. of the Vaimânika gods, 45, 164, 164 n.; description of the top of the world (place of the Siddhas) above the Sarvârtha and Îshat-prâgbhara h., 45, 211 sq.; the dwelling-places of the gods, and duration of life therein, 45, 225–9; Arûpadhâtu, highest h. of the Buddhists, 45, 415 n; Mâra rules four hs., 49 (i), 163, 163 n.; Yâma, Tushita, and other hs., 49 (i), 187, 197;—the bright abode of the holy ones, 23, 11, 19; worshipped, 23, 229;—seven hs., 6, lxx; 9, 5, 66, 71, 199, 290, 292, 303, 316; highest h. called the Throne, 6, 144; 9, 71; rolled up on the last day, 9, 55;—ten hs., 40, 254.

Heavenly, the, in man, 28, 96, 125; 39, 156, 161; 40, 142–4, 146, 176, 179, 205 sq., 280 sq.; the virtue of man is in what is H., 39, 148, 383 sq.; the development of man's H. constitution produced goodness and freedom from harm, 40, 14; the Human and the H. are one and the same, 40, 37–9, 38 n., 39 n.; the Creator recompenses men only for the use of the H. in them, 40, 205; connexion between the H. and the Human elements in man's constitution, 40, 287, 289 sq.

Heavenly lights, secret union of the, 15, 46.

Heavenly vision, the power of seeing beings pass from one existence to another, 11, 216 sqq.

Heavenly world, *see* Heaven.

Hek = Idâ, 12, 223.

Hell(s).

(*a*) H. in Indian religions.
(*b*) H. in Zoroastrianism.
(*c*) H. in Islâm.
(*d*) H. in Chinese religions.

(*a*) H. IN INDIAN RELIGIONS.

Punishment of h. for transgressions of the law, 2, 19, 166, 169 sq., 248; 7, 111, 282; 11, 17 n.; 14, 29 sq., 95; 25, 78, 84, 496, 500; 42, 171, 177, 434 sq.; the perjuror punished in h., 2, 171, 247; 7, 51, 57; 14, 204; 25, 267, 267 n., 270; 33, 93 sq., 245 sq.; the condition of outcasts is h., 2, 281; lists of h., and description of the torments inflicted in them, 7, xxix, 140–4; 10 (ii), 121; 19, 157 sq.; 45, 93–7, 279–86, 376; 49 (i), 149 sq.; the seven h. or Pâtâlas, 7, 3, 3 n.; 38, 123; carnal desire, wrath, and greed, the threefold path to h., 7, 132; 8, 116 sq.; twenty-one h., 7, 140–4; 25, lxviii, 142 sq. and n.; 33, 220; intermingling of castes and destruction of families lead to h., 8, 41 sq.; evil-doers go to h., or are reborn in h., 8, 116, 182 sq., 233, 240, 321, 378; 10 (i), 35, 35 n., 38; (ii), 41, 47, 55; 17, 100; 25, 473; 35, 124, 283, 283 n.; 45, 15, 21, 28, 31, 33, 83, 417; 46, 335; the downward course, the evil path, Niraya, 10 (i), 74–6; swallowing of hot iron balls in h., 10 (i), 86, 86 n.; he who has attained the bliss of the right view is released from the four h., 10 (ii), 38; he who is strong after conquering the pain of h., is Dhîra, 10 (ii), 91; the Buddhist saint sees both heaven and h., 10 (ii), 116; 'this h.,' the world, 10 (ii), 129; 'h. is destroyed for me,' 11, 26 sq.; the pains in the h. were allayed on the eve of Buddha's birth, 19, 345; he who causes a schism is boiled in Niraya, h., for a Kalpa, 20, 254, 268; 35, 163, 167 sq.; eight evil conditions causing sufferings in h. for a Kalpa, 20, 262 sq.; some Bodhisattvas save the creatures in the h., 21, 13; no h. in Buddha fields, 21, 194, 197, 377; 49 (ii), 12, 33, 97, 97 n.; the preacher hears

the cries of those who suffer in h., 21, 339; beings in h., brute creation, and in kingdom of Yama, 21, 233, 248, 401 sq.; h., brute creation, and Yama's realm will come to an end through Avalokitesvara, 21, 415; unworthy king sinks into h., 25, 307–9; 33, 246; a son saves his father from the h. called Put, 7, 65; 25, 354; Harmya = fiery pit, into which evil-doers are thrown, 32, 217 sq.; degree of pleasure and pain enjoyed by inmates of h., 34, 27; the fire of h. more fierce than ordinary fire, 35, 103; though they burn for hundreds of thousands of years in purgatory, beings are not destroyed, 35, 103–6; beings in purgatory are still afraid of death, 35, 206–13, 206 sq. n.; fear of h. a motive of good conduct, 35, 295; the Bhikkhu should preach of purgatory and Nirvâna, 36, 345 sq.; to h. a man-slayer sacrificed at the Purushamedha, 44, 413; the sinner, though he be a monk, will not escape h., 45, 23; fifteen places of punishment, 45, 182; seven kinds of h. and denizens of h., and duration of life in h., 45, 201, 221 sq.; denizens of h. commit sins, 45, 356; the southern region, h., and the dark fortnight are the share of the evil-doer, 45, 372, 372 n., 377; sinners fall into h. but are saved by being preached to, 49 (ii), 197; — *Andhatâmisra* h., 7, 275; 25, 159; *Asamvrita* h., 14, 95; 25, 141; *Avîki* h., 20, 264; 21, 7, 10, 337, 340; 36, 261, 263; 49 (ii), 9; punishments in the Avîki and other h. for those who scorn Buddha's Law, 21, 92, 359 sq.; Avîki h. outside the earth, 35, xl, 9, 9 n.; Avîki, the Waveless Deep, 36, 221, 221 n.; *Kâlasûtra* h., 25, 121; the *Mahâraurava* h. for those who drink spirits, 7, 175; the *Paduma* h., a punishment for backbiting, Buddha describes it, 10 (ii), 119–24; Raurava, one of the seven h., 38, 123; 48, 593; those who do not perform sacrifices go to *Samyamana*, the abode of Yama, 38, 122 sq.; *Tâmisra* h., 25, 155.

(*b*) H. IN ZOROASTRIANISM.

The Drug comes from h., 4, lxxii sq., 122, 122 n., 223; the dogs of h. (Kerberos), 4, lxxiv sq.; Spenta Ârmaiti throws him into h. who does not make gifts, 4, 31; the sinners go to h. by their own doings, 4, 66 sq., 81; lies in the north, 4, 76 n., 101, 112, 129, 209; 23, 45, 45 n.; the wicked dragged into and punished in h., 4, 218 n., 223, 247; 5, 204, 215; 18, 115; 24, 23, 81; 31, 132 sq., 141, 390; 37, 250, 272, 290 sq.; gate of h., 4, 225; 5, 15 n., 36, 109, 361; 24, 58 n., 91 sq. and n.; abode of the Evil Spirit, 4, 376; 23, 296; 24, 104; the 'endlessly dark,' 5, 4; demons and wizards hurled into, rush back to h., 5, 19, 227; 24, 9, 81; 37, 228; 47, 148; is in the middle of the earth, 5, 19; the souls of Mashya and Mashyôî in h., 5, 55; fountain from h. in Kamîndân, 5, 87; described, 5, 114; 37, 209 sq., 209 n.; punishments and misery of h., 5, 124 sq. and n., 303, 305, 350; 18, 57 sq.; 24, 51–3, 183 sq., 188, 193 sq., 200, 336; 37, 69 (frost); created by Aûharmazd, 5, 129; the way to h. through which the demons make the wicked run, 5, 161; four grades of h., 5, 294 n.; 24, 24 sq., 30 sq., 31 n.; *they should not set their minds steadfastly on h.*, 5, 350; how the wicked soul goes to h. and what it suffers there, 18, 70–4, 76; position and subdivision of h., 18, 74 sq. and n.; the gloomy abyss at the bottom of the sky, 18, 87, 259, 259 n.; there is no h. after the renovation of the universe, 18, 118; Keresâsp in h., 18, 372 sq.; next-of-kin marriage preserves from h., 18, 417; Evil-thought H., Evil-Word H., Evil-Deed H., 23, 320; the unhappiest land in which h. is formed, 24, 28; fear of h., 24, 50; how to escape from h., 24, 83 sq.; 37, 179, 426, 436, 445; escape from h. through wisdom, 24, 99; men go to h. by want of wisdom, 24, 102; what admits men to eternal h., 24, 176 sq.; h. and hellish existence by the will of God, 24, 203; worshippers sent by God to h. through a fiery river, 24, 224 sq.; escape from h. by renunciation of sins, 24, 309;

for those who are liberal towards the unworthy, 24, 343; as 'the worst life,' 31, 25, 30; the abode of the Worst Mind, 31, 64, 64 n.; the Home of the Lie, 31, 177, 184; demons rush from h. into the world, 37, 197; childlessness in h., 37, 211; gloomy existence which is horrible h., 47, 92.

(*c*) H. IN ISLÂM.

Seven divisions, doors of h., 6, lxx, 247; certain Jews believe that h. fire only touches them for a number of days, 6, 10, 49; torments of h. for the misbelievers, 6, 32, 57, 70, 165, 167, 175, 178, 180, 182 sq., 189, 193, 199, 206 sq., 216–18, 232 sq., 234 sq., 237, 242, 253, 256; 9, 5, 11, 26, 33, 44, 48 sq., 54, 61, 64, 81, 86, 124, 133, 149, 174, 177, 188, 190, 196 sq., 271, 274, 292, *293*, 294 sq., 305 sq., 329, 340, 344; the reward for killing a believer, 6, 85; the hypocrites condemned to h., 6, 91 sq.; many of the *g*inn and men predestined for h., 6, 160; frightful tortures in h., 6, 240, 244; for him who is only desirous of this life, 9, 3; the tree Ez Zaqqûm in h., 9, 7, 7 n., 170, 170 n., 220, 264; prayer to God to avert h., 9, 89; described, 9, 170; Satan and his followers shall fill h., 9, 181; mutual recriminations of the unbelievers in h., 9, 195; and its nineteen angels, 9, 309; El 'Hu*t*amah in h., 9, 341.

(*d*) H. IN CHINESE RELIGIONS.

The teaching of Purgatorial Sufferings refuted by *K*wang-ȝze, 40, 63 n. *See also* Future Life.

Hemaka, n. of a Brâhma*n*a, 10 (ii), 187, 201 sq., 210.

Hemakamâ*n*avapu*kkh*â, t.c., 10 (ii), 201 sq.

Hemavata, n. of a Yakkha, 10 (ii), 26–8.

Hemavatasutta, t.c., 10 (ii), 25–9.

Hemp, layer of, in fire-pan, 41, 252; sling of h. for gold plate, 41, 266.

Hen, *see* Parables (*c*).

Herbad Zâ*d*-sparam, *see* Zâ*d*-sparam.

Herbs, *see* Plants.

Heresy (apostasy, heretical teaching): Aharman appears on account of toleration of h., 5, lii, 233; he who performs the rites of h. will become a snake, 5, 384 sq.; is the most mischievous weapon of the fiend, 18, 106–9, 109 n.; the sin of h. and how to atone for it, 18, 136–9, 218 sq.; 24, 72, 72 n.; 37, 18, 73, 156; 47, 86, 88 sq., 96 sq.; the merit of him who saves others from it, 18, 139–41; a vice of priests, 24, 105; sects and heretical doctrines, 24, 168, 172, 193, 195; false teaching one mode of engaging in conflict, 37, 40, 40 n., 44; *see also* Ashemaogha;—heretical teaching of 'demoniac' beings, 8, 115; study of heretical books, 19, 263 sq., 264 n.; 25, 443, 443 n.; the Li*kkh*avis destroy their books of h., 19, 279; sixty-two heretical doctrines, 21, 48; heretical systems denounced, 25, 484, 484 n., 505; list of heretical views, 36, xxiii–xxv, 361 sq.; heretical opinions the cause of bad births, 45, 230 sq.; pious monk does not utter heretical doctrines nor ridicule them, 45, 327. *See also* Philosophy.

Heretics (apostates, Daêva-worshippers, Titthiyas): sins atoned for by killing a Daêva-worshipper, 4, 270; the Holy Word not to be taught to h., 4, 276 n., 277, 315; hearken not to the doctrines of h., teach him with the thrust of the sword, 4, 277, 277 n.; he who gives to the Ungodly harms Asha, 4, 297–9; he who refuses food to the heathen and the sinner is not guilty, 4, 315; killing h. a good work, 4, 371; 24, 307; 37, 346, 392; treatment of h., 24, 44, 44 n.; 37, 250 sq.; the Waters invoked against the godless h., 31, 318; proceedings against h., 37, 62; controversy with them, 37, 72, 406 sq.; assault on h., 37, 72; testimony of the orthodox and the heterodox, 37, 118; disturbers of religion, 37, 278–80; avoiding h., 37, 285 sq.; priests triumph over h., 37, 328 sq.; not being deceived by h., 37, 340; relegated to hell, 37, 345 sq.; heretical demon-worshippers, 37, 484;—Jewish doctors and Christian monks denounced, 6, 177;—Titthiyas

(Pali), ascetics adhering to various systems of philosophy, 10 (ii), x, xiii; disputatious h. do not overcome Buddha, 10 (ii), 63; call each other fools, 10 (ii), 170; a Bhikkhu who had formerly belonged to a Titthiya school, goes back to it again, 13, 177, 186 sq.; probation time and ordination of h., 13, 186–91; Bhikkhu or Bhikkhunî who joins a sect of Titthiyas, cannot be received into the order again, 13, 186 sq.; 20, 366; enter upon Vassa under an earthenware vessel, 13, 319; Buddha rebukes Bhikkhus for taking upon themselves the vow of silence as h. do, 13, 328; the wickedness of h. in the last epoch of the world, 21, 259–61; to be avoided by Bodhisattvas, 21, 263, 265; how the *G*aina should behave towards h., 22, 62 sq.; a monk or nun on a begging tour should avoid the company of h., 22, 90; not to be honoured, 25, 133, 133 n.; in a country which is subject to h., a Snâtaka shall not dwell, 25, 138; for h. no funeral libations are made, 25, 184, 184 n.; banished, 25, 381; the kings must maintain the rules settled among corporations of h. (such as Buddhist or Jain monks), 33, 153–5; he who has forsaken the order of religious ascetics, and he who has entered an order prohibited in law, are both contemptible, 33, 265; cannot be witnesses, 33, 303; Milinda mentions his dilemmas as being the expressions of h., 35, 145 sq., 153 sq., 199, 219; 36, 131; Sama*n*as and Brahmans hold forth their various nostrums, 36, 366; philosophical doctrines of the h. mentioned by *G*ainas and Buddhists, 45, xxiii–xxvii; *G*aina and Buddhist doctrines influenced by the teaching of h., 45, xxvii–xxix; many people are h. and follow heretical teachers, 45, 43; a bad *S*rama*n*a follows heretical teachers, 45, 79; practise the five wrong *s*îlas, 45, 80, 80 n.; attend the meeting of Kê*s*i and Gautama, 45, 121; are those who have chosen a wrong path, 45, 126; revilers of the sacred lore, the Kêvalins, and the Saṅgha, realize the Kilvisha-Bhâvanâ, 45, 231; will not be freed from Sa*m*sâra, 45, 239, 240 sq., 242 sq., 246, 250; see no harm in the enjoyment of women, 45, 270; a monk should expound the true doctrine about the soul to h., 45, 308 sq.; heretical teachers and the parable of the Lotus-pool, 45, 335–8; the doctrines of the h. refuted, 45, 339–47.

Hêr-Frôvag, or Âtûr-Frôbag, son of Farukhûzâ*d*, quoted, 18, 289, 289 n.

Hermaphrodites, their food forbidden, 2, 267; a Bodhisattva has no intercourse with h., 21, 264, 266; cannot be converted, 36, 177. *See also* Deformities.

Hermits (Sk. Vânaprasthas) belong to the third â*s*rama, 1, 35 n.; who in the forest follow faith and austerities, go on the path of the gods, 1, 80; life of h. is really abstinence (brahma*k*arya), 1, 131; 38, 300 sq.; studentship a necessary preliminary for the h., 2, 153, 153 n., 155; rules for h. living in the woods, 2, 155–8, 195; 7, 276–8; 8, 361 sq.; 14, 45 sq., 259, 291–4; 25, 193, 198–205, 198 sq. n.; are exempt from fare or toll, 7, 36; 25, 325; his wealth inherited by his spiritual teacher or pupil, 7, 69; food of h., 7, 171; 25, 64 sq. and n., 123, 125, 199 sq., 202 sq.; order of h., living on fruit, roots, and air, prescribed for the three twice-born castes, 8, 316; order of h., previous to the establishment of the Buddhist church, 10 (ii), xii; Buddha recommends the life of a h. to Râhula, 10 (ii), 55 sq.; the merit of the h.'s austerities and of the householder's reciting a single *Rik* are equal, 14, 130; receiving alms from h., &c., purifies from sin, 14, 327; Buddha walks alone in the forest like an elephant, 17, 308, 312–14; probationary not allowed to lead life of h., 17, 387; perform sacrifices and rites, 19, 76 sq.; life of h. not necessary for religion, 19, 97; leading a h.'s life leads to the first dhyâna, 19, 137; 21, 132 sq.; h.'s life without morality no use, 19,

260 sq.; Bhikkhunîs not allowed to adopt h.'s life, 20, 362 sq.; righteousness and sagedom are inconsistent with weak house-inhabiting men, 22, 46 sq.; dress of h., 25, 199, 201; may starve himself to death, 25, 204; h. who gained sovereignty, 25, 222; produced by quality of goodness, 25, 494; penance of h. when they have broken the vows, 38, 319; Tâoist h. eat acorns and chestnuts, and wear skins and hair-cloth, 40, 34, 93 sq.; living at home or in the forest, 44, 356; h. who returned to the state of householders, 49 (i), 100 sq. *See also* Âsramas, Holy persons, *and* Vaikhânasa.

Heroes, advantages resulting from the actions of Gâyômar*d* and other h., 24, 57–65.

Heroism, worshipped as a deity, 31, 346.

Heterodoxy, *see* Heresy.

Hetuvidyâ, *see* Philosophy.

Hexagrams: the eight triagrams of Fû-hsî, and sixty-four h., 3, xvi sq.; the sixty-four h., their names and meanings, 16, viii sq., 57–210; 'The Great Symbolism'—moral lessons derived from the h., 16, 36–8, 267–347; correspondence between the phenomena of nature and the figures of the Yî King, 16, 38–40, 348 sq., 349 sq. n., 353 sq., 354 sq. n., 358–61, 359 n., 373, 377 sq., 378 sq. n., 380 sq., 387; plates exhibiting the h. and triagrams, 16, 56; the changes of triagrams and h., 16, 219 sq. n.; on the distinction of triagrams into Yang and Yin, 16, 388, 388 sq. n., 395, 423 sq.; nine h. discussed, 16, 397 sq., 398 sq. n.; short explanations of triagrams, 16, 428–32; appendix to the Yî on the orderly sequence of the h., 16, 433–40; treatise on the h. taken promiscuously, 16, 441–4; the Khân and Lî h., 40, 295; the h. of the 'dragons on the wing,' 40, 314, 314 n.; alluded to, 40, 319 n. *See also* Symbols, *and* Yî King.

'*Hidh*r, legend of Moses and his servant in search of El 'H., 9, 21–3, 23 sq. n.

Highest Being, *see* God.

Highest good (summum bonum), according to Upanishads and Bhagavadgîtâ, 8, 16 sq.; not attained through the Vedas, 8, 16 sq., 214; attained by action, 8, 52 sq.; or 'Brahmic wealth,' the way to it, 8, 162, 162 n.; according to Buddha, 10 (ii), xvi, 43 sq.; 49 (i), 120; to be obtained by the Dhamma, 10 (ii), 54 sq.; means of attaining it, 25, lxxiii, 501–9, 511; 34, 298; consists in three things, 25, 70 sq.; the ascetic having become indifferent attains to eternal happiness, 25, 212 sq.; 'the better than the good' besought for the holy man, 31, 94, 99, 99 n.; weal and immortality, 31, 111, 119 sq.; the best creation of the bounteous spirit, 31, 148, 148 n.; the h. g. of Buddhists, the bliss of Arhatship, 35, 31, 49 sq., 146, 146 n.; 36, 356; Vessantara's only aim in giving was Supreme Enlightenment, 36, 124 sq.; 'Perfect Enjoyment' according to Tâoism, 39, 149; 40, 1–4; the four requisites for the attainment of it, 45, 15–18. *See also* Nirvâ*n*a.

Highest Person, *see* God, *and* Person.

Highest Self, *see* God, *and* Self.

High-priest, *see* Priests (*d*, *e*).

Himâlaya, 'Manu's descent' at the deluge, a peak of it, 12, 218, 218 n.; *Ri*shis and Brâhmans live in the H. mountains, 19, 78; Mount White is chief of the H., 36, 55; description of H., 36, 129. *See also* Himavat, *and* Parables (*f*).

Himapati, a demon converted by Buddha, 19, 242.

Himavat (i.e. Himâlaya), Umâ, daughter of, 1, 151, 151 n.; one of the princes of mountains, 8, 346; invoked at the house-building rite, 29, 347; Kush*th*a plants brought from it, 42, 5 sq., 415; the waters flow from it, 42, 12; salve from H., 42, 61; the holy mountain H. inhabited by *Ri*shis, 49 (i), 75.

Hînayâna, *see* Mahâyâna.

Hind, wife of Abu Sufiyân, accompanies him in war, 6, xxxvii.

Hindrances, the five 'veils' or, of lustful desire, of malice, of sloth, of pride, of doubt, 11, 182 sq., 182 n.

Hindûk, astronomical tables of, 37, xlvi sq.
Hiouen Thsang, on the Buddhist canon, 10 (i), xii; on Vasubandhu and Gu*n*aprabha, 21, xxii; believes in Buddha as a human being, 21, xxviii; translated the Vagra*kkh*edikâ, 49 (ii), xiii.
Hira*n*yadat Vaida, n.p., 1, 208.
Hira*n*yagarbha, is Brahman, 8, 186 n.; 34, lxxxiii, cix, cxxiii, 172 n.; 38, 391 sq.; 48, 748–50; world of H., 8, 333 n.; 48, 768; the disk of the sun, 12, 271 n.; 32, 6, 10; the personified Brahman and Kapila, 15, xxxviii sqq.; produced by Rudra, 15, 245, 252; a name of the Self, 15, 311; Manu, the son of H., 25, 111; the creator, 32, 1–4; 43, xiv; 48, 334; H. Prâ*g*âpatya, author of a Vedic hymn, 32, 3; a name of Pra*g*âpati, 32, 6, 10; 34, 142, 142 n.; 41, 173 sq.; is the Self of all organs, and dwells in the Brahma-world, 34, 173; lords such as H., 34, 213; the intellect of the firstborn H. is called 'the great Self,' 34, 240, 244; a subordinate causal substance, 38, 77 n.; the Self of the prâ*n*a appears as H. in his double, universal and individual, form, 38, 91; H. himself comes to an end, 38, 238; the golden germ, 41, 368; 43, 295 n.; 44, 391; a form of Vish*n*u, 48, 93; an individual being, 48, 254; created and taught the Vedas, 48, 334; promulgated the Purâ*n*as and the Yoga-sm*ri*ti, 48, 413, 529; represents the collective aggregate of all individual souls, 48, 578; differentiation of names and forms belongs to Brahman, not to H. (i.e. Brahmâ), 48, 578–83; is the first created being, 48, 749.
Hira*n*yaka*s*ipu, or King Kin-pu, born in misery on account of evil deeds, 19, 234, 234 n.
Hira*n*yake*s*in: relation between the schools of Âpastamba, H., and Baudhâyana, 2, xvi, xxiv n., xxiv sq.; 14, xxxv sq.; Satyâshâ*dh*a H., satiated at the Tarpa*n*a, 14, 253 n., 255; 30, 245; different authors of Haira*n*yake*s*a-sûtras, 25, xl; G*ri*hya-sûtra of H., 30, 133–246.
Hira*n*yanâbha, the prince of Kosalâ, 15, 283.
Hira*n*yastûpa (Âṅgirasa), a great *Ri*shi, 12, 175, 175 n.; author of hymns, 46, 24 sq.
Hira*n*yavatî, n. of a river, 11, 85.
Hirisutta, t.c., 10 (ii), 42 sq.
Hitâspa, smitten by Keresâsp, 18, 370; 23, 255, 255 n., 296.
Hitopade*s*a, and Dhammapada, 10 (i), 36 n.
Ho, brothers of that name appointed as astronomers by Yâo, 3, 32–4, 32 n.; punished for negligence, 3, 81–3; Hsî and Ho identified with *Kh*ung and Lî, 3, 257 sq. n.; sent forth the horse with the 'river map,' 27, 392 sq., 393 n.; discourse between the Spirit-earl of the H. and the Spirit-lord Zo, 39, 148, 374–84, 374 n.; animal and human sacrifices to H., 39, 220, 220 n.
Hoazarôdathhri-hanâ Parê*s*tyarô, n. of a high-priest, 5, 115, 115 n.
Hobgoblins, *see* Demons.
Ho-hsü, a primaeval sovereign, 39, 279 sq. and n., 287.
Holiness, first step in, is better than going to heaven, and lordship over all worlds, 10 (i), 48. *See also* Arhatship, *and* Purity.
Ho-lü, famous swords made for, 40, 84, 84 n.
Holy persons: use of the words bhikshu, yati, sannyâsin, 2, lx; food given by h. p. may be eaten, 2, 70, 70 n.; ascetics and hermits eat little, an Agnihotrin and a student much, 2, 123; 14, 265, 281; men who keep the vow of chastity can work miracles, procure rain, bestow children, &c., 2, 158; students, hermits, and ascetics are free from tolls and taxes, 2, 164; 7, 36; 14, 98–100, 98 sq. n.; 25, 325; intercession of a spiritual teacher, a priest, a Snâtaka, causes mitigation of punishment, 2, 166 sq.; the naish*th*ika (professed student), bhikshu (ascetic), and vaikhânasa (hermit), 2, 192, 192 n.; meritoriousness of gifts to Brâhma*n*as, *S*rotriyas, and Vedapâragas, 2, 203, 203 n.; way must be made for a Snâtaka, and even a king must make way for a *S*rotriya, 2, 211;

persons who sanctify the company at a *S*râddha, 2, 259; 14, 19 sq., 51 sq., 266 sq.; 25, 110; ascetics and those who pursue the mode of life of Brahma*k*ârins reach the indestructible seat, 8, 78 sq.; sages became great sages by living as Brahma*k*ârins, 8, 178; *S*rama*n*as (or Sama*n*as) and Brâhma*n*as, 10 (ii), xii–xiv, 14, 18, 22, 30 sq., 45, 71, 86–8, 91, 142 sq., 164, 200; 11, 13, 16 sq., 45, 48, 72, 98, 105 n., 152–4, 187, 192–9, 270, 288; 13, 97, 136; 17, 95, 125, 129; 19, 19; 20, 196; 35, 7, 10, 195; 36, 28, 127 n., 221, 266; perpetual students, hermits, and ascetics do not inherit, 14, 89, 89 n.; trading ascetics and *S*rotriyas, 14, 100; penances for hermits and ascetics, 14, 115, 115 n.; *S*rotriyas, students, and ascetics not to be witnesses, 14, 204; 25, 265, 265 n.; 33, 82, 82 n., 87 sq., 246; presents of money to be given to good Brâhma*n*as, *S*rotriyas, and Vedapâragas, 14, 240; food of hermits and ascetics, 14, 265; different kinds of ascetics and hermits, and their modes of life, 19, 72–4, 80; 49 (i), 70–8; hospitable reception of a Snâtaka or *S*rotriya, 25, 96 sq., 97 n.; purification for students, hermits, and ascetics, 25, 193; mendicants and Dîkshitas allowed to speak to women, 25, 316; hermits and ascetics produced by goodness, 25, 494; by slaying a Soma-sacrificer one becomes guilty of murder of a Brâhma*n*a, 26, 35; *Ri*shis, hermits, the chaste ones, and those who have only one wife, worshipped at the Tarpa*n*a, 30, 245; stages of saintship: Sakadâgâmins, Anâgâmins, Arahats, Pa*kk*eka-Buddhas, Buddhas, 35, 156–9; 36, 5; 49 (ii), 120 sq., 120 n., 167, 193–5; Sama*n*as and Brâhma*n*as leading a virtuous life, live for the weal of gods and men, 35, 274 sq.; he who has slain an Arhat, wounded a Tathâgata, or outraged a nun, cannot be converted, 36, 78 n.; space the resort of *Ri*shis, ascetics, and Bhûtas, 36, 316; h. p. and deceased Fathers invoked against enemies, 42, 119, 585; gods, pious men, and Fathers, 42, 126; Rakshas, serpents, pious men, Fathers, 42, 162; *one does not become a Sramana by the tonsure, nor a Brâhmana by the sacred syllable ôm, nor a Muni by living in the woods, nor a Tâpasa by wearing (clothes of) Kusa-grass and bark. One becomes a Sramana by equanimity, a Brâhmana by chastity, a Muni by knowledge, and a Tâpasa by penance*, 45, 140; he who subdues himself is to be called a Brâhma*n*a, a *S*rama*n*a, a Bhikshu, a Nirgrantha, 45, 333 sq., 355; Naish*th*ikas, Vaikhânasas or Parivrâ*g*akas, who have broken their vow are not qualified for the knowledge of Brahman, 48, 705–7; Buddhas, Pratyekabuddhas, Bodhisattvas, and Arhats, 49 (i), 188 sq.; Buddha makes millions of ascetics, disciples, Arhats, sages, &c., 49 (i), 197 sq.; Buddhas, Bodhisattvas, Âryas, *S*râvakas, and Pratyekabuddhas, 49 (ii), 1; light going out from *S*râvakas and Bodhisattvas, 49 (ii), 52, 60 sq.; elders, great disciples, and Arhats and Bodhisattvas, 49 (ii), 89 sq., 90 n.; friars, nuns, laymen and women, and Bodhisattvas, 49 (ii), 144. *See also* Ascetics, Hermits, Snâtakas, Theras, Tîrthakas, Vaikhânasa, *and* Yogin.

Holy places, or Tîrthas, 1, 144, 144 n.; 7, 205, 205 n., 256; *S*râddhas offered in h. p., 2, 255, 255 n.; 14, 55; mountains, rivers, holy lakes, places of pilgrimage, dwellings of *Ri*shis, cow-pens, and temples of the gods, are places which purify from sin, 2, 276; water from a holy lake or river to be used for the purification of a sinner, 2, 279; 14, 78; to preserve the altars of their land and grain, the duty of princes, 3, 468, 468 sq. n.; visiting Tîrthas or places of pilgrimage, 7, xxx, 13, 256–60, and notes; one about to visit a place of pilgrimage is exempt from fares or tolls, 7, 36; mortal sinners are purified by visiting all Tîrthas on earth, 7, 133, 135; one purified by visiting Tîrthas sanctifies acompany, 7, 254; the Kaabah established by Abraham, and the pilgrimage proclaimed, 9, 59; *see also* 'Hagg,

Kaabah, Mecca, *and* Mosque; so long as the Vaggians honour their shrines, so long will they prosper, 11, 4; places of pilgrimage for devout Buddhists, 11, 90 sq.; an ascetic should not care for the three Pushkaras, 14, 48; mountains, rivers, &c., destroy sin, 14, 117, 311; residing and bathing in h. p. purifies from sin, 14, 128, 136; 49 (i), 8, 22, 74; not to be entered without having cleansed one's feet, 14, 249; *K*aityas raised in honour of former Buddhas, 19, 323, 334 sq.; Vi*k*âra-bhûmi and vihârabhûmi, places for religious practices or for study, 22, 90, 96, 163, 170; festivals and feasts in honour of h. p., &c., 22, 92; near rivers, marshes, or ponds, 22, 182; the country of the Brahmarshis, 25, 32 sq.; h. p. not to be defiled, 25, 136; pilgrimages to the Ganges and the land of the Kurus, 25, 270; 33, 246; holy fields exempt from taxes, 27, 227; sacrifice offered at a *K*aitya or holy shrine, 29, 178 sq.; the bridal procession passing h. p., 30, 262; obstruction of the sanctuary of a deity forbidden, 33, 158; discussions on secret doctrines should not be carried on in h. p., 35, 139; miracles at the *K*etiyas or mounds raised over the ashes of deceased Arhats, 36, 174–6; altar with bells, 40, 31 sq.; sacrificial hall erected to *K*wang-ȝze, 40, 320–3; the Law is 'the pond,' celibacy 'the holy bathing-place' of the monk, 45, 56; h. p. of pilgrimage are ladders to heaven, 49 (i), 75; Tîrthas in Râgag*ri*ha, 49 (i), 104; *K*aityas with relics of Buddha, 49 (i), 166–8; (ii), 124, 130; holy rivers, 49 (i), 168. *See also* Altar, *and* Temples.

Holy women, *see* Nuns.

Holy Word, *see* Mãthra Spe*n*ta, Prayers, Revelation, Sacred Books, *and* Zoroastrianism.

Hôm, *see* Haoma.

Home, ceremonies for officers leaving their country, 27, 104 sq.; how one should try to stop rulers or officers from leaving their state, 27, 107; rite performed to avoid being deprived of one's h., 44, 126.

Hôm Ya*s*t, written after the death of Alexander, 4, xlviii sq., liv; translated, 31, 230–44.

Homicide (manslaughter, murder), causes loss of caste, 2, 74; 25, 444; composition paid for h. (Wergeld), 2, 78 sq. n., 285; 6, 25, 85; 14, 201 sq. and n.; 32, 356, 361; penance for committing h., 2, 78–82, 83, 90, 283–5, 292 sq.; 7, 157 sq.; 14, 107 sq., 118; 25, 444–9, 455–8, 480; law of self-defence, 2, 90 sq.; 14, 19, 200; 25, 314 sq.; 33, 285; 37, 38; punishments for h., 2, 167; 4, 44 sq.; 33, 202 sq.; assassination of a king, 2, 277; sin of killing a Brâhma*n*a, penance for it, 2, 278, 280; 7, 132, 181; 8, 389; 14, 5, 105 sq., 109, 127, 132 sq., 211, 222, 296, 299, 310, 317; 25, 270, 440 sq., 496; 33, 229 sq.; 44, *341*, 396; sin of murdering one of the faithful, 4, 33, 33 n., 103; laws about h., 6, 25, 85; 14, 201 sq.; 33, 85, 359, 363 sq.; 37, 53; sin of h., 6, 101 sq., 135; 9, 89; 42, 521 sq.; seven kinds of assassins, 7, 41; crimes of h. which are equal to killing a Brâhma*n*a, 7, 133 sq.; sin of slaying women, children, or suppliants, 7, 133 sq., 180; 25, 270, 469; slaying a sacrificer, 7, 133 sq.; 26, 35; sin of slaying a friend, 7, 134; 25, 441; crime of killing a Kshatriya, or a Vai*s*ya, or a *S*ûdra, 7, 136; he kills not and is not killed, 8, 44 sq., 123; h. is a sin, except for just cause, 9, 4 sq.; murder of a husband, of a learned Brâhma*n*a, and destruction of embryo, are the only crimes by which women become outcasts, 14, 133; revenge for bloodshed, 27, 140; punishment of parricide and regicide, 27, 195, 195 n.; slaying a mother, a father, an Arhat, excludes from conversion, 36, 78 n., 177. *See also* Abortion, *and* Slaughter.

Honesty, not acting dishonestly, part of the conduct of the good, 8, 243. *See also* Truth.

Honey, food is, 1, 162; h.-mixture (madhuparka) for the guest, 2, 120 sq., 205; 14, 49, 244; 25, 75, 96 sq., 175, 374; 29, 89, 197–200, 274 sq., 433; 30, 130 sq., 171–4, 278; 42, 81; used as a medicine, 6, 257,

257 n.; means the sun by a metaphor, 34, 256 sq.; 48, 335; *see also* Madhuvidyâ; madhugraha or h.-cup, 41, 11, 29; used with consecration water, 41, 78; not to be eaten during initiation, 41, 186; is life-sap of the sky, 41, 390; a symbol of personal agreeableness, 42, 99 sq., 277; the h.-lash of the A*s*vins, 42, 229–32, 587–91; mixed with curds and ghee for sprinkling on fire-altar, 43, 182 sq.; not to be eaten by Brahma*k*ârin, 44, 90; is a form of Soma, 44, 243; means breath, 44, 467. *See also* Food.

Hope, meditation on it as Brahman, 1, 119; personified, 26, 349.

Hôrmazd, *see* Aûha*r*maz*d*.

Horse(s), the duke of Sung comes with white hs., 3, 327; U*kk*ai*ss*ravas, chief of hs., 8, 89, 89 n.; Sindhu hs., 10 (i), 77; h.-treasure of King Sudassana, 11, 255 sq., 274, 279, 281, 286, 287; h. led in front of the fire at ceremonies, 12, 297 sq., 298 n., 299 sq. and n.; 41, 359–62; white h. the priests' fee for an oblation to Sûrya, 12, 446 sq.; h. of the h.-sacrifice fancifully identified with things in nature, 15, 73 sq.; the sea is its kin and birthplace, 15, 74; 43, 401; Buddha's white h., 19, 57, 67; 49 (i), 59–61, 67 sq., 79; the eyesight of the male h., 23, 239, 266; (white) h. is the sun, 26, 115; 41, 199, 208, 359 sq.; 44, 312; (white) h. is Agni, 26, 149; 41, 207–12, 224, 360; origin of the h. (from the waters), 26, 281; 41, 19, 146 (a*s*va), 199, 405; 43, 401–3; 44, xviii–xx, 304, 318, 329; regulations for rearing hs., 27, 275; white h. of Pedu invoked against the serpents, 29, 131, 204, 327, 330; 30, 238, 288; 42, 152 sq., 605–8; red hs. in mythology, 32, 16–27; the h. of wonderful speed of a great king, 35, 199 sq. and n.; mutilating a h., 37, 48; about hs., 37, 90 sq.; 40, 92 sq.; 41, 177, 198, 207, 360; taming of hs., 39, 140, 276–9; how they are yoked, 41, 19–21; 43, 237; are coursers and wealth-winners, smell B*ri*haspati's portion, 41, 22, 28, 209; connected with Varu*n*a, 41, 60, 162, 405; 44, xix; one of the five sacrificial animals, 41, 162, 165 sq.; searches for Agni, 41, 204 sq.; is the highest and most perfect of animals, ranks next to man, 41, 209; 44, xviii, 287, 332; sacrifices on the footprint of the sacrificial h., 41, 212; 44, 363, 363 n.; h. is the nobility, other animals the peasantry, 41, 227; 44, 303 sq., 371; seven balls of h.-dung used for fumigation, 41, 240; 44, 455; is sacred to Pragâpati, 41, 240 sq.; 44, 274, 274 n., 277 sq., 333; produced from the eye of Pragâpati, 41, 402; 44, 328, 354; the one-hoofed animal, 41, 410; charm to endow a h. with swiftness, 42, 145 sq., 507 sq.; made to smell the bricks of the fire-altar, 43, 141; as haya it carries gods, as vâgin Gandharvas, &c., 43, 401; Pragâpati in the form of a h., 43, 401; mare brings forth within a year, 44, 12; the four priests compared to four harnessed Saindhava steeds, 44, 94; prize-winning steeds sprinkled, 44, 95; mare with a foal as sacrificial gift, 44, 218, 222; impure and unfit for sacrifice is the h., 44, 274; is the most vigorous and swiftest of animals, 44, 278; sacrificial h. committed to the care of a hundred princes, 44, 288, 355; 'child,' a favourite name of the h., 44, 288; born as a runner, 44, 294; knows the heavenly world, 44, 304–6, 320; mares penned up to make the sacrificial horse whinny, 44, 306; h. belongs to all the gods, 44, 311, 332; the sacrificial h. as a great bird, 44, 315, 315 n.; draws nothing else than a chariot, 44, 317; is Brahman, 44, 318; lying down near sacrificial h. to ensure fertility, 44, 322 n.; oblation offered on a h.-hoof, 44, 339; qualities of the h. for the A*s*vamedha, 44, 353–5; Hot*ri* sings the praises of the sacrificial h., 44, 384 sq.; has no omentum, 44, 388; the head of a h. put on Dadhya*ñk* by the A*s*vins, 44, 445.

Horse-races, rules of, 37, 125; Agni invoked for victory in h.-r., 46, 16.

Horse-sacrifice, *see* A*s*vamedha.

Horvadad, or Khûrdâd (Av. Haurvatât), Genius of Health and Water, archangel, created, 5, 10, 10 n.; 23, 48; has the lily, 5, 104; attacks Tâirêv, 5, 128; guardian of the water, 5, 359, 372 sq., 377 sq.; 31, 207, 207 n., 211, 213 sq., 221 sq., 226–8; invoked and worshipped, 5, 401, 405; 23, 5, 14, 36 sq.; Khordâd Yast in praise of H., 23, 48–52; allied with Tistrya, 23, 92; intercedes for men on the day H. of the month Fravardîn, 24, 314 sq.; H., Universal Weal, and Immortality, worshipped, 31, 196, 256, 259, 325, 330, 348, 380; offended by chatter during eating, 37, 207, 207 n.; creatures live through H., 37, 291; prescribes to Zoroaster the care of water, 47, 162. *See also* Amerôdad.

Hôshâng (or Hôshyang, or Hâôshâng, Av. Haoshyangha), the Pêshdâdian, destroyed two-thirds of all creatures of Ahriman, 4, 384; primaeval monarch, 5, 58; 18, 13, 13 n.; 37, 27, 27 n.; 47, 8, 121, 128, 140; son of Fravâk, 5, 131, 131 n.; reigned forty years, 5, 149; men under his reign, 5, 186; of the early law, 18, 90; smiter of demons, 18, 200, 200 n.; 23, 224, 251, 275 sq., 292; 47, 8; the Paradhâta king, sacrifices to Ardvi Sûra Anâhita, 23, 58 sq., 58 n.; worshipped Drvâspa, 23, 111; worships Vayu and Ashi Vanguhi, 23, 251, 275 sq.; his exploits, 24, 57 sq., 57 n.; Vâêgered brother of H., 47, x; his accession, 47, xxix; the Pêsdâdian, monarch of the seven regions, 47, 35.

Hôshêdar Bâmî, son of Zarathustra, will rise from the lake Frazdânava, 23, 79.

Hôshyang, *see* Hôshâng.

Hospitality, *see* Guests.

Hotrâ Bhârati, n. of a goddess, 46, 154, 156, 187, 191 sq.

Hotri, *see* Priests (*a*).

House, of other persons not to be entered without permission or in the absence of the owners, 9, 76; teaching the ritual for choosing the site of a h., a 'low art,' 11, 199; ceremonies on leaving and re-entering the h. before and after a journey, 12, 357–60; 29, 96–8; 30, 206 sq.; rules as to h.-building for Bhikkhus, 13, 8 sq.; five kinds of dwellings allowed to Bhikkhus, 13, 173, 173 sq. n.; 20, 158; cave dwelling-places, 17, 61; ceremonies and prayers on building and entering a new h., 20, 127–9; 29, 92–6, 211–15, 345–9, 428–30; 30, xxviii, 120–4, 204–6, 285 sq., 303 sq.; 42, 140 sq., 343–8, 494; guardian deities of the h., 25, 96; 'h.-warming' feast, 27, 196; five altars of the h., 27, 313, 313 n.; consecration of a newly-built temple and palace, 28, 169 sq.; offerings to the deities of the h., 29, 319 sq.; expiation of the site of the h., every year or every season, 30, 206; sprinkling water round the h., 30, 288; celebration and blessings for the benefit of the h., 31, 352; bath and fireplace to be provided in a h., 37, 90; about dwellings and boundaries, 37, 118 sq.; about bed-places, 37, 123; offerings to the spirit of the h., 37, 209; charm to protect the h. from fire, 42, 147, 514–16; prayer and rites connected with a h. given as dakshinâ, 42, 193–6, 595–600; personified as a goddess, 42, 194 sq., 346; many living beings are killed through h.-building, 45, 204. *See also* Parables (*f*).

Householder (grihapati), duties of the, 1, 144; 2, 50 sq., 99–152, 156, 160, 196–214; 7, 189–276; 8, 216; 10 (ii), 65 sq.; 14, 42–5, 49–58, 63–75, 236–9, 243–57, 262–73, 286 sq.; 25, 128–30; 38, 296 sqq.; the state of the h. is prescribed in the Vedas, 2, 196, 196 n.; Zoroastrian ideal of a h.'s life, 4, 23, 34, 46–8; *he who does not give their share to these five, the gods, his guests, (his wife and children and others), whom he is bound to maintain, his manes, and himself, is not alive, though he breathes*, 7, 193; order of h. prescribed for all castes, 8, 316; the happiness of the h. contrasted with the happiness of the Buddha, 10 (ii), 3–5; the life of the h. condemned as compared with the Bhikkhu's life, 10 (ii), 7; 11, 187 sq.; the faith of a h., possessed of knowledge, is not lost, 10 (ii), 16; is never equal to a Muni or Bhikkhu,

10 (ii), 33–6; '*a Brâhmana is born, loaded with three debts,*' (*and further,* '*He owes*) *sacrifices to the gods, a son to the manes, the study of the Veda to the* Rishis; *therefore he is free from debt who has offered sacrifices, who has begotten a son, and who has lived as a student* (*with a teacher*),' 14, 56, 44 n., 46; nine modes of living for h. with certain vows, 14, 284–91; no end of toil and labour in the life of a h., 20, 225 sq.; strictures on the life of a h. as compared with the religious life, 22, 15–27; becoming a h., 25, 75; has five slaughter-houses, 25, 87 sq.; daily rites to be performed by a h., 25, 87–97; hs., unlearned in the scriptures, 44, 362; some hs. are superior to monks in self-control, but saints are superior to all hs., 45, 22 sq.; the dreadful âsrama of the h., 45, 39, 39 n.; even hs. go to the world of the gods by refraining from injuring living beings, 45, 259; are killers of living beings, 45, 350 sq. *See also* Âsramas.

Housewife, *see* Wife.

Hrasva Mândûkeya, n.p., 1, 253.

Hrishîkesa, n. of Krishna, 8, 38 sq., 43, 96, 121.

Hrûdu, a name (?) of Takman, 42, 3, 273.

Hsî, and Ho, appointed as astronomers by Yâo, 3, 32–4, 32 n.; punished for negligence, 3, 81–3; H. and Ho, identified with *Kh*ung and Lî, 3, 257 sq. n.

Hsî, Duke, an ode in praise of, 3, 341–6.

Hsiâ, credibility of the books of the H. dynasty in the Shû, 3, 13; period of the H. dynasty, 3, 23 sq.; the dynastic designation of Yü and his descendants, 3, 63; 'the Books of H.' translated, 3, 63–83; overthrow of H., 3, 214 sq.

Hsiâ Fû-*kh*î, charged with irregularity in sacrificial rites, 27, 403 sq. and n.

Hsiâ-hâu Shih-*kh*ang, disciple of Yüan Kû, 3, 287.

Hsiang: the Shû King comes down to King H. of the *K*âu dynasty, 3, xv; half-brother of Shun, 3, 36.

Hsiang, duke of Sung, 27, 154, 186 sq.

Hsiang-po, hated the bad, 28, 352.

Hsiang-thû, grandson of Hsieh, 3, 309, 309 n.

Hsiang Wang, or Purposeless, 39, 312, 312 n.

Hsiâo-hsin, king of the Thang dynasty, 3, 112.

Hsiâo-*k*î, famous for filial piety, met with calamity, 40, 132, 132 n.

Hsiâo King, or 'Classic of Filial Piety,' 3, xx, 449; attributed to Confucius, 3, 449 sq., 461 sq.; its date, 3, 450 sq.; its author, 3, 450 sq.; its contents, 3, 451; its recovery and preservation, 3, 452–8; criticism of it since the Thang dynasty, 3, 458–62; its genuineness, 3, 461 sq.; translated, 3, 462–88.

Hsiâo-po = Hwan, q.v.

Hsiâo-yî, king of the Thang dynasty, 3, 112.

Hsieh, minister of instruction to Shun, 3, 42 sq., 43 n., 84.

Hsieh, founder of the Shang dynasty, 3, 303; his miraculous birth, 3, 307, 307 n., 309, 309 n.; worshipped as an ancestor, 3, 308 sq.; 28, 202, 209; called 'the dark king,' 3, 309, 309 n.; assessor at the border sacrifice of *Kh*î, 27, 372.

Hsieh Tâo-hăng, story of his life, 40, 311 sq. n.; author of the inscription on the stone-tablet in the temple of Lâo-ʒze, 40, 311–19.

Hsien, lord of Kwan, 3, 154 sq., 155 n.

Hsien, king of Ho-*k*ien, what he did for the Lî King, 27, 4–6.

Hsien, duke of Ʒin, 27, 126 sq., 127 n., 165.

Hsien, duke of Wei, 27, 182 sq.; 28, 252.

Hsien-*khih*, n. of Hwang-Tî's music, 39, 348, 348 n.

Hsien Păn-fû, driving with Duke *K*wang of Lû, 27, 127 sq.

Hsien-yüan, a primaeval sovereign, 39, 287, 287 n.

Hsien-ʒze, on mourning rites, 27, 150–4; 28, 157 sq.; advises Duke Mû as to means for procuring rain, 27, 201 sq.

Hsî-*kh*î, killed by Lî Kho, 28, 294.

Hsin, sprites haunting mounds, 40, 19.

Hsin-yüan Phing, his advice disregarded by Wăn, 27, 19, 19 n.

Hsî Phăng, a sage accompanying Hwang-Tî, 40, 96; recommended by Kwan *K*ung as minister to Hwan, 40, 102, 102 n.

Hsî Shih, a famous beauty, a courtesan, 39, 184, 184 n., 354.

Hsî-sze, brother of Duke Hsî, architect of Hsî's temples, 3, 341, 346.

Hsiung, proposed to Shun as Forester, 3, 44.

Hsî Wang-mû, got the Tâo, 39, 245, 245 n.; the Royal-mother of the West, 40, 249.

Hsüan, reigned forty-six years, 3, 22; classics collected under his reign, 3, 293; 27, 6; on occasion of a great drought, he expostulates with God and all the spirits, 3, 419–23; appoints his 'great uncle' to be marquis of Shăn, 3, 423 sq. and n.

Hsüan-*kh*ing = Hsieh Tâo-hăng, q.v.

Hsüan *K*iang, princess of *Kh*î, her beauty, 3, 435 sq.

Hsüan-ming, attending spirit of *K*wan-hsü, 27, 296, 302, 306; a Tâoist teacher, 39, 247.

Hsüan Nî, a name of Confucius, 40, 314, 314 n.

Hsüan of *Kh*î, contemporary of *K*wang-ʒze, 40, 321.

Hsüan of *Kh*û, ordered the siege of Han-tan, 39, 284, 284 n.

Hsüan-yang Ʒze, author of the Yü Shû *K*ing, 40, 265.

Hsüan Ʒung, of the Thang dynasty, author of a commentary on the Hsiâo King, 3, 450, 456 sq.

Hsü Tien, at the archery trial of Confucius, 28, 450.

Hsü Wû-kwei, the recluse, and the Marquis Wû of Wei, 39, 153 sq.; 40, 91–6.

Hsü-yî, a Tâoist teacher, 39, 247.

Hsü-yü, count of *K*î, a worthy but not a True Man, 39, 239, 239 sq. n.

Hsü Yû, mourning rites for him, 28, 166; example of the 'sagely man,' 39, 127, 169 sq., 169 n., 172 n.; and Î-*r* Ʒze, 39, 255 sq.; teacher of Yâo, 39, 312; 40, 210; flees from Yâo on account of the latter's benevolence, 40, 108; refused the throne offered by Yâo, 40, 141, 149, 183; found pleasure on the north of the river Ying, 40, 161; regardless of the name, 40, 274.

Hû, proposed as Forester to Shun, 3, 45.

Hû, or *K*ung of Ʒhâi, King *Kh*ăng's charge to him, 3, 211–13.

Hû, earl of Shâo, rewarded by the king, 3, 427 sq.

Hû, the god of the Northern Ocean, 39, 267.

Hûbakht, n.p., 5, 145.

Hubal, chief of the minor gods of the Arabs, procures rain, 6, xii.

Hûd, sent as an apostle to 'Âd, 6, 145 sq., 145 n., 210 sq.; 9, 95.

Hûdînô, n.p., 5, 145.

Hufravâkhs, n.p., 23, 219.

Hûgar=Hukairya, q.v.

Hug*au*, n.p., 23, 215.

Hui, repealed the edict forbidding the keeping of old writings, 27, 3.

Hui, *see* Yen Hui.

Hui Shih, a sophist, his teaching, 39, 163; 40, 229–32, 229 n.

Hui-wăn, *see* Wăn.

Hui-ʒze, mourning rites for, 27, 143; disputations and conversations of H. and *K*wang-ʒze, 39, 134, 172–5, 172 n., 234 sq.; 40, 98–100, 137 sq., 144 sq.; the teaching of H. opposed to Tâoism, 39, 147; *K*âo Wăn, Shih Kwang, and H., 39, 186; H. and *K*wang-ʒze, 39, 391 sq.; 40, 4; *K*wang-ʒze passing by the grave of H., 40, 100 sq., 100 n.; introduces the sage Tâi Ʒin-ʒăn to King Yung, 40, 119 sq.

Hukairya: Ardvi Sûra Anâhita flows from mount H. to the sea Vouru-Kasha, 23, 52, 54 sq., 54 n., 76, 81 sq., 181; H. of the deep precipices, made of gold, 23, 174.

Hu*k*ithra, n. of a holy woman, 23, 225.

Huma, daughter of Vîstâspa, 23, 224.

Hûmâî, daughter of Freh-mâh, 5, 146, 146 n.; daughter of Vohûman, 5, 151; of the family of Vistâsp, the finest woman, 37, 220.

Hûmâî, his accession, 47, xxx, xxxii; reigns of H. and Dârâî, 47, xxviii.

Hûmân, n.p., 5, 135, 135 n.; high-priest, quoted, 18, 150, 150 n.

Humanity, benevolence, righteousness, propriety, and knowledge are

the attributes of, 27, 59; 28, 465 sq.; is the root of right, 27, 390; h. and righteousness rooted in ceremonies, 27, 413 sq.; the virtues of h., 28, 333–7, 337 n.

Human life, *see* Life.

Human sacrifice, as a penance, 2, 83, 83 n.; to procure rain, 3, 91 n.; of ancient Arabs, 6, 132 n.; Manu's wife slain as victim, 12, 29 sq.; Purushayag*ñ*a, man-sacrifice, 38, 220–2; in China, 39, 220, 220 n.; practised amongst the Aryans of India, 44, xvii sq.; the Purushamedha, and h. s. in ancient India, 44, xxxii–xlv, 403–17; Purushamedha is everything, 44, 404 sq., 406, 410, 412 sq.; the symbolical victims of the Purushamedha, 44, 413–17; men sacrificed at the Sarvamedha, 44, 419; using skulls as drinking-vessels, and other cruel rites of *S*aivas, 48, 521. *See also* Man.

Humâyaka(?), worshipper of the Daêvas, conquered by Zairi-vairi, 23, 80.

Humility, enjoined, 4, 293; 8, 326; 9, 5; 39, 52 sq., 96 sq.; is the most excellent thing in 'propriety,' 16, 80 n.; is the road to success, 16, 89 sq., 90 sq. n.; 39, 104 sq., 109 sq.; the virtue of the superior man, 16, 226, 226 sq. n., 286 sq., 287 n., 344, 362 sq.; 28, 287–90, 339 sq.; satisfaction follows from h., 16, 434, 440; a virtue of kings, 25, 222; 39, 96 sq.; the scholar distinguished by h., 28, 409; enjoined by Tâoism, characteristic of the man of Tâo, 39, 65, 67, 71, 76 sq., 119; 40, 101–4, 226 sq.; true strength in weakness and h., 39, 118 sq.; weakness is true strength, example of water, 39, 120.

Hunger, explained, 1, 99; h. is death, 15, 75; 43, 402; 44, 340; sacrifice to H., 30, 128; a hungry man consumed by his vital airs, 43, 347 sq.; a bent Yûpa is a type of h., 44, 124.

Hung Mung, questioned by Yün *K*iang about governing men, 39, 143, 300–3, 300 n., 302 n.; 40, 286 sq.

Hung Yâo, minister of Wăn, 3, 208.

Hunting, prohibited for the rich, 5, lxi, 301, 301 sq. n.; threefold use of game caught in h., 16, 190, 192 n.; a vice of kings, 25, 223; rules about h., 27, 106, 220 sq., 265, 270 sq., 294 sq., 425 sq.; 28, 230; tribute of deer to the ruler, 27, 433, 433 n.; the autumnal hunts, 28, 11. *See also* Animals (*f*).

Hunus, smitten by Keresâsp, 18, 370 sq., 370 n., 371 n.; n. of a people (?), 23, 205, 205 n.; Vî*s*tâspa took the kingly glory from the H., 23, 306.

Hû Pû-*k*ieh, a worthy, but not a True Man, 39, 239, 239 n.

Husband and wife, *see* Family, Marriage, *and* Wife.

Hûsh, *see* Immortality (draught of).

Hûshê*d*ar, *see* Aûshê*d*ar.

Hûshê*d*ar-mâh, *see* Aûshê*d*ar-mâh.

Hu*s*kyaothna, son of Frashao*s*tra, 23, 207 sq.

Husravah (Kai Khosrav), legends of, 23, 7 n., 64 n., 65 sq.; King H. invoked, 23, 7, 7 n., 15, 358; killed Franghrasyan, 23, 114 sq., 278, 304, 307, 307 n.; worships Drvâspa, 23, 115; united the Arya nations into one kingdom, 23, 115, 278; Fravashi of King H. worshipped, 23, 222; Aurvasâra flees from him, 23, 256 sq.; worshipped Ashi Vanguhi, 23, 278; the kingly glory of H., 23, 303 sq.; went alive to Paradise, 23, 327 sq., 327 n.

Hutaosa (Phl. Hûtôs), wife of Vî*s*tâspa, 23, 77 n., 116, 116 n., 224, 257, 279; 37, 300, 300 n.; 47, 71 sq. and n., 80 n.

Hûtôs, *see* Hutaosa.

Huvâsp, n. of a high-priest, 5, 115.

Huyazata, n.p., 23, 214.

Hûzavârak, n.p., 5, 140, 140 n.

Huzzâ, El 'H., Arabian tree goddess, 6, xii sq., xxvi sq.

Hû-ʒze, defeats the wizard *K*i-hsien, 39, 137, 262–5.

***Hv*âdaêna,** son of Frashao*s*tra, 23, 208.

***Hv*adhâta,** n.p., 23, 215.

***Hv*âkhshathra,** n.p., 23, 214.

***Hv*aniratha,** Sraosha drives to the Karshvar *H.*, 31, 305; is worshipped, 31, 349.

***Hv*anva*nt*,** n.p., 23, 214.

***Hv*aredhi,** n. of a holy woman, 23, 225.

Hvare-kaêshman, n.p., 23, 216, 219, 220 n.
***Hv*are*k*ithra**, son of Zarathustra, 4, 21 n.; 23, 204, 204 n.
***Hv*arenô**, *see* Aryans (glory of the), Kings (glory of the), *and* Priests (glory of the).
Hvareza, n.p., 23, 218.
***Hv*aspa**, n.p., 23, 217, 217 n.
***Hv*embya**, *see* Parsadgâ *H.*
Hvôbŏ, *see* Hvôgvi.
Hvôgvi (Hvôbŏ, Hvôv, Hvôvi), wife of Zarathustra, 5, 143 n., 144; 23, 77 n., 195 n., 224, 224 n., 266 sq.; 37, 297, 297 n.
Hvôv, *see* Hvôgvi.
Hvôva (or Hvôgva), family of, 23, 77, 77 n., 207; 31, xxvi, xxviii, 92, 94, 133, 142 sq., 185; 37, 97, 97 n.
Hvôvi, *see* Hvôgvi.
***Hv*yaonas**, tribe conquered by Vîstâspa, 23, 117, 117 n., 280, 306.
Hwan, minister of war, had a stone coffin made for himself, 27, 149.
Hwan, duke of Ȝhâo, funeral rites for him, 27, 186.
Hwan, duke of *Kh*î, introduced the use of tablets and torches, 27, 323, 420, 420 n.; stories of him, 39, 145, 150, 233 sq., 343 sq., 343 n.; 40, 7–9, 7 n., 18–20; Kwan *K*ung counsels him about the choice of a minister, 40, 101 sq.; Duke H., called Hsiâo-po, killed his elder brother, 40, 177.
Hwan, duke of Lû, his three sons put to death, 27, 421 sq., 421 n., 422 n.; rites introduced by him, 28, 10, 168.
Hwan, a man of *K*ăng, becomes a Confucian scholar, 39, 161; 40, 204 sq.
Hwân, n. of a hexagram, 16, 194–6, 261 sq., 341, 384, 438, 442.
Hwang-fû, leading minister of Yû, 3, 355 sq., 356 n.
Hwang Liâo, a sophist, debated with Hui Shih, 40, 231.
Hwang-Tî, title of the emperor of China, 3, xxv–xxix; ancient sovereign, 3, 27; 39, 338; 40, 28, 55, 96 sq., 96 n.; what H., Yâo, and Shun did for civilization, 16, 383–5; 40, 7; divine ruler of a month, 27, 280; held the place of honour at sacrifices, 28, 201 sq.; deserves ancestor worship, 28, 208; questions Kwang *Kh*ăng-ȝze about government, 39, 24, 142 sq., 297–300, 297 n.; 40, 286; a Tâoist sage, got the Tâo, 39, 193, 244, 244 n., 256, 295, 295 n., 311 sq.; 40, 58, 60; describes the Perfect Music of Hsien-*kh*ih, 39, 348–51, 348 n.; 40, 218; how he ruled the world, 39, 359; deterioration going on under his rule, 39, 370; buried at Khwăn-lun, 40, 5; the garden of H., 40, 73; the first to disturb the primaeval paradisiacal state, 40, 171–3; the Yin Fû *K*ing attributed to him, 40, 255; reasoned with Knowledge and Heedless Bluster, 40, 291.
Hwang-ȝze Kâo-âo tells Duke Hwan all about ghosts and sprites, 40, 19 sq., 19 n.
Hwan-tâu, minister of Yâo, 3, 34; rebel against Shun, 3, 41, 54; 39, 295.
Hwan Twan, a sophist, 40, 230.
Hwâ-ȝze, officer of King Yung of Wei, 40, 119.
Hymns, *see* Prayers.
Hypnotizing, an evil practice punished in hell, 45, 366 sq.

I

I (aham, ego): relation of the Self and the I, 1, xxx; 15, 85; 48, 57 sq., 61; I am all this, 1, 124; I am thou, 1, 275; I am Brahman, 1, 278; 15, 88; I am what He (the person in the sun) is, 1, 313; escape from the I, true deliverance, 19, 139; Buddha preaches on the I, 19, 190–2; Ego and Non-Ego, the spheres of the object and subject, 34, 3; the I is unreal, 48, 36–8; consciousness of the I in sleep, 48, 37, 53, 67–9; conscious subject unreal, due to the I, 48, 61–7; conscious I persists in the state of release, 48, 69–72; is a special effect of the Unevolved, 48, 72. *See also* Aham, Aha*m*kâra, Egoism, *and* Individuality.
I, n. of rivers, 3, 66, 69, 74.
Î, prince of *Kh*iung, 3, 78 sq.
Î, n. of barbarous tribes, 3, 150, 150 n.; 28, 30; 40, 220.
I, two elementary forms, 16, 12;

hexagram, 16, 114 sq., 235, 301, 435, 443.
Î, internuncius of King Fû *Kh*âi, 27, 178.
Î, a king, degeneration of rites under, 27, 421, 421 n.
Î, n. of a famous archer, 39, 227, 227 n.; 40, 36, 36 n., 88 sq., 99.
Ibairaz, the causer of strife, 5, 118.
Iblîs (Satan): legend of I. and Ibrahim, 4, 210 n.; a fallen angel, 6, lxix; refused to adore Adam, 6, 5, 138 sq., 246 sq.; 9, 8, 19 sq., 44, 181; 24, 178 n.; created from fire, 6, 139; 9, 181; allowed to tempt Adam, 6, 139; cursed, but respited till the day of judgement, and allowed to seduce men, 6, 247; 9, 181; the hosts of I. punished on judgement day, 9, 94; people of Sebâ followed I., 9, 152 sq. *See also* Satan.
Ibrahim, legend of Iblîs and, 4, 210 n.
I*d*: offering-prayer to the I*d*s, 12, 146 sq., 146 n., 153, 157, 319, 400 n.; 26, 186 n.; I*d* another name of I*d*â, 46, 217, 218.
I*d*â, or I*l*â, represents cattle, 12, 211, 219, 222 sq., 227 sq.; connected with the pâkayag*ñ*a or domestic offerings, 12, 214, 214 n., 218, 220, 230; 30, xv sq., 39; represented as a cow, 12, 216 sq. n., 224, 355; 26, 60, 415 sq.; 44, 81, 474; I., the daughter of Manu, produced from the Pâkayag*ñ*a, identified with the I. of the mystic I. ceremony, 12, 216–30; 30, 239, 239 n.; connected with Mitra and Varu*n*a, 12, 217 n., 218, 218 n., 224; 29, 296; daughter of Manu, 12, 218 sq., 224; 25, lviii–lx; 44, 81; the I. offering, 12, 221, 259, 259 n., 403, 410 n., 412, 414; 26, 92; 43, 259 sq.; 44, 121; as the Brahman priest, 12, 224 sq.; goddess invoked in Âprî hymns, 12, 400 n.; 46, 3, 8, 11 sq., 23, 29, 154, 179, 199, 237; mother addressed as I. Maitrâvaru*n*î, 15, 224; Aila, i. e. son of I., Purûravas, 19, 149; 44, 68; 49 (i), 113, 138; invoked, 26, 40 n., 209 n.; 29, 30; 41, 41, 113; the abode of I., 30, 173; Agni (Vai*s*vânara) connected with I., 41, 334; 46, 187, 191, 287 sq., 302, 375, 377; the goddess, the mighty praise, 46, 248; the nourishment coming from the cow, 46, 289 sq.
Iddhi, Pali, t.t., miraculous or supernatural power, saintship, 11, 2 n., 232 n.; 20, 424; 35, 130; the four paths to I., by which Buddha might be able to prolong his life, 11, 40 sq. and n., 54–8, 61, 63, 232 sq., 232 n.; how a Bhikkhu may obtain the power of exercising I., 11, 214 sq.; the four I. of King Sudassana, 11, 259–61, 259 sq. n.; Arhats must not display before the laity their power of I., 20, 78–81; Devadatta's I. of appearing in another shape, 20, 233 sq.; power of quick locomotion by I., 35, 126 sq.; Buddha exalts I. or saintship, 35, 199–201; Karman more powerful than I., 35, 261–3; a man may get a fruit from the summit of a lofty tree by I., 36, 94; the vehicle of I., 36, 117; Nirvâ*n*a increases the power of I., 36, 192; men of the power of I., 36, 231 sq., 231 n., 234; vows necessary to acquire the strength of I., 36, 259, 267 sq. *See also* Miracles, *and* Saintship.
Iddhipâdâ (*k*attâro), t.t., *see* Iddhi (four paths to).
Idealists and Realists, 11, 49 n.; maintain that thought only is real, 34, 401; are the Yogâ*k*âras, 34, 401 n.; 48, 510–13; controverted, 34, 418–27.
Ideas and mental impressions succeed each other as causes and effects, 34, 420, 423, 425–7; two i. cannot apprehend or be apprehended by each other, 34, 422; require an ulterior intelligent principle, 34, 424; the i. of the waking state are not like those of a dream, 34, 424 sq.
Idiots, cannot inherit, 2, 309. *See also* Diseases.
Idolators, not to be abused, lest they too speak ill of God, 6, 128; sin of feasting with i., 37, 130; legal relations between Mazda-worshippers and i., 37, 148; necessity of destroying i., 'the two-legged wolves,' 37, 151.
Idolatry, a high-priest passing away in, 5, 309; the unpardonable sin, 6, 79 sq., 88 sq., 135; denounced, 24,

15; 47, xxvi sq., 95; heresy of i., 45, 83, 83 n.; i. of Dahâk, 47, xxvi, 67.

Idols (images of gods), as sacred objects, 2, 94, 220; 7, 200, 228; 14, 55; 25, 135; 29, 364; figures of demons destroyed by Vistâsp, 5, 193, 198; five i. worshipped by the people of Noah and by the Arabs, 6, xii, cxiv; 9, 303; beasts sacrificed to i., forbidden, 6, 97; Israelites demand i. from Moses, 6, 154; are servants of God, have neither life nor senses, 6, 162; Apostles sent to every nation to say 'Serve God and avoid *Tagh*ût,' 6, 254; the Arabs set aside part of their produce for the i., 6, 255 sq.; used for ordeals, 7, 55, 60; 33, 116, 260, 262, 319; installation of the monument of a deity, 7, 92; how to clean i., 7, 101; he must not step on the shade of an i., 7, 203; 25, 149; worship of i. of Vish*n*u, 7, 208–11, 266, 269; Brâhma*n*as who subsist upon the offerings made to an i. which they attend, defile a company, 7, 252; can neither harm nor profit, 9, 57, 88; avoid the abomination of i., 9, 59; are helpless and unable to help, 9, 115, 158 sq., 186; are to God, what slaves are to the Meccans, 9, 127, 127 n.; will disclaim their worshippers on the resurrection day, 9, 159; worshipped by Buddhists, 10 (i), 32 n.; impure food not to be thrown away at a procession with i., 14, 72; Buddha i., 21, 50 sq., 76 n.; sin of worshipping i., 24, 71; daily libations to, and worship of the i., 25, 62; visited on Parva-days, 25, 153; evidence given in the presence of i., 25, 269; seats and shrines for i. in a house, 29, 348; sacrifices (by messenger) for gods at a distant sacred place, 29, 361; images of Îsâna, Mî*dh*ushî, and *G*ayanta, 30, 290 n.; court of justice to be adorned with i., 33, 280; dance, sing, &c., 42, 262; shrines of the gods worshipped by hermits, 49 (i), 74. *See also* Gods, Holy places, Ordeals, Sacred objects, *and* *Tâgh*ût.

Idol-temples, abodes of the demons, 5, 227, 229; 24, 29; destroyed by Khûsrôî, 24, 64; 37, 225; 47, xxvii, 14.

Idrîs, a prophet, 9, 31; was patient and entered into the mercy of God, 9, 53.

Ignorance, *see* Nescience.

Î-*kh*iû, *see* Phing.

Î *K*ieh, a courtier at *Kh*û, 40, 114.

Î *K*ih, minister of Thâi-Wû, 3, 207, 207 n.

I*kkh*âna*m*kala, n. of a place, 10 (ii), 108 sq.

Ikshvâku, taught yoga by Manu, 8, 58, 58 n.; B*ri*hadratha, a king of the race of I., 15, 291; *S*uddhodana, Buddha's father, monarch of the I. family, 19, 1, 94, 131; 49 (i), 71, 92, 123; could not fix a bound for the ocean, 19, 11; 49 (i), 9; a *G*aina may beg of families belonging to the line of I., 22, 92; twenty-one Tîrthakaras of the I. race appeared before Mahâvîra, 22, 218; a noble family, 22, 225; knew the kush*th*a of yore, 42, 6, 679 sq.

Ikshvâkubhûmi, the Arhat *Ri*shabha was born at, 22, 281.

I*l*â, *see* I*d*â.

Î Lî, or 'The Decorum Ritual,' 3, xviii.

Î-liâo, n.p., 40, 28–31, 104 sq., 104 n., 288 sq.

Î Liû, originated certain funeral rites, 28, 164.

'Illiyûn, the book of the righteous kept in 'I. in Paradise, 9, 324.

Illusion, *see* Mâyâ.

Ilyâ, tree in the world of Brahman, 1, 275, 277.

Immortality, obtained by highest knowledge, knowledge of Brahman or Self, 1, 35, 149, 312 sq.; 8, 103, 143, 176, 176 n., 180, 185, 187, 193, 313, 391; 15, 342; 25, 501; 30, 228; 34, lxxix sq., 275, 279; 38, 369 sq., 392; 43, 357; 44, 165, 170; 48, 18, 296 sq., 311, 386, 396, 690, 694 sq., 699, 731 sq.; the body is mortal, the Self is immortal, 1, 140 sq.; when freed from the senses, the wise, on departing from this world, become immortal, 1, 147; 8, 44; Breath or Prâ*n*a is death, life, and i., 1, 213 sq., 294; enjoyed by the gods, 1, 291; promised to those who avoid sensual pleasures, 2, 114; reached by those who keep the vow of chastity, 2, 158; 8, 153; *in thy*

offspring thou art born again, that, mortal, is thy i., 2, 159; Zoroaster asks Aûharmazd for i., 5, 1 sq., 192, 194 sq.; the seven immortal rulers, 5, 117–19, 118 n.; 18, 79 sq., 255–8, 258 n.; means for attaining i., 8, 99–102, 165 sq.; 43, 357; 48, 395 sq.; by transcending the three qualities, 8, 109 sq.; depends on self-restraint, abandonment, and freedom from heedlessness, 8, 152, 168, 182; *delusion I call death, and freedom from delusion I call i.*, 8, 152; 48, 23; depends on truth, 8, 170; there is no death, hence there can be no i., 8, 191; the Brahman is the highest goal, where one reaches i., 8, 255; he who in the moment of death becomes equable even for the space of a single exhalation, becomes fit for i., 8, 372; when the quality of goodness predominates in the unperceived, that fits one for i., 8, 373; no man granted i., 9, 48; earnestness is the path of i., 10 (i), 9; Amrita, or i., explained as Nirvâna, 10 (i), 9 n., 43; the immortal place, 10 (i), 33; the true Brâhmana has reached the depth of the Immortal, 10 (i), 93; attained by Buddha, 10 (ii), 13, 37; Buddha's disciples merged into i., 10 (ii), 38; no prospect of i. for men, 12, 290, 295, 311; obtained through a son, 14, 84; 25, 346, 354, 354 n.; Nakiketas asks for i., 15, 4; 48, 361; i. in heaven, secured by the fire-sacrifice, 15, 4; *when all desires that dwell in his heart cease, then the mortal becomes immortal, and obtains Brahman. When all the ties of the heart are severed here on earth, then the mortal becomes immortal*, 15, 23; death is unreal, i. is real, 15, 84; Yâgñavalkya instructs Maitreyî on i. as the absorption in the Self, 15, 108–13, 181–5; 48, 387; he who is free from desires, obtains Brahman, is immortal, 15, 176 sq.; how the creatures are made immortal, 18, 85; provided by the Creator, 18, 91 sq.; succession of mortals by offspring preferable to i., 18, 92 sq. and n.; through the renovation of creatures, 18, 111, 114, 118, 160, 165; men become immortal through the sacred fire, 18, 172; gates of i. opened by Buddha, 19, 178; 21, 185; resurrection and i., 23, 290–2, 307; brought by Saoshyant, 23, 308; Aûharmazd reserves it for himself, 24, 5; of the righteous in heaven, 24, 30, 81, 122; how to become fit for i., 25, 209; the sacrificer prays for i., 26, 348 sq.; of the sacrificer, 26, 449 sq.; 43, 256; 44, 119, 204, 261 sq.; Aditi, the navel of i., 30, 174; prayer for i., 30, 212; the two eternal gifts Universal Weal and I., Haurvatât and Ameretât, 31, 52, 76, 88, 111, 119 sq., 123 sq., 127, 129, 177, 181, 181 n., 308, 320; the Daêvas beguile mankind of i., 31, 54, 59; the souls of the righteous in the eternal i., 31, 128; Universal Weal and I. worshipped, 31, 196, 256, 259, 325, 330, 348, 380; Hiranyagarbha's shadow is i., and death, 32, 1, 7; bhûman is i., 34, 163, 168; i. of all effected things is a merely relative one, 34, 169; prepared by Yim, 37, 177; through good works, 37, 338 sq.; hope of i. the basis of religion, 37, 361 sq.; given to the Mazda worshipper, 37, 387; i. of ether is to be understood, like that of the gods, as a relative i. only, 38, 17; *he who dies and yet does not perish, has longevity*, 39, 75 sq.; the reward of good deeds, 40, 238, 238 n., 267 sq.; attained to by the Tâoist who has his thoughts constantly fixed on absolute Purity, 40, 270–2, 319 n.; light is i., 41, 383; 43, 238; gold bestows i. on the fire-altar, 43, 146 sq.; is man's highest form, 43, 147, 177 sq.; the highest thing of all this universe, 43, 148, 181; laid into Agni, 43, 177 sq.; the gods make their bodies boneless and immortal, 43, 178, 180; vital airs are i., 43, 178, 220; obtained by those who live a hundred years or more, 43, 299, 323 sq., 327; gained through fire-building rite, 43, 299; is the light that shines yonder, 43, 322; the immortal element distributed by Savitri, the sun, 43, 322 sq.; no one shall be immortal with the body, 43, 357; founded on death, 43, 366 sq. and n.; he who knows the mystery of the Fire-altar being Death,

reaches i., 43, 374; secured by gift of gold to the priest, 44, 350; Yim made men and cattle immortal, 47, 9; Upanishads refer to i., 48, 7; an attribute of the highest Self only, 48, 280;—*draught of i.*, Hûsh, 5, 65, 70, 126; 18, 112, 112 n., 165 n.; prepared from the Gôkar*d* (Hôm) tree, 5, 100; 24, 111, 111 n.; Hôm, the immortalizer of the living, 5, 177; Am*ri*ta or nectar, draught of i., 8, 62, 88 sq., 126, 391; water an elixir of i., 26, 374; 44, 87; Soma, the nectar of i., 26, 385 n.; 43, 251 sq., 255 sq.; sacrificial food baked by fire is immortal (or ambrosia), 41, 164; drink of i. bought for a chariot, and stored by Indra in the waters, 42, 162; nectar of i. recovered by the gods, 43, 255 sq.; the threefold divine Am*ri*ta, 43, 365. *See also* Amerôda*d*, Emancipation, Imperishable, *and* Nirvâ*n*a.

Impediments to the attainment of *G*hânas, 13, 243, 245 sq.; false doctrine about them, 17, 377 sqq.

Imperishable, the, Sk. Akshara, is immaterial, unseen, by the command of it everything is, in it the ether is woven, like warp and woof, 15, 137–9; 34, 140; is Brahman, 34, xxxv, 138, 169–71; that element in Brahman, from which the material universe springs, 34, cxix; the higher knowledge is this by which the I. is apprehended, 34, 135–8; the Indestructible is higher than the high I., 34, 136, 137, 140; *the I. is Brahman on account of its supporting all things up to ether*, 34, 169–71; cannot be the embodied soul, 34, 171; meditations on the I., 38, 238–40. *See also* Akshara.

Impermanence, of all things, *see* World (*a*).

Imprecations, at the recitation of the Veda, 1, 251; one may curse an enemy, but not a Brâhma*n*a, 1, 251, 252; by means of breath, the beam, 1, 252; one should not utter i., 12, 159; 40, 241, 243; i. against an adulterer, 15, 218; after repeating an i. one should touch water, 29, 31; against a sacrificer, in the case of mishaps during sacrifice, 44, 179, 186, 190 sq., 201; i. by which the sacrificer rids himself of his enemy, 44, 192; against enemies, 44, 266, 438, 501; Agni, a protector of sacrifices against i., 46, 96. *See also* Curse, Incantations, Oath, *and* Prayers.

Impurity: rules about i. caused by death and childbirth, 2, lvii sq., 249–54; 7, 87–94; 14, 27–30, 153, 177 sq., 180–2, 298; 15, 312; 24, 339–41; 25, 146, 162 sq., 177–87; 29, 355, 357–9; impure persons should not salute, nor be saluted, 2, 52 sq.; causes of i., 2, 55–63, 60 sq. n., 74 sq., 181 sq., 220 sq.; 7, 94–106; 14, 22–4, 30, 71 sq., 120, 171, 174, 182 sq.; 30, 19; 42, 186; children are not defiled before initiation, 2, 139 sq.; the touch of a child cannot defile, 2, 186; is a cause of interruption of Veda-study, 2, 260 sq., 264; 29, 115–17; of a corpse, 4, 26–8; 7, 94; 11, xxxix, 125 n.; 37, 256 sq.; defiling fire or earth with dead matter involuntarily is no sin, 4, 49–51; the defiling power of a corpse differs according to the rank of the being that dies, 4, 50, 58; a corpse when dried up does not contaminate, 4, 105, 105 n.; of menstruous women, 5, lx, 16, 248, 251, 261, 265, 270 sq., 276–85, 304, 333, 341 n.; 14, 32 sq., 33 sq. n.; 18, 447; 24, 270, 296, 302–5, 330, 332–4, 340, 353; 25, 179, 183; 37, 162, 187, 432, 446; caused by death, 5, lx, 245–76, 310, 319 sq., 332; 33, 373; 37, 153 sq.; caused by a serpent, 5, lx sq., 254; caused by bodily refuse and dead matter, 5, 111, 204 sq., 378; 18, 35, 39–43, 52 n., 161, 161 n., 283, 292 sq. and n., 431, 455–8; 24, 111, 335–7, 339–41, 353–5; 37, 149 sq., 153–60; caused by sexual intercourse, 6, 78, 98; 7, 94; 25, 179, 194; caused by the funeral rites, 7, 76, 94; as long as his relatives remain impure, the departed spirit finds no rest, 7, 80; exemption from i. in cases of unnatural death, &c., 7, 92 sq.; caused by shedding tears for a deceased person, 7, 93; food rendered impure, 7, 155; penances for being defiled by various causes, 7, 175, 176; when thy impurities

are blown away, thou wilt not enter again into birth and decay, 10 (i), 60; ignorance is the greatest taint, 10 (i), 61; a bad mind and wicked deeds are what defiles a man, and no outward observances can purify him, 10 (ii), 40–2; five impurities in the world, 10 (ii), 183; impure men and animals to be avoided by the Snâtaka, 29, 318 sq.; of women after confinement, 30, 56, 56 n.; defiling fire and water, 37, 108; caused by contact with deformed persons, 42, 72, 556 sq. *See also* Child (*b*), Death (*c*), Pollution, Purification, Purity, *and* Woman (*b*, *e*).

Imrân (Amram): God has chosen I.'s people, 6, 50, 50 n.; Mary, daughter of I., 9, 292.

Inanimate things, classification of, 45, 207–10.

Inauspicious objects, *see* Omens.

Incantations, dispel the effects of poison and sickness, 7, 22; reciting deadly i. from the Atharvaveda, is murder, 7, 41; women are not to practise i. with roots, 7, 110; trying to overcome another by i., a sin, 7, 137; 14, 220; one who practises i. with roots cannot be a witness, 33, 88 n.; punishment of those who practise i. with roots and spells, 33, 361; prayers and i. of Atharvaveda, *Vol.* 42. *See also* Imprecations, Prayers, *and* Witchcraft.

Incarnations of Verethraghna, 23, 231–8.

Incest, causes loss of caste, 2, 74, 280 sq., 280 n.; 25, 338; penance for committing i., 2, 82 sq., 288, 293; 7, 132; 25, 465 sq., 465 n.; a mortal crime, 7, 132, 134; 25, 441; committed by Pragâpati, 12, 209; women who must not be approached, 14, 234 sq.; definition of i., punishments for i., 33, 179 sq., 182. *See also* Guru, *and* Sexual intercourse.

Inchastity, *see* Chastity.

Inda, *Pali for* Indra, q.v.

Îndar, or Andar, demon of the religion of apostasy, 37, 253, 253 n.

Indasâla cave, gods converted at the, 36, 248.

Indestructible, *see* Imperishable.

India, geography of, 8, 222–4; 12, xli–xliii, 104 n., 105 sq.; 14, 146–8; 32, 58–61, 320, 323, 392, 397–9; 35, xlii–xlv; 36, 203 sq., 211, 249 sq., 250 n.; Âryâvarta defined, 14, 2–4; peculiarities of the Southern country and Avanti, 17, 33–40; the border countries of I., 17, 38 sq.; Pâ*th*eyyaka, 17, 146 sq. n.; countries where pure Âryan customs prevail, 25, xliv sq., 32 sq.; Sraosha comes from I. on the East, 31, 304.

Indifference towards life and death, pleasure and pain, &c., a preliminary of release, 8, 246 sq., 392 sq.; a sign of good conduct, 8, 326; the true Brâhma*n*a or Arhat is he who is utterly indifferent, 10 (i), 92–5; (ii), 151–3. *See also* Tranquillity.

Individualism, false notions of, 36, 40 sq., 40 n.

Individuality: discussion on i. and name, 35, 40–5; continued identity of the individual, and re-individualization, 35, 63–5; impermanence of i., and its being the source of pain, 35, 67; 36, 371 sq.; i. and transmigration, 35, 112 sq.; five groups of characteristic marks of i., 36, 327; the Void Supreme *versus* i., 36, 362. *See also* I (ego), *and* Self (*c*).

Indo-European folklore, 42, 313 sq.

Indra (Pali Inda, or *S*akra, Pali Sakka, or Maghavan, or Purandara).

(*a*) Names and epithets of I.
(*b*) Qualities, attributes, family, worlds of I.
(*c*) Myths, deeds of I.
(*d*) I. and Agni.
(*e*) I. and other gods.
(*f*) I. and the Demons.
(*g*) Worship of I.
(*h*) I. in mysticism and philosophy.
(*i*) I. (*S*akra, Sakka) in Buddhism and *G*ainism.

(*a*) Names and epithets of I.

Maghavan, a name of I., 1, 137–40, 150; 8, 219, 347; 10 (i), 10; 12, xi, xi n., xix; 44, 443; Vaiku*nth*a, or the person in the air, 1, 303; 15, 101; called Purandara, or the fortress-destroyer, 8, 219, 347; 45, 48, 117; thousand-eyed, 10 (ii), 58; 42, 476; 45, 48, 288; 49 (i), 5, 21; his mystic name is Arguna, 12, 285; 41, 99; of a hundredfold powers, 12, 416; 42, 95; his horses, I. Harivat, lord of the bay steeds, 12, 434; 26, 81, 399 sq., 408; 32, 14, 29, 139, 143, 179, 272; 41, 20;

46, 96; 49 (i), 61; called *S*unâsîra, 12, 446 n.; called v*ri*shan, the strong bull, 15, 47; 32, 139, 143, 145-7, 150 sq.; 42, 81; a Lokapâla, or guardian of the world, 25, 185, 216 sq.; 35, 37; the supreme guide, 26, 57 sq.; called Kau*s*ika and Gautama, 26, 82, 82 n.; I. Vim*ri*dh (Averter of Scorn), 26, 430 sq.; 44, 5 sq.; I. the Brâhma*n*â*kh*a*m*sin, 26, 433 sq.; 'a man is I.,' 30, 54; I. *Sak*îpati, husband of *Sak*î, 30, 206; 42, 95, 125 sq., 503; 49 (i), 21; the god of the bright day, whose steed is the sun, 32, 16; as a priest (purohita), 32, 42; 42, 79; the lighter up of nights, 32, 119; Narâ*s*a*m*sa, praised by men, 32, 295, 303; called 'the best song,' 32, 439; is the god of strength, 34, 99; 44, 63 sq.; I. *G*yesh*th*a, 41, 70-2; worship of I. Sutrâman (the good guardian), 41, 129, 132-5, 136 n.; 44, 213 sq. n., 224; the Vâsava, 42, 95; *S*akra or I., 42, 117 sq., &c.; as lord in the south, 42, 192; the manly Asura, 42, 380; the lord of the nobility, 43, 74; I. Pradât*ri* (the Bestower), 44, 8 sq.; I. V*ri*trahan (slayer of V*ri*tra), 44, 11; *see below* (*f*); I. Vayodhas (giver of strength or life), 44, 213 sq. n., 273, 273 n.; I. denotes a class of beings, 48, 331 sq. *See also* Mahendra.

(*b*) QUALITIES, ATTRIBUTES, FAMILY, WORLDS OF I.

Characteristics of I., 1, 167, 170; kingdom, heaven, world, or worlds of I., 1, 275; 7, 194; 12, 451; 15, 131, 337; 19, 304; 25, 157; 41, 23; 48, 747 sq.; I. in Veda, and I*n*dra in Avesta, 4, lii sq.; 5, 10 n.; 37, 253 n.; world of I. attained by a virtuous king, 7, 41; 25, 314, 321; 33, 24, 288 sq.; 49 (i), 138; the flag of I., 7, 124; 19, 91, 112, 112 n.; 49 (i), 11, 11 n., 89, 207; his horse U*kk*ai*ss*ravas, and elephant Airâvata, 8, 89 n.; his thunderbolt, 10 (i), 28; 29, 365; 30, 169 sq.; 32, 179 sq., 182; 33, 163; 34, 217 n.; 35, 35; 41, 110 sq.; 45, 48; 48, 328; Inda, the husband of Su*g*â, 10 (ii), 189; I.'s right arm, the most powerful, 12, 53; is the recipient of wealth, 12, 236; the Phalgunîs are his asterism, 12, 285 sq.; the Night (Dawn, Day) wedded to I., 12, 337; those engaged in vows are seated on the throne of I., 14, 102; 25, 185; the bliss of I., 15, 60, 61 sq. n.; appears multiform through the Mâyâs, 15, 117; 48, 435; the child of Dyaus or Heaven, 15, 221; 29, 45; 30, 199; his palace, 19, 233, 233 n.; *S*akra, n. of Indra's throne, 22, 222, 229; the king shall emulate I., the sender of rain, 25, 396; born from Ya*gñ*a and Vâ*k*, 26, 32 sq.; all the universe had submitted to I., 26, 242 sq.; man is I.-like, 26, 407; in the *S*atapatha-Brâhma*n*a, 26, 463; knows that through which no hatred may spring up amongst us, 29, 323; Sîtâ his wife, 29, 334; Ekâsh*t*akâ, his mother, 29, 342; his chariot, 32, 14, 29; Sakka is great, and he is only one, 36, 50; husbandry beneficial to I. and other gods, 41, 329; his great mill-stone, that crushes all vermin, 42, 22, 315; drinks Soma, 42, 65, 81, 89, 204, 210; 44, 233; 46, 96; the bull with a thousand horns, befriended of I., 42, 105; is always awake, 42, 106; the lovely goddess that bore I., 42, 116 sq.; the day of I., 42, 136, 551; to I. belongs the first chariot, 42, 152; the divine representative of the warlike kings of the Vedic age, 44, xxi-xxiii; the sky relates to I., 44, 241, 247; with I.'s power, 44, 253 n.; has grown in ebriety and strength, 44, 380; his wife Indrâ*n*î, 44, 474; superior power of I. and other gods due to religious merit, 48, 238; heavenly nymphs in I.'s world, 49 (i), 88; jewels on his head, 49 (ii), 50, 173, 176, 182; Indra's bow, *see* Rainbow.

(*c*) MYTHS, DEEDS of I.

Legend of I. and Vi*s*vâmitra, 1, 218 sq., 220; grants a boon to Pratardana, 1, 293; 34, 97-9, 101; fourteen Indras (chiefs of the gods), pass away in each kalpa, 7, 79; acquired immortality in all worlds, 8, 282; has measured out the six spaces, 12, 137 n.; the sacrifice-tortoise did not stand still for I., 12, 161; I. and the women, 14, 33, 61; forest-produce generated by I.,

14, 292; having become a bird, handed the Pârikshitas to Vâyu, 15, 128; in the shape of a Brahma*k*ârin interprets a dream, 19, xxi; love affairs of I., 19, 43; 25, 273 n.; 26, 81, 81 n.; 33, 99, 99 n.; 49 (i), 44; Mandhât*ri* and Nahusha occupied I.'s throne, 19, 118, 122; 49 (i), 113; first council held in '*S*akra's cavern,' 19, 335; delivers the cows, 23, 141 n.; has laid down in the tree the embryo of the sterile cow, 30, 200; created light, 32, 14; fights for the bright cows (days, clouds), 32, 14, 37, 44; whets his red weapon, 32, 18; cut off the mountain tops, 32, 101; the treasure (rain) conquered by I. from the clouds, 32, 115; has made the waters to flow freely for man, 32, 180; found the head of the horse at *S*arya*n*âvat, 32, 398; a version of the Code of Manu ascribed to I., 33, xii; offered the Vâgapeya, 41, 3; the doer of mighty deeds, 41, 105; mighty through the people, 41, 109; excluded from Soma, 41, 130 sq.; when the Soma was flowing through him, lion, wolf, and tiger sprang from him, 41, 132 sq.; makes Vasish*th*a his Brahman priest, 42, lx; puts strength into the magic plant, 42, 38 sq., 71, 280; disease shut out by I.'s command, 42, 39; was wounded, 42, 48, 310 sq.; frees from evil sorcery, 42, 51; wore a talisman, 42, 80; fastened the amulet on for strength and heroism, 42, 85; grants husbands to maidens, 42, 94, 324; heaps together goods with a rake, 42, 95, 503; chose the waters as his goddesses, 42, 146, 350; stored away the am*ri*ta in the waters, 42, 162; protects the Brâhma*n*a, 42, 169 sq., 433; though requested by I., Bheda did not present the sterile cow, 42, 179; protects the earth, 42, 200 sq.; together with the *Ri*shis, 42, 231; the sun freed by I. and Atri, 42, 294; his misdeeds, 42, 522 sq.; 43, 345 n.; cut off the head of Makha, 44, xlviii; from out of I. the gods formed the Vi*s*vagit, 44, 139; Vasish*th*a taught I. the Virâ*g*, and I. taught Vasish*th*a the expiation for the whole sacrifice, 44, 212; when his vital powers left him by the magic of Tvash*tri*, animals and plants and metals flowed from the limbs of his body, 44, 214–16; when I.'s energies departed from him, the gods restored them by means of the Sautrâma*n*î, 44, 231; the Âdâra-plants are I.'s might, 44, 451 sq.; I. and the other gods perish and are created again, 48, 331 sq.; Da*s*aratha, friend of I., 49 (i), 90; I., the lord of the winds, went to heaven through sacrifices, 49 (i), 110; his arm paralysed when raising his thunderbolt, 49 (i), 142, 142 n. *See also below (f)*.

(*d*) I. AND AGNI.

Offerings and prayers to them conjointly, 2, 299; 12, 162 n., 176, 237 sq., 350, 369, 371, 375, 377 sq., 377 n., 380, 393 sq., 402, 408 n., 419; 14, 216; 26, 199 sq., 199 n., 221, 225, 296 sq., 313, 322 sq., 428 sq.; 29, 17 n., 84, 88, 98 n., 132, 136, 161, 203, 229, 337, 337 n., 392, 415; 30, 37, 93, 175, 183 sq., 337; 41, 12, 12 n., 45 sq., 383; 42, 24, 49, 55, 58, 75, 126, 139, 173, 195, 211, 221, 231, 454; 43, 198, 274–8; 44, 75 sq. and n., 81, 392, 392 n.; 46, 263–5, 420; when the fire is in full blaze, it is I., 12, 340; are all the gods, 12, 378; 26, 225; 41, 154, 212, 285, 375; 43, 278; 44, 392; preserved the Soma for the production of creatures, 26, 151; are this All, 26, 292, 292 n.; preserved the A*kh*avâka priest for the production of creatures, 26, 317 sq.; Agni, Mitra-Varu*n*au, I. win in the race of the gods, 26, 327 n.; lay down the third layer of the altar, 41, 188, 190; 43, 41 sq.; Agni (fire) belongs to, or consists of, I. and A., 41, 212, 253, 285, 375; I. takes the Soma juice in Agni, 41, 304; Agni is like I., 41, 325; are the two arms of Pragâpati, 41, 374 sq.; they went to the heavenly world, 41, 381–3; grant life and well-being, 42, 53; Agni seizes the wizards, and I. destroys them, 42, 64; protect from all evils, 42, 81; poured love into the waters, 42, 105; deposited in the u*kkh*ish*t*a, 42, 226; B*ri*haspati,

their companion, 42, 554; 43, 134; are the best of gods, 43, 41; 44, 278; are the gold plate and the gold man of the fire-altar, 43, 342 sq.; are two arms of the fire-altar, 43, 388; behind these two deities are all the other gods, 44, 128; Agni, the greatest of Indras, 44, 489; Agni invoked to bring I. to the sacrifice, 46, 153, 316, 377; Agni identified with I., the bull among beings, 46, 186, 371; Agni on one chariot with I., 46, 237, 391; cross the waters, 46, 263; display the lights of heaven, 46, 263; killers of foes or V*ri*tras, 46, 263 sq.; the pious men, kindling Agni, strengthening I., 46, 318; has looked after Agni, 46, 367; Agni credited with the deeds of I., the conqueror of the cows and of the waters, 46, 398. *See also* Agni (*h*).

(*e*) I. AND OTHER GODS.

The king or chief of the gods, 1, 151; 8, 347; 11, 142; 12, 449 sq.; 21, 4, 69 sq., 342, 387; 22, 222 sq.; 26, 93, 433; 35, 12 sq.; 36, 130; 44, 438 n., 464; 45, 48, 288, 292; 49 (i), 121, 187, 196; (ii), 42, 90 sq.; how he obtained pre-eminence among the gods, 1, 307; 10 (i), 10; worshipped by the gods, 10 (ii), 52, 125; speaks for the gods, 12, 154; represents all the gods, 12, 168; 44, 419; surrounded by crowds of Devas, 19, 20; surrounded by the Devîs, 19, 41; fills the gods with joy, 36, 322; in a list of gods, 42, 80, 160, 221; the gods, dispatched by I., disturb the sacrifice of an enemy, 42, 90; by his brahma*k*arya, he brought the light to the gods, 42, 217; gods draw together round I., 43, 127; is equal to all the gods, 43, 140; the gods are the people of King Dharma I., 44, 370; I., entering heaven, saluted by the immortals, 49 (i), 16;—I., Agni, and Vâyu, are above the other gods, 1, 151; I., Maghavat, and Purandara as three gods, 8, 347, 347 n.; I. combines with Âdityas, Vasus, Maruts, and Vi*s*ve Devâh, 12, 264; 26, 241; 44, 479 sq.; 46, 154; Agni, I., and Sûrya superior gods, 26, 402-4; I., Agni, Savitar, B*ri*haspati invoked for long life, 42, 49; performs the new and full moon sacrifice for his brothers Agni and Soma, 44, 16; was healed by the A*s*vins and Sarasvatî, 44, 216 sq., 248 sq., 252; Agni, I., Soma, Makha, Vish*n*u, and Vi*s*ve Devâ*h* perform sacrifice, 44, 441; Agni, I., Soma invoked together, 46, 213; I., Yama, Varu*n*a, 49 (i), 197;—has created glory for the *Apsarases*, 29, 316; tried to find out who *Brahman* was, 1, 150 sq.; is Brahman, 12, 211 n.; runs away from terror of Brahman, 15, 21, 59; humbly approaches Brahman, 19, 188; 49 (i), 107; I. and Brahman, deities of a *Ri*tu-graha, 26, 320 n.; and *Brahma*n*aspati*, 42, 163, 213; *Bri*h*aspati* put the garment of immortality on I., 29, 304; I. and B*ri*haspati invoked and worshipped together, 29, 315; 42, 160; 44, 402; compact of B*ri*haspati with I. and Brahman, 42, 127; his double B*ri*haspati, 42, 596; B*ri*haspati and I., priesthood and nobility, 43, 228 sq.; *Dhât*ri has shaven the head of I., 29, 56; the *Earth* adheres to I., 42, 203; pierces the *Gandharvas* with his missiles, 42, 33 sq.; *Kris*h*na* is I. among the gods, 8, 88; the *Lord of the seat*, the friend of I., 30, 161; I. the king, the *Maruts* the people, 8, 346; 12, 334; 42, 663; 49 (i), 53, 81; calls the Maruts to his help against V*ri*tra, 12, 334; 32, 329; 41, 34, 84; invoked and worshipped with the Maruts (Marutvat), 12, 335, 399; 26, 93, 332-8, 347; 29, 314; 30, 157; 32, 14 sq., 134, 136 sq., 143, 159, 167, 210, 272 sq., 289, 340, 375; 42, 132 sq., 183, 188, 207, 663; 44, xxii sq., 207, 255 n., 382; 46, 44, 154, 237, 378; assisted by the Maruts in battle with V*ri*tra, 12, 416 sq., 417 n., 452; 26, 334 sq.; 32, 14 sq., 36 sq., 44, 46, 392; 44, 255; dialogue between the Maruts and I., 32, xii-xxi, xxiii, 179-208, 286-8; rivalry between I. and the Maruts, 32, xxiii, 286-90; the eldest among the Maruts, 32, 67; the Maruts left I. alone in the killing of Ahi, 32, 180; Maruts announce the arrival of I., 32, 209,

213; not even I. can injure the bounty of the Maruts, 32, 210; Maruts know the manly deeds of I., 32, 210; I., in the assembly of the Maruts, 49 (i), 53; identified with *Parganya*, 42, 235; prayer to I. and *Parvata*, 26, 450; was a pupil of *Pragâpati*, 1, 134–42; 34, 199; 48, 321; I. and Pragâpati, door-keepers in the world of Brahman, 1, 275 sq., 277; Pragâpati has given victory to I., 29, 280; I. and Pragâpati on the path of the gods, 38, 386; is the left arm of Pragâpati, 43, xx; enters Pragâpati with food, 43, 92; created out of Pragâpati, 44, 15; Pragâpati performs new and full moon sacrifice for I., 44, 16; *Pûshan* has shaven the beard of I., 30, 217; I. and Pûshan praised and worshipped together, 41, 54 n., 55; 44, xxv, xliv; 46, 154; I. with the *Ribhus* invoked in the Ârbhava hymn, 44, 381; at the head of the *Rudras*, 1, 41 sq.; Rudras united with I., 44, 382, 479 sq.; *Sarasvatî* distilled Soma for the sake of I.'s strength, 44, 233; *Soma*'s relation to I., 26, xvi–xx, 22; Soma praises I., 26, 247; offering to I. and S., 41, 54 n., 56; Soma, I.'s faithful companion, 44, 226; *Speech*, the goddess, uttered by I., 29, 51; the *sun* (Âditya, Sûrya) is I., 12, 181 sq., 350; 26, 96 sq., 407, 419, 438; I. and Sûrya invoked for offspring, 29, 287; protected by *Trishamdhi*, 42, 127 sq.; tries to conquer *Ushas*, 32, 145; *Varuna* opposed to I., 42, 370; is the *Vasu* of the gods, 12, 176, 176 n.; with the Vasus, 26, 122, 241; 32, 244; 42, 116; 44, 479 sq.; Soma libations for I. and *Vâyu*, 26, 265–9, 277 sq., 362, 418–21; 32, 440; 46, 154, 156; I. and Vâyu (Wind) identified, 26, 269; 44, 479 sq.; *Virâg* became I., the ruler, 42, 216; I. and *Vishnu* divided a thousand cows into three parts, 26, 62, 62 n.; Vishnu, friend of I., 26, 171 sq.; 32, 127, 133 sq.; 41, 138 sq., 396; offerings to I. and V., 41, 54 sq., 54 n., 138–42; 44, 402; share bestowed on I., lordship on Vishnu, 43, 68; I. encompassed Vishnu, 44, 443, 451 sq.; I. and *Visvakarman*, 11, 264 sq.; 26, 431 sq., 431 n.; 41, 188, 190.

(*f*) I. AND THE DEMONS.

After having killed Vritra, I. became great, 1, 157; his struggling with and slaying of Vritra, 1, 167, 170; 12, xix, 20–2, 52 sq., 164–9, 175 sq., 177 n., 180, 182, 379, 416 sq. and n., 449 sq., 452; 26, 15 sq., 15 n., 62, 265, 333–5, 399 n., 400; 29, 334, 367; 32, 127, 133 sq., 144, 180, 182, 198, 392; 41, 45 sq., 87 sq., 138 sq., 141, 178 n., 179, 332 n., 365; 42, 18, 63, 79, 81, 91 sq., 95, 126, 129, 382, 401; 43, 275; 44, 6 sq., 11, 380 sq.; 46, 34; 49 (i), 81, 113; slew Visvarûpa, Tvashtri's three-headed son, 1, 293, 293 n.; 14, 32; 41, 130–2, 134; 42, 522; 44, 213 sq.; 48, 251, 253; delivered the Arunmukhas to the wolves, killed the people of Prahlâda, Puloma, and Kâlakañga, 1, 293, 293 n.; struggle between I. and the Asuras or Dasyus, 1, 307; 12, 286 sq. and n.; 15, 342; 26, 399; 29, 342; 42, 79, 83, 118, 137, 215, 222 sq., 500, 627; 43, 192 sq.; struggle between I. and Ahi, Âtar and Azi, 4, lii; the waters his companions in the battle against Vritra, 12, 22; Trita slew Visvarûpa for I., 12, 47 sq. and n.; 44, 250 n.; drives off the Rakshas, 12, 128; 42, 9, 66; 44, 464; Indrasátru, 'foe of I.,' and Índrasatru, 'having I. for a foe,' 12, 165 sq. n., 166; perhaps Vritra would have slain I., 12, 166; 44, 250 n.; by slaying Vritra I. became a Brâhmana-murderer, 14, 32 sq., 32 n.; destroys all enemies, 30, 169; knows the demons, 30, 212; Trita smote Ahi before I., 31, 233 n.; guided past his enemies the Rakshas, 41, 73 sq.; I. and Namuki, 41, 92; 42, 256 sq., 583; 44, 222 sq.; helps to destroy the demons, 42, 65; an ally against sorcerers and spells, 42, 77 sq., 80 sq.; the Âsurî allured I. away from the gods, 42, 103, 547; conquered the Sâlâvrikas, 42, 138; the serpent slain by I., 42, 146, 154, 349; the earth sides with I., not with Vritra, 42, 203; lives with the Asuras, 42, 268; slays Arbuda, 42, 633 sq.; the repeller of

shafts, 43, 101; '*not for a single day hast thou fought, nor hast thou any enemy, O Maghavan : illusion is what they say concerning thy battles; no foe hast thou fought either to-day or aforetime*,' 44, 14; horse-sacrifice for I. Vritrahan, 44, 398 sq.; Dadhyañk's head is cut off by I. and restored by the Asvins, 44, 444 sq.; the slayer of the evil-minded, 44, 480; smiter of the demon Vala, 49 (i), 110, 110 n.; Bali, I., and Nahusha, 49 (i), 113; Asurinda, 'lord' of the Asuras, 49 (ii), 91 n.

(*g*) WORSHIP OF I.

The Mahâvrata belongs to I., 1, 167, 170; festivals of I., 2, 42; 22, 92; 29, 98, 130, 332, 415; sacrifices to I., 2, 108, 299; 12, 128 n., 129, 162 n., 164, 176–82 and n., 185, 189, 375, 377–81, 377 n., 408 n., 415 sq., 415 n.; 14, 304; 15, 337; 25, 91, 454 sq.; 26, 220 sq., 297, 313–16, 331–9, 362, 376, 429; 29, 161, 173, 326, 331 sq., 392; 30, 37, 123, 143, 243 sq., 337; 38, 259; 41, 12, 70–2, 82, 113, 116, 120–2, 129, 132–5, 136 n., 136 sq., 162; 44, 3 n., 5 sq., 8 sq., 11, 36, 62–6, 121, 142, 207 sq., 213 sq. n., 402, 443 sq., 475, 477, 490, 502; 46, 9, 44, 198, 301; prayers to I., 2, 297 n., 298; 7, 266; 11, 180; 12, 91, 96 n., 229, 434; 14, 251, 318; 15, 45, 53; 26, 122, 304, 352 sq., 376, 450; 29, 98, 130, 141, 147 sq., 182, 190, 210, 231, 233, 280, 287, 362; 30, 148 sq., 153, 159, 176–8; 41, 38, 204 sq.; 42, 9, 24, 32, 48 sq., 54, 65 sq., 89, 138, 145, 148 sq., 151, 193, 198, 204, 211, 214, 235, 353, 454, 549; 43, 198, 291; 44, 381, 479 sq.; 46, 44, 198; Veda-study to be interrupted when I.'s flag is hoisted or taken down, 7, 124; is the deity of sacrifice, 12, 110, 129, 285, 337; 26, 58, 81, 102, 137, 239, 241, 295, 314, 428; 41, 132, 137; 44, 6; prayer to I. at the fire-worship, 12, 356; invoked to cleanse from sin, 14, 250; worshipped by Sukra and Angiras, 19, 95; Soma libations for I., I. invited to the Soma, 25, 351, 351 n.; 26, 241, 285 sq., 294–7, 320 n., 397–400, 430 sq.; 32, 408; 41, 6–8; 42, 18, 66; 44, 108; red cows sacred to I., 26, 62; the Sadas or tent belongs to I., 26, 141, 145, 147; delights in songs, 26, 146; is the leader of the sacrifice, 26, 261 sq.; offerings for his two bay steeds, 26, 315, 316 n., 369–73; the unpressed Soma delighted him not, 26, 425; the Shodasin graha is I., 26, 429; oblation to I. at the wedding, 29, 32; 30, 190; invoked for (male) offspring, 29, 43, 287; 30, 190; the Brahmakârin given in charge of I., 29, 64, 79; 44, 86; offerings to I. and those belonging to I., 29, 85, 85 n., 161; animal slain for the hospitable reception of a king or father-in-law is sacred to I., 29, 88; the newly-built house sacred to I., 29, 96, 347, 349; 30, 206; 42, 140; invoked for the protection of cattle, 29, 100; 30, 87, 89; 42, 143, 367; worshipped at rites relating to agriculture, 29, 326, 331 sq., 334, 337 sq., 415; 30, 113 sq.; the Ashtakâ sacred to I., 29, 341, 341 n.; the Indraturîya offering in which the fourth oblation belongs to I., 41, 50–4; sacrifice to I. at the king's house, 41, 59 sq.; the bull his animal, 41, 60; worshipped at the king's consecration, 41, 89, 94 sq., 101 sq.; I., the controller of bodies, invoked to promote virility, 42, 32; invoked for a wife, 42, 95, 503; invoked to deprive a man of his virility, 42, 108 sq.; invoked in charms pertaining to royalty, 42, 112–23, 125–33, 329, 380, 440, 478, 510; invoked against the serpents, 42, 152–4; a shepherd's sacrifice to I., 42, 367; all beings magnify I., 43, 140, 197; the Ardhendra or 'half-Indra' libations, 43, 216, 216 n.; is the self of sacrifice, 43, 262; the he-goat, at the horse-sacrifice, goes to the seat of I. and Pûshan, 44, xxv; animal offered to I.-Pûshan, 44, xliv; worshipped at the Sautrâmanî, 44, 213 sq. n., 216–18, 221, 221 n., 224, 232 sq., 241, 243–7, 253, 256, 260–4, 273, 273 n.; by the Sautrâmanî, I. became the highest of gods, 44, 249; worshipped at the Asvamedha, 44, 281, 300, 400; the Indraless, hymnless, i.e. godless, 46, 366; invited by

sacrificers, 48, 330 sq.; festival of setting up I.'s banner, 49 (i), 11, 11 n., 89; in heaven, honoured by *S*ukra and Aṅgiras, 49 (i), 93.

(*b*) I. IN MYSTICISM AND PHILOSOPHY.

Meditation on I. as Prâ*n*a or life, 1, 219, 228 sq., 294; 15, 275; 34, 99; 48, 250–4, 256; is the sun, 1, 219; 15, 331; 43, 92; he who knows I. as the lord of all beings, having departed, becomes I. and shines in those worlds, 1, 231, 293 sq.; a name of the Self, 1, 242, 245; 15, 311; I. is truth, 1, 293; the strength of an unchaste student goes to I., 2, 294, 294 n.; the devotee feels no attachment even to I. (or, is esteemed by I. himself), 8, 250, 250 n.; is one of the ten fires at the allegorical sacrifice of the sense-organs, 8, 261; not seen by one who does not attain to the Adhyâtman, 8, 316; the presiding deity of the hands and of actions, 8, 338; Kshatriya caste (nobility) identified with I., 12, xvi–xviii, xvi sq. n., 419; 41, 3, 23–5, 89, 102; 43, 342, 344, 345 n.; the sacrificer is I., 12, xix n.; 26, 72, 97; 41, 13, 18, 56, 81, 88, 98 sq.; Trish*t*ubh metre related to I., 12, 205 n.; 43, 262, 330; 44, 106, 358; is the highest light, 12, 328; identified with the Ahavanîya fire, 12, 338; is the sacrifice, 12, 356; is might and vigour, 12, 419; 26, 220 sq.; 41, 82, 102; 44, 217, 221; mystic doctrines of the sacred syllables and I., Agni, Vâyu, and Âditya, 15, 48 sq.; in the white eye-ball, 15, 106; is the thunder, 15, 140 sq.; 44, 116; the man in the right eye is I., and his wife abides in the left eye, 15, 159, 344; 43, 369; a manifestation of Brahman, 15, 303; 34, 101 sq.; 48, 250–4, 256; identified with Purusha, 25, 513; out-breathing and in-breathing belong to I., 26, 210; *Rik*s and Sâmans are I., 26, 436; produced from *Rik* and Sâman, 26, 438; teacher says to pupil 'I.'s pupil art thou,' 29, 306; the king represented as I., 33, 217 sq.; witnesses watched by I. and other gods, 33, 245; explained as a mystic name meaning 'kindler,' 41, 143 sq.; deity and metre, 43, 53; the Virâ*g* is the world of I., 43, 94; is Vâ*k* or speech, 43, 134; 44, 16, 218; to I. belongs the vital air of the centre of the body, 44, 121; I.'s power bestowed upon the Sacrificer, 44, 181; connected with summer, 44, 247; is the mind, 44, 263; a term referring to the Highest Reality (Nârâya*n*a), 48, 522.

(*i*) I. (*S*AKRA, SAKKA) IN BUDDHISM AND *G*AINISM.

Gods, I., Asuras, &c., cried out against the injustice of killing cows for sacrifices, 10 (ii), 51; Buddha addressed as Sakka, 10 (ii), 58, 196, 202, 207 sq.; Buddha compared with I., 10 (ii), 58; 19, 71, 78; 49 (i), 21, 52, 56, 69–71, 76; the wise man is Brahman and I., 10 (ii), 117; what I. said when Buddha died, 11, 117; by the sound of his trumpet I. makes all beings silent when Buddha preaches, 11, 142; sends Vissakamma to build a palace for the king Sudassana, 11, 264 sq.; comes to hear Buddha's preaching, 13, 123; does service to Buddha, 13, 125–7, 141 sq.; 35, 12 sq.; 36, 24; 49 (ii), 90 sq., 165; *S*uddhodana and his queen compared with I. and *S*a*k*î, Buddha with the son of I., 19, 1, 51, 94; 49 (i), 92 sq.; *S*akra himself, and his attendants perish, 19, 275; Brahman and I. scatter flowers, &c., at Buddha's birth, 19, 347 sq., 350, 352; has 20,000 gods as his followers, 21, 4; entreats Buddha to teach the law, 21, 55; I. and Brahma Sahâmpati honour Buddha, 21, 69 sq.; men may be reborn as Indras, 21, 125; seats of I. gained by hearing the Dharmaparyâya preached, 21, 332, 335; honours the preacher, 21, 349; Gadgadasvara preaches under the shape of I., 21, 401; Avalokite*s*vara assumes the shape of I., 21, 411; Mahâvîra refuses a robe given by I., 22, 79 n.; causes the embryo of Mahâvîra to be removed from the Brahmanical to the Kshatriya part of Ku*nd*apura, 22, 190 sq., 225–9; honour done by I. to Mahâvîra, 22, 196–200, 223

sqq.; on his command, demons bring treasures to Siddhârtha's palace, 22, 248; a parrot brought down I. to wait upon him, 36, 6; length of life of the Bodisat as Sakka, 36, 133 n.; the problem put by Sakka, 36, 249; the Bodisat chooses a boon of I., 36, 310; enjoys perfect bliss, 36, 322; feels no discontent, 36, 323; I., in the guise of a Brâhma*n*a, tries to persuade King Nami to retain his royalty, but finally applauds his determination to become an ascetic, 45, 36–41; directs kings to renounce the world, 45, 87; Mahâvîra is brilliant like I., 45, 288; the faithful will become like I., 45, 292; outdone by the glories of the Sâkyas, 49 (i), 2; takes the new-born Buddha, 49 (i), 5; makes gifts to Buddha, 49 (i), 166 sq.; a preacher of the Law attains the throne of *S*akra, 49 (i), 185, 187; the pitcher of god *S*akra, 49 (ii), 173.

I*n*dra, the Daêva or demon, in Avesta, 4, 139, 139 n., 224; 5, 10 n. *See also* Andar.

Indrabhûti, of the Gautama gotra, the oldest disciple of Mahâvîra, 22, 265–7, 265 n., 286 sq.; 45, 41–6, 41 n.

Indradatta, one of the sixteen virtuous men, 21, 4.

Indradatta, n. of a Sthavira, 22, 288, 292.

Indradhva*g*a, n. of a Tathâgata, 21, 178.

Indradyumna Bhâllaveya, n.p., 1, 84, 87; 12, 206 n.; 43, 393, 396.

Indra*g*âlavidyâ, or magic art, trickery, 44, 368 n.

Indraketudhva*g*arâ*g*a, n. of a Tathâgata, 49 (ii), 100.

Indrâ*n*î, oblations to her at the wedding and other domestic rites, 29, 31 n., 32, 331 sq., 352, 424; 30, 114; poured love into the waters, 42, 105; the same as the person in the left eye, 43, 369; is the beloved wife of Indra, 44, 474.

Indrapuraka Kula, of the Ve*s*avâ*t*ika Ga*n*a, 22, 291.

Indriyâ*n*i, *see* Organs, Senses, *and* Spiritual sense.

Indrota *S*aunaka, quoted as teacher on ritual, 44, 393, 396.

Indu, the moon, king of shining bodies, 8, 346, 346 n.; invoked for cows and horses, 29, 346; 30, 206. *See also* Moon.

Industries: ceremonies at the preparation of silk, 27, 36; 28, 223 sq.; silk and other i. regulated, 27, 265 sq., 271; the wives look after the silkworms, 28, 239; sacred beings instruct Masyê and Masyâôî in arts and manufacture, 47, 7 sq.

Infanticide, *see* Woman (*g*).

Inference, denotes Sm*r*iti, 34, 203.

Infidels, *see* Heresy, *and* Nâstikas.

Infinite, the, *see* Bhûman.

Infinite Feelings, *see* Meditations.

Informing, sin of malignant, 7, 135; 25, 106, 163, 441.

Iṅgitamara*n*a, *see* Itvara.

Iñgitas (commotions), pain arises from the, 10 (ii), 140 sq.

Ingratitude: those who have returned evil for good, cannot be purified, 25, 469.

Inherence (samavâya): the distinction of the Vai*s*eshikas between conjunction (sa*m*yoga) and i., 34, 389 sq., 396 sq.; the connexion between the Lord and the soul and the pradhâna cannot be i., 34, 436.

Inheritance, law of, 2, xxi sq., 130–7, 302–10; 6, 25, 37, 72–5, 77, 96, 172 n.; 7, 45, 61–74; 14, xxvi, 76, 81, 84–91, 93 sq., 179 sq., 224–31, 231 sq. n., 336; 18, 183–7, 194–6; 25, lxi sq., lxi n., lxx, cii sq., cv n., 254, 345–80, 468 sq., 600 (s.v. partition); 27, 120, 120 sq. n.; 33, xv, 62 sq., 127, 135 sq., 182, 188–202, 272 sq., 338, 369–85; 37, 113, 147, 427, 485 sq.; one should not take the heritage of an outcast, 2, 88 n., 282; liability of heirs for debts, 2, 244; 25, 282 sq.; 33, 41–9, 46 n., 329; making a will, 6, 112 sq.; 37, 47; exclusion from participation, 7, 64 sq.; duties incumbent upon the heir, 7, 65; partition of property, 7, 67 sq., 70–4; collateral succession, 7, 68 sq.; succession of females, 7, 69 sq.; indivisible property, 7, 70, 74; law of i. among Buddhist Bhikkhus, 17, 243–5; inherited property of a minor or female to be protected by the king, 25, 257 sq.; partition of i. made once only, 25, 335, 335 n.;

a (pure) mode of acquiring property, a title of possession, 25, 426; 33, 53 sq., 243, 309 sq., 314; women own no heritage, 26, 367; the domestic fire to be kindled at the division of the i., 29, 13, 13 n., 271; partition deed made by brothers, 33, 305; gift of inherited property, 33, 342 sq.; a king confiscates the property of a man who has no heir, 45, 67, 67 n.; sons divide the property of an aged father, 46, 71. *See also* Sons, *and* Woman (*a, e*).

Initiation, or Upanayana, ordained for the three higher castes, 2, 1; 34, 197, 224; rules and rites for the i. of members of the three higher castes, 2, 2–6, 175–8, 182 sq.; 7, 114 sq., 119, 127; 14, 56–8, 149 sq.; 25, xxxix n., 36–42, 61 sq.; 29, 8 sq., 58–68, 58 sq. n., 187–93, 276, 303–12, 399–403; 30, xviii sq., xxv sq., 63–77, 137–61, 253, 270–5, 302 sq.; 44, xv, 86–90; is a second birth, 2, 3, 176; 14, 9 sq., 150, 210; 25, 57, 61; 42, 215; 44, 87–90; from the time of i. the child obtains the right to perform religious ceremonies, 2, 139 sq.; the duty to live in the teacher's house after i. is common to all orders, 2, 153; allowing the time for the i. to pass, a minor offence, 2, 282; second i. after penance, 2, 287; 7, 162, 178; 14, 104 sq., 115, 213 sq.; Nû zûdi, the i. of the young Parsi, 4, 122; the marriage ceremony is considered as the i. of women, 7, 90; *from the mother is the first birth; the second, from the girding with the sacrificial string. In the latter, the Sâvitrî hymn is his mother, and the teacher his father. It is this which entitles members of the three higher castes to the designation of 'the twice-born,'* 7, 119; a teacher should not initiate one whom he does not know, 7, 122; proper time for i., 7, 136; penance for omitting i., 7, 179; 25, 469; Vrâtyas, i.e. those for whom the ceremony of i. has not been performed, 7, 187, 252; 14, 58; 25, 405 sq. and n.; the leavings of funeral repasts are the share of Brâhma*n*as who have died before i., 7, 251; the girding of the wife for the sacrifice, a kind of i., 12, 72 n.; sons begotten by an uninitiated man are Vrâtyas, 14, 197; those sprung from intermixture of castes are Vrâtyas, 14, 198; one who has not received the i. shall not sacrifice, 25, 437; 30, 267; second i. as penance, 25, 460 sq., 460 n., 469; 29, 193; the patitasâvitrîka, 29, 59 sq., 187, 311 sq.; 30, 63; repeated for the study of the secret doctrines, 29, 79 sq. n.; sacrifice at the i., 29, 380; 30, 41; joining of hands at i., 30, 151; a Vrâtya cannot be a witness, 33, 87; ordeal by sacred libation not applicable for Vrâtyas, 33, 117; younger brother to be initiated at the expense of the elder brothers, 33, 197, 373; subserves the study of the Veda, 34, 198 sq., 224, 227; omitted in a certain case, 34, 227 n.; the Bodhisattva given in charge of a teacher, 36, 45; prayers at i., 42, 240, 364 sq., 381, 383, 477, 543, 551, 569; allusion to the i. rite in the Rig-veda, 46, 252, 254 sq. *See also* Anointment, *and* Dîkshâ.

Injunctions and prohibitions, what room there is for them, if there is only one internal Self of all beings, 38, 65–8; i. expressed by potential, imperative, &c., verbal forms, 38, 304.

Insanity, *see* Diseases.

Inscriptions, on the tripods with panegyrics to the ancestors, 28, 251–3.

Insight, personified, 30, 159.

Instruction: duties of a minister of i., 3, 43, 228, 251; 27, 109, 230–5; principles of learning, 3, 117; instructors of the youth, officials, 3, 169; the young should listen to the i. of their fathers, 3, 175; all depends on the early training of a son, 3, 187; a state college repaired by a marquis of Lû, 3, 337 sq., 338 n., 340; rules about systems of schools, 27, 17, 19 sq., 32, 219, 230–5, 346 n., 348 sq., 389 sq.; 28, 18, 36 sq., 82–91, 231 sq.; training of eldest sons of rulers, 27, 23, 345–53; the shû-ȝze who superintended the instruction of princes, 27, 23, 353 sq. and n.; 28, 454 sq.; of boys and girls, 27, 27, 476–9, 477 n.; competitive examinations, 27, 56; the aged nourished in the schools, 27, 240, 242,

242 n., 359–61, 464, 466 sq.; every child put under a master, 27, 312, 312 n., 327, 474; teaching is the half of learning, 28, 83; teaching of music, 28, 107, 109; training of girls before marriage, 28, 432; the i. of a young man of bad disposition, 39, 215 sq.; — the righteous should teach the wicked, 5, 124, 124 n.; duty of sending children to school, 24, 313 sq.; teaching of children, 37, 77; religious i., 37, 99, 114, 330 sq., 367; teaching the good, 37, 321; teaching of good works is performance of good works, 37, 340, 348; teaching virtue, 37, 354; — giving i. the duty of Brâhma*n*as, 8, 21–3, 218, 324, 359; the devotee shall not teach, 8, 365; as birds feed their young ones, so are disciples regularly to be instructed, 22, 58; initiation, Vedic studentship, duties of teacher and pupil, 25, 39, 42–75; teaching allowed to Brâhma*n*as only, 25, 419; religious i., one of the four requisites to reach beatitude, 45, 16; faith produced by i., 45, 154 sq. *See also* Teacher.

Intellect, *see* Intelligence.

Intelligence (buddhi), mind and self, 7, 286; is of threefold quality, 8, 125; is a name of the great Self, 8, 332; Buddha on the relation of upright conduct, earnest contemplation, and i., 11, 11, 11 n., 12, 15, 24, 28, 34, 65 sq., 70; Brahman is pure i., 34, xxv; 48, 20–3; is higher than the mind, 34, 239 sq.; higher than the i. is the great Self, 34, 240; the pervadingness of i., 38, 40; abides in the heart, 38, 45; the connexion of the soul with the i. exists as long as the soul, 38, 45–8; is the first produced, 38, 57; there are five distinctions of i., and on their account five intellectual organs, 38, 81; i. only is true and everything else untrue, 48, 22 sq.

Intercourse, *see* Sexual i.

Intermediate place, t.t., i. e. state of dreams, 38, 133.

Internal organ, and the individual soul, 34, 122 sq., 398, 398 n.; Sâṅkhyas sometimes speak of three, sometimes of one i. o. only, 34, 376; called by different names, manas, buddhi, vig*ñ*âna, *k*itta, 38, 48; if no i. o. existed there would result either constant perception or constant non-perception, or else a limitation either of the soul or of the senses, 38, 48 sq.; they co-operate with the Selfs, 38, 69; called Âtman, 38, 81. *See also* Manas, *and* Mind.

Intoxication, *see* Spirituous liquors.

Intuition, a means of knowledge, 34, 18; is the final result of the inquiry into Brahman, 34, 18; 38, 332; vouched for by scripture, 34, 101 sq.; the highest Self corresponds to the mental act of complete i., 34, 172; true knowledge is the object of immediate i., 38, 238, 295; the fruit of all meditations is to be effected through i., 38, 281; repetition not necessary to bring about i., 38, 333. *See also* Kevala.

Invisibility, that which possesses the attributes of it is Brahman, 34, xxxv, 135–42; may be an attribute of the pradhâna, 34, 136.

Involucrum of delight, 38, 202 sq.

Î-po, uncle of Hui-po, 27, 187.

Iram, founded by Sheddâd, 9, 330, 330 n.

Iran, geography of, 4, 1–10; 23, 123, 154; 31, xxvii–xxxiii; I. and other countries, 4, 260 sq.; 23, 226 sq. and n.; foreign invasions into I., 5, l sq., 201–3, 209 sq., 214–22, 232; prophecy of a period of adversity for I., 5, l sq., 201–15; more valuable than other lands, 24, 345; boundary disputes between Tûrân and I., 47, 135–7. *See also* Khvanîras.

Irânians, Arûmans, and Tûrânians, 24, 52, 52 n.

Îrân-shâh, son of Malik-shâh, author of the metrical Sad Dar, 24, xxxvii, xliv sq.

Irâvatî, or the river A*k*iravatî, 11, 167 n.; city of the Asuras, 12, 110 n.

Iron, *see* Metals.

Irrigation, canals and fords, 24, 338 sq.; 37, 127–9; charm for conducting a river into a new channel, 42, 146 sq., 348–51.

Î-r 3ze, branded and disfigured by Yâo, 39, 255 sq., 255 n.; 40, 283.

Î*s*, Lord, a more personal name for

the highest Being than Âtman or Brahman, 1, ci, 314. *See* God.
Isaac, son of Abraham, a prophet, 6, 57, 125; 9, 30, 51, 120, 172; angels announce his birth, 6, 213; I. and Jacob were of the elect, 9, 180; brings wine from paradise which Abraham offers to God, 24, 225 sq.
Isa*d*-vâstra, or Îsa*d*vâstar, or Isatvâstra, son of Zarathu*s*tra, representing the priestly class, 4, 21 n.; 5, 123 n., 142–4; 23, 204, 204 n.; 47, 106, 111, 115; Fravashi of I., worshipped, 31, 273, 273 n., 278.
Isâf, an idol on Mount Zafâ, 6, xiii.
Î*s*âna, carries the thunderbolt, 2, 298; Brâhmans pray to him, 11, 180; a name of the Self, 15, 311; *S*akra and Î. fan Mahâvîra with chowries, 22, 198; oblation to Î. for the bridegroom, 29, 32; n. of Rudra (Agni), 29, 256; 41, 160; 43, xx; with his companions, invoked at the house-building rite, 29, 347; worship of Î., his consort and his son, 29, 352; 30, 221 sq., 289–91; invoked for success in trade, 30, 178; is the Sun, 41, 160; a created god, 48, 461; alone indeed there was Nârâya*n*a, not Brahmâ, not Î., 48, 522.
Î*s*ânabali, *see* Sacrifice (*b*).
Isa*t*-vâstra, *see* Isa*d*-vâstra.
Î*s*â-upanishad, forms part of the Sa*m*hitâ of the White Yagur-veda, 1, lxvi, c sq., 309–20; quoted, 8, 415; 38, 424; 48, 775.
Isfendyâr, son of Gu*s*tâsp, made invulnerable, 47, xxiii.
Isha Âtreya, author of Vedic hymns, 46, 383, 386.
Î-shih, a Tâoist teacher, 39, 247.
Ishmael: images of Abraham and I. in the Kaabah, 6, xiii; Abraham and I. restored the Kaabah, 6, xvi, 17 sq.; Abraham's proposed sacrifice of I., 6, lxxiv; a prophet, 6, 57, 94, 125; 9, 31; was patient, and entered into the mercy of God, 9, 53; was of the righteous, 9, 180.
Ishukâra, a king, turns monk and reaches perfection, 45, 61–9.
Ishukâra, n. of a town, 45, 62.
Isi, Pali, i.e. Sk. *R*ishi, a sage, 10 (ii), x; Buddha called a perfect, a great or divine I., 10 (ii), 13, 28, 59, 79, 127, 174, 189, 194–7, 201, 208, 210; who is a great I. or Muni, 10 (ii), 34; for what reason did they sacrifice, 10 (ii), 75; forest called after the Isis, 10 (ii), 125; I. and men, Khattiyas and Brâhma*n*as, offer sacrifices to the gods, 10 (ii), 192.
Isibhatta, n. of a Thera, 17, 237.
Isidâsa, n. of a Thera, 17, 237.
Isigili mount, at Râ*g*agaha, 11, 56 sq.
Islâm, birthplace of, 6, ix; monotheism the key-word of I., 6, xlix; its monotheistic idea not new, 6, l; means 'resignation,' 6, li, lxv, 15 n.; pre-eminently a proselytizing religion, 6, li; its originality, 6, liii sq.; sketch of the creed of Mohammed, 6, lxv–lxxvi; moral code of I., 6, lxxi sq., 24 sq.; 9, 3–5, 89, 301; there is no compulsion in religion, 6, 40; the true or best religion, 6, 48 sq., 57, 89 sq.; schism and disbelief in I. reproved, 6, 58–61, 136; sincere believers and hypocrites, 6, 91 sq.; the faith of Abraham, 6, 137; who are the true believers, 6, 163; the Muslim believes in God and the last day, is steadfast in prayer, gives alms, and fears only God, 6, 175; God sent His apostle to make I. prevail over every other religion, 6, 177; the religion of the 'Hanîf, the standard religion, 6, 204; 9, 127 sq., 338; the conquests of I., 6, 237; the religion of the prophets of old, 9, 53 sq. and n.; Judaism and Christianity treated as sects of I., 9, 68 sq.; broken up into sects, 9, 206; profession of faith, 9, 237 n.; by becoming Muslims, you do not oblige God, but God obliges you by directing you to the faith, 9, 241; exhortation to believe in God and His Apostle, and to give alms, 9, 266–8, 281 sq.; prophecy that men shall join I. by troops, 9, 343; Musulmâns hostile to Persian next-of-kin marriage, 18, 424 sq.; alluded to, but hardly ever mentioned in Pahlavi writings, 24, xxv sq., 127 n., 169 n.; 47, xviii. *See also* Morality (*e*).
Island, is neither earth nor water, 44, 497 sq.
Isle of Jewels, parable of, 21, 181 sq.
Î*s*opanishad, *see* Î*s*â-upanishad.
Israel, children of, preferred by

God, 6, 6, 17; saved from Pharaoh's people, 6, 6, 153 sq., 202 sq.; 9, 93, 219; manna and quails sent down for them, 6, 7; mountain held over them, 6, 8, 12, 93, 159; manifest signs given to them, 6, 30; God made a covenant with them and chose twelve wardens, 6, 99; wander for forty years in the desert, 6, 100 sq.; worship the calf, and are punished, 6, 155 sq.; cut up into twelve tribes, 6, 157; punished for disobedience, 6, 157 sq.; their two sins, and their punishment, 9, 1 sq., 1 n.; in the promised land, 9, 12; the law first given to I. in the Book, then to Mohammed, 9, 222. *See also* Jews.

Isrâfîl, the archangel of the resurrection, 6, lxix.

Îsvand, *see* Isva*t*.

Î*s*vara (Lord, God), in the Anugîtâ, 8, 219; is the lord of all gods, Dânavas, Bhûtas, &c., 8, 354; Buddha honoured like Î., 19, 142; *G*inas with strength like Î., 19, 275; Î. and Mahe*s*vara, two gods, honour Buddha, 21, 4, 55, 349; Avalokite*s*vara assumes the shape of Î., 21, 411; worshipped for the thriving of cattle, 30, 89; the world created by Î., 45, 244; 49 (i), 100. *See also* God (*d*).

Î*s*vara-Gîtâ, the same as Bhagavadgîtâ, 8, 2; 38, 63.

Isva*t*, or Îsvand, son of Varâza, 23, 203; a priest at the renovation, 37, 262, 262 n.

Itarâ, mother of Mahidâsa Aitareya, 1, xciv, xcv.

Itihâsa, or ancient story: Anugîtâ called a purâta*n*a I., 8, 198; parables of the Upanishads referred to as I., 8, 207, 210, 226, 268, 270, 282; I. in form of dialogues related in the Anugîtâ, 8, 256, 261, 274, 277, 289, 293, 296, 303, 310; the fifth Veda, 10 (ii), 98; Bâvarî versed in the three Vedas and I., 10 (ii), 189; I. and Purâ*n*as, *see* Itihâsa-purâ*n*a.

Itihâsa-purâ*n*a, or Itihâsas and Purâ*n*as, correspond to the Atharvaveda, 1, 39 sq. and n.; mentioned along with the Vedas, the fifth Veda, 1, 109, 110, 111, 115; 15, 330 sq.; 29, 51; Brâhma*n*as should be versed in the I., 2, 215; recited at *S*râddhas and other rites, 7, 126, 235; 25, 118; 29, 248; as a branch of sacred learning, 14, 144 n.; 29, 218 sq.; as authorities on law, 14, 149 n.; satiated at the Tarpa*n*a, 14, 255; 30, 244; mentioned after the Atharvaveda, 14, 320; quoted as authorities on religion and philosophy, 34, 198, 217, 222 sq., 304, 348; 38, 235, 315; 48, 409, 460 sq., 751; are of human origin, hence do not constitute an independent means of authoritative knowledge, 34, 218; are based on mantra, arthavâda, and perception, 34, 222; 48, 330; all the four castes are qualified for acquiring the knowledge of them, 34, 229; 48, 338 sq.; known to Milinda, 35, 6; the Brâhma*n*as occupied with I., 35, 247, 247 n.; related at the Pâriplava Âkhyâna during the horse-sacrifice, 44, xxxi, 369, 369 n.; included in the daily study of the Veda, 44, 98, 98 n., 101, 101 n.; the Veda should be made to grow by I., 48, 91; their teaching about Brahman, 48, 126; are means of meditation as supporting the Veda, but not independently of the Veda, 48, 338 sq.; refer to Kapila, 48, 409.

I-tsing, translated the Vagra*kkh*edikâ, 49 (ii), xiii.

Itvara, or Iṅgitamara*n*a, *G*aina t.t., suicide by starving oneself, 22, 72, 72 n.

Î Yin, or Â-hăng, or Pâo-hăng, 'the great Sage,' Thang's chief adviser, 3, 90, 90 n., 92–103, 113, 118, 118 n., 206 sq., 207 n., 311, 311 n.; 40, 162; cook of Thang, 40, 89.

J

Jackal, *see* Animals (*k*).

Jacob, sets up a stone as a pillar at Bethel, 6, xiii; instructs his son to believe in God, 6, 18; an inspired prophet, 6, 57, 94, 125; 9, 30, 51; Isaac and J. granted to Abraham, 6, 213; 9, 120; story of the sons of J., Joseph, 6, 219–30; was of the elect, 9, 180.

Jamshê*d* = Yima Khshaêta. *See* Yim.

Japan, Sacred Books of Buddhists in, *Vol.* 49, *part* ii; Buddhist sects in J., 49 (ii), v sq., viii, xii; Sanskrit MSS. in J., 49 (ii), vii sq.

Jerusalem, destroyed by Kaî-Lôharâsp, 24, 65, 65 n.; siege of J., 'the holy place,' 47, xiii, 121, 121 n.

Jesus, picture of the virgin and child in the Kaabah, 6, xiii; regarded with particular veneration by Mohammed, 6, li; a prophet inspired, 6, lxxi, 19, 57, 94, 104, 108, 125; 9, 29, 139, 206, 269; apostles of J. rejected at Antioch, 6, cv; 9, 163 sq., 164 n.; God gave J. manifest signs, and aided Him with the Holy Spirit, 6, 12, 39; birth and infancy of J., 6, 52, 113 sq.; works miracles, 6, 52; returns to God, 6, 53, 53 n.; His likeness with God is as the likeness of Adam, 6, 53 sq.; God raised J. unto Himself, while the Jews crucified a similitude of J., 6, 93 sq.; only an Apostle of God, not the son of God, 6, 95; 9, 29; they misbelieve who say that God is the son of Mary, 6, 100, 108; disbelieving Jews cursed by J., 6, 108; the mission of J., 6, 113 sq.; the apostles ask for a table from heaven as a sign, 6, 114; denies commanding men to worship Him and His mother as gods, 6, 114 sq.; Christians rebuked for saying that the Messiah is the Son of God, 6, 177, 200; 9, 34; birth of J., the infant J. in the cradle testifies to Mary's innocence and His mission, 9, 28 sq.; the son of the Virgin Mary, 9, 53, 68, 139, 269; made a sign by God, 9, 68; not a god, 9, 215 sq., 215 n.; prophesies the coming of Mohammed, 9, 281, 281 n.; His apostles God's helpers, 9, 282; birth of J. from the Holy Spirit, 24, 229–32; temptation of J., 24, 239.

Jethro = Sho'hâib, 6, 149 n., 249 n.

Jewels, the three, Buddha, Dhamma, and Saṅgha, 10 (i), 51 sq.; (ii), xiii n., 14, 24, 37–40, 52, 79 sq., 85, 94, 117; 11, 26 sq., 79, 108, 203; 13, 84, 106, 109, 115, 187, 209; 17, 5, 96, 115; 19, 200, 200 n., 251; 20, 77 (praised in a snake-charm), 184; 35, 144, 253 sq.; 36, 83, 365, 373; 49 (i), 163, 189; (ii), 22, 25, 96 sq., 167, 174 sq., 188 n., 196; seven J. of the Law, 11, xxii, xxii n., 29 n., 61–3; King Sudassana possessed the seven j. or precious things, 11, 249 sq. n., 251–9, 274–88; gem-treasure of King Sudassana, 11, 256; j. as ornaments or bricks of the Palace of Righteousness, 11, 262, 265–7, 269 sq.; the head-jewel of Buddha, 19, 61, 61 n.; seven j., 21, 227 sq., 232, 248; 49 (ii), 34–6, 43, 63, 92–4, 92 sq. n., 119, 123, 136, 139, 141, 143, 166, 170–4, 176, 182, 185, 190, 192 sq.; j.-flowers and j.-trees in a Buddha-country, 21, 232 sq.; 49 (ii), 19 sq., 33–6, 38, 42, 94, 172 sq., 179, 184 sq., 190; bags of j. strewn over Buddha, 21, 235 sq.; different kinds of j., 22, 227, 238; the seven j. of the Buddha, 36, 220–9, 220 n.; the 'j.' of a king, commander of the army, &c. (ratna-havîmshi), 41, 58–65, 58 sq. n.; list of j., 49 (ii), 17, 33. *See also* Gems.

Jews, referred to as infidels, 5, lxi, 297, 297 n.; J. of Medînah, opposed to Mohammed, 6, xxxv, xxxvii–xxxix, lxiii; Mohammed's relation to the J., 6, xlvii; J., Christians, or Sabaeans, whosoever believe in God, will have their reward, 6, 8; charged with corrupting the Scriptures, 6, 10 sq., 10 n., 56, 79, 99, 125, 125 n.; charged with slaying their kinsmen, 6, 11; charged with killing God's prophets, 6, 12; paradise not exclusively for J. and Christians, 6, 15; disputes between J. and Christians, 6, 15; J. and Christians and idolators opposed to Islâm and reproved, 6, 16, 105–9; 9, 272 sq.; rebuked for professing Islâm and recanting it again, 6, 55 sq., 55 n.; rebuked for making certain kinds of food unlawful to themselves, 6, 58; cursed, 6, 79; punished for demanding to see God, 6, 93; punished for misbelief, and for calumniating Mary and Jesus, 6, 93 sq.; forbidden certain kinds of food on account of their sins, 6, 94, 134 sq., 263; food of the J. lawful for Muslim, 6, 97 sq.; chaste women of the J. allowed to the Muslim, 6, 98; Mohammed warned against their treachery, 6, 99; J.

and Christians not the 'sons of God,' 6, 100; to be judged by the Qur'ân, 6, 103 sq.; 9, 106; some J., guided in truth, act justly, 6, 157 sq.; dispersed, 6, 158; rebuked for saying that Ezra was the son of God, 6, 177, 177 n.; God will decide on resurrection day between J., Sabaeans, Christians, Magians, and Idolators, 9, 58; believe in the Qur'ân, 9, 98; Moses received the Book, a guidance for the J., 9, 137, 195; defeat of the Qurâi*th*ah J., 9, 142, 142 n.; believers and unbelievers among the people of the Book, 9, 269 sq.; the J. who fought against the Muslim denounced, 9, 274–7; chastisement of the J. who would not believe in the Qur'ân, 9, 274, 274 n.; rebuked for unbelief, compared to an ass bearing books, 9, 283, 337 sq.; a Jewish sect called 'the hill-serpent of the J.,' 24, 241; reference to the J. as a tribe, 47, xiii, 129 sq. *See also* Israel (children of), *and* Judaism.

Job, an inspired prophet, 6, 94, 125; was saved, 9, 52 sq.; and his wife, how he was cured, 9, 179, 179 n.

John, the glad tidings of, 6, 51; a prophet, 6, 125; birth of J., the son of Zachariah, his accomplishments, 9, 27 sq.

Jonah, or Jonas, or DHu'nnûn, saved in the fish's belly, 6, cvi, 203; 9, 53, 53 n., 173 sq.; an inspired prophet, 6, 94, 125; the chapter of J. (Qur'ân), 6, 192; 'the fellow of the fish,' 9, 295 n., 297 sq.

Joseph, his story told in proof of revelation, 6, xci, 219–31; a prophet or apostle, 6, 125; 9, 193.

Joshua = DHu'l Kifl, 9, 53 n.

Judaism, and Zoroastrianism, 4, lvii–lx; in Arabia, 6, xiv sq.; its relation to Islâm, 6, xlvii–lii, lxix; Jewish influences in the Qur'ân, 6, 5 n.; criticism of Jewish account of creation and fall of man, 24, 178 sq., 200, 208–29; Zoroastrian converts from J., 47, xiii sq., 120 n. *See also* Jews.

Judge(s), who is fit for the office of, 2, 170; 4, 255; 25, 254–6, 507; evils befalling the country through trusting a false j., 5, 323; corruption of j., 6, 27; 25, 383 n.; 33, 360 sq.; the true j. is like Aûhar*mazd* and the archangels, the false j. like Aharman and the demons, 24, 79; one quarter of the guilt of an unjust decision falls on the j., 25, 255; unjust j. fined, 25, 383; kings and j., 25, 383; 37, 422 sq.; punishment of j., illegal action of plaintiff, 37, 46; wicked and just j., 37, 73, 146, 289 sq.; duties of j., 37, 78 sq., 102; j. and guardians, 37, 250. *See also* Judicial procedure.

Judicial procedure: the constitution of a Parishad or legal assembly, 2, 44 n.; 14, 20, 144–6; 25, lii, lii n., 509–11; modes of proof, 2, 170 sq.; 33, 58–65, 96–120; law about j.p., 2, 237, 237 n.; 14, 78–83; 25, xcix, 254–90, 382 sq. and n., 594 sq.; 27, 235–8, 271, 275, 275 n., 285, 295, 356, 359, 359 n.; 33, xiii, 5–40, 233–63, 274 sq., 282–319, 386–90; 37, 36–8, 46 sq., 49–51, 53–65, 67, 70–3, 80 sq.; mode of inflicting punishments, 3, 261–4; place, ordeal, and time of appointment proffered to the plaintiff, 4, 254; judge and witness in a circle of three steps, 4, 257, 257 n.; the guilt of an offender falls on king, judge, and witnesses, if he is not punished, 14, 203; an arrow brought to the court in civil cases, thirty pounds of gold in criminal cases, 16, 103 n.; deciding doubtful legal questions, 25, lxxiii, 509–11; courts of justice, 25, 254; 33, 36–40, 277–82; ceremonies on entering a court of justice, 29, 362 sq.; 30, 178 sq., 295; plaint and answer, 33, 17, 24–34, 235–42, 288–94; arrest, 33, 17–19; the judgement, 33, 34 sq., 297 sq.; 37, 371; disputes about partition of property, 33, 198 sq., 201; how to find out thieves, 33, 224 sq.; the trial, 33, 294–7; the king decides about punishments, 36, 266, 266 n.; decision of acquittal or conviction, 37, 329. *See also* Judge, Justice, Ordeals, *and* Witnesses.

Jugglers, practices of, are the cause of bad births, 45, 230, 231 sq.

Justice: *O ye who believe! be ye steadfast in j., witnessing before God*

though it be against yourselves, or your parents, or your kindred, be it rich or poor, for God is nearer akin than either, 6, 91; enjoined, 6, 98; j. and wisdom, 18, 11 sq.; a principle of Zoroastrianism, 24, 329; king created for the attainment of j., 25, 217; *where j. is destroyed by injustice, or truth by falsehood, while the judges look on, there they shall also be destroyed. J., being violated, destroys; j., being preserved, preserves*, 25, 255; grand minister of j., and minister of crime, 27, 109 sq.; true j. better than other good works, 37, 73, 327; administration of j., *see* Judicial procedure. *See also* Rashnû.

K

Ka, or 'Who,' a name of Pragâpati, 1, 59 n.; 12, 8, 8 n.; 26, 410; 32, 3, 11–13; 41, 173, 175, 221, 346, 368; 43, 265, 265 n., 334 sq.; 44, 86, 393; is Brahman, 1, 65, 65 n.; cake offerings to Ka, 12, 395, 403; 44, 75 n., 76; purified by means of a purificatory rite other gods, 14, 331; produced everything holy, 14, 331; the Creator, 43, xiv; 49 (i), 25; the sacrificer consecrated to K., 44, 254 n.; worshipped at the horse-sacrifice, 44, 291 n., 292, 392, 392 n., 394.

Kaabah, the chief shrine of the Arabian faith, 6, xiii; history of the K. in Mecca, 6, xvi–xviii; the point to which Mohammed turned in prayer, 6, xxxv, liii; Mohammed takes possession of the K., 6, xlii; contained all the gods of the different Arabian tribes, 6, xlv; universal reverence for the K. made use of by Mohammed, 6, liii; worship of the K., 6, lxxiv sq., 111; rebuilt by Abraham and Ishmael, 6, 17 sq.; 9, 59; God has made the K., the sacred House, to be a station for men, 6, 111.

Kabandha, Âtharva*n*a, became a Gandharva, 15, 132.

Kabandhin Kâtyâyana, n. of a sage 15, 271.

Kâbul, Indian religions in, 4, 2, 6, 6 n.

Kâ*d*, n.p., 5, 145.

Kadambavâlukâ, n. of a river in Hell, 45, 94.

Kadân, epithet of Karsêvaz, 5, 135.

Kâdraveya, *see* Arbuda K.

Kadrû, queen of serpents, 12, 301 n.; legend of Supar*n*î and K., 26, 52, 149 sq. and n.; is the earth, 26, 149.

***K*aêshman**, *see Hv*are-*k*aêshman.

Kaêva, n.p., 23, 217.

Kaho*d*a or Kahola Kaushîtaki, quoted, 12, 370; questions Yâg*ñ*avalkya, 15, 129 sq.; 38, 242 sq.; 48, 657; worshipped at the Tarpa*n*a, 29, 123, 141, 220.

Kahôs = Kâûs, q.v.

Kahrkana, n. of a family, 23, 219.

Kahrkatâs, *see* Birds (*b*).

Ka*hv*aredhas, prayer for the dislodgment of, 31, 312 sq.

Ka*hv*uzi, n. of a demon, 4, 234.

Kaî, *see* Kavis.

Kaî-Apîveh, *see* Aipivanghu.

Kaî-Arsh, king of Iran, 5, 136, 136 n.; 47, 13.

Kâidhya, Sraosha, the conqueror of, 31, 301.

Kaî Gu*s*tâsp, taught by Zoroaster, 24, 170 sq.

Kaî-Kabâ*d*, *see* Kavâ*d*.

Kaî-Kâûs, *see* Kâûs.

Kaî-Kavâ*d*, *see* Kavâ*d*.

Kaikeya, *see* A*s*vapati.

Kaî-Khûsrôî, *see* Khûsrôî.

***K*aikitâneya**, *see* Brahmadatta *K*.

***K*aikitâyana** Dâlbhya, n.p., 1, 15–17.

Kaî-Kobâ*d*, *see* Kavâ*d*.

***K*ailaki**, *see G*îvala *K*.

Kaî-Lôharâsp, *see* Lôharâsp.

Kaî-Pisân, *see* Pisanah.

Kaîs, *see* Kavis.

Kaîsar, Byzantine emperor, 47, xviii, 103, 103 n.

Kai*s*orya Kâpya, n. of a teacher, 15, 119, 187.

Kaî-Spendâ*d*, *see* Spe*n*tô-dâta.

***K*aitanya**, or pure intelligence, 34, xxiv.

***K*aitraratha** forest, Yayâti in the, 49 (i), 45.

***K*aitraratha Abhipratârin**, a Kshattriya, 34, 226 sq.; 48, 341 sq.

***K*aitya**, *see* Holy Places.

Kaî-Ûs (Av. Kava Usan), created immortal, misled by Aharman, 24,

35, 35 n.; his exploits, 24, 63 sq. and n.; neglected religion, 24, 102; grandson of Kavâd, 37, 28; his reign, success, and ruin, 37, 220–3; 47, 13, 31 sq.; Aôshnar his chancellor, 47, x; Srîtô employed by him, 47, xiv, 78 n., 135–8; his accession, 47, xxix.
Kaî-Vistâsp, *see* Vistâspa.
Kaî-Vyârsh, n.p., 5, 136, 136 n.
Kâka, King Paggota's slave, the son of a non-human being, 17, 188 sq.
Kâkandaka, *see* *Ri*shigupta *and* Supratibuddha.
Kâkandaka, Yasa, son of, 20, 387.
Kâkandikâ *S*âkhâ, of the U*d*uvâ*t*ika Ga*n*a, 22, 291.
***K*akhravâk**, n. of a high-priest, 5, 115, 115 sq. n.
***K*âkhshni**, n.p., 23, 213.
Kakhshnûs, n.p., 5, 141, 141 n.
Ka*kk*âna, mentioned among the principal Thera Bhikkhus, 17, 359. *See* Bela*tth*a, *and* Mahâka*kk*âna.
***K*akkavatti** (Râgâ), *see* *K*akravartin.
Ka*kk*âyana, *see* Mahâ-K., Pakudha-K., *and* Pubba-K.
***K*âkra**, *see* Revottara.
***K*akradharas**, 'holders of wheels,' superhuman beings, 8, 232 n.
***K*akravâka** bird, 36, 340 sq.
***K*akravartin** (Pali *K*akkavatti), viz. râgâ, t.t., a king of kings or universal emperor, 8, 232 n.; 49 (ii), 26; is possessed of the thirty-two signs of a great man, and of the seven gems or treasures, 10 (ii), 100, 187; 19, xx, 320, 360; 36, 136 sq., 203; 49 (ii), 140; rise of the idea of a *K*., 11, xv, xviii sq., 92 n.; how they treat the remains of a *K*., 11, 92 sq., 125; worthy of a dâgaba, 11, 94 sq.; wonderful qualities of a *K*., 11, 98; Sudassana a *K*., 11, 252, 260 n.; Avalokitesvara assumes the shape of a *K*., 21, 411; is never born in low families, 22, 225; the wheel of victory of a *K*., 35, 162; the marvellous jewel of a *K*., 35, 177; 36, 14, 14 n., 128; the wonderful elephant of a *K*., 36, 128 sq.; fourteen attributes of a *K*., 45, 48.
***K*âkrâya*n*a**, *see* Ushasta *K*.
Kakshîvat, Usig's son, an offerer of Soma, 12, 355; born from the armpit, 19, 3; 49 (i), 6.
***K*âkshusha**, a Manu, 25, 19.
Kakudha, became an inheritor of the highest heavens, 11, 26; the spirit of K. the Koliyan appears before Moggallâna, 20, 234 sq.
Kakutstha, Kunthu perhaps a Prâkrit form for, 45, 86 n.
Kakutthâ, n. of a river, 11, 74, 82 sq.
Kâla (Time), probably identical with Vish*n*u, 7, xxix; the destroyer of all creatures, is hard to overcome, 7, 79, 81. *See also* Time.
Kâla, the king of serpents, pays homage to Buddha, 49 (i), 135 sq.
Kâla, one of the five hundred Arhats who are to become future Buddhas, 21, 198.
Kalâbu, king of Benares, former birth of Devadatta, 35, 286, 286 n.
Kalahavivâdasutta, t.c., 10 (ii), 164–7.
Kâlaka, a Nâga, converted by Buddha, 19, 245.
Kâlaka: Ârya K. of the Gautama gotra, a Sthavira, 22, 294.
Kâlaka, n. of a merchant, husband of *K*ulla-Subhaddâ, 36, 308.
Kâlaka*ñ*ga: Indra killed the people of K. on earth, 1, 293; Asuras called K., 12, 286 n.
Kâlâma, Arâ*d*a, the kinsman of, 49 (i), 123. *See also* Â*l*âra.
Kâlâmukhas, a class of adherents of Pasupati, 48, 520 sq.
Kalanda, Sudinna, the son of, 20, 374; 35, 238 sq., 238 n.
Kalandakanivâpa, n. of a place, 10 (ii), 85, 87.
Kâla*ñ*gara, n. of a mountain, 45, 57.
Kalasi, Milinda born at, 35, xxiii, 127.
Kâ*l*âsoka, fixed his capital at Pâ*t*aliputta, 11, xvi sq.
Kâlayasas, translated the Amitâyurdhyâna-sûtra into Chinese, 49 (ii), vii, xx.
Kali: 'like a gambler vanquished by K.,' 45, 22.
Kali age, *see* Ages of the World (*a*).
Kâlî, daughter of Agni, seduced by Parâsara, 49 (i), 45.
Kâlidâsa, his date, 8, 28–30, 29 n.; his theogony, 8, 220 sq.
Kâliṅga, became an inheritor of the highest heavens, 11, 26.

Kâliṅga, a relic of Buddha in, 11, 135; the king of K. cut the Bodhisattva's flesh, 49 (ii), 127, 127 n.
Kaliṅgas, art of, an occult science, 45, 366.
Kâlodayin, disciple of Buddha, 21, 198; 49 (ii), 90.
Kalpas, *see* Ages of the World (*a*).
Kalpa-sûtra, *see* *G*aina Sûtras.
Kalpa-sûtras, and Brâhma*n*as, 12, xlvii; K. and Pûrva Mîmâ*m*sâ-sûtras, their relation to each other, 34, xii.
Kâludâyi, drinks wine, 19, xiv.
Kâma, or Lust, the unchaste student's expiatory sacrifice to, 2, 86, 294; 14, 215 sq., 318; 29, 362; offerings to K., 2, 107; 14, 118; 29, 388; 30, 23; prayer addressed to K., 2, 298; 42, 220–3, 591–5; Mâra and K. identified, 10 (i), 17 n.; 49 (i), 137–9, 147; the Brahma*k*ârin of K., 29, 65; funeral oblation to K., 29, 242; worshipped at the Tarpa*n*a, 30, 244; arrow of K., the love-god, 42, 102, 311 sq., 311 n.; poured into the waters, 42, 104 sq., 535 sq., 535 n.; the Brahmans beg the sterile cow for K., 42, 176; K. or Love (creative desire) as a primordial power, 42, 223, 359, 591 sq.; a gandharva, 42, 536; a type of manly beauty, 49 (i), 37.
Kâmaduh, the miraculous cow, 45, 104.
Kâmah Bahrah, his account of the Nasks, 37, 419, 419 n.
Kamak, *see* Birds (*b*).
Kâmak-sû*d*, Av. Vouru-savô, one of the producers of the renovation, 18, 78 sq. n., 79.
Kâmak-vakhshin, Av. Vouru-nemô, one of the producers of the renovation, 18, 78 sq. n., 79.
Kamalâ, a Brâhman woman, converted by Buddha, 49 (i), 194.
Kamaladalavimalanakshatrarâ*g*asaṅkusumitâbhi*gñ*a, n. of a Tathâgata, 21, 393 sq., 396 sqq., 404.
Kamalâvatî, wife of the king Ishukâra, 45, 62; becomes a nun, 45, 67.
Kâmandakîya Nîtisâra, t.w., on the duties of a king, 25, lxix; quoted, 25, 240 n., 241 n., 243 n., 246 n.; quotes Mânava Dharma-sûtra, 25, xxxvi–xxxviii, xxxviii n.
Kama*nd*alu, a Nâga, who worships Buddha, 49 (i), 170.
Kâmarddhi, disciple of Suhastin, 22, 291.
Kâmarddhika Kula of the Ve*s*avâ*t*ika Ga*n*a, 22, 291.
Kâma*s*âstra, or Strîveda, quoted, 45, 274, 274 n.
Kâma Sûtra, *G*ayamaṅgala, commentary on it, its date, 22, 282 sq. n.
Kâmasutta, t.c., 10 (ii), 146.
Kâmbo*g*as, degraded Kshatriyas, 25, cxiv–cxvii, 412.
***K*a*m*kin**, n. of a Brâhma*n*a, 10 (ii), 109.
Kamma, *see* Karman, *and* Works (*c*).
***K*ampâ**, n. of a great city, 11, 99, 247; 17, 1, 1 n.; 45, 108; Buddha at *K*., 17, 256–84; Mahâvîra at *K*., 22, 264.
Kampila, n. of a Bhikshu, 49 (ii), 2.
Kâmpîla, Subhadrâ living in, 44, 321 sq. n.
Kâmpilya, Sambhûta born as Brahmadatta, at, 45, 57; Sa*ñ*gaya was king in the town of K., 45, 80 sq.
Kampîyikâ *S*âkhâ of the U*d*uvâ*t*ika Ga*n*a, 22, 291.
K*ãmrô*s, *see* Birds (*b*).
***K*amru**, and Amru, mythical birds, 23, 210, 210 n.
Kâmyesh*t*i, *see* Sacrifices (*b*).
Kan, speech at the battle of, 3, 76 sq.
Ka*n*abhu*g*, *see* Ka*n*âda.
Ka*n*âda, or Ka*n*abhug, founder of a philosophical school, 34, 315; his Vai*s*eshika-sûtras, 34, 384; his doctrines, 34, 386 sq., 392 sq.; 38, 5, 33, 69; 48, 425 sq., 430, 454, 544; K. and *Kh*aluya Rôhagutta, 45, xxxvii sq.; his views altogether to be disregarded by the Vedântin, 48, 500, 520.
Kâ*n*âdas, *see* Vai*s*eshikas.
Kanak-i Barzi*s*t, n.p., 5, 136.
***K*â*n*akya Kau*t*ilya**, quoted by Kâmandaki, 25, xxxvi, xxxviii n.
***K*anda**, a prince, the Bodisat born as, 35, 290.
***K*a*nd*a**, his daughters female demons, 42, 66, 301.
***K*andâbhibhû**, the 18th Tathâgata, 49 (ii), 6.
***K*andagutta**, *see* *K*andragupta.

*K*andaka, or *Kham*daka, the Bodhisattva's faithful groom, 19, 56, 60–70, 81–84, 86, 88, 91; 49 (i), 59, 62–70, 79–89.
Ka*nd*aka, a novice, commits unlawful sexual intercourse, 13, 205, 214.
Ka*nd*akâ, n. of a Bhikkhunî, 13, 214.
*K*â*nd*âla, *see* Caste (*e*, *f*).
*K*andana, the 6th Tathâgata, 49 (ii), 6.
*K*andanâ, at the head of 36,000 nuns, 22, 267.
*K*andanagandha, n. of Tathâgatas, 49 (ii), 6 sq.
*K*andanâgarî *S*âkhâ of the Uttarabalissaha Ga*n*a, 22, 290.
Ka*nd*araggisâma, n. of an author on medicine, 36, 109.
*K*andavatî, n. of a princess, 36, 18 sq.
*K*andra (Moon), worlds of, 7, 273; 15, 131; a god, 8, 219; 21, 4; Buddha mistaken for *K*. Devaputra, 19, 72; invoked for protection of the bride, 29, 41 sq., 288; expiatory oblation to *K*. who is the self of all the gods, 30, 51; 44, 505; invoked in a medical charm, 42, 10, 237. *See also* Moon.
*K*andrâ, the Soma-cow is, 26, 59.
*K*andrabhânu, the 45th Tathâgata, 49 (ii), 6.
*K*andradevaputra, deluded by a woman, 19, 44.
*K*andragupta (Pali *K*andagutta), the king, and Indian chronology, 10 (i), xxxv–xlv; the first *K*akkavatti king, 11, xviii sq., 92 n.; war between Bhaddasâla and *K*., 36, 147.
*K*andramas (Sk., Moon), and Soma, 8, 219 sq.; prayer to *K*., 14, 305; 29, 232; 42, 17, 128; is the Brahman priest, 29, 195; conquered the golden cities of the Asuras and Dânavas, 42, 85; is the Gandharva, the stars his Apsaras, 43, 231 sq.; Agni, Vâyu, Âditya, and *K*., identified with four fires, 44, 127. *See also* Moon.
*K*andraprabha, n. of a Tîrthakara, 22, 280; n. of the 47th Tathâgata, 49 (ii), 6; n. of minister at Bimbisâra's court, 49 (ii), 163.
*K*andraprabhâ, n. of the palankin prepared by Indra for Mahâvîra, 22, 197, 199, 257.
*K*andraprabhâsvararâga, n. of numerous Tathâgatas, 21, 358.
*K*andrasûrya*g*ihmîkara*n*a, the 29th Tathâgata, 49 (ii), 6.
*K*andrasûryapradîpa, n. of former Buddhas, 21, 18 sqq.; 49 (ii), 100.
*K*andravimalasûryaprabhâsa*s*rî, n. of a Tathâgata, 21, 376–83.
*K*ândrâya*n*a, *see* Penances.
*K*ang family, headship of Tâoism hereditary in, 39, 41 sq.
Ka*ñ*gana, a demon, converted by Buddha, 19, 244.
Kangde*z* (Av. Kangha), formation of, 24, 64, 64 n., 108 sq.
*K*ăng Hsüan, a Lî scholar, 27, 8.
*K*ang Î, nourished his outer man, and disease attacked his inner, 40, 17.
*K*ăng Khang-*kh*ăng, his commentary on the Shû King, 3, 9 sq.
*K*ăng-khâo, obtained twelve sacrificial odes, 3, 293, 303 sq.
*K*ang Lâo, congratulates Wăn-ȝze on the completion of his residence, 27, 196.
*K*ang Liang, a Tâoist patriarch, 39, 41 sq.
*K*angraga*k*a, an Indian sage, converted by Zoroaster, 4, liii sq.
Kăng-sang *Kh*û, his inferiority to Lâo-ȝze, 39, 153; 40, 75–8, 82 n.; worshipped by the people of Wei-lêi, 40, 74 sq.
*K*ang Tâo-ling, a Tâoist patriarch, 39, 42.
*K*ang-yang, a primaeval sovereign, 39, 287.
*K*ăng-Ȝâi, Confucius's mother, 27, 190.
*K*ang *Z*o, a sage accompanying Hwang-Tî, 40, 96.
Ka*n*ha (Pali for K*ri*sh*n*a), a name of Mâra, 10 (ii), 59, 182. *See also* K*ri*sh*n*a, *and* Mâra.
Ka*n*hâginâ, daughter of Vessantara, 36, 115, 125 n., 131.
Ka*n*hasiri, or Asita, the Isi with the matted hair, 10 (ii), 126.
Kanishka, A*s*vaghosha, a contemporary of, 19, xxx sq.
*K*aṅkama, t.t., walking-place for meditating Bhikkhus, 17, 7, 7 n., 390.

Kaṅkatîyas, *S*â*nd*ilya enjoins a rule on them, 43, 254.
Kaṅkhâ-revata, n. of a Bhikkhu, 17, 67.
***K*aṅkî,** n. of a Brâhman, 11, 167, 167 sq. n.
Kan Pan, first teacher of Wû-ting, 3, 116, 116 n., 207.
Kanuka, n. of a holy woman, 23, 225.
Ka*n*va, quoted by Âpastamba, 2, xxvii sq., 70, 88; K. Ghaura, son of Ghora, author of Vedic hymns, 32, 16, 65, 83, 97–9, 103, 420; 42, 318; 46, 32 sq., 35; helped by the Maruts, 32, 391; employed charms, 42, 23 sq., 319; slew the Rakshas, 42, 33; the descendant of N*ri*shad, blessed the magic plant, 42, 71; milked the thousand-streamed cow, 43, 203; Nâ*d*apit, hermitage of K., 44, 399 n.; the sons of K., 46, 42 sq.; K. Baudhâyana, *see* Baudhâyana;—family of Ka*n*vas, worshippers of the Maruts, 32, 63 sq.; ancient family of Vedic *Ri*shis, 32, 392; 46, 7, 33, 38 sq.
Kâ*n*va, quoted by Âpastamba, 2, xxvii sq., 70; an epithet of Baudhâyana, 14, xxxvi, xxxvi sq. n. *See also* Punarvatsa K.
Ka*n*vas, demons, who devour the embryo in the womb, 42, 36, 302 sq.
Kan Ying Phien, *see* Thâi-shang.
***K*an-ȝze,** counsels Prince Mâu of Wei, 40, 159, 159 n.
***K*âo,** eldest son and successor of King *Kh*ăng, 3, 234, 236–49.
***K*âo,** duke of Lû, 27, 318, 327, 327 n.; 28, 167, 167 n.
***K*âo** of Yin, his cruelty, 28, 31, 31 n.
***K*âo,** king of *Kh*û, and the sheep-butcher Yüeh, 40, 155–7, 155 n.
***K*âo-hsî,** ruler of Han, 40, 152 sq.
Kaosha, n.p., 23, 217.
Kâo Thang of Lû dictated parts of the Lî, 27, 3 sq.
***K*âo Wăn,** a musician, 39, 186.
***K*âo Wăn-ȝze,** his character and knowledge of men, 27, 199 sq.; introduced the playing of the Sze Hsiâ, 27, 420, 420 n.
Kâo-yâo, minister of crime to Shun, 3, 42 sq., 48 sq., 53, 57 sq., 61 sq., 258 sq.; 'the Counsels of K.' translated, 3, 53–6; famous for his wisdom, 3, 339, 339 n.
Kâo Ȝung, his supplementary sacrifice, 3, 118 sq.; was three years in subduing the Demon region, 16, 205, 207 n., 208, 209 sq. n.; did not speak for three years, 27, 179; his way of mourning, 28, 468 sq. *See also* Wû-ting.
Kâo Ȝze-kâo, mourning for his parents, 27, 136.
***K*âpâla** *K*etiya, at Vesâli, 11, 40, 44, 54.
Kâpâlas, a class of adherents of Pa*s*upati, 48, 520.
Kapardin, quoted by Râmânu*g*a, 34, xxi.
Kapasti, spell against the demon, 4, 145 sq.
Kâpeya, *see S*aunaka K.
Kapila, Vish*n*u called so, 7, 296; 34, 294; chief among the Siddhas, 8, 89; author of Sâṅkhya-sûtras, 8, 211; 34, 291; K., an Âsura, the son of Prahlâda, made the division of orders, 14, 260 sq.; mentioned in the *S*vetâ*s*vatara-upanishad, 15, xxxviii–xli; 48, 409, 412; his philosophical doctrines on soul, Pradhâna, deliverance, &c., 19, 134, 134 n.; 34, 237, 295 sq.; 48, 201, 354 sq., 357, 363, 365, 371, 374, 385, 425, 500, 520, 524, 544; *S*âriputra, a disciple of K., 19, 193; converted by Buddha, 19, 244; Sm*ri*ti of K., i.e. the Sâṅkhya-system, 34, 291; 48, 408, 480, 482, 529; his knowledge *ri*shi-like and unobstructed, 34, 292–4, 315; the dvaitavâdin, not mentioned in *S*ruti, 34, 294; blamed by Manu, 34, 295; story of his conversion, and how he converted a gang of robbers, 45, 31 sq. n.; his verses on the right conduct of monks, 45, 31–5; acknowledges sacrifices, &c., 48, 409; the great *Ri*shi, to whom Scripture, &c., refer as a person worthy of respect, 48, 409; Sm*ri*ti of K. opposed to Scripture, 48, 410 sq., 412; the city of the great K., 49 (i), 1; called Pra*g*âpati, 49 (i), 125.
Kapila, n. of the Bodisat as a Brâhma*n*a, 35, 287 sq.
Kapila, n. of an author on medicine, 36, 109, 109 n.
Kapilasutta, t.c., 10 (ii), 46 sq.

Kapilavatthu (Sk. Kapilavastu), Buddha and Sâkiyas at, 10 (ii), 186, 188; 11, 131 sq.; 13, 208–10; 19, 219, 227–30; 20, 320; 21, 294, 296; the preaching of the Buddhavamsa at K., 36, 249; described, 49 (i), 1 sq.
Kapiñgalâda, son of Vasishtha, 49 (i), 45.
Kâpîputra, n.p., 15, 225.
Kappa, n. of a Brâhmana, 10 (ii), 187, 203 sq., 210.
Kappa, or Kappâyana, or Kappiya, *see* Nigrodhakappa.
Kappamânavapukkhâ, t.c., 10 (ii), 203 sq.
Kapphina, *see* Mahâ-Kappina.
Kappina, *see* Mahâ-K.
Kapûd, *see* Animals (*i*).
Kâpya, *see* Kaisorya K., *and* Patañkala K.
Kar(a) fish, *see* Fish.
Kara Asabana, a Turanian, 23, 71, 71 n.
Karaka, a sect of mendicants, 21, 263; a *K.*-Adhvaryu cursed Yâgñavalkya, 26, 197; peculiar rites of the *K.* Adhvaryus, 26, 262 sq., 297 sq., 406 n.; 41, 171, 175; 43, 15, 129, 131; a *K.* teacher sacrificed at the Purushamedha, 44, 416; doctrines of *K.* refuted, 45, 237 sq., 237 n.
Karakandu, king of Kalinga, became a Gaina monk, 45, 87, 87 n.
Karâlaganaka, carried off a Brâhman's daughter, 49 (i), 45.
Kârambhiya, a naked ascetic, former birth of Devadatta, 35, 287.
Kârana Gana, founded by Srîgupta, 22, 291.
Karanas, *see* Veda (*g*).
Kâranas, celestial singers, 8, 232 n.; produced by Darkness, 25, 493, 493 sq. n.
Kâranâvasthâ, t.t., causal condition, 34, xxix.
Karanavat, Buddha's definition of the term, 10 (ii), 92.
Karap (Av. Karapan), idolatrous priests or priestly tribes hostile to Zoroaster, 37, 111 sq. and n., 238, 259, 279, 297, 336, 336 n.; 47, x, xiv sq., xxv, xxx, 19, 19 sq. n., 47, 50–7, 63–6, 99, 103, 107, 112 sq., 122 sq., 145–51, 163 sq.; five K. brothers, 47, xiv, 143 sq.
Kardâr-tôrâ, the Âspîgân, 47, 34, 34 n.
Karesna, son of Zbaurvant, 23, 209 209 n.
Karetô-dãsu, *see* Birds (*b*).
Karka, quoted, 12, 185 n.
Karmabhûmi, fifteen, parts of the world, 22, 195; one of the parts of the world where men live, 45, 225, 393.
Karma-kânda, and *Gñâna-kânda*, 1, lxiii, lxxx; 8, 227; systematized in the Kalpa-sûtras and Pûrva Mîmâmsâ-sûtras, 34, ix, xii; comprises Samhitâs and Brâhmanas, 34, ix; concerns the higher castes only, 34, xi; cannot lead to final release, 34, xxvii, xxix; its subject-matter, 34, 21, 24; activity depends on it, 34, 322; works enjoined in the K., 38, 184, 314 n.
Karman, Sk. t.t. (Pali Kamma), deeds, actions, works (of one existence, which bear fruit in another): soul of pious worshipper redescends with a remainder of k., 1, 81 sq.; 8, 236 sq., 240, 242 sq.; 34, lix; 38, 112–19, 398; 48, 589–92; causes the delay between the attainment of true knowledge and death and final release or union with Brahman, 1, 107 n.; 34, lxxviii; 38, 113, 117, 119, 237, 357 sq., 362 sq.; k. performed after the attainment of true knowledge, does not count, 1, 107 n.; k. and knowledge determine the state in which a being is reborn, 1, 274; *he comes to the river Vigarâ . . . and there shakes off his good and evil deeds. His beloved relatives obtain the good, his unbeloved relatives the evil he has done*, 1, 277; the Prâna does not increase by a good nor decrease by a bad k., 1, 299; k. will not cling to a man, if he surrenders all to the Lord, 1, 311, 314; the dying person says, 'Mind, remember thy deeds!' 1, 313; bears fruit even when done unintentionally, 2, 90; k. determines a man's future births, 2, 102 sq.; 7, 79–82; 8, 158, 232 sq., 321 sq.; 10 (ii), 107, 188; 11, 216 sqq., 271, 271 n.; 15, 257 sq.; 17, 109–11, 223–5; 19, 157 sq., 161, 202 sq., 223, 233; 22, 226; 25, 483–501; 35, 100 sq.; 36, 116–20,

230; 38, 114, 117, 117 n.; 41, 181, 181 n.; 45, 15, 59 sq., 82, 140; 48, 321 sq., 324, 328, 428, 487 sq., 590 sq.; 49 (i), 149–51; *the deed does not perish*, 2, 275, 275 n.; 8, 241; 10 (ii), 123; 14, 116, 310; 38, 353 sq.; 48, 149 sq., 722; outcasts are, after death, deprived of the rewards of meritorious deeds, 2, 280; *even as a calf finds his mother among a thousand cows, an act formerly done is sure to find the perpetrator*, 7, 82; sinners in hell are beaten with their deeds in a former existence, 7, 143; released from the bonds of k. the devotee is emancipated, comes to Krishna, 8, 47, 85, 101, 101 n., 246, 370; proceeds from nature, not from the soul, 8, 55, 104–6, 105 n., 106 n.; five causes of the completion of k., 8, 123, 123 n.; where the acts of one who is released from the body remain, 8, 235; beings cannot escape the effect of their own k., 8, 235, 239 sq.; 10 (i), 21 sq., 34 sq., 37 sq.; 19, 236; 36, 101; 45, 18, 30, 42, 59, 292 sq., 349; the soul takes with itself the results of good and evil k. when leaving the body, 8, 239; 38, 102; freedom from k. is not to be attained in this world, 8, 239 sq., 256 sq., 348, 348 n.; 35, 12; ruin connected with all k., 8, 245, 355; *the body is tied down by action*, 8, 307; by k. beings remain apart from the Brahman, 8, 315; as kinsmen receive a friend on his return, so his good works receive him who has done good, in the other world, 10 (i), 57; a good work is pleasant in the hour of death, 10 (i), 79; on the saint's attaining the right view, conceit and doubt and all his k. are left behind, 10 (ii), 38; to have done good deeds in a former existence, the highest blessing, 10 (ii), 44; *by work the world exists, by w. mankind exists, beings are bound by w. as the linch-pin of the rolling cart keeps the wheel on*, 10 (ii), 117; temporary effects of k., 11, 16 sq., 84; a sufficient cause for the existence of an Opapâtika, 11, 214 n.; fire-worshippers and *G*a*t*ilas hold the doctrine that actions have their reward, 13, 190 sq.; good and evil acts done in one's youth are annulled by living righteously in one's later age, 14, 176; the eternal greatness of the Brâhma*n*a is neither increased nor diminished by k., 14, 261, 274; the good deeds of a man lost, if he does not honour his guest, 15, 3; *what they said was k. (work), what they praised was k., viz. that a man becomes good by good work, and bad by bad work*, 15, 127, 176; 48, 478; is the cause of renewed existence, 15, 176; 22, 29; 34, xxvii; 38, 105, 121; 45, 43, 260, 389 sq., 389 n., 393 sq., 398; 48, 259, 313; 49 (i), 176 sq.; souls in the bonds of k., k. characteristic of souls, 15, 235; 34, 159 sq., 269; 38, 367, 369; 48, 193, 209, 215, 239, 280, 306, 313, 326, 378, 428, 459, 756–8; caused by desire, 19, 176; 25, lxvii, 29; there could be no good and evil works, if there were a God, 19, 208; if Self were the cause of the world, there could be no evil k., 19, 212; the good or evil deeds follow us as shadows, 19, 234; punishments in future births, 19, 263; 33, 262; 45, 375 sq.; he who has destroyed his k. reaches liberation, 19, 293; 45, 49, 106, 111 sq., 119, 141, 159, 161, 166, 289 sq., 297–301, 330–2; only wisdom can consume the fuel heaped up by the power of k., 19, 309; wishing gifts for which the donor expects a particular result in a future birth, 20, 9 n.; shedding the blood of a Buddha is a k. which will work out its effect in the immediate future, 20, 246; five kinds of deeds which bring about their effect in the present life, 20, 246 n.; the effect of causing a schism in the Sa*m*gha endures for a Kalpa, 20, 254, 267–71; 35, 163; the cause of diseases, 21, 130; 33, 87, 87 n.; 35, 152; accumulations of merits compared, 21, 316 sq., 317 n., 320–35; *G*ainas share the theory of k. with Buddhists and Brahmanic philosophers, 22, xxxiv; chief tenets of *G*ainism with regard to soul and k., 22, 1–3, 3 n.; knowing that misery results from action a wise man should destroy all k. and enter a

religious life, 22, 28–31, 40 sq., 75, 81; preventing the propensity to sin destroys former actions, 22, 33 sqq.; Âsrava is that by means of which k. takes effect upon the soul, parisrava that by which the influence of k. is counteracted, 22, 37 n.; those who abstain from cruelty relinquish k. and are flesh-subduing, 22, 39; diseases, death, and births, the fruit of former acts, 22, 53 sq.; a *G*aina monk should neither be pleased with nor prohibit the action of another which produces k., 22, 186–8; eight kinds of k., 22, 258; 45, 165, 165 n., 167, 172, 192–6; Mahâvîra exerted himself for the suppression of the defilement of k., 22, 262; Mahâvîra recited the fifty-five lectures on k. before he died, 22, 269; when their fourfold k. had been exhausted, Mahâvîra and other saints died, 22, 269, 275, 278, 285; k. alone follows a man to the next world, 25, lxviii, 166 sq.; ascetic makes over his good actions to his friends, his evil deeds to his enemies, 25, 212 sq.; the good k. of an ascetic or an Agnihotrin, if he dies without paying his debts, goes to the creditor, 33, 44 sq.; meritorious deeds of false witnesses lost, 33, 245; the reward of works is not the independent result of k. acting through the apûrva, but is allotted by the Lord, 34, lxv, 357–60; 38, 180–3; the shaking off of the good and evil k. takes place at the moment of the soul's departure from the body, 34, lxx sq.; 38, 225–31; even he whose k. is entirely annihilated, is yet connected with some kind of body, 34, lxxi; different degrees of pleasure the mere effects of k., 34, 27; final release not the effect of k., 34, 27 sq.; Brahman is not, like the embodied Self, subject to fruition of k., 34, 114–17, 119; not even the embodied soul is really subject to it, 34, 116; fruition of k. is the figment of false knowledge, 34, 116; Pubba-yoga = k., 35, 4; Makkhali Gosâla denies the doctrine of k., 35, 9 sq.; an impulse, the result of a previous k., 35, 18; renunciation of the monks, apparently the consequence of k., 35, 32 sq.; if there is no individuality, there are no results of good and evil k., 35, 41; *it is one name-and-form which has its end in death, and another name-and-form which is reborn. But the second is the result of the first, and is therefore not set free from its evil deeds*, 35, 71–5, 112 sq.; Sa*m*khâras, sorts of k., 35, 77 n.; eye, forms, sight, touch, sensation, longing, k., eye: a circle, 35, 80 sq.; the five Âyatanas caused by different k., 35, 100; *he does not die until that evil k. is exhausted*, 35, 103–6; good deeds are like the boat carrying stones, 35, 124; worms are born in animals by the power of evil k., 35, 151; good and evil k. bear fruit, whether he to whom they are done consents or not, 35, 152 sq.; problems of k., 35, 164 sq.; not all pain is caused by k., 35, 191–5; Pirit is a protection for those who restrain themselves from the evils of k., 35, 214, 218; the Bhikkhus who were harmed in consequence of Buddha's preaching, suffered, not through Buddha, but through their own deeds, 35, 234–7; the thief is not punished on account of some injunction of the Buddhas, but through his own deeds, 35, 256 sq.; k. more powerful than Iddhi, 35, 262 sq.; Bhikkhus who are free from evil k. can become Arhats at once, others have to perform meritorious acts, gifts, &c., 36, 92–6; beings exist either through k., or as the result of a cause, or produced by the seasons, 36, 103, 107 sq.; the k. of evil deeds made known in this life, good deeds generally rewarded in future births, virtue more powerful than vice, 36, 144–51; how k. works as a cause of death, 36, 162–6; k., the price offered in the bazaars of Buddha's 'City of Righteousness,' 36, 213, 213 sq. n., 216 sq., 220, 222, 229 sq.; evil, lust, and k. rooted out, 36, 219; wrong views of k., 36, 362; 45, 245; there is no confusion of k., because there is no extension of the acting and enjoying Self, 38, 68; souls find in the moon complete requital of their k., 38, 115; definite fruits

are attached to particular k., 38, 117; extinguished either by expiatory ceremonies or by the knowledge of Brahman or by the full fruition of their consequences, 38, 117 n.; k. whose operation is obstructed by other k. leading to fruits of a contrary nature lasts for a long time, 38, 117 sq.; some single k. are the causes of more than one new existence, 38, 118; the fruits of some k. enjoyed in this life already, 38, 118, 119; depends on conduct, 38, 120 sq.; the fruits of k., according to Gaimini, are brought about by the k. itself, 38, 182; their reaching maturity depends on place, time, and operative cause presenting themselves, 38, 328; k., the fruits of which are opposed to each other, 38, 328; the Ear created k., k. created Fire, 43, 379 sq.; right conduct and austerities produce destruction of all k., 45, xv sq., 157, 174, 249–61; Buddha taught the Akriyâvâda, Mahâvîra the Kriyâvâda, 45, xvi; the term da*n*d*a*, punishment, used for k., 45, xvii; waiting for the destruction of his k., a monk should bear all troubles, 45, 14; having shaken off the remnants of k., the pious will become an eternal Siddha, 45, 18; those who are ignorant of the Truth are subject to the pain of Sa*m*sâra consequent on k., 45, 24 sqq.; friends,relations,and possessions will not help those who suffer from their own deeds, 45, 25, 236, 260, 301 sq.; as water quits raised ground, so the sinful k. will quit him who does not injure living beings, 45, 33; how to conquer k., 45, 37 sq., 241; on the powerful influence of k., 45, 57–61, 140; King Nandana hewed down his k. like a forest, 45, 87; he who follows the Law is exempt from k. and suffering, 45, 90; a pious monk prevents the influx of k. (âsrava) through all bad channels, 45, 99, 140; the binding (bandha) of the soul by k., and annihilation of k., two of the nine truths or categories, 45, 154; influence of the observance of the 73 articles on the k., 45, 161–73; confession and repentance of sins annihilates k., 45, 162 sq.; four remnants of k. which even a Kevalin possesses, 45, 168, 168 n., 170 sq.; the gradual destruction of k., 45, 172 sq.; bad k. produced by love and hatred, 45, 174, 180 sq.; *love and hatred are caused by k., and they say that k. has its origin in delusion; k. is the root of birth and death, and birth and death they call misery*, 45, 185; the views of the Kriyâvâdins on k., 45, 242, 242 sq. n.; misery arises from wicked deeds, not from some Creator, 45, 245; all beings, even gods, &c., must suffer for their deeds, 45, 250; k. caused by unintentional sins, is annihilated through control, 45, 257 sq.; impelled by k. people do wrong, 45, 274; in hell, those whose bad k. takes effect, punish others whose bad k. takes effect, 45, 281; *whatever cruelty he has done in a former birth, the same will be inflicted on him in the Circle of Births*, 45, 286; having annihilated his k., a monk should not again mix with the world, 45, 297, 323; two kinds of k., the one of momentary existence (airyapathika) and the other lasting (sâmparâyika), 45, 298 n., 364 sq., 364 n.; has six sources, viz. the six Âsravas, 45, 316, 316 n.; denied by the Akriyâvâdins, 45, 316; men cannot annihilate their k. by new k., but by abstention from k., 45, 318 sq.; the water of the lotus-pool compared to k., 45, 338; how a monk ceases to acquire gross k., 45, 352; a monk should preach the law for no other motive than the annihilation of k., 45, 354; actions by which bad k. accrues to a man, 45, 356–63, 364 n.; *when he leaves this body and is only accompanied by his k., he, without a will of his own, goes forth from womb to womb, from birth to birth, from death to death, from hell to hell*, 45, 361; if there is a residue of k., the pious monk is reborn in one of the regions of the gods, 45, 380 sq.; those who lead a religious life according to the 13th kind of acquiring k. will put an end to all misery, 45, 388; k. is the result of every action, even of beings without

intellect or consciousness, 45, 398–405, 399 n.; *G*ainas must believe in realization and annihilation of k., 45, 407; Mahâvîra acquires no new k., 45, 413; through the taking effect of the k. movable beings become immovable and vice versâ, 45, 424; Nescience in the form of k. good and evil, 48, 88, 147, 198, 306, 756–8; k. the root of Nescience, and Nescience the root of k., 48, 127, 259, 271; the world due to k., 48, 128 sq.; Apûrva, i.e. supersensuous result of k. which later on produces the sensible result, 48, 153–5; causes connexion of soul and body, and hence implies endless suffering, 48, 215, 239, 607, 609 sq., 616; in the Sa*m*sâra state the soul's bliss and knowledge are contracted owing to k., 48, 232; inequality of creation and the creatures' experiencing pain due to k., 48, 478 sq.; *the body's being ruled by the soul is due to the unseen principle in the form of good and evil works, and has for its end the requital of those works*, 48, 523; the effect of k. exhausted only through complete enjoyment of their results, 48, 651; knowledge of Brahman destroys all k., good and evil, 48, 693; the fruits of good k. perish on the death of the devotee, 48, 724; only those good and evil works, the effects of which have not yet begun, are destroyed by knowledge, 48, 724 sq.; where there is action, there is death, 49 (i), 73; the results of k. are inconceivable, 49 (ii), 37; the obstacle of k. removed by meditation on Avalokite*s*vara, 49 (ii), 183. *See also* Lê*s*yâ, Sin, Transmigration, *and* Works (*c*).

Karma-yoga and Sâṅkhya-yoga, 8, 105, 105 n.

Kar*n*a, a Kaurava, 8, 38; 'the charioteer's son,' 8, 95 sq., 95 n.

Karpans, opposed to Righteousness, 31, 63, 140; opponents of Zoroaster, 31, 65; gave the Kine to rapine, 31, 121; their angry zeal, 31, 158; are no friends to the creatures, 31, 177, 184; Haoma invoked against Kavis and K., 31, 236.

Kâr*s*akeyîputra, n. of a teacher, 15, 226, 226 n.

Karsêvaz, n.p., 5, 135.

Karshipta, *see* Birds (*b*).

Kârsh*n*â*g*ini, quoted in the Vedânta-sûtras, 34, xix; 38, 119 sq.; 48, 591 sq.

Karshvares, seven, of the earth, 4, 213, 222, 222 n. *See also* Geography.

Kar*s*ipt, *see* Birds (*b*).

Kârtavîrya, i.e. King Ar*g*una, a descendant of K*ri*tavîrya, 8, 293.

Kart*ri*, worshipped at the Tarpa*n*a, 30, 244.

Kârttikeya, son of Bhava (*S*iva), 49 (i), 16.

Kâru*n*ika, the 75th Tathâgata, 49 (ii), 7.

***K*ârvâkas** (materialists), attack Vedas and Brâhma*n*as, 8, 214; make no distinction between soul and matter, 48, 196. *See also* Materialists.

Kâryâvasthâ, condition of an effect, 34, xxix.

Kâ*s*akr*i*tsna, quoted by Baudhâyana, 14, xl n.; quoted in the Vedânta-sûtras, 34, xix, xcix, 278–83; 48, 392, 394 sq.

Kasar*n*îla (or Kasar*n*îra), a serpent, 42, 154, 607.

Kashaka, initiated boy given in charge to, 30, 153.

Kâshâya*n*a, n. of a teacher, 15, 186, 186 n.

Kâ*s*î, kings of, celebrate the death of Mahâvîra, 22, 266.

Kasibhâradvâ*g*a, the Brâhma*n*a, reproaches Gotama with idleness, 10 (ii), 11–15; Buddha refused an alms of K., 36, 37.

Kasibhâradvâ*g*asutta, t.c., 10 (ii), 11–15.

Kâ*s*ikâ, the harlot of Kâ*s*î, went to the heaven of the gods, 49 (i), 190.

Kâ*s*is, do not keep up the sacrificial fires, 44, 401.

Kâ*s*î*s*vara, worshipped at the Tarpa*n*a, 30, 244.

Kâ*s*î-Videhas, n. of a people, 1, 300.

Kassapa, n. of a *Ri*shi, 11, 172. *See also* Ka*s*yapa, Kâ*s*yapa, Lomasa-K., *and* Pûra*n*a-K.

Kassapa, or Kassapabuddha, one of the seven Buddhas, 10 (ii), 40; 11, 163; 35, 4, 173; 36, 20–2; rain

fell on his hut, while the potter's hut remained dry, 36, 23–5.

Kassapa-gotta, of Vâsabha-gâma, wrongly expelled from the Order, 17, 256–61.

Kasupatu, son of Ara, 23, 211.

Kasvi, or Spite, the Daêva, 4, 224.

Kâsya King, *S*atânîka took away the horse of the, 44, 401.

Kasyapa, the Muni, the goddess of the Earth went to, 7, 5 sq.; K. or Pragâpati, 8, 389 n.; one of the seven *Ri*shis, 15, 106; daughters of Daksha married to K., 25, 352; the threefold age of K., 29, 55; 30, 162; worshipped, 29, 319; 30, 244; all creatures descended from K., 41, 390; slew the Rakshas, 42, 33; K.'s charm to secure perfect health, 42, 45; the eye of K., 42, 68, 403; created talismans, 42, 80; incantation of K., 42, 107, 255; the self-existing K. born from Time, 42, 225, 686; the sun, 42, 403 sq.; in the Atharva-veda, 42, 403 sq.; officiated as priest at Visvakarman's (Sarvamedha) sacrifice, 44, 421. *See also* Harita K., *and* Silpa K.

Kâsyapa (Pali Kassapa), n. of a family: Buddha exercises magical powers for the *Ga*tilas Uruvelâ K., Nadî K., and Gayâ K., who are finally converted, 13, 118–34; 19, xxiii, 183–7; 49 (i), 192; receive the upasampadâ ordination from Buddha, 13, 131 sqq.; K. of Gayâ, or Gayâ-K., a distinguished Arhat, 21, 2, 198; K. addressed by Buddha, 21, 118 sqq., 198; Buddha's prophecy about K. who is to be the Buddha Rasmiprabhâsa, 21, 142–4; Siddhârtha of the K. gotra, 22, 191, 193, 226, 255; relations of Mahâvîra belonging to the K. gotra, 22, 193, 256; Tîrthakaras of the K. gotra, 22, 218; 45, 260 n.; the Arhat *Ri*shabha belonged to the K. gotra, 22, 282; 45, 138; Sthaviras of the K. gotra, 22, 286 sq., 290, 292 sq., 294 sq.; Mahâvîra was of the K. gotra, 22, 287; 45, xxi; Kapila, son of K. of Kausâmbî, 45, 31 sq. n.; K. of Râ*g*ag*ri*ha becomes Buddha's disciple and a chief of Arhats, 49 (i), 193 sq.; Gayâ-K., n. of a Bhikshu, 49 (ii), 2. *See also* Uruvilvâ-K., Nadî-K., Kumâra-K., *and* Mahâ-K.

Kâsyapa, a Brâhma*n*a, addressed as Parantapa, 8, 205; a Brâhma*n*a who was taught by a Siddha, 8, 231–6; K. and other sages ask Brahman about final emancipation, 8, 314.

Kâsyapa, a teacher, quoted by Baudhâyana, 14, xl n., 207 sq.

Kasyapa Mârî*k*a, author of Vedic hymns, 46, 128.

Kasyapa Naidhruvi, n. of a teacher, 12, xxxiii; 15, 226.

Kasyapas and Gandharvas, 42, 210.

Kâsyapî-bâlâkyâ-mâ*th*arîputra, n. of a teacher, 15, 224 n.

Kâsyapîyâ *S*âkhâ of the Mânava Ga*n*a, 22, 292.

Kâta, n.p., 23, 218.

Kata Vaisvâmitra, author of Vedic hymns, 46, 275, 277.

Kataka, adultery of, 2, 175 n.

Katama, 'Whoever,' and Ka worshipped, 44, 254 n., 291 n., 292.

Ka*t*amoraka-tissaka, a follower of Devadatta, 20, 251.

Katâyûn was with Frê*d*ûn, 5, 133.

Kâ*th*aka, school of the Black Yagur-veda, its high antiquity, 7, xiv–xvi, xxv–xxvii; quoted in the Vâsish*th*a Dharma-sûtras, 7, xx; sacrifices recorded in a book called K., 38, 196; gives the mantras of the Asva-medha, 44, xvi.

Kâ*th*aka-Dharma-sûtra, the basis of the Vish*n*u-sm*ri*ti, 25, xxi, xxiii, lxvi, lxx.

Kâ*th*aka-G*ri*hya-sûtra, and Vish-*n*u-sm*ri*ti, 7, x–xvi, xxix, xxxi; 25, xxi, xxiii; and Mânava-G*ri*hya-sûtra, 7, xxvi, xxvii n.

Ka*th*as, their views quoted, 29, 414.

Ka*th*a-upanishad, quoted as a Yoga-sâstra, 8, 211 sq., 415; introduction and translation, 15, xxi–xxv, 1–24; quoted in the Vedânta-sûtras, 34, xlii, 249; 38, 424; 48, 775.

Kathâ-Vatthu, and Milindapañha, 36, xx–xxvii.

Ka*th*ina ceremonies, *see* Bhikkhus (*d*), *and* Sa*m*gha.

***K*athvaraspa**, n.p., 23, 217, 217 n.

Ka*t*issabha, became an inheritor of the highest heavens, 11, 26.

Katu, n.p., 23, 213.

Kâtumâ, the Sâkyas of, 35, 301 sq.
Kâturhotra, mystery of the symbolical, 8, 277–80.
Kâturmâsya, t.t., *see* Sacrifices (*i*).
Katurmukha, a mighty being, dwelling in this world, 48, 90.
Katuryugas, or four ages of the world, 7, 78.
Katushtoma, t.t., succession of chants in which four hymn-forms (Stomas) are used, 44, 329 sq. and n.
Kâtya, quoted by Baudhâyana, 14, xl, 155. *See* Utkîla K.
Kâtyâyana, author of the Vârttikas, and Yâgñavalkya, 12, xxxv–xxxix; author of the Vâgasaneyi-Prâtisâkhya, 12, xxxviii, xl; Prabhava of the K. gotra, 22, 287; honoured as teacher, 29, 141. *See also* Kabandhin K., *and* Mahâ-K.
Kâtyâyana-smriti, quotes Manu or Bhrigu, 25, cx; its date, 33, xvi.
Kâtyâyanî, and Maitreyî, the two wives of Yâgñavalkya, 15, 108, 181.
Kâtyâyanîputra, n. of a teacher, 15, 224 sq.
Kâtyâyanîya-sûtra, quoted, 25, cxix n.; 44, xxxix.
Kâu (n. of a state and dynasty): duke of *K.*, son of King Wăn, 3, xvii; the books of the dynasty of *K.* in the Shû, their credibility, 3, 12; period of the *K.* dynasty, 3, 22; 'the Books of *K.*' translated, 3, 124–272; the sacrificial odes of *K.*, 3, 313–36; troubles of Wăn and the tyrant *K.*, 16, 403; overthrown by Wăn and Wû, 27, 396; 40, 171, 173, 178; ruled with violence, 28, 418; killed the prince Pî-kan, 39, 205; bad times under Kieh and *K.*, 39, 386; perished, 40, 131; *K.* and Kieh, examples of bad men, though sovereigns, 40, 177. *See also* Kwang-ȝze, *and* Tan.
Kauda, t.t., tonsure rite, *see* Child (*b*).
Kâu-Făng, refuses Duke Âi an interview, but sends him a message, 27, 191.
Kauhalîyas, quoted, 30, 85.
Kâu-hsin, or Shâu, last sovereign of the Shang dynasty, 3, 120 sq., 123 n.; his wickedness denounced by Wû, his defeat, 3, 124–32, 135 sq.; warning to *K.* by King Wăn, 3, 410–12; King Wăn submitted to him, but not King Wû, 39, 359.
Kâu Kiang, *see* Thâi-kiang.
Kâu-kien, and his minister Kung, 40, 111, 111 n.
Kaükthasta = Kaukûsta, 26, 426 n.
Kaukûsta, gave twenty-four heifers as dakshinâs, 26, 426.
Kaula, or Kaula-karman, t.t., tonsure rite, *see* Child (*b*).
Kâu Lî, the Rites of Kâu, or Kâu Kwan, the Officers of Kâu, the first of the 'Three Rituals,' 3, xviii.
Kâu-mang, attending spirit of Thâi Hâo, 27, 250, 250 n., 257, 262.
Kaundinya, n. of teachers, 15, 118, 118 n., 186, 186 n.; 30, 245, 245 n.; K.-kulaputra, the first disciple of Buddha, 19, 172, 178; Âgñâta-K., a distinguished Arhat, 21, 2, 34, 198; 49 (ii), 2; Yasodâ, wife of Mahâvîra, belonged to the K. gotra, 22, 193, 256, 286.
Kaundinyâyana, n. of a teacher, 15, 118 n., 186 n.
Kaunthâravya, n. of a teacher, 1, 255, 258.
Kaurama, made liberal gifts to Brâhmanas, 42, 197, 690.
Kauravas, and Pândavas, battle of, 8, 2 sq., 37 sq.; Arguna, best of K., 8, 311 sq.; a noble family, followers of a king, 45, 339.
Kauravya King, Balhika Prâtipîya, 44, 269.
Kauravyâyanîputra, n. of a teacher, 15, 189.
Kâûs (Kahôs, Kaî-Kâûs, Av. Kavi Usa): legend of Neryosengh and K. who became mortal, 4, 262 sq. n.; could not escape from death, 4, 380; son of Kaî-Apîvêh, 5, 136, 136 n.; his reign of 150 years, 5, 150, 217; sacrificed to Anâhita, 23, 65, 65 n.; his chariot carried by the raven, 23, 241 sq.
Kausalika, King, his daughter Bhadrâ, 45, 50 n., 53.
Kausalya Âsvalâyana, n. of a sage, 15, 271, 276; Para Âtnâra, the K. king, 44, 397.
Kausâmbeya, *see* Proti K.
Kausâmbî, n. of a great town, 45, 102.
Kausambikâ Sâkhâ of the Uttarabalissaha Gana, 22, 290.

Kaushîtaka, *see* Kahola K.

Kaushîtaka-Grihya, *see* Sâmbavya-Grihya.

Kaushîtaki, quoted, 1, 12, 280, 285; 29, 112. *See also* Kahola K.

Kaushîtaki-brâhmana and K.-upanishad, 1, xcviii sq.; passes over Râgasûya and horse-sacrifice, 44, xvi; on the sacrifice at the building of the fire-altar, 44, xxxix; on the Pravargya rite, 44, xlvii, xlix n.

Kaushîtaki - brâhmana - upanishad, or Kaushîtaki-upanishad, 1, xcii n., xcviii–c, 269–307; belongs to the Rig-veda, 1, xcviii; two recensions of it, 1, xcix; quoted, 8, 415; 34, xlii; 38, 424 sq.; 48, 775.

Kaushîtakins, quoted by Âsvalâyana, 29, 194; have seventeen priests, 43, 348 n.

Kaushîtaki-upanishad, *see* Kaushîtaki-brâhmana-upanishad.

Kausika, n. of a teacher, 15, 118, 186; Sthaviras of the K. gotra, 22, 288, 290, 293; Ahalyâ, wife of the Rishi K., 26, 81 n.; Indra called K., 26, 82, 82 n.; K. and Kusika, 42, xxvi. *See also* Gâthin.

Kausikâ, *see* Sandhanî K.

Kausika-sûtra, quoted, 42, xix, xxiii, lvii, lxi sq.; charms in the K., 42, 233, &c.; books of the Atharva-veda not in the K., 42, 676.

Kausikâyani, n. of a teacher, 15, 119, 186, 186 n.

Kausikîputra, n. of a teacher, 15, 225.

Kausurubindi, *see* Proti Kausâmbeya K.

Kauthumas, their views quoted, 29, 414.

Kautika Gana, founded by Susthita and Supratibuddha, 22, 292; Durgaya Krishna of the K. gotra, 22, 294 n. *See also* Susthita K.

Kautsa, quoted by Âpastamba, 2, xxvii sq., 70, 88; attacks the authority of the Vedas, 8, 214; n. of a teacher, 15, 227; Sivabhûti of the K. gotra, 22, 294; soma to be bought from a K. Brâhman, 26, 474; quoted by Gobhila, 30, 97; pupil of Mâhitthi, 43, 404.

Kautsîputra, n. of a teacher, 15, 224 n.

Kautumbinî (or Kundadharî) Sâkhâ of the Uttarabalissaha Gana, 22, 290.

Kavâd (or Kaî-Kabâd, or Kaî-Kobâd), Av. Kavi Kavâta, brought up by Aûzôbô, 5, 136, 136 n.; his descendants, 5, 136 sq.; was fifteen years, 5, 150; of a glorious race, 18, 90, 90 n.; son of Farhank, 18, 171, 171 n.; Khûsrô son of K., 18, 298; ruler of Iran, founder of the Kayân dynasty, 23, 222, 222 n., 303; 24, 62 sq. and n.; 37, 28, 29 n., 224 n.; 47, 12 sq.; his accession, 47, xxix.

Kavañgara, deluded by a woman, 19, 44.

Kavârazem, n.p. 23, 207, 207 n.

Kavasha, Rishis descended from, 48, 690.

Kâvasheya, *see* Tura K.

Kâvasheyas, Rishis who only offer as a sacrifice breath in speech, 1, 265 sq., and n.

Kavâta, *see* Kavâd.

Kavi, son of Añgiras, called his elders 'little sons,' 25, 58; Somapas (manes), sons of K. (Bhrigu), 25, 112.

Kavi, n.p., 23, 213, 215, 218.

Kavî-Kavâd, *see* Kavâd.

Kavis (or Kavîgs, or Kîgs, or Kîks, or Kaîs), and Karaps, hostile priestly tribe, oppose Zarathustra, 31, 56, 64 sq.; 37, 111 sq. n., 238, 259, 279, 297, 336, 336 n.; 47, xxv, 19, 19 sq. n., 47, 64–6, 99, 107, 112, 122 sq., 163–5; hostile to the Kine, 31, 121; evil-doers, 31, 140, 183; Haoma invoked against K. and Karpans, 31, 236; ruling priests at the time of Zoroaster's birth, 47, x; Zoroaster preaches to K. and Karaps, 47, x, xxv, 50–7; demons and K., 47, 47, 98; better than an evil ruler, 47, 103.

Kâvya, a version of Manu's Code ascribed to, 33, xii.

Kayadha, Sraosha, the conqueror of the, 31, 301; prayer for the dislodgement of the K., 31, 313; the holy man who is innocent of the K., 31, 342.

Kayâns, heroes, rulers, 5, 108, 108 n.; 47, 121, 128 sq.; race and genealogy of K., 5, 130–40; glory of the K., 37, 222, 222 n., 227, 227 n., 229;

dynasty established by Kaî-Kobâ*d*, 47, 12.
Kâyasthas or scribes, *see* Caste (*a*).
***K*eh**, called Ȝze-yû, brother of Sû Shih, 40, 320 n.
***K*ekitâna**, n. of a warrior, 8, 37.
***K*elaka** *S*â*nd*ilyâyana, quoted, 43, 364.
Kena-upanishad, or Talavakâra-upanishad, 1, lxvi, lxxxix–xci, 145–53; belongs to a *S*âkhâ of the Talavakâras of the Sâma-veda, 1, lxxxix; works on the K., 1, xci; a text of the K. belonging to the Atharva-veda, 1, xci; quoted, 8, 416; 38, 425; 48, 775.
Ke*n*iya, a *G*a*t*ila ascetic, pays honour to Buddha, 10 (ii), 96–105; 17, 129–34.
***K*en *K*hin**, on sacrifices, 27, 35.
Keresâni, dethroned by Haoma, 31, 237 sq., 237 n.
Keresaokhshan, n.p., 23, 205.
Keresâspa (Keresâsp, Kerê*s*âspô, Garshâsp), the Sâmân, or Sâm (Sâhm), and Knâthaiti, 4, 6, 6 n.; killed Azi Srvara (Sruvar), 4, 259; 18, 217 n., 370 sq., 374; 24, 268, 268 n.; slays Az-i Dahâk, 5, 119 n., 235, 235 n.; 18, 78, 111, 372; 24, 110 n.; 37, 203 n.; 47, xiii, 114, 163 n.; brother of Aûrvakhsh, 5, 137, 137 n.; legends of (the soul of) K., 18, xxviii, 39, 39 n., 369–82; 37, 198 sq., 452; aided in the renovation, 18, 78; full of strength, 18, 90; 23, 326; war his husbandry, 18, 173, 173 n.; sacrificed to Anâhita, and overcame the Ga*n*darewa, 23, 63 sq. and n., 256 n.; protected by the Fravashis, 23, 194 sq., 195 n.; Fravashi of K. worshipped, 23, 223; killed Hitâspa, to avenge his brother, 23, 255, 255 n.; worships Vayu, 23, 255 sq.; seized the Glory that had departed from Yima, 23, 295; his deeds of valour, 23, 295–7; 24, 63, 63 n.; 47, 12, 12 n.; where his body lies, 24, 110; or Sâm Narîmân, 24, 268, 268 n.; the dragon-slayer K., son of Thrita, 31, 234; ruler of Iran, 37, 28; exhorted by Tûs, adopts the religion, 37, 225.
Kerê*s*âspô, *see* Keresâspa.
Keresavazda, or Kêrsêvazd, killed by Husravah, 23, 304, 304 n.; 47, 14.
Kesakambali, *see* Agita-Kesakambali.
Ke*s*ânta, *see* Hair.
Kesaraprâbandhâ, the she-goat of, 42, 170, 432 sq.
Ke*s*arin, the 65th Tathâgata, 49 (ii), 7.
Ke*s*ava (Prâkrit Kêsava), n. of K*r*ish*n*a or Vish*n*u, 7, 7; 8, 40, 49, 52, 87, 96; son of King Vasudêva, 45, 112; asked Râ*g*îmatî in marriage for Arish*t*anemi, 45, 113; Râma and K. pay homage to Arish*t*anemi, 45, 115. *See also* K*r*ish*n*a, *and* Vish*n*u.
Ke*s*avapanîya, *see* Hair.
***K*êshmak**, the whirlwind demon, 47, 28, 28 n.; the Karap *K*. attacks Zoroaster, 47, 63.
Kêsi, leader of Pâr*s*va's sect at the time of Mahâvîra, 45, xxi sq., 119–29.
Ke*s*in, K*r*ish*n*a the destroyer of, 8, 121; Rudra casts down the car of K., 42, 157, 620 sq.; the king of the K. whose samrâ*g*-cow was killed by a tiger, 44, 131–4.
Ke*s*inî, n. of a giantess, 21, 374; a demon harassing children, 30, 211.
Ketâ, identified with Agni, 29, 348.
***K*etaka**, king of Vai*s*âlî, patron of *G*ainas, 22, xii sq.
***K*etas**, Devadatta, born as a king of the, 35, 287.
***K*etiyas**, or shrines, 11, 4, 66, 40, 58. *See also* Holy places.
***K*etokhila-Sutta**, treatise on Barrenness and Bondage, on the Buddhist Order of Mendicants, 11, x, 219–34.
Ke*t*ubha, a branch of learning, 10 (ii), xiii, 98, 189.
Ketumatî, a palace in heaven, 35, 11 sq.
Kêvâ*d*, Khûsrô son of, 5, 193, 201.
Kevala, *G*aina t.t., highest knowledge and intuition, 22, 189, 201 sq., 217 sq., 258, 263, 271, 273, 277, 283; 45, 380, 418.
Kevalin (possessed of Kevala), title of Mahâvîra, 22, 201, 263; the rank of the K. higher than that of the gods, 45, 30 n.; both the nun Râ*g*îmatî and the monk Rathanêmi become K., 45, 119; even a K. possesses the four remnants of Karman, 45, 168, 168 n., 170 sq.

Kha (ether), is Brahman, 1, 65, 65 n. *See* Ether.

***Kh*abbaggiya** Bhikkhus, and Bhikkhunîs, the constant evil-doers in the Vinaya-Pi*t*aka, 13, 213 n., 213 sq., 226, 247, 249, 258, 262–5, 300 sq., 329 sq., 340 sq.; 17, 14 sqq., 17 sq., &c., 329 n.; 22, 1, &c., 9 n., 336 (Bhikkhunîs).

Khâdira-G*ri*hya-sûtra, an abridgement of the Gobhila-G*ri*hya-sûtra, 29, 371–3; text and translation, 29, 374–435.

Khadirava*n*ika, n. of a Bhikshu, 49 (ii), 2.

Khaggavisâ*n*asutta, t.c., 10 (ii), 6–11.

Khâkân, sovereign Khân of invaders from the east, 47, xviii, 103, 103 n.

***Kh*aluka** Rôhagupta, disciple of Mahâgiri, 22, 290; a *G*aina teacher, said to be the founder of the Vai*s*eshika philosophy, 45, xxxvii sq.

***Kh*a*m*daka**, *see K*andaka.

Kha*n*da-devî, son of, a follower of Devadatta, 20, 251.

Kha*n*dahâla, n. of Devadatta born as a Brâhma*n*a, 35, 290.

***Kh*andaka**, and Udâyin become Buddhist monks, 49 (i), 195.

***Kh*andakas**, offer to nourish the prince Bodhisattva, 19, 355, 355 n.

Khanda-parittâ, a protecting charm, 35, 213.

***Kh*andas**, *see* Metres.

Khandhâ, Pali t.t., the five aggregates, the cause of individuality, 11, 148 n. *See* Aggregates, *and* Skandhas.

Kha*n*dika Audbhâri, instructs the king of the Ke*s*in, 44, 131–4.

***Kh*ândogya-brâhma*n*a**, and *Kh*ândogya-upanishad, 1, lxxxvi sq.

***Kh*ândogya-upanishad**, 1, lxxxvi–lxxxix, 1–144; belongs to the Sâma-veda, 1, lxxxvi; works on the *Kh*., 1, lxxxviii sq.; quoted, 8, 416; 38, 425–7; 48, 775–7; revealed to mankind by Manu, 25, lx sq.; most of the passages discussed in the Vedânta-sûtras are taken from the *Kh*., 34, xli–xlv; creation according to *Kh*., 38, 4 sq.; Udgîtha-vidyâ of *Kh*., 38, 192–9.

Khang, honorary title of *K*âo, son of *Kh*ăng, 3, 243, 250; worshipped as an ancestor, 3, 319; funeral rites for King K., 27, 186 sq.; conferred privileges on Lû, 28, 253 sq.

***Kh*ăng**, or Sung, son of King Wû, 3, 154–6, 155 n.; his 'great announcement,' when going to put down the revolt of Shang, 3, 156–61; King *Kh*. and the foundation of the new capital of Lo, 3, 188–95; duke of *Kh*âu addresses instructions to King *Kh*., 3, 200–5; his testamentary charge and death, 3, 234–42; his five pairs of gems, 3, 239, 239 n.; operations against wild tribes on the Hwâi river in his reign, 3, 267 sq.; addressing the princes on his accession to the government, 3, 315; sacrificial ode for him, 3, 316 sq., 377; worshipped as an ancestor, 3, 319, 321, 321 n.; worships in the temple of his father, 3, 326, 328–31; suspects the fidelity of the duke of *K*âu, 3, 330; addressed by the duke of Shâo, 3, 404; what he did for the Lî King, 27, 6 sq.; his training, 27, 23, 344 sq., 351, 351 sq. n.; the duke of *K*âu governs for the young *Kh*., 27, 29; 28, 31; mourning rites for Duke *Kh*. of Thăng, 27, 187; one of the six great men, 27, 366; King Wăn who was *Kh*., 28, 60; Duke *Kh*. assisted by *K*wang Shû, 28, 252; *Kh*. and Khang conferred privileges on Lû, 28, 253 sq.; about the Tâo, 40, 292. *See also* Wăn.

***Kh*ang Hung**, on music, 28, 122; was ripped open, 39, 283, 283 n.; killed in Shû, 40, 131, 131 n.

***Kh*ang *K*î**, asked *K*ung-nî about Wang Thâi, 39, 223–6.

Khang Shû, *see* Făng.

***Kh*ang-wû Ȝze**, his conversation with *Kh*ü Ȝhiâo-ȝze, 39, 192 sq. and n.; 40, 279; questions Ȝze-lâo, 40, 121 sq., 121 n.

***Kh*ang Yü**, n. of a sage, 40, 96.

***Kh*ăng-ȝze**, on mutual love of husband and wife, 16, 313 n.

***Kh*ăng-ȝze Kâo**, tells *Kh*ing Î how he wishes to be buried, 27, 155, 155 n.

***Kh*ăn Hăng**, *see* Thien *Kh*ăng-ȝze.

***Kh*ăn Hû**, minister of Thâi-wû, 3, 207.

***Kh*ăn Kan-hsî**, wishes his con-

cubines to be buried with him, 27, 183 sq.
*Kh*ăn *Kh*ăng-ȝze, *see* Thien *Kh*ăng-ȝze.
*Kh*ăn *Kh*î-*k*î, pursues the army of Wû, 27, 185 sq., 186 n.
*Kh*anna, n. of an obstinate Bhikkhu, 11, 112 sq., 113 n.; 17, 370 sq., 374 sq.; 20, 34, 381–5.
Khan-pei, got the Tâo, and became lord of Khwăn-lun, 39, 244, 244 n.
*Kh*ăn Ȝze-khang, on burying living persons with the dead, 27, 182, 182 n.
*Kh*ăn Ȝze-*k*ü, about burying some living persons with him, 27, 181 sq.
Khâo, duke of *K*û-lü, mourning rites for, 27, 193.
*Kh*âo, succeeded to King *K*âo, 3, 250.
Khâo-fû, the Correct, his humility, 39, 161; 40, 209 sq. and n.
Khara, n. of a Yakkha, 10 (ii), 45.
Kharaskandha, a chief of demons, 21, 6.
Kharedhar, ancestor of Zoroaster, 47, 140.
Khâulah bint THa'labah, a divorced wife, appeals to Mohammed, 9, 270, 270 n.
*Kh*âyâ, or Lakshmî, the wife of Vish*n*u, 7, 3.
Khema, i.e. Nibbâna, *see* Nirvâ*n*a.
Khemâ, a nun, dialogue between her and King Pasenadi, 45, xxix.
Khettagina, Buddha's definition of the term, 10 (ii), 90.
*Kh*î, n. of a minister of Agriculture, 3, 16 sq., 42 sq., 42 n., 56–8, 124, 319 sq., 323; the son and successor of Yü, 3, 60, 76 sq.; ancestor of the *K*âu dynasty, 3, 134, 134 n.; or Hâu-*k*î, son of *K*iang Yüan, and father of husbandry, 3, 341 sq.; 341 n.; sacrificed to under the name of *K*i, 28, 208, 208 n. (cf. 3, 57). *See also* Hâu-*k*i.
*Kh*î, count of, 3, 122 sq. and n., 136–49; Ȝze-kâo's mission to the king of *Kh*., 39, 132, 210–14.
*Kh*iang, Zui wishes to resign the post of Minister of Works in favour of, 3, 43, 43 n.
*Kh*ieh, sprites haunting furnaces, 40, 19.
*Kh*ieh *Kh*âu, the vehement debater, 39, 312, 312 n.
*Kh*ieh-yû, the madman of *Kh*û, and Confucius, 39, 132, 221 sq. and n.
*Kh*ieh-yü, teaches *K*ien Wû, 39, 137, 260; described the Spirit-like man, 39, 170 sq.
*Kh*ien, *see* Sze-mâ *Kh*.
*Kh*ien Âo, offers food to the hungry during a famine, 27, 194 sq.
*Kh*ih-*k*ang Man-*kh*î, and Măn Wû-kwei converse together about Shun, 39, 324 sq. and n., 326 n.
*Kh*î Hsieh, title of a book quoted by *K*wang-ȝze, 39, 165.
*Kh*ih-wei, a historiographer, 40, 124 sq., 124 n., 138, 138 n.
*Kh*ih-Yû, the first to create disorder, 3, 27, 255, 255 n.; Hwang-Tî fought with *Kh*., 40, 171–3, 171 n.
*Kh*ih-*Z*ăn, a saying of his quoted, 3, 106, 106 n.
*Kh*î Kung, a Tâoist teacher, 40, 42.
*Kh*î Liang, his death, and mourning of his wife, 27, 188.
*Kh*in, destruction of the classical literature by the tyrant of, 3, xvii sq., 6–8, 285; speech of the marquis of *Kh*., 3, 270–2; offered sacrifices to eight spirits, 39, 41, 41 n.
*Kh*ing, the wood-carver, and his bell-stand, 40, 22 sq.
*Kh*ing Î, asks *Kh*ăng-ȝze Kâo how he wishes to be buried, 27, 155.
*Kh*ing *K*ăng *K*ing, or 'The Classic of Purity' translated and explained, 40, 247–54.
*Kh*ing-*k*î, son of King *K*ing of *K*âu, 40, 31, 31 n.
*Kh*in Hwa-lî, disciple of Mo Tî, 40, 218, 218 n., 221.
*Kh*in *K*ang, had got the Tâo, 40, 283.
*Kh*in of Hsiang-lî, a Mohist, 40, 220.
*Kh*in Shih, condoles on Lâo-ȝze's death, 39, 201; 40, 314 sq.
*Kh*iu = Confucius, q.v.
*Kh*iû, another name of *Kh*ang-wû Ȝze, 39, 192 n., 193, 195.
*Kh*iung, or Po-*kh*iung, appointed by King Mû as High Chamberlain, 3, 252 sq.
*Kh*o, killed by Lî Kho, 28, 294.
Khordâd, *see* Haurvatâ*t*.
Khorshêd, *see* Sun.
Khosrav, *see* Husravah.

Khrafstras, Zd., t.t., noxious animals, 4, 77 n. *See* Animals (*b*).
Khrû, and Khrûighni, n. of demons, 4, 145 sq., 145 n.
Khrûtâsp, Dahâk son of, 5, 131. *See also* Aurva*d*âsp.
Khshathra, Sovereign Power, 31, 5, 12, 128, 167; invoked with Ahura and other Ameshâspends, 31, 14, 19; of Ahura produces every good thing, 31, 176, 178 sq.; invoked to appear in the village, 31, 310.
Khshathra-Vairya, or Shatraver, 'Good Government,' archangel, 4, liii, 213; 5, 10 n.; 37, 291 sq., 291 n., 387, 411 sq.; inventor of knife-medicine, 4, 226 sq., 227 n.; invoked and worshipped, 4, 245; 23, 5, 14, 36 sq., 351, 353; 31, 196, 256, 280, 325, 361, 387; creature of Ahura-Mazda, 23, 31; days sacred to Kh., 23, 85.
Khshathrô*k*inah, son of Khshvôiwrâspa, 23, 212.
Khshvôiwrâspa, son of Kh*s*tâvaênya, 23, 211 sq., 225.
Kh*s*tâvaênya, n.p., 23, 211.
***Kh*û**, the correlate of Heaven at Shun's border sacrifice, 28, 201; held the place of honour at sacrifices under Yin, 28, 202; his conversation with the ruler of Fan, 40, 55 sq., 55 n.; different branches of the ruling family of *Kh*û, 40, 86, 86 n.
***Kh*ü**, Khwăn became Inspector of roads for, 40, 108, 108 n.
Khuddaka-pâ*th*a, fifteen books of, 10 (i), ix sq.
Khu*gg*a-sobhita, appointed on the jury at the council of Vesâlî, 20, 407.
Khu*gg*uttarâ, a lady who could remember her previous births, 35, 122.
Khû Hu, a Mohist of the south, 40, 220.
***Kh*ui**, a skilful maker of arrows, 39, 286 sq.
***Kh*ü Lî**, or summary of the rules of propriety, 27, 15–17, 61–119.
Khûmbîks, Frâ*d*akhshtŏ, son of, 37, 203, 203 n.
***Kh*ung**, and Lî made an end of the communication between earth and heaven, 3, 257, 257 sq. n.
Khung An-kwo, n. of an author, 3, 3, 8–11, 453 sq., 454 n., 456.
***Kh*ung-hwâ**, a name of Shun, 3, 38.
Khung *Kh*iu=Confucius, q. v.
Khung Khwei, of Wei, inscription on his tripod, 28, 252 sq., 253 n.
Khung *K*î=3ze-sze, q. v.
Kh*ung-*r, a son of Duke Hsien of 3in, 27, 126, 165–7, 167 n.
Khung-shih=Confucius, q. v.
Khung Yang, and Lâo-3ze, 40, 250.
Khung Ying-tâ, on body and soul as Heaven's gift, 3, 139 n.
Khung-3ze, *see* Confucius.
***Kh*un *Kh*iû**, or 'the Spring and Autumn,' the fifth King, work of Confucius, 3, xix sq.; in it the sage indicates his judgement, but does not argue, 39, 189, 189 n.
Khûr, invoked, 5, 402, 405.
Khû*r*dâ*d*, *see* Ho*r*vada*d*.
Khûr-*k*ashm, Av. Hvare-*k*aêshman, future apostle, 18, 14, 14 n., 78 sq. and n.
Khûrshêd, white marv, the flower of, 5, 104.
Khûrshê*d*-*k*îhar, son of Zoroaster, 5, 142, 142 n.
Khûsrô, son of Mâh-dâ*d*, a priest, 5, 194.
Khûsrô (Khûsrôî) Nôshirvân, king, son of Kêvâ*d*, the glorified one, 5, 151 n., 172 sq. n., 193, 193 n., 201; 18, xxvii, 297 sq. and n., 394, 397; 37, xlii, 410 n., 415, 415 n.; 47, xii, 127, 127 n.; his priests and councillors, 5, 194, 194 n.; organized the religion, 47, 89 sq., 89 n., 127.
Khûsrôî (Kaî-Khûsrôî, Kaî-Khusrôb, Kaî-Khûsrôv, Av. Kavi Haosravangh), one of the Kayâns, son of Sîyâvash, 5, 63, 135 sq., 136 n., 139 sq., 150, 329 n.; 18, 90, 90 n., 257, 257 n., 258 n.; 24, 64, 64 n.; 37, 28 sq., 29 n., 191 n.; his exploits, 5, 63 sq.; 37, 223–5; 47, xxvii, 14; among the preparers of the renovation of the universe, 18, 78, 78 n.; 24, 99; 37, 355, 355 n.; 47, 114; extirpated the idol-temples, 24, 15, 15 n.; advanced Mazda-worship, 37, 203 sq. and n.; appeal of K.'s Fravashi to the angel Nêryôsang, 37, 222 sq., 222 n.; his accession, 47, xxix; smote Frangrâs'yâk, 47, 116.
***Kh*ü 3hiâo-3ze**, his conversation

with *Kh*ang-wû Ȝze, 39, 192 sq. and n.; 40, 279.
Khvanîras, or Iran, a region of the earth, 5, 32 sq.; 37, 20, 20 n.; six races of men in Kh., 5, 58; Zaratûst, its spiritual chief, 5, 116; the middle portion of the earth, 5, 175; 18, 79, 79 n.; the immortal rulers of Kh., 18, 256 sq., 256 n., 258 n.; 37, 202–4; races established in Kh. and the six regions around it, 37, 26; the Mâzendarâns and Kh., 37, 216–18. *See also* Iran.
Khvâst-aîrikht, n.p., 5, 135.
Khwâi Shang, received the condolences from Duke Âi, 27, 187.
Khwăn, father of Yü, appointed by Yâo to stay the flood, 3, 16, 35, 35 n., 139 sq.; 28, 208; made a prisoner by Shun, 3, 41; the correlate of Heaven at border sacrifices, 28, 202, 202 n.
Khwăn, the unfortunate son of Ȝze-*kh*î, 40, 106–8.
Khwang-ȝze, did not see his father, 40, 180, 180 n.
Khwăn Hwun, a sage accompanying Hwang-Tî, 40, 96.
Khwei, Director of Music to Shun, 3, 44 sq., 44 n., 61; 28, 105, 105 n., 275 sq.
Khwei, Master of the Horse to Yû, 3, 356.
Khwei, son of King Wăn of *K*âo, 40, 186 sq., 186 n.
Khwei, sprites haunting hills, 40, 19. *See also* Animals (*i*).
Khwei, symbol of, a hexagram, 16, 139 sq., 140 n., 243, 243 n., 314, 314 n., 385, 436, 442.
***K*î**, ancestor of the duke of *K*âu, 3, 153; King *K*. of *K*âu was humble and reverentially cautious, 3, 203; father of King Wăn, 3, 380 sq., 380 n.; 27, 343; 28, 309; successor to King Thâi, 3, 390; associated with God at the border sacrifice, 27, 430 sq., 430 n.; 28, 202; questions put by Thang to *K*., 39, 167; took the place of his elder brother, 40, 178, 178 n.
***K*î**, Shun's minister, spread abroad a knowledge of agriculture, 3, 258.
***K*î**, count of, his correct action, 16, 135, 137 n., 242, 242 n.; feigned himself mad, 40, 131.
***K*î**, a barbarian captive of Lî, married by Duke Hsien, 27, 126, 127 n.
***K*î**, *see* *Kh*î.
***K*iâ-fû**, author of an ode of the Shih, 3, 295, 353.
***K*iâ Î**, 'The Royal Regulations' compiled after his death, 27, 18.
***K*iang**, *see* Thâi-*k*iang.
***K*iang-lü Mien**, n.p., 39, 318 sq., 318 n.
***K*iang Yüan**, mother of Hâu-*k*î, 3, 341, 341 n., 396 sq. and n.
***K*iâo Kû**, visits the dying *K*ì Wû-ȝze, 27, 162.
***K*iâ-po**, chief Administrator of Yû, 3, 356.
Kia-ti-na râga, son of Kusika, versed in heretical systems, 19, 11.
***K*ieh**, sovereign of Hsiâ, punished by Thang, 3, 84–90, 85 n., 93, 93 n., 127 sq., 215, 215 n., 221, 310, 310 n.; 27, 396; 40, 162, 178; a bad ruler, 28, 418; 39, 242, 291, 295, 380, 386; 40, 64, 136, 177; killed Kwan Lung-făng, 39, 205; perished, 40, 131.
***K*ieh**, t.w., 39, 220.
***K*ieh-ȝze**, holds that the Tâo may allow of influence, 40, 129, 129 n.
***K*ieh Ȝze-thui**, cut a piece from his thigh as food for Duke Wăn, 40, 173 sq.
***K*ien Wû**, conversation between him and Lien Shû, 39, 127, 170 sq.; got the Tâo, 39, 244, 244 n.; his interview with *Kh*ieh-yü, the mad recluse, 39, 260; and Sun-shû Âo, 40, 54 sq.
Kîgs, *see* Kavis.
***K*ih**, Grand Music-Master of Lû, arranged the Shih King, 3, 280.
***K*ih**, the robber, 39, 139, 273, 275, 285, 292, 328; 40, 285; interview between him and Confucius, 39, 157 sq.; 40, 166–76; on the principles of robbery, 39, 283 sq.; a bad ruler, 39, 295.
***K*ih-khwâi**, resigned his marquisate, 39, 380.
***K*ih-lî Yî**, teacher of *K*û Phing-man, 40, 206.
***K*i-hsien**, the wizard of *K*ăng, defeated by Hû-ȝze, 39, 137, 262–5.
***K*î Hsing-ȝze**, how he trains a fighting-cock, 40, 20.
***K*ih Tâo-ȝze**, n.p., 27, 179 sq., 179 n.

Kî Hwan-ȝze, mourning rites for him, 27, 323.
Kîk, *see* Kavis.
***K*î *K*ăn**, holds that the Tâo forbids all action, 40, 129, 129 n.
***K*î *K*âo-ȝze**, questions Măng *K*ing-ȝze, 27, 174.
***K*î Khang-ȝze**, funeral of his mother, 27, 176, 184; his error in the mourning rites, 27, 324; use of white silk in court-robes began with him, 28, 11, 11 n.
***K*î *K*heh**, describes the right course for a king, 39, 318 sq., 318 n.
***K*i *K*hih**, a Mohist of the south, 40, 220.
***K*îkhshnûs**, ancestor of Zoroaster, 47, 34, 140.
***K*î-*kh*ü**, practised the Tâo, 39, 210.
Kilâta, and Âkuli, priests of the Asuras, 12, 29 sq.
***K*î-lî**, Thâi, and King Wăn, 28, 60.
Kimbila, converted by Buddha, 17, 309-12; 19, 226, 245; 20, 228-33; 35, 163; = Kampila, 49 (ii), 2 n.
Kimîdin, a class of demons, 42, 64, 68, 159, 205.
Kimpurushas, superhuman beings, 45, 382; souls of K., 48, 198.
Ki*m*sîlasutta, t.c., 10 (ii), 54 sq.
Ki*m*vadanta, a demon harassing infants, 29, 296; 30, 211.
***K*in**, and *Kh*in, and the siege of *K*ăng, 3, 270 sq.
***K*in**, the music-master, his views about Confucius, 39, 351-4.
Kina and Sila converted by Buddha, 19, 243.
***K*înâmrôs**, mythic bird, 24, 112, 112 n.
***K*înas**, degraded Kshatriyas, 25, 412.
Kindness for k., injury for injury, k. for injury, injury for k., 28, 332; misery prevented by freedom from malice, 37, 108; injury to be recompensed with k., 39, 31, 91 sq., 106 sq.
Kindred, *see* Relatives.
***K*in(d)var bridge**, *see* *K*invat b.
Kine, *see* Cow.
King (Kings, Rulers, Sovereigns).

(*a*) In India.
(*b*) In Iran.
(*c*) In China.

(*a*) In India.

If a k. does not punish a punishable offence the guilt falls upon him, 2, 71, 82, 169, 245; 14, 101 sq., 213; 25, 309; 33, 230, 386-8, 390; Snâtaka shall not speak evil of the k., 2, 95; must keep stores for *S*ûdra guests, 2, 110, 110 n.; reception of k. as guests, 2, 120, 205; 14, 49, 244 sq.; 25, 96 sq., 97 n.; 29, 87 n., 88, 197, 273, 435; 30, 132, 277-9; duties of k., 2, 125, 161-4, 228-31, 234-49, 273 sq., 274 n.; 7, 13-23, 41; 14, 8, 82, 96-102, 199-204; 25, lxix, 216-61, 284 sq., 306-9, 313-15, 320 sq., 323, 327, 327 n., 380-400, 423, 451, 595 sq.; 33, 69, 72, 75, 117, 153-5, 157, 164, 188, 209, 215-21, 232 sq., 251, 266 sq., 296, 365; 36, 28-30, 323-5; way must be made for a k., except if he meets a Brâhma*n*a (Snâtaka), 2, 125 sq., 211; 7, 203 sq.; 14, 69, 243; 25, 55 sq.; inherits on failure of relations, except in case of Brâhma*n*a, 2, 134, 309; 7, 68; 14, 93, 179 sq.; 25, 369, 369 n.; 33, 201 sq., 380; 45, 67, 67 n.; Brâhma*n*as and k. sustain the world, 2, 214 sq. and n.; 33, 210; relation of k. and Brâhma*n*as, 2, 234 sq.; 12, 47; 14, 8, 18; 15, 89; 25, 436; 33, 220 sq.; 41, 72, 95, 106, 110; 42, 169, 171 sq.; 43, 249; 44, 286; vices of k., 2, 234 sq. n.; 25, 220, 222-4; teacher and k. guard men, therefore they must not be reviled, 2, 238; witnesses to be sworn in the presence of the gods, the k., and Brâhma*n*as, 2, 247; position of k. with regard to impurity, k. remains always pure, 2, 254; 7, 92; 25, 185 sq.; 33, 216; impurity and interruption of Veda-study caused by the death of k., 2, 263; 7, 92; 14, 208; one who assassinates a k. to be cast off, 2, 277; ministers and officials ('jewels') of k., 7, 15-17, 20 sq.; 25, xxxvii, 224-6, 229, 234-6, 234 sq. n., 238; 35, 171; 36, 40 sq., 52 sq., 124, 147, 147 n., 265 sq.; 41, 58-64 and n., 110 sq.; 42, 333; receives sixth part of subjects' demerit or merit, 7, 16; 25, lxxviii, 307; income of k., taxes, tolls, &c., 7, 16; 25, 307, 307 n., 323-5; 33, 221; his conduct in peace and war,

7, 17–20, 22 sq.; must bestow landed property and gifts of all kind on Brâhma*n*as, 7, 21 sq.; documents attested by k., royal edicts, 7, 21 sq., 46 sq.; 33, 242, 285–7, 305 sq.; just k. becomes the associate of Indra, 7, 41; 33, 288 sq.; fines paid to the k., 7, 44; cannot be a witness, 7, 48; 14, 204; 25, 265; fourteen rulers of the world pass away in each Kalpa, 7, 79; when the k. has met with an accident, Veda-study must be interrupted, and he must not eat on that day, 7, 125, 218; Lakshmî resides in the consecration of a k., 7, 299; Yama, chief among k., 8, 89; oppressions, dangers from k., 8, 207 sq.; 13, 261; 20, 312; 35, 50; 49 (i), 115; must protect Brâhma*n*as who are the bridges of piety, 8, 347 sq.; the poor and ambitious Kshatriya who wishes for the kingdom in this world, is a losing man, 10 (ii), 19; after seeing the prosperity of k., the Brâhma*n*as gradually degenerated, 10 (ii), 50; Buddha a religious k. (dhammarâgan), 10 (ii), 102; is the principal amongst men, 10 (ii), 105; must have a Purohita, 12, xiv; takes possession of what he likes, 12, 81 sq.; becomes a Mahârâgan after victory, 12, 182, 419; 26, 338; Buddha prescribes that Bhikkhus should obey k., 13, 301; money transactions stopped between the death of a k. and the coronation of his successor, 14, 15, 15 sq. n.; food of a k. who does not slay those worthy of capital punishment not to be eaten, 14, 70; the king as administrator of justice, 14, 78; 25, 253–5, 257–62, 267, 284–7, 292, 294 sq., 296, 300 sq., 303, 321 sq., 327, 327 n.; 33, 5–8, 7 n., 14–24, 35–8, 277–82, 288; 36, 266, 266 n.; property of a k. not lost by adverse possession, 14, 81; 25, 279; 33, 61 sq., 311 sq.; property given up by its owner goes to the k., 14, 81; duties of the k. on the death of his predecessor, 14, 99 sq.; his right to property not claimed, 14, 201; 25, 258–60; 33, 127, 338; sin of serving a k., 14, 298; to be informed of an adoption, 14, 335; names of great k., 15, 289; amnesty and gifts at the birth of a prince, 19, 19 sq.; k. who obtained final bliss, though householders, 19, 97; became hermits, 19, 101, 107 sq., 132; a Bodhisattva does not serve or court k., 21, 262; political circles (ma*nd*ala) to which a k. must pay attention, 25, xxxvi, 240 sq. and n., 249 sq.; branches of knowledge to be studied by a k., 25, xxxvi sq., 222; accepting gifts from wicked k., 25, lxviii, 142; *S*ûdra k., 25, 138; k. who is not descended from a Kshatriya race to be shunned, 25, 142 sq.; Snâtaka not to step on the shadow of a k., 25, 149; Snâtaka not to accept food from a k., 25, 163; is an incarnation of the eight guardian deities of the world, 25, 185 sq.; receives the sacrament of coronation, 25, 216, 216 n.; created from the particles of gods, 25, 216 sq.; divine nature of a k., 25, 217; 33, 221 sq.; obedience to the k., 25, 218, 218 n.; his duty towards learned Brâhma*n*as, 25, 221, 229 sq., 237, 239, 323, 397–9, 431, 434 sq.; 33, 346 sq.; virtues of k., 25, 222; must consult with his ministers, 25, 224 sq., 239, 251 sq.; must wed a queen, 25, 228; k.'s palace, 25, 228; his duty to fight bravely, 25, 230–3, 245–8, 399, 399 n., 427; must employ spies, 25, 235, 240, 252, 387–9, 395, 397; must give audience, 25, 239; eightfold business of k., 25, 240, 240 n.; his duty with regard to foreign policy, 25, 240–50 and n.; in his harem, 25, 251 sq.; must always protect himself against poison, 25, 251; shall pardon those who abuse him, 25, 308 sq.; k. and his relatives liable to punishment, 25, 313, 313 n.; settles the prices of merchandise, 25, 324; forgers of royal edicts punished by death, 25, 382; corrupting ministers punished by death, 25, 382; duty of k. to remove the 'thorns,' 25, 386–94; crimes committed against the k., 25, 391 sq.; seven constituent parts of a kingdom, 25, 395; resembles the four ages of the world, 25, 396; shall emulate the gods, 25, 396 sq.; their rank in the scale of creatures,

25, 494; sovereignty deserves he who knows the Veda, 25, 507; seating the k. on the throne-seat, 26, 84 sq.; 41, 35 sq., 105 sq., 108 n.; is independent, 33, 50; as witness, 33, 81, 81 n., 299–301; enemy of the k. cannot be a witness, 33, 88; an apostate from asceticism becomes the k.'s slave, 33, 137; property found belongs to k. except when found by a Brâhma*n*a, 33, 146; intercourse with a queen termed incest, 33, 179; superior value of property belonging to the k., 33, 205; must make good the loss caused by thieves not caught, 33, 206, 226; Brâhma*n*as and k. are exempt from corporal punishment, 33, 210; 41, 108; crime of insulting a k., 33, 212; authorization from the k., and payment to the k., required for gamblers, 33, 213 sq.; duties towards k., 33, 216 sqq.; whatever a k. does is right, 33, 217; appear in the forms of five gods, 33, 217 sq.; property of a k. is pure, 33, 220 sq.; by pardoning an offender a k. commits the same offence as by punishing an innocent man, 33, 229; wicked k. go to hell, 33, 246; sixth part of the booty belongs to the k., 33, 341; an enemy of the k. shall be banished, 33, 348; fine for companies conspiring to cheat the k., 33, 349; what is done by heads of corporations must be approved of by the k. as well, 33, 349; loss and gain and life depend on fate and the k., 33, 353; unjust gifts of a k., 33, 354; how k. discuss, and how scholars discuss, 35, 46; the horse of wonderful speed of a great k., 35, 199 sq. and n.; are grasping, and never give up territory, 35, 203; ministers of the k. exempt from taxation, 35, 208; punishments for assaulting the k., 35, 270; prerogatives of a k., 36, 28–30; Râ*g*asûya or inauguration of a k., 41, xi, xxiv–xxvi, 4, 42–142; 44, xv; becomes emperor by the Râ*g*asûya, 41, xxiv sq., 4; the Abhishe*k*anîya, or consecration ceremony of a k., 41, 68–113, 68 sq. n.; 43, 213 sq. n., 220, 224–6, 225 n.; 44, 511; 49 (i), 157 n.; investing of the k. with consecration garments, bow, and arrows, 41, 85–9; *the k. indeed is the upholder of the sacred law*, 41, 106; does not shave his hair, 41, 126, 128; never stands on the earth with bare feet, 41, 128 sq.; witchcraft practices necessary for the k., 42, xlvi, xlviii, li, lxvii sq.; prayers and charms pertaining to royalty, 42, 111–33, 207, 239–41, 262 sq., 325–34, 378–81, 404–6, 436–40, 477–9, 510 sq., 582–7, 631–9, 661–3; prayer and rites at the consecration of a k., 42, 111 sq., 239, 378–81; restoration of an exiled k., 42, 112, 327–30; royal marriage, 42, 498; are performers of the great *S*rauta sacrifices, 43, xvi; whatever belongs to the people, in that the chieftain has a share, 43, 160, 162; distinction between chieftain and clan, 43, 210 sq.; he alone is k. who propagates offspring, 43, 230; chieftain's power over the clan or people, 43, 241 sq., 244 sq.; keep most aloof from their wives at meals, hence vigorous sons are born to them, 43, 370, 370 n.; Varu*n*a, the divine representative of the earthly k., 44, xix; as the people bring tribute to the k., so men offer sacrifices to the gods, 44, 38; Sânnâyya offering mystically identified with royal dignity, 44, 41; Soma, the lord of k., Varu*n*a, the lord of universal sovereigns, 44, 63; A*s*vamedha performed by k., 44, 277 n., 288 sq., 396–401; clad in mail, k. performs heroic deeds, 44, 300; royal power presses hard on the people, 44, 325 sq.; do not rear cattle, 44, 326; royal power gained by the keepers of the horse at the A*s*vamedha, 44, 359 sq.; Brâhma*n*as (lute-players) sing of righteous k. of yore, 44, 363; imperial dignity is higher than the royal, 44, 461; became *G*aina monks, 45, 85–8; description of a k.'s assembly, 45, 339; description of a virtuous k., 49 (i), 22–4; a k. eats (i. e. takes the wealth of) the rich, 46, 54; some k. obtained final bliss, 49 (i), 94 sq.; are not happy, 49 (i), 118; some k. killed their fathers, 49 (ii), 163; k. of kings, *see* *K*akravartin; wives of k., *see* Queens.

(*b*) IN IRAN.

The wicked are rebels against the k., 4, 189, 192; should deserve good renown here below, and long bliss hereafter, 4, 253, 253 n.; the most excellent thing in the world is to have an Ahu and a Ratu (prince and priest), 4, 279–81, 279 n.; Kingly Glory or Glory of the Kavis invoked and worshipped, 23, 7 sq., 7 n., 11 sq., 11 n., 15, 19, 93, 286, 289–97, 302–9, 339, 358; Nairyô-Sangha dwells in the navel of k., 23, 8, 8 n., 16, 358; must possess twelve virtues, 23, 25 n.; Kingly Glory drives behind Mithra's chariot, 23, 136, 153; Kingly Glory (genius) present at the ordeal, 23, 170; ks. worship *K*ista, wishing peace for their country, 23, 268; the punishment for installing an evil k., 31, 39, 48 sq.

(*c*) IN CHINA.

Titles of Chinese k. 'Sons of Heaven,' &c., 3, xxiii, xxv–xxix, xxv n.; 27, 107 sq.; 39, 331; Recorders, Annalists, Historiographers, and clerks at the courts of Chinese k., 3, 4–6, 153, 155; mutual relation of sovereign and people, 3, 50, 58–62, 97, 102–12; 16, 296, 297 n.; called 'The One Man,' 3, 79, 89–91, 89 n., 100, 105, 107, 109, 127 sq., 130, 154, 163, 170, 178, 198 sq., 207, 213, 228, 234, 244, 253, 260, 266, 394; 27, 107; duties of a k., 3, 79 sq., 92–103, 142–4; the k. is the parent of the people, 3, 125, 144, 483; *he who soothes us is our sovereign; he who oppresses us is our enemy*, 3, 130; only the k. entitled to receive revenues, 3, 144 sq.; exhortations addressed to a k., 3, 150 sq., 166–71, 190 sq., 212 sq.; the virtue of reverence to be cultivated by a k., 3, 182, 184–7, 191; offerings made to the k. or Son of Heaven (by feudal princes), 3, 184, 184 n., 188, 191, 445 sq., 446 n.; 16, 88, 285; 39, 105 sq.; model k. (according to the Tâo), 3, 201–4; 39, 82 sq., 136 sq., 145, 259–62, 267 n.; palace of a k., 3, 236 sq. n.; installing the new k. on the death of his father, 3, 237–42; presents offered to the newly appointed k., 3, 243 sq.; 'Kinged by God,' 3, 319; prerogatives of k. with regard to certain sacrifices, 3, 405 n.; filial piety in the Son of Heaven, 3, 467 sq., 479; love rendered to the mother, reverence to the k., both to the father, 3, 470; benevolence shown by k. in their hunting expeditions, 16, 75, 76 n.; 'k.'s father' and 'k.'s mother' in Chinese = 'grandfather' and 'grandmother,' 16, 133 n.; ancient k. examined the different regions of the kingdom, 16, 292; promulgates his announcements throughout the four quarters of the kingdom, 16, 321; date of marriage to be announced to the k., 27, 78; etiquette to be observed in eating with a k., 27, 81 sq.; rules concerning a k.'s carriage, 27, 94–8; etiquette to be observed before a k., 27, 103; must not leave his gems without good reason, 27, 106; how one should try to stop a k. from leaving his state, 27, 107; announcement of a k.'s death, 27, 108; members of the royal harem, 27, 109; certain things that should not be said of k., 27, 113; sacrifices to be offered by the k., 27, 116; rules for discharging royal orders, 27, 118; mourning for a k.'s mother or wife, 27, 155; keep their coffin deposited away, 27, 156 sq.; funeral rites for k., 27, 157–61, 173–5; messages of condolence from k., 27, 163; mourning of the heir on the k.'s death, 27, 179; superiors should pay regard to popular opinion, 28, 288; the kingdom is a 'spirit-like vessel,' 39, 72; call themselves 'orphans,' 39, 82, 85; rulers of the world are to act in accordance with the spontaneity of Heaven, 39, 143, 307–14, 307 n.; the way of Heaven is to be the way of Tîs and k. and sages, 39, 144, 330 sq., 334–8; k. and sages who resigned or refused a throne, 39, 157; 40, 149–52, 161–3; what is the fullest discharge of loyalty, 39, 212; he who establishes the attributes of the Tâo is possessed of kingly qualities, 39, 310 sq.; sovereign, 'the correlate of Heaven,' 39, 312 sq., 312 n.; the right course

for a Tî or k., 39, 318 sq.; follow the pattern of Heaven and Earth, 39, 334, 346; by the grace of Heaven, 39, 338, 338 n.; three Hwangs and five Tîs, 39, 353, 353 n., 358–60, 358 n., 376, 381; how Tîs and k. arose, 40, 65; five official departments kept by a k., 40, 127; the services of Tîs and k. are but a surplusage of the work of the sages, 40, 154; troubles of a k., 40, 195; the perfection of the Sage and the k. both from the Tâo, 40, 214, 217; wickedness of opposing a k., 40, 243; Tîs and k. interfered with the minds of men, 40, 286; Chinese dynasties, Hwangs, Tîs, Wangs, 40, 316, 316 n.;—ministers and officers of Chinese k., 3, 15, 34 sq., 35 n., 42–5, 102, 114 sq., 122, 122 n., 131, 142, 158 sq., 178–80, 206–10, 220, 222–31, 223 n., 235, 235 n., 355 sq., 356 n., 384, 384 n., 422; 27, 71, 92, 109–12, 209–19, 209 n., 244–8; control over ministers, their punishment, 3, 81–3, 169 sq.; appointments on the hereditary principle, and by virtue, 3, 125; 27, 438; duties of ministers and officers, 3, 232–4, 469–71, 471 n.; 27, 221, 228, 230–9, 270; 28, 73, 344–7, 355–9; the functions of the ministers, &c., at the funeral of a k., 3, 240–2; 27, 146; names of ministers recorded on 'the grand banner,' 3, 250, 250 n.; appointment of Minister of Instruction, 3, 250 sq.; must be surrounded by good household officers, 3, 252 sq.; how ministers may remonstrate with the k., 3, 483 sq.; 27, 114; gifts of a k. to a feudal prince for services rendered, 16, 131 sq., 133 n., 241; the sage k. nourish men of talents and virtue, by them to reach to the myriads of the people, 16, 235, 235 n.; should seek to maintain union and an affectionate relation with the princes of his states, 16, 277 sq.; k. and ministers must maintain secrecy, 16, 363; k. and minister, father and son, 16, 436; 27, 121; etiquette and ceremonies at interviews between rulers and officers, 27, 86, 90, 104–6; minister's duty on the k. being ill, 27, 114; k. at the mourning rites for a minister, 27, 172; duty first, salary second, 28, 295–7; virtues of a minister, 28, 421 sq. *See also* Government, *and* Tî.

King or *K*ing, meaning 'canonical book,' 3, 2. *See* Confucius (*b*), Hsiâo K., Lî *K*î, Shih K., Shû K., *and* Yî K.

*K*ing, Duke Hsiang in attendance at the court of, 27, 186.

*K*ing *K*iang, wailing for her husband and her son, 27, 167, 167 n., 176.

Kingly Glory, *see* King (*b*).

*Kiñk*a, a Brahmin woman, swallowed by the earth for offending Buddha, 35, 153.

Kinnaras: Vish*n*u or Î*s*vara, the lord of men, K., Yakshas, &c., 8, 347, 354; accompany Buddha, 19, 348; 21, 5 sq.; K. and other superhuman beings, 21, 401; 36, 130; 45, 77, 121 sq., 382; created, 25, 15; manes of K., 25, 112; souls of K., 48, 198.

Kinship, *see* Family, *and* Relationship.

*K*inva*t* **bridge**, or bridge of Judgement, leading from this to the next world, 4, lxxiv; 5, 36, 36 n., 130, 339, 339 n.; 18, 54–6, 71, 76, 140 n., 289, 348, 348 n.; 23, 12, 20, 121 n., 339; 24, 18, 18 n., 22, 52, 52 n., 81 sq., 81 n., 101, 258, 264 sq., 278–80, 293, 297, 299, 305, 309, 316, 316 n., 319, 326, 352, 358 sq.; 31, 170, 173 sq. and n., 183; 37, 33, 33 n., 62, 62 n., 86, 94, 94 n., 100, 102 sq., 121, 160, 162 sq., 175, 191, 200, 204 sq., 240, 261, 275, 287, 309 sq., 317, 346, 360, 369, 371 sq., 387, 440, 455, 477, 487; the dog-killer will not find the way over it, 4, 156; dogs guard it, 4, 158, 272; the departed soul standing at the head of it, 4, 194, 218–20, 219 n.; made by Mazda, 4, 218 sq., 221; for all Mazda-worshippers shall a path be opened across it, 4, 276 n., 277; the soul passes over it into Paradise, and is received by Aûhar-mazd, &c., 4, 373 sq.; 31, 261, 330 sq.; 47, 152, 152 n.; judgement on the soul at the *K*. b., 5, 157 sq.

301 n., 351, 351 n., 363, 363 n., 383 n.; 37, 149 sq., 155, 155 n., 167; the *K.* b. and the path of the righteous and wicked, 18, 46–9, 46 sq. n.; 31, 132, 140; the path of the good over the *K.* b., 18, 242, 242 n., 247, 247 n.; the way made by Time, 23, 335; the *K.* b., and the Garô Nmâna of Ahura worshipped, 31, 345; bridge penalty, 37, 93; described, 37, 210.

Kirâta, n. of a tribe, 42, 153.

Kisa, Sa*m*ki*kk*a, his successor Gosâla, 45, xxix, xxxi.

***K*îshmak**, n. of a fiend, 5, 110.

***K*ista**, the impersonation of religious knowledge, worshipped, 4, 223, 223 n.; 23, 10, 18, 166, 264–9, 352; drives at Mithra's left side, 23, 153; the friends of the most right *K.*, 23, 164. *See also* *K*isti.

Kîstas, an ancient family of priests, 46, 130, 134.

***K*isti**, *K.* Vanguhi, angel of religious knowledge worshipped, 4, 222, 222 n.; 23, 11, 164, 166, 282; 31, 200, 211, 217, 344, 348; wisdom of Ahura, 31, 177, 185; the healing virtues of *K.*, 31, 347. *See also* *K*ista.

***K*î-sun**, 3ăng-3ze received a mat from, 27, 128; visits of condolence when his mother died, 27, 197.

***K*i-sun Suh**, Wû-3ze his posthumous title, 27, 162 n.

Ki*t*â Hill, Buddha and the wicked Bhikkhus of, 17, 347 sqq.; 20, 211 sq.

***K*î Thâ**, a worthy, but not a True Man, 39, 239, 239 sq. n.; withdrew to the river Kho, 40, 141.

***K*itra** and Sambhûta on the vanity of worldly pleasures, and the power of Karman, 45, 56–61; stories of *K.* and Sambhûta common to Brahmans, *G*ainas, and Buddhists, 45, 56 sq. n.

***K*itradhva*g*a**, asked Akshayamati about Avalokite*s*vara, 21, 413.

***K*itra Gâṅgyâyani**, or Gârgyâ*n*i, teaches Âru*n*i Uddâlaka and *S*vetaketu, 1, xcix, 271 sqq.

***K*itragupta**, employed by Yama as one of the superintendents of hells, 38, 123.

***K*itraratha**, chief among the heavenly choristers, 8, 89; connected with the Kâpeyas, 34, 226.

***K*îtrôk-miyân**, or *K*itrô-maînô, son of Vi*s*tâsp, n. of Pêshyôtanû, 5, 117, 117 n., 195. *See* Pêshyôtanû.

Kitrô-maînô, *see* *K*îtrôk-miyân.

***K*itta**, the householder, and the Bhikkhu Sudhamma, 17, 359–69.

***K*ittadhârâbuddhisaṅkusumitâbhyudgata**, the 31st Tathâgata, 49 (ii), 6.

***K*iû-fang Yăn**, a famous physiognomist, 40, 106, 106 n.

***K*î Wû-3ze**, appropriated the burying-ground of the Tû family, 27, 121, 122 n.; quoted, 27, 132; dying, 27, 162.

***K*i-yau**, translated a life of Buddha into Chinese, 19, xxiii.

***K*î-3ze**, an officer of King Yung of Wei, 40, 118.

***K*î-3ze** of Yen-ling, how he buried his son, 27, 192 sq., 192 n.

***K*î 3ze-kâo** at the burial of his wife, 27, 189, 189 n.

***K*'*K*hien**, translated the Sukhâvatîvyûha, 49 (ii), xxii.

Knãthaiti, the Pairika, created by Angra Mainyu, 4, 6, 6 n., 211; the witch, attached to Keresâspa, 18, 369, 369 n.

Knife, for slaughtering the horse of gold, of copper, of iron, 44, 303; k.-paths, 44, 326.

Knowledge.

(*a*) The acquiring o k.
(*b*) K. and works.
(*c*) Various kinds and objects of k.
(*d*) Characteristics of k.
(*e*) Results o k.

(*a*) THE ACQUIRING OF K.

True k. is to be obtained from a teacher, 1, 106; the fire of k. produced by two Ara*n*is, penance and sacred learning, 8, 308; one who has a bad understanding will not acquire k. even with a thousand admonitions, 8, 380; no k. without meditation, no meditation without k., 10 (i), 87; 38, 205, 332; perfect k. results from the four noble Truths, 10 (ii), 132–44; how a Bhikkhu may obtain a wonderful k. of other men's hearts, 11, 215; to give learning is the most excellent of all gifts, 14, 137; supernatural vision gained by subsisting during a year on alms, 14, 309; the five instruments of k. together with the

mind, 15, 22; impediments in the way of k., 15, 341 sqq.; how parents and rulers should deal with ignorance, 16, 64–6, 66 n.; generated by union of instinctive and acquired wisdom, 18, 409; of animals by instinct, of men by toil only, 24, 39; why an ignorant man will not learn, 24, 96 sq.; all k. depends on k. of the sacred being, 24, 140; three modes of acquiring k., 24, 140–2; the tree of k. in the garden of Eden, 24, 179, 200, 210, 218–20; when does it arise, in this life or in the next? 34, lxxvi, 228; 38, 316, 327–30; cannot be founded on reasoning, 34, 316 sq.; rests on the Veda, 34, 317; the divine eye, i.e. insight, cannot arise, when the cause is destroyed, 35, 179 sq., 184; eagerness for k., 37, 346; how k. is obtained, 37, 350; 38, 306–27, 331–7; 39, 89 sq.; 48, 414; natural wisdom and acquired k., 37, 434, 442; true k. will spring up of itself, it cannot be enjoined, 38, 163, 164 sq.; belongs to those who are bound to chastity, 38, 295; persons who are qualified for k., 38, 315 sq.; learning, childlike state, and Muni-hood are auxiliaries to k., 38, 322–4; 48, 700 sq., 708–12; the k. of creatures depends on their breathing, 40, 139, 139 n.; five kinds of obstruction to right k., 45, 172, 172 n., 193; passion and darkness antagonistic to it, goodness the cause of it, 48, 18; two kinds of k., from *S*âstras and Yoga, 48, 284; origination of true k. depends on caste, â*s*rama, and other conditions, 48, 750; seven steps leading towards the highest k., 49 (ii), 96, 96 n. *See also* Perception, *and* Teacher.

(*b*) K. AND WORKS.

Both k. and good works are necessary for overcoming death, and obtaining immortality, 1, 312 sq., 319; 38, 359, 361; 48, 699 sq.; relation of k. and works, 1, 314–20; 15, xxvi; 38, 330; 48, 9–11, 18 sq., 725–7; real salvation can be obtained by k. alone, not by good works, 1, 314 sqq.; 38, 267, 307; is superior to devotion, 8, 11 sq.; the sacrifice of k., 8, 62, 83, 83 n., 130; is inferior to devotion, 8, 73; esteemed highest, 8, 75; pious works are means of k., 8, 159, 159 n.; 34, lxxviii; 37, 321; 38, 292 sq., 306–9, 313, 315, 358–62; 48, 703; is one of the twelve great observances, 8, 167; by k. everlasting glory is attained, by action perishable worlds, 8, 179; as a mode of piety, 8, 376; understanding or k. performs the sacrifice, it performs all works, 15, 57; 48, 555; all rites performed through k., 25, 132; as long as true k. is not reached, the ordinary course of works holds on undisturbed, 34, 324; promoted by giving to the wise what is needful, 37, 371; loving religion through k., 37, 381; injunctions and prohibitions do not refer to him who has obtained perfect k., 38, 67; k. and works are the two roads for entering on the road of the gods and the road of the fathers, 38, 123–5, 234; works are co-operative for the origination of k., but not for the fruits of k., 38, 313; good works also obstruct the result of k., 38, 356 sq.; nescience, work, and former k., limiting adjuncts of the soul, 38, 367; by k. he who knows secures for himself the benefits of a performance of a thousand years, 43, 362 sq.; by k. alone fire-altars are built, 43, 380; the highest state attained by k., not by sacrificial rites, 43, 389 sq.; is not subordinate to works, but is itself beneficial to man, 48, 686–96; arises from good works, if not obstructed by other works, 48, 712 sq.; good and evil works destroyed by k., 48, 724 sq.

(*c*) VARIOUS KINDS AND OBJECTS OF K.

Threefold k., three kinds of k., k. of threefold quality, 1, 2 sq., 32 sq., 35; 7, 127; 8, 124, 331; 10 (ii), 117; 29, 16; 36, 265, 265 n.; 49 (ii), 24, 193; Paryaṅkavidyâ, or k. of Brahman's couch, 1, 276; 38, 400; science of the Adhyâtma, the chief of sciences, 8, 81 sq., 90; K*r*ish*n*a, the object of k., 8, 97; real k. is k. of Kshetra and Kshetra*gñ*a, 8, 102 sq.; act of k., object of k., result of k., and the knower,

8, 123 sq., 123 n.; 34, 418 sq., 429; Dh*ri*tarâsh*t*ra inquires of Sanatsu*g*âta about the highest k., 8, 151; the seven elements of k. (sambodhyaṅgas), 10 (i), 25, 25 n.; the Bhikkhu who falsely professes to possess the extraordinary k. of an Arhat, &c., has fallen into defeat, 13, 5; k. of the Self, in the Vedânta, and Samyaksambodhi in Buddhism, 15, lii; the higher and the lower k., 15, 27 sq.; 34, xxxi, lxxviii–xci, c, ci, cviii–cxi, cxv sq., 137 sqq.; 48, 284 sq.; false k. produced by B*ri*haspati, for the safety of Indra against the Asuras, 15, 342; degrees of transcendent k., 19, 156 sq., 160; 22, 257 n., 268, 274, 278; 36, 225–9; 49 (i), 187 sq.; supreme perfect k. is to be obtained by the one Buddha-vehicle only, 21, 41–59; thirty-seven constituents of true k., 21, 419 sq.; five kinds of k., 22, xxxiii sq.; 45, 152–4; 49 (ii), 89, 89 n.; the k. called Mana*h*paryâya, 22, 200; divine k., the chief virtue in the Tretâ age, 25, 24; the lower k., 34, lxxix, ci, 137 sq.; 38, 355, 364–404; the practical world vanishes in the sphere of true k., 34, 135, 281; 38, 340, 400; the higher k. is this by which the Indestructible is apprehended, 34, 135, 137 sq.; true k. is irrefutable, 34, 282; stages of higher k. before attaining to Arhatship, 35, 25–9, 25 sq. n.; Buddha's 'jewel of k.,' 36, 223 sq.; kinds of k., 37, 423; k. of the prâ*n*a, 38, 186 sq.; there can be no successive stages in true k., 38, 336; when true k. springs up, Scripture ceases to be valid, 38, 340; *he who knows other men is discerning, he who knows himself is intelligent*, 39, 75 sq.; *to know and yet (think) we do not know is the highest (attainment), not to know (and yet think) we do know is a disease*, 39, 113; true k. is the k. of the two elements in man, the heavenly and the human, 39, 134 sq., 236 sq.; the k. that stops at what it does not know is the greatest, 39, 190–2; *S*ruta and Avadhi k., 45, 120, 120 n.; in the form of meditation, 48, 15 sq.; six kinds of k., 49 (ii), 2; highest perfect k. (sambodhi, bodhi), 49 (ii), 9, 11–24, 27 sq., 40, 51, 68, 71, 73 sq., 101 sq., 119, 128, 133 sq., 138 sq., 141, 191, 199 sq.; transcendental k. possessed by beings in a Buddha country, 49 (ii), 12 sq., 21, 49; highest perfect k. is neither a thing nor a no-thing, 49 (ii), 118. *See also* Avadhi, Brahman (*b*), Dahara-vidyâ, Kevala, *K*ista, Meditation, Sacred Books, Sambodhi, Sciences, Self (*a*), Udgîtha-vidyâ, Vai*s*vânaravidyâ, Veda (*c*, *d*), *and* Wisdom.

(*d*) CHARACTERISTICS OF K.

K. is the cause of everything, is the Self, is Brahman, 1, 245 sq.; 48, 63; is enveloped by desire, 8, 57; is enveloped by ignorance, 8, 65; is better than continuous meditation, 8, 100 sq.; is the highest thing, 8, 312; he who understands the qualities, enjoys them, but is not attached to them, 8, 327 sq.; is the characteristic of renunciation, 8, 349; speech is k., 15, 153; is a modification of the Self, and therefore one with it, 22, 50, 50 n.; a blind mind is worse than a blind eye, an ill-informed worse than an ill-tempered man, 24, 56; of k. no one knows a superfluity, of learning and skill one cannot be deprived, 24, 80; no matter shall be undertaken without having advice from the wise and relations, 24, 349 sq.; goodness has the form of k., darkness of ignorance, 25, 490 sq.; 34, 46, 48 sq.; the power of wisdom, of *S*ruti and Sm*ri*ti, 29, 149; he who consists of k. is not the individual soul, but Brahman, 34, xxxviii, 233–6; defined, 34, 6; 48, 699; is not an activity, 34, 35 sq.; the individual soul consists of k., 34, 134; discarded by Tâoism as the cause of the decay of the Tâo, and of all evils, 39, 28–30, 49, 61 sq., 80–2, 90 sq., 108 sq., 123, 152, 198, 198 n., 288 sq., 293, 296 sq., 299; 40, 57–60, 63 sq., 73, 79, 224 sq., 285 sq., 294; the faculty of k. and the placidity blended together in the Tâoist, 39, 368 sq.; in the state of Perfect Unity men might be possessed of k., but they had no occasion for its use, 39, 369 sq.; what men know is not so much as what they do not know,

39, 377; the pursuer of the Tâo, a child who has no k., 40, 32, 35; *to know to stop where they cannot arrive by means of k. is the highest attainment*, 40, 83; is in not knowing, 40, 268, 291, 293; the nature of the Tâo, and the use of k., 40, 275–9; all k. is of the Real, 48, 119–24; is different from mere cognitions of sense, 48, 692.

(*e*) Results of k.

No evil clings to him who possesses true k., 1, 67; 7, 96 sq.; 36, 370; the goal of emancipation or immortality (union with Brahman, with Vish*n*u) reached by k., 1, 106 sq., 107 sq. n.; 7, 291; 8, 59–63, 103, 106 sq., 109, 154, 164 sq., 391 sq.; 10 (ii), 206 sq.; 11, 14, 14 n.; 14, 137 sq.; 15, 96, 273, 301; 25, 501, 501 n., 502 n., 503 sq., 508; 34, lxxx sq., 229, 281, 283, 291; 38, 101, 232, 235–8, 285–330, 369–78, 400, 419; 45, 152, 417 sq.; 48, 100; the effect of true k. compared with the ordeal of the heated iron, 1, 108 sq., 108 n.; is the throne of Brahman, 1, 277; k. as an object of contract, 4, 45 sq., 45 n.; to make the ignorant learned, one of the greatest concerns of men, 5, 394 sq.; sins destroyed by k., 8, 62, 65; 48, 722–4; fire of k. burns up all action, 8, 62, 279, 279 n.; 38, 237; the excellent sword of k. with which the tree of worldly life is cut, 8, 63, 313, 371; with the brilliant lamp of k. K*ri*sh*n*a destroys the darkness of ignorance in his devotee, 8, 87; both piety and sin destroyed by k., 8, 158; 48, 724; those who have eyes of k. see the soul going and coming, 8, 239; pure, highest k. is the wealth (given as sacrificial fee) at the allegorical sacrifice of the sense-organs, 8, 261; he who understands the qualities of darkness and passion gets rid of all dark and passionate qualities, 8, 323, 325; he who knows the names of Prak*ri*ti is released from all qualities, 8, 331; rewards of possessing k. of transcendent things, 8, 333; *there is no end for k. Therefore one whose self is tranquil, whose senses are subjugated, who is devoid of . . . egoism, is released from all sins by pure k.*, 8, 355; is the highest happiness, 8, 378, 380; when the sage has departed, there is no k., as there is no duality, 15, 112 sq., 184 sq.; 34, 280 sq.; even by k. and wisdom one cannot contend with destiny, 24, 54; purifies the intellect, 25, 187 sq.; property acquired by learning, 25, 374, 374 n.; a man dying in the possession of true k., shakes off his good and evil deeds, 34, lxx; 38, 119, 225–30, 294 sq., 357 sq.; even beings who have reached true k. may retain a body for the discharge of certain offices, 34, lxxii; 38, 235–8; the weapon of a Bhikkhu, 36, 328 sq.; true k. is not purposeless, 38, 64; alone effects the purpose of man, 38, 285, 290–306; mere k. cannot effect the purpose of man, 38, 288 sq.; its fruit does not manifest itself at a later time only as the fruits of actions do, 38, 294; it is impossible for any one who has not reached true k., to refrain from all actions, 38, 399; through true k. the expanse of names and forms which Nescience superimposes on Brahman is dissolved, 38, 401; rewards for esoteric k. of sacrificial rites or terms, 44, 5, 7, 11, 14, 21, 23, 26, 28, 35, 38–45, 48, 50, 56, 66–8, 82–7, 112, 117, 130, 140, 144, 155–7, 159, 165, 170, 177, 182, 236, 239, 246, 249, 251, 253, 264, 271 sq., 335, 337, 370, 403, 406, 443, 455, 507–10; a king presents gifts of cows to the most learned in sacred k., 44, 113, 115; heretical belief in the inefficiency of k., 45, 83, 83 n.; wrong k. the root of all pain, 48, 9; through the power of k., the subtle body persists, even when the works have passed away, 48, 650; *whatever he does with k., with faith, with the Upanishads, that is more vigorous*, 48, 682–4, 688 sq., 691.

Ko, earl of, punished by Thang, 3, 88, 88 n.

Ko*d*âla, *Ri*shabhadatta of the gotra of, 22, 190 sq., 218, 223, 226.

*K*odanâvatthu, Buddha at, 13, 267.

Ko*d*inya, disciple of Mahâgiri, 22, 290.

Koka, his father King *S*o*n*a, 44, 400.

Kokâlika, or Kokâliya, a follower of Devadatta, 10 (ii), 118–21; 20, 251, 258 sq.
Kokâliyasutta, t.c., 10 (ii), 118–24.
Kôkharêd, Av. Kahvaredha, son of Aêshm and Mânûsak, 47, 143, 143 n.
Kolañña, *see* Samana-Kolañña.
Kolita, other name of Moggallâna, 13, 149 sq.
Kotivisa, *see* Sona K.
Koliyas, of Râmagâma, claim relics of Buddha, and erect a dâgaba, 11, 132, 134.
Komârabhakka, *see* Gîvaka K.
Kondañña (Aññâta-K.), Buddha's first convert, 11, 153–5, 155 n.; 13, 97–9.
Kong-mang-tsiang, translator of the Kung-pen-K'i-King, 19, xxiv.
Konika, *see* Kûnika.
Korah (Qarûn), swallowed up by the earth for his pride, 9, 116 sq., 116 n., 121, 192.
Kosala, Brâhmanas of, come to Buddha, 10 (ii), 48; Buddha's family in the country of K., 10 (ii), 68; the beautiful city of the K., Sâvatthi, 10 (ii), 184, 186; Buddha journeying through K., 10 (ii), 74; 11, 167; K. and Videha, 12, 104 n., 106; kings of Kâsî and K. celebrate the death of Mahâvîra, 22, 266; generosity of the K. king, 36, 148. *See also* Videha.
Kosambî, n. of a great town, 10 (ii), 188; 11, 99, 247; 17, 285–308, 370–6; 20, 233–6.
Kosavigñâna, Sk., the knowledge of the chest (name of *Khând.* Up. 3, 15), 1, 49 n.
Kosha, the, a priestly race, 43, 392.
Koshthavat, one of the princes of mountains, 8, 346.
Kotigâma, Buddha at, 11, 23 sq.; 17, 104–8.
Kotika, other name of Susthita, 22, 288.
Kotivarshîyâ Sâkhâ, of the Godâsa Gana, 22, 288.
Kotthita (Mahâ K.), a principal Thera, 17, 317, 359.
Ko Yüan (or Hsüan), a worker of miracles, 40, 248; supposed author of the *Khing Käng King*, 40, 248 sq., 254.
Krafstar, Phl., t.t., 'noxious creature,' 5, lxxiii. *See also* Animals (*b*).
Krafstra-men, and Daêvas, 31, 260, 260 n.
Kraivya, the Pañkâla king, performed horse-sacrifice, 44, 397.
Kratu, a sage and a Pragâpati, 15, xlvii; 25, 14.
Kratusthalâ, a nymph, 43, 105.
Kraunkikîputrau, n. of teachers, 15, 226.
Krikkhra, *see* Penances.
Kripa, a Kaurava, 8, 38.
Krisânu, a guardian of Soma, 12, 183 n.; 26, 72; the footless archer, aimed at Gâyatrî, 26, 78 n.; 42, 401.
Krisâsva, or King Lui'-ma, reborn in heaven, 19, 234, 234 n.
Krishna, son of Devakî, instructed by Ghora Âṅgirasa, 1, 52, 52 n.; son of Vasudeva, 1, 52 n.; Vishnu is K., 7, 296; 34, cxxvi; dialogue between K. and his friend Arguna, 8, 3 sq., 40–131, 97, 197 sq., 229 sq., 254, 310–12, 393 sq.; four classes of devotees of K., 8, 11; is dear to the man of knowledge, and he is dear to K., 8, 12, 75, 129 sq.; K. says: *even those, who being devotees of other divinities worship with faith, worship me only, (but) irregularly. For I am the enjoyer as well as the lord of all sacrifices*, 8, 12, 67, 84 sq.; none hateful, none dear to him, 8, 12, 85; how men become dear to K., 8, 12, 99–102, 128 sq.; receives the sin or merit of none, 8, 13, 65; also called Hrishîkesa, hero in the Kurukshetra battle, 8, 38 sq.; destroyer of Madhu, 8, 40, 42, 231; the Deity, 8, 42 sq., 49 sq., 52–131; creator and lord of all things, god of gods, lord of the universe, 8, 58, 67, 86 sq., 90, 93–8, 97 n.; though unborn, is born age after age for the protection of the good, 8, 58 sq.; created the castes, 8, 59; not defiled by actions, 8, 59; is not the cause of actions, 8, 65; the friend of all beings, 8, 67; those who worship, meditate on K., are united with K., he is the final goal of the Yogin's devotion, 8, 69, 79 sq., 84–6, 97, 100, 127 sq.; the devotee sees K. in everything, and everything in K., 8, 71, 74 sq.; worship

of K. the highest devotion, 8, 73, 75, 83–6, 129; few know him truly, 8, 73; his lower nature divided eightfold, 8, 73 sq.; is Om in all the Vedas, 8, 74; producer, upholder, and destroyer of the universe, 8, 74; having assumed a human body, disregarded by deluded people, 8, 76, 76 n., 82 sq.; what other gods give is really given by K., 8, 76; knows everything, but him nobody knows, 8, 76; those who know K. with the Adhibhûta, Adhidaiva, and Adhiyagña know him at the time of death, 8, 77, 78 n.; he who remembers K. at the moment of death comes into his essence, 8, 78; pervades all this world, 8, 82 sq., 87 sq., 94–8; brings forth again and again all entities by the power of nature, 8, 82 sq.; is the father of this universe, the mother, the creator, 8, 83, 97; the source, seed, cause of all things, 8, 83 sq., 87, 90 sq.; is both immortality and death, 8, 84; is that which is and that which is not, 8, 84; he who knows K. is freed from sin, 8, 86; the eternal being, divine, the first god, the unborn, 8, 86 sq., 94, 96; his powers and emanations, 8, 86–91; to those who worship him he gives knowledge, 8, 87; is the supreme Brahman, the supreme goal, the holiest of the holy, 8, 87, 110, 110 n.; 48, 525; alone knows his self by his self, 8, 87; is the beginning and the middle and the end of all beings, 8, 88, 90; is Time, and Death, 8, 90, 95 sq.; shows himself in his divine form to Arguna, 8, 92–9; with faces in all directions, 8, 93, 93 n.; without end or middle or beginning, 8, 93 sq.; the inexhaustible protector of piety, 8, 94; sun and moon his eyes, 8, 94; is that which is and that which is not, 8, 96; is the great grandsire, 8, 97; is indefinable, 8, 97, 97 n.; worshipped by Arguna, 8, 97 sq.; assumes his (ordinary) four-handed form, 8, 98, 98 n.; is the Kshetragña in all Kshetras, 8, 102, 310; unswerving devotion to K. included in knowledge, 8, 103; he who knows Brahman is fit for assimilation with K., 8, 104, 107, 109; K. the father, the great Brahman the womb, 8, 107; he who worships K. becomes fit for union with Brahman, 8, 110; his is the light of the sun, the moon, and the fire, 8, 112; knows the Vedas and Vedântas, 8, 113; is placed in the heart of all, 8, 113, 129; is the fire of digestion, 8, 113; as earth supports all things, 8, 113, 113 n.; as moon nourishes all herbs, 8, 113; to be learnt from the Vedas, 8, 113 sq.; transfer of the embryo of K. from the womb of Devakî to that of Rohi*n*î, 22, xxxi n.; history of K. in *G*aina legend, 22, xxxi n.; 45, 112 n., 113 n.; in Brahma Kalpa and in the line of K., the Laukântika Vimânas are eightfold, 22, 195; Mount Gir*n*âr connected with the legend of K., 45, 115 n.; called Vishvaksena, 45, 290 n.; K. and the cowherds' wives, 49 (1), 38 n. *See also* Hari, Ka*n*ha (Mâra), Kesava, Mâdhava, Vâsudeva, *and* Vish*n*u.

K*r*ish*n*a, *see* Durgaya K.

K*r*ish*n*a Dvaipâyana, *see* Vyâsa.

K*r*ish*n*a Hârita, n. of a teacher, 1, 264.

K*r*ish*n*asakha Kula, of the *K*âra*n*a Ga*n*a, 22, 292.

K*r*ita age, *see* Ages of the world (*a*).

K*r*itañgaya, worshipped at the Tarpa*n*a, 30, 244.

K*r*itavîrya, Arguna, a descendant of, 8, 293.

Krivi, the ancient name of the Pañ*k*âlas, 7, xv sq.; 12, xli sq.; 32, 402, 407; 44, 397 sq.

Kriyâvâda, *see* Philosophy.

Krodha, worshipped at the Tarpa*n*a, 30, 244.

Kshamâsrama*n*a Desiga*n*in, K. Devarddhi, and K. Sthiragupta, Sthaviras, 22, 295.

Ksha*n*ikavâdin, *see* Philosophy.

Kshânti, *see* Resignation.

Kshântivâdin, the *R*ishi, Buddha born as, 49 (ii), 128.

Kshatra, Knighthood (personified), meditation on, 15, 195; offering to, 15, 211; Mitra the K., lord of the K., 44, 64. *See also* Caste, *and* Kshatriyas.

Kshatriyas, the warriors (caste): the K. sage Pravâha*n*a *G*aivali, and his teaching which 'belonged in all

the worlds to the Kshatra class alone,' 1, 78; the Gândharva form of marriage legitimate for K., 7, 108; the highest duties of K., 8, 43 n., 46 sq.; 25, 238; 45, 37–40; well-read K., 8, 209, 255; degraded K. tribes, 8, 222; procreated by Brâhma*n*as on K. women, 8, 295, 295 n.; destroyed by Râma, 8, 295 sq., 300; among men the K. are the rulers, 8, 345; the Nakshatra *K*itrâ advantageous for K., 12, 288; keep the Sabhya or hall fire, 12, 302 n.; *G*aina monks or nuns should not accept food in the houses of K., 22, 97; 45, 71; a bow laid on the funeral pile of a dead K., 29, 239; the K. is the best in the world of those who observe the rules of exogamous marriage, 35, 229 n.; have secret formulas handed down in a family, 35, 265; Atharva-veda and the K., 42, xxv sq.; the K.'s sacrifices, 44, xvii; this earth is the K.'s world, 44, 133; for the rule of this world the K. is consecrated, 44, 249; a K. is the consecrator of a K., 44, 253 sq.; born victorious, 44, 295. *See also* Brâhma*n*a (*e*), Caste, King, *and* Râganyas.

Kshatt*ri*, or king's chamberlain, 44, 545.

Kshemaliptikâ *S*âkhâ, of the Ve*s*avâ*t*ika Ga*n*a, 22, 291.

Kshemendra, refers to Milinda, 36, xvii.

Kshetra, Sk., t.t., what it is, and its relation to the Kshetra*gñ*a, 8, 102–6, 310, 351, 372.

Kshetra*g*a, *see* Sons.

Kshetra*gñ*a, Sk., philosophical t.t.: relation between Kshetra and K., 8, 102–6; instructed or directed by the K., 8, 284, 284 n., 288, 293; is the sun in the forest Brahman, 8, 287, 387; a symbol of the Brahman, 8, 308, 308 n.; identical with K*ri*sh*n*a, 8, 310, 393 n.; 48, 101; destruction of the K., i.e. identification of individual self with universal self, 8, 310, 310 n.; 48, 101; the Purusha is called K., and the K. perceives all the operations of the qualities, 8, 351; is devoid of qualities and eternal, not to be comprehended by any symbols, 8, 350 sq.; only the K. attains to the truth, 8, 351; he who understands piety and has his sins destroyed, &c., enters into the K., is the K., the Supreme Lord, 8, 351 sq.; unity of K. and nature, 8, 374, 377–9; knowledge of the K. forms part of all real k., 8, 379; the understanding is called K., 8, 386; senses, mind, and understanding are always joined to the K., 8, 386; he who abandons everything as fruitless is the K., 8, 390; one of the terms for soul, 25, 485 sq. and n.; 34, 122; 38, 83; 48, 63, 88 sq.

Kshetrapati (lord of the field), sacrifices to, 30, 224, 290 sq.; 41, 125; 42, 14, 288, 486.

Kshipra*m*suvana, t.t., *see* Child (*b*).

Kshipra*s*yena, *see* Birds (*b*).

Kshîrasvâmin, quotes Manu, 25, cxi sq., cxii n.

Kshudrasûktas, and Mahâsûktas, the hymns and poets of the 10th Ma*nd*ala of the Rig-veda, 1, 217.

Kshudrâtma, n. of the Graha appearing at the death of Mahâvîra, 22, 266.

Kshurikâ, Sk., 'razor,' name of an Upanishad, 15, xxvi sq.

*K*û, heir-son of Yâo, 3, 34, 60, 60 n.; proposed as Forester to Shun, 3, 44, 44 n.

Kubera, or Kuvera, also called Vai*s*rama*n*a and Vai*s*rava*n*a (Pali Vessava*n*a), a god who was formerly a man, 2, 40 n.; offerings to K. or V., 2, 151; 29, 32; 30, 243; lord of Bhûtas, Yakshas, and Rakshas, 8, 88; 35, 38; 44, 367; 49 (i), 61, 197; lord of all jewels, 8, 347; came to ask Buddha about the Dhamma, 10 (ii), 63; V. gladdened by the birth of his son Nalakûvara, 19, 20; V. produces rare and heavenly sounds, 19, 54; Pisha or V. converted by Buddha, 19, 245, 245 n.; a Lokapâla or guardian of the world, 21, 4, 373; 25, 185, 216 sq.; 35, 37; Gadgadasvara preaches under the shape of K., 21, 401; Avalokite*s*vara assumes the shape of K., 21, 411; the Ku*nd*aladharas (gods) of V., 22, 195; V. caught up the ornaments of Mahâvîra, 22, 199; demons in V.'s service bring

treasures to the house of King Siddhârtha, 22, 248, 251 sq.; disciple of *S*ântisenika, 22, 293; became lord of wealth by humility, 25, 222; the servants of K., demons harassing children, 30, 211; witnesses watched by K. and other gods, 33, 245; excellent in beauty, 45, 117, 117 n.; heavenly nymphs wait upon K., 49 (i), 16, 56; the monarch of Alakâ, 49 (i), 36; the dances of K., 49 (i), 38; god of wealth, 49 (i), 61, 193 sq.

***K*û*d*âkarman**, t.t., tonsure ceremony, *see* Child (*b*).

***K*u-fa-lan**, *see* Gobhara*n*a.

***K*û Hsî**, philosopher, on Confucius and the Shih King, 3, 280, 296–8; on Tâoism, 39, 23, 54, 56, 89; 40, 263, 272; on Phăng, 39, 167 n.

***K*û Hsin**, studied the subject of Life, 40, 16.

Kuhû, offering to, 25, 90; 41, 54 n.; 43, 264, 264 n.

***K*uh-yan-king**, t.w., 10 (i), lii.

Ku-i, *see* Gopî.

Kû *Kh*î, a sage accompanying Hwang-Tî, 40, 96.

Kula, Sk., t.t., 'family,' Ga*n*a and *S*âkhâ, 22, 288 n.

***K*ûla Bhâgavitti**, pupil of Madhuka Paiṅgya, 15, 214.

***K*ulanî**, mother of Sambhûta, when born as Brahmadatta, 45, 57.

K*ûla Sîla*m, t.c., 11, 189–91.

***K*ûlavagga**, t.c., 10 (ii), 37–66.

***K*ûlaviyûhasutta**, t.c., 10 (ii), 167–70.

***K*ü-liang**, lost and recovered his strength, 39, 256.

***K*ûlikâ-upanishad**, quoted, 48, 363 sq., 777.

***K*ulla-Panthaka**, the Elder, saying of, 36, 284.

***K*ullapatka**, n. of a Bhikshu, 49 (ii), 2.

***K*ulla-Subhaddâ**, exalts the Buddhist monk, 36, 308 sq., 316; story of *K*. and the naked ascetics, 36, 308 sq. n.

***K*ulla-vagga**, account of Buddha's death in it, and in the Mahâparinibbâna-sutta, 11, xi–xv; date of it, 11, xiii; part of the Vinaya Pi*t*aka, 13, x, xviii, xx, xxviii, xxx; account of councils in *K*., 13, xxii; translated, 17, 328–439; *Vol.* 20.

Kullûka, his commentary on the Manu-sm*ri*ti, 25, cxxxi sq., cxxxvi sq., *and passim.*

Kumâlana, and Dharmaprahrâda, 2, 98, 98 sq. n.

Kumâra, god, was formerly a man, 2, 263 n.; demon K. converted by Buddha, 19, 244; n. of a demon harassing infants, 29, 296; a form of Agni or Rudra, 41, 160; the war-god, 42, 325 sq.

Kumâra Âtreya, author of Vedic hymns, 46, 367.

Kumâra*g*îva, translated the 'Sermons of A*s*vaghosha,' 19, xxx, xxxiv sq.; Chinese translation of the Saddharma-pu*nd*arîka, by K., 21, xx sq., xxiii sq., xl–xlii; on a passage of Lâo-ȝze, 39, 76, 90; translated the smaller Sukhâvatî-vyûha, 49 (ii), vi sq.; translated the Vagra*kkh*edikâ into Chinese, 49 (ii), xiii.

Kumârahârita, n. of a teacher, 15, 119, 187, 216.

Kumâra-Kassapa, his ordination, 13, 229; the eloquent Thera, 35, 275, 275 n.

Kumâra-Kâ*s*yapa, n. of a Bhikshu, 49 (ii), 2.

Kumârila, philosopher, his date, 8, 31 sq.; quoted by Medhâtithi, 25, cxxi sq.; knew our Manu-sm*ri*ti, 25, 613.

Kumbhâ*nd*as, Virû*dh*aka surrounded by myriads of ko*t*is of, 21, 373.

Kumbhin, n. of a demon harassing infants, 29, 296; 30, 211.

Kumbhînasi, an evil demon, 42, liv.

Kummâra, n. of a village where Mahâvîra meditated on the Self, 22, 200.

Ku*n*âlâ, the river Erâvatî near it is very narrow, 22, 297.

Ku*n*âru, the handless, smitten by Indra, 43, 275.

Ku*n*da, a fiend, who is drunken without drinking, 4, 223; 23, 334.

***K*unda**, or Mahâ*k*unda, the smith, asks Buddha how many kinds of Sama*n*as there are in the world, 10 (ii), 15; serves Buddha with a meal of boar's flesh, his last repast, 11, 70–3, 83 sq.; 19, 285 sq., 285 n., 365–71; 35, 242 sq.; attends Buddha during his last hours, 11, 82 sq.;

questions Buddha about schisms, 17, 317; one of the principal Thera Bhikkhus, 17, 359; 49 (ii), 2; one of the five hundred Arhats who are to become future Buddhas, 21, 198.
***K*unda**, or Vunda, a Yaksha, 49 (i), 170 n.
***K*u*nd*adana**, a *S*âkya, converted by Buddha, 19, 226.
Ku*nd*adharî, *see* Kau*t*umbinî.
Kûndah, son of, converted, 47, 165.
Kûndak, demon, the steed of wizards, 5, 113.
Ku*nd*ala gotra, Kâmarddhi of the, 22, 291.
Ku*nd*aladharas, gods, 22, 195.
Ku*nd*apâyin, *see* Sacrifice (*j*).
Ku*nd*apura, or Ku*nd*agrâma, birthplace of Mahâvîra, 22, 190 sq., 219, 223, 252; its southern part brahmanical, the northern part Kshatriya, 22, 190 sq., 226, 228.
***K*undasutta**, t.c., 10 (ii), 15 sq.
Ku*n*di, n. of a demon, 4, 145 sq., 145 n.
***K*ung**, minister of Kâu-*k*ien, 40, 111, 111 n.; *K*. of Ȝhâi, *see* Hû.
Kung: earl of K. enjoyed himself on the top of Mount K., 40, 161, 161 n.
***K*ung Hsien** consults Ȝăng-ȝze about funerals, 27, 151.
Kung-hsî *Kh*ih, made the ornaments of commemoration at Confucius's funeral, 27, 139.
***K*ung-hui**, vindicates Thang's proceeding against *K*ieh, 3, 86–9.
***K*ung Hwan**, officer at *Kh*ăng's court, 3, 237.
Kung-î *K*ung-ȝze, appointed his younger son as heir, 27, 120.
***K*ung Khang**, of Shang dynasty, his reign, 3, 13, 23, 81.
Kung *K*iang, widow of Kung-po, refuses to marry again, 3, 434.
Kung-*k*ien *K*iâ, prevents Pan from using a mechanical contrivance for burying, 27, 184.
Kung-kung, Hâu-thû, a son of the line of, 28, 208, 208 n.
***K*ung-liang-ȝze**, on funeral rites, 27, 152.
Kung Liû, revives the house of *Kh*î, 3, 134, 134 n.
Kung-ming Î, at the mourning rites for Ȝze-*k*ang, 27, 140; questions Ȝăng-ȝze about filial piety, 28, 226.
***K*ung-nî**, *see* Confucius.
***K*ung-pen-k'i-king**, a Chinese life of Buddha, 19, xxiv sq.
***K*ung Shan-fû**, principal minister of King Hsüan, 3, 425 sq.
Kung-shû Mû, consults Ȝze-yû about mourning, 27, 151.
Kung-shû Wăn-ȝze, ascended the mound of Hsiâ, 27, 145; honorary title given to him after his death, 27, 180 sq., 181 n.
Kung-shû *Zo*, or Pan, wishes to use a mechanical contrivance for letting the coffin down into the grave, 27, 184, 184 n.
Kung-shu *Zü-zăn* falls in battle, 27, 185.
***K*ung Sui**, died in *Kh*ui, 27, 184.
Kung-sun Lung, his teaching opposed to Tâoism, 39, 147; a sophist, 39, 149, 183 n., 387–90, 387 n.; 40, 230; called Ping, his followers a philosophical school, 40, 99 sq., 99 n.
***K*ung-sun Mieh**, called Măng Hsien-ȝze, 28, 167 n.
Kung-sun Nî-ȝze, books of Lî *K*î ascribed to him, 27, 45 sq.
Kung-wang *Kh*iû at the archery trial of Confucius, 28, 450.
Kung-wăn Hsien, and the Master of the Left, 39, 131, 200.
Kung-yang *K*iâ originated a funeral custom, 28, 156.
Kung-yüeh Hsiû, a true Tâoist sage, 40, 114 sq.
***K*ung-yün**, chief cook of Yû, 3, 356, 356 n.
***K*ung Yung**, or 'Doctrine of the Mean,' 3, xx; 27, 42–4; 28, 300–29, 301 n.
***K*ung Ȝung**, or Thâi-wû, ruled seventy-five years, 3, 201 sq., 201 n., 204; his ministers, 3, 207, 207 n.
Kung-ȝze Mâu, prince of Wei, 39, 387–90, 387 n.
Kunî, demon, 24, 243 sq., 244 n. *See also* Demons.
Ku*n*ika, quoted by Âpastamba, 2, xxvii, 70.
Kû*n*ika, or Ko*n*ika, *G*aina n. of Agâtasattu, 11, 1 n.
***K*ün-*kh*ăn**, successor of the duke of *K*âu, 3, 231–4; the duke of Pî his successor, 3, 245, 249.
***K*un Mâng** and Yüan Fung dis-

course together, 39, 322–4, 322 sq. n.
Kunthu, n. of a Tîrthakara, 22, 280; a king of the Aikshvâka race, who became a Gaina monk, 45, 86, 86 n.
Kunthu, *see* Animals (*i*).
Kuntî, her son Arguna, 8, 254, 393; n. of a giantess, 21, 374 sq.
Kuntibhoga, n. of warrior, 8, 37.
Kün-yâ, appointed Minister of Instruction, by King Mû, 3, 250 sq.
Kû Phing-man, expended wealth in learning how to slaughter the dragon, 40, 206, 206 n.
Kü Po-yü, friend of Confucius, sayings of, 27, 145, 411, 411 n.; instructs Yen Ho, 39, 132, 215–17; changed his views when he was in his sixtieth year, 40, 124, 124 n.
Kuppapa*t*i*kk*asanti, Pali t.t., 10 (ii), 149.
Kûrkura, n. of the demon Kumâra who brings disease of children, 29, 297; 30, 219.
Kûr*n*a, converted by Buddha, 19, 241.
Kurukshetra, battle of, 8, 3, 37; men born in K. fight in the van of the battle, 25, 247, 247 n.; gods performed sacrifice in K., 26, 275; 44, 441; land of King Parikshit, 42, 198; Purûravas wandered all over K., 44, 70.
Kuru-land, *see* Kurukshetra.
Kuru-Pa*ñk*âlas, or Kurus and Pa*ñk*âlas, n. of a people, 1, 300; 12, xli–xliii, xlii n., 192; Brâhma*n*as of the K., 15, 121, 145; 44, 51; speech sounds higher among them, 26, 50; their kings performers of the Râgasûya, 41, 124, 124 n.
Kurus, destroyed by hailstones, 1, 18; saved, 1, 71, 71 n.; Devabhâga, Purohita of the K., 12, 377; perished by lust, 19, 125; 49 (i), 116; war between K. and Pâ*nd*avas, 19, 330; the Northern K., 49 (i), 38.
Kuru*s*rava*n*a, mentioned in the Rig-veda, 12, xli.
Ku*s*a-grass, sacred, 8, 68; 29, 69, 73, 130, 181, 184 sq., 193, 213, 247, 302, 313, 348 sq.; 30, 105; two k. blades as strainers, 25, 189; 29, 25 sq., 29, 162 sq., 270; substitute for Soma plants, 26, 422; strowing of k. grass at sacred rites, 29, 24, 24 n., 36, 55, 95, 128, 335; 30, 27, 32, 37; pounding a k. needle, 29, 46, 292; k. blade as protection, 29, 56; palace where it grows recommended for site of building, 29, 211; rings of k. network, 29, 256 sq.; girdle of k., 29, 310, 374; 30, 16; garment of k. grass, 41, 31; is pure, 41, 32, 356.
Kusala, Buddha's definition of the term, 10 (ii), 90.
Kû-sâu, father of Shun, 3, 52, 52 n.
Kusâvatî, old name of Kusinârâ, q.v.
Kûshtanô-bûgê*d*, quoted, 5, 260, 260 n., 266, 274, 295, 306.
Kush*th*a, the healing plant, personified, 42, 5.
Ku*s*ika, author of heretical treatises, 19, 11; Indra becomes K.'s son, 26, 82 n.; identical with Vi*s*vâmitra, 42, xxvi; Ku*s*ikas, or Vi*s*vâmitras, 46, 292, 294, 304; the son of K. attained that Brahmanhood which K. could not attain, 49 (i), 9.
Kusinârâ, Buddha at the city of, 10 (ii), 188; 17, 134–40; Buddha's last days and death at K., 11, 72–135, 238 sq., 247; its old name Kusâvatî, 11, 100; 11, 248; the royal city of King Sudassana, 11, 100 sq., 239, 248–51, 248 n., 254 sq., 268, 270, 274, 281, 283, 285, 287; dâgaba at K., 11, 135.
Ku*s*ri Vâga*s*ravasa, n. of a teacher, 12, xxxiii; 15, 226 sq.; 43, 390 sq., 390 n.; teacher of *S*â*nd*ilya, 43, 404.
Kûstîk, Phl., 'sacred thread-girdle,' 5, lxxiii.
Kusumâbhi*gñ*a, the 63rd Tathâgata, 49 (ii), 7.
Kusumaprabha, the 50th Tathâgata, 49 (ii), 6.
Kusumasambhava, the 43rd Tathâgata, 49 (ii), 6.
Kusumav*r*ish*t*yabhiprakîr*n*a, the 51st Tathâgata, 49 (ii), 6.
Kûtadanta, a Brahman, converted by Buddha, 19, 242.
Kû*t*adantî, n. of a giantess, 21, 374.
Kû*t*âgâra Hall at Vesâli, 11, 59 sq.
***K*u-ta-lih**, *see* Mahâbâla.
Ku*t*ika*nn*a, *see* So*n*a K.
Kutsa, quoted by Âpastamba, 2, xxvii, 70; sellers of Soma of the K.

tribe, 26, 64 n.; K. Âṅgirasa, author of Vedic hymns, 32, 424; 46, 110, 115, 120, 126, 127.
Kutsâyana, his hymn of praise to the Lord of the Universe, 15, 303.
Kuvera, *see* Kubera.
***K*û-yung,** attending spirit of Yen Tî, 27, 268, 268 n., 272, 276; a primaeval sovereign, 39, 287.
***K*wang,** duke of Lû, 3, 342; 27, 127 sq., 165, 188, 198.
Kwang, music-master of Duke Phing, 27, 179 sq.
***K*wang *K*âu,** *see K*wang-ȝze.
Kwang *Kh*ăng-ȝze, explains the Perfect Tâo to Hwang-Tî, 39, 24 sq., 142 sq., 297–300, 297 n.; 40, 286; the Yin Fû *K*ing attributed to him, 40, 255 sq.
***K*wang *K*iang,** complains of the bad treatment she received from her husband, 3, 433.
***K*wang Shû,** assisted Duke *Kh*ăng, 28, 252, 253 n.
***K*wang Thung,** duke of Lû, 40, 22 sq.
***K*wang-ȝze** of *Kh*ăn, his death, 27, 150 sq.
***K*wang-ȝze,** translations, editions, and commentaries of his works, 39, xviii–xxi, 9 sq.; believes in an early state of paradisiacal Tâoism, 39, 2 sq.; importance to Tâoism of his books, 39, 10 sq.; division of his books into three parts, their general title, 39, 11 sq.; on the death of his wife, 39, 22, 149; 40, 4 sq., 5 n.; his books are not historical, 39, 33 sq.; Sze-mâ *Kh*ien's accounts of *K.*, 39, 34, 36–8; notices on the writings of *K.*, 39, 127–63; dreamt that he was a butterfly, 39, 129 sq., 197, 197 n.; an Agnostic, 39, 129 sq., 179 n., 194–7; disputations between Hui-ȝze and *K.*, 39, 134, 172–5, 172 n., 234 sq.; 40, 98–100, 137 sq., 144; difference between the first and the other parts of his writings, 39, 138; spurious parts of his books, 39, 144–7, 149 sq., 152, 155–60, 163, 322 n.; 40, 8 n., 37 n., 49 n., 132 n., 134 n., 207 n., 212 n., 228 n., 285, 290, 295–7, 322 sq., 323 n.; compares himself to a phoenix, 39, 149, 391; knows what constitutes the enjoyment of fishes, 39, 149, 391 sq.; a skull appears to him in a dream and tells him of the happiness of death, 39, 149; 40, 6 sq.; his style, 39, 156, 158; 40, 142–4, 275, 279, 283–5, 288; how he cured King Wăn of his love of the sword-fight, 39, 158 sq.; 40, 186–91, 186 n.; the greatest teacher of Tâoism, 39, 162 sq.; 40, 226 sq., 228 n.; his writings translated, 39, 164–392; 40, 1–232; instructs Tang about Benevolence, 39, 346–8; his vast superiority to Kung-sun Lung, 39, 387–90; offered by the king of *Kh*û the charge of all within his territories, he declines, 39, 390; in tattered clothes, &c., he tells the king of Wei that he is poor but not in distress, 40, 36 sq.; in the park of Tiâo-ling, 40, 39–41, 290; his interview with Duke Âi of Lû, 40, 49 sq., 49 n.; instructs Tung-kwo Ȝze about the Tâo, 40, 66 sq.; passing by the grave of his friend, Hui-ȝze, 40, 100 sq., 100 n.; asks the loan of some rice from the Superintendent of the Ho, 40, 132 sq.; rebukes Ȝhâo Shang for pandering to the king of Sung, 40, 207, 207 n., 211 sq.; about his burial, 40, 212; invited by a ruler, compares himself to a sacrificial ox, 40, 212; analyses by Lin Hsî-*k*ung of several of the books of *K.*, 40, 273–97; list of narratives, apologues, and stories in the writings of *K.*, 40, 298–310; where and when he lived, 40, 320 sq.; a sacrificial hall erected to *K.*, 40, 320–3; not his object to deride Confucius, 40, 321 sq.
***K*wan-hsü,** divine ruler of winter, 27, 296, 296 n., 302, 306; sacrificed to by sovereigns, 28, 201 sq.; deserves ancestor worship, 28, 208; got the Tâo, 39, 244 sq., 244 n.
Kwan Î-wû, *see* Kwan *K*ung.
Kwan *K*ung, or Kwan-ȝze, was extravagant in sacrifices, 27, 402; a worthy great officer, 28, 165; originated the practice of old servants mourning for a great officer, 28, 168; chief minister of Hwan, 40, 7, 7 n., 18 sq., 101 sq., 177.
Kwan Lung-făng, killed by *K*ieh, 39, 205; 40, 131, 131 n.

Kwan Yin and Lâo-ȝze, the great masters of true Tâoism, 39, 162; 40, 225–7, 226 n.

Kwan-ȝze, *see* Kwan *K*ung.

Kwei shăn, 'spirit-like operation (of Providence),' 16, 417, 418 sq. n. *See also* Gods (*n*).

Kwo Hsiang, prefixed the titles to the later books of *K*wang-ȝze, 39, 138.

Kwo-hu-hien-tsai-yin-ko-king, a life of Buddha, 19, xxv sq.

Kwo-hu-yin-ko-king, a life of Buddha, 19, xxv.

Kwo *K*âo-ȝze, mourning on the death of his mother, 27, 175.

Kwo-ȝze Kâo = *Kh*ăng-ȝze Kâo, q.v.

***K*yavana**, was made young by the A*s*vins, 26, 272–5; a Bhârgava, or an Âṅgirasa, 42, xxvii; Vâlmîki uttered the poetry which *K.* could not compose, 49 (i), 9.

***K*yavana**, a demon harassing children, 29, 296; 30, 211.

L

Labour, the ethics of, 3, 201 sq.; 4, lxii, lxvii, 21–4, 29–31; 27, 230; l. for the king in lieu of taxes, 25, 238; debts paid by personal l., 25, 285. *See also* Work.

Labourer, must have his wages, even if he be a heathen or a sinner, 4, 315, 315 n.; law about l., servants, craftsmen, apprenticeship, 7, 37 sq.; 33, 131, 133–5; about workmen and women, 37, 123. *See also* Servants, *and* Wages.

Lâ*dh*as, Mahâvîra travelled in the country of the, 22, 84 sq.

Lâhyâyani, *see* Bhugyu L.

Lake Âra, *see* Ara.

Lakes, *see* Holy places.

Lakkha*n*a, one of the eight Brahmans who took note of the marks on Buddha's body, 36, 44.

Lakshmî, wife of Vish*n*u, 7, 8, 293 n.; the highest Brahman, the abode of L., 48, 3. *See also* *Kh*âyâ, *and* S*r*î.

Lalitâprabudhâ, her son Ya*s*oda, 49 (i), 191.

Lalita-vistara, quoted, 8, 208 n., 261 n., 275 n., 284 n., 289 n., 337 n.; Upanishads referred to in L., 8, 212; *K*akkavatti idea in L., 11, xix; the white elephant legend in L., 11, 47; Dhamma*k*akkappavattana Sutta in L., 11, 139; L. and *G*âtaka, 11, 209; Chinese translations of the L., 19, ix, xxv, xxviii, xxx, xxxv; compared with the Mahâvagga, 21, xi–xiv.

Lambâ, n. of a giantess, 21, 373.

Land, penance for selling it, 7, 177; merit of giving l., 7, 272; 14, 135, 137; false evidence regarding l., 25, 271; 33, 93.

Languages, of barbarians not to be learnt by a Brâhma*n*a, 14, 40; Vai*s*yas must understand l., 25, 401; religious instruction given in Prâkrit, Sanskrit, and local dialects, 33, 265. *See also* Speech, *and* Words.

Lan Ȝü, disciple of *K*wang-ȝze, 40, 40, 40 n.

Lâo Lâi-ȝze, the Tâoist, lectures Confucius, 40, 135 sq., 135 n., 294.

Lăo-lung *K*î, Tâoist teacher, his death, 40, 68.

Lâo Tan, *see* Lâo-ȝze.

Lâo-ȝze, his meeting and interviews with Confucius, 3, xxi; 39, 2 sq., 34 sq., 145, 339 sq.; the 'Old Boy,' 3, xxi; 39, 35 n.; 40, 313; his names Lî *R*, or Lî Po-yang, or Lî Tan, 3, xxi; 39, 34 sq., 35 n.; L. or Lâo Tan quoted, 27, 22, 325, 340, 342; L. and Confucius assist together at a burial, 27, 339, 339 n.; the Tâo Teh *K*ing of L., 39, xii–xviii; not the founder of Tâoism, 39, 1–3; date of his birth, 39, 2, 4; Sze-mâ *Kh*ien's accounts of L., 39, 4 sq., 33–6; *K*wang-ȝze on the death of L., 39, 21, 36; speaks of himself as having renounced learning and as different from ordinary men, 39, 62 sq.; teaches that injury should be recompensed with kindness, 39, 91 sq.; complains of not being understood, 39, 112 sq.; his ideal of the people being kept in a state of perfect simplicity, 39, 122 sq.; mourning at L.'s death, 39, 131, 201 sq.; his disciple, Yang Ȝze-*k*ü, 39, 137, 156, 261 sq.; 40, 147 sq., 322 sq.; sets forth the evils of government, 39, 142, 294 sq.; L. and Shih-*kh*ăng *Kh*î abuse each other, 39, 145, 340–2; instructs

Confucius about the Tâo, 39, 152, 317 sq., 354–7, 354 n., 360–2; 40, 46–9, 47 n., 63–6, 292; his disciple Kăng-sang *Kh*û, 39, 153; 40, 75–8; and Kwan Yin, the great masters of Tâoism, 39, 162; 40, 225–7, 226 n.; reproves Confucius as not being a Perfect man, 39, 228 sq.; Kwang *Kh*ăng-ȝze an early incarnation of L., 39, 297 n.; 40, 256; the 'Record,' a work of L., 39, 308, 308 n.; Po-*kh*ăng Ȝze-kâo, a pre-incarnation of L., 39, 315 n.; in charge of the library of *K*âu, 39, 339; Confucius acknowledges his inferiority to L., 39, 357 sq.; 40, 46–9, 47 n., 314; defeats Ȝze-kung, 39, 358–60; teaches Nan-yung *Kh*û how to become a Perfect man, 40, 78–82; and his disciple Po *K*ü, 40, 122–4; called Lâo *K*ün, 40, 249 sq.; deified, 40, 249 sq.; denounces sageness and wisdom, 40, 286; the stone tablet in the temple of L., by Hsieh Tâo-hăng, 40, 311–19; miracles at his conception and birth, 40, 313, 313 n., 317; his person described, 40, 313, 317; incarnations of L. at different periods, 40, 313; offices held by him, 40, 313 sq., 313 n.; recognized by Yin Hsî as 'the True Man,' and prevailed upon to write his Book, 40, 314; *Kh*in Shih condoles on L.'s death, 40, 314 sq.

Lâ*t*yâyana, *S*rauta-sûtras of, 29, 371.

Laukântikas, gods, 22, 195, 256, 272, 283.

Laupâyanas, *see* Gaupâyanas.

Lâ-vahâk, n.p., 5, 135.

Law (Dharma, religion): *there are three branches of the l. Sacrifice, study, and charity are the first, austerity the second, and to dwell as a Brahmakârin in the house of a tutor ... is the third*, 1, 35; l. is the true, there is nothing higher than the l., 15, 89; Brâhma*n*as born for the protection of sacred l., 25, 25 sq.; rules of conduct the basis of sacred l., 25, 27; l. in the highest order of beings produced by goodness, 25, 495; Dhâman, what is settled, or l., 32, 383 sq.; libations of ghee identified with l. and truth, 44, 40; l. of Buddha, *see* Dhamma; wheel of the l., *see* Wheel; l. of Zarathustra, *see* Zoroastrianism;—l. (civil, criminal), sources and authorities of the, 2, 1, 15, 15 n., 44–7, 44 sq. n., 64, 64 n., 72, 93, 171, 175, 182, 225, 237, 265, 275, 310; 14, 1–4, 17, 17 n., 143–8, 181; 25, lxvii, 30–3, 508 sq.; 30, 81, 87; 33, 6 sq., 7 n., 15 sq. and n., 280 sq., 285 sq., 387; difficult questions of l. should not be answered directly, 2, 98, 98 sq. n.; conflicting statements on l. in the Veda, 2, 135 sq.; customs to be followed when not opposed to Scripture, 2, 137, 137 n.; civil and criminal l., 2, 163–71, 238–49; 4, lxxi, lxxxii–lxxxvii, 34–49, 252–7; 7, 24–41; 14, 18 sq., 70, 80–3, 97, 101, 200–4; 25, lxix, xcix, cii–cvi, 253 sq., 257–386, 390–4; 33, 32 sq., &c.; how to decide doubtful cases, 2, 310; 25, lxxiii, 509–11; criminal l., 3, 167–70; 27, 235–8; 36, 18 sq., 149 sq.; *see also* Punishments; eighteen titles of the l., 7, xxii; 25, lxix sq., xcviii, cii, 253 sq., 386; 33, xiii, 9–13 and n., 14 sq. and n., 274, 282–4, 291, 388; taught by Vish*n*u to the goddess of the Earth, 7, 8–12; regarding documents, 7, 21 sq., 26, 44, 46–8; with regard to insults, 7, 28 sq.; with regard to threatening and bodily injury, 7, 30 sq.; about gambling, 7, 36; regarding workman and employer, 7, 37 sq.; regarding deposits, 7, 38 sq.; about false promises, 7, 39; about bribery, 7, 39; about landmarks, 7, 39; with regard to self-defence, 7, 40 sq.; three means of proof: writing, witnesses, and proof by ordeal, 7, 44; Dharma or l. is four-footed, 7, 262, 262 n.; 25, 22 sq. and n.; Sûtras and metrical treatises on l., 14, xli; difficult to find is the path of the l. towards which many gates lead, 14, 145, 145 n.; origin of the sacred l., 25, xcviii; l. of castes, districts, guilds, families, 25, 260–2, 260 n.; teachers of l. satiated at the Tarpa*n*a, 29, 220; written l. superior to prudence, 33, 15; is subtile and difficult, 33, 15 sq. *See also* Assault, Boundary disputes, Caste (*i*), Crimes, Debts, Documents, Family, Inheritance, Judicial procedure, Labourer, Ordeals, Property, Taxes, *and* Trade.

Law-books, *see* Dharma-*s*âstras, Dharma-sûtras, *and* Sm*ri*ti.
Law courts, *see* Witnesses.
Law suits, *see* Judicial procedure.
Lay-devotees, *see* Buddhist laymen.
Learning, *see* Knowledge.
Legends, ancient and 'modern,' in the Brâhma*n*as, 12, xxiii–xxv; purpose of l. recorded in the Vedânta-texts, 34, lxxv; 38, 305 sq.; the Pâriplava Âkhyâna, revolving or cyclic l. recounted every ten days during the year of the horse-sacrifice, 44, xxxi, 361–71. *See also* Tales, *and* Veda (*a*).
Lei-thing, sprites haunting dust-heaps, 40, 19.
Lêpa, n. of a rich householder and *G*aina layman, 45, 420.
Lepers, *see* Diseases.
Lê*s*yâ, *G*aina t.t., a subtile substance accompanying the soul, produced by Karman, 45, 196 n., 196–203, 230 sq.
Letters, meditations on certain classes of, 1, 257, 258, 263–5; A the first among l., 8, 90.
Levirate, *see* Niyoga, *and* Widow.
Lî, and *Kh*ung made an end of the communication between earth and heaven, 3, 257, 257 sq. n.; misgovernment of King L., 3, 407 sq., 410, 417; meaning of the term, 27, 9–11; Kings Yû and L. corrupted the ways of *K*âu, 27, 372; sprites haunting mountain tarns, 40, 19; = Po-yü, q. v.
Liar, *see* Truth.
Libations, *see* Ordeals, *and* Sacrifices.
Liberality, *see* Charity, Gifts, *and* Râta.
Liberation, *see* Emancipation, *and* Nirvâ*n*a.
Lie, *see* Truth; demon of L., *see* Demons.
Lieh Yü-khâu, *see* Lieh-ȝze.
Lieh-ȝze, a Tâoist teacher, 39, 5, 85; quotes Lâo-ȝze, 39, 116 sq.; a semi-supernatural being, example of the 'spirit-like man,' 39, 127, 168 sq., 168 n.; L. and the wizard *K*i-hsien, 39, 137, 262–6, 263 n.; did not leave his house for three years, did the cooking for his wife, and fed the pigs, 39, 137, 265 sq.; on the transrotation of births, 39, 150; 40, 9 sq., 10 n.; stories from L. in *K*wang-ȝze's books, 39, 150, 160; 40, 15 n., 16 n., 20 n., 41 n., 53 n.; L. and the warden Yin, 39, 150; 40, 12–14, 12 sq. n.; surnamed Lieh Yü-khâu, when he lived, 39, 160; 40, 53; frightened at the respect shown to him by the soup-vendors, L. is warned by Po-hwăn Wû-ȥăn, 39, 160 sq.; 40, 202–4, 322 sq.; exhibits his archery to Po-hwăn Wû-ȥăn, 40, 53 sq.; though reduced to extreme poverty, he refuses a gift of grain from the ruler, 40, 155 sq.; not great, because he had something to wait for, 40, 274.
Lien Shû, conversation between him and *K*ien Wû, 39, 127, 170 sq.
Life: how to obtain longevity, 1, 50 sq.; 39, 23–5; 40, 270–2; a Snâtaka should not imperil his l., 2, 99, 222; 14, 63; the worshipped ancestors grant long l., 3, 326, 344 sq., 366–8, 370; l. and death, 5, 314; parable of human l., 6, 195 sq.; transitoriness and misery of human l., birth, old age, disease, death, 7, 78 sq., 281 sq.; 8, 79, 103, 109, 170, 201 n., 245, 247; 10 (ii), 106–8, 147, 154; 21, 77 sq.; 25, 500 sq.; 35, 273, 275–8; 36, 196–201, 302; 37, 201 sq.; 40, 64, 174 sq.; 45, 18–20, 41–4, 81 sq., 90; the three objects of l., i. e. virtue, love, and wealth, 7, 194; 19, 117 sq.; 49 (i), 98, 108 sq., 119 sq.; A*s*vattha tree a symbol of worldly l., 8, 111, 111 sq. n.; *he who properly perceives pleasure and pain to be inconstant, the body to be an unholy aggregate, and ruin to be connected with action; and who remembers that whatever little there is of happiness is all misery; he will cross beyond the fearful ocean of worldly l., which is very difficult to cross*, 8, 245; worldly l. allegorically represented as an impassable place, 8, 284; the sustentation of l. impossible without taking l., 8, 291; by what entities live, and what is the limit of their l., 8, 311; the l. of this world like the plants that spring up and perish, 9, 19; the l. of this world is but a sport, 9, 124, 232, 268; long is l. to the foolish who do not know the true law, 10

(i), 20, 20 n.; a l. of one day is better if a man is virtuous, than he who lives a hundred years, vicious and unrestrained, 10 (i), 33; that l. is best which is lived with understanding, 10 (ii), 30; the best l. according to Buddha, 10 (ii), 30 sq.; the Âsava of l., one of the Âsavas, 11, 297 sq., 300 sq.; one does everything for l., 15, 154; is where there is a living spirit in the soul's body, 18, 53; misery of worldly l. as compared with a religious (houseless) l., 22, 15–27; Mânîchaean doctrine of l., 24, 245 sq.; different length of l. in different ages, 25, 23, 23 n.; the differences between rich and poor, low and high, &c., caused by Karman, 35, 100 sq.; eight conditions (gain and loss, &c.) to which men are subject, 36, 257, 257 n.; worldly existence subordinate to spiritual l., 37, 8 sq., 14; precautions in depositing or handling things injurious to l., 37, 124 sq.; *men come forth and live; they enter (again) and die*, 39, 92 sq.; how the Tâoist sage shows his love of l., 39, 114 sq.; is a dream and a delusion, 39, 129 sq., 194–7, 254 sq.; dangers to l. from sensual desires, 39, 150; 40, 17 sq.; full understanding of the l. of the body, and the l. of the spirit, 39, 150 sq.; 40, 11–26; is l. worth living? 39, 180 sq. and n.; how the Tâoist looks upon l. and death, 39, 238, 242 sq., 246–55; 40, 59 sq., 85 sq., 279, 291–3; is the root of death, and death is the root of l., 40, 262; the great elixir, 40, 271, 283; l. of gods longer than men's, 41, 344; l. (vital power) and vital air, 43, 141, 143; man has a l. of a hundred years, 43, 299, 323–6; 44, 220, 261, 287, 298, 311, 313, 353, 357; l. and immortality, 43, 327, 357 sq.; the meritoriousness of sacrificing one's own l., 49 (ii), 125 sq., 129. *See also* Ahimsâ, Breath, Death, Pain, Samsâra, Suicide, *and* Transmigration.

Life-winds, *see* Prânas.

Light, which shines above heaven, is the same which is within man, 1, 47; on the road beginning with l. the departed soul proceeds, 1, 68, 80; 38, 382–4, 386–9; sun and knowledge the highest l., 1, 141, 141 n.; the endless and sovereign, 4, 221, 221 n.; 23, 177; l. or deity of l. not seen but by those who attain to the Adhyâtman, 8, 316; the entity, connected with the self called eye, with objects colour, its presiding deity the sun, 8, 337, 340, 348, 350, 352; sound, touch, and colour are the three qualities of l., 8, 384; Svar, the realm of l., the gods, 12, 270 sq.; by the l. of Brahman everything is lighted, 15, 20, 37; 34, xxxvi, 192–5; sun, moon, fire, sound, and the Self, are the l. of man, 15, 162 sq.; Brahman is the light of lights, 15, 178; 34, 193 sq.; between the earth and the region of infinite l. there are the star region, the moon region, and the sun region, 23, 73 n.; the heavenly ls. oppressed by Daêvas, and helped by Fravashis, 23, 194; endless ls., highest Paradise, 23, 317, 344; is the highest Brahman, 34, xxxiv, xxxviii, 87–97, 185, 191, 231 sq.; 48, 247–9, 256; the first-born l. which has not yet become tripartite, 34, 88 sq.; the highest l. identified with the gastric fire within man, 34, 89; l. of Brahman is the cause of the manifestation of this entire world, 34, 194; the prâgña Self is the universal l., 34, 195; the l. into which the soul enters is the highest Self, 38, 407; is immortality, 41, 383; 43, 238; three ls., viz. Agni, Vâyu, and Sûrya, produced, 44, 102. *See also* Luminaries, *and* Sun.

Lightning, the person in the, is Brahman, 1, 66, 151 sq., 152 n., 303; 15, 68, 101, 192; a station on the soul's road to the sun or Brahman, 1, 68, 80; 38, 386, 389; 48, 747 sq.; its red, white, and black colours, 1, 95; the presiding deity of air (skin, touch), 8, 337, 340; no impurity for those killed by l., 25, 185; lows like a cow, 32, 81, 91 sq.; ls. go in quest of the rain, 32, 98, 103; with gory teeth, 32, 209, 222; is the spear of the Maruts, 32, 272, 274; laughing or smiling ls., 32, 280, 284, 312, 315; 46, 205; the red apple shaken from the firma-

ment, 32, 331; prayer to l. as the cause of diseases, 42, 7, 246–52; is the teat whence the shower of wealth flows, 43, 221; kindled by the stars, 43, 399; one of the six doors to the Brahman, 44, 66 sq.; coming upon a sacrificial fire, l. is a sign for the sacrificer that the gods have helped him, 44, 193; a terrible form of rain, 44, 251; gold a symbol of l., 44, 251; Agni as the fire of l., 46, 103, 105.

Lî Kho, killed Hsî-*kh*î, 28, 294.

Lî*kh*û, a primaeval sovereign, 39, 287.

Lî *Kh*wan, commentator of the Yin Fû *K*ing, 40, 255–7.

Lî *K*î, or the Record of Rites, 3, xviii sq.; translated, *Vols.* 27 and 28; translations and editions of the work, 27, xi–xiv; how Confucius and Mencius spoke of 'the Rules of Propriety,' 27, 1 sq.; three different Lî King or Ritual Books acknowledged in China, 27, 1–9; its date, 27, 2; recovery of the first two, and formation of the third Ritual Book under the Han dynasty, 27, 2–9; one of 'The Five King,' 27, 2, 14; meaning of the title, 27, 11 sq.; value of the work, 27, 12–14; brief notices on the different books, 27, 15–60.

Lî *K*î, n. of a famous beauty, 39, 191, 191 n.; became the wife of the ruler of Ʒin, 39, 194.

Li*kkh*avis, of Vesâli, noble princes, wish to invite Buddha, but are outdone by the courtesan Ambapâli, 11, 31–3; 17, 106–8; claim relics of Buddha, 11, 131; a noble family of the soldier caste, 11, 131; 45, 321, 321 n., 339; erect a dâgaba at Vesâli, 11, 134; some of them dark, some fair, some red, some white, 17, 106; preached to and converted by Buddha, 17, 108–17; 19, 244, 257–66, 257 n., 258 n.; their grief about Buddha's death, and their full conversion, 19, 274–6, 278–82; destroy their books of heresy, 19, 279; their government, 22, xii; the nine Mallakis and nine L. celebrate the death of Mahâvîra by an illumination, 22, 266; L. or Li*kkh*ivi, a mixed caste, 25, 406, 615.

Li*kkh*ivi, see Li*kkh*avis.

Lî *K*û, the man of wonderful vision, 39, 269, 274, 286 sq., 311.

Lî-lû, a primaeval sovereign, 39, 287.

Limitation, *see* Property.

Ling, duke of Wei, 27, 323; 39, 132, 215; 40, 31; takes a deformed person for his friend and adviser, 39, 233 sq.; how he came by his epithet Ling, 40, 124–6, 125 n.

Liṅga-worship, supposed to be recognized in the Pravargya, 44, xlvii.

Lin Hsî-*k*ung, his analyses of *K*wang-ȝze's books, 40, 273–97.

Lin Hui of *K*iâ abandoned his jade symbol and hurried away with his infant son, 40, 34 sq., 34 n.

Lion, *see* Animals (*a*, *k*), *and* Parables (*c*).

Literati, *see* Confucianists.

Lî Thiâo, an officer of Duke Phing, 27, 179 sq.

Liû-hsiâ Hui, brother of the robber *K*ih, friend of Confucius, 39, 157 sq.; 40, 166 sq., 166 n., 175 sq.

Liû Hsiang, president of the council convoked by Hsüan, 27, 6.

Liû *K*wang, grand historiographer of Wei, 27, 183.

Liû Mî, on the object of Tâoism, 39, 23.

Liû Zo, warns Ʒze-sze, 27, 151 sq., 152 n.

Lives, *see* Souls.

Living beings, *see* Beings.

Lo, the city of, the new capital of the *K*âu, 3, 182–4, 196, 198–200, 218, 218 n.; 'The Announcement concerning Lo,' 3, 188–95.

Logic, non-exclusive expressions, 35, 208 sq.

Logos, Vohu-manô compared with, 4, lvi sq.

Lôharâsp, or Kaî-L., Av. Aurva*d*aspa, ruler of Iran, 5, 137, 137 n.; 37, 29, 29 n.; was 120 years, 5, 150; his exploits, 24, 64 sq., 64 n.; assists Nebuchadnezzar in the siege of Jerusalem, 47, xiii, 121, 121 n.; his accession, 47, xxix.

Lohitaka, one of the *Kh*abbaggiya-Bhikkhus, 17, 329 sqq., 339, 341 sq.

Loka, Sk., world, 1, 127 n.

Lokapâlas, *see* Gods (*a*).

Lokapradîpa, n. of a Tathâgata, 49 (ii), 66.

Lokaraksha, translated the Sukhâvatîvyûha, 49 (ii), xxii.
Lokasundara, the 76th Tathâgata, 49 (ii), 7.
Lokâyata, philosophical system not allowed to the Bhikkhus, 20, 151 sq.
Lokâyatikas, adepts of Lokâyata or worldly philosophy, 21, 263; 34, 14.
Lokendra, n. of Tathâgatas, 49 (ii), 6 sq.
Lokesvararâga, the last in the list of eighty-one Tathâgatas, 49 (ii), ix, 7-10.
Lomapâda, King, sacrifice of, 36, 17 n.
Lomasa Kassapa, the Bodisat, killed animals at the Vâkapeya sacrifice, 36, 16-19.
Longevity, *see* Immortality, *and* Life.
Lopâmudrâ, wife of Agastya, 32, 288; 49 (i), 44, 44 n.
Loqmân, the Aesop of the Greeks, 9, 131 n.; his advice to his son, 9, 132 sq.
Lord (îsvara), *see* God (*d*).
Lord of Beings, Vaisvadeva offering to, 29, 320.
Lord of the Forest, *see* Trees.
Lord of the Seat, invoked at the beginning and completion of a Kânda of the Veda, 30, 161.
Lord of Treasures, invoked at the house-building rite, 29, 347.
Lo-sung and his grandson, Tâoist teachers, 39, 247; 40, 282.
Lot, a chosen (prophet) of God, 6, 125; 9, 51, 173; story of L. and the destruction of Sodom, 6, 148, 213 sq., 248 sq.; 9, 51, 96 sq., 104, 120 sq., 173, 176, 242, 257; the people of L. called him liar, 9, 61; wife of L. punished for disobedience, 9, 292.
Lotus: l.-leaf not tainted by water, 8, 64, 64 n.; 36, 189, 189 n., 222 sq., 295; l.-ponds made by King Sudassana, 11, 261-4, 261 sq. n.; l. of the heart is the same as ether, 15, 306; Buddhas and Bodhisattvas in l.-flowers, 19, 222; 21, 248; 49 (ii), 178 sq.; compared with Brahman, 34, 348; not defiled by mud, 36, 119; 49 (ii), 57; l.-flowers presented at the Dasapeya, 41, 115-17, 115 n.; l.-leaf as symbol of the womb, of speech, of the waters, 41, 215 sq., 222, 343, 363-5; 43, xx, 118 sq., 368; Agni found on a l.-leaf, 41, 360; l.-leaf in the centre of the altar-site, 41, 363-5; 43, xx, 44, 374; is the immortal light, 43, 365-8; beings living in l.-flowers in Sukhâvatî, 49 (ii), x, 62-5; l.-flowers made of gem, in Sukhâvatî, 49 (ii), 36; l.-lakes in Sukhâvatî, 49 (ii), 93 sq.; L. of the True Law, *see* Saddharma-pundarîka. *See also* Avakâ plants, *and* Parables (*e*).
Love, Krishna is L. which generates, 8, 74, 89, 89 n.; hatred never ceases by hatred, but by l. only, 10 (i), 4 sq.; *let us live happily then, not hating those who hate us! among men who hate us let us dwell free from hatred!* 10 (i), 53; grief comes from l. and affection, but those who love nothing, and hate nothing, have no fetters, 10 (i), 56 sq.; (ii), 3, 61; 19, 222; *so long as the l. of man towards women, even the smallest, is not destroyed, so long is his mind in bondage*, 10 (i), 69; the dangers of l. and friendship, 10 (ii), 6 sqq.; cultivation of l. towards all beings, 10 (ii), 24 sq.; 11, 161, 163, 201, 273; 36, 329, 356; thoughts of L., the first of the 'infinite feelings,' 11, 201 sq., 273; the feeling of l. towards all beings, as a kind of magic power warding off dangers, 17, 136; 20, 76, 249 sq.; 35, 279-83, 282 sq. n.; *for not by hatred is hatred ever appeased; by not-hatred it is appeased; this is an eternal law*, 17, 298-305, 307; the remedy against pain, 19, 265, 265 n.; by l. Sabbakâmî reached a high old age, 20, 404 sq.; the fundamental subject, 27, 389; l. of man the great thing in the practice of government, 28, 264, 268; l.-charms, 30, 269 sq.; 42, 99-105, 274-7, 311-13, 356-9, 459 sq., 512 sq., 534-6, 539 sq., 546 sq.; as the tree gives shadow to everybody, so the Bhikkhu should love friend and foe, 36, 355; l.-charms to allay jealousy, 42, 18, 106 sq., 467 sq., 547 sq., 559; *quitting your former connexions place your affection on nothing; a monk who loves not even those who love him, will be freed from sin and hatred*, 45, 32, 264. *See also* Ahimsâ, Kâma, *and* Woman (*c*).

Low Arts, practising of, one of the four stains by which Samanas and Bhikkhus are affected, 20, 389 sq.

Lû, praise odes of, 3, 336-46; privileges of the marquises of L., 27, 29; 28, 32-9; distinction conferred on the princes of L., 27, 37 sq.; 28, 253 sq., 254 n.

Lü, marquis of, on punishments, 3, 254-64; Tâoist patriarch, quoted, 39, 86.

Lû Fang-hû, quoted, 40, 293.

Lü *Kh*un-yang, or Lü 3û, q. v.

Lü *K*î, marquis of *Kh*î, master of the guards to *Kh*ăng, 3, 237, 237 n.

Lû *K*ü, philosopher, 40, 99, 99 n.

Lumbinî, garden of, where Buddha is born, 10 (ii), 125; 19, 346-50; 49 (i), 198-200.

Luminaries: worship of sun and moon (and stars), 2, 96; 5, 352; 23, 158; 24, 264, 264 n.; 37, 477; 42, 160 sq.; 47, 168 sq.; *K*wang *K*iang, being badly treated by her husband, invokes sun and moon, 3, 433 sq.; sun, moon, and stars grieved by defilement, 4, 133, 144 n.; 18, 292 sq.; 37, 160; the l. created, 5, 10-13; 18, 88; Aharman's conflict with the planets, 5, 19; seven chieftains of the planets come unto the seven chieftains of constellations, 5, 21 sq. and n.; revolve round Mount Albûrz, 5, 22-4, 35; not to be looked at by a menstruous woman, 5, 283; sun and moon the eyes of K*ri*sh*n*a, 8, 94; the sun swallows up the moon, and another swallows up the sun, 8, 189, 189 n.; the forest of the Brahman receives light from the sun and moon, 8, 387; the Iddhi of touching the sun and the moon, 11, 214; the sun, and the phases of the moon, 18, 210 sq. and n.; cause of eclipses, 18, 212 sq. and n.; 24, 132, 132 n.; friendship between sun and moon, 23, 87; stars, sun, and moon worshipped, 23, 158; motion of sun and moon and stars, 24, 90, 92 sq., 100; planets bound to the sun and moon, 24, 132; sun and moon given to hell, 24, 225, 225 n.; arrangement of sun and moon according to Mânîchaean doctrines, 24, 244 sq.; not to be looked at by a Brâhma*n*a who is impure, 25, 151; in the second order of existences caused by goodness, 25, 495; sacrifices to sun and moon, 28, 218 sq., 218 n.; the Sun and Moon got the Tâo, 39, 136, 244; pointing suddenly at the three l., and looking long at the sun and moon are offences, 40, 244; Prâ*n*a is sun and moon, 42, 219; glory of Zoroaster descends from endless light to sun, moon, stars, and fire, 47, 18. *See also* Light, Moon, Stars, *and* Sun.

Lunar, *see* Moon; l. mansions, *see* Nakshatras, *and* Stars.

Lung, Minister of Communication to Shun, 3, 44 sq., 45 n.

Lung-făng, beheaded, 39, 283. *See also* Kwan L.

Lung Lî-*kh*ăn, a minister of the Marquis Wăn of Wei, 40, 43. *See also* Kung-sun Lung.

Lun Yü, or 'Discourses and Conversations,' the first of the four Shû, 3, xx.

Lü Pû-wei, the Yüeh Ling compiled from his *Kh*un *Kh*iû, 27, 20 sq., 251 n.

Lust, spiritual bondage of passion for, 11, 225, 229 sq.; Âsava of L., 11, 297 sq., 300 sq.; painfulness and dangers of l., 17, 378 sqq. *See also* Kâma, *and* Passion.

Lute, *see* Parables (*f*).

Lü Tung-pin, or Lü 3û, q. v.

Luxury, which the Bhikkhu is to avoid, 11, 193 sq.

Lü Yen, or Lü 3û, q. v.

Lü 3û, a famous Tâoist, who wrote 'Explanations of the Tâo Teh *K*ing,' 39, xvi sq.

Lying, *see* Truth.

M

Madanapâla, and Medhâtithi's commentary, 25, cxxiv sq.

Maddaku*kkh*i at Râgagaha, 11, 56 sq.

Maddî, wife of Vessantara, 35, 174; 36, 125, 125 n.

Mâdhava, n. of K*ri*sh*n*a, 8, 38, 41, 230 sq., 252; 48, 528.

Madhu, K*ri*sh*n*a, destroyer of, 8, 40, 42, 71, 77, 231, 252.

Madhuka Paiṅgya, pupil of Yâgñavalkya, n. of a teacher, 1, 280; 15, 214; 44, 122, 149, 162; worshipped at the Tarpa*n*a, 29, 123, 220.
Mâdhuki, a teacher, quoted, 12, 300.
Madhu*kkh*andas Vai*s*vâmitra, author of Vedic hymns, 1, 162; 32, 441; 46, 2.
Madhuparka, Sk., t.t., honey-mixture, *see* Honey.
Madhura, a chief Gandharva, 21, 5.
Madhurasvara, a chief Gandharva, 21, 5.
Madhuvidyâ, the mystic doctrine of the sun as honey, communicated by Dadhya*k* to the A*s*vins, 12, xxxiv; 15, 113–17; 26, 277; 34, 216 sq., 256 sq.; 38, 233; 44, 444 n., 471; 48, 335–7, 369.
Mâdhyamas, the poets of the second to the ninth Ma*nd*ala of the Rig-veda, 1, 215.
Madhyamâ *S*âkhâ, founded by Priyagantha, 22, 292 sq.
Mâdhyamikas, or Nihilists, believe that everything is void and nothing whatever is real, 34, li, 5 n., 401 n.; 48, 106, 514.
Mâdhyandinâyana, n. of a teacher, 15, 186.
Mâdhyandinîya-brâhma*n*a-upanishad, 15, xxx.
Madhyântika, follows after Ânanda, 19, xi, xiv.
Madman, excluded from inheritance, 2, 133; 14, 89; 33, 194; to be maintained by the king who takes his property, 14, 100; not responsible for criminal acts, 36, 18 sq.
Madras, n. of a people, 15, 132.
Mâdrî, wife of Pâ*nd*u, 49 (i), 45.
Magadha, Buddha in, 10 (ii), 11, 67, 188; people of M. annoyed at Buddha and the Bhikkhus, 13, 150 sq.; fever delivered over to the M., 42, 2, 446, 449.
Mâgandiya, offered Buddha his daughter for a wife, 10 (ii), 159–62; finds fault with Buddha, 36, 183.
Mâgandiyasutta, t.c., 10 (ii), 159–62.
Magga-brahma-*k*ariya*m*, the system developed in the Noble Eightfold Path, 11, 16 n.
Maggadesakas = Maggadesins, q.v.
Maggadesins, a kind of Sama*n*as, 10 (ii), xiii, 15 sq.
Maggadûsins, a kind of Sama*n*as, 10 (ii), xiii, 15 sq.
Magga*ggh*âyins = Maggadesins, q.v.
Magga*g*inas, a kind of Sama*n*as, 10 (ii), xiii, 15 sq.
Magga*g*îvins, a kind of Sama*n*as, 10 (ii), xiii, 15 sq.
Ma*ggh*ima-Nikâya, a Tevi*gg*a Sutta in the, 11, 159; *K*etokhila Sutta in the M., 11, 221; quoted, 36, xxiii, 54, 83 sq.; Lomaha*m*sana Pariyâya of M. quoted, 36, 331.
Ma*ggh*ima Sîla*m*, the middle paragraphs on conduct, 11, 192–5.
Mâgha, Buddha converts him, 10 (ii), 80–5.
Mâghasutta, t.c., 10 (ii), 80–5.
Maghavan, a king who became a *G*aina monk, 45, 85, 85 n.
Maghavat (°an), *see* Indra.
Magi, or Magians, and magicians confounded, 4, xxxix n.; forbidden to cross the sea, 4, xl; the only true priests of Mazdeism, 4, lxiii; enforce the sacredness of water and earth, 4, lxxvii; God will decide between Jews, M., and other faiths, 9, 58; insulter of a M. among the evil-doers, 31, 318; gifts to M. men, 37, 397.
Magic (art), learnt from Hârût and Mârût, 6, 14, 14 n.; Buddhist and *G*aina monk should not practise it, 10 (ii), 176; 45, 105; hostile m., 25, 85; in a list of arts and sciences, 35, 6; 44, xxxi; developed in modern Tâoism, 39, xii, 42, 44; practised by the Traidhâtavî offering, 41, 140 sq.; m. is the Veda, 44, 368, 368 n. *See also* Indragâlavidyâ.
Magic rites, human blood offered in, 2, 68 n.; penance for performing m. r. with intent to harm, 2, 85, 295; 7, 178 sq.; m. powers of the raven's feather, 23, 231, 241–3, 241 n.; making water round a runaway servant, 29, 350 sq.; to obtain different ends, 30, 306 sq.; m. veil, making invisible, 44, 70 n.; performed at the A*s*vamedha, 44, 368; practised by heretical monks, 45,

133 n., 363; a monk who, by m., carries off all women he sees, 45, 383 n. *See also* Plants, Samâdhis, Spells, Vows, *and* Witchcraft.

Magician, in Egypt, 6, 151 sq.; false and flattering speech is like the m.'s art, 19, 300 sq.; Brahman compared with a m., 34, xxv, xciv n.; multiform creations exist in m., 34, 353; illusive state of consciousness produced by m. by means of mantras, drugs, &c., 48, 75. *See also* Witchcraft.

Magog, *see* Gog.

Magundî, daughters of, female demons, 42, 66, 301.

Magûs, interpreted as 'men without ears,' 23, 4 n.

Mâh, his flower, 5, 104; invoked, 5, 402, 405; M. Yast, 23, 88–91; M. Nyâyis, 23, 349, 355 sq. *See also* Moon.

Mahâbala, king of Hastinâpura, became a *G*aina monk, 45, 88, 88 n.

Mahâbâla, or *K*u-ta-lih, translated the Siu-hing-pen-k'i-king, 19, xviii.

Mahâbhârata, passages of the Vish*n*u-smr*i*ti found in, 7, xxviii sq.; the Bhagavadgîtâ a genuine portion of the M.? 8, 2–6; references to M. by Bâ*n*a, 8, 28; Sanatsugâtîya loosely connected with the story of the M., 8, 135 sq.; passages quoted in Pa*ñk*atantra and Mahâbhâshya, 8, 138–41, 139 n.; the Anugîtâ in the A*s*vamedhaparvan of the M., 8, 197–206; passages of M. found in other works, 8, 203; M. and Manu-smr*i*ti, 8, 203, 226; 25, xiv, xvi, xxxviii, lx, lxxii–xci, xciv, xcvii sq., cvii, cxiv, cxvi; 33, xii, xv; M. and Dhammapada, 10 (i), 6 n., 16 sq. n., 36 sq. n., 51 n., 53 n., 54 n., 58 n., 61 n.; M. and *S*atapatha-Brâhma*n*a, 12, xxx, xxxii, xliii; M. and Baudhâyana Dharma-sûtra, 14, xli; passage of *S*vetâ*s*vatara-upanishad in the M., 15, xli; quoted, 25, xxxiv n.; 38, 375, 427; 48, 241, 400, 410, 528 sq.; legends of Manu in the M., 25, lxv; allusions to legends of the M., 25, lxxii n., lxxx, 222 n., 331 n., 352 n., 398 n., 399 n., 425 n., 478 n.; quotes a Dharma*s*âstra of Manu, 25, lxxv–lxxix; on Dharma*s*âstras, 25, xcvi, cvi n.; Bhârata and M. satiated at the Tarpa*n*a, 29, 220; Vedântic portions in the M. referred to by Bâdarâya*n*a, 34, cxxvii; there is one universal Self according to the M., 34, 295; the Atharva-veda in the M., 42, li–liv; horse sacrifice in the Â*s*vamedhikaparvan of the M., 44, xxvi–xxxiii; human sacrifices in the Sabhâparvan of the M., 44, xxxvi n.; Bhârata-Sa*m*hitâ in a hundred thousand *s*lokas, the Mokshadharma chapter quoted, 48, 528; philosophical systems recommended in the M., 48, 529 sq.

Mahâbhâshya, mentions Upanishads as part of Vedic literature, 8, 212; geography of India known to M., 8, 223.

Mahâbhi*gñ*â*gñ*ânâbhibhû, former Buddha, his sixteen sons, 21, xxix, 153–80, 183–7; how the numbers of his disciples increase, 21, 173 sqq., 186 sq.

Mahâbhûta, Sk., t.t., the five gross elements, 15, 296. *See also* Elements.

Mahâdamatra, worshipped at the Tarpa*n*a, 29, 123.

Mahâdeva, n. of Rudra, 29, 256; offering to him at the *S*ûlagava, 29, 352; invoked against the enemies, 42, 133; when the Agnihotra milk belongs to M., 44, 81.

Mahâdhanaka, a former birth of Devadatta, 35, 288 n.

Mahâdharma, n. of a Kinnara king, 21, 5.

Mahâ*g*a*gñ*u, n. of a *R*ishi, 14, 309, 309 n.

Mahâgandharâ*g*anirbhâsa, the 24th Tathâgata, 49 (ii), 6.

Mahâgiri, n. of a Sthavira, 22, 287; his eight disciples, 22, 289 sq.

Mahâgu*n*adhara, the 61st Tathâgata, 49 (ii), 7.

Mahâgu*n*adharabuddhiprâptâbhi*gñ*a, the 28th Tathâgata, 49 (ii), 6.

Mahaitareya, n. of a *R*ishi, 1, xcvii n.; worshipped at the Tarpa*n*a, 29, 123, 141, 220; M.-upanishad, *see* Upanishads (*a*).

Mahaka, and Ka*nd*aka, two novices who commit sodomy, 13, 205.

Mahâka*kk*âna, questions Bûddha about the behaviour in case of schisms, 17, 317. *See also* Ka*kk*âna.

Mahâ-Ka*kk*âyana, Sk. Mahâ-Kâtyâyana, pleads for special rules for the Bhikkhus in the Southern country and in Avanti, 17, 32–40; converted by Buddha, 19, 244; an eminent Arhat, 21, 2; 49 (ii), 90; Subhûti, Mahâ-K., Kâ*s*yapa, and Maudgalyâyana address Buddha, 21, 98 sqq., 144 sq.; Buddha's prophecy about M., who is to be the Buddha *G*âmbûnadaprabhâsa, 21, 147–9; Gopâla's mother gave a meal to the Elder M., 36, 146; quoted, 36, 282.

Mahâkalpa, its duration, 7, 78.

Mâhâ*k*amasya, n.p., taught the syllable Mahas, 15, 48.

Mahâkaphila, *see* Mahâ-Kappina.

Mahâ-Kappina (*or* Kappina, *or* Kapphi*n*a, *or* Mahâkaphila), n. of an eminent Arhat, 13, 247 sq.; 17, 317, 359; 21, 2, 2 n.; 49 (ii), 2, 90; one of the five hundred Arhats who are to become future Buddhas, 21, 198.

Mahâ-Kassapa, Sk. Mahâ-Kâ*s*yapa (Kassapa, Kâ*s*yapa), president of the First Council, immediately after the death of Buddha, 10 (i), xii; 20, 370–8; on Buddha's death and funeral, 11, xi sq.; 14, 126–9; 19, 323; 20, 370 sq.; is too venerable for Ânanda, 13, 228; going to the Uposatha, 13, 254; his robe, 17, 230; questions Buddha about the behaviour in case of schisms, 17, 317; successor of Buddha, 19, xi, xiv; conversion of Kâ*s*yapa Agnidatta (Eggidatta), i.e. M., 19, 197–201, 197 n.; a distinguished Arhat, 21, 2; 49 (ii), 2, 90; Subhûti, Kâtyâyana, M., and Maudgalyâyana address Buddha, 21, 98 sqq.; repeats the parable of the poor son of the rich man, 21, 108; saying of M. the Elder, 36, 330; Buddha exalts M. the Elder, 36, 340.

Mahâ-Kâ*s*yapa, *see* Mahâ-Kassapa.

Mahâ-Kâtyâyana, *see* Mahâ-Ka*kk*âyana.

Mahâkaushîtaka, satiated at the Tarpa*n*a, 29, 220.

Mahâkaushîtaki, worshipped at the Tarpa*n*a, 29, 123, 141.

Mahâ-Kaushîtaki-brâhma*n*a, in the *S*âṅkhâyana-sûtra, 44, xvi, xxxiii n., xliv, xlv n.

Mahâ-Kaush*th*il(y)a (Pali Ko*t*-*th*ita), an eminent Arhat, 21, 2; 49 (ii), 2, 90. *See also* Ko*tth*ita.

Mahâkautuka, his daughter Eka-*s*â*m*gî, 49 (i), 198.

Mahâkâya, one of the Garu*d*a chiefs, 21, 6.

Mahâketu, the 69th Tathâgata, 49 (ii), 7.

Mahâ Ko*tth*ita, *see* Ko*tth*ita.

Mahâ *K*unda, *see* *K*unda.

Mahâmaṅgalasutta, t.c., 10 (ii), 43 sq.

Mahâ-Maudgalyâyana, *see* Moggalâna.

Mahâmeru, n. of a Tathâgata, 49 (ii), 99.

Mahâ-Moggalâna, *see* Moggalâna.

Mahânâga, a title of Arhats and Buddhas, 49 (ii), 2–4.

Mahânâma, a distinguished Arhat, one of the first converts of Buddha, 11, 155 n.; 13, 100; 20, 224 sqq.; 21, 2; 49 (ii), 2.

Mahânâma, author of the Mahâva*m*sa, 10 (i), xiv–xx; 36, xviii sq.

Mahânâma, king of Ceylon, 10 (i), xv–xx.

Mahânanda, *see* Nanda.

Mahânârâya*n*a-upanishad, of the Taittirîyas, 15, xxvii; quoted, 48, 777.

Mahân Deva*h*, n. of Rudra (Agni), 41, 160.

Mahâpadesâ, Pali t.t., the four Great References or Authorities, 11, 66–70, 66 n.

Mahâpadma, a king who became a *G*aina monk, 45, 86, 86 n.

Mahâpadma, the elephant which supports the world, 49 (i), 17, 17 n.

Mahâ Paduma, prince, the Bodisat as, 35, 290.

Mahâpa*g*âpatî Gotamî, questions Buddha how she is to behave towards the litigious Bhikkhus, 17, 317 sq.; foster-mother of Buddha, 19, 355, 359 sq.; 20, 322, 380; 36, 51 sq.; entreats Buddha to allow women to enter the homeless state, 20, 320–7; questions Buddha as to the regulations for the Order of Bhikkhunîs, 20, 326–9; at the head of 6,000 nuns, 21, 3.

Mahâpaiṅgya, worshipped at the Tarpa*n*a, 29, 123, 220.
Mahâ - parinibbâna - Sutta(nta), 'The Book of the Great Decease,' 11, ix, xxix–xlviii, 1–136; date of the M., 11, x–xx, 19 n., 67 n., 92 n.; title and divisions of the M., 11, xxxii sq.; summaries and parallel passages from other parts of the Tipi*t*aka, in the M., 11, xxxiii–xxxvi; Chinese translation of the M. or of works based on it, 11, xxxvi–xxxix; 19, 251 n., 257 n., 365; legend of Mahâ Sudassana in the M., the *G*âtakas, and the Mahâ-Sudassana-Sutta, 11, 288 sq.
Mahâparinirvâ*n*a, *see* Nirvâ*n*a.
Mahâ Patâpa, King, Devadatta as, 35, 290.
Mahâprabha, n. of a Tathâgata, 49 (ii), 100.
Mahâpra*g*âpatî, *see* Mahâpagâpatî.
Mahâpra*gñ*â-pâramitâ-sûtra, Va*g*ra*kkh*edikâ, a portion of the, 49 (ii), xiii.
Mahâpratibhâna, a Bodhisattva Mahâsattva, 21, 4, 228 sqq., 255.
Mahâpûr*n*a, one of the Garu*d*a chiefs, 21, 6.
Mahârâ*g*a, a class of gods, 7, 293 sq. and n.; Bali offering to M. at the house-building rite, 30, 123. *See also* King.
Mahâratnaketu, n. of a Tathâgata, 49 (ii), 100.
Mahâratnapratima*nd*ita, n. of an aeon, 21, 66.
Maharddhikas, gods, 22, 195.
Maharddhiprâpta, one of the Garu*d*a chiefs, 21, 6.
Mahâr*k*iskandha, n. of a Tathâgata, 49 (ii), 100.
Mahârûpa, n. of the sphere in which the Buddha Mahâbhi*gñ*â*gñ*ânâbhibhû appeared, 21, 153.
Mahâ*s*âla *G*âbâla, Aupamanyava, n.p., 43, 331, 393, 395.
Mahâsambhava, n. of a Buddha-field, 21, 354 sq.
Mahâsena, a god, reborn as Nâgasena, 35, 11–14.
Mahâsthâma, and Avalokite*s*vara, 49 (ii), 176, 179, 197; meditation on M., 49 (ii), 184–7, 200.
Mahâsthâmaprâpta, a Bodhisattva Mahâsattva, 21, 4, 354–60; 49 (ii), 52.
Mahâsudar*s*a, a king, who retired into the forest with his wife, 49 (i), 87 sq.
Mahâ-Sudassana, a king of kings, whose royal city was Kusâvatî, 11, 100. *See also* Sudassana.
Mahâ-Sudassana *G*âtaka, translated, 11, 237–41, 288 sq. n.
Mahâ-Sudassana-Sutta(nta), the Legend of the Great King of Glory, 11, x, xiv, 99 n., 101 n., 235–89.
Mahâsûktas, and Kshudrasûktas, the hymns and poets of the tenth Ma*nd*ala of the Rig-veda, 1, 217.
Mahâsuvratâ, at the head of the female lay votaries under Arish*t*anemi, 22, 278.
Mahat, Sk., t.t., of Sâ*m*khya philosophy, *see* Great One.
Mahâtamâlapatra*k*andana - kardama, the 62nd Tathâgata, 49 (ii), 7.
Mahâte*g*as, one of the Garu*d*a chiefs, 21, 6.
Mahaudavâhi, worshipped at the Tarpa*n*a, 29, 123, 220.
Mahâ-vagga, of Sutta-nipâta, 10 (ii), 67–145.
Mahâ-vagga, of the Vinaya-pi*t*aka, prophecy of the future greatness of Pâ*t*aliputta in the, 11, xv, 19 n.; M. and Mahâ-parinibbâna-Sutta, 11, xxxiv; translated, 13, 71–355; 17, 1–325.
Mahâva*m*sa, t.w., on the Tipi*t*aka, 10 (i), xii sqq.; its date, 10 (i), xiii; founded on the Sinhalese A*tth*akathâs, 10 (i), xiii, xvi sq.; its author Mahânâma, 10 (i), xv–xx; account of Buddhaghosa in the M., 10 (i), xxi sqq.; Assagutta and the Vattaniya Hermitage in the M., 36, xviii sq.
Mahâvana, at Vesâli, 11, 59 sq.
Mahâvideha, Mahâvîra's parents will reach Nirvâ*n*a in, 22, 194.
Mahâvikrâmin, a Bodhisattva Mahâsattva, 21, 4.
Mahâvîra, date of his death, 10 (i), xli sq.; founder of the *G*aina church, his birthplace and parentage, 22, x–xv; his connexion with the feudal aristocracy, a cause of his success, 22, xiii; his names Vardhamâna, *G*nât*ri*putra, Nâtaputta, 22, xiv sq., xv n., 192–4, 249, 255 sq.; life of M., 22, xv–xviii, 189–202, 217–70; a contemporary of Buddha, 22,

xvi; 45, xiv; life of M. and life of Buddha compared, 22, xvii sq.; story of his birth, the removal of his embryo from the womb of the Brâhma*n*î Devânandâ to that of the Kshatriyâ*n*î Tri*s*alâ, 22, xxxi, xxxi n., 189–92, 217–56; description of the austerities and the mendicant life of M., and his indifference to pain, 22, 79–87; dwelling-places of M., 22, 82; travelled in Lâ*dh*a, 22, 84 sq., 84 n.; meditated free from sin and desire, 22, 87; plucked out his hair in five handfuls, 22, 189, 199, 217, 259; reaches Nirvâ*n*a, resp. Kevala, and becomes an Arhat, a *G*ina, a Kevalin, 22, 189, 201 sq., 217 sq., 258, 263 sq.; the five important events of his life happened in Uttaraphalgunî, 22, 189, 217 sq.; in Svâti he obtained final liberation, 22, 189, 218, 264 sq.; his various kinds of transcendent knowledge, 22, 190, 191, 200, 219, 229, 257, 263 sq.; his early childhood, 22, 192 sq.; his life as a prince of Videha, 22, 193 sq., 256; his relations and family connexions, 22, 193 sq., 256; gives away his property and retires from the world, thereby causing a great stir among the gods, 22, 194–200, 257–9; resolves to neglect his body for twelve years, 22, 200 sq., 260–3; teaches the five great vows, 22, 202–10, 212; 45, 121 sq., 434 sq.; the last of the Tîrthakaras, predicted by former Tîrthakaras, 22, 225 sq.; prisoners set free and great entertainments arranged in Ku*nd*apura at the birth of M., 22, 252 sqq.; wore clothes for a year and a month, then went about naked, 22, 259 sq.; the ideal ascetic, 22, 260–3; places where he spent his rainy seasons, 22, 264; became a Siddha, a Buddha, a Mukta, finally liberated, 22, 264 sq.; events happening on the death of M., 22, 265–7; his death in Svâti, 22, 269; had nine *G*a*n*as and eleven Ga*n*adharas, 22, 286 sq.; was of the Kâ*s*yapa gotra, 22, 287; 45, xxi; how he kept the Pa*gg*usan, 22, 296; declared the rules of the Paryusha*n*âkalpa, 22, 311; the Arhat *G*ñâtr*i*putra, of Vai*s*âli, who possessed highest knowledge and faith, 45, xv sq., 27, 261, 301, 304; a doctrine of Pâr*s*va ascribed to M. by Buddhists, 45, xxi; called an Aggivêsana, i.e. confounded with Sudharman by Buddhists, 45, xxi; his Syâdvâda established in opposition to Sa*ñg*aya's Agnosticism, 45, xxvii; relation between M. and Gosâla Makkhaliputta, 45, xxix–xxxii; forbade the use of clothes, which Pâr*s*va allowed, 45, xxx; his success in propagating his creed, 45, xxxii; declared the twenty-two troubles which a monk must conquer, 45, 8–10, 15; when M. spoke, he was understood by all creatures whatever their language, 45, 8 n.; describes the death of the ignorant man, 45, 21; addresses a sermon to his disciple Indrabhûti, 45, 41–6; Pâr*s*va and M., *S*vetâmbara and Digambara sects, 45, 119 n., 119–29; his disciple Gautama, i.e. Sudharman, 45, 120; preaches on the seventy-three articles by which final beatitude is reached, 45, 158, 173; on the fate of heretics, 45, 239; describes the hells, 45, 279; praise of M., the omniscient great sage, 45, 287–92; how to become a M., or a Great Hero, who is omniscient, does not die, and is not born again, 45, 329–32; first wandered about as a single monk, and then went about teaching his doctrines to many people, 45, 409; Go*s*âla compares M. with a merchant, and is rebuked by Ârdraka, 45, 413 sq. *See also* *G*ina.

Mahâviyûhasutta, t.c., 10 (ii), 171–4.

Mahâvrata, the Great Rite, the last day of the Gavâmayana, a sacrifice lasting a whole year, 1, xcii sq., xcix, 157–99, 258, 260; 26, 427 n., 429–32, 429 sq. n.; 43, xxv–xxvii, 282–9, 282 sq. n., 342, 342 n., 346–9; 44, 165, 167, 167 n.; is for the attainment of Brahman, 1, 162; belongs to Indra, 1, 167, 170; is Brahman, 1, 169; the Hot*ri* priest sitting on a swing at the M., 1, 172–6; the most important day of the Soma sacrifice, 1, 224 n.; restrictions as to teaching the M. ceremony, 1, 266–8; formerly one of the three

great rites of the Sattra, 44, 139 n., 144, 159 sq., 167.
Mahâvrishas, n. of a people, 1, 57 n., 58; 42, 1 sq., 446, 448.
Mahâvyûha, n. of the age of the Buddha Rasmiprabhâsa, 21, 142.
Mahâvyûha, the 57th Tathâgata, 49 (ii), 7.
Mahâyagña, *see* Sacrifice (*b*).
Mahâyâna, school of Buddhism, its doctrine on the person of Buddha, 21, xxviii; the Saddharma-pundarîka an exposition of the M. system, 21, xxxii; the distinguishing features of the M. system from the Hînayâna doctrines, 21, xxxiii sq.; why victorious over the Hînayâna, 21, xxxvii; the instrument of the Law of the perfect Buddha, 49 (i), 184; Buddhist M. texts, *Vol.* 49 (ii); tenets of Mahâyâna metaphysics, 49 (ii), xiv–xix.
Mâh-ayâr, n.p., 5, 147.
Mâh-bôndak, n.p., 5, 147.
Mâh-bûkht, n.p., 5, 147.
Mâh-dâd, n.p., 5, 145, 194.
Mahendra, n. of a mountain, 8, 346.
Mahendra, god, Sânnâyya offered to, 12, 182; 30, 337; the special deity of a gatasrî, 12, 183 n.; oblations to M., 12, 408 n., 419; 30, 123; 44, 76 n., 77; Soma libation (Mâhendra-graha) for M., 26, 338, 404; 41, 13, 17 sq., 41, 81, 113; Indra became M. after slaying Vritra, 26, 338; worshipped at the new and full moon sacrifices, 29, 173, 392; 30, 37; Mahêndras enjoy themselves on Mount Meru, 45, 288.
Mahendra, prince, his invasion of Ceylon, 8, 223.
Mahesvara, fell in love with the daughter of Himâlaya (Umâ, Pârvatî), 19, 150; announces to the Devas the birth of Buddha and admonishes them to pay homage to him, 19, 361 sq.; Îsvara and M., two gods, each followed by 30,000 gods, 21, 4; M. and Îsvara entreat Buddha to teach the law, 21, 55; Brahma, Îsvara and M., and Indra, 21, 349; Avalokitesvara assumes the shape of M., 21, 411; worshipped before the ordeal by poison, 33, 260. *See also* Siva.
Mâhesvaras, *see* Saivas.
Mâhesvarî, or Pârvatî, or Umâ, the chief of all females, 8, 219, 347, 347 n.
Mahî, n. of a river, 10 (ii), 3.
Mahî, a goddess, invoked in Âprî hymns, 46, 8, 11 sq., 154, 377.
Mahidâsa Aitareya, author of the Aitareya-brâhmana and Âranyaka, 1, xciii–xcv; lived 116 years, 1, 51; quoted, 1, 212 sq., 231.
Mahiddhi, Brâhmans pray to, 11, 180.
Mahikerus, n. of a family (?), 46, 42 sq.
Mahiman, cup of Soma, 44, 391, 394.
Mahinda, son of Asoka, Buddhist missionary in Ceylon, 10 (i), xiii, xxiv sq. *See also* Mahendra.
Mahishî, t.t., the king's first wife, 41, 238; 44, 386 sq.
Mâhissatî, n. of a town, 10 (ii), 188.
Mâhitthi, n. of a teacher, 15, 227; 41, 175; 43, 105–8, 271, 404.
Mahopanishad, quoted, 48, 522.
Mahosadha, Amarâ, the faithful wife of, 35, 294–7.
Mahraspand, *see* Mãthra Spenta.
Mahrkûs, a wizard, destroyed by the Dâhmân Âfrîn, 47, xii, xxxi, 108, 108 n.; the winter of M., 47, 9 sq.; a devastator, 47, 126. *See also* Mahrkûsha.
Mahrkûsha, the demon who sends the deathly winters, 4, 251, 251 n. *See also* Mahrkûs.
Mâhvand-dâd, quoted, 5, 215 sq., 216 n.
Mâh-vindâd, copied the Dînkard, 37, xxxiv–xxxvi, xxxviii.
Mâhya, the monthly festivals, worshipped as deities, 31, 198, 205, 210 sq., 216, 220, 224, 368, 379.
Maiden, *see* Marriage, *and* Woman (*a*, *b*, *e*).
Maidhyâirya, worshipped, 31, 198, 205, 210, 216, 220, 225, 335, 338, 368, 370, 372.
Maidhyô-mâh, the Spitâma, a follower of the law of Ahura, 31, 186.
Maidhyô-maungha, first disciple of Zarathustra, 23, 203; his son Ashastu, 23, 209; the younger, 23, 219.
Maidhyô-shema, worshipped, 31,

198, 205, 210, 216, 220, 224, 335, 338, 368, 372.

Maidhyô-zaremaya, worshipped, 31, 198, 205, 210, 216, 220, 224, 335, 338, 368 sq., 372.

Maî*d*ôk-mâh, Zoroaster relates the incidents of his birth to, 37, 226 sq.; disciple of Zoroaster, 37, 230; praise of M., 37, 298.

Maighika Kula, of the Ve*s*avâ*t*ika Ga*n*a, 22, 291.

Mainyô-i Khar*d*, refers to next-of-kin marriage, 18, 398 sq. *See also* Dînâ-î Maînôg-î Khira*d*.

Maithilas, suffered destruction, 49 (i), 116.

Maitra, converted by Buddha, 49 (i), 190; his daughter Gopikâ, 49(i), 198.

Maitra, *see* Love.

Maitrâvaru*n*a, *see* Priests (*a*).

Maitrâvaru*n*î, *see* I*d*â.

Maitrâya*n*a - brâhma*n*a - upanishad, *see* Maitrâya*n*îya-upanishad.

Maitrâya*n*îputra, *see* Pûr*n*a M.

Maitrâya*n*îya-sa*m*hitâ, quoted, 38, 427; gives the mantras of the A*s*vamedha, 44, xvi.

Maitrâya*n*îya - upanishad, or Maitrâya*n*a-brâhma*n*a-upanishad, or Maitri-upanishad, 1, lxx; 8, 418 sq.; 15, xliii–lii, 285–346; M. and Manusm*ri*ti, 25, xliv sq., lxxiii; Mâyâ in the M., 34, cxvii n., cxxi n.; quoted, 38, 427; 48, 458.

Maitreya, preserves the Buddhist scriptures, 19, xv; n. of a Bodhisattva Mahâsattva, 21, 4, 8–16, 22 sq., 28 sq., 286–99, 311, 316, 328; 49 (i), 180; (ii), 2; called Agita, 21, 18 sq.; recites stanzas in honour of Buddha, 21, 314; resides among the Tushita gods, 21, 436.

Maitreya, questions Parâ*s*ara, 48, 92.

Maitreya-upanishad, t.w., 15, xliv–xlvi.

Maitreyî, wife of Yâ*gñ*avalkya, taught by her husband, 15, 108–13, 181–5; 34, 274 sqq.; 48, 387, 395 sq. *See also* Sulabhâ M.

Maitreyî-brâhma*n*a, the story of Yâ*gñ*avalkya and Maitreyî, 15, xlvi; 38, 305 sq.; 48, 385 sq., 388, 395 sq.

Maitri, or Maitra, n. of a sage, 15, xlvii, 290 sq.

Maitri-upanishad, *see* Maitrâya*n*îya-upanishad.

Maitrîya, told by Buddha to turn the wheel of the law, 49 (i), 173 sq., 173 n.

Makha, deity, initiated boy given in charge to, 30, 154; is the sacrifice, 41, 233; 44, 443, 450–8; Indra cut off the head of M., which is restored by the Pravargya, 44, xlviii, 450–8; performs sacrifice, 44, 441; is Vish*n*u, 44, 443; worshipped at the Pravargya, 44, 460; is the sun, 44, 460.

Makkhali Gosâla (M. of the cowpen, or Go*s*âla Makkhaliputra), n. of a teacher, 10 (ii), xii, 86 sq.; 11, 106; 35, 8–10; 45, xxii sq., 409–14; an Arhat possessed of Iddhi, 20, 79; relation between him and Mahâvîra, 22, xvi, xviii; 45, xxix–xxxii; his doctrines refuted, 45, ix, 245, 245 n.; system of Fatalism ascribed to him, 45, xxv sq.

Ma*kkh*ikâsa*nd*a, Sudhamma and *K*itta at, 17, 359.

Mâkshavya, n. of a teacher, 1, 247.

Maku*t*a-bandhana, a shrine of the Mallas where the cremation of Buddha's body is to take place, 11, 124 sq., 129.

Maku*t*adantî, n. of a giantess, 21, 374.

Mâlâdhârî, n. of a giantess, 21, 374.

Mâlâlaṅkâravatthu, t.w., 11, xvi sq., 32 n., 82 n.; based on the Mahâparinibbâna-Sutta, 11, xxxii.

Male, and female created, 8, 244 n.; 16, 435; ruler over females, 8, 346, 346 n.; 43, 230; m. organ, 44, 19; m. and female, *see also* Woman (*f*).

Mâlik, the keeper of hell, 9, 217, 217 n.

Malimlu*k*a, n. of a demon harassing infants, 29, 296.

Malkôs, the deluging rain of, 18, 109, 109 n.; 24, 59, 59 n.; will arise, 24, 268.

Mallakis, instituted an illumination on the death of Mahâvîra, 22, 266.

Mallas (Mallians): Pukkusa, a young Mallian, 11, 75, 75 n.; Sâla grove of the M., 11, 81, 85, 247; come to take leave from Buddha, 11, 101–3; 19, 285–90; informed of Buddha's death, their grief, they perform obsequies, 11, 121–31; 19, 321–5; claim relics of Buddha, and erect a

dâgaba, 11, 133, 135; 19, 325–34; establish a compact that whosoever did not welcome Buddha should pay a fine, 17, 135.

Malli, n. of a Tîrthakara, 22, 280.

Mallikâ, the queen, the fame of her good deeds reached to the gods, 35, 172; a flower girl, became chief queen, 36, 146.

Mâluṅkyâ-putta, his question not answered by Buddha, 35, 204–6.

Mâlyaka Kula, of the *K*âra*n*a Ga*n*a, 22, 292.

Mâlyavat, n. of a mountain, 8, 346.

Mamaka, perhaps n.p., 46, 29.

Mamatâ, *R*ishi Dîrghatamas, the blind son of, 46, 170, 171; sons of M., 46, 332; daughter of the Maruts, 49 (i), 44.

Man (men, mankind), is a creature of will, 1, 48; is sacrifice, 1, 50 sq., 223; 38, 220 sq., 265; 44, 19 sq.; water in the fifth 'libation' called M., 1, 77–9; consists of sixteen parts, 1, 97 sq.; 44, 19 sq.; the abode of Brahman, 1, 205 sq.; *and in m. again the self develops gradually, for he is most endowed with knowledge.... By means of the mortal he desires the immortal—thus is he endowed*, 1, 222; *m. is the sea, rising beyond the whole world. Whatever he reaches, he wishes to go beyond. If he reaches the sky, he wishes to go beyond. If he should reach that (heavenly) world, he would wish to go beyond*, 1, 223; is fivefold, i. e. consists of the five elements, 1, 223; 43, 326 sq.; the body of m. represented as the whole world, 1, 249; most highly endowed, noblest of all creatures, 3, 125, 476; 37, 238; receives body and soul from Heaven, 3, 139 n.; all m. are good at first, 3, 234, 410 sq., 411 n., 425 n.; 16, 356, 357 n.; as a microcosm, 4, 191 n.; origin or creation of m., 5, 10; 8, 387; 18, 197–9, 224 sq.; 24, 58; 37, 25 sq.; 41, 402; 43, 403; on the nature and varieties of m., 5, 52–9; varieties of human monsters, 5, 59, 59 sq. n.; fire in m. and animals, 5, 61 sq.; how the black-skinned negro arose, 5, 87; three material, and eleven immaterial things in m., 5, 355, 355 n.; the three greatest concerns of m., 5, 394 sq.; m. were one nation once, 6, 30; soul of m. is enveloped in six sheaths, three of which come from the father, and three from the mother, 7, 171 n.; K*r*ish*n*a is the ruler of m. among m., 8, 89; action the characteristic of m., 8, 348; birth, growth, and death of m. are proofs of resurrection, 9, 56 sq.; creation, conception, birth, death, and resurrection of m., 9, 65 sq., 196 sq., 312; lives even longer than a hundred years, 12, 272; fifteen parts of m., 15, 41; duty of m., in what it consists, 15, 51 sqq.; compared with a tree, 15, 149 sq.; is the altar on which the Devas offer food, 15, 208; Heaven and Earth and m., 'the three Powers,' 16, 351, 351 sq. n., 402, 402 sq. n., 423 sq., 424 n.; 28, 115, 115 n., 300 sq., 301 n., 319, 319 n.; 40, 258–60; flesh of m. must not be eaten by Bhikkhus, 17, 84 sq.; why m. are created, and what they ought to do, 18, 25 sq.; created as a guardian of the creatures, 18, 88; three kinds of m., 24, 82 sq.; dwelling of understanding, intellect, seed, and wisdom in m., 24, 89 sq.; the chief of m. is he who is wise, religious, and true, 24, 107; four capabilities in m., 24, 119; good and bad influences in m., 24, 133, 160 sq.; design in the organization of the human body and soul, 24, 143–5; Iblîs refuses to do homage to the first m., 24, 178, 178 n.; did evil arise before or after or with m.? 24, 187 sq., 194 sq.; punishments for stealing m., 25, 310; 33, 227, 362 sq.; is impure by speaking untruth, 26, 8, 16; the highest of animals, 26, 210, 407; 41, 402; consists of body, animal soul, and intelligent soul, 27, 36; 28, 220–2; 39, 21–3, 316, 316 n.; 40, 251; stages of a m.'s life, and characteristics of each stage from childhood to old age, 27, 65 sq.; the seven feelings of m., 27, 379 sq.; likes and dislikes of m., 27, 380; *m. is the heart and mind of Heaven and Earth, and the visible embodiment of the five elements*, 27, 380–2, 382

sq. n.; propriety and righteousness the great elements for m.'s character, 27, 388; *of all that Heaven produces and Earth nourishes, there is none so great as m.*, 28, 229; good m. and women worshipped, 31, 253, 257, 385 sq.; mutual service of m., cattle, and sacred beings, 37, 265; m.'s place among other m. in the world, 39, 131 sq., 203; can a m. be without desires and passions? 39, 134, 234 sq.; being in harmony with m. is called the Joy of M., 39, 144, 332; influence of external things on m. cannot be determined beforehand, 39, 155; 40, 131 sq.; the difficulty of knowing the mind of m., and nine methods of testing it, 39, 161; 40, 209; six classes of men described, 39, 363 sq.; is only one of myriads of existences, 39, 376; inconstancy of m.'s lot, 39, 377; birth and life of m., 40, 64; spirits residing in m., 40, 236, 236 n.; striding over a m., a wicked act, 40, 243; harmony of Heaven and M., 40, 257–64; m.'s body is the house of the breath, the mind the lodging of the spirit, 40, 270; flayed by the gods, and his skin put on the cow, 41, 31, 31 n.; belong to Vish*n*u, 41, 54; lives up to a hundred years, 41, 93, 135, 405; 44, 261, 275; has a hundred powers, 41, 93, 135; 44, 275; m.'s thought taken by the sun, 41, 130; one of the five animals to be sacrificed at the building of the fire-altar, 41, 162, 165 sq., 177, 404 sq., 407, 409; *m. is born into the world made by him*, 41, 181, 181 n.; a sham-m. substituted for m. at sacrifice, 41, 197, 197 n.; is a fathom high, 41, 309; is Pragâpati, 41, 309; life of m. shorter than that of gods, 41, 344; tends upwards by his vital airs, 41, 368; is not held down by food or breath, 41, 379; clay is m.'s human form, 41, 382; have their birth-place in the west, 41, 389; five races of m., 42, 201, 204; 43, 269; in the list of cattle, 43, 38; cattle are his food, 43, 335; m. at the end of sexual union becomes apathetic, 43, 370; serve the person in the eye under the name of 'wealth,' 43, 373; is born thrice, through birth, sacrifice and death, 44, 23 sq.; why the limbs of m. are tripartite and furnished with two joints, 44, 77; sacrifice to m., one of the 'five great sacrifices,' consisting in presents to guests, 44, 95; the Year is M., 44, 144 sq., 168 sq.; Sacrifice, M., and Pragâpati do not exceed one another, 44, 165 sq.; from the Sacrifice M. (the Purusha, Agni-Pragâpati, and the Sacrificer) is born, 44, 259–64; does not know rightly the way to heaven, 44, 305; are the people of Manu Vaivasvata, 44, 361; is twenty-one-fold (ten fingers, ten toes and the body), 44, 378; to be born in the state of m., the first requisite to reach beatitude, 45, 15 sqq.; are of ten kinds, 45, 17; live either in Karmabhûmi, or in Akarmabhûmi, or on the minor continents, 45, 224 sq.; only m. can obtain perfection, 45, 331, 331 n.; on the generation of the different classes of m., and how they feed, 45, 393 sq., 393 n.; human birth is a rare chance for a living being, 45, 42 sq.; *but see also* Transmigration; souls of m., 48, 198. *See also* Animals (*d*), Creation, Life, Male, Manu, Mashya, Purusha, *and* Superior Man.

Mâna, another name of Agastya, 46, 182, 184. *See also* Mândârya.

Mânadantavya, quoted, 29, 389.

Mana*h*paryâya, a kind of transcendent knowledge, 22, 200, 268 n.

Manaka, *S*ayyambha, father of, 22, 287.

Manas, Sk., mind or internal organ, 34, xxiii, xxvi, li, lxxix, cxxi, 175, 239, 376 n., 398 n., 440; 38, 14, 16, 27, 33, 48, 65 n., 69, 81 sq., 84, 89 sq., 260, 336, 411, 413–15; 48, 162, 169, 188, 210, 356 sq., 481, 497, 570–2, 577. *See also* Internal organ, *and* Mind.

Mânas, the people of Mâna or Mândârya, 32, 289, 291.

Manasâka*t*a, a Brâhman village in Kosala, 11, 167, 169, 185 sq.

Mânasî and her image *K*âkshushî, 1, 276.

Manasvin, n. of a Nâga king, 21, 5.

Manât, a stone worshipped by

Arabian tribes, 6, xii sq.; the divinity of M. recognized and again denied by Mohammed, 6, xxvi sq.
Mânatantavya, n. of a teacher, quoted, 30, 28, 28 n.
Mânatta, t.t., penance, when unlawful, 17, 270 sq.; regulations about the m., 17, 397–418, 420–39. *See also* Sa*m*gha (disciplinary proceedings).
Mânava, *S*aryâta, the, 26, 273.
Mânava Dharma-*s*âstra, *see* Manu-sm*ri*ti.
Mânava Dharma-sûtra, converted into our Manu-sm*ri*ti, 25, xix sq., xxii–xlv, lxv–cvi.
Mâ*n*ava-gâmika, n. of a god, 36, 55.
Mânava Ga*n*a, founded by *R*ishigupta Kâkandaka, 22, 292.
Mânava-G*ri*hya-sûtra, and Kâ*th*aka-G*ri*hya-sûtra, 7, xxvi, xxvii n.; M. and Manu-sm*ri*ti, 25, xxiii, xxxviii–xl; on marriage by purchase, 25, xciii.
Mânavâ*k*ârya, author of Mânava-sûtras, 25, lxiii, lxiii n.
Mânavas, home of their school, 25, xlv.
Mânava *S*râddhakalpa, and Manu-sm*ri*ti, 25, xl–xliv.
Manâvî, wife of Manu, 12, 29 sq.; 25, lx.
Ma*nd*âkaka, n. of a demon, 30, 220.
Mâ*nd*alikas, mothers of, wake up after seeing one of the fourteen auspicious dreams, 22, 246.
Mandapâla, married Sârangî, 25, 331, 331 n.
Ma*nd*ârava, *see* Flowers.
Mândârya, son of Mâna, *R*ishi of hymns to the Maruts, 32, 181, 183 sq., 203, 206, 211, 273, 280.
Mâ*nd*avya, n. of a teacher, 15, 227; 29, 141; worshipped at the Tarpa*n*a, 29, 122, 220; declared a thief by unjust trial, 33, 16, 16 n., 285; pupil of Kautsa, 43, 404.
Mandha, *see* Mândhât*ri*.
Mândhât*ri* (Mandha), miraculously born from the forehead, 19, 3; 49 (i), 6; obtained the half of *S*akra's throne, and was not satisfied, 19, 118, 122; 49 (i), 113; typical great king, 19, 221, 275; went up to heaven, even in his human body, 35, 172; 36, 146; bow of M., 49 (i), 108.
Ma*nd*ikaputra, n. of a Sthavira, 22, 286.
Ma*nd*ikukshi *K*aitya, n. of a park, 45, 100.
Ma*nd*u, worshipped at the Tarpa*n*a, 29, 122; honoured as teacher, 29, 141.
Ma*nd*ûka, a god, conversion of, 36, 249.
Mâ*nd*ûkâyani, n. of a teacher, 15, 227; 43, 404.
Mâ*nd*ûkâyanîputra, n.p., 15, 225.
Mâ*nd*ûkeya, n. of a teacher, 1, 247 sq., 251, 252; two teachers, father and son, 1, 248; Hrasva M., 1, 253, 257, 265; quoted, 29, 25, 28, 83; worshipped at the Tarpa*n*a, 29, 123, 220.
Mâ*nd*ûkîputra, n.p., 15, 225.
Mâ*nd*ûkya - upanishad, quoted, 8, notes to 79, 247, 251, 259, 324, 376.
Manes, *see* Ancestors, Fathers, Fravashis, Souls, *and* Spirits.
Man-fû, of Ȝâu, his mother told Confucius the grave of his father, 27, 124.
Măng Hsien-ȝze, his excessive mourning, 27, 129 sq.; mourning rites for him, 27, 154; quoted, 28, 167, 167 n., 423.
Măng-hû, uncle of Wăn, 27, 152.
Măng *K*ing-ȝze, on funeral rites, 27, 174.
Mango Grove, at Pâvâ, 11, 70, 82 sq.
Măng Phî, nephew of Wăn, 27, 152.
Măng-sun Ȝhâi, how he behaved on the death of his mother, 39, 253–5; obtained the Tâo, 40, 283.
Mañgudhva*g*a, n. of a Tathâgata, 49 (ii), 99.
Mañ*g*ughosha, *see* Mañ*g*u*s*rî.
Mañ*g*ûshakas, *see* Flowers.
Mañ*g*u*s*rî, or Mañ*g*ughosha, a Bodhisattva Mahâsattva, 21, 3 sq., 8–29, 248–50, 363; 49 (ii), 90, 161, 161 n.; taught the daughter of the Nâga-king Sâgara the Lotus of the True Law, 21, 250–4; Buddha explains to him the rules of conduct for a Bodhisattva, 21, 262–80; the prince royal, 21, 394, 396 sq., 399, 404.
Mañ*g*usvara = Mañ*g*u*s*rî, 21, 16; Tathâgatas, called M., 49 (ii), 71.

Măng-ȝze, a eunuch, composed an ode of the Shih, 3, 295.
Măng Ȝze, record of her death, 28, 298.
Măng Ȝze-fan, n. of a Tâoist, 39, 250, 250 n.
Mânî, doctrines of, criticized, 24, 243, 243 n.
Ma*n*ibhadra, disciple of Sambhûta-vigaya, 22, 289.
Mânichaeans, *see* Manicheism.
Manicheism, a heresy of Zoroastrianism, 4, xlvi; *of a mixed law are those of the Sinik congregation* (M.?), 5, 296, 296 sq. n.; criticism of its doctrines, 24, xxv, xxviii, 170, 243–51.
Mânih, a heretic, 37, 278 sq., 278 n.; 47, 88 n., 126, 126 n.
Mâ*n*i*k*ara, n. of a demon, invoked, 29, 364.
Ma*n*ikûlaka, a village headman, asserts that gold and silver was not allowed by Buddha, 20, 391 sq.
Mân Kâu-teh, and Ȝze-*k*ang converse together on right conduct, 40, 176–80.
Mankind, *see* Man.
Mankura, attendant on Milinda, 35, xix, 47 sq.
Manmatha, god of love, 42, 311.
Manobhirâma, n. of a Buddha-field, 21, 150.
Mano*gñ*a, a chief Gandharva, 21, 5.
Mano*gñ*a*s*abdâbhigar*g*ita, n. of the aeon in which Ânanda is to be a Buddha, 21, 206.
Mano*gñ*asvara, a chief Gandharva, 21, 5.
Manotâ, a deity, offering to, 26, 203, 393.
Man-sacrifice, *see* Human sacrifice.
Mânsarspend, *see* Mâthra Spe*n*ta.
Manslaughter, *see* Homicide.
Mantha, or mash offering, a rite, performed to obtain greatness, 1, lxxv sq., 75 sq.; 15, 209–15.
Manthâlagautama, a Bhikshu, seduced by Bâlamukhyâ, 49 (i), 38 sq.
Manthin, is the moon, 26, 278 sq.; Soma libations for *S*ukra and M., 26, 278–88, 316, 332, 409; 41, 111 sq.; 44, 209 sq.
Mantî, one of the eight Brâhmans who took note of the marks on Buddha's body, 36, 44.
Mâ*n*tî, n. of a teacher, 15, 119, 187.
Mantra-Brâhma*n*a, and Gobhila-G*ri*hya-sûtra, 30, 3–11.
Mantrapâ*th*a, and Âpastambîya-G*ri*hya-sûtra, 30, 249.
Mantras: 'I know the M. only, the sacred books, I do not know the Self,' 1, 110; are contained in a name, 1, 112, 114; M. for the funeral oblations, 1, 83, 83 n., 84, 84 sq. n., 86; sacraments for women without M., 7, 114; 25, 330, 330 n.; only the flesh of beasts that has been consecrated with M. may be eaten by Brâhma*n*as, 7, 169; M. for the *S*râddha ceremonies and oblations, 7, 232–7 and notes, 239, 240, 250 n.; sacrifices without M. are no good, 8, 119, 119 n.; how to know where a M. ends, 29, 375; the M. used at G*ri*hya ceremonies, their date and metre, 30, ix–xiv, xxx, xxx n., xxxv; M. used for rites for which they have not been composed, 30, 114 n.; how the M. have to be recited, 30, 318–20; definitions of M. and Brâhma*n*as, 30, 323–5; rules about the recitation of M. at sacrifices, 30, 325–9, 345, 350 sq., 353, 359 sq.; certain M. and Brâhma*n*a passages met with in the beginning of some Upanishads, do not belong to the brahmavidyâ, 34, lxx; 38, 222–5; M. and arthavâdas as authorities on the gods, 34, 198, 203, 217, 219 sq., 223, 304, 348, 355; do not constitute an independent means of authoritative knowledge for anything, 34, 218; though subserving other purposes, are also independent means of knowledge, 34, 220–2; have occasionally to be explained in a secondary sense, 34, 318; Nâgasena wants Roha*n*a to teach him the best 'Mantra,' 35, 19 sq.; stories about men who obtained new bodies, in M. and arthavâdas, 38, 235; M. which are enjoined in one *S*âkhâ or Veda are taken over by other *S*âkhâs or Vedas also, 38, 273 sq.; on the non-return of the released soul, 38, 418 sq.; relation between M. and sûtras, 42, 480; the thoughtful men find the hidden Agni by reciting M. or spells, 46, 61; Veda

study analogous to the recital of M., 48, 6. *See also* Charms, Māthras, *and* Prayers (*a*, *b*).

Mantra-upanishads, 15, xxvi, xxxii, xliii.

Manu, revealed Upanishads to mankind, his offspring, 1, 44; 25, lx sq.; taught by Pragâpati, teaches mankind, 1, 144; quoted as authority, 2, lxi; 14, 314, 319; 29, 89; 48, 414; divided his estate amongst his sons, 2, 135; 14, 224; 25, lvii, lxi; revealed the *S*râddha ceremony for the salvation of mankind, 2, 140; fourteen Ms. pass away in each Kalpa, 7, 79; quoted by Kâlidâsa, 8, 30; the doctrine of devotion taught by the Sun to M. who communicated it to Ikshvâku, 8, 58, 58 n.; four ancient Ms., 8, 86, 86 n.; legend of M. and his bull with the Asura-killing voice, 12, 29 sq., 29 n.; Agni kindled by M., 12, 116; 46, 33; *see also* Manus; worshipped with sacrifice, 12, 133; 30, 142; 41, 250; legend of M., his daughter I*d*â, and the deluge, 12, 216–21, 224; 26, xxx sq.; 42, 679 sq.; 44, 81; M. and Dhât*ri* perform the punarâdheya, 12, 314 n.; quoted by Vâsish*th*a, 14, xvii–xx, xxvii, 4, 16, 26, 52, 60, 64, 105, 123, 127; 25, xxxii–xxxiv; prose quotation from M., 14, xviii sq.; a great authority on law in ancient as in modern times, 14, xx; prosperity prevailed in the world on the birth of M.'s son, 19, 22; lamented for his son, 19, 92; 49 (i), 90; son of Brahman Svayambhû, 25, xii, lvii, lxi, lxiv, 19, 19 n., 26; quoted in the Manu-sm*ri*ti, 25, xiii, 103, 116, 145, 175, 192, 208, 275, 278, 284, 291, 297, 303, 305, 313, 359, 365, 384, 416, 419; identified with the supreme soul, 25, xiii sq., lvii, lxiv, 512; was omniscient, 25, xiii, 30; a king, 25, xiii, lviii sq., lxiv, 222; the Pragâpati M. a great sage, 25, xiii sq., lvii, lxiv, 330, 419; 33, 263; 41, 250; 49 (i), 90; *all M. said is medicine*, 25, xiv, xvi, lx sq.; 34, 294; 48, 412; credited with the revelation of Mantras, 25, xvi, lx sq.; father of mankind, founder of social and moral order, hence credited with the authorship of legal maxims, 25, xxxiv, lvii sq., lxi–lxiv, lxxv; M. Vaivasvata, son of Âditya Vivasvat, 25, lvii, 19; 49 (i), 90; inventor of sacrificial rites, 25, lix; quoted by Yâska, 25, lxi sq., lxi n.; produced by Virâg, 25, lxiv, 14; seven Ms., 25, lxiv sq., 14, 14 n., 19; creates ten sages, 25, lxiv sq., 14; quotations from a *S*âstra of M. in the Mahâbhârata, 25, lxxv–lxxix; 33, xv; M. Prâ*k*etasa quoted in Mahâbhârata, 25, lxxvi sq., lxxvi n.; conversation between M. and B*ri*haspati, 25, lxxix; a divine being, asked by the sages to expound the law, 25, 1 sq.; Manvantara, the period of a M., 25, 22; M. Svâyambhava, original author of the Manu-sm*ri*ti, 25, 26, 28, 509, 513; 33, xi sq., 2, 2 n.; M. and other sages, children of M., the son of Hira*n*yagarbha, 25, 111; Bh*ri*gu, son of M., 25, 170; allotted to women impure desires, 25, 330; they have ploughed through Sarasvatî under M., 29, 338; M. and the goddess I*d*â connected with Pâkayag*ñ*as, 30, xv sq.; Father M. acquired health and wealth by sacrifices, 32, 193, 422; chose the medicines of Rudra, 32, 427, 433; quoted by Nârada, 33, xiv, 100, 116, 227–31; the law of M. superintended by the guardians of the world, 33, 109; any Sm*ri*ti text opposed to M. has no validity, 33, 274, 387; quoted by B*ri*haspati, 33, 316, 369, 375, 385; mentioned in *S*ruti, 34, 294, 294 n.; blames the doctrine of Kapila, 34, 294 sq.; recommends reasoning, 34, 315; the doctrine of pradhâna accepted by M., 34, 394; charms against hostile demons practised by M., 42, 67; remedies chosen by Father M., 42, 679; King M. Vaivasvata whose people are men, 44, 361, 362 n.; the Earth is M.'s mare, 44, 466; his sacrificial grass, 46, 13; Agni caused the sky to roar for M., 46, 22; the gods have placed Agni for M., 46, 32; the divine host, the Gh*ri*ta-sprinkling offspring of M., 46, 42 sq.; Agni among the offspring of M., 46, 64; primaeval sacrificer,

46, 96, 99, 206; Agni was born in M.'s firm law, 46, 137; Mâtari*s*van has brought Agni to M., 46, 137; Vâmadeva understood, 'I am M. and the sun,' 48, 253, 618; teaches Brahman as the universal cause, 48, 409 sq.; the golden age of M., the son of the Sun, 49 (i), 19; Vasus and Ms., 49 (i), 197; Laws of M., Code of M., *see* Manu-sm*ri*ti.

Manus (or Manu), Agni established by, 46, 8–11, 38, 230, 412; Agni sacrificed for M., 46, 24, 194, 275; M. and Manusha, Nahus and Nahusha, 46, 28; Agni inflamed by M. in the abode of I*d*, 46, 217; Agni, the Purohita of M., 46, 232; together with the people of M. Agni spreads out the sacrifice, 46, 232 sq.; Agni belonging to M., 46, 256, 287 sq.; the sacrificer, 46, 316. *See also* Manu.

Mânû*s*, n.p., 5, 137; 47, 128.

Mânû*s*ak, sister of Mânû*sk*îhar, 47, 143.

Mânû*s*-i Khurshê*d*-vînîk, n.p., 5, 134.

Mânûs-khûrnâk, ancestor of Zoroaster, 47, 34, 140.

Mânû*s*-khûrnar, or Mânû*s*-Khvârnar, ancestor of Zoroaster, 5, 134, 134 n.; 47, 34, 128, 140.

Mânû*sk*îhar (Zd., Manu*s*-*k*ithra), king, descendant of Frê*d*ûn, ancestor of Zoroaster, 5, 134, 134 n., 136, 138, 141 sq., 145 sq.; 37, 28, 28 n.; 47, xxix, 11, 11 n., 34, 121, 128, 135 n., 140; used the Frât river for irrigation, 5, 78; made captive by Frâsîyâ*v*, 5, 135; all Môbads from the family of M., 5, 147; reigned 120 years, 5, 150; the steed of M., 5, 182; addressed by Spenda*r*ma*d*, 5, 329, 329 n.; 24, 350, 350 n. (Minô*k*ihar); 37, 468; has both wisdoms, 18, 90, 90 n.; avenged the slaughter of Aîrî*k*, 24, 52 n., 61 sq., 61 n.; race of M., 37, 29 sq.; coming of M., 37, 267; the Aûsikhshes descended from demon of Wrath, and a sister of King M., 47, xiv; Spenda*r*ma*d* appears at the court of King M., 47, xiv, 134; his sister Mânû*s*ak, 47, 143; ancestor of Râgh and Nôdar, 47, 147.

Mânû*sk*îhar, son of Yûdân-Yim, author of the Dâ*d*istân-î Dînîk, pontiff of Pârs and Kirmân, 5, xlii, 147 n.; 18, xiii sq., xxii, 3 sq., 3 n., 276, 323, 357, 359; his Epistles, 18, xiii–xv, xxv–xxviii; 37, xlvi sq.; MSS. of his writings, 18, xiv–xix; date of his writings, 18, xiv, xxvii sq.; his style, 18, xix sq.; his Epistles translated, 18, 277–366; his epistle to the good people of Sîrkân, 18, 279–324; his epistle to his brother Zâ*d*-sparam, 18, 325–58; threatens to leave Iran, 18, 349 sq., 353; his epistle to all of the good religion in Iran, 18, 359–66; controversy between M. and Zâ*d*-sparam, 18, 455.

Manu*s*-*k*ithra, son of Airyu, 23, 222, 222 n. *See* Mânû*sk*îhar (1).

Manu-sm*ri*ti, or Mânava Dharma-*s*âstra, quoted in the Maitrâya*n*îya-upanishad, 1, lxx; based on an older Dharma-sûtra, 2, ix sqq. note; 14, xviii–xx, 26 n.; 25, xviii–xlv; M. and Vish*n*u-sm*ri*ti, 7, xxii–xxvii, xxxii; belongs to a school of the Black Yagur-veda, 7, xxv–xxvii; doctrines of Bhagavadgîtâ compared with M., 8, 20–4, 27; its relation to the Mahâbhârata, 8, 203, 226; 25, lxxiv–xci, xciv, xcvii sq., cvii, cxiv, cxvi; verses from M. in the Dhammapada, 10 (i), 33 n., 36 sq. n.; translated, *Vol.* 25; origin of M. according to Hindu tradition, 25, xi–xviii; is Bh*ri*gu's version of the Institutes of the Sacred Law proclaimed by Manu, 25, xi–xiii, xvii, xcii, xcv sq., cvi, cvi n., cx, 19, 26, 28; heads the lists of Dharma-*s*âstras, 25, xvi; quoted by Vâsish*th*a, 25, xxii, xxxi–xxxiv; proofs of its later origin, 25, xxiii–xxxi; conflicting opinions on certain points stated in it, 25, xxiii sq.; its author knew Dharma-*s*âstras, 25, xxv sq.; authorities quoted in it, 25, xxvi–xxx; perhaps quoted by Gautama, 25, xxxiv sq.; perhaps quoted by *S*âñkhâyana, 25, xxxv sq.; quoted by Kâmandaki, 25, xxxvi–xxxviii; the work of a special law school, not of a Vedic school, 25, xlv–lvi; converted into a metrical Sm*ri*ti by a special school of lawyers, 25,

xlv–lvi; claims the allegiance of all Hindus, 25, xlv, lv sq.; a school-book, 25, liv sq.; more systematic than any Dharma-sûtra, 25, liv sq.; free from sectarian influences, 25, lv; to be taught by Brâhma*n*as, and to be learnt by all Âryas, 25, lv, 26, 26 n., 32; advantages of studying it, 25, lv, 513; chosen for conversion into a Sm*ri*ti on account of the myths and legends of Manu, 25, lvi–lxv; reason for its high veneration, 25, lvii; old and new parts of the work, 25, lxvi–lxxiii; sources of the matter added to the old Mânava Dharma-sûtra, 25, lxxiv–xcii; alludes to legends of the Mahâbhârata, 25, lxxx; quotations from a B*ri*hat M., and V*ri*ddha M., and from M. not found in our Sm*ri*ti, 25, xcii, xcvi sq.; contradictory passages in it, 25, xcii–xciv; not the last link in a long chain of metrical Manu-sm*ri*tis, but the immediate offspring of the old Mânava Dharma-sûtra, 25, xcii–cvi; Paura*n*ic stories on recasts of M., 25, xcvi; anterior to other metrical Sm*ri*tis, 25, xcix–cvi; its language, 25, cv; its probable date, 25, cvi–cxviii; 33, xvi; its commentaries, 25, cvii sq., cxviii–cxxxviii; B*ri*haspati-sm*ri*ti a Vârttika on M., 25, cviii–cx; 33, 271–5; referred to in inscriptions, 25, cxiii sq.; V*ri*ddha or B*ri*hat M. later than Bh*ri*gu's Sa*m*hitâ, 25, cxvii; translations of it, 25, cxviii, cxxxviii; merit of studying it, 25, 26; its contents, 25, 27 sq.; revealed, 25, 511; compared with other law-books, 25, 515–82; known to Kumârila, 25, 613; M. and Nârada-sm*ri*ti, 33, xi–xvi; four versions of M., 33, xi sq., 2 sq., 274; Nârada's account of the M., 33, 1–4, 1 n.; opposed to the Sâṅkhya-sm*ri*ti, 34, xlvii, 291; quoted, 38, 427; 48, 777; inculcates practical religious duty, 48, 409, 411.

Mânutantavya, *see* Saumapa M.

Măn Wû-kwei and *Kh*ih-*k*ang Man-*kh*î converse on the Lord of Yü (Shun), 39, 324 sq. and n.

Mânya, i.e. son of Mâna, *see* Mândârya.

Măn-yin Tăng-hăng, employed as a teacher by Thang, 40, 117.

Manyu, Wrath, sacrifices to, 2, 86; 29, 388; 30, 23; n. of Kâma, 42, 223, 594; Rudra produced from M., 43, 157.

Mâo Hăng, his text of the Shih King, 3, 288.

Mâo *K*ang, his text of the Shih King, 3, 288 sq., 297.

Mâo Ȝhiang, a famous beauty, 39, 191, 191 n.

Mâra, the Evil One, the 'tempter,' or 'evil spirit,' will overthrow the sensual man, 10 (i), 5; bridle your mind, to escape from the bonds of M., 10 (i), 12; one should attack M. with the weapon of knowledge, 10 (i), 14, 19; his flower-pointed arrow, 10 (i), 17, 17 n.; Buddha conquers M. and his armies, 10 (i), 44 n.; (ii), *69–72*, 94, 103, 106; 13, 113 sq., 116; 19, xxii sq., 147–56, 316, 318, 364; 36, 27, 55, 60, 212; 49 (i), 157, 183; the wise conquer M. and his train, 10 (i), 48; those who enter the eightfold way are freed from the bondage of M., 10 (i), 67; crushes those who do not overcome thirst, 10 (i), 80; by meditation a man will cut the fetter of M., 10 (i), 82 sq.; king of death, devil; 10 (ii), x; existence the realm of M., 10 (ii), xv; tempts Dhaniya, 10 (ii), 5; (worlds of) gods, Mâras, and Brahmans, 10 (ii), 14, 30, 45, 96, 142 sq.; called Ka*n*ha, 10 (ii), 59; the wise having conquered all association with M., do not go to rebirth, 10 (ii), 135; by those that have entered the realm of M., the Dhamma is not perfectly understood, 10 (ii), 145; Lust, Delight, Thirst, the daughters of M., 10 (ii), 159; 19, 147 sq., 150; 49 (i), 137, 160–3; the hosts of M. described, 19, 150–2; those who have seen the Dhamma do not fall into the power of M., 10 (ii), 204; *for whatever they grasp after in the world, just by that M. follows the man*, 10 (ii), 205; Ânanda possessed by M., 11, 41; tries to persuade Buddha to die, 11, 42–4, 43 n., 52 sq.; one of the eight kinds of assemblies, 11, 48; world of M., 11, 72, 187, 288; the wheel of the

empire of Truth set rolling by Buddha, cannot be turned back by M., 11, 154; Brahmâ assists Buddha in his conflict with M., 11, 164; the hosts of M. are dispelled, when the real nature of things becomes clear to the meditating Brâhma*n*a, 13, 78; M. or Death, 13, 113 sq.; alone grieved by the birth of Buddha, 19, 6, 6 sq. n.; Buddha mistaken for the 'sixth M.,' 19, 72, 72 n.; the Devarâ*g*a M. grieves when Buddha reaches Bodhi, 19, 165; M. Pi*s*una requests Buddha to pass to Nirvâ*n*a, 19, 267, 267 n.; M., the god of desires, dwells in heaven, 19, 267 sq. n.; alone rejoices at Buddha's death, 19, 308; 20,000 damsel attendants on M. proceed from the Kâmaloka heavens to wait upon the mother of Bodhisattva, 19, 354; Bodhisattvas, after conquering the Evil One, strike the drum of the law, 21, 13; *S*âriputra when first hearing Buddha is afraid that it might be M. in the disguise of Buddha, 21, 63 sq.; M. and his followers will receive the true law under the Buddha Ra*s*miprabhâsa, 21, 143; the Buddha Mahâbhi*gñâ*-*gñ*ânâbhibhû defeats M., 21, 155; the triple world assailed by M., and conquered by Buddha's followers, 21, 275; defeated by the keeper of the Lotus of the True Law, 21, 391 sq.; preachers protected from M. and his followers by Samantabhadra, 21, 433; avoiding M. one is liberated from death, 22, 29; exerting himself in the rule of truth a wise man overcomes M., 22, 33; how M. one day could prevent Buddha from receiving alms, 35, 219–23; is great, and he is only one, 36, 50; Bhikkhus reverenced by Mâras, 36, 120; a servant of M. tempts Gotama with the wheel-treasure, 36, 136 sq.; Ms. or evil spirits even long for the righteous man, 36, 221; the Bhikkhu will remove the bonds of M., 36, 324; individuality the food of evil and the Evil One, 36, 372; originated Mâyâ, hence the world appears uneternal, 45, 244, 244 n.; his sons, Confusion, Gaiety, and Pride, 49 (i), 137; his vain attempts to disturb Buddha meditating at the foot of the Bodhi tree, 49 (i), 137–47; identified with Kâma, 49 (i), 137–9, 147; sons of M. who favoured the side of truth, 49 (i), 158, 158 n.; attacks of M. on the Buddha, 49 (i), 160–4; called Namu*k*i, 49 (i), 162, 164; the Arhat conquers the hosts of M., 49 (i), 177. *See also* Ka*n*ha.

Mârakâyikas, the sons or angels of Mâra, 21, 391 sq., 433.

Mâ*r*aspend, father of Âtû*r*pâ*d*, 5, 104, 145, 147, 404 sq.; 37, 30; 47, 87 sq.

Mar*d*ân-farukh, son of Aûha*r*ma*zd*-dâ*d*, author of *S*ikand-gûmânîk Vigâr, 24, xxv–xxvii, 120 sq., 120 n.

Mar*d*ân-vêh, n.p., 5, 146 sq.

Mar*d*-bû*d*, quoted, 5, 267, 267 n.

Mard-shah, or Shah-mard, author of the Sad Dar, 24, 255 n.

Mare, *see* Horse.

Mârgandak, n.p., 5, 139 sq.

Mârga*s*îrsha festival, *see* Serpents.

Marhayâ, *see* Mashya.

Mârî*k*a, *see* Kasyapa.

Marî*k*i: K*r*ish*n*a is M. among the Maruts, 8, 88; a sage and Pragâpati, 25, 14, 19; Manes descended from M., 25, 111 sq.

Marka, and *Sand*a, two Asura-Rakshas, 26, 279–84; a demon harassing infants, 29, 296; 30, 211; M. and *Kand*a, 42, 301.

Mârka*nd*eya remodelled the Manusm*r*iti, 25, xvii, xcv; 33, xi, 2 sq., 2 n.

Market, *see* Trade.

Marriage.

(*a*) Choice (Intermarriage, Forbidden degrees, Marriageable age, Order of m. in family, Number of wives, Election of bride and groom).
(*b*) Law of m.
(*c*) History of m. (Forms of m., Re-marriage Duty and Meritoriousness of m.).
(*d*) Hindu m. ceremonies.
(*e*) Chinese m. ceremonies.
(*f*) Parsi m. ceremonies.

(*a*) CHOICE (INTERMARRIAGE, FORBIDDEN DEGREES, MARRIAGEABLE AGE, ORDER OF M. IN FAMILY, NUMBER OF WIVES, ELECTION OF BRIDE AND GROOM).

Opinions about m. with a *S*ûdra female, 2, 69, 258; 14, 6; 25, xxvi sq., xxvii n., 78 sq., 104; inter-

marriage of castes, 2, 308 sq.; 5, 206; 7, 67, 106; 25, 75, 77–9, 83, 86; intermarriage with idolaters forbidden, 6, 33; m. with slave girls, 6, 75 sq.; *the ancient Brâhmanas did not marry a woman belonging to another caste, nor did they buy a wife; they chose living together in mutual love after having come together*, 10 (ii), 49; intermarriage with outcasts, 14, 58, 58 n., 68, 109; 25, 37, 105; sin of intermarrying with wicked people, 14, 130; 25, 384; an excellent wife may be acquired from a base family, 25, 72 n., 73; wives of different castes, their standing, 25, 342 sq.; m. of cripples, idiots, eunuchs, outcasts, 25, 373, 373 n.; children from wives of different castes, 25, 402–5, 402 sq. n., 407–9, 412, 416–18, 416 sq. n.; confusion of castes through m. with women who ought not to be married, 25, 407; rules about intermarriage, 28, 63, 63 n.; the Khattiya the best in the world of those who observe exogamous m., 35, 229 n.; a wife to be given only to a Mazda-worshipper, 37, 66 sq.;—forbidden degrees, 2, 127, 127 n., 196 sq.; 6, 75; 7, 106 sq.; 14, 42, 146, 146 n., 216 sq.; 25, 75–7 and n., 466, 466 n.; 27, 203; 28, 297 sq.; 30, 82; 33, 166, 287, 389; next-of-kin marriage (Khvêtûk-das) in Zoroastrianism one of the good works, 4, 98 sq., 98 n.; 5, 212 sq., 307, 388 sq., 389 sq. n.; 18, 225, 232, 387, 387 n., 391; 23, 332; 24, 26, 26 n., 74; 31, 250; 37, 273 sq., 273 n., 288, 288 n., 392, 431, 445; 47, x, xxv sq., 51–3, 166 sq.; m. between blood-relations, 12, 238, 238 sq. n.; texts on next-of-kin m., 18, xxviii sq.; next-of-kin m. of the first man and woman (mashya mashyôi), 18, 105, 105 n.; 37, 365; 47, 6; origin of next-of-kin m., 18, 199–201, 199 n.; meaning of Khvêtûk-das or next-of-kin m., 18, 389–430; breaking off a next-of-kin m., a heinous sin, 24, 71; the youth given in m. to his kin, 31, 342;—proper age of m., 2, 196, 272 sq.; 14, 314; 25, 343 sq., 344 n.; 27, 65, 65 n., 478; 30, 82, 186; 33, 169 sq., 170 sq. n.; maiden allowed to choose a husband, in case of her relatives neglecting to marry her, 2, 272; 7, 109, 109 n.; 14, 91 sq., 314; 25, 343 sq.; 33, 169; maidens married early, 31, 92; child-m., 35, 74;—the order in which brothers and sisters must marry, 2, 130, 257 sq., 272; 7, 136, 177; 14, 4, 103, 103 n., 217, 329; 25, 103 sq., 107 sq., 442; 44, 414; m. of a younger sister, 16, 181 sq., 183 sq. n.; expiation for m. of a younger brother before an older, 42, 164 sq., 521, 523–8;—number of wives, 2, 126, 126 n.; 7, 106, 111 sq.; 14, 5 sq.; 29, 277; division of inheritance among sons born by several wives, 2, 304 sq.; Shun's m. to the daughters of Yâo, 3, 36 sq.; about accepting the child of a handmaid, 5, 323 sq., 323 n., 344 sq.; harem of King Sudassana, 11, 239, 274, 276 sq.; position of a concubine improved by a son, 16, 170, 171 sq. n.; feudal prince marries nine ladies, one of them to be the proper wife, 16, 183 sq. n.; younger sister married off in a position ancillary to the real wife, 16, 334 sq., 335 n.; when the first wife dies, a man may marry again, 25, 198; wives and concubines, 27, 109, 161, 164, 181, 189, 457, 471–3, 479; 28, 44, 47–52, 47 n., 54 sq., 137–9, 380, 380 n.; the son of a concubine did not preside at the sacrifices, 27, 223; 28, 457; polyandry in the Veda (?), 32, 277; want of harmony among wives and concubines, one of the troubles of common people, 40, 195; *she who is first taken to wife is the consecrated consort*, 41, 238; why a single man has many wives, 43, 230;—a man should not marry a girl who has no brothers, 2, 305; marriageable women to be sought for wealth, 6, 76; fine for giving a blemished damsel in m., without indicating her blemish, 7, 29; general advice as to choice of a wife, 7, 107; 14, 7, 42; 25, 76 sq.; 29, 21; 30, 186; vile men are to marry vile women, vile women vile men, 9, 73, 76; Bhikkhus must not give advice as to taking and giving

in m., 11, 199; 19, 296; 36, 287; one should not marry a bold or resolute female, 16, 154, 250, 271, 272 n.; duty of choosing a wife of character, 24, 10 sq.; a girl of the same surname not to be married, 27, 78; election of bride and bridegroom, betrothal, 29, 164; 30, 42 sq., 256–8; 33, 165 sq., 165 n.; examination of the bridegroom with regard to his virile, 33, 166–9; qualities of a bridegroom, 33, 171 sq.; faults of a maiden, or of a suitor, 33, 172 sq.; charms for obtaining a husband, 42, 94 sq., 322–5, 491; charm for obtaining a wife, 42, 95, 502 sq.

(*b*) Law of m.

Law about m., 2, 196–200; 6, 71 sq.; 7, 38; 25, 291, 291 n., 294 sq.; 33, 164–77; 37, 66, 106, 113 sq.; an untruth spoken at the time of m., is venial, 2, 291; 14, 83; 25, 273; law of divorce, 5, 306; 6, 33–7, 75; 9, 145 sq., 270 sq., 279 sq., 288 sq.; 18, 406 sq.; 25, 341 sq.; 27, 457, 457 n.; 28, 44 sq., 57, 57 n., 170 sq.; 33, 183 sq.; the m. portion, dowry of a maiden, 6, 71 sq.; 33, 53 sq., 243, 309; the heir bound to marry unmarried sisters, 7, 64; the persons by whom a girl may be given in m., 7, 109; 25, 195; 33, 169; divorced wives not unlawful to marry, 9, 138 sq. and n., 144, 144 n.; property given to a wife after m. by her husband's family, 14, 81; the son of a pregnant bride, 14, 87, 228; families are degraded by neglect of lawful m., 14, 175; unjustly forsaking a wife, 25, 120; once only is a maiden given in m., 25, 335, 336 n.; 33, 171, 171 n.; betrothal binding, except when bride blemished, 25, 335, 340, 340 n., 345; mourning for a divorced mother, 27, 122; 28, 42, 381, 381 n.; newly married men exempted from official duties, 27, 374; 39, 231, 231 n.; announced to the king, 28, 167, 167 n.; one about to marry must not be arrested, 33, 18; wife allowed to take another husband in case of impotency, 33, 168 sq.; m. dissoluble on discovering a blemish in the husband, 33, 184; one about to marry must not be put under restraint, 33, 288; wickedness of breaking up projected marriages, 40, 240. *See also* Wife, *and* Woman (*a*).

(*c*) History of m. (Forms of m., Re-marriage, Duty and Meritoriousness of m.).

Eight forms or rites of m., 2, xix–xxi, 127 sq., 128 n., 132 sq., 197, 200; 7, 69, 107–9; 14, 6 sq., 205–8; 25, xxxix n., lxxvii sq., 371; 29, 166 sq.; 33, 171, 173 sq., 191; lawful and unlawful m. rites, 2, 130 sq.; 25, xxiv, 79–83, 79 n.; a bride is given to the family, 2, 166; m. by purchase, fee (*s*ulka) taken at an Âsura or Ârsha wedding, 2, 306; 7, 69 sq., 69 n., 108; 14, 7, 7 n.; 25, xciii sq., 79–82, 84 sq., 291, 291 n., 294 sq., 318, 344 sq.; 33, 53, 53 n., 171 sq. and n., 194, 343; 35, 74, 74 n.; wives acquired by contract, 4, 45 sq., 45 n.; five kinds of m., 5, 142, 142 sq. n.; m. by capture, 7, 108; the son of a female married according to the Brâhma-rite, sanctifies the company, 14, 19; against sale of daughters, 25, 345; buying a concubine, 27, 78; 28, 297 sq.; in the age of Shăn Năng people knew their mothers, but did not know their fathers, 40, 171; lineage through the mothers amongst the evils of heresy, 47, 88 sq.; *see also* Niyoga, Widows, *and* Woman (*a*);—position of son of re-married woman, 2, 258; 25, 104, 109, 359, 363, 363 sq. n., 369, 369 sq. n.; re-marriage of widows allowed, 6, 35 sq.; Hindu law about re-marriage of widows and virgin brides, 7, 62; 14, 92, 314 sq.; 25, 196 sq., 339 sq., 340 n.; 33, 287; definition of the term 're-married woman,' 14, 86; re-marriage of wives of emigrants, 14, 92 sq.; re-marriage of women who have left an impotent man, 14, 228; low estimation of 're-married' women, 25, 107; 33, 174 sq., 174 n.; a widow may not marry again, 27, 439, 439 sq. n.; when a second m. is permitted, 33, 184 sq.; re-marriage of widows, and polyandry practised in some countries, 33, 389;—a virtuous king will not treat

with contempt wifeless men and widows, 3, 165, 202 sq., 475; the solitary and widows laid their complaints before the great Tî, 3, 258; dignity of m., 4, 34, 46 sq.; giving a virgin in m., one of the good works, 4, 175; duty of marrying for men and women, 5, 322 sq.; 24, 278; duty of marrying the single, servants and handmaidens, 9, 77; householder's duty of taking a wife, 15, 51, 91; 25, 128, 198; the worst deed, when men prevent maids from marrying and bringing forth children, 23, 281; king's duty to wed a queen, 25, 228; king to deliberate on bestowing his daughters in m., 25, 240; father's duty to give daughter in m., 25, 328; 33, 367 sq.; 37, 66, 148; promoting m., the duty of rulers, 27, 392; m. and relationship, in the different ages of the world, 39, 359 sq.

(*d*) Hindu m. ceremonies.

After m. husband and wife must perform the rites prescribed for household life, 2, 99; anniversary of the wedding day celebrated, 2, 100 sq. and n.; begging allowed to defray the expenses of m., 2, 123, 203; 14, 240; 25, 430 sq.; reception of the bridegroom as a specially honoured guest, 2, 205; 14, 49, 244 sq.; 29, 435; 30, 132; one of the forty sacraments, 2, 216 sq.; a man should not shave in the year of his m., 2, 220 n.; to defray the expenses of a wedding, money may be taken forcibly from *S*ûdras and others, 2, 273; ceremony at the m. of an appointed daughter, 2, 305; 14, 86; the m. ceremony is considered as the initiation of women, 7, 90; 25, 42; m. ceremony begins with the Nândîmukha *S*râddha, 7, 92 n.; impurity cannot arise during a m. ceremony, 7, 93; Hindu m. ceremonies, 7, 106; 14, 6; 25, 81 n., 83, 195, 195 n.; 29, 20–46, 164–72, 276–90, 380–5; 30, xxv sq., 42–52, 186–99, 253, 255–65, 267 sq., 270, 300 sq.; 33, 165, 174 sq., 190; way must be made for a bride and a bridegroom, 7, 203; 14, 69; 25, 55; Lakshmî resides in the m. ceremony, and in the bridegroom, 7, 299; preparatory m. rites, 10 (ii), 99; 29, 31–4; betrothal, gift with a libation of water, 14, 6; 25, 82, 336 n., 340 n.; impure food not to be thrown away at weddings, 14, 72; wedding feasts in the house of the husband, or the bride's father, 22, 97; sacred fire kindled at the wedding, 25, 87; 29, 12, 12 n., 20, 43, 270; 30, 14 sq.; betrothal the cause of husband's dominion, 25, 195; benedictory texts recited, 25, 195, 195 n., 294 sq.; sacrifice to Pragâpati at weddings, 25, 195, 195 sq. n.; the seven steps, 25, 294 sq.; 29, 38; nuptial texts applied to virgins only, 25, 294 sq.; gifts made at m., 25, 370 sq., 374, 374 n.; 29, 285; 33, 129 n., 342 sq.; auspicious times for m., 29, 20 sq., 277; 30, 255 sq.; wooing, betrothal, 29, 21 sq.; 30, 255, 258; 45, 113; bride's bath, 29, 31 sq.; a dance, 29, 32; joining of hands, 29, 35, 167, 283, 382 sq.; 30, 45, 47, 189, 259; circumambulation of the fire, 29, 37 sq.; treading on the stone, 29, 37 sq.; exorcism of the bride, 29, 41 sq., 44, 288 sq.; 30, 197; taking the bride home, 29, 39–44, 287 sq., 382 sq.; 30, 47–50, 193, 261–5; 42, 196; rites of the fourth day, 29, 44, 288 sq.; 30, 51 sq., 197 sq., 267 sq.; 42, 546; ceremonies at the cohabitation, 29, 45 sq.; 30, 51 sq., 199 sq., 267 sq.; 42, 276; m. ceremonies analogous to Upanayana rites, 29, 64 n., 65 n.; the bride sacrifices, 29, 169; 30, 191; cow killed at a wedding, 29, 276; 45, 114; comes after the Samâvartana, 29, 379 sq.; Âgya oblations at the wedding, 30, 41; m. ceremonies to be learnt from women, 30, 255; celebrated with Atharvanic rites, 42, lv; prayers at m. rites, 42, 96, 252 sq., 275 sq., 276 n., 498 sq., 503, 532, 546; amulets worn by bride and bridegroom, 42, 275 sq., 276 n.; bath of the bridegroom, 45, 113. *See also* Sacrifices (*b*).

(*e*) Chinese m. ceremonies.

New name assumed on m. by a man, 3, 265, 465 n.; 27, 79, 79 n.; divination and other ceremonies to determine the auspiciousness of a m.,

3, 381, 381 n.; 16, 65; m. of a young lady a good omen, 16, 178, 180 sq. n., 257 sq., 258 n.; the goose in Chinese m. ceremonies, 16, 181 n.; improper m., 16, 183 n.; Chinese m. ceremonies, 27, 26, 78, 438–42; 28, 172, 297–9, 299 n.; meaning of m. ceremonies, 27, 55; 28, 428–34; a betrothed girl wears strings hanging down her neck, 27, 77, 77 n.; wedding presents, 27, 78, 439 sq.; when a daughter is promised in m., she assumes the hair-pin, 27, 79; brides accompanied by two ladies to the harem, 27, 100 sq. and n.; language used in sending daughters to different harems, 27, 119; sacrifice of the emperor to 'the first match-maker,' 27, 259; course to be taken if m. rites are interrupted by mourning, 27, 320–3, 321 n.; 28, 162; the new wife presented and m. announced in the ancestral temple, 27, 322, 355, 358; sacrifices at m., 27, 322, 441 sq. and n.; going to meet the bride, 28, 141; is seeking assistance for sacrificing, 28, 238; importance of m. ceremonies, 28, 259, 264–6; *the ceremony of m. was intended to be a bond of love between two (families of different) surnames, with a view, in its retrospective character, to secure the services in the ancestral temple, and in its prospective character, to secure the continuance of the family line*, 28, 428.

(*f*) Parsi m. ceremonies.

Prayers when going to seek a wife, 5, 392, 392 n.; 37, 174; m. customs, 18, 405 sq., 405 n.; m. song for the nuptials of Zarathustra's daughter, 31, 187–94; sin of giving a woman to one when engaged to another, 37, 70; bride conveyed to her husband's house, 37, 100; merit of a woman giving herself to a righteous man, 37, 204 sq.

Marrow, symbolism of, 43, 20, 327, 387; 44, 169.

Mârtânda, the cast off and unformed son of Aditi, 26, 12 sq.

Martial Law, *see* War.

Marudevî, mother of the Arhat *Ri*shabha, 22, 281 sq.

Mârût, a fallen angel, 6 xiv, 14, 14 n.

Marut, n. of B*ri*hadratha Aikshvâka, 15, xlvii, 290, 328.

Maruts.

(*a*) Names, epithets, attributes, appearance of the M.
(*b*) Their horses (deer) and chariots.
(*c*) Deeds of M., M. myths.
(*d*) M. and other gods.
(*e*) Worship of M., and their relation to men.

(*a*) Names, epithets, attributes, appearance of the M.

They are the people (vi*s*) of the gods, the Vai*s*yas, the peasants, 8, 346; 12, xvii sq., xvii n., 334, 387, 393, 398 sq., 401 sq.; 26, 220 sq., 396 sq.; 41, 13, 34, 61, 84, 84 n., 99 sq., 102, 125; 42, 663; 49 (i), 53, 81; 43, 210, 212 n.; 44, xxii, 409, 466; seven troops of M., consisting of seven each, 12, 387, 387 n.; 32, 313, 318; 41, 102; 42, 207 (thrice seven); 43, 212; they sport and sing, are singers, or musicians, 12, 416 sq., 417 n.; 32, 14, 45, 53, 56, 63, 76 sq., 82, 95, 107, 121, 126, 138, 159, 169, 171 sq., 209 sq., 312–14, 340, 343, 352 sq., 369, 416; are ever young, 32, xxiii, 341, 343 sq., 374; are the storm-gods, 32, xxiii sq., 63 sq., 81 sq., &c.; the word M. meaning 'gods,' 32, xxiii sq.; etymology of 'Marut,' 32, xxiv–xxvi; Marut and Mars, 32, xxv sq., 277; assume the form of new-born babes, 32, 14, 36 sq.; not originally gods, became deified, 32, 37, 53; called Vi*s*ve Devâs, 32, 53, 55; are war-like gods, with daggers, spears, rings, and golden ornaments, 32, 63, 71, 106 sq., 111 sq., 120, 126 sq., 130, 159, 162, 169, 209 sq., 230, 279, 283, 295, 307, 312 sq., 319, 326, 333, 337, 340, 343, 352, 363, 369, 373 sq., 379, 392, 400–2, 412, 417; 46, 22; host, the manly host of the M., 32, 63, 67–70, 82, 95, 106, 126, 145, 148, 209, 312 sq., 320, 325, 338, 363 sq., 369, 373, 382, 391, 401, 412; 46, 80, 326; compared to birds (hawks, swans), 32, 76, 159, 169, 179, 210, 348, 373, 386, 401, 412; called Rudras, 32, 97, 106, 126, 209, 296, 325, 340, 352, 364, 391, 400; are strong and powerful 32, 97 sq., 106–8, 159, 197, 273, 325; are joyful, wise, the sages, 32,

106; 46, 22, 293; the roarers, roar like lions, 32, 106 sq., 159, 210, 369; 46, 292; the chasers of the sky, 32, 107, 154, 333, 363; shine like the heavens with their stars, 32, 159 sq., 295, 299; their names, 32, 167; 43, 213; as wild boars with iron tusks, 32, 169, 176 sq.; all of the same age, dwell in the same nest, 32, 179; are strong and bounteous, 32, 210, 240 sq., 293; shining like snakes, 32, 293; golden-breasted, 32, 295 sq., 299, 333, 340, 416; golden-jawed, 32, 295, 301 sq.; brilliant like fires, 32, 295; terrible like wild beasts, 32, 295; are they called Dasagvas? 32, 296, 306 sq.; the constant wanderers, 32, 296; with the clouds as if with glittering red ornaments, 32, 296, 307 sq.; with their birds, 32, 319, 321; called Vasus, 32, 334, 374, 378, 386, 412; like wild bulls, 32, 337, 390, 402; obtained their immortal name, 32, 340; are lords of Am*ri*ta, 32, 343; are like red horses, like heroes eager for battle, 32, 347; Evayâmarut, 32, 363–5; flame-born, 32, 369; strong, wild, furious, 32, 373 sq., 400 sq.; play about like calves, 32, 374; fleet like racers, 32, 374; with sun-bright skins, 32, 387; of reddish hue, 32, 390, 395; called *Ri*bhukshans, 32, 390 sq., 395, 400; the strong hunters, 32, 392; called Âdityas, 32, 412 sq.; like priests, like kings, like youths of the hamlets, 32, 416; are like winds, 32, 416; M., Vasus, Âdityas, &c., 34, 202, 216; the all-knowing M., 41, 20; the lords of the northern region, 43, 102; givers of rain, fire-tongued increasers of *Ri*ta, 46, 38, 292.

(*b*) Their horses (deer) and chariots.

Spotted deer or horses, their animals, 12, 242; 32, 63, 70 sq., 107, 126, 159, 164, 209, 295, 302, 325, 343, 346, 352, 373, 392, 401; 46, 293; drive on chariots, 32, xxiii, 63, 82, 337 sq., 352, 356 sq., 391, 401; the cloud, one of the horses of the M., 32, 20; ride on horseback, 32, 43, 356, 358; they crack their whips, 32, 63, 72, 187, 279; come on quick, strong-hoofed, golden-hoofed steeds, 32, 64, 81 sq., 93, 343, 356, 392; harness the spotted or fallow deer or horses to their chariots, 32, 97, 102, 126, 180, 196, 296, 312, 319, 325 sq., 333, 336, 340, 408; 46, 292; lead about the powerful horse, the cloud, to make it rain, 32, 106, 116 sq., 126; lightning stands on the seats of their chariots, 32, 107; carry casks or buckets (clouds) on their chariots, 32, 159, 161; come on red or tawny horses, which hasten their chariots, 32, 169, 337, 340; come on chariots charged with lightning, 32, 169; thunder, the noise of their chariots, 32, 173; carry weapons on their chariots, 32, 210, 340; from the tires of their chariot-wheels streams gush forth, 32, 280; unharness their horses, 32, 289; wash their horses, 32, 295, 300, 347; cut the mountain asunder with the tire of their chariot, 32, 313; mount their chariots, 32, 319 sq.; move along on quick well-broken horses, 32, 333; when they went in triumph, the chariots followed, 32, 333–5; possessed of good horses and chariots, 32, 340; on golden chariots, 32, 340; harness the winds as horses to the yoke, 32, 344; the rushing chariots of the roaring M. come forth, 32, 363; their carriage, even without deer, without horses, passes between heaven and earth, 32, 369; golden chest on the chariot of the M., 32, 400, 404 sq.

(*c*) Deeds of M., M. myths.

The M. scorched, trod V*ri*tra, 12, 409; 32, 392; practised penance, 25, 475; stood in the Asvattha tree, 29, 331; 32, 329; 41, 34, 84; hurl the thunderbolt, 32, xxiii, 293, 325; toss the clouds across the surging sea, 32, 53; their birth, 32, 63, 76, 295, 299, 319, 373, 382; send rain, 32, 63 sq., 81, 106 sq., 126, 159, 169, 176, 209, 280, 282, 284, 295, 319 sq., 326, 333, 343 sq., 393, 412; 41, 328; 43, 170; the cows of the M., 32, 81; the shakers, they shake the earth, even mountains, 32, 97 sq., 101, 106, 112 sq., 159, 209, 273, 278 sq., 325, 340, 379, 382, 390, 400 sq.; made wind and lightnings,

32, 106; slayers of the demon, 32, 106, 111; have established their seat in the sky, 32, 126; have made heaven and earth to grow, 32, 126, 129 sq.; drunk of Soma, 32, 127; strike the fiend with their lightning, 32, 154; their gory-toothed lightning, 32, 209, 222; lightning and thunder, their companions or wives, 32, 272–6; lightnings, their spears, 32, 272, 274; have uncovered the cows by blowing away the cloud, 32, 295, 298 sq.; spring, like rushing bulls, over the dark cows, 32, 312; come from heaven, from the sky, even from near, 32, 319; hold lightnings in their hand, 32, 325, 392; shake the red apple from the firmament, 32, 326; carrying waterskins, fill the well, 32, 326, 379; their milch-cows are never destroyed, 32, 333; have measured the sky with their strength, 32, 333; go round heaven and earth, 32, 334; clothed in rain, 32, 340; 46, 292; dwell on high mountains, 32, 341 sq., 344, 409; dim the eye of the sun with streams of rain, 32, 347; shake the heavenly bucket, 32, 348; in the highest, in the middle, in the lowest heaven, 32, 352; the sons of an excellent mother, 32, 356, 359; bring together heaven and earth, 32, 368, 371, 391 sq., 400, 403; drive away darkness, 32, 374; mount up to the firmament from the abyss of Nir*ri*ti, 32, 382; sow the mist, 32, 390; bring together the great waters, the sun, and the thunderbolt, 32, 391 sq.; spread out, or hold asunder, or join, heaven and earth, 32, 408 sq.; take delight in sweet nourishment, 42, 207; where they wish to lay the Gârhapatya, 43, 118; the troop of the M. is the air-world, 43, 236; they make the mountains tremble, 46, 292.

(*d*) M. AND OTHER GODS.

M. with Soma at their head, 1, 42 sq.; K*ri*sh*n*a is Marî*k*i among the M., 8, 88; seen within K*ri*sh*n*a, 8, 92; alarmed at the greatness of K*ri*sh*n*a, 8, 94; are the princes among the Ga*n*as, 8, 346; Dyutâna, son of the M., 26, 144; Ûrdhvanabhas, son of the M., 26, 198, 198 n.; their mother P*ri*s*n*i, their father Rudra, 32, xxiii, 73, 81, 106 sq., 126, 144 sq., 280, 285, 295 sq., 299 sq., 313, 340 sq., 343, 347 sq., 352, 368–73, 375, 382, 390 sq., 400 sq., 408, 422 sq.; 42, 132 sq., 207; 46, 292; when the M. had joined Indra they took their holy names, 32, 14, 37, 159, 166 sq.; the tall bulls of Dyu, 32, 106, 110 sq.; when Vish*n*u saved the Soma, the M. sat down like birds on the altar, 32, 127, 133–7; mighty sons of Heaven, 32, 154 sq.; their wife Rodasî, 32, 272–7; compared to Somas, 32, 279, 282 sq., 416; Trita a friend of the M., 32, 296 sq., 305, 325, 392; men of Svar, men of Dyu, 32, 326; Rodasî stands on the chariot of the M., 32, 338, 369; Vish*n*u invoked in company with the M., 32, 363–5; M. invoked with other gods, 32, 375, 386, 408; Rudra invoked with the M., 32, 386–9, 419; servants of Dyu, 32, 401, 405 sq.; sons of Sindhu, 32, 416; prayer to Rudra, Father of the M., 32, 426–8; Vâyu, their father, Dyu, their mother, 32, 444, 448; the Marut-eyed gods in the north, 41, 49; Âditya, Brahma*n*aspati, and the M., 42, 126; the Rudras are united with the M., 42, 135; all the M., and all the gods, 42, 184; the honey-lash of the A*s*vins, the child of the M., 42, 230; share of the Âdityas, lordship of the M., 43, 68; their relation to Indra and to Varu*n*a, 44, xxii sq.; curds offering to Varu*n*a and the M. at the second seasonal sacrifice, 44, 75 n., 76; Âpyas, Sâdhyas, Anvâdhyas, and M., the divine guardians of the sacrificial horse, 44, 359; Bhâratî and other goddesses among the M., 46, 154, 156; Mamatâ, daughter of the M., 49 (i), 44; Heaven without the lord of the M., when V*ri*tra was slain, 49 (i), 81; *see also* Indra, *and* Rudra;—Agni invoked in company with the M., 14, 216; 32, 53, 68 sq., 82, 94, 337, 339, 352–4, 369, 392 sq., 399; 46, 292 sq., 307; are like Agni, 32, 416; 46, 292; born after the law of Agni, 46, 22; the bright ones, i.e. the M., did service to Agni, 46, 82, 84; Agni turns away the anger

of the M., 46, 109; Agni (the roaring of the flames) compared with the M., 46, 130, 138, 157, 303, 341; Agni identified with the host of M., 46, 187, 191; Agni invoked to bring the host of the M. to the sacrifice, 46, 198, 316; Agni strengthened by the M., 46, 266; sing to Agni a pleasant song, 46, 268; cling to Agni, 46, 273; have adorned themselves for Agni's glory, whose offspring they are, 46, 371, 373.

(*e*) WORSHIP OF M., AND THEIR RELATION TO MEN.

Offerings to the M., 2, 202; 12, 387 sq., 394, 396–9, 402 sq.; 25, 91; 29, 86, 331; 32, 106, &c.; 41, 60 sq., 102; 43, 208–14; 44, 75, 75 n., 336 n.; the vital spirits of a student who breaks the vow of chastity go to the M., 2, 294, 294 n.; devourers of foes, 12, 397; 32, 106; offerings to the M. Sântapanâ*h*, G*ri*hamedhina*h*, and Krî*d*ina*h*, 12, 408 n., 409–17, 410 n.; 44, 76, 76 n.; a pure offering to the pure M., 14, 186; prayer to the M., 14, 318; the person in the wind worshipped as the unconquerable army of the M., 15, 101; the hosts of M. entreat Buddha to teach the law, 21, 55; worshipped by the student who has broken his vow, 25, 454 sq.; 29, 362; animal sacrifices for the M., 26, 220 sq.; 41, 13 sq., 125 sq.; 44, 402; deity of a *Ri*tu-graha, 26, 320 n.; are not oblation-eaters, 26, 396 sq.; embryo offered to the M., 26, 396 sq.; invoked at the Ash*t*akâ, 29, 207; invoked for protection, 29, 280, 344; sacrifice to the M. at rites relating to agriculture, 29, 326; 30, 113 sq.; eat what is not sacrificed in the fire, 29, 331, 331 n.; were ploughers, exuberant givers, 29, 338; if thou belongest to the M., I buy thee for the M., 30, 53; worshipped at the Tarpa*n*a, 30, 243; hymns to the M., *Vol.* 32; invoked in battle against enemies, 32, 97 sq., 107 sq., 369, 375, 386; 42, 121 sq., 132 sq.; invoked at the third Soma libation, 32, 122 sq.; did not originally enjoy divine honours, 32, 166 sq.; give wealth and protection, 32, 326 sq.; good warriors come from the M., 32, 343; their bolt kills cattle and men, 32, 374; worshipped as house-gods, 32, 374, 377, 387, 389; strike the sinner with their thunderbolt, and forgive sin, 32, 379, 382; kill the enemy with the thunderbolt, 32, 386; invited to drink Soma, 32, 386, 408 sq.; liberal givers of Soma (rain), 32, 400; medicines of the M., 32, 402, 407; invoked for prosperity, 42, 48; grant life and well-being, 42, 53; invoked against disturbers of holy rites, 42, 90; invoked in a love-charm, 42, 104; invoked at the restoration of an exiled king, 42, 112, 328; call the king to the throne, 42, 113; invoked at the building of a house, 42, 140; invoked to make the horse fleet, 42, 146; song of praise to the M., 42, 151, 548; rites to the M. performed to cure leprosy, 42, 266 sq.; deities and metres, 43, 53, 331; were the guardsmen of King Marutta, 44, 397; a Vai*s*ya sacrificed to the M. at the Purushamedha, 44, 413; invoked at the Pravargya, 44, 466; invoked by hosts and troops, 46, 292; invited to sit down on the sacrificial grass, 46, 418.

Marutta Âvikshita, the Âyogava king, performed a horse-sacrifice, 44, 397.

Mary, the Virgin, daughter of Imrân, brought up by Zachariah, 6, 50 sq.; 9, 292; the Virgin mother of Jesus, 6, 51 sq.; Jews calumniated M., 6, 93; legend of M., annunciation, birth of Jesus, 9, 28 sq.; called the sister of Aaron, 9, 29; the Spirit breathed into the Virgin M., 9, 53; M. and her son made a sign by God, 9, 68.

Mar'zapân, a copyist of the Dînka*rd*, 37, xxxv.

Mâsapûrikâ *S*âkhâ of the Uddeha Ga*n*a, 22, 290.

Mashîkh, *see* Messias.

Mashya (Marhayâ, Mâshya, Masîyâ, Masyê) and Mashyôî (Mâshyôî, Marhîyôih, Mashyana), the first human pair, progenitors of mankind, 4, lviii; 5, 53–9, 53 n., 149; 18, 197–200, 199 n., 225, 402, 411 sq., 416; 37, 26, 26 n.; 47, 6 sq., 6 n.; they grew up from the earth, 5, 120, 183

sq., 183 n.; 47, xxix; their resurrection, 5, 123; sprung from the seed of Gâyômard, 5, 130; 18, 105, 105 n.; 47, 35, 121, 140; sowing of corn from their bodies, 37, 103.

Mashyana, *see* Mashya.

Mashyôî, *see* Mashya.

Masîyâ, *see* Mashya.

Masvâk, n.p., 5, 146.

Masyê and Masyâôî, *see* Mashya.

Mâtalî, knows amrita as a remedy, 42, 162, 629.

Mâtaṅga, a *Kandâla*, was reborn in the Brahma world, 10 (ii), 23.

Mâtarisvan, used in the sense of prâna or spirit, 1, ci, 311; 15, 276; 42, 219; n. of Vâyu, the wind, 1, 150, 311; 41, 221; 42, 53, 205, 216; 'M.'s cauldron,' the atmosphere, 12, 186, 186 n.; invoked at the marriage, 29, 278; Agni became manifest to M., 46, 22, 157; M. brought Agni to Bhrigu, to Manu, 46, 52, 137, 241, 256; produced Agni by attrition, 46, 74, 77 sq., 147, 173 sq., 256; Agni called M., 46, 119, 123, 241, 292, 294; has established Agni on earth, 46, 230; when he has been shaped in the mother, Agni becomes M., 46, 303.

Mate, *see* Wife.

Materialists, assert that a Self separate from the body does not exist, 34, lxxiv; 38, 269; consider intelligence to be a mere attribute of the body, 34, 368; do not admit the existence of anything but the four elements, 38, 270; doctrines of m. refuted, 45, ix, 236 sq., 339–43; their doctrines as described by Gainas and Buddhists, 45, xxiii sqq. *See also* Kârvâkas.

Mâthara, gotra, Sthaviras of the, 22, 287, 289, 293 sq.

Mâthava, the Videgha, and his family priest Gotama Râhûgana, 12, xli sq., 104–6, 104 n.; 26, xxix.

Mãthras: the Drûg overthrown by the M. of Ahura's doctrine, 31, 110, 118; the holy M. of Ahura guide the way through Righteousness, 31, 110, 119; Zarathustra proclaims the M. of Ahura-Mazda, 31, 172 sq.; the M. with their good ceremonies worshipped, 31, 360. *See also* Prayers (*d-f*), *and* Revelation.

Mãthra-Spenta (Mânsarspend), the Holy Word, invoked and worshipped, 4, 236 sq.; 23, 12, 19 sq., 165 sq., 271, 285; 37, 192, 192 n.; meat-offering for him, 5, 337, 337 n.; takes best the unseen Drug away, 23, 160; is the soul of Ahura-Mazda, 23, 199; Fravashi of M. worshipped, 23, 200; the all-knowing, who hates the Daêvas, the friend of Ahura-Mazda, 23, 227; the Bounteous M., the revelation given against the Daêvas, worshipped, 31, 199 sq. and n., 206, 211, 217, 221, 225, 256, 259, 272, 277, 328, 349, 355, 362, 385; is the word well spoken, 31, 266.

Mãthravâka, a great confounder of heresies, 23, 208, 208 sq. n.; his son Vahmaêdâta, 23, 213.

Mathurâ, or Sauryapura, 45, 112 n.

Mâtikâs, Buddhist texts, 13, 272 sq.; 17, 285, 288, 345, 413.

Matipatrikâ Sâkhâ of the Uddeha Gana, 22, 290.

Matrô and Matrôyâô = Mashya and Mashyôî, q. v.

Mâtsya, knew the Kushtha plant, 42, 6, 681.

Matsya Sâmmada, king, water-dwellers, his people, 44, 369.

Matsyas, fight in the van of the battle, 25, 247, 247 n.; Dhvasan Dvaitavana, king of the M., 44, 398.

Matta-kundali, conversion of, 36, 249.

Matter and souls constitute the body of the Lord, 34, xxviii; unevolved (avyakta) and gross m., 34, xxviii sq.; m. constitutes the body of the Self, 48, 358. *See also* Samskâras.

Mâu, prince of *K*ung-shau, though he had not attained to the Tâo, had an idea of it, 40, 159 sq., 159 n. *See also* Kung-ȝze Mâu.

Maudgalya, *see* Nâka M.

Maudgalyâyana, *see* Moggalâna.

Mauna, t.t., Sk., vow of silence, taciturnity, is abstinence, 1, 131; m. or restraint of senses, 8, 119, 119 n., 161–3, 161 n., 163 n., 168, 173; Muniship, state of Muni, 34, lxxvi; 38, 322 n., 323.

Mauryaputra, n. of a Sthavira, 22, 286.

Mauryas, *see* Moriyas.

Maushikîputra, n. of a teacher, 15, 224 n.

Mâya, the mysterious wisdom of the Divine Benevolence, 31, 94, 99.

Mâyâ, mother of Buddha, 19, xix, 1; 49 (i), 3-5, 7; dies after birth of Buddha and is born in heaven, 19, 23, 23 n., 87, 353; 49 (i), 19 sq.

Mâyâ (Illusion): creation is M., the creator mâyin, 15, xxxvi; theories of M. and Evolution in the Vedânta, 15, xxxvii; as the creating power, 15, xxxvii sq.; 34, cxvii n.; Indra appears multiform through the Ms., 15, 117; Prak*ri*ti (nature) is M., and the Lord the ruler of M., 15, 252; 48, 125 sq., 138 sq., 364, 367, 397; M. the principle of illusion, 34, xxv, lx, xcvi sq., 243, 256 n., 329, 371; 38, 133 sq.; the appearance of the world due to M. or Avidyâ, 34, xxv, 345; cannot be called sat nor asat, 34, xxv, 243; constitutes the upâdâna, 34, xxv; belongs to Brahman as a *s*akti, 34, xxv, 362; modifies itself into all the individual existences, 34, xxv; bodily organs and mental functions, the offspring of M., 34, xxvi; the non-enlightened soul is unable to look through it, 34, xxvi; the material world merged into non-distinct M., 34, xxvi; he whose soul has been enlightened withdraws from the influence of M., 34, xxvii; the world is not unreal M., 34, xxx; Brahman becomes a personal God through M., 34, xxx; soul is Brahman in so far as limited by the unreal upâdhis due to M., 34, xxx; is wonderful nature (Râmânu*g*a), 34, lxi; doctrine of M. unknown to Bâdarâya*n*a, 34, xci-xcvii, c; is of a non-intelligent nature, and the world springs from Brahman as being associated with M., 34, xciii; doctrine of M. not in the Upanishads, 34, cii, cxvi-cxxi, cxvii n., cxxv; the highest Lord may assume a shape formed of M., 34, 81; the nature of the Lord is M. joined with time and karman, 34, 357 n.; in consequence of the Lord's conjunction with M. the creation is unavoidable, 34, 357 n., 369; not a Buddhist conception, 36, 141 sq. n.; emitted by the omniform Nârâya*n*a, 38, 157; Mâra originated M., hence the world appears uneternal, 45, 244, 244 n.; through beginningless M. diversity is seen in Brahman, 48, 22; things seen in dreams are M., 48, 86, 602; the real meaning of M., 48, 125 sq.; the Lord manifests himself by M., 48, 241; cessation of M. through meditation on and union with God, 48, 364; lord of M. creates everything, 48, 368, 400, 406, 469; men intent on their duties pass beyond M., 48, 411; there is no distinction between M. and Nescience, 48, 441 sq. *See also* Delusion, Nature, Nescience, *and* Prak*ri*ti.

Mâyâvâda, theory of illusion, 34, xcviii.

Mâyâvâdin, one who holds the theory of illusion, 34, cxx.

Mâyu, n.p., 23, 217.

Mâ Yung, a compiler of Lî books, 27, 7 sq.

Mâzainya, fiends, spells, a weapon to smite them, 4, 126; 23, 33.

Mâzana, spell against the Daêvas of, 4, 141, 141 n.

Mazda, meaning of, 31, 104 sq. n.; M. worship, *see* Zoroastrianism.

Mazdag, or Mazdak, or Mazdîk, son of Bâmdâ*d*, a heretic, 5, 194, 194 n., 201, 201 n.; 37, 257 n.; 47, 88, 88 n., 89 n.

Mazdayasna, or a worshipper of Mazda, 4, li.

Mazdayasna, n.p., 23, 216.

Mazdeism, Zoroastrianism called so, 4, xiii.

Mazdîk, *see* Mazdag.

Mãzdrâ-vanghu, n.p., 23, 215.

Mâzendarâns, rain the seed of the, 24, 244 sq.; war with the M., 37, 216-18. *See also* Demons.

Mâzînikan, *see* Demons.

Meals: rules about the preparation of food for daily m., 2, 104 sq.; rules about daily m. of householders, 2, 109 sq., 122 sq.; 7, 221; 14, 49-51, 239-42, 245, 263-6; 29, 387 sq.; 30, 21-4; two m. in winter, three in summer, 4, 256, 256 n.; Pra*g*âpati ordained that men should eat only in the evening and morning, 12, 361 sq.; invitations to m. which a Bhikkhu may accept, 13, 41-3; 17, 72-6, 89-92; m. of a

king, 25, 251 sq. *See also* Eating, *and* Food.

Mean: king should set up the standard of the m. before the people, 3, 88; the correct course of the due m., 16, 150, 219, 281, 304, 305 n., 307, 316, 320 sq., 331, 333 n.

Measures, Persian, 5, 98, 98 sq. n.; of distance, 37, 51 n., 56, 56 sq. n., 67, 67 n.; span and cubit, the cubit is the arm, 41, 200; finger-breadth the lowest m., 43, 300; measuring the fire-altar, 43, 305–12. *See also* Weights.

Meat, *see* Animals (*e*).

Mecca, the sacred city of the Arabs, seat of the Kaabah, 6, xvi sq., xlv; war between M. and Medînah, 6, xxxv–xlii; turn (at prayer) thy face towards the Sacred Mosque, 6, 20 sq.; the first House founded at M., 6, 58; 'the mother of cities,' 6, 126; 9, 205; Abraham prays that M. might be a sanctuary, 6, 242 sq.; 9, 124; 'the safe land,' 9, 336, 336 n.; pilgrimage to M., *see* 'Hagg; Sacred Mosque of M., *see* Mosques.

Mêdârya Gotra, Udaka of the, 45, 420.

Medhâganana, t.t., *see* Child (*b*).

Medhâtithi Kâ*n*va, n. of a *Ri*shi, author of Vedic hymns, 1, 9; 32, 54; 46, 7, 35; Indra carries off M., 26, 81, 81 n.

Medhâtithi, his commentary on the Manu-sm*ri*ti, 25, cvii sq., cxviii–cxxvi, cxxviii–cxxx, cxxxiv; a Kasmîrian, 25, cxxiii sq., cxxiv n.; refers to the Nârada-sm*ri*ti, 33, xii, xviii.

Medhyâtithi, n.p., 46, 32 sq., 35 sq.

Medicaments, *see* Medicine.

Medicine, origin of, 4, lxx, 225–7; spells more powerful than the m. of lancet and drugs, 4, lxxx; three (five) kinds of m. (holiness, the Law), the knife, herbs, and sacred spells, 4, 87, 87 n., 225–8; 23, 44; men become skilled in m. in the age of Hûshê*d*ar-mah, 5, 233; on m. to be used by Bhikkhus, 13, 174; 17, 41–61, 65 sqq., 68, 76 sq., 89, 97, 144 sq., 221–5; 20, 77, 154; one should beget offspring through the application of m. and prayers, 14, 273; castration and surgical operations near the anus, and clysters forbidden to Bhikkhus, 17, 77–80; Buddha allows store-houses to keep drugs in, 17, 121; Mahâvîra never used m., 22, 86; Gaina monk must not take m. without asking leave of his superior, 22, 306; wisdom requisite for understanding m., 24, 102; dead matter used as m., 24, 336; rules about taking m., 27, 114; 37, 48; storing of medicinal herbs, 27, 271; treatment of wounds, 35, 211; saving criminals worthy of death for medical purposes, 37, 53; curing defective sight, 37, 123; treated in the Nasks, 37, 437, 447; urine as a cure for scrofulous sores, 42, 19, 489; salve as a protector of life and limb, 42, 61 sq.; urine, Rudra's m., 42, 138; use of m. forbidden to Gaina monks, 45, 97; spells and roots as m., 45, 103; knowledge of m. disclosed by Zoroaster, 47, 75 sq. *See also* Parables (*f*), *and* Physicians.

Medînah, the city of YaTHrib, 6, xxxiv; Mohammed at M., 6, xxxiv sq.; war between Mecca and M., 6, xxxv–xlii; the Muslims besieged by the confederate army at M., 9, 138–42, 138 n., 140 n., 142 n.; warning to the infidels and hypocrites of M., 9, 148, 284 sq. *See also* YaTHrib.

Meditation.

(*a*) M. on Brahman, the Lord, the Self.
(*b*) M. of Buddhist and Gaina monks.

(*a*) M. ON BRAHMAN, THE LORD, THE SELF.

Two kinds of m., the brahmopâsana and the pratîkopâsana, 1, 201; rules about m., for the ascetic, 7, 281, 287–91; 15, 241 sq.; 25, lxix, 209–13, 211 n.; *whatever he meditates upon, that is obtained by a man (in a future existence): such is the mysterious power of m.*, 7, 289; m. at time of death, 8, 78, 390; a means of attaining to K*ri*sh*n*a, 8, 79, 84, 100; silent m. superior to all sacrifices, 8, 89, 89 n.; some by m. see the self in the self, by the self, 8, 105; leads to unity with Brahman, 8, 128; 11, 201 sq., 201 n.; persons made to appear by mystic m., 8, 136, 150; by exclusive m., the devotee attains concentration of mind, 8, 248, 251; by m. he reaches greatness, 8, 332;

the Sannyâsin who wishes to attain to final emancipation, should meditate on one point, 8, 368; some Brâhma*n*as recommend m., others sacrifice and gifts, 8, 376; purifies from sin, 14, 128; the results of practising m. or Yoga, 15, 242; discussions as to whether certain m. (vidyâs) have to be combined or to be kept apart, 34, lxvii sq., lxx, lxxii sq., lxxv; 38, 184–96, 216–22, 240–9, 277–9, 281–4, 303–5; m. on constituent parts of sacrifices, are not to be considered as permanently requisite parts of the latter, but are valid for all *S*âkhâs, 34, lxxiv; 38, 252–6, 272–4; 48, 629 sq., 675–7; m. on the Self must be repeated again and again, 34, lxxvi; 38, 331–7; is to be carried on in a sitting posture, 34, lxxvii; 38, 349 sq.; 48, 720 sq.; may be carried on at any time, and in any place, favourable to concentration of mind, 34, lxxvii; 38, 350 sq.; ms. are to be continued until death, 34, lxxvii; 38, 351 sq.; 48, 721 sq.; is an action, knowledge is not, 34, 35; the threefoldness of m., 34, 102–6, 272; 48, 253 sq.; m., as taught in the Vedânta-texts, is possible only if the soul is an agent, 38, 52; presentation before the mind of the highest Self is effected through m., 38, 171 sq.; as a means of the knowledge of the highest person, 38, 204 sq.; twofold m. on the oneness of the Self, 38, 244 sq.; ms. are themselves acts, but not subordinate members of the sacrifices, 38, 256, 348; owing to the might of the m. on the unity of pra*n*ava and udgîtha, the Hot*ri* sets right any mistake he may commit in his work, 38, 282; ms. subserve the end of man, not of sacrifice, 38, 283; ms. of priest and sacrificer, the fruit belongs to him who carries out the m., 38, 320 sq.; m. and knowledge identical, 38, 332; 48, 715 sq.; on the udgîtha viewed as the sun, 38, 333; by the application of m. the soul departs by the vein passing through the skull, 38, 377 sq.; enjoined by Vedânta-texts, 48, 13 sq., 179 sq., 681; the term explained, 48, 14 sq.; abstention and the other six auxiliary means of m., 48, 17, 261, 284; true mode of m., 48, 363; as a mental sacrifice on the altars of mind, speech, &c., 48, 668–73; at the time of m. the Self of the devotee is of the nature of the released Self, 48, 673–5; the Upako*s*ala, the *S*â*nd*ilya, the Vai*s*vânara m., the m. on the Self of bliss, on the Imperishable, and other ms., 48, 679; a purification of the sacrificer's mind, 48, 686 sq. *See also* Brahman (*b*), Cognitions, Knowledge, Worship, *and* Yoga.

(*b*) M. of Buddhist and *G*aina monks.

Without knowledge there is no m., without m. there is no knowledge, 10 (i), 87; Buddha on the relation of upright conduct, m., and intelligence, 11, 11, 11 n., 12, 15, 24, 28, 34, 65 sq., 70; four *Gh*ânas or stages of m., 11, 61, 62 sq. n.; 36, 143; nine stages of m. preceding Buddha's Nirvâ*n*a, 11, 114 sqq., 115 n.; 19, 307; m. (samâdhi) in Buddhism, corresponds to Faith in Christianity, 11, 145; the four Appama*ññ*as or Brahma-vihâras, 'infinite feelings' of Love, Pity, Sympathy, Equanimity, 11, 201 sq., 201 n., 272 sq., 273 sq. n., 285, 285 n.; the ecstasy of contemplation, one of the conditions by which a Bhikkhu obtains his desires, 11, 210–18; the 'Great Complex' a kind of m., 11, 267 n.; stages of mystic m. or superhuman conditions (*gh*âna, vimokkhas, samâpattis), 13, 235 sq., 245 sq.; 19, 138 sq., 138 n.; 35, 52; 49 (i), 128 sq.; Bhikkhus walk up and down when meditating, 17, 6 sq., 17, 17 n.; 36, 9; list of ms., 21, 420, 424 sq.; its characteristic marks, 35, 60 sq.; the advantages of m., 35, 196–8; compared with a state of dream, 36, 161; subjects for m., 36, 212 sq.; Buddha's 'jewel of m.,' 36, 222 sq.; Bhikkhus addicted to m., 36, 238; emancipation the flower of m., 36, 312; enjoined for the Bhikkhu, 36, 372; the Bhâvanâs (*G*aina t.t.) ms. conducive to the purity of the soul, 45, 69, 69 n.; pure m. on the law, the sixth kind of internal austerities, 45, 179 sq.; the

soul purified by m. on the vanity of life and the world, 45, 329 sq., 329 n.; the m. called the Arouser of all worlds, 49 (i), 173; m. on Sukhâvatî and Amitâyus, 49 (ii), 169–99. *See also Gh*âna, *and* Samâdhis.

Mê*d*ôk-mâh, or Mê*d*yôk-mâh, n. of a Zoroastrian teacher, commentator, 5, 243, 243 n., 245, 245 n., 249 sq., 268, 292; 18, 299–305, 299 n., 312–15, 332 sq., 336 n., 361, 449, 449 n.

Mê*d*yôk-mâh, Zaratûst's first disciple, 5, 141 sq., 141 n., 145, 187. *See also* Maidhyô-m*a*ungha, *and* Mê*d*ôk-mâh.

Mêdyômâh, an author of the Sad Dar, 24, xxxvii.

Mê*d*yômâh, first cousin of Zoroaster, who converts him, 47, xv, xxx, 155, 155 n., 163 sq.; Aharûbô-stôtô, son of M., 47, 166.

Megha, disciple of Suhastin, 22, 291.

Meghadundubhisvararâ*g*a, n. of a Tathâgata, 21, 399 sq.

Meghakâlî, female attendant of Mâra, 19, 153; 49 (i), 144.

Meghasvarapradîpa, n. of a Tathâgata, 21, 178.

Meghasvararâ*g*a, n. of numerous Tathâgatas, 21, 179, 358.

Mei Ȝeh, presented a copy of the Shû to the emperor Yüan, 3, 9; author of a commentary, 3, 10.

Mekhalîyikâ *S*âkhâ of the U*d*uvâ*t*ika Ga*n*a, 22, 291.

Memory, as Brahman, meditation on, 1, 119; confusion, want of m., 8, 51, 320; discussion on m., 35, 120–3.

Menâ, or Menakâ, Indra in love with, 26, 81 n.; a nymph, 43, 106.

Menander, or Milinda, 35, xviii–xxiii.

Mencius, the works of, the second of the four Shû, 3, xx; quotes the Shû King, 3, 2; on old historical documents, 3, 5; on chronology, 3, 21–3; on the records of the Shû, 3, 213; his acquaintance with the Shih King, 3, 285; his doctrine of the goodness of human nature, 3, 425 n.; 16, 357 n.; on the interpretation of old Chinese poems, 16, xv; on husband and wife, 16, 313 n.; how he spoke of the Lî *K*î, 27, 1 sq.; on the four constituents of human nature, 27, 10; parts of 'the Royal Regulations' taken from M., 27, 18 sq.; on man, 27, 383 n.; on benevolence being man, 28, 269 n., 312 n.; a contemporary of *K*wang-ȝze, 39, 36; on human nature, 39, 147; M. and Hui-ȝze, 39, 172 n.; attacked Mih-ȝze, 39, 182 n.; the scholar of Ȝâu, honourably mentioned as a teacher, 40, 216, 216 n.

Me*n*daka and his family converted by Buddha, 17, 121–8.

Mendicants, religious, *see* Ascetics, Bhikkhus, *G*aina monks, Holy persons, Parivrâ*g*akakas, *and* Sannyâsins.

Menstruation, *see* Purification, *and* Woman (*b*, *e*).

Mental impressions, the variety of ideas is due to, 34, 420, 420 n.; their existence is not possible on the Bauddha view, 34, 425–7; internal cognition cannot be their abode, 34, 426 sq.

Merchant, *see* Parables (*f*), *and* Trade.

Mercy, genius of, invoked, 23, 5, 14, 36 sq.

Merezîshmya, n.p., 23, 219.

Merit, *see* Karman.

Meru, the first-born of mountains, 8, 354; the gods dwell on the tops of M., 10 (ii), 125; 12, 110 n.; description of M. or Sudar*s*ana, the best of all mountains, 45, 288 sq.; blazing M. at the end of an aeon, 49 (i), 143.

Merudhva*g*a, n. of a Tathâgata, 49 (ii), 99.

Merukalpa, n. of a Tathâgata, 21, 178.

Merukû*t*a, n. of Tathâgatas, 21, 178; 49 (ii), 6.

Meruprabhâsa, n. of a Tathâgata, 49 (ii), 99.

Merupradîpa, n. of a Tathâgata, 49 (ii), 100.

Messiah, traditional Semitic belief in the coming of a, 6, xxx, 1; criticism of the Christian doctrine of the M., 18, 107 sq. and n.; 24, 229–38; M. or Mashikh, an extender of belief, 47, 126. *See also* Buddha (*j*), *and* Saoshya*nt*(s).

Metals, under the protection of Shatvaîrô, duties regarding them,

5, 375 sq.; origin of m., 18, 199, 199 n.; 24, 58; 25, 189, 189 n.; 44, 215; similes of iron, 36, 198 sq.; 45, 269; charm with lead, against demons, 42, 65 sq.; why lead is soft and, while being like gold, not worth anything, 43, 92; lead is a form of both iron and gold, 44, 219; knives of gold, copper, iron, 44, 303 sq.; admonitions about the use of m., 47, 161. *See also* Gold.

Metaphysics, *see* Philosophy.

Metârya, n. of a Sthavira, 22, 286.

Metres: speculations on the number of metrical feet, and the peculiar virtues of different m., 1, 50 sq., 159–62, 172, 180 sq., 183 sq., 186, 187 sq., 193–6, 209 sq., 227–9; 34, 93–5; Anush*t*ubh is speech, 1, 158, 184, 194; 12, 171; 43, 137, 140, 144, 269, 277, 291, 328; 44, 89, 244, 353; Gâyatrî, Trish*t*ubh, *G*agatî, and Virâg are all m., 1, 180 sq.; Trish*t*ubh is the man, Anush*t*ubh the wife, and they make a couple, 1, 182; the person of the m., 1, 259; Trish*t*ubhs as sign of antiquity, 7, xvii, xxiii sq., xxix; versification of Sanskrit works, and chronology, 8, 15 sq.; ritualistic and mystic (symbolic) application of the m., 12, 11, 11 n., 59 n., 60, 60 n., 79 sq., 80 n., 82 sq., 91, 91 n., 175, 194–6, 195 n., 205–7, 232–6, 252, 269 sq., 292, 297, 307 sq., 333, 354 sq., 390; 26, 21, 23–5, 27, 59, 65 sq., 68, 74 sq., 87–9, 91, 112 sq., 120, 166 sq., 171, 226, 229 sq., 230 n., 245, 250 sq., 303 sq., 314–16, 328–30, 362, 380, 383 sq., 389 sq., 399 sq., 416–21, 450; 29, 198 sq.; 41, 31, 40, 40 n., 44, 64, 91, 103 sq., 120 sq., 167–70, 183, 193, 196, 201–3, 218–20, 232–5, 241, 253, 266, 271, 276 sq., 307, 316–18, 323, 337, 339, 341, 352 sq., 353 n., 358, 366, 398, 407 sq., *414*, *416 sq.*; 42, 112, 186, 208 sq., 212, 646 sq.; 43, 12, 50–4, 57 sq., 70, 83, 85, 87–91, 94, 108–16, 120, 134, 137, 140, 142, 164 sq., 174, 178, 197, 204–6, 211 sq., 226, 243, 247, 262, 265, 268 sq., 277, 279, 300, 307 sq., *327–31*, 352–4, 352 n., 356, 360, 384–7, 390; 44, 3, 26, 55, 65, 106, 151, 153, 155 sq., 161 sq., 170 sq., 255 sq., 256 n., 379, 402 sq., 476, 497, 549 sq.; Gâyatrî-Agni-Brâhma*n*as, Trish*t*ubh-Indra-Kshatriyas, 12, 96, 96 n.; are cattle, the cattle of the gods, 12, 232, 234; 26, 369–72; 41, 414; 43, 36–40, 45 sq., 51 sq., 79 sq., 87, 110, 115; 44, 26, 221, 376 n.; represented as birds, 12, 242 n.; 44, 173; offerings to the deified M. (*Kh*andas), 14, 63; 29, 321, 325; connected with different quarters, 15, 338–40; m. employed in the sacred books of the *G*ainas, 22, xli sq.; brought forth by Kadrû, 26, 150; seven m., 26, 213, 230 n.; 43, 277, 277 n., 314; 44, 154; 46, 168; are the limbs of Garutmat (?), 29, 49; different m. for different castes, 29, 59 n., 66; worshipped at the Tarpa*n*a, 29, 121, 219; worshipped at the Upâkara*n*a, 29, 221; Vedas with the m., invoked in danger, 29, 232; the m. of the Mantras in the G*ri*hya-sûtras, 30, ix–xiv, xxxv–xxxvii; m. of the Gâthas, 31, 91 sq.; all the sacred m. worshipped, 31, 328; metrics and prosody of the Rigveda-sa*m*hitâ, 32, xxxvii sq., lii, lxxvii–cxxv, 83, 91, 99, 170 sq., 324; 46, 68 sq., 98, 131 sq., 166; names of m. derived from choregic movements, 32, xcv–xcvii, cxii, 316 sq.; speculations as to the origin of the m., 32, cxi; 43, 4, 6, 8, 10 sq., 14 n.; statements about the order of succession of m. supplementing each other, 38, 225, 228; of the Asuras and of the Devas, 38, 228, 228 n.; m. of Chinese poetry, 40, 315 sq.; the divine ladies, 41, 243; in the Atharva-veda, 42, 296, 444; identified with deities, 43, 32, 53; regions identified with the m., 43, 45 sq.; Trish*t*ubh is the thunderbolt, is energy, vital power, 43, 193; 44, 222, 311, 404, 408, 411 sq.; deities of m., 43, 330 sq.; 44, 312 sq.; fire-altar identified with the m., 43, 384–6; created, 43, 403; abide here on the new moon day, 44, 2; sacrificial formulas of the seasonal sacrifices in Trish*t*ubh, *G*agatî, and Anush*t*ubh m., 44, 78; the Anush*t*ubh and Gâyatrî Sâvitrî, 44, 89, 89 n.; are divine creatures born from the mouth, 44, 90; by

means of the m. the sacrifice is performed, 44, 154; there are three m., 44, 155; a m. does not collapse from excess or deficiency of a syllable, 44, 157; by means of the B*ri*hatî the gods reached heaven, 44, 172; cattle related to the B*ri*hatî, 44, 221, 371; the *G*agatî is this earth, 44, 245; the hair is the m., 44, 249, 448; by means of the *G*agatî he secures cattle, 44, 252, 284, 408; horse of the Anush*t*ubh character, 44, 304; Anush*t*ubh the highest of m., 44, 332; Trish*t*ubh is the vigour in Indra, 44, 358; certain m. for each of the three Soma pressings, 44, 444; 46, 301; Gâyatrî, Trish*t*ubh, *G*agatî, and the three worlds, 44, 494 sq.; Anush*t*ubh, 44, 518; Ati*kkh*andas, 44, 379, 497, 522; B*ri*hatî, 44, 526; Dvipadâ, 44, 530; Ekapadâ, 44, 531; *G*agatî, 44, 534; Gâyatrî, 44, 535; Kakubh, 44, 543; Paṅkti, Padapaṅkti, 44, 554; Sa*m*stubh, Samudriya, 44, 567; Satob*ri*hatî, 44, 569; Svarâ*g*, 44, 576; Trikakubh, Trish*t*ubh, 44, 578; irregularities of m. in *G*aina verses, 45, 39 n. *See also* Gâyatrî, Numbers, *and* Virâ*g*.

Mettagû, n. of a Brâhma*n*a, 10 (ii), 187, 193–5, 210.

Mettagûmâ*n*avapu*kkh*â, t.c., 10 (ii), 193–5.

Mettasutta, t.c., 10 (ii), 24 sq.

Metteyya, the Buddha to come, 35, 225, 225 n. *See also* Tissa M.

Mettiya, one of the *Kh*abbaggiya Bhikkhus, 20, 9–17, 118.

Mettiyâ, falsely accuses Dabba of having defiled her, 20, 13 sqq.

Miâo, lord of, 3, 51 sq. and n., 54; people of M. rebels against Shun, 3, 61; wickedness of the M., their punishment, 3, 255–60.

Michael and Gabriel, 6, 13, 13 n.

Mî*dh*ushî, n. of a goddess, 30, 290 n.

Midian, Sho'hâib sent as an apostle to, 6, 148–50; 9, 121; punishment of the people of M., who disbelieve in Sho'hâib, 6, 183, 214–16, 249, 249 n.; 9, 61, 97, 176, 242.

Migadâya, a hermitage at Benares, 11, 146, 153 sq.

Migâra, *see* Visâkhâ, mother of M.

Mihir, *see* Mithra.

Mih-ȝze, his followers, the Mohists, 39, 182, 182 n.

Mikâ'îl, guardian angel of the Jews, 6, lxix.

Milinda, King, conversations between him and Nâgasena, 11, 112 n.; 35, xii, xiv, xvi sq., 1, 40–302; 36, 1, &c.; the Greek Menander, 35, xviii sq.; coins of M., 35, xviii, xx–xxii; Greek and Roman writers on M., 35, xix sq.; was he a Buddhist? 35, xxi–xxv; his date and birthplace, 35, xxiii, 127; previous births of M. and Nâgasena, 35, 4–6; his greatness and wisdom and love of disputation, 35, 6–13, 23, 29 sq.; confutes Âyupâla, 35, 30–3; goes to meet Nâgasena, 35, 37–40; makes presents to Nâgasena, 35, 134 sq.; longs for the higher life of the recluse, 35, 135; studies the Buddhist Scriptures and becomes a lay disciple of Nâgasena, 35, 137–44; 36, 373 sq.; takes the Buddhist vows, 35, 138; mentioned by Kshemendra, 36, xvii; gives up his kingdom and becomes an Arhat, 36, 374; builds a Vihâra, 36, 374; 'Questions of M.,' *see* Milindapañha.

Milindapañha, the date of Buddha's death in the, 11, xlvii sq.; translation, *Vols.* 35 and 36; translated into Pali, 35, xi, xlv; Sinhalese version of the M., 35, xi–xiii; as a work of art, 35, xii, xvii sq., xxiv, xlviii sq.; 36, xxvii; Buddhaghosa's references to M., 35, xiv–xvi; a work of great authority about A.D. 430, 35, xvi; its date, 35, xvi, xxiii, xxv–xlv, 248 n.; MSS. and edition of the text, 35, xvi sq.; the author of the M. knew the Pi*t*akas, 35, xxvii–xlii; countries and persons mentioned in the M., 35, xlii–xlv; its language, 35, xlv–xlviii; its relation to the Tipi*t*aka, 35, 196 n., 293 n., 298 n.; 36, 19 n., 144 n., 176 n., 304 n.; Chinese versions of the M., 36, xi–xv; references to it in other works, 36, xvii–xix; M. and Kathâ Vatthu, 36, xx–xxvii.

Milk: dadhi-gharma, libation of hot m. mixed with sour m., 26, 336 n.; 44, 502 sq.; as m. transforms itself into curds, so Brahman is the cause of the world, 34, 346 sq.; used with

consecration water, 41, 78 sq.; is breath, 41, 245; 43, 200; laid in the female, 41, 245, 311; sour m. (curds, whey, dadhi) is life-sap and belongs to Indra, 41, 374 sq., 389 sq.; 43, 201; fire-altar sprinkled with sour curds mixed with honey and ghee, 43, 182 sq.; sour m. represents cattle, 43, 203; is seed, the earth a womb, 44, 180; cups of m. and Surâ, 44, 225, 228; is vital air and food, and prosperity, 44, 237 sq.; cups of m. offered, 44, 240 n., 241. *See also* Animals (*e*), *and* Parables (*f*).

Milk-ocean, Vish*n*u in the, 7, 6 sqq.; a vision of the m., 22, 236 sq.

Milky Way, *see* Stars.

Millenniums, *see* Ages of the World.

Mîmâ*m*sâ, its two branches, pûrva and uttara, 34, ix; the word already employed in the Brâhma*n*as, 34, x; vast literature connected with it, 34, xi; its various means of proof, 34, xli; the Vedânta-sûtras as well as the Pûrvâ-Mîmâ*m*sâ-sûtras are throughout M., 34, xlv; the earlier part of the M. teaches works, the latter part knowledge of Brahman, 48, 5, 19; what it aims at, 48, 6 sq.; M.-theory, as opposed to the Vedântin view, 48, 148–53. *See also* Philosophy.

Mîmâ*m*sâ-*s*âstra, a short name for the Pûrva-Mîmâ*m*sâ-*s*âstra, 34, xi.

Mîmâ*m*sâ-sûtras, different from other Sûtras, 34, xiii; not intelligible without a commentary, 34, xiii sq.

Mind (manas, internal organ): meditation on m. as Brahman (n.), 1, 53, 112, 152; 15, 65; 34, xxxiv sq., 107–16; the subtilest portion of earth becomes m. in man, 1, 96–8; 38, 366; breath as the causal substance of m., 1, 99; 38, 366; speech is merged in the m., m. in breath, at death, 1, 100 sq., 107 sq.; 38, 364–7; 48, 729; is the self, is the world, 1, 112; is difficult to restrain and fickle, 8, 71; K*r*ish*n*a is the m. among the senses, 8, 88; as the instrument of knowledge, m. is the upholder of the body, 8, 261 sq.; 41, 270; first words are produced, and the m. runs after them, 8, 262; whether speech or m. is superior, 8, 263 sq.; 26, 54 sq.; there are two minds, immovable and movable, 8, 264; relation of m. and sense-organs, 8, 268–70, 337; 38, 365 sq.; m. and understanding, as husband and wife, 8, 310; the five Prâ*n*as, speech, m., and understanding make up the eight constituents of the universe, 8, 336; the moon its deity, m. is the moon, 8, 338; 43, 11, 333; 44, 31; when everything is absorbed into the m., the pleasures of worldly life are not esteemed, 8, 341; the characteristic of m. is thought or meditation, 8, 348–50; the pole of the wheel of life, 8, 355; the truth about m., understanding, senses, &c., must be understood by the Sannyâsin, 8, 368; is the ruler of the five elements, 8, 385 sq., 385 n.; relation between m. and individual soul, 8, 386; 34, 104, 107, 118 sqq., 175; the pupil of the Kshetra*gñ*a, 8, 394; libations to M. and Speech, 12, 124–7; dispute between M. and Speech, decided by Pra*g*âpati, 12, 130 sq., 130 n.; m. and speech are the two libations of the Agnihotra, 12, 332; difference between m. and buddhi, 15, xiv, xiv n.; the triad of m., speech, breath, 15, 93–7; Pradyumna identical with it, 34, xxiii, 440; is the abode of the power of cognition, 34, 105; abides in the heart, 34, 175; is superior to the sense-objects, 34, 239; intellect is higher than the m., 34, 239 sq.; presupposes the existence of an aggregate of atoms, viz. the body, 34, 403 n.; speech, breath, and m. presuppose fire, water, and earth, 38, 78 sq.; has all things for its objects and extends to the past, the present, and the future, 38, 81; on account of the plurality of its functions we find it designated as manas or buddhi or aha*m*kâra, or *k*itta, 38, 81; has five functions, 38, 89 sq.; accompanies the soul when leaving its body, 38, 102; six and thirty thousand different energies of the m. identified with the fire-altars, the cups, &c., 38, 265; Lâo-ȝze describes the m. of man, 39, 294 sq.; by the m. everything is gained here,

41, 100; 44, 507; gods created from union of M. and Speech, 41, 149; m. is Sarasvat, speech is Sarasvatî, 41, 398; the first of vital airs, 41, 402 sq.; 43, 337; 44, 504; fashioned from the wind, 43, 6; speech, daughter of the m., created by the m., 43, 11, 376 sq.; as a Gandharva, 43, 233; the ultimate cause of the universe, 43, 374–80; created, 43, 402; libation to M., 44, 28, 32, 33, 35 sq.; m. and speech, while being one and the same, are distinct from each other, 44, 46 sq.; Hot*ri* and Adhvaryu priests are speech and m., 44, 136. *See also* Manas, Organs, Prâ*n*as, Psychology, *and* Senses.

Mindfulness, or sati, 11, 145; part of the higher wisdom, 11, 306; its characteristic mark, 35, 58–60.

Minerals, origin of, 5, 183.

Ming, the correlate of Heaven at border sacrifices, 28, 202, 202 n.; deserves ancestor worship, 28, 209.

Minô*k*ihar, *see* Mânû*sk*ihar.

Min-ȝze, a disciple of Confucius, 39, 232.

Miracles, worked by holy men, 2, 158; Hûshê*d*ar makes the sun stand still, 5, lii, 231 sq., 233 n.; at the birth of Vahrâm the Vargâvand, 5, 221; Christian m., 6, 113 sq.; God could send a sign if He pleased, 6, 119; worked by Moses, 6, 157; 9, 35 sq., 92 sq., 100, 111; people ask for signs, 6, 195; 9, 46; the splitting asunder of the moon, 9, 255 n.; Buddha on m., 10 (i), 63 n.; 21, 421; worked by Buddha, 10 (ii), 14, 101; 11, xviii, 18, 21, 48 sq., 74 sq.; 13, 105–7, 119–22, 127–31, 133 sq.; 17, 83 sq., 95, 104, 219; 19, 185, 185 n., 222, 222 n., 240, 251 sq.; 20, 243–50; 21, xxx sq., 237 sq., 281–6, 364–8; 49 (i), 167, 170, 194, 196–9; in connexion with Buddha's death, 11, 44, 86 sq., 123 sq., 128–30; 19, 268 sq., 307 sq.; in Buddhism, 11, 46 sq. and n., 155; Nâga King Mu*k*alinda protects Buddha, 13, 80; gods render service to Buddha, 13, 83, 125–7; at the foundation of the Kingdom of Truth, 13, 97 sqq.; the gods come to hear Buddha's preaching, 13, 122–4; Buddha understands the thoughts of others, 13, 124 sq.; 17, 192; supernatural power of suddenly disappearing, 14, 309; worked by Buddhist saints, 17, 2–4, 64 sq., 76 sq.; 19, 189; 20, 7 sq., 394; 21, 396; Buddha's miraculous appearance and disappearance, 17, 7, 9; miraculous powers possessed by Me*nd*aka and his family, 17, 121–4; a person poised in the air by supernatural power, not to be considered as completing a Sa*m*gha, 17, 269 sq.; attending the birth of Buddha, 19, xix, 2–7, 13, 344–64; 49 (i), 4–8; on Buddha's reaching Bodhi, 19, 146 sq., 156, 163 sq.; 21, 160 sq.; 49 (i), 155–7; converts suddenly transformed into Bhikshus, 19, 197, 197 n.; flying through the air, crossing a river without a boat, 19, 260; celestial beings open the gate of the Sîtavana for Anâthapi*nd*ika, 20, 181 sq.; Revata, by the divine ear, hears what people at a distance say, 20, 396; apparition of the seven-jewelled Stûpa in the sky, 21, xxx, 227–40; Abhi*g*ñâs or magical powers of Arhats, 21, 1 sq. n.; there are always m., when Buddhas are about to preach, 21, 16–29, 223, 225; miraculous powers (indriyas, balas), constituents of Bodhi, 21, 79; men who possess transcendent faculties and the triple science, compared to small plants, 21, 125; saints endowed with magical powers, emitting rays, 21, 126 sq.; a ray darts from Buddha's brow, and Buddhas appear in myriads of worlds, 21, 231–6, 393; Bodhisattvas rise into the sky on lotuses, 21, 248 sq.; rain of heavenly flowers, &c., and heavenly music in honour of Buddha, 21, 313, 315 sq., 378; performed by the Act of Truth, 21, 384 sq.; 35, 180–5, 180 n., 185 n.; two princes convert their father by performing m., 21, 421 sq., 426; performed by King *S*ubhavyûha, 21, 426, 428; displayed on the arrival of Samantabhadra in the Saha-world, 21, 431; attending the birth of Mahâvîra, 22, 189–92, 217–56; produced by the gods when Mahâvîra retired from the world and reached highest knowledge, 22,

195-202, 257-9; dry passage over a river, 23, 72; no m. in the Gâthas, 31, xxvi; happening at the birth of Nâgasena and other events of his life, 35, 14 sq., 22, 29; 36, 373; two reasons why Buddhas do not work m., 36, 24 sq.; why there are m. at the graves of some Arhats, 36, 174-6; the double m. at the foot of the Ga*nd*amba tree, 36, 247; the m. of the manifestation to the world, 36, 248; worked by Ko Yüan, 40, 248; in the legendary history of Zoroaster, 47, xi, xiv sq., xxi-xxiii; at the birth of Zoroaster, 47, 17-33, 35, 122, 139-43; connected with the childhood of Zoroaster, 47, 35-46, 122 sq., 145-51; birth of apostles from a maiden, 47, 105 sq., 111, 115; on Buddha's departure from home, 49 (i), 60 sq., 68 sq., 85 sq.; during Buddha's battle with Mâra, 49 (i), 141; Pâramitâs, miraculous powers, 49 (ii), 12; appear on Buddha finishing his description of Sukhâvatî, 49 (ii), 72; the six supernatural faculties, 49 (ii), 193. *See also* Flowers, Iddhis, *and* Omens.

Mîrak the Âspiyân, and Zîyânak Zardâhim, the first pair, 5, 131, 131 n.

Miriam, sister of Moses, and the Virgin Mary confused, 6, 50 n.

Mirror, the person in the, as Brahman, 1, 304; does not manifest the face, 48, 67; M. of Truth, *see* Truth. *See also* Parables (*f*).

Misbelievers, rebuked, 6, 2-4, 22; are fellows of the Fire, 6, 40; no repentance accepted from m., 6, 57 sq. *See also* Faith.

Miscarriage, *see* Child (*b*).

Misfortune, *see* Nir*ri*ti.

Mithilâ, kingdom of Ganaka, 8, 304; Mahâvîra at M., 22, 264; Nami, king of M., 45, 36.

Mithra (Mit*r*ô, Mihir), the da*n*hupaiti of all dahyus, 4, xlix; Avestic M. and Vedic Mitra, 4, lii; an Aryan God, 4, lxiv; the Sun, making the earth fertile, 4, 23, 23 n.; a lie unto M. a heinous crime, 4, 49; Rashnu, M., and Sraosha, the three judges of the departed, 4, 89 n.; 23, 168; 24, 18, 18 n., 258, 280, 361; invoked by Zarathu*s*tra, 4, 214, 258; the god with beautiful weapons, reaches the all-happy mountain, 4, 218; of the rolling country-side comes to meet the departed soul, 4, 373; all violets are his, 5, 104; the lord of wide pastures, invoked and worshipped, 5, 228 sq., 232, 402, 405; 23, 5, 5 n., 14, 36, 38, 86 sq., 166, 294, 350 sq.; 31, 319; 37, 183, 183 n., 210; watches over promises, and is an account-keeper of sin and good works, 18, 33, 33 n., 66; 37, 155, 155 n.; of the wide pastures, of the thousand ears, and of the myriad eyes, 23, 9, 17, 119-22, 130, 141-58; 31, 196, 204, 209, 215, 219, 223, 256, 271, 276, 324, 326, 337, 340, 346, 351, 379-81; lord of wide pastures, opened a wide way to Ti*s*trya, 23, 95, 103; expiatory rites connected with the worship of M., 23, 119, 151 sq., 151 n.; Mihir Ya*s*t, devoted to M., 23, 119-58; the god of heavenly light, 23, 119, 122 sq., 131 sq., 136, 143 sq., 157; guardian of truth, preserver of contracts and oaths, 23, 119 sq., 124-6, 128-30, 135, 137, 139 sq., 146 sq.; means 'contract,' 23, 120 n., 149 sq.; is truth-speaking, 23, 121; as a god of the battle-field, 23, 122, 128-31, 145, 148 sq.; not identical with the sun, 23, 122 n., 143; eight friends as spies of M., 23, 130, 130 n.; makes the waters flow and the plants grow, 23, 134; drives along on his chariot drawn by four steeds, 23, 136, 138, 152-5, 157; invoked by all beings, 23, 140 sq.; swinging in his hands a club, 23, 144, 154; guards and maintains the creation of Mazda, 23, 145; the warrior of the white horse, 23, 145; his virtue and wisdom, 23, 146 sq.; the weapons of M., with which he smites the Daêvas, 23, 154; lord of all countries, 23, 157 sq.; M., Rashnu, and Spe*n*ta-Ârmaiti, accompany Mazda, 23, 181; a worshipper of M. shall become a mighty ruler, 23, 184; the Fravashis, along with M. and Rashnu, help in battle, 23, 191; Fravashi of M. worshipped, 23, 200; the lord of wide pastures, increases the excellences of countries, 23, 202; Verethraghna goes along with M. and Rashnu, 23, 244; brother of Ashi Vanguhi, 23, 274;

has piercing rays, 23, 327, 329; M. and Rashnu Razista, 23, 342; follows the sun in its course, 23, 349; Mihir Nyâyis, prayer to M., 23, 349, 353–5; will smite the demons, 24, 33; angel of the sun's light, 24, 96; breach of promise called M.-drug, 24, 287 sq.; the province-ruler, worshipped, 31, 199, 205, 210, 216, 220, 225; Ahura and M. worshipped, 31, 199, 199 n., 205, 210, 216, 220, 225; prayer to M. to defeat Wrath and Lethargy, 37, 219; at the renovation of the universe, 37, 235; punishes the sinner, 37, 278. *See also* Sun.

Mîtôkht, the liar, evil spirit, 5, 107 sq.; 18, 95 sq., 95 n.

Mitra, in Veda, and Avestic Mithra, 4, lii; in the Anugîtâ, 8, 219 sq.; the emancipated sage is M., 8, 220 sq., 345; one of the ten fires at the allegorical sacrifice of the sense-organs, 8, 261; the presiding deity of Apâna and the organ of excretion, 8, 338; when the flame of the fire gets lower and lower it is M., 12, 341; prayers and offerings to M., 14, 247; 15, 45, 53; 26, 24; 29, 274; 41, 125, 244, 244 n.; 44, 281, 385; 46, 13, 418; protects him who performs the twilight devotions, 14, 249; identified with the excretions of the Âtman, 25, 512; oblation to M. at the wedding, 29, 32; the firm, powerful eye of M., 29, 61; 30, 148; the Brahma*k*ârin identified with M., 29, 64; worshipped at the hospitable reception of a friend, 29, 88, 198; invoked at the house-building rite, 29, 214; of truth, invoked for protection, 29, 280; 'M. art thou by rights,' says the teacher to the pupil, 30, 151; invoked at the Upanayana, 30, 151; Agni and M., 32, 94; 46, 158, 387; invited to the Soma, 32, 408; sacrifice to M. and B*ri*haspati at the Râgasûya, 41, 66–8; is the Brahman, and the sacrifice, 41, 67; is every one's friend, 41, 68; offering to M. Satya, 41, 71; is the breath, 41, 230 sq.; a Vasu, 41, 231; 42, 116; the worlds are protected by M., 41, 245; husbandry beneficial to M. and other gods, 41, 329; sun, the eye of M., 41, 408; invoked in a medical charm, 42, 10, 237; saves from premature death, 42, 50 sq.; invoked to remove evil bodily marks from a woman, 42, 109; in a list of gods, 42, 126, 160; worshipped at the Mitravindâ sacrifice, 44, 62–6; lord of the Kshatra, bestows noble rank, 44, 63 sq.; expiatory oblation to M., 44, 207; Agni is like M., 46, 38, 46, 100, 186, 193, 202, 333, 341 sq., 371, 373, 389, 401; M. and Aryaman invited to the morning service, 46, 38; Agni is M., friend of the gods, 46, 109, 112, 119, 240 sq., 371; is glorious through Agni, 46, 148; 'human clans going to settle M.,' 46, 202, 204; Agni brings M. to the sacrifice, 46, 316; Agni announces man's sin to M., 46, 325; the laws of M., 46, 335; M. and Varu*n*a, *see* Varu*n*a (*c*).

Mitrâtithi, n.p., 46, 36.

Mitravindâ, *see* Sacrifice (*j*).

Mit*r*ô, *see* Mithra.

Mit*r*ô-aîyyâr, son of Mahmâ*d* of Ispahân, 24, xxvi, 122 sq. and n.; questions of M. answered, 24, 162 n.

Mitrô-akâvî*d*, n.p., 5, 146.

Mit*r*ô-*â*pân, n. of a scribe, 37, xxxviii.

Mit*r*ô-khûrshê*d*, Dâ*d*istân-î Dînîk, a reply to an epistle from, 18, xxii, 3.

Mitrô-tarsah, n.p., 5, 137.

Mitrô-varâ*z*, n.p., 5, 146.

Mle*kkh*a, *see* Barbarians, *and* Caste (*e*).

Mo and Yang have not hit on the proper course, 39, 329.

Mobeds or Parsi priests, *see* Priests (*d*).

Moderation, secures long life and success, 39, 102 sq.

Moggalâna or Mahâ-M., Sk. Maudgalyâyana, or Mahâ-Maudgalyâyana, died at Kusinârâ, 11, 238; procures, with the help of a Nâga, edible stalks of lotuses for Sâriputta, 17, 76 sq.; questions Buddha about the behaviour in case of schisms, 17, 317; an Arhat, and foremost disciple of Buddha, 17, 359; 20, 79; 21, 2, 98 sqq., 144 sq.; 49 (ii), 90, 164 sq., 201; relates the early history of Buddha, 19, xviii; his conversion, 19, 196; the spirit of Kakudha the Koliyan appears before M. telling him the thoughts of De-

vadatta, 20, 234 sq.; finds out and turns out an evil-doer who defiles the assembly at the Pâtimokkha, 20, 300 sq.; Buddha's prophecy about M. who is to be a Buddha, 21, 149–51; though possessed of Iddhi, was beaten to death with clubs, 35, 261–3; saying of M., 36, 369; possessed of miraculous power, 49 (ii), 31 sq.; teaches Bimbisâra the eight precepts, 49 (ii), 162 sq.; Sâriputta and M., *see under* Sâriputta.

Moggaliputta Tissa, *see* Tissa.

Mogharâ*g*amâ*n*adapu*kkh*â, t. c., 10 (ii), 208.

Mogharâ*g*an, n. of a Brâhma*n*a, 10 (ii), 187, 208, 210; saying of M. the Elder, 36, 359 sq., 360 n.

Mohammed, reprehends and abjures idol worship, 6, xii sq., 121, 123; God sent His Apostle to men and *g*inns to make Islâm prevail over every other religion, 6, xiv, xxvii, 66, 177; 9, 55; adopts the titles 'Hanîf and Muslim, 6, xvi, 117; his ancestors, 6, xvi–xviii; his birth, 6, xviii; life of M., 6, xviii–xliv; his children, 6, xix; M. and his wives, 6, xix, xxix, lxxvi; 9, 142–8, 142 n., 143 n., 144 n., 233 n., 240 n., 290 sq., 290 n.; his appearance and character, 6, xix sq.; his revelations, 6, xx–xxiii; 9, 9, 9 n., 14, 16, 43, 46, 229; hysterical symptoms of M., 6, xx sq.; his mental struggles, thoughts of suicide, 6, xxi sq.; mocked at, 6, 245; 9, 48 sq., 87, 90; encouraged against misbelievers, 6, 250; helped by mortals to compose the Qur'ân, 6, 261; is to dispute and to punish kindly, 6, 264; is but a mortal, 9, 11, 26, 83 sq., 199; exhorted to be patient, 9, 45; his first followers, chiefly men of the lowest ranks, 6, xxiii sq., xlvi; attitude of his fellow citizens towards the new doctrine, 6, xxiv sq.; hostility of the Meccans against M. and his followers, 6, xxiv–xxxiii; his compromise with the Qurâi*s*, 6, xxvi sq.; his family placed under a ban by the Qurâi*s*, 6, xxviii; his marriage with Zâinab, the divorced wife of Zâid, 6, xxix; 9, 139 n., 144, 144 n.; his flight to Tâ'if, 6, xxx; his negotiations with the inhabitants of YaTHrib, 6, xxx–xxxiii; his miraculous 'Night Journey' from Mecca to Jerusalem, 6, xxxi sq.; 9, 1, 1 n., 7, 7 sq. n.; plots against M. frustrated by God, 6, xxxiii, 166; his flight (Higrah) with Abu Bekr, to YaTHrib, 6, xxxiii sq.; his war against the Meccans, 6, xxxv–xlii, 165 n.; wounded in battle, 6, xxxviii; writes letters to the great kings and emperors of the world, to embrace his faith, 6, xl; marries a Coptic slave girl Mary, 6, xl; 9, 290 sq., 290 n.; master of Mecca, 6, xlii; destroys the idols in the Kaabah, 6, xlii; his military enterprises, 6, xlii–xliv; his 'Farewell Pilgrimage' to Mecca, and his death, 6, xliv; the secret of his success, 6, xliv sq.; could he read or write? 6, xlvii; 9, 122; styles himself En Nebîy el' ummîy, 6, xlvii; his relation to Jews and Christians, 6, xlvii sq., lxxxii, 53; not acquainted with the originals of the Jewish and Christian Scriptures, 6, xlviii sq.; neither 'possessed' (a madman), sorcerer, soothsayer, poet, nor impostor, 6, lvi, 160; 9, 46, 69, 84, 151, 156, 167, 169, 247 sq., 250, 295, 298, 300, 322; at Mecca and at Medînah, 6, lxii sq.; *g*inns preached to and converted by M., 6, lxx, cx; 9, 228, 304 sq., 304 n.; 'the Apostle of God,' 'the seal of the prophets,' 6, lxxi; 9, 145, 237 sq., 237 n.; belief in and obedience to God and the Apostle, 6, lxxi, 50, 56 sq., 68, 74, 80–2, 105, 163, 165, 183; 9, 79 sq., 143 sq., 148 sq., 232, 241, 287; 'there is no prophet after me,' 6, lxxi; denounces the 'hypocrites,' 6, lxxxviii sq., 172–92; Satan suggests a wrong reading to M., acknowledging the chief idols of the Qurâi*s*, 6, xcix, xcix n.; 9, 62 n.; his compromise as to Al 'Huzzâ, Allât, and Manât, 6, cxii; 9, 2 2; the death of M. should not discourage believers, 6, 63; asked for a proof of his prophetic mission, 6, 68 sq., 68 n.; 9, 7, 11; will intercede for the believers, 6, 81; *whoso obeys the prophet he has obeyed God*, 6, 83; inspired like other prophets before him, 6, 94 sq.; a witness, a warner and

herald of glad tidings, 6, 100, 120, 161, 205 sq., 233, 237; 9, 12, 80, 88, 107, 112 sq., 135, 145, 154, 156, 159, 162 sq., 180 sq., 199, 210, 225, 234, 287, 289 sq., 294; had M. been an angel, he would have come in the guise of man, 6, 116; does not say that he is an angel, 6, 120; is not to repulse believers, 6, 121; the coming of M., 'the illiterate prophet,' foretold, 6, 156 sq.; humiliation of one who would not acknowledge M. as the prophet, 6, 159 sq., 159 n.; the coming of the 'Hour' only known to God, 6, 161; his expedition against the caravan from Syria under Abu Sufiân, 6, 163 sq., 164 n.; miraculous victory at Bedr, 6, 164 sq., 165 n., 171, 171 n.; *see also* Bedr; brotherhood between those who fled with M. and the inhabitants of Medînah who gave him refuge, 6, 171 sq., 172 n.; the Muhâgerîn who fled with M. are highest in rank with God, 6, 175; aided by God in the battle of 'Honein, 6, 176, 176 n.; M. and Abu Bekr in the cave, helped by God, 6, 179; found fault with for his use of the alms, 6, 181; builds the mosque of Qubâ', 6, 188 sq., 188 n.; God will stand by His Apostle, 6, 191 sq.; misbelievers deem him a sorcerer, 6, 192; 9, 225; sent to assert the unity of God, 6, 235–7; 9, 26, 180 sq., 199, 247; God his witness against misbelievers, 6, 238; sent to warn the Meccans, 9, 61; to be addressed respectfully, 9, 82; cannot make the deaf hear, but only those who believe in God's signs, 9, 106, 130; meeting of M. and Moses during the 'night journey,' 9, 137, 137 n.; warned against misbelievers and hypocrites, 9, 138; struggle with the confederate army at Medînah, 9, 138–42, 138 n., 140 n., 142 n.; is nearer of kin to the believers than themselves, 9, 139; his wives are the mothers of the believers, 9, 139; set a good example to the Muslim, 9, 141; privileges granted to M. in the matter of women, 9, 146; how the Muslim should behave towards M., 9, 147 sq.; God and His angels pray for M., 9, 148; accused of imposture, 9, 157; came with the truth, and verified the apostles, 9, 169; bidden to serve God, the first of those resigned, 9, 183; shall die, like other mortals, 9, 185; Meccans say that if M. had been a man of consideration they would have believed, 9, 213; said to be taught by others, or mad, 9, 218; Israel received the Book, and then M. the Qur'ân, 9, 222; God pardons the sins committed by M., 9, 233, 233 n.; those who swear allegiance to M., swear allegiance to God, 9, 234; his expedition of 'Hudâibîyeh, and against the Jews of Khâibar, and the truce of 'Hudâibîyeh, 9, 235–7; prohibited by the Qurâis from the pilgrimage to Mecca, 9, 236 sq.; believers not to raise their voices above the voice of the prophet, 9, 238 sq. and n.; inspired by Gabriel, the vision of his 'night journey' not a delusion, 9, 251 sq., 251 n.; secret plottings against the Apostle punished in hell, 9, 271 sq.; Jesus prophesies the coming of M., 9, 281, 281 n.; denounced by an insolent opponent, 9, 295 sq.; bidden to preach, 9, 305 sq., 308; reproved for frowning on a poor blind believer, 9, 320, 320 n.; how God cared for M., 9, 334 sq.; God expanded his breast, 9, 335, 335 n.; his first call to 'read' the Qur'ân, 9, 336.

Mohammedanism, *see* Islâm.

Mohism, represented as an erroneous form of Tâoism, 39, 162; 40, 217–21, 218 n.; modifications and development of it, 39, 162; 40, 221–5.

Mohists hold that all should be loved equally, 40, 178; wear skins and dolychos cloth, 40, 220. *See also* Confucianists.

Moksha, *see* Emancipation, *and* Salvation.

Moksha *S***âstras**, quoted, 38, 158.

Moliya Sîvaka, *see* Sîvaka.

Momentariness, Bauddha doctrine of universal, 34, 403 n., 407, 408, 413–15, 427.

Monasteries (Convents), mentioned in the Yâ*gñ*avalkya-sm*ri*ti, 7, xxi; fools wish for lordship in m., 10 (i), 22; a Sâvaka is to seek for a m., 10 (ii), 65; Ânanda went out from

the m., 11, 35, 315; merit acquired by gifts of m., 21, 14; he who occupies himself with sacred writ need not build m., 21, 321 sqq., 324 sq. *See also* Vihâras.

Money, coined, referred to by the term nâ*n*aka, in the Yâg*ñ*avalkya-sm*r*iti, 7, xxi; the Vaggian Bhikkhus allow the use of gold and silver, 20, 386; Buddha does not allow the use of m. for Bhikkhus, 20, 387–92, 399, 413. *See also* Gold.

Money-changing, as a profession, 13, 201.

Money-lending, allowed to Brâhma*n*as, 2, 228; legal interest for m., 2, 241–3 and n.; subsisting by m., an offence, 7, 139; the occupation of Vai*s*yas, 25, 325; as a mode of acquiring property, 25, 426 sq. *See also* Usury.

Monism, *see* Advaita.

Monks: Vasso Rules of *G*aina and Buddhist m. founded on rules of the Dharma-sûtras, 2, lx; Christians rebuked for introducing monkery, 9, 269; monk's robe sacrificed, 30, 127; monasticism in China, 39, 42 sq.; celibacy enforced on m. and nuns in modern Tâoism, 39, 44; Tâoist m. called 'Plumaged guests,' 40, 319, 319 n. *See also* Bhikkhus, *G*aina Monks, *and* Holy Persons.

Monotheism, *see* Islâm.

Monsters, *see* Animals (*i*).

Months: six m. when the sun goes to the north, a stage on the soul's road after death, 1, 80; 8, 81, 255; 48, 745; the sacred m. of the Arabs, 6, 27 sq. and n., 31, 172, 178; Mârga*s*îrsha the first of m., 8, 90; are threefold, 8, 330; begin with bright fortnight, 8, 352; wheel of life measured by m., and half-m., 8, 356; the 8th, 15th, 23rd days of the m. under the rule of Ahura and the Amesha-Spe*n*tas, 23, 6 sq. n.; names of the m., 26, 321 sq.; have sixty days and nights, 41, 184; created, 43, 74; M. and Half-m. worshipped as deities, 44, 142. *See also* Moon, Sacred Times, Seasons, Time, *and* Year.

Monuments, set up as testimonials of good conduct in China, 3, 247, 247 n.

Moon.

(*a*) M. the Heavenly Body.
(*b*) New and Full M.
(*c*) M. as a Deity, Worship of M.
(*d*) World of M.

(*a*) M. THE HEAVENLY BODY.

Its red, white, and black colours, 1, 95; the tides connected with the m., 5, 44, 44 n., 171 sq., 172 n.; K*r*ish*n*a is the m. among the lunar mansions, 8, 88; the juicy m. nourishes all herbs, 8, 113, 113 n.; one of the ten fires at the allegorical sacrifice of the sense-organs, 8, 261; is the first of Nakshatras, of heavenly bodies, 8, 346, 346 n.; 10 (ii), 105; 45, 138, 290, 313; the black spots in the m., 12, 64, 278 n.; Indra made the m. out of the Soma taken from V*r*itra's body, 12, 167; the cause of destiny, 18, 215; produced by union between Soma and the water, 26, 438; sacrifice, while the m. has a halo, by one who is desirous of flocks, 30, 118; rises when begged to do so, 36, 319; created, 41, 149; the golden ship with golden tackle (the m.?) moves upon the heavens, 42, 4 sq., 6, 415, 679 sq.; the bull with a thousand horns, 42, 373; as weather-prophet, 42, 533 n.; is food, is the year, is all living beings, 43, 54; the food or joy of the sun, 43, 335, 399; kindled by the sun, 43, 399; the hare in the m., 44, 10; is that heavenly dog who watches the Sacrificer's cattle, 44, 10–12; shines less than the sun, for its shine has been taken from it, 44, 130; a piece of silver representing the m., 44, 196; greatness of Pra*g*âpati in the Nakshatras and the m., 44, 394; a body consisting of am*r*ita, 48, 585, 588.

(*b*) NEW AND FULL M.

The wise m., who orders the seasons, when it is born consisting of fifteen parts, 1, 274; fasting, sacrifices, and other observances on Parvan, i. e. full and new m. days, 2, 86, 100, 104; 12, 172, 180; 13, x; 14, 61, 159, 287, 327; 25, 152 sq.; 29, 16–18, 172–6, 290, 389–93, 425, 427, 431; 30, 25–40, 265, 332–8; on the days of full and new m. Veda-study must be interrupted,

2, 263; 14, 210 sq.; 29, 142, 414; 30, 80; the phases of the m. are indications of time, 6, 27; worship of Vish*n*u on the days of full m. and new m., 7, 156; one must not use tooth-picks on the day of new m., 7, 198; new and full m. worshipped, 10 (ii), 110; 31, 198, 205, 210, 216, 220, 224; the times for new and full m. ceremonies, 12, 1 sq.; demons roam about on full and new m. days, 14, 210; 42, 65, 256 sq.; hair, &c., cut on new and full m. days, 14, 300; waning and waxing m., 23, 89 sq., 89 n.; chastity for Snâtakas on new and full m. days and on the fourteenth, 25, 149; men feel joy on seeing the full m., 25, 396 sq.; offerings and ceremonies on the first day of the m., 27, 156; 28, 3 sq.; prayers on seeing the new m., 30, 179; out of the new m. the sacrifice is spread, 41, 180; rites of the new m. night, 42, 35, 408; is fifteenfold, waxes and wanes during fifteen days, 43, 62; four phases of the m. personified, 43, 264, 264 n.; Pragâpati-Sacrifice is the Year, the night of new m. its gate, the m. is the bolt of the gate, 44, 1; new m., why it is the proper time for laying down the sacred fires, 44, 1 sq.; all the nights of the waxing m. concentrate in the full m. night, all the nights of the waning m. in the night of new m., 44, 21; full m. and new m. identified with sun and m., earth and sky, &c., 44, 30 sq.; is born again and again, 44, 315; sepulchre to be made at new m., 44, 423. *See also* Sacred Times, *and* Sacrifices (*b*, *j*).

(*c*) M. AS A DEITY, WORSHIP OF M.

The Person in the m. as Brahman, 1, 66, 303; 15, 101; by Vyâna the ear is satisfied, and thereby the M. and the Quarters are satisfied, 1, 90; invoked for protection, 29, 280, 349; rites and prayers addressed to the M., for the life of (new-born) children, 1, 285-8; 29, 396; 30, 56 sq.; the M., who protects the creatures during night, to be worshipped by the Snâtaka, 2, 96; offering to the M., 2, 108; to be worshipped at the *K*ândrâya*n*a, 2, 300; joint invocation to the Waters and the M., 4, 230, 232 n., 233; keeps in itself the seed of the bull, 4, 233, 233 n.; 5, 179; 23, 8, 8 sq. n., 16, 88-91, 176, 355; 31, 199, 210, 216, 225, 256; meat-offering to the M., 5, 337; he must not look at the m., while unclean, 7, 220; a form of K*r*ish*n*a, 8, 97; the m. together with the fire, upholds all beings, 8, 257; is the mind, or the presiding deity of the mind, 8, 338; 15, 81; 43, 363; 44, 133; the presiding deity of the tongue and taste, 8, 350; adore not the m., but God, 9, 202; worship of the m., 11, 174; 14, 305; 19, 26; 24, 96, 358; 30, 243; relates to Soma, 12, 169; Soma is the m., and the m. the food of the gods, 12, 176 sq., 176 n., 181, 362, 380; 44, 6, 9 sq., 34; V*r*itra is the m., 12, 180, 182; 41, 45, 45 n.; lives together with the Nakshatras, 12, 269 n.; the Brahman priest identified with the m., 15, 123; 44, 135; one of the Vasus, 15, 140; 44, 116; a manifestation of Brahman, 15, 303; 44, 317; a name of the Self, 15, 311; prayers to the M., 23, 88-91, 349, 355 sq.; Ti*s*trya protects the M., 23, 93; not to void urine against the m., 25, 137; a Lokapâla or guardian deity of the world, 25, 185, 216 sq.; cursed by Daksha, 25, 398, 398 n.; genesis of the m., 27, 381, 381 n.; worshipped by the bridegroom, 30, 194; worshipped by the student, 30, 277; lord of constellations, 36, 55, 55 n.; mentioned before the sun, 36, 127 sq. and n.; is a mighty lord, 36, 318, 318 n.; the m. and the All-gods, 41, 150; is Pragâpati, 41, 160; 43, xxi sq.; Sinîvâlî and Anumati, phases of the m., 42, 461; the typical bridegroom, 42, 498; Soma, the M., 43, xxi; 44, 135; Speech fashioned from the m., 43, 11; deity and metre, 43, 53; deity and brick of fire-altar, 43, 91; who knows the M.? 44, 390; the M. begat Budha on B*r*ihaspati's wife, 49 (i), 45. *See also* Anumati, Indu, *K*andra, *K*andramas, Luminaries, Mâh, Sinîvâlî, *and* Soma.

(*d*) WORLD OF M.

The departed sacrificer goes from

the sun to the m., from the m. to the lightning, 1, 68, 80, 80 sq. n., 273 sq.; 8, 240; 15, 272 sq.; 34, cvii, 108, 110, 112, 114, 121–5; 48, 593; can a man, after he has been in the m., be born again? 1, 83 n.; is the door of heaven, 1, 274; 42, 646; from the m. the seed was brought, gathered up in an active man, and brought to a mother, 1, 274 sq.; by the *K*ândrâya*n*a penance a Brâhma*n*a goes to the world of the m., 2, 302; 14, 326; Yagus guides to the m. world, 8, 20; path to the m. from which the souls return, 8, 81; the gate of the world of the fathers, 12, 267 n.; the light of the fathers, 12, 361; the world of the fathers, 15, 209; a vision of the m., the beloved of Rohi*n*î, 22, 234 sq.; the world of the m. attained by gifts and penance, 25, 165, 475; the heart (of the earth?) that dwells in heaven, in the m., 30, 212; the soul's ascent to, and descent from the m., 38, 101–32; the body of the soul in the m. consists of water, 38, 114, 115, 127; one of the six doors to the Brahman, 44, 66 sq.; evil-doers do not, after death, ascend to the m., 48, 592–6; those who die during the southern progress of the sun, go to the Fathers and the m., 48, 741–3.

Morality.

(*a*) In Brâhma*n*ism.
(*b*) In Buddhism and *G*aina Religion.
(*c*) In Zoroastrianism.
(*d*) In Chinese Religions.
(*e*) In Islâm.

See also Good Works, Righteousness, Sin, *and* Virtue.

(*a*) In Brâhma*n*ism.

Neither right nor wrong would be known, if there were no speech, 1, 111; what is right and what is wrong, we understand by understanding, 1, 115; moral laws, common to all castes, 7, 13; by forgiveness of injuries the learned are purified, by liberality, those who have done forbidden acts, 7, 97; moral precepts, especially for Snâtakas, 7, 224–31; 25, 150 sq., 153–8; Lakshmî resides in good and pious men and women, 7, 300 sq.; moral conduct leads to tranquillity and immortality, 8, 101 sq.; 15, 11; classification of sins, sinful dispositions, good works, and virtues, 8, 166–70, 181–5; one should ever and always be doing good, 8, 191; rules of conduct for the four âsramas, a system of m., 8, 358–68; 14, 49; sixfold mode of life of a Brâhma*n*a, 8, 359 sq., 359 n.; good conduct more important than study of the Veda and sacred rites, 14, 34 sq.; rules of conduct for Brâhma*n*as, 14, 38–40; moral precepts for the householder, 14, 138, 237; cling to the good, do not choose the pleasant, 15, 8 sq.; moral duties of man, 15, 51–3; why spiritual merit should be accumulated, 25, lxviii, 166 sq.; means of attaining supreme bliss, 25, lxxiii, 501–9, 511; merit and demerit distinguished at the creation, 25, 13; moral conduct of the ascetic, 25, 207; the tenfold (moral) law, 25, 215, 215 n.; *abstention from injuring (creatures), veracity, abstention from unlawfully appropriating (the goods of others), purity, and control of the organs, Manu has declared to be the summary of the law for the four castes*, 25, 416; remembering the results of deeds in future life, one should always be good in thoughts, speech, and action, 25, 477, 483–5; why people confound good and bad, 26, 228, 228 n. *See also* Karman, *and* Qualities.

(*b*) In Buddhism and *G*aina Religion.

Moral precepts, especially for Bhikkhus, 10 (i), 3–95; (ii), 24 sq., 28, 54 sq., 65 sq., 175–80; 11, 6–11, 28, 38 sq., 61 sq., 84, 91, 188, 210, 218, 221–34, 303–6; do to others as you would be done by, 10 (i), 36 sq.; 22, 50; *not to commit any sin, to do good, and to purify one's mind, that is the teaching of (all) the Awakened*, 10 (i), 50; Buddha's definition of an outcast, 10 (ii), 21–3; the exemplary life led by the ancient Brâhma*n*as, 10 (ii), 48–50; *great is the fruit, great the advantage of earnest contemplation when set round with upright conduct*, 11, 11, 11 n., 12, 15, 24, 28, 34, 65 sq., 70; the *K*ûla Sîla*m*, the Ma*gg*h*i*ma Sîla*m*, and the Mahâ Sîla*m*, 11, 189–200, 189 n.; six Precepts of King Sudassana, 11, 253;

Buddhist m., and the classification of offences in the Vinaya, 13, xxiv sqq.; ten precepts for novices, 13, 211 sq.; the fivefold loss of the wrong-doer, and the fivefold gain of the well-doer, 17, 99 sq.; Buddha gives an exposition of his moral teaching, 17, 110–16; 19, 234–6; moral conduct, the source of all that is good, 19, 259–65; 21, 427 sq.; 35, 52–4; following the moral precepts as taught by Buddha is one way leading to enlightenment, 21, 49; the ten (moral) conditions of heart, 35, 173 sq.; moral conduct, the root and essence of Buddha's teaching, 35, 187–90; list of twelve kinds of men who pay no respect, 35, 250; good men live for the benefit of gods and men, 35, 274 sq.; motives for moral conduct, 35, 295; difference between breach of moral law and offences against Rules of the Order, 36, 98–100; ten sorts of individuals who are despised in the world, 36, 139 sq.; right conduct (sîla) for laymen, Bhikkhus, and Arhats, 36, 220 sq. and n.; *G*aina ethics based on primitive animism, 45, xxxiii; moral conduct, one of the four roads to final beatitude, 45, 152, 158–61, 163, 169–72; moral conduct produces destruction of Karman, its five subdivisions, 45, 157; orthodox *G*aina views about m., 45, 406–9; the five and eight precepts of Buddha, 49 (ii), 162, 162 n., 192 sq., 196. *See also* Pâramitâs.

(*c*) In Zoroastrianism.

Practical m. of Zoroastrianism, 4, lxii; the three perfections, good thoughts, good words, good deeds, 4, 197, 199, 246 sq., 287–9, 357 (the best sacrifice), 375 sq.; 5, 54, 226, 226 n.; 18, 12, 14, 18, 33 sq., 54–6, 121, 125, 172, 179, 285, 384 sq., 387; 23, 22, 266–8, 312 sq., 316–18, 342–5; 24, 20, 30, 42, 78, 118, 270, 321; 31, 213 sq., 213 n., 223, 243, 247, 265 sq., 282 sq., 285, 321, 342, 359; 37, 20, 174, 196 sq., 229, 265, 270, 273, 308, 415 sq., 460 sq.; 47, 157, 159; think of the hour of death in doing what is good and abstaining from what is bad, 18, 275, 275 n.; the most powerful prayer is that recited to renounce evil thoughts, evil words, and evil deeds, 23, 313; 31, 361; Ahura-Mazda, the inspirer of good thoughts, 31, 108, 113; good thoughts, words, and deeds are thought, spoken, and done with intelligence, 31, 390; the weak man should be good, 37, 105; good thoughts, good words, good deeds—the food of Aûharmazd, 37, 242 sq.;—the three best things: worship of Ahura, worship of the fire, and respect shown to the righteous, 4, 292 n., 293; of two men, the wiser and more truthful is chief, 5, 90; the earth pleased by moral conduct, displeased by sin, 5, 376 sq.; moral purification for the sacred ceremonial, 18, 166, 172; men misled by demons, 18, 271; do by others as you would be done by, 18, 271; 37, 51; moral precepts for the preservation of body and soul, 24, 9–16, 25 sq.; the ten happiest lands, 24, 27 sq., 27 n.; the ten unhappiest lands, 24, 28 sq., 28 n.; the highest pleasures, 24, 41; who is truly rich, and who is truly poor, 24, 70 sq.; moral rules and precepts, 24, 77–9; man's own fiends: greediness, wrath, lust, disgrace, discontent, 24, 82; spiritual armour and weapons requisite for attaining to heaven and escaping from hell, 24, 83 sq.; the man most conversant with good and evil, 24, 106 sq.; the man who is chief over his associates, 24, 107; prayer that the soul may advance in good, 31, 326; best and worst actions, 37, 107; necessity of scrutinizing actions, 37, 121 sq.; the utilizers and misusers of life, 37, 177; five storeholders of perfect excellence, 37, 180; advice to mankind, 37, 244 sq.; *let no one practise ill-perpetrated deeds, even though in a wilderness when far from publicity, nor in distress, O Spîtâmân! because Aûharmazd, the observer of everything, is aware of them*, 37, 266; understanding good and evil through Vohûman, 37, 320 sq.; virtuous conduct advances religion, 37, 323–7; all excellence is both root and fruit, 37, 351 sq.; happy is he from whom

there is no mischief, 37, 386; ideal moral life in the future existence, 37, 393-7; ten admonitions as to religion, 47, 167, 167 n., 169 sq. *See also* Dualism.

(*d*) In Chinese Religions.

Moral precepts to be followed in government, 3, 47; moral laws are from Heaven, 3, 55 sq., 169; God has conferred a moral sense even on inferior people, 3, 89 sq.; noble sentiments of King Thang, 3, 90 sq.; 'the Great Symbolism' a means of imparting moral instruction, 16, 36-8, 267-347; there is a soul of good even in men who seem only evil, 16, 319, 320 n.; moral lessons derived from the hexagrams of the Yî, 16, 389-94, 408-21; the scholar a pattern of moral conduct, 27, 51 sq.; 28, 402-10; development of m. from highest antiquity, 27, 65; in life we should be of use to others, 27, 155; the seven lessons of m., 27, 230, 248; duty of government to teach m., 27, 230 sq. and n.; music and ceremonies conducive to m., 27, 388-90; 28, 95-116, 125-9; filial piety the source of all m., 28, 226-9, 268 sq., 269 n.; *what you do not like when done to yourself, do not do to others,* 28, 305 sq.; the long dress symbolical of moral conduct, 28, 396; cultivation of the person the root of m., 28, 411 sq., 416 sq.; moral teaching of Tâoism, 39, 30-3, 381-4; pattern of moral conduct to be got from the Tâo, 39, 82 sq.; the 'three precious things' of Tâoism, 39, 110 sq.; what is good should be practised without any regard of fame, 39, 130 sq., 198, 198 n., 201, 201 n.; 40, 176-85; Shăn Tâo, in his system of Tâoism, disregarded right and wrong, 40, 224 sq.; the way of a good man, and his reward, 40, 237 sq. *See also* Tâoism.

(*e*) In Islâm.

The moral duties of the Muslim, 6, lxxi sq., 24 sq.; 9, 3-5, 89, 301; *verily, God bids you do justice and good, and give to kindred (their due), and He forbids you to sin, and do wrong, and oppress; He admonishes you, haply ye may be mindful!* 6, 260; return good for evil, 9, 202; patience and forgiveness enjoined, 9, 209. *See also* Islâm.

Mora-parittâ, a protecting charm, 35, 213.

Moriyas (people) of Pipphalivana take the embers of Buddha's funeral pile and erect a dâgaba, 11, 134, 135.

Mortar and pestle, symbolism of, 41, 393-6, 400; 43, 2 n.

Mosadhamma, Pali, t.t., the dyad that what the world considers true, is false, 10 (ii), 131, 142 sq.

Moses, and the golden calf, 6, 6, 12 sq., 93, 155 sq.; 9, 40-2; God gave M. the Book, 6, 7, 12, 125, 136; 9, 1, 50, 68, 86, 112, 137, 172, 203; 24, 208; strikes the rock, 6, 8, 157; ordains the slaughter of a cow in expiation of murder, 6, 9, 9 n.; questioned, 6, 15; a prophet, 6, 19, 57, 125; 9, 30 sq., 139, 206; 'he with whom God spake,' 6, 39, 39 n., 94; Jews ask M. to show them God, 6, 93; bade the children of Israel enter the Holy Land, and they hesitated, 6, 100 sq.; sent to Pharaoh with signs, the plagues of Egypt, 6, 151-4, 201-3, 216, 238 sq.; 9, 12, 90-3, 107-12, 121, 192-5, 214 sq., 247, 318 sq.; communes with God, receives the tablets of the Law, 6, 154 sq.; 9, 30 sq.; story of M. and his servant in search of El '*Hidh*r, 9, 21-3, 23 sq. n.; God appears to M. in the fire and sends him to Pharaoh, 9, 35-7, 100, 111; burnt his tongue with a live coal, 9, 36 n.; thrown into the sea, and restored to his mother, 9, 36 sq.; slays an Egyptian and flees to Midian, 9, 37, 110; M. and Aaron go to Pharaoh, their contest with the Egyptian magicians, 9, 37-9; leads the children of Israel across the sea, Pharaoh's people drowned, 9, 40; Covenant on Mount Sinai, miracle of the manna and the quails, 9, 40; was called a liar, 9, 61, 68; exposed in the river, watched by his sister, nursed by his mother, 9, 108 sq.; marries the daughter of Sho'hâib, 9, 110; came with signs to Korah and Pharaoh, 9, 121; meeting of Mohammed and M. in heaven, 9,

137, 137 n.; annoyed and disobeyed by the people, 9, 149, 281; was given the guidance, 9, 195; the Book of M. before the Qur'ân, 9, 225; fulfilled his word, 9, 253; revelation in the books of Abraham and M., 9, 329; Jesus not come to destroy the law of M., 24, 242 sq.

Mosques, the Muslim places of worship, 6, lxxii; injustice of prohibiting God's m., 6, 16; men are to go to m. decently clad, 6, 140; immunity for those with whom a league was made at the Sacred M., 6, 173; giving drink to the pilgrims and repairing to the Sacred M. not equal to professing Islâm, 6, 175, 175 n.; it is not for idolators to repair to the m. of God, 6, 175 sq.; the M. of Qubâ' preferred to the M. built by the Beni *Gh*anm in opposition to Mohammed, 6, 188 sq., 188 n.; those who prevent men from visiting the Sacred M. will be punished, 9, 58; the m. are God's, 9, 305.

Mother: he who desires the world of the ms., by his mere will the ms. come to receive him, 1, 127 sq.; the student who returns home shall give everything to his m., 2, 27; *a m. does very many acts for her son, therefore he must constantly serve her, though she be fallen*, 2, 88; is chief among all venerable persons (Gurus), 2, 192; of female relations only m. saluted by embracing her feet, 2, 209; the m. only impure on the birth of a child, 2, 251; 14, 28 sq., 180; 25, 178, 178 n.; right of inheritance of m., and after m., 2, 306; 7, 73; 14, 89, 230; 25, 371, 378; love rendered to the m., reverence to the ruler, both to the father, 3, 470; highest amercement for insulting a man by using bad language regarding his m., 7, 28; son not to pay debt for m., nor m. for son, 7, 45; girl may be given in marriage by the m., 7, 109; pleasant in the world is the state of a m., 10 (i), 79; all creatures exist through the protection of their ms., 14, 44; does not become an outcast for her son, 14, 67; sons born without ms., 14, 180; an outcast m. must be supported without speaking to her, 14, 230; offspring, the secret union of m. and father, 15, 46 sq.; naming people after their m.'s name, 20, 125 n.; two princes crave the permission of their m. before they join the Buddha, 21, 420–3; prayer for the protection of a m., 23, 341; student first to beg food of his m., 25, 39; how the student salutes maternal relations, 25, 54; reverence due to m., 25, 57, 71 sq., 154, 157; prayer to expiate the sin of one's m., 25, 330 sq. and n.; 30, 227; father more important than m., 27, 315 sq.; without being taught ms. know the wants of their infants, 28, 417; a son who does not support his m. to be punished, 33, 368; a m. being guardian of her son's father, 37, 148; a m. bears her son in her lap, 41, 232; hymns containing the names of the ms., 42, 518 sq.; m. and child, *see* Child. *See also* Family, Parents, *and* Woman (*b*, *e*).

Mo Tî, or Mo-ʒze, a great heresiarch, 39, 270, 270 n., 287, 360; his followers, the Mohists, 40, 99 sq.; a truly noble scholar, 40, 177; his system, 40, 218–21, 218 n. *See also* Mih-ʒze.

Mountains (hills), worshipped, 3, 39, 39 n., 70 sq., 74, 134 sq., 317 sq., 318 n.; 27, 225, 407; Shun raised altars upon twelve hills, 3, 40; spirit sent down from the m. to produce the birth of Fû and Shăn, 3, 423 sq. and n.; creation or origin of m., 5, 29 sq., 174 sq.; 18, 213 n.; on the nature of m., list of m., 5, 34–41, 34 n.; the water protecting m., 5, 67, 67 n.; the chief of m., 5, 89, 91; fires formed on m., 5, 186; prayers for blessing from m. and hills, 5, 392; idols standing on m., 6, xiii; Mount Qâf, the abode of the ginn, 6, lxx; Zafâ and Merwah, m. near Mecca, may be compassed by pilgrims, 6, 22, 22 n.; are auspicious places for *S*râddhas, 7, 260; Meru and Himâlaya, first of m., 8, 88 sq., 222, 354; lists of m., 8, 222–4, 346; 49 (ii), 60; oath by Mount Sinai, 9, 336; the symbol of a m., 16, 216 sq., 217 n.; symbolical of resoluteness, 16, 271; fabulous m., 18, 117; 23, 174 sq.; Ushi-darena

and other sacred m., worshipped, 23, 33, 33 n., 321 sq., 358; 31, 200, 200 n., 206, 211, 217, 221, 225 sq., 259, 272, 277, 291, 329, 336 sq., 340, 391; description and worship of the m., 23, 286–9; the use of m., 24, 98; the mother of a new-born infant shall not cast her eyes upon a hill, 24, 277; a Snâtaka shall not reside long on a m., 25, 138; rites performed on m., 27, 216–18, 410; 30, 125; 31, 302; the salve coming from the Trikakud Himavat m., 30, 168; m. and clouds, 32, 57; *K*ien Wû, spirit of Mount Thâi, 39, 244, 244 n.; Khwăn-lun m. in Thibet, the fairy-land of Tâoists, 39, 244 n.; 40, 70, 70 n.; no m. in Sukhâvatî, 49 (ii), 36. *See also* Hara Berezaiti, Himâlaya, Holy places, *and* Ushi-darena.

Mourning, *see* Funeral rites.

Mo-yeh, a famous sword, 39, 249, 249 sq. n.

Mo-ʒze, *see* Mo Tî.

M*rid*a, n. of Rudra, 29, 256.

M*ri*gâ, mother of Bala*s*rî, 45, 88.

M*ri*gâputra, or Bala*s*rî, a prince who becomes a *G*aina monk, and reaches Nirvâ*n*a, his description of hell, 45, 88–99.

M*rikkh*aka*t*ikâ, the drama, and Nârada-sm*ri*ti, 33, xvii; the judicial proceedings in the M., 33, 27 sq. n., 276.

M*ri*ktavâhas Dvita Âtreya, author of a Vedic hymn, 46, 405.

M*ri*tagangâ, n. of a river, 45, 57.

M*ri*tyu, or Death, or Yama, 15, 2–24; worshipped at the Tarpa*n*a, 30, 244; invoked against the enemies, 42, 133. *See also* Death.

M*ri*tyu Prâdhva*m*sana, teacher of Atharvan Daiva, 15, 120, 187.

Mû, King, appointed *K*ün-yâ as Minister of Instruction, 3, 250 sq.; appoints *Kh*iung his High Chamberlain, 3, 252 sq.; Penal code under King M., 3, 254–64.

Mû, Duke, Marquis of *Kh*in called so, 3, 270 sq.; Odes of the Shih ascribed to him, 3, 407, 410; three worthies buried with Duke M., when he died, 3, 443 sq.; death of the mother of Duke M. of Lû, 27, 126; Hsien-ʒze consulted by him, 27, 150; sends a message of condolence to *Kh*ung-*r*, 27, 165–7, 167 n.; asked Ʒze-sze about mourning, 27, 173; questions Hsien-ʒze about means to procure rain, 27, 201; speech of M., 28, 421; Pâi-lî Hsî, his minister, 40, 50, 50 n., 89; his famous horses, 40, 175, 175 n.

Mû*g*avats, Rudra invoked to depart beyond the, 12, 443; n. of a distant people, 42, 1 sq., 446, 446 n., 448, 711.

Muhâ*g*erûn, the Mecca immigrants in Medînah called so, 6, xxxiv; believers who fled with Mohammed, 6, lxii, 172 n.; the M. who fled with Mohammed promised Paradise, 6, 187, 254.

Muhammadanism, *see* Islâm.

Mûidhi, spell against the demon, 4, 145 sq.

Mu*k*alinda, or Mu*k*ilinda, Nâga-king, protects Buddha from the storm, 13, 80; 49 (i), 164 sq.

Mu*k*anna, the veiled prophet of Khorassan, 6, xlv.

Mu*k*ilinda, *see* Mu*k*alinda.

Mukta (emancipated one), Mahâvîra became a, 22, 265.

Mukta*kkh*atra, the 66th Tathâgata, 49 (ii), 7.

Mukta*kkh*atrapravâtasad*ris*a, the 37th Tathâgata, 49 (ii), 6.

Muktakusumapratima*nd*itaprabha, the 20th Tathâgata, 49 (ii), 6.

Mukti, Sk., t.t., *see* Emancipation, *and* Salvation.

Mukunda, feasts at festivals of, 22, 92.

Mûlâya pa*t*ikassanâ, t.t., a kind of disciplinary proceedings, when unlawful, 17, 270 sq.

Mulûk-ut-tavâif, petty local sovereigns in Iran, 4, xli, xliv, xlix sq.

Munâfiqûn, or 'hypocrites,' the disaffected class in Medînah, 6, xxxiv, lxiii.

Mu*nd*aka, or 'shaveling,' term of reproach for Buddhist mendicants, 15, xxvii.

Mu*nd*aka-upanishad, quoted, 8, 420; 38, 427 sq.; 48, 777 sq.; is a Mantra-u., 15, xxvi, xliii; its title, 15, xxvi sq.; translated, 15, 24–42; and the rite of carrying fire on the head, 38, 186, 189 sq.; explained, 48, 282–7.

Mu*nd*ibha Audanya, discovered the atonement for the slaying of a Brahman, 44, 341.

Mu*ñg*a-grass, *see* Plants.

Muni, is not he who observes silence, but the wise man, 10 (i), 65 sq., 66 n.; Buddha's definition of a M., 10 (ii), 33–6, 91, 162–4, 174, 199 sq.; the life of a M., or the state of wisdom (moneyya), 10 (ii), 128–31, 177–80; when a Brâhma*n*a becomes a M., 15, 130; he who knows the Self, becomes a M., 15, 179. *See also* Ascetics, *and* Holy persons.

Munisutta, t.c., 10 (ii), 33–6.

Munisuvrata, n. of Tîrthakara, 22, 280; 45, 86 n.

Mû-po, *K*ing *K*iang wailing for, 27, 167, 176.

Mûrakas, *see* Demons.

Murdâd, *see* Amerôda*d*.

Murder, *see* Homicide.

Musâilimah, Mohammed's rival, 6, xlv.

Music, power of, 3, 44 sq., 61; appointment of a Director of M., 3, 44 sq.; musical instruments, 3, 45, 59, 61, 61 n.; 11, 268, 270; 27, 217–19, 219 n.; 28, 31, 35–7 and n.; 35, 84, 93; m. and poetry, 3, 45, 275 sq.; used in the service of a ruler, 3, 59, 61; 27, 222; 28, 2, 4 sq., 274 sq.; reformed by Confucius, 3, 284; the Grand Music-Master as a collector of poems, 3, 291–3; 27, 216, 216 n.; accompanying the rites of ancestor-worship, 3, 300 sq., 304 sq., 304 n., 319, 323 sq. and n., 328, 367 sq. and n., 374 sq., 400; employed at sacrifices, ceremonies, and religious services, 3, 371; 16, 287, 288 sq. n.; 27, 273 sq., 348, 408, 411, 413, 418–20, 442 sq. and n.; 28, 32 sq., 210, 213 sq., 241, 253 sq., 330, 350; employed to make people harmonious and benignant, 3, 474, 482; war m., 8, 38 sq.; Sâma-veda full of m., 8, 88 n.; protests against m. and dancing, 8, 208; devotion to m., belongs to the quality of passion, 8, 325; the Hindu Gamut, 8, 385; worship of relics of Buddha by m. and songs, 21, 51; heavenly m. on a Buddha's attaining highest enlightenment, 21, 156 sq., 183; homage paid to the Buddha by m., 21, 400; musical performances to celebrate the birth of Mahâvîra, 22, 253 sq.; a recreation of kings, 25, 252; treatises on m., 27, 30–2, 38; 28, 92–131, 97 sq. n., 255; suspended during mourning, 27, 103, 130, 130 n., 132, 142 sq., 159 sq., 179 sq., 322; 28, 162, 164; regulations about m., 27, 106, 273, 273 n.; instruction in m., 27, 232–4, 255, 269 sq., 345 sq., 349, 389 sq., 478; 28, 74, 84 sq.; using licentious m. punished with death, 27, 237; every month has its special m., 27, 250, 250 n., 258, 262, 268, 272, 276 sq., 281, 283, 287, 291, 296, 302, 306; festival in honour of the inventor of m., 27, 261; concert at the end of spring, 27, 266; at court entertainments, 27, 271; concert of wind instruments at the end of winter, 27, 293, 308, 308 n.; at the feasting of the aged, 27, 360 sq.; five notes, 27, 382; 28, 111; 39, 55, 269, 269 n., 274, 279, 286, 328; blind musicians, 27, 385, 407; 28, 36 sq., 37 n.; the Son of Heaven moves in his virtue as a chariot, with m. as a driver, 27, 391; m. and archery, 27, 424; 28, 398 sq., 448 sq.; musical girdle-pendants, 28, 18 sq., 18 n.; use of the drum, 28, 90; *virtue is the strong stem of man's nature, and m. is the blossoming of virtue*, 28, 112; old and new m., 28, 116–21; the object of ceremonies and m., 28, 224–6; discarded during purification, 28, 239 sq.; to be versed in ceremonies and not in m.—and vice versa—is one-sidedness, 28, 275 sq.; a ruler must know the principles of ceremonies and m., 28, 278; 'm. that has no sound,' 28, 279 sq.; the harmony of humanity, 28, 409; at drinking festivals, 28, 441; the 'notes' of the Earth, 39, 177 sq., 177 n.; 'the Mulberry Forest,' and 'the *K*ing Shâu, pieces of m., 39, 199; grand m. not appreciated by the people, like common songs, 39, 327; the Perfect M. gives an idea of the Tâo, 39, 348–51, 348 n.; as a result of the Tâo, 39, 369; different kings had different kinds of m., 40, 8, 8 n., 26, 218; Lû *K*ü illustrates his philosophy by tuning two citherns and striking

different notes, 40, 99 sq., 99 n.; cultivated by Confucius, 40, 193; Mo-ȝze wrote a treatise 'Against M.' and denounced m., 40, 218 sq.; began to be practised when the Tâo was laid aside, 40, 284 sq.; m. and ceremonies in the age of perfect virtue, 40, 312; drums beaten at sacrificial rites, 41, 23 sq., 26; spell put in the drum, 42, 77; hymns and verses to the battle-drum, 42, 117, 130–3, 204, 436–40; lute-playing at the horse-sacrifice, 44, 285–7, 356 sq., 359, 362–70, 372; lute-player, flute-player, and other musicians sacrificed at the Purushamedha, 44, 417.

Muslim, title adopted by Mohammed, 6, xvi; their flight to Abyssinia, 6, xxv sq.; God made a covenant with them, 6, 98 sq.; believe in the faith of Abraham, 9, 65; quarrels between parties of the M., 9, 239 sq.

Mû*s*par, the thievish (comet?), 5, 22, 22 n.; leader of planets, 5, 113 sq., 113 n.; comet considered as a witch, 24, 132, 132 n.

Mutanebbî, 'the would-be prophet' and poet, 6, xlv sq.

Mûtazalîk, Mohammedan schismatics, 24, 195, 195 n.

Mû-yê, a famous sword, 40, 84, 84 n.

Myazd, Parsi t.t., sacred feast, 18, 155.

Myazda, the lord, worshipped, 31, 351.

Mysticism, mystic powers, mystic doctrines, mystics: Hari or K*rish*n*a*, the lord of the possessors of mystic power, 8, 93, 131; early Buddhist m., 11, x, 207–18; the answer of early Buddhism to the mystics, 11, 207; a mystery for the Bodhisattvas, 21, 58; *try to understand the mystery of the Buddhas, the holy masters of the world*, 21, 59; the doctrine of the one Buddha-vehicle not to be taught to everybody, 21, 91 sq., 95–7; the mystery expounded by the Tathâgata is difficult to understand, 21, 121 sq.; the Saddharmapu*n*d*a*rîka is the transcendent spiritual esoteric lore, 21, 219, 221. *See also* Iddhis, Secret Doctrines, *and* Tâoism.

Myths: worship derived from mythic conceptions, 4, lxxiii–lxxv.

N

Nabhas, n. of one of the three Agnis, 26, 118, 118 n.

Nabhasaspati, the lord of the cloud, 42, 141, 499.

Nâbhi, patriarch, father of the Arhat *Ri*shabha, 22, 281 sq.

Na*d*a Naishadha, carried King Yama to the south, 12, 338, 338 n.

Nâ*d*apit, *S*akuntalâ conceived Bharata at, 44, 399.

Na*dh*r ibn al' 'Hareth, purchased Persian legends and preferred them to the Qur'ân, 9, 131 sq., 131 n.; challenges the truth of Islâm, 9, 300 n.

Nadi, brother of Kâ*s*yapa, converted by Buddha, 19, 185–7.

Nâdika, n.pl., Buddha at, 11, 24–8.

Nadî-Kâ*s*yapa, one of the five hundred Arhats who are to be future Buddhas, 21, 2, 198; 49 (ii), 2. *See also* Kâ*s*yapa.

Nâ*d*îs, Sk., t.t., veins or arteries, *see* Arteries.

Nâga, a n. of Buddha, 10 (i), 77 n.; (ii), 195; an eminent man, an Arahat, 10 (ii), x, 90, 106; n. of Sthaviras, Ârya N. of the Gautama gotra, 22, 290, 294.

Nâgâbhibhû, n. of Tathâgata, 49 (ii), 6, 66.

Nâgabhûta, a Kula of the Uddeha Ga*n*a, 22, 290.

Nâgaputra, disciple of Mahâgiri, 22, 290.

Nâgara, father and mother of, converted by Buddha, 19, 245.

Nâgâr*g*una, founder of the Mahâyâna school of Buddhism, 35, xxv sq.; wrongly identified with Nâgasena, 35, xxv sq., xxvi n.

Nâgas (snake-gods, dragons), Ananta chief among, 8, 89; have relics of Buddha, 11, 135 sq.; the N. Mu*k*alinda protects Buddha, 13, 80; 49 (i), 164 sq.; Buddha conquers the fire of the N. in Kassapa's room, 13, 119–22; 19, 183–5; a N. procures edible stalks of lotuses for Moggallâna, 17, 76 sq.; pay homage to the new-born Buddha, 19, 4 sq., 350; rejoice at Buddha's escape from the palace, 19, 58; Gods and N. rejoice on Buddha's reaching Bodhi, 19, 146 sq., 163 sq.; friends

of Buddha, 19, 152–5, 247; 49 (i), 7 sq., 8 n., 141, 164 sq., 169 sq., 191; converted by Buddha, 19, 243, 245 sq.; weep for Buddha's death, 19, 308; protect Stûpas, 19, 336 sq.; N.-women with half their body visible at the birth of Buddha, 19, 344 sq.; dwell in the ocean, 20, 302, 305; the daughter of the N.-king Sâgara (Ocean) changes her sex to become a Buddha, 21, xxx, 250–4; enumeration of the great N.-kings, 21, 5; voices of gods and N. heard by the preacher, 21, 339; show honour to the preacher, 21, 347, 349; creation of N. and Sarpas, 25, 15; Dhara*n*endra, the best of N., 45, 290; the N.-king entering the cave of Nandâ, 49 (i), 4; guardians of treasures, 49 (i), 151. *See also* Snakes, *and* Superhuman Beings.

Nâgasena, conversations between King Milinda and, 35, xii, xiv, xvi sq., 1, 40–302; 36, 1, &c.; not identical with Nâgâr*g*una, 35, xxv; and Patañ*g*ali, 35, xxvi sq.; previous births of Milinda and N., 35, 4–6; birth story of N., 35, 11–16; educated as a Brahman, 35, 17 sq.; is taught by Roha*n*a and admitted into the Order, 35, 18–24; gradually reaches Arhatship, 35, 25–9; the head of a body of disciples, his greatness and wisdom, 35, 34–9; receives a Vihâra and other presents from Milinda, 35, 134 sq.; 36, 374; a N. mentioned in the Bharhut Tope, 36, 377.

Naggati (Nagna*g*it), king of Gândhâra, became a *G*aina monk, 45, 21, 87, 87 n.

Nâgila, disciple of Va*g*rasena, 22, 288.

Nagna*g*it, *see* Naggati.

Nahâtaka, Pali for Snâtaka, q.v.

Nahus, n. of an Aryan tribe, 46, 28.

Nahusha (Nung-Sha), got power to rule the heavens, 19, 122; perished through want of humility, 25, 222; Agni, the clan-lord of the N., 46, 23; prayer for the offspring of N., 46, 393; Yayâti, the son of N., 49 (i), 18; Indra, Bali, and N., 49 (i), 113; in heaven with Indra, 49 (i), 113.

Naidhruvi, *see* Ka*s*yapa N.

Nâîkîyas, the demon, his doings, 5, 106 sq.

Naïla, an idol on Mount Marwâ, 6, xiii.

Nail-paring, *see* Body.

Naimishîya-sacrificers, the Udgât*ri* of the, 1, 6.

Nairyô-sangha, messenger of Ahura-Mazda, is with the righteous souls, 4, 220, 237 sq., 237 n.; dwells in the navel of kings, 23, 8, 8 n., 16, 358; companion of Mithra, 23, 132; worshipped along with Sraosha, 23, 162; Fravashi of N. worshipped, 23, 200; converse with N., the tall-formed, 23, 339; worshipped, as connected with Fire, 31, 258, 258 n.; worshipped, 31, 298, 331, 345, 353, 381; identical with Narâ*s*a*m*sa, 46, 10.

Naishadha, *see* Na*d*a N.

Naish*th*ika, t.t., he who has lapsed from his duties, 48, 705–7. *See also* Brahma*k*ârin, *and* Holy persons.

Nâkahê*d*, *see* N*a*unghaithya.

Nâka Maudgalya, n. of a teacher, 14, xl, 234; 15, 51, 216; 44, 201; converted by Buddha, 49 (i), 193.

Nakedness of ascetics, 10 (ii), 41; *see also G*aina monks; rising at night and showing his person naked, an offence, 40, 244.

Na*k*iketas, legend of Yama and, 15, xxi sq., 1–24, 342; 34, 247–52; 38, 123; 48, 269–71, 361 sq.; gives himself away as a sacrificial reward, 42, 424.

Nâki*s*îyyâ, *see* N*a*unghaithya.

Nakshatra, Ârya N. of the Kâ*s*yapa gotra, a Sthavira, 22, 294.

Nakshatrarâ*g*a, n. of a Tathâgata, 21, 4; 49 (ii), 100.

Nakshatrarâ*g*asaṅkusumitâbhi*g*ña, n. of a Bodhisattva, 21, 376–92, 394.

Nakshatras (lunar mansions, constellations), auspicious for *S*râddhas, 7, 242–4; moon, the prince among N., 8, 346, 346 n.; have *S*rava*n*a as the first, 8, 352; the forest of the Brahman is adorned with planets and N., 8, 387; suitable N. for setting up the sacred fires, 12, 282–8; offerings to the N., 14, 252 sq.; 29, 52, 86, 339; 30, 58 sq.; 44, 296; worlds of the N., 15, 131; called the eighth of the Vasus, 15, 140; determine the path of the sun, 15,

316; produced by Goodness, 25, 494; list of the N. and their presiding deities, 29, 53 sq.; images of N. made at the *K*aitra festival, 29, 132; the Ash*t*akâ sacred to the N., 29, 206; invoked for protection, 29, 280; auspicious N. for marriage, 30, 255 sq.; twenty-seven N., 41, 19 n.; 43, 383, 383 n.; the Rohi*n*î N. means self, offspring, and cattle, 44, 2; greatness of Pra*g*âpati in the N. and the moon, 44, 394; single N. belong to the Fathers, 44, 423; expiatory oblation to the N. which are a place of abode for all the gods, 44, 505 sq. *See also* Moon, *and* Stars.

Nakshatra-vidyâ, or astronomy, 1, 110 sq., 115.

Nakula, the Pâ*nd*ava, 8, 39.

Nala, his gambling, 25, lxxi, lxxx, 381 n.

Naladî, n. of an Apsaras, 42, 33.

Nâlagâma, Sâriputta born at, 11, 238.

Nâlâgiri, n. of an elephant, 20, 247-50; 35, 298 n.

Nâlaka, the sister's son of Asita, advised by Asita to follow Buddha, 10 (ii), 127 sq.; converted by Buddha, 10 (ii), 128–31; 49 (i), 191.

Nâlakasutta, t.c., 10 (ii), 124–31.

Nalakûvara, or °kûbara, son of Vai*s*rava*n*a, 19, 20; 45, 117, 117 n.; 49 (i), 16.

Nâlandâ, Buddha at, 11, 12–15; Mahâvîra at N., 22, 264; n. of a suburb of Râ*g*agr*i*ha, 45, 419 sq.

Nâmadheya or Nâmakara*n*a, t.t., name-giving rite, *see* Child (*b*).

Nâmarûpa, t.t., name and form, *see* Name.

Name(s): Fire, Sun, Moon, Lightning are mere ns., 1, 95 sq.; meditation on the n. as Brahman, 1, 110 sq.; the n. of a superior person not to be pronounced by an inferior, 2, 188 sq. and n., 209; ns. and characteristics of all things, 8, 352, 352 n.; having understood n., let the Muni cross over the stream, 10 (ii), 148; a Muni, delivered from n. and body, disappears, 10 (ii), 198; kings and other persons in Buddhist writings scarcely ever mentioned by their real ns., 11, 1 n.; metronymics, 12 xxxiv sq., xxxv n.; sacrificer addressed by his ordinary n. and Nâkshatra n., 12, 251 n.; when a man dies, the n. does not leave him, for the n. is endless, 15, 126; mystical power of God's ns., 23, 21; auspicious and inauspicious n., 25, 76 sq.; 30, 257; a Brâhman, if he prospers not, shall take a second n., 26, 154; n. of maturity and n. taken at marriage, 27, 55, 79, 79 n., 438; rules about avoiding the mention of certain ns., 27, 93, 100 sq., 113, 239; 28, 17 sq., 161, 168; an orphan son not to change his n., 27, 102; honorary ns. conferred on officers, 27, 128, 144; n. of the deceased avoided, 27, 190; honourable n. after death, 27, 438; 28, 339; auspicious ns. for certain things to be used by a Snâtaka, 29, 317 sq.; n. to be used by the pupil when saluting his teacher, 29, 400; 30, 65; the two ns. of a student pronounced at the Upanayana, 30, 150, 150 n.; discussion on n. and individuality, 35, 40–5; the two secret ns. applied to the deva-abode of Brahman and to its bodily abode, 38, 216–18; giving of n. frees from evil, 41, 159; ns. of Agni mentioned, to gratify him, 43, 219; he who is consecrated comes to have two ns., 43, 247; even if two enemies, on meeting together, address one another by n., they get on amicably together, 44, 288; all things are merely ns., 49 (ii), xv; n.-giving ceremony for the child, *see* Child (*b*); ns. of girls, *see* Woman (*b*);—*name*(*s*) *and form*(*s*) (nâmarûpa) developed by the Sat, 1, 95; 34, 267; the universe is evolved or becomes manifest by n. and f., 1, 132 sq. n.; 8, 164; 15, 87; 34, 233, 242, 268, 357; 38, 98; ether is the revealer of ns. and fs., 1, 143; are contained in the Brahman, 1, 143; 34, 125; the wise Bhikshu cuts off the desire for n. and f. and overcomes suffering, 10 (i), 58, 86, 86 n.; (ii), 59, 93, 179, 205; one of the Buddhist Nidânas, 10 (i), 58 n.; (ii), 166, 191; 35, 79; mean individual existence, 10 (ii), xv; 34, xxv; the delusion of n. and f., the root of sickness, 10 (ii), 91;

the world of men and gods dwells in n. and f., 10 (ii), 143; a seeing man will see n. and f., 10 (ii), 173; are born from Brahman, 15, 29; triad of n., f., and work, 15, 99; evolution of n. and f. is the work, not of the individual soul, but of the Lord, 34, lix, lxiii; 38, 96–100; are the object of Brahman's knowledge before the creation, 34, 50; presented by Nescience, 34, 140, 282, 328 sq., 345, 369; 38, 64, 140, 401, 402; on account of their equality, there is no contradiction to the eternity of the Veda in the renovation of the world, 34, 211-16; the world periodically divests itself of them, 34, 212; Brahman only is different from n. and f., 34, 232 sq.; whether n. and f. abide in the individual soul, 34, 277–9; non-existence of the effect previous to its production only means the state of n. and f. being unevolved, 34, 333; the element of plurality characterized by n. and f., 34, 352; meaning of the term, 34, 404, 404 n.; 35, 76 sq.; is that which is reborn in consequence of Karman, 35, 71–5, 112 sq.; the apparent world of n. and f. to be dissolved by knowledge, 38, 162 sq.; deposited in the u*kkh*ish*t*a, 42, 226; Brahman (neut.) descends into this world by means of n. and f., 44, 27 sq.

Nami, n. of a Tîrthakara, 22, 280; dialogue between King N. who retires from the world, and Indra, 45, 35–41; king of Videha, became a *G*aina monk, 45, 87, 87 n., 268.

Namu*k*i, a name of Mâra, 10 (ii), x, 69, 71; 49 (i), 162, 164; an Asura, demon killed by Indra, 32, 111; 41, 92, 135; 42, liv, 256 sq., 583; 44, 216, 222 sq., 232; minister of Padmottara, *G*aina representative of the demon Bala, 45, 86 n.

Namûn, son of Spend-shê*d*, 37, 30, 30 n.

Nanârâsti, son of Paêshatah, 23, 213.

Nanda, n. of a Brâhma*n*a, 10 (ii), 187, 199–201, 210; 35, 153.

Nanda, the *S*âkya, and his mother, converted, 13, 210; 19, 226, 243; N. or Mahânanda, an eminent Arhat, 21, 2; 49 (ii), 2, 90.

Nanda, the king, fought for the sake of a beautiful woman, 19, 330; the royal family of N., 36, 147.

Nanda, n. of a Nâga-king, 21, 5.

Nanda, at the head of the lay votaries, under Arish*t*anemi, 22, 278.

Nandâ, n. of a Buddhist nun, 11, 25.

Nandabalâ, the herdsman's daughter, refreshes the Buddha who is exhausted by fasts, 19, 144 sq.; 49 (i), 135.

Nandahara, god, produces visions which cause Buddha to become an ascetic, 19, xx sq.

Nandaka, an ogre who laid hands on Sâriputta was swallowed up by the earth, 35, 152 sq.

Nandamâ*n*avapu*kkh*â, t.c., 10 (ii), 199–201.

Nandana, n. of Indra's beautiful park, 45, 100, 104, 288, 288 sq. n., 290; 49 (i), 35.

Nandana, king of Kâ*s*i, became a *G*aina monk, 45, 87, 87 n.

Nandana, author of commentary on Manu-sm*ri*ti, 25, cxxxiii–cxxxv.

Nandanabhadra, disciple of Sambhûtavigaya, 22, 289.

Nandapa*n*d*i*ta, author of commentary on the Vish*n*u-sm*ri*ti, 7, xxxii–xxxvi.

Nanda Va*kkh*a, Gosâla, the successor of, 45, xxix, xxxi.

Nandavana, the heavenly forest, 19, 37.

Nandika, his daughters the first Buddhist nuns, 49 (i), 192.

Nandika, or Nandiya, n. of a Bhikshu, 17, 309–12; 49 (ii), 2, 2 n.

Nândika (Pr. Nandigga), a Kula of the Uddeha Ga*n*a, 22, 290.

Nandin, a poor Brâhman, converted by Buddha, 49 (i), 170.

Nandî*s*vara, a god who was formerly a man, 2, 40 n.

Nandita, of the Kâ*s*yapa gotra, a Sthavira, 22, 295.

Nandivardhana, eldest brother of Mahâvîra, 22, 193, 256.

Nandiya, the monkey king, a Bodisat, 35, 287. *See also* Nandika.

Nandupananda, the *S*âkya, converted, 19, 226.

Năng, *see* Shăn Năng.

Nan Hwa *K*ăn *K*ing, general title of *K*wang-ʒze's works, 39, 11 sq.

Nan-kung *K*ing-shû, carried his treasures with him when he went to court, 27, 149.

Nan-kung Kwo, minister of Wăn, 3, 208.

Nan-Kung Mâo, officer at *Kh*ăng's court, 3, 237.

Nan-kung Thâo, his wife mourns for her mother-in-law, 27, 129.

Nan-kwo ʒze-*kh*î, and his disciple Yen *Kh*ăng ʒze-yû, 39, 156, 176–8, 176 n.; 40, 145 sq., 145 n.; his son Khwăn, 40, 106–8.

Nan-po ʒze-*kh*î, n. of a Tâoist sage, 39, 219; 40, 103 sq., 104 n.

Nan-po ʒze-khwei, wishes to learn the Tâo, 39, 245, 245 n.; and Nü Yü, 40, 282.

Nan-yung *Kh*û, inquires about the method to become a perfect man, 40, 77–81, 77 n.

Naotara, Vistauru, son of, 23, 71, 206, 206 n.; the N. family worshipped Anâhita, 23, 77, 77 n.; legend of Turanians and Ns., 23, 280 sq. and n.

Napâ*t*-apăm, *see* Apăm Napâ*t*.

Naptya, n.p., 23, 206.

Nârada, dialogue of Sanatkumâra with, 1, 109–25; 8, 17; 34, 166 sq.; 48, 300, 527; calls K*r*ish*n*a the first god, 8, 87; chief among divine sages, 8, 89; dialogue between N. and Devamata, 8, 274 sq.; both N. and Pabbata rejoice at Buddha, 10 (ii), 94; remodelled the Manusm*r*iti, 14, xi sq., xvi, 2, 2 n.; 25, xcv sq.; 33, 274; on the Manusm*r*iti, 25, xv, xvii; 33, 1–4, 1 n.; a sage and a Pragâpati, 25, 14; his repute as a legal writer, 33, xxi; a doctor of medicine, 36, 109, 109 n.; instructed by the omniform Nârâya*n*a, 38, 157; assumed a new body, 38, 235; in the Atharva-veda, 42, 172, 175 sq., 178, 435; Hari*s*candra told by N. to vow his son to Varu*n*a, 44, xxxvi.

Nârada-sm*r*iti, its relation to the Manu-sm*r*iti, 7, xxv; 25, xcii, xcv sq., xcix, ci–civ, cvii; 33, xi–xvi, 4, 4 n.; its date, 25, cvii; 33, xvi–xviii; compared with other Sm*r*itis, 33, xvi sq., 274 sq.; compared with the drama M*r*ikkh*akat*ikâ, 33, xvii; translation of the N., editions, MSS., and commentaries, 33, xix–xxii, 1–232; quotations from N., 33, xxi sq., 233–67.

Naradatta, one of the sixteen virtuous men, 21, 4; nephew of *S*uddhodana, 49 (i), 15, 15 n.; converted by Buddha, 49 (i), 194.

Narâ*s*a*m*sa, a name or form of Agni, 12, 136, 136 n.; 32, 439; 46, 10, 303; offerings to N., 12, 233 sq., 235, 321; 26, 154, 154 n.; is the air, 12, 234; worshipped in Âprî hymns, 26, 186 n.; 46, 8–10, 198, 377; n. of Indra, 32, 303; mixes the sacrifice with honey, 46, 153.

Nârâ*s*a*m*sa, fathers, 44, 211.

Nârâ*s*a*m*sî-Gâthâs, to be studied, 44, 98.

Nârâya*n*a, is Vish*n*u, 7, 296; a name of the highest Self, 8, 219, 280 sq.; 15, 311; 34, 440; 48, 240, 279, 282; the counterpart of the Buddha of the Saddharmapu*nd*arîka, 21, xxvii; a name of Brahman, 25, 5, 5 n.; 34, xxxi n.; 48, 240, 256, 521, 530 sq., 667; the omniform N. instructed Nârada about Mâyâ, 38, 157; Purusha N., 44, 173, 403, 410; the one God and Creator, 48, 133, 207, 227, 229, 239, 242, 280, 359, 404, 461, 469, 522; alone existed before creation, not Brahmâ, nor *S*iva, 48, 240, 472, 767; free from all evil, 48, 279; from N. there was born the Four-faced One, 48, 335; assumes the form of the world, 48, 410, 461; to be meditated on, 48, 411; of infinite nature, eternal, 48, 461; is alone the operative and the substantial cause of the world, 48, 521; Pra*g*âpati, &c., refer to the supreme Reality established by the texts concerning N., 48, 522; declared the Pa*ñk*arâtra doctrine, 48, 529–31; the thunderbolt (?) of N., 49 (ii), 17 sq. *See also* God.

Nârâya*n*a, author of Manvarthaviv*r*iti, 25, cxxviii–cxxx.

Nârâya*n*abha*tt*a, author of Dîpikâs on several Upanishads, 15, x–xii.

Naremana*u*, epithet of Keresâsp, 18, 369, 369 n.

Narêmân Hôshang, his account of the Nasks, 37, 428, 428 n.

Narendra, the 74th Tathâgata, 49 (ii), 7.

Narendrarâ*g*a, n. of a Tathâgata, 49 (ii), 67.

Narsih, son of Vîvanghâû, 5, 118; one of 'the Rashnû of *K*înô,' 5, 130 sq., 130 n.

Nas, *see* Nasu.

Nâsadîya-sûkta, quoted, 38, 85.

Na*s*âk, one of the first women, 5, 58.

Nâsatya, goes round the earth, 46, 325, 328; the Ns. or the A*s*vins, 46, 358; compared with Av. N*a*unghaithya, 5, 10 n.

Nâsî, Sk., t.t., explained, 34, 153.

Nasks of the Zend-Avesta, fragments of the, 4, 243–386; quoted in the Shâyast lâ-shâyast, 5, lxiii sq.; Dâmdâ*d* N., 5, 177, 177 sq. n., 181, 181 n., 325, 341, 345; 37, 465 sq., 465 n.; Stû*d*gar N., 5, 191 sq. and n., 319, 319 n., 352; Hâ*d*ôkht N., 5, 224, 225 sq. n., 347, 351, 356; Pâzôn N., 5, 311, 311 n.; Nihâ*d*ûm N., 5, 315 sq. and n., 325, 345; Spend N., 5, 316 sq. and n., 340, 343, 345, 350; Dûbâsrû*g*ê*d* N., 5, 320 sq. and n.; Hûspâram N., 5, 323–5 and n., 339, 342, 344 sq., 360; 18, 194, 194 n.; Sakâ*d*ûm N., 5, 326 sq. and n., 339, 343 sq., 364; 18, 309–12, 309 sq. n.; Bagh N., 5, 327 sq. and n.; *K*îdra*s*t N., 5, 329 sq., 329 n.; Ratû*s*tâîtîh N., 5, 330, 330 n.; the N. quoted by Mânû*s*kîhar, 18, xxiv; legend about Keresâspa in Sû*d*kar N., 18, 370–2; account of the N. in the Dînka*rd*, 37, xxix sq., xxxviii–xlvi, 1–397; the twenty-one N., 37, xxix, xl; classification, names, and divisions of the N., 37, 3–10; details of the N. from the selections of Zâ*d*-sparam, 37, 401–5; details of the N. from Dînka*rd*, 37, 406–18; details about the N. from Persian Rivâyats, 37, 418–47; the archangels come to the reciter of the first N., 37, 428 sq., 438; N. fragments translated, 37, 451–88.

Nasr, Arabian god, worshipped under the shape of an eagle, 6, xii; 9, 303.

Nâstikas, or infidels, 8, 378 n. *See also* Nihilists, *and* Scepticism.

Nasu (Nas, Nasû*s*, Nasru*s*t), the Drug, vanishes before Zarathu*s*tra, 4, 225; demon of corruption, entering the corpse, 5, 111, 245 sq., 245 n., 259, 259 n., 320 n., 331 sq., 331 n.; 18, 39, 39 n., 42 n., 292 sq. and n., 438–42, 445, 454; 23, 49–51; 24, 296, 296 n., 313; destroyed by ablution, 5, 299, 299 n.; to keep the N. from the body, one of the three duties of men, 5, 394. *See also* Drug.

Nâtaputta, *see* Mahâvîra, *and* Niga*nth*a N.

Ñâtikas, the *G*ñâtr*i*ka Kshatriyas to whose clan Mahâvîra belonged, 22, x sq.

Nature, phenomena of, symbolical of human qualities, 3, 147 sq. and n.; 16, 408, 417; male and female parts of n., 5, 61; actions proceed from n., not from the soul, 8, 55, 104–6, 105 n., 106 n.; all beings follow n., 8, 55 sq., 56 n.; n. only works, not the Lord, 8, 65; Kr*i*sh*n*a brings forth the entities by the power of n., 8, 82, 82 n.; functions of n. and spirit, 8, 104 sq. and n.; the qualities born from n., 8, 107, 107 n.; relations between n. and Kshetra*g*ña, 8, 377–9; considered as the cause of everything, 15, 260; correspondence between the phenomena of n. and the figures of the Yî King, 16, 38–40, 348 sq., 349 sq. n., 353 sq., 354 sq. n., 358–61, 359 n., 373, 377 sq., 378 sq. n., 380 sq., 387; analogy of phenomena of n. to social and political changes, 16, 245, 245 n.; constant change of rest and movement in n., 16, 355 sq., 357 n.; the presence and operation of God in n., 16, 425–7, 426 n.; fire, wind, water, earth are mutual causes and effects, 18, 120; the theory of self-n. or svabhâva refuted, 19, 208–11, 208 sq. n., 293 sq., 293 n.; the Great Mother, 21, 371 n.; extraordinary phenomena of n., 25, 15; sacrifices to phenomena or spirits of n., 27, 36; 28, 203, 209, 218, 218 n.; masculine and feminine phenomena in n., 27, 55; 28, 433 sq.; ceremonial usages suggested by the course of n., 27, 59;

28, 465 sq.; worship of hills, forests, streams, meres, 27, 256; 31, 291; Heaven and Earth, and the processes of n., 27, 380-4, 387 sq.; phenomena of n. represented by music, 28, 111; phenomena of n. symbolically represented by guest and host at the drinking festival, 28, 436-8 and n., 442-5, 444 n.; to be imitated by man, 39, 340; the regularity and noiselessness of the phenomena of n., 39, 345 sq. and n.; operation of the Tâo in n., 40, 63 sq.; n. and soul without beginning, 48, 140, 365. *See also* Heaven (*a*), Pradhâna, Prak*ri*ti, *and* Tâo.

N*a*unghaithya (Av.), Phl. Nâkahê*d* and Nâki*s*îyyâ, and the Nâsatya or A*s*vins, 4, liii; spell against the demon N., 4, 139, 139 n.; the Daêva, 4, 224; one of Aharman's archdemons, 5, 10, 10 n.; 18, 319, 319 n.

Nâûnghas, Tarômat is, 5, 128, 128 n.

Nâvâsutta, t.c., 10 (ii), 52 sq.

Navavâstva, n.p., 46, 33, 36.

Nayâzem, n.p., 47, 34, 34 n.

Nebuchadnezzar, his siege of Jerusalem, 47, xiii, 120 sq.

Nectar (am*ri*ta), *see* Immortality, draught of.

Ne*g*amesha, prayer to, 29, 48, 181.

Nemi, perished through want of humility, 25, 222.

Nemôvanghu, son of Vaêdhayangha, 23, 210.

Neo-Platonism, and Zoroastrianism, 4, xv, lv-lvii.

Nera*ñg*arâ, n. of a river, 10 (ii), 69; 11, 52 sq.

Neremyazdana, son of Âthwyôza, 23, 211.

Neriosengh, *see* Nêryôsang.

Nêrôksang, *see* Nêryôsang.

Nêryôsang (Neryosengh, Nêrôksang), angel, messenger of Aûha*r*maz*d*, 4, 262 sq. n.; 5, 224, 224 n., 226, 235; 47, 11, 11 n., 23, 23 n., 34, 129, 129 n., 140; kept charge of Gâyômar*d*'s seed, 5, 53, 53 n.; watches the seed of Zaratû*s*t, 5, 144; 23, 195 n.; the promoter of the world, 37, 222 sq., 222 n.; sent to Vi*s*tâsp, 47, 70 sq.; Zoroaster's connexion with Aûha*r*maz*d* through Yim and N., 47, 139 sq.

Nêryôsang (Neriosengh), son of Dhaval, author of Sanskrit versions of the Yasna and of Pahlavi texts, 4, xxv; 5, 305 n.; 24, xx-xxii, xxiv, xxx-xxxvi.

Nêryôsang, a teacher, quoted, 5, 305, 305 n.

Neryosengh, *see* Nêryôsang.

Nescience, or Ignorance (Sk. avidyâ, a*gñ*âna, Pali avi*gg*â), is the source of all evil and suffering, 10 (ii), 134; 13, 75-8, 75 sq. n.; is the head, knowledge, &c., cleave it, 10 (ii), 189, 206 sq.; with n. is the world shrouded, 10 (ii), 190; the Âsava of n., 11, 298, 300 sq.; in Brahmanic philosophy and Buddhism, 13, 76 n.; the appearance of the world due to it, 34, xxv, 135, 155; 38, 294; avidyâ, Sk. t.t., means n. as to Brahman, 34, lxxix, xcvii sq., cxv, 62; 38, 83 n.; superimposition is n., 34, 6; perception, &c., have for their object that which is dependent on n., 34, 7; n., the seed of the Sa*m*sâra, destroyed by knowledge of Brahman, 34, 14, 31, 300; 38, 68 sq., 370; 48, 9, 11, 23 sq., 54, 66, 681, 748, 750; all difference fictitiously created by n., 34, 32; 48, 25, 193, 195, 197; the limiting adjunct, consisting of the organs of action, presented by n., 34, 134; 38, 67, 153, 156, 367; 48, 566; names and forms presented by n., 34, 139 sq., 282, 328 sq., 345, 357, 369; 38, 64, 67, 140, 163, 401 sq.; the conception that the body and other things are our Self, constitutes n., 34, 157, 244; from it there spring desires, aversions, fear and confusion, 34, 157, 167; compared to the mistake of him who in the twilight mistakes a post for a man, 34, 185; the unreal aspect of the individual soul, as different from the highest Self, is a mere presentation of n., 34, 189, 241, 244, 251 sq.; 38, 68, 139, 173, 179, 340; 48, 100 sq.; by means of n. the highest Lord manifests himself in various ways, 34, 190, 352; the causal potentiality is of the nature of n., 34, 243; the elements and the sense organs the product of n., 34, 281; the effects both at the time of creation and reabsorption

are the mere fallacious superimpositions of n., 34, 312, 357 n.; view of the plurality of existence due to n., 34, 355; 48, 9, 22 sq., 102–19, 180; cannot be the cause of inequality, as it is of a uniform nature, 34, 360; the relation of causes of suffering and of sufferers is the effect of n., 34, 380; in the Vaiseshika-sûtra, 34, 392 sq., 393 n.; Bauddha doctrine of n., 34, 404–9, 404 n., 423; 48, 502 sq.; is the root of time, 35, 79, 81; the rising from deep sleep is due to the existence of potential n., 38, 48; the conditions of being agent and enjoyer presented by n. only, 38, 54, 55; the soul being engrossed by n. identifies itself with the body, &c., and imagines itself to be affected by pain which is due to n., 38, 63–5; the soul when leaving its body takes n. with itself, 38, 102; the Lord is everlastingly free from n., 38, 149; a soul which has freed itself from n. can impossibly enter into phenomenal life, 38, 149; the primaeval natural n. leaves room for all practical life and activity, 38, 156; the bondage of the soul due to n. only, 38, 174; final release consists in cessation of n., 48, 9, 11, 70 sq., 271, 438; put an end to by Vedânta-texts, 48, 10 sq., 39; consciousness is non-contradictory of n., 48, 50; does not originate, is the substrate of changes, 48, 54; what it is, 48, 72; souls engrossed by n. in the form of good and evil works (Karman), 48, 88–90, 101, 147, 198, 306, 756–8; individual soul the abode of n., 48, 98; taught neither by Scripture nor by Smriti and Purâna, 48, 124–9; cannot belong to Brahman, 48, 131; not terminated by cognizing Brahman as the Universal Self, 48, 145–7; the root of all error, 48, 161; owing to n., Brahman is viewed as connected with the world, 48, 176; produces the organ of egoity, 48, 182; Brahman, the substrate of beginningless n., 48, 215 sq.; beginningless n. the root of Karman, 48, 259; obscures the true nature of the soul, 48, 271; Brahman's true nature cannot be obscured by n., 48, 393; Brahman connected with n. the cause of the world, 48, 429, 445; all effects are based on n., 48, 432; souls the abode of n., souls and n. like seed and sprout, 48, 436 sq.; a special n. for each soul, 48, 438 sq.; no distinction between Mâyâ and n., 48, 441 sq.; objections to the theory of Brahman's nature being hidden by n., 48, 445–53; Brahman by being conscious of n. experiences unreal bondage and release, 48, 494; the individual soul due to n., 48, 543; five kinds of n., 49 (i), 126 sq. *See also* Ignorance, Karman, *and* Mâyâ.

Nether world, *see* Hell.

Nêvak-tôrâ, the Âspîgân, 47, 34, 34 n.

New-moon, *see* Moon.

New Testament, no historical connexion between Tipitaka and, 11, 165 sq.

Nibbâna, *see* Nirvâna.

Nidâna, of the Bhâllavins, quoted, 14, 3 sq. and n.

Nidânas, the twelve, Buddhist doctrine of the chain of causes and effects, 11, 141, 208 sq.; 13, 75–8, 75 n., 85, 146; 34, 404 sq., 407–10, 410 n.; 35, 79, 81, 81 n.

Nieh, known as King Yû, a worthless ruler, 3, 265. *See* Yû.

Nieh Khüeh, was a perfect man, 39, 172 n.; disciple of Wang Î, 39, 190–2, 190 n., 259; 40, 279; teacher of Hsü Yû, 39, 312; 40, 108; asks Phei-î about the Tâo, 40, 61 sq., 291.

Nie-hsü, n. of a Tâoist teacher, 39, 247.

Nî-fû, posthumous title of Confucius, 27, 159, 159 n.

Niganthа-Nâtaputta, n. of a teacher, 10 (ii), xii, 86 sq.; 11, 106; accuses Buddha of not believing in the result of actions, 17, 109; an Arhat possessed of Iddhi, 20, 79; and King Milinda, 35, 8.

Niganthas, Sk. Nirgranthas, a sect of naked ascetics, 10 (ii), x, xiii; 21, 263; disputatious N. do not overcome Buddha, 10 (ii), 63. *See also* Gaina monks, *and* Holy persons.

Nîgâs-afzûd-dâk, n.p., 5, 146.

Nighandu, vocabulary, 10 (ii), 98, 189.

Night: the soul of the departed

goes from smoke to n., from n. to dark half of the moon, 1, 80; 8, 81; 15, 209; the sage is awake when it is n. for other beings, 8, 51; day and n. of Brahman, 8, 79 sq.; day and n. a pair, 8, 276 sq. n., 277; day and n. are threefold, 8, 330; ends with the sun's rising, 8, 354; the N. wedded to Indra, 12, 337; day and n. are Pragâpati, hence it is right to unite in love by n. only, 15, 273; the two goddesses N. and Dawn, mothers of Agni, and of *Ri*ta, 26, 186 n.; 41, 272 sq.; 43, 201; 46, 8, 74, 76, 114-16, 119, 153, 167 sq., 193, 198 sq., 239 (the two D.), 268 sq., 377; the Ash*t*akâ sacred to the N., 29, 206; invoked for protection, 29, 348; 32, 357, 362; unites, 43, 88, 326; day and n. created, 44, 14; means peaceful dwelling, 44, 285; secret is the n., 44, 433; the gods have made n. and dawn of different shape and colour, 46, 89. *See also* Day, *and* Ûrmyâ.

Nigrodha, former birth of the Bodisat, 35, 289 sq.

Nigrodhakappa, Thera who attained Nirvâ*n*a, 10 (ii), 57-60.

Nihâ*g*, a Tûrk, wounded Sâm, 5, 119, 119 n.

Nihilism, belongs to the quality of darkness, 8, 320; Buddhism not n., 36, 191 n.; *s*ûnyavâda, hypothesis of a general void, 38, 14; theory of n., 49 (i), 130, 132; emptiness of everything, the highest wisdom, 49 (ii), 147-9, 153 sq. *See also* Nothingness.

Nihilists (*S*ûnyavâdin), maintain that everything is void, 34, 401; are the Mâdhyamikas, 34, 401 n.; Bauddhas so called, 34, 415; are contradicted by all means of right knowledge, 34, 427; are Akriyâvâdins, 45, 317, 317 n.

Nihîv, demon of terror, 18, 96.

Nika*t*a, reached the highest heavens, 11, 26.

Nikâyas, the Buddhist canon divided into five, 10 (i), ix sq.; a man to whom the N. had been handed down, 17, 345. *See also* Tipi*t*aka.

Nikhshahpûr, councillor of King Khûsrô Nôshîrvân, 18, 397.

Nîla, one of the princes of mountains, 8, 346.

Nilavâsi, n. of a Thera, 17, 238.

Nimi, the king, went up to heaven even in his human body, 35, 172; 36, 146; Vasish*th*a cursed by N., 38, 235.

Nimi, the 56th Tathâgata, 49 (ii), 7.

Nimi-videha, legend of, 49 (i), 137 n.

Nimrod, and Abraham, 6, 40 sq.

Nine, *see* Numbers (*b*).

Nipu*n*i, a demon harassing children, 30, 211.

Nîrang, Zd. t.t., washing with ox's urine, 4, lxxiii.

Nîrangistân, *see* Zend-Avesta.

Niraya, *see* Hell.

Nirgranthas, *see* Niga*nth*as.

Nir*ri*ti, student who has broken his vow of chastity shall offer an ass to, 2, 85, 289; 14, 215; 25, 454 sq.; 29, 361; offerings to N., 14, 118, 193; 30, 330; 41, 43 sq., 43 n., 65; the region of N. (south-west), 25, 452; sin, power of evil, misfortune, personified, 32, 88; 41, 319, 322; 42, 82; Maruts mount up to the firmament from the abyss of N., 32, 382, 385; Soma and Rudra drive away N., 32, 434; the altar of N., 41, 319-25; homage to N., 41, 321 sq.; is the earth, 41, 322; charm to release a patient from N., 42, 14 sq.; invoked against evil demons, 42, 36; the lap of N., i.e. destruction, 42, 49, 52 sq., 564 n.; 44, 71, 71 n.; driven away, 42, 57, 187; invoked against enemies, 42, 90, 92; ominous birds, the messengers of N., 42, 166 sq.; the golden-locked N. worshipped, 42, 173; receives a share of the sacrifice, 42, 183, 617; throwing a stone towards N.'s quarter, 43, 171; altar for warding off N., 43, 361; in a list of gods, 49 (i), 197.

Nirukta, of Yâska, 8, 226; 14, xvi; 38, 428.

Nirvâ*n*a (Pali Nibbâna).

(*a*) What is N.?
(*b*) The attainment of N.

(*a*) WHAT IS N.?

N. is highest tranquillity, 'the quiet place,' the tranquil state, 8, 212, 215, 247 n.; 10 (i), 86, 88;

(ii), 24; 11, 118; 13, 91; 19, 181, 189, 203, 224, 273, 273 n., 279, 288, 304; 35, 119 n., 198; 'the other shore,' i. e. N., 10 (i), 24 sq. and n., 89; (ii), 4; is unconditioned freedom, 10 (i), 27 sq., 27 sq. n.; the Eternal, the Immortal (amata), 10 (i), 43, 87; 19, 222 sq. n., 337; 36, 84 n., 190, 190 n.; long-suffering the highest N., 10 (i), 50; the highest happiness, 10 (i), 54 sq.; (ii), x, 10, 44; 36, 230; 45, 99; 49 (ii), 9, 43, 148, 154; the Ineffable, 10 (i), 57; the unchangeable place, 10 (i), 58; (ii), xv, 33, 213; means extinction, 10 (ii), x, xvi, 57-60, 178, 198; 19, 177, 273 n.; 21, 403; 35, 106 sq.; the destruction of desire, 10 (ii), 10, 34, 197, 201 sq., 206; 19, 203, 203 n., 294; the end of birth and destruction, 10 (ii), 34; a saint described as 'seeing N.,' 10 (ii), 58; Buddha sees what is exceedingly pure, i. e. N., 10 (ii), 77, 127; *what is not false, the N., that the noble conceive as true*, 10 (ii), 143; Khema, security, i. e. N., 10 (ii), 155, 171; 11, 233; freedom from upadhis is N., 10 (ii), 195, 201; seclusion = N., 10 (ii), 196; N., the destruction of decay and death, is the matchless island for those who stand in the middle of the water, 10 (ii), 203 sq.; realized in this life, is one side of Arhatship, the supreme goal of the higher life, 11, 39, 39 n., 110, 207, 218, 243 sq., 293, 312; 35, 41, 78; 36, 84 n., 181 n.; the diadem of N., 11, 62 n.; the N. or utter passing away of the Buddha, as the going out of a lamp, 11, 81, 118; 19, 275, 275 n., 287 sq., 371; 35, 144-53; 49 (ii), 13; the state of the Anâsava the same as N., 11, 97 n.; the great ambrosial N., 11, 241; the cessation of the Saṅkhâras, 11, 241, 243; doctrine of N. difficult to understand, 13, 85; Buddha says, 'I have gained coolness and have obtained N.,' 13, 91; the state where all sorrow ceases, 13, 146; 19, 181; 21, 56 sq.; Buddha conceives the idea of N., preaches N., 19, 51, 168; 21, 45, 48, 56 sq., 63, 121; the great *R*ishi's house, 19, 163; the condition of the original first cause, 19, 271 n.; only in N. is there joy, 19, 309, 309 n.; praises of Tathâgata's N., 19, 309-22; 'and after this present life there will be no beyond,' for him who attains to Arhatship, 20, 385 n.; Buddha only makes a show of N., in reality he is not subject to N., 21, xxv sq.; Bodisatship versus N., 21, xxxiv; N. and *G*îvanmukti, 21, xxxiv n.; when one becomes Buddha, then one will be completely extinct, 21, 63; *deliverance from birth, decrepitude, disease, and death is inseparably connected with N.*, 21, 71; there is only one N. for all beings, 21, 129, 180 sq.; by a device, Buddha teaches to beings not far enough advanced that N. to which they are attached, 21, 180-3, 189 sq.; the fancied and the real N., 21, 201-4; the place, the city of N., 21, 275; 36, 117, 202-5, 213, 257; Buddha announces final extinction though himself he does not become finally extinct, 21, 303 sq.; Buddha's doctrine of N. opposed to the Brahmanic theory of the Âtman, 22, xxxiii; Mahâvîra reaches the N., supreme knowledge, called Kevala, 22, 201 sq.; *the nectar waters of the teaching of the N. of the truth*, 35, 35; N. and Parinirvâ*n*a to be distinguished, 35, 78 n.; how can those who do not receive N. know what a happy state N. is? 35, 108; the nature of N., 36, 103-8, 186-95; N. itself is all bliss, though there is pain incurred by those who are in quest of N., 36, 181-5; false explanation of suññatâ, 36, 191 n.; on the sweet couch of N.'s peace let him rest, 36, 283, 283 n.; individuality and the Void Supreme, 36, 362; agnosticism prepared the way for Buddha's doctrine of N., 45, xxviii sq.; *N., or freedom from pain, or perfection, which is in view of all; it is the safe, happy, and quiet place which the great sages reach*, 45, 128; N. or perfection, moksha or deliverance, 45, 156 n., 372, 427; *he should cease to injure living beings whether they move or not, on high, below, and on earth. For this has been*

called the N., which consists in peace, 45, 271, 311; the flying up of the big lotus in the parable of the lotus-pool compared to N., 45, 338; a monk should preach cessation of passion, N., purity, simplicity, humility, freedom from bonds, 45, 354; puts an end to all future births, 49 (i), 162. *See also* Brahma-nirvâna, Death (*b*), Emancipation, Immortality, *and* Transmigration.

(*b*) THE ATTAINMENT OF N.

N. is the reward of earnestness, 10 (i), 9, 9 n., 11; 11, 9; 36, 353; Bhikshu is to strive after N., 10 (i), 22; (ii), 61; 11, 7 sq.; 21, 36; 36, 360; those who are free from all worldly desires attain N., 10 (i), 35, 37; (ii), 178 sq.; 11, 84; 19, 298; the four steps in the path that leads to N., 10 (i), 48 n.; who strive after N., their passions come to an end, 10 (i), 58; attained by the noble eightfold path, 10 (i), 67 n., 69; 11, 147 sq.; 13, 94–7; the untrodden country, reached by the tamed man, 10 (i), 77; *having cut off passion and hatred, thou wilt go to N.*, 10 (i), 86; by meditation and knowledge one approaches N., 10 (i), 87; 21, 135 sq., 138–41; 36, 224; Bhikkhu leaves this and the further shore, 10 (ii), 1–3; exertion is the beast of burden that carries Buddha to N., 10 (ii), 13; he who delights in N., is a Maggagina Samana, 10 (ii), 16; Buddha taught the excellent Dhamma leading to N., 10 (ii), 31, 39; 21, 171, 275; for one who has seen the state of N., it is impossible to conceal a sin committed, 10 (ii), 39; Buddha's meditation for the sake of acquiring N., 10 (ii), 69; 19, 307; 49 (i), 53; '*who except the noble deserve the well understood state (of N.)? Having perfectly conceived this state, those free from passion are completely extinguished*,' 10 (ii), 145; although near N., the Muni should not think himself the best, 10 (ii), 157; how the gods can attain to it, 11, 163; how to be obtained, 11, 233, 233 n.; 19, 75, 75 n.; 36, 195–205; 49 (i), 174, 177–9; results from acts of charity, 19, 215; Buddha desires N., fixes the time of his N., 19, 249, 267–9, 274 sq., 283, 283 n.; the passage in the boat of wisdom from this world to N., 19, 251; disciples of Buddha, and Arhats reach N., 19, 295, 336; 21, 128; 49 (i), 172, 192; (ii), 27; Buddhas reach final N., 21, 8, 21 sq., 26 sq., 67, 363 n., 382; the four Noble Truths and the way to N. preached to disciples, 21, 18, 355; 49 (i), 175; roused by Buddha's N., or established in N., 21, 34; the Arhats, &c., think that on reaching N. they will also acquire the transcendent powers of Buddha, 21, 35; Arhats before and after reaching N., 21, 43; some acquire the knowledge of the four great truths, others become Pratyekabuddhas and Bodhisattvas, for the sake of their own complete N., 21, 80; Buddha does not teach a particular N. for each being, but causes all beings to reach complete N. by means of his own complete N., 21, 81; to be reached by the vehicle of Buddha, 21, 90; Subhûti and other Arhats fancied they had attained N., but they never longed to be Buddhas, 21, 98 sq., 107, 113 sq.; men who walk in the knowledge of the law which is free from evil after the attaining of N., 21, 125; for the complete N. of the Tathâgatas Buddha created all this, 21, 300; Buddha reveals a state in which N. has not yet been reached, 21, 301; men would not obey Buddha's word, unless he enter N., 21, 308, 403; the three good methods of entering N. (by suicide), 22, 68 n., 74 n., 78; Mahâvîra's parents, after being born as gods, will reach final N., 22, 194; Mahâvîra lived walking the path of N. and liberation, 22, 200 sq.; of the Arhat *R*ishabha, 22, 285; from birth till attainment of N., 35, 5; Nâgasena had obtained N., 35, 36; the righteous receive N., 35, 107; 45, 16, 46, 243, 372; beings who cannot attain to insight into Truth and N., 36, 176 sq.; why children under seven years of age cannot attain to N., 36, 177–81; the result of Karman,

36, 230; Buddhist laymen attain to N., 36, 244-50, 253-5; keeping the vows necessary for attaining to N., 36, 255-61, 267; the Bhikkhu should preach of purgatory and N., 36, 345 sq.; *those who through perfect knowledge have dispelled all mental darkness and are devoted to the eternally perfect N. do not return*, 38, 419; the Law (of Gainas) leads to N., 45, 99, 427; an ascetic who has ceased to act will enter the path of N., 45, 111; an ascetic who has reached N., is called a true Brâhma*n*a, 45, 139; Mahâvîra the best of those who have taught the N., 45, 290; *a sage setting out for the real good (viz. Liberation), should not speak untruth; this (rule, they say,) comprises N. and the whole of carefulness*, 45, 309; one should not maintain that some beings are qualified for N., and some are not, 45, 406 n.; reached by means of the six mudrâs, 48, 520 sq.; opposed to the objects of life, 49 (i), 108; Mâra tries to persuade Buddha to enter N. at once, 49 (i), 160; Buddha tranquil like one who has entered N., 49 (i), 161; Buddha's mind guided by the conduct which leads to N., 49 (i), 162; promised to Buddha by Mâra, 49 (i), 164; obtained by bathing in a holy river, 49 (i), 168; Buddha, the guide showing the way to N., 49 (i), 183; Bodhisattvas work for the attainment of N., 49 (ii), 16; beings in Sukhâvatî are always constant in truth, till they have reached N., 49 (ii), 44; Buddhas helping people to attain Parinirvâ*n*a, 49 (ii), 52; attained by knowing the virtues of a Buddha, 49 (ii), 70; all beings must be delivered in the perfect world of N., 49 (ii), 114, 132; the path that leads to N., 49 (ii), 126, 130; there is no knowledge, no obtaining, no not-obtaining of N., 49 (ii), 148, 154.

Nishâdas, and the four castes, 34, 262; a N. (one of the wild aboriginal tribesmen) sacrificed at the Purushamedha, 44, 414. *See also* Caste (*e, f*).

Nishadha, n. of mountain, 45, 289, 289 n.

Nîshahpûhar, or Nikhshâpûr, or Nîvshahpûhar, or Nîshâpûr, n. of a town, 18, xiv, 180 n., 325 sq. n., 344 n.

Nîshahpûhar, or Nîvshahpûhar, priest and councillor of King Khûsrô Nôshirvân, 18, xxvii sq., 297 sq. and n., 325.

Nishekakarman, t.t., *see* Child (*b*).

Nissâlâ (?), n. of a female demon, 42, 66, 300 sq.

Nissaya, Pali t.t., relation between teacher and pupil, *see* Teacher (*b*).

Nissaya-kamma, Pali t.t., act of subordination, *see* Sa*m*gha.

Nissita (the dependent), for it there is vacillation, hence the n. cannot overcome sa*m*sâra, 10 (ii), 141.

Nityaparinirv*ri*ta, n. of a Tathâgata, 21, 178.

Nityodyukta, n. of Bodhisattvas, 21, 4; 49 (ii), 90.

Nivar, n.p., 5, 146.

Nîvara*n*â, Pali t.t., 'hindrances,' 11, 182 n.

Nîvê*d*i*s*, brother of Zoroaster, 47, 144.

Nivika (Nîvîk), descendants of, smitten by Keresâsp, 18, 370, 372; 23, 296; 37, 198, 198 n.

Nîyâ*z*, demon of want, 5, 110; 18, 96.

Niyoga, t.t., appointment of widows, levirate, Kshetraga sons, law about, 2, xix-xxi, 131 sq. and n., 165 sq. and n., 270 sq., 306; 7, xxiv, 61, 61 sq. n.; 14, xxvi sq., 84 sq., 90 sq., 93, 226 sq., 229, 234; 25 xxiv, xciii sq., cv n., cix, 105, 108, 197, 333-40, 349 sq. and n., 356, 359-61, 360 sq. n., 369, 369 n., 373 n.; 33, xv, 175, 181-3, 192-5, 195 n., 200, 272, 369; difference made between 'father' and 'begetter,' 2, 196, 196 n.; N. at a living husband's request, 2, 271; Kshatriyas produced by Brâhma*n*as on Kshatriya women, 8, 295, 295 n.

Nizî*s*tô, demon, opposes the departed soul, 24, 17.

Nmânya, chief of the house-lord, worshipped, 31, 197, 205, 209, 215, 220, 224, 250 sq., 250 n., 259, 278, 387 sq.

Noah, parallels to the story of, in the Avesta, 4, lviii sq.; sent as an apostle or prophet, and saved from deluge in the ark, 6, lxxi, 50, 94,

125, 144 sq., 183, 200 sq., 207–10, 239; 9, 51 sq., 66 sq., 94 sq., 119, 139, 171, 206, 255 sq., 269; story of N.'s son, 6, 209 sq.; was a thankful servant, 9, 1; many generations destroyed after N., 9, 3; called a liar by his people, 9, 61, 66 sq., 86, 176, 190, 242; the people of N. punished, 9, 193, 247, 254; wife of N. punished for disobedience, 9, 292; preaches in vain to the unbelievers, 9, 302–4.

Nobility, *see* Castes, *and* Kshatra.

Noble Ones, i.e. Buddhas, Pa*kk*eka-buddhas, Arahats, &c., 11, 217, 217 n., 297, 300.

Nô*d*ar, n.p., son of Mânû*sk*îhar, 5, 118, 134, 136, 146; 37, 29, 29 n.; 47, xiv, 29, 29 n., 40, 44, 146 sq.; village of the Nô*d*ars, 47, 80, 80 n.

No*d*arîgâ, brother of Zoroaster, 47, 144.

Nodhas Gautama, author of Vedic hymns, 32, 106, 109, 124 sq.; 46, 46, 48, 50, 52.

Nôktargâ, n. of a sorcerer, 5, 138.

Non-being, *see* Asat.

Non-duality, *see* Advaita.

Non-Ego, notion of, 34, 3.

Non-entity, non-existent, *see* Asat.

Non-Existence, all things come from, 40, 85 sq. *See* Asat.

Non-human beings, *see* Demons.

Non-sentient, the, *see* Pradhâna.

Nôsâî Bûrz-Mitrô, quoted, 5, 307.

Nôshirvân, *see* Khûsrô.

Nothingness, wishing for, 10 (ii), 184, 197 sq.; the bonds of pleasure do not originate in n., 10 (ii), 207; the idea of n., 11, 52; Buddhist theory of n. refuted, 48, 514–16.

Novices, ten precepts for, 13, 211 sq.; punishments inflicted on unruly n., 13, 212–15; a Bhikkhu must not draw the n. of senior Bhikkhus over to himself, 13, 214. *See also* Ordination, *and* Sekha.

N*rik*akshas, expiatory oblations to, 44, 210.

N*ri*ma*n*i, n. of a demon harassing infants, 29, 296.

N*ri*shad, Ka*n*va, descendant of, 42, 71.

N*ri*si*m*ha - Tâpinî - upanishad, quoted, 8, 20, 79 n., 85 n., 93 n., 105 n., 112 n., 142 n., 152 n., 157 n., 163 n., 170 n., 171 n., 186 n.

Nü-kwa, the organ of, 28, 37, 37 n.

Numbers.

(*a*) N. in general, and large n.
(*b*) N. from two to twenty.

(*a*) N. IN GENERAL, AND LARGE N.

Speculations on n., 1, 159 sq., 165, 171 sq., 182 sq., 185 sq., 193 sq., 223–7, 257 sq.; eighty thousand sages, 2, 158; large n. (84,000, &c.) in Buddhist literature, 11, 239, 263 n., 274 sqq., 278–88; 17, 1 sqq., 90, 93, 171 sq.; 19, 344, 348, 351–4; 21, 1–7, 9, 11, 13, &c., 153 sq., 241, 241 n., 281 sqq., 299 sq., 383, 383 n.; 49 (ii), 2, 5, &c., 91 n., 111, 111 n.; n. in Sâṅkhya philosophy and in the *S*vetâ*s*vatara-upanishad, 15, xli sq., 232 sq., 260; n. of arteries, 15, 105; n. of the gods, 15, 139 sq.; use of n. in connexion with the figures of the Yî and the practice of divination, 16, 365 sq, 366–9 n.; vast n. in the lives of the *G*inas, 22, 267 sq., 274, 278–85; connected with the seasons of the year, 27, 250, 250 sq. n., 258, 262, 268, 272, 277, 281, 283, 287, 291, 296, 302, 306; numerical distinctions in ceremonies, 27, 397 sq.; odd and even n., 27, 419, 419 n., 436; 29, 209, 238; 44, 423, 423 n.; numerical categories, 40, 330 sq.; five and fifty, seven and seventy, nine and ninety, in a charm, 42, 19, 472; fifty-three sorceries, and hundred performers of sorcery, and seven charms, 42, 38, 672; one hundred and one, 42, 168, 170, 565; categories of n. from one to thirty-three, 43, 73–6; a thousand means everything, 43, 147, 304; 44, 348; life of a thousand years, 43, 362; highest and lowest n., 43, 172; there are twelve months in the year, five seasons, and three worlds, and the sun the twenty-first, 44, 150; offerings to the n. from one to a hundred and one, 44, 297 sq., 297 n.; symbolism of n., *see also* Metres.

(*b*) N. FROM TWO TO TWENTY.

Categories of *two*, 28, 484;—*three* virtues, 3, 140, 144 sq., 144 n.; triads of things, 8, 330 sq., 15, 93 sq., 99, 257; threefold is the

sacrifice, 12, 32, 62 sq., 83, 86, 96, 127; 26, 35, 38, 81, 145 sq., 166, 200 sq., 291; the number three in the Nâ*k*iketa rite, 15, 5; 'three years,' i. e. a long time, 16, 164 n.; food, or cattle, is threefold, 26, 28, 172; categories of three, 28, 483 sq.; three forms of evil, 39, 313 n., 314; three poisons (greed, anger, stupidity), 40, 251; what is threefold belongs to the gods, 41, 21; the three distances, the three ethers, 42, 92; thirty-three, 42, 102, 539; 43, 76; 44, 164; three in magic, 42, 165, 526; Agni has three heads, three tongues, bodies, &c., 46, 167, 281; the threefold song, 46, 293, 295;—*four* classes of the people, 3, 229; the four tribes, the fourteen worlds, with all the n. of beings, multiplied eighty-four times, 15, 297; categories of four, 28, 476;—*five* duties, punishments, courses of honourable conduct, relationships, and ceremonies, 3, 38–40, 43, 48 sq., 55 sq. and n.; 39, 335, 335 n., 349; 40, 178 sq., 179 n.; five seasons, 3, 55; 12, 192, 280; 26, 24, 166; 44, 405; five colours, musical notes, six pitch-tubes, eight kinds of musical instruments, 3, 59; 27, 382; 39, 328 sq., 351; five orders of nobles, and relations of society, 3, 136 sq., 228, 251; five elements, personal matters, dividers of time, sources of happiness, 3, 139–42, 140 sq. n., 142 n., 149; 27, 382; 40, 258 sq., 270; five pairs of gems, 3, 239, 239 n.; fivefold is the sacrifice, 12, 16, 16 n., 142, 144, 192, 280; 15, 50, 91; 26, 24, 166; 44, 405, 452; cattle are fivefold, 12, 219, 228; *whatever exists is fivefold,* 15, 50; five beings, 15, 178, 178 n.; categories of five, 28, 475; five viscera, 39, 294 sq.; five forms of superciliousness, 40, 210; five mountains, 40, 317; five tribes of men, 42, 92; 44, 399; *see also* Five-people; fifteenfold is the thunderbolt, 44, 300 sq., 350; fifteen sets of victims at the A*s*vamedha, 44, 308;—*six* occasions of suffering, six deplorable conditions, 3, 140, 149; 40, 184; divided and undivided lines of the hexagrams indicated by the numbers six and nine, 16, 58, 58 sq. n.; categories of six, 28, 482; six elemental influences, 39, 301, 301 n.; six Extreme Points and five Elements belonging to Heaven, 39, 346; six things that obstruct the course of the Tâo, 40, 87 sq.; six confines of the world of space, 40, 96 sq., 128; six faculties of perception, 40, 139, 139 n.; six parties in the social organization, 40, 178 sq., 179 n.; six repositories of the person, 40, 210 sq.; six desires, 40, 251;—*seven, see separately;*—*eight* objects of government, 3, 140–2; 27, 230, 248; eight tribes of the Mân, 3, 150; 28, 30; eighty in the fire-ritual, 12, 347 n.; eight abodes, worlds, gods, persons, 15, 149; eight months of spring, 27, 250, 251 n., 258, 262; eight sacrifices, 27, 431; categories of eight, 28, 474; eight qualities, 39, 188 sq.; eight delights, 39, 293; men are liable to eight defects, and the conduct of affairs to four evils, 40, 196 sq.; eight extreme conditions, 40, 210; thrice-eighty sâman-singers, 42, 89, 296 sq.; the year is eighteenfold, 43, 66; eighty means food, 43, 92, 112 n., 161, 223; symbolical significance of eight, 43, 190;—*nine* services to be accomplished by a ruler, 3, 47 sq.; nine branches of kindred, 3, 54, 88; nine virtues, 3, 54 sq., 221; nine divisions of 'the Great Plan,' 3, 137–49; nine, a favourite n. with Yü, 3, 138; nine tribes of the Î, 3, 150; 28, 30; nine regions, 3, 307, 307 n., 310; 39, 304, 304 n., 376; 40, 317; nine to 99,999 diseases, 4, 236–40; categories of nine, 28, 479 sq.; nine openings, and six viscera, of the body, 39, 180; 40, 259 sq.; ninety navigable streams, 42, 74; nine and ninety, 42, 172; sixteen nineties, 44, 288; ninety strongholds of the Dâsas, 46, 263;—*ten* evil ways, 3, 94, 94 n.; Buddha possessed of ten Noble States, ten Powers, understands ten Paths of Kamma, and possesses ten attributes of Arhatship, 13, 141 sq.; categories of ten, 28, 483; ten-ten means

many times, 43, 3; — categories of *twelve*, 28, 484; twelve, 42, 165, 524, 528; all this (universe) consists of *sixteen* parts, 44, 302, 302 n., 384, 410; *twenty-one*, *see* Seven.
Nuns, *see* Ascetics, Bhikkhunîs, *and* *G*aina monks and nuns.
Nü Shang, minister of the Marquis Wû of Wei, 40, 91–3.
Nü Yü, an old man with the complexion of a child, 39, 24; a great Tâoist teacher, 39, 245; 40, 282.
Nû zûdi, *see* Initiation.
***N*ya**, n. of a lake in the world of Brahman, 1, 131, 132 n.
Nyagrodha, converted by Buddha, 19, 241.
Nyagrodha tree, *see* Trees.
Nyarbudi: prayer to Arbudi and N. for help in battle, 42, 123–6, 129, 631–4, 637.
Nyâya, *see* Philosophy.
Nyâya-sûtra, quoted, 38, 428; 48, 162.
Nymphs, *see* Apsaras.

O

Oath(s), false, crime of perjury, 2, 170 sq.; 4, 34, 46, 48 sq.; 5, 207, 207 n.; 9, 234; 33, 91 sq.; 37, 155; witnesses to be charged on o., 2, 247; 25, 273 sq., 273 n.; 33, 91; lady swears by the sun that she is sincere in her affection, 3, 440; formula on taking an o., 4, 49 n.; sin of perjury extends to nine generations, 4, 266 sq.; occurring in the Qur'ân, 6, lxii; make not God the butt of your o., 6, 33; expiation for inconsiderate o., 6, 109 sq.; 9, 290 sq., 290 n.; warning against breaking o., 6, 260 sq.; false o. permissible, 25, 273; prescribed in the Veda, 25, 288, 288 n.; as a means of proof, 33, 97–100, 97 n.; o. for light cases, ordeals for heavy crimes, 33, 100; when to be administered, 33, 225 sq., 314 sq., 337, 352, 359.
Obedience, *see* Sraosha.
Objects, and subjects, their mutual relation, 1, 298 sq.; 34, 3 sq., 104–6, 378 sq.; o. are beyond the senses, 34, 239, 244; mind is superior to the o., 34, 239.
Obsequies, *see* Funeral rites.
Obstacles, *see* Hindrances.
Occult sciences, *see* Divination, Omens, *and* Witchcraft.
Occupations, *see* Caste (*a*), *and* Professions.
Ocean, and rivers produced, 5, 28 sq.; 8, 192; nature and origin of o., lakes, rivers, 5, 41–5, 169–73; explanation of the tides, 5, 44, 44 n., 171 sq., 172 n.; the three-legged ass in the o., 5, 67–9; chief among waters, 8, 89, 346, 354; 36, 55; 41, 75 sq.; dialogue between Kârtavîrya and the O., 8, 293 sq.; this world as far as the o., 8, 296; eight astonishing and curious qualities of the o., 20, 301–5; corpses thrown out by the o., 20, 303; 35, 259; 36, 70 sq., 191, 303; can never be filled, nor exhausted, 20, 304; 36, 120; 39, 323, 375; made salt by a Brâhma*n*a, 25, 398, 398 n.; long-lived through the rivers, invoked to give long life to the new-born child, 29, 294; Vedic Indians acquainted with the o., 32, 57–61; there is only one o., 36, 50; monsters and dragons in the o., 36, 298; the Southern O. the Pool of Heaven, 39, 164, 167; flows round the world from left to right, 41, 301; 43, 169; the cloudy o. is the sky, 43, 235; those who enter a sacrificial session for a year cross an o., 44, 145 sq.; the aerial o., name of the wind, 44, 479. *See also* Parables (*f*), Sea, *and* Vourukasha.
Offences, *see* Crimes, Punishments, *and* Sins.
Offspring, *see* Child, *and* Sons.
Oghati*nn*a, 'saved from the flood,' t.t., a Bhikkhu who has escaped from the five fetters (senses), 10 (i), 86.
Ogres, ogresses, *see* Demons, *and* Pi*s*â*k*as.
Ogress-ridder, a name of the wind, 44, 479.
Ohod, battle of, 6, 61, 61 n., 64 sq., 66 n.
Okkâka, King, slays animals for sacrifices, 10 (ii), 50 sq.; the Sâkya son, an offspring of O., 10 (ii), 186.

O-lâi, put to death by King Wû, 40, 131, 131 n.

Old age: way must be made for an aged man, 7, 203; the reward of him who reveres the aged, 10 (i), 33, 33 n.; the virtuous man is an elder, not he whose head is grey, the latter is called 'old-in-vain,' 10 (i), 64; paying of reverence and apportionment of the best seat and water and food, shall be according to seniority, 20, 191–6; reverence to the aged, 25, 52, 55, 58 sq., 221; 28, 62, 216, 230–2; aged people not to be insulted, 25, 151; king to treat kindly the aged, 25, 322 sq.; feasting and cherishing the aged, 27, 23, 27, 239–44, 240 n., 287 sq., 347 sq., 359–62, 418, 464–70; 28, 124; rules and laws concerning o. a., 27, 66, 78, 228; rules for juniors in their intercourse with elders, 27, 67–71, 73 sq., 76, 80 sq., 96; 28, 439 sq.; centenarians visited by the sovereign, 27, 216; three classes of old men in the college, 27, 385; three grades of o. a., 37, 176, 176 n.;—the devotee works for, attains to release from o. a. and death, 8, 77, 109, 151, 170, 187, 249 sq., 349; the misery of birth, o. a., death, disease, 8, 103, 233, 247, 289, 356; 10 (i), 37; 25, 209, 212; seat of Vish*n*u free from o. a., 8, 194; the cause of birth, death, and o. a., 8, 371. *See also* Death (*b*), Disease, *and* Etiquette.

Old things, used at funeral rites, 44, 439.

Old times, Siddhas belong to, 8, 314.

Om, sacred syllable, meditations on, 1, xxiii-xxvi, 1–17, 133; 15, 281–3, 301, 320–5; 34, lxviii, 171–4; 38, 193 sq., 196–9, 283; 48, 314, 664, 682–5; means ether, 1, xxv; 15, 189; explanation of O. and the Udgîtha, 1, 1 n.; issued from the Vyâh*r*itis, 1, 35; is all this (universe), 1, 35; 15, 50; 34, 169 sq.; O. (yes) is true, Na (no) is untrue, 1, 230; pronounced at the beginning and end of a lecture in the study of the Veda, 2, 48 sq., 183 sq.; 7, 126; Veda recitation is separated from profane speech by O., 2, 48 sq.; is Brahman, 7, 183; 8, 79, 163 n., 282 sq.; 14, 278, 316; 15, 10, 50, 189; 25, 45; K*r*ish*n*a is O., 8, 74, 83, 89; O., tad, sat is Brahman, 8, 120 sq., 121 n.; is the Veda, the essence of the Veda, 8, 163 n., 353; 14, 283, 316; 15, 189; 25, 149, 149 n., 483; is essential in recitation of Sâman hymns, 12, 100, 100 n.; to pronounce O. is the best mode of reciting the Veda, 14, 46; great merit of repeating O., 14, 126; by meditating on it one becomes one with Brahman, 14, 283 sq., 283 n.; 15, 301, 343 sq.; 34, 170; O. is the bow, the Self is the arrow, Brahman is the aim, 15, 36; the pra*n*ava (= O.) a means of perceiving the Self, 15, 237; all ceremonies to begin with O., 15, 337; O. and Vyâh*r*itis accompanying suppressions of the breath, 25, 211; pra*n*ava, the drawing out of the syllable ôm, 26, 88, 88 n.; is truth, 26, 331, 331 n.; is common to the three Vedas, 38, 282 sq.; O. not to be placed in a wrong place, 44, 385; one does not become a Brâhma*n*a by O., 45, 140; meditation with Aum, i.e. O., on the highest Person, 48, 311 sq.; Yama's instruction about O., 48, 362. *See also* Sacred syllables, *and* Udgîtha.

'Omâiy-yat ibn Abi Zalt, prophesied the coming of Mohammed, 6, 159 n.

Omar ibn el *'Hatt*âb converted by Mohammed, 6, xxiv, xlvi; the first to think of editing the Qur'ân, 6, lvii.

Omens (Omina and Portenta), forboding death, 1, 261–3; causing interruption of the study of the Veda, 2, 33–46, 260–4; 7, 124 sq.; 14, 64–7, 208–11; 25, 145–9; 29, 115, 142, 323 sq., 414; 30, 80 sq.; penances for, rites for averting, evil o., 2, 129 sq., 184, 236, 236 n.; 7, 20; 25, 152; 29, 83, 100, 136–40, 224–6, 231, 366 sq., 405 sq., 425; 30, 81, 127 sq., 180–4, 253, 268 sq., 296 sq., 306 sq., 326; 42, 166–8, 262 sq., 474 sq., 555 sq., 564 sq.; the life of the mother of a person who eats at the Tishya ceremony will be shortened, 2, 149; a Snâtaka shall speak about unlucky things

as lucky, 2, 221; auspicious things to be passed with the right turned towards them, 2, 225 sq. and n.; a king must listen to the advice of interpreters of o., 2, 236; crowing of a hen in the morning indicates subversion of the family, 3, 132; evil o., 3, 355; 7, 200–3, 217 sq.; 8, 40, 365 n.; 18, 280, 280 n., 326; appearance of a pair of phoenixes, a good o., 3, 406, 406 n.; King Yû blamed for disregarding evil o., 3, 428; prayers recited at sneezing, yawning, and sighing, 5, 352, 352 n.; 20, 152 sq.; 24, 265 sq.; 37, 452; houses not to be entered from behind, 6, 27, 27 n.; auspicious things and persons (in which Lakshmî resides), 7, 298–301; approaching from the right, a good o., 9, 169; the Bhikkhu must refrain from the interpretation of o., 10 (ii), 60, 176; 11, 196–9; 20, 152; knots as o., 12, 73, 73 n.; 26, 134, 146; tuck of a garment sacred to the Manes, 12, 435, 435 n.; an ascetic shall not live by explaining o., 14, 48; 25, 208; if a man sees himself in the water, he should recite a certain verse, 15, 216 sq.; auspicious and inauspicious lineal figures, *Vol.* 16; the miracles at Buddha's birth good o., not portents, 19, 7 sq.; white cloth spread out for good luck by a woman who had had a miscarriage, 20, 129; knowledge of o., the last of the seventy-two sciences, 22, 282; thunder a dangerous o., 27, 260; rules for wind, thunder, rain, 28, 5; occurring to a wedding procession, 29, 40 sq., 170 sq.; 30, 49 sq., 258, 262; birth of twin-calves inauspicious, 29, 100; 42, 145, 359–61; a weather-prophet not fit to be a witness, 33, 88; interpreters of evil o. termed 'open thieves,' 33, 360; interpretation of o., the business of Brahmans, 35, 247 sq.; danger from ill-omened speaking, 37, 129; prodigies, a ewe lambing and a quail hatching in the house, 40, 107; when the axle of the chariot creaks, that voice is demoniacal, 41, 291; amulets against the consequences of evil o., 42, 82; Rudra invoked against evil o., 42, 156, 619; the black bird defiles the sacrifice, 42, 186; cry of birds a good o., 42, 312; the 'seven *Ri*shis' obscured by a nebulous mass or comet, 42, 390, 563; not looking backwards, 44, 205, 267; good and bad o. from the glowing of the Gharma (pot at the Pravargya), 44, 468, 485; he who puts his faith in prognostics will be born an Asura, 45, 231; lucky and unlucky marks of the body, *see* Body. *See also* Divination, Eclipses, Miracles, *and* Trees.

Ommâiyet ibn '*H*alf, tries to induce Mohammed to give up his poorer followers, 9, 17 n.

Omnipotence depends on the omnipotent ruler being the cause of all created things, 34, 132.

Omniscience, 'all-knowing' denotes death, and is the same as nescience, 21, 118 n.; obtained by a hermit's life, 21, 132 sq., 139 sqq.; Buddha has raised o. in the Arhats, who do not know it, 21, 202; ascribed to the Pradhâna, 34, 46 sq.

Onahâ, Pali t.t., 'obstacles,' 11, 182 n.

Opapâtika, Pali t.t., a being sprung into existence without the intervention of parents, such as the higher devas, 11, 213 sq. n.

Opposites, pairs of, such as heat and cold, pleasure and pain, &c., 8, 48, 48 n., 60, 63, 74 n., 76, 111, 160, 167 n., 168 n., 233, 246 sq., 257, 292, 351, 357 sq., 366, 369 sq., 379. *See also* Pain, *and* Pleasure.

Oracles: the Bhikkhu should not apply himself to the interpretation of sleep and signs, or of the cry of birds, 10 (ii), 176; how to find out the qualities of a girl one intends to wed, 29, 165; 30, 42 sq., 257; what the sacred fires prophesy for the deceased and his son, at the funeral, 29, 242 sq. *See also* Divination.

Oral tradition, as an authority for the true teaching of Buddha, 11, 67–70.

Ordeal(s), by the heated hatchet, to find out a thief, 1, 108 sq., 108 n.; 34, 323 n.; a means of ascertaining the truth, as part of judicial pro-

cedure, 2, 125, 170; 4, 254, 299, 299 n.; 7, xxiv; 33, xiii, 100–21, 120 n., 123 n., 286, 297, 312, 334, 359; 37, 130, 284; 47, xi; by fire and melted metal, by heated gold, 4, xxxviii, xlvii, 371, 371 n.; 5, 199, 199 n., 376, 376 n.; 7, 53, 55, 57–9; 23, 361, 361 n.; 24, 171, 171 n.; 25, 274, 274 n.; 31, 39, 51, 182 n.; 33, 8 n., 9, 108–11, 119 sq., 254–6, 277–80, 318; 37, 187, 324 sq., 368; 42, 294–8; oath taken before the boiling water, 4, 46, 46 n., 49, 49 n.; you can bribe the judge, but not the o., 4, 298 sq. and n.; property seized in consequence of o., 4, 339; Lake Frazdân does not receive what an unrighteous man throws into it, 5, 86; six hot o., 5, 360; 37, 477 sq.; rules regarding the performance of o., 7, 52–61; 25, xcix, ci sq.; 37, 55 sq., 58 sq., 61, 63, 70, 105, 144 sq.; by poison, 7, 53, 55, 60; 18, 102 sq. n.; 33, 114–16, 248, 260 sq.; by water, 7, 53, 55, 59 sq.; 25, 274, 274 n.; 33, 111–14, 256–9, 318; by sacred libation, 7, 53–5, 60 sq.; 33, 116–18, 247 sq., 261–3, 318, 347, 384; by the balance, 7, 53–7; 33, 100–8, 251–4, 317; 44, 45 n.; Rashnu invoked at o., 23, 168–77, 170 n.; calamity befalling a witness within seven days after his evidence has been taken, a proof of guilt, 25, 273; 33, 246; are sometimes made nugatory by artful men, 33, 13; divine proof or o., when to be resorted to, law about o., 33, 30 sq. and n., 96–9, 247–63, 295, 315–19; 37, 403; the o. by grains of rice, 33, 118 sq., 318; by the ploughshare, 33, 316, 318 sq.; by Dharma and Adharma, 33, 319; sacred-twig and heat o., 37, 48; wizards tried by o., 37, 144; Gâthas for an o., 37, 205, 205 n.; ritual of o., 37, 246, 329 sq., 371 sq., 385; thirty-three o. instituted by Zoroaster, 47, 74; blessedness of o., 47, 82; heretics do not establish o., 47, 89; Zoroaster subjected to o. by the archangels, 47, 158 sq. *See also* Idols, Judicial procedure, Oath, *and* Woman (*a*).

Orders, *see* Â*s*ramas.

Ordination (Upasampadâ, Pabbaggâ), of Buddhist friars, 10 (ii), x; 11, 110 sq. n.; 13, 114 sq., 168–70, 208 sq., 228–34; 17, 33 sq., 38 sq.; 35, 42; Parivâsa or Probation, rules before the o. of heretics, 13, 14, 186–91; 17, 270 sq., 384–93, 395 n.; no one must confer the o. on a person without being asked to do so, 13, 170 sq.; he who ordains a person must tell him the four Resources, i. e. the food, clothes, dwellings, and medicines allowed to Bhikkhus, 13, 172–4; a chapter of ten Bhikkhus required for the o. service, 13, 175; only a learned, competent Bhikkhu who has completed at least ten years may confer the o., 13, 175–8; cases of admissibility of o., 13, 182–6; persons who shall not receive the pabbaggâ or upasampadâ o., 13, 191–9, 215–17, 219–25, 230–3; the proper age for receiving o., 13, 201–5, 229; no one shall confer the pabbaggâ o. on a son without his parents' permission, 13, 210; no one shall ordain two novices, 13, 205; exception to this rule, 13, 210 sq.; no animal shall receive the o., and if it has received it, it shall be expelled, 13, 219; newly ordained Bhikkhu should not go out without a companion, 13, 234 sq.; the o. of Bhikkhus who had been temporarily expelled, 13, 236–8; pabbaggâ o. must be performed also during the rainy season, 13, 320 sq.; not to be performed by an incomplete Sa*m*gha, 17, 268 sq.; when unlawful, 17, 277–80; Bhikkhus by whom o. is not to be performed, 17, 337, 340, 372, 386; second o. of a Bhikkhu who, when under probation, threw off the robes, 17, 419, 422–31; after having been trained for two years in the Six Rules, Bhikkhunîs are to ask leave for the upasampadâ o. from both Sa*m*ghas, 20, 324; Bhikkhunîs receive the upasampadâ o. from Bhikkhus, 20, 327; rules for the upasampadâ o. of Bhikkhunîs, 20, 349–55, 360–2; when Buddha attained Bodhi, this was his o., 35, 118; things necessary for admission into the order, 36, 96, 96 n.

Organic beings, four classes of, 38, 126.

Organs, cannot accomplish anything without self-consciousness, 1, 296–8; five o. of perception, five o. of action, the mind belongs to both, and the understanding is the twelfth, 7, 286; 8, 336 sq.; 25, 46 sq.; 38, 81; 48, 577; the eleven o., which are produced from egoism, 8, 258 n., 336; the seven or ten o. as the seven or ten priests, 8, 259 sq., 261, 266 sq.; seven o. (nose, tongue, eye, skin, ear, mind, understanding), are causes of emancipation, 8, 278; seven o., as seven large trees in the 'Forest' Brahman, 8, 285 sq. and n.; o. of the slain victim enter earth, water, sun, quarters, and sky, 8, 290; dialogue between Alarka and the seven o., 8, 296–300; the o. of action, as connected with the self and the objects, and their presiding deities, 8, 338; relation of o., senses, and elements, 8, 349 sq.; the good householder is not thoughtlessly active with his o., 8, 359; restraint of external o. the duty of an ascetic, 8, 364; mystic doctrines of the seven o. of the head and the seven *Ri*shis, 15, 105 sq.; controlling the o. of sensation and action, 25, lxvii, 43, 46–9, 51, 62, 65, 151, 167, 198 sq., 205, 207–9, 207 n., 211 sq., 215, 222, 453, 474 sq., 491, 501; symbolical performance of the five great sacrifices in the o., 25, 132, 132 n.; creation and reabsorption of the o. of the soul do not interfere with the creation, &c., of the elements, 34, liii; 38, 26–8; drawn inward in sleep, 38, 136; the o. of the body and the divinities are non-different, 38, 257; why the gods made the *nose* a partition between the eyes, 43, 369; the *nostrils* are the path of the breath, 44, 263. *See also* **Prâ*n*as**, Psychology, *and* Senses.

Oriental Alphabets, transliteration of, 1, xlviii–lv.

Ormazd, *see* Ahura-Mazda, *and* Aûha*r*ma*zd*.

Orphans, *see* Charity.

Ô*s*dâ*s*târ, *see* Ushidarena.

Othmân ibn Affân, converted by Mohammed, 6, xxiii; the Caliph O. fixed the text of the Qur'ân, 6, lix.

Outcast, *see* Caste (*e*).

Owl, *see* Birds (*b*).

Owokhm, n. of a demon, 5, 132, 132 n.

Ox, sacred to Agni, 12, 297, 297 n., 322; *in the ox is our strength, in the ox is our need; in the ox is our speech, in the ox is our victory; in the ox is our food, in the ox is our clothing; in the ox is tillage, that makes food grow for us*, 23, 247, 247 n.; flesh of o. not to be eaten, 26, 11; cow and o. support everything here, 26, 11; black o. ensures rain, 26, 78; is of Agni's nature, 26, 390; 41, 355, 360; 44, 438; tired out by drawing the cart, 41, 257; ruddy ox-hide, 41, 355; is vigour, 43, 38; Râganya shooting arrows at two o.-hides, 43, 283 n.; is born as a draught (animal), 44, 294; the mourners, returning from the funeral, hold on to the tail of an o., 44, 438, 438 n. *See also* Bull, *and* Parables (*c*).

P

Pabbâ*g*aniya-kamma, t.t., Act of Banishment, *see* Sa*m*gha.

Pabba*gg*â, Pali t.t., *see* Ordination.

Pabba*gg*âsutta, t.c., 10 (ii), 67–9.

Pabba*g*ita, Pali t.t., Sk. Pravragita, one who has given up the world, pilgrim, 10 (i), 89; (ii), x; 11, 146 n.; a careless pilgrim only scatters the dust of his passions more widely, 10 (i), 75. *See also* Bhikkhus.

Pabbata and Nârada rejoice at Buddha, 10 (ii), 94.

Padhânasutta, t.c., 10 (ii), 69–72.

Pa*d*îragtarâspô, grandfather of Zaratû*s*t, 47, 20 sq., 20 n., 34.

Padma, founder of the Âryapadmâ Sâkhâ, 22, 293.

Padmâ, goddess of fortune, 25, 217, 217 n.; lotus-goddess, 49 (i), 40.

Padmabimbyupa*s*obhita, the 53rd Tathâgata, 49 (ii), 6.

Padmagulma, n. of a heavenly region, 45, 57.

Padmakhanda, forest, Buddha retires to, 49 (i), 35.
Padmaprabha: Sâriputra is to be the future Buddha P., 21, 64–9.
Padmaprabha, n. of a Tîrthakara, 22, 280.
Padmasrî, n. of a Bodhisattva Mahâsattva, 21, 4, 399–403, 405, 429.
Padmavrishabhavikrâmin, a future Buddha, 21, 67 sq.
Padmila, disciple of Vagrasena, 22, 288.
Padmôttara, father of Vishnukumâra, 45, 86, 86 n.
Padramgôs, to be corrected to Ptolemêôs, 37, xlvi sq.
Paduma, *see* Hells (*a*).
Paêsanghanu, the holy maid, 23, 225.
Paêshatah Paitisrîra, n.p., 23, 203, 213, 216.
Paêsis, a n. of the Drug, 23, 308.
Paêtrasp, n.p., 47, 34.
Pagâpati, Pali for Pragâpati, q. v.
Paggota, king of Uggenî, cured by Gîvaka, the physician, 17, 186–90.
Paggusan, *see* Rainy Season.
Pahlavas, mentioned in Manu-smriti, 25, cxiv–cxvii; degraded Kshatriyas, 25, 412, 412 sq. n.
Pahlavi, inscriptions deciphered, 4, xxi; language, writing and pronunciation, 5, xi–xxii; 18, xx–xxii; to be taught to priests only, 24, 360.
Pahlavi texts, and Avesta, 5, ix–xi; their date, 5, xlvi n.; 18, xxvii sq., 297 sq. n.; their extent, and how far they represent the mediaeval Zoroastrianism, 5, lxvii sq.; difficulty of translating them, 5, lxx sq.; Nîrangistân, 'code of religious formulas,' 5, 206, 206 n., 227.
Pâi, duke of, contended for Khû, which led to his extinction, 39, 380.
Pâi = Ʒze-shang, q. v.
Paigavana, *see* Sudâs P.
Paila, worshipped at the Tarpana, 29, 122, 149, 220.
Pâi-lî Hsî, a cattle-feeder, and minister to Mû of Khin, 40, 50, 50 n., 89.
Pain, and pleasure alike to the devotee, 8, 110; threefold source of p., 8, 159, 159 n.; pleasure and p. inconstant, 8, 245; the effect of attachment, 8, 250, 250 n.; of the quality of passion, 8, 292 n., 301 n.; mankind pierced by the arrow of p., 10 (ii), 55; origin of p., 10 (ii), 193–5; by destruction of the Âsavas there is an end of all p., 11, 300, 307; the chain of cause and effect, cause and end of p., 35, 79, 82 sq.; destruction of p. by Nirvâna, 35, 106 sq.; removal of p. the aim of renunciation, 35, 124; caused not only by Karman, 35, 191–5; Buddha finds out the origin and stopping of p., 49 (i), 152–5; five worldly sufferings (birth, old age, sickness, death, parting), 49 (ii), 169, 169 n. *See also* Opposites, Pleasure, *and* Truths (the four noble).
Paiṅgi, worshipped at the Tarpana, 30, 245, 245 n.
Paiṅgîputra, n. of a teacher, 15, 224 n.
Paiṅgi-rahasya Brâhmana, t.w., 34, 122.
Paiṅgi-upanishad, t.w., 34, xxxv n., 161.
Paiṅgya, *see* Madhuka P.
Pairika, a female demon, symbolizes idolatry, 4, 6; spell against the P., 4, 145 sq., 145 n.; the P. Knãthaiti, 4, 211; put to flight by sacrifices, 31, 257; the waters worshipped for the defeat of the cheat P., 31, 322; —*generally plur.*: the fire kills Yâtus and P., 4, 115; spell against Yâtus, P., and Gainis, 4, 229, 235, 241; Yâtus and P., 23, 16, 24, 26, 43, 50, 57, 59, 65 sq., 86, 97, 105, 128, 134, 161, 223, 232, 247, 252, 292 sq.; in the shape of shooting-stars, afflicted by Tistrya, 23, 95 sq., 95 n., 104; Mithra, the withstander of the P., 23, 126; Fravashis invoked against P., 23, 208; Pitaona, attended by many P., killed by Keresâspa, 23, 296.
Pairistîra, n.p., 23, 210, 210 n.
Pairi-urvaêsm, n. of a demon, 5, 132, 132 n.
Pairs, of every species, created, 8, 244; such as good and evil, day and night, 8, 276 sq.; of opposites, *see* Opposites.
Paitidrâtha, n.p., 23, 210.
Paîtirâsp (Paîtiraspô), ancestor of

Zoroaster, 5, 140 sq., 140 n., 145; 47, 140.
Paitisha, the most Daêva-like amongst the Daêvas, 4, 224, 224 n.
Paitishahya, worshipped, 31, 198, 205, 210, 216, 220, 224, 335, 338, 368, 370, 372.
Paityarsvant, n.p., 23, 210.
Pâka, the Daitya, 22, 222.
Pâkayagña, son of Idâ, n. of a teacher, 30, 39.
Pâkayagña, t.t., *see* Sacrifice (*i*).
Pâkîna-vamsa-dâya, Buddha at, 17, 309–12.
Pâkittiya, Pali t.t., *see* Sins (*b*).
Pakkeka-Buddha, is worthy of a dâgaba, 11, 93 sq., 93 n. *See also* Buddha (*j*), *and* Holy persons.
Pakudha-Kakkâyana, n. of a teacher, 10 (ii), xii, 86 sq.; 11, 106; 35, 8; an Arhat possessed of Iddhi, 20, 79; his materialistic philosophy, 45, xxiv sq.
Palâgala, t.t., courier of a king, 41, 64.
Pâlâgalî, t.t., a king's fourth wife, of low caste, 44, 313 n., 349, 387.
Palâsa tree, *see* Trees.
Pali, old Vedic forms in, 10 (ii), xi sq.; P. Suttas, *see* Suttas, *and* Tipitaka.
Pâlita, a merchant, father of Samudrapâla, 45, 108.
Palmistry, *see* Divination.
Pâmsava, *see* Asat P.
Păn, superintendent of officers' registries, 27, 154; or Kung-shû Zo, 27, 184, 184 n.
Pândava, n. of a mountain at Râgagriha, 10 (ii), 68; 49 (i), 106.
Pândavas, and Kauravas, battle of, 8, 2 sq., 37 sq.; 19, 330; Buddha like the P. in heroism, 49 (i), 106.
Pandita, Buddha's definition of a, 10 (ii), 90 sq.
Pându, Arguna, son of, 8, 229 sq., 255; incurred death by having intercourse with his wife, 49 (i), 45.
Panduka, one of the *Kh*abbaggiya-Bhikkhus, 17, 329 sqq., 339, 341 sq.
Pândubhadra, disciple of Sambhûtavigaya, 22, 289.
Păng 3û, the long-lived, 39, 146, 364.
Pânini, his date, 8, 33; 12, xxxv–xxxix; and the Vaiyâkaranas, 25, 1 sq.; the sûtras of P., and the Paribhâshâs, 30, 312; quoted, 38, 428; 48, 69, 778.
Panis, Agni concealed by the, 12, 245.
Paññitabhûmi, Mahâvîra at, 22, 264.
Pañkadasî, quoted, 34, xcii.
Pañkaganâh, five-people, 34, xl, 257–62, 258 n. *See* Five-people.
Pañkâgnividyâ, knowledge of the five fires, a text, so called, 1, 274; 34, lxxxiii, cviii; 38, 187. *See* Fire.
Pañkâlakanda, n. of a teacher, 1, 255.
Pañkâlas, or Pâñkâlas, Svetaketu in the assembly of, 1, 76; Kurus and P. in Vedic literature, 7, xv sq.; 12, xli–xliii, xlii n.; Brâhmanas of the Kurus and P., 15, 121, 145; Pravâhana Gaivali in the settlement of the P., 15, 204; fight in the van of the battle, 25, 247, 247 n.; kings of P., 44, 397, 400; 45, 58, 60 sq.; were formerly called Krivis, 44, 397 sq.; enormous offering-gifts received by the Brâhmanas of the P., 44, 398. *See also* Kuru-Pañkâlas.
Pan-kăng, removes the capital from the north of the Ho to Yin on the south of it, 3, 103–12.
Pâñkarâtra, the followers of the, i. e. the Bhâgavatas, 34, 442; system of P. explained in the Mahâbhârata, 48, 528 sq.; declared by Nârâyana, 48, 529–31; Sâṅkhya, Yoga, Vedas, and Âranyakas together are called P., 48, 530. *See also* Bhâgavatas.
Pañkarâtra-sâstra, 'a great Upanishad,' the work of Vâsudeva himself, 48, 528.
Pañkarâtra-tantra, sets forth the Bhâgavata theory, is authoritative for the Vedântin, 48, 524–31.
Pañkasikha, Kapila, and Âsuri, 15, xl; a heavenly being, converted by Buddha, 19, 242; a Smriti writer, 34, 291 n.
Pañkatantra, and Mahâbhârata, 8, 139, 139 n.
Pañkavimsa-brâhmana, *see* Tândya-mahâbrâhmana.
Pâñki, n. of a teacher, 12, 61, 61 n., 300.
Pannapattiyâ, *see* Pûrnapatrikâ.
Pantheism: Vishnu as all-god, 7, 287–91, 298–301; Vaipulya doctrine of Buddhism is pure p., 19, xi.

Pâo-hăng, *see* Î Yin.
Pâo-hsî=Fû-hsî, q. v.
Pâo Shû-yâ, friend of Kwan *K*ung, 40, 101 sq., 101 n.
Pâo-sze, female favourite of Nieh, 3, 265.
Pao-yun, translator of the Fo-pen-hing-king, 19, xxviii.
Pâo 3iâo, committed suicide, 40, 173, 173 n.
Pao-3ze, stood till he was dried up, 40, 180.
Pâpâ, Mahâvîra died at, 22, 264, 269.
Pâpak, Ardashîr son of, 5, 137, 151.
Papa*ñk*a, Pali t.t., delusion, 10 (ii), 175.
Para Â*t*nâra, Kausalya king, offered a horse-sacrifice, 44, 397.
Parâbhavasutta, t.c., 10 (ii), 17-19.
Parables (Allegories, Similes).

(*a*) Their occurrence in general.
(*b*) P. and similes referring to agriculture.
(*c*) P. and similes referring to animals.
(*d*) The king in p. and similes.
(*e*) Plants (and trees) in p. and similes.
(*f*) Other p. and similes arranged alphabetically according to catchwords.

(*a*) THEIR OCCURRENCE IN GENERAL.
P. illustrating the rewards of charity, 6, 41 sq.; struck out by God, 6, 234, 241, 243 sq., 258; 9, 78, 185; illustrating the soul's entrance into the foetus, 8, 242; the desert of life, and the forest of Brahman, 8, 284-8; Buddha teaches by p., for men are ready to catch the meaning of what is taught under the shape of p., 21, 129; p. illustrating Buddha's preaching, and his attitude towards the good and the wicked, 35, 235-7; a wife conciliates her husband with what belongs to him—a royal barber pleases a king with a golden comb belonging to the king—a novice serves his teacher with alms belonging to the teacher—so Buddha is pleased by parables preached by himself, 35, 302; illustrating the greatness of Nirvâ*n*a, 36, 178-80, 189-95; showing the advantages of keeping the vows, 36, 255-61; [sixty-seven (and thirty-eight) similes of Arhatship, 36, 275-373; illustrating the antagonism between Tâoism and knowledge, 39, 30; illustrating the advantage of being useless, 39, 132, 217-22; allegory of 'the State of Established Virtue,' 40, 30 sq.; list of narratives, apologues, and stories in the writings of *K*wang-3ze, 40, 298-310; showing the difficulty of performing the duties of a monk, 45, 92 sq.; illustrating the principal *G*aina doctrines, 45, 123-8.

(*b*) P. AND SIMILES REFERRING TO AGRICULTURE.
Simile of the barley reapers to illustrate the use of reasoning and wisdom, 35, 51; the farmer who stops ploughing and sowing is aware that his granary is not filled—so he who is not to be reborn, is aware of the fact, 35, 65 sq.; ripe grain is guarded from water, but when it is green, it is given water (no remedy for one whose allotted time has come to an end), 35, 215; the Karumbhaka grass does not disgrace the healthy rice (backsliders not the religion of Buddha), 36, 73 sq.; some men get the seed to grow without a fence, others have to make a fence (some become Arhats at once, others only after recitation, &c.), 36, 93; the Kumudabha*nd*ikâ corn grows quickly, the much more valuable rice takes six months to grow (virtue lasts longer than vice), 36, 148 sq.; the crop dying for want of water, or destroyed by worms, or by a hail-storm (comp. premature death of men), 36, 171-3; the husbandman removes weeds, &c., before he ploughs and sows (the vows taken before attaining to Nirvâ*n*a), 36, 269 sq.

(*c*) P. AND SIMILES REFERRING TO ANIMALS.
Jews compared to an *ass* bearing books, 9, 283; the man who defiled an ass, because it was his own, 24, 189 sq.; the *bee* and the honey—individual soul and fruit in future birth, 8, 188, 188 n., 190; understanding and egoism, the two *birds*, 8, 371, 371 n.; two birds, inseparable friends, cling to the same tree, 15, 38, 251; the two birds on the

tall tree and the low shrub, and their shadows, 35, 127 sq.; an owl, when a phoenix went passing overhead, looked up to it and gave an angry scream, 39, 391; how a certain ruler tries to treat a bird like a man with feasts and music, 40, 8 sq., 26; a mantis pounces on a cicada, a large bird takes its opportunity to secure them both, *K*wang-ʒze might have shot the bird, but lets it alone, 40, 39–41; men abandoning worldly pleasures compared to birds, 45, 67 sq.; the life of monks like the life of pigeons, 45, 91 sq.; the crane produced from an egg, and the egg produced from a crane: the same with desire and delusion, 45, 185; birds of prey carrying off young birds: so unprincipled men will seduce a novice, 45, 324; a man taking a cripple on his cart, does a meritorious act, though he puts the *bullocks* to pain (causing sorrow by making gifts), 36, 116 sq.; the behaviour of bad bullocks put before a car compared to the behaviour of bad pupils, 45, 149–52; Buddha persuaded by the p. of the seed and of the *calf* to forgive Sâriputta and Moggallâna, 35, 301 sq.; the misbelievers shall not enter into Paradise until a *camel* shall pass into a needle's eye, 6, 142; the city guard and the *cat*, 11, 14; story of the hunchback catching *cicadas* on the point of a rod, 40, 14 sq. and n.; heretics compared to *deer* who dread safe places, but are not afraid of traps, 45, 240 sq.; the boy who, finding the Black *Dragon* asleep, takes a pearl from under his chin, 40, 211; young *elephants* who imitate the old ones, Devadatta emulating Buddha, 20, 260 sq.; *see also* Elephants; story of the goby *fish* who wanted a pint of water and is promised a stream when it will be too late, 40, 133; story of the scion of Zăn who caught the huge fish, after fishing for a whole year in the Eastern Sea, 40, 133 sq.; men abandoning worldly pleasures—as the fish Rohita breaks through a weak net, as the herons fly through the air, 45, 66; the *frog* of the dilapidated well, bragging before the turtle of the Eastern Sea, 39, 388 sq.; *gnat* and Udumbara tree, 8, 374, 379; the *hen* and her chickens, 11, 233, 233 n.; the hen and the egg—an endless series, 35, 80; hens without a cock, 39, 263, 263 n.; Milinda compares himself to a *lion* put in a golden cage, 35, 135; simile of lion, 36, 338–40; a keeper of *monkeys* proposes to give them in the morning three and in the evening four measures: they are angry; he gives them in the morning four and in the evening three: they are satisfied, 39, 185; the monkey dressed up as a duke, 39, 354; the monkey happy among the branches of high trees, but distressed among prickly trees and thorns, 40, 36 sq.; a starved *ox* might be tied up, an excited ox will escape (the ordinary man, and the Arahat), 36, 76 sq.; how the clever cook of King Wăn-hui cuts up an ox, 39, 130, 198–200; *pigs* sucking at their dead mother, 39, 230; *rams* butting together, 35, 92 sq.; the ram fed with rice to be killed: so the ignorant man sins and enjoys pleasures, to gain hell, 45, 27 sq.; the *snail* with two horns on which are the kingdoms called Provocation and Stupidity, 40, 119 sq.; worldly pleasures abandoned—as a *snake* casts off the slough, 10 (ii), 1–3; 45, 66, 98, 253; the man whom a poisonous snake approaches even for the sake of curing him, is yet afraid of it—so beings in hell are afraid of death, 35, 212; the man who kills a serpent by destroying an anthill, 35, 234 sq.; the effect of snake poison removed by a snake charmer (comp. premature death), 36, 168 sq.; as the snake gathers dust (both on and in its body): so the fool accumulates sins by acts and thoughts, 45, 21; the *spider's* house, 9, 121; the spider with its thread (everything coming from the Self), 15, 105; the Sannyâsin draws in his senses, as a *tortoise* his limbs, 8, 342, 366; the purblind tortoise and the attainment of the condition of a human being, 35, 291 sq.;—the *khwei* desires to be like the *millipede*, the millipede like the *serpent*, the

serpent like the wind, 39, 148, 384 sq.; *mosquito* employed to carry a mountain, a *millipede* to gallop as fast as the Ho runs, 39, 389; using a carriage and horses to convey a *mouse*, trying to delight a *quail* with the music of bells and drums, 40, 26; why *foxes* and *leopards* are killed, 40, 29. *See also* Animals (*k*).

(*d*) THE KING IN P. AND SIMILES.

Parable of the king who rewards his warriors, bestowing at last his crown jewel on the most deserving —just as Buddha rewards those who struggle for him, keeping the crown jewel (omniscience) for the last, 21, xxx, 274–80; the king, his treasurer, and his confidential adviser—to illustrate mindfulness, 35, 59 sq.; the whole army with the king as its chief—meditation the summit of all good qualities, 35, 60 sq.; the king and his servant, 35, 76, 93; 36, 53 sq.; the king's treasurer, 35, 94; the king who tells his sons they might abandon parts of the empire, in order to test them, 35, 203; the criminal sent for by the king to be released is yet in fear of the king—so beings in hell are afraid of death, 35, 212; the low man who were to gain a kingdom would soon be deprived of it (unworthy members of the Order return to the lower state), 36, 69 sq., 262 sq.; a low man becoming king cannot bear the dignity (layman becoming an Arhat dies), 36, 97 sq.; a king raises a tax and thereout bestows a gift (comp. Vessantara's gift causing sorrow), 36, 117 sq.; the bliss of sovranty and the previous sufferings in war (comp. the bliss of Nirvâ*n*a and the previous pain incurred by the quest of Nirvâ*n*a), 36, 183 sq.; he who, being worthy, takes the vows, compared to a king, 36, 265 sq.; a prince who wants to escape is helped by his servant threatening him with a switch, 40, 321; the king who lost his kingdom by eating a mango fruit: worldly pleasures and divine life, 45, 28 sq.; the king's son in the golden dungeon, 49 (ii), 63 sq.

(*e*) PLANTS (AND TREES) IN P. AND SIMILES.

Life like the plants that spring up and perish, 9, 19; the minds of men compared with the movements of a giant *bambû*, 35, 155–8; a *jasmine* bush is not disgraced by the fallen-off flowers (Buddha's religion not by backsliders), 36, 73; water fallen on a *lotus* flows away, 8, 289, 374, 379; 36, 70; the beings of this world compared to the different lotuses in a pond, 13, 88; the lotus flower produced in mud and water, but does not resemble the mud or water, 35, 117; the world a lotus-pool, the people lotuses, 45, 335–8, 355; as the soft fibres are extracted from the *Muñga grass*, so is the devotee's self extracted from the body, 8, 249; *sandal wood* is not disgraced by a portion of it being rotten (Buddha's religion not by backsliders), 36, 74; a good word like a good *tree* whose root is firm and whose branches are in the sky: a bad word like a felled tree, 6, 241; worldly life represented as a great tree, which is eternal, and the seed of which is the Brahman, 8, 313, 370 sq.; the Creator compared to an orchard-owner, 24, 134–6; worshippers of Buddha compared with trees, 35, 151; a tree may be in full fruit, yet the fruits cannot be enjoyed until they have fallen (Buddha is omniscient, yet reflects), 35, 161 sq.; the trunk of a mighty tree is not shaken, though the branches may wave (the body, but not the mind of an Arahat suffers), 36, 77; a fruit from a high tree fetched by means of Iddhi (Arhatship attained at once), 36, 93 sq.; of the large calabash, the salve, and the large Ailantus tree, showing that nothing is really useless, 39, 128, 172–5; the *Vanishing Root* which makes men invisible (the magic power of love), 35, 281.

(*f*) OTHER P. AND SIMILES ARRANGED ALPHABETICALLY ACCORDING TO CATCHWORDS.

The *acrobat* first clears the ground before he shows his tricks—so is good conduct the basis of all good

qualities, 35, 53; sticks, &c., cannot stand in the *air* (conversion cannot take place without a cause), 36, 79 sq.; untrained *archers* miss the mark, so fools cannot realize the religion of Buddha, 36, 71 sq.; training in archery comp. training for Nirvâ*n*a, 36, 253 sq., 369–72; the *architect* of a town begins by clearing the site—the recluse by good conduct, 35, 53; Buddha an a., his doctrine a city he has built, 36, 208–43; the small *army* breaking up a large one—perseverance, 35, 57; the various parts of an a. working for the same end—so all the five good qualities, 35, 62; thinking powers of the Buddhas like an excellent *arrow*, discharged by a powerful man on a fine stuff, 35, 159; the a. that does not reach its aim (comp. premature death), 36, 169; a man in whose body sticks an a., does not extricate it, and the arrow goes deeper and deeper in the flesh: so the deceitful man who does not confess his sin, 45, 362; heretics, *blind* men led by the blind, 11, 173 sq. and n.; 15, 8, 32, 343; 45, 241 sq., 295; the blind-born man who is first cured, then believes he sees and knows everything, but is shown that he knows nothing, finally acquires transcendent knowledge—so the creatures blind with infatuation are led to Nirvâ*n*a, 21, xxix, 129–41; blind man who had caught hold of the ox's tail, 34, 55; a blind man, though he have a light, does not see: the heretics, 45, 317; good deeds are like the *boat* carrying stones, 35, 124; the b. that can bear only one man (the world can bear only one Tathâgata), 36, 48; pushing along a b. on the dry land, 39, 353; a b. colliding with an empty vessel, 40, 31; a blind-born man getting into a leaky b. is drowned—so are heretics whirled round in the Sa*m*sâra, 45, 243, 314; the *burglar* caught in the breach of the wall by his own work: a man cannot escape the effect of Karman, 45, 18; the *carpenter*, 35, 96; one *cart* following the other (habit), 35, 91; two full c., the load of one piled up on the other (so would the world be with two Buddhas), 36, 49; if two smashed cars were to unite there would be at least one fit for driving, 44, 198; the man in a *cave*, protected from rain, 35, 281 sq.; simile of the *chariot* yoked with vicious horses (senses), 1, 234; 8, 187; 15, 241; 34, 121, 239 sq., 244, 246; 48, 355 sq., 370; going on foot, and driving in a carriage (progress of the man of understanding and the man devoid of it), 8, 380–2; simile of the ch. and its parts, 35, 43 sq.; the body the chariot, the mind the *charioteer*, the organs the reins, &c., 1, 142 n.; 8, 338 n., 386; 15, 12 sq., 292–5, 301; 48, 638 sq.; as the ch. who leaves the smooth highway repents — so the fool who transgresses the Law, 35, 102 sq.; 45, 22; Pirit compared with a mother who chastises her *child*, 35, 218 sq.; a mother brings forth the ch. that is already there (Buddha brings to light the teaching of former Buddhas), 36, 15; toys given to *children* before a task is appointed to each of them, 36, 32 sq.; parents and ch. (Buddha and the Order), 36, 52 sq.; the *child-wife* who, when grown up, is carried off by another; the latter punished, for the grown-up girl is derived from the child (Karman), 35, 74; a *circle* —illustrating the endlessness of the past, 35, 80; the *city* which denied God's favours, 6, 262; the embodied spirit within the c. with nine gates, 8, 65, 65 n., 317 sq.; 15, 247; the c. with one gate, 35, 90 sq.; the guardian of a c., 35, 95; a man condemned to *death*, but let off with having his hand or foot cut off, 35, 166 sq.; six brothers are sentenced to d., one is spared, the father rejoices: the householder who abstains from slaughter of animals as he cannot spare the six kinds of living beings, 45, 421 sq., 421 n., 424; the *copper vessel* beaten into shape, 35, 96; as a *coward* takes to flight in battle, so the unworthy recoils from the restraints of Buddha's religion, 36, 72; *cymbals* clashing together, 35, 93; the man escaped from a spot

filthy with *dirt* (Nirvâ*n*a the clean place), 36, 198; the sage under the influence of his heavenly constitution: compared to the *drunkard* who is unconscious of any injury under the influence of drink, 40, 13 sq.; Arahats compared with the *Earth* who is not afraid of people digging into it, &c., 35, 299; it is not the fault of the e., if a man falls by running with too great a haste (austerities overdone), 35, 61 sq.; Buddha compared with the e., 35, 150 sq., 258 sq.; the man who is satiated cannot *eat* any more (the world cannot bear more than one Buddha), 36, 48 sq.; yolk and *egg*-shell dependent one on the other—so name and form, 35, 76 sq.; the hard things eaten by females are destroyed, but not the *embryo* in their womb, 35, 104 sq.; the man who has freed himself from *enemies* (realization of Nirvâ*n*a), 36, 197 sq.; parable of the burning house, to exemplify the skill of the good *father* (Buddha) in saving his children, 21, xxix, 72–90; the parable of the rich f. whose son has gone astray and become poor and wretched; how the f. gradually leads him back to self-respect and happiness—just as the wise f. Buddha, 21, 98–115; 36, 52 sq.; the young man who claims to be the f. of the centenarian—Buddha and the Bodhisattvas, 21, 294 sq., 297; parable of the *fire*, and of the storm-cloud, 6, 3; by abandoning fancies he obtains Nirvâ*n*a, like f. devoid of fuel, 8, 247; the sparks coming from the f. (everything coming from the Self), 15, 105; the custom of putting up five pots full of water as a fire-extinguishing apparatus; sinfulness extinguished by the five organs of moral sense, 35, 67 sq.; of the f. left burning, which sets the neighbour's field on fire, and the lamp which sets the village on fire—illustrations of Karman, 35, 72 sq.; f. and flames, 35, 114; he who seizes a fiery mass of metal intentionally is less burnt than he who seizes it inadvertently, 35, 129; Buddha compared to a f. set alight and gone out, 35, 146 sq.; discourse on the simile of the burning f., 35, 234; f. cannot burn in water (conversion cannot take place without a cause), 36, 80; f. goes out by the exhaustion of the fuel, or by a rain shower (premature death), 36, 166 sq.; the world consumed by the f. of love and hatred—as by a conflagration of a forest animals are burned, 45, 67; a pot filled with lac will melt in the f.: so monks are lost through intercourse with women, 45, 274 sq.; a starving man turning away from a largesse of *food* (backsliders turning away from the largesse offered by Buddha), 36, 65 sq., 68; it is not the fault of the f. if a man dies from indigestion (laymanship, not Arhatship, at fault, if the layman dies by becoming an Arhat), 36, 97; the seed developing *fruit*, and seed taken from the fruit—an endless series, 35, 79, 82; Karman illustrated by various seeds producing all kinds of f., 35, 100 sq., 113, 120; f. fall in fullness of time, or out of season (death), 36, 162 sq.; Buddhism compared to a mighty *furnace* with a continual supply of fuel, 35, 188; the man escaped from a blazing fiery f. (Nirvâ*n*a the cool place), 36, 196 sq., 199; the *gambler* who hazards all dice, 35, 103; as the gamester throws down his dice, so Varu*n*a lays down his laws, 42, 88, 391; a clever gambler casts K*ri*ta, not other dice: so the sage adopts the Law of the Saviour, 45, 256; the man who has a *gem* bound within his garment, and does not know it—like some Arhats, 21, 201–4; faith, illustrated by the water-cleansing magic g., 35, 54 sq.; there is no need of polishing a pure diamond g. (so no restraint for the Buddhas), 36, 7; the lost g. of sovranty (the teaching of former Buddhas), 36, 14 sq.; renunciation like the wish-conferring g., 36, 58 sq.; a wish-conferring g. is not disgraced by a roughness on one side (Buddhism not by backsliders), 36, 74; Nirvâ*n*a compared with the *gods* called 'Formless Ones,' 36, 186 sq.; *guide*

in the woods who does not know the way (false philosopher), 45, 241; peeping at the *heavens* through a tube, aiming at the earth with an awl, 39, 389; some men do a business themselves, others need *help* (some become Arhats at once, others by means of recitation, &c.), 36, 94; a man may go up the *Himâlaya*, but cannot bring the Himâlaya here (Nirvâ*n*a), 36, 105; the man thrown into a trough of *honey*, 35, 88; mind without senses is like a *house* without a door, 8, 270; the world a h. on fire, 19, 53, 103; 45, 90 sq.; 49 (i), 54; a falling h. supported by a prop—thus perseverance is a support, 35, 57; the apex the top of the h.—meditation, 35, 60; hs., trees and plants, pots, music, fire, images—do not spring up suddenly, but gradually, 35, 83–6; life compared with a redhot *iron*, which cannot be taken hold of in any place, 36, 198 sq.; if you do not give up false doctrines you will repent of it, as the man did who carried iron believing it to be silver, 45, 269; final beatitude, an *island* in the sea of Sa*m*sâra, 45, 313; people wandering through a dense forest to the *Isle of Jewels*, and their guide who makes a magic city appear to give them some repose—so Buddha with fancied and real Nirvâ*n*a, 21, 181–3, 187–9; men setting out on a *journey* take provisions: why not take provisions on the journey to the world beyond, 4, 378 sq.; the man who for the sake of one *Kâkinî* loses a thousand Kârshâpa*n*as: worldly pleasures and divine life, 45, 28 sq.; the bliss of *knowledge* and the inconvenience undergone in the pursuit thereof, 36, 184 sq.; teacher full of wisdom compared to a *lake* full of water, 22, 49; a *lamp* lighting up a house—so is wisdom, 35, 62 sq., 67; the l. which burns the night through is the same and yet not the same in the three watches of the night—so is the continuity of a person, 35, 64; the letter written, when the l. is lit, remains after the lamp is extinguished: reasoning ceases, and knowledge remains, 35, 67; a man lighting a l. from another l., 35, 111; l. gives light, but remains luminous itself (Self compared with it), 48, 59; as one goes into a dark place with a *light*, so those who wish for the supreme go with the light of knowledge, 8, 379 sq.; a *lost thing* found—a jungle cleared—Buddha rediscovers the lost teaching of the Buddhas, 36, 15; the man in *love* with a woman whom he does not know, 11, 175 sq.; man compared to a *lute*, 1, 263 sq.; the lute the strings of which are too much stretched or too loose, 17, 8; the baby and the grown-up *man* are the same, and yet not the same individual—compare the continuity of a person when reborn, 35, 63; the sick man is yet subject to fear of *medical* instruments, &c. (so beings in hell are in fear of death), 35, 211 sq.; a sick man wants emetics, &c. (so for the wicked only restraint in food is enjoined, not for the Buddhas), 36, 7; oil given to patients before purges are administered, 36, 33; the parable of the Three *Merchants*, each travelling with his capital: the capital is human life, the gain is heaven, 45, xlii, 29 sq.; the *milk* is not the same, and yet the same, as the curds, the butter, and the ghee—comp. the continuity of a person, 35, 65, 75; the *mirror*—the body, darkness—sleep, light—the mind, 36, 158, 160; Buddhism compared to a stainless m. that is constantly polished, 35, 189; *mother-of-pearl* mistaken for silver, 34, 4 n., 5, 43; as a *needle* with its thread is not lost, so the soul possessing the sacred lore is not lost in the Sa*m*sâra, 45, 170; as the *ocean* remains unmoved, though all waters enter and fill it, so the devotee, 8, 51; as rivers run into the o., 8, 95, 307; the o. of this world, 8, 100, 179, 179 n., 245, 343; like billows in the o., 8, 388; the eight qualities of the o., and the eight qualities of the Sa*m*gha, 20, 301–5; 35, 131–4, 259; 36, 70 sq.; the man who crosses the shallow brook, but hesitates before the mighty o. (Pa*kk*eka-Buddhas),

35, 158 sq.; a man can cross the o., but cannot bring the other shore here (Nirvâ*n*a realized, but no cause), 36, 105; Nirvâ*n*a as unfathomable as the sea, 36, 186 sq.; drop of water on the blade of grass, and the o.: as human compared with divine pleasures, 45, 30 sq.; Buddha compared to a *physician*, 21, 304–6, 309; 35, 116, 165, 168 sq., 240; the ph. with the five kinds of drugs, 35, 68 sq.; the sick man who goes to a skilled ph. but will not allow himself to be cured (backsliders), 36, 64 sq., 67 sq.; training of a ph., comp. training for Nirvâ*n*a, 36, 254 sq.; the man rescued from a *pit* full of dead bodies (Nirvâ*n*a), 36, 197; the man preparing *poisons*, and the man preparing ghee, honey, &c., 35, 94 sq.; he who eats poison without knowing it, dies; who walks into fire unawares, is burnt; a man bitten by a snake unawares, is killed;—an unconscious sin prevents conversion, 36, 80 sq.; the *potter* makes different pots out of the same clay, so there are disciples, Pratyeka-Buddhas, and Bodhisattvas, though there is only one Buddha-vehicle, 21, 129, 136; the *proud man's garden* destroyed while that of the humble man flourished, 9, 18 sq.; the *quarrel* between the sense-organs, 1, 72–4, 72 n., 290; 8, 207, 268–70; 15, 202 sq., 274; the *rain* pouring down on all plants, exemplifying Buddha's preaching for the benefit of all creatures, 21, xxix, 119–27; the man who has lost his way finds a *refuge* at last (Nirvâ*n*a), 36, 200; the *rich man* is not poor, though he may not have food ready in his house at any time (Buddha, though omniscient, reflects), 35, 161; the *river* of which the senses are the banks, the agitation of mind the waters, and delusion the reservoir, 8, 344; the man praying to the further bank of a r. to come over, 11, 178–80; the man who wants to cross a r. while bound by a strong chain, or covering himself up with a veil, 11, 180–2; the brave man who jumps over the over-flowing brook—illustration of faith, 35, 56 sq.; *robbers* lying in ambush, caught by the king (Buddha and Mâra), 35, 222 sq.; Time or Days (Nights) represented as r., 45, 63–5; the emancipated Bhikkhu compared to a *rock* unshaken by wind and rain, 17, 12 sq.; seed cannot grow on a slab of r. (conversion of a sinful layman impossible), 36, 79; a blade of grass broken by a heavy r. placed on it (layman dies by becoming an Arhat), 36, 97; the penumbrae and the *shadow*, 39, 196 sq.; 40, 147; the man who tried to run away from his sh., 40, 197; *shipowner* who has become wealthy, goes to distant countries (thirteen vows, preparation for future bliss), 36, 269; of the *slave*, and of the dumb man, 6, 258; Buddha compared with the *sound* of a drum that has died away, 35, 149; the s. of a brazen vessel interrupted, if the vessel is touched (comp. premature death), 36, 170 sq.; the man making a *staircase* up to something unknown, 11, 177; four obstructions of the *sun* and moon, and four stains by which Sama*n*as and Brâhmans are affected, 20, 389; as s. and moon shine upon all men, so is Buddha impartial in educating all creatures, 21, 128, 136; the sun—the body, the veil of fog—sleep, the rays—the mind, 36, 160; the parable of the three *swords* told by *K*wang-ȝze, 40, 189–91; the *syrup* or sauce with its ingredients, 35, 97 sq.; it is not the fault of the bathing *tank* (Buddha's doctrine) if the dirty man turns away without bathing in it, 36, 63 sq., 66 sq.; a large t., when its supply of water has been stopped, gradually dries up: so is the Karman of a monk annihilated by austerities, 45, 174; relation of senses and mind is like that of *teacher* and pupil, 8, 269; the *thief* who says that the fruit he has taken is different from that which the owner put in the ground, 35, 72, 112; pain caused by extracting a *thorn*, with good intentions, 35, 169; the *warrior* with the five javelins, 35, 69; the *water* sloping down, 35, 89 sq.; Buddhism compared to a reservoir with a con-

stant supply of fresh w., 35, 187 sq.; a dry log of wood cannot be revived by pouring w. over it (there is no Pirit to prolong the life of one whose allotted period has come to an end), 35, 214; a tiny drop of w., and a mighty rain shower (vice and virtue), 36, 154 sq.; goodness compared to a pool of clear w. with the w. coming and flowing away constantly, 36, 155 sq.; tranquillity exemplified by the surface of a pool of still w., 39, 232, 331, 366; principles of good government illustrated by a *well*, 16, 164–6, 166 sq. n., 253, 253 n., 327; the man who causes a w. to be dug in arid land, who at last is certain that water is near—like the Bodhisattvas, 21, 221, 224; you do not begin to dig a w. when you feel thirsty, nor set to work to have fields ploughed when you feel hungry, nor make a fortress when the battle is set in array against you, 35, 102, 125 sq.; the *wheel* of worldly life described, with its spokes, &c., 8, 355–8; Buddha compared to a mighty *wind* that has died away, 35, 147–9; a mighty storm cloud dispersed by the w. (comp. premature death), 36, 167 sq.; sense-organs compared with *windows*, 35, 86 sq.; the famous beauty who frowns imitated by the ugly *woman*, 39, 354; the body is like a *wound*, 35, 115.

Paradhâtas, or Pêshdâd, kings of the first Iranian dynasty, 4, 226 sq., 226 n.

Paradise, of the Holy Ones, 4, 220 sq., 220 n., 221 n.; good deeds reach P., 4, 247; every man is born, so that on death he may have P. as his reward, 4, 375; Haurvatâ*t* and Ameretâ*t* reward the holy ones in P., 23, 31, 31 n.; the beautiful abodes of the Amesha-Spe*n*tas, 23, 42 sq.; Good-Thought P., Good-Word P., Good-Deed P., 23, 43, 43 n., 317, 344; bliss of P., 23, 336 sq., 340 sq.; *see also* Aîrân-vêg, Future Life (*a*), *and* Garô-nmânem;—happiness of P., 6, 69 sq., 74; P. for the Muhâgerîn, 6, 175; P. for the believers, 9, 225 sq.; *see also* Future Life (*d*);—paradisiacal state of the world on the birth of the Bodhisattva, 19, 20–3; 49 (i), 17–9; Saha world described as a kind of p., 21, 232 sq.; *see also* Ages of the World, Buddha-fields, *and* Sukhâvatî;—paradisiacal chaotic state or state of Perfect Unity, and its gradual deterioration, 39, 369–71; *see also* Tâo.

Pârâ*g*ika, t.t., explanation of it, 13, 3 n.; sins termed p., or bringing about defeat, 13, 3–6; summary of the P. rules, 20, 374–6; a deliberate lie a P. offence, 35, xli; a layman who has unawares committed a P. offence, cannot be converted, 36, 78–81, 78 n. *See also* Sins (*b*).

Paramârtha, translated the Vagra*k-kh*edikâ into Chinese, 49 (ii), xiii.

Parama-sa*m*hitâ, quoted, 48, 526 sq.

Paramâtman, the highest Self, *see* Self.

Parama*tth*akasutta, t.c., 10 (ii), 152–4.

Paramesh*th*in, taught by Brahman, 15, 120, 188; P. and the Sun, 41, 188 sq., 190; in a list of gods, 42, 80; splendour in Pragâpati, in P., 42, 84; extended the thread of the sacrifice, 42, 208; prayer to P., 42, 209 sq., 665; Pragâpati P., 42, 215; Time supports P., 42, 225, 686; a layer of the fire-altar laid down by means of P., 43, 130, 142; son of Pragâpati, 44, 15 sq.; oblation to P. to support the Soma-sacrifice, 44, 206.

Pâramitâs, the six (five) perfections of a Buddha, 21, 243, 246, 249, 316, 318 sq., 355, 419; 49 (ii), 127. *See also* Miracles, *and* Morality.

Parâ*s*ara, son of Sârasvata, 19, 10, 10 n.; the *Ri*shi P. deluded by a woman, 19, 44; 49 (i), 45; V*ri*ddha P. reached final deliverance, 19, 139; 49 (i), 130; worshipped at the Tarpa*n*a, 30, 244; quoted as Sm*ri*ti author, 48, 72, 90, 92, 284, 406, 410, 474, 478, 564, 593.

Parâ*s*ara *S*âktya, author of Vedic hymns, 46, 55, 58, 62, 65, 68, 71, 75, 83, 89.

Pârâ*s*ara, n. of a great ascetic, 45, 269, 269 n.

Pârâ*s*arîkau*nd*inîputra, n. of a teacher, 15, 224 n.

Pârâsarîputra, n. of a teacher, 15, 224 n., 225.
Pârâsarya, author of a Bhikshu-sûtra, 8, 32 sq.; n. of teachers, 15, 118, 118 n., 119, 186 n., 187.
Pârâsaryâyana, n. of teachers, 15, 119, 186, 187.
Pâraskara-Grihya-sûtra, Stenzler's edition and translation of, 29, 263-8; translated, 29, 269-368.
Parasurâma, story of, in the Anugîtâ, 8, 221.
Parâvasu, a Hotri of the Asuras, 12, 137.
Pârâvata, 'distant people,' an Aryan border clan, 32, 316.
Pârâyanavagga, t.c., 10 (ii), 184-213.
Pârâyanika, n. of a Bhikshu, 49 (ii), 2.
Pardon, law about pardoning criminals, 2, 167 sq., 245.
Pârendi (Parendi), follows Tistrya, 23, 104; on her light chariot, follows Mithra, or Ashi Vanguhi, 23, 136, 330; goddess of treasures, 23, 270; chief of women, goddess of riches, invoked, 31, 251, 346.
Parents, to keep them by begging is permitted, 2, 123; food of a person cast off by his p. forbidden, 2, 267; must not be treated improperly under any circumstances, 2, 282, 282 n.; respect due to p. and teachers, 4, 370 sq.; father, mother, and spiritual teacher, are three Atigurus, equal to the three Vedas, gods, worlds, fires, 7, 128 sq.; crime of abandoning one's p., 7, 135; 25, 104 sq., 321, 442; serving mother and father, part of the conduct of the good, 8, 243; the duty of supporting aged p., 10 (ii), 18, 21 sq., 66; 30, 186; father who has committed a mortal sin must be cast off, mother does not become an outcast to her son, 14, 67; father more venerable than teacher, and mother more venerable than father, 14, 68; have power to give, abandon, or sell children, 14, 75, 335; sin of disobedience towards p., 14, 298; the p. alone, or the mother alone, impure on account of birth, 14, 180; Bhikkhu allowed to make a gift of robes to his p., 17, 232; fine for defaming p., 25, 302; rights of p., 33, 51, 190; one who quarrels with his father is unfit to be a witness, 33, 89; father is not liable to be punished for the crime of his son, 33, 212; there can be no lawsuit between father and son, 33, 234; numerous kings have killed their father, but none their mother, 49 (ii), 163. *See also* Family, Father, *and* Sons.
Parganya, god of rain, 1, 30; 26, 78; 34, 358; is the altar on which the Devas offer Soma, 1, 78 sq.; 15, 207; if Samâna and mind are satisfied, P. and lightning are satisfied, 1, 90 sq.; or rain, the uniter of earth and heaven, 1, 249; rains, 12, 241 n.; 30, 73; 41, 412; 42, 52; 44, 295; offerings and prayers to P., 12, 386 n.; 29, 86, 320, 326, 341; 30, 113 sq.; 42, 161; 44, 402; clings to man by the water in the eye, 15, 105 sq.; identified with Prâna, 15, 275; 42, 623 sq.; the bull (Soma?) reared by P., 26, xiv; is the Udgâtri priest, 29, 195; the Cloud, 32, 92, 94 sq.; 46, 105; air manifests itself in the form of P., 34, 229; Bhava is P., 41, 160; Agni as P., 41, 277 sq., 277 n.; his mother Prithivî, 42, 8, 233-5; the father of the arrow, of hundredfold power, 42, 10, 236 sq.; favours the plants, 42, 43; the brilliancy of P. transferred on the king, 42, 116; Vâta and P. invoked against the serpents, 42, 153; the earth is the mother, P. the father, 42, 200, 204; Indra and P. identified, 42, 235; sends his rain-messengers, 42, 588; the boon-bestower, 43, 107 sq.; Amrita offered in P. becomes rain, 48, 585.
Paribbâgaka, Pali t.t., a wandering mendicant, 10 (ii), x; Buddha's definition of a P., 10 (ii), 92 sq.; the same as Sk. Parivrâgaka, q. v.
Parihâsaka, a Kula of the Uddeha Gana, 22, 290.
Parikara, *see* Sura P.
Parikshit, King, Kuru-land, the kingdom of, 42, 197 sq., 691 sq.
Pârikshita, *see* Ganamegaya P.
Pârikshitas, or Pârikshitîyas, a royal race supposed to have vanished from the earth, 15, 127; Ganame-

*g*aya, Bhîmasena, Ugrasena, *S*ruta-sena, are the P., 44, 396, 396 n.
Pârileyyaka, Buddha at, 17, 312–14.
Parinibbâna-Sutta, Chinese translations of, 10 (i), xxxi; the First Council not mentioned in the P., 10 (i), xxxi. *See also* Mahâ-parinibbâna-Sutta.
Parinirvâ*n*a, *see* Nirvâ*n*a.
Pâriplava, *see* A*s*vamedha, *and* Legends.
Parishad, *see* Judicial procedure.
Parisrava, *G*aina t.t., explained, 22, 37 n.
Parisrut, *see* Spirituous liquors.
Pârisuddhi, t.t., *see under* Uposatha.
Parittâ = Pirit, *see* Charms.
Parivakrâ, a Pâñ*k*âla king offered sacrifice at, 44, 397.
Parivâsa, t.t., probation, *see* Ordination, *and* Sa*m*gha.
Parivrâ*g*akas, who do not yet know the Highest Brahman go the path of the gods, 1, 80; sect of P., 21, 263; state of life of P., 48, 705. *See also* Ascetics, Holy Persons, *and* Paribbâgaka.
Parivr*i*ktâ, t.t., third or discarded wife of a king, 44, 387.
Pâriyâtra, n. of a mountain, 8, 346.
Pariyonahâ, Pali t.t., 'entanglements,' 11, 182 n.
Parôdar*s*, *see* Birds (*b*).
Parôdasma, son of Dâ*s*tâghni, 23, 218.
Par*s*adgâ *Hv*embya, chief of Pê*s*yânsaî, 5, 117 sq. and n.
Parsha*n*ta, son of Ga*n*darewa, 23, 217.
Parsha*d*-g*a*u, or -gâvô, *see* Parsha*t*-gau*s*.
Parsha*t*ga*us*, or Parsha*d*-g*a*u, son of Frâta, 23, 203, 219; disciple of Zoroaster, 37, 230; 47, xi; his bull cured with Hôm-water by Zoroaster, 47, 57 sq. and n.
Parshad-tô*r*â, Zoroaster goes to, 47, xxv.
Pârsh*n*i, n. of a protecting demon, 29, 335.
Parsis, Zend-Avesta, sacred book of the, 4, xiii; religion of the P., called Dualism, or Mazdeism, or Magism, or Zoroastrianism, or Fire-worship, 4, xiii; their numbers in Persia and India, 4, xiii sq. and n.; Âṅgirasa, one of the four Vedas of the P., 42, xx. *See* Zoroastrianism.
Par*s*tva, n.p., 5, 146.
Pâr*s*va, Mahâvîra's parents were worshippers of, 22, 194; life of the Arhat P., 22, 271–5; the four vows of P. and the five vows of Mahâvîra mixed up by the Buddhists, 45, xxi, 121 sq., 434 sq.; a historical person, 45, xxi; allowed the use of clothes, 45, xxx; relation between the followers of P. and those of Mahâvîra, 45, xxxi sq., xxxii n., xxxiii, 119 n.; a *G*ina, an Arhat, a prophet of the Law, his disciple Kê*s*i, 45, 119 sq.; discussion between Kê*s*i and Gautama about the merits of P.'s and of Mahâvîra's law, 45, 119–29; Udaka, a follower of P., converted by Gautama to Mahâvîra's creed, 45, 420–35.
Partition of property, *see* Family, *and* Inheritance.
Paru*kkh*epa Daivodâsi, author of Vedic hymns, 32, 446; 46, 131, 138.
Parushnî and *S*ipâlâ, two rivers, 42, 29.
Parvan days, *see* Moon (*b*).
Parvata, prayer to Indra and, 26, 450.
Pârvatî, or Mâhe*s*varî, or Umâ, 1, 151 n.; 8, 219, 347, 347 n.
Paryagnikara*n*a, t.t., *see* Fire.
Paryaṅka-vidyâ, 'knowledge of (or meditation on) the couch (of Brahman),' 1, 276; 38, 230, 232 sq.
Paryusha*n*âkalpa, n. of a lecture declared by Mahâvîra, 22, 311.
Pâsâ*n*aka *K*etiya, the Rock Temple, 10 (ii), 188, 209.
Pasenadi, king of Kosala, 13, 321 sq.; 20, 209; 45, xxix.
Pashang, Aghrêra*d*, son of, 5, 117, 135.
Passion: men adhere to p., created by the demons, without thinking of death, 4, 376 sq.; wrath, born from p., 8, 57; the devotee in whom the quality of p. is suppressed, 8, 70, 342, 363, 369; the body full of p., 8, 343; ps. or thirty-six channels, 10 (i), 80, 80 sq. n.; freedom from p. defined, 35, 119. *See also* Anger, *and* Qualities.
Pa*s*ubandha, *see* Animal sacrifice (*b*).
Pâ*s*upatas, a sect of adherents of Pa*s*upati, 7, xxix sq., 202, 202 n.;

48, 520, 523; their system contrary to the Veda, 48, 523; P. doctrine is of human origin, 48, 529; P. doctrine is not to be rejected absolutely, 48, 531.

Pasupati, n. of Rudra, 12, 201; 29, 256; 41, 159; sacrifices to P., 29, 130, 203, 352; 30, 221 sq.; 43, 152; P. or Siva, according to the Saivas, the operative cause, 34, 435; a form of Agni, 41, 159; 43, xx; Rudra and P. invoked, 42, 161; lord of cattle, 42, 171; promulgator of Pâsupata doctrine, 48, 520–3, 529. *See also* Rudra, *and* Siva.

Pasupurodâsa, *see* Animal sacrifice (*b*).

Pasûra, n.p., 10 (ii), 159.

Pasûrasutta, t.c., 10 (ii), 157–9.

Pâtakhsrôbô, king of the Arabs, 47, x, xxv, 12 sq. and n.

Patala, a demon, converted by Buddha, 19, 244.

Pâtâla, *see* Hell (*a*).

Pâtaligâma, n. of a town (afterwards called Pâtaliputta, q. v.), Buddha at, 11, 15–21; 17, 97–104; a fortress built at P., 11, 18–21.

Pâtaliputta, Sk. Pâtaliputra, the town of Patna: Mahâ-parinibbâna-Sutta probably composed before P. had become the capital of Magadha, 11, xv–xvii, 19 n.; Buddha's prophecy concerning P., 11, 18, 19 n.; 17, 101 sq., 102 n.; 19, 249–51, 249 n.; council of P., 19, xii sq., xvi, xxxvii; the 'Gautama gate' and 'Gautama ford' at P., 19, 251 sq.; the eleven Aṅgas collected by the Saṅgha of P., 22, xliii; Asoka park in P., 35, 26, 28 sq.; Asoka and the courtesan Bindumatî at P., 35, 182 sq.

Patañgali, author of Yoga-sûtras, 8, 9 sq., 211, 248 n.; author of Mahâbhâshya, his date, 8, 19, 32, 223; Mahâbhârata and P.'s Mahâbhâshya, 8, 138–41, 139 n.; mountains mentioned by P., 8, 346 n.; P. and Satapatha-brâhmana, 12, xxix; refers to Dharma-sûtras, 25, li sq.; quotes Manu, 25, cxii, cxii n.; Nâgasena not P., 35, xxvi sq.; the arguments of Buddha, P., and others are mutually contradictory, 48, 425.

Patañkala Kâpya, n.p., 15, 127, 132.

Pâtava, *see* Revottara.

Path, *the noble eightfold*, taught by Buddha, as the fourth of the Noble Truths, 10 (i), xlviii sq.; 11, ix, xxi, 16 n., 27, 61, 63, 106 sq., 107 n., 149 sq., 300; 13, xii, 95 sqq.; 36, 369; leads to the quieting of pain, to Nirvâna, 10 (i), 52, 67–9; 11, 147 sq.; 13, 94–7; true salvation by the n. e. p., not by rites and ceremonies, 11, 21 sq., 22 n.; the Buddhist ideal of the perfect life, 11, 143–5; must be walked by the gods, even by Brahmâ, 11, 163; those walking in the n. e. p. called the Noble Ones, 11, 217 n.;—the good and evil p., Buddhist t.t., 10 (i), 7, 7 n., 75 sq.; the way to the other shore, 10 (ii), 210; the Bauddha instruction as to the p., 34, 411; the p. across Samsâra leading to liberation taught by Mahâvîra, 45, 310 sq.; P. of Duty, *see* Tâo; p. of the fathers, of the gods, *see* Future Life (*b*).

Pathana, nine sons of, killed by Keresâspa, 23, 295, 295 sq. n.

Pâtheyyaka Bhikkhus, of Western India, 17, 146 sqq., 146 sq. n.

Pathi Saubhara, n. of a teacher, 15, 119, 187.

Pâthya, the bull, kindled Agni, is the Mind, 41, 218.

Pathyâ Svasti, a genius of wellbeing and prosperity, 26, 49 sq., 49 n.; oblations to P. S., 26, 386 sq.; 44, xlii sq.; is speech, 26, 386 sq.; wife of Pûshan, 42, 331.

Pâtihârakapakkha, Pali t.t., consists of eight parts, 10 (ii), 66.

Patikka - samuppâda, Pali t.t., knowledge of the Chain of Causation, 11, 209.

Pâtimokkha, Pali t.t., Sk. Prâtimoksha, rules of, 10 (i), xxx, xxxiv; 11, 188; 36, 220; the oldest collection of moral laws of the Buddhists, 10 (i), 50 sq. n.; its origin and importance, 13, ix–xv; divided into Bhikkhu-p. and Bhikkhunî-p., 13, xiii sq.; not included in the Tipitaka, 13, xiv sq.; an old commentary of the P. contained in the Sutta-vibhaṅga, 13, xv–xix; meaning of the word, 13, xxvii sq.; translation of the P., 13, xxxvi sq., 1–69; disrespectful behaviour of Bhikkhus

during the recitation of the P., 13, 50 sq.; regulations concerning the Uposatha ceremony and the recitation of the P., 13, 239–97; various ways of reciting the P., 13, 260 sqq.; must be recited in an audible voice, 13, 265 sq.; laymen and certain Bhikkhus must not be present at the recitation of the P., 13, 266, 295–7; 35, 232, 264–8, 264 n., 265 n.; the Thera is master of the P., 13, 266–8; recitation of P. in the case of unlearned Bhikkhus, 13, 267 sq., 272–4; after re-establishment of concord among the Sa*m*gha, 17, 322; Buddha enjoins reverence and obedience to the P., 19, 296; knowledge of P. rules required of a Bhikkhu who is to judge upon conduct of other Bhikkhus, 20, 50 sq., 317; legal and illegal exclusion from P. ceremony, 20, 299–319; the P. ceremony for Bhikkhunîs, 20, 330 sq., 338 sq.; the five recitations of the P., 36, 215.

Pa*t*isâra*n*iya-kamma, t.t., Act of Reconciliation, *see* Sa*m*gha (disciplinary proceedings).

Pati*tth*âna, of A*l*aka, 10 (ii), 188.

Patka, n. of a Bhikshu, 49 (ii), 2.

Patna, *see* Pâ*t*aliputta.

Pâtrapâ*n*i, demon harassing infants, 29, 296; 30, 211.

Patriarchs, *see* Pra*g*âpatis.

Pât-srôbô, king of the Arabs, 37, 28, 28 n.

Paul, the 'high-priest,' his words quoted, 24, 237.

Paulkasas, *see* Caste (*f*).

Pau*m*sâyana, *see* Dush*t*arîtu P.

Pau*nd*ras, became V*ri*shalas, 8, 295.

Paurâ*n*ikas, refutation of their views about creation, 45, ix, 244 sq., 247, 247 n.

Paura*s*ish*t*i, *see* Taponitya P.

Paurukutsya, *see* Trasadasyu.

Pâûrvâ*g*îryâ, grandfather of Aôshnôr, 18, 171, 171 n.

Paurvikâ, daughter of Râhula, 49 (i), 198.

Paushkarasâdi, *see* Pushkarasâdi.

Paushkara-sa*m*hitâ, quoted, 48, 525.

Pautimâshîputra, n. of a teacher, 15, 224.

Pautimâshya, n. of a teacher, 15, 118, 185 sq.

Pautimâshyâya*n*a, n. of a teacher, 15, 118 n.

Pâvâ, the city of wealth, 10 (ii), 188; Buddha at P., 11, 70–2; 19, 285, 285 n.; the Mallas of P., 11, 133; Dâgaba at P., 11, 135.

Pavamânîs, poets and hymns of the 9th Ma*nd*ala of the Rig-veda, 1, 217, 217 n.

Pâvana, etymology of, 15, 310.

Pavâra*n*â, *see* Rainy Season.

Pâvârika, mango grove, at Nâlandâ, 11, 12, 14.

Pavattinî, t.t., *see* Teachers (*b*).

Payanghrô-makh*s*ti, n.p., 23, 214.

Pâyâsi, the Râ*g*anya, addressed by Kumâra Kassapa, 35, 275.

Pâzinah, n.p., 23, 214.

Peace: the Bhikkhu is to be a p.-maker, a lover of p., impassioned for p., 11, 190; *G*aina monks and nuns must avoid all quarrels and dispute, for 'p. is the essence of monachism,' 22, 309; Âkh*s*ti, genius of P., worshipped, 23, 4, 4 n., 13, 35, 37, 164, 249; 31, 345, 353; the consort of P., 29, 346; inward p., *see* Tranquillity.

Pearl, and its shell, 42, 62, 383 sq.; hymn strung as a p. on a thread, 44, 173; gold ps. woven into the hair of sacrificial horse, 44, 313.

Peasantry, *see* Caste.

Pê*dh*âla, father of Udaka, 45, 420.

Pedu, his white horse that slays serpents, 29, 131, 204, 327, 330; 30, 238, 288; 42, 152 sq., 605–8. *See also* Horse (white).

Pei-a, a class of sprites, 40, 19.

Pei-kung Shê, collector of taxes for Duke Ling of Wei, 40, 31 sq., 289.

Pei-măn *Kh*ăng, n.p., 39, 348.

Pe*n*âhikâ bird, 36, 342 sq.

Penal Law, *see* Law, *and* Punishments.

Penances (Sk. Prâya*sk*itta), enjoined when a mistake occurs during sacrifice, 1, 69 n.; 12, 27, 45, 56, 214 sq.; 26, 411–13, 411 n., 422 sq.; for those who have missed the initiation rite, and for those whose ancestors have not been initiated, 2, 4–6; 14, 58; rules about p., 2,

67, 67 n., 78–92, 125, 274–302; 7, 138–40, 149–86; 14, xxxiii, 30, 31 sq. and n., 73, 91, 95, 102–35, 145, 148 sq., 157 sq., 161, 182 sq., 185, 202, 204, 211–23, 232, 235, 239, 241, 248, 266, 294–333; 25, 430, 430 n., 435, 438 sq., 444–82, 601; 29, 120, 136–40, 224 sq., 361 sq., 376, 393; 33, 56, 157, 180; for touching or speaking to or looking at a *K*â*n*d*â*la, 2, 103; for various offences, 2, 129 sq.; 7, 175–80; for unlucky omens, 2, 184 sq.; doubts about the efficacy of p., 2, 274 sq.; 14, 116, 310; secret p., 2, 291–6; 14, xxi–xxv, 124–35, 320–2; K*rikkh*ra and *K*ândrâya*n*a (lunar) p., 2, 296–302; 14, 113, 122–4, 132, 223, 303–7, 323–6; 25, 172, 202, 438, 452, 454 sq., 458, 462–4, 466 sq., 469, 471, 473–5; for intercourse with a woman during her sickness, 4, 206–8; for perjury, 7, 50; 14, 83; for impurity, 7, 88 sq., 93–5; the Tapta-K*rikkh*ra or 'hot p.' prescribed for one concerned with the death or funeral of a suicide, 7, 93; no p. allowed to women apart from their husbands, 7, 111; various p. for students, 7, 120 sq., 130; 25, 63 sq., 70, 70 n.; 29, 83; for offending a teacher, 7, 130; for the nine principal degrees of crime, 7, 133, 135, 138–40; for killing animals, 7, 138, 158–61; the Mahâvrata or 'great observance' for one who has committed homicide, 7, 157 sq.; the Govrata p. for one who has killed a cow, 7, 158 sq.; for eating forbidden food, 7, 162–9; 25, 164, 172; for theft, 7, 172 sq.; for illicit sexual intercourse, 7, 174 sq.; he who associates with one guilty of a crime must perform the same p. as he, 7, 175; for selling certain articles, 7, 177 sq.; half of every p. for old men, youths, women, and sick persons, 7, 180; he who has done p. must not be taxed with his offence, 7, 180; 33, 210; for secret sins, 7, 180–4; 25, 476, 476 n., 479–82; by pious gifts bestowed on Brâhma*n*as, 7, 264–70, 272; bathing, &c., in the month of Kârttika purifies from every sin, 7, 265; p. performed under false pretence go to the demons, 7, 275; fruit of p. obtained by devotion, 8, 81; performed by Pra*g*âpati wishing to create, 12, 323; of an outcast, 14, 77 sq.; prescribed for a king, 14, 101 sq.; upright Brâhma*n*as accomplish their desires even without p., 14, 329 sq.; a monk who has offended should repent and do p., 22, 48; a Snâtaka must not dictate a p. to a *S*ûdra, 25, 141; should not be used as a pretext for committing sins, 25, 159 sq. and n.; hermit may live according to the *K*ândrâya*n*a p., 25, 202; those who perform p. for mortal sins shall not be branded, 25, 383 sq.; for teaching *S*ûdras, sacrificing for them, or accepting gifts from them, 25, 425; for neglecting sacred fires, 25, 438; for unintentional sins, 25, 439; why p. must be performed, 25, 440 sq.; for the slayer of a Brâhma*n*a, 25, 444–9, 449 n.; atonement by death, 25, 445, 446 n., 451 sq.; subsisting on alms, 25, 445, 455, 467, 481; for minor offences, 25, 453–73; description of the principal p., 25, 473–5; prayer to Vish*n*u, if the sacrificer breaks his vow of silence, 26, 35; prayer to Agni, p. for break of vow, 26, 45; P. personified, 26, 150; for the study of the Âra*n*yakas, 29, 143 sq., 147 sq.; p. for accidents to a king's chariot, &c., 29, 287 sq.; for omitting sacrifices, 30, 39, 203; prescribed for religious men, 33, 362; for violated women, 33, 367; K*rikkh*ra p. for hermits and mendicants who have broken their vows, 38, 319; expiation in case the fire-pan breaks, 41, 263; p. if the fire goes out, 41, 263–5; charms in expiation of sin and defilement, 42, 163–8, 473–5, 483–5, 521–9, 555 sq., 564 sq.; by fasting, 43, 255 sq. *See also* Asceticism, Austerity, Expiatory rites, Sa*m*gha, *and* Sin.

Pentateuch, concordance between Avesta and, 4, lviii sq.; P. and Qur'ân, 9, 112 sq. *See also* Sacred Books.

Pentecost, the day of, and the Foundation of the Kingdom of Righteousness, 11, 141 sq.

Perception, understanding based on, 1, 121; p. based on belief, 1, 122; experience the result of p., 8, 57 n.; sevenfold p. due to earnest thought, 11, 9; denotes Scripture, 34, 203; possible without the body as in dreams, 38, 272; conflict between p. and Scripture, 48, 24–6, 30, 73–8; reveals to us non-differenced substance only, 48, 30 sq.; of two kinds: non-determinate and determinate, 48, 41; does not reveal mere Being, but difference, 48, 44–6; as a source of knowledge, 48, 162; organs of p., *see* Organs.

Perethu-afzem, n.p., 23, 219.

Perethuarsti, n.p., 23, 206.

Perfect: the p. one (the Brahman), 8, 173, 251; the p. is raised out of the p., 8, 186, 186 n.; the p. self, 8, 248, 248 n.; the Perfect Man, *see* Holy Persons.

Perfection, not attained by mere renunciation, 8, 52; attained by action, 8, 54, 100; devotee works for and attains p., 8, 72 sq., 79, 127; he who abandons scripture does not attain p., 8, 117; how a Siddha attains to p., 8, 233 sq., 314, 384, 393; reached by penance and concentration of mind, 8, 300, 388 sq.; on moral p., 28, 236 sq., 318–21; may be reached by women, men, hermaphrodites, orthodox, heterodox, and householders, 45, 211; description of the life of perfected souls, 45, 211–13; absurdity of trying to attain p. by abstaining from salt, by ablutions, or by tending the fire, 45, 294 sq.; if all beings were to reach p. the world would become empty: or, not all beings are qualified for p., 45, 406, 406 n. *See also* Emancipation, *and* Pâramitâs.

Pericardium, a place of deep sleep, 38, 142, 144 sq.

Periods, *see* Ages of the World.

Perjury, *see* Oath, *and* Witnesses.

Perseverance, impossible without self-restraint, 8, 51; p. in pursuit of knowledge, 8, 114; its characteristic marks, 35, 57.

Persians (Pârasîkas) conquered Syria, 9, 125 n.; matches with a mother occur among the P., 33, 389.

Person, *see* Purusha.

Pêsdâd, Hôshâng the, 24, 57 sq., 57 n.

Peshana, worshipper of the Daêvas, enemy of Vîstâspa, 23, 79, 306.

Peshî, n. of a woman (?), 46, 366, 369.

Peshô-*K*angha, the corpse-burier, conquered by Zairi-vairi, 23, 80.

Peshô-tanu, Peshôtan, *see* Pêshyôtanû.

Pêshyôtan(û), or Peshô-tanu, or Peshôtan, son of Vistâsp, 5, li, 117, 137, 142, 142 n.; 47, 70, 70 n., 81, 127, 127 n.; restores the Mazdayasnian religion and becomes high-priest, 5, li sq., 224–30, 231 n., 232 sq.; an arranger of the world, 18, 90, 90 sq. n.; one of the seven immortals, 18, 257 sq. and n.; 23, 329, 329 n.; 37, 203, 203 n.; called *K*itrag-miyân (*K*itrô-mêhônŏ), 37, 285, 285 n.; 47, xii, 104 sq., 104 n.; a producer of the renovation, 37, 437, 437 n.; birth of P., 47, xi sq., 76 sq.; made immortal, 47, xxiii. *See also* *K*itrôk-miyân.

Phalgumitra, of the Gautama gotra, a Sthavira, 22, 294.

Phâlguna, n. of Arguna, 8, 394.

Phalika-sandâna, n. of a Thera, 17, 238.

Phăng, *see* Birds (*b*).

Phăng Măng, a famous archer, 40, 36, 36 n.; a Tâoist professor who did not know the true Tâo, 40, 223–5.

Phăng Yang, called Zeh-yang, 39, 154.

Phăng-ȝû, Tâoist patriarch, lived more than 1,800 years, 39, 24, 167, 167 n.; got the Tâo, 39, 136, 245, 245 n.; did not live out his time, 39, 188.

Pharaoh, and Moses, punishment of P. and his people, 6, 6, 47, 151–4, 169 sq., 201–3, 216, 239; 9, 12, 40, 91–3, 107–12, 121, 192–5, 214 sq., 218 sq., 247, 257, 298, 318 sq., 327, 331; Moses sent to P. with signs, 9, 36 sq., 100; Moses and Aaron before P., 9, 37–9, 68; claims to be a god, 9, 91; 'P. of the stakes' called the apostles liars, 9, 176, 176 n.; rejected the prophet, 9, 242, 307; the good wife of P., 9, 292.

Phassa, Pali t.t., touch; pain and pleasure arise from it, 10 (ii), 136, 166.

Pheî-î, a perfect man, 39, 172 n.; teacher of Wang Î, 39, 312, 312 n.; instructs Nieh *Kh*üeh about the Tâo, 40, 61 sq., 291.

Phî, grand-administrator of *Kh*ăn, 27, 179.

Phien, the wheelwright, and Duke Hwan, 39, 343 sq.

Phî-î, *see* Pheî-î.

Philo Judaeus and Zoroastrianism, 4, lv–lvii.

Philosophy, Âpastamba knows the Pûrva-Mîmâ*m*sâ (called Nyâya by him) and the Vedânta, 2, xxviii sq., 121; Bhagavadgîtâ anterior to systems of p., 8, 7–13; Sâṅkhya and Yoga in the Bhagavadgîtâ, 8, 27, 47, 47 n., 52, 63 sq., 74 n.; causes of action according to the Sâṅkhya system, 8, 123, 123 n.; no system of p. in the Sanatsugâtîya, 8, 144 sq.; Buddha sees no good in p., but seeks for inward peace, 10 (ii), xii, xiv, 157–9, 160–3, 167; 11, 194 sq., 293 sq., 298 sq.; 35, 205 sq.; sixty-three systems of p. at the time of Buddha, 10 (ii), xiii, 93; the Bhikkhu has shaken off the dogmas of p. and is therefore independent, 10 (ii), 148–50, 152–4; no one is purified or becomes a Muni by p., 10 (ii), 150 sq., 199 sq.; the different schools of p. contradict each other, constantly exciting strife in the world, 10 (ii), 167–74; the systems of other teachers than Buddha are void of saints, 11, 106–8; summing up of various systems of p., 15, 232 sqq. and n.; Vedânta and Sâṅkhya systems, 15, 250 n.; metaphysical speculations, 19, 105–9; 49 (i), 99 sq.; psychology and metaphysics of Ârâ*d*a Kâlâma, 19, 133–41; 49 (i), 124–32; Hetuvidyâ *s*âstras, works on the explanation of causes, 19, 209, 209 n.; preachers of the Lotus of the True Law will have no pleasure in worldly p., 21, 438; p. in Manu-smr*i*ti, 25, lxxiii; science of dialectics to be learnt by the king, 25, 222, 222 n.; systems of p. not based on the Veda denounced, 25, 505; a logician and a Mîmâ*m*saka among the members of a legal assembly, 25, 510; Nyâya p., 34, 15 n.; systems of p. known to Milinda, 35, 6; of Buddhism, 36, 361 sq., 362 sq. n.; philosophical controversies, 39, 128 sq., 176–97; Tâoist and other Chinese systems of p., 39, 162 sq.; 40, 214–32; five schools of p., 40, 99 sq.; philosophical hymns in the Atharva-veda, 42, xxix, xl, lxvi; heretical doctrines of p. discussed from the *G*aina point of view, 45, ix, 235–47; the Kriyâvâda held by the *G*ainas, the Akriyâvâda by the Buddhists, 45, xvi, xxv, 83 n., 318 sq.; systems of p. mentioned in *G*aina and Buddhist writings, 45, xxiii–xxvii; relation between *G*ainism and the Vai*s*eshika system, 45, xxiv sq., xxxv–xxxviii; Ksha*n*ikavâdins and *S*ûnyavâdins, 45, xxv; the system of Fatalism described in *G*aina and Buddhist writings, 45, xxv sq.; Agnosticism (Ag*ñ*ânavâda) as described in Buddhist writings, 45, xxvi; influence of heretical systems, esp. Agnosticism, on *G*aina and Buddhist doctrines, 45, xxvii–xxix; Vedânta, Sâṅkhya, and *G*aina metaphysics, 45, xxxiii sq., 153 sq.; Mahâvîra had mastered all systems of p., 45, 291; criticism of the four creeds: Kriyâvâda, Akriyâvâda, Vinayavâda, and Ag*ñ*ânavâda, 45, 315–17; refutation of Materialists, Vedântins, and Fatalists, 45, 339–47, 417 sq., 417 n.; there are 306 systems of p. all teaching final beatitude: but their adherents do not abstain from injuring living beings, and are therefore subject to the Sa*m*sâra, 45, 385–7; how philosophers treat one another, 45, 411 sq. *See also* *G*ñânakâ*nd*a, Heretics, *K*ârvâkas, Lokâyatikas, Pûrva-Mîmâ*m*sâ, *and* Vedânta.

Phing, or Î-*kh*iû, King, delivers the charge to Marquis Wăn, 3, 22, 265–7; the banished son of King Yû, bewails his fate, 3, 360.

Phing, Duke, drinking with Kwang and Lî Thiâo, 27, 179 sq.

Phoenix, *see* Birds (*b*).

Phû-î-ȝze, an ancient Tâoist, 39, 259, 259 n.

Phû-yau-king, Chinese translation

of Lalita-Vistara, 19, ix, xxv; specimen of the expanded Sûtra P., 19, 344–64.

Physicians must practise on Daêva-yasnas before treating Mazdayasnas, 4, li; law regarding p., their duties and fees, 4, lxx n., 85–7; 7, 39; 37, 48, 116–18, 117 n., 158 sq.; kinds of p., 4, 87, 87 n.; 37, 360 sq.; Buddhist and *G*aina monks and Brahmans must not be p., 10 (ii), 176; 11, 199 sq.; 19, 296; 42, xxxix sq.; 45, 71; how a p. cures a blind-born man, 21, 130 sq.; excluded from *S*râddha feasts, 25, 103, 109; food not to be accepted from p., 25, 162 sq.; fined for bad treatment, 25, 392 sq.; how p. treat a wound, 35, 168 sq.; should find out the age of the patient before curing his disease, 35, 272; description of a good p., 36, 67; a list of famous p., 36, 109; the training of a p., 36, 254 sq.; social position of p., 42, xxxix sq., xlviii, l, liv; wizard p., 47, 30. *See also* Medicine, *and* Parables (*f*).

Pî, proposed as forester to Shun, 3, 44.

Pî, duke of, successor to *K*ün-*kh*ăn, 3, 245–9.

Piâo, eulogy of the Lord of, 39, 351, 351 n.

Piâo-shih, the ode of, 40, 37.

Pîdha, n. of a family, 23, 219.

Pien Suî, when Thang offers him his throne, commits suicide, 40, 162.

Pien-ȝze informs Sun Hsiû about the perfect man, 40, 25.

Piety (dharma), is it destroyed by sin, or sin by p.? 8, 158 sq.; actions accumulate as long as the p. which dwells in concentration of mind has not been learnt, 8, 242; a means to reach final emancipation defined, 8, 242 sq.; characteristics of p., 8, 348 sq.; various modes of p., 8, 375–7; personified, *see* Âramaiti.

Pi*g*avana, Sudâs, son of, 25, 222.

Pihu*nd*a, n. of a sea town, 45, 108.

Pî-kan, his heart cut out by *K*âu-hsin, 3, 128 sq.; 16, 19 n.; 39, 205, 283; 40, 37, 131, 174, 180; Wû raised a mound over P.'s grave, 3, 136; 28, 123.

Pîlâ, n. of an Apsaras, 42, 33.

Pilgrim, *see* Pabbagita.

Pilgrimages, *see* 'Hagg, *and* Holy places.

Pilindava*kkh*a, suffers from various diseases, 17, 53, 55 sqq.; story of P. and the park-keeper's daughter whose grass chumbat he turned into chaplet of gold, 17, 61–5; stores up medicines presented to him, 17, 65 sq.

Pilindavatsa, an eminent Arhat, 21, 2.

Piliyakkha, Prince Sâma killed by, 35, 280 sq.

Pi*nd*ola Bhâradvâ*g*a, an Arhat, displays his power of Iddhi, 20, 79–81; sayings of P. B. the Elder, 36, 335, 345.

Ping, *see* Kung-sun Lung.

Piṅgiya, the great Isi, 10 (ii), 187, 209–13.

Piṅgiyamâ*n*avapu*kkh*â, t.c., 10 (ii), 209.

Pin-mâu *K*iâ, converses with Confucius about music, 28, 121–4.

Pippalâda, n. of a teacher, 15, xlii, 271, 284.

Pipphalivana, Moriyas of, 11, 134.

Pîrân Vîsah, head of the Vîsah family, 5, 135, 135 n.; 23, 67 n.

Pirit, *see* Charms.

Pisâ*k*as (ogres), created, 7, 4; 8, 387; 25, 15; eat flesh, 7, 171; 25, 176; extol the emancipated saint, 8, 345; P. and other demons, 8, 354; 42, 205; marriage rite of the P., 25, 79–82; a *S*râddha at which friends are entertained, instead of Brâhma*n*as, is an offering to the P., 25, 101, 101 n.; their food and drink, 25, 450; produced by Darkness, 25, 494; thieves reborn as P., 25, 496; driven away from the bride, 30, 188; children sucked out by P., 30, 200; charm against the P., 42, 34–7, 68, 407–9; 44, 368 n.; the flesh-devouring P. driven away, 42, 57, 187, 190; destroyed by lead, 42, 65; cure of possession by P., 42, 290 sq., 302; a *G*aina monk abused as 'a very devil (P.) of a dirty man,' 45, 51; female cane-worker sacrificed to the P. at the Purushamedha, 44, 414; souls of P., 48, 198. *See also* Demons, *and* Superhuman beings.

Pisanah or Kaî-Pisân, n. of a king, 5, 136 sq., 136 n.; 23, 222, 222 n.
Pisha, i.e. Vais*r*ava*n*a, converted by Buddha, 19, 245, 245 n.
Pisina, king of Iran, 23, 303.
Pi*s*una, a name of Mâra, 19, 147 sq. *See* Mâra.
Pi*t*akas, three, *see* Tipi*t*aka.
Pitâmaha, quoted by B*ri*haspati, 33, 318.
Pitaona, with the many witches, 18, 370; killed by Keresâspa, 23, 296.
Pit*ri*s, *see* Fathers.
Pit*ri*ya*gñ*a, Sk., 'Sacrifice to the Fathers,' *see* Fathers.
Pitrya, rules for the sacrifices for the ancestors, 1, 109, 110, 111, 115.
Pity, *see* Ahi*m*sâ, Compassion, *and* Sympathy.
Planets, evil influences of the seven, 5, 113 sq.; 24, 34, 38; worship of the p., 7, xxi; the sun is the prince among p., 8, 346; simultaneous occurrence of particular conjunctions of the p., 18, 333–5; seven p. assist Aharman, 24, 55, 76; opposed to the good constellations, 24, 163. *See also* Stars.
Plants.

(*a*) Origin and nature of p., healing p., p. as living beings.
(*b*) Holy and magic p., p. in worship and mythology.

(*a*) ORIGIN AND NATURE OF P., HEALING P., P. AS LIVING BEINGS.

Creation of p., 5, 10, 30 sq.; fire in p., 5, 61 sq.; 43, 184; origin and nature of p., 5, 99–105; 25, 16; barley seed is the first among p., 8, 353, 353 n.; created by Pragâpati, 12, 323; when the light of the moon waxes warmer, p. grow, 23, 90; the best grains and fruit, 24, 46; wheat, the chief of grains, 24, 108; the essence of p. is water, the essence of water are p., 26, 142; are the pith of the earth, 26, 451; created for the kine, 31, 152, 156; grow thrice, in spring, in the rainy season, and in autumn, 41, 340; shoot out a hundredfold and a thousandfold, 41, 340; that which consists of all p. is all food, 43, 224; honey is the essence of p., 44, 90; how all kinds of p. come into existence, and how they feed, 45, 388–92; *see also* Parables (*e*);—healing p. brought by Ahura-Mazda, 4, 225–7, 227 sq. n.; 5, 18; healing or medicinal p., 5, 31, 45, 66, 90, 99–101, 103, 176; 18, 262 sq., 265; 31, 292; 37, 165; 41, 341 n.; 42, 3, 19–21, 30–4, 36, 55–8, 302, 369, 376, 385, 408–10, 419–23, 464–6, 470, 516, 536; five esculent p., 27, 272, 272 n.; gathering medicinal p., 37, 18, 130; created for the subjugation of disease, 37, 116; prayers to the kush*th*a-plant to destroy fever, 42, 4–6, 441 sq., 414–19, 676–81; dark p. curing leprosy, 42, 16, 267–9; poisonous p. on the mountains, 42, 26, 375, 378;—crime of and penance for cutting trees, shrubs, creepers, &c., 7, 137, 161 sq.; 25, 459, 459 n.; 28, 250; 37, 108; injury done to long-living bodies, i.e. p., 22, 7; sin of injuring p., 22, 9–11; 25, 443; 36, 100; 45, 293; are living beings with reason, &c., 22, 10; 45, 293; experience pleasure and pain, 22, 11; p. destroyed for sacrifices are reborn in higher existences, 25, 175; souls of trees, bushes, creepers, grasses, &c., 48, 198. *See also* Ahi*m*sâ.

(*b*) HOLY AND MAGIC P., P. IN WORSHIP AND MYTHOLOGY.

Darbha grass is 'free from evil, 1, 173; sacred twigs, and other sacred p., 18, 164 sq. and n.; the branch Hadhânaêpata lifted up at the sacrifice, offered to the Fire, 31, 274–6, 316, 320 sq., 350; the Dûrvâ grass, 41, 187 n., 379–81; 43, 2 n.; layer of mu*ñg*a-grass in the fire-pan as womb, 41, 251; holy p. mixed with the water at the anointing of a king, 42, 378; *see also* Âdâra, Arka, Avakâ, Baresma, Barhis, Darbha, Dûrvâ, Ku*s*a, Sacrifice (*b*), *and* Trees;—magic p., 42, 40–4, 80, 137 sq., 219, 305, 305 n., 356 sq., 507, 578–82, 675, 702 sq.; charms with p. against demons and sorcerers, 42, 68–72, 77, 393–404, 429, 556; magic p. used against curses, 42, 91, 285 sq.; magic p. bestowing a husband, 42, 94 sq., 325; used with love-charms, 42, 99–103, 107 sq., 354 sq., 513, 534; used with battle-

charms, 42, 117 sq., 583 sq.; water-p., and a frog, used with charms to ward off fire, 42, 147, 514 sq.; used against snake poison, 42, 154, 606–8; —prayers and offerings to herbs and trees, 2, 107; 12, 333; 29, 219, 347, 388; 30, 22, 154; 41, 340 sq. n.; 42, 119, 160; 44, 81, 87, 206; Waters and P. invoked and worshipped, 4, 245; 23, 8, 16, 26, 53, 193 sq., 199, 227, 356; 26, 216 sq., 292; 29, 306; 31, 199, 206, 210, 217, 220, 225, 249, 257–9, 329, 362, 382, 385, 389; 32, 375; 44, 266, 438; the evil spirit's conflict with the p., 5, 17 sq., 30 sq., 176 sq.; origin of p. from the primaeval ox, 5, 45 sq., 177–9; purification of polluted trees, corn, fruits, 5, 274–6; not to be looked at by a menstruous woman, 5, 283; duties with regard to water and p., the counterparts of Horvada*d* and Amerôda*d*, 5, 373, 377 sq.; Waters and P. assist Ti*s*trya, 23, 95, 99, 101; Waters, P., Fravashis come for help, drive along with Mithra, 23, 26, 145; the seeds of all p. on the tree of the eagle, 23, 173, 173 n.; Fravashi of the p. worshipped, 23, 200; Waters and P. rejoice at Zarathu*s*tra's birth, 23, 202; the p. Ḫadhânaêpata offered to the Waters, 31, 208, 223; the p. Hadhânaêpata worshipped, 31, 270 sq.; the mothers of Agni, 41, 224, 227 sq., 294; the wives of the gods, 41, 242; are related to Soma, Soma their king, 41, 340; 42, 14, 44, 55, 162; 44, 135, 206; invoked as divine beings, 42, 3, 160, 162; their parents, 42, 20 sq., 30, 41–3, 97, 419–21, 465, 579; the food of Agni, the offspring of the waters, 42, 42; called mothers, 42, 581; the hair of the earth, 43, 208; as Apsaras, Agni's mates, 43, 231; p. and trees, the food of Agni, 43, 335; p. and trees, the hair of the sacrificial horse (Pra*g*âpati), 43, 401; certain p. arise from parts of the body of the bewitched Indra, 44, 214–16; offering to Grass and Lotus, 44, 336; the Fathers are the world of the p., 44, 429; *S*amî plant gives peace (*s*am), Vara*n*a plant wards off (var) sin, Apâmârga plant wipes away (apa-marg) sin, 44, 436–8, 437 n.; care and propitiation of p., 47, 162, 168. *See also* Amerôda*d*, Haurvada*d*, Hom, *and* Trees.

Plato, Platonic ideas in Zoroastrianism, 4, lv.

Pleasure(s), devotee does not long for, 8, 47, 50, 66, 322, 341; are the source of misery, 8, 66; celestial p. of gods, 8, 84; higher and lower p., 8, 240, 287; produced from union of Udâna and mind, 8, 275, 275 n.; of the quality of Goodness, 8, 300 sq.; what is p.? 8, 311; are of the quality of passion, 8, 324 sq.; the end of p. is grief, the end of grief is p., 8, 354 sq.; 10 (i), 56; the dangers of sensual p., 10 (ii), 8 sqq., 146 sq.; 19, 121–30; 45, 62–9; 49 (i), 112–19; what the world considers p., is really pain, and vice versâ, 10 (ii), 143 sq.; vanity of worldly p., 45, 58–61; are the cause of love and hatred, and a hindrance to final beatitude, 45, 187–92; p. and pain, 48, 152–5; *see also* Opposites, *and* Pain; nothing is in itself of the nature of p. or pain, 48, 390; what are called p. are merely remedies for pain, 49 (i), 116–18.

Pledge, *see* Property.

Pleiades, *see* Stars.

Poetry, the expression of earnest thought, 3, 45, 275 sq.; p. and music, 3, 45, 275 sq.; Brâhma*n*as sing about the gifts, Râ*g*anyas about the victories of the sacrificer, 44, 286 sq.

Poets, sinful liars, on whom the devils descend, 9, 99.

Po-hwang, a primaeval sovereign, 39, 287.

Po-hwăn Wû-*ȝ*ăn, warns Lieh-*ȝ*ze in vain, 39, 160 sq.; 40, 202–4, 202 n.; a famous Tâoist teacher, 39, 226; 40, 53 sq.

Po-î, minister to Shun, 3, 44, 44 n., 258; a pattern of justice, 3, 259; died to maintain his fame, 39, 139, 273, 275; a worthy, but not a True Man, 39, 239, 239 sq. n., 375 sq.; declines to take office at the court of Wû, 40, 163–5; died of starvation, 40, 173.

Poison, *see* Ordeals, *and* Parables (*f*).

Po-kâo, mourning rites for, 27, 134 sq., 134 n.

Po *Kh*ang-*kh*ien, a historiographer, 40, 124 sq., 124 n.

Po-*kh*ăng 3ze-kâo, appointed prince of a state by Yâo, resigned the principality, 39, 315, 315 n.

Po-*kh*in, son of the duke of *K*âu, 3, 267–70; 27, 29, 345, 351, 351 sq. n., 372 n.; entered military service during mourning, 27, 342, 342 n.

Po-*kh*iung, *see* *Kh*iung.

Pokkharasâti, n. of a Brâhma*n*a, 10 (ii), 109, 110; 11, 167 sq., 168 n., 170.

Po *K*ü, disciple of Lâo-3ze, 40, 122 sq.

Po-lâo, the first tamer of horses, 39, 140, 276 sq., 276 n., 279; 40, 284.

Politics, rules of diplomacy, 39, 213 sq. *See* King, *and* Rulers.

Pollution, penance for, 2, 289 sq.; 4, 202 sq.; 14, 118, 300; purification after it, 14, 174; sin of causing p., 37, 45; calamities caused by p., 37, 158, 446; abstinence from p., 37, 432. *See also* Impurity, Nasu, *and* Purification.

Polygamy, *see* Marriage.

Portents, *see* Divination, *and* Omens.

Pôrûdakhstôîh, or Pôrûdakhshtŏ, Ashavazang, his son, 18, 256, 256 n.; 37, 203, 203 n.

Pôru*k*îst, daughter of Zoroaster, 5, 142; 37, 299 sq., 299 n.; 47, 166 n.

Pôrûshâsp(ô), *see* Pouru*s*aspa.

Pôsaha, Prâkrit t.t. = Pali Uposatha: duties of *G*aina laymen on P. fasts, 45, xviii sq., 23, 23 n., 39, 383 sq., 428 sq.

Posâla, n. of a Brâhma*n*a, 10 (ii), 187, 207, 210.

Posâlamâ*n*avapu*kkh*â, 10 (ii), 207 sq.

Positions of Mastery, eight, 11, 49–51.

Possession, *see* Property.

Potala and Potalaka, demons converted by Buddha, 19, 244.

Potter, *see* Parables (*f*).

Pouru-bangha, son of Zaosha, 23, 218.

Pourudhâkh*s*t(i), son of Kh*s*tâvaênya, father of Ashavazd(ah), 5, 118, 118 n.; 23, 70 sq., 71 n., 211 sq., 211 n., 225.

Pouru-*g*îra, n.p., 23, 221.

Pouru*k*ista, daughter of Zarathu*s*tra, 23, 204 n., 224; 31, 191.

Pouru*s*aspa, Phl. Pôrûshâsp(ô), father of Zarathu*s*tra, 4, 211, 225, 255, 371; 5, 82; 23, 58; 31, 235; 47, 20 sq., 23, 25–31, 34–44, 122 sq., 139, 143–55; his genealogy, 5, 140 sq.; son of Vînâsp, 5, 146; was rich in horses, 23, 326, 328.

Pouru*s*ti, son of Kavi, 23, 213.

Poverty, and the proper use of wealth, 24, 42 sq.

Power (bala), meditation on it as Brahman, 1, 116; mystic p. of K*r*ish*n*a, 8, 76, 92 sq., 98, 131; the five moral powers (pa*ñk*a balâni), 11, 61, 63; 35, 52 sq.; transcendent p., *see* Miracles.

Po-yü, or Yü, Shun's minister, 3, 42 sq. and n., 258.

Po-yü, or Lî, son of Confucius, 27, 131, 131 sq. n.

Prabhâkara, n. of a Tathâgata, 49 (ii), 6, 100.

Prabhâsa, n. of a Tathâgata, 21, 199.

Prabhâsa, n. of a Sthavira, 22, 286.

Prabhava, n. of a Sthavira, 22, 287.

Prabhûtaratna, a Tathâgata, appears in the seven-jewelled Stûpa in order to hear the Lotus of the True Law, 21, xxx, 227–40, 248 sq., 283; Buddha and P. exhibit miracles, 21, xxxi, 313, 364–8, 397; identical with Devadatta (?), 21, 246 n., 247; Gadgadasvara greets the extinct Buddha P., 21, 398 sq.; Avalokite*s*vara shares his gift with Buddha *S*âkyamuni and P., 21, 412; Buddha restores the Stûpa of P., 21, 441.

Prabhuvimita, the golden hall in the world of Brahman, 1, 131, 132 n.

Pradakshi*n*a, t.t., *see* Circumambulation.

Pradâna*s*ûra, a Bodhisattva Mahâsattva, 21, 4, 372, 394, 404.

Pradhâna, t.t. of Sâṅkhya philosophy, the material cause of the world, 8, 244 sq.; 34, 291; 48, 200 sq., 281–3, 308–10, 414, 417, 428, 482–4; after perceiving the Brahman, the devotee understands

the P., 8, 253; a name of Prak*ri*ti, 8, 331; he who understands the P., is emancipated, 8, 370; meditated upon by sages, is void of smell, taste, colour, touch, sound, 8, 382; is unperceived, 8, 382; not an independent power, but the power (*s*akti) of the Deva, 15, xxxv sq.; the perishable P. is ruled by the imperishable Hara (God), 15, 235 sq.; Brahman compared to a spider drawing threads from the P., 15, 263; the thinking Purusha abides within P. (nature), 15, 313; how the perception of P. takes place, 15, 314; the Sâṅkhya doctrine of the P. as the cause of the world refuted, 34, xxxii, xlvi, l, xciii, cxvii, 16, 16 n., 46 sq., 47–64, 70 sq., 135 sq., 139–42, 237–41, 238 n., 252, 257–60, 263, 290, 296, 313 sq., 353 sq., 363–81, 437 sq.; 48, 200–8, 354–407, 475; the Upanishads teach nothing like the P., 34, cxix, 252; figuratively spoken of as thinking, 34, 52 sqq.; cannot be designated by the term 'Self,' 34, 55–60; the internal ruler is not the P., 34, 132 sq.; absolute bliss cannot result from P., 34, 138; the abode of heaven, earth, &c., cannot be the P., 34, 154, 157 sq.; the supporting of all things up to ether cannot be the work of the P., 34, 170 sq.; denoted by 'the Undeveloped,' 34, 238, 245 sqq.; by the term P. the Sâṅkhya understands the antecedent condition of the world, 34, 242; is something to be cognized, 34, 246; is not spoken of as an object of knowledge, 34, 246 sq.; not mentioned among the subjects of discussion in the colloquy between Yama and Na*k*iketas, 34, 247–52; is not denoted by a*g*â, 34, 252–7; why it is treated in the Vedânta-sûtras, 34, 288 sq., 317; assumed by the Yoga-sm*ri*ti, 34, 296; non-intelligent P. cannot be the cause of intelligent soul, 34, 308; 48, 205; is the state of equilibrium of the three gu*n*as, 34, 353, 364 n., 366 sq.; 48, 201; arguments of the Sâṅkhyas for the threefold P., 34, 364; is not intelligent, therefore cannot produce the world, 34, 367–71; 48, 484–6; does not modify itself spontaneously, 34, 371 sq.; absence of a purpose on the part of the P., 34, 372 sq., 374; the soul may move the P. as the lame man moves the blind one, or as the magnet moves the iron, 34, 373 sq.; the theory of P. adopted by Manu and other adherents of the Veda, 34, 394; Lord acts as ruler of the P. and of the souls, and P., soul, and Lord are of mutually different nature, 34, 434–7; of infinite duration, 34, 438; the same as sa*m*sâra, 34, 439; through P. the souls obtain enjoyment and release, 38, 69; Vish*n*u as P., 48, 93; is perishable, 48, 139; independent of Brahman, 48, 413; the master of the P. and the souls, the lord of the gu*n*as, 48, 469; God not the ruler of P., 48, 522 sq.; 'Brahman' used in the sense of P., 48, 533.

Pradhva*m*sana, n. of a teacher, 15, 120, 187.

Pradyumna, Vâsudeva, Saṅkarsha*n*a, and Aniruddha, 11, 267 n.; a manifestation of the highest being, 34, xxiii, 441 sq.; cannot spring from Saṅkarsha*n*a, 34, li, 441–2; a form of Vâsudeva, denotes the mind (manas), 34, 440; Aniruddha cannot spring from P., 34, 441 sq.; the internal organ so called by the Bhâgavatas, 48, 524–6.

Pra*g*âpati.

(*a*) P. a supreme God and creator; the Pra*g*âpatis.
(*b*) Other mythological conceptions of P.
(*c*) Worship of P.
(*d*) P. as a teacher.
(*e*) P. in philosophy and mysticism.

(*a*) P. A SUPREME GOD AND CREATOR; THE PRA*G*ÂPATIS.

Is the father of gods, (men), and Asuras, 1, 4; 12, 54, 54 n., 59, 110, 144, 153, 198, 265, 279, 286, 370; 15, 78, 189; 26, 31, 105, 135, 142, 301; 41, 1, 254, 256, 289, 387; 43, xvii, 59 sq., 193, 257; 44, 22, 105, 152, 423, 429; brooded on the worlds, and from them Sacrifice, and the sacred syllables, proceeded, 1, 35; called Ka, 1, 59 n.; *see also* Ka; created the three worlds, the three lights (Agni, Vâyu, and Sûrya),

and the three Vedas, 1, 70; 44, 102 sq.; the seed of P. are the Devas, 1, 205; 41, 194 sq.; 43, 220; the creator, 2, 160; 12, xviii, 173, 196 n., 205 n., 296, 322–7, 342, 384–91; 15, 97, 272 sq., 292 sq.; 25, 173 sq., 330, 400; 26, 213 sq., 302, 429 sq.; 34, 203 sq.; 38, 206; 41, 80 sq., 112, 145–61, 173, 250, 252, 299, 312, 346, 359, 402, 407, 412; 42, 217; 43, 3–12, 32 sq., 67, 71–6, 289 sq., 304, 350, 361; 44, 12–15; 48, 540; a form of K*r*ish*n*a, 8, 97; he who had been first created, created all creatures, 8, 244; fixed a limit of time for the migrations of creatures, 8, 244; the presiding deity of the generative organ, 8, 338; is lord of all peoples, 8, 347; the god above all other gods, 8, 353; 43, xx, 76; created all this by the mind only, 8, 388; as a boar, P. creates the earth, 12, 280 n.; 44, 451, 451 n.; created Agni, 12, 283, 283 n.; produced creatures, food, &c., by means of sacrifice, 12, 445; 41, 47, 283, 286 sq.; P., Hira*n*yagarbha, and Brahman Svayambhû, 15, xxxix; is the highest Brahman, 15, 190, 303; 41, 353; 43, xxiv; 44, 409, 409 n.; Brahman produced P., P. the Devas, 15, 191; milked out the sacred syllables from the three Vedas, 25, 44; having created beings, felt himself exhausted, and strengthened himself by sacrifices, 26, 217–21; draws to himself everything here, 26, 307; seasons produced from P., 26, 318; is the bull, the male, the bestower of seed, 26, 360, 368 sq.; there are thirty-three gods, P. is the thirty-fourth, 26, 411; 41, 9, 79; 44, 151, 211; over and above the three worlds, 26, 424; rules over the procreation of children, 29, 45; 30, 200; 42, 97 sq., 357, 461; the sons of P., the serpents, 29, 204; called Hira*n*yagarbha, 32, 6, 10; birth of P., whose body is this threefold world, 34, 142; 44, 458 n.; Agni, or the gods, restored the relaxed P., 41, 150–4, 168–70, 174 sq., 312–14, 319, 345, 367, 374, 377, 380, 394, 396, 414; 43, 28, 31, 36, 42, 54, 60, 142, 157, 229, 238 sq., 270, 282, 341; is the great god, 41, 160; he created by means of the Vish*n*u-strides, 41, 276, 283, 286 sq.; is both the gods and men, 41, 290; Vi*s*vakarman (the all-former) is P., 41, 311, 378; 43, 28, 37, 233; amulet created by P., 42, 86; produced Gandharvas and Apsaras, 43, 229; Father P., 43, 309, 312 sq.; constructs himself a body so as to contain the whole threefold lore, 43, 352–4; Agni, Indra, Soma, and Paramesh*th*in Prâgâpatya created out of P., 44, 15; creates *S*rî, 44, 62; was becoming heated (by fervid devotion), whilst creating living beings, 44, 62; fashioned for himself a body by means of the seasonal sacrifices, 44, 74–8; by the womb of woman P. bore creatures, 44, 114; made the worlds firm and steadied, 44, 126; creates and performs sacrifices, 44, 239, 284; the most vigorous of the gods, 44, 278; created the Virâg, 44, 310; trees from which the twenty-one sacrificial stakes are made, originated from parts of P.'s body, 44, 373 sq.; behind P. are all the gods, 44, 393; evolved names and forms by means of the Veda, 48, 332; creates the *R*ishis gifted so as to see the Mantras, 48, 332 sq.; the supreme reality (Nârâya*n*a), 48, 522;—Pragâpatis (*plur.*), the patriarchs, or creators of the world, 8, 354, 387 n.; the P. Manu, 25, xiii, lvii, lxiv, 419; 41, 250; ten lords of created beings produced by Manu, 25, 14; seven Ps., Manvantaras, 25, 19; Nârada reckoned among the Ps., 33, 2 n.

(*b*) OTHER MYTHOLOGICAL CONCEPTIONS OF P.

Hall of P., 1, 143; world of P., on the path of the gods, 1, 275; 8, 389, 389 n.; 14, 309; 15, 131, 172, 176, 337; 25, 157; 38, 386; 48, 747–9; Indra and P., doorkeepers in the world of Brahman, 1, 275 sq., 277; Sûrya, son of P., 1, 313; his incest with his daughter, 12, 208–13, 209 n., 284 n.; 41, 159 n.; 44, 36 n.; M*r*iga*s*îrsha is the head or body of P., 12, 284 sq., 284 n.; performs sacrifices, 12, 303, 323, 331, 375 sq.; 41, 256; 44, 239,

280, 289, 448; identified with Agni, 12, 386; 41, xxvii, 144, 148, 151, 153, 165, 167–9, 172 sq., 174, 183, 240 sq., 245, 284, 290, 309, 313, 330, 341, 353, 377, 386; 43, xvii, xix–xxiii, 66, 189 sq., 229, 234; 44, 275 n.; Savit*ri* is P., 12, 386; 44, 174; delivers his creatures from Varu*n*a's noose, 12, 391, 393–5, 398 sq., 404, 408, 445; Snâtaka reaches the highest abode of P. Paramesh*th*in, 14, 160; bliss of P., 15, 60 sq., 61 sq. n.; sprung forth from the sacrifice, 26, 28; man is nearest to P., 26, 341; 41, 31; gives Dakshi*n*âs, 26, 347; the G*ri*hapati of the gods, 26, 452 n.; abused, 26, 452 sq. n.; has given victory to Indra, 29, 280; the court and the assembly, the two daughters of P., 29, 362 sq.; 42, 138; the Brahman's son, 30, 194; a guardian of the world, 35, 37; the Lord of Speech, 41, 5; Soma and Surâ belong to P., 41, 8; is Heaven and Earth, 41, 28; identified with Soma, the moon, 41, 28, 178; 43, xxi sq., 349–52, 354; is Vâyu, 41, 152, 175 sq., 176 sq. n.; is both father and son of Agni, 41, 153 sq., 168–70, 360; 43, xx, 206; searches for the hidden Agni, 41, 161 sq., 215; saw the earth as the first layer of the altar, 41, 187, 190; birth of P., 41, 252; kindled Agni, 41, 284; the Bharata is P., 41, 292; assumed the form of a tortoise, 41, 390; wants to slaughter animals, 41, 401, 408; delivers from death and evil, 42, 55; 43, 67–71; in a list of gods, 42, 80, 126; splendour in P., in Paramesh*th*in, 42, 84; the first-born of *Ri*ta, supplies what is wanting to the earth, 42, 206; Time, the father of P., 42, 224 sq.; his voice is the thunder, 42, 230–2; Agni and Indra his arms, 43, xx; covets Agni's forms, 43, xx; conceived as man, and animal, 43, xxi; the Orderer and the sun, 43, xxii, 263 sq.; confounds Death, 43, 77; beset by evil, 43, 83; his food, 43, 87 sq.; the last of the gods entering heaven, 43, 113 sq., 117; Rudra produced from P. and Manyu, 43, 157; assuming the form of a chariot enclosed Gandharvas and Apsaras, 43, 229, 234; desirous of gaining these worlds fashioned the fire-altar, Mahad uktham and Mahâvrata, 43, 285 sq.; made immortal, 43, 289–94; 'The golden P.,' 43, 295, 295 n.; desirous of going up to heaven, 43, 299; the one person made out of seven persons became P., 43, 304, 312, 315; the well-winged eagle, 43, 305; afraid of death, 43, 350; overpowered by death, practises austerities for a thousand years, 43, 361; his session of a thousand years, 43, 361–3; born from the golden egg, 44, xiv, 12; the horse originated from P.'s eye, 44, xix, 328, 354; Yudhish*th*ira, at the horse sacrifice, shone like a second P., 44, xxvii; was the first to slaughter five victims (man, &c.) at the building of the fire-altar, 44, xxxviii; was born with a life of a thousand years, 44, 13; injured by the shafts of Varu*n*a, 44, 36 sq., 36 n.; the gods resort to Father P. to dispel the darkness spread by the Asuras, 44, 91 sq.; slaughtered the sun as sacrificial animal, 44, 128 sq.; poured forth the life-sap of the horse, 44, 292, 308; assigned the sacrifices to the gods, 44, 295; *G*amadagni (*Ri*shi) is P., 44, 302; desires to gain the world of the gods and the world of men, 44, 306; desired to be great and more numerous, whence he offered the Mahiman cups of Soma at the A*s*vamedha, 44, 327; lute-players sing of the Sacrificer along with P., and thereby make him share the same world with P., 44, 372 sq.; lord of the Earth, 44, 466; a being of great merit, 48, 237.

(*c*) WORSHIP OF P.

Prayers to P., 1, 21; 7, 86 n.; 11, 180; 26, 253, 376; 29, 344, 347; 30, 151; 41, 20 sq., 385; 42, 149, 161, 204; 44, 328 n.; hymn, not definitely addressed to any deity, is supposed to be addressed to P., for P. is indefinite, 1, 169; worship of, offerings to P., 2, 108, 202, 299; 7, 279; 12, 124 n., 159 sq.; 14, 307; 15, 212; 25, 90, 205; 29, 19, 28, 84, 98, 121, 141, 149, 161, 161 n., 219, 287, 290, 319, 321, 381,

387 sq.; 30, 22, 58, 91, 123, 142, 145, 158, 161, 188, 196, 203, 236, 243, 254; 33, 376; 41, 250; 44, 3, 143, 183, 206, 391, 394; reception of guests represented as a sacrifice to P., 2, 117 sq.; 29, 88; oblation to P. at the wedding, 2, 305; 25, 195, 195 sq. n.; 29, 32, 279, 283 sq., 289; 30, 49; part of the hand sacred to P., 7, 198; 25, 40; offerings to P. made with a low voice, 12, 131, 170; Muhûrta sacred to P., 14, 63, 90; the horse of the A*s*vamedha belongs to P., 15, 77; 43, 404; 44, xviii, xx, xxiii sq., 274, 274 n., 277 sq., 291 n., 295, 314, 319, 333, 336; invoked for offspring, 15, 221; 29, 171, 180 sq., 344; 30, 199; marriage rite of P., 25, 79–82; a horse sacred to P. as sacrificial fee, 25, 438, 438 n.; animal sacrifice for P., 26, 429, 429 n., 441, 443 sq.; 29, 88, 360; 41, xxiv, 14–17, 171–86; 44, 127, 383 n., 393, 405, 409, 417; student given in charge to P., 29, 189, 306, 401; 30, 66; 44, 86; the Ash*t*akâ sacred to P., 29, 206 sq., 341, 341 n.; 30, 97; connubial intercourse after the Samâvartana sacred to P., 29, 223; vow belonging to Agni together with P., 29, 229; the milkings of P., 29, 342 sq. n; Udumbara tree sacred to P., 30, 122; parasol (of Snâtaka), 'P.'s shelter,' 30, 169; he who offers the Vâgapeya becomes P.'s child, 41, 32, 33 n.; goats are of P., 41, 35; informed of the king's consecration, 41, 89; prayer to P. at the consecration, 41, 97; the Agni*k*ayana belongs to P., 41, 179; 43, xviii, xviii n.; invoked in a charm to promote virility, 42, 31; he who gives the sterile cow to the Brahmans, does not estrange himself from P., 42, 179; he-goat offered to P., 44, xxxviii sq., 371, 371 n.; the Vyâh*ri*tis relate to P., 44, 313 sq.; victims to P. at the Purushamedha, 44, 408 n.; the dead body placed in the deity P., 44, 433 sq.

(*d*) P. AS A TEACHER.

List of teachers beginning with Brahman and P., 1, 44, 144; 15, 227; 43, xviii, 401; the quarrelling senses went to their father P., who acts as umpire, 1, 73; 8, 271 n.; instructs Indra and Viro*k*ana, teaches the true Self, 1, 134–42; 34, 183–91, 199; 48, 321–4, 328, 608, 673, 675, 757, 760; praises the order of the householder, 2, 160; decides the dispute between Mind and Speech, 8, 263 n., 265; 12, 130 sq., 130 n.; instructs gods, 8, 282 sq.; 25, 164; 43, 175; 44, 103; ordains for all beings their mode of life, 12, 361 sq.; utterances about laws and customs ascribed to P. (author of a Sm*ri*ti?), 14, xvii sq., 23, 71–3, 248, 266, 309, 323, 331 sq.; 25, 335, 452, 455, 473; 33, 197; created the law by his austerities, 25, 479; decides quarrels between gods, 26, 267; the *Ri*shi of a Kâ*n*d*a, 30, 242; the great inspirer of devotion, 41, 194; the Ara*n*yenû*k*ya belongs to P., 43, 212; first saw the A*s*vamedha, and the Purushamedha, 44, xlii, 127, 275, 347; from out of P. the gods formed the Mahâvrata, 44, 140; tells Purusha Nârâya*n*a to sacrifice, 44, 172 sq.; declares that the soul has the power of realizing all its wishes, 48, 602; Kapila called P., 49 (i), 125.

(*e*) P. IN PHILOSOPHY AND MYSTICISM.

P. is the self, 1, 245; 15, 311; 26, 419, 424; 34, 142 sq. n.; 43, xxiv; is the year, 1, 265; 12, 62, 62 n., 98, 135, 144, 173, 198, 198 n., 265, 309, 346; 15, 95, 272, 317; 26, 37, 251, 301, 318, 408, 425 sq.; 41, 1, 1 n., 8, 13, 30 sq., 57 sq., 119, 152, 158, 173–5, 386; 43, xxii sq., 30, 49, 62–6, 70 sq., 76, 127, 264, 281, 313, 321–7, 347, 349–52, 356–8, 403 n.; 44, xiv, 1, 15, 344, 432 n., 506; the emancipated sage is P., 8, 219–21, 345; one of the ten fires at the allegorical sacrifice of the sense-organs, 8, 261; is the truth, 8, 315; 26, 285; is not seen by one who does not attain to the Adhyâtman, 8, 316; the Mahat is P., 8, 334; is the sacrifice, 12, 8, 8 n., 62, 62 n., 143, 210, 309, 386; 15, 140 sq.; 26, 37, 251, 302, 341, 406, 408 sq.; 41, 1, 1 n., 8 sq., 17, 30 sq., 72 sq., 79–82, 112, 118 sq., 215; 43, xxi; 44, 1, *22*, 105, 107, 116, 205, 344, 406 n., 454

sq., 484, 506; is undefined, represents all deities, 12, 160, 160 n.; 41, 179, 215; 43, 37; 44, 183, 484, 506; is speech, 12, 171; 41, 24; 44, 353; is the highest light, the heavenly world, 12, 269, 269 n., 328; the sacred fire is P., 12, 346, 349; is the devatâ of the person in the seed, 15, 145; is everything here, 15, 190; 26, 411; 41, 2 sq., 8, 15, 33; 44, 405; is the heart, 15, 190; identified with the month, day and night, and food, 15, 272 sq.; is prâ*n*a or breath, 15, 275; 26, 408; 41, 192; 42, 219; called Vi*s*va, is the Person who makes the body intelligent, 15, 292, 304; uttered the world in the words Bhû*h*, Bhuva*h*, Svar, 15, 308; the gross body of P., 15, 308 sq.; in the sun, 15, 318; Om is Brahman and P., 25, 45, 45 n.; the father is the image of P., 25, 71; identified with (Purusha's) organ of generation, 25, 512; identified with Purusha, the Man, 25, 513; 41, 366; 43, xv, xxiv; the lord of thought and speech, 26, 17, 17 n.; the she-goat is P.'s kind, 26, 71; the Soma plant called P., P. is King Soma, 26, 248, 248 n.; 44, 205; the Udgât*ri* is P., 26, 327; offers himself or is offered up as a sacrifice, 26, 327 n.; 43, xv–xvii, xxi, 304 sq.; goats and sheep like P., 26, 407; everything here is after P., 26, 408; the A*ms*u graha is P., 26, 423–6; 44, 105; he who sacrifices for a year is as P., 26, 430; the mystical syllable hiṅ of P., 29, 298; is seventeenfold, 41, 8, 14 sq., 22, 24 sq., 31, 34, 37, 40, 79, 118, 174; 43, 62, 76, 190, 347 sq.; 44, 170, 301, 352, 384; represents productiveness, 41, 15 sq.; is father and mother, 41, 28; is mysterious, 41, 89; P. and Ushas, master and mistress of the house, 41, 158; is the three worlds and the quarters, and the fourth beyond, 41, 192 sq.; 43, xx; 44, 4; he who builds a house is a P. on high, 42, 194; P. Paramesh*th*in and the Brahma*k*ârin (the sun), 42, 215 sq.; is in the u*kkh*ish*t*a, 42, 226, 228; speculations about P. the Lord of Creatures or generation, 43, xiv–xxvii; the Sacrificer identified with P., 43, xv–xvii, xix–xxiv, 1 sq. n., 32, 57 sq., 67, 76 sq., 85–92, 291–5, 300, 300 n., 309, 313–15, 321–7, 341, 355 sq.; 44, 314 n., 322 n., 406 n., 432 n.; play on the word pra*g*â in P., 43, xvi; the Year, as Death, 43, xxiii, 356–8; is Mind, 43, xxiv; identified with the Veda, 43, xxvi; identified with Agni or the fire-altar, 43, 13, 28–31, 42, 49, 54, 57, 70 sq., 92, 127, 159 sq., 181, 270, 281, 290 sq., 309, 312 sq.; 44, xiv; became a metre, 43, 36 sq.; is eighteenfold, 43, 66; P.'s layer (of the fire-altar), 43, 81; identified with the *Kh*andasyâs, 43, 114; 'Heart of P.,' a Sâman hymn, 43, 180, 180 n.; consists of sixteen parts, 43, 189; is all the sacrificial animals, 43, 299 sq.; the metres in relation to P., 43, 327–30; is the sacrificial horse, the universe, 43, 401, 401 n.; 44, xlvii sq., 274 n., 314 n., 322 n.; spoke at the end of a year, 44, 12 sq.; six portions of P. in the new and full moon sacrifice, 44, 52, 54; is the body, 44, 105; there must be no questioning beyond the god P., 44, 117 n.; as the year P. is twenty-fourfold, 44, 141 n.; how is it that Sacrifice, Man, and P. do not exceed one another? 44, 165 sq.; the A*s*vamedha is P., 44, 301, 352 sq., 375; is both defined and undefined, both limited and unlimited, 44, 454 sq. *See also* Purusha.

Pra*g*âpatî Gautamî, *see* Gautamî.

Pra*g*âpati Kratu, n. of a saint, 15, xlvii, 291, 295 sq., 299.

Pra*g*âpativâkya, in the *Kh*ândogya-upanishad, 34, lxiii.

Pra*g*âthas, the poets of the 8th Ma*nd*ala of the Rig-veda, 1, 216; receive a libation at the Tarpa*n*a, 29, 122.

Pra*gñ*â, *see* Self-consciousness.

Pra*gñ*âkûta, n. of a Bodhisattva, 21, 248–54.

Pra*gñ*â-pâramitâ, transcendent wisdom preached by Buddha, 49 (ii), 111, 124 sq., 127, 139, 147–9, 153 sq.

Pra*gñ*â-pâramitâ-h*ri*daya-sûtra, the larger and the smaller, translated, 49 (ii), xii, xx, 145–54.

Prahlâda, Indra killed his people in heaven, 1, 293; chief among demons, 8, 89, 89 n.

Prahlâda, Kapila, the son of, 14, 260; saying of P., 48, 253.
Pra*k*etas, a sage and Pragâpati, 25, 14; P. Âṅgirasa invoked for protection from evil, 42, 163, 484 sq.
Prâ*k*îna gotra, 22, 287 sq.
Prâ*k*îna*s*âla Aupamanyava, n. of a *Ri*shi, 1, 84, 86; 38, 274, 276; 43, 393 n.; 48, 288, 290.
Prâ*k*înayogîputra, n. of a teacher, 15, 226.
Prâ*k*înayogya, Satyayag*ñ*a Paulushi addressed as P., 1, 86; n. of a teacher, 15, 49, 118.
Prakramas, t.t., certain oblations at the A*s*vamedha, 44, 282 n., 363, 364 n., 365–70.
Prak*ri*ti, or Pradhâna, or Nature, t.t. of Sâ*m*khya philosophy, 8, 245 n.; 34, xxx; 48, 480 sq.; the unperceived P. is the sprout from the seed of the tree of worldly life, 8, 313, 313 n.; the five gross elements developed from the P., 8, 318 n.; names and attributes of P., 8, 331, 331 n.; 48, 526; is the three qualities in equilibrium, 8, 331 n.; is beginningless and eternal, 8, 351 n.; 48, 399; the physical manifestations of P. beyond the domain of worldly life, 8, 355 n.; ignorance is the same thing as P., 8, 357 n.; the Purusha feeds on the food supplied by P., 15, 313; mutual relation of P. and soul, 34, lxxxiii; 48, 490–5; the Unevolved, 48, 62; evil qualities connected with P. denied of Brahman, 48, 78, 81; merged in the highest Self, 48, 88; Self connected with the different effects of P., 48, 89; is Mâyâ, 48, 125 sq., 139, 364; differences due to P., 48, 127; the Self not an effect of P., 48, 240; dependent on Brahman, 48, 363–5, 396; is agâ the P.? 48, 365–70; exists in a twofold state, being either cause or effect, 48, 368; a non-intelligent principle, the causal substance of the material universe, 48, 370, 396, 399; soul, the ruler of P., 48, 378; the Lord creates this world in so far only as guiding P., 48, 397; denotes Brahman in its causal phase when names and forms are not yet distinguished, 48, 399; P. and soul constitute the body of Brahman, 48, 406; creation results from connexion of P. and soul, 48, 424 sq., 490, 492; by the attributes of P. actions are wrought, 48, 553. *See also* Pradhâna, Unevolved, *and* Unperceived.
Pralaya, t.t., reabsorption of the world into Brahman at the end of each kalpa, 34, xxix, liv, xciv, 382 n., 386–9, 391; 38, 47, 371, 392. *See also* Ages of the World (*a*), *and* World (*b*).
Pramâda Dâsa Mitra, on God and Brahman, 15, xxxviii.
Pramandanî, n. of an Apsaras, 42, 33.
Pramlo*k*antî, n. of an Apsaras, 43, 106.
Prâ*n*a, *see* Breath, Life, *and* Prâ*n*as.
Prâ*n*abh*ri*t, Sk., t.t., individual soul, 34, 158.
Prâ*n*âgnihotra, *see* Prâ*n*as (*b*).
Prâ*n*as (breaths, breathings, life-winds, vital airs, organs of sense and action).

(*a*) Number of P.
(*b*) The five breathings.
(*c*) The P. as organs of sense and action.

(*a*) Number of P.

Meditation on the fivefold Sâman as the P., 1, 25 sq.; five P. or senses identified with Vasus, Rudras, and Âdityas, 1, 50; there are nine or ten P., the tenth being the vital self, 1, 184, 184 n., 186; 12, 140; 26, 25; 41, 50, 93, 135, 183, 196, 218, 296 sq.; 43, 164 sq. (identified with Agni), 243, 309; 44, 24, 137, 150, 153; are twelvefold, seven in the head, two on the breast, three below, 1, 194, 196; seven vital airs in the head, 26, 17; 41, 241, 340, 402 sq.; 43, 277, 314, 329; 44, 203, 235, 291, 488, 506; their number, 38, 79–84, 94; 48, 570–2; by the six vital airs the self is able to exist, 41, 270; 44, 262, 468 sq.; four vital airs in the head, undefined number in the body, 41, 331; bestowing the ten vital airs on Agni (the fire-altar), 43, 1–22, 2 n.; fivefold in the head, 43, 190; 44, 36; are the ten Rudras, 44, 116; called the ten heroes, 44, 238.

(*b*) The five breathings.

Vyâna is a combination of prâ*n*a and apâna, 1, 7; the five breathings, viz. prâ*n*a, vyâna, apâna, samâna,

udâna, 1, 46 sq., 223; 15, 148; 29, 295; 34, 342; 38, 86, 89; 41, 336 sq., 339; 48, 466 sq., 574 sq.; Prâ*n*âgnihotra, five Agnihotra oblations to Prâ*n*a, &c., 1, 89–91; 14, 262–4, 266, 304 sq.; 38, 249–52; 44, 321, 378; offering of the P., 8, 61 sq.; their movements in the body, 8, 237 sq.; produced from food, 8, 238; from the Brahman the P. proceed, and into it they enter, 8, 258; speech produced by means of the P., 8, 263–6; speech dwelt between prâ*n*a and apâna, 8, 264; Prâ*n*âyâma or restraint of P., 8, 266 n.; the five P. as five priests, 8, 270; death met with on the exhaustion of the P., 8, 270; the five P. appeal to Brahman to decide who is the greatest amongst them, 8, 271–4; when a creature is born, which of the P. comes into existence first? 8, 274–7; there are three P. (prâ*n*a, udâna, vyâna) in man, 8, 331; 12, 20, 99; 15, 196, 198; 26, 17, 210, 252–8, 255 n., 260, 262–5, 323, 358 sq., 366; 41, 317; 43, 236 sq., 402; 44, 89 sq., 246, 321, 467, 470, 499; the five P. are joined to the inner self, and together with speech, mind, and understanding make the eight constituents of the universe, 8, 336; two or three vital airs (prâ*n*a, udâna, &c.), 12, 19 sq. and n.; the Samidhs identified with the P., 12, 152; the rays of the sun extend down to the P., 12, 343; prayer to the five P., 14, 299, 299 n.; the Vyâh*r*itis as the breathings, 15, 49; Prâ*n*a, Apâna, Vyâna form the body of the Self, 15, 55, 308; identified or connected with the quarters, 15, 160, 338–40; the origin, entry, place, the fivefold distribution (Apâna, &c.), and the internal state of the Prâ*n*a, 15, 276–8, 293 sq.; eating, a sacrifice to the P., 15, 312; are born of the mind, 26, 39; identified with deities, 26, 39; 41, 273; grahas are the vital airs, 26, 298 sq., 301, 419–21, 424; created seven persons or souls, 41, 144, 144 n.; assuming the form of a bird, the P. became Pragâpati, 41, 157, 157 n.; in-breathing and out-breathing protect life, 42, 49 sq., 52 sq., 57, 60; bricks of the fire-altar identified with P., 43, 60, 82, 90; up-breathing and in-breathing identified with full and new moon, 44, 31; fore-offerings and after-offerings represented as out-breathings and off-breathings, 44, 43, 43 n.; navel the channel of central breathing, 44, 58; Mitra is in-breathing, Varu*n*a is off-breathing, 44, 269; oblations to in-breathing and off-breathing, 44, 378.

(*c*) THE P. AS ORGANS OF SENSE AND ACTION.

In dreamless sleep the P. become absorbed in the prâ*n*a (breath) alone, 1, 58, 307; the quarrel of the P., viz. breath, speech, eye, ear, mind, 1, 72–4; 8, 207; 15, 201–4, 274 sq.; 34, lxx, 304; 38, 88 sq., 186 sqq., 200, 211, 215, 309; 48, 572, 574; all senses are breath, therefore they are called the P. or breaths, 1, 74; 15, 97 sq.; 48, 577 sq.; meditation on P. as identified with the hymns of the Rig-veda and their poets, 1, 214–18; after having become one, the P. perceive speech, form, sound, thought together, but breath alone is self-consciousness, 1, 294 sq.; absorption of the other P. into breath, at the time of death, 1, 295 sq.; 15, 126; the seats of the P., 7, 285; the P., the tongue, the mind, and the qualities of goodness and passion make up the manifestations as individual entities, 8, 292, 292 n.; offerings to the P. (breath, speech, &c.), 15, 210 sq.; 44, 504, 506; prâ*n*a, vital air, a generic name denoting the sense-organs, and the manas, 34, lix, 261, 269 sqq.; 38, 65 n., 93 sq., 96; their origination, 34, lix; 38, 74–9; 48, 568–70; they are minute, 34, lix; 38, 84; 48, 572 sq.; are superintended and guided in their activity by special divinities, they are independent principles, not mere modifications of the chief vital air, 34, lix; 38, 91–6; 48, 586 sq.; do not depart from the body, 34, cxii; the word 'person' applied to them, 34, 261; the instance of the P. illustrates the identity of cause and effect, 34, 342 sq.; the individual soul is the sustaining principle of the P., 34, 361; 38, 367 sq.; difference of scriptural

statements regarding them, 38, 3, 74–9; called graha, seizers, 38, 79, 83; although guided by divinities, are yet connected with the individual soul, 38, 92 sq.; are not functions of the chief vital air, 38, 94; when a new body is obtained, they also go from the old body to the new one, 38, 105; at the time of death the P. go to the other gods, 38, 105 sq.; do not depart from the embodied soul of him who knows Brahman, 38, 372 sq.; are *Ri*shis, 41, 143, 333; 43, xxi n., 60, 122, 174, 185; 48, 568 sq.; Pra*g*âpati produces creatures by union with the P., the life-sustaining gods, 43, 32, 34; put into the body of Agni (the fire-altar), 43, 51, 54–61, 90 sq., 136, 138–44, 149, 209–12, 214, 220; identified with Agni, 43, 70; assist Pra*g*âpati in the creation, 43, 72–6; are the highest of all this universe, 43, 149; the Sâmans are P., and the P. are immortality, 43, 177 sq.; are the gods among the gods, 43, 185 sq., 304; are the immortal element, 43, 220; food conveyed to them, 43, 347 sq.; mind, speech, and the other P., 43, 376–9; work incomplete without P., P. incomplete without work, 43, 379; the mouth is the extreme end of the P., 44, 76; speech, breath, eye, and other P., 44, 174; imperishable are the P., 44, 174; the sacred fires identified with them, 44, 190; the bearer of P., i.e. the individual soul, 48, 298, 554 sq.; the rule of the soul and the presiding divinities (Agni, &c.) over the P. proceeds from the will of Brahman, 48, 575–7; all P. are 'organs' except the vital breath, 48, 577 sq.; soul, when passing out from the body, followed by the P., 48, 586. *See also* Organs, *and* Senses.

Prâ*n*asa*m*vâda, Sk., the quarrel of the senses, 1, 72 n.; 34, lxx. *See also* Prâ*n*as (*c*).

Prâ*n*ata Kalpa, the tenth world of the gods, 22, 271.

Pra*n*ava, t.t., the drawing out of the syllable Om, *see* Om.

Prâ*n*avidyâ or prâ*n*asa*m*vâda, t.c., 1, 72 n., 234 n., 236; 34, lxviii; 38, 200 sq., 212. *See* Prâ*n*as (*c*).

Pra*n*îtâ*h*, *see* Water (*b*).

Prâptasena, the 44th Tathâgata, 49 (ii), 6.

Pra*s*âst*ri*, *see* Priests (*a*).

Prasena*g*it, king of Ko*s*ala, 19, 213, 213 n., 230–40.

Praska*nn*va Kâ*n*va, author of hymns addressed to matutinal deities, 46, 37, 39, 42 sq.

Pra*s*na-upanishad, quoted, 8, 20 and notes on 65, 79, 81, 123, 152, 166, 176, 259, 271, 390 sq.; 34, xliii; 38, 428; 48, 778; translated, 15, xlii sq., 269–84.

Pra*s*navâhanaka Kula of the Kau*t*ika Ga*n*a, 22, 292.

Prâ*s*nîputra Âsurivâsin, n.p., 15, 226.

Prâta*h*savana, *see* Sacrifice (*i*).

Pratâpavat, the 2nd Tathâgata, 49 (ii), 6.

Pratardana, the son of Divodâsa, came to the abode of Indra, instituted the inner Agnihotra, 1, 283, 293 sqq.; 34, 97–9, 101; 38, 305 sq.; 48, 250–4.

Pratibimbavâda, Sk., t.t., the doctrine that the soul is a reflection of the Self in the buddhi, 34, lviii, xcvii sq.

Pratibodha, the watchful divinity, or the Sage Watchful, 42, 54, 60, 571.

Prâtîbodhî, n. of a wife of Hrasva Mâ*nd*ûkeya, 1, 253.

Pratîdar*s*a *S*vaikna performed the Dâkshâya*n*a sacrifice, 12, 376; P. Aibhâvata questioned by Suplan Sâr*ñ*gaya, 44, 239, 239 n.

Pratihart*ri*, *see* Priests (*a*).

Pratî*k*îna, 'back-hurler,' the descendant of Aṅgiras, 42, 73, 603.

Pratîkopâsana, *see* Meditation.

Pratikrama*n*a, *G*aina t.t., expiation of sins enjoined by Mahâvîra, 45, 434 sq., 434 n.

Prâtimoksha, *see* Pâtimokkha.

Prâtipîya, *see* Balhika P.

Pratiprasthât*ri*, *see* Priests (*a*).

Prâtitheyî, *see* Va*d*avâ P.

Prât*ri*da, n.p., 15, 194.

Pratyânîka, King, oblation (at the wedding) to, 29, 32.

Pratyavaroha*n*a, *see* Serpents.

Pratyekabuddhas, the vehicle of the, 21, 10, 78–80, 88 sq.; men who covet the state of P. compared to

mean plants, 21, 126; hospitality towards P. and Bodhisattvas, 21, 318, 318 n.; the four P., Nami, &c., 45, 35 n., 87 n.

Pravâha*n*a *G*aivali, prince of Pa*ñk*âla, questions *S*vetaketu, 1, 15–17, 76 sq.; 12, xlii; 15, 204–9; 48, 585.

Pravara, *see R*ishis, and Sacrifice (*i*).

Pravargya ceremony, at Soma sacrifice, 38, 222–4; 41, 355; 43, 187 sq.; 44, 441–510; its history and significance, 44, xlvi–l; sacrifice shattered by the death of the samrâ*g*-cow, atonement for it, 44, 131–4, 131 n.; the names Gharma, P., Mahâvîra, Samrâ*g* explained, 44, 442 sq.; a mystery taught by Dadhya*ñk* to the A*s*vins, 44, 444; to be kept secret, 44, 445, 458 n.; the P. is the sun, 44, 445 sq., 452 sq., 457, 460, 466 sq., 469, 472–4, 477, 481 sq., 484 sq., 501; he who teaches or partakes of the P. enters that life and that light, 44, 458, 468, 472, 478, 493, 504, 510; observance of P. is the same as Creation, 44, 458, 458 n., 468, 472, 478, 493, 504, 510; the head of the sacrifice, 44, 461; called Emperor (Samrâ*g*) as distinguished from King Soma, 44, 461, 461 n.; is the wind, 44, 475; must not be performed at one's first Soma-sacrifice, and not for anybody and everybody, 44, 490; the P. is the year, the P. is everything, 44, 491, 507 sq.; sacrifices at which a P. may be performed, 44, 491; how it is distinguished from other sacrifices, 44, 491–3; arrangement of sacrificial apparatus in form of human body, 44, 499 sq.; is Agni, Vâyu, Âditya, and is all sacrifices, 44, 508 sq.; to be studied in the forest, 48, 644 sq. *See also* Sacrifice (*j*).

Pravra*g*ita, *see* Pabba*g*ita.

Prâya*n*îya, °yesh*t*i, *see* Sacrifice (*i*).

Prayantika, a Brahma*k*ârin, converted by Buddha, 19, 242.

Prâyas*k*itta, Sk., t.t., *see* Penances.

Prayasvanta Âtreya, author of a Vedic hymn, 46, 410.

Prayers.

(*a*) Indian p. in general.
(*b*) Indian p. for certain occasions.
(*c*) Certain Indian p. (alphabetically arranged).
(*d*) Zoroastrian p. in general.
(*e*) Zoroastrian p. for certain occasions, to certain divinities.
(*f*) Certain Zoroastrian p. (alphabetically arranged).
(*g*) Chinese p.
(*h*) P. in Islâm.

See also Charms, Curse, Exorcisms, Imprecations, Speech, *and* Spells.

(*a*) Indian p. in general.

All sacrifices are contained in the hymns, 1, 112, 114; fired by hope does memory read the hymns, 1, 119; hymn of triumph, of one who has reached the world of Brahman, 1, 143; 'rich in p.,' an epithet of Sarasvatî, 1, 165; p. will not save a man who is in the bonds of death, 7, 82; those who neglect their p. defile a company, 7, 253; one intent upon saying p. sanctifies a company, 7, 254; an ascetic must not pronounce a benediction, 7, 280; the taint of p. is non-repetition, 10 (i), 61; worthlessness of hymns and sacrifices, 10 (ii), 41 sq.; the Brâhma*n*as, having composed hymns, went to the king to advise him to offer sacrifices, 10 (ii), 50 sq.; the teaching of p. for fire-sacrifice, a low art, 11, 199 sq.; spoken p. and thought p. convey the sacrifice to the gods, 12, 124 sq.; a student reciting p. shall stand in the day-time and sit down at night, 14, 42; more efficacious than sacrifices, 14, 128; 25, 45 sq.; great meritoriousness of reciting p., 14, 128 sq.; the fivefold obeisance to the Arhats, &c., is the best benediction, 22, 217, 224 sq.; sacraments for females without p., 25, 42; the muttering of a sacrificial formula is an occult form of sacrifice, 26, 20; p. are also sacrifices, 29, 159 sq.; sacrificial objects hallowed by p. must not be tossed about, 30, 331; gods delight in p., and p. delight in gods, 32, 86, 179; Sumati=p., 32, 219–21; *Sam*sa means blessing or curse, or p. of praise, 32, 270 sq.; p. also are conducive to knowledge of Brahman, 38, 316; 48, 704; effect of p., 41, 235, 235 n.; ceremonies with and without p., 41, 341 sq.; p. is thought, 41, 352; sacrifices purified by p., 42, 211 sq.; fire of Rohita kindled by p., 42, 213;

list of p. and liturgies, 42, 226–8; by singing praises and sacrificing the gods do everything, 43, 73; p. and metres, 43, 330 sq.; hymn of praise is food for the gods, 44, 232; unsuccessful in the sacrifice is what is performed without a formula, 44, 276; praises and hymns necessary for final beatitude, 45, 159, 164; Agni invoked to announce to the gods 'this our newest efficient Gâyatra song,' 46, 16; *be magnified, O Agni, through this spell (brahman), which we have made for thee with our skill or with our knowledge*, 46, 24; worshipper expects reward for his p., 46, 46, 52, 327; the Aṅgiras have broken even fortresses by their hymns, 46, 74; Agni invoked to prosper the p., 46, 108, 303; p. compared with horses, 46, 164; p. compared to a cow yielding milk, 46, 194, 197; increase, strengthen the god, 46, 228, 240, 259, 391, 413; Agni is like a worshipper bearing the lights of p., 46, 259 sq.; Agni invoked for assistance in spells and hymns, 46, 266, 281, 350, 352; Agni gives wealth for p., 46, 300; Agni is the first-born son of the sacred spell, 46, 304; Agni has laid the p., like a burden, on the worshipper, 46, 335; godless people called 'hymnless,' 46, 366; the poet has fashioned his hymn like a workman a chariot, 46, 367; Agni led by p. and sacrifices, 46, 380; salvation (Sukhâvatî) obtained by p., not by works, 49 (ii), 98 sq., 98 n., 102; Lord of p., *see* Brahma*n*aspati.

(*b*) INDIAN P. FOR CERTAIN OCCASIONS.

P. to secure the life of sons, and at rites of conception, childbirth, &c., 1, 49 sq., 285–8, 286 n.; 14, 273; 15, 220–4; 29, 46–57, 180–6, 287, 290–300, 394–9; 30, 52–63, 208–18; for a man when his end approaches, 1, 52 sq., 261, 313 sq., 313 n.; 15, 199 sq.; hymns to be recited at the Mahâvrata ceremony, 1, 157–72, 176–99, 202–4; at rites connected with the study of the Veda, 1, 246; 29, 143–50, 218–22, 322 sq., 325, 368; 30, 73–8, 161, 242 sq., 245 sq.; recited by a man who, speaking in an assembly, does not please, 1, 264; to the Prâ*n*as, 1, 281 sqq.; 14, 262–4; for travelling and returning home from a journey, 1, 288; 29, 96–8, 231; at expiatory rites, 2, 85 sq., 275 sq. and n.; 7, 153–5; 14, 250–2; 15, 312; 25, 272, 272 n., 330 sq. and n.; 44, 179–81, 188 sq., 191–6, 206–11; addressed to Rudra and his hosts, 2, 96; 12, 440–3; 29, 255–9, 352–4; 30, 92 sq., 221–4; daily p., 2, 105; 25, 151 sq.; 30, 19–22; at the Vaiṣvadeva ceremony, 2, 106–9, 106 sq. n., 109 n.; of a teacher, 2, 114; 15, 47 sq.; to the dead at funeral oblations and rites for the manes, 2, 138 n.; 7, 86, 86 n.; 11, xlii sq.; 12, 364–9, 426–36; 14, 267–70; 25, 123; 29, 103 sq., 107, 109–11, 206 sq., 239, 241–3, 246, 251–5, 355–7, 355 n., 421–4; 30, 106–13, 225–36; 44, 205, 430–4, 437–40; to be recited inaudibly by the hermit, 2, 157; twilight devotions (sandhyâ), morning and evening p., 2, 187, 187 n.; 7, 116 sq., 229; 12, 344 n.; 14, 126 sq., 163, 245–9, 246 n.; 25, 42, 44, 48 sq., 70, 70 n., 143, 252; 29, 74, 225 sq., 286 sq.; at penances, 2, 279, 287, 289–301, 289 n., 291 n., 295 n.; 7, 88, 93, 97, 121, 149, 151, 161, 165, 175 sq., 178 sq., 181–6; 14, 102 sq., 110 sq. and n., 116 sq., 120, 122, 125–9, 132, 134 sq., 215–17, 222, 294–302, 304–6, 316–22, 327 sq., 330; 25, 44, 48 sq., 63, 439, 454, 457, 459, 459 n., 467, 470, 476, 476 n., 479–82; 29, 287 sq.; for bathing, 7, 205–7; at the worship of Vish*n*u, 7, 208–10; p. muttered at sacred places confer eternal bliss, 7, 256; at rites for the protection of cattle, 7, 261 sq.; 29, 99–101, 215 sq., 258 sq., 354; 30, 87 sq., 184–6; 42, 143–5, 150, 303 sq., 351 sq., 359–61, 412–14, 490, 493; in praise of Vish*n*u, Indra, and B*ri*haspati, 7, 266; at Soma sacrifices, 12, 11, &c.; 26, 54, &c.; 42, 18, 562; at the preparation of the sacrificial fires, the Agnihotra libations and other rites of fire-worship, 12, 2, 275, 293, 298, 298 n., 300–2, 307 n., 317–22, 335–7, 346 n., 349–60, 389 n.; 29, 133 sq.; 30, 201–3, 267; on taking the vow of abstinence, 12, 3 sq.; at

the choosing of priests, 12, 6 sq.; 29, 193–7; at preparatory rites to a sacrifice, 12, 7 n., 11–175; special p. for Brâhma*n*as and Kshatriyas, 12, 35, 35 n.; p., rites, and knowledge of rites by which a sacrificer defeats enemies, 12, 35–7, 53, 57 sq., 66, 69, 97, 113, 130, 132 n., 139, 149 sq., 154 sq., 158 sq., 171, 182, 199, 236 sq., 269 sq., 298 sq., 340, 409, 416 sq.; 26, 119, 123, 142 sq., 171, 217, 243, 251 sq., 255, 262, 433; 41, 53 sq.; for new and full moon sacrifices, 12, 175–273; 29, 173–5; 42, 18, 559; benedictions for offspring, cattle, long life, health, and prosperity, 12, 226 sq.; 42, 47–63, 81, 220, 306 sq., 309, 341 sq., 364 sq., 381, 383, 455, 551 sq., 569 sq., 573, 623, 625, 668 sq.; 43, 108 sq., 109 n.; Hot*ri* invokes blessings on the sacrificer, 12, 248–56; at the Varu*n*apraghâsa sacrifice, 12, 397–407; for the ceremony of adoption, 14, 76, 76 n.; at the readmission of an outcast, 14, 78; at rites of purification, 14, 160–2, 161 sq. n., 191, 195 sq.; 25, 183, 183 n., 188; to the sun for a sick person, 14, 215; invocations to gods, *Ri*shis, &c. &c., at the Tarpa*n*a, 14, 252–6; enjoined for ascetics, 14, 275–83; on departing from one's home, 14, 286, 289; at rites securing success, 14, 323, 333; at the horse-sacrifice, 15, 123 sqq.; 44, 276–82, 282 n., 287 sq., 292–5, 297 sq., 304 sq. and n., 311–14, 316–36, 329 sq. n., 348 sq., 351–3, 356–9, 375–82 (Stotras and *S*astras), 384–7, 391, 394; to Agni, Vâyu, Âditya, and Brahman, 15, 334 sq.; certain hymns connected with certain quarters, 15, 338–40; Buddha receives the *G*etavana with a p., 19, 231, 231 n.; hymns in praise of Buddha, 19, 352 sq., 357–9, 362–4, 368–70; 49 (ii), 162, 164; recitations of Bhikkhus as a protection to Buddha when his life is threatened by Devadatta, 20, 246 sq.; praises of Sthaviras, 22, 295; at meals, 25, 39 sq., 170, 173 sq.; morning p., 25, 153; 29, 19 sq.; at wedding rites, 25, 195 sq., 195 n.; 29, 21–46, 164 sq., 167–71, 277–90, 380–5; 30, 42–52, 187–99, 33, 165; p. that destroy poison, 25, 251; at the Dîkshâ, 26, 5–11, 14, 16–29, 33 sq., 37 sq., 41–5; 44, 122; at hair shaving or cutting, 26, 6 sq., 7 n.; 29, 301–3; at animal sacrifices, 26, 162–217; 29, 176–8; at domestic ceremonies, 29, 19, &c., 30, 19, &c.; at the Upanayana ceremony, 29, 61–8, 188–93, 304–8, 400–2; 30, 64–7, 142–60; 44, 86 sq.; addressed to Agni, 29, 75 sq.; 42, 18, 559; 46, 1, &c.; at ceremonies relating to the Brahma*k*ârin, 29, 75 sq., 90–2; at house-building rites, 29, 92–6, 213–15, 345–9; 30, 123 sq., 204–7; 42, 140 sq., 343–8; at agricultural rites, 29, 98 sq., 126 sq., 215, 331–8; 30, 93 sq.; 42, 141 sq., 486, 499, 541; at the Ash*t*akâs, 29, 102–5, 206 sq., 341–4, 417–24; 30, 98–110; for the ceremony performed when crossing water, 29, 127; for serpent worship, 29, 127–32, 201 sq., 204 sq., 257, 327–30, 338–41; 30, 90 sq., 94–6, 237–41; for the consecration of tanks, wells, ponds, and gardens, 29, 134–6; to avert evil omens, 29, 136–40, 224–6, 231; 30, 81, 180–4; recited before the performance of a sacrament, 29, 164; at the reception of guests, 29, 198–200, 273–6; 30, 129–31, 171–5; on mounting a chariot, and the like, 29, 209–11, 362–6; at the Samâvartana, 29, 228 sq., 313–16; 30, 83 sq., 162–71; for averting danger and misfortune, 29, 231–3, 247–50, 366 sq.; 30, 118 sq.; before battle, 29, 233–5; at connubial intercourse, 29, 290; to Indra and the Maruts, 29, 331 sq.; to the waters, 29, 349 sq.; to prevent a servant from running away, 29, 351; to Kâma or Lust, 29, 362; for one who cannot pay a debt, 30, 113; for the obtainment of special wishes, 30, 114–20, 124–8; 43, 340; for various magic and auspicious rites, 30, 176–9; to the moon, 30, 179; charms against diseases, 30, 219 sq.; 42, 59–62, 339, 341, 406, 456, 473; for rain, 32, 181; for health and wealth (*s*ám yó*h*), 32, 193 sq.; at ordeals, 33, 105 n., 106 sq., 106 n., 108 n., 109 sq., 111 n., 113–16, 119 sq., 253–5, 258–61, 319, 319 n.; recited by a widow, 33, 381; at the Vâga-

peya sacrifice, 41, 6 sq., 18–41; at the king's consecration, 41, 71–112, 133–5; 42, 111, 239; at the building of the fire-altar, 41, 154, 155 sq., 167–9, 193, &c.; 43, 3–12, 21, &c.; imprecations against demons, sorcerers, and enemies, 42, 64–93, 237 sq., 256 sq., 285, 295, 298, 334 sq., 389–404, 456–8, 475 sq., 495 sq., 544 sq., 602 sq.; diseases and misfortunes conjured upon others, 42, 66, 301; imprecations against enemies, 42, 88 sq., 117–33, 167 sq., 191, 201, 214, 221–3, 592, 660; 43, 105 sq., 155, 165 sq., 171; incantation to make a woman sterile, 42, 98, 545; incantations against a rival or co-wife, 42, 107 sq., 252–5, 354–6; for deliverance from calamity to all the gods, 42, 160–2, 628 sq.; wrong committed through imprecations, 42, 163; imprecations against the oppressors of Brâhma*n*as, 42, 169–72, 184, 430–6; for victory in a debate or assembly, 42, 644; at the seasonal sacrifices, 44, 78 sq., 78 n., 79 n.; night-hymns and day-hymns recited at sacrificial sessions, 44, 92; at the Sautrâma*n*î sacrifice, 44, 223–8, 230–4, 236–9, 242–5, 250–9, 264–8; at the Purushamedha, 44, 409 sq.; at the Pravargya sacrifice, 44, 449–60, 462–89, 494–507; for wealth and for liberal givers, 46, 88 sq., 420 sq. (dânastuti); liturgical verses addressed to the sacrificial post, 46, 252–5; repeating the name of Buddha Amitâbha secures salvation, 49 (i), viii sq., 1; muttered by hermits before the shrines of the gods, 49 (i), 74; Gâthâs in praise of the Buddha Lokes*v*ararâga, 49 (ii), 7–9; Gâthâs in praise of Buddha countries and Buddhas, 49 (ii), 22–4, 70 sq.

(*c*) CERTAIN INDIAN P. (ALPHABETICALLY ARRANGED).

The *Adhrigu* litany, 26, 188; 44, 385 sq., 385 n.; the *Agnish*t*oma* and Agnish*t*oma-Sâman, 41, xiii sq., 12, 127; 43, 252, 287, 289; 44, 147, 376; the *Âgur*-formulas uttered at the new and full moon sacrifice, 44, 32 sq. and n.; the *Âgya-s*a*stra*, 26, 323 n., 325–31; the *anuvâkyâs* or invitatory p. and the *yâgyâs* or offering p., 12, 117–20, 119 n., 135 n., 202 n., 387, 411–14, 416; 26, 105, 254 sq.; 44, 25 sq., 54 sq., 63–6, 247 sq., 262, 302; offering-formulas and *anumantra*n*as*, 44, 40, 40 n.; the *Âprî* verses, forming the offering-p. at the fore-offerings of the animal sacrifice, 12, 400 n.; 26, 185 sq. and n.; 41, 169, 173 sq., 183 sq.; 44, 129, 244, 244 n., 302, 519; 46, 8–12, 153–6, 179 sq., 191 sq., 198–201, 236–9, 377 sq.; the *âpti* formulas, 41, 29 sq.; *Â*s*vina*s*astra* and morning-litany, 44, 92–4; *Avakâ*s*a* formulas, 26, 409; *Âvid* formulas by which gods are informed of the king's consecration, 41, 89 sq.; the *Bahishpavamâna* stotra, 26, 275 sq., 307 n., 309–11, 309 n., 310 n., 311 sq. n., 315; 44, 173; chanting the *Brahma*s*âman*, 26, 433–6; *gâyatra* songs, 46, 104, 154, 180; *gâyatrî*, *see* Sâvitrî; *Grâva-stotra*, praise of the stones at the pressing of Soma, 26, 332 n.; the *Idâ*, Sûktavâka, &c., 44, 37, 42 sq.; the k*aturhot*ri formulas, 26, 452, 452 n.; the *Kayâ*s*ubhîya* hymn serves for mutual understanding, 1, 170; the *k*l*ipti* formulas, 41, 30 sq.; *Mahad uktham*, the Great Litany, 43, 110, 110 sq. n., 112 n., 113, 113 n., 167–9, 168 n., 222 sq., 273, 278; the Great Litany recited after the building of the fire-altar, 43, 281–9, 286 n., 298, 342, 342 n., 346–9, 366 sq.; *Mahânâmnî* hymns in the Aitareya-âra*n*yaka, 1, xciii, xciii n.; the *Mahâvrata Sâman* and Great Litany chanted at the Mahâvrata, 43, xxvi sq., 278, 281 n., 282–9, 282 sq. n., 286 n., 298, 342, 342 n., 346–9, 366 sq., 367 n.; the *Marutvatîya* hymn for the noon-libation of the Mahâvrata, 1, 166–72; the *mât*r*inâmâni* hymns, 42, 399; *Nârâ*s*âm*s*âni*, recitals in praise of pious men, at the Purushamedha, 44, xxxii, xlii; the *Nigadas*, 12, 114 n., 202 n.; the *Nishkevalya-*s*astra* at the Mahâvrata ceremony, 1, 172–97, 218–35; *Nivids*, solemn formulas of invocation, 12, 114 n.; 15, 139; 46, 119, 122; the *Pañka*d*a*s*a-stoma*, 26, 167; *Parimâda*

Sâmans, 43, 288, 288 n.; the *Patnî-samyâgas*, 44, 25, 37, 42–4; the Abhyâroha of the *Pavamâna* verses, and other Stotras, 15, 83 sq.; the Pavamâna chants, during which the Soma becomes clarified, 26, 307–11, 315, 315 n., 332 n., 333, 333 n., 336 n., 357 n., 360 n.; 44, 235; *Pâvamânî* verses means of purification, 2, 5 sq.; *Praishas* of the Maitrâvaru*n*a priest, 46, 10; morning-prayer (*prâtar-anuvâka*) on the day of the Soma feast, 26, 226–32, 229 sq. n.; 41, xviii; 43, 249, 249 n.; 44, 92–4; *G*aina monk should recite the *Pratikramana-sûtra*, 45, 148 sq.; hymn to be chosen for the *pra-uga*, 1, 161–5; *Pravara* mantra by which Agni is invited to assist the sacrificer as Hot*ri*, 12, 114–20, 114 n.; *Pri*s*h*tha consisting of seven elements, 44, 2, 170 sq.; 46, 335, 337 sq.; *Puro'nuvâkyâ* and Praisha and offering formula, 44, 391; *Puroru*k formula, 44, 391, 391 n.; *Sâmidhenî* verses, recited at the kindling of fire, 12, 96–114, 120–4, 120 n.; 26, 13; 30, 345; 41, 167 sq., 172, 174, 183 sq.; 44, 24 sq., 35, 39 sq., 65, 350, 352, 355–8; *Samish*t*ayagus*, 44, 44; the *Sam-yuvâkas* or 'All-hail' blessings, 12, 254 sq. and n.; 26, 371, 371 n.; 44, 29, 37, 42–4; the *Sarpanâma* formulas, 41, 369–71; the *S*atarudriya, p. to Rudra, 43, 150–81, 298; *Satya Sâman*, the true hymn, 41, 363, 363 n.; *Stotras* and *S*a*stras* at the allegorical sacrifice of concentration of mind, 8, 280; the different Stomas or forms of chanting stotras, 26, 308 sq. n., 313, 313 n.; Stotras or hymns of the Udgât*ri*, and *S*astras, songs of praise, recited by the Hot*ri*, 26, 323 sq. n., 325 sq. n., 326 sq. n., 336 sq. n., 339, 339 n., 361 n., 368–70 n., 373, 375, 387, 397 sq. n., 401, 401 n., 405 sq. n., 418 n., 451 sq., 451 n.; Stotras are taught in the three Vedas, and so also the meditations resting on them, 38, 282 sq.; Stotras and *S*astras, Sâmans and Stomas, at Soma sacrifices, and sacrificial sessions, 41, xii–xxiv, 8 sq. n., 11 n., 12 n., 15 sq. n., 41, 41 n., 69 n., 81, 91, 113, 118, 127 sq. and n., 274, 376; 43, 246, 252, 252 n.; 44, 152 sq., 156–9, 163–7, 170 sq., 395–401, 405, 418–20; Sâmans and Stomas, used at the Agni*k*ayana, 43, 4–14, 20, 26, 43, 59–70, 77–81, 85, 92–4, 100, 143–6, 192, 217 sq., 220, 319; seven Stomas, 43, 277, 314; all the gods, &c., all the Stomas (hymn forms), all the P*ri*sh*th*as abide here on new moon day, 44, 2; the *Subrahmanyâ* litany, 25, 351, 351 n.; 26, 81–3, 230 n., 455; the *Sûdadohas* verse, 1, 187–93, 194 n.; 41, 301, 305–7, 307 n., 316, 322, 348, 354, 366, 369, 376, 379, 381, 383, 386, 389, 393, 396, 398, 407; the *Sûkta-vâka*, 44, 37, 42–4; he who knows the *Sûryâ hymn* shall receive the bride's shift, 29, 38, 171; *Uttara-Nârâyana litany* at the Purushamedha, 44, 412; the *Vaisvadeva* hymn at the Mahâvrata ceremony, 1, 197–9; the *Vâmadevya* hymn, 8, 277, 277 n.; knowledge of it, 38, 310; the *Vâtsapra* hymn and rite at the building of the altar, 41, 261, 283–90; 43, 298; *yâgyâs, see above* anuvâkyâs. *See also* Mantras, Sacred syllables, Sâman, Sâvitrî, Uktha, Veda, *and* Yagus.

(*d*) ZOROASTRIAN P. IN GENERAL.

Blessings pronounced by priests, 4, 86, 86 n.; spells (the Holy Word) heal better than the knife, or herbs, 4, 87, 87 n.; 23, 44; priests who know the Holy Word, perform the rite of purification, 4, 123; chanting the Gâthas and saying p., the duty of Zoroastrians, 4, 195, 287, 383; 5, 212 sq., 380 sq., 381 n.; 23, 316, 320 n., 344; 37, 35, 192; the Holy Word shall keep away the evil, 4, 232–4; rules for the priest with regard to the recitation of p. and singing of the Gâthas, 4, 317–31; 37, 195 sq.; the limits of the five Gâthas (Gâhs), 4, 331–7, 331 n.; the poor who recite p. celebrate the festival, but the rich who sacrifice, and do not recite p., do not celebrate it, 4, 337–9; 'stimulator of religious formulas,' a god, 5, 228; sin of interrupting p. by chatter, 5, 287 sq., 288 n., 290–3, 291 n., 321; 24, 11, 11 n., 283 sq., 283 n.; 37,

182, 182 n., 192, 192 n., 207, 477; when and why p. should be addressed to angels and archangels, 5, 312–14; inward p., 5, 321; 18, 134, 134 n., 135 n.; 37, 332; must be properly recited, not mumbled, 5, 327 sq., 370 sq., 370 n.; 24, 106; 37, 479 sq.; mystic signification of Gâthas and other p., 5, 352–69; how men are led to meditation and p., 18, 124, 124 n.; the sacred girdle a token of worship at p., 18, 124 sq.; prostrations during p., 18, 124 n.; 'the precinct of p.,' the place used for a ceremony, 18, 163; sin of not repeating the full grace before drinking, 18, 233–6, 233 n.; blessings and curses in word and thought, 23, 12, 12 sq. n., 20; the awful cursing thought of the wise, a genius, 23, 136, 153, 170, 191; the power of p. or spells against Daêvas and other fiends, 23, 160–2; 31, 382; blessing and curse, gâthas, p., and spells worshipped as deities, 23, 285; 31, 200, 206, 211, 217, 221, 226, 227 sq., 293–5, 326 sq., 331, 337, 340, 349, 361, 363 sq., 381 sq.; how the homage and glorifying of the sacred beings are to be performed, 24, 95 sq.; good works of no use unless performed with the authority of p., 24, 266 sq., 267 n.; 'the metric feet of zealous worship,' 31, 174; a p. of Zarathustra, 31, 230; p. and sacrifices offered to the gods, 31, 350 sq.; effectual invocation, 37, 196; those who pray become righteous, but not if they are wishful sinners, 37, 197; benefit of the liturgy, 37, 240 sq., 248, 333; perfection of p., 37, 298; the words of Zaratûst the best p., 37, 397.

(*e*) ZOROASTRIAN P. FOR CERTAIN OCCASIONS, TO CERTAIN DIVINITIES.

P. to Ahura-Mazda, 4, xlvii, 283, 293; 31, 28, &c.; formula of repentance, 4, lxxxvi; Earth pleased by p. to Mithra, 4, 23; formula on taking an oath, 4, 49 n.; morning p. to smite the Daêvas, 4, 197, 199; recited to atone for sins, 4, 202 sq.; the Word of Mazda, Zarathustra's weapon against Angra Mainyu, 4, 208, 212; 31, 312 sq.; Zarathustra repels the demons by singing sacred words, 4, 208–10; addressed to a tree, 4, 215; at purificatory rites, 4, 216 sq.; 18, 307, 307 n., 309, 309 n., 316 sq.; invocations of the creation of Ahura-Mazda, of the gods, &c., 4, 220–4; invocations for the protection of the family, addressed to the waters and the sun, moon, and stars, 4, 230–4; praise of the bull, 4, 231; invocation to the rain as a healing power, 4, 231; recited while putting on new clothes, 4, 245; Thraêtaona invoked against brigands, 4, 245 sq.; morning and evening p., 4, 246 sq.; for the benefit of a member of the family who is traveling, 4, 248; connected with sacrificial rites, 4, 248–50; 37, 94 sq.; benedictory formulas, 4, 369; 24, 269, 269 n.; on killing a serpent, 4, 371; for salvation in Paradise, 4, 386; recited by Gâyômard, 5, 18; about p. to be recited by a menstruous woman, 5, 277 sq., 278 n., 281; 24, 303 sq., 303 n.; for tying the sacred girdle, 5, 286, 286 n.; 18, 128, 130–3, 131 n.; at fire worship, 5, 299, 299 n., 333, 333 n., 371; when making water, 5, 318, 318 n.; 24, 317; Gâthas not to be recited over the dead, 5, 318; begging forgiveness for a person who has passed away, 5, 319 sq.; an Avesta to be recited by an unmarried man, 5, 323, 323 n.; on lying down and getting up, 5, 325 sq.; at the morning ablution, 5, 347; 24, 296, 313, 338; recited at sneezing, yawning, and sighing, 5, 352; 24, 265 sq.; 37, 452; Gâthas and Mãthras, and p. of blessings, for the propitiation of the Yazads, 18, 61, 61 n.; 31, 208, 213 sq., 223, 259, 270 sq., 274–6; before and after eating, 18, 133–6; 24, 282–5; 37, 167, 182 sq.; at the consecration of a sacred cake, 18, 141–5, 143 sq. n.; 24, 314, 316 sq.; liturgies at the sacred ceremony, 18, 160 sq., 166–9; at the Bareshnûm ceremony, 18, 437, 442–4, 447–54, 448 n.; to Ardvi Sûra Anâhita for success in battle, 23, 84; for help, joy, and every bliss to Mithra, 23, 120 sq., 126–8, 133 sq., 138 sq., 142 sq., 144, 148 sq., 155; to the

Fravashis to avert dangers, &c., 23, 185–230; occasions when p. are recited, 23, 311–13; for the protection of the mother and the newly born child, 23, 341; daily and monthly p. to sun and moon indispensable, 24, 264, 264 n.; to Ashi Vanguhi for earthly goods, 23, 272 sq.; benedictions (âfrîngân) in honour of the departed souls, 24, 273 sq.; recited when disposing of nail-parings, 24, 275 sq., 275 n.; anything agreeable to be saluted with 'in the name of the sacred being,' 24, 276 sq.; recited to frighten away demons, 24, 292, 292 n.; no daily p. (Nyâyises) enjoined on women, 24, 320 sq.; duty of thanksgiving, 24, 328 sq.; daily p. to sun, moon, and fire, 24, 341, 357 sq.; 37, 168; recited before sleeping and when restless, 24, 348 sq.; recited after a death, 24, 351 sq.; p. of Zarathustra for the people, 31, 5, 12 sq.; for Grace and for the Words of Revelation, 31, 14–24; to Haoma to drive away death and other evils, 31, 236 sq., 238–40, 243 sq.; for sanctity and its benefits, 31, 292 sq.; for the dwelling of the sacrificer, 31, 310–12; the well-timed p. for blessings as it rules in the order of p., 31, 351; benediction of the priest on giving legal decision, 37, 61; nightly p., 37, 163; at cohabitation, 37, 208 sq.; comfort for the spirit of the liturgy, 37, 296.

(*f*) Certain Zoroastrian p. (alphabetically arranged).

Âfrîgân Dahmân, a p. recited in honour of the dead, 23, 192 sq., 193 n.; 24, 283, 298; 31, 367–75; 37, 219 sq., 219 n.; the *Âfrîn Dahmân*, a p. of blessing on the house, 4, 289, 289 n., 291; the *Ahuna Vairya* (Ahunavar) p., or Honover, 4, 100, 100 n., 251, 263, 287, 287 n., 355; 5, 157–9, 158 sq. n., 346 sq.; 18, 65 n.; 23, 23, 30 sq., 30 n., 36, 39, 42, 47, 49, 52 sq., 84 sq., 87, 89, 91, 109 sq., 118, 142, 158 sq., 163–7, 169, 178, 230 sq., 248 sq., 262, 268, 282 sq., 285, 287, 308, 328, 355–8, 361; 37, 5 sq. and n., 166, 172–4; 482 sq.; 47, xxvi, 69; libations without the Ah. flow to the benefit of the Daêvas, 4, 347; the Evil Spirit confounded by Aûharmazd's uttering the Ah., 5, 8 sq., 8 n.; 23, 274 sq.; 37, 11, 11 n.; when and how the Ah. and Ashem-vohû p. are to be recited, 5, 390–3; 37, 208 sq.; the Ah. is the best fiend-smiter, with it Zoroaster confounds the demons, 23, 160, 305; 37, 254 sq.; 47, xxv, 7, 58–60, 62 sq.; Ah. the divine word of Aûharmazd, 24, 65, 65 n.; 31, 264; the Ah. worshipped, 31, 227 sq., 253, 266, 281, 309; the Ah. first sung by Zarathustra, 31, 235, 235 n.; 37, 231; commentary (Zand) on the Ah., 31, 259–66; 37, 231 sq., 231 n., 453–61, 464; by chanting the Ah. the soul passes over the *Kinvat* bridge, 31, 261; prelude to the chief recital of the Ah., 31, 280 sq.; Ah. and other p. come to Sraosha, 31, 303; Ah., Ashem-vohû, and Yênhê hâtãm, 31, 312 sq., 336, 339; the wise offerings of the Ah., 31, 354; Ah. and other great p. extolled, 31, 393; the twenty-one words of the Ah., and the twenty-one Nasks, 37, xxix, xl, 7, 7 n., 9, 10 n., 12 n., 13 sq. n., 15 n., 19 n., 23–5 n., 31 n., 34 n., 35 n., 74 n., 92 n., 121 n., 152 n., 166 n., 169 n., 173 sq., 428, 433; the Ah., the first saying of revelation, 37, 13, 13 n.; the Ah. smites the fiends and heals, 37, 160, 165 sq. and n.; Ah. recited when spilling food after sunset or to the north, 37, 207, 207 n.; embodying the Ah., 37, 261; details about the Ah., 37, 303–8; Ah. a symbol of the Nasks, 37, 401–3, 404 n.; effect of reciting the Ah., 37, 451; the new-born Zoroaster utters the Ah., 47, xiv, 142, 142 n.; the power of the *Airyama-ishyô*, 4, 247; 23, 41, 43–7; 37, 302 sq., 403, 404 n., 405, 405 n.; the Ai. worshipped, 31, 293, 293 n., 337, 340, 380; the Ai. the greatest of all p., 31, 390; the *Ardibehist Yast* recited every day, 23, 41; *Asha-Vahista* p., 23, 356 sq.; the prayer *Ashem-vohû*, Praise of Asha, the epitome of religion, 4, 289, 376, 376 n., 383; 5, 75, 75 n., 212 sq. and n., 289, 333, 347; 23, 22, 30, 34 sq., 39–41, 48, 52 sq., 84 sq., 87 sq., 91 sq., 109 sq.,

118 sq., 158 sq., 168, 178, 180, 230 sq., 248 sq., 263 sq., 269, 282 sq., 285 sq., 309 sq., 328–31, 333 sq., 337, 339 sq., 345, 350, 353, 355 sq., 358, 361; 31, 281 n.; 37, 11 n., 175, 175 n., 308 sq.; eulogy of the Ash., 23, 311–13; Ash. recited by a dying person, 24, 309; different value of Ash. on different occasions, 24, 343 sq.; commentary (Zand) to the Ash., 31, 266–8; 37, 232 sq., 461–3; Ash. worshipped, 31, 268; the *Fshûshô-mãthra*, 31, 303, 306–8, 306 n., 310; *Hâdôkht* and Dvâzdah-hômâst, 5, 224–7, 229; the *Ithâ* and Ashem-vohû, 5, 285, 285 n., 291–3; *Khûrshêd Nyâyis*, or 'salutation of the sun,' 5, 297 sq. n.; the *Mãthra Spenta*, the healing Word, 4, 251; the *Nîrang-i Kustî* or sacred girdle formulas, 18, 383–8; *Nyâyis*, begging p., *Sitâyis*, p. of praise, 23, 349; *Sîrozâh*, a liturgy composed of thirty invocations, 18, 144 n.; 23, 1 sq.; the *Staota Yêsnya* p., 23, 335, 356 sq.; Yasts, Sîrôzahs, Nyâyis, 23, 1, &c.; *see also* Yasnas, *and* Yasts; the *Yathâ-ahû-vairyô*, 5, 162, 318, 346; Yath. recited when Hôm is given to the new-born child, 24, 287; the *Yênhê hâtãm* p., 5, 214 n.; 31, 222, 228, 268 sq., 281 n.; 37, 175 sq. and n., 233 sq., 309 sq., 463 sq.; the four best p., 37, 219 sq. and n. *See also* Mãthras, *and* Zendavesta.

(*g*) CHINESE P.

Tan's p. for the life of Wû deposited in 'the metal-bound coffer,' 3, 151–6, 154 n.; p. to Heaven, 3, 187 sq., 317, 317 n.; Tan prays to the spirits of Wăn and Wû for *Kh*ăng's prosperity, 3, 194; a declaration in the form of a p., 3, 195; sacrificial odes to royal ancestors, 3, 303–36; the Father of Husbandry invoked for rain and against insects, 3, 371 sq.; p. for the aged, 3, 401; exorcism employed to expel the bad, 16, 190, 192 n.; for a prosperous year, 27, 254, 300; for success in agriculture, 27, 264, 273 sq.; for blessing to the people, 27, 278; p. and sacrifices to the seas, rivers, &c., 27, 303 sq., 304 n.; 28, 205; at ancestral worship, 27, 370–3, 373 n.; instituted by the ancient kings, 27, 385; the object in sacrifices is not to pray, 27, 403, 403 n.;—officer of p. at sacrifices, 3, 366 sq.; 'Grand-minister of p.,' one of the six grandees, 27, 109; officer of p. accompanies the ruler at mourning rites for a minister, 27, 172; officers of p. the first to assume mourning, 27, 194, 194 n.; officers of p. in the ancestral temple, 27, 301, 373, 385; the officer of p. the medium of communication between the spirit and the sacrificer, 27, 301, 444, 446; officer of p. who used the Shang forms, 28, 144, 148, 189; officer of p., exorcist and blesser at funeral rites, 28, 187, 189, 194; the representative of the dead and the officer of p., 39, 170; honours and costume of the officer of p., 40, 18.

(*h*) P. IN ISLÂM.

Call to p., 6, xxiv, xxxiv, lxxii, 106; Kaabah the point to which Mohammed turned in p., 6, xxxv; rosaries used by the Muslim when repeating the names of Allah, 6, lxviii; 9, 13 n.; regular p. prescribed, 6, lxxi sq., 2, 87, 140; p. for guidance, 6, 1; Muslim to be steadfast in p., 6, 6, 11, 15, 24, 44, 105, 159, 163, 173–5, 183, 235, 242; 9, 60 sq., 65, 78, 80, 99, 128, 131, 133, 143, 160, 209, 272, 301, 329, 338; the qiblah or point fixed to which Muslim turn at p., 6, 20 sq., 20 n.; in danger, 6, 22, 22 n.; God answers p., 6, 26; 9, 208; rules about saying p., 6, 36 sq.; believer's p., 6, 46; p. for the believer, 6, 70; believers must not pray when drunk or polluted, 6, 78; precautions to be taken against an attack during p., 6, 86 sq.; stated times for p., 6, 87, 218; 9, 308, 313 sq.; ablutions before p., 6, 98; morning and evening devotions, and p. at night, 6, 121, 163; 9, 9 sq., 45, 89, 126, 145, 196, 244, 251; *call on your Lord humbly and secretly*, 6, 144, 163; 9, 81; hypocrites perform not p. save lazily, 6, 180; for the dead, 6, 185; Mohammed is to pray for confessed sinners, 6, 188; Israelites pray to God for deliverance from Pharaoh, 6, 202; Abraham's p. to God, 6, 242 sq.; 9, 94; man prays for evil,

and is ever hasty, 9, 2; neither to be said openly, nor to be murmured, 9, 13; Ishmael used to bid his people p. and almsgiving, 9, 31; the name of God to be mentioned over cattle when slaughtered, 9, 60; prayer forbids sin and wrong, 9, 122; Solomon's remorse for neglecting his evening p., 9, 178 n.; Muslim are to leave off traffic, to say p., 9, 283 sq.; *woe to those who pray and who are careless in their p.*, 9, 342; invocations to God against the evils of the night, witches, and devils, 9, 344 sq.

Preachers of the law of Buddha have to be honoured even more than Buddha himself, and they are always helped by Buddha, 21, xxx, 213–26, 326 sq.; to abuse a p. is a graver sin than to abuse Buddha himself, 21, 216, 218, 225; rules of conduct for p. of Buddha's law, 21, 262–73; coquetry of p., 21, 264; how the (Buddhist) p. is to be dressed and to appear personally, 21, 269 sq.; reward of the p. of Buddha's law who follows all the precepts of Buddha, 21, 274–80, 336–53; incantation against those who attack a p., 21, 374 sq.; Samantabhadra promises to protect the p., 21, 431–5; qualities of p. of the Lotus of the True Law, 21, 437 sqq. *See also* Arahat.

Preaching: persons to whom a Bhikkhu should not preach the Dhamma, 13, 65–7; Bhikkhus should recite the Dhamma when assembling on the Uposatha days, 13, 241; monks who are entitled to preach, 13, 262; 45, 313, 319, 419; discourse delivered by an Arhat in the presence of Buddha, 17, 10–13; the Dhamma may be intoned, but must not be sung, 20, 72; great meritoriousness of hearing and accepting the p. of the law, 21, xxx, 328–35; *G*aina monk should preach the law to all creatures, 22, 60 sq.; thanksgiving discourses by Buddhist friars at the end of meals, 35, 16, 16 n., 25; the Bhikkhu's duty to preach Dhamma, 36, 345; a monk should preach the law for no other motive than the annihilation of Karman, 45, 354; how a monk should preach the Law, 45, 410–13; p. the Law more meritorious than gifts to Buddha, 49 (ii), 119, 124, 126, 129 sq., 139, 144. *See also* Buddha (*f*).

Precious things, *see* Jewels.

Predestination, doctrine of, inculcated by Islâm, 6, lxxv. *See* Fate.

Pregnancy, *see* Woman (*b*, *e*).

Presents, *see* Gifts.

Pretas, i. e. the ghosts, the departed spirits, find no rest and return to visit relatives, as long as these remain impure, 7, 80; worship of P. is of the quality of darkness, 8, 118; are hungry and thirsty, 19, 92; sufferings of beings in the state of P., 19, 158–60; a tear shed on *S*râddha food sends the food to the P., 25, 118; sinners reborn as P., 25, 497, 499, 499 n.; 36, 261–4; four kinds of P., 36, 151; ghosts of evil-doers, 36, 165; beings born in the P. world cannot attain to insight into the Truth, 36, 176 sq.; no pretaloka or realm of P. in a Buddha country, 49 (ii), 12, 33, 97 n.

Pride is of the quality of darkness, 8, 320; act virtuously, but do not pride yourself on your virtue, 40, 41. *See also* Humility.

Priests.

(*a*) Number and classes of p. in India.
(*b*) Functions, duties, and qualifications of Indian p.
(*c*) Rights and privileges of p. in India, honour due to them.
(*d*) Position (authority, fees, &c.) of Parsi p.
(*e*) Duties and functions of Parsi p.

N.B. For Chinese p. *see* Officer of prayers *under* Prayers (*g*), *and* Society.

(*a*) Number and classes of p. in India.

The different offices of the Brahman, Adhvaryu, Hot*ri*, and Udgât*ri* p., 1, 2 sq., 3 n., 12, 284; 12, 8; 41, 141 sq.; office, duties, and knowledge of Udgât*ri* p., 1, 14 sq., 18–21, 33 sq.; 38, 194 sq., 197, 321; 44, 305 sq., 305 n., 579; the Brahman priest performs the sacrifice in his mind, the Hot*ri*, Adhvaryu, and Udgât*ri* priests by words, 1, 69, 69 n.; rank, knowledge, duties, office of Brahman p., 1, 71 sq., 259; 41, 22, 24, 141; 43, 192; 44, 45, 104, 135, 211 sq., 213 n., 277, 391, 459, 483, 503; the Purohita or domestic p. of a king, the king's duty to chose one, his rank, &c., 2, 125, 235 sq.;

7, 20; 12, xii, xiv; 14, 96, 200; 17, 295 sq.; 19, 93; 25, 228, 494, 494 n.; 29, 179, 233–5; 30, 278; 33, 280; 35, 233; 41, 59, 94, 110, 259 sq.; 42, 610; 44, 371; 49 (i), 91; Brihaspati is the Purohita of the gods, 8, 89; 44, 258; the ten or seven sense-organs as ten or seven sacrificial p., 8, 261, 261 n., 266 sq., 270; the Prâ*n*as (Prâ*n*a, Apâna, &c.) as five p., 8, 270; 15, 280; the universe enveloped by the four Hot*ri*s, viz. instrument, action, agent, and emancipation, 8, 278; the p. at the allegorical sacrifice of concentration of mind, 8, 280; dialogue between an Adhvaryu and an ascetic, 8, 289–93; the four classes of p., 12, xx–xxii, 383; 43, 103; the Adhvaryus and the Yagur-veda, 12, xxii, xxv; 29, 14; the Agnîdh or Âgnîdhra, 12, 8, 55; 26, 148; 41, 119, 122, 142; 43, 169, 192; 44, 44, 137; the A*s*vins are the Adhvaryus of the gods, 12, 16, 53; 43, 23; the Pravara, or choosing of the divine and human Hot*ri*, 12, 95, 95 sq. n., 114–20, 131–8; 26, 183 sq. and n.; Adhvaryu and Hot*ri* at the kindling of the fire, 12, 95 sq.; seven Hot*ri*s or p., 12, 223, 223 n.; 26, 148 n.; 43, 205; 44, 390; 46, 168, 206–8, 236, 238, 259 sq., 318, 322; the divine and human Adhvaryus, 12, 225, 225 n.; 46, 98; the two divine Hot*ri*s, 12, 239 sq., 244 sq., 244 n., 247, 260, 404 n., 405, 436 sq.; 26, 186 n.; 46, 8, 11, 153 sq., 179, 199, 237, 377; the Pratiprasthât*ri* subordinate to the Adhvaryu, 12, 401; 41, 111; 44, 137, 232, 321 n.; election of Hot*ri* does not take place at the sacrifice to the Manes, 12, 427; a p. who is to be a Sâma-singer must have a good voice, 15, 83; temple-p. excluded from *S*râddha feasts, 25, 103, 109; the A*kk*hâvâka priest excluded from drinking Soma, 26, 151, 317 sq., 317 n.; the Adhvaryu is the head of the sacrifice, 26, 276; the Soma cups of the fire-p., 26, 286–8 and notes; the *k*aturhot*ri* formulas, 26, 452, 452 n.; the Brahman priest at domestic sacrifices, 29, 340, 346, 375 sq.; 30, 29–31, 29 sq. n., 38; the p. and the four Vedas, 30, 320 sq.; 42, lv sq., lviii, lxiv sq.; 44, 103 sq.; Homas are always performed by the Adhvaryu, 30, 323; Vahni meaning p., 32, 38, 40–3; the five Hot*ri* p., 32, 297; the Hot*ri* invokes the gods, 32, 374; the Hot*ri* rejoices in the Soma libation, 32, 408, 411; three kinds of p.: hereditary, appointed by the sacrificer, officiating out of friendship, 33, 126, 339; Adhvaryu, his duties, knowledge, fees, &c., 38, 240; 41, 108, 119, 122, 142; 43, xxiv, 23, 181, 181 n., 282, 340; 44, 45, 57 sq., 136, 245, 348, 350, 503; 46, 340; Hot*ri* p., his seat, rank, offices, &c., 38, 282; 41, 108 n., 142, 219, 358; 44, 45, 136, 245, 459 sq., 504; the B*ri*haspatisava, installation of a Purohita, 41, xxiv sq., 4 n., 34 sq., 34 n.; Nesh*tri*, 41, 10, 31, 119; 44, 137, 321 n.; the Brahman p., his fees, 41, 29, 108, 119, 122, 141; 44, 350; fees of Hot*ri* p., 41, 119, 122, 142, 219; presents to the different p., 41, 119; Brâhma*n*â*kk*h*am*sin, 41, 119; 44, 136; Atharvan, Añgiras, and Bh*ri*gu are fire-p., 42, xxiii, xxvii; the Purohita or king's chaplain an Atharvan, 42, xlvi, xlviii sq., li, lviii, lxi sq., lxvii–lxxi, 128, 379, 405, 632; the Brahman p., an Atharvavedin, 42, lviii–lxi, lxii–lxxi; Hot*ri* and Udgât*ri* engaged in the Mahâvrata, 43, xxiv–xxvi; office of Adhvaryu, and other p. at the Agni*k*ayana, 43, 336 sq., 337 n., 339 sq., 346, 363 sq., 373; sixteen officiating p., 43, 348, 348 n.; sadasya a seventeenth p., 43, 348 n.; the Maitrâvaru*n*a p., 44, xxii; 46, 10; four p. compared to four harnessed steeds, 44, 94; six offering-p. (Hot*ri*s) required for the animal sacrifice, 44, 121 sq. and n.; the Brahman is the moon, 44, 135, 317 sq.; Pot*ri* under the Brahman, Prastot*ri* and Pratihart*ri* under Udgât*ri*, 44, 136 sq.; 48, 26; Grâvastut, 44, 137; Adhvaryu and Pratiprasthât*ri* purify the sacrificer, 44, 230; the Brahman p. is the heart of the sacrifice, 44, 245; Brahman or Udgât*ri* sings Sâmans at the Sautrâma*n*î, 44, 255–7, 255 n.; he who will fetter the horse (for the sacri-

fice) must announce it first to the Brahman, 44, 277 sq.; Hot*ri* sings the praises of the sacrificial horse, 44, 384; the Brahman p. is the highest seat of speech, 44, 391; the Hot*ri* is the sacrifice, 44, 460; the Brahman is the best physician among the officiating p., 44, 483; Agni as Hot*ri* or Purohita p., 46, 1, 6, 8, &c.; *see* Agni (*q*); Agni is Adhvaryu, Hot*ri*, Pra*s*âst*ri*, Pot*ri*, &c., 46, 96, 98 sq., 108 sq., 111, 186, 189, 303, 348 sq.; with the five Adhvaryus the seven p. watch the footstep of the bird (Agni), 46, 249; the Hot*ri* is called the carrier (of the gods), 46, 281 sq.; the Hot*ri* called upon to sacrifice, 46, 303.

(*b*) FUNCTIONS, DUTIES, AND QUALIFICATIONS OF INDIAN P.

Procession of p., 1, 21; 26, 305 n., 306; may perform sacrificial acts without knowing their hidden meaning, 1, 36; 38, 254; duties of the various p. at the sacrifice, 1, 69, 69 n.; 12, *passim*, 138–43, 145 sq., 236–56, 236 n., 274–6, 297, 298 n., 392 sq. n., 396, 400–6, 411, 413, 431 sq.; 14, 193–5; 15, 122–5; 26, *passim*; 30, 331 sq.; 41, *passim*; 43, *passim*, 191 sq., 194 sq., 282–4, 288 n., 298; 44, *passim*, 93 sq., 459; places of the p. at the Mahâvrata ceremony, 1, 174 sq.; only Brâhma*n*as may be, and Brâhma*n*as shall be p., 2, 124; 8, 359; 12, 25, 25 n.; 26, 129 sq.; 30, 321; requirements of an officiating p., 7, 122; 25, 56; those only who possess true knowledge and serenity of mind, are true p., 10 (i), 7 sq., 8 n.; sacrificing p. who slay innocent cows, blamed, 10 (ii), 51; sacrifices and the priesthood, 12, ix–xix; ceremony of choosing the p., 12, 6 sq., 375; 26, 107; 29, 193–7; what blessings the p. invoke at the sacrifice, that is for the sacrificer, 12, 77, 77 n., 253; keep up the tradition as to the sacrifice, 12, 140 sq.; p. who neglect Veda-study and sacrifices become outcasts, 14, 68; sin of sacrificer falls on negligent p., 14, 101; 25, 309, 309 n.; excommunication of an outcast in the presence of p., 25, 468; blameworthy p. make the ship of sacrifice sink, 26, 311; at domestic sacrifices, 29, 163; 30, 138 sq.; Brâhma*n*a recites prayers at ordeals, 33, 105 n., 107, 108 n., 109; chief judge at an ordeal like an officiating p. at a sacrifice, 33, 250; sacrificers of the same family employ p. of the same family, 34, 226; the fruit of meditations in which the p. is the agent goes to the sacrificer, 38, 321; Brahman, the priesthood, created, 43, 73; the sacrificer is the body of the sacrifice, the officiating p. the limbs, 43, 280; 44, 236; order in which the p. are initiated for the sacrificial session, 44, 135–8; Brahmodya or theological discussions between p., as part of ceremony, 44, 314, 388–91; the p.'s colloquy with the king's wives at the horse-sacrifice, 44, 324–6, 386 sq.; seated around the king at the horse-sacrifice, 44, 360 sq.; Brâhma*n*a p. insult a *G*aina monk, and are punished by Yakshas, 45, 51–4; Ârdraka's dialogue with a Vedic p., 45, 417; have established Agni and pressed Soma, 46, 42, 52; Praisha, t.t. of the sacrificial commands of one p. to another, 46, 164, 165; meditations on elements of the sacrifice, to be performed by the p., not by the sacrificer, 48, 707 sq.

(*c*) RIGHTS AND PRIVILEGES OF P. IN INDIA, HONOUR DUE TO THEM.

Crime of slaying initiated p., 2, 79, 81; received as guests, 2, 120, 205; 14, 49, 245; 25, 96, 97 n.; 29, 87 n., 88, 197, 273, 276, 435; 30, 132, 279; Daiva marriage for p., 2, 127, 197; 7, 107; 14, 6, 205; 25, 80; 29, 166; 33, 173 sq.; reverence towards one who has performed the Dîksha*n*îyesh*t*i of a Soma sacrifice, 2, 188; how to be honoured, 2, 209; 12, 276; 14, 67, 155; sacrificing a means of livelihood for Brâhma*n*as, 2, 227, 227 n.; he who forsakes p. becomes an outcast, 2, 282; ignorant p. must be forsaken, 2, 282; Lakshmî resides in officiating p., 7, 299; the 'man-gods,' 12, 86 n.; carry the sacrifice to the gods, 12, 92; are repellers of the Rakshas, 12, 93; consequences of cursing a Hot*ri*, 12, 122–4; must be satisfied

on the completion of the sacrifice, 12, 208; 'the Brahman's portion' at the new and full moon sacrifice, 12, 212–15, 213 sq. n.; when chosen, the Hot*ri* becomes non-human, by touching the earth he becomes human at the end of the sacrifice, 12, 255 sq.; garments used at an expiatory rite given to p., 12, 406 sq.; eat the sacrificial food, 12, 415, 437; Snâtaka must not go to a sacrifice, except when chosen as a p., 14, 62; on property obtained for performing sacrifices, 14, 81; impurity on the death of officiating p., 14, 177; 25, 182; take inheritance of people who die without legitimate heirs, 14, 179; funeral rites for p., 14, 182; costume of p., 14, 186–8; quarrels with p. to be avoided, 25, 157; rule over the world of the gods, 25, 157; breach of contract between sacrificer and p., 25, 321; where wise p. perform the sacrifice, that is the best sacrificial ground, 26, 2 n., 3; Tânûnaptra, covenant between the sacrificer and his p., 26, 93–7, 93 n., 100; they strengthen the sacrifice, 26, 101; the Brâhma*n*a or p. has power over cattle, 26, 219 sq., 220 n.; guilt of oppressing p., 26, 258; prepare for the sacrificer another self in yonder world, 26, 341; any p. can be a Brahman now, 26, 434, 434 n.; judges and p. compared, 33, 289; to be punished by admonition only, 33, 387; auspicious dialogue between the Brahman and the king, 41, 108–10, 108 sq. n.; the p. (*ri*tvig) are the seasons (*ri*tu), 44, 38, 44 sq., 246, 259; how the sacrificer's welfare depends on the p.'s modes of offering, 44, 56–60; the priest *S*aulvâyana taught by a householder, 44, 61 sq.; through the p. the sacrifice is made to prosper, 44, 231; the p. called buffaloes, 44, 231; cups of liquor drunk by the p. at the Sautrâma*n*î, 44, 245–7; brace up the sacrificer to energy, 44, 256; greatness of Pragâpati entered the great sacrificial p., 44, 275, 275 n.; four regions belonging to the four p., 44, 402, 412; partake of the residue of the Gharma, 44, 489 n.; feeding learned p., a householder's duty, 45, 62 sq., 137, 137 n.; *may he with the help of his p. become a gainer*, 46, 16; the wise poets, i. e. p., protect Agni and search for him, 46, 167. *See also* Brâhma*n*as, Dakshi*n*âs, *and* Holy persons.

(*d*) Position (authority, fees, &c.) of Parsi p.

Ardashîr, both a king and a p., 4, xli; a house with a (domestic) p. within, the Zoroastrian ideal, 4, 23; pay by blessings, 4, 86, 86 n., 132; stipends, fees, gifts due to p., 4, 132 sq.; 18, 28 n., 145–51, 201–9, 242 sq., 245–55, 245 n.; 37, 101, 422, 440; 47, 91; Vohunazga dog compared with the p., 4, 161, 161 n.; on the unworthy Âthravan, 4, 193; as the Ahû (prince) is excellent, so is the Rahu (p.), 4, 279–81, 280 n.; 31, 212 sq., 222, 228, 230, 253–5, 281, 309, 323, 343, 372, 381; Zoroastrian priesthood hereditary, 4, 313 n.; in partnership, assemblies, associations, 4, 315 n., 341; 37, 92 sq., 114 sq.; any one of the faithful, even a woman or a child, may be a p., 4, 327; are the authorities on all religious questions, 5, 74, 309; 18, 9, 19, 296 sq., 316–20; 24, 7, 145, 257, 359; 37, 285, 460; necessity and worthiness of high-p., 5, 109, 339; 37, 192, 231–3, 244, 479; spiritual chieftains of the regions of the earth, 5, 115 sq.; family of the Môbads, 5, 142, 142 n., 145–8; Isa*d*vâstar, chief of p., 5, 142; good and bad p., 5, 206 sq.; 23, 155 sq.; 37, 20; Pêshyôtanû becomes high-p., 5, 229 sq.; atonement ordained by and confession to be made to p., 5, 290 n., 300 n., 301–7, 354, 363; 24, 95, 289, 308, 353; 37, 41; high-priest passing away in idolatry, 5, 309; initiation of p., 5, 315, 315 n., 354, 354 n.; 18, 234, 234 n., 236; meat-offering to the fravashi of p., 5, 337; submission to p. enjoined, 5, 385; 24, 78; 37, 94, 295; 47, 170; troops maintained by high-p., 18, xxvii, 290, 290 n., 346 sq.; pontiffs, p., high-p., judges, and other religious leaders, 18, 6; high-p. provided in every age for the protection of creatures, 18, 51;

how p. may obtain a livelihood, 18, 153–5; about precedence among p. of different knowledge, at a sacred feast, 18, 155–9; creation of the 'shape of the fire-p.,' 18, 198, 198 n.; accusations against p., 18, 354 sq. and n.; good work of keeping p. in food and clothing, 18, 422; the glory of the p., that cannot be seized, 23, 7 n., 11 sq., 11 n., 19, 286, 297–302, 309; Ahura-Mazda called Âthravan, 23, 27; Zarathus*trôtema, chief of p., 23, 149, 149 n.; the Zarathus*trian's duty with regard to p., 23, 330 sq., 331 n.; kind regard for the good, i.e. the p., a good work, 24, 27; authority of p. and kings requisite for inflicting punishment of death, 24, 267; sins made high-p. necessary, 24, 268; p. and relations appoint an adopted son for a childless man, 24, 280; for each man an angel is stationed on the right-hand side, and two angels for the p., 24, 283; *G*âda*n*gôî ceremony to be performed for p. and high-p., 24, 285 sq., 285 n.; every man of fifteen years must take a high-p., whom he must obey, 24, 288–90; no good work possible unless ordered by a high-p., 24, 290; parents and p. must not be distressed, 24, 301 sq.; 37, 483; garments, as gifts for a departed soul, to be given to p., 24, 351 sq.; Pahlavi must be taught to p. only, 24, 360; *G*aini would beguile both fire-p. and Haoma, 31, 243; chief of fire-p. invoked, 31, 251 sq.; the Zaotar, Hâvanan, Âtarevakhsha, and other p., worshipped, 31, 383, 385; difference of sin in p., 37, 46; as judges, 37, 54, 58, 61 sq., 67 sq., 80, 195; law about property of p., 37, 60; priestly dwellings, 37, 118 sq.; p. and their disciples, 37, 120 sq., 145, 341, 356, 368; providing a high-p., 37, 148, 274; selection of high-p., 37, 166 sq.; complaint of a high-p. dying in an out-district, 37, 178, 451; loss of merit from want of a p., 37, 183; three grades of ceremonial according to the p. employed, 37, 192; impure recitation, when not made by p., 37, 195; souls praise the soul of a virtuous high-p., 37, 209; merit of a good p., 37, 260 sq.; the Zôti and assistant p. at the renovation, 37, 261 sq. and n.; high-p., the tongue of a spiritual lord, 37, 282 sq.; maintained by the husbandmen, 37, 286; instruction only by p., 37, 314; wealth necessary for maintaining p., 37, 319 sq.; enlarging the priestly assembly, 37, 322 sq.; triumph over apostates, 37, 328 sq.; men and sheep to be kept as property through a p., 37, 332; indicate the way to yonder world, 37, 335; predominance of high-p., 37, 339; praise of priestly-controlled action, 37, 343; rulers exist for maintaining p., 37, 409; tithe to the p. and king, 37, 425, 443, 457; their fate at the collapse of the sovereignty of Iran, at the end of millennium, 47, 92 sq., 96; beneficence of p., 47, 100; necessary for the care and propitiation of the earth, 47, 162. *See also* Magi, *and* Society.

(*e*) DUTIES AND FUNCTIONS OF PARSI P.

The Ratu and Sraoshâ-varez prescribe penalties, 4, 57 sq. and n., 92; names of the different p. engaged in the sacrifices, 4, 65, 65 n., 80; the Ratu directs the funerals, 4, 98; Âthravan says prayer, 4, 100; have to undergo the Barashnûm purification before the sacrifice, 4, 122 sq.; punishment of the cleanser who does not know the rites of cleansing, 4, 134–6; implements used by p., 4, 172 sq., 193 sq.; the p. officiating out of his house, 4, 305–11; women and children as assistant-p., 4, 307–9, 307 n., 327, 339, 365; 5, 332 sq., 332 n.; 37, 95; the student p., 4, 311–15; duties of Zaotar and Râspî (assistant) p., 4, 315–21; 5, 128, 128 n.; rites performed by p. in a state of sin, 4, 325–7; the Frabaretar brings the libations, the Hâvanan prepares the Haoma, 4, 347; functions and places of the p. at the sacrifice, 4, 351–5; 18, 166 sq.; five dispositions of p., 5, 74, 74 n.; 47, 167–9; regulations about corpse fixed by p., 5, 94; mouth-veil to be worn by p., 5, 333 sq.; choice of p. for purification rites, 5, 347–9, 347 n.; righteous-

ness and truthfulness required of p., 5, 348; duties of p. and disciples, 18, 151–3, 244 sq. and n.; 24, 67 sq.; 37, 16 sq., 16 n., 20; their position at the ceremonial, 18, 163; the Âthravans and their pupils beg knowledge of Anâhita, 23, 74; Aêthrapati, Hamidhpati, p., 23, 208, 208 n.; the Âthravans of the countries, itinerant p., 23, 228, 228 n., 268, 268 n., 299, 332; the seven p., 23, 332; must teach the Avesta correctly, 24, 359 sq.; litany spoken by the Zaotar and Ratu, 31, 212 sq., 222, 228–30, 246 n., 253–5, 309, 323, 341–3; the Zaotar calls all the p., 31, 341 sq. and n.; regulations for p., 37, 92–4; teaching disciples, 37, 93; sins of p., 37, 93, 95; position and duty of p. at sacred ceremonial, 37, 94 sq.; sin of employing or being an improper Zôti, 37, 194; *thy high-priest is he whose own religion is pure*, 37, 278; proceedings of the Zôti or chief priest at ceremonies, 37, 292 sq., 293 n.

Prishâtaka or *S*iva, offering to, 29, 203; P. festival, *see* Cattle.

Prish*t*i*k*ampâ, Mahâvîra stayed at, 22, 264.

Pri*s*ni (cow, cloud), mother of the Maruts, 32, xxiii, 73, 81, 126, 280, 285, 295 sq., 299 sq., 313, 340, 343, 347, 352, 359, 368, 371, 373, 390 sq., 408; 42, 132, 207; in the plural, the clouds, 32, 390, 395; plants, children of P., 42, 43; Agni, the winged (son?) of P., 46, 193, 196; the good name of P., 46, 335 sq.

P*ri*thâ, Arguna, son of, 8, 229–31, 254–6, 281, 311 sq.

P*ri*thin Vainya was consecrated (king) first of men, 41, 81.

P*ri*thivî, Earth, invoked to unite the deceased with his ancestors, 7, 86 n.; one of the Vasus, 15, 140 sq.; 44, 116; the wife of P*ri*thu, 25, 335, 335 n.; with Agni invoked in danger, 29, 232; mother or wife of Parganya, 42, 8, 200, 204. *See also* Earth (*c*).

P*ri*thu, King, born from the arm of Ve*n*a, 19, 2; 49 (i), 6; gained sovereignty by humility, 25, 222; P*ri*thivî, wife of P., 25, 335, 335 n.

Prîtidharmika Kula, of the *K*âra*n*a Ga*n*a, 22, 292.

Priyadar*s*ana, n. of an aeon, 21, 400, 419.

Priyadar*s*anâ, the name of A*n*oggâ, Mahâvîra's daughter, 22, 194, 256.

Priyagantha, founder of the Madhyamâ *S*âkhâ, 22, 293.

Priyakâri*n*î, other name of Tri*s*alâ, 22, 193, 256.

Priyamedha, and the Priyamedhas, connected with the Ka*n*vas, 46, 42 sq.

Priyavrata Rauhi*n*âyana on prayer, 43, 340.

Probation, *see* Sa*m*gha.

Procreation, *see* Generation.

Prodigies, *see* Omens.

Professions or occupations: persons following certain p., whose food must not be eaten, or who may not be invited to *S*râddhas, 2, 67–9, 71, 257 sq., 265–7; 14, 69, 71; 25, 103–7, 109, 161–4; contemptible and unlawful p., 7, 137, 148, 163 sq., 252 sq.; 15, 341 sq.; 25, 142, 265 sq., 442 sq., 494, 494 n.; to be avoided by the Bhikkhu, 11, 191, 195–200; Brâhma*n*as following forbidden p. to be treated like *S*ûdras, 14, 17, 175; sins committed by following certain p., 14, 219, 219 n.; adultery with wives of minstrels and actors not punishable, 14, 233; dancers, athletes, butchers, &c., shunned by Bodhisattvas and preachers, 21, 263, 265 sq., 438; *G*aina monk may beg of royal families, cowherds' families, Vai*s*ya, barbers', carpenters', *t*akurs', and weavers' families, 22, 92; instruction for the p., 27, 235; people following certain p. cannot be witnesses, 33, 86–9; property of stage players free of duty, 33, 127; astronomers, physicians, and priests to be honoured by the king, 33, 288; laws relating to various kinds of p., 33, 340 sq.; quacks, low artists, jugglers, punished as 'open thieves,' 33, 360 sq.; wrestlers, tumblers, jugglers, &c., forming secret societies, 35, 266, 266 n.; list of all sorts and conditions of men living in a great city, 36, 209–11; distribution and acquire-

ment of fortune, 37, 179; minstrels, heralds, actors, and men of many other p. among the symbolical victims of the Purushamedha, 44, 413–17; of women, 44, 414 sq. *See also* Actors, Artisan, Arts, Astronomers, Castes, Low arts, *and* Physicians.

Property, law about it, 2, 168–70, 231 sq.; 7, 19 sq., 30, 34, 36 sq., 40 sq.; 14, 80–3; 33, 264 sq.; 37, 57–65, 68, 70, 72, 74, 80 sq., 102, 106, 112 sq., 138–43, 147 sq.; modes of acquiring p., 2, 231 sq.; 25, 426; 33, xiii, 52–5, 242 sq.; law about finds and lost p., 2, 231 sq.; 14, 18; 25, 258 sq. and n.; 33, 146; confiscation of p. for an habitual offender, 2, 241; law of limitation, 2, 243, 243 sq. n.; 14, 81; 25, 279; 33, 60–2, 205 n., 238 sq., 243 sq., 310–14; law regarding p. of orphans and idiots, 6, 71 sq.; 9, 5; trusts to be paid to their owners, 6, 80; he who injures p. incurs a heavier penalty than he who injures animal life, 7, 173; three kinds of p., 7, 189 sq.; crime of destroying p., 8, 41 n., 159; not to be acquired by the ascetic and monk, 8, 364 sq.; 11, 192; p. of minors and unprotected females to be protected, 14, 79 sq. and n., 81, 229 sq.; 25, 257 sq. and n.; deposit and pledge, a title of the law, 25, ciii, 253, 278–80, 278 n., 279 n., 286–9; 33, 61, 63, 65, 120–3, 128, 144, 265, 330, 332–5; punishment required for the protection of ownership, 25, 219; seizure of p. by king, 25, 223; law about treasure-trove, 25, 259 sq. and n.; 37, 134–6, 136 n.; law about damage done to p., 25, 304–6, 391–3; p. of slaves, wives, and sons, 25, 326 sq.; 33, 136 n., 138; indivisible p., 25, 379, 379 sq. n.; appropriating p. to prevent starvation allowed, 25, 433 sq.; possession as a means of proof, 33, 58–65; once only the family p. is divided, 33, 171; acquired by study, 33, 191; law about p. in land and boundary disputes, 33, 266; law about p. and possession, 33, 309–14; sale without ownership, 33, 334–6; value of and damage done to p., animate and inanimate, 37, 86, 136 sq.; about selling p., 37, 98; sequestration law, 37, 131–4, 136; keeping men and sheep as p., 37, 332; prayer to Pûshan, to find lost p., 42, 159 sq., 542; no idea of p. in a Buddha country, 49 (ii), 13, 43, 55; partition of p., *see* Inheritance. *See also* Trade, *and* Woman (*a*, *g*).

Prophecy, *see* Divination.

Prophets, *see* Apostles, *and* Holy persons.

Propriety, reverence and gravity and careful speech essential in, 27, 61 sq.; rules of p. and moral conduct, 27, 61–70; marks the distinction between men and brutes, 27, 64 sq.; p. and righteousness, 27, 388 sq.; the rules of p. serve as instruments to form men's characters, 27, 395; good government secured by p. and righteousness, 28, 462 sq.

Prosh*th*apadâs, oblation to, 29, 331.

Prosperity, goddess of, 41, 324. *See also* Bhûti.

Prostitutes, may be killed without penance, 2, 286; what dogs have in common with p., 4, 166 sq., 167 n.; the evil caused by the p., she may be killed, 4, 205 sq. and n., 279; Vaidehakas live by keeping dancing-girls and other p., 7, 67; crime of living by prostituting one's own wife, 7, 137; 33, 88 n.; food of a p. impure, 7, 155, 163; 14, 70, 298; 25, 161, 163; laws about p., 7, 174, 176, 200; 10 (ii), 19; 33, 129 sq. n., 143, 266; punishment of the whore and the whoremonger, 9, 73; slave girls not to be compelled to be p., 9, 77, 77 n.; the courtesan Ambapâli, 11, 30–3; 17, 105–8; thirty friends sporting with their wives, one of them with a p., 13, 116 sq.; novice must not frequent the society of p., 13, 189; towns flourishing through courtesans, 17, 171 sqq.; Bhikkhunîs bathing together with courtesans, 17, 222 sq.; dancing-girls, 17, 349; concubines and courtesans unfit to be adopted, 18, 191; a Bhikkhunî is not to keep courtesans, 20, 343; a courtesan who becomes a

Bhikkhunî, 20, 360; a Bodhisattva must have no intercourse with whores and whoremongers, 21, 266; not allowed to partake of sacrifices, 23, 109, 244; p. procuring abortion, hateful to Ashi Vanguhi, 23, 280 sq.; sin of going to p., 24, 73; subsistence by the gain of p., 25, 142; clever p. are 'thorns,' 25, 388; brothels watched by soldiers and police, 25, 389; Haoma invoked against the body of the harlot, 31, 239; prostitution of widows, &c., among heretics, 33, 155 n.; different classes of women termed 'punarbhu' (re-married) and 'svairi*n*î' (wanton), 33, 174–6; king must not confiscate ornaments of p., 33, 215; are punishable as 'open rogues,' 33, 223, 360 sq.; the courtesan Bindumatî, 35, 182–4; p., swingers and jumpers, slave girls of bullies, 36, 211, 211 n.; sin of ill-treatment of a courtesan, 37, 211, 211 n.; p. sacrificed to Desire and Fun at the Purushamedha, 44, 413, 417; women of evil conduct go to hell, 46, 335; Hôm-water not for a satisfier of p., 47, 57; the demons and the p. withdrawn from mankind, 47, 59; Kâ*s*ikâ, the harlot of Kâ*s*î, 49 (i), 190.

Proti Kau*s*âmbeya Kausurubindi, pupil of Uddâlaka Âru*n*i, 44, 153, 153 n.

Proverbs: 'consult the gatherers of grass and firewood,' 3, 408, 408 n.; 'when a tree falls utterly, while its branches and leaves are yet uninjured, it must first have been uprooted,' 3, 412; 'there is no wise man who is not stupid,' 3, 413; 'the little ant continually exercises the art of amassing,' 28, 84; 'the hunter who hits a game that has already been hit,' 33, 159, 159 n.; 'he went to Yüeh to-day, and arrived at it yesterday,' 39, 181, 181 n.; 'the poor wine of Lû gave occasion to the siege of Han-tan,' 39, 284; 'when sages are born great robbers arise,' 39, 284; 'when the lips are gone, the teeth are cold,' 39, 284; 'no better than a man who asserts that his own mother never had any children' (said of one who contradicts himself), 48, 43, 58, 186, 415; 'a man blind from birth undertaking to guide another blind man,' 48, 50; example of the unreal: 'a horn of a hare,' 48, 433, 453, 508 sq. *See also* Parables.

Psalms, quoted, 9, 55.

Psychology: mind, intellect, the individual Self, and the indiscrete (avyakta) are 'that which exceeds the senses,' 7, 286; creation of mind, soul, organs, &c., 25, 6 sq., 7 sq. n., 9 n., 10 n., 21 n.; internal organ, soul, intellect, 25, 47, 188; definition of terms for 'soul': Self, Kshetra*g*ña, &c., 25, 485–7 and n.; Buddhist p., 35, 86–99, 132–4. *See also* Organs, *and* Soul.

Ptolemêôs, astronomical tables of, 37, xlvi sq.

Pubba Ka*kk*âyana, n. of an author on medicine, 36, 109.

Pubbârâma, n. of a country, 10 (ii), 131.

Pubbe-nivâsa-ñâ*n*a, Pali t. t., knowledge of Past Births, 11, 209, 215 sq.

Public buildings and places to be watched by soldiers and police, 25, 389; damage done to them, 25, 391–3.

Public rest-houses, *see* Rest-houses.

Puggala Paññatti, quoted in Milindapañha, 35, xl, 21.

Pukkusa, a young Mallian, a disciple of Â*l*âra, converted by Buddha, 11, 75–80, 75 n.

Pû Kwo, spearman of Duke *K*wang, 27, 127.

Pulaha, a sage, and a Pra*g*âpati, 25, 14.

Pulastya, a sage, and a Pra*g*âpati, 25, 14; Â*g*yapas (manes), offspring of P., 25, 112; teacher of Parâ*s*ara, 48, 92.

Pû-liang Î, had the abilities of a sagely man, but had to learn the Tâo, 39, 245 sq.

Puloma, Indra killed the people of P. in the sky, 1, 293.

Pu*m*savana, t.t., *see* Child (*b*).

Punabbasu, and Assagi, two wicked Bhikkhus, 17, 347–57; 20, 211 sq.

Punarvasu, creator, destroyer of sin, 2, 297.

Punarvatsa Kâ*n*va, author of Vedic hymns, 32, 391, 394.

Pu*nd*ravardhanîyâ *S*âkhâ, of the Godâsa Ga*n*a, 22, 288.

Puñgikasthalâ, a nymph, 43, 105.

Punishments: corporal p. of students forbidden, 2, 191; Brâhma*n*as exempt from opprobrious p., 2, 216; the five inflictions and other p. instituted by Shun, 3, 40 sq., 40 n., 43; five p., 3, 48 sq., 56, 255 sq. and n., 259–62, 261 n., 264, 481; 28, 99, 99 n., 353, 384; 39, 335, 335 n.; Shun's great justice in the infliction of p., 3, 49; different kinds of banishment, 3, 75 sq.; traitors have their noses cut off, 3, 110; on the infliction of p., penal law, 3, 167–70, 254–64; 16, 101 sq., 102 sq. n., 293 sq.; 25, 382–6; 27, 235–8, 235 n., 259, 288; 37, 54; death inflicted for drunkenness, 3, 178 sq.; the end of p. is to make an end of punishing, 3, 233; corporal p. and fines according to Mazdean law, 4, lxxxii–lxxxvi; capital p., 4, lxxxiv–lxxxvii, 27 sq., 77, 113, 113 n., 134 sq., 135 n.; 7, 24, 26; 18, 223 sq., 224 n.; 24, 267, 310; 36, 17; 37, 52 sq., 78; 39, 116 sq.; p. for burying a corpse, 4, 32 sq.; for breach of contract, 4, 34, 38 sq.; for different kinds of assault, 4, 34, 40–5; for transgressing the laws of purity, 4, 62, 68–70, 75, 82 n., 92, 121 sq.; for throwing clothes on a corpse, 4, 102 sq.; for unnatural sin, 4, 103, 104 sq. n.; for illicit sexual intercourse, 4, 188 sq.; 24, 267; 25, 317 sq., 318 n.; criminals burnt alive, 4, 271; p. for neglecting the celebration of the Gâhânbârs, 4, 329; scale of offences and p., 5, 239–41 and n., 242 n., 256, 258 sq., 261–3, 265 sq., 268 sq., 272, 282 sq., 288 sq., 289 sq. n., 291, 294 sq., 298, 334 sq. and n., 379 sq. and n.; kinds of p., 7, 24–41; 25, 275 sq., 308; 35, 239 sq., 254–7, 269 sq., 276–8, 277 n.; 36, 145, 145 n., 147, 150, 262; wisdom and caution of the superior man in the use of p., 16, 335, 337, 343; draught of wine given to one who is to be tortured and executed, 19, 280, 280 n.; people stoned for not wearing the sacred thread-girdle, 24, 310; p. for theft and robbery, 24, 326–8; 25, 307–14, 390–2, 394; 35, 236; 37, 75; the Lord created his own son, Punishment, the protector of all creatures, 25, 218–20; king's duty to inflict p., 25, 218–20, 306–9, 313–15, 320 sq., 327 n., 377, 380–7, 389–94, 397, 423, 451; official convicted of stealing slain by an elephant, 25, 259; for perjury, 25, 275; fines, 25, 277, 282, 382; various corporal p. for seizing property under false pretences, 25, 288, 288 sq. n.; cruel p. inflicted on *S*ûdras, 25, 302–4; rules about corporal p., 25, 306; p. for adultery, 25, 315, 318–21, 332, 497; riding on a donkey for crimes of unchastity, 25, 318; p. for gambling, 25, 380–2; branding, 25, 383 sq.; 28, 250; prisons to be near a high-road, 25, 393; penal laws differ according to rank, 27, 90, 90 n.; ceremonies of an officer going into exile, 27, 104; inflicted in the market-place, 27, 215; criminals cast off, 27, 215 sq.; exile and exclusion from office, 27, 232–4; inflicted on the ruler's kindred, 27, 356, 359, 359 n.; madmen not guilty of capital offence, 36, 18 sq.; mutilation a p. for crimes, 39, 133, 223 n., 227 sq. *See also* Judicial procedure.

Pu*nn*a, or Pu*nn*aka, the hired servant, a devout Buddhist, 35, 172; attained to the dignity of a Se*tth*i, 36, 146.

Pu*nn*â, the slave girl, the fame of her good deeds reached even to the gods, 35, 172.

Pu*nn*a*g*i receives ordination from Buddha, 13, 110 sq.

Pu*nn*aka, the slave, *see* Pu*nn*a.

Pu*nn*aka, n. of a Brâhma*n*a, 10 (ii), 187, 192 sq., 210.

Pu*nn*akamâ*n*avapu*kkh*â, t.c., 10 (ii), 192 sq.

Punnapattiyâ, *see* Pûr*n*apatrikâ.

Puns, *see* Etymologies.

Pu*n*yabhadra, disciple of Sambhûtavi*g*aya, 22, 289.

Pupil, *see* Teacher.

Purâbhedasutta, t.c., 10 (ii), 162–4.

Pura*m*dara = Indra, q. v.

Purâ*n*a, adheres to the Dhamma

and Vinaya as he had heard it from Buddha, not acknowledging the rehearsal of Râ*g*agaha, 20, 380 sq.

Pûra*n*a-Kassapa, n. of a teacher, 10 (ii), xii, 86 sq.; 11, 106; an Arhat possessed of Iddhi, 20, 78 sq.; questioned by King Milinda, 35, 8 sq.; his materialistic doctrines, 45, xxiii.

Purâ*n*as: Itihâsa-purâ*n*a, and Veda, authority of P. as scripture, 1, 40 n., 43 n.; 42, 229; 44, 369, 369 n.; 48, 460, 751; Âpastamba's quotations from P., 2, xxix–xxxii, 70 sq., 158, 160; date of the P., 2, xxx sq. n.; 8, 14, 14 n.; 25, xci n.; 49 (ii), xxii; Bhavishyat-p. quoted, 2, 160; a Brâhma*n*a should be skilled in reciting legends and P., 2, 215; an authority on law, 2, 237; 33, 280; Phala*s*ruti in the P., 8, 143; legends of P. and of the Brâhma*n*as, 12, xxiv; pre-eminence of Manu's teaching acknowledged in P., 25, xiv, xvi sq.; legends of Manu in the P., 25, lxv; allusions to legends of P., 25, lxxii n.; Skanda, Bhavishya, and other P. and Manu-sm*ri*ti, 25, lxxiii, cvi, cx sq., 78 n.; date of Matsya-p., 25, cxi; to be recited at *S*râddhas, 25, 118; on past and future Kalpas, 34, 361; Atharva-veda in the P., 42, lv sq.; Mârka*nd*eya-p., 42, 435; do not teach the doctrine of one non-differenced Substance, 48, 86–102; promulgated by Hira*n*yagarbha, 48, 413; the writers of P. attribute consciousness to rivers, hills, the sea, &c., 48, 416. *See also* Itihâsa, Itihâsa-purâ*n*a, *and* Sacred books.

Purandhi, goddess, gives the bride to the husband, 29, 282; 30, 189; the Morning, 32, 444, 447; Liberality of the gods personified, 46, 186, 190.

Purification, rules about impurity and the rites of, 2, 54–9, 60 n., 62, 66 sq., 178–82, 226; 4, lxx–lxxxi, 32–4, 49–85, 87–102, 105–15, 119–55, 185–92, 213–17, 220 n., 264 sq., 272, 274, 284 sq.; 14, 20–5, 36 sq., 160–77, 183, 187–96, 287; 25, 136, 140 sq., 152, 177–94; 37, 442; by bathing in one's clothes, 2, 253; the Ghosel, a means of p., 4, lxxxi, 106 n.; the Barashnûm, 4, lxxxi, lxxxi n., 63 n., 64 n., 87 n., 99 n., 106 n., 107 n., 114 n., 120 n., 122–42, 220 n., 236, 240 n.; 5, 205, 247, 247 n., 262 n., 319 n., 320 n., 347–9 and n.; 18, xxix, 241, 241 n., 284 n., 292–8, 308, 327 n., 330 n., 340 n., 343 n., 360–6, 424, 431–55, 458 n.; 23, 48, 50 sq., 339, 341, 353; punishments for defiling fire, water, earth, 4, lxxxiv sq.; modes of p. for clothing and other articles when polluted by dead matter, 4, 65 sq., 79–81, 83–5, 92 sq., 216 sq.; 5, 273–6; 24, 354 sq.; of the man defiled by the dead, 4, 105–13; p. after touching a corpse in the wilderness, 4, 119–22; 18, 455–8; the Sî-shu p., 4, 120 n.; means of p., 5, lx, 245–76, 310, 319 sq., 332; 7, 96–106; 25, 187 sq., 191, 206, 206 n.; choice of priests for p. rite, 5, 347–9, 348 n., 349 n.; by water or sand, 6, 78, 98; does not come from philosophy, but from indifference to this world, 10 (ii), 150–2; by touching water, 12, 2 sq. and n.; after a rite in honour of Rudra, 12, 443; water and fire as means of p., 14, 60; 19, 135; of food, 14, 72; disputes about p. the subject of the Epistles of Mânû*s*kîhar, 18, xxv sq.; cleansing the mouth after meals, 18, 133–6; ceremonial p. at sacrifices, 18, 162–8, 171–3; Zâ*d*sparam's heresy regarding the p. ceremony, 18, 282–6, 284 n., 292–365; ceremonial p. cleanses the soul, 18, 284 sq. and n.; plan of Bareshnûm Gâh, 18, 435; by means of water and gômêz, 23, 336, 336 n.; why the Bareshnûm p. is incumbent on every man and woman, 24, 296–8; ablutions and sipping water, 25, 39–41, 43, 151, 183, 193 sq.; judge and witnesses enter the court being purified, 25, 269; by means of sacred grass, 26, 16–18; three days of p. preceding sacrifices, 27, 448; sipping water, &c., explained, 29, 374 sq.; 30, 17–19; necessary after inauspicious sacrifices and sacrificial acts, 30, 330; duty of priests with regard to p., 37, 93; warming bull's urine by the fire, 37, 126; required for Vedic works, with a view to the origination of know-

ledge, 38, 314; purificatory charm, 42, 556; Sautrâma*n*î a means of p., 44, 234–6; cleansing from dead matter, menstruation, and bodily refuse to be understood by priests, 47, 168. *See also* Ablutions, Impurity, *and* Purity.
Purigîvana, converted by Buddha, 19, 243.
Purimatâla, n. of a town, 22, 283; 45, 57.
Purity: *when the food is pure the mind becomes pure*, 1, 125; 48, 702; laws of p. in Zoroastrianism, 4, lxii, lxiv, lxvii; meaning of p. and impurity in the Avesta, 4, lxxii; *p. is for man, next to life, the greatest good*, 4, lxxii, 56, 141; p. or holiness the best of all good, 4, 216, 299; 23, 22, 30, 34, 39, &c.; things which are always pure, 7, 103 sq.; 14, 132 sq., 170; 25, 191; p. and p. of heart of devotee, 8, 103, 114, 119; p. a duty of Brahmans, 8, 126, 359 sq.; part of the conduct of the good, 8, 162, 243, 326; sacred objects not to be touched or looked at by one impure, 25, 151; is of the quality of goodness, 25, 491; 'The Classic of P.,' 40, 247–54; during the twelve hours of the day let the thoughts be constantly fixed on absolute p., 40, 269–72. *See also* Impurity, *and* Purification.
Pûr*n*a, son of Maitrâya*n*î, converted by Buddha, 21, 3, 191–8; 49 (i), 190, 194; (ii), 2, 162 sq.
Pûr*n*a*k*andra, a Bodhisattva Mahâsattva, 21, 4.
Pûr*n*apatrikâ (Punnapattiyâ, or Panna°, or Sunna°, or Suvanna°), *S*âkhâ of the Uddeha Ga*n*a, 22, 290.
Pûr*n*ibhadra, *see* Pu*n*yabhadra.
Purohita, *see* Priests (*a*).
Purtarâspô, ancestor of Zoroaster, 47, 139.
Pûr-tôrâ, ancestor of Frê*d*ûn, 5, 132 sq., 132 n.; 47, 34.
Pûru, conquered by Bharata in battles, 41, 292.
Pûru Âtreya, author of Vedic hymns, 46, 401, 403.
Puru*g*it, n. of a warrior, 8, 37.
Purukutsa, the Aikshvâka king, performed a horse-sacrifice, 44, 397.
Purumî*lh*a Vaidada*s*vi, n.p., 32, 356, 358–62.
Puru*n*îtha *S*âtavaneya, n.p., 46, 50.
Purûravas and Urva*s*î, the two ara*n*is, 12, 389 n.; 26, 91; P. or Aila (son of I*d*â), grandchild of Soma, became a madman, 19, 149; 49 (i), 138; myth of Urva*s*î and P., 26, 91, 91 n.; 42, 521; 44, xiv, 68–74, 68 sq. n.; 49 (i), 113; son of I*d*â introduced three sacrificial fires, 30, xvi, xvi n.; a solar hero, 32, 307 sq.; throws himself into the lap of Nir*ri*ti, 42, 564 n.; the well-doing P., 46, 22.
Pûrus, n. of a clan, 46, 49.
Purusha, the Person: a P. not human leads the departed to Brahman, 1, 68, 80, 80 n.; the Self when free of the body is the highest P., 1, 141; as Creator, 1, 210–12; 34, cxxiii sq.; 43, xiv; 48, 201 sq., 333 sq.; created from the water, 1, 238; is the year, and its essence the sun, 1, 259; meditation on P., the embodied Self and the universal Soul, 1, 305; 7, 287–91; 38, 205; a day of P., 7, 78; offering of flowers to P., while muttering the Purushasûkta, 7, 206 sq.; there is nothing imperishable except P., 7, 290; Vish*n*u is P., 7, 291, 296; knows the Kshetra, therefore is he called Kshetra*gñ*a, 8, 351; the truth about the unperceived, the P., &c., to be understood by the Sannyâsin, 8, 368; beyond the Undeveloped there is the P., beyond the P. there is the goal, the highest road, 15, 13, 22; 34, cxix, 237 sq.; 38, 205; not larger than a thumb, the P. dwells in the heart of man, 15, 16, 23, 35, 246 sq.; 34, xxxvii, 195–8; the highest P. is Brahman, the Immortal, 15, 19; 25, 6, 6 n.; 34, xxxv–xxxvii, 171–4, 195–8; 43, 400; 48, 4, 39, &c.; the eternal and true P. reached by knowledge of Brahman, 15, 32 sq.; the heavenly P. is without body, pure, higher than the Imperishable, 15, 34; 34, cxix, 298; the lord of the world as the P. who has his source in Brahman, 15, 38; the Ps. in the sun, moon, lightning, &c., worshipped as Brahman, 15, 100–3;

appearance of the P., 15, 107; 38, 167–9; the bright, immortal P. in all beings and things is the same as the Self, the Immortal, Brahman, the All, 15, 113–17, 245–8; 48, 334, 356; Yâ*gñ*avalkya on the p. in the earth, in love, in the colours, in ether, &c., the principle of every self, 15, 142–5; the golden P., the lonely bird, 15, 165; 43, xxiv, 400; P. under the form of mind is light, within the heart, and small like a grain of rice or barley, 15, 192; he who knows the great P. passes over death, 15, 245; 48, 686; with a thousand heads, eyes, feet, 15, 247; 44, 410; the P. of sixteen parts within the body, 15, 283 sq.; is Pra*g*âpati, called Vi*s*va, who makes the body intelligent and is the driver thereof, 15, 291 sq.; 43, xxiv; is Agni Vai*s*vânara, 15, 294; 43, 398; when all things perish, he becomes one with the P., 15, 302; Pradhâna (nature) and the P. (the thinking subject), as food and feeder, 15, 313 sq.; seven Ps., 25, 11, 11 n., 613; 43, xv n.; the P. in the heart sees everything, 25, 269 sq., 269 n.; the supreme Male, 25, 512; individual soul (in the Sâṅkhya sense), 34, xxx, xl, xlvi, 36, 45, 238 n., 370; is not the original Brahman but an effect, may be called the internal Self of all beings, 34, 142; puri*s*aya, the person dwelling in the castle (of the body), 34, 172, 178; is higher than the senses and everything else, 38, 204 sq.; is hard to know, and to be reached by sharp minds only, 38, 205; became Pra*g*âpati, 41, 144; the one P. made out of seven Ps., 41, 144; 43, 205, 304 sq.; P.-Pra*g*âpati is related to the herbs, 41, 340 sq. and n.; the Ps. in the sun, in the eye, and in the gold man of the Fire-altar, 43, xxii, 466–74; the Agni-like, Arka-like, Uktha-like P., 43, 398 sq.; the fire-altar, as representing P.-Pra*g*âpati, 44, xiv; P.-Pra*g*âpati born from golden egg, 44, 12; P. Nârâya*n*a exhorted by Pra*g*âpati to sacrifice, 44, 172 sq.; has entered into five things, 44, 389, 389 n.; P. Nârâya*n*a desiring to overpass all beings, beheld the Purushamedha, 44, 403; Virâ*g* born from P., and P. from Virâ*g*, 44, 403 sq.; is the wind, 44, 407; P. Nârâya*n*a litany, 44, 410; the inner ruler of Agni, &c., pleased by sacrifices to Agni and other gods, 48, 155; the body of the highest P., 48, 202; Pradhâna and all its effects and the individual souls have their Self in P., 48, 359; release consists in attaining to the highest P., 48, 625–8; knowledge or meditation originated through the grace of the Supreme P., 48, 699; hymn to P., *see* Purusha-sûkta; in the eye, in the lightning, in the moon, in the sun, *see* Eye, Lightning, Moon (*c*), *and* Sun. *See also* God, Man, *and* Soul.

Purushamedha, *see* Human sacrifice.

Purushanti, n.p., 32, 360 sq.

Purusha-sûkta, hymn to Purusha, of the Rig-veda, 1, lxvi; 7, 206 sq.; 8, 280 n.; 25, 480; 43, xiv sq., xv n.; 44, xx, 410.

Purusha-vidyâ (i. e. meditations on Purusha) of the Taittirîyaka and of the *Kh*ândogya-upanishads, 38, 220–2.

Purushottama, the Highest Man, a name of Buddha, 21, 44.

Pûrvâ*k*âryâs, 'ancient teachers,' quoted by Râmânu*g*a, 34, xxi.

Pûrvâ-Mîmâ*m*sâ, system of philosophy, its early existence, 2, xxviii sq., 121; 25, xlvii, xlvii n.; 34, ix; systematizes the Karmakâ*nd*a, 34, ix; inquiry into active religious duty its subject, 34, 10; means of proof made use of in the P., 34, 17 sq. and n.; 38, 262 sq.

Pûrvâ - Mîmâ*m*sâ - sûtras and Kalpa-sûtras, their relation to each other, 34, xii; the Vedânta-sûtras presuppose them, 34, xiii. *See also* *G*aimini-pûrvamîmâ*m*sâ-sûtra.

Pûrva*s*kitti, is a nymph, 43, 108.

Pû*s*, demon of avarice, 5, 110 sq., 110 n.

Pûshan, a name of the sun, 1, 313; 15, 199; worshipped at the ceremony of setting a bull at liberty, 7, 261; 29, 101; 'with the hands of P.,' the distributor of portions to the gods, 12, 16, 42, 53, 213; 26,

136, 141, 167, 181, 239; 29, 63, 198; 30, 232; 41, 39, 53, 63, 63 n., 201, 214; 43, 228; 44, 449, 474; the Hotri invokes the help of P. for his work, 12, 135; how P. became toothless, 12, 210 sq.; cattle belong to P., 12, 314 n.; 41, 55 sq.; 43, 75; 44, 346; offerings and prayers to P., 12, 386, 402, 418 sq.; 26, 22–4, 24 n.; 29, 64, 86, 398; 38, 309; 41, 38, 62 sq., 82, 113, 116, 125; 42, 160; 44, 34 n., 62–6, 207, 291 n., 293, 346, 486; is this earth, 12, 418 sq., 418 n.; 26, 57; 41, 205; 44, 300, 352; related to the *S*ûdra caste, 15, 89; the mouth of the true (Brahman) is covered with a golden lid, which P. is invoked to open, 15, 335; represents or means cattle, 26, 22 sq., 219; 41, 82, 89 sq., 113, 116; 43, 195; 44, 293; lord or guardian of paths, 26, 57; 29, 86; 42, 135, 495; 44, 352 sq.; the speed of P. is the wind, 26, 205; 44, 474 sq., 486; animals esp. goats sacrificed to P., 26, 219; 44, xxv, xliv, 300; porridge offered to P., 26, 315, 316 n.; 44, 75, 75 n., 352 sq.; is rich in kindred, 29, 27; worshipped at the wedding, 29, 32, 44, 169 sq., 279, 285; 30, 45 sq., 190, 194; invoked at the Upanayana, 29, 64, 188; 30, 66, 151; invoked to protect the house, 29, 97; invoked for the protection of cattle, 29, 99, 354; 30, 89, 184 sq.; 41, 52 n.; 42, 143; invoked in dangers, 29, 226; has shaven B*ri*haspati's head or beard, 30, 61, 217; where P. dwells, 30, 218; has braided hair, 32, 424; offering to Agni and P., Indra and P., and to P., 41, 54 n., 55 sq.; informed of the king's consecration, 41, 89 sq.; husbandry beneficial to P., 41, 329; Aryaman and P. invoked for easy parturition, 42, 99, 243 sq.; among the Vasus, 42, 116; prayer to P. for finding lost property, 42, 159 sq., 542; invoked to wipe off sins on the abortionist, 42, 165 (bis), 526 sq.; bestows a thousand cows as sacrificial reward, 42, 198; Pathyâ Svasti, wife of P., 42, 331; goat of P., 42, 421 sq.; Aditi's share and P.'s lordship, 43, 69; is the protector of all this world, 43, 195; invoked for cattle and good fortune, 44, 63; wealth, the lord of wealth, bestows wealth, 44, 64, 326; the heads of P., 44, 253 n.; protector of travellers, watcher of men, 44, 293; Indra accompanied by P., 46, 154; Agni said to be P., 46, 187.

Pushkarasâdi, teacher, quoted, 2, xxvii sq., 70, 88; 30, 154.

Pushpadanta, *see* Suvidhi P.

Pushpadantî, n. of a giantess, 21, 374.

Pushpadhva*g*a, n. of a Tathâgata, 49 (ii), 67.

Pushpâkara, the 33rd Tathâgata, 49 (ii), 6.

Pushpa*k*ûlâ at the head of nuns, under *G*ina Pâr*s*va, 22, 274.

Pushpâvatîvanarâ*g*asaṅkusumitâbhi*gn*a, the 32nd Tathâgata, 49 (ii), 6.

Pushpottara, Vimâna, from which Mahâvîra descended, 22, 190, 218.

Pushyagiri of the Kau*s*ika gotra, a Sthavira, 22, 293.

Pushyamitra, grandson of A*s*oka, 19, xiv sq.

Pushyamitrika Kula of the *K*âra*n*a Ga*n*a, 22, 292.

Pûtadaksha, author of a Vedic hymn, 32, 410.

Pûtîka, *see* Âdâra.

Pûyi*s*n-shâ*d*, n.p., 5, 147.

Puzzles, about the dawn, 42, 204, 667 sq.; relating to Agni, 46, 114 sq. *See also* Riddles.

Q

Qadr, t.t. meaning of, 9, 337 n.

Qâf, Mount, 6, lxx.

Qâinuqâh, Jews of, 6, xxxvii, 68 n.; 9, 276 n.

Qarûn, *see* Korah.

Qâsim, El, Mohammed's son, 9, 343 n.

Qiblah, t.t., the point to which one turns in prayer, 6, liii, 20, 202.

Qiyâs, 'Analogy,' 6, lxvi.

Quails, sent to the people of Moses, 6, 7.

Qualities, eight good, of the soul, 2, 217 sq.; crimes and bad qu. that make one contemptible, 7, 137, 148,

163 sq., 252 sq., 275 sq.; moral qu. of Buddha, 10 (ii), 26 sq.; good and bad qu. of admissible and inadmissible witnesses, 33, 302 sq.; the five good qu., viz. good conduct, faith, perseverance, mindfulness, meditation, 35, 51–62, 68 sq.; moral qu. and mental habits, which make up Arhatship and Buddhism, 35, 58, 58 n.; moral qu. of the Bhikkhu, 36, 303, 309 sq.; the 'eight qu.' in discussions, 39, 188 sq.; are inherent in one substance, 45, 153, 153 n.;—*the three Gunas or qu.* of Goodness (sattva), Activity (ragas), and Darkness (tamas) in nature and in moral life, 7, 287 n.; 8, 17, 48, 75, 276, 292, 318; 25, lxxiii, 2, 16, 489–95; 34, 28, 46, 48 sq., 254, 353; 48, 365, 475; the body is endowed with ragas (passion), 7, 283; Purusha Vish*n*u destitute of the three qu., 7, 288, 290; difference from qu. and from actions, 8, 55, 55 n.; produced from nature (prak*ri*ti or mâyâ), 8, 104 sq., 107, 107 n.; 15, xxxvi; bind down the soul in the body, 8, 107 sq.; influence of the three qu. in this life and hereafter, 8, 108 sq.; he who transcends the three qu. attains immortality, 8, 109 sq., 344; classification of actions according to the three qu., 8, 117–21; three qu. in all entities, 8, 122, 124–6; are the foes in this world, 8, 300 sq. and n.; of darkness and passion, 8, 302, 390; 15, 298 sq.; what are the qu.?, 8, 311; their characteristics, virtues and vices belonging to each of them, and their consequences in future births, 8, 319–31; 15, 257; never exist separately, but always mixed up, 8, 328–31; the middle qu., i. e. passion, dominant in Kshatriyas, 8, 345; the qu., created again and again, are non-intelligent, 8, 351; the wheel of life sustained by the qu., 8, 356; Brahman devoid of qu., 8, 369; attainment of Yoga and final emancipation depends on the qu. of goodness, 8, 373 sq.; 34, 46, 49; works endowed with the three qu., 15, 260; God, the lord of the three qu., 15, 265; the Self concealed in the cloak of the three qu., 15, 295; represented in Rudra, Brahman (m.), and Vish*n*u, 15, 303 sq.; food is composed of the three qu., 15, 313; all things in the world are fettered by qu. or gu*n*as, 19, 210; heretical systems based on Darkness or ignorance, 25, 505, 511, 511 n.; knowledge an attribute of the gu*n*a of Goodness, 34, 46, 48 sq.; why they are called white, red, and black, 34, 253; the pradhâna is the state of equilibrium of the three qu., 34, 353, 367, 370; are the three constituent elements of the pradhâna, 34, 364 n., 366 sq.; absolute independence, their essential characteristic, 34, 374 sq.; the gu*n*a Passion cannot be that which causes suffering, 34, 379; the gu*n*a Darkness is eternal, 34, 380. *See also* Morality.

Quarters: in the East the seed of the gods springs up, 1, 176; demons come from the north, 5, 318, 318 n.; are one of the ten fires at the allegorical sacrifice of the sense-organs, 8, 261; are the presiding deity of space and connected with ear or sound, 8, 337, 340, 350; 15, 81; 43, 10, 363; 44, 133; East or North, the first of all qu., 8, 347, 354, 354 n.; East the qu. of the gods, North (West) qu. of men, South qu. of ancestors, 12, 63, 187, 243, 270, 422; 26, 1–4, 146, 165; 41, 329, 329 n., 389; 42, 186, 188, 192 sq.; 43, 226 sq.; 44, 424; five qu. and their deities, 12, 382 sq.; 26, 50 sq.; 41, 152, 152 n.; 42, 113; invoked and worshipped as goddesses, 12, 382 sq.; 29, 232, 320 sq., 348; 30, 171, 194, 213 sq., 277; 42, 161 sq.; 43, 193, 245 sq.; 44, 140, 143, 505; the wind entered the qu., 12, 385; North, Rudra's quarter, 12, 438 sq.; all the qu. are all the prâ*n*as, 15, 160; Vâyu the child of the Qu., 15, 221; South the region of brightness, 16, 426; Soma desires to consort with the qu., 26, 245 sq.; game sacrificed to the four qu., 27, 295; special colours and weapons for the qu., 27, 328, 328 n.; weeping, spitting, urinating, and reviling forbidden when facing the north, 40, 244; king, at consecration, made to ascend the qu., 41, 91; five

qu. represented by five dice, 41, 107 sq., 107 n.; sacrifice (Pañkabila) for the appeasement of the qu., 41, 120–3; four qu. the four corners of the earth (or the sun), 41, 155, 242; 44, 498; nine or ten qu., 41, 196, 296 sq.; 43, 26 sq., 43–6, 91; four and four, 41, 203; North-east, qu. of both gods and men, 41, 229, 252; 44, 359; by means of the four qu. the gods carried Agni, 41, 268; four or six, 41, 268 sq.; 42, 68, 196; East, Agni's region, 41, 291; decline, weakness, sickness in the North, 41, 348; are the seven hotrâs, 41, 368; four goddesses, the consorts of the wind, 42, 14; are the heavenly world, 43, 9 sq.; identified with the metres, 43, 45 sq.; their names, 43, 46; Agni is the ten qu., 43, 70, 164, 263, 263 n.; the qu. and their rulers, 43, 100–3; ten qu., five on each side of the sun, 43, 104; gods and Asuras contending for the qu., 43, 193, 195, 198, 200; the goddesses Anumati, &c., are the qu., and the qu. are deities, 43, 264 sq.; seven qu., 43, 277, 314; beheld (or discovered) by the gods, 44, 16–18; four qu. belong to the four priests, 44, 402; Northern qu. especially sacred, 49 (i), 75.

Qubâ', mosque of, first place of public prayer in Islâm, 6, 188 sq., 188 n.

Queen, is one of the king's jewels, 41, 60; lies down near the sacrificial horse, 44, 321 sq. and n. *See also* King, Rulers, *and* Women.

Quiescence, Quietness, Quietism, *see* Nirvâ*n*a, *and* Tranquillity.

Qurâi*dh*ah, Jews of, 6, xxxviii sq.; 9, 274 n.

Qurâis, tribe of, 6, xvi, xxvi, xxviii, xxxiii, xlix, lix, 97 n., 165 n., 249 n.; 9, 17 n., 62 n., 69 n., 236 n., 254 n., 320 n.; their prosperity, 6, liii, lxi; 9, 342.

Qur'ân, its early portions genuine rhapsodies of an enthusiast, 6, xlvi; Jewish and Christian influences on it, 6, xlvii–lii, lxix, 5 n.; its influence on the Arab mind, 6, l; not a formal and consistent code of morals, 6, lii; its language and style, 6, liv sq., lxxvi sq., 43 n.; nothng like it in Arabic literature, 6, lv sq.; division of the Q. in Sûrahs, verses, &c., 6, lvi, lxv; means 'a reading,' is also called 'the discrimination,' 6, lvii; 9, 83; how it was written down, 6, lvii sq.; its arrangement, 6, lviii; different dialects and various readings in the Q., 6, lviii sq.; its text fixed by Othmân, 6, lix; Sûrahs revealed at Mecca, and those revealed at Medînah, 6, lix–lxv; chronological arrangement of Q., 6, lix–lxv; mysterious letters at the beginning of Sûrahs, 6, lxiv sq.; 9, 175 n., 295 n.; names of the Q., 6, lxv; revealed by the archangel Gabriel, 6, lxix, 13; 9, 98; revealed in the 'night of power' during Rama*dh*ân, 6, lxxiii, 26; 9, 218, 337; translations of the Q., 6, lxxvii–lxxx; abstract of the contents of the Q., 6, lxxxi–cxviii; not composed by Mohammed, but revealed by God in Arabic, 6, cviii, 46, 83, 117, 136, 138, 182, 185, 192, 194, 206, 219, 232, 261; 9, 10–13, 43, 98, 122, 160, 162, 182, 190, 199, 203 n., 205, 210 sq., 258, 300; a confirmation of former Scriptures of Moses, 6, cviii, 46, 254 sq.; 9, 112 sq., 203, 203 n., 225, 228; a guide, a warning, glad tidings, a mercy to believers, 6, 2, 257, 260; 9, 2, 13 sq., 34, 83, 99, 106, 117, 131, 162, 167, 178, 184, 186, 205, 210; some verses decisive, others ambiguous in the Book, 6, 47; ask not about painful things till the whole Q. is revealed, 6, 111; a special revelation to the Meccans, 6, 125 sq.; when the Q. is read, listen thereto and keep silence, 6, 163; Meccans challenged to bring a sûrah like it, 6, 197; *this Q. could not have been devised by any beside God*, 6, 197; God a witness at reciting a Q., 6, 199 sq., 199 n.; confirms the unity of God, 6, 205; were the Q. to convulse nature, some would not believe, 6, 236; the original ('the Mother of the Book') is with God, 6, 237; 9, 211; revealed to bring men from darkness into light, 6, 238; the 'Seven of the Repetition,' opening chapter of the Q., 6,

249, 249 sq. n.; those who dismember the Q. punished, 6, 250; the Holy Spirit brought the Q. down from the Lord, 6, 261; a reader of the Q. to take refuge with God from Satan, 6, 261; verses of the Q. abrogated, 6, 261; unbelievers cannot understand the Q., 9, 6; mankind and *G*inns together could not produce the like of it, 9, 10; revelation of the Q. not to be hurried, 9, 43, 311, 313; men mock at the Q., as a 'jumble of dreams,' forged by Mohammed, 9, 46; called old folks' tales composed by mortals, 9, 83; objection that it was revealed piecemeal, 9, 86, 86 n.; decides disputed points for the Jews, 9, 106; Mohammed bidden to recite the Q., 9, 107, 122; no doubt in the revelation of the Q., 9, 135; reward of those who recite the Q., 9, 160; oath by the Q., 9, 175; an Arabic Q. with no crookedness therein, 9, 185; punishment of those who mock at the Q., 9, 201; 'the Book inscribed upon an outstretched vellum,' 9, 248; not to be touched by the unclean, 9, 265; power of the Q., 9, 277; to be recited by night, 9, 306–8; allusion to doctrines of the Q., 24, 173 n., 178 n., 192 n., 194 n. *See also* Revelation.

Quzâi, an ancestor of Mohammed, 6, xvii.

R

Race, racing: the gods ran a r., 12, 370 sq.; 26, 327 n.; 41, 1 sq.; the r. of the Maruts, 32, 63, 75, 77, 159, 209; chariot-r. at the Vâgapeya, 41, xxiv, 17–29.

Races, *see* Caste (*e*), *and* Man.

Râ*g*a, *see* King.

Ragâ, daughter of Mâra, 10 (ii), 159.

Râ*g*agaha, or Râ*g*ag*ri*ha, Buddha at, 10 (ii), 67, 80, 85, 87; 11, 1–12, 55–7; 13, 136–51, 205–7, 239, 267 sq., 298, 302; 17, 1, 68, 78, 97, 171, 207 sq.; 19, 111 sq., 187; 20, 4, 66, 157, 220, 236, 390, 392; 21, 1; 49 (i), 104 sq.; (ii), 1 sq., 147, 161; a great town, 11, 99, 239, 247; Dâgaba over the remains of Buddha at R., 11, 134; Council of R., 13, xxi; 20, 370–85; Buddhist elders and Bhikkhus at R., 13, 172, 201, 253 sq.; Pilindava*kkh*a's mountain cave at R., 17, 61; the courtesan Sâlavatî installed at R., 17, 172; festival on the mountain-top at R., 20, 71, 168; Mahâvîra at R., 22, 264, 311; the eleven Ga*n*adharas of Mahâvîra died at R., 22, 287; discourse between Gautama and Udaka at Nâlandâ, a suburb of R., 45, 419 sq.

Ra*g*an, n.p., 5, 141, 141 n., 146; 47, 34 n.

Râ*g*anya, nobleman or warrior, at the Vâgapeya and Râ*g*asûya performs rites, such as shooting arrows, &c., 41, 25, 29, 83, 114 n.; the bow his strength, 41, 89; drinks Surâ, 44, 233; is a form of noble rank, 44, 286; the battle is his strength, 44, 287; born as one heroic, skilled in archery, a mighty car-fighter, 44, 294 sq.; a R. lute-player sings on wars and battles of the king at the A*s*vamedha, 44, 364, 364 n. *See also* Caste.

Râ*g*a-paramparâ, or lists of kings in the Ceylon chronicles, 11, xlvi sq.

Ra*g*as, Sk. t.t., Passion, *see* Qualities.

Râ*g*astambâyana, *see* Ya*gñ*ava*k*as R.

Râ*g*asûya, t.t., Soma sacrifice at the inauguration of a king, 15, 89; 41, xi, xxiv–xxvi, 4, 42–142; 42, 661 sq.; 44, xv–xvii; Brâhma*n*as are not qualified for the R., 34, 218; 38, 266; to be offered by a prince who wishes to become the ruler of the whole earth, 34, 222, 222 n.; avesh*t*i, an offering at R., 38, 266; the Pa*ñk*avâtîya offerings at the R., 41, 48–50, 48 n.; Da*s*apeya, part of the R., 41, 113–26; R. and Vâgapeya, 43, 213 sq. n., 225 sq., 225 n., 246 n., 298; a great state function with religious elements, 44, xv; called Varu*n*a's consecration, 44, xix; story of *S*una*h*sepa recited at the R., 44, xxxiv; *S*una*h*sepa to be offered at the R., 44, xxxv.

Râ*g*a-yoga, t.t., consisting in mere control of the mind, 8, 300 n.

Râgh, who he was, 47, xiv; provinces of R. and Nô*d*ar (proverb about R. and Nô*d*ar), 47, 146 sq.

Râghavânanda, his commentary on the Manu-smr*i*ti, 25, cxxxii sq.

Raghu, Sumitra left the son of, 49 (i), 66.

Râ*g*îmatî turns nun and reaches highest perfection, 45, 113–19, 113 n., 116 n.

Râ*g*yapâlikâ *S*âkhâ of the Ve*s*avâ*t*ika Ga*n*a, 22, 291.

Rahasya-brâhma*n*a of the Tâ*nd*ins and the Paiṅgins (the *Kh*ândogya), 38, 220.

Râhu, the monster who swallows sun or moon at eclipses, 1, 143, 143 n.; 8, 224; 10 (ii), 76, 83; 25, 146; 35, 38; 36, 321; 49 (i), 96; a chief of demons, 21, 6.

Râhûga*n*a, *see* Gotama R.

Rahûga*n*as, a branch of the Gotamas, 46, 102.

Râhula, Buddha's only son, 10 (ii), 55; 19, 28, 90, 229, 366; 36, 355; 49 (i), 24, 65, 88, 96; Buddha recommends the life of a recluse to R., 10 (ii), 55 sq.; Subhaddâ, the queen, was formerly his mother, 11, 241; asks his father for his inheritance, whereupon Buddha orders Sâriputta to confer the pabba*gg*â ordination on his son, 13, 208 sq.; questions Buddha about schisms, 17, 317; mentioned as one of the principal Thera Bhikkhus, 17, 360; 49 (ii), 2, 90; an eminent Arhat, 21, 3; Ânanda and R. distinguished as Buddha's attendants, 21, 205; Buddha's prophecy about R. who is to be a future Buddha, 21, 209 sq.; is always to be the son of Buddhas, 21, 209 sq.; saying of R., the Elder, 36, 290, 297, 360; Buddha exhorts his son R., 36, 312, 312 n., 317; his daughter Paurvikâ, 49 (i), 198; turns Buddhist monk and Arhat, 49 (i), 199 sq.

Râhulasutta, t.c., 10 (ii), 55 sq.

Raibhya, n. of a teacher, 15, 118 n.

Raikva with the car, and *G*âna*s*ruti Pautrâya*n*a, 1, 55–8, 55 n., 57 n.; 48, 338–42; a *S*ûdra, 34, 223–6; possessed the knowledge of Brahman, 38, 315; 48, 704, 716.

Raikva-par*n*a villages in the country of the Mahâvr*i*shas, 1, 58.

Rain, offered by the Devas on the altar earth, 1, 79; food depends on r., 1, 117; 8, 54; 25, 89; prayer to the r. as a healing power, 4, 231; is produced by sacrifices, 8, 54; prayers and rites to produce r., 12, 43 sq., 56–8, 143, 184, 189, 241–3, 331; r. and food produced by friendship of heaven and earth, 12, 196, 196 n., 241, 241 n.; rites symbolical of the production of r., 18, 170 sq. and n.; produced by Tî*s*tar, 18, 264–9, 264 n.; 23, 92–109; 24, 133, 133 n.; origin of r., 24, 101, 112, 112 n.; 26, 196; the seed of the Mâzendarâns (demons), 24, 244 sq.; produced from the sun, 25, 89; if the oxen of the Soma-cart are black, there will be much rain that year, 26, 78; plants produced by r., by eating plants sap originates, from sap seed, from seed beasts, 26, 182; means for procuring r., 27, 201 sq. and n.; by observing the *S*akvarî-vrata, a Brahma*k*ârin can produce r. according to his wish, 30, 73; sent by the Maruts, 32, 63 sq.; the offspring of the cloud, 32, 78; the milk of the clouds, 32, 106, 116; three kinds of r., 35, 171; 'grass-dogs' used in ceremonies to procure r., 39, 50 sq.; the bad man reviles the r., 40, 242; water poured out at the altar-site signifies r., 41, 335–7; smoke goes up from this world and produces r. in yonder world, 41, 383; produced by Prâ*n*a, 42, 218 sq., 623 sq.; put into the fire-altar, 43, 35; the arrows of the Rudras, 43, 164 sq.; means food, 43, 219; 44, 136; Paramesh*th*in (or Par*g*anya) rains, 44, 15; when it rains, everything is in accordance with the law, when there is drought, the stronger seizes upon the weaker, 44, 18; produced by sprinkling water behind the altar, 44, 82; falling of r. on the Agnihotra-milk a good omen, 44, 187; sky, r., was the first conception, 44, 315; when the rs. overflow, all the gods and all beings subsist

thereon, 44, 507; rites for the liberating of r., 47, 76. *See also* Parganya, *and* Waters.

Rainbow, called 'Indra's bow,' 2, 96, 221; 7, 299; 14, 62, 242; 29, 318; its cause, 18, 210; imperfect and perfect r., 25, 15, 15 n.; must not be pointed out to anybody, 25, 138; 40, 244.

Rainy season (Sk. varshâ*h*, Pali Vassa or Was), ascetic must not change his residence during the, 2, 193, 193 n.; 8, 363; 14, 260; regulations for the residence of Bhikkhus during the r. s. (keeping Vassa), 2, 193 n.; 13, 298–324; 17, 147 sq.; 35, 23 sq.; year (varsha) named from it, 12, 315 sq. and n.; when interruption of keeping Vassa is permitted, 13, 274, 285, 302–17; special rules about the r. s. due to Ahi*m*sâ, 13, 298 sq., 300; two periods of the r. s., 13, 299 sq., 300 n.; allowed and unallowed places for keeping Vassa, 13, 317–19; rules about the Pavâra*n*â ceremony at the end of the r. s., 13, 325–55; 17, 147 sq., 268 sq., 288–91, 338, 340, 373 sq., 386 sq.; proper days for the Pavâra*n*â ceremony, 13, 330 sq.; Pavâra*n*â should not be held in an assembly of Bhikkhus before a Bhikkhunî, 13, 337; Pavâra*n*â ceremony, regulations for it in times of danger, 13, 337–40; Bhikkhus guilty of an offence excluded from Pavâra*n*â, 13, 340–9, 351 sq., 354 sq.; in Isha or September, 14, 35 n.; Ka*th*ina ceremony after r. s., 17, 149 sq.; rules about robes given to Bhikkhus while keeping Vassa, 17, 217–20, 234–40, 248–53; allotments of lodging-places in the Vihâra take place after the Pavâra*n*â ceremony, 20, 204; duties of Bhikkhunîs with regard to Pavâra*n*â, 20, 323, 356–8; rules about the r. s. (Paggusan) for *G*aina monks and nuns, 22, 136 sq., 296–311; what householders do in the r. s., 22, 296; in the r. s. living beings, grass, seeds, &c., frequently come forth, 22, 308; an Ash*t*akâ celebrated in the r. s., 29, 345, 345 n.; Bhikkhus spend Was with friends, 36, 36; is the offspring of the eye, 43, 8; consists of months Nabhas and Nabhasya, 43, 48. *See also* Seasons.

Raivata, a Manu, 25, 19.

Raivata, a seer, skilled in sorcery, converted by Buddha, 49 (i), 194.

Raivataka, n. of a mountain, 45, 115, 115 n.

Râk, son of Dûrâsrôb, 5, 138, 141 n.; R. and Nô*d*ar, 47, 29, 29 n., 40, 44.

Râkâ, invoked at the Sîmantonnayana, 29, 181; 30, 55, 208; invoked at the *S*râva*n*a ceremony, 29, 412; offerings to R., 30, 124; 41, 54 n.; 43, 264, 264 n.

Rakhshas, the iniquitous act like them, 31, 249.

Rakkhasas, *see* Râkshasas.

Raksha of the Kâ*s*yapa gotra, a Sthavira, 22, 294.

Râkshasas, or Rakshas (devils, goblins), Bali-offering to the, 2, 107, 107 n.; 29, 388; 30, 23; created, 7, 4; 8, 387; 25, 15; penance and vows performed under false pretence go to the R., 7, 275; 25, 160; delusive nature of Asuras and R., 8, 83; Kubera, chief of Yakshas and R., 8, 88; 44, 367; worship of Yakshas and R. of the quality of passion, 8, 118; bands of R. extol the emancipated saint, 8, 345; Vish*n*u is the ruler of snakes, R., &c., 8, 347; Î*s*vara, the lord of gods, Dânavas, snakes, R., &c., 8, 354; cried out against the injustice of killing cows for sacrifices, 10 (ii), 51; prayer to the R. on touching water, 12, 3 n.; charms against the R., 12, 7; 41, 371 sq. and n.; 42, 33, 36–8, 57, 69, 280–4; the R. forbade (raksh) the gods to sacrifice and set up fires, 12, 8 sq., 35, 69, 126, 297; repelling the R. at sacrificial rites, 12, 12, 16, 24 sq., 31, 36, 38, 45 sq., 69, 92 sq., 158, 185, 189 sq., 220–2, 298, 352, 364 n., 365; 26, 15 sq., 28, 34, 74, 76–80, 99, 131, 136–40, 142, 158, 165, 167–70, 174–6, 186 sq., 193 sq., 206, 225, 233, 253, 283, 289, 328, 380; 41, 49, 51–4, 80, 92, 199, 357, 359, 371–3; 42, 187, 190; 43, 308; 44, 463–5; Asuras and R. crushed by the roaring of Manu's bull, 12, 29 sq.; Araru was an Asura and R., 12, 57; are enemies of Indra, who beats

them off towards the South, 12, 128; 41, 74, 92; 42, 9; Agni repels the R. at the sacrifice of the gods, 12, 157 sq.; 42, 58; 46, 104, 367 sq.; refuse of rice and blood of victim are the share of the R. at sacrifices, 12, 265 sq.; 26, 193; 44, 125, 125 n.; sacrifice offered by the unchaste student to the R., 14, 118, 215; ablution after worship of R., 14, 193; 29, 31; 30, 330; marriage rite of the R., 25, 79–82; 29, 167; consume the food eaten by unworthy guests at *S*râddha, 25, 107, 118 sq.; manes of R., 25, 112; destroy a funeral sacrifice not protected by a Vai*s*vadeva offering, 25, 113; are associates of the night, 25, 127; 41, 361 sq.; using animals for other but sacrificial purposes is a proceeding worthy of R., 25, 174; compelled by fear to yield enjoyments, 25, 219; who worships aged men, is honoured even by R., 25, 221; their food and drink, 25, 450; produced by darkness, 25, 493; sinners who are reborn as Brahma-r., 25, 497, 497 n.; pursue women, 26, 35; Agni's holy name, unviolated by R., 26, 119; Soma afraid of R., 26, 157; move about the air rootless and unfettered, 26, 189, 194, 253; threaten the animal victim, 26, 209, 209 n.; Âdityas are afraid of R., 26, 350, 352, 355; exorcism of R. threatening the place of confinement, 29, 49; satiated at the Tarpa*n*a, 29, 219; among the pa*ñk*aganâ*h*, 34, 262; prayer for protection from the R., the evil-doers, 41, 26; the coursers, swallowing the dragon, the wolf, the evil spirits, 41, 27; suck out the creatures, 41, 49, 51; water unimpaired by the R., 41, 84 sq.; gods afraid of the R., 41, 191, 199; 43, 104 sq., 316; 44, 453, 462, 467, 478; Agni protected from the R., 41, 208, 212 sq.; threaten Agni, 41, 228, 241 sq., 266, 334, 361; smitten by the gods, 41, 357, 359; the cause of madness, 42, 32; demons of disease, 42, 34; magic plants drive away the R., 42, 42, 71; slain by an amulet, 42, 62, 80, 96; mar the sacrifice, 42, 90; invoked upon the enemies, 42, 125 sq.; R., serpents, pious men, Fathers, 42, 162; sacrifice to the gods frustrated by sacrifice to the R., 42, 557; propitiatory hymn protecting the fire-altar from R., 43, 275, 316; the Asura-R., i.e. the Asuras, 44, 95; repelled by the singing of Sâmans, 44, 496 sq.; their weapons are real, 48, 125; souls of R., 48, 198. *See also* Asuras, Demons (*b*), *and* Superhuman beings.

Rakshovidyâ, science of demons, 44, 368 n.

Ram, *see* Parables (*c*), *and* Sheep.

Râm, yellow chrysanthemum, the flower of, 5, 104; invoked, 5, 403, 405; funeral cake dedicated to the spirit R., 24, 351. *See also* Vâê.

Râma, one of the eight Brahmans who took note of the marks on Buddha's body, 36, 44.

Râma (Baladeva), son of King Vasudêva, 45, 112; pays homage to Arish*t*anêmi, 45, 115.

Râma Aupatasvini, quoted, 26, 425.

Râma, Da*s*aratha's son, hero of Râmâya*n*a, 19, 65, 82, 95, 107; 49 (i), 90, 93, 101; for Sîtâ's sake, killed the demon-spirits, 19, 330; highest being becomes manifest in R., 48, 525; R. and Râma, the son of Bh*r*igu, pleased their father, 49 (i), 95.

Râma *G*âmadagnya, killed his mother, 2, 175 n.; chief among warriors, 8, 90, 90 n.; kills all Kshatriyas, 8, 294 sq.; admonished by his grandfathers, engaged in fearful penance, 8, 300; the *R*ishi R. perished because of lust, 19, 123; the *R*ishi R. fought against Da*s*aratha, 19, 330.

Râma Mârgaveya, a *S*yâpar*n*îya priest, 43, 345 n.

Râmagâma or Râmagrâma, the Koliyas of, 11, 132; stûpa of R., 11, 134 sq.; 19, 336 sq.

Râmagupta, a great ascetic, 45, 269.

Râma *Hv*â**stra**, the god that gives food its savour, 4, 23, 23 n.; invoked and worshipped, 23, 5, 5 n., 9 sq., 14, 17 sq., 34, 36, 38, 119, 158; 31, 196, 204, 209, 219, 223, 256, 271, 276, 323, 337, 340, 379–81; 37,

183, 183 n.; connected with the Moon, 23, 88; Râm Yast devoted to R. and Vayu, 23, 249–63; has fullness of welfare, 23, 327.
Ramak-tôrâ, ancestor of Frêdûn, 5, 132; the Âspîgân, 47, 34, 34 n.
Râman *Hvâstra*, *see* Râma *H.*
Râmânuga, on the Bhagavadgîtâ, 8, 30 sq., 35, 66 n., 84 n., 89 n., 90 n., 107 n., 112 n., 116 n., 124 n., 346 n., 378 n.; followed Baudhâyana, 8, 32; 34, xxi sq.; his Vedântasâra, 34, xvi; his *S*rî-bhâshya, 34, xvi sq., xxii, xxxi n.; *Vol.* 48; his relation to *S*aṅkara, 34, xvii, xxii sqq., xli–xlvi, lxxxv–ci, cxxiii sq., cxxvi; 48, ix sq.; quotes a series of ancient teachers in his Vedârthasaṅgraha, 34, xxi sq.; sketch of his philosophical system, 34, xxiv, xxvii sqq.; chief points in which R. and *S*aṅkara agree and differ, 34, xxx sq., xxxiii–xl, xlviii–li, lxii–lxvi, lxviii–lxxiv, lxxvi–lxxix, lxxxi–lxxxvi, cxii, cxiv, cxviii n., cxxi; approves of the system of the Bhâgavatas, 34, li sq.; on the relation of the individual soul to Brahman, 34, liii sq., lviii; according to R., the soul is of minute size and a knowing agent, 34, liv–lvii; on the activity of the soul, 34, lvii; on dreams, 34, lx sq.; denies the distinction of the two Brahmans and the doctrine of Mâyâ, 34, lxi, xci, cii; on the combination of the senses with the manas, &c., on the death of the vidvân, 34, lxxix; on the immortality of him who knows Brahman, 34, lxxix, lxxx; denies the distinction between a higher and a lower knowledge, 34, xci.
Râmânugas, their sect occupies a pre-eminent position among the Vaish*n*ava sects, 34, xvii; closely connected with the Bhâgavatas, 34, xxii sq.; their fundamental text concerning the soul's fate after death, 34, cxxi sq. *See also* Bhâgavatas.
Râmaputta, *see* Uddaka R.
Râmâya*n*a and Dhammapada, 10 (i), 36 n.; horse-sacrifice in the R., 44, xxix;—R. of Tulsidâs, 34, cxxvii sq.
Ra*n*añgaha, the 27th Tathâgata, 49 (ii), 6.
Râ*n*âyanîyas, Khilas of the, quoted, 34, lxx; 38, 218–20; 48, 643; Upanishad of the R., 38, 219.
Rangûstar, brother of Zoroaster, 47, 144.
Ransom, to be paid for Vessantara's children, 36, 131.
Rantideva, or Antideva, 49 (i), 101 n.
Rao*k*as-*k*aêshman, n.p., 23, 216, 219, 220 n.
Rapithwina, worshipped, 31, 197, 201, 204, 209, 215, 219, 223, 373, 381 sq.; the R. ritual, 31, 367, 374 sq.
Rapti, or A*k*iravatî, 11, 167 n.
Rasâ, the distant river, 32, 1, 8; Avestic Ra*n*hâ, a kind of Okeanos, 32, 320, 323.
Rasâstât, Thoughtfulness, a genius, 23, 11, 282; worshipped, 31, 200, 211, 217, 226.
Rasâtala (lower region), the earth sunk into, 7, 3, 8.
Rashn, *see* Rashnu.
Rashn-rêsh, n. of an apostate, 47, 12, 84 sq. and n.
Rashnu, or Rashn, or Rashnû, or R. Razista, or Rashn Râst, Genius of Truth and Justice, 4, 49; 5, 213 n.; 23, 327; comes to meet the departed soul, 4, 89 n., 373; stationed at the *K*invat bridge, 4, 272; 5, 383 n.; dog-rose, the flower of R., 5, 104; 'the R. of *K*înô,' 5, 130 sq. and n.; the just, 5, 228; 37, 72 sq., 72 n., 278; weighs good works and sins in his golden scales, 5, 241 sq. n.; 18, 33, 33 n., 61 n., 92 n., 282; 24, 18, 18 n., 22; 37, 155, 155 n.; funeral cake to R., 5, 383; 18, 61, 61 n.; 24, 351; invoked, 5, 402, 405; 23, 6, 9, 15, 17, 36, 38, 40, 164, 166, 168–78 (Rashn Yast), 283; Mithra and R. take the account of the soul's action, 18, 66; 24, 258, 280, 319, 361; frees from demons, 23, 50; liars who escape Mithra fall into the hands of R., 23, 129; companion of Mithra, 23, 139, 145, 152, 342; the unholy priest displeases R., 23, 156; one of the three judges of the departed, 23, 168; invoked at ordeals, 23, 168–77; Mithra, R., Spe*n*ta-Ârmaiti, with Ahura-Mazda,

23, 181; the Fravashis along with Mithra and R. help in battle, 23, 191; Fravashi of R., worshipped, 23, 200; Verethraghna goes along with Mithra and R., 23, 244; brother of Ashi Vanguhi, 23, 274; the most just, invoked and worshipped, 31, 198, 205, 209, 215, 220, 224, 256, 319, 326, 345, 351, 388; the Rashnus having the seed of fire in them, 31, 358, 358 n.; supremacy of R. the righteous, 37, 80; ceremonial of R., 37, 183.

Ra*s*miprabhâsa, a future Tathâgata, 21, 142–4.

Ra*s*mi*s*atasahasraparipûr*n*adhva*g*a, a future Buddha, 21, 257 sq.

Râspî, *see* Priests (*d*).

Rass, the people of ar R. punished for disbelief, 9, 86, 86 n., 242.

Râstare-vagha*nt*, n.p., 23, 209.

Râta, Genius of Charity, made by Mazda, 4, 215, 215 n.; 23, 338; 37, 227, 227 n.; the good R., with eyes of love, invoked, 23, 5, 14, 36 sq., 330.

Ratanasutta, t.c., a Sutta of the Suttanipâta, 10 (ii), 37–40; a Pirit or protecting charm, 35, 213.

Ratha, Ârya, founder of the Ârya*g*ayantî *S*âkhâ, 22, 293.

Rathag*ri*tsa, is a spring-month, 43, 105.

Rathanêmi makes love to Râ*g*îmatî, but is converted by her, and both reach highest perfection, 45, 116–19, 116 n.

Rathantara hymns, *see* Sâman.

Rathaprota is a rainy month, 43, 106.

Rathasvana is a summer-month, 43, 106.

Rathau*g*as is a spring-month, 43, 105.

Rathavîti Dârbhya, n.p., 32, 357–60, 362.

Rathe*k*itra is a summer-month, 43, 106.

Râthîtara, *see* Satyava*k*as R.

Râthîtarîputra, n.p., 15, 225.

Rati, Lust, daughter of Mâra, 49 (i), 139.

Ratipratipûr*n*a, n. of the period of the Buddha Tamâlapatra*k*andanagandha, 21, 150.

Râti-sâ*k* gods, accompany Agni at the sacrifices, 46, 188.

Ratnâbhibhâsa, the 55th Tathâgata, 49 (ii), 7.

Ratnahavî*m*shi, t.t., 'jewel-offerings' at king's consecration, 41, 58 sq.

Ratna*k*andra, a Bodhisattva Mahâsattva, 21, 4; the 52nd Tathâgata, 49 (ii), 6.

Ratnâkara, one of the sixteen virtuous men, 21, 4; n. of a Tathâgata in the East, 49 (ii), 66.

Ratnaketu, the 71st Tathâgata, 49 (ii), 7.

Ratnaketurâ*g*as, future Buddhas so called, 21, 210–12.

Ratnakusumasampushpitagâtra, n. of a Tathâgata, 49 (ii), 100.

Ratnamati, son of a former Buddha *K*andrasûryapradîpa, 21, 19.

Ratnapâ*n*i, a Bodhisattva Mahâsattva, 21, 4.

Ratnaprabha, n. of a god and a Bodhisattva Mahâsattva, 21, 4.

Ratnaprabhâsa, n. of the period of the Buddha *S*a*s*iketu, 21, 145.

Ratnasambhava, n. of *S*a*s*iketu's Buddha-field, 21, 145.

Ratna*s*ekhara, king, who spares one of six brothers sentenced to death, 45, 421 n.

Ratna*s*rî, the 72nd Tathâgata, 49 (ii), 7.

Ratnate*g*obhyudgata, n. of a Tathâgata, 21, 431 sq.

Ratnâvabhâsa, n. of the aeon of the Buddha Dharmaprabhâsa, 21, 195, 197.

Ratnavi*s*uddha, the world where the Tathâgata Prabhûtaratna is, 21, 229.

Ratnina*h*, t.t., recipients of the 'Jewel offerings' at a king's consecration, 41, 58 sq. n., 65, 108 n.

Ratnotpala*s*rî, n. of a Tathâgata, 49 (ii), 101.

Ra*tth*apâla, n.p., 11, 260 n.

Ratu, *see* Priests (*d*).

Ratu: the holy gods and the great R., 4, 250.

Ratus, the chiefs of creation, ruled by the Gâthas, 4, 222, 222 n.

Ratû*s*tar, brother of Zoroaster, 47, 144.

Rauhi*n*âyana, n. of a teacher, 15, 118 n.

Raurava, *see* Hell (*a*).

Râva*n*a, a Brâhma*n*a with ten heads, 42, 374 sq.

Rava*nt*, n.p., 23, 217.

Raven, *see* Birds (*b*).

Reabsorption of the world into Brahman, *see* Pralaya, *and* World (*b*).

Real and Unreal, 34, 4.

Realists and Idealists, 11, 49 n.; maintain the reality of everything, 34, 401; the Sautrântikas and the Vaibhâshikas are the R., 34, 401 n.; controverted, 34, 402–18.

Reasoning stands nearer to perception than *S*ruti, 34, 299; its relation to the sacred texts, 34, 299 sq., 314–17; only a subordinate auxiliary of intuitional knowledge, 34, 307; the assertion that r. has no foundation rests on r. only, 34, 315; recommended by Manu, 34, 315; the want of foundation constitutes the beauty of r., 34, 315 sq.

Rebha, n.p.? 46, 136.

Rebirth, *see* Transmigration.

Recluse, *see* Hermits, *and* Holy persons.

Recompense, *see* Karman, *and* Works (*c*).

Reflection (dhyâna), earth, sky, heaven, water, mountains, gods, and men reflect, 1, 114; meditation on r. as Brahman, 1, 115.

Regicide, *see* Homicide, *and* Rulers.

Regions, *see* Quarters, *and* World.

Relationship, five orders of, 3, 43; nine branches of r., 3, 54, 88; 'the hundred houses,' or chambers in a hundred family residence, 3, 333, 333 n.; degrees of r. and period of mourning, 4, 148–54; religion to be preferred to ties of r., 6, 175 sq.; real ties of r. to supersede the tie of sworn brotherhood, 9, 139; degrees of consanguinity and affinity in China, 27, 202–8 and Tables 1–6. *See also* Family, *and* Relatives.

Relatives, father-in-law, and uncles received as guests, 2, 120, 205; 14, 49, 244 sq.; 25, 96, 96 n.; 29, 87 n., 88, 197, 273, 435; 30, 132, 279; the terms sagotra, sakulya, sapi*nd*a, and samânodaka defined, 2, 127 n., 250, 250 n.; 7, 87; 14, 28, 177 sq., 178 sq. n.; 25, 74, 178, 180 sq., 186 sq., 366 sq. and n., 368 n., 468; impurity on birth and death of Sapi*nd*as and Samânodakas, 2, 251, 251 n.; 25, 177–82, 186 sq.; 29, 244 sq. and n.; those who do not cast off r. guilty of mortal crimes, and those who forsake blameless r. become outcasts, 2, 280; 25, 384, 442, 442 n.; Sapi*nd*as, Sagotras, and Samânapravaras inherit on failure of sons, 2, 305 sq.; 25, 366 sq.; believers should not ask forgiveness for the idolators, though they be their r., 6, 189; two kinds of Bandhu and Sakulya, 7, 68, 68 n.; who are to be honoured as Gurus, 7, 129; how to be saluted, 14, 67, 155; not to be fed at *S*râddhas, 14, 267; 25, 101 sq.; to be informed of an adoption, 14, 335; Mithra (contract) between r., 23, 149 sq.; to help in illness, 24, 69; quarrels with near r. should be avoided, 25, lxviii, 157 sq.; maternal uncle, aunt, grandfather, 25, 39, 54, 96, 102, 157, 182; respect due to to r., 25, 54 sq.; marriage with (female) Sapi*nd*â forbidden, 25, 75, 466; defamation of r., 25, 302; Niyoga with Sapi*nd*â, 25, 356; names to be given to r., 27, 118; r. who should wear mourning for each other, 27, 146 sq., 146 n.; 28, 42, 42 n., 44, 55; regulations about a ruler and his r., 27, 354–9; rights of eldest cousins, 27, 458 sq.; assembly of r. at ancestral rites, 28, 293; love of kindred, the greatest exercise of benevolence, 28, 312 sq.; liability of r. for debts contracted by members of a family, 33, 41–6, 48, 329; king must maintain the rules settled among assemblages of r., 33, 153–5; who are inadmissible witnesses, 33, 302 sq.; property not lost to r. by long possession, 33, 310 sq.; authority for inquiry into the sin of r., 37, 77; loyalty towards r., 40, 242 sq. *See also* Etiquette, *and* Guru.

Release, *see* Emancipation, *and* Salvation.

Released, the, one who has reached union with Brahman, 8, 288 sq.; for the r. there is no fear anywhere, 8, 292; the r. soul, *see* Soul (*d*).

Relics, *see* Buddha (*l*), *and* Stûpas.

Religion, the good, *see* Zoroastrianism.
Religious acts (duties, works), *see* Sa*m*skâra, *and* Works.
Religious hunter (Dharmavyâdha), 34, 228.
Religious instruction, *see* Brahma*k*ârin, Instruction, *and* Teacher.
Religious merit, *see* Karman, *and* Works.
Religious student, *see* Brahma*k*ârin.
Re*n*â, female disciple of Sambhûtavi*g*aya, 22, 289.
Renovation of the universe, *see* World (*b*).
Renunciation and pursuit of actions, 8, 63; r. and tranquillity belong to knowledge, 8, 103; true r. defined, 8, 121 sq., 127; is penance, and a means to attain knowledge of the Brahman, 8, 312, 369; man of understanding practises r., giving prominence to knowledge, 8, 349; as a mode of piety, 8, 376; what is the object of r. of Buddhist monks? 35, 31 sq., 49 sq.; sensations, pleasant and painful, connected with r., 35, 71; destruction of sorrow, the aim of r., 35, 101–3, 124; advantages of r., 36, 58 sq.; ten bonds on account of which men do not renounce the world, 36, 139; fruits of Sama*n*aship gained by r., 36, 360. *See also* Sin (*c*).
Repentance, *see* Sin (*c*).
Resignation (kshânti), three kinds of, 49 (ii), 51. *See also* Islâm.
Resources, the four, of religious life, 13, 172–4.
Rest-houses, public, built by pious people, 11, 15 sq., 25 n.; 17, 98 sq.; 22, 126 sq.; Bhikkhu may take one meal at r., 13, 37, 37 sq. n.
Restraint, penance, sacrifice, are the feet of the Brâhmî-upanishad, 1, 153; of senses, 8, 51, 53, 57, 86, 99, 126, 162, 232, 242, 248, 251, 257, 282, 336, 358; of the self in the self, 8, 392. *See* Self-restraint.
Resurrection, the world of, the happy day of, 4, 81 n., 82 n., 147, 203, 211 n., 247, 247 n., 381; 5, 8; 18, 13, 38, 45, 70, 73, 110, 213 n., 378, 382; 37, 420 sq., 446 sq.; r. and renovation of the universe, under Sôshyans, 5, lii, 9, 9 n., 33, 120–30, 196, 235; 37, 431; those who have no part in the r., 5, 384 sq.; the place whence r. will take place, 5, 386 sq., 386 n.; the day of judgement, 6, 6, 140 sq., 243 sq.; 9, 9, 19, 29 sq., *85*, 114 sq., 185, 188 sq., 216, 220, 254 sq., 255 n., 257 sq., 262, *299*, *301 sq.*; threats and terrors, warnings of r. day, 6, 66, 69 sq., 159, 199, 216, 244, 252 sq.; 9, 54–7, 66, 72, 130, 218, 222–4, 248 sq., 251, 307–11; God will assemble the believers on r. day, 6, 84, 117; unbelievers doubt in r. and are punished in hell, 6, 254; 9, 6, 84, 105, 154–6, 168, 286; 37, 193; every nation shall have a witness against it on the day of r., 6, 259 sq.; each man shall have a book on r. day with an account of his deeds, 9, 3; all cities destroyed before the day of judgement, 9, 7; retribution on r. day, 9, 11; proofs of r., 9, 32, 56 sq., 241 sq., 246; 18, 99–113; descriptions of r. day, 9, 42 sq., 189 sq., 314 sq., 317–26, 329–31, 338–40; just balances will be placed on the r. day, no soul shall be wronged, 9, 49; the kingdom shall be God's on judgement day, 9, 62 sq.; r. called old folks' tales, 9, 70; the beast that shall appear on r. day, 9, 106; punishments on r. day, 9, 112; the dread hour when the father shall not atone for his son, nor the child for its parent, 9, 134 sq.; as God quickens the earth by rain—so shall the r. be, 9, 158, 164; the sudden coming of the judgement day, 9, 165 sq.; the infidels regret on r. day, 9, 187; God the only judge on r. day, 9, 192; the very skins of the unbelievers bear witness against them on judgement day, 9, 200 sq.; the quickening of the earth a sign of r., 9, 202, 211; smoke shall cover the heavens on r. day, 9, 218; the two recording angels, death and r., the last judgement, 9, 243–5; creation and r. of man, 9, 328; the hope of all good creations, 18, 5; 37, 246; mankind continues till the r., 18, 76 sq.; fifty-seven years of the r., 18, 79; the wicked purified at the r., 18, 111 n., 114–16, 115 n.; *in revelation it is said*

that every dead body is raised up, both of the righteous and of the wicked; there is none whom they shall abandon to the fiend, 18, 222 sq.; made by Verethraghna, 23, 238–40; immortality of the world after r., 23, 290–2, 307; r. and future existence, 24, 15, 61, 63 sq., 74, 81 n., 82 sq., 99, 104, 207, 225, 258, 336; 37, 440; wicked souls remain in hell until r., 24, 25; three nights' punishment at the r., 24, 51, 51 n.; demonstrated by the death of Christ, 24, 232 sq.; denied by the Mânîchaeans, 24, 246; belief in r., 27, 193; let the dead arise, 31, 391; foretold by Aûharma*zd*, 47, 163. *See also* Future Life (*a*, *d*), Saoshya*n*t, *and* World (*b*).

Retribution, *see* Future Life, Karman, *and* Works (*c*).

Revata, sends a robe to Sâriputta, 17, 251 sq.; questions Buddha about schisms, 17, 317; one of the principal Thera Bhikkhus, an Arhat, 17, 360; 21, 2; 49 (ii), 2, 90; won over by Yasa, R. takes an active share in convening the council of Vesâlî, and is one of the referees, 20, 397–414; Vaggian Bhikkhus try in vain to win R. by gifts, 20, 400 sqq.

Revatî, at the head of 318,000 female lay votaries, 22, 267 sq.

Revatika, n. of a park at Dvârâvatî, 22, 277.

Revelation, not claimed for the sacred books of Confucianism, 3, xv;—Avesta, r. of the law (dînô) by Ahura to Zarathu*s*tra, in questions and answers, 4, lviii sq., lxx–lxxii, lxxii n., 2, 11, 22, &c., 208, 212; 23, 24, 24 n., 202; 24, xvii, 170; 37, 3–6, 9, 258, 413; mountain of the holy questions, i. e. of conversations between Ormazd and Zoroaster, 4, 240, 240 n.; many works of wisdom can only be conceived through the Holy Word, or r., 4, 296 n., 297; defined, 5, 4; quoted, appealed to, 5, 8, 15, 25, 41, 46, 52, 60 sq., 63, 65, 73–5, 83, 85, 88–91, 105, 115, 120, 149, 161, 183 sq., 354, 393; 18, 11, 15, 21, 25 sq., 30, 41, 75, 125, 127, 129, 133, 148, 150, 223, 227 sq., 282, 288, 292, 295, 332, 338 sq., 341, 360 sq., 378, 422 sq.; 23, 127, 133; 24, 52 sq., 59, 258 sq., 261 sq., 267, 271, 273, 277 sq., 281–3, 287 sq., 290 sq., 293, 295, &c.; is not wanting in completeness, but our understanding, 18, 7, 9 sq.; priest keeps the Ma*zd*a-worshipper in accordance with r., 18, 19; Avesta revealed, not the Pahlavi commentaries, 18, 215 n.; arrangement and restoration and benediction of r., 18, 322; Zarathu*s*tra prays for r., 31, 16, 23 sq., 78, 82, 90, 108–21; Mãthras and Gâthas delivered to Zarathu*s*tra by Ahura, 31, 37, 43, 123, 126, 176, 179; 37, 406 sq.; Zoroaster questions Ahura-Mazda as to the future, 31, 38 sq., 48–50; all that Zarathu*s*tra said, inspired by Ahura, 31, 134, 144; Zarathu*s*trian r. given against the Daêvas, 31, 199 sq. and n.; reciting the r., 37, 245, 330; Nasks sent down by God, 37, 419–21; *see also* Ahura-Mazda (*c*);—first and second r. of Mohammed, 6, xx–xxiii; Mohammed's marriage with Zâinab sanctioned by a r., 6, xxix; Mohammed's wife cleared from suspicion by a r., 6, xxix; Mohammed reconciles his wives to his marriage with Mary by a r., 6, xl; the pious to believe in r., misbelievers doubt in r. and are punished, 6, 2, 24, 138, 191, 197 sq., 263 sq., 206; 9, 176; Jews say that they believe in what God revealed to *them*, 6, 12; belief in what has been revealed to Abraham, Ishmael, Isaac, Jacob, Moses, and Jesus, 6, 19; angels bear witness to what God revealed, 6, 95; Jews to be judged by what God has revealed, 6, 103 sq.; had the r. been a book on paper, idolators would have disbelieved it, 6, 116; Moses receives the tablets of the Law from God, 6, 154 sq.; Jews inherited the Book, 6, 158 sq.; unbelievers call r. old folks' tales, 6, 166, 252; Mohammed dare not change the r., 6, 194; story of Joseph, a proof of r., 6, 219, 230 sq.; God can annul or confirm any part of r., 6, 237; for every period there is a book revealed, 6, 237; the

people of the Book to be treated mildly, 9, 122; God will vindicate the truth of His r., 9, 207 sq.; hypocrites ask for the r. of a Sûrah, 9, 231; *see* Qur'ân;—disclaimed by Buddha, 19, 170 n.; Manu-smr*i*ti revealed by Brahman, 25, xii, xv, xvii, 19; Vishnu-smriti a r. of the god Vish*n*u, 25, xxi; *S*ruti or r., the Veda, 25, 31; the Veda is eternal, though *Ri*shis are makers of hymns and sections, 48, 332 sq. *See also* *S*ruti, Upanishads (*a*), *and* Veda (*f*).

Revenge, King Dîghîti dissuades his son Dîghâvu from, 17, 298–305.

Revottara Pâ*t*ava *K*âkra Sthapati, a priest, 44, 236, 269–72.

***Ri*bhu,** n. of one of the *Ri*bhus, 44, 381; Agni called *R.*, 46, 187, 191, 240, 243, 382.

***Ri*bhukshans,** Maruts so called, 32, 390 sq., 395, 400.

***Ri*bhus,** worshipped at the Tarpa*n*a, 30, 243; became immortal, 32, 36 sq., 166 sq.; constructed the chariot of the A*s*vins, 42, 20, 389; the wagoners, 42, 73, 603; the evening Soma pressure for the *R.*, 42, 231; share of the *R.* and lordship of the Vi*s*vedevas, 43, 69; a *R.* formed of the *G*agat metre bears the sacrificer to well-being, 44, 173; viz. *Ri*bhu, Vibhvan, Indra, Vâ*g*a, invited to the sacrifice, 44, 381; to the *R.* a furrier sacrificed at the Purushamedha, 44, 415; Savit*ri* accompanied by *R.*, Vibhus and Vâ*g*as, 44, 480.

Rice, different kinds of, 41, 69 sq.; its origin, 44, 216. *See also* Parables (*b*).

Riddles, propounded by Angra Mainyu to Zarathu*s*tra, 4, 208, 210, 210 n.; Âpattis not subject to legal questioning are sot-âpatti and samâpatti, 20, 44; of the sorcerer Akhtya, 23, 72 sq. and n.; r. and similes of Arhatship, 36, 275–373, 282 n. *See also* Brahmodya, *and* Puzzles.

Right (and left): the son walks round his father keeping his r. side towards him, 1, 292; left hand prized on occasions of festivity, r. hand on occasions of mourning, 39, 73 sq.; r. side of animal is the stronger, 43, 115; rightward or sunward way, 43, 136, 139, 147; Adhvaryu priest steps past the altar, keeping his left foot before the r. one, 44, 56 sq. and n. *See also* Omens.

Right Conduct, *see* Morality, Righteousness, *and Ri*ta.

Righteousness, he is not mighty, &c., who is not mighty, &c., in, 4, 297; the righteous and the wicked distinguished on resurrection day, 5, 123–7; Aûhar*mazd* considered r. as a destruction of the fiend, 5, 183; r. is the one thing which is good, 5, 335; the righteous man a counterpart of Aûhar*mazd*, 5, 373 sq.; there is a hope for everything but wickedness, everything will lapse except r., 5, 396; righteous feelings belong to good conduct, 8, 326; righteous life is the worthiest homage of the Tathâgata, 11, 87; a life of r., the first of the conditions by which a Bhikkhu obtains his desires, 11, 207, 210–18; palace and lake called 'R.' of King Sudassana, 11, 239, 265–70, 274, 277, 278, 281, 285, 287; deviation from established course allowed in what is conventional and ceremonial, but not in the matter of r., 16, 202, 204 n.; righteous man better than all creatures, spiritual or worldly, 18, 11–15; why a righteous man is created, and how he should act, 18, 15–20; why a righteous man is great, 18, 20 sq.; r. and sagedom are identical, 22, 46; propriety and r. the great elements for man's character, 27, 388 sq.; humanity and r. rooted in ceremonies, 27, 413 sq.; r. arises from affection between husband and wife, father and son, 27, 440; rites promote r. and humility, 28, 219 sq.; benevolence and r., instruments of a ruler, 28, 257; r. is perfect excellence, 37, 11 sq. and n., &c.; three kinds of righteous men, 37, 149; cause and effect of r., 37, 168; happiness comes from r., 37, 176; propitiation of the righteous is the best thing, 37, 188; *righteous action is the desire of the soul, and also the gifts which they give away*, 37, 193; superiority of

the righteous man, 37, 231; what is r., 37, 233; benefit of worship and r., 37, 241; rewards and tokens of r., 37, 269 sq.; *r. is the best of religions*, 37, 271; reward of liberality and r., 37, 282; Zoroastrianism the religion of r., 37, 286 sq., 344; teaching r., 37, 314; the way of r., 37, 347; thinking about r., 37, 358; r. produced by complete mindfulness, 37, 379 sq.; way of r. not concealed, 37, 380 sq.; giving delight to him who is a right-living poor man, 37, 383 sq.; assisting the world through r., 37, 387 sq.; *rectitude assists a man like a regiment a thousand strong*, 37, 409; dominion is for r., 37, 462; Zoroaster a seeker of r., 47, xxvi, 49, 51, 53; Zoroaster's 'eternal statement' about reverencing the righteous, 47, 44; praise r., 47, 69; reverence for r., 47, 150; benevolence and r., *see* Benevolence. *See also* Islâm, Morality, *and* Virtue.

Righteous Order, *see* Asha.

*Rig*umati, disciple of Sambhûtavigaya, 22, 289.

*Rig*upâlikâ, n. of a river, 22, 201, 263.

Rig-veda, or *Rig*-veda-sa*m*hitâ, or *Rik* (*Rik*as), Agni or fire in, 1, xxii; religious notion of sin in R., 1, xxii; germs of Upanishad doctrines found in R., 1, lxvi; breath identified with the hymns of the R. and their poets, 1, 214–18; arrangement of hymns in R., 1, 214 n.; 12, xvi, xx–xxii; 29, 113 n.; 32, xli sq.; 46, 17 sq., 104, 216, 293, 297, 310, 361, 395 sq.; date of R. and Prâti*s*âkhyas, 1, 214 n.; 32, xxii, xlv, li, 60; speculations on the recitation of the Sa*m*hitâ, Pada, and Krama texts, 1, 247, 250 sq., 253–6, 265; texts of R. quoted, 8, 224, 277 n., 284 n.; 25, 63, 183, 183 n., 272, 480–2, 482 n.; 38, 428 sq.; 44, 223, 397, 445; 48, 778; Brâhma*n*as recite the verses in the same way as they were recited by their authors, the ancient *R*ishis, 11, 172 sq.; efficacy of priestly invocations and sacrifices in hymns of R., 12, x sq.; caste in R., 12, xii; priests in R., 12, xv; allusions to Kurus and Pa*ñk*âlas in R., 12, xli sq.; portions of it going by the name of Upanishad, 15, xxxii; of what use is the R. to him who does not know the Self? 15, 251; Brâhma*n*a useless who does not know the *Rik*as, 25, 59; is sacred to the gods, 25, 148; Brâhma*n*a who retains in his memory the R. is not stained by guilt, 25, 482; a miscellaneous production, 26, xviii; *Rik*, the (female) Hot*ri*, 26, 247, 327; the hymns of R. belong to Indra and Agni, 26, 429, 429 n.; *R*ishis, authors of R., 29, 122 sq., 219 sq.; 46, 33 sq.; methods of translation and interpretation, 32, ix–xxii, xxix–xli; value of Sâya*n*a's commentary, 32, xxix–xxxi, xxxiv, xliv, xlvi, lxviii–lxxi; editions of R. and Sâya*n*a's commentary, 32, xxxi sq., xliii–cxxv; metrics and prosody of R., 32, xxxvii sq., lii, lxxvii–cxxv, 83, 91, 99, 170 sq., 324; the Sa*m*hitâ and the Pada texts, 32, xlii sq., xliv, xlviii, li sq.; 46, 69, 71, 79, 145; importance of Prâti*s*âkhya for R. text, 32, xliv sq., xlviii–liii, lv–lvii, lxxii, lxxv, lxxviii–ci, cvii, cxiii sq., cxvi; Vâlakhilya hymns of R., 32, xlvi–li; the Sarvânukrama*n*î, 32, lxviii–lxxi, lxxviii; old mistakes in the text, 32, lxxi–lxxvii; hymns of R. translated, *Vols*. 32 and 46; ancient and modern hymns, 32, 3–6; mythology of the R. to be kept distinct from that of other Vedas, 32, 260 sq.; bibliography of works on R., 32, 540–9; highest Self is *Rik*, 34, 79; lower knowledge comprises the R., 34, 137, 138; pra*n*ava belonging to R. is connected with udgîtha belonging to Sâmaveda, 38, 282 n.; Atharva-veda and R., 42, xxx sq.; R. and the horse-sacrifice, 44, xvii, xxiv; Nârâ*s*a*m*sâni, verses or hymns of the R., recited at the Purushamedha, 44, xxxii; story of Purûravas and Urva*s*î in R., 44, 70–2, 72 n.; the *Rik* verses are the Veda, 44, 362; at the time of the Anukrama*n*î, all real knowledge as to authors of the hymns of the first Ma*nd*ala lost, 46, 24 sq.; later additions to the hymns of R., 46, 301, 304, 421, 424; later hymns of R., 46, 304. *See also* Veda.

Rik, *Rik***as**, *see* Rig-veda.

*Rik*î**ka**, an ancestor of Râma, 8, 295.

Rinañgaya, worshipped at the Tarpa*n*a, 30, 244.

Rishabha, Arhat, life of the, 22, 281–5; had five names, 22, 282; the first Tîrthakara, 45, 71 n.; the first *G*ina, of the Kâsyapa Gotra, addresses his sons, 45, 249, 260, 260 n., 261 n. *See also* Kâsyapa.

Rishabha Vaisvâmitra, author of Vedic hymns, 46, 267, 269.

Rishabha Yâgñatura, king of the Svikna, 44, 250, 399 sq.

Rishabhadatta, Devânandâ, wife of the Brâhma*n*a, 22, 190 sq., 218, 220–3, 226.

Rishabhasena, at the head of the Srama*n*as in *R*ishabha's time, 22, 284.

Rishidatta, disciple of Susthita and Supratibuddha, 22, 293.

Rishidattika Kula, of the Mânava Ga*n*a, 22, 292.

Rishigupta Kâkandaka, founder of the Mânava Ga*n*a, 22, 292.

Rishiguptika Kula, of the Mânava Ga*n*a, 22, 292.

Rishipâlita, disciple of Sântisenika, 22, 293.

Rishis (sages, seers), are not born in the Kali Yuga, 2, xviii, xl sq., 19, 19 n.; one should not marry a woman belonging to the same Gotra, or descended from the same *R.* ancestors, or from the same Pravaras, 2, 127 n., 196; 7, 106, 106 sq. n.; 14, 42; 33, 166, 166 n.; committed no sin by transgressions of the law, but men of later times must not imitate them, 2, 132, 175, 175 n.; the seven *R.* as creators, 2, 160; 42, 179–83, 204; the bodies of the great *R.* became stars, 2, 160; daily libations and other offerings to the *R.*, 2, 195, 201; 14, 63, 238; 25, 62, 132; 29, 192; dwellings of *R.*, sacred places, 2, 276; 14, 117, 311; the seven *R.*, 7, 4, 4 n., 153; 8, 86, 281; 14, 309; 15, 106; 30, 244 (their names); 33, 99; 42, 52, 161, 179–83; 43, xv n., 73 (created), 205, 207, 211 sq., 250, 250 n., 267, 267 n.; 44, 397; 46, 80, 225, 312 sq.; *see also* Stars; royal and Brahmanical *R.* have perished by the action of Kâla, 7, 79; man owes a debt to the *R.*, viz. Veda study, which is the sacrifice to the *R.*, 7, 194, 194 n.; 12, 190 sq., 190 n.; 14, 56, 259, 271; 25, 89, 169; 49 (i), 100; *see also* Debts (the three), *and* Sacrifice (*h*); royal *R.* learnt yoga from Ikshvâku, 8, 58; gods and *R.*, the emanations of K*r*ish*n*a, 8, 86; all *R.* worship K*r*ish*n*a, 8, 87, 94; Bh*r*igu and Nârada chiefs among *R.*, 8, 89; are within K*r*ish*n*a, 8, 93; he is called the highest *R.* who understands the Brahman, 8, 173; by self-restraint, &c., one becomes a *R.*, not by dwelling in the forest, 8, 173, 173 n., 282; question Pragâpati, resp. Brahman about final emancipation, 8, 282 sq., 314; are subject to delusion, 8, 322; the great *R.* also extol the emancipated saint, 8, 345; attained the godhead by means of penance, 8, 388; are the authors of Vedic hymns, Vedas seen by or revealed to them, 11, 172 sq.; 25, 477, 479; 29, 70–2 and n.; 34, 213, 223; 48, 332 sq.; Agni the Hot*ri* introduced to the *R.* and gods, 12, 115, 115 n.; Agni praised by *R.*, Vipras (bards), and Kavis (sages), 12, 116; how they obtained the sacrifice from the gods, 12, 160–3; how they reached safely the night, 12, 352; accomplished what they wanted by the sacrifice, 12, 370; part of the hand sacred to the *R.*, 14, 25, 166; to carp at the teaching of the *R.* is to destroy one's soul, 14, 62; honoured as guests with madhuparka, 14, 244 sq., 244 n.; satiated at the Tarpa*n*a rite, 14, 254 sq.; 29, 115, 121–3, 219 sq., 223; 30, 79, 244; reached their high station by 'the ladder of the gods,' 14, 309; world of *R.* obtained by reciting hymns, 15, 90; Prâ*n*a is the true work of the *R.*, 15, 275; Prâ*n*a is the only *R.*, 15, 276; names of ancient *R.* in Pali, 17, 130; the *R.* Asita comes and departs by the way of the wind, 19, 18; 49 (i), 14; were seduced by women, 19, 39 sq., 43–5; 49 (i), 38 sq.; forests of the Himâlaya, the favourite resort of Brahmanical, royal and divine *R.*, 19, 78; 49 (i), 75; Buddha called a great *R.*, 19, 147, 163, 281, 281 n.; a hermit

may fall into ruin, a householder may become a *R.*, 19, 239; possessed of magical powers, 19, 352; 21, 131; different degrees of sages, 22, 268, 274; Manu creates ten *R.*, who again create seven Manus, 25, lxv, 14 sq.; the great *R.* approach Manu, 25, 1; country of Brahmarshis, 25, 32 sq.; Ârsha marriage rite of the *R.*, 25, 79–82, 85; 29, 166; Manes descended from Marî*k*i and other *R.*, 25, 111 sq.; desert a country ruled by a wicked king, 25, 220; even the great *R.* took oaths, 25, 273, 273 n.; 33, 98 sq. and n.; great *R.* of the Brâhma*n*a caste made substitutes for principal rules, 25, 435; penances adopted by gods, *R.*, and Manes, 25, 473, 475; caused by Goodness, 25, 495; learnt sacrificial rites from the gods, 26, 21, 36, 39, 46, 101; Brâhma*n*as, the descendants of the *R.*, 29, 62, 62 sq. n.; 42, 175; 44, 195 sq. (represent all deities); adoration to gods, *R.*, Manes, and men, 29, 150; if the newly married abstain for one year, a *R.* will be born, 29, 171; at opening and concluding ceremonies of Veda study, 29, 221, 321, 325; 30, 161, 161 n., 242, 266 sq.; the vow belonging to Agni together with the *R.*, 29, 229; invoked to give long life to the new-born child, 29, 294; cannot perform sacrifices, hence are not entitled to the study of the Veda, 34, 197 n.; are entitled to acquire knowledge, 34, 199; knowledge of the *R.* necessary for the performance of a sacrificial action, 34, 213 sq.; cannot be qualified for meditations connected with *R.*, 34, 217; we have no right to measure by our capabilities the capability of *R.*, 34, 223; Sâṅkhya*s*âstra composed by a *R.*, 34, 291 sq.; create many things by their mere intention, 34, 347 sq.; in Chinese Buddhism and in Tâoism *R.* are immortal, 40, 238 n.; were the non-existent from which creation started, 41, 143; 48, 568 sq.; the years, the *R.*, the truths, 41, 168; gods and *R.*, 41, 189 sq.; represent the vital airs, 41, 333; 43, xxi n., 60, 100, 122, 174, 185, 267, 267 n.; 48, 568 sq.; charms found by *R.*, 42, 29; stanzas, the milk of the *R.*, 42, 73; Indra together with the *R.*, 42, 231; *Ri*shis' layer (of the fire-altar), 43, 81; are the first-born Brahman, 43, 100–3; when the *R.* performed sacrifice, the Gandharvas came and criticized it, 44, 29; Agni makes the mortal *R.*, 46, 24; Agni compared to a *R.* uttering sacred shouts, 46, 57; the seven *R.* or Aṅgiras, sons of the Dawn and Heaven, breaking the rock in which the cows are imprisoned, 46, 308 sq., 313 sq., 318, 322; go to heaven, 49 (i), 19 sq.; a *R.* stepping from a heavenly chariot, 49 (i), 22; Nahusha made the *R.* bear his litter, 49 (i), 113; Purûravas wished to take gold from the *R.*, 49 (i), 113. *See also* Holy persons, *and* Isi.

***Ri*shisvâdhyâya**, a treatise quoted, 29, 72.

***Ri*shya*s*ri*ṅ*ga**, seduced by a woman, 19, 39, 39 n.; 49 (i), 39.

***Ri*ta** (Right, Order): the departed sage says, 'I am the first-born of *R.*,' 15, 69; the Self the enjoyer of *R.*, 15, 295; Aditi, the wife of *R.*, 32, 261; the gods release the *R.* (divine order of the universe) from darkness, 42, 15; *R.* or universal order, supports the earth, 42, 199; Pragâpati, the first-born of *R.*, 42, 206; Agni the guardian of *R.*, 46, 1, 259, 282; the divine gates, the increasers of *R.*, 46, 8, 153; Agni kindled on behalf of *R.*, 46, 32; Agni born from or in or according to *R.*, 46, 33, 54, 161, 181, 281; Maruts, the increasers of *R.*, 46, 38; Agni in the lap, in the womb of *R.*, 46, 54, 220; the gods followed the laws of *R.*, 46, 54; the stream of *R.*, 46, 61, 63, 147; serving the *R.*, 46, 61, 64; the instigations of *R.*, the thought of *R.*, 46, 64; Agni penetrated by *R.*, 46, 70; the Aṅgiras founded the *R.*, 46, 74; the lowing milch-cows of *R.*, 46, 88; a sacrifice conforming to the great *R.*, 46, 95; Agni swells with the milk of *R.* and is led on the straightest paths of *R.*, 46, 103, 137; Agni in the sphere or abode

of *R.*, 46, 148, 248, 412; Night and Dawn, the young mothers of *R.*, 46, 153, 377; Agni the charioteer of *R.*, 46, 158, 229, 350; streams of *R.* hidden at the birthplace of Agni, 46, 160, 161 sq.; Agni is intent upon *R.*, 46, 164; the gods rejoiced in the song of *R.*, 46, 170; Agni Vai*s*vânara, increaser of *R.*, 46, 228; Agni loves many aspects of *R.*, 46, 240; the two long-maned, red horses of *R.*, that swim in ghee, 46, 244; the thoughts of the worshippers go along the path of *R.*, 46, 263; priests, eager to set to work the *R.*, 46, 297, 299; the host (of the seven *Ri*shis?) came forth in the womb of *R.*, 46, 308; our human fathers (the seven *Ri*shis), aspiring after *R.*, 46, 308 sq., 318; Agni has harnessed the two steeds of *R.*, 46, 316, 319; the brilliant dawns have shone out *R.*, 46, 318; the wise have held up the *R.*, 46, 318; the sacrifice, one of the chief manifestations of *R.*, 46, 325, 328; by *R.* the waters have sped forward, 46, 326; with *R.* Agni has been anointed, 46, 326; the *R.* of the cow (milk) ruled by *R.*, 46, 326, 329; by the *R.* the Aṅgiras have broken the rock, 46, 326; the abode, foundation of *R.*, 46, 336, 343; Agni has spread over heaven and earth according to *R.*, 46, 364; Agni knows *R.*, 46, 372; Agni has grasped the rein of *R.*, 46, 382; Agni as connected with *R.*, 46, 393 sq.; by *R.* they have supported the supporting *R.*, 46, 399; Agni implored for favour, wealth, and *R.*, 46, 410.

***Ri*tañgaya**, worshipped at the Tarpa*n*a, 30, 244.

Rites, *see* Auspicious rites, Ceremonies, *and* Works.

***Ri*tu**, *see* Seasons.

Rivâyat, on next-of-kin marriage, 18, 414–26, 428; extracts from Persian R., 37, 418–47.

River(s): simile of r. and sea, 1, 102; 34, 277–9; two r. in the world of Brahman, 1, 275–7; worshipped, 3, 39, 39 n., 134 sq., 317 sq., 318 n.; 27, 225; 29, 127; origin of r., 5, 28 sq., 172 sq.; nature of r., list of r., 5, 74–85; chiefs of r., 5, 89 sq.; rules about crossing r., 7, 203; *S*râddhas performed on the banks of holy r., confer eternal bliss, 7, 256–60; ocean the prince among r., 8, 346; feast of the Gaṅgâ and Mahî, 17, 25; 20, 359; the cause of r. beds, 18, 213 sq.; names of r., 20, 301 sq., 304; 32, 320, 323; 35, 171; 36, 304 sq.; why r. were created, 24, 98; Snâtaka must not swim over a r., 25, 141; a r. made pure by its current, 25, 188; invoked for bliss, 32, 423; 46, 143; the seven r., 42, 25, 375; 43, 211 sq.; 46, 75, 219, 224; expiatory oblation to the stream at Soma-sacrifice, 44, 211; in hell, 45, 280; Dâît (Av. Dâitya), a mythic r., 47, 25, 25 n.; wonderful r. in Sukhâvatî, 49 (ii), 37–9. *See also* Holy places.

Robbery, *see* Theft.

Rodasî, wife of the Maruts, 32, 272–7, 284, 338, 357, 369; and Eileithyia, 32, 277 sq.

Ro*g*a, the Malla, converted by Buddha, 17, 135–9; 35, 282 n.; a friend of Ânanda's, 17, 228.

Rohagupta, *see Kh*aluka R.

Roha*n*a, disciple of Suhastin, 22, 290; teacher of Nâgasena, 35, xxv, 13–24.

Rohi*n*î, moon beloved by, 22, 235; divinity of the cows, 42, 7, 265; wife of Rohita, 42, 210, 661, 665 sq.; wife of King Vasudêva, 45, 112; wife of Soma, 49 (i), 44.

Rohita, the red sun, prayer for sovereign power addressed to, 42, 207–14, 661–8; the divine R., 42, 265; identified with Time, 42, 683.

Rohita, son of Hari*sk*andra, 44, xxxiv sq.

Romaka, Romans (?), v. l. Râmaka, 14, xxv, 94 n.

Rosaries, Buddha worshipped with, 49 (i), 191.

Rôshan, Pahlavi writer, quoted, 5, 216, 216 n., 256, 267, 272; 24, xxvi sq., 120 n., 169, 169 n., 189.

Rôshanô-*k*ashm, Av. Rao*k*as-*k*aêshman, among the producers of the renovation, 18, 13, 14 n., 78 sq. and n.

Royal, royalty, *see* King.
Rû*d*astâm, or Rustam, 5, 139 n., 140, 140 n.
Rudra.

(*a*) R. in mythology.
(*b*) Worship of R.
(*c*) The Rudras (plur.).

(*a*) R. IN MYTHOLOGY.
Is not lord of mountains, but lord of clouds, 1, 151 n.; acquired a splendid abode, after performing penance, 7, 153; in the Anugîtâ, 8, 219; presiding deity of egoism, 8, 338; is Î*s*vara, 8, 354 n.; legend identifying R., the god of cattle, with Agni Svish*t*ak*ri*t, 12, 199–202, 201 n., 206 sq.; 44, 338 sq.; Agni identified with R., 12, 201 sq.; 26, 343 n.; 41, 51, 64, 159–61; 43, 156, 158, 160, 169 sq., 172, 201; 46, 17, 19, 187, 191, 228, 325, 327, 371, 373; *S*arva, Bhava, Pa*s*upati, R., Agni, names of R., 12, 201 sq., 201 n.; his name inauspicious, 12, 202, 211, 211 n.; lord of beasts, rules over cattle, 12, 206 sq., 212, 300 n., 439, 441; 26, 58 sq., 153; 29, 280; 41, 52 n., 205; 44, 229 sq.; pierces Pragâpati who had committed incest, 12, 209 sq., 209 n., 213; Bhûtavat = R., 12, 284 n.; when the fire is kindled, and there is nothing but smoke, it is R., 12, 340; a violent, hostile deity, 12, 340; 26, 153; 29, 258; 44, 229 sq.; R. Tryambaka, 12, 408 n., 441; 32, 387, 389; the north his region, 12, 438 sq.; 43, 158; 44, 488; cross-roads his favourite haunt, 12, 439; bestows husbands on the maidens who worship him, 12, 441; clings to man by the red lines in the eye, 15, 105; the one God, supporter of the gods, creator of the world, 15, 244 sq., 252–4; 32, 436; dweller in the mountains, 15, 245; 43, 150, 152 sq.; gave birth to Hira*n*yagarbha, 15, 245, 252; Prâ*n*a identified with R., 15, 275; is a manifestation of the highest Brahman, 15, 302, 303, 324; that part of the Self which belongs to tamas is R., 15, 304; is called Bhargas, 15, 310; a name of the Self, 15, 311; together with the Vasus, 26, 59; 'R. is the universe,' 29, 367; father of the Maruts, 32, xxiii, 73, 81, 106, 126, 144 sq., 295 sq., 299 sq., 313, 340 sq., 348, 352, 368 sq., 372 sq., 375, 382, 400 sq., 422 sq., *426–8*; called v*ri*shan, 32, 144; gives health and wealth, 32, 193, 419, 422; with the Rudras, 32, 244; Maruts, men of R., 32, 341; divine physician, brings medicines, 32, 407, 419 sq., 422, 426 sq., 434, 436; 42, 389; 43, 151; like the sun, like gold, 32, 419; the best Vasu among the gods, 32, 419; the red boar of the sky, 32, 422; his hair is braided, 32, 422, 424; wielder of the thunderbolt, 32, 426, 436; most beautiful, and strongest, 32, 426; tawny, with beautiful cheeks, 32, 426–8; decked with golden ornaments, 32, 427; the bright tawny bull, 32, 427; sits in his chariot, 32, 427, 432 sq.; with sharp weapons, 32, 436; in consequence of a boon being granted to R., Sanatkumâra was born again as Skanda, 38, 235; the son of Pragâpati and Ushas, 41, 159; urine, the remedy of R., 42, 10, 19, 138, 488 sq.; his arrow inflicts disease, 42, 11, 19, 488 sq., 506; lord of the beings, 42, 66, 604; in a list of gods, 42, 80; with black crest of hair, 42, 138, 155; his missiles threaten cattle, 42, 144; is thousand-eyed, 42, 155, 157, 402, 619; 43, 157; the archer, the slayer of Ardhaka, 42, 155, 620; his howling dogs, 42, 158; the long-haired, shouting hosts of R., 42, 158; punishes him who withholds the sterile cow from the Brahmans, 42, 179; cow slain by R., 42, 253, 253 n.; lord of thieves and robbers, 42, 390; 43, 152; has a brown horse, 42, 422; colours attributed to R., 42, 586 sq.; Trisha*m*dhi weapon, and R.'s lightning, 42, 637; gods afraid of R., 43, 156 sq.; origin of the hundred-headed, hundred-quivered R., 43, 157; R. the chief, Rudras the peasants or clansmen, 43, 159; the R.-like powers of the Maruts (?), 46, 82, 84; the man-killer, 46, 325; martial R., the giver of offerings, 46, 326, 328; Brahman and R. in the train of Buddha, 49 (i), 198. *See also* Hara, Î*s*âna,

Mahâdeva, Pasupati, Sarva, Siva, Tryambaka, *and* Ugra.

(*b*) Worship of R.

Prayers addressed to R., 2, 96, 297 sq., 297 n.; 12, 3 n.; 14, 264, 298; 29, 101, 255–9, 280, 366 sq.; 30, 181; 43, 159–69; offerings to R., 2, 108; 14, 304; 15, 252, 254; 29, 388; 30, 25; 41, 50–2, 63 sq., 97 sq.; 44, 210; is the recipient of refuse, 2, 110; 41, 51, 71; offering to R. Tryambaka, 12, 408 n., 437–44; purification required after prayers or offerings to R., 14, 193; 29, 31; 30, 330; feasts at festivals of R., 22, 92; R. received the cow as Dakshinâ, 26, 348; worshipped at the Kaitra festival, 29, 132; worshipped by a sick person, 29, 137; Sûlagava sacrifice to R. and his wife, 29, 163, 255–8, 351–3; 30, 221–4, 289–91; hymns addressed to R., 29, 353 sq.; 32, 419–39; Yagñavâstu, a regular sacrifice to R., 29, 391 sq.; 30, 37; Âsvayuga sacrifice to R., 29, 415; 30, 92 sq.; invoked against evil demons and enemies, 30, 179; 42, 37, 120; worship of the hosts of R., 30, 222 sq., 290 sq.; worshipped at the Tarpana, 30, 244; hymn to the Maruts and R., 32, 386–9; lord of animal sacrifices, 32, 419 sq.; worshipped in company with Soma, 32, 434 sq.; 41, 65 sq.; offering to R. Pasupati, 41, 70 sq.; appeased by the priest for the king, 41, 110; worshipped in charms against fever, 42, 3, 11, 506; prayer to R. under his various names, 42, 155–9, 406 sq., 618–22; R. and Pasupati invoked, 42, 161; entreated to depart to the Mûgavants, 42, 446 n.; the Satarudriya offerings to R., 43, 150, 156–69, 171 sq., 174; the Satarudriya, prayers to R. in all his forms, 43, 150–5; blood milked of the Agnihotra cow, offered to R., 44, 183 n.; fire of a firebrand belongs to R., 44, 201; cattle is shielded from R. by the Svishtakrit oblations of blood, 44, 338 sq.; worshipped at the Pravargya, 44, 488.

(*c*) The Rudras (plur.).

The noon-libation belongs to them, 1, 35 sq., 50; 44, 173, 443, 480 n.; Sâman addressed to R., 1, 36; with Indra at their head, 1, 41 sq.; 44, 382; Sankara chief of R., 8, 88; seen within Krishna, 8, 92; alarmed at the greatness of Krishna, 8, 94; Tvashtri is the prince of R., 8, 346 sq.; invited to sit on the Prastara, 12, 93; (eight) Vasus, (eleven) R., and (twelve) Âdityas, three classes of gods, 12, 135, 239; 26, 350, 411; 34, 202, 216; 41, 241, 246, 264; 42, 161; 43, 75; 44, 116, 291 n.; 46, 42, 45; eleven R., explained as the ten vital breaths and Âtman, 15, 140 sq.; rise in the South, are lords of southern region, 15, 339; 43, 101; the Manes of grandfathers, 25, 127; practised penance, 25, 475; Soma with the R., 26, 93; Varuna invoked with the R., 26, 122; Soma libation for Indra with the R., 26, 241; invoked, 29, 198, 207, 344, 347; 43, 25; 44, 312; 46, 253; the cow, or Aditi, the mother of the R., 29, 199, 275; 30, 131, 174; 'if thou belongest to the R., I buy thee for the R.,' 30, 53; worshipped at the Tarpana, 30, 243; Maruts called R., 32, 97, 106, 126, 209, 296, 325, 340, 352, 364, 391, 400; 44, 382; Rudra with the R., 32, 244; 43, 159–69; eleven R. created, 41, 149 sq.; having mixed the earth, they kindled the great light, 41, 231; fashioned the air, 41, 234; help in battle, 42, 119; are united with the Maruts, 42, 135; origin of the R., 43, 33, 157; deities and metres, 43, 53; share of the Vasus, lordship of the R., 43, 68; where they wish to lay the Gârhapatya, 43, 118; hover by thousands around Rudra, 43, 151, 155; offering to the R. of the terrestrial world, the air-world, and yonder world, 43, 155, 158–65; the rain, their arrows, 43, 164 sq.; Indra accompanied by Vasus and R., 44, 479; Rudra praised by the R., 44, 488; invited to the sacrifice together with Agni, 46, 281.

Rudrâ, the Soma-cow is a, 26, 59.

Rudradatta, commentator on Âpastamba's Sûtras, 30, 313.

Rudradeva, Purohita, Bhadrâ his wife, 45, 50 n.

Rudraka, or Udraka, 49 (i), 132 n.,

169; seven hundred disciples of R. become Buddhist monks, 49 (i), 194.
Rudrâ*n*î, offering to, 29, 352.
Rudras, *see* Rudra (*c*).
Ru*k*aka, the best of circular mountains, 45, 289, 289 n.
Ruler, internal, *see* Antaryâmin.
Rulers: worship of ancient r. deified and presiding over the seasons of the year, 3, xxviii sq.; 27, 250, 250 n., 257, 262, 268, 268 n., 272, 276, 280, 283, 283 n., 286 sq., 291, 296, 296 n., 302, 306; 'The Royal Regulations,' book of Lî *K*î, 27, 18 sq., 209–48; training of princes, 27, 23, 345–53; their caps and dresses, 27, 27 sq.; 28, 1–3; rites in 'The Hall of Distinction' for audiences, &c., 27, 28–30, 328, 420 sq.; 28, 28–31, 34, 124, 231; king offers the united sacrifice to all ancestors, 27, 30 sq.; 28, 60 sq.; ploughing of special fields by r., 27, 36; 28, 222, 231, 239, 338; are the parents of the people, 27, 41; 28, 278 sq., 340 sq., 340 n., 419 sq.; virtue of the founders of the three dynasties, 27, 41; 28, 281–3; mourning and funeral rites for r., 27, 188–90, 189 n., 193 sq., 202, 222 sq., 325, 331–5, 354 sq., 357; officers without salary, 27, 189, 189 n.; wailing of the r., when a sad disaster occurred to the army, 27, 190; how r. gain the confidence of the people, 27, 191 sq.; punishment of a regicide, 27, 195, 195 n.; territories of a son of Heaven and the nobles, 27, 209 sq., 212 sq.; their symbols of distinction, 27, 214 sq.; feudal princes have to send missions to the emperor, 27, 216; emperor's tour of inspection, 27, 216–18, 324, 416 sq., 426, 426 sq. n.; 28, 232; gifts of r. to officers and vice versa, 27, 238; 28, 21–3, 69; succession, 27, 248, 366; regulations for the emperor for every season, 27, 251 sq., 258 sq., 263 sq., 269, 273, 277, 281, 284, 287, 292, 297, 302, 307; duty of r. to stimulate the husbandman's work, 27, 270; ancestor-worship of the emperor taking a journey, 27, 326; sacrifices interrupted by death of king or queen, 27, 329–31; r. and minister, like father and son, or heaven and earth, 27, 351–3; 28, 103 sq.; punishments inflicted on the r.'s kindred, 27, 356, 359, 359 n.; rules of propriety for r. and ministers, 27, 374 sq., 380, 391, 397, 420–3; 28, 6 sq.; son of Heaven forms a ternion with Heaven and Earth, 27, 377 sq.; 28, 256 sq.; prerogatives and duties of r., 27, 378 sq., 379 n.; 28, 1–9, 61 sq., 315 sq., 324, 354–6; distinction in ceremonial for r., 27, 397 sq., 400; ceremonies at the king's reception of the nobles, 27, 419 sq., 419 n.; minister cannot serve two r., 27, 420 sq.; tribute offered by princes to the r., 27, 433, 433 n.; rules for officers in attendance on r., 28, 17; emperor 'the One man,' 28, 26; the r.'s duty towards his ancestors and kindred, 28, 60–7; feast to be given by r. to his kindred, 28, 64 sq.; duties of r. with regard to sacrifices, 28, 204–7, 231; benevolence and righteousness the instruments of r., 28, 257; ceremonies when one r. visits another, 28, 274 sq.; in the sky there are not two suns, nor in a state two r., 28, 285, 467; ceremonies to show the distinction of r. and subjects, 28, 285 sq.; a son is not styled r. until the mourning rites are finished, 28, 294, 294 n.; emperor cannot be received as a guest, 28, 295; r. and people are like heart and body, 28, 359 sq.; virtues required of r., 28, 419–24; duties of king and queen, 28, 432 sq.; mourning for king and queen as for father and mother, 28, 434;—divine glory of (Iranian) r., 5, 138, 138 n.; five chieftainships, 5, 358 sq., 358 n., 365, 367, 391; 37, 459 sq.; worldly r. are to promulgate the good religion, 18, 12 sq.; the seven immortal r. of Khvanîras before the coming of religion, 18, 255–8, 258 n.; 37, 202–4 and n.; good king is equal to angels and archangels, bad king to Aharman and demons, 24, 44 sq.; the best and worst conversation for r., 24, 50 sq.; the worst ruler, and the good ruler, 24, 69; 37, 250 sq., 409; serving good r., 24, 78; 37, 306, 315, 322; death punishment

inflicted on the authority of priests and kings, 24, 267; thirty-three chieftainships, spiritual and worldly, 37, 18; monarchs from Gâyômard to Zaratûst, 37, 26–9; frontier governors and r., 37, 48; fitness for sovereignty, 37, 70, 379 sq.; necessity and worthiness of r. and high-priests, 37, 192, 231 sq., 457; 47, 170; sovereignty provided by Aûharmazd, 37, 243, 322, 332; desire for good r., 37, 294 sq.; telling r. the truth, 37, 332; true and virtuous statements in a well-established sovereignty, 37, 337 sq.; benefit of sovereignty, 37, 357; sovereignty good through Mazda-worship, 37, 412; about kings and judges, 37, 422 sq.; tithe to r., 37, 425, 443. *See also* King.

Rules of conduct, *see* Morality.

Rûpakâs, phantoms, sprites, 42, 125, 636.

Rûpas, the form-possessing people, go to rebirth, 10 (ii), 141 sq.

Rûpinî, wife of Samudrapâla, 45, 108.

Rusamas, n. of liberal bestowers of sacrificial gifts, 42, 197, 690.

Rûstâm, son of Gûstâsp, 37, xxxvi.

S

Sa'ad ibn Waqqâz, converted by Mohammed, 6, xxiii.

Sabaeanism, or the worship of the hosts of heaven, the religion of the Arabs, 6, xi, xv.

Sabaeans, believe in God, 6, 8, 107; God will decide between Jews, S., and other creeds, 9, 58.

Sabaras, art of, an occult science, 45, 366.

Sâbaras, became Vrishalas, 8, 295.

Sabarasvâmin, his date, 8, 32; quotes Manu, 25, cxii; quoted, 38, 268.

Sabbadinna, attendant on Milinda, 35, xix, 47 sq.; called Dinna, 35, 87.

Sabbakâmî, pupil of Ânanda, eldest Arhat at the council of Vesâlî, appointed as referee, 20, 404–14.

Sabbamitta, a distinguished Brahman, teacher of the Bodhisattva, 36, 45.

Sabbâsava-sutta, t.c., on 'All the Âsavas,' principles of Buddhist Agnosticism, 11, x, 291–307.

Sabbath, punishment for transgressing upon it, 6, 8 sq., 79, 158; compact of the S. day, 6, 93; ordinance of the S., 6, 263. *See also* Pôsaha, *and* Uposatha.

Sabhiya, is instructed and converted by Buddha, 10 (ii), 85–95.

Sabhiyasutta, t.c., 10 (ii), 85–95.

Sabhya, an ascetic, converted by Buddha, 49 (i), 191.

Sacraments, *see* Samskâra.

Sacred beings, *see* Gods.

Sacred Books, their character and importance, 1, ix–xx, xxxviii, xl, xlii; what translations of s. b. are and what they are not, 1, xx–xxxviii; lists of sacred literature, and branches of knowledge, 1, 109–11, 110 n., 115; 7, xxxi sq., 126, 254; 10 (ii), 98, 110, 189; 14, 19; 15, 330 sq.; 22, 221; 29, 218 sq., 218 n.; 42, xxx n., xxxvi–xxxviii, xli, xliv sq., xlvii, lii; 44, 98, 98 n., 101, 101 n.; Veda, Itihâsa, Purâna, and Dharmasâstra, &c., to be recited at Srâddhas, 7, 235; 25, 118, 118 n.; one who has studied s. b. sanctifies a company, 7, 254, 254 n.; 14, 19; great religious merit of reading s. b., 7, 301 sq.; oral tradition of s. b., 11, xxii sq.; a Bhikkhu versed in the traditions, a custodian of the Dhamma, of the Vinaya, and of the Mâtikâs, 13, 272 sq.; 17, 285, 288, 345, 413; one who knows the Mîmâmsâ, the Aṅgas, and a teacher of the sacred law belong to a legal assembly, 14, 20; Srâmanaka-sûtra contains rules for the hermit, 14, 45, 45 n.; Bhikshu-sûtras alluded to, 14, 115, 115 n.; no one but a son or a pupil shall be instructed in the Institutes of Sacred Law, 14, 124; studying the Institutes of sacred law purifies from sin, 14, 132; Ârâda quotes from Sûtras and Sâstras, 19, 133, 137; reciting s. b., a false expedient for final rescue, 19, 135; studying the Sûtras and Sâstras leads to enjoyment of dhyâna, 19, 137; Buddha warns his followers not to hold what is not in Sûtra, Dharma, or Vinaya, 19, 283 sq.; the true

and hidden meaning of Buddha's sayings should be grasped, while holding to letter is the way of foolish teachers, 19, 284; not to know the Sûtras and the *S*âstras, is to be devoid of wisdom, 19, 285; those who preach and study, read or copy the Dharmaparyâya, are destined for supreme enlightenment, have always to be honoured, and are always helped by Buddha, 21, xxx, 213–26, 320–7; those who occupy themselves with the Dharmaparyâya, need not build Stûpas and monasteries or perform acts of charity, 21, 321 sqq.; worship of s. b., 21, 375; 29, 122; 49 (i), 186; king before giving judgement, should listen to the exposition of Purâ*n*as, codes of law, and rules of polity, 33, 280; knowledge derived from s. b., 45, 152; faith produced by study of Sûtras and Aṅgas, 45, 154 sq.; study of s. b., among the articles necessary for perfection, 45, 159, 165 sq., 170, 185, 328; study, fivefold, one of the 'internal austerities,' 45, 179; copying s. b. meritorious, 49 (i), 186; (ii), 68 sq., 129; of Mahâyâna Buddhism, 49 (i), 199; (ii), xxiv sq.;—Zarathu*s*tra invokes the glorious Holy Word, 4, 213 sq.; imperfect state of Zoroastrian s. b., 37, xxix;—Scriptures ('The Book') given to Moses and Aaron, 6, 7, 12; 9, 50, 172, 195; Jews charged with corrupting the Scriptures, 6, 10 sq., 10 n.; belief in the Book, a dogma of Islâm, 6, 24; 'those who have the Reminder' (O. and N.T.) asked to confirm the Qur'ân, 6, 254 sq.

Sacred Cord, *see* Costume.

Sacred Duties, *see* Works.

Sacred feasts (myazd), 5, 388 sq., 389 n.; priests entertained at s. f., 18, 155–8. *See also* *S*râddha.

Sacred objects: fire, sun, water, wind, a Brâhma*n*a, cows, images of the gods, moon, 2, 94, 220; 14, 36; fire, water, earth, cow, trees, 4, lxii, 133; Snâtaka to turn his right hand towards them, 25, 135; not to be defiled, 25, 136 sq.; eight s. o., 33, 221 sq.; gold, cow-dung, or blades of sacred grass to be held by a witness, 33, 302.

Sacred places, *see* Holy places.

Sacred syllables: sound Him is Brahman, 1, 176; 29, 298; the Stobha syllables in singing the five Sâmans, 1, 226, 226 n.; Vasha*t* and *S*rausha*t*, sacrificial calls, 2, 45 sq.; 8, 324; 12, 88 sq., 88 n., 138, 141 sq., 144, 151, 171, 171 n., 191, 193 sq., 197 sq. and n., 235 sq., 239, 246, 246 n., 261, 319, 374, 382, 400–5, 411–14, 416, 427–31, 436; 15, 193; 25, 49, 49 n.; 26, 42, 107 sq., 183, &c.; 30, 341; 41, 17, 68, 73, 113, 135; 42, 84, 99, 128, 243; 43, 202, 211, 221, 230, 284, 341–3 (Vausha*t*), 343 n., 346, 348; 44, 3, 23, 26, 26 n. (Vausha*t*), 170, 258 sq., 277, 277 n., 391, 394, 464 n., 478, 482 sq., 502; 46, 22; Vyâh*ri*tis, Om, Satya, 2, 183 sq.; *S*ûdra may obtain permission to use the exclamation namas for his prayer, 2, 233 sq.; hiṅ, hi*m*, 12, 100 sq., 325; 26, 291, 375, 420; 44, 282, 306, 306 n.; five sacrificial utterances, 12, 142–4, 142 sq. n.; Om, Vasha*t*, Mahâvyâh*ri*tis worshipped at the Tarpa*n*a, 29, 121, 219; the s. s. hum of the cattle, 30, 215; Evayâmarut, 32, 363–5; sacrificial calls Ve*t* and Vâ*t*, 43, 183 sq., 220 sq., 231; 44, 478; nine utterances of impulsion (certain sacrificial formulas), 44, 24; Vasha*t* uttered over cattle, 44, 45; *S*rausha*t*, its tone, 44, 58–60; when the wind blows, when it lightens, when it thunders, when it rumbles—these are the four Vasha*t*-calls at the 'sacrifice to the Brahman' (Veda-study), 44, 99;—the three *Vyâhritis*, i.e. the three sacred 'words' bhûr bhuva*h* svar, and Om, 2, 45 sq., 183; 7, 182 sq.; 12, 2, 296 sq., 300 sq., 357; 14, 322; 15, 306–10; 25, lxvii, 43–6, 211, 479 sq.; 26, 37, 455; 43, 145 sq. and n.; 44, 12, 259, 313, 523; mistakes made at sacrifices remedied by the Vy., 1, 68 sq. n., 70–2; 44, 103 sq., 180; the three Vy. are the three Vedas, 1, 177 sq.; Vy. and Om. pronounced at beginning and end of Veda recitation, 2, 183 sq.; 25, 43 sq.; 29, 119, 144, 222, 322, 402; 30, 67, 154 sq., 273; mystic doctrines of

the Vy., and the syllable Mahas, 15, 48 sq., 192, 211; origin of Om and Vy., 25, 44; Vy. produced from the three Vedas, 44, 102 sq.; Vy. mean all this universe, 44, 253; *see also* Om;—Svadhâ is food of the fathers, 1, 33; 43, 373; 44, 96, 138, 234, 423; sacrificial exclamations Svâhâ (for gods) and Svadhâ (for fathers), 2, 45 sq., 48; 8, 324, 324 n.; 12, 148, 148 n., 150 sq., 153, 303, 324; 15, 193; 26, 19, 42 sq., 196, 252, 375, 397, 437; 29, 29; 30, 40, 339; 41, 407 sq.; 42, 177, 660; 43, 158 sq., 161, 166, 183, 205, 211, 221, 230, 235, 267; 44, 48, 96, 277, 277 n., 327, 388, 478; 46, 9, 154, 180, 199, 237; 49 (ii), 149, 154; children must not repeat prayers beyond pronouncing Svadhâ, 2, 186; the svâhâ ceremony, 8, 324, 352, 366, 370; Svâhâ is food, 41, 261; 43, 159.

Sacred Times: king should set out on an expedition in the months of *K*aitra and Mârga*s*îrsha, 7, 18, 18 n.; conjunctions favourable for gifts and fasts, 7, 157; 'the Night of Power,' 9, 337; the twilights, the full moon and new moon, the beginnings of the seasons, are the joints (parvan) of the year, 12, 173; the proper time for setting up the sacred fires, 12, 274, 282–91, 315 sq.; 30, 15; when the sacred fire is to be churned, 12, 295; times for ancestral worship, 12, 362 sq.; auspicious times for sacrifices, 12, 369 sq., 383 sq., 447 sq.; 25, 122, 126 sq.; 29, 374; 30, 13; 41, 178–82; on the day of the winter solstice the ancient kings shut the gates of the passes from one state to another (to stop all business), 16, 297, 298 n.; days sacred to the sun, 23, 85; auspicious t. for initiation, and other domestic ceremonies, 25, 35, 35 n.; 30, 137, 186, 204, 251; times when Veda-study is to be interrupted, 25, 49, 147; 29, 414; unfavourable days, 27, 239; regulations for the vernal equinox, 27, 259 sq.; abstinence enjoined for midsummer, 27, 275; celebration of the winter solstice, 27, 299 sq., 300 n., 304 sq.; ceremonies performed at certain times of the year, 30, xxvii sq.; dancing and singing on the last day of the moon or of the year, forbidden, 40, 243 sq.; bawling out or getting angry on the first day of the moon or in the early dawn, forbidden, 40, 244; it is wicked to inflict punishments at the eight terms of the year, 40, 244, 244 n.; the auspicious time, when Buddha mounted the throne of the Law, 49 (i), 173. *See also* Months, Moon (*b*), Sabbath, Seasons, *and* Time.

Sacred twigs, *see* Baresma, *and* Plants (*b*).

Sacrifice, Sacrifices.

(*a*) General rules and classifications.
(*b*) Sacrificial apparatus (utensils, vessels, materials, &c.).
(*c*) Duty of sacrificing, results of s.
(*d*) Relative value or worthlessness of s., symbolical s.
(*e*) The s. and the gods.
(*f*) The sacrificer at s. in India.
(*g*) Science of s. in India (s. and the Veda, s. and higher knowledge, s. personified in mysticism and legend).
(*h*) Indian domestic (G*ri*hya) s.
(*i*) Indian *S*rauta (Soma) s. and its rites.
(*j*) Forms of Indian Soma s.
(*k*) Details of Zoroastrian s.
(*l*) Details of s. in China.
(*m*) Arabian s.

(*a*) GENERAL RULES AND CLASSIFICATIONS.

Duties of priests at s., 1, 69, 69 n.; 12, xx sq.; 37, 292 sq., 293 n.; enumeration and classification of s., 1, 223; 2, 217, 217 n.; 7, 190–3; 8, 61 sq., 184 sq., 184 n.; 12, xlviii, 26, 26 n.; 14, 56, 237, 258, 261; 25, 132 sq., 200, 200 n.; 27, 397, 414, 414 sq. n.; 29, 15, 15 n.; 30, 357–9; 42, 226–8; 44, 390; 46, 85; general rules about s., 2, 101; 14, 193–5, 245, 256; 23, 75 sq., 108 sq., 244 sq., 333 sq.; 25, 603; 27, 92, 116 sq.; 29, 17 n., 22–31, 35, 38, 139 sq., 162–4, 269 sq., 374–9, 380 sq., 390–2; 30, xxvi sq., 13–19, 27–41, 138–46, 158, 251–5, 266 sq., 299 sq., 315–71; 31, 318 sq.; 37, 94–7; rules about invitations to s., 2, 259; strong drink forbidden during s., 4, 321–3; proper and improper libations, 4, 345–51; 23, 75 sq.; offerings to be made, while looking at the fire and the Baresman, 4, 347; have to be interrupted during period of

impurity, 7, 87; s. offered with faith are good, offered from a desire of fruit bad, 8, 16, 118–22; are threefold (three Gu*n*as), 8, 330; preparations for s., 10 (ii), 99; 12, 6–47; 26, 3 sq.; 46, 340; Roman s., 12, x; development of sacrificial ceremonial, and the priests, 12, x–xix; treatises on s., 12, xlvii sq.; 27, 35–8; 28, 201–54; 34, xii; preparation of the altar, 12, 47–94; there must be no s. without a sacrificial fee (dakshi*n*â), 12, 48 sq.; 44, 7, 9, 11 sq., 108; human s., animal s., and vegetable s., 12, 49–52 and n.; penance for unlawful s., 14, 132; gods only enjoy pure s. when offered with faith, 14, 172 sq., 186; rules about purification at s., 14, 187–96; eighteen s. (?), 15, 31; performed in the bright half, or in the dark half of the month, 15, 273; proper mode of celebrating the ceremonial (ya*z*i*s*n), 18, 159–73; ritual studied by *S*rautîs and Yâ*gñ*ikas, 25, xlviii sq.; Brâhma*n*as to be entertained at s. to gods and manes, 25, 99–111, 113 sq., 113 n., 133; 29, 15 sq.; alms must be given at s., 25, 431, 431 n.; what is human is inauspicious at a s., 26, 2, 4, &c., 41, 85; five s. of the house, 27, 116, 225, 300, 329, 376, 385 sq.; rules about s. taught in schools, 27, 347; higher and lower s., 27, 406, 406 n.; morning auspicious for all kinds of s., 29, 16 sq.; performing s. a means of livelihood for the Snâtaka, 29, 124; *S*rauta- and G*ri*hya-s., 29, 159, 159 n.; interrupted after a funeral, 29, 358; substitutes for proper s., 30, 39 sq.; definition of ya*gñ*a, s., 30, 315; s. of Âgya is understood by the term *g*uhoti, 30, 322; rules about the Darvihomas, 30, 339–41; the principal s., Prak*ri*tis and Vik*ri*tis, 30, 345–9, 354 sq., 361–3; some s. performed for the obtainment of special wishes, others as sacred duty, 30, 356 sq.; words meaning 'work, toil' used for s., 32, 165 sq.; property acquired by sacrificing, 33, 53; twenty-one s. allowed for some mixed castes, 33, 187 n.; punishment for those who disturb s., 33, 223 sq.; offerings made before administering an ordeal, 33, 250 sq., 252, 254, 256, 260; performed in different ways by members of different Vedic Schools, 34, x; ish*t*i, sacrificial oblation, 38, 108–10, 259, 353 n.; s. purified by prayers, 42, 211 sq.; sacrificial rites performed from west (left) to east (right), 43, 107; 46, 219, 224, 244, 279 sq., 340; Govinata form of s., 44, xxx; the Dakshi*n*â cows stand to the south of the altar, 44, 17; sacrificial fee, *see* Dakshi*n*â; expiatory s., *see under* (*b*) and (*i*) *below*; to the Manes, *see* Ancestor worship, *and* Funeral rites. *See also* Ceremonies, Fire (*d*–*g*), Karmakâ*n*d*a*, *and* Priests, *and besides separately* Animal s., A*s*vamedha, *and* Human s.

(*b*) Sacrificial apparatus (utensils, vessels, materials, etc.).

Udumbara wood, its advantages for s., 1, 173; respect shown to the sacrificial food by the Hot*ri* priest, 1, 175 sq., 175 n.; how to clean defiled sacrificial implements, 2, 62; 4, 50, 61 sq.; 7, 98 sq.; 14, 169; 25, 189; food fit or unfit for s., 2, 68, 138 sq.; 14, 69 sq., 72; 25, 123; begging allowed for sacrificial purposes, 2, 123, 204; 14, 240; 25, 430; for the purposes of s., any gifts from members of any caste may be accepted, 2, 265, 273; 7, 188; 14, 70; property destined for s. shall not be divided between heirs, 2, 310; 25, 379, 379 sq. n.; at s. spirituous liquors should be employed, 3, 174–7, 174 sq. n.; sacrificial millet, 3, 341 sq., 365, 439; 27, 293; the most trivial things accepted in s., 3, 431; sacrificial implements: log of wood, Baresma, milk, mortar, fire, Haoma, 4, 22 sq., 136, 136 n., 214 sq., 214 n., 365–7; libations of defiled water attract the Drug, 4, 94, 94 n.; sacrificial implements, the weapons with which Zarathu*s*tra repels the creatures of Angra Mainyu, 4, 208, 212; preparation of the *g*îvâm (milk and hôm), and the holy water or Zaothra, 4, 248–50; 5, 357 sq., 357 n.; gifts of wood, offerings of Baresman exalt the Righteous, 4, 285; the darûn

(draonô), a little cake tasted by the priest at the end of the Srôsh darûn, 4, 321, 321 n.; what property is accepted for s., 4, 339–41; offerings to be made on the Baresman, 4, 349 sq.; consecration of the sacred cakes (drôn), 5, 283–5, 283 sq. n., 292, 307, 307 n., 312, 332 sq., 338 sq., 369–71, 370 n.; 18, 141–5, 234, 236, 240 sq.; 24, 46, 46 n., 314–17; 37, 94, 394, 477; putrid meat and hairy cakes and butter unfit for s., 5, 332, 332 n.; the sacred feast (myazd), 5, 346 sq., 362, 388 sq., 389 n.; 18, 155–8, 243, 245 sq., 426; 24, 273 sq., 283, 298; 31, 368–72; 37, 132; penance for eating food destined for s., 7, 166 sq.; 25, 170, 170 n., 173, 475; he must not make an oblation to the gods or to the manes with water collected at night, 7, 210; materials for s., which are to be avoided, 7, 210 sq.; Brahma*k*ârin should eat leavings of s., 8, 360; sacrificial vessels and other utensils, 12, 10–16, 18–27, 30, 34, 34 sq. n., 38 sq., 42, 44, &c., 67 sq. and n.; 15, 214 sq., 293 sq.; 18, 163–5, 170; 26, 158 sq.; 27, 104, 115, 244, 299; 30, 323, 331, 360 sq.; 38, 253–6, 253 n., 284, 287 n., 321, 347, 347 n.; 46, 121 sq.; butter and Soma, the two kinds of oblations, 12, 193; no tax on s., 14, 100; water-pot not to be used for s., 14, 164; a sincere worshipper is not startled into letting go his ladle and cup of sacrificial spirits, 16, 173, 256; even in s. two baskets of grain only may be presented, 16, 246, 247 n.; sacrificial food for the gods must be cooked, 16, 255, 255 n.; 26, 38; remainder of a s. is called amr*i*ta, 25, 128; fish used for s., 25, 172; property may be appropriated for sacrificial purposes, 25, 313, 432 sq.; property begged for s. must not be used for other purposes, 25, 435; Kapâla or potsherds in which the cakes are baked, 26, xxvii–xxix; provision for s. by taxation, 27, 294, 308 sq.; the student's cord, girdle, &c., sacrificed in water, 29, 84; sacrificial implements burnt with a dead body, 29, 237, 240 sq.; 44, 203 sq.; Zaothras, Baresman, and other implements of s. worshipped, 31, 203, 208, 229, 270 sq., 276, 309, 321, 331, 346 sq., 349, 381, 385; gods worshipped with Zaothra and Baresman, 31, 203–8, 213 sq., 223, 253, 255, 270 sq., 274 sq., 298, 338–41, 345, 350, 354, 374 sq.; Zoroastrian worshippers partake of the meat offering, 31, 228 sq.; Haoma cups at s., 31, 243, 246; milk-offering and libation, 31, 257; fire worshipped with Baresman, 31, 314 sq.; water, mighty at s., 32, 106, 110; 38, 105, 108 sq.; clarified butter is sacred, 33, 222; the spirit of the sacred cake attacks the demons, 37, 197; remnants of food not used at s., 39, 67; sacrificial ladles, dipping-spoons, 41, 53, 192, 373; 43, 204, 214; 44, 56 sq., 60 sq.; 46, 45–8, 153, 160, 164, 228, 252 sq., 340, 354, 363; pavitra, strainer, filter, 41, 84; 44, 235; sphya, sacrificial wooden sword, 41, 110 sq.; kumbhî, pot, sthâlî, caldron, 41, 135, 270; 44, 220, 234 n.; sacrificial food which is baked is immortal, 41, 164; the u*kk*ish*t*a, the leavings of the s., as a primordial principle, 42, 226–9, 629–31; Sânnâyya (mixture of milk and sour curds) is royal dignity, 44, 41; the gods satisfied by milk, ghee, Soma, fat, and honey offerings, 44, 96–8; ghee is s., 44, 236 sq.; pressing-stones, 44, 243, 486; deified objects connected with the s., 46, 8–12; spreading the Barhis or sacrificial grass, 46, 24, 92, 153 sq., 228, 289, 391; worshipper fits out the s. as a vehicle, 46, 289 sq. *See also* Baresma, Barhis, *and* Costumes.

(*c*) Duty of sacrificing, results of s.

S., study, and charity, the duties of the householder, 1, 35; 8, 114, 340; 48, 695, 700; s. and prayers, enjoined by the Veda, hence of greatest merit, 2, 159; 8, 62; 38, 274 sq.; king's duty with regard to s., 2, 161, 236, 236 n.; 25, 228, 307; one of the eight objects of government, 3, 142; extinction of s. means the overthrow of a state, 3, 214, 214 n., 393, 393 n.; to maintain

their s., the duty of inferior officers, 3, 471, 471 n.; duty of making offerings to the angels, 5, 342 sq.; enjoined by the Creator, 8, 53; this world is fettered by all action other than that for s., 8, 53 sq.; s., the cause of production and development of all things, is named action, 8, 77; one of the twelve great observances, 8, 167; the highest of initiatory ceremonies, 8, 347; the high-caste householder's duty to perform s., 8, 358 sq.; 14, 43 sqq., 56, 199, 224, 261 sq., 271; 25, 24, 419 sq.; 38, 298; some Brâhma*n*as recommend s., others meditation, others gifts, 8, 376; Buddha recommends offerings to the gods, 11, 4, 20, 20 n.; 17, 103; a Brâhma*n*a who offers s. in the three sacred fires is worthy to receive gifts, 14, 39; a debt to the gods, 14, 56; 49 (i), 100; families are degraded by neglect of s., 14, 175; in order to offer s., wealth must be acquired, 15, 91; 25, 434; performance of s., chief virtue in the Dvâpara age, 25, 24; established by the ancient kings, 27, 385; *s. is the greatest of all things*, 28, 244; s. and hymns besides morality, 31, 71, 76; enjoined by the gods, 32, 238 sq.; the end of s. obtained by austerity, fervour, faith, s., and oblations, 44, 441;—*with the successful s. the sacrificer gets on; yes, having sacrificed, he becomes better*, 1, 69; are performed with a desire for heavenly rewards, for those who offer s. go to the world of the gods (but are reborn again), 2, 117, 140; 8, 84; 12, 254 sq., 260 sq.; 15, 31; 25, 29, 307; 26, 342 sq., 345, 348 sq.; 38, 111 sq., 162, 182; 41, 345; 44, 160; 48, 26, 681; 49 (i), 110; in reward of their s. the gods went to heaven, 2, 140; he who performs certain s., sanctifies the company, 7, 254; 14, 19; offering of burnt-oblations in sacred places (Tîrthas) confers eternal bliss, 7, 256; those who eat leavings of s. are released from sin, 8, 53, 62; *the oblation which is properly thrown on the fire, goes toward the sun; from the sun comes rain, from rain food, from food living beings*, 8, 54; 15, 337; 25, 89; fruit of s. obtained by devotion, 8, 81; a means for attaining to Brahman, 8, 164 sq., 164 n.; 25, 34, 34 n.; spirits of earth and air protect men who both day and night bring their offerings, 10 (ii), 37; all that exists is made to take part in the s., for those who do not take part in the s. are forlorn, 12, 139 sq., 333; 26, 154 sq.; *he who sacrifices, doubtless, sacrifices with a desire that he also may obtain a place in the world of the gods. That s. of his then goes forth towards the world of the gods: after it follows the fee which he gives (to the priests), and holding on to the priests' fee (follows) the sacrificer*, 12, 252, 266; king obtains the sixth part of the merit acquired by Brâhma*n*as through s., 14, 8; 25, 307; those who mutter prayers and offer s. will never perish, 14, 129; advantage of s. to the sacred beings, 18, 159–61; 37, 150–2; he who performs good s. will reign in Paradise, 23, 341; selling the rewards for s., 25, 163; are for the good of this world, 25, 175; Brâhma*n*as sanctified by s., 25, 308; due performance of s. frees from guilt, 25, 479; *he who has sacrificed, shares in the world of bliss*, 26, 151 sq.; the s. is a ship bound heavenwards, 26, 311; blessing, i.e. perfection, obtained by s., 28, 236 sq.; s. and sacrificial fee protect the house, 29, 348; those who do not perform s. descend to the abode of Yama, suffer there torments, and then again reascend to this world, 38, 122 sq.; 48, 592–6; everything can be obtained by a long sacrificial session for a year or more, 41, 140; father procures blessings for the son by s., 42, 89; 46, 13; is a blessing, 43, 107; powers bestowed by Soma-s., 43, 299, 356; s. forms the body of the sacrificer in yonder world, 44, 23, 35–8, 273, 273 n.; offering s., a second birth, 44, 23; modes of offering by which a priest promotes the sacrificer's welfare, 44, 56–60; successful issue of the sacrificial food, 44, 66–8; everything and to every one he offers (at the Sarvamedha), in order to gain

everything, 44, 420; wishing for glory and food men enter upon s., 44, 441; offspring and cattle the reward of s., 44, 504; for him who walks in righteousness the s. is anointed with honey, 46, 179; purify the mind, 48, 700, 703; only through the propitiation of the gods, s. can bring about their results, 48, 720.

(*d*) Relative value or worthlessness of s., symbolical s.

Are useless for attainment of salvation, 1, ci; 8, 16, 47 sq., 84, 367; 10 (ii), 41 sq., 192 sq.; 34, 197 n.; 49 (i), 120 sq., 126; performers of s. proceed, after death, on the path of the fathers, not of the gods, 1, 80; 15, 96; 34, 27; 38, 121–6; 48, 588–92; s. can procure a limited beatitude only, and are a hindrance to real salvation, 1, 314 sq.; 8, 185; should be avoided at the Tishya ceremony, 2, 150; officiousness in s. is called irreverence, multiplying ceremonies leads to disorder, 3, 116; sowing corn, a religious act equal to the recitation of 10,000 sacrificial formulas, 4, 30, 30 n.; Ahura-Mazda offended by the s. of a thief, or liar, 4, 283–5; s. without knowledge is no piety, 4, 347, 347 n.; good thoughts, words, and deeds, the best s., 4, 355–7, 355 n.; ceremonial worship (yazisn) of mortal sinners who have not confessed, has no value, 5, 302; burnt-offerings will not save a man who is in the bonds of death, 7, 82; prayers more efficacious than s., 7, 183 sq.; 14, 128; 25, 45 sq.; Krishna cannot be seen by means of s., 8, 98 sq.; s. without Mantras condemned, 8, 119; 44, 276; are acts belonging to the quality of passion, 8, 324 sq., 324 n.; end in destruction, 8, 355; ascetics renounce s., 8, 366; 14, 260; 25, 205; God does not wish men to provide Him with food, 9, 248; good works, gifts of food, homage paid to the righteous, are better than s., 10 (i), 32; 14, 245; 19, 260 sq.; 49 (i), 23; eight persons that are praised by the righteous, Buddha's disciples, are worthy of offerings, 10 (ii), 38; Mâra tempts Buddha with a religious life and performing s., 10 (ii), 69; Buddha's discussion with Bhâradvâga on s., and those who are worthy of s., 10 (ii), 74–9; classed with divination, witchcraft, and other 'low arts' and 'lying practices,' forbidden to the Bhikkhu, 11, 196, 199; rejected as belonging to worldly existence, 13, 138; prayers and Veda study equivalent to s., 29, 159 sq.; the gifts to Ahura are the actions of the pious, 31, 80, 83; truth better than a thousand horse-s., 33, 93; a son is better than a hundred s., 33, 93; superiority of asceticism to s. shown, 45, 55 sq.; the 's.' of the monk described, 45, 55 sq.; what the true s., and true Brâhmanahood consists in, 45, 136–41; being causes of sin, s. cannot save the sinner, 45, 140;—performed in thought only by a man living in the forest, 1, 51 sqq., 51 n.; there are two ways of the s., by mind and by speech, 1, 69; 38, 57; five 'libations' of the Devas on the five 'altars': heaven, Parganya, earth, man, woman, 1, 78 sq.; 38, 103; *the first food which a man may take is in the place of Homa*, 1, 89; fired by hope does memory perform s., 1, 119; what people call s. is really abstinence (brahmakarya), 1, 131; breath in speech offered, 1, 266; oblations of ghee offered to the deities Speech, Breath, Eye, Ear, Mind, and Knowledge, 1, 281 sq.; allegorical s. of the Prânas or senses, 8, 61, 260 sq., 276 sq.; 14, 138; 15, 91; s. of Brahman with Brahman in Brahman, 8, 61; Gapa (silent meditation) the chief of s., 8, 89, 89 n.; the s. of concentration of mind, 8, 279 sq.; by performing a mental s. at which meditation is the fire, truthfulness the fuel, patience the oblation . . . ahimsâ the sacrificial cake . . . a wise man goes to heaven, 14, 139; offering to the Vital Airs or to the soul, 14, 262–4, 266, 280, 299; eating represented as a s. of the Self to the Self, 15, 312 sqq.; by protecting his subjects the king performs a kind of sacrificial session, 25, 307; judicial proceedings compared with s., 33, 298;

Dhamma-yûpa, the 'sacrificial post' of truth, and the s. of truth, 35, 35; meditation as a mental s. on the altars of mind, speech, &c., 43, 375–80; 48, 668–73; libations to Mind and Speech, 44, 28, 28 n., 32.

(*e*) The s. and the gods.

To whatever deity an oblation is offered, hunger and thirst are co-partners in it, 1, 240; offerings to Vish*n*u, 7, 208–11; Lakshmî resides in s., 7, 299; *the Creator, having in olden times created men together with the s., said: 'Propagate with this.... Please the gods with this, and may those gods please you. Pleasing each other, you will attain the highest good. For pleased with the s., the gods will give you the enjoyments you desire. And he who enjoys himself without giving them what they have given, is, indeed, a thief,'* 8, 53; place of Agni, Indra, and Vi*s*ve Devâs, in different s., 12, xviii sq. and n.; gods subsist on s., that is their food, 12, 66 sq.; 32, 303; 41, 1; 43, 12; 44, 22; 46, 283; gods rejoice about Zarathu*s*tra's birth, at the prospect of receiving s., 23, 202; gods consume offerings through the mouth of a Brâhma*n*a, 25, 25; fire (Agni) carries the offerings to the gods, 25, 167; 43, 124; s. to Pragâpati performed by the ascetic, 25, 205; invisible is the s., invisible are the gods, 26, 18 sq.; gifts offered to Ahura in return for his blessings, 31, 83; who is the God to whom we shall offer s.? 32, 1 sq., 11–13; to the Maruts, 32, 106, 126, 154, 209–11, 272, 279, 286–8, 295–7, 305, 312 sq., 334, 364, 373 sq., 379, 386 sq., 390 sq., 401, 408–13; s. to Agni and the Maruts, 32, 352–4; to Rudra, 32, 422 sq.; to Vâta, 32, 449; a god may divide himself into many forms and enter into relation with many s., 34, 200; Gandharvas devour oblations, 42, 33 sq., 410 sq.; Indra protects the s., 42, 214; oblations to Kâma, 42, 220 sq.; the s. is the self of all beings, of the gods, 43, 103, 216; 44, 504; *for whatever deity an oblation is prepared that is a deity, but not one for whom no oblation is prepared,* 43, 207, 240, 245 sq.; offerings to the gods, compared to tribute brought by the people to the king, 44, 38; Soma-s. divided among Vasus, Rudras, and Âdityas, 44, 443; Agni and s., 46, 1, 6 sq., 8, 13, 31–3, 92, 108–10, 129 sqq., 206, 380; offerings of ghee made to Agni, 46, 3, 6, 92, 386, 397, 423; 'let us sacrifice to the gods, if we can,' 46, 17; Agni assists at the s., 46, 22, 24, 95, 100, 138, 153, 194, 279, 391; gods and goddesses sit down on the sacrificial grass, 46, 24, 153 sq., 289, 391; Agni, the beautifier, the beacon of s., 46, 37, 52; Agni watches s., 46, 96, 137; Narâ*s*a*m*sa mixes the s. with honey three times a day, 46, 153; Tanûnapât invoked to measure out the s., 46, 153; by s. men make Agni their father, brother, son and friend, 46, 187; Agni identified with sacrificial food, 46, 293, 295; Agni goes thrice round the s., 46, 340, 360; worshipper prepares food for Agni thrice a day, 46, 354; A*s*vins invited to s., 46, 358 sq.; Agni with all the gods invited to the sacrificial feast, 46, 418; s. offered to Agni and other gods, please the highest Person, 48, 155; gods come to the s., 48, 330 sq.; God, in the form of gods and pit*ri*s, enjoys s., 48, 411 sq., 487; are nothing else but means to propitiate deities, 48, 626; offerings made to Buddha, 49 (i), 166.

(*f*) The sacrificer at s. in India.

Dreaming of a woman during s. forbodes success of sacrificer, 1, 76; wife's share in performance of s., 2, 126, 126 n.; 25, 78 sq., 342–4; 41, 31 sq., 65; 44, 313, 321–3, 349, 472; *see also* Wife (*a*); women, children, and persons not initiated, must not offer s., 2, 139, 186, 270, 270 n.; 7, 111; 25, 161, 196; permitted for all castes in times of distress, 2, 211 sq.; s. of hermits, 2, 156 sq.; 8, 362; 10 (ii), 184; 19, 76 sq.; 25, 199 sq.; persons (women, multitude of men) for whom a Brâhma*n*a should not perform s., 2, 257; 7, 252; 14, 219, 219 n.; 25, 103, 106, 106 n., 161; 29, 224 sq.; 33, 87; 42, xl n., li; sin of sacrificing for unworthy persons, 2, 274;

7, 136, 155, 178 sq.; 14, 115, 122, 130, 239, 310; 25, 442; no impurity for those engaged in s., 7, 92; 14, 102; 25, 185; crime of killing one engaged in a s., 7, 133 sq.; s. at the ceremony of entering the order of ascetics, 7, 279; 14, 275-8; s. performed by the wicked, are s. only in name, 8, 116; lord of s. is the sacrificer, 12, 15, 44, 187; 26, 378; sacrificer is the victim, 12, 49 n.; s. is a man, i. e. represents the sacrificer himself, 12, 62, 78 sq., 78 n.; 26, 25, 25 n., 126 sq., 135, 139 n., 148 sq., 248, 248 n., 357 n.; 44, 298, 484, 504; the god and the sacrificer barter food and drink, 12, 416; Snâtaka must not go to a s., except as a priest, 14, 62; 25, 138; in so far as man sacrifices, he is the Devas, 15, 90; mortal sinner excluded from s., 25, 384; gods accept the offerings only of Brâhma*n*as who are purified by austerities, 25, 479; sacrificers caused by Goodness, 25, 495; foot of sacrificer used for measuring the high altar, 26, 119; Maruts sacrifice on the height of heaven, 32, 325, 328; one about to offer s. must not be arrested, 33, 18; one who makes illicit s. cannot be a witness, 33, 87; performed separately by a divided family, 33, 370 sq.; animals, gods, and *Ri*shis do not perform s., 34, 197 n.; *S*ûdra unfit for s., 34, 224; performed even by priests who do not know the divinities of the s., 38, 254; sacrificer is Indra, 41, 13, 18; 43, 94; 44, 245; sacrificer, sprinkled with remains of offerings, 41, 38; Agni is the sacrificer, 41, 212; 43, xv sq., 146 sq., 186, 197, 201, 253, 262; s. and sacrificer invoked as divine beings, 42, 161; mystic connexion between s. and sacrificer, 43, xvi sq., 94, 279 sq.; 44, 26 sq., 38; sacrificer flies up to heaven in shape of the altar, 43, xxi sq.; sacrificer is Death, 43, xxiii; gods do everything with praise and s., 43, 73; sacrificer thrust out from his world by wrong procedure at s., 43, 94; sacrificer is with the Vi*s*ve Devâs, with the gods, 43, 124, 202, 270; never-ending circle: sacrificer — gods — cow — sacrificer, 43, 221; Agni-consecration of sacrificer, 43, 225-9; sacrificer the body of s., the priests its limbs, 43, 280; 44, 236; God offered s. to one another, Asuras into their own mouths, 44, 22; when the *Ri*shis were performing s., the Gandharvas came nigh and criticized it, 44, 29; death of sacrificer, 44, 197-205; the burning of the dead sacrificer in his fires, a s., 44, 204; the s. prospers through the priests, through the s. the sacrificer, 44, 231; sacrificer in heaven, 44, 231, 259, 303; *whosoever sacrifices, sacrifices after becoming, as it were, a Brâhmana*, 44, 348; sacrificer or presser of Soma, 46, 325; knowledge of s. only required of householders, 48, 698.

(*g*) SCIENCE OF S. IN INDIA (S. AND THE VEDA, S. AND HIGHER KNOWLEDGE, S. PERSONIFIED IN MYSTICISM AND LEGEND).

The s. is founded on, contained in, as great as the triple Veda, 1, 2 sq., 38 sq., 112, 114; 30, 317 sq., 323-5; 41, 139 sq.; depends on the syllable Om, 1, 2 sq.; there is no s. corresponding to the Atharva-veda, but the Itihâsa-purâ*n*a takes the place of it, 1, 39 sq. and n.; the portion of the alms which the Brahma*k*ârin gives to the teacher is his daily s., the teacher representing the deity, 2, 14; Veda recitation an everlasting s. to Brahman, 2, 45 sq.; 25, 49; Veda-study to be interrupted on the occasion of a s. to men, 2, 263, 263 n.; Vedas always concerned with s., 8, 54; studentship compared to a sacrificial session, 14, 156; 29, 305, 305 n.; 44, 49; Vedic texts on s. to be studied, 25, 213, 213 n.; the texts belonging to whatever s. he repeats, that s. a man is considered to have offered, 29, 220; every s. must be preceded by the knowledge of the *Ri*shi of the mantra used, 34, 213 sq.; the s. is of Virâ*g*, of Gâyatrî, nature, 44, 153 sq.; Âprî hymns and the s., 46, 8 sqq., 153 sqq., 179 sq., 198 sqq., 236 sqq., 377 sq.; depends on the three fires and is revealed in the Veda, 48, 285;—s. is more powerful when

joined with knowledge, 1, 3, 36, 36 n.; whatever is acquired for the next world by s. perishes in the case of him who knows the Self, 1, 127; performance of s., followed by a desire for knowledge, 1, 200 sq.; s. and Brahman, the twofold path, knowledge of Brahman being the true path, 1, 201, 201 n.; 8, 60–2; K*ri*sh*n*a worshipped by the s. of knowledge, 8, 83 sq., 130; required as conducive to knowledge, 8, 147; 15, 41 sq., 179, 287; 34, lxxv; 38, 306–9, 313–15, 327 n.; 48, 9 sq., 699, 709–12; knowledge cannot be obtained by s., 15, xxvi; performance of s. leads to rebirths, while knowledge of Brahman leads to immortality, 15, 30–3; 43, 389 sq.; *understanding performs the s., it performs all acts*, 15, 57; 48, 555; relative value of s. and knowledge of the soul, 25, 501–4 and n.; 34, cvii; Vikalpa, an optional proceeding in the details of s. not allowed in the *G*ñânakâ*nd*a, 34, xi; meditations on subordinate members of the s., 34, lxxvi, 199; 38, 192, 192 n., 222–5, 252–6, 281 sq., 320 sq., 345–9; 48, 664 sq., 675–7, 682–5, 707 sq.; cognitions compared with s., 38, 280; who is better, the self-offerer, or the god-offerer? 44, 38; *such, indeed, are the wilds and ravines of s., and they (take) hundreds upon hundreds of days' carriage-drives; and if any venture into them without knowledge, then hunger or thirst, evil-doers and fiends harass them*, 44, 160; those who knew Brahman, busied themselves chiefly with s., 48, 688; —man identified with s., 1, 50 sq., 223; 38, 220 sq., 265; 44, 19 sq., 155; Vâyu, the Wind, is the s., 1, 68 sq.; 26, 378; s., penance, restraint, are the feet of the Brâhmî-upanishad, 1, 153; fivefold is the s., 1, 223; 12, 16, 16 n., 142, 192, 280; 15, 91; 26, 24, 70, 88, 166, 241, 306, 390; 41, 249; 44, 125, 154, 405, 452 sq.; everything exists through s., 2, 214 sq. n.; 26, 155; s. represented as Vish*n*u, 7, 1–3, 9, 294; 44, 442; created, 8, 53, 120; 25, 12, 12 n.; 42, 225; 43, 403; K*ri*sh*n*a identical with all s., 8, 83, 83 n.; identical with Purusha-Pra*g*âpati, 12, 8; 44, xviii, xx, 22, 454 sq., 484, 506; legends of the gods and the personified s., 12, 23, 140, 160–2; 26, 89, 231, 235; 44, 270 sq.; threefold is the s., 12, 32, 62 sq., 83, 86, 96, 127; 26, 35, 38, 81, 145 sq., 291; 44, 475, 501; is seventeenfold, 12, 143; the Dîkshâ, all s. and sacrificial fees come from the Highest Person, 15, 35; at the offering of which libation do the waters speak with a human voice? 15, 205, 207 sq.; Prâ*n*a and the s., 15, 275, 280; legend of Ya*gñ*a and Vâ*k* (S. and Speech), 26, 30–3; the outbreathing of s. personified in Soma, 26, 248, 248 n.; represented as a bird, 26, 264 sq.; S. (personified) is long-lived through sacrificial fees, invoked to give long life to the new-born child, 29, 294; has seven threads, 32, 253; s. supports the earth, earth the seat of s., 42, 199–201, 203 sq.; sacrificial rites symbolical of cosmogonic and theosophic theories, 43, xiii–xxvii; creation originating from s., 43, xiv; primaeval s. of Purusha or Pra*g*âpati, 43, xiv sq.; Ya*gñ*a or S. a Gandharva, 43, 232 sq.; all s. are a hundred and onefold, 43, 325; fire is the womb of the s., 44, 3; homage to the S. (personified), 44, 29; personified, its head, breath, eyes, &c., 44, 35–7, 124; the S. is the Year, 44, 38 sq., 154; the s. is cattle, 44, 116; how is it that S., Man, and Pra*g*âpati do not exceed one another? 44, 165 sq.; couples (male and female) belonging to a s., 44, 240; is speech, 44, 343, 349; is the navel of the world, 44, 390; is a sphere especially pervaded by the power of *Ri*ta (Right), 46, 297, 299; parts of s. fancifully identified with parts of human body, 48, 643 sq.

(*b*) INDIAN DOMESTIC (G*RI*HYA) S.

Oblations of ghee offered by one who wishes to become dear to any man or woman, 1, 282 sq.; *there are five great s., and they, indeed, are great sacrificial sessions,—to wit, the s. to beings, the s. to men, the s. to the Fathers, the s. to the gods, and the s. to the Brahman*, 2, 47 sq. and n., 201,

217; 7, 193 sq., 211–17; 8, 216, 358; 14, 256 sq.; 25, 87–97, 127 sq., 132, 198 sq.; 29, 217, 271, 271 n., 319; 30, xx; 44, 95 sq.; 48, 17; student who has broken his vow of chastity offers an ass to Nirriti like a Pâkayagña, 2, 85; 14, 215 sq.; 29, 361 sq.; at the anniversary of the wedding-day, 2, 100 sq. and n.; Vaisvadeva ceremony, burnt-oblations and Bali-offerings made from the daily meals, 2, 104–9, 202 sq.; 7, 146, 192 sq., 220; 8, 216; 12, 245 sq., 245 n., 329 sq.; 14, 49 sq., 239 sq.; 22, 99; 25, 90, 90 n., 95, 95 n., 97, 124, 199; 29, 84–7, 89 sq., 133, 161 sq., 290 sq., 319–21, 387 sq.; 30, 22–5, 266 sq.; reception of a guest represented as a s. to Pragâpati, 2, 117 sq.; s. to Kubera to attain prosperity, 2, 151, 151 n.; hermit shall offer the five great s., 2, 195, 195 n.; 7, 276 sq.; 14, 259; 25, 199; Madhuparka offered to guests at s., 2, 205, 207; 30, 132; Sûdra may offer the Pâkayagñas, 2, 234; offerings at marriage rites, 2, 305; 14, 205; 25, 195, 195 sq. n.; 29, 22–32, 34 sq., 37, 41–4, 167–71, 279–83, 287–9, 380–5; 30, 45–52, 187 sq., 190 sq., 196–8, 253, 259–68; 42, 96, 498; sprinkling the ground round the altar and putting fuel on the fire, duties of the student, 7, 116; the (four, seven) Pâkayagñas, 7, 183 sq. and n., 190 sq.; 25, 46, 46 n.; 29, 12, 12 n., 15, 15 n., 20, 159, 163, 176, 276, 375; 30, xv sq., xxii–xxiv, xxiii n., 254; s. to the waters on crossing water, 7, 203; 29, 127; offerings to gods and manes after having bathed, 7, 206 sq.; by bathing he becomes entitled to perform the offerings to the Visve Devâs, 7, 207; domestic s. on the Parvan or new and full moon days, 7, 230; 14, 159; 25, 152; 29, 17 sq., 136, 172–6, 290, 389–93; 30, 27–40, 196, 265, 332–8, 345, 361–3; 42, 559; 46, 108, 111; at the letting loose of a bull, 7, 261; 29, 353–5; oblations in the fire with prayers addressed to Vishnu on the full moon day of the month Pausha, 7, 266; Brahmakârin must offer s. to the fire, and make libations of water to satisfy the deities, 8, 360 sq.; Kâmyeshtis or s. for the fulfilment of a special wish, 12, 97 sq., 143, 163 sq.; 29, 223 sq., 226, 426–8, 431 sq.; 30, 114–20, 124–9, 177 sq., 267, 356 sq.; Idâ connected with the Pâkayagñas, 12, 214, 214 n., 218, 220, 230; at ceremonies connected with study of Veda (Upâkarana, Utsarga, Anupravakanîya), 14, 63; 29, 73 sq., 112 sq., 191, 221–3, 321 sq., 405; 30, 74–6, 75 n., 161, 242, 266 sq.; burnt-offerings at the ceremony of adoption, 14, 76, 335 sq.; daily libations to gods, Rishis, and manes, 14, 238; 25, 62; 30, 246; the Tarpana or satiating of gods, Rishis, &c., with water libations at the end of course of Veda-study, 14, 252–6; 29, 3 sq., 115, 120–3, 149, 219 sq., 223, 325; 30, 79, 243–6; s. to be performed on entering a new mode of life, 14, 285 sq.; as rites securing success, 14, 323, 331–3; all s. are useless without the Vaisvadeva ceremony, 15, 31; Sthâlîpâka offering connected with conception, 15, 220; interpreters of dreams make offerings (bali) to the house-gods, 22, 245; offerings to house-gods made at birth ceremonies, 22, 255; 45, 371; at Ashtakâ festivals, 25, 152; 29, 102–5, 206–9, 341–4, 417–24; 30, 97–110; libations of water to the gods, 25, 203; s. at domestic ceremonies, *Vols.* 29 and 30; general division of domestic s., 29, 30 sq., 159, 159 n.; at the Upanayana ceremony, 29, 61, 68, 188–93, 306, 380; 30, 64, 138–46, 158, 253, 271, 273; of a teacher on initiating a student in the secret doctrines, 29, 79; at house-building ceremonies, 29, 92–6, 213, 215, 345–7, 429 sq.; 30, 122–4, 204–6, 286; 42, 141, 344; for protection of cattle, 29, 100 sq., 410; 30, 88 sq., 185 sq.; 42, 143, 303, 360; at serpent worship (Srâvana and Mârgasîrsha or Âgrahâyanî rites), 29, 127–32, 201–5, 327–30, 338–41, 411–13, 416 sq.; 30, 89–92, 94 sq., 238–40, 287–9; on the Âsvayuga full moon day, 29, 130, 203, 332 sq., 415; 30, 92 sq.; at the consecration of ponds, wells,

tanks, and gardens, 29, 134-6; oblations made before the performance of s., 29, 164; outline of the Pâkayagña ritual, 29, 172-6; connected with charms for averting danger, disease, and other evils, 29, 224 sq., 232, 432; 30, 118 sq.; 42, 17, 32, 261, 505, 519; to be performed by one who has been restored to health, 29, 236; to prevent death in the family, 29, 248-50; to Rudra to cure cattle diseases, 29, 258 sq.; Vrâtya-stoma s., whereby a patitasâvitrîka becomes fit for initiation, 29, 312; to prevent a servant from running away, 29, 351; at the beard-cutting, 29, 380; Yagñavâstu ceremony, 29, 391 sq.; 30, 37; daily and monthly s., 30, xxvii; for one who cannot pay a debt, 30, 113; Sthâlîpâka to Indrânî, 30, 114; at the Samâvartana, 30, 161 sq., 253, 275 sq.; at the reception of guests, 30, 174; to make husband and wife love each other, 30, 269; Îsânabali and offerings to Kshetrapati, 30, 289-91; s. to Agni and Pragâpati on the appointment of a daughter, 33, 376; oblation to the sun, the heavenly dog, to cure disease, 42, 13, 500 sq.; oblation offered to destroy evil demons, 42, 36, 64 sq., 475; oblation to save one from death, 42, 49; charm to frustrate the s. of an enemy, 42, 90, 557; for the suppression of enemies, 42, 92, 476, 495 sq.; for the welfare of a child, 42, 109; s. before battle, 42, 119 sq., 122, 128 sq., 132, 325, 439, 510, 582, 632; to allay discord among kinsmen, 42, 135 sq.; for success in trade, 42, 148 sq., 352-4; Bali offerings to the earth, 42, 207; of persons wishing to obtain a husband or wife, 42, 323, 491, 502; a shepherd's s. to Indra, 42, 367; Bali offerings to Sahasrâksha, 42, 473; the Grihamedhas, 43, 298; offerings to Heaven and Earth, Vâyu and Sûrya, to recover anything that is lost, 44, 347; offered to gain wealth, 46, 316 sq.; Sandhyâ ceremony, an item of virtuous conduct, 48, 592;—expiatory s. for offences committed, 2, 85 sq., 86 n., 275, 275 n., 284, 287, 289-91, 293-302; 7, 153-5, 181; 12, 398 sq., 406 sq.; 14, 58, 106, 110 sq. and n., 116-18, 120, 125, 128, 130, 134, 148 sq., 204, 211 sq., 215 sq., 217, 222, 295 sq., 297-9, 301 sq., 303-11, 318 sq., 321, 328, 330; 25, 435, 445, 445 n., 454 sq., 471, 472 n., 475 sq., 481 sq.; 29, 134, 136-40, 224 sq., 406; Vaisvânarî Ishti, an expiatory s., 7, 192; 25, 435; self-sacrifice to Death as a penance, 14, 106; offerings to Sarasvatî in expiation of falsehood, 25, 272; expiatory s. for evil omens, 29, 406; 30, 81, 184; 42, 166; expiatory s. before cohabitation, 30, 197 sq.; penance for omitting half-monthly s., 30, 203; at auspicious and expiatory rites, 30, 253, 295-7; 45, 371; expiatory formula for imperfections in s., 42, 164, 528; offering on having a bad dream, 30, 183 sq.; 42, 484;—s. for the sake of cattle, *see* Cattle; connected with conception and birth of children, *see* Child (*b*); agricultural s., *see* Agriculture (*c*).

(*i*) INDIAN *S*RAUTA (SOMA) S. AND ITS RITES.

Soma-s. is the most perfect of s., 1, 223; who is obliged to offer Soma-s., 7, 192; Havis-s. and Soma-s., 12, 141 sq.; Soma-s. performed by the seven Hotris, 12, 223, 223 n.; other s. given up for Soma-s., 12, 447 sq., 447 n.; younger brother must not offer *S*rauta-s. before the elder, 14, 329; annual Soma-s., 25, 133; Soma-s. in the *S*atapatha-brâhmana, 44, xiv; some perform animal s. without, others with Soma, 44, 122 sq.; at Soma-s. fire burns on the eight altars called Dhishnya, 46, 325, 328;—when a man hungers, thirsts, and abstains from pleasures, that is the *Dîkshâ* or initiatory rite of Soma-s., 1, 51; the Dîkshâ represented as a new birth, 1, 52; 25, 61; the Dîkshanîyeshti, or consecration offering, 1, 75 sq.; 26, 12-25; 43, 258, 258 n.; when initiated to *S*rauta-s., the performers shave their hair, 2, 37; food of a Dîkshita, i.e. one who has performed the initiatory ceremony of a Soma-s., not to be eaten, 2, 68; 7, 163; 14, 69; 25, 161; how to salute the

Dîkshita, 2, 210; he must not step on the shade of the Dîkshita, 7, 203; 25, 149; Dîkshita must avoid connubial intercourse, 7, 222; men who have performed the initiatory ceremony of a Soma-s. are not impure through death, 14, 177; vows to be kept by the Dîkshita, 14, 195 sq.; Dîkshâ abides in the True, 15, 147; Dîkshita must not be addressed by his name, 25, 53 sq., 53 n.; the Audgrabha*n*a libations at the Dîkshâ, 41, 249–51; the gods crush the head of him who during a sacrificial session speaks evil of the initiated sacrificer, 44, 149; the fast-observance the head, the initiation the body of the s., 44, 240; *see also* Dîkshâ;—the three Savanas, i.e. the morning, midday, and evening pressings or libations of Soma-s., 1, 35–7, 50 sq.; 12, xviii sq., xviii n.; 26, 222 sq., 249 sq., 249 n., 289, 291, 293 sq., 299, 314–16, 325 sq. n., 329 sq., 340, 350, 357, 362, 399; 32, 390, 394; 42, 231, 590; 43, 144; 44, 155; 46, 300 sq.; the Upasads, and the Pravargya, 1, 51; 26, 104–11, 104 sq. n.; 41, 116–19, 116 sq. n., 355; 43, 259, 316–18 and n., 320; 44, 43 sq.; 48, 654; the Pravara, or choosing of the Hot*ri*, 12, 95, 95 sq. n., 114–20, 131–8; the two libations (âghâra) of butter, 12, 95, 124–31; 41, 172, 172 n.; Prayâgas or fore-offerings, 12, 138–59, 202, 390, 404, 418, 427 sq., 445; 26, 13, 184–90, 210; 38, 255, 274 sq., 274 n., 287, 313, 331; 43, 259 sq.; the after-offerings (Anuyâgâs), 12, 151, 202, 390, 404, 404 n., 418, 424, 436, 445; 26, 13, 210–15, 229; 43, 259 sq.; the two butter-offerings (âgyabhâga) to Agni and Soma, 12, 159–75; the T*ri*tîya Savana, or evening pressing, 12, 204 sq., 204 n.; 26, 350–74; 46, 203; the Samish*t*ayagus, 12, 390, 390 n., 406, 418, 445; 26, 13, 374–6; 41, 185; 43, 257–62, 265; the Patnîsa*m*yâgas, 12, 405 sq.; 26, 13, 52, 446; the Mahâhavis or Great Oblation, 12, 408 n., 417–20, 417 n.; preparatory rites of Soma-s., 14, 302, 302 n.; 26, 226–38; 43, 181–8, 241–9; 46, 219; the Prâya*n*îyesh*t*i, or opening s. at Soma-s., 26, 47–52, 48 n., 85; 41, 325 sq.; 43, 258 sq., 259 n.; concluding rites of Soma-s., Avabh*ri*tha bath, Udayanîyâ, and offering of barren cow, 26, 48, 48 n., 51 sq., 85, 373 n., 374–97; 43, 262, 266; *S*amyuvâka, I*d*â offering, 26, 52; 43, 259; the offering with gold, and homage to the Soma cow, 26, 52–63; the Vaisargina offerings and leading forward of Agni and Soma, 26, 155–62; the Prâta*h*savana, or morning pressing, 26, 238–331; the Mâdhyandina-Savana or midday pressing, 26, 297, 331–49; 42, 18, 562; Pâtnîvata cup, or libation of Soma with the water mixed with it, 26, 365–9, 365 n.; the Apsushomâ*h*, or Soma draughts in water, 26, 373 sq.; the A*ms*u-graha representing Pragâpati, 26, 423–6; 44, 105; Prâya*n*îya and Udayanîya Atirâtra, 26, 427 n., 454 sq.; 43, 254, 254 n.; Grahas or Soma libations, 26, 432 sq., 432 n.; 43, 282; the Sattrotthâna or rising from the session, 26, 446–52; Soma libations to Indra and Vâyu, 32, 440 sq., 444–6; udbhid, 34, 261, 261 n.; 'mental' cup, offered on the tenth day of Soma-s., 38, 260 sq., 263, 266 sq.; the Ukthya, second Soma-day, 41, xiv–xvi; 44, 298; A*ms*u and other libations of Soma at the Vâgapeya, 41, 5–11; Udavasânîyesh*t*i or completing oblation, 41, 87, 115; 43, 269, 269 n.; Soma libations at the Râgasûya, 41, 133–5; Kuntâpa-hymns at prolonged Soma-s., 42, 689; the drawing of the cups (Grahas) and litanies at the building of the fire-altar, 43, 4–14, 20; at the installation and consecration of Agni, 43, 207–41; Vasor dhârâ or 'shower of wealth,' procuring prosperity, 43, 213–16, 221–4, 298; Râsh*t*rabh*ri*t oblations, 43, 229–33; oblations to the Divine Quickeners (Devasû), 43, 246–9, 246 n.; Sutyâ, Day of Soma-s., 43, 249–71, 320; by the after-offerings the sacrificer overcomes his enemies, 44, 43; the Adâbhya cup of Soma at the Soma-s., 44, 105–8; offering of the two Mahiman cups of Soma at the A*s*vamedha, 44, 327 sq., 391, 394; *see also* Soma (*a*);—expiations

for making good mishaps during the Soma-s., 26, 305–7, 411–13, 411 n.; 41, 264 sq.; 44, xiv, 29 sq., 103 sq., 131–4, 187–96, 205–13; expiatory s. connected with the Agnihotra, 44, 178–96; expiatory rites at the Asvamedha, 44, 289, 341, 345–7; expiatory rites connected with the Pravargya, 44, 504–10; Râkshasas driven from the s., *see* Râkshasas.

(*j*) FORMS OF INDIAN SOMA-S.

Soma-offerings at the end of the year, 25, 133; *S*rauta-s. for those fallen in battle, 25, 186, 186 n.; different kinds of Soma-s., 26, 236 sq., 312 sq., 397 sq. n., 402 sq. n., 423, 423 n., 426; 41, xii–xxv, 11 sq. and n.; Sattras, long sacrificial sessions lasting a year or more, 26, 389, 389 n., 402 sq. n.; 44, 135–77; Soma-s. to Agni and the Maruts, 32, 53 sq., 62; Sava-libations (Saptasûrya, to *S*ataudana libation) offered in the one fire of the Âtharva*n*ikas, 38, 189 sq.; 48, 631; supernumary rites are the Agni*k*ityâ, Râ*g*asûya, Vâ*g*apeya, and Asvamedha, 41, 246, 246 n.; Soma-s. and fire-worship connected, 41, 342 sq.; Soma-oblation to Indra, as the slayer of the Rakshas, 42, 66, 458; oblation offered by a king desiring glory, 42, 117, 478; a Soma-s., and the cooking of a porridge as a fee to the Brahmans, 42, 179–93, 610–18, 645–55; the s. of Rohita, 42, 213; an 'all-offered' s., 43, xiv, xiv n.; the first layer of fire-altar is the Soma-s., 43, 298; a Soma-s. for Pra*g*âpati, 43, 348; how the regular s. are uninterrupted though the performers of a year's sacrificial session become initiated for a year, 44, 175–7; the Soma-s. uninterrupted by the Soma-pressings at the Sattra, 44, 177; the Pravargya is the Agnihotra, the New and Full-moon s., the Seasonal s., Animal s., Soma-s., 44, 509 sq.;—Soma-s. at the king's consecration (*Abhishek*a*n*î*ya*), 41, 68–142; the king consecrated at the midday Soma-feast, 41, 80 sq.; all forms of s. wrought in the king's consecration garments, 41, 86, 86 n.; the great *S*rauta-s. performed by rulers or chiefs, 43, xvi;—the *Agnish*t*oma*, 26, 299–301; 41, xii–xiv, 11 sq.; 42, 589; 43, 287 n.; 44, 140 n.; Agnish*t*oma, the first Soma-day at the horse-sacrifice, 44, 295, 295 sq. n.;—penance for *Ahîna* s., 7, 178 sq. and n.; 25, 471, 471 n.;—the *Aptoryâma*, 41, xx–xxiii;—the *Atirâtra*, 26, 398, 427 n., 454 sq.; 41, xvii–xx, 127 n., 128; 46, 44; Sho*d*asin-cup at the Atirâtra-sacrifice, 34, 262 sq.; 38, 188;—*Atyagnish*t*oma*, 26, 398 n.; 41, xvii;—the *Darsapûrnamâsa* or new and full moon s., 7, 191; 12, 1–273, 369, 373–83, 407, 433, 443 sq.; 13, x; 25, 132, 200; 26, 40, 40 n.; 38, 255, 275, 287 n., 309, 309 n., 313, 324; 41, 45, 47 n.; 43, 297, 299, 356; 44, xiv, 1–12, 15–45, 52–6, 175; special preliminary rites of the new moon s., 12, 175–90; chief offerings at new and full moon s., 12, 190–230; the after-offerings (anuyâ*g*as) at the new and full moon s., 12, 230–73; the Patnîsa*m*yâ*g*as at the new and full moon s., 12, 256–62, 256 n.; Dâkshâya*n*a s., a modification of the new and full moon s., 12, 374–83; 44, 5; Anvârambha*n*îya ceremony at Darsapûr*n*amâsa, 29, 18, 18 n.; symbolism of new and full moon s., 44, 2–4; new and full moon s. to be offered for 30 years, 44, 4 sq.; two messes of rice, one for Sarasvat on the full moon, and one for Sarasvatî on the new moon, 44, 32 sq., 35 sq.; the new and full moon s. represented as a sort of horse-s., and all benefits accruing from the latter claimed for the former, 44, 33–5;—the *Dvâdasâha* or twelve days' performance, 26, 402–10, 402 sq. n., 418–21, 418 n.; 38, 413; 48, 763 sq.;—*G*â*madagnya-ahîna-s.*, 38, 240, 240 n.; 48, 654;—*Gavâm ayana*, a sacrificial session extending over twelve months, 26, 426–55; 44, xiv;—the *Gosava* sacrifice, 29, 251;—*G*y*otish*t*oma*, form of Agnish*t*oma, 34, xxxviii, xliv, 54 sq., 57, 87–93; 38, 185, 185 n.; 43, 287–9;—the *K*â*turmâsyâni* or seasonal s., 2, 36; 12, 173, 383–451; 25, 133; 41, 46–8; 43, 297, 299,

356; 44, xiv, 74–9, 176, 309, 309 n., 383, 393, 402; 48, 149, 155; the Vaisvadeva, the first of the Kâturmâsya-s., 12, 383–91; 41, 47; 44, 74, 74 n., 78, 289 sq. and n., 291 sq.; the Varunapraghâsa offerings, 12, 391–407; 41, 47 sq.; the Sâkamedhâh or third seasonal s., 12, 408–51; 41, 48 sq.; 44, 76, 76 n.;—the *Kesavapanîya*, 41, 126–8, 126 sq. n.;—the ayana of the *Kundapâyins*, a great s. lasting a whole year, 38, 250, 250 n., 251, 314;—*Mahâvrata* ceremony must not be performed for another, except a father or a teacher, 1, 260 sq., 266 sq. n.;—the *Mitravindâ*-s., its origin and fruit, 44, 62–6;—the *Prishthya-shadaha*, an accelerated Soma-feast, 44, 171;—the *Sahasradakshina Trirâtra*, or s. of three pressing-days with a thousand cows as the priests' fee, 26, 414–18, 414 n.;—the *Satarudriya*, or 425 oblations to Rudra, 43, 150, 156–69, 171 sq., 174, 320;—the *Satâtirâtram*, or sacrificial session of a hundred Atirâtra-s., 44, 91–5; origin, purpose, and peculiar rites of the *Sautrâmanî*-s., 12, 165, 165 n.; 44, 213–73; the Sautrâmanî, 41, xxvi, 129–38; 42, 112, 328 sq., 329 n., 591; 44, xiv, 223, 239–48, 262, 264, 270; Sautrâmanî is a Brâhmana's s., 44, 260;—the *Shodasin*, 26, 397–402; 38, 228; 41, xvi sq.;—the *Sunâsîr(î)ya*, 12, 444–51; 41, 48 sq.; 44, 77 sq., 77 n.;—the *Tâpaskita*, an accelerated Soma-feast, substitute for the performance of a thousand years, 44, 171 sq.;—the *Traidhâtavî* ishti, or the completing oblation of the Râgasûya and other s., 41, 138–42; 44, 412;—the *Trishamyukta* or triply connected s., 41, 54–7, 54 n.;—the *Vâgapeya*, 26, 167; 41, xi, xxiii–xxv, 1–41, 246; 42, 508; 43, 223–5; 44, 254; 46, 408; Brihaspatisava, part of the Vâgapeya, 38, 223 sq., 223 n.; Vâgapeya is superior to Râgasûya, 41, 4; 43, 225;—*Vishuvat* day, the middle of a Sattra, 2, 77; 44, 139, 144, 158–60, 165–7, 177;—the *Visvagit Atirâtra*, 43, 320 sq. and n. *See separately* Mahâvrata, Pravargya, Râgasûya, *and* Sarvamedha.

(*k*) Details of Zoroastrian s.

S. to Sraosha, 4, 136, 136 n., 223; 23, 162–7; to atone for the murder of a water-dog, 4, 170 sq.; to the good waters, 4, 210, 255, 335, 337; to the Fire, 4, 217, 223; 31, 313–16; to Saoka, 4, 237 sq.; to Waters and Plants, 4, 245; to Thraêtaona, 4, 246; for the benefit of a member of the family who is travelling, 4, 248; prayer and s. to Ahura-Mazda, 4, 283; 23, 25 sq.; 31, 80, 83; s. and prayers to Ahura and the Fire, 4, 293; offerings for the Gâhânbârs, 4, 337–43; Sôshyans performs a Yazisn ceremony, 5, 126; death occurring during the sacred ceremony (yazisn), 5, 255–7, 257 n.; the simplest form of worship (yast), 5, 338 sq.; to all the divinities of the Sîrôzah, 23, 13–20; to the Amesha-Spentas, 23, 31, 37 sq.; 37, 394; to Asha-Vahista, 23, 47; to Haurvatât, the seasons and the years, 23, 49, 51 sq.; to the Waters and Ardvi Sûra Anâhita, 23, 54–84, 357; 31, 320–4, 320 n.; s. to the Sun enable men to withstand the demons, 23, 86 sq.; to the Moon, 23, 90 sq.; to Tistrya, the star, 23, 93–109; offered to Gôs Drvâspa, 23, 111–18; to the Sun, Mithra, and other gods, 23, 120–58, 351–5; the first, the next, the middle, and the highest s., 23, 165, 165 n.; to the Fravashis, 23, 185 sq., 188, 190, 192 sq., 197, 228; to Verethraghna, 23, 231–48; to Vayu, 23, 249–63; to Kista, 23, 264–9; to Ashi Vanguhi, 23, 270–82; to the awful kingly Glory, and to the priestly Glory, 23, 289–309; to Âtar, 23, 359–61; Yasna, the chief liturgy of the Zarathustrians, 31, 195; liturgies at Zoroastrian s., 31, 195–230, 253–9, 270–84, 290 sq., 309 sq., 320–32, 335–64, 379–88, 391 sq.; all the Yazads worshipped, Hôm Yast recited at the time of Hâvani, 31, 201, 207, 211, 217, 222, 226, 231; offerings (meat, fruits, liquids, &c.), for the propitiation of gods, 31, 207 sq., 211–14, 222, 226–9, 270 sq., 274–6, 320 sq., 350; Myazdas offered to Maidhyô-zaremaya, &c., 31, 368–72; proper

times for the ceremonials of various deities, 37, 183 sq. and n.; offerings to the spirit of the house, 37, 209; offerings to the sacred beings, 37, 481; offering to Fire for the welfare of an embryo, 47, 30.

(*l*) Details of s. in China.

S. performed by Shun, to God, gods, and spirits, 3, 39; to spirits of land and grain, hills, forests, streams, meres, 3, 70 sq., 74; 27, 256; 28, 101; bad rulers overturn the temples and extinguish s., 3, 80; sincerity the chief thing in s., 3, 99; 16, 158, 159 n., 160, 162 sq., 164 n., 206, 207 sq. n., 346; 27, 26, 416–18, 416 sq. n., 428–30, 434–7, 435 n.; 28, 292; victims devoted to the spirits of heaven and earth, stolen and eaten, 3, 123, 126; Shâu neglects the s., 3, 128 sq., 132; offered after a successful war, 3, 134; s. of rulers and princes, king must pay attention to s., 3, 137, 163, 186, 192, 197; 27, 107 sq., 218, 220, 222, 225–7, 372 sq.; 28, 3 sq.; offered in a new city, 3, 190; the order of ministers at s. to be regulated by the king, 3, 190, 192; winter s., 3, 195; 27, 296 sq., 300, 300 n., 302–4, 306 sq., 307 n.; regulated by the Minister of Religion, 3, 228, 228 n.; pieces of the Shih King sung at s., 3, 277 sq.; s. to God at stated seasons, 3, 302; at the summer and winter solstices, 3, 302, 420 n.; seasonal s., 3, 305 sq., 305 n., 316, 321, 323 sq., 331–3, 342 sq., 343 n., 366, 420 n., 422 n., 488; 27, 226, 323, 329; 28, 33 sq., 249 sq.; spring s., 3, 320 sq., 321 n., 342 sq., 343 n.; 16, 158, 159 n., 160, 206, 207 n.; 27, 251, 251 n., 258 sq., 261, 261 n., 262–4, 418; 28, 210, 213; autumn s., 3, 342 sq., 343 n.; 27, 283, 287, 291, 293, 418; 28, 210, 213, 253, 271 sq.; to the great God, 3, 343, 343 n.; Wăn sacrificed to God and the Father of War, 3, 392; *K*iang Yüan sacrificed that her childlessness might be taken away, 3, 396 sq., 396 n.; founded by Hâu-*k*î, 3, 398 sq. and n.; prerogatives of sovereigns with regard to s., 3, 405 n.; offered to spirits during a drought, 3, 419 sq., 419 n.; to the spirits of the four quarters and of the land, 3, 422; offerings to the spirit of the road, 3, 425 sq., 425 n.; 27, 314; s. of a lamb to the Ruler of Cold or the Spirit of the Ice, 3, 445, 445 n.; s. to Hâu-*k*î as the correlate of Heaven, 3, 477, 477 n.; worshipper washes his hands before offering s., 16, 99, 230; king shall employ his virtues in presenting offerings to God, 16, 150; music employed at s., 16, 287, 289 n.; 28, 101, 119 sq.; the ancient kings presented offerings to God, 16, 341, 342 n.; the great Border s. to Heaven and Earth, 27, 26, 416 sq. and n., 427–31; 28, 167, 201 sq., 204, 217 sq., 253, 271 sq., 311; different rites under different dynasties, 27, 26, 443 sq.; are merely expressions of gratitude, 27, 35–7; 28, 201 n., 218; reverence the important thing in s., 27, 36, 141; 28, 210–15, 250 sq.; s. and the ten relationships of men, 27, 37; 28, 245–9; to spiritual beings on occasions of supplication, thanksgiving, &c., 27, 64, 64 n.; offering to the 'father of cookery' at meals, 27, 79 sq., 80 n., 106; 28, 7 sq., 20 sq., 38; when sacrificing, one should not speak of what is inauspicious, 27, 103; on the first day of the moon, 27, 156; places of s. destroyed by Wû, 27, 178; to be suspended on the death of a high minister, 27, 184; when passing a place of s. one should dismount, 27, 185; to the hills and rivers offered by a ruler on his tour of inspection, 27, 216 sq.; summer s., 27, 269, 269 n., 272–4, 274 n., 277, 281; 28, 253, 271 sq.; drinking to one another at s., 27, 317 sq.; place of honour at s., 27, 323; causes of interruption of s., 27, 329–31; thanksgiving sacrifice *K*â, 27, 364, 364 n., 431–4, 432 n.; extravagance and niggardliness in s., 27, 402; the object in s. is not to pray, 27, 403, 403 n.; one, three, five, and seven libations, 27, 412, 412 n.; the great quinquennial s., 27, 412 sq.; at the Shê altars, 27, 424 sq.; for the purpose of prayer, or of thanks-

giving, or of deprecation, 27, 448; women attend at s., 27, 477 n., 479; 28, 170 sq.; no avoiding of names at s., 28, 18; demeanour at s., 28, 26, 74 sq., 77, 79–81; offering to the father of charioteering, 28, 78 sq.; fish offerings, 28, 78, 78 n.; at the beginning of school lessons, 28, 84; to the waters, 28, 91; to heaven and earth, 28, 99; s. at the equinoxes, 28, 218 sq. and n.; in the suburb to heaven and sun and moon, 28, 218 sq. and n.; in the Hall of Distinction, 28, 231; on purification as preparatory to s., 28, 239 sq.; three things important at s., 28, 241 sq.; servants and assistants at s., 28, 249; days for s. fixed by divination, 28, 349–51; at hospitable receptions, 28, 439–41; archery trials at s. of a ruler, 28, 451 sq.; sons shall offer s., though not to the Highest Object, 39, 97 sq.; offered to tutelary spirits of the land, 39, 382; a sacrificial libation made of a cup of wine, 40, 104.

(*m*) ARABIAN S.

Mohammed is to offer s. from his abundance, 6, cxviii; 9, 342 sq.; what is sacrificed to idols, forbidden to eat, 6, 97; portions of tilth and cattle set apart for Allah and other deities by the Arabs, 6, 132 sq., 132 n.; offered at the Kaabah, 9, 59 sq., 59 n.

Sacrificer, *see* Sacrifices (*f*).

Sacrificial fee, *see* Dakshi*n*â, *and* Priests (*c*, *d*).

Sadânvâs, female demons, 42, 62, 66 sq., 301.

Sadâparibhûta, n. of a Bodhisattva, 21, xxxi, 356–62.

Sadasaspati, worshipped at opening and concluding ceremonies of Veda study, 14, 308; 29, 221, 321 sq.; 30, 242, 266 sq.

Sad Dar, t.w., not a Pahlavi text, 24, xxxvi; prose and metrical versions, their authors, 24, xxxvii, xliii–xlv, 255 sq. n.; its contents, 24, xxxvii sq.; MSS. and versions of it, 24, xxxix–xlv; S. or 'The hundred subjects,' translated, 24, 255–361.

Saddharma-pu*nd*arîka, the 'Lotus of the True Law,' t.w., dramatic character of it, 21, ix sq.; one of the Mahâvaipulya-sûtras, 21, x; relative dates of the metrical (Gâthâ) and the prose portions of S., 21, xviii–xx; Chinese translations of S., 21, xix–xxiv, xl–xlii; its date, 21, xx–xxii; Burnouf on S., his translation of it, 21, xxiv sq., xxxvii sq.; its general character, 21, xxiv–xxviii, xxxii; how far it represents orthodox Buddhism, 21, xxviii sq.; summary of its contents, 21, xxix–xxxii; a Tathâgata appears to hear the preaching of the S., 21, xxx, 229–40; Buddha relates by what merits he acquired the S., 21, xxx, 243–6; promise of Bodhisattvas, disciples and nuns to preach the S. after Buddha's Nirvâ*n*a, 21, xxx, 255 sq., 258–61, 363 sq.; glorification of the S. as the best of all Sûtras, 21, xxxi, 242, 386 sqq., 391 sq.; expounded by a Buddha, 21, 174 sq., 186 sq.; difficulty of keeping and preaching the S. illustrated, 21, 240–2; he who will preach the S. after Buddha's extinction, will be the leader of the sons of the Tathâgata, 21, 242 sq.; whoever hears the chapter on the apparition of the Stûpa in the S., will be born in the Buddha-fields, 21, 248; daughter of a Nâga-king has fully grasped the S., therefore becomes fully enlightened, and changes her sex, 21, 250–4; preaching of S. is the last and most precious gift bestowed by Buddha on his disciples, 21, 274–80; the merit of preaching the Lotus of the True Law illustrated by the story of Sadâparibhûta, 21, 356–62; *in this Dharmaparyâya I (Buddha) have succinctly taught all Buddha-laws (or Buddha-qualities), all the superiority, all the mystery, all the profound conditions of the Buddhas. Therefore, young men of good family, you should, after the complete extinction of the Tathâgata, with reverence keep, read, promulgate, cherish, worship it*, 21, 367, 369; meritoriousness of preaching and keeping the S., 21, 368–71, 377–9, 386, 388–92; one of the Samâdhis, 21, 393; great merit of writing, reading, and studying it, 21, 435 sqq.; those who preach and

hear it will become Buddhas, 21, 438 sq.; punishments for those who scoff or ill-treat preachers and hearers of S., 21, 439.
Saddhivihârika, Pali t.t., fellow monk, *see* Teacher (*b*).
Sadhanah, n.p., 23, 214.
Sâdhîna, king, went up to heaven even in his human body, 35, 172; 36, 146.
Sâdhyas, genii, with Brahman at their head, 1, 43; alarmed at the greatness of K*r*ish*n*a, 8, 94; begotten from the Highest Person, 15, 35; rise in the north, 15, 339; created, 25, 12, 12 n.; Somasads, the manes of the S., 25, 111; made substitutes for the principal rules, 25, 435; in the second order of existences caused by Goodness, 25, 495; worshipped at the Tarpa*n*a, 29, 219; 30, 243; a class of gods, 34, 216; help in battle, 42, 119, 585; divine guardians of the sacrificial horse, 44, 359; to the S. a tanner is sacrificed at the Purushamedha, 44, 415. *See also* Superhuman beings.
Sa*d*vâstarân, the assembly of, 5, 123, 123 n.
Saêna, n.p., *see* Sênô; n. of a family, 23, 219.
Saêna, or Sîmûrgh, mythic bird, 23, 173 n., 210 n., 241 n., 242.
Saêni, n. of a Daêva, 23, 49 sq., 49 n.
Sâgala, n. of the town of the Yonakas, where Milinda was king, 35, 1–3, 6, 10, 12, 23, 30, 34, 36, 48; 36, 373.
Sagara, son of Ikshvâku, could control the tide of the sea, 19, 11; made a bound for the ocean, 49 (i), 9.
Sagara, a king who became a *G*aina monk, 45, 85, 85 n.
Sâgara (Ocean), n. of a Nâga-king, story of his daughter, 21, xxx, 5, 250–4.
Sâgarabuddhidhârin, i.e. Sâgaravaradharabuddhivikrî*d*itâbhig*ñ*a, q.v.
Sâgarameru*k*andra, the 41st Tathâgata, 41 (ii), 6.
Sâgaravarabuddhivikrî*d*itâbhig*ñ*a, the 22nd Tathâgata, 49 (ii), 6.
Sâgaravaradharabuddhivikrî*d*itâbhig*ñ*a, future Buddha, who was formerly Ânanda, 21, 206–8.
Sâgata, Buddha's attendant, works miracles, 17, 2–4.
Sag-dîd, Zd. t.t., 'the look of the dog,' 4, lxxii sq., lxxxi. *See also* Dog, *and* Funeral rites (*c*).
Sages, *see* Holy persons, Muni, *Ri*shis.
Sagga, Pali for Sk. Svarga, *see* Heaven (*d*).
Sagotra, t.t., *see* Relatives.
Saha, or Sahâ, *see* Saha-world.
Sahadeva, the Pâ*nd*ava, 8, 39.
Sahadeva, Somaka, son of, 46, 360 sq.
Sahadeva Sâr*ñg*aya, n. of a teacher, also called Suplan, 12, 376; 44, 239, 239 n.
Saha*g*anyâ, a nymph, 43, 106.
Sahaka: Brahmâ was, in the time of Kassapa Buddha, a Bhikkhu named S., 11, 163 sq.
Sahâmpati, and Agni sahaspati, 21, 5 n.
Saharakshas, a messenger for the Asuras, 12, 110 sq.; 26, 115.
Sahasrâksha, worshipped at the Tarpa*n*a, 29, 121, 149; the thousand-eyed deity, 42, 163, 474.
Saha-world, in which Buddha appeared, 21, 179, 230, 232 sq., 253 sq., 321, 366; 49 (ii), v, x, 52 n., 61, 102; the creatures wicked and perverse in the S., 21, 256; Bodhisattvas springing up from the earth, their place in the S., 21, 281–92; has ups and downs, consists of earth and mountains, 21, 394 sq. *See also* Paradise.
Sâhm, *see* Sâm.
Sahya, one of the princes of mountains, 8, 346.
*S*a**ibya**, n. of a warrior, 8, 37.
*S*a**ikshas**, t.t., novices who are still under training, striving for Arhatship, 21, 71.
*S*a**ilâli**, n. of a teacher, 44, 393.
*S*a**ilini**, *see* *G*itvan *S*.
Saints, five degrees of, viz. Arhats, Liberated Ones, Religious Guides, Religious Instructors, all S. in the world, 22, 217, 278, 284; obeisance done by *S*akra to *G*inas, Arhats, &c., 22, 224 sq.; male and female s. worshipped, 31, 268, 358–60, 381; are superior to all householders in self-control, 45, 22. *See also* Arhat, *G*inas, Holy persons, Muni, *Ri*shis, Theras, *and* Tîrthakara.

Saintship, stages of, viz. the Threefold Wisdom, the Heavenly Vision, Having entered upon the Stream, and the Pothugganikâ Iddhi, 20, 230; degrees of s., Sotâpanno, Sakadâgâmin, Anâgâmin, Arhatship, 20, 305. *See also* Arhatship, Holy persons, *and* Iddhi.

Sairima, Airya, and Tûra, the three sons of Thraêtaona, 4, lix.

***S*aitân**, *see* Satan.

Saitava, n. of a teacher, 15, 118, 118 n., 186, 186 n.

***S*aiva** ascetics, adherents of Pa*s*upati, wear the hair platted and gathered up in a knot, 10 (i), 39 n.; their doctrines, 34, 435; 45, 245 sq., 245 n.; 48, 520 sq.; theory of *S*. contrary to the Veda, 48, 523.

***S*aivya**, *see* Satyakâma.

Sa*k*a, the Nirgrantha, converted by Buddha, 19, 244.

***S*âka**, worshipped by the Snâtaka, 30, 166.

Sakadâgâmin, t.t., Bhikkhus who on their first return to this world will make an end of sorrow, 21, 25; how the Bhikkhu may become a S., 11, 213. *See also* Saintship.

***S*akadhûma**, ruler of the stars, 42, 160, 532 sq.

***S*âkalya**, meditation taught by, 1, 248 sq.; Sthavira *S*., 1, 257, 265; dialogue between Yâg*ñ*avalkya and Vidagdha (the shrewd) *S*., on the gods and the one God, 15, 139–49; 44, 115–17; Vidagdha *S*. says that the heart is Brahman, 15, 157 sq.; worshipped at the Tarpa*n*a, 29, 123, 141, 220.

***S*akambhara**, n. of the demon of diarrhoea, 42, 1, 445 sq.

Sâkamedhâ*h*, t.t., third seasonal sacrifice, *see* Sacrifice (*j*).

***S*âkapû*n*i**, worshipped at the Tarpa*n*a, 29, 123.

***S*akas**, mentioned in Manu-sm*ri*ti, 25, cxiv sq., cxiv n., cxvii; degraded Kshatriyas, 25, 412.

***S*aka*t*amukha**, a park outside the town Purimatâla, 22, 283.

***S*âkâyanins**, quoted, 43, 363.

***S*âkâyanya**, saint, dialogue between him and B*ri*hadratha, 15, xlvii, 287 sqq., 326–9.

Sâketa, n. of a great town, 10 (ii), 188; 11, 99, 247; 36, 249.

Sâkha and Nigrodha, former births of Devadatta and the Bodisat, 35, 289 sq.

Sakhar, n. of a devil who takes away Solomon's ring, 9, 178 n.

***S*âkhâs**, t.t., 'branches' (of Veda), i. e. Vedic Schools, *see* Veda (*g*).

Sa*k*î, wife of Indra, 19, 1; 29, 33; 42, 95, 125 sq., 503; 49 (i), 21.

Sâkiyas, or Sakyas, or *S*âkyas, Buddha's family, 10 (ii), 69; claim relics of Buddha, 11, 131 sq.; S. by birth, who have been heretics, may be ordained without a parivâsa being imposed on them, 13, 191; *S*uddhodana, king of the S., 19, 1; 49 (i), 2 sq.; princes of S. tribe become Bhikkhus, 19, 226; 20, 224–33; are renowned for pride, 20, 230.

Sakka, *see* Indra.

Sa*kk*aka: disputation between Buddha and S., the son of a Niga*nth*a, 45, xxiii; his account of the conduct of the A*k*elakas, 45, xxxi.

Sa*k*-*k*id-ânanda, Brahman defined as, 34, xcii.

***S*akra**, *see* Indra.

Sak*ri*dâgâmin, Sk.=Sakadâgâmin, q. v.

***S*akti**, Mâyâ belongs to Brahman as a, 34, xxv.

***S*akti**, a woman of great Brâhmanical power, converted by Buddha, 49 (i), 194.

***S*âktya**, *see* Gaurîviti *S*., *and* Parâ*s*ara *S*.

Sakulya, t.t., *see* Relatives.

***S*akuntalâ**, Apsaras, conceived Bharata, 44, 399.

Sakyamuni, *see* Buddha.

***S*âkyas**, Sakyas, *see* Sâkiyas.

***S*âlagrâm**, the sacred stone in which Hari is contemplated, 34, 114, 126, 178.

Sâla grove of the Mallians, 11, 81, 85, 103 sq., 122, 247.

Sâla*g*ya, city, in the world of Brahman, 1, 275, 277.

Sâlaka, *see* Animals (*i*).

***S*âla-king**, Amitâbha shines as the, 21, 417.

***S*âlankâyanîputra**, n. of a teacher, 15, 224 n.

Sâlavatî, courtesan of Râgagaha, mother of *G*îvaka, the physician, 17, 172 sq.

Sâlâvrikas, conquered by Indra, 42, 138, 306.
Sâlendrarâga, n. of a Tathâgata, 21, 429; 49 (ii), 101.
Sâlha, n. of a Bhikkhu, who attained to Arahatship, 11, 25; Brahmâ appeared to confirm his wavering faith, 11, 164; takes his stand against the theses of the Vaggian Bhikkhus, and is confirmed by a deity, 20, 401; appointed on the jury at the council of Vesâlî, 20, 407.
Sâlî, mother of Maudgalya, 49 (i), 193.
Sâlîki, quoted by Baudhâyana, 14, xl n.
Sallasutta, t.c., 10 (ii), 106–8.
Salm, son of Frêdûn, 5, 133 sq., 133 n.; 37, 28; S. and Tûg defeated by Mânûskîhar, 24, 61; 47, 11, 11 n.
Sâlmalî tree, in hell, with sharp thorns, 45, 94; 'my own Self is the S. t.,' 45, 104; most famous of trees, 45, 290.
Salmân, the Persian, referred to in the Qur'ân, 6, xlviii.
Salt, melted in water, simile, 1, 104 sq.; the savour of the sky and the earth, also cattle, 12, 278, 278 n.; bags of s. thrown up to the sacrificer at the Vâgapeya, 41, 33 sq.; means cattle, 41, 33, 299 sq., 343; saline soil is the amnion of fire, 41, 302, 344; means seed, 44, 426.
Saluting, *see* Etiquette.
Sâlvas, Salvas, Sâlvas, n. of a people, 30, 280; 43, 344; 49 (i), 101.
Salvation: Buddha answers a Yakkha's question as to s., 10 (ii), 27 sq., 30 sq.; is only to be found in the three jewels, Buddha, Dhamma, and Sangha, 10 (ii), 36–40; in which one is no longer liable to be reborn, 11, 25 sq.; attained by the Mirror of Truth, 11, 26 sq.; '*decay is inherent in all component things! Work out your s. with diligence!' This was the last word of the Tathâgata!* 11, 114; Buddha's teaching a scheme of s. by self-culture and self-control, 11, 142 sq.; how to obtain final s., 11, 213; 45, 355, 380; is universal for believers, 31, 93, 98; eternal s. of the saint, 31, 359; is the best thing, a sage by restraining his senses brings it about, 45, 313; only men can obtain final s., 45, 331, 331 n. *See also* Emancipation.
Sâlyâ, mother of Sâriputra, 49 (i), 193.
Sâm, i.e. Sâma Keresâspa, became immortal, wounded by Nihâg, slew Dahâk, 5, 119, 119 n.; his descendants, 5, 137, 139 sq., 139 n. *See also* Keresâspa the Sâmân.
Sâma, prince, was killed by Piliyakkha, 35, 280 sq.; Devadatta born as S., 35, 288.
Samâ, goddess of zealous devotion, worshipped, 29, 334.
Samâdhi, Pali t.t., contemplation or meditation, 11, 145; the S. Sarvarûpadarsana (sight or display of all forms), 21, 378; enumeration of S., 21, 393 sq. *See also* Faith, *and* Meditation.
Sâmâga, in his field Mahâvîra reached Nirvâna, 22, 201, 263.
Sâmak, son of Masyê and Masyâôî, 47, 8.
Samâkâra, a book of the Âtharvanikas treating of Vedic observances, 38, 189.
Sâmân, primaeval ruler, 47, 121.
Sâman, melody: meditations on the (fivefold, sevenfold) S., 1, 16 sq., 23–8; 15, 82 sq.; Stobhâksharas used in the S. hymns, 1, 22; on the different tones employed in singing the S. hymns, 1, 33 sq.; the Brihat consists of hundred verses, and is made by Bharadvâga, 1, 189 sq., 190 n.; the Rathantara hymns, made by Vasishtha, consist of hundred verses, 1, 189 sq., 189 n.; the Brihat is man, the Rathantara is woman, 1, 190; Stomas and S. connected with the Nishkevalya-sastra, 1, 224–7 and n.; S. and Samhitâ connected, 1, 254; S. verses represented as parts of the throne and couch of Brahman, 1, 277 sq.; Rig-veda and Yagur-veda not to be studied while the sound of S. is heard, 2, 38, 261; 7, 125; 8, 20; 14, 66, 208; 25, 148; 29, 116, 116 n., 324; Brihat, chief among S. hymns, 8, 90, 90 n.; are pure, 8, 145, 180; Brihat, Rathantara, and Vâmadevya S. in the ritual, 8, 180; 12, 196, 196 n.,

222, 222 n., 298 n., 299 n.; 26, 339 n.; 29, 209 sq., 363 sq.; 30, 170; 41, xx–xxiii, 196, 274; must be sung at sacrifices, 12, 100; no S. hymn sung at the worship of Varu*n*a, 12, 406; he who meditates on Om, is led up by the S. verses to the Brahma-world, 15, 282; 48, 311; *the S. is the truth, the S. is born of the gods*, 26, 97; is a repeller of evil spirits, 26, 380; 44, 496 sq.; the highest self is S., 34, 79; meditation on the fire as S., 38, 345–9; the term S., 41, xiii; thrice eighty S.-singers, 42, 89, 297; singing S. round the altar, 43, 177–81; is the essence of all the Vedas, 44, 255, 370; means lordship and imperial sway, 44, 255; Agni has proclaimed the great, doubly-powerful S., the prayer, to the worshipper, 46, 335, 337. *See also* Prayers (*c*), *and* Sâma-veda.

Samâna, *see* Prâ*n*as.

Sama*n*a (Pali t.t. = Sk. *S*rama*n*a), 'ascetic,' 10 (ii), x: not by tonsure and other outward acts is a man a S., but by extinction of desires, 10 (i), 62 sq., 65; (ii), 89; 35, 251 sq.; etymologized as 'a quiet man,' 10 (i), 65, 65 n., 89; pleasant is the state of a S., 10 (i), 79; four kinds of S., 10 (ii), xiii, 15 sq.; Buddha is a S., 10 (ii), xiv, 12; blessing of intercourse with S., 10 (ii), 44; Bhikkhus admonished to remove as chaff those that are no S., 10 (ii), 47; philosophical disputations among S., 10 (ii), 158, 167–70; much-talking S., 10 (ii), 177; a S. may, by intense meditation, cause an earthquake, 11, 45 sq.; S. = brâhma*n*â or Brâhmans by saintliness of life, 11, 105 n.; Sakyaputtiya S., the oldest name of the Buddhist fraternity, 13, xii; there are many sorts of S., 22, 128, 128 n.; Mahâvîra called S., 22, 193, 255; wandering teachers, 35, 7, 7 n.; twenty qualities of Sama*n*aship, 35, 230 sq.; difference between a guilty layman and a guilty S., 36, 82–4; four fruits of Sama*n*aship, 36, 297. *See also* Ascetics, *and* Holy persons.

Sama*n*a Kola*ññ*a, king of Kali*n*ga, 36, 81.

Samânapravara, t.t., *see* Relatives.

Sâma*n*era (Buddhist novice), Thera is always accompanied by, 11, 102 n.; disciplinary proceedings against S., who speaks against Buddha's doctrine, 13, 48 sq.; offices and ceremonies for which S. is disqualified, 13, 275, 296; 17, 269, 419; 20, 215 sq., 266; one of the seven classes of persons, 13, 303–11; Mânatta discipline for a Bhikkhu who, having committed offences, becomes a S., 17, 426, 430; struck with tooth-sticks, 20, 147 sq.; superintendent of S., 20, 223; may be left in charge of the sleeping-places, 20, 282 sq.

Sâma*ññ*a, 'priesthood,' 10 (i), 8 n.

Sâma*ññ*a-phala-sutta, Buddhist text, 10 (i), 8 n.; when and where it was spoken, 20, 377.

Samânodaka, *see* Relatives.

Samantabhadra, the Bodhisattva, mounted on a white elephant, 21, xxxi, 431–9.

Samantagandha, the Wind, a god, 21, 4.

Samantakusuma, god, pays homage to Buddha, 49 (i), 159.

Samantaprabhâsa, future Buddhas of the name of, 21, xxx, 198–204.

Samâpatti, *see* Meditation (*b*).

Samappadhâ*n*â (*k*attâro), Pali t.t., —fourfold great struggle against sin, 11, 63.

Sâmarîy, makes the golden calf, 9, 40 sq., 40 n.

Sâmas (Semites?), Thrita, the most helpful of the, 31, 233, 233 n.

Samâvartana, ceremony of the (student's) 'returning' (from the teacher), or the bath taken at the end of studentship, 2, 32; 8, 358; 25, 50, 73; 29, 91 sq., 223, 226–30, 312–19, 407–9; 30, 82–5, 161–75, 253, 275–7; precedes the marriage, 29, 379 sq.; setting up the domestic fire after S., 30, 14 sq.

Samavâya, Sk. t.t., *see* Inherence.

Sâma-veda: meditation on special parts of the S. ceremonial, 1, 28–33; expiatory Mantras from the S., 7, 185 sq.; sound of S. unholy, 8, 20; K*ri*sh*n*a is the S. among the Vedas, 8, 20, 88; schools of S., 12, xxvi,

xxvi n.; is sacred to the manes, 25, 148; followers of the S. quoted by Âpastamba, 30, 285; the pra*n*ava belonging to the *Ri*g-veda is connected with the S. meditation on the udgîtha, 38, 282 n.; a certain mantra of the S. to be recited in the Yagurveda style, 48, 654. *See also* Sâman, Udgîtha, *and* Veda.

Sâmavidhâna, in the Gautama-Dharma-sûtra, 2, 296–9, and n.

Samaya (annihilation) is the principal thing, 10 (ii), 167.

***S*ambara**, an evil demon, 42, liv; 46, 49.

***S*âmbavya**, author of G*ri*hya-sûtra, 29, 257 n.

***S*âmbavya-G*ri*hya-sûtra**, quoted, 29, 3 sq.; its relation to *S*âṅkhâyana-G*ri*hya-sûtra, 29, 6–9.

Sambhava, n. of a Buddha-sphere, 21, 153.

Sambhava, n. of a Tîrthakara, 22, 280.

***S*ambhu**, a name of the great self, or the highest Brahman, 8, 219, 332; 15, 311; 48, 667; pierced by the arrow of the love-god, 49 (i), 139.

Sambhûta, dialogue between *K*itra and, 45, 56–61; stories of *K*itra and S. in various births common to Brahmans, *G*ainas, and Buddhists, 45, 56 sq. n.

Sambhûta Sâ*n*avâsî, n. of a Thera, 17, 238; joins Yasa in convening the council of Vesâlî, and becomes one of the referees, 20, 394–407.

Sambhûtavi*g*aya, n. of a Sthavira, 22, 287; his twelve disciples and seven female disciples, 22, 289.

Sambodhi, the holy eightfold Path leading to, 13, 94–7. *See also* Knowledge.

***S*âmbu** Aṅgiras, the kush*th*a plant, thrice begotten by, 42, 6, 678.

Sambuddha, the perfectly enlightened, title of the Buddha, 10 (ii), 186–8, 190, 212 sq.

Sa*mg*ayin**, an ascetic, converted by Buddha, 49 (i), 191.

Sa*m*gha, Buddhist Church, the Order (of monks): happy is peace in the S., 10 (i), 52; the thoughts of the disciples of Gotama are always set on the S., 10 (i), 71; those who have formerly been followers of another doctrine, have to remain four months on probation (parivâsa) before being accepted in the S., 10 (ii), 94 sq.; 11, 109; 13, 188; amongst those that wish for good works and make offerings the S. is the principal, 10 (ii), 105; 17, 134; religious service in the S., 11, 16; worthy of honour, of hospitality, of gifts, and of reverence, &c., 11, 27; Buddha explains to Ânanda that the S. was not dependent on him, 11, 36–9; 35, 225; the S. allowed by Buddha to abolish after his death all the lesser and minor precepts, 11, 112; 35, 202–4; he who has doubts in the S. is not free from spiritual barrenness, 11, 224, 228 sq.; penitential meetings in the S., 13, x sq.; an organized brotherhood from the first, 13, xi sq.; sins which require formal meetings of the S., 13, 7–15; how the Bhikkhu is to behave towards one not received into the higher grade of the S., 13, 32 sq.; property of the S., 13, 34, 52; 17, 143; 20, 209–12; a person under twenty years of age must not be admitted to the higher grade in the S., 13, 46; misbehaviour of a Bhikkhu in a regularly constituted S., 13, 52; disciplinary proceedings against Bhikkhus by the S., 13, 68 sq., 161 sq., 306 sqq.; 17, 276–84, 329–83; the S.'s permission must be asked for having the new-coming Bhikkhus shaved, 13, 201; the two S., viz. that of Bhikkhus and that of Bhikkhunîs, 13, 256 n.; 17, 253 sq.; 20, 343 sq., 352; validity and invalidity of formal acts of the S., 13, 277–9; 17, 256–84, 290 sq.; an extraordinary Uposatha may be held for the sake of composing a schism in the S., 13, 297; it is a grievous sin to cause divisions in the S., 13, 316 sq.; for the sake of concord among the S., Pavâra*n*â may be held on another day but the Pavâra*n*â day, 13, 337, 337 n.; on the apportioning of food in times of scarcity, 17, 70 sq., 74–8, 118; 20, 220 sq.; distributions of robes for the S., the Ka*th*ina ceremonies, 17,

146–70 and notes, 234–40, 248–55; a Bhikkhu possessed of five good qualities, to be officially appointed by the S. for receiving robes, 17, 200 sq., 203 sq.; property left by deceased Bhikkhus belongs to the S., 17, 243–5; unlawful and lawful expulsion from the S., 17, 256–62, 272 sq., 274 sq., 283 sq., 291; there are five kinds of S., 17, 268 sq.; persons who cannot protest against official acts of the S., 17, 271; schisms in the S., 17, 285–325; 19, xi–xvi; 20, 265–7; regulations about re-establishment of concord and ending a schism, 17, 320–5; the Bhikkhu worthy of the leadership in affairs of the S., 17, 323–5; formal acts of the S. must not be carried out against Bhikkhus who are not present, 20, 1 sq.; settlement of disputes among the S., 20, 1–65; appointment of a regulator of lodging-places and apportioner of rations, 20, 5 sq., 221–3; proceeding for the acquittal of one conscious of innocence, 20, 16–18, 57 sq.; the taking of votes in the S., 20, 24–7, 56 sq.; no voting must be taken when a schism in the S. is likely to arise, 20, 27; the Tassa-pâpiyyasikâ-kamma, or proceeding in the case of the obstinately wrong, 20, 28–31; settlement of disputes by Ti*n*avatthâraka or 'the covering over as with grass,' 20, 31–4, 61, 64 sq.; four kinds of legal questions to be settled by the S., 20, 35–45; two kinds of settlement of legal questions: proceeding in presence, and proceeding by majority of the S., 20, 45–65; proceeding on confession of guilt, 20, 61–4; proceedings of the S. as to 'turning the bowl down' in respect of a layman who has committed certain offences, 20, 119–25; appoints Bhikkhus as overseers when a Vihâra is being built, 20, 189–91; probation and penance, 20, 195 sq.; office of overseer of buildings, 20, 212–16; the Act of Proclamation against Devadatta, 20, 239 sqq.; dissensions in the S. caused by Devadatta, 20, 251–6; eight qualifications for an emissary, 20, 261 sq.; results of Kamma brought about by causing a schism in S., 20, 267–71; will not brook association with an evil-doer, but cast him out just as the ocean throws out a dead corpse, 20, 303; points to be considered if a Bhikkhu intends to take upon himself the conduct of any matter to be decided in the S., 20, 313–15; the higher penalty, 20, 381; laxer rule on the carrying out of official acts discussed at the council of Vesâlî, 20, 386, 398, 411; the Act of Reconciliation, 20, 388; the Act of Suspension, 20, 393 sq.; any one can leave the S. when he likes, 35, 20, 20 n.; reasons for which people join the S., 35, 49 sq.; in what sense there can be no schism, 35, 227 sq.; why reverence must be shown even by converted laymen to members of the S., 35, 229–33; Buddha greater than the S., but gifts should be given to the S. rather than to the Buddha, 36, 51–6; laymen are admitted into the S., though they may become backsliders, 36, 63–75; rules for members of the S., 36, 98–100, 98 n., 99 n.; why did not the Buddha promulgate all the rules of the S. at once? 36, 109–11; causing a schism, and furtively attaching oneself to the S., are offences preventing conversion, 36, 177; Bhikkhus versed in the Regulations of the S., 36, 236; Bhikkhu should dwell under the shelter of the S., 36, 343; the first members of the S., 49 (i), 172; Buddha, Dhamma, and S., *see* Jewels, the three. *See also* Bhikkhunîs, Bhikkhus, Buddha (*b*), Mânatta, Ordination, Penances, Sâvaka, Sekha, *and* Uposatha.

Sâ*mg*îvî-putra, n. of a Vâgasaneyi teacher, 12, xxxii–xxxv; 43, xviii, 404.

Sa*mgñâ*, *see* Name.

Sa*mgñâ*skandha, group of verbal knowledge, 34, 402, 402 n.

Sa*m*grahîtri, t.t., king's charioteer, 41, 62, 104.

Sa*m*hitâs or unions, the secret doctrine of the, 15, 46 sq. *See also* Veda.

Sa*m*hitâ-upanishad of the Aitareya-

âra*n*yaka, 1, 266, 266-8 n.; S., or Sâ*m*hitî-upanishad of Taittirîyaka, 15, xxviii; of the Âtharva*n*as, 48, 191.

Sâmidhenî verses, *see* Prayers (*c*).

Samita, disciple of Si*m*hagiri *G*âtismara, 22, 293.

*S*a*m*kara, *see* *S*añkara.

Sa*m*kâ*s*ikâ *S*âkhâ of the *K*âra*n*a Ga*n*a, 22, 291.

Sa*m*khâra, Pali t.t. (Sk. Sa*m*skâra), plur. Sa*m*khârâ, one of the five Khandhas (Skandhas), meaning of the word, 10 (i), 54 sq. n.; 11, 242 sq.; all compound things, the material world, 10 (ii), x; Bhikkhu skilled in the knowledge of the cessation of the S., 10 (ii), 62, 180; 36, 336; pain arises from the S. (matter), 10 (ii), 134 sq.; transitoriness of all S. or component things, 11, 288 sq.; productions, their number, 13, 76 sq. n.; impression, affection, 34, 404 n.; 'confections,' for them time is not, 35, 77, 77 n.; rise from Ignorance, 35, 79; come to be by a process of evolution, 35, 83-6.

Sâ*m*khya, *see* Sâñkhya.

Sâ*m*k*ri*ti A*m*tideva, Brahmarshi and king, 49 (i), 101, 101 n.

Sammâ, Pali t.t., the Life that's Right, 11, 107 n.; difficulty of rendering it, 11, 143 sq.

Sâmmada, *see* Matsya S.

Sammâparibbâ*g*aniyasutta, t.c., 10 (ii), 60-2.

Sammeta, Mount, Pâr*s*va died on the summit of, 22, 275.

Sa*m*nyâsin, *see* Sannyâsin.

Sampalita of the Gautama gotra, a Sthavira, 22, 294.

Samprati, grandson of A*s*oka, converted by Suhastin, 22, 290 n.

Samrâ*g*, a name of the Self, 15, 311.

Samrâ*g*-cow, t.t., the cow which supplies the milk for the Pravargya, 44, 131-4, 131 n.

Sa*m*sâra, t.t., the endless cycle of birth, action, and death, or transmigration, 10 (ii), x; 22, 11; 34, xxix; caused by desire, 10 (ii), xv sq.; crossing the stream of S. and conquering birth and death, 10 (ii), 89; 45, 31-5, 37 sq.; he who has overcome S., is a saint, a Brâhma*n*a, 10 (ii), 115 sq.; the causes of pain are the cause of S., by destruction of the causes, a Bhikkhu is liberated from S., 10 (ii), 132-45; 45, 141; the world a field in which the Lord spreads out one net after another (S.), 15, 255; represented under the idea of a lake or slough, 22, 20 n.; Veda furnishes the means of escaping from endless S., 34, xxvii; release from S. according to *S*añkara and Râmânu*g*a, 34, xxxi; Nescience, the seed of the entire S., 34, 14; 38, 68 sq.; 48, 311; non-eternal, of a fleeting, changing nature, 34, 27; beginningless, 34, 212, 214, 420; 38, 60; gradually all souls are released from it, 34, 439; the pradhâna which is ruled by the Lord and which modifies itself for the purposes of the soul is what is meant by S., 34, 439; the sufferings of S., 35, 278; 45, 93-7, 103; is only due to the qualities of buddhi and other limiting adjuncts being wrongly superimposed upon the Self, 38, 43 sq., 46-8; and moksha result from the highest Lord, 38, 58 sq.; the Lord afflicted by the pain caused to the soul by its experience of the S., 38, 63; nine qualities of the Selfs constitute the S., 38, 69; the manner in which the soul together with its subordinate adjuncts passes through the S., 38, 101-32; threefold fruits of action in the S., viz. pain, pleasure, and a mixture of the two, come from the Lord, 38, 180 sq.; the Self which stands outside the S., 38, 288; scriptural declarations of the S., 38, 371; would be impossible on the assumption of the soul being either a part, or an effect of, or different from Brahman, 38, 397; because the S. depends on works, it does not follow that the S. will cease when works are absent, 38, 398; *birth is misery, old age is misery, and so are disease and death, and ah, nothing but misery is the S., in which men suffer distress*, 45, 90; the manifold chances of S., 45, 15 sq.; fool subject to the pain of S., 45, 24 sqq.; soul is driven about in the S. by its good and bad Karman,

45, 43; as merchants go over the sea, so the monks will cross the flood of S., 45, 271, 311; those who injure living beings will wander about in the beginningless and endless wilderness of the fourfold S., 45, 387; opposed to final release, 48, 71; Yoga, the remedy of S., 48, 89; *from Brahmâ down to a blade of grass, all living beings that dwell within this world are in the power of the S. due to works*, 48, 90; *the S. state consists in the possession of name and form, which is due to connexion with non-sentient matter, such connexion springing from good and evil works*, 48, 298. *See also* Life, *and* Transmigration.

Sa*m*skâra, Sk., Brâhmanical t.t., purificatory rite or ceremony, forty sacraments by which members of the three higher castes are sanctified, 2, 215–17; 8, 358, 358 n., 361; 25, 32–42, 32 n., 56; 34, 33, 227; 38, 120 n., 286, 286 n., 287 n., 347 n.; he who is sanctified by the S. but destitute of moral qualities will not reach heaven, 2, 218; prescribed for *S*ûdras, 2, 232 sq. n.; *S*ûdra shall not receive S., 14, 25 sq.; 25, 429; 34, 227; to be performed with the sacred domestic fire, 14, 236, 236 sq. n.; for women without sacred texts, 25, 330, 330 n.; peace of sacred fire at S., 29, 20; oblations made before the performance of S., 29, 164; auspicious time for S., 29, 164; allowed for certain mixed castes, 33, 187, 187 n.; performed by one of undivided brothers, 33, 198 sq.; *see also* Sacrifice (*b*); —Annaprâ*s*ana, 2, 139; Godâna, 2, 187; the S. for a new-born child to be performed for an outcast when readmitted, 14, 78, 78 n.; Pu*m*savana and similar S. performed for males, 14, 105 sq. n., 106. *See also* Child (*b*), *and* Initiation.

Sa*m*skâra, Sk., Buddhist t.t., = Pali Sa*m*khâra, q. v.

Sa*m*skâraskandha, the group of impressions, 34, 402, 402 n.

***S*â*m*tanu**, lost his self-control from love, 49 (i), 138 sq., 138 n.

Samudda-datta, a follower of Devadatta, 20, 251.

Samudra, father of A*s*va, 44, 302.

Samudrapâla, a merchant's son, turned monk, 45, 108–12.

Samudravi*g*aya, father of Arish*t*anemi, 22, 276; 45, 112.

Sa*m*varga-knowledge, or S.-vidyâ, 34, 224–6; 38, 19, 196.

Sa*m*varta, though not following the duties of Â*s*ramas, became a great Yogin, 38, 315; 48, 704.

*S*a*m***vatya**, quoted by Â*s*valâyana, 29, 257, 257 n.

Sa*m*yadvâma, a name of the highest Self, 34, 125, 128, 130; 48, 272.

Samyaksambodhi of Buddhism, and knowledge of the Self in the Upanishads, 15, lii.

Sa*m*yamana, *see* Hell (*a*).

*S*amyu Bârhaspatya, invented the *s*am-yos formula, 12, 255 sq., 255 n.

Sa*m*yutta-Nikâya, Dhamma-*k*akkappavattana-sutta in, 11, 139 sq.; quoted, 35, xxix–xxxi, xxxiii–xxxvi, 56, 194 sq.; 36, 55, 290, 298, 302, 319, 337, 340, 345, 354; repeaters of the S., 36, 231.

***S*amyuvâkas**, *see* Prayers (*c*), *and* Sacrifice (*i*).

***S*ân**, n.p., 5, 135, 135 n.

Sana*g*a, n. of a teacher, 15, 120, 188.

Sanaka, a mighty being dwelling in this world, 48, 90.

Sanâru, n. of a teacher, 15, 120, 188.

Sanâtana, n. of a teacher, 15, 120, 188; = Sanatsu*g*âta, q.v.

Sanatkumâra, instructs Nârada about the Self, 1, 109–25; 8, 17; 34, 166 sq.; 48, 300; is called Skanda, 1, 125; Sanatsu*g*âta the same as S., 8, 135, 141, 149 n., 150 n.; Buddha compared with S., the son of Brahmadeva, 19, 24; 49 (i), 21; a son of Brahman's mind, was born again as Skanda, 38, 235; waiting on Indra in heaven, 49 (i), 53.

Sanatkumâra, n. of a king of Hastinâpura, 45, 60, 60 n., 85, 85 n.

Sanatsu*g*âta, the Sanatsu*g*âtîya, a dialogue between him and Dh*ri*tarâsh*t*ra, 8, 135 sq., 149–94; quoted, 48, 23. *See also* Sanâtana.

Sanatsu*g*âtîya, episode of Mahâbhârata, 8, 135–8; compared with Bhagavadgîtâ, 8, 135, 137, 142, 144–8; commented on by *S*a*n*kara, 8, 135,

137 sq., 148; its text, 8, 137 sq.; its date and position in Sanskrit literature, 8, 138–48, 203; its style, metre, and language, 8, 142–4; no system of philosophy in it, 8, 144 sq.; its relation to the Veda, 8, 145–7; translated, 8, 149–94; S. and Anugîtâ, 8, 227; quoted, 48, 23.

Sanavâsa, successor of Madhyântika as head of the Buddhist Church, 19, xii, xiv.

Sâ*n*avâsî, *see* Sambhûta S.

Sanctity, *see* Ashi Vanguhi.

***S*a*nd*a**, and Marka, two Asura-Rakshas, 26, 279–84; demon harassing infants, 29, 296; 30, 211.

Sandhyâ, *see* Prayers (*b*), *and* Sacrifice (*b*).

***S*â*nd*ikera**, demon harassing children, 30, 211.

***S*â*nd*ilîputra**, n. p., 15, 225.

***S*â*nd*ilya**, his teaching of Brahman, 1, 48; 34, cxv; 48, 679; *see* *S*â*nd*ilya-vidyâ; his relation to the *S*atapatha-brâhma*n*a, 12, xxxi–xxxiv; 43, xviii; n. of teachers, 15, 118, 118 n., 119, 186, 187; pupil of Vâtsya, 15, 227; did not find highest bliss in the Vedas, 34, 443; quoted, 41, 414; 43, 254, 279, 295, 345, 345 n.; complete *S*. fire-altar, 43, xviii, 167, 222, 272, 274; sum total of the wisdom of *S*., 43, xxiv, 400, 400 n.; pupil of Ku*s*ri, 43, 404; promulgator of the Pañ*k*arâtra doctrine, 48, 526 sq.

***S*â*nd*ilya**, n. of a Sthavira, 22, 294, 294 n.

***S*â*nd*ilya-vidyâ**, t.t., meditation of *S*â*nd*ilya on Brahman, 1, 48 n.; 34, lxvii, lxxv, cxiv, 91; 38, 187, 214, 216 sq., 219, 233, 266; in the Agnirahasya and in the B*ri*had-âra*n*yaka, 48, 641 sq.

***S*â*nd*ilyâyana**, quoted, 43, 273.

Sâṅgamana, *see* Ana*s*nat S.

Sañgaya, charioteer, relates to Dh*ri*tarâsh*t*ra the events of the battle of Kurukshetra, 8, 3, 37–43, 92, 96, 98, 130, 136.

Sañgaya Bela*tth*iputta, n. of a teacher, 10 (ii), xii, 86 sq.; son of the Bela*tth*i slave-girl, 11, 106; 35, 8; Sâriputta and Moggallâna as followers of S., 13, 144, 148 sq.; 250 followers of the ascetic S. converted by Buddha, 13, 148–51; an Arhat possessed of Iddhi, 20, 79; his doctrine of Agnosticism, 45, xxvi sq., xxix.

Sañgaya, King, converted by the monk Gardabhâli, 45, 80–8; belongs to the Gotra of Gotama, 45, 83.

Sañgaya, a Brahman who met death for his son's sake, 19, 92 n.; 49 (i), 90 n.

Saṅghâdisesa, *see* Sin (*b*).

Saṅghapâlita of the Gautama gotra, a Sthavira, 22, 294, 294 n.

Saṅgharakkhita Sâma*n*era, when attaining to Arhatship, shook the palace of the king of the gods with his big toe, 11, 46 n.

Saṅgharaksha, author of a life of Buddha, 19, xxviii sq.

Saṅghavarman, translated the Amitâyu*h*-sûtra and Sukhâvatî-vyûha into Chinese, 49 (ii), vi, xxii.

Sang Hû, *see* Ʒze-sang Hû.

Sañgikâ-putta, a young Brahman, son of the Sañgika woman, 20, 125 sqq.

Sâñgîvîputra, n. of a teacher, 15, 226 sq.

Săng-kia-lo-c'ha-sho-tsih-fo-hing-king, a life of Buddha, 19, xxviii sq.

San Î-shăng, minister of Wăn, 3, 208.

Saṅkalpa, Sk. t.t., will, conception, &c., 1, 112 n.; meditation on S. or Will as Brahman, 1, 112 sq., 113 n.

Saṅkappo, Pali t.t. (= Sk. saṅkalpa), aims or aspirations, 11, 144 sq.

***S*aṅkara**, god: K*ri*sh*n*a is *S*. among the Rudras, 8, 88; offering to *S*., 29, 203; n. of Rudra, 29, 256; author of a version of Manu's code, 33, xii; a form of Vish*n*u, 48, 93.

***S*aṅkara**, or *S*aṅkarâ*k*ârya, his commentaries on the Upanishads, 1, lxxi, lxxiv sq.; 15, x; his authority for the text of the Upanishads, 1, lxxi sq., lxxiii sq., xcvii, xcix; 15, xii sq.; his date, 8, 27; 25, cxi, cxi sq. n.; his commentary on the Sanatsugâtîya, 8, 135, 137 sq., 148; acquainted with the Anugîtâ, 8, 197, 201–4, 226; Upanishads referred to by *S*. in his commentary on the Vedânta-sûtras, 15, ix, ix n.; 38, 421–30; quoted by Medhâtithi, 25,

cxxi sq.; importance of his commentary on the Vedânta-sûtras, 34, xiv; his authority above doubt and dispute for the Indian Pa*nd*it, 34, xv; how far he represents the true Vedânta-doctrine, 34, xvii sq.; *S.* and Râmânu*g*a, 34, xvii, xxii sqq., xxviii, xxx sq., xli–xlvi, li sq., lxxxv–ci; 48, ix sq.; his whole system hinges on the doctrine of the absolute identity of the individual soul with Brahman, 34, xx; refers to other commentators, 34, xx; his school acknowledges Vedântic teaching of a type essentially different from their own, 34, xxi; preceded by Drami*d*a, 34, xxii; sketch of his philosophical system, 34, xxiv–xxvii; no tendency among his followers to keep their doctrines secret, 34, xcix; his doctrine faithfully represents the teaching of the Upanishads, 34, cxxi sq.; his mode of interpretation with regard to Upanishads, 34, cxxii–cxxv; philosophy of *S.* nearer to the teaching of Upanishads than Sûtras of Bâdarâya*n*a, 34, cxxvi; translation of his commentary cannot be combined with an independent translation of the Vedânta-sûtras, 34, cxxviii.

***S*aṅkara-bhâshya,** i.e. the commentary of *S*aṅkarâ*k*ârya on the Vedânta-sûtras, translated, *Vols.* 34 and 38.

***S*aṅkarânanda,** his commentaries on the Upanishads, 1, lxxi, lxxvii; 15, x.

Saṅkarsha-kâ*nd*a, text quoted, 38, 259.

Saṅkarsha*n*a, n. of a deity, 11, 267 n.; a manifestation of the highest being, 34, xxiii, lii, 441 sq.; originated from or is a form of Vâsudeva, 34, li, 440; is the individual soul, 34, 440; 48, 524–6; cannot spring from Vâsudeva, nor can Pradyumna spring from S., 34, 441 sq.; proclaimed Mâdhava in agreement with the Sâtvata law, 48, 528 sq.

Sâṅkarsha*n*a, text quoted, 48, 666.

Saṅkassa, n. of a city in heaven, 36, 248.

***S*aṅkha,** a demon harassing children, 30, 287.

Saṅkhârâ, *see* Sa*m*khâra.

***S*aṅkha*s*ataka,** at the head of 159,000 lay votaries, 22, 267.

***S*âṅkhâyana,** *see* Suya*gñ*a *S.*

***S*âṅkhâyana-âra*n*yaka** and Kaushîtaki-upanishad, 1, xcix.

***S*âṅkhâyana-G*ri*hya-sûtra** possibly refers to Mânava Dharma-sûtra, 25, xxxv sq.; Suya*gñ*a *S*âṅkhâyana its author, 29, 3–5; its relation to the *S*rauta-sûtra of *S*âṅkhâyana, 29, 5 sq.; the fifth and sixth books later additions, 29, 9–11; translated, 29, 12–150.

***S*âṅkhâyana-sûtra** (i.e. *S*rauta-sûtra) explains Râ*g*asûya and A*s*vamedha in two chapters in Brâhma*n*a style, 44, xvi; on the Purushamedha, 44, xxxiii, xli–xliii, xliv; on the sacrifice at the building of the fire-altar, 44, xxxix; on the offering to *G*umbaka, 44, xxxix sq.

Sâṅkhya, system of philosophy: Vish*n*u-sm*ri*ti knows only Yoga and S., 7, xxiv; attempts in Vish*n*u-sm*ri*ti to reconcile tenets of S. with Vaish*n*ava creed and Yoga, 7, xxviii; the 24 or 25 entities or categories of S., 7, 287 sq. n.; 8, 368 n., 373 n.; 34, 257–60; 48, 371–4, 530; Vish*n*u is the teacher of the S., 7, 296; in Upanishads, 8, 8; in Bhagavadgîtâ, 8, 8, 27, 47; S. and Yoga are one, 8, 63 sq., 372 n.; doctrines of S., 8, 74 n., 286 n., 372 n., 386 sq. n., 392 n.; 25, 3 n., 4 n., 7 n., 21 n., 495 n.; 34, 28; 38, 33, 86, 103; 48, 355, 358–60, 480–4; Prak*ri*ti or Pradhâna and purushas (souls) of the S., 8, 313, 332 n.; 34, xxx, 301; 48, 282 sq., 298; doctrines of S. refuted, 8, 383 n.; 34, xl, 288 sq., 297 sq., 363 sq., 374 n.; 34, xxxix–xlviii, xciii, 15 n., 237–89; 38, 69 sq.; 45, ix, 237, 407 n.; 48, 354–407, 424 sq., 427, 480–95; *S*vetâ*s*vatara-upanishad an Upanishad of the S.? 15, xxxiv–xlii; meaning of the word S., 15, xxxv; God as the cause which is to be apprehended by S. (philosophy) and Yoga (religious discipline), 15, 264; S. and Yoga maintain duality, do not discern the unity of the Self, 34, 298; S. and Sassata-vâdâ, 36, xxv; S. and Yoga are mere Sm*ri*ti, not of scriptural character, 38, 381; athe-

istic and theistic S., 48, 396; conflicting with the Veda, 48, 426; the Pañkarâtra in harmony with S. and Yoga, i.e. the concentrated application of knowledge and of works, 48, 528; in the Mahâbhârata, 48, 529–31; not to be rejected absolutely, 48, 531. *See also* Philosophy, Pradhâna, Qualities, *and* Sâṅkhyas.

Sâṅkhya-kârikâ, and its commentary Sâṅkhyatattva-kaumudî quoted, 8, 240 n., 258 n., 265 n., 286 n., 291 n., 319 n., 321 sq. n., 329 n., 331 n., 334 n., 337 n., 351 n., 356 n., 371 n., 380 n., 382 n., 391 n.; 25, 21 n.; 38, 429; 48, 778.

Sâṅkhyas, or adherents of Sâṅkhya philosophy: path of S. and Yogins, 8, 52; Sesvara-S. admit the existence of a highest Lord, but postulate a pradhâna besides, 34, xl; are anxious to prove that their views are warranted by scripture, 34, xlvi; S., Vedântins, and Upanishads, 34, cxvii; are in harmony with the Veda, in their description of the soul as free from all qualities, 34, 298; the objections raised by the S. against the Vedânta doctrine apply to their view also, 34, 313 sq.; charge the Vedântins with contradictions, 34, 376–8; are Akriyâvâdins, 45, ix, 237, 316 n.; maintain absolute inactivity of the purusha, 45, 399 n.; Ekadandin or S., 45, 417 n.; carry on philosophical investigations apart from the Veda, 48, 346.

Sâṅkhya-sâra of Vigñâna Bhikshu, quoted, 8, 197, 201 sq., 204, 219, 244 n., 285 n., 300 n., 317 n., 327 n., 332 n., 334 n., 337 n., 338 n., 373 n., 390 n., 392 n.

Sâṅkhya-sâstra or Sâṅkhya-smriti, quoted, 8, 123, 123 n.; 34, 247, 258, 284 n., 296; conflicting claims of S. and other Smritis, 34, xlvii, 290–6; refuted, 34, 132 sq.; the Pradhâna assumed by the S., 34, 158; 48, 414; the three entities (the great principle, the Undeveloped, the soul) in the S., 34, 238; taught by Kapila, 34, 291 n.; knowledge of the S. does not lead to highest beatitude, 34, 298; its use and its relation to the Vedânta, 48, 409.

Sâṅkhya-sûtras, quoted, 8, 190 n., 268 n., 321 n., 331 n., 332 n., 334 n., 339 n., 354 n., 368 n., 392 n.; 38, 429; relation of Anugîtâ to S., 8, 210 sq., 215, 332 n.

Sâṅkhya-Yoga, *see* Philosophy, Sâṅkhya, *and* Yoga.

Saṅkoka, t.t., contraction or non-manifestation of intelligence, 34, xxix.

Sâṅkritîputra, n.p., 15, 225.

Sâṅkritya, n. of a teacher, 15, 118.

San-miâo, chief of, punished by Shun, 3, 41; people of S. dealt with by Shun, 3, 45.

Sannyâsin or parivrâg, the religious mendicant, 1, 35 n.; the same as the Buddhist Bhikkhu, 15, li sq. *See also* Ascetic, *and* Holy persons.

Sântâ, seduced the *Ri*shi *Ri*shyasriṅga, 49 (i), 39.

Sânti, n. of a Tîrthakara, 22, 280; 45, 85 sq., 85 n.

Sânti, wife of Atharvan, 42, xxi n.

Sântisenika, disciple of Ârya Datta, 22, 293.

Santushita, a guardian of the worlds, 35, 37.

Santuttha, became an inheritor of the highest heavens, 11, 26.

Saoka, Genius of the good eye, with eyes of love, 4, 221, 221 n., 237 sq.; 23, 4, 4 sq. n., 13, 30, 35, 37, 42, 48; present at the ordeal, 23, 170.

Saokanta, golden instrument on Mount, 23, 4, 13, 35, 37, 352, 352 n.

Saoshyant (Saoshyãs, Saoshyôs, Sôshyans, Sôshâns), Keresâspa destroyed by, 4, 6 n.; the unborn son of Zoroaster, the last of the apostles, who will destroy Ahriman and cause resurrection, 4, 211, 211 n., 381; 5, 33, 33 n., 121, 123, 125–7, 144, 144 n., 355; 18, 13–15, 13 sq. n., 78 n., 79, 91, 170, 299, 299 n., 369, 417, 444; 23, 165, 165 n., 167; 24, 64, 64 n., 99; 37, 34, 34 n., 260, 285, 355 sq.; 47, xxxi, 15, 15 n., 17, 112, 114–18, 115 sq. n., 125, 127, 156; millennium of S., 5, lii, 235, 235 n.; 24, 15, 15 n.; 47, xiii; his greatness, 18, 21; the last man, 18, 60, 60 n.; birth of the Saviour S., 23, 195 n., 224 n., 226 n.; 47, xxxi; Fravashi

of S. worshipped, 23, 211, 215, 220 sq., 227; 31, 279, 279 n.; son of Vîspataur-vairi, 23, 307 sq.; the Daêna of the S., 31, 124, 129; the Faith of the S. which Ahura will found, 31, 189, 191; proclaimed by Mazda, 31, 266, 266 n.; the S. who smites with victory, worshipped, 31, 309; the Mãthra of the S., 31, 339; Khûsrôî's meeting with S., 37, 225; saying of S., 37, 386; the smiter and developer, 37, 390; the 57 years of S., 37, 405;—the Saoshyants (plur.), assistants and forerunners of S., preparers of the renovation of the universe, the great saints of Mazdeism, 4, 247, 247 n.; 5, 119, 126 sq.; 18, 77–80; 23, 220, 220 n., 270 sq., 271 n., 291 sq., 306 sq.; 31, 250; Ameshôspentas and S. worshipped, 4, 291, 291 n.; 31, 362; are not yet born, 23, 184, 189, 197; revealed precepts of the S. or Saviours, 31, 82, 89; the salvation-schemes of the S., 31, 131, 135 sq.; the saving S., the vicegerents of the Immortals upon earth, 31, 152 sq., 158 sq.; are summoned to the sacrifice, 31, 343; the holy S. and the Bountiful Immortals, 31, 344; the innate thoughts of the S. presented with the Haomas, 31, 350; the worshippers are the S. of the provinces, 31, 352 sq.; use the Airyemâ-ishyô prayer, 31, 390.

Sapendârmad, *see* Spenta-Ârmaiti.

Sapinda, *see* Relatives.

Sapindîkarana, *see* Srâddha.

Sappasondika, mountain cave at Râgagaha, 11, 56.

Sâptarathavâhani, pupil of Sândilya, 43, 295.

Saptaratnâbhivrishta, the 60th Tathâgata, 49 (ii), 7.

Sarah, promised a son, 6, 213.

Saramâ, the two hounds, her sons, 29, 241; mother of Kumâra or Kûrkura, 29, 297; the four-eyed bitch, mother of Yama's dogs, 42, 68, 404; found the strong stable of the cows, 46, 83.

Sârameya, the dog-demon, causing epilepsy of children, 30, 219 sq.

Sârandada Temple (Ketiya) at Vesâli, 11, 4, 40, 58.

Sârangî, wife of Mandapâla, 25, 331, 331 n.

Saranyû, wife of Vivasvat, 25, lvii.

Sarasvat, oblations to, 12, 7; 29, 18 n.; 44, 32; is the Mind, 44, 32, 35 sq.

Sârasvata, his son Po-lo-sa (Parâsara?), 19, 10, 10 n.

Sarasvatî, n. of a river, 32, 58-61; 46, 287; water from it used for the king's consecration, 41, 73 sq., 73 n., 79 sq.

Sarasvatî, goddess of speech, 8, 264; 41, 74, 80; offerings and prayers to S., 12, 7, 260 n., 386, 400 n., 402, 418; 26, 22 sq., 315, 316 n.; 29, 18 n.; 41, 82, 113, 115, 125; 44, 32, 62–6, 75, 75 n., 291 n., 293, 475; the sacrifice-tortoise did not stand still for S., 12, 161; is Speech, 12, 418; 26, 22, 218 sq., 313, 429; 41, 39, 82, 113, 115, 132; 44, 32, 35 sq., 263, 293, 475 sq.; invoked at the ceremony of name-giving, 15, 223; offerings to S. to expiate falsehood, 25, 272; animal victim for S., 26, 218 sq., 313, 313 n., 429; 41, xviii, xxiv, 12 sq., 129, 132–5, 136 n.; 44, 216–18, 300; morning prayer to S., 26, 229 n.; a name of the cow, 26, 415; 44, 474, 476; invoked by the Brahmakârin, 29, 83; 30, 159; invoked to give intelligence, 29, 182, 308; 30, 153; song to S. at the wedding, 29, 283; they have ploughed through S. under Manu, 29, 338; invoked, 29, 347, 350, 378; 30, 19, 142, 151, 253; 41, 38; 42, 23, 32, 139, 173, 454; invoked at marriage rites, 30, 189; invoked for conception, 30, 199; knows the prayers, 32, 221; Mind and S. (speech), the two Sârasvata, 41, 398; three S., 42, 27, 512; divine physician, 42, 389; by the support of S. Vâk, 43, 228; hymns to Yama and S. at the Purushamedha, 44, xliv; bountiful S. grants favours, 44, 63 sq.; is healing medicine, 44, 216 sq.; is the breath, 44, 218; worshipped at the Sautrâmanî, 44, 213 sq. n., 221 n., 224, 233, 241, 243–7, 253, 261–3, 273 n.; helps Indra in slaying Namuki, 44, 222 sq., 232; air relates to S., 44, 241, 247; Asvins and S. heal Indra with

the Sautrâmanî, 44, 249, 252, 253 n.; invoked in Âprî hymns, 46, 8, 11 sq., 154, 179, 199, 237, 377; Agni identified with S., 46, 187, 191; the son of S. proclaimed the lost Veda, 49 (i), 9, 9 n.

*S*âriputra, *see* Sâriputta.

Sâriputta (Sk. *S*âriputra), is to be the successor of Gotama Buddha, 10 (ii), 103; 36, 273 sq.; instructed by Buddha, conversations between S. and Buddha, 10 (ii), 180-3; 11, 12-14; 17, 315-19; 21, 30-59; 36, 331; 49 (ii), 91-102; called Upatissa, or Tishya, 11, 1 n.; 21, 89; born at Nâlagâma, died at Kusinârâ, 11, 238; confers ordinations on a Brâhma*n*a from whom he has received a spoonful of food, 13, 169; ordains young Râhula, 13, 208 sq.; a family devoted to the special service of S., 13, 210 sq.; Ânanda wishing to give a robe to S., 17, 213 sq.; Revata sends a robe to S., 17, 251 sq.; an Arhat and foremost disciple of Buddha, one of the principal Theras, 17, 359 sq.; 21, 2; 36, 374; 49 (ii), 90; 'The Questions of *S.*' in the Chinese Tripi*t*aka, 19, xiii-xv; converted by Buddha, 19, 193-5; 49 (i), 193; a friend of Anâthapi*nd*ada, 19, 216 sq.; appointed to proclaim Devadatta throughout Râgagaha, 20, 240 sq.; is worthy to be an emissary, 20, 261; prophecy of Buddha regarding *S.*, who is to be the Buddha Padmaprabha, 21, xxix, 64-9; his rejoicing on attaining Arhatship, 21, 60-4; legend of *S.* and the daughter of the Nâga-king who changes her sex, 21, 252-4; sayings of S., 35, 70, 145, 237 sq.; 36, 284, 287, 292-4, 299, 302, 329, 332, 349, 355, 357, 366, 372; the ogre Nandaka laid hands on S. and was swallowed by the earth, 35, 152 sq.; was in different births a relation of the Bodisat, 35, 292; even S. did not attain to Arahatship without discipleship, 36, 95, 95 n.; Pu*nn*aka, the slave, gave a meal to S., 36, 146; instructed by Âryâvalokite*s*vara, 49 (ii), 147-9, 153 sq.;—*S. and Moggallâna*, Kokâliya abuses them, 10 (ii), 118 sq.; their ordination, 13, 144-51; S. converted by Assagi, converts Moggallâna, 13, 144-7; S. and M. go to Buddha, 13, 147-51; S. suffering from fever attended to by M., 17, 76 sq.; S. and M. ordered by Buddha to carry out the Pabbâganiyakamma, 17, 352 sq.; the two most eminent followers of Buddha, 19, 196; 20, 154; 49 (ii), 2; animosity of the followers of Assagi and Punabbasu against S. and M., 20, 211 sq.; Buddha exalts S. and M. against Devadatta, 20, 238 sq.; sent out to convert the followers of Devadatta, they bring them back to the Order, 20, 256-9; dismissed by Buddha, 35, 257 sq. and n., 301 sq.; S. rejects a medicine and food offered by M., 36, 36, 288 n.; formerly adherents of Sa*ñ*gaya, 45, xxix.

Sâriputtasutta, t.c., 10 (ii), 180-3.

***S*ârîraka-Mîmâ*m*sâ**, or *S*ârîraka-*s*âstra, i.e. Vedânta, q.v.

***S*ârîraka-Mîmâ*m*sâ-sûtras**, another name for Vedânta-sûtras, 34, xiv n., 9.

***S*ârkarâkshyas**, meditate on the belly as Brahman, 1, 206.

***S*armish*th*â**, altercation between her and Devayânî, 14, xli.

Sâr*ñ*gaya, *see* Suplan S.

Sarpa-vidyâ, the science of serpents or poisons, 1, 110 sq., 115; 44, xxxi, 367, 367 n.

Sarsaok, *see* Animals (*i*).

Sarshapâru*n*a, n. of a demon harassing children, 29, 296; 30, 211.

Sârû, *see* Sauru.

***S*arva**, n. or form of Rudra, 2, 298; 12, 201; 29, 256; 43, 152; compared with Av. Sauru, 5, 10 n.; offering to *S.*, at the *S*ûlagava, 29, 352; 30, 221; 41, 159; Bhava and *S.* invoked, 42, 56, 75, 119; the blue-necked, white-throated *S*arvas, below the earth, 43, 155. *See also* Bhava, *and* *S*iva.

Sarvabuddhasandar*s*ana, n. of a Buddha-field, 21, 400.

Sarvalokabhayâ*g*ita*kkh*ambita-tvavidhva*m*sanakara, n. of a Tathâgata, 21, 179.

Sarvalokadhâtûpadravodvega-pratyuttîr*n*a, n. of a Tathâgata, 21, 178.

Sarvamedha, t.t., 'All-Sacrifice,'

44, xlv, 417–21; is supreme among sacrifices, 44, 418; is everything, 44, 420.

*S*arvâ*n*î, offering to, 29, 352.

Sarvânnabhûti, Bali offering to, 25, 92 n.; 29, 86.

Sarvârthadar*s*a, n. of a Tathâgata, 49 (ii), 101.

Sarvârthanâman, a Bodhisattva Mahâsattva, 21, 4.

Sarvârthasiddha, the Vimâna, *Ri*shabha descended from it, 22, 281.

Sarvârthasiddha, n. of Buddha, 49, (i), 19.

Sarvarûpasandar*s*ana, n. of a meditation, 21, 403 sqq.

Sarvasattvapriyadar*s*ana, the Bodhisattva, who burns himself in honour of the Buddha, 21, xxxi, 376–85; Gautamî, the nun, is to become the future Buddha S., 21, 256 sq.

Sarvasattvatrât*ri*, n. of a great Brahma-angel, 21, 161.

Sarvasattvo*g*ahârî, n. of a giantess, 21, 374.

Sarvâtmabhûti, Bali offering to, 25, 91, 91 sq. n.

***S*aryâta**, the Mânava, and the *Ri*shi *K*yavana, 26, 272–5.

***S*aryâti**, Indra drank Soma at the sacrifice of the son of, 26, 336.

Sasa Âtreya, author of a Vedic hymn, 46, 412.

Sâsân, n.p., 5, 137 sq. and n.

Sâsânians, rulers of Iran, 5, 151, 151 n.; 37, 29 sq., 29 n.

Sasarama*t*a*m*ka, a demon harassing children, 30, 219.

***S*a*s*iketu**, a future Tathâgata, 21, 145.

S*âst*ri, a name of the Self, 15, 311.

***S*a*s*îyasî**, Tarantamahishî, a liberal woman, 32, 358–60, 362.

***S*astras**, *see* Prayers (*c*).

***S*âstras**, *see* Sacred Books.

Sat, Sk. t.t., 'Being,' 'that which is,' τὸ ὄν, the beginning of all things, Âtman identified with it, 1, xxx sq., 93, 124 n.; 15, xvii–xix; 34, cv sq., cxviii; 38, 96, 209 sq.; cannot be translated in English, 1, xxxii sq.; everything in this world was produced by the union of the S. with the elements, 1, xxxiii sq.; is called parâ devatâ, 'the highest being' (not 'deity'), 1, xxxiv, 94 n.; called a*n*iman or 'subtile essence,' 1, xxxiv sq.; produces fire, 1, 93; 38, 20–2; enters into the elements and reveals names and forms, 1, 94 sq.; 34, 267; is the highest substance or subject, the Brahman, 1, 98 n.; 34, 332; 38, 19 sq., 142, 144, 160; nothing is true but the S., 1, 133 n.; what is different from the gods and the senses that is S., 1, 278; *he became sat and tyat*, 15, 58; 38, 25, 167; Not-being and S. are in the highest heaven, in the lap of Aditi, 32, 246; born from Not-being, 32, 246 sq.; Mâyâ cannot be called S., 34, xxv; the thought of the S. not to be understood in a figurative sense, 34, 54; release is taught of him who takes his stand on the S., 34, 55–7; Pradhâna is not denoted by the term S., 34, 57–60; comprises the Self as well as the Non-self, 38, 210, 210 n.; is the root of the world, is the only object of cognition, 38, 396; is alone real, 48, 32 sq.; whether S. and Consciousness are one, 48, 33, 47; affected with difference, 48, 40; perception does not reveal mere S., i.e. Brahman, 48, 44–6. *See also* Entity, *and* True, the.

Sâtâgira, n. of a Yakkha, 10 (ii), 26 sq.

***S*atakratu**, n. of Indra, 8, 219.

Satan, or *S*aitân, a fallen angel, fell from paradise because he refused to adore Adam, 6, lxix, 5; suggests a wrong reading to Mohammed, 6, xcix; 9, 62 n.; follow not the footsteps of S., 6, 23, 30, 134; pelted with shooting stars, 6, 50 sq. n.; evil ascribed to S., 6, 65, 67; men warned against S., 6, 78, 140; leads men into error, 6, 81, 83, 120; 9, 101, 121; fight against the friends of S., 6, 82; wine and gambling are S.'s work, 6, 110; makes people forget, 6, 123, 223, 223 sq. n.; 9, 21; made a breach between Joseph and his brethren, 6, 230; will desert the misbelievers, 6, 241; patron of the unbelievers, 6, 256; 9, 231; the pelted one, has no power over believers, 6, 261; an open foe to man, 9, 6, 166; respited till resur-

rection day, and allowed to tempt men, 9, 8; a rebel against God, 9, 30; tempts Adam, 9, 44; tries to tempt the prophets, 9, 62; leaves man in the lurch, 9, 86; calls the infidels to the torments of hell, 9, 133; opponents of the Apostle are the crew of S., 9, 273. *See also* Iblîs.

*S*atânîka Sâtrâ*g*ita, seized the sacrificial horse of Dh*ri*tarâsh*t*ra, 44, xxx; performed a horse-sacrifice, 44, 400 sq.

*S*atapatha-brâhma*n*a, its two recensions, 12, xxviii–xxx, xxxix sq., xliii–xlvi; its several portions, 12, xxix–xxxv, xlvi; quoted as 'Vâgasaneyaka,' 12, xxxix sq., xl n.; geographical and ethnical allusions in the *S.*, 12, xli–xliii; books i and ii translated, *Vol.* 12; B*ri*had-âra*n*yaka-upanishad of the *S.*, 15, xxx; the vocabulary of the Buddhist scriptures and that of the *S.*, 21, xvi sq.; on creation, 25, 2 n.; books iii and iv translated, *Vol.* 26; its accentuation, 34, 258 n.; quoted, 38, 429; 48, 778; books v to vii translated, *Vol.* 41; books viii to x translated, *Vol.* 43; list of teachers of the *S.*, 43, xviii; books xi to xiv translated, *Vol.* 44; *S.* and Vâgasaneyi-sa*m*hitâ, 44, xiii.

*S*atar*k*in, the poets of the first Ma*n*d*a*la of the Rig-veda, 1, 214 sq.

*S*atarudriya, *see* Prayers (*c*), *and* Sacrifice (*j*).

Satatasamitâbhiyukta, n. of a Bodhisattva Mahâsattva, 21, 4, 336 sqq.

*S*atâtirâtra, *see* Sacrifice (*j*).

*S*ataudana, *see* Sacrifice (*j*).

Satavaêsa, *see* Satavês.

*S*âtavaneya, Puru*n*îtha, 46, 50.

Satavâyês, *see* Satavês.

Satavês, Phl., Zd. Satavaêsa, n. of a constellation, 5, 12, 13 n.; western chieftain of constellations, 5, 12, 21; 24, 109, 109 n., 131; the Gulf of S., 5, 43 sq., 43 n.; revolves round Hûgar, 5, 89 sq., 90 n.; powerful S. worshipped, 23, 9, 16, 92, 109; makes the waters flow and the plants grow, 23, 96, 96 n., 101, 190 sq.

*S*atayâtu, epithet of Vasish*th*a, 14, xii, 140.

Sati, Pali t.t., mindfulness, 11, 145.

Satippa*tth*ânâ, Pali t.t., four Earnest Meditations, 11, 62 n.

Sâtrâ*g*ita, *see* *S*atânîka S.

Sâtrâsâha, *see* *So*n*a* S.

*S*atru, n. of a demon harassing infants, 29, 296; 30, 211.

Sattambaka *K*etiya, at Vesâli, 11, 40, 58.

Sattapa*nn*i cave at Râ*g*agaha, 11, 56 sq.

Sattee, *see* Widows (self-immolation of).

Satthâ, *see* Teacher.

Sattra, *see* Sacrifice (*j*).

Sattva, Sk. t.t., Internal organ, 34, 122 sq., 161; Goodness, *see* Qualities.

*S*atvâharân, to be corrected to Shat*r*o-ayârân, 37, xlvi sq.

Sâtvata doctrine, its purport is to teach the worship of Vâsudeva, 48, 529.

Satvat-Matsyas, n. of a people, 1, 300.

Satvats, Bharata seized the horse of the, 44, 401.

Sâtvata-sa*m*hitâ quoted, 48, 525.

Satvavat, worshipped at the Tarpa*n*a, 30, 244.

Satya, Sk. t.t., the true, the real, Âtman identified with it, 1, xxx sq., xxxiii, 130; 15, 311; *see* True (the), *and* Truth; one of the Heavens, *see* Satyaloka.

Satyabhedavâda, t.t. for the teaching of Au*d*ulomi, 34, 278 n.

Satyakâma *G*âbâla, taught by Gautama as to Brahman, 1, 60–4, 75; 15, 157, 308; 34, cv, 228; 48, 311, 313, 343; son of a female slave, 1, 60; teacher of Upako*s*ala, 1, 64; pupil of *G*ânaki Âyasthû*n*a, 15, 214; a Brâhma*n*a, 25, 403 n.; quoted on ritual, 44, 392.

Satyakâma, *S*aivya teacher, 15, 271, 281.

Sâtyaki, n. of a hero, 8, 39.

Satyaloka, or world of the (lower) Brahman, 8, 234 n.; 34, 181.

Satyâshâ*dh*a Hira*n*yake*s*in, *see* Hira*n*yake*s*in.

Satya*s*ravas, worshipped at the Tarpa*n*a, 30, 244.

Satyavâha Bhâradvâ*g*a, Aṅgir told the knowledge of Brahman to, 15, 27.

Satyavakas Râthîtara, n. of a teacher, 15, 51.
Satyayagña Paulushi, n.p., 1, 84, 86; 26, 2, 2 n.; Prâkînayogya, 43, 393 sq.
Sâtyayagñi, *see* Somasushma S.
Sâtyâyana, honoured as teacher, 29, 141.
Sâtyâyani, quoted, 43, 21, 363.
Sâtyâyanins, quoted, 48, 726.
Sâu, prince, flees to escape the danger of being made ruler of Yüeh, 40, 151 sq.
Saubhara, *see* Pathi S.
Saubhari, a being endowed with special powers, 48, 331, 447.
Sâudâ, wife of Mohammed, 6, xxix.
Saudâmanî, the lightning so called, 45, 113.
Saudhanî Kausikâ, converted by Buddha, 49 (i), 198 sq.
Saudharma(n), Kalpa and heavenly abode, 22, 222, 229; 45, 291.
Saudyumni, patronymic of Bharata, 44, 399.
Saugâmi, satiated at the Tarpana, 29, 220.
Saukarâyana, n. of a teacher, 15, 186, 186 n.
Saukeya Prâkînayogya, instructed by Uddâlaka Âruni, 29, 58 sq. n.; 44, 79–85.
Saul (Tâlût), chosen by God to be king of Israel, 6, 37 sq.
Saulbâyana, *see* Udanka S.
Saulvâyana, n. of a priest, 44, 61 sq.
Saumapa Mânutantavya, n. of two teachers on ritual, 30, 28 n.; 44, 392.
Saumya, a Ganadhara of Pârsva, 22, 274.
Saunaka, author of last books of Aitareya-âranyaka, 1, xciii, xcv sq.; teacher S. Kâpeya, 1, 58 sq.; 34, 226; 48, 342; householder S. asks Angiras for the knowledge of Brahman, 15, 27; 48, 284; in a line of teachers, 15, 118 n.; quoted, 25, xxvi sq., 78; 29, 253, 259; 34, 213; 48, 101, 758; works of S. and Âsvalâyana, 29, 153–8; satiated at the Tarpana, 29, 220; S. Svaidâyana fights the priest Uddâlaka Âruni in a disputation, 44, 50–6. *See also* Âsvalâyana *S.*, Atidhanvan *S.*, *and* Indrota *S.*
Saunaka-smriti based on Grihya-sûtra, 25, xxii.
Saunaki, worshipped at the Tarpana, 29, 123.
Saunakîputra, n. of teacher, 15, 224 n.
Saundikeya, n. of a demon harassing infants, 29, 296.
Saungha, n.p., 23, 218.
Saungîputra, n.p., 15, 225.
Saunu (?), established on the throne of Suddhodana, 49 (i), 199 sq.
Saurâshtrikâ Sâkhâ of the Mânava Gana, 22, 292.
Sauripura, Arishtanemi born at, 22, 276.
Saurpanâyya, n. of a teacher, 15, 118 n., 186 n.
Sâuru, or Saurva, or Sârû, or Sôvar, n. of an arch-demon, 4, lii, 139, 139 n., 224; 5, 10, 10 n.; 18, 319, 319 n.; the Indian Sarva or Siva, 4, lii sq.; opposed to wearing the sacred girdle, 37, 182, 182 n.
Sauryapura, Vasudeva and Samudravigaya, kings of, 45, 112, 112 n.
Sauryâyanin Gârgya, n. of a sage, 15, 271, 279.
Sausromateya, *see* Ashâdhi S.
Sautaptikâ Sâkhâ of the Uttarabalissaha Gana, 22, 290.
Sautasomî, converted by Buddha, 49 (i), 198 sq.
Sautrâmanî, *see* Sacrifices (*j*).
Sautrântikas, a school of Buddhists, Realists, 34, 401 n.; 48, 510.
Sauyâmi, worshipped at the Tarpana, 29, 123.
Savahis, worshipped, 31, 349.
Sâvaka, Pali t.t., a follower or disciple of Buddha, 10 (ii), x, 63–5.
Savana, *see* Sacrifice (*i*).
Savanghavâk and Erenavâk, daughters of Yima, ravished by Azi Dahâk, 23, 62, 62 n.; delivered by Thraêtaona, 23, 113, 255, 277.
Sâvanghi and Vîsya, the holy and masters of holiness, 23, 23, 23 n.; worshipped, 31, 196, 196 n., 201 sq., 204, 207, 209, 212, 215, 219, 223, 254, 367, 379 sq.
Sâvar, demon, 5, 106 sq.; smitten by Shatvaîrô, 5, 128.
Savara, a city of outcasts, 35, 267.

Sâvatthî (Pali), Sk. *S*râvastî, n. of a great town in Kosala, where Buddha often dwelt, 10 (ii), 17, 20, 43, 48, 62, 72, 118, 131, 184, 186–8; 11, 99, 210, 223, 247, 296; 13, 210 sq., 302, 325 sq.; 19, 213, 218; 36, 247; on the A*k*iravatî, 11, 167 n.; Buddha at S. in the *G*etavana, 17, 24, 36, 41, 76, 143, 146 sqq., 216, 314 sqq., 329, 351, 363, 377, 384, 397; 20, 1, 130, 191, 272, 299, 335, 388; 49 (ii), 89–91, 89 n., 111 sq.; Mahâvîra at S., 22, 264; Ke*s*î and Gautama at S., 45, 120.

Sâvayasa, *see* Âshâ*dh*a S.

Saviour, *see* Buddha (*j*), *and* Saoshya*n*t.

Savit*ri*, god.

(*a*) Mythological character of S.
(*b*) Worship of S.

(*a*) MYTHOLOGICAL CHARACTER OF S.

The food of the divine S., 1, 76; the Brahman (priest) of the gods, 12, 6 sq.; the impeller of the gods, 12, 16, 21, 42, 52 sq., 76 sq., 134, 184 sq., 211, 213, 215, 337, 356, 386, 418; 26, 45, 66, 129 sq., 136, 141, 167, 170, 181, 213, 221, 232, 239, 435 sq.; 41, 2, 4 sq., 23, 25 sq., 39, 53, 61, 69, 82, 84, 109, 109 n., 113, 115, 136, 193, 201, 214, 244; 42, 221; 44, 462; the golden-handed, 12, 32, 40; 42, 168; God S. bakes the sacrificial cake, 12, 46, 46 n.; 'S.'s arms,' 12, 92; Varu*n*a's noose bound by Gracious S., 12, 262 n.; is Pra*g*âpati, the intermediate progenitor, 12, 386; 44, 174; brought Agni above the earth, 15, 238; the eternal, the adorable light of S., 15, 253; etymology of S., 15, 310; a name of the Self, 15, 311; dwells in time, 15, 317; bestower of wealth, 26, 45; 44, 63; represents cattle, 26, 49; is the sun, 26, 50, 358; 41, 61, 193, 195, 223, 273; 43, 305; to him belongs the western region, 26, 50; is all the seasons, 26, 358; Pra*g*âpati has created, S. shaped the embryo, 29, 45; wisdom raised by S., 29, 50; has shaven the beard of Soma and Varu*n*a, 29, 56, 185, 302; 30, 217; 'at the impulse of god S.,' 29, 63, 280; 30, 232, 241; 43, 228; 44, 253 n., 258, 449, 474; gives the bride to the husband, 29, 282; 30, 189; governs one of the seasons, 29, 343; where S. dwells, 30, 218; after having for thousands of yugas performed the office of watching over these worlds, S. enjoys the condition of release in which he neither rises nor sets, 38, 236; Agni is like S., 41, 325; 46, 32, 88, 90, 115, 340; one of the divine purohitas, 42, 79; in a list of gods, 42, 80; conquered this light, 42, 85; his daughter Sûryâ, 42, 95, 503; S. and Agni envelop the sun, 42, 210; 'May I, like S., be lovely,' 42, 212; brown horse of S., 42, 422; share of S. and lordship of B*ri*haspati, 43, 69; the sun-rayed, golden-haired, 43, 195; enjoyed by all men, 43, 203; quickens, 43, 249; distributes the immortal element among creatures, 43, 322; connected with the rainy season, 44, 247; healed the form of Indra, 44, 252; is this earth, 44, 284; leads the sacrificial horse to the heavenly world, 44, 319; 48, 599; is fair-fingered, 44, 358; ever helpful, friend of the house, 44, 381; speeds the sacrifice, 44, 409; inspires to prayers, 44, 409; vouchsafes a place in the earth for the deceased man's bones, 44, 431; purifies the burial-place, 44, 432; Agni united with S., 44, 469 sq.; wind identical with S., 44, 480; accompanied by the *Ri*bhus, Vibhus, and Vâ*g*as, 44, 480; Agni is the god S., 46, 187; has sent his light upwards (so that the sun rises), 46, 356, 358.

(*b*) WORSHIP OF S.

Prayers to S., S. invoked for food, &c., 1, 21; 12, 188; 14, 250; 15, 312; 26, 17 sq., 376, 435; 29, 26, 66 sq., 163, 198, 274, 286, 301 sq., 378 sq., 398; 30, 19, 33, 61, 81, 142, 188, 204, 253; 41, 18, 38, 244 sq.; 42, 48 sq., 54, 109, 123, 140, 143, 149, 160; 44, 64; offerings and prayers to S., 12, 56–8, 386, 402, 418; 14, 803; 25, 152; 26, 24, 24 n., 49, 66 sq., 129 sq.; 30, 68, 244; 41, 4 sq., 61, 82, 113, 115, 125, 136 sq.; 43, 266, 347; 44, xlii, 62–6, 75, 75 n., 77 n.,

206, 221 sq., 221 n., 260 sq., 263 sq., 409, 433, 462, 464; verses in praise of S., 15, 238–41; the Soma made over to S. for protection, 26, 160; animal victim for S., 26, 221; morning prayer to S., 26, 232; 46, 38 sq.; Soma libations for S., 26, 356–9; 41, 251; invoked at the Upanayana, 29, 64, 188; 30, 66, 68, 150 sq.; student given in charge to S., 29, 90, 231, 306, 401; 30, 66; 44, 86; pupils studying Âranyaka texts look at S., the Sun, 29, 145; invoked to give intelligence to the new-born child, 29, 182; invoked to bestow insight, 29, 308; study of Veda interrupted on the day sacred to S., 30, 78 sq.; Soma libations to S. Satyaprasava, S. Prasavitri, S. Âsavitri, 41, 69, 71; 44, 34 n., 284 n., 355–8; the Sâvitra libations at the building of the fire-altar, 41, 190–6; every mortal seeks the friendship of S., the divine Guide, 41, 251; invoked to promote virility, 42, 32; invoked for a husband, 42, 95; invoked at the consecration of a king, 42, 111; deity of Ushnih metre, 43, 330; worshipped at the Asvamedha, 44, 280, 283–5, 286 n., 355–8, 364, 371 n.; invited to the sacrifice together with Agni, 46, 281.

Sâvitrî or Gâyatrî, i.e. the verse Rig-veda III, 62, 10 addressed to the god Savitri, is learnt for the sake of all the three Vedas, 2, 2; 25, 149, 149 n.; recited at the initiation rite, hence 'S.' also used in the sense of 'upanayana,' or 'initiation,' 2, 176, 176 n.; 7, 119, 127, 179; 14, 58; recitation of the S. at rites, 2, 184, 184 n.; 7, 101; 15, 213; 29, 120; merit of muttering it, 7, 182–4, 265; is the first of all branches of learning, 8, 353, 353 n.; Buddha about the Sâvitti (= S.) of the Brâhmanas, 10 (ii), xiii, xiii n., 75, 105; 17, 134; is the mother at the 'second birth,' i.e. initiation, 14, 9; 25, 61; ceremony of 'entering the S.' performed on entering the order of ascetics, 14, 274, 274 n.; deified and worshipped, 14, 308; 29, 219, 221; 30, 244; teaching the S., 15, 197 sq.; 29, 66 sq., 190, 193, 306, 402; 30, 67, 154 sq., 273; 44, 87–90; worship of Sun and Breath with the S., 15, 306, 309 sq.; Sûryâ S., or Ushas, 42, 661. *See also* Initiation.

Sâyakâyana, *see* Syâparna S.

Sayampabhas, gods, 10 (ii), 66.

Sâyana, his commentaries on the Upanishads, 1, lxxi; as a student of law, 25, xlix sq.

Sayha, n.p., 36, 18.

Sâyuzdri, father of Ashavazdah and Thrita, 23, 71, 212.

Sayyambha, n. of a Sthavira, 22, 287.

Scepticism (natthikaditthi), sin of, 10 (ii), 41; syâdvâda or s., 34, 431. *See also* Faith.

Schism, *see* Heretics, *and* Samgha.

Scholar, Confucius describes the character and style of life of a, 27, 51 sq.; 28, 402–10. *See also* Knowledge.

Schools, *see* Instruction.

Sciences (branches of knowledge), enumeration of, 1, 109–11, 110 n., 115; 2, xxvii; 8, 315; 15, 27, 111, 153, 184; 22, 221, 282; 25, 131 sq. and n.; 35, 6, 6 n.; 48, 284; Arthasâstra, the knowledge which Sûdras and women possess, 2, xxxii, 171, 171 n.; ministers are told to study antiquity as a preparation for entering on their duties, 3, 229 sq.; ascetic shall not try to get alms by casuistry and expositions of the Sâstras, 14, 48; which are required of members of a legal assembly, 14, 143 sq.; brought forth from Brahman, 15, 111, 184; which are to be studied by a king, 25, xxxvi sq., 222; arts and s. practised by Brahmans, 35, 247 sq.; texts on snake-science, demonology and magic art related at the horse-sacrifice, 44, xxxi; weak Sramanas have recourse to worldly s., 45, 266; which teach the destruction of living beings, 45, 298; s. of astrology and divination, 45, 317. *See also* Knowledge, Sacred Books, *and* Vedângas.

Scribes or Kâyasthas, *see* Castes (*a*).

Scripture, ordinances of, 8, 117–20; Kâsyapa had learnt the S. relating to all duties, 8, 231; quoted as authority, 8, 239, 314; oral tradition must harmonize with S. to be authoritative, 11, 67–70; allows

argumentation, 34, 17; S. and intuition as means of knowledge, 34, 18; Brahman the source of S., 34, 19–22; the means of knowing Brahman, 34, 20–47, 288, 350–2, 355; 38, 339; 48, 161–74, 255; aims at action, 34, 20 sq.; not the source of Brahman, 34, 22; because it is directly stated in S. therefore Brahman is the cause of the world, 34, 61–4, 306, 317; intuition vouched for by S., 34, 101 sq.; nowhere makes statements regarding the individual soul, 34, 160; Brahman is the special topic of S., 34, 160, 265 sq.; 48, 174–200, 255 sq.; in order to be authoritative, is independent of anything else, 34, 203; Smr*i*ti depends on S., 34, 203, 440; may sometimes have to be taken in a secondary sense, 34, 318; its authoritativeness denied by the Bauddhas, 34, 412; the production of the omniscient Lord, and omniscience of the Lord based on S., 34, 437; our only authority on supersensuous things, 38, 4; 48, 426; our knowledge of what is duty and the contrary of duty depends entirely on S., 38, 131; ceases to be valid when true knowledge springs up, 38, 340; is of greater force than Perception, 48, 24–6, 30; rests on endless unbroken tradition, 48, 25 sq.; how scriptural texts are to be reconciled, 48, 26 sq., 138–45; not stronger than Perception, 48, 73–8; is more loving than even a thousand parents, 48, 204, 662; aims at comforting the soul afflicted by pain, 48, 216; enjoins meditation, 48, 252; Smr*i*ti, when contradicted by S., is of no account, 48, 408; on which its authoritative character depends, 48, 414; the highest authority among the means of knowledge, 48, 435, 473 sq.; authority of S., Smr*i*ti, Itihâsa, and Purâ*n*a, 48, 460, 751. *See also* Sacred Books, *S*ruti, Tipi*t*aka, Upanishads, *and* Veda.

Sea, going to, a custom peculiar to the north, 14, 146; s. voyages forbidden, 14, 217, 217 n.; 25, 105; is the kin and birthplace of the horse, 15, 74; 43, 401; flow and ebb, 18, 89; merchants trading by s., 25, 282, 282 n.; the s., the child of the reed, worshipped, 29, 127; is the womb of the waters, 41, 416; expiatory oblation to the S., 44, 211. *See also* Ocean.

Seasons, speculations on the, 1, 25, 30 sq.; year has six s., 1, 186; 12, 62, 198, 281, 309, 321, 368, 421, 435; 26, 101, 109, 166, 248, 289, 294, 383, 408; 41, 31, 124, 206, 220, 244, 269, 271, 351; 43, 64 sq., 96, 228, 318–20, 322; 44, 88, 154, 168, 246 sq., 287, 323, 402, 406, 431; moon, the ordainer of the s., 1, 274, 274 n.; the departed says: I am a season, and the child of the s., 1, 275, 278; regulation of the s. for agriculture by Yâo, 3, 32–4; the five elements that regulate the s., 3, 77, 77 n.; winter created by Angra Mainyu, by the Daêvas, 4, 4, 10, 224; seven months of summer, and five of winter, 4, 260; spring, best of s., 8, 91, 91 n.; have winter as the first, 8, 352, 352 n.; worshipped, 12, 79 sq.; 23, 5, 14, 36–8, 49, 52; 28, 203; 31, 198, 210 sq., 216 sq., 220, 225, 336, 339; 44, 142; cause living beings to be produced, and plants to ripen, 12, 92; five s. in the year, 12, 98, 98 n., 142, 144, 192, 280, 317, 382 sq.; 26, 16, 21, 24, 50, 70, 88, 166, 241, 251, 408; 41, 8, 152, 172, 198, 232, 293, 307 sq., 333, 335, 372; 42, 58, 209; 43, 62 sq., 96, 120, 147, 163, 184, 191, 204, 240, 253; 44, 13, 37, 125, 150, 154, 168, 291, 375, 402, 405, 452; Prayâga offerings and the s., 12, 146–8, 159; description of winter, 12, 153; how the S. obtained their share in the sacrifice, 12, 155–7; are the doors of the year, 12, 159; three s. represent the gods, three the fathers, 12, 289, 420; three s., 12, 290; 43, 322; 44, 88, 247, 445; connected with the castes, 12, 290 sq.; 41, 91; 44, 347 sq.; the sun is all the s., 12, 316; the divine coursers are the s., 12, 382 sq.; the fathers are the (six) s., 12, 431, 435; 43, 243 sq., 244 n.; he who sacrifices the *K*âturmâsya offerings, becomes a s., and as such goes to the gods, 12, 444; the s.

and the quarters, 15, 338–40; 41, 91, 120 sq.; where the demon of winter is most predominant, 24, 86; six s. worshipped together with the manes, 25, 115; sacrifices at the end of s., 25, 133; on the last nights of the s. Veda-study must be interrupted, 25, 148; the s. ascended with the sun to heaven, 26, 309 sq.; *Ri*tu-grahas, or Soma libations to the s., 26, 318–24, 319 sq. n., 407 sq.; regulations for spring, 27, 249–67; 'the inauguration of spring,' 27, 253–5, 253 n.; regulations for summer, 27, 268–81; 'inauguration of summer,' 27, 269; the four s. and the four cardinal points, 27, 281 sq.; regulations for autumn, 27, 283–95; 'inauguration of autumn,' 27, 284; regulations for winter, 27, 296–310; 'inauguration of winter,' 27, 297 sq.; invoked as divine beings, 29, 206 sq., 339; 42, 162; 'the cow with the five names, the five s.,' 29, 342 sq.; sacred to Pra*g*âpati, 30, 97; beings produced by the s., 36, 103, 107 sq.; number of s., 36, 112 sq., 113 n.; ruled over by Savit*ri*, 41, 40 n.; Prayu*g*â*m* havî*m*shi by which the anointed king yokes the s., 41, 123 sq.; seven s., 41, 249, 254, 295, 358; 43, 63, 65 sq., 96, 163, 177, 205, 211, 277, 314, 320; by the six s. the year is linked to the moon, 41, 269; the All-gods are the s., 41, 311; the gods are the s., and from them the herbs grow in spring, rainy season, and autumn, 41, 339 sq.; consist each of two months, 41, 386; 43, 29, 48 sq., 70 sq., 105–8, 126 sq.; Madhu and Mâdhava, the spring, which is the earth, 41, 386; by s. the age of embryo and man is computed, 41, 386 sq.; origin of s., s. created, 43, 4, 6, 8, 10 sq., 14 n., 74, 125; 44, 13; summer is the part between earth and atmosphere, 43, 29; by union with the s., Pragâpati produces creatures, 43, 32; rainy season and autumn are the air-world and the middle of the year, 43, 49; winter is the space between air and heaven, between waist and head, 43, 70 sq.; bricks of the fire-altar identified with s., 43, 90 sq., 125–9; come and go, 43, 91; in each s. is the form of all s., 43, 126; the year is joined and everything fits in by means of the s., 43, 126; Tapas and Tapasya, the two dewy s., 43, 126; are on this side of the sky and the sun, upwards from the earth, 43, 128; are deranged for him who dies, 43, 129; ten s., 43, 165; dying man changes to the s. he dies in, 43, 244 n.; priests mystically identified with the s., 44, 38, 44 sq.; forest fires occur in spring, in winter cattle waste away, 44, 45; the sun is the light of the s., 44, 149; all the s. are first, all of them intermediate, and all of them last, 44, 248; the year is the bull among the s., 44, 276; different birds sacrificed for spring, summer, and rainy season, 44, 382 sq., 383 n.; animal sacrifice of the s., 44, 402; sepulchre to be made in autumn or summer, 44, 423. *See also* Festivals, Rainy Season, Sacred times, Sacrifice (*j*, *l*), Time, *and* Year.

Sebâ, Solomon and the queen of, 9, 101–3; ruin of the town of S., 9, 150 n., 152 sq., 153 n.

Secret doctrines, mentioned after the Vedas, as connected with Brahman, 1, 40; Brahma-upanishad, the s. d. of the Veda, 1, 44; *the gods love what is mysterious*, 1, 242; 15, 159; 41, 144, 146 sq., 149, 270, 365, 367, 380, 395; 43, 156, 158, 175, 179, 363 sq., 372, 398; he who recites to another that self which consists of sight, &c., has no luck in what he has learnt, he does not know the path of virtue, 1, 260; 'Brâhma*n*a' in the sense of s. d., 1, 264, 264 n.; restrictions as to teaching the Sa*m*hitâ-upanishad, 1, 266, 266–8 n.; secret ordinances, 7, 11, 11 n.; (Buddha says:) *I have preached the truth without making any distinction between exoteric and esoteric doctrine: for in respect of the truths, Ânanda, the Tathâgata has no such thing as the closed fist of a teacher, who keeps some things back*, 11, 36; 35, 204; teaching the secret penances, 14, 124, 322; only to be taught to a son or a pupil, 15, 267, 326; special ob-

servances connected with the study of s. d., 29, 76–83, 141–50; where and with whom s. d. should not be discussed, 35, 138–41; a teacher should keep nothing secret from his disciple, 35, 142, 142 n.; the recitation of the Pâtimokkha and the Vinaya Pi*t*aka are kept from laymen, but they are not s. d., 35, 264–8; sin of disclosing s. d., 37, 130; Pravargya ceremony must not be taught to any and every one, 44, 445. *See also* Mysticism, Teacher, *and* Upanishads.

Secret rites, *see* Witchcraft.

Sects, costume of different, 7, 202 n.; views held by different s., 8, 375–7; lists of religious s., 8, 376 sq. n.; 35, 266, 266 n.; leaders of many s. dwell at Sâgala, 35, 3; followers of all s. frequent the court of a king, 36, 266. *See also* Âgîvikas, Heresy, Heretics, *and* Karaka.

Seduction, *see* Woman.

Seed, origin of, 1, 205, 243 sq.; food turned into s., 8, 238 n.; body made up of s. and blood, 8, 241; from desire s. is produced, 8, 275; apâna wind, as connected with objects, is s., 8, 338; water abides in s., and s. in the heart, 15, 147; s. of man and tree compared, 15, 150; prayer on shedding s., 15, 216; offences with regard to s. (corn), 25, 394; is produced from the whole body, 41, 349, 353 n.; is white, speckled, moist, 41, 351 sq.; is twenty-five-fold, 41, 353, 353 n.; is virile power, 41, 354; is cast silently, 41, 358; 43, 208; 44, 179; only he who has testicles sheds s., 41, 384; why the s. of the boy and the old man is not productive, 44, 53, 56; from s. everything is generated, 44, 179 sq. *See also* Parables (*f*).

Seers, *see R*ishis.

Sê*g*, fiend of annihilation, 5, 110; a fiend in the house, threatening infants, 24, 294, 294 n.

Sekha, Pali t.t., a novice or student, 10 (ii), x, 182.

Sela, the Brâhma*n*a, goes to meet Buddha, discovers his thirty-two signs, and is converted, 10 (ii), 98–106; 35, 253; 36, 25.

Selasutta, t.c., 10 (ii), 96–106.

Self (Âtman).

(*a*) Knowledge of S.
(*b*) Highest S. or Brahman, and individual s. or Soul.
(*c*) Individual s.
(*d*) The Highest S.

(*a*) Knowledge of S.

Âtman best translated by S., 1, xxix, xxxii; salvation obtained by knowledge of the S., 1, 110, 312; 2, 154; 8, 126; 15, 24; 25, 501, 501 n., 502 n., 503 sq., 508; 34, 98, 167, 250; 38, 285–306; is hidden in the Veda, 1, 110 n.; there is freedom in all the worlds for those only who have discovered the S., 1, 127; *the S. which is free from sin, free from old age, from death and grief, from hunger and thirst, which desires nothing but what it ought to desire, and imagines nothing but what it ought to imagine, that it is which we must search out, that it is which we must try to understand. He who has searched out that S. and understands it, obtains all worlds and all desires*, 1, 134–42; 48, 314; by the S. we obtain strength, by knowledge we obtain immortality, 1, 149; meditation on the S. which is conscious, 1, 305; *he who beholds all beings in the S., and the S. in all beings, he never turns away from it*, 1, 312; knowledge of the Âtman, the highest object, to be sought after, 2, 75–8, 75 sq. n., 154; 14, 47, 261; various meanings of Âtman, 8, 11; self-restraint necessary for S.-knowledge, 8, 51; by concentration of mind he sees the S. in the S., 8, 105, 105 n., 248 sq., 250, 344; through egoism one does not attain to union with the S., 8, 153; knowing the Supreme S. is identical with becoming it, 8, 156, 156 n., 164 sq.; 38, 138 sq.; difficulty of knowing the S., it cannot be gained by the Veda, nor by understanding, nor by much learning, 8, 247, 385; 15, 8 sq., 11, 40, 87; 48, 617; meditation on the S. as existing in all things, 8, 312; 25, 210, 511–13, 511 sq. n.; 34, 171–4; 43, xxiv, 400; 48, 179 sq.; names of the great S., 8, 332; 15, 310 sq.; the great S., the heart of all beings, is resplendent in the emancipated sage, 8, 345; he who understands

the S. which is uncreated, changeless, unmoving, &c., becomes immortal, 8, 367, 391; 15, 14; discussion on the S., by Buddha, 13, 100 sq.; Yama explains the true nature of the S. to Na*k*iketas, 15, 8–17; 34, 248; *the wise who, by means of meditation on his S., recognizes the Ancient, who is difficult to be seen, who has entered into the dark, who is hidden in the cave, who dwells in the abyss, as God, he indeed leaves joy and sorrow far behind*, 15, 10; everything is known by the S., 15, 15 sq., 87; 34, 275; by the light of the one S. everything is lighted, 15, 19 sq.; the subtle S. is to be known by thought, interwoven with the senses, 15, 39; must be gained by truthfulness, penance, right knowledge, and abstinence, 15, 39–41; everything is perceived and known in the S., 15, 110 sqq., 183 sq.; to be described by No, no, 15, 148 sq., 160, 180, 185; 48, 396; *whoever has found and understood the S. that has entered into this patched-together hiding-place, he indeed is the creator, for he is the maker of everything, his is the world, and he is the world itself*, 15, 178; dialogues on the S., 15, 290–317; knowledge of S. required to reap full reward of sacred rites, 25, 213, 213 n.; knowledge of Supreme S. to be learnt by the king, 25, 222; pupils of the sacred doctrines turn their minds to the S., 29, 147; in its primary meaning it refers to what is intelligent only, 34, 56; is not destroyed, but by means of true knowledge there is effected its dissociation from the mâtrâs, 34, 281; how is it known at all if it is not the object of perception? 34, 368; knowledge of S. is self-established, 38, 14; those who do not know the S. are objects of enjoyment for the gods, 38, 111; knowledge of the unity of the S. established in the *S*ârîraka-Mîmâ*m*sâ, 48, 9; S. and Nescience are one, 48, 54; defined, 48, 72; the S., meaning 'cognition,' appears as a thing, 48, 118; represented as a man, for the sake of meditation, 48, 293.

(*b*) Highest S. or Brahman and individual s. or Soul.

Identity of the individual s. with the Highest S. or with Brahman, 1, xxv, xxx, 101–9, 125 sq. n., 135 sq., 138, 140; 8, 156 sq. and n., 193 sq.; 14, 264, 264 n., 278; 15, 113–17, 176, 178–81, 245–8, 290 sq.; 34, xx, xxvii, xxx, xxxiv sq., 14 sq., 30 sq., 36, 41–3, 45, 51, 104 sq., 113, 115 sq., 155, 161, 185, 190, 190 n., 198, 233–5, 240 sq., 249–51, 277–83, 295, 320–30, 377, 381; 38, 30 sq., 33 sq., 42 sqq., 65–8, 73, 138–40, 146, 174–80, 208 sq., 244 sq., 288, 291, 335, 337–40, 396 sq., 399 sq.; 48, 10, 23 sq., 98 sq., 102, 126, 191, 203, 238 sq., 351, 467, 655 sq., 659, 687, 717 sq.; the *S*â*nd*ilya-vidyâ, 'he is my s. within the heart, smaller than a corn of rice . . . greater than the earth . . . he my s. within the heart, is that Brahman,' 1, 48; 15, 11; 43, 400; 48, 315; relation of the Supreme S. (paramâtman) or Brahman and individual s., 1, 84; 8, 55, 92, 103, 111; 15, 235; 25, 486–8 and n.; 34, xix, lvii sqq., xcvii–c, cxxi sq., 37, 59 sq., 112 sq., 115, 118–23, 130, 161, 185–7, 190, 233, 249–52, 277–83, 278 n., 441; 38, 61–73, 138, 149, 173–5, 240 sq., 407 sq.; 48, 98 sq., 141, 257–65, 393, 459, 559, 561 sq.; the living s. suffers pleasure and pain on earth, not the Highest S., 1, 95 n.; individual s. a shadow or reflection of Highest S., 1, 95 n.; 34, xcvii; 38, 68 sq.; *let him know that the person within all beings, not heard here, not reached, not thought, not subdued, not seen, not understood, not classed, but hearing, thinking, seeing, classing, sounding, understanding, knowing, is his S.*, 1, 263; the departed says to Brahman: 'Thou art the S. What thou art, that am I,' 1, 278; individual s. part of Brahman or the Supreme S., 8, 31, 112, 186, 186 n.; 34, xxv, lviii, xcvii sq.; 38, 61–3, 396 sq.; 48, 191, 195 sq., 558–67; the Brahman dwells only in the s. of a man of high vows, 8, 180; God and the s., the two divine principles, 8, 187, 187 n., 192, 192 n.; the S. is placed in the ether, in the heavenly

city of Brahman, 15, 37; 34, 175; the S. in the universe and in man is the antaryâmin, puller or ruler within, 15, 132–6; 48, 101, 132, 226, 279, 607–11, 655; how to obtain union with the H. S., 15, 299–302; the Sun as the outer S., and Breath as the sinner s., 15, 305–12; individual ss. derived from the creator's S., 25, 8, 8 n.; 48, 88 sq.; to attain complete union with the Supreme S., the aim of the hermit, 25, 203 sq., 203 n.; Brahman appears to be broken up into gîvas or individual ss., 34, xxv; the individual soul has Brahman for its S., 34, xxvi, 23; 48, 133 sq., 141; individual s. or ss. (connected with pradhâna or matter) constitute the body of the Highest S. or of Vishnu, 34, xxviii; 48, 93, 128, 130, 132, 138–45, 242, 253, 307 sq., 312, 406, 435–7, 469 sq.; the characteristics of the released s. are similar to those of Brahman, 34, xxx; discussions as to whether certain terms or descriptions are meant for Highest S. or individual s., 34, xxxii–xxxiv, xxxix sq., lxix, 64–289; 38, 54, 205–11; 48, 257–353; difference and non-difference of the Lord (Brahman) and the individual s., 34, xxxix, xlviii sq., 69–77, 81, 114–16, 183–91, 277 n., 278 n., 281 sq., 318–20, 343–6; 38, 68 sq., 149, 339 sq.; 48, 427 sq.; in its activity the s. is dependent on the Lord who impels it with a view to its former actions, 34, lvii; 38, 58–61; imperfections and suffering of the s. are not Brahman's, 34, lxii–lxiv; 48, 406, 563 sq., 607–11; released ss. participate in all the perfections and powers of the Lord, with the exception of the power of creating and sustaining the world, 34, lxxxv; 38, 415–18; 48, 214 sq.; although eternally unchanging and uniform, the H. S. reveals itself in a graduated series of beings, 34, 63; the real, innermost s. and secondary ss., 34, 64–6, 68, 72; difference of soul and Highest S. due to limiting adjuncts, viz. body, &c., 34, 104, 281 sq.; 38, 340; 48, 100 sq.; *the 'two entered into the cave' are the individual soul and the H. S., for the two are intelligent ss. and therefore of the same nature*, 34, 118–23; Brahman in the city of the s., 34, 178; the Lord acts as the ruler of the pradhâna and of the ss., and the pradhâna, the ss., and the Lord are of mutually different nature, 34, 329, 434 sq.; Brahman is superior to the s., 34, 345; different states of the s. and the nature of Brahman, 38, 101, 133–83; bondage and release of the s. result from the wish of the Supreme Person, 38, 138 sq.; 48, 603; relation of the Highest S. to individual s. has to be viewed like that of the snake to its coils, or that of light to its substratum, 38, 173 sq.; Highest S. and individual s. referred to by 'the two birds, inseparable friends,' &c., and by 'the two drinking their reward,' &c., 38, 240 sq.; the light into which the soul is said to enter is the Highest S., 38, 407; lordly power of the other ss. depends on the highest Lord, 38, 416–18; man fashioned from Pragâpati's s., 41, 402; Brahman or Highest S. is different from the s., 48, 98 sq., 209–37, 242, 468 sq., 658; in state of release individual s. enters into the Brahman and attains its true nature, 48, 192, 323, 351; supreme bliss cannot belong to the individual s., but only to the Highest S., 48, 213; the Person within the sun and within the eye different from the individual s., 48, 237–42; only Brahman, but not the individual s. (not even when released) is identical with the world, 48, 261; the meditating s. recognizes itself as being of the nature of Brahman, 48, 269; individual ss. modes of the highest Brahman, 48, 271, 406, 469 sq.; creation results from connexion of Prakriti and s., 48, 282, 490, 492; activity of the soul depends on the Highest S., 48, 356, 556–8; the enjoying s. the cause of the world, 48, 378; ss. are one with Brahman in so far as they are its effects, 48, 391 sq.; Brahman abides within the s. which thus constitutes Brahman's body, 48, 392, 394, 469 sq.; mutual relation of s.

and Prak*ri*ti, 48, 490–5; though all ss. are equal as being parts of Brahman, yet there is difference (of caste, &c.) on account of the connexion with a body, 48, 564 sq. *See also* Purusha.

(*c*) INDIVIDUAL S.

Breath, speech, and mind require the support of the living s. (*g*îvâtman) before they can act, 1, xxxiv; the person in the eye is the s., 1, 67, 135; 34, 124, 129 sq.; the Sat enters into the elements with the living s., 1, 94 sq.; pervaded by the living s., the tree lives, 1, 103; *this body indeed withers and dies when the living s. has left it, the living s. dies not,* 1, 103, 103 n., 140 sq.; 8, 252; without the instrument of the mind, the s. cannot act or enjoy, 1, 112 n.; the ether within the heart is the s., free from sin, free from old age, from death and grief, &c., 1, 127; 38, 247–9; inner s., of the size of a thumb, abides or is hidden in the (cave of the) heart, 1, 129; 8, 192, 333; 15, 11, 163, 277, 340; 25, 41, 41 n.; 38, 38 sq., 45, 175; 48, 604 sq.; is a bank and boundary, so that these worlds may not be confounded, 1, 130; 15, 179, 340; viewed as the reflexion in the water, 1, 136–8; wanders about in dreams, 1, 138 sq.; 15, 163, 165; 38, 49 sq., 56; in deep sleep, 1, 140; 38, 141–7; 48, 205 sq.; pleasures of the s. when free of the body, 1, 140, 141 n.; relation of s. to the body, 1, 141 n.; 48, 136–8; sees the pleasures of the Brahma-world through his divine eye, i.e. the mind, 1, 142; he who knows, let me smell this, let me say this, let me hear this, let me think this, is the s., the senses are only instruments, 1, 142; the living s. is as large as heaven and earth, 1, 185; gradual development of the thinking s. in living beings, 1, 222 sq.; three dwelling-places of the s. in man, 1, 242; Prâ*n*a is the s. of pra*g*ñâ (the self-conscious s.), 1, 299 sq.; the one s., though never stirring, is swifter than thought; it stirs and it stirs not; it is far, and near; both inside and outside of all this, 1, 311 sq.; the s. of man is imperishable, without beginning, immaterial, pure, wise, free from sin, old age, &c., passing all thought, immutable, omnipresent, 1, 312; 7, 82 sq.; 8, 44–6; 15, 10 sq., 340; 34, 79; 38, 29–33; 48, 63; parable of the s. as a charioteer, the body being the chariot, the senses being the horses, 7, 231; 15, 12 sq.; 34, 121; 48, 269, 355 sq.; the self-restrained, embodied s. in the city of nine portals, 8, 65, 65 n.; man's own s. is his enemy and his friend, 8, 67 sq.; immaculate s. not the agent of actions, 8, 105 n., 106, 123; 34, 33; inner s. void of symbols, immovable, pure, free from all pairs of opposites, 8, 160; inner s., of the size of a thumb, is always migrating in consequence of its connexion with the subtle body, 8, 190; how the s., getting rid of nature, abandons the body produced from it, 8, 235, 252 sq.; whence am I, and whence are you? 8, 311; restraining the s. in the s., one becomes emancipated, 8, 372, 392; subdue thy s., 10 (i), 45 sq.; s. is the lord of s., s. is the refuge of s., 10 (i), 45 sq., 87; created by Pragâpati, 12, 296; *the knowing s. is not born and dies not,* 15, 10; 48, 479, 524; the s. of a thinker is like pure water poured into pure water, 15, 17; fate of the s. at the time of and after death, 15, 18 sq., 173–7; Om is the bow, the s. is the arrow, Brahman is the aim, 15, 36; is pure and like a light within the body, 15, 39; inner s. consists of food, breath, mind, understanding, bliss, and has the shape of man, 15, 55–62, 68; *unseen, but seeing; unheard, but hearing; unperceived, but perceiving; unknown, but knowing. There is no other seer but he, there is no other hearer but he, there is no other perceiver but he, there is no other knower but he. This is thy s., the ruler within, the immortal. Everything else is of evil,* 15, 136, cf. 129, 138 sq.; the person who is the principle of every s., 15, 142–5; abides in the Breath, 15, 148; surrounded by senses (Prâ*n*as), 15, 163, 179; compared to the fire by the two

ara*n*is, 15, 236 sq.; wanders about in every body, 15, 292, 295; the enjoyer of *ri*ta (good works), 15, 295; pure s. and elemental s. (Bhûtâtmâ), 15, 295–9; the taking of food represented as a sacrifice of the s. to the s., 15, 312 sqq.; the four conditions of the s.: the person in the eye, in dream, in deep sleep, and he who is above the sleeper, 15, 345 sq.; Buddhist denial of s. or individuality, 19, xxxiii, 204 sq., 273; 49 (ii), 117–44; 'the s. called son,' 29, 295, 298; 30, 211; the soul looks for its true s. in the body, &c., 34, xxvi; the existence of a s. different from the body proved, 34, lxxiv, 424; 38, 268–72; the interior s. is the object of the notion of the Ego, 34, 5; the interior s. is the witness of all the modifications of the internal organ, 34, 9; passages about the non-transmigrating s., 34, 25 sq.; neither joined to the gross body, nor to the subtle body, 34, 28 n.; embodied s. is purified by certain ritual actions, 34, 33; its true nature is nothing either to be endeavoured after or to be avoided, 34, 36; how far the s. can be considered as the agent in sacrifices, 34, 42; the personal s. of a deity may be called an intelligent S., 34, 99; as the ruler of the organs of action the embodied s. is connected with the mind, 34, 107; the golden person is in the embodied s., 34, 112; the cognitional s. is not immortal, 34, 130; the effects of nescience, desire and works, ascribed to it, 34, 130; embodied s. is, by means of merit and demerit, the cause of the origin of the complex of things, 34, 136; has the qualities of Selfhood and intelligence, but not those of omniscience and similar qualities, 34, 158, 268; one and the same divine s. may assume several forms at the same time, 34, 200; words like âditya, &c., convey the idea of certain divine ss., 34, 219; in the individual s. of a dreaming person, there exists a multiform creation, 34, 352 sq.; 38, 133 sq., 137 sq.; though devoid of motion, the s. may yet move other things, 34, 369; relation of object and subject cannot exist in it, 34, 378 sq.; is one and permanent, 34, 424; *as the nature of the s. is eternal presence, it cannot undergo destruction even when the body i reduced to ashes; nay we cannot even conceive that it ever should become something different from what it is*, 38, 15; nine qualities of the s., according to the Vai*s*eshikas, 38, 69; the passages about it having true wishes and other qualities, have to be combined, 38, 247–9; not different from the body, according to the materialists, 38, 269; transmigrating s. as the object of cognition, 38, 288; it is the agent in seeing and hearing, is successively apprehended as the inward s. of all the outward involucra beginning with the gross body, and finally ascertained as of the nature of intelligence, 38, 335; men wrongly superimpose upon it the attribute of being made up of many parts, such as the body, the senses, &c., 38, 336; wrong conceit of the s. being subject to pain, 38, 336 sq.; released s. manifests itself in its own nature, 38, 405 sqq.; love, play, and the like cannot be ascribed to the action of the s., 38, 410; one's own s. is the doer and undoer of misery and happiness, according as one acts well or badly, 45, 104; a wicked s. commits sins, though the individual be unconscious of the operations of his mind, speech, and body, 45, 399 sqq., 399 n.; the s. different from the 'I,' 48, 37 sq., 57 sq., 61, 72; the abode of knowledge, 48, 63; the s. which dwells in the different bodies of gods, men, &c., is of one and the same kind, 48, 96 sq.; different from, but conscious of the organ of Egoity, 48, 182; the s. of non-sentient beings, 48, 243, 245; the bodiless and knowing s. is immortal, 48, 321, 392. *See also* Soul.

(*d*) THE HIGHEST S.

Âtman, the S., is the cause of everything, 1, 124, 236–41; 15, 85–91, 105, 329 sq.; 34, 53–6, 274, 286; 38, 209 sq.; knowledge, and

all that is produced by knowledge, that is, the whole world, is the S., 1, 124, 245 sq., 312; 15, 111 sq., 184 sq., 249 sq.; 26, 420; he who loves the S., and delights in the S., becomes a Svarâg, 1, 124; the Sat is the S., 1, 124 n.; 34, 4 n.; 38, 209 sq.; 48, 89, 203; *that serene being which, after having risen from out this earthly body, and having reached the highest light (self-knowledge), appears in its true form, that is the S.*, 1, 129 sq., 141; worshipped, sacrifices to S., 1, 136 sq.; 2, 293; 15, 88, 90; 25, 503 sq. and n.; the S. abides in everything, and all beings abide in the S., 8, 71; 15, 13, 116; 38, 242 sq.; K*ri*sh*n*a is the S. seated in the hearts of all beings, 8, 88; Supreme S. not tainted by action, 8, 106; 38, 288; the Highest S. pervading the three worlds, supports the destructible and the indestructible, 8, 113; the pure great light which the gods worship, 8, 186; moving about above the waters, the Supreme S. does not raise one leg, 8, 189, 189 n.; the absolute, Supreme S., 8, 248, 310, 367, 394; *he is not to be grasped by the eye, nor by any of the senses. Only by the mind (used) as a lamp is the great S. perceived. He has hands and feet on all sides; he has eyes, heads, and faces on all sides; he has ears on all sides; he stands pervading everything in the world*, 8, 253, 332; above the S. is the Unperceived, 8, 317, 385; from the Prak*ri*ti the great S. was first produced, 8, 332 sq.; mythological deities, the Lord, and the H. S., 15, xxxiii sq.; Brâhma*n*as and Kshatriyas and all things are but food to the H. S., 15, 11, 340; 34, 116–18; the one S. is not contaminated by the misery of the world, 15, 19; differentiation of the one S., 15, 19; the S. is the Bright, the Immortal, 15, 24; is 'the True of the True,' 15, 105; what we love, when loving husband, wife, &c., is really the S. which is everything, 15, 109 sq., 182 sq.; 34, 274; 48, 385–90; *this S. is the lord of all beings, the king of all beings*, 15, 116, 179, 340; 34, 131 sq.; the S. who is within all, is he who breathes (Prâ*n*a), 15, 128 sq.; 34, 230 sq.; 48, 569 sq.; is a mass of knowledge, its nature is pure intelligence, 15, 176, 179; 22, 50, 50 n.; 34, 185 sq., 276, 281; 48, 38, 60, 89, 100 sq.; everything rests in the H. S., 15, 280 sq.; this immortal S. is like a drop of water on a lotus-leaf, 15, 296; the S. being one, becomes three, eight, eleven, twelve, infinite, 15, 304; the S. and the Sun remain as long as the egg of the world, 15, 337; all creatures are woven within the S., 15, 340; the H. S. identified with *S*ambhu, Bhava, Rudra, and other gods, 15, 340 sq.; 34, xxiii, 440; 44, 116; he who abides in the fire, in the heart (breath), and in the sun, they are one and the same, 15, 341, 343; H. S. cannot be the cause of the world, 19, 211 sq.; 45, 343–5, 343 sq. n.; reason or the intelligent S., the real deity of the Upanishads, 21, xxvii; Manu identified with the Supreme S., 25, xiii sq., lvii, lxiv, 512; the world is the body of the H. S., 34, xxx; 48, 227, 295; H. S. is higher than everything, 34, lxix; 38, 204 sq.; Pradhâna cannot be designated by the term 'S.,' 34, 55–60; the individual soul goes to the S., 34, 59 sq.; the person in the eye, in the disk of the Sun, is the H. S., 34, 63; 48, 237–42; is ânandamaya, or consisting of bliss, 34, 66–8, 70–7; 48, 209–37; is *Rik*, Sâman, Uktha, Yagus, Brahman, 34, 79 sq.; the qualities of having true desires and true purposes attributed to the H. S., 34, 110; is free from Karman and the enjoyment of its fruits, 34, 117, 119 sq.; 48, 420; immortal, eternally unchanging, unseen, unheard, 34, 132, 281; organs of action may be ascribed to it, 34, 132; there can be one S. only, 34, 135, 282 sq.; 38, 69–73, 172; the Person called the internal S. of all beings, 34, 142, 171–4, 205; may be represented as the Gârhapatya-fire, 34, 150; the H. S. as the mere witness, i.e. the pure S., non-related to the limiting conditions, 34, 150; is the abode of heaven, earth, &c., 34, 161; is free of the activities of

seeing, &c., 34, 168 sq.; the qualities of being the True, of resting in its own greatness, of being omnipresent, and of being the S. of everything, can belong to the H. S. only, 34, 169; corresponds to the mental act of complete intuition, 34, 172; that after which sun, moon, &c., are said to shine is the H. S., 34, 192-4; the word 'light' denotes the H. S., 34, 195; 38, 407; with reference to the heart the H. S. is said to be of the size of a span, 34, 196-8; is the end of the journey, the highest place of Vish*n*u, 34, 239; is higher than the intellect, 34, 240; the great S. may denote the intellect of the first-born Hira*n*yagarbha, 34, 240; the calm, i. e. the H. S., 34, 241; is the intelligent soul of the Sâṅkhyas, 34, 241, 259; is above all attributes, 34, 249; is the centre of the whole world with the objects, the senses and the mind, it has neither inside nor outside, 34, 276; the S. makes itself, which is possible owing to modification, 34, 287; is not affected by the world-illusion, 34, 312; the one unchanging witness of the three states, the creation, subsistence, and reabsorption of the world, 34, 312; there results from the *G*aina doctrine non-universality of the S., 34, 431 sq.; appears in manifold forms, 34, 440; 38, 66-8; the nature of the S. is eternal presence, 38, 15; is not an effect, 38, 15; is not the shaper of dreams, 38, 137 sq.; the creation of the worlds was accomplished by some inferior Lord, different from, and superintended by the H. S., 38, 206; not to be contemplated in the symbol, 38, 340-2; Pra*g*âpati identified with the S., 43, xxiv; the Supreme S. has entered into the Year (of the sacrificial session), 44, 167; different from matter, 48, 96; *he of whom the Unevolved is the body, of whom the Imperishable is the body, of whom Death is the body, he is the inner S. of all things*, 48, 202; fire is his head, his eyes the sun and the moon, the regions his ears, &c., 48, 287, 289; abides, as Vai*s*vânara, in the body of living creatures, 48, 291, 357; 'not born, he is born in many ways,' 48, 297; bodiless among bodies, 48, 424; activity of soul depends on H. S., 48, 556-8; *who dwelling in the S. is different from the S., whom the S. does not know, whose body the S. is, who rules the S. from within, he is thy S., the inward ruler, the immortal one*, 48, 557. *See also* Brahman, God (*d*), *and* Purusha.

Self-concentration, *see* Meditation.

Self-conquest: *the strong man is he who overcomes himself*, 16, 309 n.; 39, 75; to conquer one's self is the best victory, 45, 38 sq.

Self-consciousness (pra*gñ*â), the organs and parts of the body cannot accomplish anything without it, 1, 296-8; s. or egoism, the feeling 'this is I,' 8, 102 n., 322 n., 333 n., 336 n., 338; subtle elements of material things proceed from s., 34, 376.

Self-control, of ascetics, 8, 48, 126 sq., 246, 366; want of s., 8, 183, 236; energy in s., indispensable in order to reach beatitude, 45, 15-18. *See also* Self-restraint.

Self-correction is the happiness of the small man, 16, 391.

Self-culture: a Bhikkhu who has doubts in the system of S. (Sikkhâ), is not free from spiritual barrenness, 11, 224, 229.

Self-defence, *see* Homicide.

Self-existent, *see* Svayambhû.

Selfishness, grief and avarice come from, 10 (ii), 154 sq.

Self-restraint, *is the best instrument of purification; s. is the best of auspicious objects; by s. he obtains anything he may desire in his heart*, 7, 231; devotion not to be attained without s., 8, 9, 21, 50, 60 sq., 64, 66-70, 103, 127, 182, 250; what real s. is, 8, 67, 168; is mental penance, 8, 119; defects of s., 8, 170. *See also* Restraint, *and* Senses.

Self-sacrifice, *see* Suicide.

Semen, *see* Seed.

Se-na, *R*ishi, his daughters give milk to the Bodhisattva exhausted by austerities, 19, xxi sq.

Senâ (or E*n*â), female disciple of Sambhûtavi*g*aya, 22, 289.

Sena*g*it, is a winter-month, 43, 108.

Senagit, n. of a king, whose son reached final bliss, 49 (i), 95.

Senâpati, Buddha visits the village of, 19, xxvii.

Senika, disciple of *S*ântisenika, 22, 293.

Seniya, *see* Bimbisâra.

Sênô, or *S*ênô, *S*ênôv, Av. Saêna, son of Ahûmstu*t* (Hûmstûv), disciple of Zoroaster, a priest at the renovation, 23, 203, 203 n.; 37, 230, 262, 262 n.; the times of *S*., 37, 406; admonitions of the righteous *S*., 37, 410 n.; a high-priest, 47, xi, 83, 83 n., 85 n.; priestly college established by *S*., 47, xxviii; his date, 47, xxx sq.; an upholder of the religion, 47, 166.

Sensations, different kinds of, 35, 70 sq.; defined, 35, 93; dependent on Karman, 35, 100.

Senses, worshipped at the Dîkshâ by one who lives in the forest, 1, 75; relation of s. and elements, 1, 96–8; 8, 342 sq., 348–50, 352, 382–5; are only instruments, 1, 142; when freed from the s. the wise, on departing from this world, become immortal, 1, 147; Brahman directs the s., but is independent of them, 1, 147 sq.; eye, ear, mind, speech, breath, as five deities, 1, 185; speech is not intertwined with the other seven s. of the head, 1, 196; quarrel, as to pre-eminence, of the s., 1, 206 sq., 290 sq.; 15, 97 sq.; when breath departs, the s. also depart with it, 1, 223; compared to harnessed horses drawing about the body, 1, 233; 7, 231; 8, 187, 386; 49 (i), 22; the deities (mind, speech, eye, ear) bring an offering to Prâ*n*a, 1, 280, 281; the contacts of the s. (external objects) are not permanent, 8, 44; restraining the s. necessary for attaining tranquillity and release, 8, 50 sq., 57, 242, 246, 248, 251, 266 n., 362; sacrificing the s. in the fire of restraint, 8, 61; who controls the s. is not tainted by actions, 8, 64; the embodied self in the city of nine portals, 8, 65, 65 n.; enjoyments of the s. sources of misery, 8, 66; mind, chief of s., 8, 88; the ten s. and five objects of sense, included in the Kshetra, 8, 102; the soul presides over the five s. and the mind which issue from nature and return to it, 8, 112, 112 n.; relation of s. to one another, and of mind and s., 8, 268–70; five s., the fuel for the fire connected with the Brahman, 8, 286; the sprouts in the holes of the tree of worldly life, 8, 313, 371; the ten s., and the one sense (mind), 8, 317; 38, 65 n.; contact of objects of sense with the s. is the source of delusion, 8, 335; the s. and the objects of s., and the five great elements to be placed together, and held by the mind, 8, 341; desire, wrath, &c., are got rid of by restraint of s., 8, 344; the group of s., the bonds of the wheel of life, 8, 355; the ascetic draws in his s. as a tortoise his limbs, 8, 366; the Supreme Self cannot be reached by the s., 8, 367; the Sannyâsin understands the s. and the objects of the s., 8, 368; the different kinds of sound, touch, colour, taste and smell, 8, 383–5; five s., the five fetters, to be cut by the Bhikshu, 10 (i), 86; 11, 181; he whose s. are trained, and longs for death, is called subdued, 10 (ii), 89; s. and Âsavas, 11, 301–3; are different from the Self, 15, 22; eight grahas, 'seizers' or s. and atigrahas or objects of sense, 15, 125 sq.; 34, cxi sq., 239; 38, 79, 83, 369; gather round the Self at the time of death, 15, 173 sq.; 38, 102; nature of s., 15, 329; are our greatest foes, 19, 297; renouncing all attachments to the objects of s., the fifth great vow of the *G*aina, 22, 208 sqq.; five s. known through the Veda, 25, 505; the objects are beyond the s., 34, 239, 244; relation of the s. and their objects is based on the mind, 34, 239; elements and s., the product of Nescience, 34, 281; Sâṅkhyas enumerate sometimes seven s., sometimes eleven, 34, 376; 38, 82 sq.; 'the abode of the six' (s.), in Bauddha terminology, 34, 404, 405 n.; produced from name and form, 35, 79; are not interchangeable, 35, 86–9, 98 sq.; action of s. by contact, sensation, idea, thought, &c., 35, 86–9,

92–8, 132–4; thought and s., 35, 89–92; six doors, the s., 36, 351, 370; though the soul is intelligent, the s. are not useless, 38, 34; are the cause of the perception of the sense-objects, 38, 95; the word prâ*n*a is secondarily applied to the s., 38, 96; all s., i.e. their functions, are merged in mind, on the departure of the soul, 38, 365 sq.; the s. and elements of him who knows Brahman are merged in Brahman, 38, 376 sq.; it is better to satisfy the belly than the s., 39, 55 sq.; classification of animate beings according to the number of s. (two, three, four, five), 45, 219 sqq.; 'Five-people,' the five s., 48, 373 sq.; gods enter into s. as their superintendents, 48, 417. *See also* Mind, Organs, Parables (*f*), Prâ*n*as, Self-restraint, Speech, *and* Touch.

Sensuality, and asceticism are the two extremes to be avoided, 11, 146 sq.; sensual pleasures, *see* Pleasure.

Serpents, *see* Snakes.

Servants, rites to prevent them from running away, 29, 350 sq.; 30, 175–7, 296; there can be no lawsuit between master and s., 33, 234; disputes between master and s., 33, 273 sq.; law regarding master and s., 33, 298, 343–6; warriors, the highest class of s., 33, 345; s. refusing to do their work, 'open thieves,' 33, 360. *See also* Labourers, Slaves, *and* Wages.

***S*esha**, Vish*n*u's serpent, 7, 7.

***S*eshadravyâ**, n. of a bathing-hall at Nâlandâ, 45, 420.

***S*eshavatî**, granddaughter of Mahâvîra, 22, 194, 256.

Setavya, n. of a town, 10 (ii), 188.

Seth and Enoch, the prophets of Sabaeanism, 6, xi; the Kaabah restored by S., 6, xvi.

Seven directors (in astronomy), 3, 39, 39 n.; s.-shrined temple of ancestors, 3, 102, 102 n.; penalty of twice s. head of small cattle, &c., 4, 175; s. pairs of men from Mâshya and Mâshyôî, 5, 57 sq.; s. powers of the demon Aeshm, 5, 108; s. planets, 5, 113 sq.; s. spaces of the earth, 5, 175; 29, 341; 31, 303; story of the S. Sleepers of Ephesus, 9, 14–16; s. conditions of welfare, 11, 2–7; s. jewels of the Law, 11, 29, 61–3; *but see also* Jewels; s. sacred places at Vesâli, at Râgagaha, 11, 40, 56–8; s. treasures of a king of kings, 11, 63, 251–9, 288; 21, 348 n.; 36, 136, 203; s. classes of gods, 11, 154 n.; s. ramparts and s. rows of palm-trees in King Sudassana's town, his elephant s.-fold firm, 11, 249 sq., 254, 254 n.; s. kinds of instruments, 11, 268, 270; s. or thrice s. stalks of purifying grass, 12, 84 n.; 26, 17; s. troops of or thrice s. Maruts, 12, 387, 387 n.; 32, 313, 318; 41, 102; 42, 207; 43, 209, 212; s. worlds, regions, worlds of gods, 15, 31, 35; 43, 277, 314; Agni has s. tongues, s. rays or reins, s.-tongued horses, s. forms, 15, 31; 46, 167, 244, 246, 343 sq.; s. senses, s. lights, s. kinds of fuel, s. sacrifices, 15, 35; s. kinds of food, 15, 91; vital airs (Prâ*n*as, s. organs of the head), 15, 105 sq.; 41, 241; 43, 212, 277, 314; 44, 291; s. kinds of wisdom, 17, 224; *see also* Wisdom; Vîrâf's s. sisters, 18, 397 sq.; new-born Bodhisattva takes s. steps, 19, 3 sq. and n., 350; 49 (i), 6; on a s.-gemmed ladder Buddha descends from heaven, 19, 241; s. Buddhas, 20, 77; ceremony of taking s. steps, 26, 58 sq. and n., 141; 29, 38, 169 sq., 283 sq., 382; 30, 46, 191 sq., 259; s. metres, s. formulas, s. domestic and s. wild animals, 26, 213, 226, 230 n.; 43, 211 sq., 277; s. days' fasting and looser vigil, 27, 133; 28, 240, 292; s. days' mourning after king's death, 27, 194, 202; 28, 143, 164, 373; ruler of second class has s. symbols, 27, 215; king coffined on seventh day and interred in seventh month, 27, 222; s. lessons of morality, 27, 230, 248; s. classes of grooms, 27, 294; s. feelings of man, 27, 379; mourning term of s. months, 28, 46, 46 n.; s. regulations in teaching, 28, 84 sq.; s. dynasties, 28, 204, 204 n.; s. sacrifices and altars for the king, 28, 206; three times s. barley corns, 29, 394; 30,

52, 269; 42, 236; s. priests or Hotris, s.-fold Hotriship, 30, 193; 46, 236, 238, 249, 303; s.-fold oblation, 30, 202, 202 n.; s. human females (serpent demons?), 30, 238; sacred number s., 32, 252; 41, xvii; s. Âdityas, 32, 252 sq.; s. treasures, 32, 434; 46, 363; s. circles, &c., at the ordeal by fire, 33, 109–11, 254 sq.; s. portions of the Buddhist canon mentioned by Asoka, 35, xxxvii sq.; number s. in the story of Nâgasena, 35, 14, 16, 22, 24, 45 sq.; s. classes of minds, 35, 155; earth shook s. times at Vessantara's largesse, 35, 170 sq., 178; s. acts of devotion which bare fruit even in this life, 35, 172; s. kinds of men who die out of time, 36, 163; s. jewels of the Buddha, 36, 220–9, 220 n.; man has s. orifices, 39, 267; s. precious organs in the body, 40, 272; person Pragâpati consists of s. persons, 41, 144 sq.; s. times s. means many times, 41, 241; 43, 209; sun is ekavi*ms*a, the twenty-first, 41, 265, 265 n., 308; 43, 62; 44, 331, 333–5, 378, 402; twenty-one bricks, &c., of fire-altar, 41, 316; s. layers of fire-altar, 41, 358; 43, 277; s. rivers, 42, 25, 375; 43, 211 sq.; 44, 437; 46, 83, 219, 224 sq.; Varu*n*a's toils, s. by s., threefold, 42, 88; s.-fold spectral brood, 42, 124; s.-fold strength of cattle, 42, 187; Rohita has a thousand and s. births, 42, 211; Time with s. reins and s. wheels, 42, 224, 682 sq.; s. honies of the whip (of the A*s*vins), 42, 232; s. and twenty-one in magic and sacrificial rites, 42, 305, 542; 43, 205, 211 sq., 277, 314; s. rays of the sun, 42, 514; from Pragâpati's body the deities departed in a s.-fold way, 44, 289 sq.; s. tribes of men, 44, 401; thrice s. steps or places laid down in Agni, 46, 82, 85; s. kind mothers of Agni, 46, 147; s. young wives (rivers or waters) made Agni grow, 46, 219, 224; s. sounds, 46, 220, 225, 248; the s. strong ones, 46, 237, 239; the s.-headed song, 46, 240, 242 sq.; s. friends were born for the bull Agni, 46, 308; the s. or three times s. highest names of the cow or the Dawn as the mother of the cows, 46, 309, 314; the P*r*ish*th*a consisting of s. elements, 46, 335; s. horses carry the Sun, 46, 356; s. blessings, 49 (i), 170; world Sukhâvatî adorned with s. terraces, 49 (ii), 91; dungeon with s. walls, 49 (ii), 161; s. *Ri*shis, *see Ri*shis; s. seasons, *see* Seasons.

Sexual intercourse between Aryans and low caste individuals, sin of, 2, 74 sq., 87, 88 n., 278, 281; with female friends of a Guru causes loss of caste, 2, 74; sin of illicit and unnatural s. i., penances and punishments for it, 2, 85, 239, 239 n., 248, 257, 287 sq., 291 sq., 295; 5, 210, 301 n.; 6, 76; 7, 134 sq., 138, 174 sq., 181; 9, 4, 89; 14, 104, 109 sq., 118, 122, 213, 218 sq., 235, 300, 319, 328 sq.; 18, 216–27; 24, 71; 25, 106, 317 sq., 318 n., 441 sq., 444, 465–7, 466 sq. n.; 29, 224 sq.; 33, 88 n., 168 n., 179 sq.; 37, 71, 100, 111, 160–2, 164, 177; 40, 241; 45, 428; Snâtaka shall not have s.i. in water, 2, 94; unnatural crime, and self-pollution, are mortal sins, 4, lxxxvi sq., 7, 103 sq.; 24, 267 sq.; forbidden during pregnancy, 4, 177; forbidden with a woman during her sickness, 4, 188, 206; 5, 282; 14, 59; 25, 135; sinfulness of sodomy and paederasty, 4, 269; 5, 384 sq.; 31, 183; 37, 185 sq.; paederasty in Sodom, 6, 148; 9, 96, 104, 120; torment for the sin of fornication doubled in the case of the prophet's wives, 9, 143; forbidden with a woman who has just miscarried, 12, 131; sodomy committed by two novices, 13, 205; violator of a Guru's bed will suffer from skin diseases in future birth, 14, 109; 25, 440; fornication is a vice of kings, 25, 223; betrothal with deflowered bride not binding, 25, 340; sons of pregnant bride or of unmarried daughter, 25, 359, 363; one enslaved on account of s. i. with a female slave, 33, 135 n., 136 sq., 137 n.; forbidden in certain places, 33, 178; punishments for s. i. with a maiden, 33, 179; indecent assault on another man's wife, a heinous

offence, 33, 202 sq.; false evidence concerning connexion with a female, 33, 244; a Nirgrantha should not occupy places frequented by women, cattle, or eunuchs, 45, 74; Karman which results in carnal desire for women or eunuchs, 45, 162;—rules about and duty of connubial intercourse, 2, 97, 100, 102, 113, 200, 221 sq.; 6, 33; 7, 222; 10 (ii), 49; 14, 36, 44, 61, 96, 107, 210, 215, 215 n., 224, 287, 315; 25, lxvii, cxxviii, 83 sq. and n., 149; 29, 124, 289 sq., 385; 30, 51 sq., 268; 33, 368; abstinence from it during mourning, 2, 254; 28, 192; prayers recited at cohabitation, 5, 392 n.; 23, 312; 30, 199 sq., 268; 37, 174, 208 sq.; allowed on the night of a fast, 6, 26; forbidden on a pilgrimage, 6, 28; husband's duty to approach his wife in due season, 7, 176; 25, 328, 328 n.; only allowed with wives or slaves, 9, 65, 301; the Muni or Bhikkhu must abstain from s. i., 10 (ii), 35, 128, 156 sq., 176; 13, 4, 234 sq.; 20, 374; Buddha's contempt for s. i., 10 (ii), 159 sq.; the woman lies on the left side of the man, 12, 10; symbolical references to s. i. in the ritual, 12, 194, 257 sq., 261 sq., 277, 281, 334, 336, 377 sq., 381, 386, 388 sq., 395 sq., 398; 26, 61, 90 sq., 131, 212–15, 318, 327 sq., 365–9, 437 sq.; 41, 15, 56, 171, 179 sq., 192, 199, 211 sq., 215, 219 sq., 222, 239 sq., 248 sq., 254, 349, 384 sq., 391; forbidden after a *S*râddha, 14, 54 sq.; in the night of and with garments worn at conjugal intercourse Veda-study must be interrupted, 14, 65; 25, 147; 29, 117; to take place by night, not by day, 15, 273; one of the four stains by which Sama*n*as and Brâhmans are affected, 20, 389 sq.; unknown in Sukhâvatî, 21, 417; he who is clever, should not seek after s. i., 22, 42; *G*aina monks abstain from s. i., hence women believe that by having intercourse with such a monk they will have a strong and beautiful son, 22, 124; the *G*aina's fourth great vow to renounce s. i., with its five clauses, 22, 207 sq.; husband not to approach the wife for forty days after childbirth, 24, 340; abstention recommended, 25, 177; bathing prescribed after it, 25, 194; three days' abstinence from conjugal intercourse after marriage, 29, 43; garbhâdhâna (conception) rites, 29, 45 sq.; connubial intercourse after the Samâvartana sacred to Pragâpati, 29, 223; ceremony for success in connubial intercourse, 30, 295 sq.; fourteen kinds of impotency, 33, xiii, xx, 166–9; gifts made for s. i., 33, 129; local customs regarding s. i., 33, 287; forbidden after animal sacrifice at the building of fire-altar, 41, 185 sq.; takes place in secret, 41, 229; charm to promote virility, 42, 31 sq., 369–71; charm to deprive a man of his virility, 42, 108 sq., 538 sq.; symbolized by the churning of fire, 42, 346; how the sacrificer becomes fit again for s. i. with a human woman, 43, 270; to be avoided in new and full moon night, 44, 22 n.; stipulations of Urva*s*î, regarding s. i., 44, 68 sq.; the teacher who initiates a Brâhma*n*a must refrain from s. i., 44, 90; is an Agnihotra offering, 44, 114; symbolical s. i. between queen and sacrificial horse, 44, 386. *See also* Chastity, Generation, Impurity, Incest, *and* Woman.

Seyyasaka, n. of a stupid, incorrigible Bhikkhu, 17, 343 sqq., 384 n.

Shadow, meditation on the person that is in the, 1, 305. *See also* Parables (*f*).

Sha*d*vi*ms*a-brâhma*n*a quoted, 34, 219.

Shâh-nâmeh, legends of it preferred to the Qur'ân, 9, 131 n.; legends of S. and Avesta legends, 23, ix, 58 n., 60 n., 62 n., 63 n., 64 n., 66 n., 67 n., 69 n., 70 n., 71 n., 79 n., 80 n., 114 n., 208 n., 221 n., 222 n., 224 n., 237 n., 241 n., 254 n., 286, 292 n., 327 n.; 37, 220 n., 221 n.

Shahpûhar, priest, his son Yûdân-Yim, 18, xiii, 289.

Shâhpûhar (Shahpûr) I, his share in the formation of the Avesta, 4, xxxviii, xlvi, xlviii; reign of King S., 5, 199, 199 n.; 37, 278 n., 414, 414 n.

Shâhpûhar (Shahpûr) II, checked the sects of Zoroastrianism, 4, xxxviii, xlvi sq.; Bahak, his high-priest, 4, 145, 145 n.; Âtûr-pâd, his high-priest and minister, 24, 171, 171 n.; 37, 10 n., 30 n.; son of Artakhshatar, collected Pahlavi writings, 37, xlii, 414 sq., 414 n.; his reign, 47, xxxiv sq.

Shahrêvar, *see* Khshathra-Vairya.

Shăn, Duke Hsî, a marquis of Lû, 3, 337–40.

Shăn, *see* Ʒăng-ʒze.

Shang, books of the dynasty of, in the Shû, 3, 13, 84–123; period of the S. dynasty, also called Yin or Yin-S., 3, 22 sq., 84, 103, 308 n.; ruin of the S. dynasty, 3, 120–3, 216 sq.; conspiracy of Wû's brothers with the son of the tyrant of S. against *Kh*ăng, 3, 154 sq., 155 n., 156–61; sacrificial odes of S., 3, 303–13; 40, 158. *See also* Yin.

Shang-fû, Wû's principal counsellor, 3, 382, 382 n.

Shang Tî = Tî = God, 3, xxiii–xxv.

Shang Yang pursuing the army of Wû, 27, 185 sq.

Shang Yung honoured by King Wû, 3, 136.

Shăn-hsiang, son of Ʒze-*k*ang, 27, 132 sq., 189, 189 n.

Shan *K*üan refuses the throne offered by Shun, 40, 150, 183.

Shan-ming, a Tâoist teacher, 39, 247.

Shăn-năng, 'father of agriculture,' 3, 323, 396, 398 n.; 27, 432; invoked for rain, and against noxious insects, 3, 371 sq. and n.; his work for civilization, especially husbandry, 16, 383, 386 n.; deified as Yen Tî, 27, 268 n.; a primaeval sovereign, 27, 370 n.; 39, 287; deserves ancestor-worship, 28, 208, 208 n.; deterioration going on under his rule, 39, 370; words of Sui-zăn and S., 40, 7; method of S. and Hwang-Tî praised, 40, 28; disciple of Lăo-lung *K*î, 40, 67 sq., 68 n.; a king according to the Right Way, 40, 164, 171.

Shan Pâo, recluse, killed by a tiger, 40, 17.

Shăn Phei, his text of the Shih King, 3, 286.

Shăn-shăng, 'the Reverential Heir-son' of Duke Hsien, his tragic death, 27, 126 sq., 127 n.

Shăn Tâo, taught an erroneous system of Tâoism, 40, 223–5, 223 n.

Shăn-thû *K*iâ, a cripple, and a Tâoist sage, 39, 226–8.

Shăn-thû Tî, a worthy, but not a True Man, 39, 239, 239 sq. n.; drowned himself, 40, 141, 173, 173 n.

Shăn-ʒze would not defend himself, 40, 180, 180 n.

Shâo Hâo, divine ruler of autumn, 27, 283, 283 n., 287, 291.

Shâo *K*ih and Thâi-kung Thiâo discourse about the Tâo, 40, 126–30, 126 n.

Shâo-lien, his demeanour at mourning, 28, 153 sq., 154 n.

Shâo-shih, Confucius his guest, 28, 171.

Shapîgân, original of Parsi scriptures in the treasury of, 37, xxxi, 413 sq., 413 n.

Shapîr-abû, maiden mother of Aûshê*d*ar-mâh, 47, 111, 111 n.

Shatraver, *see* Khshathra-Vairya.

Shat*r*ô-*a*yâr, a copyist of the Dînka*rd*, 37, xxxv sq., xlvi sq.

Shatvaîrô (Shat*r*yôvair, Shatvêr), archangel, created, 5, 10; has the basil-royal, 5, 104; smites Sâvar, 5, 128; genius of metal, 5, 359, 365, 365 n., 372 sq., 372 n., 375 sq.; 18, 434, 434 n.; 47, 161; invoked, 5, 401, 405.

Shâu, king of Yin, became abandoned to drunkenness, 3, 204; punished, 3, 222; cruelties of S., king of Shang, 16, 19 sq. and n. *See* *K*âu-hsin.

Shâu-ling, young learners of, had forgotten all they had learnt there, when they arrived in Han-tan, 39, 389 sq., 390 n.

Shâyast lâ-shâyast, account of its contents, 5, lix–lxiii, lxvii; its date, 5, lxiii–lxvii, 297 n.; MSS. of it, 5, lxiii–lxvi; or the Proper and Improper, translated, 5, 237–406; to be known by priests, 18, 146, 146 n., 156.

Shechina: the ark with the S. sent down to the believers for victory, 6, 38, 38 n., 176, 179; 9, 233, 236 sq.

Shê*d*ak, n.p., 5, 135, 135 n.
Shê*d*âspîh of the Kilsyâkîh, a fiend representing Christianity, 5, 215 sq. and n., 223.
Shê*d*âspô, destroyed by Pêshyôtanô, 47, xii; the ecclesiastical Arûman, 47, xviii, 104, 104 n.
Sheddâd, son of 'Âd, chastisement of, 9, 330 n.
Sheep: rams butting together, 35, 92 sq.; manslaughter by a s. 37, 67; sacrifice of a s., 37, 95, 99; 41, 156, 162, 165 sq.; sin of slaughtering a s., 37, 206; merit of the increase of s., 37, 331 sq.; s. and men, 37, 376 sq.; ewe is this earth, 41, 156; how created, 41, 402, 411; 43, 38; 44, 215; is sacred to Varu*n*a, 41, 411; ram is vigour, 43, 38; vicious ram an unclean animal, 44, 178; malted barley bought with s.'s wool, 44, 219; fable showing that the ewe excels other animals in maternal love, 45, 270 n.
Shemig-abû, maiden mother of Aûshê*d*ar, 47, 105 sq.
Shih, *see* Shih King.
Shih, duke of Shâo, grand-guardian at the court of King *Kh*ăng, 3, 181–8, 205–10, 404; 28, 363.
Shih, n. of a clever artisan, 39, 217–19; 40, 101.
Shih-hû, farmer of, refuses the throne offered by Shun, 40, 150.
Shih Hwang Tî, of *Kh*in, his edict forbidding to hide and keep old writings, 27, 3.
Shih-*kh*ăng *Kh*î and Lâo-ȝze abuse each other, 39, 145, 340–2.
Shih *Kh*î-ȝze, successor to Shih Tâi-*k*ung, 27, 181.
Shih Khwang, n. of a musician, 39, 269, 274, 286 sq.
Shih King or Book of Poetry, meaning of the name, 3, xv sq., 275 sq.; its date, 3, 276, 296; its contents, 3, 276–8; parts of a religious character, 3, 277 sq.; classification of pieces from their form and style, 3, 278 sq.; what Confucius did for it, 3, 280–4; existed before Confucius, 3, 281–3; recovered after the fires of *Kh*in, 3, 285; three different texts, 3, 285–7; a fourth text, that of Mâo, 3, 288 sq., 297; genuineness of the recovered text, 3, 289; collection of its odes for governmental purposes, 3, 290–5; why it is so small and incomplete, 3, 293 sq.; its interpretation, 3, 294 sq.; the writers of the odes, 3, 295 sq.; authorship of the preface, 3, 296 sq.; odes translated, 3, 299–446; form and style of odes, allusive pieces, 3, 322; singing of its odes, 28, 129 sq., 130 n.
Shih Kwang, a music-master, 39, 186.
Shih-nan and Î-liâo, 40, 288 sq.
Shih Tâi-*k*ung, choice of his successor, 27, 181.
Shih-wei got the Tâo, and by it wrought wonders, 39, 135, 244, 244 n.; park of S., 40, 73, 73 n.
Shih Ȝhiû, an officer of Wei, a righteous man and good ruler, 39, 269, 269 sq. n., 274, 287, 295; classed together with the robber *K*ih, 39, 292, 328; 40, 285; came as a messenger to Duke Ling of Wei, 40, 125.
Shin-t'ung-yaou-hi-king, Chinese translation of the Lalita-vistara, 19, xxx.
Ships, a hundred cubits long, on the great ocean, 36, 90; similes of the s., the anchor, the mast, the pilot, the sailor, 36, 297–302.
Shîrtashôsp, n.p., 5, 146.
Sho*d*a*s*akalâvidyâ, Sk., the knowledge of the sixteen parts of Brahman, 1, 60 n.; 38, 233.
Shoes, of boarskin, 41, 102; he who has performed Râ*g*asûya shall never stand on ground without s., 44, 129.
Sho'hâib, sent as an apostle to Midian, 6, 148–50, 214–16; 9, 97, 121; = Jethro, 6, 249 n.; Moses marries his daughter, 9, 110.
Shooting stars, *see* Stars.
Shrine, *see* Holy places.
Shû, Zui wishes to resign the post of Minister of Works to, 3, 43, 43 n.; son of Kung-shû Wăn-ȝze, 27, 180.
Shû, a poor and deformed man, 39, 132, 220 sq.
Shû, god of the Southern Ocean, 39, 267 sq.
Shû, *see* Shû King.
Shui, the clever artisan, 39, 151; 40, 23 sq., 23 n.

Shû-*kh*î, a worthy, but not a True Man, 39, 239, 239 sq. n.; declines to take office at the court of Wû, 40, 163-5; died of starvation, 40, 173.

Shû King, the Book of Historical Documents, 3, xv, 1 sq.; 'The four S.' or Books of the Four Philosophers, 3, xx; an existing collection of documents before Confucius, 3, 2 sq.; number of documents in it, 3, 3 sq.; its sources, 3, 4-6; its recovery after the destruction by the tyrant of *Kh*in, 3, 7-11; its genuineness, 3, 10 sq.; credibility of the records in it, 3, 12-20; translated, 3, 31-272.

Shû-*k*ung *Kh*ien on mourning rites, 27, 200.

Shû-*k*ung Phî instructs his son 3ze-liû on mourning rites, 27, 200, 200 n.

Shun of Yü, spoken of as Tî, 3, xxvii-xxix, 256; 28, 343 sq.; records of the reign of S. in the Shû later and more legendary, though based on ancient documents, 3, 13-15; becomes Yâo's minister, 3, 14; 39, 331; a historical personage, 3, 19; period of Yâo and S., their good reign, 3, 24-7; 39, 359, 386; 40, 183, 279; appointed by Yâo to assuage the inundation, and to be his successor, 3, 35 sq., 38; 39, 315; his dynastic designation Yü, 3, 37; 'The Canon of S.' translated, 3, 37-45; his great virtues, 3, 38; 28, 339; meaning of his names, 3, 38, 38 n.; his excellent administration and government, 3, 38-45, 258 sq.; 28, 302, 343 sq., 343 n., 418; his death, 3, 45; conversations between S. and his ministers, 3, 46-8, 57-62; appoints Yü to be his successor, 3, 48-51; 27, 396; 39, 359, 380; charges himself with his parents' guilt, 3, 52, 52 n.; his anxiety about Hwan-tâu and the lord of Miâo, 3, 54; Yâo and S. the ideals of kings, 3, 118; 39, 282, 319; 40, 120; Yâo and S. established a hundred officers, a crowd of ministers, 3, 227; 40, 171; called Hwang Tî, 3, 256, 256 n.; restrained and extinguished the people of Miâo, 3, 256 sq.; Hwang-Tî, Yâo, and S., their work for civilization, 16, 383-5; his three wives not buried in the same grave with him, 27, 132, 132 n.; made the lute with five strings, 28, 105, 105 n.; his sacrifices, 28, 201; deserves ancestor-worship, 28, 208; his great filial piety, 28, 308; ways of Yâo and S. handed down by Confucius, 28, 326; disturbed the world by his benevolence and righteousness, 39, 139, 272, 295, 295 n.; dialogue between Yâo and S., 39, 190; acted according to the Tâo, 39, 210; a sovereign, and a perfect man, 39, 225; was not equal to the ruler of the line of Thâi, 39, 259; served Phû-î-3ze as his master, 39, 259 n.; instructs Yâo as to what a king ought to be, 39, 338; Yâo and S., the lords of Thang and Yü, 39, 370, 370 n.; the ways of Hwang-Tî, Yâo, and S., 40, 7; when about to die, instructs Yü, 40, 35 sq.; did not trouble his mind about death, and therefore was able to influence others, 40, 50, 50 n.; his palace, 40, 73; Yâo and S. did not benefit the world, the greatest disorder was planted in their times, 40, 76 sq., 76 n.; an example of the grasping and crooked, 40, 109 sq.; proposes to resign his throne to 3ze-*k*âu *K*ih-po, Shan *K*üan, and a farmer of Shih-hû, 40, 149 sq.; offers his throne to the northerner Wû-*k*âi, 40, 161 sq.; Yâo and S. possessed the whole kingdom, 40, 170; was not filial, 40, 173; banished his half-brother, 40, 178; had his Tâ Shâo music, 40, 218; and *Kh*ăng about the Tâo, 40, 292. *See also* Yâo, *and* Yü.

Shû-*r*, famous cook, 39, 274, 274 n.

Shû-shan the Toeless, a Tâoist sage, 39, 228 sq.

Shû-sun Thung, a scholar of *Kh*in, 27, 19, 19 n.

Shû-sun Wû-shû, an officer of Lû, 27, 146; 28, 156, 156 n.

Shû Tan, brother of King Wû, 40, 163.

Shû-yü and *K*âo Wăn-3ze, 27, 199.

Siau-pen-k'i-king, a life of Buddha, 19, xxiii.

***S*ibi**, or Sivi, King, gave away his own flesh or his eyes in charity, 19, 159; 35, 179–85; 36, 378; 49 (i), 151.

***S*ibinta**, worshipped at the Tarpa*n*a, 30, 244.

Siddhânta, i.e. *G*aina canon, *see G*aina Sûtras.

Siddhârtha, name given to Buddha, 19, 23.

Siddhârtha, father of Mahâvîra, 22, x sq.; Tri*s*alâ, wife of the Kshatriya S., of the Kâ*s*yapa gotra, of the clan of the *Gñ*ât*ris*, 22, 191, 226, 228, 239–56; his other names *S*reyâ*m*sa and *G*asa*m*sa, 22, 193.

Siddhârtha Vana, n. of a park, 22, 283.

Siddhas, Kapila, chief among the, 8, 89, 89 n.; praise K*r*ish*n*a, 8, 94, 96; are invisible, possess extraordinary powers, 8, 232, 235 n.; 35, 181, 181 n.; Kâ*s*yapa instructed by a S., 8, 232–6; see with a divine eye the soul, departing from the body and coming to the birth, 8, 239; final emancipation understood by the S., 8, 314; Mahâvîra became a S., 22, 264; satiated at the Tarpa*n*a, 29, 219; pious monks will after death become eternal S., 45, 8, 18, 167 sq.; through the law of chastity, the S. have reached perfection, 45, 77; thirty-one qualities of S., 45, 183; who the S. or perfected souls are, where and how they live, 45, 211–13; souls of S., 48, 198; beings born as S. on account of religious merit, 48, 238. *See also* Holy persons, *and* Superhuman beings.

Si*gg*în, register of the wicked in hell, 9, 324, 324 n.

Si*g*ill, Es-S. rolls up the books of human fates, 9, 55, 55 n.

Sîha, general-in-chief of the Li*kkh*avis, a follower of the Niga*nth*a sect, is converted by Buddha, 17, 108–17; 45, xvi.

***S*ikand-gûmânîk Vi*g*âr** or 'doubt-dispelling explanation,' by Mar*d*ânfarukh, object of the work, 24, xxv–xxviii; its age, 24, xxvi sq.; MSS. and versions of it, 24, xxviii–xxxvi; translated, 24, 117–251.

***S*ikha*n*d*in**, n. of hero, 8, 39.

***S*ikhin**, n. of a Brahma angel, 21, 5 n., 169. *See* Brahma *S*ikhin.

Sikkhâ, *see* Self-culture.

***S*îkshâ**, the pronunciation of the Veda, chapter on, 15, 45–53. *See also* Sciences.

***S*ikshâ-vallî**, in the Taittirîyaka-upanishad, 15, xxvii sq.

Sila, converted by Buddha, 19, 243.

Sîla, Pali t.t., right conduct, 11, 159, 188 n., 189–200. *See also* Morality.

***S*îlâgarbha**, a *K*aitya so called, 49 (i), 167 sq.

***S*ilaka *S*âlâvatya**, n.p., 1, 15–17.

Silence, *see* Mauna, *and* Speech.

***S*ilpa** Ka*s*yapa, n. of a teacher, 15, 226.

Silver, originated from Agni's tears, 12, 322 n.; 'white gold,' i.e. s., representing the moon, 44, 196; gold and s. plates at sacrificial rites, 44, 251, 462; as the priests' fee, 44, 357. *See also* Metals, *and* Money.

Sîmantonnayana, *see* Child (*b*).

Si*m*ha, of the Kâ*s*yapa gotra, a Sthavira, 22, 294.

Si*m*ha, a Bodhisattva Mahâsattva, 21, 4; n. of a Tathâgata, 49 (ii), 7, 66 sq., 100.

Si*m*hadhva*g*a, n. of a Tathâg ta, 21, 178.

Si*m*haghosha, n. of a Tathâgata, 21, 178.

Si*m*hagiri *G*âtismara, n. of a Sthavira, 22, 288, 293.

Si*m*ha*k*andrâ with five hundred nuns, 21, 360.

Si*m*hamati, n. of a Tathâgata, 49 (ii), 7.

Si*m*hasâgarakû*t*avinanditarâ*g*a, n. of a Tathâgata, 49 (ii), 6.

Similes, *see* Parables.

Simplicity: to keep people in a state of s. and ignorance, the ideal of Tâoism, 39, 78 sq.

Sîmûrgh, *see* Saêna.

Sin(s).

(*a*) Definition, origin, consequences of s.
(*b*) Classification of s.
(*c*) Atonement, Repentance, Renunciation of s.

(*a*) DEFINITION, ORIGIN, CONSEQUENCES OF S.

The religious notion of s. in the

Rig-veda, 1, xxii; he who learns that a man has committed a s. should not be the first to make it known, but he shall not invite him to dinners given at religious ceremonies, 2, 75; food of sinners not to be eaten, 2, 190, 267; 14, 69–71; 25, 161–4; created by Angra-Mainyu, 4, 5–9; s. and merit compared as to their results in future life, 4, 270 sq., 281, 281 n.; evil demons produced by s., 5, 113; s. is what is against the will of Aûhar*mazd*, 5, 157; new-born child not to be shown to a sinful person, 5, 322; *whoso commits a crime, he only commits it against himself*, 6, 88; God has only prohibited sinful actions, 6, 140 sq.; causes of s., 8, 56 sq.; 22, 3–14, 51 sq.; Kâ*s*yapa was conversant with merit and s., 8, 232; men reborn in uncomfortable and harassing states in consequence of s., 8, 233, 321; 10 (ii), 47; what is s.? 8, 311; each soul is to bear the burden of its own s., 9, 3, 253; what is s. according to Buddha, 10 (ii), xv sq., 40 sq.; destiny and sinfulness, 18, 215 sq.; he who comprehends the causes of s. is a sage, 22, 2 sq.; results of s., retribution, 25, lxviii, 155 sq.; 37, 45 sq., 68; sinful acts and qualities, marks of the qualities of Activity and Darkness, 25, 491; there is more merit than demerit, 35, 128 sq.; 'your s. will find you out,' 35, 295, 295 n.; misery arises through sinfulness, 37, 35 sq.; abettors of s., 37, 72; pregnancy of the fiend due to certain s., 37, 164, 207; there would be no s. if the soul were not embodied, 37, 200; committed by the gods, 42, 32, 520; disease caused by one's own s. or that of parents, 42, 41, 59, 293 sq.; V*ri*tra is s., which ever keeps him from well-being and virtue, 44, 11; care taken at funeral rites that the deceased man's s. should be restricted or not made manifest, 44, 422, 425–8, 435–7; no s. in a Buddha country, 49 (ii), 14, 40. *See also* Crimes, Karman, Morality, Nir*ri*ti, *and* Transmigration.

(*b*) Classification of s.

Five deadly s., 1, 83 sq.; 2, 277 sq.; 14, 4 sq.; 35, 41; 49 (ii), 73, 192, 197, 197 n.; Abhi*s*asta, one who has committed the five great s., and loses his caste, 2, 74, 79, 79 n., 91 sq., 190, 190 n., 267, 267 n., 275; 14, 69, 119, 122, 182; 25, 64, 162; *see also* Caste (*e*); lists of s. according to their greatness, classes of s., 2, 280–3; 4, lxxxiv–lxxxvii; 14, 4 sq., 296, 298, 313 sq.; 17, 316; 18, 33 n., 230 sq. and n., 235 sq. n., 426; 25, 441–4, 484; 35, 268–70; 37, 62, 62 n., 103 sq., 104 n., 107 sq., 154 sq., 192; 42, 521 sq., 524, 528; 45, 366–77; s., which cause loss of caste, 2, 280–2; 14, 217–19; that cannot be expiated, 2, 281; 25, 469; which are minor offences (upapâtaka), 2, 281; 14, 4 sq., 219; five s. that make one a Peshôtanu, 4, 176 sq.; classification of s., their punishments, and counterbalancing of s. by good works, 5, lx, 239–41 and notes, 242 n., 256, 258 sq., 261–3, 265 sq., 268 sq., 272, 282 sq., 288 sq., 289 sq. n., 291, 294 sq., 298, 300 sq. and n., 304–8, 307 n., 315 sq., 318 sq., 322, 326, 326 n., 334 sq. and n., 340 sq., 379–81; committed in the period of adversity, 5, 202–10; abominable s. to be avoided, 6, 135; those who have done evil in ignorance will be forgiven, 6, 263; *he who destroys life, who speaks untruth, who in this world takes what is not given him, who goes to another man's wife; and the man who gives himself to drinking intoxicating liquors, he, even in this world, digs up his own root*, 10 (i), 61; twelve kinds of s., 10 (ii), 17–19; 45, 356–64, 387 sq.; he who has attained the bliss of the right view is incapable of committing the six deadly s., or to conceal them when committed, 10 (ii), 38 sq.; the s. termed sa*m*ghâdi-sesâ, or requiring formal meetings of the Order, Mânatta penance for them, 13, 7–15; 17, 397–439; the s. termed aniyatâ, or undetermined, 13, 16 sq.; the s. termed nisaggiyâ pâ*k*ittiyâ, involving forfeiture, 13, 18–31; the s. termed pâ*k*ittiyâ,

requiring expiation, 13, 32–55; Pâkittiya offence of reopening disputes once settled, 13, 46, 51; 20, 47, 54, 61, 63 sq.; the s. termed Pâtidesaniyâ, that ought to be confessed, 13, 56 sqq.; matters connected with discipline (sekhiyâ dhammâ), 13, 59–67; Dukkata offences not embodied in the Pâtimokkha, 13, 166 sqq., 174, 175, 194, 196–9, 205, 210, 213 sq., 225, 226, 231, 246 sq., 250, &c.; 17, 15, &c.; 20, 2, &c.; five or seven classes of s., 13, 244, 244 n.; 20, 36; s. committed on the day of Uposatha, 13, 282–6; moral transgressions, transgressions against the rules of conduct, and heresy, reasons for inhibiting Pavâranâ, 13, 343 sq.; which make men impure, 14, 220; committed by torturing animals, 17, 25; which occasion the Tagganiya-kamma, 17, 335–7; for which the Pabbâganiya-kamma is enjoined, 17, 347–9, 355 sq.; which cause the disciplinary proceeding by Patisâraniya-kamma, 17, 365 sq.; (seven) heinous s., 18, 216–19; 37, 148, 164, 206; list of thirty s., 24, 71–3; atonement of unintentional s., 25, xxiv, 439; 37, 39, 148; which make persons unworthy to be guests at Srâddhas, 25, 103–9; mortal sinners cannot be witnesses, 25, 265, 265 n., 268; 33, 86–90; punishments for mortal s., 25, 383–5, 496; Pârâgika and Pâkittiya offences, 35, xli; contradiction as to s. committed in ignorance, 35, 129, 224 sq.; s. committed by those who are immoderate in food, 36, 5; s. on account of which conversion cannot take place, 36, 177; difference of s. in priests, 37, 46; Tanâpûhar s., 37, 67; 47, 54 sq.; aggravated by deceit, 37, 71; of children, 37, 77; various s. due to reverence for the demons, 37, 181 sq.; s. of greediness, 37, 196; heinous s. do not obliterate other s., 37, 197; against the gods, 42, 44; mental s., 42, 163; Buddha and Mahâvîra on s. of the body and s. of the mind, 45, xvi sq.; three ways of committing s., by one's own activity, by commission, by approval, but there are no s. committed intentionally, 45, 243; thirty-three s., 47, 134, 134 n., 164, 164 n.; five Ânantarya s. (which bring immediate retribution), 49 (ii), 15.

(*c*) Atonement, Repentance, Renunciation of S.

S. is destroyed by knowledge, 1, 84, 293 sq.; 8, 292 n., 355, 378; 38, 355; 48, 722–4; doubts about s. being effaced by penances, 2, 274 sq.; reciting sacred syllables and prayers frees from s., 4, lxxxvi; 25, 44, 48 sq.; 42, 44, 163–6, 521–8; 44, 265 sq.; confession and renunciation of s., atonement for s., 4, lxxxvi, 33 sq., 57 sq. and n., 103 sq., 266; 5, lxi, 281, 290, 290 n., 300–8, 310, 354, 363, 371 n., 396; 18, 35, 37, 137–9, 223, 223 n., 231 sq., 236, 384 sq.; 24, 95 sq., 258 sq., 305 sq., 308 sq., 348 sq.; 37, 16, 41, 41 n., 45–7, 52, 63, 68, 103 sq., 115 sq., 146, 167; repentance of s. delivers before God, but not before man, 4, lxxxvi, 28; atoned for by repentance, 4, 135; 9, 89, 187 sq., 208, 291; 14, 176; 16, 163, 165 n.; 24, 308 sq., 353; 47, 170; balanced by good works, 4, 269–71; 5, 350 sq.; 9, 89; 18, 30–2; 37, 336; destroyed by penance, and austerities, 8, 288, 389; 14, 176, 313 sq.; 25, 439, 478 sq.; means of purification from s., 8, 314; 25, 477; the emancipated sage released from s., 8, 358, 372, 394; 38, 353–6; by getting rid of the qualities of passion and darkness, a man gets rid of all s., 8, 390; whose s. are extirpated from the root, he will wander rightly in the world, 10 (ii), 61; Dhamma destroys s., 10 (ii), 64; the fourfold great struggle against s., 11, 61, 63; disciplinary proceedings against Bhikkhus guilty of or suspected of certain offences, 13, 340–9, 351 sq., 354 sq.; offenders who have received punishment due to them become pure, 14, 101; 25, 309; Brâhmanas who perform the sacred rites and study the Veda are not tainted by s., 14, 129–31, 248 sq.; *to commit no s. is better than retribution and renunciation of s.*, 18, 139;

renunciation of s., as a preparation for sacrifices, 18, 166; atoned for by next-of-kin marriage, 18, 424; *this is the advantage of the discipline of the noble one, that he who looks upon his s. as s., and makes amends for it as is meet, he becomes able in future to restrain himself therefrom*, 20, 122 sq.; rules about one Bhikkhu warning another in respect of s. committed by him, 20, 315–19; not to repent a s. committed, is a second folly, 22, 42; forgiven by priests, 24, 289, 353; proper fasting is abstaining from s., 24, 348; no intercourse with persons who have not atoned, 25, 469; penances for secret s., 25, 476, 476 n., 479–82; cast away at the purificatory bath, 26, 385; wiped out with the help of gods and sacrifices, 26, 385; 44, 38; punishment of certain s., 37, 18, 205; harm of unrenounced s., 37, 45 sq., 62; inquiry into s. of relatives, 37, 77; wiped away by the good religion, 37, 154; controllers of s., 37, 194; the best thing for mankind is purification from s., 37, 286; repenting s. is changing calamity into blessing, 40, 245 sq.; charm against the consequences of s., 42, 72, 82; all s. redeemed by the A*s*vamedha, 44, 328, 396; repentance, confession, and expiation of s. are necessary for perfection, 45, 158 sq., 162–4; expiation and confession of s., described as internal austerities, 45, 179; he commits a twofold s., who obstinately denies what he has done, 45, 275; who confess and expiate their s., are born as gods, 45, 384; Pratikrama*n*a, or expiation of s. by various processes, 45, 434 n.; Agni invoked to release from s. before Aditi, 46, 354; expiated by meditating on Sukhâvatî, 49 (ii), 172, 175, 177, 179, 185; expiated by recitation of Mahâyâna-sûtras, 49 (ii), 195; expiated by uttering the name of Buddha, 49 (ii), 195, 198, 200; expiatory offerings for s. committed, *see* Sacrifice (*b*). *See also* Confession, Good Works, *and* Penances.

Sindhu: people of the S. favoured by the Maruts, 32, 402, 407; Maruts sons of S., 32, 416; queen of the waters, 42, 12 sq.; the river Indus, 42, 40; 46, 38, 41, 54, 57; invoked, 46, 110, 115, 127.

Sineru, there is only one, 36, 50; is immovable, 36, 120.

Singing, at sacred rites, 29, 48, 181, 283, 293; 30, 41, 50, 280; 44, xxxi, 285 sq., 356, 362 sq.; Snâtaka allowed s., 29, 317. *See also* Music.

Sinîvâlî, invoked for conception, 15, 221; 30, 52, 199; 42, 98, 461; offerings to S., 41, 54 n.; 43, 264, 264 n.; is speech, 41, 231; fashions, 41, 231 sq.; invoked in a cattle charm, 42, 143, 304; her hair-dress, 42, 538. *See also* Moon (*c*).

***S*îpâlâ**, n. of a river, 42, 29.

Sîra (plough), as agricultural deity, 12, 445 sq. n.

***S*irarddhi**, disciple of Mahâgiri, 22, 290.

Sirimâ, n. of a courtesan, 36, 249.

Sîrozâh, *see* Prayers (*f*), *and* Zend-avesta.

Sîsara, father of Kumâra, who brings disease of children, 29, 297.

Sîsarama, n. of a demon harassing children, 30, 220.

***S*ish*t*as** (learned Brâhma*n*as), their tradition to be followed as authority on law, 2, 44 sq. and n., 64, 64 n.; 14, 143 sq., 147; 30, 81, 87. *See also* Brâhma*n*as.

Sister, *see* Woman (*b*).

***S*i*s*u Âṅgirasa**, story of, 14, 155.

***S*i*s*upâla**, K*r*ish*n*a's victory over, 45, 261, 261 n.

Sîtâ, her father *G*anaka, 12, xliii; for her sake, Râma killed the demons, 19, 330; sacrifice to S. at agricultural rites, 29, 326 sq., 333–6; 30, 113 sq.; wife of Indra, 29, 334; not born in the ordinary way, 38, 125.

***S*îtala**, n. of a Tîrthakara, 22, 280.

Sîtavana, grove at Râ*g*agaha, 11, 56 sq.

Sîtâyi*s*, *see* Prayers (*f*), *and* Zend-avesta.

Siu-hing-pen-k'i-king, a Chinese life of Buddha, 19, xvii–xxii.

***S*iva**, Umâ, wife of, 1, 151 n.; a sacred word, 2, 301; his name *S*arva, and Avestic Saurva, 4, lii sq.; 5, 10 n.; is the ruler of creatures,

8, 219, 347; as a name of Rudra, 12, 201 n.; 15, 252 sq.; 29, 256; the Person (purusha) is Bhagavat, is the omnipresent *S.*, 15, 246; 'the happy one,' who also creates the elements, 15, 259; Mahe*s*vara rejoiced when beholding his six-faced child, 19, 20; Gadgadasvara preaches under the shape of *S.*, 21, 401; sacrifice to *S.*, 29, 203; Vidyâdharas, attendants of *S.*, 35, 217 n.; the disease *S*ûla due to the trident of *S.*, 42, 506; slays Andhaka, 42, 620; not acknowledged as supreme god in the *G*aina-sûtras, 45, 102 n.; Nârâya*n*a alone existed, not Brahmâ, nor *S.*, 48, 240; a term referring to the Highest Reality (Brahman, Nârâya*n*a), 48, 522, 667; or Bhava, 49 (i), 16; has a bull for his sign and is immovable in his vow, 49 (i), 104; Brahman, Vish*n*u, and *S.*, 49 (i), 196 sq., 200; moon of *S.*, 49 (ii), 8; the palace of Mahe*s*vara Deva or *S.*, 49 (ii), 166. *See also* Î*s*âna, Mahe*s*vara, *and* Pa*s*upati.

***S*ivâ**, mother of Arish*t*anemi, 22, 276; 45, 112.

***S*ivabhûti**, of the Kautsa gotra, a Sthavira, 22, 294.

Sîvaka, n. of a Yakkha, 20, 181 sq.

Sîvaka: Buddha addresses Moliya S., 35, 195.

***S*ivasa*m*kalpa**, an Upanishad, in the Vâgasaneyi-Sa*m*hitâ, 1, lxvi.

Siveyyaka, a kind of cloth, 17, 190, 190 n., 193 sq.

Sivi, *see* *S*ibi.

Sîyah-tô*r*â, *see* Sîyâk-tôrâ.

Sîyâkmak (or Sîyâmak) and Na*s*âk, one of the first seven pairs of men, 5, 58 sq.; son of Mâshya, 5, 130; 47, 35, 127, 127 n., 140; Fravâk, son of S., 5, 132; primaeval ruler, 47, 121.

Sîyâk-tôrâ, ancestor of Frê*d*ûn, 5, 132; 47, 34.

Sîyâmak, *see* Sîyâkmak.

Sîyâvakhsh, Av. Kavi Syâvarshân, son of Kâî-Ûs (Kâî-Kâûs), king of Iran, 5, 136, 136 n., 224, 226; 18, 90, 90 n.; 23, 222, 222 n., 303; 24, 64, 64 n.; 47, 14; formed Kangdez, 18, 257, 257 n.; father of Husravah (Khûsrôî), 23, 114 sq., 278, 304; 37, 28; of beautiful body, 23, 326.

Siyâvakhsh, an author of the prose Sad Dar, 24, xxxvii.

Skanda, called Sanatkumâra, 1, 125; 38, 235; chief among generals, 8, 89; feasts at festivals of S., 22, 92; worshipped at the Tarpa*n*a, 30, 244; son of Agni, 49 (i), 12.

Skandhas, Buddhist t.t., the five aggregates or constituent elements of being, 10 (i), 54, 54 sq. n., 87; 22, xxxiii; 34, 402 sq.; 35, 42-4, 82; 49 (ii), 147, 153. *See also* Aggregates, *and* Khandhâ.

Skandila, president of the council of Mathurâ, 22, 294 n.

Skâraya*t*-ratha, n.p., 23, 210.

Skins of animals, *see* Animals (*e*), *and* Antelope.

Sky, first created by Aûharmaz*d*, 5, 10; attacked by the evil spirit, 5, 17, 25, 167 sq.; three parts of the s., 18, 86-8, 94, 94 n., 126 sq., 127 n., 220, 220 n.; 24, 17 n.; nature and material of the s., 18, 259-62; 24, 36, 36 n.; invocation and sacrifice to the sovereign S., 23, 10, 18, 34, 136, 334, 352; Fravashi of the s. worshipped, 23, 200;—union of S. with the sun, 41, 149, 188 sq.; the s. or the udder of the s. is the waters, 41, 216, 284; 44, 492; fashioned by the Âdityas, 41, 234; is Pragâpati's head, 41, 313, 317; sheds seed in the form of rain produced by smoke (steam), 41, 383; the seat of waters, 41, 416; is blissful, 43, 88; deity and brick of fire-altar, 43, 91; the firmament or heavenly world, the third luminous back of the s., 43, 93, 100, 122, 198, 250, 304; is the left wing of fire-altar and universe, 43, 179; is the higher abode, 43, 202 sq.; the stars are its hair, Âditya the man, 43, 208; steadied by clouds and stars, 44, 126; relates to Indra, 44, 241; was the first conception, 44, 315, 389; was afraid of being injured by the heat of the Pravargya, 44, 467; is yellow, 44, 467; a place of abode for all the gods, 44, 505; laughing of the s., the lightning, 46, 203, 205. *See also* Heaven.

Sky-flowers, example of an imaginary thing, not objects of consciousness, 48, 50, 55, 77, 532.

Slander, Brâhma*n*as speaking ill of others dwell in hell, 8, 182 sq.; the Bhikkhu abstains from s., 11, 190; sin of s., 13, 9 sq., 32; 24, 9, 305 sq., 356 sq.; 37, 45.

Slaughter, stories illustrating the sinfulness of, 8, 288-96; necessary for the sustentation of life, 8, 291; refraining from s. is the duty among all duties, 8, 291; is of the quality of passion, 8, 324. *See also* Ahi*m*sâ.

Slaves must not be stinted, 2, 122 sq.; division of s. among co-heirs, 2, 304; 25, 357; 33, 382; slavery in Islâm, 6, lxxv sq.; mutilated by branding, &c., 6, 89, 89 n.; those whom their right hands possess, 6, 257 sq.; law with regard to s., 7, 37, 43; 33, 131 sq.; female s. are indivisible property, 7, 74; 25, 379, 379 sq. n.; period of impurity for wives and s., 7, 89; stealing s., men and women, 7, 172; 25, 464; 33, 228; female s. not to be compelled to prostitution, 9, 77, 77 n.; to be allowed to purchase their freedom, 9, 77; s. and children to ask permission before entering a private apartment, 9, 81; as s. to the Meccans, so are the idols to God, 9, 127, 127 n.; Mohammed allowed to marry s. girls, 9, 146, 301; a Bhikkhu must not get s., 11, 191; cannot be witnesses, 24, 78; 33, 86; quarrels with s. to be avoided, 25, 157 sq.; may, exceptionally, be witnesses, 25, 267; may be beaten, 25, 306; conversing with female s. of others, 25, 317; seven, or fifteen kinds of s., 25, 326, 326 n.; 33, xiii, 135-9; have no property, 25, 326 sq.; offspring of s. belongs to the owner of the s.-girl, 25, 336; son begotten on female s. inherits, 25, 364; sin of selling oneself, 25, 442, 442 n.; transactions of s. invalid, 33, 50, 145; ordeal by sacred libation not applicable for s., 33, 117; ceremony at the emancipation of s., 33, 138 sq.; illegal use of a female s. belonging to another, 33, 264 sq., 344; possession of s., 33, 311 sq.; given as gifts, 36, 121, 124, 131; 47, 55, 55 n.; the children of Vessantara could not become s., 36, 126-30; servants and s., 36, 209 sq., 210 n.; mentioned among other property, 36, 254; ill-treatment of s., 37, 41; litigation with s., 37, 58; selling of men, 37, 63; seizure of human beings to work off a debt, 37, 142; evils of slavery, 47, 89, 89 n. *See also* Woman (*a*).

Sleep, true nature of soul in state of, 1, 98 sq.; 15, 163-73, 279 sq.; 34, 59 sq.; 48, 205 sq., 379, 383 sq., 606, 755, 757, 765 sq.; in deep s. the self is absorbed in the highest Self, in the Brahman, 1, 98 n., 140; 15, 167-71, 280; 48, 318, 352, 606; in deep s. the soul enters into the arteries of the heart and obtains the light of the sun, abides within Brahman in the heart, 1, 133, 306; 15, 103-5; 34, lxi, 180, 273, 350; 38, 54 sq., 141-7, 176, 210; 48, 604 sq.; in dreamless s., speech, eye, ear, and mind are all absorbed in the one prâ*n*a, breath, 1, 295, 307; 8, 112 n., 268 n.; 38, 136; 43, 332; 48, 577; rules about sleeping, 2, 17 sq., 97 sq., 129, 225, 290; 7, 223 sq.; 8, 236, 360 n.; 11, 191, 193; 14, 4, 102 sq., 118, 237; 17, 226; 19, 298 sq.; 25, 70; 26, 3 sq., 44, 46; God takes men to Himself during s., 6, 122; Prâ*n*a and Apâna do not forsake a person in s., 8, 258, 259 n.; senses show the mind objects in s. (dreams), 8, 269; s., sloth, and delusion, 8, 301, 320; state of s., an intermediate state between this world and the other, 15, 164 sq., 165 n.; prayers recited when going to s. and rising, 23, 312 sq.; the Mazda-made S. worshipped, 31, 346, 346 n.; the soul awakening from s. is the same that went to s., 34, lxi; 38, 147-9; 48, 605 sq.; what Scripture says about absence of all specific cognition, refers either to deep s. or final release, 34, lxxxv; 38, 145, 414 sq.; activity of sense-organs interrupted during s., 34, 85, 86, 163, 168; 43, 372; vital air remains awake in deep s., 34, 162-8; bliss or serenity attaches to deep s., 34, 163, 164, 168, 182; a kind of dissolution and origination takes place in the sleeping and the waking states, 34, 212; the highest Self different from the

individual soul in the state of deep s., 34, 233–6; the undeveloped principle is a universal s. in which are lying the transmigrating souls destitute for the time of the consciousness of their individual character, 34, 243; doctrine about the soul conveyed by the waking of the sleeping man, 34, 269, 273 sq.; the case of the reabsorption of the world compared with that of deep s., 34, 312; in deep s. a man's mind has returned home, 36, 159 sq.; 'monkey's s.,' a dozing state, 36, 161, 162 n.; the absence of intelligence in deep s. is only due to the absence of objects, but the soul remains intelligent even in deep s., 38, 33, 34 sq., 47 sq., 336 sq.; the rising from deep s. is due to the existence of potential avidyâ, 38, 48; the soul wanders about in the state of s., 38, 49 sq.; the state of swoon is half-coincidence with deep s., 38, 151 sq.; in deep s. the elements are merged in Brahman in such a way as to continue to exist in a seminal condition, 38, 371; sleeping-charm, 42, 105 sq., 372; S., the immortal child of the gods, invoked to avert evil dreams, 42, 167; consists in the union of the persons in the right and left eye, 43, 370–2; in deep s. the idea of 'I' is absent, but the consciousness of the self persists, 48, 37 sq., 40, 52 sq., 67–9; no consciousness in deep s., 48, 545, 550 sq., 606; cessation of pain and pleasure in deep s., 48, 737.

Sloth, appertains to the quality of darkness, 8, 301; devotee should be without s., 8, 361, 378, 389; is a spiritual bondage, 11, 227, 231.

Smell, ten kinds of, 8, 383 sq.

Smoke, is the breath of sacrifice, 41, 240; is seed shed by the earth, and becomes rain, 41, 383; is the vigour of fire, 43, 250.

Sm*ri*ti, or traditional literature, of secondary authority only, 1, lxvii; means Dharma*s*âstra, 25, xxv, 31; S. such as the Manu-s. opposed to the Sâṅkhya-s., 34, xlvii, 290–6; Kâpila S. or S. of the Sâṅkhyas, 34, 132 sq., 291; 48, 408; in order to be authoritative, S. depends on Scripture (*S*ruti), 34, 145 sq., 203, 291 n., 293 sq., 297 n., 440; 38, 211–14; 48, 119, 408–12, 460; if the doctrine of Brahman being the cause of the world be accepted, is there any room for S.? 34, 290–9; men who are unable to ascertain the true sense of *S*ruti, rely on S., 34, 292; Sâṅkhya and Yoga are S. only, without scriptural authority, 38, 381; does not teach the doctrine of one non-differenced substance, 48, 86–102. *See also* Dharma*s*âstras *and* Scripture.

Snakes, dreams of, forbode daughters, 3, 350; legends of dragon-slaying, 4, lii; 31, 233 sq.; creation of s., 4, 4; 12, 384; 42, 154; killing s. a good act, 4, 171, 371; 5, 109 sq.; disease comes from the (poison of) s., 4, 226, 226 n.; Az-i Dahâk, the three-headed fiend of s. origin, 4, 258 sq.; 5, lii, 233, 233 n.; 31, 233, 233 n.; Srôbar or Azi Srvara, the horned s., slain by Keresâsp, 4, 259; 18, 217, 217 n., 370 sq., 374, 381; 23, 295, 295 n.; 24, 63, 268, 268 n.; 37, 185, 198, 199 n.; 47, 12; pollution caused by s., 5, lxi, 254; Aharman as a s., 5, 17, 160 sq.; s.-like fish, 5, 66; animals which kill s., 5, 72; Gô*k*îhar burns the s. in the melted metal, 5, 129, 129 n.; charms and medicines for those bitten by s., 5, 182, 182 n.; 17, 59; 20, 75–7; 42, 27–30, 147 sq., 151–4, 368 sq., 425–8, 461–3, 487 sq., 552–5, 605–8; he who performs the rites of apostasy will become a s., 5, 384 sq.; penances for killing s., 7, 160; 25, 457 sq.; the s. demons Taksha and Upataksha worshipped, 7, 212; Vâsuki chief among s., Ananta chief among Nâgas, 8, 89, 89 n.; celestial s. within K*ri*sh*n*a, 8, 93; all s. are hated in the world, 8, 281 sq.; have natural inclination to biting, 8, 282; s., gods, and sages approach Pragâpati for instruction about the highest good, 8, 282 sq.; evil-doers reborn as s., 8, 321; is the middle quality (passion) among dwellers in holes, 8, 345; the highest among reptiles, 8, 353; simile of s.

casting off its skin, 10 (ii), 1–3; 22, 212; 44, 38; 45, 66; 48, 311; V*ri*tra was a s., 12, 166; hymn of the queen of s. (Kadrû, or the earth), 12, 301 sq., 301 n.; 26, 451, 451 n.; a s., in the shape of a youth, becomes a Bhikkhu, manifests his true nature in sleep, and is expelled, 13, 217–19; manifest their true nature during sexual intercourse and in sleep, 13, 219; the dragon a symbol of 'the superior man' and 'the great man,' 16, 57 sq., 59 sq. n., 409–14, 412 n.; the s.-king Supassa asks Buddha to forbid eating s. flesh, 17, 86; the s. winged around Dahâk, 18, 110, 110 n.; subdued by charms of snake-charmers, 19, 266, 299; 35, 38, 212, 213 n., 215 sq.; 36, 168 sq.; 44, 367; four royal breeds of s., 20, 76; girdles made like the head of a s., 20, 143; danger of s. in houses, 20, 166, 174, 272 sq.; girdle of s., 20, 233; Gadgadasvara assumes the shape of a great s., to preach the Lotus, 21, 401; Avalokite*s*vara protects from Nâgas and s. emitting flames, 21, 414 sq.; feasts at festivals of s., 22, 92; A*z*i Dahâka, the storm-cloud 'snake,' 23, 60 n., 75, 75 n.; against the evil done by s., the Fravashi of Thraêtaona is worshipped, 23, 221; Adam seduced by a s., 24, 179, 210–12, 219 sq.; manes of s.-deities, 25, 112; must never be despised, 25, 150; s. deities yield enjoyment from fear of punishment, 25, 219; the west belongs to the s., 26, 4; the fore-edge of the Dîkshita's cloth belongs to the s., 26, 10; feud between men and s., 26, 379; worshipped at the Tarpa*n*a, 29, 121, 219; worship of s. at the *S*râva*n*a and Âgrahâya*n*î (rainy season) ceremonies, 29, 127–32, 201–5, 327–31, 338–41, 411–13, 416 sq.; 30, 89–92, 94–7, 124, 237–41, 287–9; 42, 639 sq.; blood of sacrificial animal assigned to s., 29, 257; Ahi budhnya, the dragon of the deep, 29, 331; 41, 96, 96 n.; invoked at house-building rite, 29, 347; Rudra dwells among the s., 30, 181; Haoma invoked against the Dragon, 31, 239; the two foes who meet the Dragon demon-made, 31, 257; the Dragon Daêva-made opposed by sacrifices, 31, 322; s. surrounded by Garu*d*as, 35, 38; the 'poem of love to the s.,' 35, 282 n.; the Bodhisattva a s. king, 35, 287; similes of s., 36, 348 sq.; 45, 68, 92; sinfulness of the s. Srôbar by witchcraft, 37, 111, 111 n.; birds kill the s. which are produced by the demons, 37, 196; the boy who stole a pearl from under the chin of the Black Dragon when he was asleep, 39, 161; 40, 211; Confucius has seen the dragon coiled up in Lâo-ȝze, 39, 358; the s. desires to be like the wind, 39, 384 sq.; wounded s. healed by a lord of Sui brings him a large pearl, 40, 154 n.; 'slaughtering the dragon' means 'learning the Tâo,' 40, 206, 206 n.; killing s. forbidden, 40, 244; the coursers, swallowing the dragon, 41, 27; are neither worms nor non-worms, 41, 90; 'those that crawl on their belly' driven away, when sweeping the ground for the Gârhapatya, 41, 298; worshipped by the Sarpanâma formulas, 41, 369–71; know healing plants, 42, 43, 580; ichneumon tears the serpent, and joins him together again, 42, 103, 540; invoked against enemies in battle, 42, 119; s. and other superhuman beings, 42, 125 sq., 162; the cloud-s. slain by Indra, 42, 146, 349; as guardians in the six regions, 42, 192 sq.; the pure earth starts in fright away from the s., 42, 203; earth invoked against the s., 42, 204 sq.; Vyâla = s.? 42, 447 sq.; Arbuda and Arbudi, s., 42, 633; 44, 367; Rudra invoked against s., 43, 151; the s. serve the Person in the eye under the name of 'poison,' snake-charmers under the name of 'snake,' 43, 373; people flock from all sides to see a great s., 44, 40; s. deities gratified at the Agnihotra, 44, 82; a stronger has driven a great s. from its own place, the lake (parable), 44, 92; is he who creeps along the path, 44, 390; blockhead sacrificed to s. at the Purushamedha, 44, 414; do not stir in the presence of Supar*n*a, 45, 68; do not shut

their eyes, 45, 92; Gandhana-s. suck the poison from the wound they have inflicted, 45, 118, 118 n.; different kinds of s., huge s., 45, 394, 394 n.; Agni, the roaring s., 46, 103, 105; s. on the Hôm tree, killed by the Fravashi of Zaratûst, 47, 24; example of the rope mistaken for a s., 48, 23 sq., 32 sq., 47, 66, 73, 75, 148 sq., 180 sq., 184 sq., 191, 217, 433; imagination of being bitten by a s., owing to the nearness of the s., 48, 75; the relation of the world to Brahman is like that of the s. to its coils, 48, 618–21; live on air, 49 (i), 72; the s. Kâla pays homage to Buddha, 49 (i), 135 sq.; the s. *S*esha, 49 (i), 197. *See also* Ahi, Dahâka, Nâgas, Sarpavidyâ, Superhuman beings, Uragas, *and* Vâsuki.

Snaoya, n.p., 23, 203.

Snâtaka, i.e. 'he who has bathed' after completing his studentship, 2, 92 n.; honour due to the S., 2, 93; 25, 75, 75 n.; duties and rules of conduct for S., 2, 93–9, 218–26; 7, 179, 224–31; 14, 59–63, 158–60, 239–43; 25, 130–69, 472; 29, 123–6, 230, 316–19, 409 sq., 433; 30, xxxiv sq., 85–7; how to be received as guests, 2, 120; 14, 49; 29, 87 n., 88, 92, 197, 273, 435; 30, 132, 171–5, 277; way must be made for a S., even by a king, 7, 203 sq.; 14, 69; 25, 55 sq.; three kinds of S., 7, 203 n.; 29, 310 sq.; 30, 86; qualities through which one becomes a true S. (Nahâtaka), 10 (ii), 89 sq.; 45, 140; must be supported by householders, 25, lxviii, 133 sq.; a S. becoming a hermit, 25, 198; gifts must be made to S., 25, 431; *a great being indeed is a S.*, 29, 230; auspicious rite performed by S., 30, 128; the sun shines through the splendour of S., 30, 165; hairs from the navel of a S. used for a charm, 42, 477; a S. or a Brahma*k*ârin initiates the Unnet*ri* for the sattra, 44, 137; he who always feeds two thousand S. will become a god, 45, 417. *See also* Holy persons, Morality (*a*), Teacher (*a*), *and* Woman (*b*).

Snâvidhaka, killed by Keresâspa, 18, 370; 23, 296 sq., 297 n.

Sneezing, explained, 24, 265 sq. *See also* Omens.

Sobhari, n. of a clan, 32, 400, 403–5; S. Kâ*n*va, a poet, 32, 401, 403.

Sobhya, prayer addressed to, 2, 297 n., 298.

Society, three classes of, viz. priests, warriors, and husbandmen, 4, 21 n., 58 sq., 65, 78, 80, 166; 5, 142, 186; 18, 215; 23, 201, 201 n., 327, 329, 332; 31, 343; intermarriage between different classes of s., 5, 206; four classes of s., priests, warriors, husbandmen, and artisans, 5, 357, 357 n., 360, 365; 24, 67–9, 105 sq., 118 sq.; 31, 252, 265; 37, 308, 424 sq., 459 sq.; 47, 9, 15, 46 sq., 148 sq.; disreputable professions, 7, 186–9; 25, 387 sq. and n.; origin of social distinctions, 16, 436; social constitution of Zoroastrian Iran, 23, 119, 149 sq., 149 n.; ranks and classes of s., 23, 332; 31, 385 sq.; property of nobles and the people, 37, 92; natural superiority, 37, 97 sq. *See also* Castes, *and* Professions.

Sodom, destruction of, 9, 96 sq., 104, 120 sq., 246.

Sodomy, *see* Sexual intercourse.

Sôg-tô*r*â, the Âspîgân, 47, 34.

Soittiyâ, *see* Sautaptikâ.

Sôk-tôrâ, ancestor of Frê*d*ûn, 5, 132, 132 n.

Soldiers, the highest class of servants, 33, 134.

Solitude, is wisdom, 10 (ii), 129–31; one of the conditions by which a Bhikkhu obtains his desires, 11, 210–18.

Solomon, rules over the ginns, and has power over nature, 6, lxx; 9, 52, 52 n., 151, 151 sq. n.; it was not S. who disbelieved, but the devils, 6, 14, 14 n.; an inspired prophet, 6, 94, 125; David and S. give judgement about a field, 9, 52, 52 n.; taught the speech of birds, marches with ginns, birds, and men, through the valley of the ant, and converts the queen of Sebâ, 9, 100–3; his death discovered by a worm, 9, 151, 152 n.; legends of S., 9, 178 sq. and n.; the wind and the devils subjected to him, 9, 179.

Solstices, *see* Sacred Times.

Soma.

(*a*) The S. plant and drink.
(*b*) S., the god, in mythology.
(*c*) Worship of god S.

(*a*) The S. plant and drink.

S. offered by the Devas on the altar Parganya, 1, 78 sq.; Asvattha tree showering down S., in the world of Brahman, 1, 131, 132 n.; the buying of the (king) S., 2, 68; 26, 49 sq., 53 sq., 56, 63–75, 152, 442 sq., 445, 474; 30, 329 sq.; 41, 9, 117 sq. and n., 181 sq., 342; 43, 256; sin of selling S., 2, 257; 7, 177; 14, 5, 12, 69, 115; 25, 105, 105 n., 109, 421; 33, 57, 57 n.; the 'drinker of S.,' i.e. S. sacrificer, 2, 273; 14, 13, 137; 49 (i), 22; drinking S. purifies from sin, 2, 276; 8, 84; 14, 117; the waters are the first to drink S., 12, 21; the S. pressing, 12, 26; 42, 131, 180 sq., 438 sq., 440; 46, 42 sq., 148, 153, 317; Agni brings S. to the sacrifice, 12, 118; how Indra obtained the S. juice in spite of Tvash*tri*, 12, 164 sq.; 44, 214; prepared for Indra and other gods, gods drink S., 12, 176–80; 32, 127, 154, 386, 408 sq., 440; 44, 216; 46, 38 sq., 42 sq., 110, 128, 148, 263, 285, 291, 304, 358; strengthening the S., 12, 178, 178 n.; 26, 100–4, 100 n.; clarifying King S. with a strainer, 12, 187; mixed with milk and honey, 12, 189; 32, 444 sq.; 42, 143, 351; means seed (semen), 12, 258, 386; 26, 84, 100, 160, 214, 235, 260; is sacred to Fathers, 12, 364; 26, 50, 363, 363 n.; vessels do not become impure through S., 14, 164, 169; its place at sacrifices, 14, 193 sq. and n.; purified by Ka, 14, 331; the divine food or supreme oblation, 15, 314; 25, 123; 26, 84, 218 sq.; 41, 258; 43, xxi; 44, 54, 217, 222, 242; S. and Hôm, 18, 164 n.; persons who are allowed to drink S.-juice (perform S. sacrifices), 25, 432 sq., 432 n.; the spirituous liquor, and the plant, 26, xii sq., xxiv–xxvii; identified with Indra's thunderbolt or its barb, 26, xvii sq., 108, 108 n.; what is moist in the S. is of S.'s nature, 26, 49; hospitable reception given to King S., 26, 51, 54 n., 85–92; 41, 118, 342, 355; 44, 491; represents offspring, 26, 68; Gandharvas, the guardians of the S., 26, 72, 150–2; the bought S. an embryo, 26, 73, 76; procession and entrance of King S., 26, 75–85, 442 sq., 445; is in the mountains, 26, 77; is said to fly away having become a falcon, 26, 80; Vasativarî, Ekadhanâ, and Nigrâbhyâ waters mixed with S., 26, 102, 102 n., 147, 222–6, 231–3, 232 n., 235–8, 240, 242 sq., 244 n., 247, 257 n., 293 sq.; construction of S.-carts and sheds, and preparation of the pressing-place, &c., 26, 126–55, 128 n.; he who presses S. kills him, 26, 239 sq., 243, 251, 340, 363 n.; 44, 2; became sacrificial food for the gods, 26, 242, 245 sq., 258 sq.; 44, 16; etymology of S., 26, 246; vessels used at the S. pressing, 26, 259 n.; mountains and stones his body, 26, 314; the nectar of immortality, 26, 385 n.; 43, 251 sq., 255 sq.; 44, xlviii sq., 223; substitutes of S.-plants, 26, 421 sq.; 44, 451 n.; 48, 120; S. Pavamâna, the udder of Ash*t*akâ, 29, 103; called vahni, 32, 40; called dânu, 'liquid, rain,' 32, 115; Vish*n*u saved the S., and the Maruts sat down around it, 32, 127, 133–7; Maruts compared to S. drops, 32, 279, 282 sq., 416; Maruts givers of S. (rain), 32, 400; how much property required to drink S. juice, 33, 129; flowing through Indra, the S. became a tiger, 41, 81, 92; Sautrâma*n*î heals excess in S.-drinking, 41, 129 n., 131 sq., 137, 137 n.; Nir*ri*ti visits him who does not offer S., 41, 321; birth (sûti) and S. pressing, 42, 99, 243; the house a receptacle for S., 42, 194 sq.; Rudra, lord of the S. plant, 43, 154, 162; King S. offered in the fire, then drunk, 43, 251 sq., 256 sq.; Agni supported by offering S., 43, 274; for a year S. should be pressed, 43, 320; streams of S. flow at a sacrificial session, 44, 94, 95; by the buying of S. plants they sacrifice to S. and become S., 44, 140; is cattle, 44, 217; the Surâ-liquor mixed with S. and made a form of

S., 44, 223 sq., 226 sq.; S.-juice is the seed of the vigorous steed, 44, 390 sq.; is the sacrifice, and the Pravargya is its head, 44, 461, 502; when S. overflows, all the gods and all beings avail themselves thereof, 44, 510; Agni protects those who offer S., 46, 24; kept over night, 46, 43 sq.; may the chariot of him who presses S. be to the front, 46, 109; washing of the S., 46, 150; mixed with water, i.e. the waters of the cloud, 46, 264; with threefold admixture, 46, 420, 422. *See also* Sacrifice (*i, j*).

(*b*) S., THE GOD, IN MYTHOLOGY.

At the head of the Maruts, 1, 42 sq.; King S. is the moon, the food of the gods, 1, 80, 287, 303; 8, 219 sq.; 12, 176, 176 n., 181, 362, 380; 15, 207; 26, xiii–xvi; 30, 179, 194; 41, xxvii, 229, 355, 355 n.; 42, 62, 103, 161; 43, xxi; 44, 6, 9 sq., 34, 135, 135 n.; 48, 588; presiding deity of water (tongue, taste), 8, 337, 340; lord of Nakshatras, 8, 346 n.; is the lord of herbs and trees, 8, 346, 346 n.; 29, 280, 294; 41, 340; 42, 14, 44, 55, 162, 189; 43, 76; 44, 135, 135 n.; is the king of Brâhma*n*as, 8, 347; 14, 8; 30, 208; 41, 72, 95; 43, 249; Indra, S., and Agni, 12, xix; 26, 22; 42, 117, 122, 222; 44, 441; 46, 213; Gâyatrî as a falcon carries off the S. from heaven, 12, xxiv, 183 sq., 183 n.; 233, 452; 26, xiv, xix–xxiii, xx sq. n., 52–4, 58, 71 n., 78, 88, 149–52, 241, 329, 422; 42, 331 sq., 580 sq., 43, xxi, 46 n.; 44, 122; Indra made the moon out of S., 12, 167; represents all the gods, 12, 168; what is moist relates to S., dry to Agni, 12, 169, 175; the moon, the night, and the waning half moon relate to S., 12, 169; black related to S., white to Agni, 12, 175; established the fire and became glorious, 12, 313; with the aid of S. the gods slew V*ri*tra, 12, 418; women belong to S., 14, 133; gave women cleanliness, 14, 233; the person in the moon worshipped as the king, clad in white raiment, 15, 101, 103; is the deity in the Northern quarter, 15, 147; 42, 188, 193; rises from the *S*raddhâ libation of the Devas, 15, 207; 48, 588; S. and the vital breaths, offshoots of Brahman, 15, 335; kingdom of S. gained by Uktha, 15, 337; daughters of Daksha married to S., 25, 352, 352 n.; myth of S., S. in *S*atapatha-brâhma*n*a, 26, xi–xxiii, 469, 572; his divine personality vague, 26, xii, xv sq.; his intercourse with the waters and plants, and his own regeneration, 26, xiii, xiii n., 438; the sun connected with S., 26, xiii–xvi; marriage of S. and Sûryâ, 26, xiv; 42, 503; as the bright ether, 26, xv; is Indra's friend, 26, xvi–xx; 41, 134; 44, 226; 46, 96; his descent in showers of rain, 26, xvi, xix–xxiii; slayer of V*ri*tra, and 'cow-giver,' 26, xvii; relation between S. and Agni, 26, xviii sq.; 42, 135; and the lightning, 26, xix–xxiii; tuck of the garment sacred to S., 26, 29; to him belongs the Southern region, 26, 50; is a god, is Lord of beings, is in heaven, 26, 70, 79 sq., 160 sq., 239, 243, 250, 314; the king, lord of kings, 26, 79 sq. and n.; 29, 293; 44, 63, 461, 461 n.; is the nobility, 26, 87, 227 sq.; 41, 102; with the Rudras, 26, 93; various identifications of S., 26, 100; Agni the day, S. the night, 26, 108; afraid of the Rakshas, 26, 157; = sacrifice = Vish*n*u, 26, 160; 44, 205; was V*ri*tra, 26, 239, 265–9, 271, 314, 371; his light in the heavens, on earth, and in the air, 26, 242; born from the *Rik*, 26, 247; had oppressed B*ri*haspati and had to be purified, 26, 258 sq.; Varu*n*a struck King S. in the eye, 26, 281; begotten by B*ri*haspati, 26, 366; the child of the waters, 26, 384; is rich in wives, 29, 27; Savit*ri* shaved the beard of King S., 29, 185, 302; 30, 217; deity of sesamum, 29, 251; the bride belongs first to S., 29, 278 sq.; 30, 44, 190; 33, 171 n.; 42, 254, 323; B*ri*haspati has given the (Brahma*k*ârin's) garment to King S., 30, 147; where S. dwells, 30, 218; the Fathers, friends of S., 30, 225, 229, 231; 42, 89 sq.; the *Ri*shi of a Kâ*n*d*a*, 30, 242; as a red

horse, 32, 18, 24; V*ri*shan, strong or fertilizing, an epithet of S., 32, 142, 146-8, 150; the king appears as S., 33, 217 sq.; is truth, prosperity, light, 41, 8, 29; the S.-eyed gods above, 41, 49; S. and Rudra freed the sun from darkness, caused by Svarbhânu, 41, 65 sq.; is everything, 41, 131 sq.; 44, 509; identified with Agni, 41, 224 n.; is breath, 41, 354; the imperishable, red drop, 41, 405; Kush*th*a, the friend of S., 42, 5 sq.; rendered poison powerless, 42, 25; the lord in the watches of the night, 42, 30; the brother of curative plants, 42, 32; with his rays (or shoots), grants life, 42, 53, 570; pearl born from S., 42, 62; one of the divine purohitas, 42, 79; fastened the amulet on unto perfect hearing and seeing, 42, 85; makes maidens lovely, 42, 94; King S. and the mountains, 42, 112, 329; the waters support Agni and S., 42, 146 sq.; charm born of S., 42, 148; removes the poison of snakes, 42, 154; is the Brâhma*n*a's heir, 42, 170, 431 sq.; rules in the west, 42, 186; as a teacher, 42, 216; Pragâpati (year-Agni) is King S., the moon, 43, xxi, 349-52, 354; 44, 205; repeller of shafts, 43, 102; Vai*s*vânara as S.'s splendour, 43, 396; created out of Pragâpati, 44, 15; S. the leader of the S., 44, 107; Brahman (m.) with S. for his leader, 44, 318; the people of King S. Vaish*n*ava are the Apsaras, 44, 366; Agni, a performer of worship like S., 46, 54; the red young child of Heaven, 46, 360, 362; Rohi*n*î, wife of S., 49 (i), 44. *See also* Agni (*b*), Indra (*e*), Indu, *and* Moon (*c*).

(*c*) WORSHIP OF GOD S.

Offerings to S., 2, 299; 12, 150, 256 n., 258, 386, 401 sq., 411, 413 sq., 418; 14, 308; 15, 211; 25, 90 sq.; 26, 49, 157, 363 sq.; 29, 27, 32, 339; 30, 34, 123, 143, 158, 260; 41, 82, 85, 113 sq., 116 n., 118, 120-2, 125; 44, 62-6, 74 n., 75; Vedic worship of S., Avestic worship of Haoma, 4, lii; 26, xi sq., xvi, xxiv; 31, 230 sq.; offerings to the Fathers, accompanied by S., and to S. Pit*ri*mat, i. e. S. accompanied by the Fathers, 7, 84; 12, 364, 421, 421 n., 427-9; 14, 268; 29, 421; 30, 106, 226; Brâhmans pray to S., 11, 180; Agni, Indra, and S. at sacrifices, 12, xix; offerings to Agni and S., 12, 159-75; 25, 90; 26, 386; 29, 174, 390; 30, 254; 44, 16, 36 sq., 54; *see also* Agni (*b*); worshipped in worshipping Agni Indumat, 12, 319 sq.; oblation to S. before a *S*râddha, 25, 114; prayers to S., 26, 45; 29, 280, 314; 30, 151, 166, 178; 32, 419, 434 sq.; 41, 28, 38, 94, 354; 42, 1, 44, 75, 123, 133, 149, 183, 443; 44, 65; animal victim for S., 26, 218 sq.; 44, xxv, 280, 300; King S. asked to descend to the people, 26, 228; invoked for the protection of a child, 29, 54, 294; 30, 215; offerings to S. Vanaspati and those belonging to S., 29, 84 sq., 85 n., 161; 41, 70 sq., 102; worshipped at the Tarpa*n*a, 29, 121; 30, 243; song in praise of S., 29, 181; barley grains bought from, or for King S., 30, 53, 269; offerings to Agni and S., Indra and S., and to S., 41, 54 n., 56 sq.; offerings to S. and Rudra, 41, 65 sq.; 43, 153 sq.; invoked in a charm to obtain a husband, 42, 94; invoked for royal power, 44, 63; he offers S. to S., 44, 107 sq.; expiatory oblation to S. at the Soma-sacrifice, 44, 208. *See also* Indra (*b*).

Somabhûta, a Kula of the Uddeha Ga*n*a, 22, 290.

Somadatta, his son, a Kaurava, 8, 38.

Somadatta, disciple of Bhadrabâhu, 22, 289.

Somadeva, quotes Manu, 25, cxi.

Somâhuti Bhârgava, author of Vedic hymns, 46, 203, 207, 210, 211.

Somaka, Sahadeva's son, 46, 360 sq.

Soma-sacrificer, *see* Holy persons.

Somasads, sons of Virâ*g*, the manes of the Sâdhyas, 25, 111.

Soma*s*ushma Sâtyaya*g*ñi, his meeting with King *G*anaka, 12, xliii; 44, 112 sq.; quoted as a teacher, 44, 354, 395.

Soma*s*ushmâya*n*a, worshipped at the Tarpa*n*a, 30, 244.

Soma-world, as the reward of meditation on Om, 15, 282.

Somayâ*g*in, third name to be given to children, 30, 215.
Son of Heaven, *see* Rulers.
Son(s), a meditation which secures the life of, 1, 49 sq., 49 n.; substitutes for legitimate s., 2, xix–xxi, 132 n., 271, 307 sq. and n.; 7, 61–5; 14, 84–8, 90 sq., 226–9; 25, cix, 359–65, 367 n., 403 n.; 33, 192–5, 200 sq., 369, 375 sq.; whether s. of an Abhi*s*asta may mix with Âryas, 2, 91 sq.; belong to the begetter, 2, 131 sq.; number of ancestors saved by s. springing from the different marriage rites, 2, 200; rights of s. of an appointed daughter (putrikâ), 2, 305; 25, cix, 77, 352–5 and n.; legal position of s., 7, 35, 45, 63–5, 67 sq., 70–3; 25, 605 sq.; adopted, 7, 63; 25, 355, 359, 362; *see also* Adoption; bought, 7, 63; 25, 359, 363; duty of begetting s., 7, 65, 260; 25, 34, 354 sq.; 33, 375; *the father obtains immortality, if he sees the face of a living s.*, 7, 65; 14, 84; 25, 346, 354; impurity on the death of s. other than a s. of the body, 7, 91; sin of abandoning a s., 7, 135; 25, 321, 442; illegitimate s. defile a company, 7, 252; giving away of s., s. an invalid gift, 8, 169; 33, 128, 342; great love for s., 13, 210; daughter's s. sanctifies the *S*râddha, 14, 54; s. born without mothers, as Agastya and Vasish*th*a, 14, 180, 180 n.; of wives of different castes, 14, 225 sq.; 25, 357–9, 364; 33, 371 sq., 374, 376; world of men can be gained by a s. only, 15, 95 sq.; are bliss, 15, 157; 43, 161; two kinds of s. born by wives of other men, 25, 108; king to deliberate on keeping his s. from harm, 25, 240; father must not pay the debt of his s., but s. must pay that of his father, 25, 282 sq.; 33, 41 sq., 45, 263, 327–9; s. has no property, 25, 326, 374; Kshetra*g*a s., and their rights, 25, 333–7, 349 sq. and n., 356, 359–61, 360 sq. n., 365 n., 366 n., 367 n., 369, 369 n., 373 n.; s. (put-tra) delivers his father from the hell Put, 25, 354; respect to be shown to s., 28, 266; rite to be performed by one who wishes a son to be born, 29, 253; only the eldest s. is independent, 33, 50; a s. is better than a hundred offerings, truth is better than a hundred s., 33, 93; oaths by the heads of s., 33, 315; duties of s. towards deceased father, 33, 376 sq.; if one brother has a s., all are declared to have male offspring, 33, 385; if one wife has s. all are declared to have male offspring through that s., 33, 385; father may deposit his s. as a pledge, 36, 122; birth and care of a s., 37, 100, 110, 122; irreverent s. disinherited, 37, 147; prayer of the king, at the consecration, for his s., 41, 97, 97 n.; kind as a father to his s., 43, 25, 206; are more selfish to the father, than the father to the s., 43, 59 sq.; in early life s. subsist on father, the reverse in later life, 44, 157; lovingly touch their father when he comes home from abroad, 44, 204; father and s. part in times of peace, 44, 308, 308 n.; there will be no better world for men without s., 45, 62; as a tree without branches, a bird without wings, &c., so is a man without his s., 45, 66. *See also* Child, Family, Father, Inheritance, Parents, *and* Woman (*b*).
So*n*a Ko*l*ivisa, a delicate Se*tth*i's son, who becomes an Arhat, 17, 1–14.
So*n*a Ku*t*ika*nn*a, pupil of Mahâ Ka*kk*âyana, 17, 32–40.
*So*n*a* **Sâtrâsâha**, Pâ*ñk*âla king, performed horse-sacrifice, 44, 400.
So*n*avâsî, another n. of Sambhûta Sâ*n*avâsî, 20, 394 n.
Songs, *see* Gâthâs, Singing, *and* War.
So*n*uttara, father of Nâgasena, 35, xxv, 14, 17.
So*n*uttara, a Nesâda, Devadatta born as, 35, 286.
Sophists, their theory of everything being jaundiced, denounced, 24, 149 sq., 149 n.
Sorcerers in Egypt, 6, 201 sq.; profession of s. condemned, 15, 341; 31, 318; 33, 360 sq.; spells against s., 21, 372, 374; 31, 313; 42, xxii, 38, 59, 61, 64 sq., 82, 159, 237 sq.; accompany the king at the mourning rites for a minister, 27, 172 172 n.; employed to brush the bier, 27, 187, 187 n.; Daêvas and s. ab-

jured, 31, 249; exorcists charm devils, 35, 38; magicians and s. enumerated in a list of superhuman beings, Yakkhas, &c., 36, 101; will be born in hell, 45, 366 sq., 430; Agni burns down s., invoked against s., 46, 6, 32 sq., 96, 103, 331. *See also* Magician, Witchcraft, *and* Zan*d*as.

Sorcery, *see* Witchcraft.

Sôshâns, Sôshyans, *see* Saoshya*n*t.

Sôshâns or Sôshyans, n. of a Zoroastrian teacher, 5, 243 sq., 243 n., 259, 261 n., 265 sq., 274 sq., 279, 295; 18, 299–302, 299 n., 312, 316, 333, 336 n., 361.

Soshyantîhoma, t.t., *see* Child (*b*).

Sotâpatti, Buddhist t.t., the first step in holiness, 10 (i), 48 n.

Sottiya, *see* Srotriya.

Soul.

(*a*) Views of different sects and schools about the nature, size, &c., of the s.
(*b*) S. and body.
(*c*) Mythological aspect of s., its fate after death, worship of ss.
(*d*) Effects of good and evil works on the s.; the released s.

(*a*) VIEWS OF DIFFERENT SECTS AND SCHOOLS ABOUT THE NATURE, SIZE, ETC., OF THE S.

The living (*g*îva) s. returns, in deep sleep, to Brahman or the Highest Self, 1, 98 n.; 34, xxvi, lxi, 60, 273; 38, 54, 141–9, 176, 210; 48, 205 sq., 317 sq., 379, 383 sq., 604 sq.; is imperishable, immortal, 4, 373; 8, 244; 12, 310 sq.; 34, 37, 133, 438; 38, 28 sq.; 48, 310; fires like three breathing ss., 5, 62–4; God made you spring from one s., 6, 127; 9, 182; theory of s. rejected by Buddhism, 8, 26 n.; 11, 142, 162, 214 n., 294, 299 sq.; 19, 140 sq., 199 sq., 261 sq., 264, 264 n., 294; 34, 403, 406; 35, 40–5, 67, 86–9, 111, 268 n.; 36, xxi, 137; 49 (i), 177; presides over the senses and the mind, rules the organs of action, 8, 112, 112 n.; 34, 102, 133; its three seats (this world, the next world, and the womb), 8, 239 sq., 239 n.; *that living s. is to be known as part of the hundredth part of the point of a hair, divided a hundred times, and yet it is to be infinite. It is not woman, it is not man, nor is it neuter; whatever body it takes, with that it is joined* (*only*), 15, 257; characteristics of *anima* and *animus* known from the Yî King, 16, 354, 355 sq. n.; creation of the s., 18, 17; s. and life, 18, 59, 59 n.; the cause of birth and death, 19, 106 sq.; discussions and theories of philosophers on the s., 19, 134–6, 135 n., 142; 34, liii, 248, 276 sq.; 36, xxi–xxv; 38, 3, 28–73; 45, 83, 83 n.; 49 (i), 99 sq., 125–32, 176; *see also* Psychology; tenets of *G*ainism with regard to s., 22, xxxiii, 1–3, 3 n.; 34, 428, 428 n.; 45, xix, 84 sq., 84 n.; *G*aina belief in numberless ss., 22, 3 n.; 45, xxxiii, xxxvi sq.; ss. in the six classes of living beings, 22, 3–14, 80 sq., 103–10, 202; 45, 42 sq., 146; water (rain-drops) possessed of s. according to the *G*ainas, 22, 301 n.; 36, 85–91; 45, xix; five faculties of the s., 23, 197 sq., 198 n., 228, 230; meditation of ascetics on the s., 25, 169, 207, 491; the s. is the witness of the s., the supreme witness of men, 25, 269; heart is the s., 26, 201; can go everywhere, 27, 193; consciousness, s., and Fravashi, 31, 294; Bhâgavata theory of Sankarsha*n*a, the individual s., 34, xxiii, 440; 48, 524–6; individual or personal s. or *g*îva, 34, xxv sq.; bound up by mâyâ, 34, xxvi; 48, 126; is intelligent, pure intelligence, 34, xxvi, lv sq., xcvii, 53, 103, 133 sq.; 38, 33–5, 39–43, 45–8, 367 sq.; 48, 425, 438, 491; is an agent, 34, xxvi, lvii, xcvii, 104, 160; 38, 49–58; 48, 553–6; is the enjoyer and sufferer, 34, xxvi, 104, 133, 160, 376 n., 378–80; 48, 365, 553; is connected with limiting adjuncts (upâdhi), founded on name and form as presented by Nescience, hence becomes limited in knowledge and power, 34, xxvi, 139 sq., 171, 241, 244, 277–9; 38, 42–5, 140, 367, 402; 48, 436 sq., 690; *see also* Upâdhi; in the pralaya state the ss., free from upâdhis, lie in deep slumber, and are not joined to material bodies, 34, xxvi, xxix; according to Râmânu*g*a, 34, xxx sq., liii sq., xcvii; meant by the serene being, 34, xxxvi, 188, 191; is permanent,

eternal, not produced from Brahman at the time of creation, 34, liii; 38, 29–33; 48, 140, 392, 478 sq., 540–4; is gña, the Knower, 34, liv, 159; 38, 33–5; 48, 544–53; is of atomic (anu) size, like the point of an awl or a goad, 34, liv, xcvii, 113, 175; 38, 35–45, 397; 48, 326, 546–8, 551, 690, 764; is all-pervading, not anu, 34, liv sqq.; 38, 35–49, 402; its intermediate state, i. e. the state of dreams, 34, lx; 38, 133–41; 48, 601–4; its state of swoon, 34, lxi; 38, 149–52; 48, 606 sq.; manifests itself through its own self, in its own nature, 34, lxxxiii; 38, 405–7; the s. of the pious effects its desires by mere determination, 34, lxxxiv sq.; 38, 410 sq.; the subject of the Upanishads, 34, 36 sq.; cannot be denied, 34, 37; 48, 556; is eternally unchanging, pure, and free, 34, 37; 48, 425, 491; is the Self, 34, 37, 54, 103, 361; characteristic marks of s. and chief vital air, 34, 102–6; Sattva and Kshetragña, or internal organ and individual s., 34, 122 sq.; 38, 83; is non-pervading, not omnipresent, 34, 158; how far Scripture refers to s., 34, 160; 38, 400 sq.; cannot be denoted by akshara, 34, 171; mind constitutes its limiting adjunct, 34, 175; every s. carries on the course of its practical existence by means of seeing, hearing, cognizing; otherwise existence would be impossible, 34, 186, 322; its nature before the rise of discriminative knowledge, 34, 186 sq., 189; as such is real, 34, 189 sq.; its different states, in deep sleep, swoon, &c., 34, 191; 38, 133–52; 48, 656; highest Self different from the s. in the states of deep sleep and departing, 34, 233–6; Sâṅkhya views about it, 34, 238, 259, 298, 301, 370, 372–4, 379 n., 436–8; 38, 33; 48, 385 sq., 481; is the support of prâna, hence may itself be called prâna, 34, 270; no separate creation of the s., 34, 279, 441; 38, 396 sq.; Sâṅkhyas assume a plurality or separateness of ss., 34, 295; 48, 494, 562, 565; according to the Vaiseshikas intelligence is not essential to the s., 34, 388 n.; 38, 33; conjunction cannot take place between atoms, s., and internal organ, 34, 398, 398 n.; Pasupati taught the five categories to the end of breaking the bonds of the animal, i. e. the s., 34, 435; there is no s. in the breath, 35, 48 sq.; the s. alone sees the events of spiritual existence, 37, 200; is not divided, but only appears divided, 38, 30, 32; s. and intelligence represented as separate, viz. as the agent and the instrument of action, 38, 42; tied by the senses (grahas), 38, 83; chief vital air is subordinate to s., 38, 88; vital airs are connected with the s. which is the Lord of the aggregate of instruments of action, 38, 92 sq.; compared to a caterpillar, 38, 103; is self-luminous, 38, 141; essentially non-connected with the worlds that appear in the waking and in the dreaming state, 38, 146; breath is merged in it, 38, 367 sq.; according to Yoga-system, 38, 414; 48, 413; vital airs created seven persons (purusha) or ss., 41, 144, 144 n.; is incorporeal, and therefore eternal, 45, 64; definition of s., and its characteristics, 45, 153; one of the nine categories, 45, 154; lêsyâ, a subtile substance accompanying the s., 45, 196 n., 203; the Materialists' doctrines about the s., 45, 339 sqq.; each individual possesses five 'bodies,' audârika, &c., 45, 406 sq. and n.; Gainas maintain that Gîva and Agîva exist, 45, 407; individual ss. of gods, Asuras, Gandharvas, &c., men, beasts, and plants, 48, 198; in its purified state, 48, 209; the individual s. is as insignificant as a glow-worm and, through its connexion with a body, liable to endless suffering, 48, 209, 262 sq., 469, 690; the bearer of Prânas, 48, 298; its true nature is abundant bliss, 48, 302; is neither a causal substance nor an effect, 48, 371; the character of a god or man belongs to the s. only, 48, 422; ss. are not numberless, 48, 444, 452; aggregate of ss. from Brahmâ down to blades of grass created, 48, 473; a witness, enjoying and cognizing, 48, 492;

three kinds of ss. according to the *G*ainas, 48, 516; of atomic size, and yet infinite, 48, 548; its true nature not manifested in the sa*m*sâra state, 48, 602; the s., though fundamentally free from evil, yet is capable of connexion with evil, 48, 653; in deep sleep and death unconscious, 48, 765 sq.; s. and God (Highest Self, Brahman), *see* Brahman (*f*), *and* Self (*b*). *See also* Purusha, *and* Self (*c*).

(*b*) S. AND BODY.

The righteous Zoroastrian is a believer in body and s., 4, 375; created before the body, 5, 53 sq., 64; whoever appeals for the body is not able to save the s., 5, 211; actions for the s. and actions for the body, 5, 395; is called 'the Knower of the field,' i.e. of the body, 7, 286 sq.; how the s. falls away from the perishable body, 8, 237; eternal s. preserves the life-winds in the body, 8, 238, 238 n.; how the s. enters the foetus in the womb, 8, 241 sq.; how the s. moving about carries the body, 8, 252; sees the self come out from the body, 8, 253; on being born in the body the s. becomes united with all evils, when departing it leaves all evils behind, 15, 163 sq.; leaves the body in dreams, 15, 165; s. of the body, the master of its house, 18, 53; distinguished from the spirit of the body, 18, 53–5, 54 n.; more important than the body, 24, 5 sq.; how to preserve both body and s., 24, 9–16, 25 sq.; body, animal s., and intelligent s. constitute man, 27, 36, 381; 28, 220–2; requires a body in order that knowledge may arise, 34, 51; is in the body only, 34, 111 sq.; 38, 93; Sâṅkhya cannot admit a real connexion of s. and body, 34, 379; is the body the sufferer of pain, or the s.? 34, 379; 38, 64, 65; endeavour (which is required for action) originates when the s. is connected with the internal organ which abides in the body, 34, 387; size of s. the same as that of body, 34, 431–4; questions about s. and body not answered by Buddha, 35, 205 sq., 361; desires of body and s., 37, 193; if the s. were not embodied, there could be no sin, 37, 200; the s. blesses the body when righteous, and curses it when wicked, 37, 207 sq.; abides in the heart, but pervades the entire body like sandal-ointment, or as light, 38, 38–42; 48, 548 sq., 765; its knowledge and lordship are hidden on account of its connexion with the body, 38, 139 sq.; 48, 603, 609; the ruler of the body and senses, 38, 367; works cause the connexion of the s. with the body, 38, 369; 48, 607, 609 sq.; embodied s. and body viewed as non-different, 38, 374; the entering of one s. into several bodies is like the multiplication of the flame of a lamp, 38, 413 sq.; individual ss. not distinguished as gods, men, &c., but only the bodies, 48, 328; may enter a body other than its own, 48, 420; the s. taking the prâ*n*as moves about in its own body, according to its pleasure, 48, 554 sq.

(*c*) MYTHOLOGICAL ASPECT OF S., ITS FATE AFTER DEATH, WORSHIP OF SS.

Its ascent to and descent from the moon, with a remainder of former deeds, which determine the new birth, 1, 80–2; 15, 209; 34, lix sq.; 38, 101–32; 48, 589, 592–4, 596–600; the ss. descending from the moon, have no consciousness, until they actually attain a new birth, 1, 83 sq. n.; after shaking off all good and evil works, the s. of him who knows Brahman passes with the subtle body to the world of Brahman, stages of the s. on its way, 1, 235; 34, lxxxii; 38, 382–9; 48, 648–51, 728–54; fate of s. after death, the two roads to the world of the gods and of the fathers, 1, 271–9 and notes; 48, 589–92; shooting-stars, the ss. of good men falling from heaven, 2, 96 n.; Fravashis and ss. of the saints worshipped, 4, 349; 31, 214, 275, 278 sq., 279 n., 351; begs the body not to throw her into hell, 4, 375 sq.; comes out from the body of the dead, 5, 163; Siddhas see the s. departing from the body and coming to it at birth, 8, 239; of what description is the s.

when it leaves the body? 8, 252; no mention of the passage of a s. from the earth to heaven, in Buddhism, 11, 165; anointing the cake with ghee means bestowing a s. on it, 12, 438 sq. and n.; offering to the s., best of sacrifices, to be performed by householders, 14, 262–4, 299; worship of the s., identified with Brahman, 14, 278; ascetic sacrifices in his s., 14, 280; journey of the s. from this world through wind, sun, and moon, to the world where there is no sorrow, no snow, 15, 193; passes through three kinds of rays either to the world of Brahman, or to the mansions of the gods, or to this world, 15, 328 sq.; account rendered by the s. of its good and bad works, 18, 28, 31–3, 47, 50, 54, 56, 60, 62 sq., 66, 71; 24, 50, 82 sq.; when dogs and birds tear the corpse, is the s. aware of it? 18, 36–8; food of ss. in heaven and hell, 18, 66 sq. and n., 72; 24, 21 sq., 21 n., 25; relation of ss. to this world, 18, 67–9; angels, ss., and guardian spirits, 18, 120; saving the s. by gifts to the priest, 18, 150 sq. and n.; purpose of the ceremony for the living s., 18, 237–42, 237 n.; 24, 318–20; ceremonial purification cleanses the s., 18, 284 sq. and n.; ss. of animals and of holy men and women, worshipped, 23, 229; 31, 288, 381; fate of the s. after death, 24, 16–25; ss. of the righteous are the happiest, 24, 66; 'treasurers' of the s., the female spirits who meet it after death, 24, 137, 137 n.; departed ss., when not properly worshipped, complain to Hôrmazd, 24, 274; departed ss., when properly worshipped, protect their former friends, 24, 274; ss. require gifts of garments, 24, 351; body and animal s. go downwards, the intelligent spirit is on high, 27, 369, 444; offerings for the contentment of each man's s., 31, 209, 223; ss. of the dead find delight in works of Asha, 31, 256; Fravashi of the s., 31, 273, 273 n.; sacrifice to the worshipper's own s. and Fravashi, 31, 309, 331, 350; when passing out of the body at the time of death, s. remains invested with the subtle material elements which serve as an abode to the prâ*n*as, 34, lix; 38, 101–12; 48, 584–9; fate of s. of him who possesses the lower knowledge or no knowledge of Brahman, 34, lxxix, lxxxi sq., cvii; 38, 364–404; the s. of him also who knows the highest Brahman departs from the body, 34, lxxxi; is enveloped in the subtle body until it reaches the river Vigarâ, 34, lxxxi n.; when it departs from the body all specific cognition vanishes, but the Self is not destroyed, 34, 281; immortal progress of the s., 37, 275; Zaratû*s*t receives the s. of him who gives thought to religion, 37, 330 sq.; every one making his own s. immortal, 37, 394; accompanied by the chief vital air, the sense-organs and the mind, and taking with itself Nescience, moral good or ill-desert, and the impressions left by its previous existences, the s. leaves its former body and obtains a new body, 38, 102; 48, 586; goes enveloped by water, 38, 103–10, 112, 127; ss. are the food of the gods, on account of their not knowing the Self, 38, 110–12; when it descends from the moon, it enters into similarity (not identity) with ether, air, smoke, mist, cloud, and rain, 38, 126–8; passes through the stages of its descent in a not very long time, 38, 128; when descending, the ss. enter into plants animated by other ss., they do not undergo pleasure and pain in that condition, 38, 129–31; after having entered into plants, s. enters into conjunction with one who performs the act of generation, 38, 131 sq.; is to be meditated upon as the sun, 38, 244; the s., with the breath, goes to the elements, 38, 368 sq.; the abode of the s. when about to depart is the heart, and the point of it is lighted up, 38, 377 sq.; is led by the 'person not a man' to the lower Brahman, 38, 389–402; on the passing away of the effected world of Brahman the ss. go together with the ruler of that world to what is higher than that, 38, 391 sq.; flies swiftly to a distance, 42, 8; 'Thy s. I hold

fast in thee,' 42, 56; is not at rest at night, 42, 462; combination of material existence, guardian spirit, and s. of Zaratûst, 47, 17 n.; ss. go to the best existence, 47, 147 sq.; *people, by looking into the open eye of a person, determine whether the living s. remains in him or is departing*, 48, 272; s. becomes Brahman, when departing from the body, 48, 392; the ss. of those who do not perform sacrifices do not ascend to the moon, 48, 592–6; perfected ss., *see* Siddhas. *See also* Ancestors, Ancestor Worship, Beings, Fathers, Fravashis, Future Life, Spirits, *and* Transmigration.

(*d*) EFFECTS OF GOOD AND EVIL WORKS ON THE S.; THE RELEASED S.

Ss. of the wicked become Daêvas, 4, 104, 104 n.; rewards of departed s., 4, 115–19; he has gained nothing, who has not gained the s., 4, 370; salvation of the s. created by Ormazd, 4, 375; no s. compelled by God beyond its capacity, 6, 135, 142; 9, 69; each s. to bear its own burden, 6, 137; 9, 159, 183; the s., dropping out of the body, is surrounded by its own actions, 8, 239; whoso does right does it for his s., 9, 118, 203, 222; every s. recompensed for what it has earned, 9, 222, 310; 24, 137; internal organ is purified by truth, s. by sacred learning and austerity, understanding by knowledge, 14, 24, 165, 287; 25, 188; description of the liberated s., 22, 52; who worships the Sun, benefits his own s., 23, 86; the fiends tremble at the perfume of the righteous s., 23, 335; who is able to preserve his s., is most complete in wisdom, 24, 77; duty towards one's own s., 24, 78 sq.; Aharman strives to injure the s., 24, 88; the appliances of the s., 24, 118, 145; necessity of preserving the s. from defilement, 24, 166 sq.; actions (Karman) determine the future embodied existences of the s., 25, 485–9; 34, xxvi, xxix, 159 sq., 269; 48, 135, 313, 321, 324, 478; is the charioteer driving on through transmigratory existence and final release, 34, 121, 241; cannot be the guiding principle of the ad*r*ish*t*a, as at the time of pralaya its intelligence has not yet arisen, 34, 388; gradually all ss. obtain release from Sa*m*sâra, 34, 439; deliverance of the s., 37, 30; the ss. praise the s. of a virtuous high-priest, 37, 209; provision for the s., 37, 291; guarded from hell by reciting the Ahunavair, 37, 305 sq.; on account of its non-extension, there is no confusion of the results of actions, 38, 68; ascend to the moon for the purpose of finding there a complete requital of their works, 38, 115; the s. of him who knows Brahman does not depart, 38, 372–5; its fetter (bad qualities), the cause of worldly existence, 45, 64; taking the form of a straight line, the s. develops into its natural form and obtains final beatitude, 45, 173; Karman binds all ss. and the whole s., 45, 195 sq.; 48, 239, 259, 326, 350, 459; what causes the bondage of the s., 45, 235 sq.; expanded by a good work, 47, 149; connexion of s. with works without beginning, 48, 193; its bliss and knowledge in the Sa*m*sâra state contracted owing to Karman, 48, 232, 280; Agâ is enjoyed by the s. controlled by Karman, 48, 367; work, whether meritorious or the contrary, belongs to the individual s. only, 48, 378; steeped in ignorance and misery, saved through meditation on Brahman, 48, 394; that the s. experiences pleasure and pain is due to Karman, 48, 428; the ss. and their deeds form a stream which has no beginning, 48, 429, 497;—opinions about the characteristics of the released s., 34, xix, xxx, lxxxiv; 38, 408–10; 48, 100 sq.; released s. is non-separate from Brahman, 34, lxxxiv, 157 sq., 180 sq.; 38, 173–5, 407 sq.; released s. is either embodied or disembodied according to its wish and will, 34, lxxxv; 38, 410–13; how the released s. can animate several bodies at the same time, 34, lxxxv; 38, 412–15, 414 n.; absence of all specific cognition on the part of the released s., 34, lxxxv; 38, 414 sq.; released ss. do not return to new forms of embodied existence, 34,

lxxxv, 243; 38, 418 sq.; 48, 770 sq.; released s. reaches the sun, 34, 232; released s. is without another lord, 38, 411; released s. possesses a mind (manas), 38, 411; has the released s. a body and senses? 38, 411–13; the enjoyment only of the released s. and the highest Lord is equal, 38, 418; released s. attains only to the same attributes as the highest Self, but does not become one with it, 48, 98 sq., 160, 758 sq.; released s. produces no effects, is not an agent, 48, 172; highest Brahman imparts to released s. infinite bliss, 48, 198 sq.; released s. takes no part in the world-business, 48, 350; s. in the state of Release, and size of the s. are permanent, 48, 520; superior existence of the released s., 48, 755–71; released s. is all-knowing, 48, 765; the released s. does not share Brahman's power of creating and ruling the world, 48, 766–71.

Sound, meditation on, 1, 304 sq.; ten forms of s., 8, 385.

Sôvar, *see* Sâuru.

Sovereigns, *see* Kings.

Sovereignty, over the three worlds, 8, 40, 307; verses about s., 8, 302 sq. *See also* Khshathra.

Space (Sk. âkâ*s*a), one of the eight parts of K*r*ish*n*a, 8, 73, 156 n.; sound the quality of s., 8, 74, 343, 348, 350, 352, 384 sq.; atmosphere always remains in s., 8, 82, 368; 34, 413; the all-pervading s. is not tainted, 8, 106, 289 n.; named womb, 8, 260; s. or deity of s. not seen but by him who attains to the Adhyâtman, 8, 316; the first entity, as connected with the self called ear, as connected with objects of sound, its presiding deity the quarters, 8, 337, 340; land, water, and s., the three seats for all entities, 8, 339; worldly life moves in s. and time, 8, 356; some sects believe in the existence of time and s., others do not, 8, 375; the eternal or boundless and sovereign luminous s., 23, 12, 20; one of the three non-existences of the Bauddhas, 34, 410, 412 sq.; is mighty, therefore there is only one, 36, 50; is not the result of any cause, 36, 103, 107; compared with Nirvâ*n*a, 36, 192 sq.; qualities of s., 36, 316 sq.; is Pragâpati, 43, 62; is invisible, 44, 17; as a substance, 45, 153, 207 sq. *See also* Ether.

Spaênyasp, n.p., 5, 135, 137.

S*p*ânsnâyô*s*, two sons of, 37, 218 sq. and n.

Sparnak, n.p., 5, 140.

Spazg, demon of slander, 5, 111.

Species: the individuals only have an origin, not the s., they are eternal, 34, 202 sq.; words connected with the s., not with the individuals, 34, 202 sq.

Spectacles, public, Bhikkhu refrains from witnessing, 11, 192.

Spê*d*-tôrâ, ancestor of Frê*d*ûn, 5, 132.

Speech: the subtilest portion of fire becomes s., 1, 96–8; is merged in the mind, at death, 1, 100 sq., 107 sq.; 38, 364 sq.; 48, 728 sq.; if there were no s., neither right nor wrong would be known, 1, 111; meditation on s. as Brahman, 1, 111; 15, 152 sq.; makes us understand the Vedas and everything else, 1, 111; is the breath's rope, the names the knots, 1, 209; is (the root of) everything here, by s. everything is done and gained, 1, 255; 25, 168; 34, 346, 381; 43, 12, 365; 44, 16, 161, 507; s. and breath swallow each other, s. is the mother, breath is the son, 1, 256; breath in s., and s. in breath offered as a sacrifice, 1, 266; an eminent female, 8, 90; the s. which causes no sorrow, 8, 119; actions, &c., of body, s., and mind, 8, 123, 128, 177 n., 184 n., 185, 257, 366; one of the organs or vital airs, 8, 261; 43, 190; 44, 246; lord of s. looks up to the mind, 8, 262, 262 n.; how s. comes into existence first, and mind afterwards, 8, 263–6; 44, 262 sq.; never speaks after hard exhalation, 8, 264 sq.; meditation on s. as a cow, 8, 265; 15, 193; the five Prâ*n*as, together with s., mind, and understanding make the eight constituents of the universe, 8, 336; relates to all the gods, 8, 338; words are the characteristic of s., 8, 348; the four kinds of well-spoken language, 10 (ii), 72 sq.; what the s. of the Bhikkhu is to be, 11, 190; re-

straining of s. at or between certain sacrificial rites, 12, 12, 26 sq., 188, 214, 359 sq.; 26, 19, 34–8, 45–7, 240, 289 sq., 448, 453–5; 41, 342; *see also* Mauna; libations to Mind and S., 12, 124–7, 129; 44, 28, 32 sq., 35 sq.; dispute between Mind and S., decided by Pragâpati, 12, 130 sq., 130 n.; mind and s. are the two Agnihotra libations, 12, 332; the secret union of the body, 15, 47; Death and S. produce the year, 15, 76; triad of mind, s., breath, 15, 93–7; 38, 78 sq.; *speaking is the progeny of thinking*, 24, 215; upheld by the mind, 26, 54 sq.; four grades of s., 26, 268; called graha, 26, 432; *Rik* and Sâman are S. and Mind, 26, 437, 439; distinction of names and forms originates from s. only, 34, 352; ill-omened speaking, 37, 129; *see* Chatter; acts under the guidance of Agni, 38, 91 sq.; lord of s. is Pragâpati, 41, 5; by his Mind Pragâpati entered into union with S. and created Vasus, Rudras, and Âdityas, 41, 149 sq.; s. and breath, s. is based on vital air, 41, 151, 192; 43, 15; speaks truth and untruth, divine and human, 41, 200; 43, 257; speaks as far as a span's distance, 41, 200; there is a keen edge to s. on one or both sides, 41, 200, 200 n.; consists of four syllables (vâ*k* and akshara), 41, 203; is a spade, 41, 215; is of the body, is a mahishî (consecrated queen), 41, 239; three kinds of s., 41, 239; is healing medicine, 41, 341; by s. gods conquered Asuras, 41, 387; bears what is desirable, 41, 388; breath the male or mate of s., 41, 391; 43, 285; the mind's daughter, fashioned from the moon, 43, 11; is the *Ri*shi Vi*s*vakarman, 43, 12; lordship bestowed on s., 43, 67; gods made s. their milch-cow, 43, 173; by s. one gets into trouble, 43, 210; is Agni, the Fire-altar, 43, 332, 364 sq.; is yonder sun, 43, 365; Mind created S., S. created Breath, 43, 376 sq.; Pragâpati created s., and by s. everything else, 43, 403; mind and s. are the same and yet distinct, 44, 46, 218; Adâbhya cup of Soma identified with s., 44, 105 sq.; Hot*ri* is s., Adhvaryu mind, 44, 136; life and the gods depart from those who at the sacrifice speak impure s., 44, 387, 541; is worship, 44, 470, 476; all s. has informing power with regard to actions only, 48, 148–56; sacred s., *see* Prayers. *See also* Senses, Vâ*k*, *and* Words.

Spells, against enemies and the Drug, 4, lxxiii, lxxv, 100 sq., 112 sq., 125 n., 126, 129 sq., 133 sq., 136–48, 213 sq., 250 sq.; curative s., 4, lxxx, 225 sq., 228–30, 235–41; 45, 103; s. against the demons produced by shavings of hair, and parings of nails, 4, 191 sq.; plants defiled by magic s., 12, 370, 373; sacrifices used as s. against enemies, 14, 187, 193; water poured out in the direction in which an enemy dwells with a s., 14, 250; dhâra*n*îs or talismanic words for the protection of preachers, 21, xxi, xxxi, 371–5, 434 sq., 439; preacher of the Lotus of the True Law obtains magical s. in his dreams, 21, 278; name of Avalokite*s*vara acts as a s. in all anxiety, and makes pernicious s. revert to whence they come, 21, 406, 414; evil s. worked out by the foe of Mithra, 23, 125, 125 n.; used in a law-court, 29, 362 sq.; food may be made poisonous by evil s., 35, 218; the Bodhisattva a *Kand*âla who knows a s. producing fruits out of season, 35, 284; teaching s., tricks, &c., a means of getting alms, employed by bad monks, 45, 133 n.; fate of those who practise s. and besmear their bodies with ashes for the sake of amusement or power, 45, 231; for killing living beings, 45, 298; pious monk does not use s., 45, 327; those who practise magic arts by means of s., will be born in hell, 45, 366 sq.; Agni upholds the sky by his efficacious s., 46, 61; Agni invoked to protect from evil s., 46, 138, 170, 372; power of s., 46, 194; knowledge of Dhâra*n*îs possessed by beings in Buddha-countries, 49 (ii), 19, 190. *See also* Prayers, *and* Witchcraft.

Spênâk-maînôk, Phl. for Av. Spe*n*ta-Mainyu, 5, 3 n.

Spendamat, Phl. for Spe*n*ta-Mainyu,

q.v.; confounded with Spendarmad, 5, 365 n.
Spendarmad, *see* Spenta-Ârmaiti.
Spend-dâd, son of Vistâsp, 5, 137 sq., 137 n., 150; 47, 83, 83 n.; converted, 47, 125.
Spend-shêd, n.p., 37, 30, 30 n.
Spengaghra, demon of draught, smitten by the lightning, 4, 223, 223 n. *See* Spêngargâk.
Spêngargâk = Spengaghra = Aspengargâk, 5, 28 n.; fire in a cloud which stands opposed to S., 5, 62.
Spenta, n.p., 23, 217.
Spenta-Ârmaiti, Phl. Spendarmad, means 'Humility,' 4, liii; 5, 10 n.; genius of the earth, 4, lxvii, lxxvii, 13 sq., 213; 5, 197 sq., 198 n., 203, 209, 211, 359; 18, 198, 198 n.; throws him into hell, who does not make gifts to the faithful, 4, 31; man delivered unto S., 4, 203, 203 n.; look of a courtesan withers one-third of the strength of S., 4, 205; daughter and wife of Ahura-Mazda, 4, 213 sq., 213 n.; 18, 392 sq. and n., 396, 401, 415 sq.; 37, 273 n., 274, 365 sq., 393; the archangel, created, 5, 10; kept charge of one portion of Gâyômard's seed, 5, 53, 53 n.; has the musk flower, 5, 104; seizes on Tarômat, 5, 128; 18, 270, 270 n.; received the gold of the dead Gâyômard, 5, 183; admonishes Mânûskîhar, 5, 329, 329 n.; 24, 350; 37, 468; meat-offering to S., 5, 336; confounded with Spendamat, 5, 365 n.; protector of earth and virtuous woman, how to be propitiated, 5, 372 sq., 376 sq., 377 n.; invoked for blessing in procreation, 5, 401, 405; Gâyômard begets Mashya and Mashîyôî on S., 18, 401 sq.; invoked and worshipped, 18, 437, 444; 23, 5, 14, 36 sq.; creature of Ahura-Mazda, 23, 31, 33; helps against foes and fiends, 23, 32; Mithra, Rashnu, and S., with Ahura-Mazda, 23, 181; the milk of the good S., 23, 341, 341 n.; offended by a corpse buried in the ground, 24, 294 sq.; offended by walking barefoot, 24, 307; offended by the corpse of an unthankful person, 24, 329; complete mindfulness through S., 37, 194, 194 n., 291 sq.; righteous souls protected by S., 37, 291; the pious give S. to Aûharmazd, 37, 334, 341; the desire of S., 37, 386 sq.; Zoroaster tempted by a fiend in the guise of S., 47, xi, 62 sq., 63 n.; at the court of Mânûskîhar, 47, xiv, xxix, 134; protects Zoroaster, 47, 145; orders the institution of priests, 47, 161 sq.; Zoroaster indicates his religion as complete to S., 47, 163.
Spenta-Mainyu, and Amesha-spentas, 4, 139 n.; spirit of prosperity, 5, 3 n.; part of Vayu belongs to S., 23, 10, 18, 34, 250, 250 n., 262; creatures of S., 23, 106 sq.; 31, 354; Angra-Mainyu gives way to the blows of S., 23, 183; as a creator and maintainer of the world assisted by the Fravashis, 23, 187; invoked, 23, 351, 353; gifts of S., the Good Spirit, 31, 83, 83 n.; the spirit of Ahura-Mazda, 31, 145; the stars, S.'s creatures, 31, 199, 210, 216, 225; Yasna offered to all the holy creatures of S., 31, 201, 211, 226, 280, 349; the wicked excluded from the creatures of S., 31, 229; worshipped, 31, 308.
Spentâmainyu, the Gâtha, 31, 145–75.
Spentô-dâta, or Kaî Spendâd, adopted Zoroastrianism, 23, 207, 207 n.; 24, 171, 171 n.
Spentô-khratu, n.p., 23, 213.
Spentô-khratvau, a high-priest, 47, 83 sq.
Spenzagar, demon of thunder, 24, 133, 133 n.
Spêtô-tôrâ, the Âspîgân, 47, 34.
Sphota, grammatical t.t., is the word, 34, 204–6, 204 n.; is eternal, 34, 206; its assumption gratuitous, 34, 209 sq.
Spider, as it emits out of itself the threads of its web, so Brahman creates the world, 34, 348; simile of the s., 36, 351. *See also* Parables (*c*).
Spingauruska, conquered by Vîstâspa, 23, 117, 280.
Spirit, functions of nature and, 8, 104 sq. and n.; *the supreme s. in this body is called supervisor, adviser, supporter, enjoyer, the great lord, and the supreme self also*, 8, 105, 105 n. *See also* Breath, *and* Purusha.

Spirits, of earth and air listen to a sermon on salvation, 10 (ii), 37–9; Kakudha appears after his death as a s. to Moggallâna, 20, 234 sq.; the preacher hears the yells uttered by the s., 21, 339; evil deed cannot be kept secret from s. (fairies, dryads, &c.), 35, 295, 295 n.; abide here on new moon day, 44, 2. *See also* Ancestors, Ancestor Worship, Ghosts, Gods, *and* Superhuman beings.

Spirit Tablets, *see* Ancestor Worship (*d*).

Spiritual insight, or Vipassanâ, one of the conditions by which a Bhikkhu obtains his desires, 11, 210–18.

Spiritualism, in Buddhism, 11, 208.

Spiritual sense, five organs of, 11, 61, 63.

Spirituous liquor, drinking of, forbidden, is a high crime or mortal sin, 2, 63, 74, 188, 188 n., 280; 6, 32, 110; 7, 26, 132, 134; 8, 279, 389; 10 (i), 61; (ii), 18, 66; 11, 253; 13, 44; 14, 5, 105; 25, 383, 441, 494; 44, 233, 260; 48, 702; penance for drinking surâ or any s. l., 2, 82 sq., 87, 287, 287 n., 293; 7, 162, 181; 14, 127, 132, 213 sq., 296, 299; 25, 449–51, 449 n., 450 n., 460 sq., 460 n., 480; drinkers of s. l. excluded from *S*râddha, 2, 257; 25, 105; being abandoned to drink, Hsî and Ho neglected the duties of their office, 3, 81 sq.; the people of Yin (Shang) ruined by indulgence in s. l., 3, 122; on the proper use of s. l., and the disastrous consequences of drunkenness, 3, 171–9; wine and other s. l. in China, 3, 172 sq.; employed at sacrifices, 3, 174–7, 174 sq. n.; 27, 408, 443, 445–7, 447 sq. n.; 28, 141, 293; offered to the departed spirits or their personators, 3, 194, 241 sq., 300, 304 n., 306, 323, 332, 365, 367–70, 375, 386 sq., 387 n., 401, 403; 28, 293; used by a king for making presents, 3, 267; 27, 119; vice of drunkenness, 3, 359, 411, 414, 414 n.; drinking festivities, 3, 374 sq. and n.; 27, 56, 271, 271 n., 299, 316 sq., 317 n.; 28, 435–46, 455–7; 37, 150; two bottles of s. l. offered by the people of Pin to their ruler, 3, 445; drinking wine forbidden during the sacrifice, 4, 321–3; 37, 94; three kinds of s. l. are unclean for the higher castes, ten kinds for the Brâhma*n*as only, 7, 95 sq.; defiles vessels, &c., 7, 97, 102 n., 164 sq.; 25, 190; women who drink s. l. denounced, sin of intercourse with them, no funeral libation for them, wives who drink may be deserted, &c., 7, 137; 14, 112 sq.; 25, 184, 329, 341 sq., 444; crime of smelling s. l., 7, 138; 25, 444; Brâhma*n*as, esp. women, who drink s. l. reborn in hell or as low animals, 7, 175; 14, 112; 25, 496; drinker of s. l. will have black teeth in future birth, 14, 109; 25, 440; Brâhma*n*as drink rum in the north, 14, 146, 146 n.; distilleries of s. l. are impure, 14, 170; punishments for drinking Surâ, 14, 201; 25, 383, 496; 33, 229 sq.; about selling wine to foreigners and infidels, 18, 176 sq.; sin of drunkenness, 18, 177–80; 37, 180; unfermented toddy not allowed to Bhikkhus, 20, 386, 399, 412; drinking of s. l. one of the four stains by which Sama*n*as and Brâhmans are affected, 20, 389 sq.; advantages of moderate drinking of wine, 24, xvii, 46–8; evils of immoderate drinking, 24, 48 sq.; food of one intoxicated not to be eaten, 25, 161; abstention recommended, 25, 177; drunkenness a vice of kings, 25, 223; money due for s. l. not to be paid by heir, 25, 282; 33, 329; sellers of s. l. banished, 25, 381; not to be sold by Brâhma*n*as, 25, 421; regulation of drinking-habits, 27, 81; 28, 106 sq.; regulations about preparation of s. l., 27, 303; 28, 141; drinking to one another at sacrifices, 27, 317 sq.; 'the dark spirit' (water) more valuable than s. l. for sacrifices, 27, 435, 435 n.; Surâ given to women at the wedding, 29, 32; debts contracted for s. l. not to be paid, 33, 45; drinkers of s. l., inadmissible witnesses, 33, 303; forbidden gift, 36, 121; Surâ means untruth, misery, darkness, 41, 8, 29; Surâ cups offered at the Vâgapeya, 41, 8–11, 29; Parisrut liquor bought from a eunuch, 41, 9 sq.; one who drinks s. l.

talks as one who enjoys himself, 41, 130; origin of Parisrut, 41, 131; 44, 215; Parisrut and Surâ at the Râgasûya, 41, 133, 134 n.; offered to Fathers from pitcher with holes, 41, 135 sq.; libations of Surâ made at the Sautrâmanî sacrifice, 42, 578; 44, 213 n., 216, 223–33, 223 sq. n., 236, 241, 245, 260, 269–72; cups full of fiery liquor poured out in the palace of Ganamegaya, 44, 95; Surâ (matured liquor), the essence of food, waters, and plants, 44, 215, 225, 232 sq., 242; preparation of Surâ, 44, 223 sq.; Surâ contributes to joy, 44, 227 sq., 233; Surâ a form of Soma, 44, 233; Surâ purifies the sacrificer, 44, 236. *See also* Soma.

Spitâma, n.p., 23, 204.

Spîtâmân (Spîtâm), ancestor of Zoroaster, 5, 141, 141 n.; 47, 34, 140.

Spitâmas, the family of Zarathustra, 31, 133, 142, 190 sq., 190 n.; 37, 281, 299, 299 n.

Spitâmi, daughter of Zarathustra, 31, 191.

Spiti, son of Uspãsnu, 23, 216, 216 n.

Spîtîyôs, son of Spânsnâyôs, 37, 218 sq. and n.

Spîtôîd-i Aûspôsînân, or Spîtôîs Uspãsnaos, n. of a high-priest, 5, 115, 115 n.; 37, 219 n.; comes to Frashôstar in search of wisdom, 47, 81, 81 n.

Spîtôîs, *see* Spîtôîd.

Spîtûr, or Spityura, one of 'the Rashnû of Kînŏ,' 5, 130, 130 n.; with Dahâk, cut up Yim, 5, 131; 23, 297, 297 sq. n.

Spring, *see* Seasons.

Sprites, invoked upon the enemies, 42, 125. *See also* Superhuman beings.

Sraddhâ, Sk., Faith: a S. libation offered by the Devas in heaven, 1, 78, 81 n.; Gamadagni has brought a wreath to S., 30, 168. *See* Faith.

Srâddha, Sk. t.t., funeral oblation and funeral meal: anxiousness of continuance of S., and the laws about substitutes for legitimate sons, 2, xix sq.; Veda-study interrupted after having eaten S. food, 2, 39 sq., 43, 263, 265; 14, 64 sq., 209; 25, 110, 146 sq.; 29, 115 sq., 118, 142, 323; teacher, student, Snâtaka shall not eat S. food, 2, 113; 7, 117, 167; 25, 462 sq. and n.; 29, 318; the S. revealed by Manu for the salvation of mankind, 2, 140; 25, lix sq., lx n.; times when S. should be performed, 2, 140–2, 146 sq.; 7, 240–6; 14, 51, 55 sq., 55 n.; 25, 97, 125–7, 125 sq. n.; rules for the performance of S., 2, 140–51, 255–9; 7, 232–63; 14, 51–6, 266–70; 25, 97–127, 606 sq.; 29, 106–12, 250–5; 30, 225–31, 305; substances which should be offered at S., 2, 142 sq., 150 sq.; 7, 246–9; 25, 98, 124 sq.; persons to be invited to S., 2, 143 sq., 146, 148, 255 sq., 259; 7, 251–5; 25, 64 sq., 98–111, 113 sq., 116–24, 133; persons who defile the company at S., 2, 145, 256–8, 267, 281; 25, 100, 103–10; rules for the daily S., 2, 147 sq.; 25, 87–90, 127; monthly S., 2, 150 sq.; 25, 97 sq., 97 n., 127; 29, 106; 30, 111 sq., 225, 292 sq.; to be offered also by Sûdras, 2, 233; 25, 164; by whom, and to whom S. are to be offered, 2, 256; 7, 239 sq.; 25, 328 sq. n., 352 sq., 355; animals slain for, and meat eaten at S., 2, 270, 270 n.; 14, 54; 25, 150; Ekoddishta S. for a recently deceased person, 7, 75 sq., 83–5; 25, 121 n., 146; 29, 108 sq., 246, 357–9; *the dead person and the performer of the* S. *are sure to be benefited by its performance. Perform the* S. *always, therefore, abandoning bootless grief. This is the duty which should be constantly discharged towards a dead person by his kinsmen; by mourning a man will neither benefit the dead nor himself,* 7, 80; Sapindîkarana, or ceremony of investing a dead person with the rights of a Sapinda, 7, 80, 85–7; 25, 121, 121 n.; 29, 109 sq., 138 sq.; offerings at S. made in trenches, 7, 84, 238 sq.; monthly S. during the first year after the decease of a person, 7, 85, 86; a S. to be performed on the anniversary of the deceased relative's death, 7, 86; Nândîmukha S. at the beginning of the marriage ceremony, 7, 92 n.; food offered at a S. is impure, 7, 155; 14, 298; penance for eating

of a S. repast consisting of raw food, 7, 168; after having partaken of a S., given a S., or been invited to a S., he must avoid connubial intercourse, 7, 222; S. of the gods, and S. of the manes, 7, 232, 251 sq.; new moon S., and S. on Ash*t*akâs and Anvash*t*akâs, 7, 233, 238–41; 34, 297 n.; rewards obtained by the performance of S., 7, 241–6, 256, 260; 25, 98, 126 sq.; one should avoid wrath, shedding tears, and being in a hurry when performing S., 7, 248; should be performed in an enclosed place, 7, 250; food for the manes must not be placed upon a chair, nor touched with the foot, nor sneezed upon, 7, 250; details about the S. repast, 7, 250 sq.; fit and unfit countries and places for S., 7, 255–60; a S. with sesamum, on the full moon day of the month Mâgha, 7, 266; sacred texts repeated at S., 7, 301; 15, 14; survivals of Brâhmanic S. in Buddhist funeral feasts and gifts, 11, xliii sq., 131–5; enumerated among public spectacles to be avoided by the Bhikkhu, 11, 192; fragments of S. meals are for the Manes of those who have died childless, 14, 52 sq.; to be offered by the heir, 14, 87, 87 n.; 33, 375–80, 385; *G*aina monks should not accept food at S., 22, 92, 97; disposal of the cake offerings, 25, xxiii sq., 123 sq.; the Mânava *S*râddhakalpa and Manusm*ri*ti on S., 25, xl–xliv; results of inviting sinners to S., 25, lxvii, 107–9; number of guests at S., 25, 98 sq.; different kinds of S., 25, 122, 122 n.; 29, 250, 251 n.; offered to three ancestors, 25, 366; Âbhyudayika S. for joyful occasions, 29, 110–12; 30, 110 sq.; all ceremonies accompanied by an Anvâhârya S. (?), 30, 13, 13 n.; a S. in the rainy season, 30, 231; persons excluded from S. cannot be witnesses, 33, 86; local customs with regard to feeding Brâhma*n*as at S., 33, 389 sq. *See also* Ancestor Worship.

*S*rama*n*a, *see* Sama*n*a.

Sraosha, or Srôsh, obedient attention, angel of Obedience, 4, 89 n.; 18, 443; 31, xix, 69, 74, 127, 127 n.; comes to meet the departed soul and guides it to heaven, 4, 89 n., 373; 31, 15, 20, 20 n.; Rashnu, Mithra, and S., the three judges of the departed soul, 4, 89 n.; 18, 33, 33 n.; 23, 168; 24, 18; 37, 155, 155 n.; invoked and worshipped, 4, 101, 101 n., 136, 223, 230, 241; 5, 139, 402, 405; 31, 69, 74, 197, 205, 208 sq., 212–15, 218, 220 sq., 222, 224, 226 sq., 254, 256, 271, 274 sq., 280, 319 sq., 325 sq., 345, 351–3, 358, 387 sq.; 37, 219; the Genius of Active Piety, and his holy bird, 4, 196–200, 196 sq. n.; first tied the Baresma and sacrificed to Ahura, 4, 196 n.; dialogue between the holy S. and the Drug, 4, 200–4; wields the club against the fiends, 4, 214; 5, 402, 405; 37, 279; pious, sovereign S., 4, 274; red chrysanthemum belongs to S., 5, 104; attacks Aeshm, 5, 128, 128 n.; 24, 33; Behrâm fire an assistant of S., 5, 185; messenger of Aûhar*m*az*d* to mankind, 5, 224, 224 n., 226, 235; 31, 95 sq., 101 sq.; the vigorous, 5, 228; comes three times to defend mankind against demons, 5, 366, 366 n.; ceremonial of S. during three days after a death, 5, 382–4; 18, 59–63, 240 sq.; 24, 310, 351; 37, 183; protects the soul from demons during three days after death, 5, 382, 382 n.; 18, 60; 24, 17, 17 n., 19 sq., 318 sq.; Vohûman in the thoughts, S. in the words, Ar*d* in the actions, 18, 18 sq., 18 n.; 'the season of S.,' 18, 23 n.; takes the account of sin and good works, 18, 60, 66; dedication to S., 18, 447 sq.; who makes the world grow, invoked, 23, 6, 15, 40; the incarnate Word, invoked, 23, 9, 17, 36, 38, 159–67, 332, 339; comes for help and joy, 23, 26, 30; brings the liar into the power of Mithra and Rashnu, 23, 129; companion of Mithra, 23, 132, 145; praise and worship of S. in the Srôsh Ya*s*ts, 23, 159–67; 31, 296–306, 297 n.; Fravashi of S. worshipped, 23, 200; Fravashis invoked together with S., 23, 227; brother of Ashi Vanguhi, 23, 274; is tall and victorious, 23,

327; is lord and king of Aîrân-vêgô, 24, 87, 87 n.; abode of S., 24, 110; 31, 302 sq.; opposed to wrath, 24, 161 n.; propitiated by prayers said before and after meals, 24, 284; Zoroaster prays to be led by S., 31, 97, 103–5; invoked to spread delight and peace in the house, 31, 240; obedience, opposed to deaf disobedience, 31, 243; first worshipped Ahura and the Ameshô-spentas, 31, 298 sq.; not one of the Ameshô-spentas, 31, 298 n.; sits among the Ameshô-spentas, 31, 300, 300 n.; a guardian of the homes and tribes, 31, 301 sq., 311; worshipped by Haoma, 31, 302; drawn by four racers, 31, 304; let S. be here for the worship of Ahura-Mazda, 31, 357; at the resurrection of the universe, 37, 235; S. and Vohûmanô protect Zaratûst, 47, 39, 146; qualities of S., 47, 85 n.

Sraoshâ-varez, *see* Priests (*e*).

Sraumatya, quoted, 43, 363.

Srauta-sûtras rest on Sruti, Grihya-sûtras on Smriti, 30, xvii; relation between S., Grihya-sûtras, and Dharma-sûtras, 30, xxix–xxxv.

Srâvakas, *see* Holy persons.

Sravana, a Nakshatra, worshipped, 29, 127, 327; 30, 91.

Sravanâ or Srâvana ceremony, *see* Snakes.

Srâvastî, *see* Sâvatthî.

Srâvastikâ Sâkhâ of the Vesavâtika Gana, 22, 291.

Srenika, or Sren(i)ya, *see* Bimbisâra.

Sreyâmsa, n. of Mahâvîra, 22, 193, 256; n. of a Tîrthakara, 22, 280; n. of a lay votary, 22, 284.

Srî, or Lakshmî, goddess of Fortune, wife of Vishnu, praised by the Earth, 7, 297 sq.; colloquy of the Earth and *S.*, 7, 297–301; dwells in all good and auspicious things and persons, 7, 298–301; is wedded to kings, 12, 377; Indra invoked to bring *S.*, the woolly, with cattle, 15, 47 sq.; the anointing of the goddess *S.*, a lucky vision, 22, 219, 232 sq.; Bali offering to *S.*, 25, 91; 29, 86; good wives are *S.* or goddesses of fortune, 25, 332; springs from Pragâpati, and is dismembered by the gods, 44, 62–5.

Srî-bhâshya, title of Râmânuga's commentary on the Vedânta-sûtras, 34, xvi sq.; translated, *Vol.* 48. *See* Râmânuga.

Srîdhara, a Ganadhara of Pârsva, 22, 274.

Srîgarbha, n. of a Bodhisattva, 21, 22, 27.

Srîgupta, disciple of Suhastin, 22, 291.

Srîkûta, the 21st Tathâgata, 49 (ii), 6, 67.

Srîkutaka, or Srîguptaka, converted by Buddha, 19, 241 sq.

Sriñgaya, the son of Devavâta, 46, 360 sq.; his son Suvarnanishthîvin, 49 (i), 90.

Sriñgayas (n. of family): Suplan Sârñgaya, 12, 376; Devabhâga, Purohita of the S., 12, 377; the S. Vaitahavyas, 42, 171, 433 sq.; Revottaras Pâtava expelled by the S., restores King Dushtarîtu to the dominion over the S., 44, 269, 272.

Srîraokhshan, n.p., 23, 205.

Srîrâ-vanghu, n.p., 23, 215.

Srîsaok, *see* Animals (*i*).

Srît, or Srîtô, daughter of Zoroaster, 5, 142; 47, 166.

Srît, n. of a teacher, 5, 404.

Srîtak, n.p., 47, 140.

Srîtô, hero, presents a chariot to the soul of Vistâsp, 47, xi, 77–81, 78 n., 126; kills the miraculous ox who decides boundary disputes, 47, xiv, xxix, 32, 135–8, 136 n.

Srôbar, or Srôbŏvar, *see* Snakes.

Sronadanta, converted by Buddha, 19, 243.

Srôsh, *see* Sraosha.

Srôsh Yast, *see* Yasts.

Srotriya, t.t., a learned Brâhmana, definition of, 2, 115, 115 n.; reception of *S.* as guest, portions of daily food to be given to *S.*, 2, 205 sq.; 14, 50; 25, 97, 133; 29, 86; king must support and treat kindly *S.*, 2, 228; 25, 237, 322 sq.; may settle difficult questions of law, 2, 310; 25, xlviii sq.; Buddha's definition of a Sottiya, i.e. *S.*, 10 (ii), 92; a Brâhmana in whose family there is no *S.*, is like a Sûdra, 14, 33 sq. and n.; property of a *S.* not lost by being enjoyed by others, 14, 81; 25, 279; Veda-study to be interrupted,

and impurity, on the death of a *S.*, 14, 208; 25, 182; 29, 245; they never say to a *S.* 'Thou art destitute of offspring,' 14, 210; a *S.* who is without sin and without desires, enjoys highest bliss, 15, 172; seniority among *S.*, 25, 55; descendants of *S.* sanctify a company, 25, 110; only *S.* entitled to sacrifice, 25, 161; niggardly *S.* worse than liberal usurer, 25, 164; are exempt from taxes, 25, 237; cannot be made a witness, 25, 265; fined for not inviting another *S.* to a festival, 25, 322; king and *S*rotriya are the upholders of sacred law, 41, 106; theologians, accepting no gifts, present at the A*s*vamedha, 44, 370.

***S*rutabandhu,** one of the Gaupâyanas, 46, 415.

***S*rutasena,** a Pârikshita, offered horse-sacrifice, 44, 396.

Srûta-spâdha, n.p., 23, 213.

Srûta*t*-fedhri, the virgin mother of Ukhshya*t*-ereta, 23, 195 n., 226, 226 n.

***S*ruti,** Sanskrit t.t. for divine revelation, 1, xiii; Upanishads belong to *S.*, 1, lxvii; meaning of *S.* inferred from Sm*ri*ti, 34, 145 sq.; the highest authority, 34, 291 n., 293 sq., 297 n.; 38, 211–14, 262 sq.; men who are unable to ascertain the true sense of *S.*, rely upon Sm*ri*ti, 34, 292; supersensuous matters cannot be perceived without *S.*, 34, 293; if in conflict with other means of right knowledge, has to be bent, so as to accord with the latter, 34, 299; teaching of *S.*, 48, 119, 120. *See also* Revelation, Scripture, Upanishads, *and* Veda.

Srûtvôk-spâ*d*âk, Av. Srûtô-spâd*a*u, high-priest, 47, 83 sq., 83 n.

Srûvô, *see* Animals (*i*).

Srvara, *see* Snakes.

Stages of life, *see* Â*s*ramas.

Staotar-Vahi*s*tahê-Ashyêhê, n.p., 23, 211, 211 n., 225.

Staota Yêsnya, *see* Zend-Avesta.

Stars, invoked and worshipped, 2, 108; 14, 252 sq.; 30, 243, 277; 42, 161; bodies of great sages become s., 2, 160; 8, 240; 12, 269 n.; 39, 245, 245 n.; 41, 244; to be examined about wind and weather, 3, 149; appeal to the s. of heaven, which are mentioned by name, 3, 362–4; Ti*s*trya, the bright and glorious star (of rain), and other s. invoked, 4, 222, 222 n.; 23, 9, 16; joint invocation to waters and s., 4, 230, 232 n., 234; seed of waters, earth and plants in the s., 4, 234, 234 n.; 23, 9, 16, 104, 106, 175 sq. and n.; size of s., 4, 254, 254 n.; the constellation s. and those also not of the constellations, produced by Aûhar*ma*z*d*, 5, 10–12, 12 n.; twenty-eight lunar mansions, 5, 11, 11 n.; are a specimen of a warlike army, 5, 12; every month is the owner of one constellation, 5, 25 sq.; influence of Jupiter and Saturn on life and death, 5, 165 sq.; Tî*s*tar and Avrak, constellations of the Zodiac, 5, 168 sq.; appearance of s. and periods of the day, 5, 371; position of the sun and constellations, 5, 397–400; worship of s. among the Sabaeans, 6, xi; signs of Zodiac guarded from the devils who are pelted with shooting s., 6, 245; 9, 305; he must not look at the s., while unclean, 7, 220; God the Lord of Sirius, the Dog-star, 9, 254; Sirius worshipped by the Arabs, 9, 254 n.; oaths by the s., 9, 326–8; divine female beings, 12, 269 n.; 41, 243 sq.; legend of the K*ri*ttikâs and the seven *Ri*shis, 12, 282 sq.; *see also Ri*shis; the Pleiades as barricades keeping the fiends from the uppermost sky, 18, 94, 94 n.; the great Graha, called Kshudrâtma, entered the natal asterism of Mahâvîra in the night of his death, 22, 266 sq.; the Haptôiri*n*gas (Ursa Major), 23, 9, 16, 97, 97 n.; good and bad s., belonging respectively to the worlds of Ahura-Mazda and Angra-Mainyu, 23, 89 n., 92, 176, 176 n.; 24, 127–38; demons flying about as worm-s. or shooting-s., 23, 95 sq., 95 n.; Vana*n*t, Ti*s*trya, Haptôiri*n*ga, and other s., 23, 175 sq. and n.; Fravashis watch over the Haptôiri*n*ga s., 23, 194; twelve signs of the Zodiac, 24, 34, 38, 245, 245 n.; 47, 124; duties and influence and motion of s., 24, 90–3; are guardian spirits, 24, 92; comet, the evil

being Mûspar, 24, 132, 132 n.; destiny allotted by the constellations, auspicious and inauspicious, 24, 227 sq.; 31, 28, 28 n.; 37, 421, 445; 40, 236, 313, 317; the meshes of the Dîkshita's cloth belong to the s., 26, 10; bridegroom shows the bride the polar-star and other s., 29, 43, 285 sq., 383 sq.; 30, 47 sq., 263; bride and bridegroom worship the s., 29, 170; 30, 194–6; polar star worshipped as Brahman, 30, 194 sq.; the s. which are Spenta-Mainyu's creatures, worshipped, 31, 199, 199 n., 205, 210 sq., 216 sq., 220, 225 sq., 256, 308, 329, 383; the body of Ahura-Mazda, 31, 285; interpretation of s., 37, 429, 433 sq.; Nasks on s., good and evil, 37, 437, 440, 447; Wei-tâu, the Great Bear, got the Tâo, 39, 136, 244, 244 n.; the Milky Way not to be traced to its beginning or end, 39, 170, 170 n.; spirit-rulers residing in the Great Bear, 40, 236, 236 n.; spitting at shooting s. forbidden, 40, 244; origin of s., 41, 149; 43, 361; expiatory charm for a child born under an unlucky s., 42, 109 sq., 517 sq.; deities and bricks of fire-altar, 43, 91; the hair of the sky, 43, 208; as Apsaras, the mates of the Moon, 43, 232; kindled by the moon, 43, 399; are Vasus, 44, 116; the region between the rising of the seven *Ri*shis (Ursa Major) and the setting of the sun in the quarter of the living, 44, 425; there are no s. in Sukhâvatî, 49 (ii), 43. *See also* Luminaries, Moon, Nakshatras, Omens, Planets, *and* Sun.

Steer, *see* Bull.

Sthâlîpâka, *see* Sacrifice (*b*).

Sthapati, *see* Revottara.

Sthavira *S*âkalya, n. of a teacher, 1, 257, 265.

Sthaviras, Elders, among *G*aina monks, 22, 286–95, 297, 306; 45, 149. *See also* Theras.

Sthiragupta, *see* Kshamâ*s*rama*n*a S.

Sthûlabhadra, n. of a Sthavira, 22, 287, 289.

Stipi, son of Rava*nt*, 23, 217.

Stiva*nt*, n.p., 23, 216.

Stobhâksharas, or syllables used in the musical recitation of Sâman hymns, speculations on them, 1, 22, 26–8.

Stoma, *see* Prayers (*c*).

Stones, worshipped by Arabs, 6, xii sq., xv; *see also* Kaabah; ceremony of treading on a s., 29, 168, 282 sq., 357, 381; 30, 45 sq., 146, 188, 260 sq., 272; placed to bar off death, 29, 248; sprinkling the fire-altar from a s., 43, 169–71; why s. are hard and not fit for eating, 43, 170; variegated s. set up as symbol of sun, vital air and vital power, 43, 195 sq., 243, 360 sq.

Storehouses, and store-rooms for robes, of Buddhist monks, 17, 119–21, 128 sq., 201 sqq.

Stories, *see G*âtakas, *and* Tales.

Storm, lightning and thunder celebrate God's praise, 6, 233. *See also* Wind.

Stotra, *see* Prayers (*c*).

Strîdhana, t.t., wife's separate fortune, *see* Woman (*a*).

Strîveda, though acquainted with it men get into the power of women, 45, 274.

Student, studentship, *see* Brahma*k*ârin, Holy persons, *and* Teacher (*a*).

Study, *see* Veda (*c*).

Stûpas, or Thûpas, or Topes, or Dâgabas, memorial burial-mounds, date of the earliest, 11, xvii sq.; to be erected at the four cross-roads for *K*akkavatti kings and Buddhas, 11, 93, 125 sq.; mounds in which the bones and ashes of the deceased are to be placed, 11, 93 n.; persons worthy of S., and the use of S., 11, 93–5; erected over the relics of Buddha in eight parts of India, 11, 131–6; 19, 334 sq.; A*s*oka raised 84,000 S., 19, 336 sq.; wonderful apparition of a seven-jewelled S, disclosing the frame of the expired Tathâgata Prabhûtaratna, 21, xxx, 227–40, 283, 364–8, 404, 441; S. containing the relics of extinct Buddhas appear in the Buddha-fields, 21, 8; building of S., and worship of relics in S., 21, 15, 50–2, 147–51, 247; 36, 230, 280 sq.; numerous S. were erected over the relics of Buddhas, 21, 27, 382 sqq.; different kinds of S., 21, 50; the

world of the Buddha Dharmaprabhâsa will be full of S., 21, 195; Buddha-shrines without relics to be erected where the Dharmaparyâya is preached or studied, 21, 220, 324, 327, 367; Devadatta's body shall remain as one mass within a S., 21, 247; those who are occupied with sacred writ need not build S., 21, 321 sqq., 324 sq.; erected for King Milinda, 35, xx; the wise are to be honoured like S., 36, 375; Buddha built a round S., 49 (i), 199.

Stuta-*s*astras, Sk. t.t., hymns sung and recited at sacrifices, 1, 51.

Sû, duke of, a minister of crime, 3, 225, 225 n.

Subâhu, receives the upasampadâ ordination from Buddha, 13, 110 sq.; n. of a Bhikshu, 49 (ii), 2.

Subâla-upanishad, quoted, 48, 778.

Subandhu, one of the Gaupâyanas, 46, 415.

Subbhabhûmi, Mahâvîra travelled in, 22, 84.

***S*ubha**, a Ga*n*adhara of Pâr*s*va, 22, 274.

Subhadda, Sk. Subhadra, his disloyalty the chief cause of the First Council, 10 (i), xxxi; rejoices at the death of Buddha, 11, xi sq., xiv, 127, 127 n.; converted by Buddha, became an Arhat, 11, 26, 103–11; the Bhikkhus S., the Brâhman, and S., the barber, different persons, 11, 127 n.; 17, 140 n.; raises objections against the rules prescribed by Buddha, 17, 144 n.; 20, 371; interview of the heretic S. with the dying Buddha, 19, 290–5; 35, 186–9; reaches Nirvâ*n*a before Buddha, 19, 295.

Subhaddâ, queen of Mahâ Sudassana, 11, 239 sqq., 274, 276–84, 276 n.; 36, 249. *See also K*ulla S.

Subhadrâ, son of, a hero, 8, 37, 39.

Subhadrâ, or Subhadrikâ, a wicked woman living in Kâmpîla, 44, 321 sq. n.

Subhadrâ, n. of a female lay votary, 22, 284.

Subhâsitasutta, t.c., 10 (ii), 72 sq.

***S*ubhavyûha**, King, was converted by his sons, 21, xxxi, 419–30; becomes the Buddha *S*âlendrarâ*g*a, 21, 429.

Subho*g*a, one of the eight Brahmans who took note of the marks on Buddha's body, 36, 44.

Subhûti, n. of an eminent Arhat, 21, 3, 98 sqq.; 49 (ii), 2; Buddha's prophecy about S. who is to be the Buddha *Sas*iketu, 21, 144–7; saying of S. the Elder, 36, 315, 323; conversation between Buddha and S., 49 (ii), 112–44.

Subjects, *see* Objects.

Subrahma*n*yâ liturgy, *see* Prayers (*c*).

Substance, contradictions in the Vai*s*eshika doctrine about it, 34, 394 sqq.; definition of s. and the six kinds of s., viz. Dharma, Adharma, space, time, matter, and souls, 45, 153 sq., 207 sq. *See also* Upadhi.

Subtle body, *see* Body.

Sûdadohas verse, *see* Prayers (*c*).

Sudar*s*ana, mountain, invoked at the house-building rite, 29, 347. *See* Meru.

Sudar*s*ana, a Nâga prince, 49 (i), 169.

Sudar*s*anâ, eldest sister of Mahâvîra, 22, 193, 256.

Sudar*s*anâ, n. of the palankin of the Arhat *Ri*shabha, 22, 283.

Sudâs, perished through want of humility, 25, 222, 222 n.; Vasish*th*a swore before S., son of Pigavana, 25, 273, 273 n.; gave one hundred thousand cows as the sacrificial fee, 30, 38 sq.

Sudassana, king of kings, a Bodisat, legend of, 11, 239–41, 248–89; legend of S., a spiritualist's sun-myth, 11, 244 sq.; his four marvellous powers, 11, 251, 259–61; his seven precious things, 11, 251–9.

Sudatta, after death, became a Sakadâgâmin, 11, 25; one of the eight Brahmans who took note of the marks on Buddha's body, 36, 44.

Sudatta, n. of Anâthapi*nd*ada, 19, 201 n., 202 n.; 20, 182.

Sudda, Pali, for Sk. *S*ûdra, q.v.

***S*uddhara*s*miprabha**, n. of a Tathâgata, 49 (ii), 100.

Suddha*tth*akasutta, t.c., 10 (ii), 150–2.

***S*uddhipanthaka**, disciple of Buddha, 49 (ii), 90.

Suddhodana, Pali Suddhodana, father of Buddha, 13, 208 sqq.; 19, 1, 6, 18, 20, 25–8, 91–4; 36, 45; 49 (i), 2–25, 81, 89–91, 195–200.

Sudhamma, n. of a Bhikkhu, 17, 359–69.

Sudhanvan Âṅgirasa has become a Gandharva, 15, 127.

Sudharma, n. of a Kinnara king, 21, 5; n. of a Brahma-angel, 21, 167.

Sudharmâ, assembly hall of the gods, 21, 342, 345; 22, 222.

Sudharman, chief apostle of Mahâvîra, 22, xvi, 1; a Sthavira and Gaṇadhara, 22, 286 sq.; died after the Nirvâṇa of Mahâvîra, 22, 287; an Agnivaiśyâyana, confounded with Mahâvîra, by Buddhists, 45, xxi; followers of Pârśva converted by S. Gautama to the creed of Mahâvîra, 45, 119–29, 420–35.

Sudinna, the Kalanda, subject of the first Pârâgika, 20, 374; called a useless fellow by Buddha, 35, 237–41.

Sûdras, caste of: knowledge which S. and women possess a supplement of the Atharva-veda, 2, xxxii, 171, 171 n.; 42, xlix; food touched or left by S. is impure, 2, 60 sq., 61 n., 75; 14, 73; 25, 162; food of S. not to be eaten, 2, 67, 147; 7, 192; 14, 29 sq., 38 sq., 69, 298; 25, 162–4, 193; 29, 318 sq.; killing S. minor offence, 2, 83; 7, 161; 14, 118; 25, 444; cohabitation with S. females causes loss of caste, fines and penance for it, 2, 85; 14, 218, 218 n., 313, 319, 328; 25, 320 sq.; shall eat the remainder of the ass-offering to Nirṛti, 2, 85; Snâtaka must not see, nor visit, nor journey with S., nor teach or do anything for S., nor live in countries inhabited or ruled by S., 2, 98, 220; 7, 199, 227 sq.; 25, 138, 141, 151, 402 n., 614; 29, 318 sq.; may be employed for washing the feet of a guest, 2, 115; S. who live by washing the feet, exempt from taxes, 2, 164; sacred rites without reciting sacred texts allowed to S., 2, 232 sq. n.; 25, 429; their duties and occupations, 2, 233; 25, 24, 325, 327, 401, 423, 428–30; money may be taken (by fraud or force) from S. to defray the expenses of a wedding or a religious rite, 2, 273; 25, 327, 433; mortal sin of sacrificing for S., or sacrificing accepting money from S., 2, 277 sq.; 7, 252 sq.; 14, 77; 25, 106, 109, 435, 438 sq.; offence of entertaining a S., 7, 34; S. who has given false evidence, must feed ten cows for one day, 7, 50; S. and the law of inheritance, 7, 73; 14, 88; 25, 358, 364; must never carry out a deceased member of a twice-born caste, 7, 75; 25, 187; funeral oblations for S., 7, 86; serving a S. renders unworthy to receive alms, causes loss of caste, 7, 139; 14, 218; 25, 444; S. whose food may be eaten, 7, 188 sq.; 25, 164, 168; Vidura, born a S., refrains from speaking on esoteric doctrines, 8, 136, 150; shall not milk the cows at a sacrifice, 12, 186 n., 330 n.; carpenters (Rathakâras) who are S. admitted to initiation and to Srauta sacrifices, 14, xxxviii sq.; characteristics of S., 14, 38; in case of any doubt about the qualifications of an adopted son, he shall be set apart like a S., 14, 76; marriage with a S. female, 14, 88; 25, xxvi sq., xxvii n., 78 sq., 83, 86, 104; Veda must not be recited before, nor sacred rites performed for S., 14, 95; 25, 144; 29, 116 sq.; *a S.-wife who belongs to the black race is espoused for pleasure, not in order to fulfil the law,* 14, 96; during certain penances and rites one shall avoid speaking to S., 14, 124, 305, 323; rules for S. employed by Âryas (as cooks), 14, 174 sq., 174 n.; created from the feet of Brahman, 14, 199; 25, 14, 24; are not allowed to teach nor to be taught the Veda, 15, 341; 25, 104; 33, 356; 34, xxxvii, 197 n., 223–9; 48, 337, 343; may reside anywhere, 25, 33; names suitable for S., 25, 35; time of impurity after death, and mode of purification for S., 25, 41, 182, 186, 193; rules of saluting S., seniority among S., 25, 53, 55, 58; he who is not initiated is on a level with the S., 25, 61; may marry wives of their own caste only, 25, 77, 358; marriage

rite for *S.*, 25, 83; are not guests, but fed, 25, 95; sin of dallying with *S.* female when invited to *S*râddha or studying a vrata, 25, 111, 121, 467; 30, 76; Sukâlins, the manes of *S.*, 25, 112; giving remnants of a *S*râddha meal to *S.*, a crime, 25, 121; deceiving *S.*, 25, 160; how to be buried, 25, 184; are to work for the king, 25, 238; must not be judges, 25, 255 sq.; a kingdom where *S.* are numerous soon perishes, 25, 256, 256 n.; *S.* give evidence for *S.*, 25, 266; special rules for *S.* of administration of oath and examination as witness, 25, 269 sq., 274; punishments of *S.* for crimes (assault, adultery, defaming) against members of higher caste, 25, 301–4, 319; guilt of *S.* in case of theft, 25, 313; created to be slaves, 25, 326; cannot be initiated, 25, 402; not worthy to receive sacraments, 25, 429; cannot commit offence causing loss of caste, 25, 429; produced by Darkness, 25, 493; *S.* who neglects his duty becomes a Preta in next birth, 25, 499; sell Soma, 26, 64 n.; acts performed by a *S.* (servant) at a funeral, 29, 239; the ass is a *S.* by birth, 29, 366; sacred fire not to be taken from the house of a *S.*, 29, 385; excluded from sacrifices and ceremonial purifications, 34, 224, 227–9; 41, 66 sq., 66 n.; 48, 337, 342 sq.; the word *S.* etymologized, 34, 225 sq.; Agni removed from the *S.* caste, 41, 226; Takman (fever) entreated to go to the *S.*-females, 42, 2; Agîgarta, father of *S*unah*s*epa, reproached for not abandoning the ways of a *S.*, 44, xxxv; the Pravargya must be performed whilst not coming into contact with *S.*, 44, 446; woman, *S.*, dogs, and crows are untruth, sin, darkness, 44, 446; not qualified for the knowledge of Brahman, 48, 337–47; allowed to hear Itihâsas and Purâ*n*as, 48, 338; reason why *S.* might be qualified for cognition of Brahman, 48, 343–7. *See also* Caste (*e, f*).

Sudyumna, Manu's son, 49 (i), 90 n.

Suffering, *see* Pain, *and* Truths (the four noble).

Su*g*â, wife of Inda or Indra, 10 (ii), 189.

Sugata, *see* Buddha.

Su*g*âtâ, a devout woman, obtained final salvation, 11, 25; daughter of Senâpati, 19, xxvii; one of the first Buddhist nuns, 49 (i), 192.

Sugata*k*etanâ, a leader of female lay devotees, 21, 360.

Su*g*âtavaktra, satiated at the Tarpa*n*a, 29, 220.

Sugrîva, M*ri*gaputra's father king in the town of, 45, 88.

Suhail ibn 'Amr, concluded truce with Mohammed, 9, 237 n.

Suhasta, a guardian of Soma, 26, 72.

Suhastin, n. of a Sthavira, 22, 288; his twelve disciples, who gave rise to numerous Kulas and *S*âkhâs, 22, 290 sqq., 290 n.

Sui, the pearl of the marquis of, 40, 154, 154 n.

Suicide as a penance, 2, 82, 89, 283, 288; 14, 104 sq., 108, 213; he who commits s. becomes an Abhi*s*asta, 2, 89; 14, 119; no funeral libation and no period of impurity for those who commit s., 2, 250; 7, 93; 14, 119; 25, 184; symbolical self-sacrifice, 2, 293; by hanging oneself, 4, 77; 8, 237; penance for one who has been concerned with the death or funeral of a s., 7, 93; inciting a man to s., a kind of destruction of life, 13, 4; penances for intended or attempted s., 14, 119 sq.; by entering the fire the world of Brahman is gained, 14, 136, 136 n.; self-sacrifice in honour of a Buddha highly recommended for a Bodhisattva, 21, 379 sq., 385 sq.; recommended to *G*aina monks, 22, 68–78, 68 n., 70 n., 72 n., 74 n.; 45, 147, 175 sq.; special places for *G*ainas committing religious s., 22, 182; *G*aina monk is not allowed to commit religious s. without asking leave of his teacher or superior, 22, 307; voluntary death the befitting end of a hermit's life, 25, 204, 204 n., 212; promise to die for a friend, 27, 69, 69 n.; why Buddha prohibited s., 35, 273–5; denounced, 40, 141, 295; committed by Tâoist sages, 40, 162 sq., 165; three methods of the sage's 'death with one's will,' 45, 24, 24 n.

Sui-zăn, the first ruler who broke up the Primal Unity, 39, 370, 370 n.; words of S., 40, 7.

*S*uka, the son of Vyâsa, travelled to the sphere of the sun, 38, 375.

Sukanyâ, daughter of *S*aryâta, wife of *K*yavana, 26, 273–5.

Suke*s*as Bhâradvâga, n. of a sage, 15, 271, 283.

Suketâ (good-will?), identified with the sun, 29, 348.

Sukhâkara = Sukhâvatî, q. v.

Sukhâvatî, the Land of Bliss, the paradise or Buddha-country of Amitâbha, where there are no women, and existence is by apparitional birth, 21, 389, 417; 49 (ii), v, viii, 28; its Paurâ*n*ik prototype, 49 (ii), xxii; description of S., 49 (ii), 1, 33–44, 49–59, 61–5, 91–8; those who think of the Tathâgata are after death born in S., 49 (ii), 45 sq.; beings who are born in S., 49 (ii), 55–9, 66–72, 98–102, 188–99; how to obtain it, 49 (ii), 166–99. *See also* Buddha-fields, *and* Paradise.

Sukhâvatî - vyûha, and Mahâ-Sudassana - Sutta, 11, 246; the larger and the smaller S., sacred books of Buddhists in Japan, 49 (ii), v–xii, xxii sq.; the larger S. translated, 49 (ii), 1–75; the smaller S. translated, 49 (ii), 87–103.

Sû*k*iloma, Yakkha, threatens to harm Buddha, if he cannot answer his questions, 10 (ii), 45.

Sû*k*ilomasutta, t.c., 10 (ii), 45 sq.

*S*ukra: B*ri*haspati became *S*., 15, 342; son of Aṅgiras, 19, 10; 49 (i), 8; worships Indra, 19, 95; 49 (i), 93; is the sun, 26, 278 sq., 324 sq., 338, 407, 419 sq.; Soma libations for *S*. (and Manthin), 26, 278–88, 316 n., 324 sq., 332, 338, 407–9, 419–21; 41, 111; 44, 209.

Sûktavâka, *see* Prayers (*c*).

Sukurkura, a demon harassing children, 30, 219. *See also* Kûrkura.

Sula, converted by Buddha, 19, 241.

Sulabhâ Maitreyî, worshipped at the Tarpa*n*a, 29, 123, 220; entered into the body of *G*anaka, to carry on a discussion with him, 38, 237.

*S*û**lagava**, *see* Animal Sacrifice (*b*), *and* Cattle.

Sulasâ, female lay votary, 22, 267 sq.; a courtesan, 36, 249.

Sumana, appointed on the jury at the council of Vesâlî, 20, 407; the garland maker, a devout Buddhist, 35, 172; 36, 146 sq., 249.

Sumanobhadra, disciple of Sambhûtavi*g*aya, 22, 289.

Sumantra left Râma in the forest, 19, 65, 65 n.

Sumantu, worshipped at the Tarpa*n*a, 29, 122, 149, 220.

Sumati, son of Mâra, 19, xxii.

Sumati, son of a former Buddha *K*andrasûryapradîpa, 21, 19.

Sumati, n. of a Tîrthakara, 22, 280.

Sumati, son of Bh*r*igu, author of a version of Manu's Code, 25, xvii, xcv; 33, xi, xiii sq., 3, 3 n.

Sumeru swayed by the birth of Buddha, 19, 5, 5 n.; chief of mountains, 19, 9; Buddha compared with S., 19, 221, 221 n., 276, 276 n.

Sumerukalpa, n. of a Tathâgata, 49 (ii), 6, 101.

Sumitra, left the son of Raghu, 49 (i), 66.

Summum bonum, *see* Emancipation, Highest Good, *and* Nirvâ*n*a.

Sumukha, perished through want of humility, 25, 222.

Sun.

(*a*) The s. as a heavenly body.
(*b*) The s. in mysticism and symbolism.
(*c*) The s. in mythology; world of the s.
(*d*) Sacredness and worship of the s.

(*a*) THE S. AS A HEAVENLY BODY.

Connexion between the rays of the s. and the arteries of the heart, 1, 132–4; Hûshê*d*ar makes the s. stand still for ten days at the end of millennium, 5, lii, 231 sq., 233 n.; 47, xii sq., 105–7, 110–12, 114–16; revolution of the s. round Mount Albûrz, 5, 22–4, 23 n.; position of the s., and lengths of midday and afternoon shadows, 5, 397–400; is the first among shining bodies, 8, 346, 346 n., 352 sq.; 10 (ii), 105; 14, 196; light of s. is the source of colours, 8, 352; magic power of being able to touch the s., 11, 214; hard to look at is the s. in autumn, 11, 268; is the cause of time, 15, 316; 42, 683; Buddha compared with the s., 19, 3; description of a

s.-rise, 22, 241 sq.; 32, 14, 16; as the s. draws water with his rays, so the king draws taxes, 25, 396; in the beginning the s. was on earth, 26, 309; eclipse of the s., 27, 328–30, 328 n., 338 sq.; body of s. made for the creation of the Ameshô-spentas, 31, 262; s.-rise an image of the creation, 32, 10; the chief of planetary orbs, 36, 55; why does the s. at times shine with diminished heat? 36, 111–13, 113 n.; moon mentioned before the s., 36, 127 sq. and n.; qualities of the s., 36, 320–2; essence of waters contained in s., 41, 7; s.-rain, 41, 76; watery s.-motes, 41, 79 sq.; created, 41, 148; through time the s. rises, 42, 225, 687; moves from left to right, 43, 136; is smooth and round, 43, 180; is variegated, has the air for his seat, and is half-way from this earth, 43, 196; when the s. sets, it enters the wind, 43, 333; the s. is motion, everything moves as soon as he rises, 43, 337; everything is baked by the s., 43, 352; floats along the waters, 43, 368 n.; mightily shineth the towering form of the ball, yonder burning s., 44, 107; not rivalled by any one, 44, 354; no one can turn him back, 44, 359; is four-cornered, the four quarters being his corners, 44, 498; suns revolve round Meru, 45, 288, 288 n.; cows lowed and men shouted at sight of s., 46, 57, 68; rays of s. present also during the night, 48, 739 sq. *See also* Luminaries, Omens, Parables (*f*), Planets, *and* Stars.

(*b*) THE S. IN MYSTICISM AND SYMBOLISM.

Breath (the inner Self) and s. (the outer Self) identified, 1, 7, 214, 219; 15, 305–12; the golden person within the s., 1, 13 sq.; 41, 367; person in the s. and person in the eye identified, 1, 15; 15, 191; 43, 368 sq., 371, 374; yonder s. is the twenty-first, or twenty-onefold, 1, 28; 41, 265, 308; 43, 62, 163; 44, 37, 150, 150 sq. n., 291, 305 n., 331 n., 333, 375, 378, 402; meditation on the s. as the honey of the Devas, 1, 38–44; 34, 216, 256 sq.; 48, 335, 368–70; meditation on the s. or Person in the s. as Brahman or Highest Self, 1, 54 sq., 66, 302 sq.; 15, 61, 68, 100, 134, 306, 317 sq., 338–41; 34, 63, 112; 41, 366; 43, 94; 44, 388, 459 sq.; if Prâ*n*a is satisfied, the eye is satisfied, and thereby s. and heaven are satisfied, 1, 89; *what I am (the worshipper), that is he (s.); what he is, that am I*, 1, 220, 313; 15, 335; *the s. is the self of all that moves and rests*, 1, 221, 259, 261; 2, 297 n.; *the door of the True is covered with a golden disk*, 1, 313; the s. as a Brahma*k*ârin, 8, 178; 42, 214–17, 626–8; one of the ten fires at the allegorical sacrifice of the sense-organs, 8, 261; only seen by one who attains to the Adhyâtman, 8, 316; the light in the s. is goodness, the heat passion, the eclipse is darkness, 8, 329 sq.; is all the seasons, 12, 316; the Agnihotra is the s., 12, 327; rays of the s. extend down to the vital airs, 12, 343; s. or man in the s. is death, 12, 343 sq.; 38, 267; 43, 366 sq.; 44, 26; is the eye of creatures, the eye of the world, 15, 19; 44, 346; 49 (i), 62; the s. the essence of the material, the person in the s., the essence of the immaterial, 15, 107; golden Person in the s. is the self in the lotus of the heart, 15, 134, 306; 34, 81; Ahar, secret name of Person in the s., 15, 192; the spirit of all creatures, 15, 272; the Self is the s., hidden by the thousand-eyed golden egg, 15, 311; is the cause of new births, of heaven, of emancipation, 15, 329; Brahman, the essence of the s., 15, 335; the Self and the s. remain as long as the egg of the world, 15, 337; the symbol of the s. appearing above and 'within' the earth, 16, 241, 242 n.; the s. or Ether, and Mind or Reason, the two supreme beings of the Upanishads, 21, xxvii; a vision of the s., 22, 235; is the lotus of the sky, 26, 277; is the soul of the movable and immovable, 26, 343; is Suketâ ('good-will'?), 29, 348; soul to be meditated upon as the s., and the s. as the soul, 38, 244; truth is the same as the s., 41, 265; 44, 457; gold plate and gold

man represent the s. and the man in the s., 41, 265-7, 272; 43, 366-74; eye from the s., 42, 56; 43, 8; 44, 133; the rising or setting s. takes away the strength of those who are asleep, 42, 93, 521, 544 sq.; Prâ*n*a identified with the s., 42, 220, 623, 624 sq.; the eye goes to the s., 42, 418; deity and metre, 43, 53; represented in the bricks of the fire-altar, 43, 80; variegated stone set up on the fire-altar as symbol of the s., 43, 195-7; black cow with white calf symbolical of night and s., 43, 200; a chariot as symbol of the s., 43, 234 sq.; the year is the same as the s., 43, 313, 363; established in the seven-syllabled Brahman, 43, 314 sq.; the Pravargya is the s., 43, 317 sq., 320; 44, xlviii, 138; the immortal element, 43, 322, 326 sq., 366; speech is yonder s., 43, 365; fire-altar built on the immortal light of the s. (represented by the lotus-leaf), 43, 365 sq.; *Rik*-verses the orb, Sâman-tunes the light, Yagus-formulas the man in the s., 43, 365 sq.; orb, light, and man in the s. are identical with the white in the eye, the black in the eye, and the man in the eye, 43, 368; encircled by 360 navigable streams, 43, 388; the sacrificial horse as the representative of Agni-Pragâpati, the S., 44, xviii; the Vasha*t*-call is yonder shining s., 44, 26; gold a type or form of the s., 44, 125, 195; the s. slaughtered by Pragâpati as sacrificial animal, 44, 128 sq.; by performing the Pravargya offering they sacrifice to S. (Âditya) and become s., 44, 141; fire (Agni) and s. (Âditya), the two lights of these worlds, 44, 149, 405; the sacrificer is the s., 44, 248; established on the B*ri*hatî the s. shines, 44, 256, 256 n.; is the divine Kshatra, the glory, the supreme lordship, the realm of light, 44, 291; is spiritual lustre, 44, 314 sq.; yonder s. is the A*s*vamedha, 44, 333, 375, 378; the sacrifice is the s., 44, 442, 446; by means of Agni and S. (Âditya) the sacrificer ascends to heaven, 44, 473; is a web-weaver, 44, 484; meditation on the s., to obtain a vision of Sukhâvatî, 49 (ii), 169 sq. *See also* Purusha.

(*c*) THE S. IN MYTHOLOGY; WORLD OF THE S.

Is the deity of the udgîtha, 1, 20; all beings are dependent on the s., 1, 26 sq.; migration of the s. through the worlds of gods, 1, 41-3, 43 n.; protects the creatures during the day, 2, 96; the undying, swift-horsed s., 4, 232; 5, 231 sq., 231 n.; 18, 15, 15 n.; 23, 8, 16, 85-7, 122, 122 n., 177, 199, 327, 349-54; prior to K*ri*sh*n*a, 8, 58; K*ri*sh*n*a is the beaming s. among the shining bodies, 8, 88; attacks of Râhu on the s., 8, 224, 303, 303 n.; the presiding deity of light (eye, colour), 8, 337, 340, 350; legend of King Sudassana a s.-myth, 11, 244 sq.; is the repeller of evil spirits, 12, 92; relates to Agni, 12, 169; is Indra, 12, 181 sq., 328; seven rays of the s., 12, 271 n.; 19, 327; 42, 514; is Self-existent, the best ray of light, 12, 271; rays of the s. as heavenly cows, 12, 271, 271 n.; took their energy from the Nakshatras, 12, 288; northward and southward movement of the s. suitable for gods and fathers resp., 12, 289 sq.; night envelops the s. as an embryo, 12, 328; rays of the s. are the All-gods, 12, 328; 26, 325; 44, 194, 196; Pragâpati identified with the S., and the man (purusha) in the s., 12, 328; 43, xxii, 264; 44, 375, 378; is the light of the gods, the moon the light of the Fathers, 12, 361; Agni is the s., 12, 409 n.; 41, 152; 43, 195; 46, 167 sq.; cows are children of the s., 14, 135; purified by Ka, 14, 331; chariot of the s., 15, 256; 42, 53, 570; the father with five feet, with twelve shapes, giver of rain, 15, 273; as a gold-coloured bird, a swan, an eagle, 15, 332; 41, 281; 42, 220, 401, 623-5; 46, 242; the Yen-tsz' cave, hiding-place of the s., 19, 313, 313 n.; men and gods could not withstand the Daêvas, if the s. did not rise, 23, 86; has a bright face and a dark one, 23, 143 n.; observes all good creatures with kind eyes, 24,

122; divides days and nights, 25, 20; a guardian of the world, 25, 185, 216 sq.; the eye of Mitra, Varu*n*a, and Agni, 26, 343; 41, 408; 43, 363; is footless, yet able to walk, 26, 380; called graha or 'seizer,' 26, 432 sq.; is the house-lord of the seasons, 26, 453 n.; the gods have released the s. from darkness and from the seizing demon, 30, 213; 42, 15, 294; Daêva-worshippers blaspheme the S., 31, 55, 62; the s. of the rapid steeds, the eye of Ahura-Mazda, 31, 199, 199 n., 210, 216, 225, 256, 271, 276, 324, 360; the s. as a (red or white) horse, 32, 14, 16–20, 279; 35, 199 sq. n.; 41, 208, 359–61; 43, 250; 44, 312, 501; Arusha, the red morning-s., 32, 20–3; the eye of the s., 32, 347; the s. and the other divinities are mere differentiations of prâ*n*a, 34, 269; stricken with darkness by Svarbhânu, 41, 65 sq.; the S. and the Âdityas, 41, 149 sq. n., 150; the S. with the dappled horse, 41, 334; strings these worlds to himself on a thread, 41, 360, 360 n.; 43, 141; Agni in the s., 41, 383; 43, 239 sq.; 46, 70, 229; the heavenly dog, 42, 13, 500 sq.; as the slayer of unseen vermin, 42, 23 sq., 315, 318; has given (the ants) as a remedy against poison, 42, 27; at his rising the s. removes pains, 42, 47, 600; by means of breath the gods aroused the s., 42, 51; Rohita, the red s., 42, 207–14, 661–8; the bay steeds of the s., 42, 210–12, 661 n.; as a tortoise, and a hermit, 42, 403; regent of the heavens, 43, xx; is the all-embracer, 43, 8, 106; is the holder of the air, supporter of the regions, and ruler of beings, 43, 28, 62; wields the thunderbolt, 43, 85; is the last Vi*s*vagyotis, 43, 129 sq.; is of unimpaired strength, 43, 134; revolves round the worlds, 43, 134; animates all this universe, 43, 142; the heart of Pragâpati, 43, 180 sq.; the s. the foundation of Pragâpati (the fire-altar), 43, 354 sq.; Vai*s*vânara as the s., 43, 396; the eater of the moon, 43, 398 sq.; kindled by the wind, 43, 399; as the horse of Varu*n*a, 44, xix sq.; when the s. (Âditya) sets, all the gods follow him, 44, 113; yonder s. walks singly, 44, 314, 388; who knows the birth-place of the great s.? 44, 390; is the remover of evil, 44, 426; the cut-off head of Vish*n*u became yonder s., 44, 442; Brahma*n*aspati is the s., 44, 453; is Yama, Makha, 44, 460; the father of thoughts, the lord of the creatures, 44, 469; is the child of the gods, 44, 469; sustainer of the sky and of heat, and of the gods, the immortal, born of heat, 44, 470; the never-resting guardian, 44, 470; lord of all worlds, of all thought, of all speech, 44, 471; wanders on paths hither and thither, 44, 471; guards the gods, 44, 471; our father, 44, 472; is the divine ruler, hence protects human rulers, 44, 496; when yonder s. overflows all the gods subsist upon him, 44, 508; Savit*ri*, the rising s., 46, 39; the lover of the Dawn, 46, 67 sq.; rules over wealth, 46, 75; Vai*s*vânara unites with the s., 46, 127; meant by 'the great impeller'? 46, 178; ascended to the wide plains, beholding right and wrong deeds among the mortals, 46, 309; the mighty s., the quick Aditi, 46, 326, 329; *the rays of the s. have shaken the darkness, and have sunk it into the waters like a hide. Unsupported, unattached, spread out downwards-turned—how is it that he does not fall down? By what power of his does he move? Erected as the pillar of Heaven he protects the firmament,* 46, 356; Varu*n*a and Mitra make the s. rise, 46, 356; seven young fallow mares carry the s., 46, 356; the all-observer, 46, 356; Agni has found the s., 46, 397 sq.; the Person within the s. is different from the soul, viz. the highest Self, 48, 237–42; Manu, the son of the S., 49 (i), 19; surrounded by Apsaras, 49 (i), 40; *see also* Savitar, *and* Sûrya;—the departed goes from the year to the s., from the s. to the moon, 1, 68, 80, 134; 15, 328 sq.; is the door of the world of Brahman, 1, 134; 44, 66 sq.; world of the s.

gained by the giver of horses or cows, 7, 273; 25, 165; the solar sphere the seat of men who perform meritorious actions, 8, 240; the gate of the world of the gods, 12, 267 n.; rays of the s. are the righteous departed, 12, 269, 269 n.; is the final goal, the safe resort, of those who know Brahman and have reached final release, 12, 271 sq.; 15, 273; 34, 232; 44, 37, 167; 48, 739 sq., 745; world of the s. gained through a son's grandson, 14, 84; 25, 354, 354 n.; souls of the wise pass through the S. to where the immortal Person dwells, 15, 32; kingdom of s. gained by long sacrifices, 15, 337; 26, 426 sq.; reward in the s., the most kindly-regarding and swiftest, 37, 359 sq.; dying during the northern progress of the s. is more excellent, 38, 380; departed soul follows the rays also during the southern progress of the s., 38, 380; the connecting link or hinge for the worlds, 41, 269, 269 n.; the s., the world of immortality, 42, 53.

(*d*) SACREDNESS AND WORSHIP OF THE S.

Whenever the s. rises and sets, shouts of hurrah arise, and all beings arise, and all things which they desire, 1, 55; worship of the s., as a penance, 1, 285; 2, 298; 14, 295, 305; 30, 197; easing nature, spitting, micturating, &c., forbidden while facing the s., 2, 94; 25, 136 sq.; 29, 319; 42, 214; 44, 447; invoked and worshipped, prayers and offerings to the s., 2, 108, 298; 4, 23 n.; 5, lxi, 297–9, 297 n., 394; 11, 174; 15, 213, 249, 317 sq., 338–41; 25, 38, 63; 26, 253 sq., 342 sq.; 29, 99, 145–8, 205, 211, 224 sq., 249, 280, 320 sq., 426 sq.; 30, 117–20, 127, 156 sq., 243, 270; 33, 118; 42, 13, 132, 222, 500 sq.; 44, 142, 412, 469–72; looking at the s. a penance, 2, 290; 14, 121; 25, 183; a lady swears by the bright s. that she is faithful to her lover, 3, 440, 440 n.; corpse laid out on the Dakhma, so as to behold the s., 4, lxxviii, lxxviii n., 54, 75, 75 n., 87 sq.; joint invocation to the waters and the s., 4, 230–3, 232 n.; rays of the s. are purifying, 7, 96, 102; 12, 21; 25, 187; 26, 18; he must not look at the s. while unclean, 7, 220; K*r*ish*n*a taught devotion to the s., 8, 58; adore not the s., but God, 9, 202; worshipping the s., classed with witchcraft and other 'low arts' to be avoided by the Bhikkhu, 11, 199; Agnihotra connected with the s., 12, 327–9; is made to rise by kindling the fire, 12, 328; 46, 326, 330, 379, 381, 403 sq.; Snâtaka must not look at the s., 14, 60, 242; 25, 135; 29, 123, 317; sick person worships the s., 14, 215; worshipped by ascetics, 14, 278, 280; is not contaminated by external impurities, 15, 19; prayer addressed to the s. by a dying person, 15, 199 sq.; Khôrshê*d* Ya*s*t and Nyâyi*s* devoted to the s., 23, 85–7, 349–53; purifies earth and water, 23, 86; s. and Mit*r*ô worshipped, 24, 96; must not shine on fire, 24, 334 sq.; salutation of the s., three times every day, 24, 358; burnt-oblation reaches the s., whence rain is produced, 25, 89; sacrifice at the solstices, 25, 133; morning s. to be avoided by Snâtaka, 25, 139, 139 sq. n.; Vasatîvarî water taken for the s., 26, 223 sq.; exorcisms addressed to the s., 26, 433; sunwise motion or turning round in accordance with the course of the s., 26, 440; 41, 329 sq. and n., 359, 372 sq.; *see also* Circumambulation; the chief object at the border sacrifice, 27, 427, 427 n.; ceremonies on an eclipse of the s., 28, 433; Brahma*k*ârin given in charge of the s., 29, 64, 79; looking at the s. before continuing Veda-study after an interruption, 29, 118; the Ash*t*akâ sacred to the s., 29, 206; bride worships the s., 29, 284; child when taken out for the first time, made to look at the s., 29, 298; Brahma*k*ârin made to look at the s., 29, 305; student worships the s., 29, 314; 30, 83 sq., 162 sq., 274; A*s*vattha tree sacred to the s., 30, 122; shall not shine on the student on the day of the Samâvartana, 30, 165, 275; a sacred object, 33, 222; by practising

liberality the s. is benefited, 37, 326; expiatory rite when the s. sets on the sacred fire, 44, 194 sq.; hymns addressed chiefly to the rising s., 46, 356 sq., 358 sq.

*S*una, and Sîra, ploughshare and plough, as tutelary deities of agriculture, 12, 445 sq. n.

*S*una*h*sepa, legend of, 12, xxiv; 14, xiii sq., 87 sq.; 32, 255, 257; 41, 95 n., 109 n.; 42, 241; story of *S.*, and human sacrifice in ancient India, 44, xxxiv–xxxvi; *S.* Âgîgarti, *Ri*shi or author of a hymn, 46, 14, 17; loosed from the sacrificial posts, 46, 366 sq.

*S*una*m*kuri, n. of a protecting demon, 29, 335.

Sunandâ, leader of female lay votaries, 22, 274.

Sûnâparantas, converts made on the occasion of the, 36, 249.

*S*unâsîr(î)ya, t.t., *see* Sacrifice (*j*).

Sunda and Upasunda, two Asuras fighting against each other, 19, 125; 49 (i), 116.

Sundara-Nanda, an eminent Arhat, 21, 3.

Sundarânanda, converted by Buddha, 49 (i), 198.

Sundarî, a *Ri*shi seduced by her, 19, 39.

Sundarikâ, n. of a river, 10 (ii), 74.

Sundarikabhâradvâ*g*a, a Brâhma*n*a, converted by Buddha, 10 (ii), 74–80.

Sundarikabhâradvâ*g*asutta, t.c., 10 (ii), 74–80.

Sung, *see* *Kh*ăng.

Sung Hsing and Yin Wăn, founders of a modified system of Mohism, 40, 221–3, 221 sq. n.

Sun Hsiû, a man of weak intelligence, 39, 151; 40, 24–6.

Sunîdha, a chief minister of Magadha, 11, 18–21; 17, 101 sqq.

Sunnapattiyâ, *see* Pûr*n*apatrikâ.

Suññatâ, t.t., 'Void,' *see* Nirvâ*n*a (*a*).

Sûn*ri*tâ, the Dawn, 32, 444, 446; invoked at the Pravargya, 44, 478.

Sun-shû Âo was thrice chief minister, and did not feel elated, and thrice dismissed without manifesting any sorrow, 40, 54 sq., 54 n., 104 sq., 104 n.

*S*ûnyavâda, *S*ûnyavâdin, *see* Nihilism, *and* Nihilists.

Supar*n*a and Âsurî, 42, 16, 268 sq.

Supar*n*as, created, 25, 15; manes of S., 25, 112; produced by Darkness, 25, 493.

Supar*n*î and Kadrû, legend of, 26, 52, 149–52, 149 n., 150 n.

Supâr*s*va, paternal uncle of Mahâvîra, 22, 193, 256; n. of a Tîrthakara, 22, 280.

Supassa, the serpent king, asks Buddha to forbid eating serpents' flesh, 17, 86.

Superhuman beings: Bali-offerings to the G*ri*hâs, Avasânas, Avasânapatis and all creatures, 2, 107 n.; Bali offering to s. b. walking about at night, 2, 203; Mohammedan angelism and demonology, 6, lii; world inhabited by human and s. b., 6, lxx; invisible Siddhas and celestial singers, 8, 232; lists of s. b., 8, 345, 347, 354, 387; 15, 289; 36, 101, 130; 45, 318, 382; 49 (ii), 30, 60, 70; Râkshasas and Pi*s*â*k*as roam about on Parva-days, 14, 210; Yâtudhânas and Pi*s*â*k*as steal the food intended for the manes, 14, 269; demons, Yakshas, and Rakshas converted by Buddha, 19, 243–6; Devas, Nâgas, Gandharvas, Kinnaras, Mahoragas, Asuras accompany Buddha's mother to the Lumbinî garden, 19, 348; gods, Nâgas, and other s. b. forming a Buddha's audience, 21, 5 sq., 69 sq., 162, 213, 222 sq., 225, 253, 376, 383, 412, 431, 442; description of horrible beings haunting an old house (the world), 21, 83 sq.; demons, ghosts, &c., the consequence of there being no Buddha, 21, 170; sounds uttered by demons, &c., 21, 339; the preacher discerns gods and demons by his smell, 21, 344 sq.; demons, Nâgas, Garu*d*as, &c., show honour to the preacher, 21, 347, 349; gods, Nâgas, and other s. b. worship Buddha by strewing heavenly flowers, garments, &c., 21, 365 sq.; the giantesses pronounce talismanic words for the protection of preachers, 21, 373 sqq.; no ghosts nor demons in a certain Buddha-field, 21, 377;

Mârakâyikas, Nâgas, goblins, imps, 21, 391; Gadgadasvara preaches to demons, Garu*d*as, Kinnaras, under the shape of these beings, 21, 401; island of giantesses, 21, 407; Avalokite*s*vara assumes the shape of all kinds of s. b., 21, 411; ocean the abode of s. b., 21, 413; Avalokite*s*vara protects from s. b. who try to hurt men, 21, 414; Garu*d*as and Nâgas carry Mahâvîra's throne, 22, 198; manes of Daityas, Dânavas, &c., 25, 112; Siddhas, Sâdhyas, Vipras, Yakshas, and other s. b. worshipped at the Tarpa*n*a, 29, 121; day-walking and night-walking beings, and Rakshas worshipped at the Vai*s*vadeva, 29, 162; the white one with the black teeth, the lord of bad women, demons dwelling in the village or forest, 29, 290; Asuras, Garu*d*as, Yakkhas, Nâgas—beings living in water, 35, 175 sq.; 45, 295; Titans, Garu*d*as, Nâgas, Yakshas, 36, 116; a Bhikkhu reverenced by Nâgas and Yakshas, 36, 120; s. b. who got the Tâo, and were raised to spirits of mountains, &c., 39, 135 sq., 244 sq. and n.; Hwan's encounter with a ghost, his officer tells him all about the different kinds of sprites, 40, 18–20, 19 n.; Arbudi invoked, to make the enemies see all kinds of spooks and sprites, 42, 125 sq.; gods, Dânavas, Gandharvas, Yakshas, Râkshasas, and Kinnaras pay homage to a chaste monk, 45, 77; gods, Dânavas, Gandharvas, Yakshas, Râkshasas, Kinnaras, and Bhûtas assemble to see Kê*s*i and Gautama, 45, 121 sq.; the Bhaumêyika and Vyantara gods are Asuras, Nâgas, &c., and Pi*s*â*k*as, Bhûtas, &c., 45, 225 sq.; must all suffer for their deeds and are subject to transmigration, 45, 250, 318; injury done to living beings for the sake of Nâgas, Bhûtas, or Yakshas, 45, 357; praise Buddha, 49 (i), 157–9; where Buddhism is preached, there shall be no fear of gods, Nâgas, Yakshas, 49 (i), 188; s. b. with the gods, men, evil spirits, and genii, 49 (ii), 72, 102; Devas, Nâgas, and Yakshas worship Buddha, 49 (ii), 201. *See also* Demons, Goblins, *and* Gods.

Superhuman condition, *see* Meditation.

Superhuman powers, *see* Iddhi.

Superimposition, explained, 34, 3 n., 4–9; 38, 197; is Nescience, 34, 6; mutual s. of Self and Non-Self, 34, 7–9; endless s., the cause of individual souls appearing as agents and enjoyers (of the results of their actions), 34, 9; s. of something higher upon something lower is the rule, 38, 343 sq.

Superior Man, represses what is evil and gives distinction to what is good, in sympathy with the Heaven-conferred nature, 16, 285, 286 n.; holds the course of the due mean, 16, 290, 291 n., 292; helps the people and nourishes his own virtue, 16, 290 sq., 291 n.; is perfectly sincere, leaving the question of happiness and calamity to Heaven, 16, 299 sq. n.; four virtues practised by the s. m., 16, 408; state of equilibrium and harmony exhibited by the s. m., 27, 43 sq.; 28, 300–29, 301 n.; description of the s. m., 27, 86, 350, 394; 28, 325–31, 333, 335–40, 345, 347–9, 351 n., 354, 358–62, 413–19, 478. *See also* Morality (*d*), *and* Tâo (*c*).

Superstition, *see* Omens.

Suplan, *see* Sahadeva Sâr*ñ*gaya.

Suppabuddha, the Sâkyan, swallowed up by the earth, for offending Buddha, 35, 153.

Suppiya, ascetic, the Brahma*g*âla spoken concerning him, 20, 376.

Suppiyâ, a devout laywoman, cuts a piece of flesh from her thigh, to procure broth for a sick Bhikkhu, 17, 80–5; 35, 172; 36, 146.

Supratibuddha Kâkandaka, n. of a Sthavira, 22, 288, 292.

Supratish*th*ita*k*âritra, n. of a chief Bodhisattva, 21, 284.

Supreme Being, *see* God.

Supreme Bliss, *see* Emancipation.

***S*ura**, a name of one A*s*vaghosha, 19, xxxi.

***S*ûra**, famed feats of the grandson of, 49 (i), 9.

Surâ, *see* Spirituous liquors.

Surabhi, mother of kine, 44, 438 n.

Sûrâk, n.p., 5, 135.
*S***ûrakû***t***a**, the 26th Tathâgata, 49 (ii), 6.
Sura Pari*k***ara**, a king of the *K*etas, former birth of Devadatta, 35, 287, 287 n.
Suras ('gods'), and Asuras created, 7, 4; and Asuras carry Mahâvîra's throne, 22, 198; Indra chief of the S., 22, 222; *G*inas and S. come to the turning of the wheel of the law, 49 (i), 173.
*S***ûrasena**, men born there fight in the van of the battle, 25, 247, 247 n.
*S***ûravîra** Mâ*nd*ûkeya, *see* Mâ*nd*ûkeya.
Surgery, *see* Medicine.
Sûrô-yazata, n.p., 23, 215.
Sûrya, the Sun, son of Pra*g*âpati, 1, 313; 15, 199; in a list of gods, 8, 219; 21, 4; 42, 160, 205; Agni, Vâyu, S., gods of earth, air, sky, 12, 327; 44, 291 n.; Agnihotra libation to S., 12, 327, 334–7; 29, 161, 161 n.; is the light when the sun rises, 12, 335; Agni has attained to S.'s lustre, 12, 352; is the scorching sun that governs the world, 12, 446; offerings to S., 12, 446 sq.; 26, 263, 427–9; 29, 121, 149; 30, 51; 44, 77, 77 n., 127, 300, 346 sq., 505; prayers to S., 14, 305; 25, 183, 183 n.; 26, 224, 253; 29, 41 sq., 190, 287 sq.; 41, 38, 94, 112; 42, 10, 17, 31, 47, 60, 203, 211, 237; 43, 143; 44, 432; identified with Prâ*n*a, 15, 275; etymology of S., 15, 310; Buddha mistaken for god S., 19, 72; his chariot drawn by seven horses, 19, 313, 313 n.; 33, 14 n.; Soma's marriage with S.'s daughter, 26, xiv; invoked to ward off evil spirits, 26, 77; 29, 44; the god-born light, the son of the sky, 26, 83; given as sacrificial gift to the Aṅgiras, 26, 114; Agni, Indra, and S., superior gods, worshipped, 26, 402–6; morning oblation for S., 29, 19, 172, 287, 386; 30, 20, 197, 266; celestial serpents belonging to S., 29, 328 sq.; Sâmans, S., heaven, eye, 30, 152 sq.; lord of celestial beings, highest light, 30, 237; 42, 53, 60, 116; 43, 131, 240; the soul of the movable and immovable, 41, 408; fastens the amulet on with which he conquers the directions of space, 42, 85; Soma and S., 42, 103; the bull with a thousand horns, 42, 105, 373; brilliancy of S. transferred upon a king, 42, 116; Rohita and S., 42, 210, 214; *S. (the sun) surveys the sky, S. the earth, S. the waters. S. is the single eye of being: he has ascended the great heavens*, 42, 212; is the Gandharva, his Apsaras are the sun-motes, 43, 231; Agni made to ascend the terrestrial world, Vâyu the air, S. the sky, 44, 27; Sâma-veda produced from S., 44, 102; Agni, Vâyu, and S., the three lights, 44, 102; Faith, the daughter of S., 44, 226; delivers from sin, 44, 265; the highest light, is the heavenly world, 44, 267, 502; sacrificed as an animal, 44, 320; is all the gods, 44, 419, 505; worshipped at the Pravargya, 44, 460; in the glowing Mahâvîra pot Agni shines with S., 44, 469 sq.; one of his rays called the rain-winner, 44, 478; Vâmadeva: 'I am Manu, I am S.,' 48, 253. *See also* Sun (*c*).
Sûryâ, the Sun-bride, wedding of, 29, 283; 42, 202; Rodasî compared to S., 32, 272; Savitar's daughter, bride of A*s*vins, 42, 95, 503; Ushas or S., 42, 661, 666; S. hymn, *see* Prayers (*c*).
Sûryagarbha, one of the sixteen virtuous men, 21, 4.
Sûryaka, the enemy of the fish, shot by the arrow of Kâma (Mâra), 49 (i), 138, 138 n.
Sûryodana, the 11th Tathâgata, 49 (ii), 6.
Susa*m***sthita**, one of the sixteen virtuous men, 21, 4.
Susârthavâha, one of the sixteen virtuous men, 21, 4.
Sûshan and Sûsha*n*â, deities of parturition, 42, 99, 244 sq.
Sushe*n***a** is a winter-month, 43, 108.
Sû Shih, styled Ʒze-*k*an, and Tung-pho, his notice of the Sacrificial Hall to *K*wang-ʒze, 40, 296, 296 n., 320–3, 320 n.
*S***ushkabhri***ṅ***gâra**, quoted, 1, 283.
*S***ush***n***a**, the Dânava, is the pupil of the eye, 26, 14 sq.

Susravas Kaushya, n. of a teacher, 30, 244; 43, 390.
Susthita Kautika, n. of a Sthavira, 22, 288, 292.
Susunâga removed the capital of Magadha to Vesâli, 11, xvi sq.
Sutambhara Âtreya, author of Vedic hymns, 46, 392, 394, 395, 397.
Sutanu, perhaps synonym of Râgîmatî, 45, 117 n.
Sûtas, caste of, 2, 198; 14, 94, 197 sq.; 25, 404 sq., 407; are charioteers, 25, 413; court-minstrels and chroniclers, 41, 60, 111.
Sutasravas, n. of a teacher, 30, 244.
Sutegas, the head of Vaisvânara, 38, 275 sq.
Sûtras, metrical Smritis derived from, 2, ix sqq. n., x sq.; date of the S. period, 2, xviii sq.; style of S., 7, xvii; 11, xxiii; originally composed for a single Vedic school, 14, xiv; date of the Mahâvaipulya and the simple Buddhist S., 21, x–xiv; satiated at the Tarpana, 29, 220; are 'short aphorisms constituting in their totality a complete body of doctrine upon some subject,' 34, xi, xiii; all S. aim at conciseness, 34, xiii; peculiarity of the philosophical S., 34, xiii sq. *See also* Dharma-sûtras, Grihya-sûtras, Kalpa-sûtras, Sacred Books, Srauta-sûtras, Suttas, *and* Vedânta-sûtras.
Sûtrâtman = Pragâpati, 34, 142 n.
Sutta-Nipâta, Purânas mentioned in the, 8, 14 n.; quoted, 8, 14 n., 19 n., 24 n., 36, and notes to 40, 45 sq., 48–51, 56, 59 sq., 62–6, 68–70, 79, 88 sq., 101, 103, 105, 108 sq., 111 sq., 114, 118, 121; 36, 285, 313, 358, 363 sq.; its language, 10 (ii), xi sq.; contains remnants of Primitive Buddhism, 10 (ii), xi–xvi; translated, *Vol.* 10 (ii); Sona pleases Buddha by reciting the Atthakavagga of the S., 17, 37. *See also* Tipitaka.
Suttantas, t.t., older name for Suttas, 13, xxix sq. *See* Suttas, *and* Tipitaka.
Suttas, Pali texts of Buddhist canon, translated into Singhalese, 10 (i), xiv; translations of S., *Vols.* 10 (ii) and 11; 11, xxiv–xxvii; age of S., 11, x–xx; their authorship, 11, xx; their teaching, and the original teaching of Buddha, 11, xx sqq.; stock phrases and repetitions in them, 11, xxii–xxv; peculiar use of the words Dhamma, S., and Suttanta, 13, xxviii sqq. *See also* Tipitaka.
Suvannapattiyâ, *see* Pûrnapatrikâ.
Suvarnagarbha, the 67th Tathâgata, 49 (ii), 7.
Suvarnanishthîvin, son of Srimgaya, 49 (i), 90.
Suvarnaprabha, the 14th Tathâgata, 49 (ii), 6.
Suvidhi Pushpadanta, n. of a Tîrthakara, 22, 280.
Suvikrântavikrâmin, one of the sixteen virtuous men, 21, 4.
Suvîrina, n. or epithet of the dog-demon harassing children, 30, 219.
Suvisuddha, n. of the world of the Buddha Dharmaprabhâsa, 21, 195, 197.
Suvrata, at the head of the lay votaries, under Pârsva, 22, 274; Ârya Dharma of the S. gotra, 22, 294; ordained Vishnukumâra, 45, 86 n.
Suwâ'h, an idol worshipped by the Arabs, 6, xii; 9, 303.
Suyagña Sâṅkhâyana, author of the Sâṅkhâyana-Grihya-sûtra, 29, 3–5, 123; honoured as teacher, 29, 123, 141, 220.
Suyâma, a guardian of the world, 35, 37.
Suyâma, one of the eight Brahmans who took note of the marks on Buddha's body, 36, 44.
Sû Ʒze-kau, *see* Sû Shih.
Svabhâva, t.t., various meanings of it, 8, 11.
Svadhâ, *see* Sacred syllables.
Svâdhyâya, t.t., daily reading of Veda, *see* Veda (*c*).
Svâgata, one of the five hundred Arhats who are to become future Buddhas, 21, 198; n. of a Bhikshu, 49 (ii), 2.
Svâhâ, *see* Sacred syllables.
Svaidâyana, *see* Saunaka S.
Svaikna, *see* Pratîdarsa S.
Svaitreya, n. of a victorious hero, 46, 407.
Svalominî, a demon harassing children, 30, 211.

Svâna, guardian of Soma, 26, 72.
*S***vapâka**, *see* Caste (*e*).
Svar (sun-light), Maruts, men of, 32, 326.
Svarâ*g* (an autocrat or self-ruler): he who loves, and delights in the Self, becomes a S., 1, 124; Virâ*g* and S., 30, 167; metre, 41, 364; 43, 385.
Svarbhânu, the Âsura, struck the sun with darkness, 41, 65 sq., 406 n.; 42, 294.
Svarga world, *see* Heaven (*d*).
Svar*g*it Nâgna*g*ita or Nagna*g*it, the Gândhâra, quoted, 43, 21.
Svâro*k*isha, a Manu, 25, 19.
Svastika, one of the celestial regions, 22, 190.
Svastika, a poor Brâhman, converted by Buddha, 49 (i), 192.
Svastika, ornament, 48, 434, 447.
Svâtikârî, sacrifice to, at the ploughing rite, 29, 326.
Svayambhû, the Self-existent, offering to, 14, 308; Brahman is S., 15, 120, 188; *Ri*shi of a Kâ*n*da, 30, 242; quoted as authority on law, 33, 227; ocean, the delight of S., 45, 49; created the world, 45, 244; sleeps on the ocean, 45, 290; prayers to S., 49 (i), 25; worshipped by Buddha, 49 (i), 200. *See* Brahman.
*S***veta**, one of the princes of mountains, 8, 346.
*S***vetadîpa**, 'the white island,' the abode of Bhagavat, 7, 156.
*S***vetaketu** Auddâlaki Âru*n*eya, and his father Uddâlaka Âru*n*i, legend and dialogue, 1, xxxiii–xxxvi, 76 sq., 92–109; 15, xiv sqq., 1 n.; 34, cv, cxviii; 38, 210; 48, 583, 585; taught by *K*itra Gâṅgyâyani, 1, 271 sqq.; quoted, 2, xxviii, xl–xlii, 50; 26, 100, 314; 43, 333–6; 44, 40, 90; became similar to *Ri*shis by study of the Veda, 2, 19, 19 n.; teacher of Yâ*gñ*avalkya, referred to by Âpastamba as 'modern,' 12, xli; mentioned in the Mahâbhârata, 12, xliii; King *G*anaka meets with and questions *S*., 12, xliii; 44, 112 sq.; and the Kshatriya sage Pravâha*n*a *G*aivali, 15, 204; possessed esoteric knowledge, 44, 147; desirous of final release, 48, 203.
*S***vetâ***s***vatara** proclaimed Brahman to ascetics, 15, 266.
*S***vetâ***s***vatara-upanishad**, quoted, 8, 432; 38, 429; 48, 778 sq.; its position in the Upanishad literature, 15, xxxi–xlii; is it a sectarian Upanishad? 15, xxxiii sqq.; translated, 15, 228–67; Mâyâ in the *S*., 34, cxvii n., cxxi n.
*S***vikna**, n. of a people, 44, 239 n., 250, 400.
Swallow, *see* Birds (*b*).
Swan maidens, nymphs swimming about as, 44, 70.
Swoon, nature of it explained, 34, lxi; 38, 149–52; is half-union or half-coincidence with deep sleep, 38, 151 sq.; a half-way approach to death, 38, 152; 48, 606 sq. *See also* Sleep.
*S***yâpar*n*a** Sâyakâyana, n. of a teacher, 15, 186, 186 n.; 43, 274, 344, 344 sq. n.; was the last to slaughter five victims at the building of the fire-altar, 41, 171; 44, xxxviii.
*S***yâva**, *see* *S*yâvâ*s*va.
Syâvarshân(a), *see* Sîyâvakhsh.
Syâvâspi, n.p., 23, 213.
*S***yâvâ***s***va** Âtreya, author of a Vedic hymn, 32, 312, 314, 321, 328, 335, 339, 342, 345, 349, 354, 356, 358; legend of *S*., 32, 359 sq.
Syllables, sacred, *see* Om, Sacred syllables, Stobhâksharas, *and* Vyâh*ri*tis.
Symbols, of royalty, 3, 58 sq.; 27, 214 sq.; natural phenomena as s. of human qualities, 3, 147 sq. and n.; royal s. used at ancestral sacrifices, 3, 154, 420, 420 n.; inner self is void of s., 8, 160, 160 n., 309, 351, 367; with numerous s. only one knowledge is approached, 8, 307, 307 n.; s. of the Brahman, 8, 308; lineal figures, their origin and explanation, in the Yî King, 16, 9–26; lineal figures employed for divination, 16, 20 sq.; the 'Treatise on the S.,' 'the Great Symbolism,' 16, 35–8; good fortune and bad indicated by the s. of the Yî King, 16, 350 sq., 351 n.; the Ho map and the Lo writing, 16, 374, 376 n.; symbolism in wearing the sacred thread-girdle, 18, 122 sq., 122 n., 125, 129–34;

24, 268–70; Hôm a s. of the birth and understanding of the apostles, 18, 170; the jade-symbol, 27, 59; 28, 459 sq., 463 sq.; pratîkopâsana, meditation in which Brahman is viewed under a s., 34, lxxvii; 38, 340–5; only those who do not take their stand on s. are led to the world of Brahman, 38, 402–4. *See also* Hexagrams, *and* Yî King.

Sympathy, one of the four 'infinite feelings,' 11, 201 sq., 273. *See also* Love, *and* Morality.

Syûmarasmi Bhârgava, author of Vedic hymns, 32, 414, 418.

Sze of Pâo, King Yû's concubine, raised to be his queen, 3, 356, 356 n., 360.

Sze-mâ Hsiang-zû, officer and author, 27, 19.

Sze-mâ *Kh*ien, his accounts of Confucius as the author of the Kings, 3, 3, 280–3; 16, 28; his accounts of Lâo-ʒze, 39, 4 sq., 33–6; his accounts of *K*wang-ʒze, 39, 34, 36–8.

Sze-thû *K*ing-ʒze of Wei, mourning at his death, 27, 174 sq.

T

Taciturnity, *see* Mauna.

Tadvana, a name of Brahman, 1, 152, 152 n.

Tâ*g*, Azi Dahâka, a descendant of, 4, xlix sq.

Ta*gg*aniya Kamma, t.t., act of rebuke, *see* Bhikkhus (*c*).

***T*â*gh*ût**, idols and demons of the ancient Arabs, 6, 40, 79, 81 sq., 106, 254; 9, 184. *See also* Idols.

Tâham, n.p., 5, 146.

Tahmûrâf, *see* Tâkhmôrup.

Tahmuras and the Deluge, 4, 384 n.

Tâ Hsio, or 'Great Learning,' the third of the Shû, 3, xx.

***T*â'if**, n.pl.: tribe of the Thaqîf at *T.* defeated by Mohammed, 6, xlii sq.

Tâi *Kh*ăng, reduced the Lî *K*î to forty-six books, 3, xix.

Tâîrêv, *see* Tauru.

Tâi Shăng, a Lî scholar, 27, 6 sq.

Tâi Teh, a Lî scholar, reduced the Lî *K*î to eighty-five books, 3, xix; 27, 7–9.

Taittirîya-âra*n*yaka, Ândhra recension of, 2, xxxvi sq.; quoted, 8, 432; 38, 429; 44, xlvii; 48, 779; T. and Taittirîyaka-upanishad, 15, xxvii.

Taittirîya-brâhma*n*a, quoted, 8, 261 n., 262 n., 266 n.; 38, 429; 44, xxxiii n., xxxix, xl n.; 48, 330; legend of Na*k*iketas in the T., 15, xxi sq.; treats of the horse-sacrifice, 44, xvi.

Taittirîya(ka)-upanishad, quoted, 8, 432 sq.; 34, xlii; 38, 429 sq.; 48, 779 sq.; introduction to T., 15, xxvii–xxx; translated, 15, 43–69.

Taittirîyas, *see* Veda (*g*).

Taittirîya-sa*m*hitâ, quoted, 38, 429; 48, 779; gives mantras of the Asvamedha, 44, xvi.

Tâi ʒin-zăn, n. of a Tâoist sage, 40, 119 sq.

Takhma, n.p., 23, 204.

Takhma Urupa, *see* Tâkhmôrup.

Tâkhmôrup, or Takhma Urupa, or Tahmûrâf, son of Vîvanghat, made Ahriman his steed, 4, 384, 384 n.; 5, 130, 130 n.; 23, 252, 252 n., 292 sq.; 47, xxv, 8; Av. Takhmôurupa, a primaeval sovereign, 5, 62; 18, 13, 13 n.; 47, 121, 128; reigned thirty years, 5, 149; a smiter of Aharman, the demon, 18, 90, 90 n., 200, 201 n.; brother of Yima, killed by Angra-Mainyu, 23, 60 n.; is well-armed, 23, 326; his exploits, 24, 58 sq. and n., 60 n.; second ruler of the earth, 37, 27, 27 n.; his accession, 47, xxix.

Tâ-*k*î, wife of King *K*âu-hsin, 3, 130, 130 n.

Takkasilâ, n. of town, where *G*îvaka is trained by a famous physician, 17, 174 sq.

Takman, demon of fever, 42, 1–6, 273, 442, 445, 449.

Takshaka, n. of a Nâga-king, 21, 5; T. Vaisâleya worshipped at the Âgrahayana festival, 29, 131; worshipped at a rite against poison, 42, 374 sq., 374 n., 425.

Takshan, recites for Âru*n*i who wished to obtain holy lustre, 12, 335.

Tâ-kwei, a personification of the Great Tâo, 40, 96, 96 n.

Talavakâra-brâhma*n*a and Kena-upanishad, 1, lxxxix sq.

Talavakâra-upanishad, i.e. Kena-upanishad, 1, lxxxix; translated, 1, 145-53.

Tales: of a strange prophet, who bids Moses not question anything he may do; he scuttles a ship, kills a boy, and builds up a tottering wall; Moses desires an explanation, which the stranger gives, 6, xcv; 9, 21-3, 23 sq. n.; the Bhikkhu refrains from mean talk, such as t. of kings, demigods, ghost-stories, &c., 11, 194; list of worldly things forming the subject of t., 11, 194; 17, 20 sq.; of Pilindava*kkh*a, who changed the grass chumbat on the head of the park-keeper's daughter into a chaplet of gold, 17, 61-5; of Me*nd*aka and his miraculous powers, 17, 121-4; of *G*îvaka and his wonderful cures, 17, 172-94; of Dîghâvu who would not revenge the murder of his parents, 17, 293-305; Buddha tells many amusing and instructive t., by means of which he teaches the law, 21, 120; Tri*s*alâ, in order that her good dreams should not be counteracted by bad dreams, remained awake by means of hearing auspicious t. about gods and religious men, 22, 240; telling t. after the funeral, 29, 248, 357; told on festival nights, 30, 29; of a Dânava who, to guard his wife, put her into a box and swallowed it, 35, 216 sq.; of a Vidyâdhara who committed adultery with a queen, was caught, and became invisible, 35, 217; of the parents who ate their only child in the desert, 36, 282 n.; purpose of t. told in the Vedânta texts, 38, 305 sq.; 48, 697 sq.; the pâriplava t. told at the horse sacrifice, 38, 305 sq.; 44, 361-71, 361 sq. n.; of the man who was so taken with the charms of a one-eyed courtesan, that he thought other women had an eye too many, 39, 233 n.; of Kapila, who was converted, and converted a gang of robbers, 45, 31 sq. n.; of a friar who, by magic arts, carries off every woman he sees, 45, 383 n.; told for soothing children and sick persons, 48, 198, 199 sq. *See also* *G*âtakas, *and* Parables.

Tal'hah, converted by Mohammed, 6, xxiii.

Tâ-lien and Shâo-lien, their demeanour at mourning, 28, 153 sq., 154 n.

Talisman, *see* Amulets.

***T*âlût**, *see* Saul.

Tamâlapatra*k*andanagandhâbhi-*gñ*a, n. of a Tathâgata, 21, 178.

Tamas, *see* Qualities.

Tâmasa, a Manu, 25, 19.

Tambayak, n. of a demon, 5, 132, 132 n.

Tâmraliptikâ *S*âkhâ, of the Godâsa Ga*n*a, 22, 288.

Tan, prays to the three ancestors for the life of his brother Wû, and the prayer is deposited in 'the metal-bound coffer,' 3, 151-6; generally called 'the Duke of *K*âu,' famous in Chinese history, 3, 152; T. and the building of the city of Lo, 3, 165, 181-5, 185 n., 188-91; wishes to retire into private life, but the young king *Kh*ăng charges him to remain in office, 3, 191-4; King *Kh*ăng sends him a present, 3, 194 sq., 194 n.; gives instructions to *Kh*ăng, 3, 200-5, 219-25; 27, 23, 344 sq., 351, 351 sq. n.; addresses 'Prince Shih,' 3, 205-10; his memory cherished by the people, 3, 232; what he accomplished with the people of Yin, 3, 246 sq., 249; author of odes of the Shih, 3, 295, 317 sq., 347, 377, 407, 444; appointed as marquis of Lû, 3, 342; sacrifices introduced by T., 3, 476 sq. and n.; 16, 289 n.; Yî King ascribed to King Wăn and his son T., 16, xiii, xvi-xix, 5 sq., 10, 26 sq., 35 sq., 57, 58 n., 63 n., 351 n., 397 n.; continues the work of his father on the lineal figures, 16, 21-5; treatise on the Symbolism of the Hexagrams, and of T.'s explanations of the several lines, 16, 267-347; the Yüeh Ling wrongly ascribed to him, 27, 20; receives the feudal lords in audience, 27, 28 sq.; 28, 29-31, 29 n.; one of the six great men, 27, 366; his institutions corrupted, 27, 372 sq. and n.; assisted King Wû in attacking *K*âu, 28, 31;

the princes of Lû sacrifice to T., 28, 32–4; did most meritorious service for the kingdom, 28, 253 sq., 339; killed his brother, 40, 178, 178 n.

Tâ*n*d*ya, quoted, 41, 153; 43, 132 n.

Tâ*nd*ya-mahâbrâhma*n*a, quoted, 38, 430; 44, xvi; 48, 342.

Tang, the minister of Shang, questions *K*wang-ȝze about Benevolence, 39, 346–8.

Tăng Ling-ȝze, a Mohist of the south, 40, 220.

Ta*n*hâ, Pali t.t., Sk. t*r*ish*n*â, Thirst or Desire, Craving, the cause of transmigration and pain, by its destruction man becomes free, 10 (i), 80–4; (ii), 137 sq.; 11, 149 n.; personified as daughter of Mâra, 10 (ii), 159; the wise cross the ocean of T. without rafts, 11, 21 sq., 22 n.; destroyed by the destruction of the Âsavas, 11, 307. *See also* Desire, *and* Truths (four noble).

***T*aṅka**, quoted by Râmânuga, 34, xxi; quoted as the vâkyakâra, 34, xxii; 48, 15–18, 24, 99, 138, 317.

***T*aṅkana**, a savage hill tribe, 45, 268.

Tanmâtrâs, t.t. of Sâṅkhya philosophy, the five elements, sound, touch, form, taste, smell, 8, 387 n.; 15, 296.

Tansar, the high-priest, gathered the fragments of the Avesta, 4, xxxviii, xli–xlv, xlviii; a member of the Platonic sect, 4, lv.

Tantra, or Sâṅkhya*s*âstra, 34, 291, 291 n.

Tanûnapât, n.d., form of Agni, offerings and prayers to, 12, 146 sq., 146 n., 152, 157, 319, 400 n.; 46, 10, 153, 303; covenant of T., 26, 93–7, 93 n., 100; is the wind, the witness of living beings, 26, 94–6; worshipped by Âprî verses, 26, 186 n.; 46, 8–10, 179, 236; Agni is called T. as the Asura's germ, 46, 303. *See also* Agni (*d*).

Tanvasar, chancellor of A*r*takhshatar, 47, xii, xxxiv, 85–7, 85 sq. n.

Tâo, Duke, condoles with Yû Zo, 27, 165; mourning rites for Duke T., 27, 174; death of the mother of Duke T., 27, 189.

Tâo, the.

(*a*) Meaning and characteristics of the T.
(*b*) Its working, its power and influence.
(*c*) The T. as a pattern of morality; possessing and knowing the T.

(*a*) MEANING AND CHARACTERISTICS OF THE T.

Meaning of the term T., 3, xxi sq.; 39, 12–15, 41, 67–9; T. and Logos, 3, xxii; Thâi *K*î identified with the T., 16, 376 n.; or 'ideal method,' 16, 377, 379 n.; Thien T., 'the Way of Heaven,' 27, 39 sq.; 28, 268; its relation to Tî or God, 39, 16, 18 sq.; 'the T. of Heaven,' 39, 16 sq., 89, 119, 121, 123; the T. or Path of duty of Confucius, 39, 29; there is nothing before the T., it might seem to have been before God, 39, 49 sq., 60, 68 sq., 84, 135, 243, 243 n.; the strength of its weakness, exemplified by water, 39, 52 sq., 83, 87, 118–20, 148; its freedom from all preoccupation and purpose, 39, 54 sq.; the Equable, the Inaudible, the Subtle, the One, 39, 57 sq.; its mysteries comprehended by the masters of old, 39, 58 sq.; used to signify 'spirits and men,' 39, 67 sq.; gravity and stillness, attributes of the T., 39, 69; the unchanging T. without a name, and the operating T. with a name, 39, 74 sq.; all-pervading is the Great T., 39, 76; is the most valuable thing, 39, 105 sq.; not a Personal name, 39, 129 sq., 134 sq.; is 'The Lord of Life,' 39, 130 sq.; is 'that in which there is no element of falsehood,' 39, 133, 224, 224 n.; is 'the great and most honoured Master,' 39, 134, 236, 241 n.; 40, 280; is Tranquillity amid all Disturbances, 39, 136, 246; 40, 282; *vacancy, stillness, placidity, tastelessness, quietude, silence, and non-action;—this is the Level of heaven and earth, and the perfection of the T. and its characteristics*, 39, 144, 331, 364 sq.; the presence and power of the T. cannot be communicated by words, 39, 152; 40, 42–6; the characteristics of the T. fully set forth by *K*wang-ȝze, 39, 152; 40, 57–73; grand description of the T., 39, 154, 243 sq.; 40, 112 sq., 112 n.;

cannot be described by any name —neither speech nor silence is sufficient to convey the notion of It, 39, 154 sq.; 40, 126–30, 126 n., 130 n.; heaven as a synonym of T., 39, 178 n., 182 n., 185 n., 196, 196 n., 229 n., 234 n., 278 n.; 40, 61 n.; the true 'Governor,' according to *K*wang-ʒze, 39, 179 n.; the Great T. does not admit of being praised, 39, 189; is 'The Heavenly Treasure-House,' 'The Store of Light,' 39, 190; the Central Element of our nature, 39, 198; the ever-during Thing, 39, 242 sq., 242 n.; that Itself on which all things depend, and from which every transformation arises, 39, 243; no one knows Its beginning, no one knows Its end, 39, 245, 382; 40, 293; the perfect T. explained by Kwang *Kh*ăng-ʒze, 39, 297–300; always One, and yet requiring to be modified, 39, 305; the Way of Heaven, and the Way of Man, 39, 306, 306 n.; admits of no substitute, 39, 348; the Perfect Music illustrating the T., 39, 348–51, 348 n.; stupidity akin to the T., 39, 351; Lâo-ʒze instructs Confucius about the T., 39, 354–7; aimlessness of the T., 40, 51, 51 n.; the Complete, the All-embracing, the Whole, the One, 40, 66 sq.; cannot be known or named, 40, 68–70; personified as 'Non-entity,' 40, 70, 70 n.; characteristics and attributes of the T., 40, 84 sq., 105 sq., 267, 280; Tâ-kwei, a personification of the T., 40, 96 n.; the T. as described by the robber *K*ih, 40, 174 sq.; *the T. is the course by which all things should proceed,* 40, 201; the Grand Unity, the Grand Purity, the Grand Rest, 40, 206 sq.; is twofold: the Pure and the Turbid, Motion and Rest, 40, 250 sq.; the Perfect T. cannot be heard and seen, can only be described by Itself, 40, 265 sq.; is in heaven and earth, 40, 267; the nature of the T. and the use of knowledge, 40, 275–9; is originally one, 40, 277, 291; the Mind, the T., the Heavenly, and the Human are simply One, 40, 281; the Root and Origin, 40, 290 sq., 293, 313, 316; was before Heaven and Earth, 40, 290, 293; is It existing or non-existing? 40, 291–3; cannot be called a 'Mystery,' 40, 292; Its omnipresence, 40, 292; praised, 40, 319. *See also* God (*b*), *and* Heaven (*a*).

(*b*) ITS WORKING, ITS POWER AND INFLUENCE.

Genesis of all things, under the guidance of T., 39, 21; the T. as promotive of longevity, 39, 23–5, 51, 146, 298 sq., 299 n., 331, 364; acts as a kind of talisman, 39, 25 sq., 99; proceeds by contraries, 39, 26, 31, 48, 78, 83–6, 88, 102, 106–8, 112 sq., 123 sq.; 40, 262–4; growth of knowledge caused the decay of T., 39, 28–30; the Author of all things, the Creator, the Originator of heaven and earth, the Mother of all things, 39, 47, 67 sq., 82–4, 94 sq., 247–50, 256; 40, 28, 205, 205 n., 249, 288, 290; its operation is quiet and unceasing, 39, 50; 'the spirit of the valley,' a name for the activity of the T., 39, 51; produces all things, but does not claim them as its own, 39, 54, 76 sq., 93 sq.; its silent, but all-powerful operation in nature, in man, and in government, 39, 59 sq.; an antidote against decay and death, 39, 60, 92 sq.; production of material forms from the T., 39, 64 sq.; its non-active and yet all-efficient operation, 39, 70, 79, 106 sq.; 40, 88, 127, 129 sq., 262; its relation to the world, 39, 75; the Great Image of the invisible T., its inexhaustible efficacy for the good of the world, 39, 77; comprehends and rules all Lâo-ʒze's teaching, 39, 112 sq.; all creatures find their happiness in T., 39, 127, 164–7; the panacea for the evils of controversy, 39, 129, 181–5, 196, 196 n.; the characteristics of the T. and their influence on man, 39, 133, 223–35, 225 n., 231 n.; the author of all the transformations of things, 39, 133, 224, 224 n.; how the T. lifts men above deformities of the body and all calamities, 39, 136, 247–9, 255–8; the greatness of the T. in its spontaneity, when it has obtained complete dominion over man, 39, 145, 148 sq., 374–85; its

characteristic inaction or passionless and purposeless action, 39, 149; 40, 3 sq., 59; doing nothing the essential condition of the T., 39, 161, 261 n.; is injured by disputations, 39, 186; is self-existent, produced heaven and earth, was before all things, independent of space and time, 39, 243 sq. and n.; a great founder, heaven and earth a great melting-pot, 39, 249 sq.; *He gives to all things their blended qualities, and does not count it any righteousness; His favours reach to all generations, and He does not count it any benevolence; He is more ancient than the highest antiquity, and does not count Himself old; He overspreads heaven and supports the earth; He carves and fashions all bodily forms, and does not consider it any act of skill; —this is He in whom I find my enjoyment*, 39, 256, 332; overspreads and sustains all things, 39, 309; if there were not the T., there would be no life, 39, 310; its universal comprehension and unfathomableness, 39, 342; nothing can be effected without the T., 39, 361; the Great T. has no name, no passions, no bodily form, but It produced everything, 40, 249.

(*c*) THE T. AS A PATTERN OF MORALITY; POSSESSING AND KNOWING THE T.

Paradisiacal state of simplicity under the guidance of the T., 39, 26–8, 139–41, 277–80, 287–90; cultivation of the person according to the T. the best qualification for the highest offices, 39, 56 sq., 97 sq.; the full possessor of the T. is like heaven, 39, 60, 111 sq.; end of the paradisiacal state when 'the Great T.' ceased to be observed, 39, 60–2; 40, 312 sq., 316 sq.; possession of the T. confers intelligence and might, 39, 65 sq., 75 sq.; what is not in accordance with the T. soon comes to an end, 39, 73, 99; affords a pattern of moral conduct, 39, 82 sq., 96, 309 sq.; practice of the T. conduces to contentment and happiness, 39, 88 sq., 151; 40, 31–6; the world can only be won by the T., not by learning, 39, 90 sq.; those who conduct government according to the Great T. contrasted with those who rule in a spirit of ostentation and by oppression, 39, 96 sq.; he who has in himself the attributes of the T. is like an infant, 39, 99; the man of T. is humble and retiring, the noblest man under heaven, 39, 100; government according to T. is alone effective, 39, 100–5, 108 sq., 136, 259–62, 267 n.; the guarding of the T. ensures long life, with vigour and success, 39, 103; nothing is useless, if used Tâoistically, 39, 128; 40, 27 sq.; the passionless performance of duty, the method of the T., 39, 130, 198–201; is the Master of the T. still 'a man'? 39, 134, 234 sq.; the True Man of T. knows the difference between the Heavenly (= Tâoistic) and the Human in man, 39, 134 sq., 236 sq.; the True Man or the Master of T., 39, 135, 236–43, 237 n.; ancient personages and superhuman beings who got the T., 39, 135 sq., 244 sq.; genesis of the knowledge of the T., 39, 136, 246 sq. and n.; knowledge of the T. makes men superior to the infirmities of age, 39, 136, 245 sq.; to be found only in a spirit-like energy working imperceptibly and controlling all phenomena, 39, 145; what really belongs to man is the T., sufficient for his happiness, 39, 155; they who possess the T. refuse worldly honours, even a throne, 39, 157; 40, 149–65; is to be loved more than Heaven, 39, 241 sq. and n.; he who has the T. looks upon death not as a calamity, 39, 249–55; unity with the mysterious Heaven, or the Great Pervader, the aim of the Tâoist, 39, 255, 257; to be good means to possess the qualities of the T., 39, 274 sq.; even in the non-action of the Master of the T. there are things he must do, 39, 305 sq., 305 n.; without comprehending the T., no course can be pursued successfully, 39, 306; the ancients who ruled according to the T. did nothing, and everything was done, 39, 307 sq.; pure simplicity of the

Embryonic Age possessed by the Master of the T., 39, 319–22; Heaven must be understood first, then the T., 39, 336; four other steps to be taken before speaking to the Great T., 39, 337; cannot be learnt from books, 39, 343 sq.; how moral qualities appear as results of the T., 39, 369; Yâo and Shun left the T. and substituted the Good for it, pursuing the course of Haphazard Virtue, 39, 370; the sages who preserved the T. in their own persons, 39, 371 sq.; looked at in the light of the T. all things are serviceable, and all things are unserviceable, 39, 379 sq.; do not by the Human extinguish what is Heavenly, guard the T., this is reverting to your True Nature, 39, 384; let your abode be in the T. and its Attributes, 40, 28; enjoying oneself with the T. in the land of Great Vacuity, 40, 31; he who possesses the T. and its Attributes cannot be in distress, 40, 36 sq.; those who know the T. do not speak of it; those who speak of it, do not know it, 40, 58; *to exercise no thought and no anxious consideration is the first step towards knowing the T.; to dwell nowhere and do nothing is the first step towards resting in the T.; to start from nowhere and pursue no path is the first step towards making the T. your own*, 40, 58; put away all that obstructs the free course of the T., 40, 87 sq.; the rule of the T. to be followed by sovereigns, 40, 119 sq.; not to be taught to everybody, 40, 200; those who possess the T., do not know it, 40, 205; to know the T. and not to speak of it is the way to attain to the Heavenly, 40, 205 sq.; 'slaughtering the dragon' means 'learning the T.,' 40, 206 n.; the method of the T. as opposed to other methods employed in the regulation of the world, 40, 214; the perfect system of the T. in antiquity, 40, 214–18, 221, 223, 225, 227; how the system of the T. was gradually obscured and torn in fragments, 40, 216 sq.; how to become a Possessor of the T., 40, 251–3, 282 sq.; those who hold the attributes of the T. and display them, are not Possessors of the T., 40, 253; the reason why all men do not obtain the True T., 40, 253 sq.; they who understand the True T. obtain it and abide in Purity and Stillness, 40, 254; for Heaven now to give life and now to take it away is the method of the T., 40, 260; sincerity the first step toward the T., 40, 266 sq.; to be one with the T. is the True Forgetfulness, 40, 267; by acquiring the True T., the stupid become wise and the coarse become fine, 40, 268; after the T. was abandoned, people began to practise benevolence, righteousness, ceremonies, and music, 40, 284; enjoyment in the T. only to be found by 'emptying one's self,' 40, 288 sq.; Lâo-ȝze's aim to lead men back to the T., 40, 314. *See also* Morality (*d*).

Tâoism described as rationalism, 3, xxi; Sacred Books of T., 3, xxi sq.; 39, xii–xxii; historical phases of T., 3, xxii; 39, 162 sq.; 40, 214–28, 322; its relation to Buddhism and Confucianism, 3, xxii; 39, xi sq., 1–3; 40, 288; Sung philosophy more Tâoistic than Confucian, 16, xvi; Tâoist influence in the Yüeh Ling, 27, 20 sq.; Tâoistic element in the Lî Kî, 27, 24, 45, 364–7, 364 n., 365 n., 367 n., 387 sq. n.; 28, 344 n.; and occult sciences, 39, xii, 42, 44; later phases of T., 39, xii, 96, 135, 237 n.; 40, 295; its relation to Confucianism, 39, xv sq., 1–3, 33, 132, 139, 141; 40, 152; older than Lâo-ȝze, 39, 1–4; chief points of belief in T., 39, 12–33; T. and Buddhism, 39, 23, 33, 35 n., 42–4, 111, 129, 131, 155, 197 n., 313 n.; 40, 139 n., 238 n., 266, 288, 293; its moral teaching, 39, 30–3; old T. not a religion, 39, 41; worship of the 'Three Pure Ones,' 39, 43; dreams of Tâoists about the elixir vitae and life-preserving pills, 39, 103; definitions and illustrations of the perfect Tâoist, 39, 127 sq., 168–71, 192–4; non-action the essence of T., 39, 137, 142–4, 264–6, 291–8, 302 sq., 305 sq., 330–8; opposed to benevolence, righteousness, arts,

and all culture, 39, 139–41, 268–90, 292 sq., 295 sq., 305 sq., 328 sq., 328 n.; the Ruling Powers do nothing, but those subordinate to them act, 39, 144, 334–8; antagonism of T. to Confucianism, 39, 144 sq., 147, 242 n.; 40, 192–201; 'vulgar learning' contrary to the principles of T., 39, 147, 368–73; 'Perfect Enjoyment,' what is it? 39, 149; 40, 1–4, 107; transrotation of births in T. and Buddhism, 39, 150; 40, 10n.; the distress of those who disallow the great Tâoist principle of doing nothing, 39, 154; 40, 97 sq., 98 n.; the principle of doing nothing and thereby accomplishing everything, 39, 154; 40, 104–6, 104 n., 285–8, 291–3, 314; submission to what is beyond our knowledge and control, the highest issue of T., 39, 248, 258, 258 n.; the usefulness of what is of no use, 40, 137 sq.; the stages attained to by a Tâoist disciple, ending with the attainment of the Great Mystery, 40, 146; longevity as the aim of T., 40, 235 sq., 236 n., 270–2; its mysticism, 40, 247 sq., 257. *See also* Humility, Morality (*d*), *and* Philosophy.

Tâoist sage (True Man of Tâo, Perfect or Great Man), symbolized by the dragon, 16, 57 sq., 58 sq. n., 409–11, 412 n., 416 sq.; his firm and correct course finally leads to success, 16, 83–5, 85 n., 86, 252, 252 sq. n.; by humility he will be successful, 16, 89 sq., 90 sq. n.; it is advantageous to meet with him, 16, 141–3, 143 n.; his course is like that of the earth, 16, 214, 215 n.; sages, by their spirit-like ability, invented the diagrams of the Yî for divination purposes, 16, 372 sq., 374 n.; the sages who made the Yî were independent of it, 16, 404, 406 n.; the sage and the Spirit-man, 28, 317–20, 317 sq. n., 320 n., 323, 325; the accomplished Tâoist as 'the Perfect Man,' 'the Spirit-like Man,' and 'the Sagely Man,' 39, 127 sq., 168–71, 192–4, 323 sq.; 40, 140, 214 sq., 274 sq.; certain Tâoist sages who are crippled or deformed, and yet perfect men, 39, 133, 223–34; characteristics of the True Man or the Master of the Tâo, 39, 135, 146 sq., 151, 153, 236–43, 237 n., 364–7; 40, 25 sq., 28, 33 sq., 42 sq., 48 sq., 53–5, 75–84, 88–90, 105 sq., 110, 115–18; when he employs his mind, it is a mirror, 39, 137, 266; how to become a perfect man, 39, 153, 246, 256 sq.; 40, 48 sq., 77–82; the superior man, he who does nothing, 39, 293 sq.; 40, 60 sq., 286 sq.; contrasted with ordinary philosophers, 39, 303–5; how he acts in accordance with the Tâo, 39, 309 sq.; after living a thousand years, he ascends among the Immortals, 39, 313 n., 314; sages, the uncrowned kings, 39, 331 sq.; the perfect man who has comprehended the Tâo, 39, 342; those whom the ancients called 'Retired Scholars,' preserved the Tâo in their own persons, 39, 371 sq.; he has no thought of self, 39, 378 sq.; he is the Great Conqueror of all, 39, 385, 385 n.; the courage of the T. s., 39, 386; his attainments under the influence of his 'Heavenly constitution,' 40, 12–14; the contemplation of the process of beginning and ending of all things, is the delight of the T. s., 40, 46–8, 47 n.; sages, like rulers in court, keep their face to the south, 40, 75, 75 n.; specimens of true men of Tâo, 40, 91–4, 93 n., 114 sq.; 'Heavenly Master,' title of a chief of Tâoism, 40, 97, 97 n.; he leaves no traces of his conduct, 40, 138; he only is able to enjoy himself, 40, 138 sq., 295; his happiness, 40, 160 sq.; the sagely man rests in what is his proper rest, 40, 205; the sage is not at war in himself, 40, 206, 206 n.; the True Man possesses both the True Knowledge and the Tâo, 40, 280–3. *See also* Morality (*d*).

Tâo *K*ih, *see K*ih.

Tao-sing, assisted in the Chinese translation of the Vinaya, 19, xxvi.

Tâo Teh *K*ing, or 'the Tâo and its characteristics,' t.w., Lâo-ȝze's treatise, 3, xxi sq.; editions, commentaries, and translations of it, 39, xii–xviii, 6–8; a genuine production of Lâo-ȝze, 39, xiv, 4–9; its historical elements very vague, 39, 2;

division into parts and chapters, 39, 8 sq.; hardly a historical allusion in it, 39, 33; translated, 39, 45–124; its superiority to other books, 40, 314.

Tap, demon of fever, 18, 95.

Tapas, Sk. t.t., translated by 'brooding,' 15, 28 n.; Buddha's teaching on T., 17, 111, 113 sq.; creative fervour, 42, 199, 214–17, 224 sq., 686. *See also* Asceticism, Austerity, Devotion, *and* Penance.

Tâpasa, n. of disciple of Vagrasena, 22, 288.

Tâpasa, n. of disciple of *S*ântisenika, 22, 293.

Tâpasas, *see* Ascetics, *and* Holy persons.

Tâpa*sk*ita, t.t., *see* Sacrifices (*j*).

Tapoda, n.pl., grove at Râ*g*agaha, 11, 56 sq.

Taponitya Paura*s*ish*t*i, n. of a teacher, 15, 51.

Taprê*v*, demon, business of, 5, 107.

Taptak*rikkh*ra, *see* Penances.

Tapussa, and Bhallika, two merchants, the first lay-disciples of Buddha, 13, 81–4.

Târâ, wife of B*ri*haspati, 49 (i), 45 n.

Târâga*n*a, n. of a great ascetic, 45, 268, 268 n.

Taranta Vaidada*s*vi, n.p., 32, 356, 358–62.

Târkshya, is an autumn month, 43, 107; T. Vaipa*sk*ita or Vaipa*s*yata, King of Birds, 44, 369, 369 n.; the sun-horse, 49 (i), 62. *See also* Târukshya.

Tarômat, or Târôkmat, demon of disobedience, 5, 107; is Nâûnghas, smitten by Spenda*r*ma*d*, 5, 128, 128 n.; the fiend, opposes the angel Spenda*r*ma*d*, 18, 270, 270 n.; 37, 263 sq., 263 n.

Tarpa*n*a, *see* Sacrifices (*b*).

Târukkha, n. of a Brâhma*n*a, 10 (ii), 109, 110; 11, 167, 167 sq. n., 169 sq.

Taruksha, worshipped at the Tarpa*n*a, 30, 244.

Târukshya, n. of a teacher, 1, 254.

Taste, six forms of, 8, 384.

Tâ Tâi = Tâi Teh, q. v.

Tathâgata, *see* Buddha (*a*, *j*).

Tâ Thâo, the Grand Historiographer, 40, 124 sq., 124 n.

Tâ-thing, a primaeval sovereign, 39, 287.

Tâthrava*nt*, an enemy of Vî*s*tâspa, 23, 79, 117, 280, 306.

Ta-tseu-sui-ying-pen-k'i-king, t.w., a Chinese life of Buddha, 19, xxiii sq.

Tattooing of wild tribes in China, 27, 229.

Tat tvam asi, *see* Brahman (*f*).

Tâûîrê*v*, *see* Tauru.

Tauru, Av., Phl. Tâîrê*v*, or Tâûîrê*v*, or Tâûr*v*ŏ, spell against, 4, 139, 139 n.; one of the six demons of Aharman, 5, 10, 10 n.; 18, 319; attacked by Horvada*d*, 5, 128; propitiated by walking barefoot, 37, 182, 182 n.

Taurvasa horses, 44, 400.

Taurvâti, n.p., 23, 213.

Taurvi and Zairi, demons, 4, 224.

Tâûr*v*ŏ, *see* Tauru.

Tauvilikâ, female demon of disease, 42, 30, 466.

Tâvati*m*sa-devâ, *see* Gods (*j*).

Taxes, duties, and tolls, law about, 2, 164, 228 n., 229-31; 14, 8, 97, 98–100, 98 n., 100 n., 199 sq.; 25, 323–5; 27, 227 sq., 271, 294, 301; 33, 126 sq.; regulated by Yü, 3, 63–75; a tenth of the field produce is annually levied, 3, 370, 370 n.; law regarding fares and tolls, 7, 36; exemption from t., 25, xxxiii, xxxiii n., 248 n., 322; 33, 219; 35, 208; king to settle t. and duties, 25, 229, 234, 236–8; arrears of t. need not be paid by the heir, 25, 282; king's share in kind, 25, 386 sq.; to be collected by the king, 25, 396, 427 sq. and n.; tithe to priests and kings, 37, 425, 443.

Tâ*z* and Tâ*z*ak, ancestors of the Arabs, 5, 58; son of Fravâk, 5, 132; brother of Hôshâng, 37, 27 sq.

Tâ*z*ak, wife of Tâ*z*, 5, 58.

Teacher, teachers and pupils, religious instruction.

(*a*) Guru or t. of the Veda in Brâhma*n*ism.
(*b*) In Buddhism and *G*aina religion.
(*c*) In Zoroastrianism.
(*d*) In China.

(*a*) Guru or t. of the Veda in Brâhma*n*ism.

Only knowledge which is learnt from a t. (â*k*ârya) leads to real good, 1, 64, 64 n.; 48, 275; attention on a tutor (or spiritual guide), the basis

of belief, 1, 122; attention on a tutor based on the performance of sacred duties, 1, 122; duties of student (Snâtaka, householder) towards his t., 1, 144; 2, 3, 7, 11-32, 49 sqq., 111-13, 111 n., 183-5, 188-93; 8, 176-8, 360; 14, 10 sq., 40-2, 152-8; 25, 43, 51, 65-9; 29, 119, 124 sq., 191; 33, 131-3; 44, 50; succession of t. and pupils considered as a spiritual family, 2, 26 n.; on the fee to be given to a t., 2, 27 sq.; 14, 124, 322; 25, 73 sq., 92; 29, 82 sq., 230; 30, 156; 44, 66; students go to several t. to learn the several Vedas, 2, 27, 27 n., 28; duties of t. towards religious students, 2, 31 sq., 113 sq.; 25, 42 sq., 59; how to behave towards fallen t., 2, 88; hospitable reception of t., 2, 120, 205; 25, 96, 96 n.; 29, 87 n., 88, 197, 273, 435; 30, 132, 279; begging for t., for t.'s fee, allowed, 2, 123, 203; 25, 430; right to inherit of t. and pupils, 2, 134; 14, 179; 25, 367, 367 n.; he who initiates and he who teaches the Veda is called t., 2, 176; who is more venerable, t. or parents, 2, 192; 7, 127 sq.; 25, xxiv, 56 sq. and n., 61; when one may study under a t. who is not a Brâhma*n*a, 2, 211; 25, 72 sq.; teaching the duty of and a means of livelihood for Brâhma*n*as, 2, 227, 227 n.; 8, 359; 25, 24, 401 sq., 419 sq., 424 sq.; the t. and the king guard men, therefore they must not be reviled, 2, 238; death of t., impurity caused by it, and funeral rites for dead t., 2, 252; 7, 91 sq., 96; 14, 67, 182; 25, 181 sq., 184; 29, 244 sq., 344, 358; 42, 528; sin of casting off one's t., 2, 282; 25, 104, 442; those t. who do not impart instruction or commit mortal sins must be forsaken, 2, 282; definitions of the terms 'teacher' (â*k*ârya), 'sub-teacher' (upâdhyâya), and guru, 7, 121 sq., 127; 14, 20; 25, 56; reverence towards and venerability of t., 7, 129-31; 8, 103, 119, 243; 14, 124; 25, lxvii, 56 sq., 61, 71 sq., 149, 154, 157; one must not step on the shade of a t., 7, 203; birth through a t. more important than birth from father and mother, 8, 175-7; pupil is like the shadow of the t., 8, 312; lists of t., lines of t., 12, xxxi-xxxv, xxxiii n., xxxiv n.; 15, 118-20, 185-8, 213 sq., 224-7; 29, 141; 43, xviii, 404; the t. is the father, the Sâvitrî the mother, at the 'second birth,' 14, 9 sq., 209 sq. and n.; the sacred fire represents the t., when the t. dies, 14, 40 sq.; t. who neglect Veda-study and sacrifices become outcasts, 14, 68; the t. is ten times more venerable than a sub-teacher, 14, 68; behaviour towards t.'s t., and t.'s son, 14, 68; 25, 67 sq., 74; leavings of a t. may be eaten, 14, 71; sin of pupil falls on negligent t., 14, 101; 25, 309; penance for a t. on the death of a student, 14, 118; sin of teaching wicked people, 14, 130; penances for t., 14, 214; staying in the house of a t. after having finished studentship, a sin, 14, 220; associating with outcast t. or pupil is sinful, 14, 239; rites securing success may be performed only for a t., father, or mother, besides oneself, 14, 331; secret union of t. and pupil, 15, 46; prayer of a t. that Brahman-students may come to him, 15, 47 sq.; pupils approaching the t. with fuel in their hands, 15, 271; 44, 53 sq.; behaviour towards t.'s wives, 25, 68 sq., 74; life-long service to a t., 25, 73 sq.; the pupil must not pay fee, but give presents to t., 25, 73 sq., 104; Snâtaka receives hospitable reception from t., 25, 75, 75 n.; not called a guest, 25, 95; entertained at *S*râddhas, 25, 102; offences against t., 25, 103, 154, 302, 441 sq.; *S*ûdra t. and those who instruct *S*ûdras excluded from *S*râddha, 25, 104; sin of teaching for a stipulated fee or learning from a paid t., 25, 104, 442; pupil may be beaten to be corrected, 25, 154, 306; is the lord of the world of Brahman, 25, 157; quarrels with t. to be avoided, 25, 157; falsely accusing or abusing one's t. a mortal sin, 25, 303, 441, 441 n., 448; students guard their t., his house, &c., 26, 151; ceremony performed by the t. at the betrothal, 29, 22; pupil and t. descendants of the same *R*ishi, 29, 62

sq. n.; the student's costume, a gift to the t.. 29, 92; list of t., worshipped at the Tarpa*n*a, 29, 123, 149, 220, 223; 30, 244 sq.; rules for the t. when beginning instruction in the secret doctrines, 29, 141; water libations to the t., 29, 325; 30, 79; the t. is independent, the student dependent, 33, 50; property acquired by religious instruction, 33, 53; men deprived of potency by the curse of a t., 33, 167; intercourse with wife of a t. termed incest, 33, 179; *see also* Incest; there can be no lawsuit between t. and pupil, 33, 234; obedience of pupil towards t. falling under the law of master and servant, 33, 344; *G*anaka gives Yâ*gñ*avalkya a hundred cows for his esoteric doctrine regarding the Agnihotra, 44, 46; whether the t. of a Brahma*k*ârin may carry on sexual intercourse or not, 44, 90. *See also* Brahma*k*ârin, Guru, Holy persons, *and* Initiation.

(*b*) In Buddhism and *G*aina religion.

On choosing a good and learned t., 10 (ii), 52 sq.; t. of the Dhamma to be honoured, 10 (ii), 54; he who has doubts in the t. (satthâ) is not free from spiritual barrenness, 11, 223 sq., 228; an upa*gg*h*â*ya must be appointed at the ordination, 13, 151–4, 170, 222; 36, 96, 96 n.; duties of a pupil (saddhivihârika) towards an upa*ggh*âya, 13, 154–63; 36, 184 sq., 310; duties of an upa*ggh*âya towards his saddhivihârika, 13, 163–5; dukka*t*a offences committed by misconduct of saddhivihârikas and upa*ggh*âyas towards each other, 13, 165–8; when a t. might turn away a saddhivihârika, 13, 166–8; duties of an antevâsika towards his â*k*ariya, and vice versa, 13, 178–180; difference between â*k*ariya and upa*ggh*âya, 13, 178 sq. n.; only a learned, competent Bhikkhu who has completed at least ten years, may receive a young Bhikkhu as his antevâsika, 13, 181; nissaya, or relation between t. and pupil, rules concerning its admissibility or cessation, 13, 181–6, 206 sq., 226–8; 17, 337, 337 n., 340, 372; knowledge of Dhamma, Vinaya, and Pâtimokkhas, required of a t., 13, 184 sq.; persons unfit to be upa*ggh*âyas, 13, 222 sq.; Bhikkhus should not travel without permission from their â*k*ariyas or upa*ggh*âyas, 13, 272; respect to be shown by Bhikkhus to their t. (â*k*ariyas and upa*ggh*âyas), 17, 18; t. and pupils must wait upon each other in sickness, 17, 241 sq.; the duties of an â*k*ariya and of an upa*ggh*âya are not subjects of a legal question of business, 20, 45; instructors (pavattinî) for Bhikkhunîs to be appointed, 20, 350 sqq., 351 n.; the thesis that anything be permissible for a Bhikkhu in following the practice of his upa*ggh*âya, 20, 386, 398, 411; Ga*kkh*as or lists of t. in *G*aina books, 22, xxxvi sq.; how a *G*aina monk or nun should behave when wandering with their t. or master, 22, 146; a *G*aina monk is not allowed to go out or do anything without asking leave of the t. or sub-t., or Sthavira, or Ga*n*adhara, &c., 22, 306 sq.; a t. should be like a father, 35, 142 sq.; twenty-five virtues of a t., 35, 142 sq.; ten virtues of a lay-disciple, 35, 143 sq.; honour due to a t. though he be only a novice, 36, 334; how a *G*aina pupil should behave towards his t., 45, 1–8; the *G*aina monk's duty towards t., 45, 78, 142–9; bad pupils compared to unmanageable bullocks, 45, 149–52; a *Kh*admastha or a *G*ina, as t., 45, 155, 155 n., 157; obedience and reverence to t. among the articles necessary for perfection, 45, 158 sq., 162 sq., 184; serving the t., one of the internal austerities, 45, 179, 179 n.; duties of *G*aina novices towards t., and duties of t. towards novices, 45, 324–8; he who has learned from a *S*rama*n*a or Brâhma*n*a even one noble truth only, will reverence him like a deity or a sacred shrine, 45, 433. *See also* Bhikkhus (*c*), *G*aina monks, Preachers, *and* Preaching.

(*c*) In Zoroastrianism.

Contracts between pupil and t., 4, 45 sq.; 23, 150; student and teaching priest, 4, 311–15; fees of t.,

4, 315; respect due to parents and t., 4, 370 sq.; spells to be taught only to a son, a brother, or a pupil, 23, 51, 243; to be obeyed, 24, 78; unfriendliness of a t. towards a disciple, 37, 51; t. and disciple in legal proceedings, 37, 59; duty of aiding a disciple, 37, 80; duties towards t., 47, 169.

(*d*) IN CHINA.

Rules of conduct for pupils towards t., 27, 70, 74 sq.; duties of pupil towards t. the same as of a son towards his father, 27, 121; offerings to the t., 27, 347-9, 349 n.; *hence it is from the t. indeed that one learns to be a ruler, and the choice of a t. demands the greatest care; as it is said in the Record, 'The three kings and the four dynasties were what they were by their t.,'* 28, 88; honour due to the t., 28, 88; masters of schools in China receive their pupils in the courtyard, 40, 40 sq., 40 n.; wickedness of being angry with t., 40, 241.

Teaching, *see* Teacher.

Tegas, Sk., how to be rendered properly, 1, 93 sq. n.

Teka, n. of a demon harassing children, 30, 219.

Tekula and Yame*l*u, two Brâhmans who had become Bhikkhus, 20, 149 sq.

Temples, to be passed with one's right turned towards them, 2, 226; 29, 125; in the vicinity of a t. the Veda must not be studied, 7, 124; he must not eat in a t., 7, 221; a builder of t. enters the dwelling-place of that deity to whom he has erected a t., 7, 271; Lakshmî resides in t., 7, 299; Pâsâ*n*aka *K*etiya, the Rock Temple, n. pl., 10 (ii), 188; with embroidered flags, 19, 198; t. and statues erected to their prophets by Buddhists and *G*ainas, 22, xxi; built where boundaries meet, 25, 298; balance for ordeal erected in sight of a t., 33, 104; associations formed for the erection of t., 33, 348; cities adorned with t., 36, 209; shrines of gods adorned with flowers, 36, 211 n.; *see also* Holy places, Idols, Idol-temples, *and* Sârandada T.;—t. restored by Duke Hsî, 3, 341, 346; Than-fû raised a t. to the spirits of the land, 3, 384, 385 n.; t. to Lâo-ʒze, 40, 311 sq. n., 317-19; ancestral t., *see* Ancestor Worship (*d*).

Tevi*gg*a, Pali t.t., Sk. traividya, 'learned in the three Vedas,' title of Buddha, 11, 159; the T. compared to the Scribes and Pharisees of the New Testament, 11, 160; in what sense used as an epithet of Buddhist Arhats, 11, 161 sq.

Tevi*gg*a-Suttanta, 'The Discussion on Knowledge of the Three Vedas,' Sutta of the Dîgha Nikâya, 11, x; translated, 11, 157-203; treats of Sîla, or Right Conduct, 11, 159.

Tevi*gg*a-va*kkh*agotta-sutta, of the Ma*gg*hima-Nikâya, 11, 159.

Thâi, *see* Than-fû.

Thâi Hâo, divine ruler of spring, 27, 250, 250 n., 257, 262.

Thâi Khang, a bad ruler, deplored by his five sons, 3, 78-80.

Thâi *K*iâ, grandson and heir of Thang, Î Yin gives instructions to him, 3, 92-103; kept by minister Î in the palace of Thung near the grave of the former king, 3, 95, 97; or Thâi ʒung, successor to Thang, 3, 303.

Thâi-*k*iang, or *K*iang, wife of Than-fû, 3, 383, 383 n., 387 sq. and n.

Thâi-kung, and his descendants buried in *K*âu, 27, 131; commentator of the Yin Fû *K*ing, 40, 255 sq.

Thâi-kung Thiâo and Shâo *K*ih discourse about the Tâo, 40, 126-30, 126 n.

Thâi-kung *Z*ân converts Confucius to Tâoism, 40, 32-4, 32 n., 289.

Thâi Mâu, reigned seventy-five years, 3, 23; canonized as *K*ung ʒung, worshipped as an ancestor, 3, 303, 305 sq.

Thâi-po, eldest son of King Thâi, 3, 390, 390 n.

Thâi-shang Kan Ying Phien or tractate of actions and their retributions, 39, xxi sq., 38-40; translated, 40, 235-46.

Thâi Sze, wife of Wăn, 3, 388, 388 n.

Thâi Tien, minister of Wăn, 3, 208.

Thâi-wang Than-fû, leaves his kingdom for the wild tribes of the North, to avoid war, 40, 150 sq., 150 n.

Thâi-wû, *see* *K*ung ʒung.

Thâi-zăn, the virtuous wife of *K*î of *K*âu, and mother of King Wăn, 3, 380 sq., 380 n., 387.

Thamûd, people of, reject Zâli'h who was sent unto them with the sign of the she-camel, 6, 146 sq., 147 sq. n.; 9, 7, 242; 'Âd and T., 6, 183; 9, 121; punished for disbelief in the mission of Zâli'h, 6, 211 sq., 239; 9, 86, 96, 103 sq., 176, 200, 247, 254, 256, 298, 327, 331, 333; or El '*H*agr, 6, 249 n.; called their prophet liar, 9, 61.

Than-fû, great-grandfather of Wû, 3, 124; 28, 309; called 'King Thâi,' founder of the state of *K*âu, 3, 134, 134 n.; canonized as King Thâi, 3, 152 sq., 316; 28, 60; was humble and reverent, 3, 203; 28, 283; among the descendants of Hâu-*k*î, 3, 342; his settlement in *K*âu, building of temples and palace, 3, 382–5, 389; Shun was not equal to him of the line of Thâi, 39, 136, 259 sq.

Thang, or Thien-yî, or *Kh*ăng Thang, the Successful, founder of the Shang dynasty, 3, 13, 84, 303; the Book of Th. in the Shû King, 3, 31–6; surnamed Ȝze and Lî, 3, 84; summons his people against *K*ieh of Hsiâ, 3, 84–6, 127 sq.; *K*ung-hui's 'announcement' justifying T.'s proceedings against *K*ieh, 3, 86–9; noble character and sentiments of T., 3, 87 sq., 90 sq., 91 n., 93 sq., 96, 98 sq., 310 sq.; 28, 281; his Announcement, inaugurating the new dynasty, 3, 89–91; his self-sacrifice to assuage a draught, 3, 91 n.; his death, 3, 92; ancestor of the Count of Wei, 3, 162; a model king, 3, 176, 221 sq.; punished and destroyed the sovereign of Hsiâ, 3, 197, 215; had Î Yin as his minister, 3, 206; sacrifice offered by one of his descendants to T., 3, 304 sq.; appointed by God, to regulate the boundaries of the kingdom, 3, 307 sq.; changed the appointment of the line of Hsiâ, 16, 254; one of the six great men, 27, 366; dethroned *K*ieh, 27, 396; 40, 178; worshipped as an ancestor, 28, 202, 209; inscription on his bathing-tub, 28, 415; questions put by T. to *K*î, 39, 167, 167 n.; had recourse to the force of arms, 39, 359; he and Wû contended for the sovereignty, 39, 380; 40, 73; seven years' draught in the times of T., 39, 388; made Î Yin his cook, 40, 89; followed Măn-yin Tăng-hăng as his master, 40, 117; proposes to resign his throne, 40, 141, 162 sq.; Th. and Wû set up as Sons of Heaven, yet their posterity cut off, 40, 170 sq.; banished his lord, 40, 171, 173; had his Tâ Hû music, 40, 218. *See also* Yâo.

Than Kung, the Book named after him, 27, 17, 120.

*TH*aqîf, submit to Mohammed on condition of being allowed to retain their idol Allât, 9, 9 n.

That art thou, *see* Brahman (*f*).

That which is, *see* Sat.

That which is not, *see* Asat.

Theft, sin of, especially stealing gold of a Brâhma*n*a, causes loss of caste, 1, 83 sq.; 2, 74, 280; 7, 133 sq.; 8, 389, 389 n.; 14, 5, 201, 218; 25, 383; *see also* Brâhma*n*a (*d*); ordeals applied in cases of th. and robbery, 1, 108 sq.; 33, 98, 316, 319; 34, 323 n.; thief set at liberty heaps his guilt on the king, 2, 71, 82; penances for th. (esp. of gold of Brâhma*n*a), 2, 82 sq., 293; 7, 172 sq., 181; 14, 108, 127, 132, 213, 296, 299; 25, 448, 448 n., 451, 463–5, 480; definition of th., 2, 88; to keep off danger from thieves, a king's chief duty, 2, 162; law about th., 2, 163, 167, 169, 232, 240, 244 sq., 248; 7, 136; 25, 253, 267, 306–14; 33, 204–6, 223–32, 266 sq., 359–63; 37, 51, 56, 58–60, 69 sq., 74–7, 99; thieves defile the company at a *S*râddha, 2, 256; 25, 103; cases when it is allowed to take money from *S*ûdras and others (by fraud or force), 2, 273; punishments for th. and robbery, 6, 102; 7, 26, 31 sq., 36; 14, 101, 201; 25, 390–2, 394, 496–9; 35, 256 sq., 290; 37, 121; appropriating land or a deposit belonging to a Brâhma*n*a, is a crime equal to the th. of gold, 7, 134; refraining from th., part of the conduct of the good, 8, 243; is of the quality of passion, 8, 324; one of

the five principal sins, 10 (i), 61; all sort of th. to be avoided, 10 (ii), 65 sq.; *ye shall not take that which has not been given*, 11, 189, 253; 13, 235; the Bhikkhu who commits th., falls into defeat, 13, 4; penalties for th. with and without violence, 24, 326–8; punishment of officials for stealing, 25, 259; stolen property must be restored, 25, 260; thieves, robbers, burglars are 'thorns,' 25, 387; punishments for th. in future births, 25, 440; various kinds of th., 25, 441, 443 sq., 443 n.; is sinful bodily action, 25, 484; violating truth, a kind of th., 33, 95, 95 n.; clandestine sale of stolen articles, is considered as th., 33, 144 sq.; robbers of human beings and quadrupeds, 37, 427; charm against robbers, 42, 147 sq., 367; he who takes away land may be slain as an assassin, 45, 19. *See also* Judicial procedure.

Theogony, *see* Gods (*b*).

Theopompus, and Zoroastrianism, on the periods of the world, 4, liv.

Theosophists, not Buddhists, 35, 268 n.

Thera-Gâthâ, t.w., quoted in Milindapañha, 35, xli.

Thera-paramparâ, or lists of Elders in the Ceylon chronicles, 11, xlvii.

Theras, Buddhist t.t., Elders, senior priests, 10 (ii), x; the Bhikkhus' duties towards Th., 11, 6; as authorities for the true teaching of Buddha, 11, 66–70; never go about in public alone, but are always accompanied by a Sâma*n*era, 11, 102 n.; young Bhikkhus must follow the order of the Th., 13, 268, 271. *See also* Preachers.

Thief, *see* Parables (*f*), *and* Theft.

Thien, *see* God (*b*), *and* Heaven (*a*).

Thien Ho, marquis of *Kh*î, 40, 103, 103 n.

Thien Kăn, his interview with 'a nameless man,' 39, 137, 260 sq.

Thien Khâi-*k*ih, has an interview with Duke Wei of Kâu, 39, 150; 40, 16 sq.

Thien *Kh*ang, killed his ruler and usurped the state, 40, 177, 177 n.

Thien *Kh*ăng-ȝze, killed the ruler of *Kh*î and stole his state, 39, 282, 282 n.

Thien Mâu, of *Kh*î, violated a treaty with King Yung of Wei, 40, 118, 118 n.

Thien Phien, a Tâoist professor who did not know the true Tâo, 40, 223–5.

Thien ȝze-fang, at the court of the Marquis Wăn of Wei, 39, 151 sq.; 40, 42 sq.

Third Place, *see* Future Life (*b*).

Thirst, explained, 1, 100; sacrifice to Th., 30, 128. *See also* Ta*n*hâ.

Thou art that, *see* Brahman (*f*).

Thought, thoughts: harbouring evil th. belongs to the quality of passion, 8, 323; the characteristic quality of mind is th., 8, 348, 350; all that we are is the result of our th., 10 (i), 3 sq.; guard your th., 10 (i), 12–15; th., word, and deed, 10 (i), 28, 28 sq. n., 59, 85, 87, 90; 11, 10; relation between th. and the senses, 35, 89–92; good th., *see* Morality (*c*).

Thoughtfulness, dams the streams of desire, 10 (ii), 190 sq.

Thoughtlessness, opp. to earnestness, 10 (i), 9–11.

Thraêtaona, and Traitana, 4, lii; his three sons Airya, Sairima, and Tûra, 4, lix, 255; 23, 222 n.; smote Azi Dahâka, 4, 9, 9 n., 226, 245; 23, 61, 113, 242, 254 sq., 277, 294, 307; 31, 233, 233 n.; the functions of Thrita ascribed to Th., 4, 226; invoked against brigands, 4, 245 sq.; invoked in spells and incantations, 4, 246; 23, 69 n.; Th. and Trita, 12, 48 n.; 42, 523; delivers Savanghavâ*k* and Erenavâ*k*, 23, 61 sq.; sacrifices to Ardvi Sûra Anâhita, 23, 61 sq.; Vafra Navâza flung up in the air by Th., 23, 68 sq. and n.; as inventor of magic, 23, 69 n.; worships Drvâspa, 23, 113; Fravashi of Th. worshipped, 23, 221; 31, 389 sq.; worships Vayu, 23, 254 sq.; worships Ashi Vanguhi, 23, 277; seized the glory that had departed from Yima, 23, 294; is fiend-smiting, 23, 326; son of Âthwya, 31, 233, 233 n., 389 sq.; 42, 523. *See also* Frê*d*ûn.

Thread-girdle, *see* Costume.

Three, *see* Numbers (*b*).
Three Jewels, *see* Jewels.
Threshold, Buddha's room to be entered without crossing it, 17, 137; the mother of a new-born child must not step on a th. in the dwelling, 24, 277, 339; an officer should enter the palace without treading on the th., 27, 71; bride shall not stand on the th., 30, 193, 263.
Thrimithwant, son of Spitâma, 23, 204, 204 n.
Thrit, son of Aêvo-saredha-fyaêsta, 23, 218.
Thrita, the inventor of the herbs-medicine, 4, 225–7; one of the first priests of Haoma, 4, 226; the Sâman, father of Keresâsp, 18, 369; 31, 233 sq.; 47, 136 n.; son of Sâyuzdri, 23, 71, 212; 47, 78 n.
Thritak, n.p., 5, 134; 47, 34.
Thriti, daughter of Zarathustra, 23, 204 n., 224.
Thunder, meditation on the person in the, as Brahman, 1, 303; th. and rain symbolical of political disorder, 16, 215 sq., 216 n.; the emblem of great power, 16, 309, 309 n.; th. and rain symbolical of forgiveness on the part of a conqueror, 16, 316, 317 n.; Indra is th., and th. is thunderbolt, 44, 116. *See also* Omens.
Thunderbolt, chief among weapons, 8, 89; the prâna is a raised th., 34, 229–31; used to denote 'cause of fear in general,' 34, 230 sq.; is fifteenfold, 41, 413; 43, 37, 62, 85 sq.; 44, 300 sq., 350, 384; drives off the evil-doer, 43, 37; strength means th., 43, 64; 44, 384; is wielded by the sun, 43, 85 sq.; Indra drives off the Asuras with it, 43, 193; Indra is the th., 44, 116. *See also* Indra (*b*).
Thunderstorm, shooting arrows at, 32, 400, 404 sq.; how it arises, 40, 132; Agni in the th., 46, 103. *See also* Storm.
Thûpas, *see* Stûpas.
Tî and Shang Tî meaning God, 3, xxiii–xxix; 16, xix sq., 51 sq.; 39, 202 n.; as title of Chinese sovereigns, 3, xxiii, xxv–xxix; the title T. and Hwang Tî, 3, 256, 256 n.; the relation of the Tâo to T. or God, 39, 16, 18 sq.; Tîs and Kings regard Heaven and Earth as their Author, 39, 333. *See also* God (*b*), *and* Kings (*c*).
Tî, behaved rudely in mourning, 27, 177.
Tidasapura, *see* Gods (*j*).
Tides, *see* Ocean.
Tiger, *see* Animals (*k*).
Tî I consults Ȝze-hsiâ about mourning, 27, 151.
Tî *Khû*, deserves ancestor worship, 28, 208.
Time, Wăn of Wei praised for his regard to auspiciousness of, 3, 436 sq., 436 n.; boundless T. invoked, 4, 213 sq.; 23, 10, 18, 34, 334, 352; the departed soul enters the way made by T., 4, 218; produced by Aûharmazd, 5, lxx, 160; reckoning of t., year, months, and seasons, 5, 23 sq., 91–7 and n., 149–51; names of angels ascribed to the thirty days of the Parsi month, 5, 103 sq. n.; the decree of appointing T., 5, 165; Hâsar, measure of t., 5, 308, 308 sq. n.; beginning of the morning watch determined, 5, 371; lengths of midday and afternoon shadows, 5, 397–400; days of the Parsi month, 5, 406 n.; divisions of t., 7, 77 sq.; 15, 316 sq.; 25, xii, lxxxiii sq., 19 sq.; 44, 168 sq.; is without either beginning or end, 7, 78; highest self unlimited by t. and space, 8, 45, 45 n., 186; day, bright fortnight, six months of the northern solstice on the path to Brahman, 8, 80 sq.; night, dark fortnight, six months of southern solstice, on the path to the moon, 8, 81; Krishna is T. (Kâla, king of death), 8, 89 sq. and n.; Mârgasîrsha, chief among months, 8, 90, 91 n.; day, night, months, half-months, years, seasons, conjunctions, are all threefold (of the three Gunas), 8, 330; is threefold, past, present, and future, 8, 331; the wheel of t. which rotates in this world, 8, 343, 355 n., 356; day was first, then night, months have the bright fortnight first, of Nakshatras is Sravana, of seasons the winter first, 8, 352; some say both t. and space exist, others deny it, 8, 375; *who knows the morrow of man?* 12, 291; considered by some as the cause of everything,

15, 260; is Breath and a manifestation of the highest Brahman, 15, 302; the fire of the sun, called t., 15, 306; the sun is the cause of t., the year is the visible form of t., 15, 316 sq.; *from t. all beings flow, from t. they grow; in t. they obtain rest; t. is visible (sun) and invisible moments,* 15, 317; descent of good and evil spirits from 'boundless T.,' 18, xxiv; cannot be the cause of the world, 19, 211; Gaina eras and periods of t., 22, 189 sq., 218, 262, 262 n., 265, 265 n.; 45, 143 sq. and n., 200–3; personified as Zurvân, 24, 245, 245 n., 248; created, 25, 12; past, present, and future known by the Veda, 25, 505; divination about the proper t. for undertakings, 27, 94; characteristics of every month of the year, 27, 249 sq., 249 n., 257 sq., 262, 268, 272, 276 sq., 280 sq., 283, 286 sq., 291, 296, 301 sq., 306; reckoning of t. by the heavenly bodies, 27, 381–4; Day-lords, Month-lords, and Year-lords worshipped, 31, 202 sq., 207, 212, 217, 221, 226; t. which exists, and t. which does not, 35, 77–82; infinite t., 35, 79–82; periods of day and year, 37, 17, 19; longest and shortest days and Parasangs, 37, 67; day of twelve hours in China, 40, 269–71; prayers to Kâla or T. as a primordial power, 42, 224 sq., 681–8; T. in the shape of its unit, the Year, takes its part in the primaeval sacrifice, 43, xv; the fire-altar identified with the year, 43, 21; the year is the same as this world, 43, 49; divisions of the year, 43, 167, 167 n., 221 sq.; as a substance, 45, 153, 207 sq.; the Parsi calendar, 47, xlii–xlvii; Vishṇu as T., 48, 93; not an independent substance, 48, 518; is inseparably connected with all things, 49 (i), 97 sq. *See also* Ages of the World, Kâla, Months, Old Times, Sacred Times, *and* Year.

Timi, mighty beings dwelling in the ocean, 20, 302, 305.

Timiṅgala, mighty beings dwelling in the ocean, 20, 302, 305.

Timitimiṅgala, mighty beings dwelling in the ocean, 20, 302, 305.

Ting, the Shih from the time of King Wăn to that of, 3, xvi.

Ting of Kû-lü, on punishment of a parricide, 27, 195, 195 n.

Tipiṭaka, date of the, 10 (i), x–xlv; 35, xxxvii sq.; Buddhist canon settled at the First Council, 10 (i), xii; finally settled at the Second Council, of Vesâlî, 10 (i), xii, xxxix; handed down by oral tradition, 10 (i), xii sq., xxiv sq.; 13, xxxii–xxxvi; Buddhaghosa's translation of the Commentaries on the Pali T., 10 (i), xxii; short abstract of the T., 10 (i), xxvii–xxix; First Council of Râgagaha, and Second Council of Vesâlî, mentioned in the T., 10 (i), xxix; no mention of the Third Council of Pâṭaliputta, found in the T., 10 (i), xxix sq.; the term T. or Piṭaka, not met with in the Buddhist canon itself, 10 (i), xxxii; its three portions, and its three subjects, 10 (i), xxxii sq.; summaries and parallel passages in the T., 11, xxxiii–xxxvi; the word Piṭaka not used by the side of 'scripture' in the Mahâ-parinibbâna-sutta, 11, 67 n.; no historical connexion between T. and the New Testament, 11, 165 sq.; liturgical texts excluded from the T., 13, xiv sq.; Chinese translations of the T., 19, xxxiv; some Bhikkhus are repeaters of the Suttantas, others are in charge of the Vinaya, others preach Dhamma, 20, 6; the word of the Buddhas must not be put into Sanskrit verse, but the Bhikkhus are to learn it each in his own dialect, 20, 150 sq.; eighty-four thousand divisions of the T., 21, 241, 241 n.; quotations from the T. in the Milindapañha, and their importance, 35, xxvii–xlii; extent of the T., 35, xxxvi sq.; quotations from T. in Milindapañha, different from our text of the T., 35, xl–xlii; parts or whole of the T. learnt by Nâgasena, 35, 21 sq., 28 sq., 34; 36, 244; earliest mention and meaning of the term, 35, 28 n.; statements in the Milindapañha referring to traditions later than the T., 35, 196 n., 293 n., 298 n.; 36, 19 n., 43–6 notes, 144 n., 176 n., 304 n.; there is only one 'canon of

the Buddhist Scriptures,' 36, xv–xvii; importance of the Dîgha and Ma*gg*h*ima Nikâyas, 36, xxiii; its nine divisions (navangâni), 36, 92, 92 n.; what is the use of recitation of the Scriptures to Bhikkhus? 36, 92–6; Suttantas the market-place, Abhidhamma the crossways, Vinaya the judgement hall, in the city of Righteousness, 36, 212; teachers and preachers of different parts of the T., 36, 231, 235–9, 237 n.; discourses of Buddha, at which numbers of celestial beings were converted, 36, 247–9; 'the Elders who collected the Scriptures,' 36, 286; a Bhikkhu shall study the Abhidhamma, the Vinaya, and the Suttas, 36, 306; Ekuttara Nikâya quoted, 36, 324; Lakkha*n*a Suttanta quoted, 36, 346. *See also* Âgamas, Buddhist Sacred Books, Dhammapada, Ma*gg*h*ima-Nikâya, Sa*m*yutta-Nikâya, Sutta-Nipâta, Suttas, *and* Vinaya-Pi*t*aka.

Tîr, *see* Ti*s*tar.

Tiridates, a Magian, brother of Valkhash, 4, xxxix sq., xxxix n.

Tîrônakathwa of the Uspaê*s*ta-Saêna house, 23, 219.

Tîrthakara, t.t., used by Buddhists and *G*ainas, 22, xx; 34, 429; *G*aina theory of former T., and Buddhistic theory of Buddhas, 22, xxxiv sq.; after 23 T. of the Ikshvâku, Kâ*s*yapa, Hari, and Gautama gotras had appeared, Mahâvîra was born, 22, 218; epochs of the intermediate T., 22, 280; called 'Buddhas,' 45, 314 sq., 314 n.; the eyes of the world and its leaders, 45, 318; called 'Tathâgatas,' 45, 320, 320 n. *See also* *G*ina, *and* Saints.

Tîrthas, *see* Hand, *and* Holy places.

Tîrthikas, or Titthiyas, *see* Heretics.

Tîs, *see* King (*c*).

Tishya, the star, bestows wealth, 32, 326, 331.

Tishya, *S*âriputra addressed as, 21, 89; the 38th Tathâgata, 49 (ii), 6.

Tishyabhadra, disciple of Sambhûtavi*g*aya, 22, 289.

Tissa, Buddha foretells his future birth, 35, 6; the Elder T. known by his writings, 35, 110; Moggaliputta T. Thera, author of the Kathâ Vatthu, 36, xx sq.

Tissametteyya, n. of a Brâhma*n*a, 10 (ii), 156, 187, 191 sq., 210.

Tissametteyyamâ*n*avapu*kkh*â, t.w., 10 (ii), 191 sq.

Tissametteyyasutta, t.c., 10 (ii), 156 sq.

Ti*s*tar, or Tîr (Phl.), Av. Ti*s*trya, the rain-god, 4, 55 n.; the constellation Sirius, chieftain of the east, leader of stars, 5, 12, 12 n., 13 n., 21; 23, 92; 24, 90 sq. and n., 131; fights Apaosha and other Evil Spirits and sends rain, 5, 25–8; 23, 92–109; 24, 133, 133 n.; assumes the forms of a man, a horse, and a bull, 5, 26 sq., 26 n., 169; 23, 93, 93 n., 96, 98–100, 99 n., 106; sends rain, 5, 31 sq., 176; 23, 92–109, 173 n.; seizes water from the ocean, produces rain, defeats Apâôsh, 5, 69; 18, 264–9, 264 n.; 24, 112, 112 n.; sends rain on the plants, 5, 100; the violet his flower, 5, 104; opposes Aharman in his contest with the water, 5, 168–71; invoked and worshipped, 5, 402, 405; 23, 9, 16, 92–109, 285, 351 sq., 354; 31, 199, 210, 216, 225, 256, 280; Yim in the water of T., 18, 418, 418 n.; to increase the star T., 23, 34; Tîr Ya*s*t devoted to T., 23, 92–109; a protector from hostile hordes and all plagues, 23, 108 sq.; Mithra's face flashing with light like the face of the star T., 23, 157; divides the waters, 23, 249 n.; the bright, glorious star T. moves on equally, 23, 284.

Ti*s*tar-yâr, n.p., 24, 256.

Ti*s*trya, *see* Tîstar.

Titans, *see* Superhuman beings.

Tithe, *see* Taxes.

Titles, applied to and used by chiefs of regions, provinces, and of barbarous tribes, 27, 110 sq., 113; 28, 26 sq.; applied to wives of kings, princes, &c., 27, 112 sq.

Titthiya, *see* Heretics.

Tittira, worshipped at the Tarpa*n*a, 30, 245.

Tî-yî, father of *K*âu-hsin, 3, 176, 176 n.; all sovereigns from Thang to T. attended to the sacrifices, and were virtuous, 3, 197, 216; King

T.'s rule about the marriage of his younger sister, 16, 82, 83 sq. n., 182, 184 n., 335.
Tîsyarsti, n.p., 23, 206.
Todeyya, n. of a Brâhma*n*a, 10 (ii), 109; 11, 167, 168 n.; the two T., disciples of Bâvarî, 10 (ii), 187, 202 sq., 210.
Todeyyamâ*n*avapu*kkh*â, t.c., 10 (ii), 202 sq.
Tolerance, and intolerance, *see* Heretics.
Tolls, *see* Taxes.
Tombs, prayers at, 6, 185. *See also* Funeral rites, *and* Holy places.
Tonsure, *see* Child (*b*), *and* Hair.
Toothpick, how it is to be cut, 5, 323, 344, 344 n.; 24, 278.
Topes, *see* Stûpas.
Tortoise, its shell used for divination, 3, 50 sq., 104, 112, 120, 138, 140 n., 145 sq., 145 n., 153 sq., 157–61; 40, 136 sq., 137 n.; *see also* Divination (*a*); supposed to live on air, 16, 115 n.; princes set great store by the t., 27, 397; knows the future, 27, 413; is the most valuable of gifts, 27, 420; simile of the t., 36, 288–90, 352 sq.; spirit-like t.-shell worshipped in *Kh*û, 39, 390; killing t. without reason an offence, 40, 244; the marvellous t., 40, 294; how created, 41, 147; a t., representing heaven and earth, put down on the fire-altar, 41, 389 93; 43, 2 n., 358, 392 sq.; Kasyapa the sun as a t., 42, 403.
Tôsar, high-priest, what he did for the Parsi scriptures, 37, xxxi; summoned by Artakhshatar to expound Zoroastrianism, 37, 414.
Touch, is of twelve descriptions, 8, 384. *See also* Phassa.
Toys, children's, list of, 36, 32 sq.
Trade, law relating to, 6, 44 sq.; 7, 35 sq., 38; 25, 323–5; 27, 289 sq.; 33, 144–53; 37, 98; lawful occupation of, obligatory on Vaisyas, 8, 127; 14, 199; 25, 24, 325, 327, 400 sq., 419 sq.; buying and selling, belong to the quality of passion, 8, 323; articles which a Brâhma*n*a must never sell, even when resorting to t., 14, 12–14; 25, 103, 105, 421 sq.; 33, 57 sq.; customs with regard to t. peculiar to the north, 14, 146, 146 n.; forbidden to Brâhma*n*as, 14, 218; 25, 86, 109, 272; lawful and forbidden articles of sale, 14, 221, 313; sin of speculating upon prices with corn, 18, 174–6; about selling wine to foreigners and infidels, 18, 176 sq.; about bargains in wheat, 18, 180–2; in cattle, 18, 182 sq.; development of t. in the time of the Manu-sm*r*iti, 25, ci; permitted as a means of subsistence to Brâhma*n*as, 25, 129, 421 sq.; king must learn the theory of trades and professions, 25, 222; sale without ownership, a title of the law, 25, 253, 289 sq.; 33, 272 sq.; concerns among partners, a title of the law, 25, 253, 291 sq.; 33, 124–7, 336–41; rescission of sale and purchase, a title of the law, 25, 253, 294 sq.; void and fraudulent sales or purchases, 25, 283; 33, 336; adulteration of merchandise, 25, 290, 393, 440; punishments for dishonesty in t., 25, 323, 387, 393 sq.; 33, 360; permitted to Kshatriya in time of distress, 25, 422; property which must not be sold, 25, 442; 27, 238; rites and sacrifice for success in t., 30, 126, 177, 296; 42, 490; king must maintain the rules settled among the guilds and corporations of trades, 33, 153–5; rescission of purchase and sale, 33, 350 sq.; rules of the market, 37, 124; in products of animals, 37, 139–42; buying up supplies, 37, 141; a merchant's prayer, 42, 148 sq., 352–4, 532, 619. *See also* Property, Taxes, Usury, *and* Weights.
Tradition, *see* Sm*r*iti.
Traidhâtavî, t.t., *see* Sacrifice (*j*).
Trailokavikrâmin, a Bodhisattva Mahâsattva, 21, 4.
Trairâsika *S*âkhâ, founded by *Kh*aluka Rohagupta, 22, 290.
Traitana and Thraêtaona, 4, lii.
Traiva*n*i, n. of a teacher, 15, 119, 186 n., 187.
Traividya, t.t., learned in the three Vedas, *see* Tevigga, *and* Veda (*b, d*).
Trance, in it the body is there, yet the mind inactive, 36, 160.
Tranquillity (indifference, abandonment of all action), constant equability with regard to what is agree-

able and disagreeable, 8, 47 sq., 60, 65, 71, 103, 325 sq., 366; ideal of t., its characteristics, 8, 49–52, 101 sq., 433; obtained through knowledge, 8, 63; attained by devotion, 8, 65, 67; is a means for final emancipation, 8, 67–70, 110, 246; obtained through devoutly worshipping K*ri*sh*n*a, 8, 85; t. and equability are from K*ri*sh*n*a alone, 8, 86; a natural duty of Brâhma*n*as, 8, 126; part of the conduct of the good, 8, 243; is the eternal Brahman, 8, 277; the shade of the tree intelligence, 8, 286 sq.; equability and t. are of the quality of goodness, 8, 372 sq.; some sects extol t., others action, 8, 376; the nature of t. is as when one sees a dream, 8, 392; blessedness of t. and retirement from the world, 10 (i), 24–30, 55; 20, 231–3; the perfect peace of the true Brâhma*n*a or Arhat, or accomplished Muni, 10 (i), 92–5; (ii), 177–80, 196 sq.; sweetness of seclusion and t., 10 (ii), 43; only from t., or inward peace, comes purity, 10 (ii), 159–62; Buddha's definition of a calm Muni, 10 (ii), 162–4; the Muni who has laid down his burden and is liberated, not belonging to time, not dead, not wishing for anything, 10 (ii), 173 sq.; the Bhikkhu is to strive for t., 10 (ii), 174–7; he who is calm and free from desire, crosses over birth and old age, 10 (ii), 193, 199–207; wonderful calmness of mind of Buddha, 11, 76–9; quietude of heart, one of the conditions by which a Bhikkhu obtains his desires, 11, 210–18; a preacher must always be in a peaceful state, 21, 268–71; t. amid all disturbances obtained by the Tâo, 39, 136, 246; constant stillness and rest, the aim of Tâoism, 40, 252 sq. *See also* Desires, Indifference, Nirvâ*n*a, Peace, *and* Renunciation.

Transliteration, of Oriental Alphabets, 1, xlviii–lv; of Chinese names, 3, xxix sq.

Transmigration, men are born in higher or lower castes according to their deeds, 1, 82; 2, 102 sq., 126; 25, 401, 412, 435; the moon sends the departed down as rain upon this earth, and according to his deeds and his knowledge he is born again here as an animal, or as a man, or as something else, 1, 83 n., 274; caused by not knowing (Brahman), knowledge frees from re-birth, 1, 107 sq. n.; 8, 59; 15, 40; 34, 41–3; 48, 9, 259; re-birth after death called the third birth, 1, 244; new round of births of those who follow the path of the fathers, 1, 272 n.; the sages who desired offspring obtained 'burial-grounds,' i.e. new births, 2, 158, 158 n.; determined by actions (Karman), 2, 238; 7, 82; 8, 105, 116, 232 sq., 241, 302; 11, 16 sq.; 15, 175 sq.; 17, 100; 25, 483–501; 34, xxvi sq.; 36, 230; 48, 597–600; *those who are born are sure to die, and those who have died are sure to be born again*, 7, 79; 8, 233; the departed will receive the *S*râddha, whether he has become a god, or an inmate of hell, or an animal, or a human being, 7, 80; the imperishable and immutable self of man puts on new bodies, as a man puts on new clothes, 7, 82 sq.; re-births in animals and other effects in future births as punishments for sins, 7, 144–7, 276; 14, 13, 30, 108 sq., 208, 221; 25, lxxiii, 66 sq., 94, 109, 109 n., 111, 155, 160, 174 sq., 197, 332, 422, 435, 440 sq.; 26, 11; 33, 94; 49 (ii), 175; after suffering torments of hells and passing through animal bodies, sinners are born as human beings afflicted with diseases, 7, 147–9; whatever a man takes from others, of that he will be bereft in every future birth, 7, 173; recollection of former existences obtained by certain Mantras or Sâmans or other means, 7, 186; 11, 215 sq.; 14, 134; 25, 152; rebirth as god, man, or animal, according to the property used for the obsequies, 7, 189; rewards in future births, for gifts bestowed on Brâhma*n*as, 7, 265, 269; 14, 136 sq.; the misery of the Sa*m*sâra or t., 7, 282; 19, 156–60; 21, 77; 25, 16, 500 sq., 513; 34, xxvi sq., xxix sq.; 36, 285; 49 (i), 148–51; birth the fruit of acts, freedom from births the summum bonum, 8, 47–9; the

devotee is released from the shackles of repeated birth and death, 8, 49, 313; Arguna has passed through many births, 8, 59; meritorious acts lead to birth in good families, 8, 72 sq.; all worlds return, but after attaining to K*r*ish*n*a there is no re-birth, 8, 79 sq., 107; sacrificers go to the world of the gods, whence they are re-born again, 8, 84; future births depend on the prevalence of the three qualities, 8, 105, 108 sq., 321 sq., 325; one should seek the seat from which those who go there never return, 8, 111 sq.; driven on by egoism, avarice, thirst, carelessness, foolish men undergo again and again birth and decay, 8, 153 sq., 302; 10 (i), 78, 80-4; 15, 13; 22, 18-20; the Siddha perceives the t. of souls, 8, 232; Siddhas, saints, Arhats, and Buddhas, remember previous births, 8, 234; 10 (ii), 116; 35, 122 sq.; 49 (i), 148; (ii), 12 sq., 49, 53; *all beings are constantly distracted with birth and death, and ... are seen abandoning their bodies, or entering the womb on the exhaustion of their previous actions*, 8, 237; those who perform actions (Karman) and rejoice in this world are born again and again, 8, 378; 22, 37 sq.; no new births are in store for the Arhat, the Buddha, the Muni, 10 (i), 28; (ii), 25, 27, 34; 17, 9 sq.; 20, 385; some people are born again, others go to hell, or heaven, 10 (i), 35, 35 n.; *looking for the maker of this tabernacle, I shall have to run through a course of many births, so long as I do not find (him); and painful is birth again and again. But now, maker of the tabernacle, thou hast been seen; thou shalt not make up this tabernacle again*, 10 (i), 42 sq.; 35, 275 n.; he who is free from guilt, will not enter again into birth and decay, 10 (i), 60; he who has destroyed the germs of new births, is a true Brâhma*n*a (Arhat), 10 (i), 94 sq.; those who understand the noble truths will not have to take the eighth birth, 10 (ii), 38; *the old is destroyed, the new has not arisen, those whose minds are disgusted with a future existence, the wise who have destroyed their seeds (of existence, and) whose desires do not increase, go out like this lamp*, 10 (ii), 39; the wise who know whence sin arises, drive it away, they cross over this stream that is difficult to cross, with a view to not being born again, 10 (ii), 46, 167; a wicked Bhikkhu, having gone to calamity, from womb to womb, from darkness to darkness, after passing away, goes to pain, 10 (ii), 47; liberation from t. is Nirvâ*n*a, 10 (ii), 57-60; an Ariya is one who is not re-born, 10 (ii), 92; having abandoned sensual pleasures, let him cross the stream, and go to the other shore, 10 (ii), 146, 148, 194 sq., 200 sq.; foolish men desire reiterated existences, 10 (ii), 147 sq., 160, 162, 196 sq.; a Brâhma*n*a who does not depend on philosophical views, having gone to the other shore, does not return, 10 (ii), 153 sq.; *he for whom there is no death and no re-birth, how can he tremble or desire anything?* 10 (ii), 172; leave the body and desire behind that thou mayest never come to exist again, 10 (ii), 209; is due to not understanding the four Noble Truths, 11, 23 sq.; 17, 104 sq.; he who possesses the Mirror of Truth, is not liable to be re-born as an animal, or a ghost, or in any place of woe, 11, 26 sq.; the gods liable to t., 11, 163; Buddha's knowledge of past and present births, 11, 209; how the Bhikkhu can be freed from re-birth, 11, 213; how a Bhikkhu may obtain the super-human power of seeing beings pass from one existence to another, 11, 216 sqq.; a Brâhma*n*a who eats the food of a *S*ûdra will be re-born as a pig or a *S*ûdra, 14, 38 sq.; freedom from future births is certain for the ascetic, 14, 47, 274; bad wives re-born as animals, 14, 112; 25, 332; freedom from t. through final liberation acquired by learning, 14, 137; according to their work and to their knowledge, some enter into organic beings, others into inorganic matter, 15, 19; how do men come back to this world? 15, 204, 209;

he who performs works, migrates through his works, led by the three Gu*n*as, and following the three paths, 15, 257 sq.; the elemental self (bhûtâtmâ), overcome by bright and dark fruits of action, enters on a good or bad birth, 15, 295–300; by the dim rays of the sun a man travels on helplessly, to enjoy the fruits of his actions here, 15, 329; thoughts alone cause the rounds of birth, 15, 333; it is difficult when born to be born as a human being, 19, 369; 45, 15 sq., 42 sq., 249, 294, 331; a vision of beings leaving one state of existence to be born in another, 21, 10; through lust men are tormented in the six states of existence and people the cemetery again and again, 21, 48, 54; punishments in hell and t. of those who scorn Buddha's law, 21, 92–5; after hearing Buddha's law, beings are re-born, as gods or men, Indras, Brahmas, &c., 21, 125; the three misfortunes: being born in hell, among beasts, and in Yama's kingdom, 21, 248; *G*ainas share the belief in t. with Buddhists and Brâhmanic philosophers, 22, xxxiii sq.; he who does not comprehend the causes of sin is re-born to pain, 22, 2 sq.; men, gods, hell-beings are produced by regeneration, 22, 11; Mahâvîra, when he had reached Kevala, saw all conditions of beings in their different births, 22, 263 sq.; monks who follow the rules prescribed for the rainy season will not be born again, or be born once, or twice, but never more than seven or eight times, 22, 310 sq.; of the soul into vegetable or animal seed, 25, 17 sq., 18 n.; the perpetual student will not be born again in this world, 25, 74; plants and animals destroyed for sacrifices, are re-born in higher existences, 25, 175; an ascetic shall meditate on t. and recompense, 25, 209–12; acts which cause continuation of existence, and such as ensure cessation, 25, 503; debtor re-born as slave in the house of the creditor, to repay the debt, 33, 44; false witness will be re-born as a woman, 33, 92; the origin, &c., of the world cannot proceed from a being subject to t., 34, 17; sinful beings are re-individualized, sinless ones are not, 35, 50; neither as the same nor as another is a man re-born, 35, 63–5; a man who will not be re-born, is aware of the fact, 35, 65 sq.; he who will not be re-born, feels bodily, but not mental pain, 35, 69 sq.; that which is re-born is name-and-form, 35, 71–5; if one dies with craving for existence he will be re-born, if not, not, 35, 75 sq.; where there are beings who will be re-born, there time is, 35, 78; the virtuous man re-born in heaven, the wicked in hell, 35, 93–5; there can be re-birth without t., 35, 111; t. and individuality, 35, 112 sq.; he who is about to be re-born knows that he will be born, 35, 113; explained, 35, 120; re-birth takes place with the quickness of thought, 35, 127 sq.; meeting of all kinds of beings in various t., 35, 292; Buddhism does not teach t. of souls, 36, 142 n.; keeping the vows is like a boat carrying to the other shore of the ocean of t., 36, 256; the 'faggots' (the body) consumed, while the 'fire' (the animating spirit) is transmitted elsewhere, 39, 131, 202, 202 n.; a Tâoist statement of the transrotation of births, 39, 150; 40, 9 sq., 10 n.; caused by the Tâo, 39, 249, 249 n.; the pious monk becomes on leaving this body, either a Siddha, or a god, 45, 8; the fool's death happens many times, the sage's death at best only once, 45, 20; souls gain human birth through four causes, 45, 30 n.; the various births of *K*itra and Sambhûta, 45, 56 sq. and n.; Bh*ri*gu's sons abandoned the world, hoping to escape the Wheel of Births, 45, 62; M*ri*gâputra remembers his former birth, 45, 89; Samudrapâla crossed the ocean-like flood of worldly existence and obtained exemption from t., 45, 112; influence of the observance of the seventy-three articles on the t. of the soul, 45, 161–73; the duration of the Lê*s*yâs in mundane existence (as denizens of hell, brutes, men, and gods) detailed, 45,

201–3; conditions of the soul at the time of death causing good or bad births, 45, 230–2; knowing the endless circle of births, a wise man should wait for his decease, practising self-control, 45, 286; the faithful will either make an end of their mundane existence, or become like Indra, 45, 292; all beings subject to t., men seduced by their senses and by women are born again and again, 45, 318; the evil-doer wanders from womb to womb, from birth to birth, from death to death, from hell to hell, from pain to pain, 45, 377; *G*ainas should believe in the fourfold circle of births, 45, 408; *G*ainas and Vedântins hold the same views about t., 45, 417; beings now movable will become immovable beings, and it will never happen that either movable or immovable beings should die out, 45, 421–33; all living souls from Brahmâ down to the blade of grass, experience the fruits of action, 48, 156; the Lord hurls the evil-doers perpetually into t. and into demoniac wombs, 48, 558; embodiment in non-moving beings the result of evil deeds, 48, 599. *See also* Death (*b*), Heaven (*d*), Karman, Life, Sa*m*sâra, Soul (*c*, *d*), *and* Works (*c*).

Trapusha, a merchant who worships Buddha, 49 (i), 166 sq.

Trasadasyu Paurukutsya, author of a Vedic hymn, 46, 420 sq.

Travelling, rules relating to it, 7, 199–204; ceremonies for one travelling from home, 24, 315 sq. *See also* Child (*b*), Fire (*d*), *and* Sea.

Trayastri*m*sa, *see* Heaven (*b*).

Trayî Vidyâ, *see* Veda (*b*).

Treasure-trove, *see* Property.

Trees, live, pervaded by the living Self, 1, 102 sq., 103 n.; the cleanser delights the t., 4, 133; spell to purify t., 4, 144; the holy t. invoked, 4, 221; healing plants grow round the tree of eternal life, 4, 226; the chief of t., 5, 90 sq.; t. as omens, prayers and ceremonies on passing boundary t. and well-known large t., 7, 200; 14, 171; 25, 135; 29, 367; 30, 49, 122, 181, 262, 269; worshipped, 7, 213; 25, 91; 31, 362; 49 (i), 191; merit of planting t., 7, 270 sq.; list of t. which are the princes among t., 8, 346; the great tree of Brahman, 8, 370 sq., 370 n.; sacred t. as refuge, 10 (i), 51; the t. suitable for sacrificial purposes, 12, 90; 26, 38, 38 n.; tree-deities, 13, 126; 49 (i), 168 sq.; fruit t. and flowering t. not to be injured, 14, 97; people believe that life dwells in t., 17, 22; tree-Devas appear with half their body visible at the birth of Buddha, and worship the infant Bodhisattva, 19, xix, 345, 349; houses in t., 22, 145; a *G*aina monk should not point at sacred t. with his fingers, 22, 145; boundaries marked by t., 25, 298; fine for injuring t., 25, 304, 304 n.; prohibitions against cutting down t., 27, 256, 259, 265, 270, 274, 278; only to be felled at the proper season, 28, 227 sq.; with a new chariot one should drive round a widely-known tree, 29, 210; certain t. sacred to different gods, 30, 122; t., i.e. the dryads, talk, 35, 241 sq.; Arhats compared with t., 36, 355; a stolen tree, 37, 71; felling t., lawful and unlawful, 37, 120, 127; stories of wonderful t. which are useful by being useless, 39, 132, 217–20; *K*wang-*3*ze shows the use of an apparently useless large tree, 40, 27; crime of employing poison to kill t., 40, 241; branches of certain t. used for making sacrificial bowls, 41, 67, 83 sq.; amulets from certain t., 42, 81–8, 605; Soma lord of t., 43, 76; created, 43, 76; the green-haired and gold-haired t. worshipped, 43, 151, 154; certain t. from which stakes are made, originated from parts of Pra*g*âpati's body, 44, 373–5; pegs of different t. fixed on making the tomb, 44, 436 sq.; Yakshas living in t., 45, 50 n., 51; the tree invoked in the Âprî hymns, the sacrificial post, 46, 9, 12, 180, 237, 239; ritual acts referring to the sacrificial post and tree-worship, 46, 253 sq.; Buddha, a tree of paradise, 49 (i), 157; meditations of Buddha under several t., 49 (i), 165; —El 'Huzzâ worshipped under the form of an *acacia* tree, 6, xii; *see*

also Huzzâ; the *Asvattha* tree (*ficus religiosa*) showering down Soma, in the world of Brahman, 1, 131, 132 n.; Asvattha, chief among t., 8, 89, 89 n.; Asvattha, symbol of the course of worldly life, 8, 111, 111 sq. n., 189, 189 n., 313, 313 n., 370 n.; Asvattha leaves used for salt-bags, 41, 33; Maruts stay on the Asvattha, 41, 34, 84; the Asvattha tree, the seat of the gods in the third heaven, 42, 4, 6, 415 sq.; Asvattha tree as a charm against enemies, 42, 91 sq., 334 sq.; honour secured by Asvattha, 44, 215, 220; tomb should not be made near Asvattha and certain other t., 44, 427 sq.; Asvattha or Par*n*a t. the abode (of seeds or herbs?), 44, 433; the t. that yield up *Baresma*, worshipped, 4, 214 sq. and n.; 23, 158; he who has injured a *Bodhi* (Bo) tree, cannot be converted, 36, 78 n.; the holy Bodhi tree, 49 (i), 198; (ii), 200 n.; the Bodhi tree of Sukhâvatî described, 49 (ii), 49–51; the *Gambû* tree Sudarsanâ, the abode of the presiding deity (Anâd*ri*ta), 45, 48 sq., 48 n.; the *Gôkar*d tree and the tree of all seeds growing in the middle of the sea Vouru-kasha, 4, 55, 55 n.; 5, 31, 65–7, 91, 100, 100 n., 118, 161, 176; 18, 256, 256 n., 258 n.; 23, 173, 173 n.; 24, 112, 112 n.; 37, 202, 202 n., 358; the *Gôkereno* or white Hôm yielding the elixir of immortality, 18, 164, 164 sq. n.; 37, 165, 165 n.; *Ilyâ* tree in the world of Brahman, 1, 275, 277; *Kârshmarya* tree repels the Rakshas, 41, 373 sq.; the sacred tree *Manorama* in Mithilâ, 45, 36 sq.; the long-lived t. *Ming-ling* and Tâ-*kh*un, 39, 166 sq.; the *Nâga* t., 36, 130, 130 n.; simile of the infinitesimal seeds of the fruit of the *Nyagrodha* tree (Indian fig), 1, 104; sweet drink secured by Nyagrodha t., 44, 216, 220; why Nyagrodha t. grow downwards, and why the cotton-tree is the largest among t., 44, 317, 317 n.; an *oak-tree* used as an altar for the spirits of the land, 39, 217–19; *Palâsa* (*butea frondosa*) is the Brahman, is Soma, 12, 90, 90 n.; 41, 53, 83, 229, 258; 44, 221; Palâsa branch used for sweeping sites of altars and burial-places, 41, 298, 343; 44, 430; sacrificial stakes to be made of Palâsa and other t., 44, 123, 373–5; *Parna* or Palâsa and other holy t. used for magic rites, 42, 37–41, 114, 280 sq., 291, 331 sq., 463; Par*n*a branch used for driving away calves at new moon, 44, 8; origin of Par*n*a tree, 44, 122 sq.; the *Plaksha* the first of all immovable entities, 8, 354; *Samî* appeases, 43, 202; *Udumbara* (*ficus glomerata*) contains vital sap of all other t., means substance, food, strength, 41, 35 sq., 256 sq., 267 sq., 373–5, 393–5; 43, 189, 203; 44, 215, 220, 448; Udumbara wood used at Vâgapeya and coronation for throne-seat, and water-vessel, &c., 41, 35 sq., 73, 83, 104; Udumbara tree sides with the gods, the other t. with the Asuras, 41, 256 sq.; Udumbara produces fruit equal to that of all other t., and is always moist, 41, 257; Udumbara jar used for sowing seed on Agnikshetra, 41, 337; etymology of Udumbara, 41, 395; pieces of firewood of Udumbara, 43, 189, 191, 203; offering-ladle of Udumbara, 43, 214; origin of Udumbara, Asvattha, and Nyagrodha t. from Indra's flesh, skin, and bones, 44, 215 sq.; tree of *Wisdom*, 36, 81; the *Zaqqum* tree of hell, *see* Hell (*c*). *See also* Parables (*e*), Plants, *and* Vanaspati.

Tretâ age, *see* Ages of the World.

Triagrams, *see* Hexagrams.

Trial, *see* Judicial procedure.

Tribes: men of wild, low, aboriginal t., sacrificed at the Purushamedha, 44, 416.

Tridhâtu, n. of a teacher, worshipped at the Tarpa*n*a, 30, 244.

Trikakud, Mount, formed out of the eye of V*ri*tra, 26, 15 sq.; salve from Mount T., 42, 61 sq., 381 sq.

Trikavya*m*gikâ, a female ascetic, converted by Buddha, 49 (i), 191.

Trikû*t*avat, one of the princes of mountains, 8, 346.

Trimûrti, the gods Brahman, Vish*n*u, and Siva, 7, xxii, 128; 15, 304, 308.

T*rin*abindu, n. of a teacher, worshipped at the Tarpa*n*a, 30, 244.

Trinaskanda, Maruts invoked for the people of, 32, 293.

Trisalâ, the Kshatriyânî mother of Mahâvîra, 22, xii sqq., 191 sq., 226, 228–51; her other names Videhadattâ and Priyakârinî, 22, 193, 256.

Trisanku, poet, teaching of the Veda by, 15, 51 sq.

Trisarana, or Buddha, Dharma, Sangha, 10 (i), 51 n.

Trishamdhi, invoked for help in battle, 42, 126–9, 632, 637.

Trishnâ, *see* Tanhâ.

Trishtubh, *see* Metres.

Trita, an Âptya deity, 12, 47–9, 48 n.; slew Visvarûpa for Indra, 12, 47 sq. and n.; 44, 250 n.; T. and Thraêtaona, 31, 233 n.; Maruts weaken those who are weakening T., 32, 296; a friend of the Maruts, 32, 297, 305, 325, 392; Trita or T., the scapegoat of the gods, 42, 165, 521–8; in heaven blows upon Agni like a smelter, 46, 387; Dvita and T., 46, 406.

Trita, *see* Trita.

Tritsus, wear braided hair, 32, 424.

Trivarsha, n. of a teacher, worshipped at the Tarpana, 30, 244.

Trivrishan, father of Tryaruna, 46, 420 sq.

Troy (Ἴλιος, vîlu), siege and conquest of, 32, 44.

True, the (sat or satyam, τὸ ὄντως ὄν), is Âtman and Brahman and all this, 1, xxx sq., xxxiii, 130, 278 sq.; 15, 58, 190 sq., 311, 335; 34, cix, 167, 267; 38, 216 sq., 234; when a man sleeps, he becomes united with the T., 1, 98 sq., 98 n.; 34, 350; 38, 210; *all these creatures, my son, have their root in the T., they dwell in the T., they rest in the T.*, 1, 100; creatures, when they have become merged in the T. (either in sleep or in death), and when they have come back from the T., know not that they are merged in the T., or have come back from it, 1, 101 sq.; *now that which is that subtile essence (the root of all), in it all that exists has its self. It is the T. It is the Self, and thou, O Svetaketu, art it*, 1, 101–9; though you do not perceive it, exists, 1, 105; is our real home, 1, 106 sq. n.; he who understands the T., declares the T., 1, 121; is the abode of the Brâhmî-upanishad, 1, 153; the door of the T. is covered with a golden disk (the sun), 1, 313; by the T. the way of the gods is laid out, by which the sages proceed to the highest place of the True One, 15, 39; 'True of the T.,' a name of Brahman or the Self, 15, 105, 108; 38, 171; rests on the eye, on life (prâna), 15, 197; identified with the person in the sun, 15, 199 sq.; there is only one vidyâ of the T., 34, lxxii; 38, 245–7; *ativâdin* is one who declares something beyond by means of the T., 34, 163, 165 sqq.; its secret names, ahar and aham, 38, 246. *See also* Sat.

Trust, *see* Property.

Truth: speaking the t. a proof of being a (true) Brâhmana, 1, 60; 8, 171; *what is true (Om) is the flower and fruit of speech.... Therefore one should not say what is untrue, but guard oneself from it*, 1, 230; when promises need not be kept, 2, 204; speaking the t., a penance, an observance, a vow, 2, 277, 297; 12, 4, 273; 25, 476; 29, 319; 44, 240; 48, 301, 303; sin of, and penance for, speaking untruth, 2, 290 sq.; 7, 135, 139, 176; 25, 155, 444; is the best thing, the highest virtue and duty, 4, lxii; 5, 396; 10 (ii), 30; 25, 156; 33, 93; 37, 282–4; falsehood the chief of all sins, 4, 35 n.; 5, 396; 10 (i), 61; 24, 322 sq.; truthfulness required of a priest, 5, 348; the all-importance of t., 7, 51 sq.; the mind is purified by t., 7, 97; 14, 165, 287; 25, 188; 33, 93; one purified by veracity, sanctifies a company, 7, 254; ascetic to utter speech purified by t., 7, 280; 25, 207; truthfulness one of the twelve great observances of a Brâhmana, 8, 167–70, 182; the world rests on t., immortality depends on it, 8, 170; 33, 93 sq.; 48, 540; is the Sastra at the allegorical sacrifice of concentration of mind, 8, 280; what is t.? 8, 311, 314; those whose final goal is concentration of mind, are full of t., 8, 315; the Brahman

is the t., penance is the t., Pragâpati is t., the entities are born from t., the universe is the t., 8, 315; is of the quality of goodness, 8, 325, 373; only the Kshetragña attains to the t. which is great and transcendent, 8, 351; veracity, the duty of householder, Brahmakârin, hermit, and ascetic, 8, 360, 362, 364; the ascetic understands all t., 8, 366–8; abandoning both t. and falsehood, a creature is emancipated, 8, 370; cutting the tree of worldly life with the sword of knowledge of t., 8, 371; *ye shall speak no lie*, 10 (ii), 65 sq.; 11, 253; *t. verily is immortal speech, this is a true saying*, 10 (ii), 73; what the world considers true, is false, what the world considers false, is true, 10 (ii), 142 sq.; *for the t. is one, there is not a second*, 10 (ii), 168 sq.; if an elect disciple possesseth the Mirror of T. he may be assured of final salvation, 11, 26 sq.; the Bhikkhu always speaks the t., 11, 190; gods are the t., man is the untruth, 12, 4, 16; 26, 63, 238; the eye is t. (what one sees is true), 12, 78; 26, 285; he who speaks the t., worships the fire, 12, 312 sq.; only by not speaking at all one speaks no untruth, 12, 313, 452; by a deliberate lie, a Bhikkhu commits a pâkittiya sin, 13, 32; Buddha rebukes Upananda for not keeping his word, 13, 322; cases when speaking untruth is permitted, 14, 83; miracles performed by the mystic Act of T., 21, 384 sq.; 35, 180–5, 180 n., 185 n.; *that is t. beyond doubt, what has been declared by the Ginas*, 22, 49 sq.; four kinds of speech: t., untruth, t. mixed with untruth, neither t. nor untruth, 22, 150; the Gaina's second vow to renounce all lying, with its five clauses, 22, 204 sq.; how Mithra punishes the liar, 23, 119 sq., 124–6, 128–30, 135, 137, 139 sq., 146 sq.; good for all the world, 24, 26; the speech of him is most proper who speaks t., 24, 77; the power of t., 24, 120, 323 sq.; the worst sin of breaking a promise, 24, 287 sq.; 37, 195; to be sincere and true, a principle of Zoroastrianism, 24, 329; is entire in the Krita age, 25, 22, 22 n.; *truthfulness is better than silence*, 25, 45; no untruth must be uttered at a Srâddha, 25, 117 sq.; who is dishonest in speech, is dishonest in everything, 25, 168; necessity of speaking t. in a court of justice, 25, 254; witnesses admonished to speak the t., 25, 268–71; falsehood allowed for pious ends, 25, 272; speaking untruth verbal sin, 25, 484; man is impure in that he speaks untruth, 26, 8, 16; whosoever walks in the way of the gods, walks in the way of t., 26, 344; truthfulness and harmony 'the things advantageous to men,' 27, 380, 388, 393; prayer addressed to Brahman and T., 29, 150; on new and full moon days let him strive to speak the t., 30, 28; for truthful speech Ahura-Mazda rules with absolute sway, 31, 39, 51; Zoroaster abjures the sin of dishonesty and lying, 31, 69, 73; Snâtaka must always say the t., 35, 150; what kind of sin is a deliberate lie? 35, 268–70; keeping and breaking promises, 37, 69; necessity for maintaining the t., 37, 72 sq.; a t. that is wicked, 37, 149; self-injury of a liar, 37, 193 sq.; Âstâd and Mitrô watch over t., 37, 210; promises must be kept even with the wicked, 37, 210 sq.; fire assisted by t., 37, 355; supports the earth, 42, 199; the gods hold fast to t., the Asuras to untruth, 43, 257; he who speaks t. prospers in the end, 43, 257 sq.; is the threefold lore, 43, 258, 258 n.; libations of ghee identified with law and t., 44, 40; ghee is t., t. sacrificed in faith, 44, 46; *one rule the gods indeed keep, to wit, the t.: let him therefore speak nothing but the t.*, 44, 85, 447; the purificatory bath at the 'sacrifice to the Brahman,' i.e. the Veda-study, is t., 44, 96; those of old became glorious, t.-speaking and faithful to their vow by the three great rites, 44, 144; 'at the first age of the t.' (?), 44, 276; whatever untruth man speaks here is unmixed with earth, as it were, 44, 446; the righteous one is t., and the sun is the t., 44, 457; the divine

order is the t., 44, 498; the best of true speeches is that which causes no distress, 45, 290 sq.; 't.,' i.e. Buddhist religion, *see* Dhamma. *See also* Arstât, Rashnu, *and* Satya.

Truthfulness, *see* Truth.

Truths, the Four Noble, viz. pain, the origin of pain, the destruction of pain, and the eightfold holy way, 10 (i), 52, 67, 67 n.; (ii), 132–45; 11, ix, 148–50 and notes; 13, 95–7; 19, 177; 21, 172 sq., 185; 49 (i), 175; those who understand the f. n. t. will not have to take the eighth birth, 10 (ii), 38; the Bhikkhu must know the f. n. t., 10 (ii), 62; part of the original doctrine of Buddha, 11, xxi sq.; 13, xii; *when these n. t. are grasped and known the craving for existence is rooted out, that which leads to renewed existence is destroyed, and then there is no more birth*, 11, 23 sq.; 17, 104 sq.; four truths (dhammâ) different from the f. n. t. (sakkâni), 11, 64 sq., 64 n.; were discovered by Buddha alone, they were not among the doctrines handed down, 11, 150–2; by the knowledge of them, Buddha became free from re-birth, 11, 152 sq.; and the Âsavas, 11, 294, 301; and doctrine of Nidânas, 13, 75 n.; people acquire the knowledge of the f. n. t. for the sake of Nirvâna, 21, 18, 80; attained by the Act of Truth, 35, 182; if a man does not attain to the perception of the f. n. t., his being born as a man was in vain, 35, 239; followed by the Bodisat for immeasurable aeons of the past, 36, 143; the antidotes made known by Buddha, 36, 217; in their triple order, in their twelvefold form, 36, 298. *See also* Buddhism (*a*).

Tryambaka, cakes sacred to, 30, 98. *See also* Rudra.

Tryaruna, worshipped at the Tarpana, 30, 244; the son of Trivrishan, a liberal lord, author of a Vedic hymn, 46, 420 sq.

Tû, younger brother of the duke of Kâu, father of Hû, 3, 211.

Tubbâ'h, fate of the people of, 9, 219, 242.

Tûg, son of Frêdûn, 5, 133–5, 133 n., 137; 37, 28; Salm and T. defeated by Mânûskhar, 24, 61; 47, 11, 11 n.

Tû Khiâo, mourning rites for his mother, 27, 153.

Tû Khwai, the clever cook of Duke Phing, 27, 179 sq.

Tûla, a demon harassing children, 30, 219.

Tû Lin, preserved parts of the Shû King, 3, 9.

Tulsidâs, Râmâyan of, 34, cxxvii sq.

Tûmâspa, n.p., 23, 221; Aûzôbô, son of T., 47, 11.

Tumiñga, *see* Aupoditeya.

Tun, grandson of Count of Wei, 27, 120; son of Duke Âi, 27, 188.

Tuṅgikâyana, n. of a gotra, 22, 287.

Tung-kwo Shun-ȝze, a Master of the Tâo, teacher of Thien Ȝze-fang, 40, 42 sq., 42 n., 66 n.

Tung-kwo Ȝze, perplexed about the Tâo, 40, 66 sq., 292.

Tung-kwo Ȝze-khî = Nan-kwo Ȝze-khî, q. v.

Tung-pho, *see* Sû Shih.

Tung Wû, a Tâoist teacher, 40, 103.

Tung-yê Kî recklessly drives his exhausted horses, 39, 151; 40, 23, 23 n.

Tûra, Airya, and Sairima, the three sons of Thraêtaona, 4, lix; Frârâzi, son of T., 23, 217.

Tûrak, n.p., 5, 135, 137.

Tura Kâvasheya, n. of a teacher, 12, xxxi sq.; 15, 227; 43, xviii; built a fire-altar for the gods at Kârotî, 43, 279; received teaching from Pragâpati, 43, 404.

Turanians, conflict between them and Naotaras, 23, 280 sq. and n.; disputes between T. and Iranians, 24, 52, 52 n.; 47, 135–7; there is hope even for the T. enemies of the Zarathustrians, 31, 133, 141, 141 n.; converts to Zoroastrianism, 31, 188.

Tûr-î Aûrvâîtâ-sang, n.p., 18, 413, 413 n.

Tûr-î Brâdar-vakhsh, or Brâdrô-rêsh the Tûr, or Brâdrôk-rêsh, or Brâd-rêsh, a Karap, enemy of Zoroaster, 5, 195 sq. and n.; 47, 20 n., 40–3, 143 sq.; one of the seven heinous sinners, 18, 218, 218 n.; 37, 111, 111 n.; slew Zaratûst, 24, 267 sq., 267 n.; 47, 44 sq. n.,

77 n., 126; destroyed a righteous man, 37, 185.
Turks, 'Turkish demons with dishevelled hair,' 47, xviii, 94, 104.
Turvasa, helped by the Maruts, 32, 391; called from afar through Agni, 46, 33, 36.
Turvîti, n.p., 46, 33, 36.
Tûryaghosha, the 19th Tathâgata, 49 (ii), 6.
Tûs, Zd. Tusa, son of Nô*d*ar, 5, 119; among the preparers of the renovation of the universe, 18, 78, 78 n.; struggle between T. and the sons of Vaêsaka, 23, 66–8, 66 sq. n.; T. and Khûsrôî, 37, 224, 224 n.; exhorts Keresâsp, 37, 225.
Tusa, *see* Tûs.
Tushita, or Tusita, *see* Heaven (*b*).
Tusnâmaiti, n. of a holy woman, 23, 225.
Tutelary Spirits, *see* Gods (*n*).
Tutha is the Brahman, 26, 344.
Tuttha became an inheritor of the highest heavens, 11, 26.
Tuvatakasutta, t.c., 10 (ii), 174–7.
Tvâshtra, *see* Âbhûti T., *and* Visvarûpa T.
Tvashtri, god, Indra slew Visvarûpa, the three-headed son of, 1, 293; 12, 47, 164–6; 41, 130; 42, 522; 44, 213 sq., 248; 48, 251, 253; in the Anugîtâ, 8, 219; is the prince of the Rudras, 8, 346 sq.; invoked and worshipped by offerings, 12, 256 n., 258; 26, 320 n.; 29, 280; 30, 151, 244; 41, 113, 115 sq., 125; 44, 62–6, 291 n., 293; fashions the cast seed into the embryo, 12, 259; 26, 177, 367; 42, 97; dispenser of boons, invoked, 12, 268; 26, 374, 376; why all forms belong to T., 12, 314, 314 n., 317; Vritra, the son of T., 14, 32; the honey of T., and the madhuvidyâ, communicated by Dadhyañk, 15, 117; invoked for conception and male offspring, 15, 221; 30, 199, 210; 42, 48, 97; 44, 472; 46, 154, 156, 199, 237; is lord of beasts, of cattle, 26, 180, 202; 42, 143; 44, 64 sq., 472; worshipped by Âprî verses, 26, 186 n.; 46, 377; invoked at and worshipped by animal sacrifices, 26, 210; 41, 162; 44, 300; invoked together with Vishnu, 26, 376; invoked and worshipped at the wedding, 29, 32; 42, 96; the fashioner of living forms of cattle, 29, 280; 41, 113, 115; 44, 64 sq., 293; 46, 179; the camel, the son of T., 29, 366; turned the thunderbolt, 32, 127, 137; with the mothers, 32, 244; lays speed into the horse's feet, 41, 20; 42, 146; the ewe sacred to Varuna and T., 41, 162, 406, 411; T.'s charm against jealousy, 42, 18; is preparing a wedding for his daughter, 42, 51, 364–6; the first-born T. invoked, 42, 160; the carpenter, 42, 189; invoked for beauty, 44, 63; seeing his son slain, brought Soma for witchery, and withheld it from Indra, 44, 248; the seminal, the multiform, 44, 293; the foremost, all-shaped god, 46, 9; father of Agni, 46, 114, 116, 248, 251; Agni, being T., grants abundance in heroes, 46, 186.

U

Uda, or Aû*d*ak, demon, 5, 109; 37, 212 sq. n.
Udaî, ancestor of Dahâk, 5, 132, 132 n.
Udaka, son of Pê*d*hâla, a follower of Pârsva, is converted by Gautama to the creed of Mahâvîra, 45, 420–35.
Udakakandra, the 34th Tathâgata, 49 (ii), 6.
Udalâkâsyapa, n.d., sacrifice to, at the ploughing rite, 29, 326.
Udamaya, n. of teacher, worshipped at the Tarpana, 30, 244.
Udâna, *see* Prânas (*b*).
Udaṅka Saulbâyana says that life is Brahman, 15, 153 sq.
Udanya, or Udanyu, father of Mundibha, 44, 341 n.
Udara-sândilya, n.p., 1, 17.
Udavasânîyâ, °yeshti, Sk. t.t., completing oblation, 26, 389 sq., 389 n.; 41, 115, 139; 43, 269, 269 n.; 44, 402. *See also* Sacrifices (*i*).
Udaya, n. of a Brâhmana, 10 (ii), 187, 206, 210.
Udayamânavapukkhâ, t.c., 10 (ii), 206 sq.
Udâyana, or Uddâyana, king of

Sauvîra, became a *G*aina monk, 45, 87, 87 n.
Udayanîyâ, Sk. t.t., completing offering, 44, 402; *but see* Sacrifice (*i*).
Udâyi, a Bhikkhu, had a crow's voice, 13, 266; commits a Sa*m*ghâdisesa offence, 17, 397–408; inhibited the exhortation of Bhikkhunîs, and then went away, 20, 336 sq.
Udâyin, tries in vain to make the Bodhisattva enjoy worldly pleasures, 19, 38–46; son of *S*uddhodana's minister, converted by Buddha, 19, 227; 49 (i), 37–9, 43, 195 sq.; Buddha addresses U., 36, 4, 6.
Uddaka Râmaputta, one of the teachers to whom Gotama attached himself after his pabba*gg*â, 13, 89 sq.; 36, 46.
Uddâlaka Âru*n*i Gautama, n. of a teacher, 1, xxxiii, 44; 15, 216; 34, cv, cxv, cxviii; 38, 276; dialogue between U. and his son *S*vetaketu, 1, xxxiii–xxxvi, 92–109, 271; 12, xli; 15, 1 n.; knows the Self called Vai*s*vânara, 1, 84 sq., 88; 43, 393 n.; 48, 288; taught by *K*itra Gâṅgyâyani, 1, 271–3; teacher of Yâ*gñ*avalkya, 12, xlii; 15, 132–6, 213, 226; 48, 280; quoted, 12, 14; 26, 82, 413; 44, 37, 182; wished to obtain holy lustre, 12, 335 sq., 335 n.; Âru*n*i Auddâlaki Gautama, father of Na*k*iketas, 15, 1 n.; instructs *S*au*k*eya Prâ*k*inayogya on the Agnihotra, 29, 58 sq. n.; 44, 79–85; was a householder, and yet taught his son, 38, 288; challenges the Brâhma*n*as to a disputation, they choose *S*aunaka Svaidâyana for their champion, U. Â. becomes *S*aunaka's pupil, 44, 50–6; teacher of Proti Kau*s*âmbeya, 44, 153.
Uddâlakâyana, n. of a teacher, 15, 186.
Uddâyana, *see* Udâya*n*a.
Uddeha Ga*n*a, founded by Ârya Roha*n*a, 22, 290.
Uddha*m*soto, *see* Ûrdhva*m*srotas.
Udena *K*etiya, n.pl., at Vesâlî, 11, 40, 57 sq.
Udena, a king and lay devotee, 13, 302; the ladies of King U. pay homage to Ânanda who preaches to them, 20, 382; questions Ânanda as to how the Bhikkhus dispose of robes, &c., given to them, 20, 383 sq.; how Gopâla's mother became the chief queen of U., 36, 146.
Udgât*ri*, *see* Priests (*a*, *b*).
Udgîtha, t.t., explained, 1, 1 n.; meditations on the U., 1, 1–17; 15, 78–84; 34, lxxiv; 38, 247, 252–6, 272–4, 282 sq., 282 n., 292, 303–5, 321, 333, 345–9; 48, 8 sq., 19, 633–6, 664 sq., 676, 691, 696 sq., 707 sq.; the U. of the dogs, 1, 21; is the Pra*n*ava, 15, 307; U. and Âditya (the sun), 34, lxxvii; 38, 333, 346 sq. and n.; ether is the U., 34, 83; U. and Udgât*ri*, 38, 197; never used to denote the syllable Om in its connexion with the *Ri*g-veda and Ya*g*ur-veda, 38, 199; the best of all essences, 48, 696 sq. *See also* Om, *and* Sâmaveda.
Udgîtha-vidyâ in the B*ri*had-âra*n*yaka and in the *Kh*ândogya-upanishad, 34, lxviii; 38, 192–9.
Udraka Râmaputra, the philosopher, Buddha's meeting with, 19, 131, 131 n., 142; 49 (i), 132, 132 n.; was dead, when Buddha began to preach, 19, 167 sq.
Udumbara, *see* Trees.
Udumbarikâ *S*âkhâ of the Uddeha Ga*n*a, 22, 290.
U*d*uvâ*t*ika Ga*n*a, founded by Bhadraya*s*as, 22, 291.
U*gg*enî, n. of a town, 10 (ii), 188.
Ugra, n. of Rudra, offerings to, 29, 256, 352; 30, 221 sq.; 41, 159 sq. n. of Vâyu, 41, 160.
Ugradeva, n.p., 46, 33, 36.
Ugras, a class of Kshatriyas, 45, 71, 71 n., 321, 339. *See* Caste (*e*).
Ugrasena, a Pârikshita, offered horse-sacrifice, 44, 396; father of Râ*g*îmatî, 45, 113 n.
Ugrâyudha, killed by Bhîshma, 49 (i), 113 sq.
Ûhâ, n. of a river in the Himâlaya, 35, 109.
Ukha, n. of teacher, worshipped at the Tarpa*n*a, 30, 245.
Ukhshan, son of Vîdi-sravah, 23, 215, 215 n.
Ukhshya*t*-ereta, the Saviour born of Srûta*t*-fedhri, forerunner of Saoshya*n*t, 23, 195 n., 220, 220 n., 226 n. *See* Aûshê*d*ar.
Ukhshya*t*-nemah, Saviour born of

Vanghu-fedhri, forerunner of Saoshya*n*t, 23, 195 n., 220, 226 n. *See* Aûshê*d*ar-mâh.

Ukhshyei*n*ti, wife of Staotar-Vahi*s*tahê-Ashyêhê, 23, 225.

U*kk*ai*hs*râvyakar*n*aka, father of the demons, harassing children, 30, 212.

U*kk*anâgarî *S*âkhâ, of the Kau*t*ika Ga*n*a, 22, 292 sq.

Ukkhepaniya-kammas, t.t., Acts of Suspension, *see* Bhikkhus (*c*), *and* Sa*m*gha.

Uksh*n*orandhra, ox-hole, the cloud (?), 32, 392, 396 sq.

Uktha, Sk. t.t., hymn, song of praise, 1, 206; 41, xiv–xvi; the senses strove to be the U., 1, 206 sq.; meditation on the U. as identical with the three Vedas, 1, 283 sq.; meditation on the U. as Brahman, or the highest Self, 1, 283 sq.; 34, 79; the Âgnimâruta U., 12, 209, 209 sq. n.; speculations on the triad U., Sâman (song), Brahman (prayer), 15, 99; meditation on the U., Yagus, and Sâman, 15, 195; U. is Agni, 43, 399.

Ukthya, t.t., *see* Sacrifice (*i*).

Ullaga*kkh*a (or Ârdraka*kkh*a), a Kula of the Uddeha Ga*n*a, 22, 290.

Ulûkhala, n. of a demon harassing infants, 29, 296; 30, 211.

Umâ, daughter of Himavat, tells Indra who Brahman is, 1, 151; the goddess U. (Mahe*s*varî, Pârvatî) is the best of all females, 8, 219, 347, 347 n.; *S*ambhu's mistress, 49 (i), 139, 139 n. *See also* Mahe*s*varî.

Umm Salmâ, wife of Mohammed, 6, 70 n.

Unbelief, and Belief, represented as two women, 44, 110–12.

Unbelievers, *see* Heresy, *and* Heretics.

Unborn (ag*a*): the u. (female), and the u. (male) being producing offspring, 15, 250. *See also* Agâ.

Unchastity, *see* Chastity.

Uncle, *see* Relatives.

Uncreated: he who knows the U., is the greatest of men, 10 (i), 29.

Understanding (vig*ñ*âna), by it we understand what is right and wrong, good and bad, &c., 1, 115; meditation on u. as Brahman, 1, 115 sq.; 8, 338 sq.; 15, 57, 65; based on perception, 1, 121; mind and u. as husband and wife, 8, 310; a name of the great Self, 8, 332; the five Prâ*n*as, speech, mind, and u., make up the eight constituents of the universe, 8, 336; the twelfth of the organs, 8, 337; impelling the six senses, with Brahman as the presiding deity, 8, 338 sq.; determination is the characteristic of u., 8, 348–50; the spoke of the wheel of life, 8, 355; the supreme self not reached by u., 8, 367; the truth about mind, u., egoism, &c., to be understood by the Sannyâsin, 8, 368; the trunk of the tree of worldly life, 8, 371; u., and egoism, the two birds in a tree, 8, 371 n.; is above egoism, 8, 385; proclaims the mind's power, 8, 386. *See also* Vig*ñ*âna.

Undeveloped, the, or the Unevolved, or the Unperceived principle (Avyaktam, Sk. t.t.), 8, 80, 96 n., 317, 318 n., 350 sq., 350 n., 439; 34, xxviii, xxxix, 237–42, 238 n., 241, 245, 252; is the source of the worlds, and also the end of everything, 8, 80, 354, 372; 48, 483; the universe is pervaded by K*ri*sh*n*a in an u. form, 8, 82, 193; those who meditate on the U., attain to K*ri*sh*n*a, 8, 100; the great elements, egoism, the understanding, the U., the senses, &c., are the Kshetra, 8, 102, 102 n.; 48, 403; is the seed of the tree of worldly life, 8, 313, 371; consisting of the three qualities, 8, 331; *from the U. was first produced the great self*, 8, 332; the truth about egoism, the U., Purusha, &c., to be understood by the Sannyâsin, 8, 368; when the quality of goodness predominates in the U., one attains immortality, 8, 373; the U. is of the nature of seed and a product, 8, 382; is the Pradhâna, 8, 382; 34, 238, 238 n.; 48, 354 sq.; a development of the U. is the Mahat, 8, 382; the U. is above the self, and above the U. is the being, 8, 385; the forest of the Brahman begins with the U., 8, 386; the devotee enters the highest world, which is the U., 8, 390; beyond the Great, there is the U., beyond the

U. there is the Person, 15, 13, 22; 34, 237 sq., 243 sq.; 48, 354–8; means the body, and not the pradhâna, 34, xxxix, 237–52; that element in Brahman, from which the material universe springs, 34, cxix, 243; is the body in the simile of the chariot, 34, 239; 48, 357–9; means the subtle body, 34, 241 sq., 244; 48, 358; is Nescience, 34, 244; is not mentioned as an object of knowledge, 34, 246; the Aha*m*kâra or I an effect of the U., 48, 62, 72; the U. is merged in the Imperishable, 48, 125.

Unevolved, the, *see* Undeveloped.

Ungrateful, penance for being, 7, 177.

Unity and diversity of the Brahman and the world, 8, 374, 374 n.; the true sense of U. and denial of duality, 48, 351–3; *but see* Brahman (*d–g*), Self (*b*), Soul (*b*), *and* World (*a*).

Universal Soul, *see* Self (*b, d*).

Universal Weal, *see* Horvada*d*.

Universe, *see* World.

Unperceived, *see* Undeveloped.

Unseen principle, Sk. ad*r*ish*t*a, t.t. of the Sâṅkhya and Vai*s*eshika philosophy, 34, li, 382, 406; 38, 75, 115, 137 n., 166; the u. p. and the activity of the Lord are the operative causes of the world, 34, 382; the motion in the atoms is due to it, 34, 387, 388; is it to be considered as inhering in the soul or in the atom? 34, 388; according to the Sâṅkhyas, abides in the pradhâna, 38, 70; is of the nature of religious merit or demerit and acquired through mind, speech, and body, 38, 70; refutation of the Sâṅkhya and Vai*s*eshika doctrines of the u. p., 38, 70–3; is due to the non-particular conjunction of the Selfs with the internal organs, 38, 70 sq.; the limitation of actions and their results cannot be caused by it, 38, 70 sq.

Untruth, *see* Truth.

Upâdâna, t.t., 'grasping,' the source of the five Khandhas, the cause of pain, 10 (ii), 138; 11, 148 n.; the material cause of the world, 34, xxv.

Upâdhi, t.t., limiting adjuncts of the soul, 34, xxvi, xxx, lvii, lxii, lxiv, xcv, cxxi; 38, 153. *See also* Brahman (*b*), Mâyâ, *and* Soul (*a*).

Upadhi, Buddhist t.t., the elements of existence in the world, 10 (i), 94 n.; (ii), x, 150; 13, 85 n.; pain arises in the u., 10 (ii), 5, 133, 194 sq.; the Bhikkhu is not to see any essence in the U., 10 (ii), 60, 62; overcome by Buddha, 10 (ii), 94, 106, 186; freedom from U. or Nibbâna, 10 (ii), 201; when he has become free from U., the pilgrim finds in sin no pleasure, 17, 37 sq. *See also* Nirvâ*n*a.

Upa*ggh*âya, *see* Teacher (*b*).

Upagupta, successor of *S*anavâsa, 19, xii, xiv.

Upaka, a naked ascetic belonging to the Â*g*îvaka sect, meets Buddha, 13, 90 sq.

Upâka, or Upagana, a young Brahman, Buddha's meeting with, 19, 168–71, 168 n.

Upa*k*ara, other name of Pari*k*ara, 35, 287 n.

Upâkara*n*a, or Upakarman, *see* Veda (*c*).

Upakâ*s*inî, a demon harassing children, 30, 211.

Upako*s*ala Kâmalâyana, taught by the sacred fires, 1, 64–7; 34, cv, cviii, 126 sq.; 48, 273–7, 679.

Upako*s*ala-vidyâ, 'the Upako*s*ala meditation,' teaches first Brahman as the cause, and then its various forms, 1, 64 n.; 38, 219, 233–5; 48, 679.

Upakurvâ*n*a, Sk. t.t., the Brahma*k*ârin for a certain time only, 38, 318 sq.

Upâli, the barber, the Vinaya ascribed to him by tradition, 13, xii sq.; 20, 374–6; examines men who wish to become Bhikkhus, 13, 217, 220; questions Buddha about Vinaya regulations, 17, 276–80, 276 n., 317, 322 sq., 391 sq., 395; 20, 265–71, 313–19; one of the principal Thera Bhikkhus, 17, 360; son of Atalî, converted by Buddha, 19, 227; praised by Buddha as a teacher of the Vinaya, 20, 206 sq.; story of U. the barber who becomes a Bhikkhu together with the Sâkya princes, 20, 229 sq.; 35, 163; saying of U. the Elder who carried the Rules of the Order in his head, 36, 368.

Upâli, the Nirgrantha, converted by Buddha, 19, 242; 45, xvi sq.

Upâli, a young boy of Râgagaha with sixteen other young boys, become ordained, 13, 201 sq.

Upananda, n. of a Nâga king, 21, 5.

Upananda, disciple of Sambhûta-vigaya, 22, 289.

Upananda Sakyaputta, of the Sakya tribe, and his two novices Ka*nd*aka and Mahaka, 13, 205, 214; U. and King Pasenadi of Kosala, 13, 321 sq.; food given to the Sa*m*gha by a family with especial reference to the venerable U., 17, 75; spends the rainy season in one place, accepting a share of robes in another, 17, 238 sqq.; causes quarrels, 20, 198, 204 sq.; U. and the precept by which gold and silver were forbidden by Buddha, 20, 392; an eminent Arhat, 21, 3.

Upanayana, *see* Initiation.

Upanishad, t.t., meaning of the word, 1, lxvi, lxxix–lxxxiv; a hymn of the Rig-veda called 'U.,' 1, lxvi; the word U. used with different meanings in the Upanishads themselves, 1, lxxxii sq.; means doctrine, 1, 136 sq.; secret vow, 1, 280 sq.; with the U. as the bow, hit Brahman, 15, 36; secret meaning, mystic import, 15, 46; 38, 216; 43, 339, 363 sq.; 44, 155, 155 n.; true name and doctrine of the Self, 15, 105; revelation, 15, 330; the Pu*m*savana and similar rites called 'U.,' 30, xxi n.; the Pañ*k*arâtra called a great U., 48, 528; *whatever he does with knowledge, with faith, with the U., that is more vigorous*, 48, 682 sq., 684, 688. *See also* Upanishads.

Upanishad-brâhma*n*a, a name of the *Kh*ândogya-brâhma*n*a? 1, lxxxviii; the last book of the Talavakâra-brâhma*n*a, 1, xc.

Upanishads.

(*a*) The U. literature.
(*b*) The teaching of the U.

(*a*) THE U. LITERATURE.

Persian translation of the U., 1, lvii sq., lviii n.; Anquetil Duperron's translation of the Upanishads, 1, lviii–lxi, lxxxviii, xci; Rammohun Roy and the U., 1, lxii–lxv; place of the U. in Vedic literature, 1, lxv–lxvii; 8, 211 sq.; 15, xxxii; the germs of the doctrines of the U. go back to the hymns of the Rig-veda, 1, lxvi; form a body of revealed truth (*S*ruti), 1, lxvii; 34, xi, ciii; different classes of U., 1, lxvii–lxx; their date, relative age, 1, lxvii, lxix sq.; 8, 19; 15, xxxii sq.; list of the U. chiefly studied in Bengal, 1, lxviii n.; the twelve U. explained by Vidyâra*n*ya in his Sarvopanishad-arthânubhûti-prakâ*s*a, 1, lxviii; number of U., 1, lxviii sq.; language and metres of the U., 1, lxix, lxxii sq., 148 n.; 8, 15 sq.; principle on which the passages from them have been selected and arranged in the Vedânta-sûtras, 1, lxix; 34, xli–xlvi; critical treatment of the text of the U., 1, lxxi–lxxix; 15, xxiii–xxv; difficulty of translating the Upanishads, 1, lxxix; 15, xii–xx; works on the U., 1, lxxxiv sq., lxxxviii, xci, xcvii; principal part of the sacred science, to be studied, 2, 111, 111 n.; Bhagavadgîtâ and U., *see* Bhagavadgîtâ; relation between the Sanatsu*g*âtîya and the U., 8, 135, 141–7, and notes to 152–76, 178–81, 184–94; relation of Anugîtâ to the U., 8, 197, 200, 207–12, 215, 224, 226 sq.; not revealed by God, 8, 227; instruction received after studying the U., 8, 251 n.; quoted, 14, 281; list of U. to which *S*a*n*kara refers in his commentary on the Vedânta-sûtras, 15, ix, ix n.; *S*a*n*kara's commentaries on the U., 15, x; 34, xv; list of smaller U., 15, xi sq.; *G*anaka Vaideha knows the Vedas and U., 15, 159; historical groundwork of the U., 15, 161 n.; an Âryan must study the Veda with the Rahasyas, i. e. U., 25, 56, 56 n., 60; Vedânta, i. e. U. to be studied, 25, 59 n., 213, 213 n., 215; rules for the study of Âra*n*yakas and U., 29, 141–50; the teachers of the U. belong to different sections of Brâhmanical society, some of them are even Kshattriyas, 34, ciii; the Atharva-veda in the U., 42, xl–xliii; are of no use, 48, 346 sq.; *see also* Scripture, Secret doctrines, *and* *S*ruti:—MS. of the *Aitareya-upa-*

nishad, discovered by Dr. Bühler, 1, lxxviii sq.; Aitareya-upanishad and Aitareya-âra*n*yaka, 1, xci-xcviii, 155-268, 236; Aitareya-upanishad called Bahv*ri*ka-brâhma*n*a-upanishad, 1, xcii; the Bahv*ri*ka or Mahaitareya-upanishad, different from the Aitareya-upanishad proper, 1, xcv-xcvii, 200; works on the Aitareya-upanishad, 1, xcvii sq.; three Upanishads in the Aitareya-âra*n*yaka, 1, 200; the Sa*m*hitâ-u., or the third Âra*n*yaka of the Aitareya-âra*n*yaka, 1, 247 n.; Ânanda-vallî and Bh*ri*guvallî in the *Âtharvana*-u., 15, xxviii; *Atmabodha*-u., modern, 1, 52 n.; *Muktikâ*-u., 15, xliv; *Sarvasâra*-u., 1, xcvii; *Vâruny*-u., 15, xxviii; *Veda*-u., means Brahma-u., 34, 94; *Yâgñiki*-u., 15, xxvii. *See separately* Atharva*s*iras, Brahma-upanishad, Brâhmî-u., B*ri*had-âra*n*yaka-u., *G*âbâla-u., Garbha-u., Gopâlatâpanî-u., Î*s*â-u., Ka*th*a-u., *Kh*ândogya-u., Kaushîtaki-brâhma*n*a-u., Kena-u., Kshurikâ, *K*ûlikâ-u., Mâdhyandinîya-brâhma*n*a-u., Mahânârâya*n*a-u., Mahopanishad, Maitrâya*n*îya-u., Maitreya-u., Mâ*nd*ûkya-u., Mantra-u., Mu*nd*aka-u., N*ri*si*m*ha-Tâpinî-u., Paiṅgi-u., Pra*s*na-u., Râ*n*âyanîyas, Sa*m*hitâ-u., Subâla-u., *S*vetâ*s*vatara-u., Taittirîya-u., *and* Talavakâra-u.

(*c*) THE TEACHING OF THE U.

Their highest object, the recognition of the self in man as identical with the highest Self or Brahman, 1, xxv, xxx; 34, cxxi sq., 128, 317; 48, 3, 39, 174, 200; Schopenhauer and the U., 1, lix-lxii, lxiv; their teaching about knowledge and works, 1, 314-20; are the couch of Vish*n*u, 7, 3; no philosophical system in them, 8, 8, 13; 34, ciii-cxv; summum bonum according to U., 8, 16 sq.; doctrines of the U., and Buddhism, 15, xxvii, li sq.; rites for the welfare of the embryo, for securing male offspring, and birth ceremonies, treated of in the U., 15, 222 n.; 29, 179; Brahmâ knows this, which is hidden in the U., in the Vedas, as the Brahma-germ, 15, 256; recognize two supreme beings, 21, xxvii; to be studied to attain union with the supreme soul, 25, 203, 203 n.; recitation of U. frees from guilt, 25, 482; U. and Âra*n*yakas constitute the *G*ñânakâ*nd*a, 34, x; differing theories claim to be founded on the U., 34, xviii; their teaching according to *S*aṅkara, 34, xxiv-xxvii, cv-cxiv; their teaching according to Râmânuga, 34, xxvii-xxxi, cii; meditation on the Lord in the way prescribed in the U. leads to final emancipation, 34, xxix; to guard the U. against misinterpretations on the part of the Sâṅkhya, was the task of the Vedântin, 34, xlvi; what is the relation in which those parts of the U. stand to each other which enjoin identical or partly identical meditations? 34, lxvi sq.; different accounts of the U. as to the stations of the way which leads the vidvân up to Brahman, 34, lxxxii, cvii-cxi; 38, 382-6; the philosophy of the U., its relation to Bâdarâya*n*a, *S*aṅkara, and Râmânuga, 34, ci-cxxvii; doctrine of Mâyâ not in the U., 34, cxvi-cxxi; the soul comprehended by the U. only, 34, 36 sq.; Mantras and passages referring to sacrifices which occur in the U., cannot be viewed as supplementary to the vidyâs of the U., 38, 222-5; Mantras and sacrificial works occur in the U., because they have to be studied in the forest as well as the vidyâs, 38, 225; 48, 644 sq.; stories met with in U., their purpose, 38, 305 sq.; 48, 697 sq.; the brahma-vidyâ in the U., 42, lxiii sq., lxvi, lxix; refer to immortality, 48, 7; doctrine, proclaimed by all U., that the entire world forms the body of Brahman, 48, 135; the way of the soul of him who has heard the U., 48, 277; declare the gods to have bodies, 48, 328; knowledge, in the sense of the U., different from cognition of sense, 48, 692. *See also* Brahman (*b*).

Upapâtaka, *see* Sin (*b*).

Upasads, Sk. t.t., *see* Sacrifice (*i*).

Upâsaka, Pali t.t., a lay devotee, 10 (ii), x. *See* Buddhist laymen.

Upasampadâ, Pali t.t., Ordination, q. v.

Upâsanâ, or upâsana, Sk. t.t., devout meditation, 34, lxxviii, cxiv, 22; 38, 203 n., 253 n. *See* Meditation (*a*).

Upasena Vaṅgantaputta, ordained a saddhivihârika one year after his own ordination, 13, 175 sq.; practised the thirteen vows, 36, 268 n., 270 sq.; sayings of U., the Elder, 36, 289, 326, 328 sq., 331; converted by Buddha, 49 (i), 192.

Upasîva, n. of a Brâhma*n*a, 10 (ii), 187, 197–9, 210.

Upasîvamâ*n*avapu*kkh*â, t.c., 10 (ii), 197–9.

Upa*s*ruti, a demon harassing children, 29, 296; 30, 211.

Upastuta, n.p., 32, 152 sq.; 46, 32 sq., 35 sq.

Upasunda and Sunda, Asuras, 49 (i), 116.

Upatishya *S*âriputra, *see* Sâriputta.

Upatissa, called Dhamma-senâpati, or Sâriputta, 11, 1 n.; 13, 149 sq. *See* Sâriputta.

Upavakt*ri*, *see* Priests (*a*, *b*).

Upavâ*l*a, *see* Uvâ*l*a.

Upâva*n*a, n. of a Bhikkhu, 11, 87 sq.

Upavarsha, a Mîmâ*m*saka teacher, quoted by *S*abarasvâmin, 8, 32; his views quoted and discussed, 34, xxxvii, 206 sq.; 38, 268.

Upavasatha, Sk. t.t., *see* Fasting (*a*).

Upavattana of Kusinârâ, 11, 81, 85, 103 sq., 122, 247.

Upave*s*i, pupil of Ku*s*ri, 15, 226.

Upavîra, demon harassing children, 29, 296; 30, 211.

Uposatha, Pali t.t. (the same as Sk. upavasatha), Buddhist 'Sabbath day,' 11, 251 sq., 251 n., 254 n.; the Pâtimokkha repeated on the U. day, 13, x sq., 1, 241–6; Bimbisâra suggests to Buddha the institution of U., 13, 239 sq.; regulations concerning the U. ceremony and the recitation of the Pâtimokkha, 13, 239–97; the U. service is to be held by the complete fraternity of one residence, 13, 247, 249 sq., 253–8, 278; Arhats also should come to the U. service, 13, 247–9; rules about the boundaries for common residence and communion of U., 13, 249 sq., 253–8; about the hall in which the U. service is to be held, 13, 250–3, 270–2; lawful and unlawful U. services, 13, 258–60; how to fix and to make known the day of U., 13, 268–70; the number of Bhikkhus to be counted on U. day, 13, 269; regulations about Bhikkhus who cannot be present at the U., 13, 274–8; regulations concerning a mad Bhikkhu who may or may not be present at the U., 13, 278 sq.; how the U. is to be held by an assembly of less than five Bhikkhus, or by a single Bhikkhu, 13, 280–2; regulations about confessions of offences committed on U. day, 13, 282–6; cases of incomplete assemblies at U. services discussed, 13, 286–94; without the observance of the U. no one can reach prosperity, 35, 291; restrictions as to going from one residence to another on U. day, 13, 294 sq.; the pârisuddhi declaration of a pârivâsika should not be accepted, 13, 297; a special U. allowed if a schism among the fraternity has been composed, 13, 297; exceptional U. held, in order to avoid quarrels with regard to the Pavâra*n*â ceremony, 13, 350 sq.; regulations about holding U. with an expelled Bhikkhu, 17, 288–91; after re-establishment of concord among the Sa*m*gha, 17, 322; objections against a Bhikkhu's taking part in the U., 17, 338, 340; a Bhikkhu under disciplinary proceedings cannot raise objections against a regular Bhikkhu's taking part in the U., 17, 373; Bhikkhus placed on probation, allowed to share in the U., 17, 386; a Bhikkhu placed on probation, must announce the fact at U. meetings, 17, 387; duties of Bhikkhunîs with regard to the U. ceremony, 20, 323; not to be held with a Bhikkhunî who has been inhibited from the Exhortation, 20, 336; laxer rule about holding U. discussed at the council of Vesâlî, 20, 386, 398, 410; Sama*n*as keep the U. day, 36, 83; meritoriousness of observance of

the U., 36, 145, 150, 155, 230. *Compare* Pôsaha.
Uposatha, n. of the elephant king of a *K*akkavatti, 36, 128 sq.
Uppalava*nn*â, n. of a Bhikkhunî, 20, 334.
Uprightness, *see* Righteousness.
Uragas, serpents, created, 7, 4. *See also* Snakes.
Uragasutta, t.c., 10 (ii), 1–3.
Uragavagga, t.c., 10 (ii), 1–36.
Ûrdhva*m*srotas (Pali, Uddha*m*soto), Buddhist t.t. for one who has reached the world of Av*ri*has, 10 (i), 57, 57 n.
Ûrdhvanabhas, n. of Vâyu, son of the Maruts, 26, 198, 198 n.
Urine, *see* Bull, Easing nature, Medicine, *and* Nîrang.
Ûrmyâ, the night, invocation to, 32, 357, 362. *See also* Night.
Urûdhaya*nt*, the holy maid, 23, 225.
Urûdhu, son of Pouru-dhâkh*s*ti, 23, 212.
Urugadhasp, n.p., 47, 34.
Ururvi*g*a, n.p., 5, 143, 143 n.
Uruvelâ, n.pl., Buddha at, 13, 74, 116, 118–34.
Uruvelâ Kassapa, *see* Kâ*s*yapa, *and* Uruvilvâ-Kâ*s*yapa.
Uruvilvâ-Kâ*s*yapa (Sk.), or Uruvelâ Kassapa (Pali), praises Buddha's doctrine, as compared with sacrifices, &c., 13, 137–9; a distinguished Arhat, 21, 2; one of the five hundred Arhats who are to become future Buddhas, 21, 198; converted by Buddha, 49 (i), 192; n. of a Bhikshu, 49 (ii), 2. *See also* Kâ*s*yapa.
Urva*d*-gâ, n.p., 5, 146.
Urva*d*-gâi-frâ*s*t, n.p., 5, 138, 138 n.
Urvâkhshaya, brother of Keresâsp, 18, 370; 23, 255, 255 n.; son of Thrita, 31, 234.
Urvarâ (the field), worshipped as a goddess, 29, 334.
Urva*s*î, the lower ara*n*i, 12, 389 n.; 26, 91; 46, 305; mother of Vasish*th*a, 14, xii, 140; legend of U. and Purûravas, 26, 91, 91 n.; 32, 307 sq.; 42, 521; 44, xiv, 68–74; 49 (i), 113; an Apsaras, 42, 411; 43, 108; the Urva*s*îs, i.e. the Apsarases such as U., 46, 318, 323 sq.
Urvata*t*-nara, the ruler in the Vara of Yima, 4, 21, 21 n.; son of Zarathu*s*tra, 5, 118; 23, 204, 204 n.; the younger, 23, 219.
Usa, *see* Kâûs.
Usadhan, son of Mazdayasna, 23, 216; king of Iran, 23, 222, 222 n., 303.
U*s*anâ, n. of a *Ri*shi, 32, 392, 397.
U*s*ânâ, n. of the Soma plant, 26, 314.
U*s*anas, chief among the discerning ones, 8, 91, 91 n.; dialogue between the daughters of U. and V*ri*shaparvan, 14, xli, 237, 237 sq. n.; the world of U., 14, 308; Dharma*s*âstra of U. quoted, 25, xxvii, xxvii n.; quotes a Sûtra of Manu, 25, xxxv; line of battle invented by U., 29, 234.
Usenemah, n.p., 23, 225.
Ushah, the cock lifts up his voice against the mighty, 4, 197, 197 n., 199.
Ushahina, n.d., worshipped, 31, 197, 202, 205, 209, 215, 219, 224, 387.
Ushas, the Dawn, morning prayer to, 26, 229 sq. n.; Bali to U., at the Vai*s*vadeva, 29, 320; invoked, 29, 343; 42, 161; 46, 281; Indra tries to conquer U., 32, 145; is the mistress, Pra*g*âpati the master of the house, 41, 158 sq.; invoked in a charm to promote virility, 42, 31; U. and the rising sun dispel the evils of the night, 42, 318; or Sûryâ, Sûryâ Sâvitrî, or Dyu, 42, 661; the red one, the Dawn, awakening all beings to welfare, goes along on her chariot, 46, 358 sq. *See also* Dawn, *and* Sûryâ.
Ushasti *K*âkrâya*n*a, a sage, ate unlawful food, when in danger of life, but refused to drink, 1, 18–21; 38, 311; 48, 701; questions Yâ*gñ*avalkya about Brahman, 15, 128 sq.; 38, 242 sq.; 48, 656–8.
Ushi-darena (Ô*s*dâ*s*târ), Mount, seat of holy happiness, worshipped, 23, 11, 19, 33, 33 n., 283, 286, 309, 321 sq. *See also* Mountains.
Us-hindu, Mount, in the sea Vouru-Kasha, 23, 101, 101 n.
Ushmapas (gods) alarmed at the greatness of K*ri*sh*n*a, 8, 94.

Ushnih, *see* Metres.
Usig, Kakshîvat, son of, 12, 355; family of priests who have first established Agni, 46, 52 sq., 137, 139, 182, 202, 205, 228 sq., 271 sq., 341, 371; Agni called the U. of the gods, 46, 233, 261, 297; the U. have opened the mountain-prison of the cows, 46, 309.
Usig, the, and the Karpan gave the kine to rapine, 31, 121.
Usînaras, n. of a people, 1, 300.
Usinemah, n.p., 23, 212.
Usmânara, son of Paêshatah Paitisrîra, 23, 203, 216.
Usnâka, n.p., 23, 214.
Uspaêsta-Saêna, n. of a family, 23, 219.
Uspâsnu, n.p., 23, 216.
Ustavaiti, n. of a holy woman, 23, 225; the Gâtha U., 31, 91–144.
Ustâzanta, n.p., 23, 214.
Ustra, son of Sadhanah, 23, 214.
Usurers, *see* Usury.
Usury, penance for, 2, 87; usurer not to be invited to a Srâddha, 2, 258; 25, 103, 109; sin of u., 4, 33, 33 sq. n., 103; 6, 44, 62; 9, 128; 25, 442; 33, 89; law about u. and lawful interest, 14, 14–16, 15 sq. n., 175; 25, 280, 280 sq. n.; 33, 65–8; food of usurer not to be accepted, 25, 161, 163 sq.; Brâhmanas who are usurers, 25, 272; usurers connected with magic art, 44, 368, 368 n. *See also* Money-lending.
Ut, name of the person within the Sun, 34, 78, 79.
Utathya, Gautama son of, 25, xxvi sq., xxvi n., 78; husband of Mamatâ, 49 (i), 44 n.
Utayuti Vit-kavi, son of Zighri, 23, 219.
Utkîla Kâtya, author of Vedic hymns, 46, 272, 274.
Utkrishta gotra, Vagrasena of the, 22, 288.
Utopias, *see* Paradise.
Utpalaka, n. of a Nâga king, 21, 5.
Utsarga, *see* Veda (*c*).
Uttamaugas, n. of a warrior, 8, 37.
Uttaptavaidûryanirbhâsa, the 30th Tathâgata, 49 (ii), 6.
Uttara, attendant Bhikkhu of Revata, bribed by the Vaggian Bhikkhus, 20, 402 sq.
Uttara, disciple of Mahâgiri, 22, 289.
Uttarabalissaha Gana founded by Uttara and Balissaha, 22, 289.
Uttarakurâ, n. of the palankin of Arishtanemi, 22, 277.
Uttara-kuru, n. of a rich town, 35, 3; one of the four great continents, 35, 130.
Uttaramati, one of the sixteen virtuous men, 21, 4.
Uttara-Mîmâmsâ(-sûtras) systematizes the Gñânakânda, 34, x; later than the Pûrva-Mîmâmsâ, 34, x; another name for Vedânta-sûtras, 34, xii, xiv, xiv n.
Utthânasutta, t.c., 10 (ii), 55.
Uvâla, the obstinately wrong Bhikkhu, 20, 27–31.
Uvarî, converted by Buddha, 19, 245.
Uzava, son of Tûmâspa, 23, 221, 221 n.
Uzayêirina, the holy lord of the ritual order, worshipped, 31, 197, 201, 204, 209, 215, 219, 224, 383.
Uzya, son of Vanghu-dhâta, 23, 215.

V

Vâd, n.d., the Wind, has the orange-scented mint, 5, 104; meat-offering to V. the righteous, 5, 337, 337 n.; invoked, 5, 403, 405. *See also* Wind.
Vada, n. of a religious book, 42, xx.
Vadak, mother of Dahâk, 18, 217, 217 n., 228, 228 n.; 47, 32, 136; produced evil progeny, 37, 185, 185 n.
Vadast, a Karap, 47, 143, 144 n.
Vadavâ, and Sûrya, 49 (i), 138 n.
Vadavâmukha, a Rishi, made the ocean salt, 25, 398 n.
Vadavâ Prâtitheyî, worshipped at the Tarpana, 29, 123, 220.
Vaddha, the Likkhavi, falsely accuses Dabba, the Mallian, of immorality, his punishment, 20, 118–25.
Vadhaghna, *see* Dahâka.
Vadhût, the holy maid, 23, 225.
Vâdhyoga, *see* Gihvâvat V.
Vâê, *see* Vayu.
Vâêbûkht, n.p., 5, 146 sq., 146 n.

Vâêdhayangha, n.p., 23, 210.
Vaêdi*s*t, Vaêdî*s*tô, an ancestor of Zoroaster, 47, 34, 140.
Vaêdvôi*s*t, a Karap preached to by Zaratû*s*t, 47, 20 n., 55–7.
Vâêgere*d*, brother of Hôshâng, 47, x, 8; cultivator and cherisher of the world, 47, 128.
Vaêsaka, struggle between Tusa and the sons of, 23, 66–8, 67 n.
Vaêta*nd*-i Râghinôi*d*, n.p., 5, 136.
Vafra Navâza, when flung up in the air by Thraêtaona, worshipped Anâhita, and came down unhurt, 23, 68 sq. and n.; reached the distant Rangha, 23, 326, 328.
Vâ*g*a, n.d., one of the *Ri*bhus, 44, 381; Savit*ri* accompanied by *Ri*-bhus, Vibhus, and Vâ*g*as, 44, 480; plur., a name of the Maruts (?), 46, 292, 294.
Vâ*g*apeya, *see* Sacrifice (*j*).
Vâ*g*asaneya, *see* Yâ*gñ*avalkya.
Vâ*g*asaneyins, quoted, 34, 146, 148; of the Kâ*n*va and Mâdhyandina branch, 48, 278 sq., 281, 373; Vai*s*vânara-vidyâ of the V. (B*ri*had-âra*n*yaka-up., 5, 9), 48, 290 sq.
Vâ*g*asaneyi-Sa*m*hitâ, Î*s*â-upanishad and *S*ivasa*m*kalpa in the, 1, lxvi; quoted, 38, 393; V. and *S*atapatha-brâhma*n*a, 44, xiii sq.; on the Purushamedha, 44, xxxiii n.
Vâ*g*a*s*ravas, n. of a teacher, 12, xxxiii, xxxiii n.; 15, 226; 43, 390 n.; worshipped at the Tarpa*n*a, 30, 244.
Vâ*g*a*s*ravasa, n. of a teacher, 12, xxxiii; father of Na*k*iketas, 15, 1. *See also* Ku*s*ri V.
Vâgereza, n.p., 23, 213.
Va*gg*abhûmi, Mahâvîra travelled in, 22, 84.
Va*gg*ians, Agâtasattu's war against, and Buddha's prophecy about them, 11, 1–4; the ministers of Magadha build Pâ*t*aliputta, in order to repel the V., 11, 18 sq.; 17, 101; the V. Bhikkhus of Vesâlî, their ten theses relaxing the rules for Bhikkhus rejected by the council of Vesâlî, 20, 386–414.
Vaggumudâ, n. of a river, 20, 375.
Vâ*g*î, n.d., invoked at the house-building rite, 29, 347, 347 n.
Vâ*g*in, n. of a teacher, worshipped at the Tarpa*n*a, 30, 244.
Vâ*g*iratna, n. of a teacher, worshipped at the Tarpa*n*a, 30, 244.
Va*g*ra, n. of a Sthavira, 22, 288; disciple of Si*m*hagiri, 22, 293.
Va*g*rabâhu, a royal sage, 19, 97; 49 (i), 94.
Va*g*ra*kkh*edikâ, t.w., a philosophical Mahâyâna-sûtra, 49 (ii), xii–xix; translated, 49 (ii), 111–44.
Va*g*ranâgarî *S*âkhâ of the *K*âra*n*a Ga*n*a, 22, 291.
Va*g*rapâ*n*i, n.d., Avalokite*s*vara assumes the shape of, 21, 411.
Va*g*rasena, n. of a Sthavira, 22, 288, 293.
Va*g*ravâlukâ, n. of a river in hell, 45, 94.
Va*g*rî *S*âkhâ of the Kau*t*ika Ga*n*a, 22, 292.
Va*g*uttarâ, converted by Buddha, 19, 245.
Vahidhrôs, n.p., 5, 146.
Vahi*s*tôi*s*ti, a Gâtha, 31, 187–94.
Vahmaêdâta, son of Mãthravâka, 23, 213.
Vahman, the Amshaspand, intercedes for the soul, 4, 373 sq.
Vâhrâm, angel, his flower, 5, 104; the mighty, the victorious, 5, 228, 403, 405; the fire in which is V. (Varahrân), 18, 65, 65 n.; the strong (Verethraghna) V. co-operates with the departed soul, 24, 17.
Vâhrâm, son of Mâh-vindâ*d*, 37, xxxvi.
Vâhrâm Gôr, Sassanian king, 5, 200 sq., 200 n.
Vâhrâm-shâ*d*, n.p., 5, 147.
Vâhrâm the Var*g*âvand, or Shahpûr, miracles at his birth, 5, li, 221, 221 n.; destroys the fiendish races, 5, li sq., 223, 228 n., 229, 231 n., 232.
Vâi, *see* Vayu.
Vaibhâshikas, 'Realists,' a school of Buddhists, 34, 401 n.; 48, 510.
Vaibhrâ*g*a, a royal sage, 19, 97; 49 (i), 94.
Vaidabh*ri*tîputra, n. of a teacher, 15, 226 n.
Vaidada*s*vi, *see* Purumî*lh*a V., *and* Taranta V.
Vaidarbhi, Bhârgava, n. of a sage, 15, 271, 274.

Vaideha, caste, 25, 404 sq., 407, 409 n., 410 sq., 411 n., 413; *G*anaka V., *see G*anaka.
Vaidehî, chief consort of Bimbisâra, 49 (ii), v, 161–5; is instructed in the meditations on Buddha Amitâyus, 49 (ii), 165–99; obtains highest perfect knowledge, 49 (ii), 199.
Vai*d*ûryagarbha, the 68th Tathâgata, 49 (ii), 7.
Vai*d*ûryanirbhâsa, the 16th Tathâgata, 49 (ii), 6.
Vai*g*avâpa, n. of a teacher, 15, 118 n.
Vai*g*avâpâyana, n. of a teacher, 15, 118 n., 119.
Vai*g*ayanta, palace of the gods, 21, 342, 345.
Vaikar*n*a, n.d., invoked at the marriage rite, 29, 278.
Vaikhânasa, Sk. t.t., a hermit, 2, 192, 192 n.; 48, 705.
Vaikhânasa *S*âstra, *see* Vaikhânasa-sûtra.
Vaikhânasa-sûtra, or the Institutes of Vikhanas on the duties of hermits, is the *S*râma*n*aka-sûtra, 2, 155 n., 192 n.; 14, 259, 293; V. and Baudhâyana Dharma-sûtra, 14, xxxiv; quoted, 25, xxvii–xxix, 202, 203 n.
Vaiku*n*t*h*a, n. of Vish*n*u, 7, 295. *See also* Indra (*a*).
Vainas, *see* Caste (*f*).
Vainâ*s*ika, i.e. Bauddha, 34, 414, 415.
Vaipa*s*kita, *see* Târkshya.
Vaipa*s*yata, *see* Târkshya.
Vairo*k*anara*s*mipratima*nd*ita, n. of a Buddha-field, 21, 393, 396, 419.
Vairo*k*anara*s*mipratima*nd*itarâ-ga, was in a former birth the queen Vimaladattâ, 21, 429 sq.
Vai*s*âlî, *see* Vesâlî.
Vai*s*ampâyana, relates the story of the Mahâbhârata, 8, 150 sq., 229 sq.; worshipped at the Tarpa*n*a, 29, 122, 149, 220; 30, 245.
Vai*s*âradyaprâpta, n. of a Tathâgata, 49 (ii), 67.
Vai*s*eshikas, school of philosophy, non-difference of cause and effect defended against them, 34, xlix, 320–43; refutation of their tenet that the world originates from atoms set in motion by the ad*r*ish*t*a, 34, l sq., 381–400; 48, 517; their belief in a non-intelligent soul, 34, liv; 38, 33–5; 48, 552; teach that the Lord is the operative cause of the world, 34, 17 n., 435; their argument against the Vedântins, 34, 381; difficulties with regard to their six categories, 34, 394 sqq.; their doctrine may be called semi-destructive or semi-nihilistic, 34, 401, 401 n.; refutation of their doctrine of many Selfs, 38, 70; their opinion that the mind only proceeds to the new abode of fruition, 38, 104; forerunners of the V., their doctrine refuted, 45, ix, 237 sq., 343; views of the V. philosophy of Ka*n*âda, refuted, 48, 430–67, 495–500. *See also* Philosophy.
Vai*s*eshika-sûtras, quoted, 38, 430.
Vaish*n*ava, *see* Soma (*b*).
Vaish*n*ava sect, the Vish*n*u-sm*r*iti recast by an adherent of the, 7, xxvii–xxxii; the most important of Hindu sects, 34, xvii.
Vaish*t*apureya, n. of a teacher, 15, 118 n.
Vai*s*rama*n*a, *see* Kubera.
Vai*s*rava*n*a, *see* Kubera.
Vai*s*vadeva, t.t., *see* Sacrifice (*h*, *j*); V. hymn, *see* Prayers (*c*).
Vai*s*va*m*tara hermitage, Buddha goes to the, 49 (i), 122.
Vai*s*vânara, *see* Agni (*d*).
Vai*s*vânaranirghosha, n. of a Tathâgata, 49 (ii), 100.
Vai*s*vânara-vidyâ, or knowledge of Agni Vai*s*vânara, 8, 259; 38, 187, 233, 249, 292, 400; 48, 629 sq., 632.
Vai*s*vâvasavya, patronym. of a Hot*r*i, 43, 333.
Vai*s*ya: the sacred fire should be fetched from the house of a V. rich in cattle, 29, 13 sq. and n.; takes part in chariot race, 41, 29; sprinkles king from A*s*vattha vessel, 41, 84; hired to drink the Surâ-liquor, 44, 233; son of V. woman not anointed, 44, 326. *But see* Castes.
Vaitahavyas, perished when they devoured the cow of the Brâhma*n*a, 42, 170, 432.
Vaitâlika, a dreadful mountain in hell, 45, 285.
Vaitâna-sûtra, of the Atharva-veda, treats of the horse sacrifice, &c., 44, xvi; on the Purushamedha, 44, xxiii, xxiii n., xli, xliii–xlv.

Vaitara*n*î (Pali Vetara*n*î), a river in hell, 7, 141 n.; 10 (ii), 124; 44, 438 n.; 45, 95; 'my own Self is the river V.,' 45, 104; difficult to overcome, 45, 270; description of it, 45, 280.
Vai*tt*abhatîputra, n. of a teacher, 15, 226.
Vaivasvata, n. of Yama, 15, 3, 3 n. *See also* Manu, *and* Yama.
Vaiyâghrapadîputra, n. of a teacher, 15, 225.
Vaiyâghrapadya, Indradyumna Bhâllaveya addressed as V., 1, 87; Bu*d*ila Â*s*vatarâ*s*vi addressed as V., 1, 87. *See also* Aupoditeya.
Vâ*k* or Speech, mentioned in a list of teachers, 15, 226; legend of Yag*ñ*a and V., 26, 30–3; sent by the gods to fetch Soma from the Gandharvas, 26, 53–8; the Soma cow identified with V., 26, 54, 56–63; legend of V. who became a lioness, 26, 114–16, 119 sq., 123 sq.; Supar*n*î = V., 26, 149; prayers to V., 26, 189; 29, 51, 299; 41, 38; metres produced from V., 26, 226; Agni associated with V., 26, 365 n., 367 n.; the one-thousandth cow given at the Trirâtra is V., 26, 414, 414 sq. n.; the triple Veda the thousandfold progeny of V., 26, 436; 41, 140; 44, 343 n.; the pith of V. wished to desert the gods, 26, 450 sq.; is this earth, 26, 450 sq.; the voice of thunder, in the company of the Maruts, 32, 272, 275; victim for V., 41, 15; Sarasvatî V. the leader, yoke-fellow of Thought, 41, 39, 80, 173; offering for B*ri*haspati V., 41, 70; world of V., 41, 145, 192; waters created out of V., 41, 145 sq., 192; the Aṅgiras-like deity, 41, 154; from V. Vi*s*vakarman begat living beings, 41, 407; V. Virâg, daughter of Kâma, 42, 221, 593; escaped the gods and settled in the trees, 42, 437; speaks, 43, 323, 366; Indra is V., 44, 16; when the sacrifice is complete, V. is wholly gained, 44, 343; is the goddess Gladness, 44, 453. *See also* Sarasvatî, Speech, *and* Voice.
Vaka Dâlbhya, n.p., 1, 6, 21.
Vâ*k*aknavî, *see* Gârgî V.
Vâ*k*aspati, n.d., Lord of Speech, 8, 262 n.; 26, 250; Kapila and V., 19, 134, 134 n.; V. Vi*s*vakarman, 26, 431; invoked, 26, 452 n.; Pragâpati, the Lord of Speech, 41, 5; prayer to V., 42, 209, 665; 44, 122. *See also* Vâkpati.
Vakhsh, n.p., 5, 146.
Vakkali, was delivered by faith, 10 (ii), 212 sq.
Va*kkh*aliggа, *see* Vâtsalîya.
Vakkula, one of the five hundred Arhats who are to become future Buddhas, 21, 198; disciple of Buddha, 49 (ii), 90.
Vâkpati, Lord of Speech, 8, 262 n.; *see* Vâ*k*aspati.
Vakula, an eminent Arhat or Bhikshu, 21, 2; 49 (ii), 2.
Vâkyakâra, *see* *T*aṅka.
Vala, demon, undone by B*ri*haspati, 42, 193, 596.
Valabhi, the *G*aina council of, under Devarddhi, 22, xxxvii sqq.
Valâhassa *G*âtaka, 11, 255 n.
Valâkâkau*s*ika, n. of a teacher, 15, 186 n.
Vâlakhilyas, dialogue between them and Pragâpati Kratu, 15, xlvii, 291–302; sages who had left off all evil, who were vigorous and passionless, 15, 291; have, through Brahma-knowledge, gone to the road of Brahman, 15, 326; tried to create other gods, 25, 398 n.; by means of the V. the gods ranged over these worlds, 43, 56.
Valkhash, or Valkhas, the Askânian, Vologeses I, Parthian king, collected the remnants of the Avesta, 4, xxxvii–xli, xlviii, lxv; 37, 413, 413 n.; 47, 82 n.
Vallî, Sk., 'creeper' used in the sense of 'chapter' in Upanishads, 15, xxiii.
Vâlmîki, follows after Vyâsa, 19, 11; uttered the poetry which *K*yavana could not compose, 49 (i), 9.
Vâmâ, mother of Pâr*s*va, 22, 271.
Vâmadeva, n. of a *Ri*shi, 11, 172; author of Vedic hymns, 1, 215; 46, 310, 319, 327, 333, 337, 341, 344, 349, 351, 353, 355, 357, 358, 361; became immortal, 1, 244, 246; the *Ri*shi V. says 'I was Manu, I was the sun,' 15, 88; 38, 238; 48, 252 sq., 618; saved himself from starva-

tion, 25, 424; worshipped at the Tarpa*n*a, 29, 122, 220; honoured as teacher, 29, 141; had obtained intuition of his identity with Brahman and everything in the universe, 34, lxv; 38, 37, 37 n., 101; 48, 71; became Brahman in his mother's womb, 38, 328; B*ri*haduktha, son of V., 44, 302; Agastya and V., seeking Râma, 49 (i), 93, 93 n.

Vâmadevya, *see* Prayers (*c*).

Vâmaka, n. of a *Ri*shi, 11, 172.

Vâmakakshâya*n*a, n. of a teacher, 15, 227; quoted, 41, 314; instructed by *S*â*nd*ilya, 43, 345, 345 n.; pupil of Vâtsya, 43, 404.

Vâmanî, a name of the highest Self, 48, 272.

Vanand, Zd. Vana*nt*, constellation, chieftain of the south, 5, 12, 13 n., 21; 24, 91, 91 n., 131; meat-offering to the star V., 5, 336; the star V. worshipped, 23, 9, 16, 97, 97 n., 351; the V. Ya*s*t, 23, 310.

Vana*nt*, *see* Vanand.

Vânaprastha, t.t., Sk., the forester, or hermit, *see* Hermits.

Vanâra, n.p., 23, 205.

Vanasavhaya, n. of a town, 10 (ii), 188.

Vanaspati, 'lord of the forest,' offerings to, 26, 208 sq.; 29, 352; 44, 3 n., 253 sq., 336 n. *See* Soma (*c*).

Va*n*daremaini, brother of Arega*t*-aspa, fights against Vî*s*tâspa and Zairi-vairi, 23, 80 sq., 80 n.

Vand-Aûha*r*ma*zd*, n. of a teacher, 5, 246 sq., 257, 371.

Vandî*d*-khîm, epithet of Pêshyôtanû, 5, 229, 229 n.

Vanfraghe*s*n, son of Yim, 5, 133, 133 n.

Vaṅgantaputta, *see* Upasena V.

Vanghu-dhâta, son of *Hv*adhâta, 23, 215.

Vanghu-fedhri, the virgin mother of Ukhshya*t*-nemah, 23, 195 n., 226, 226 n.

Vaṅgîsa, desires to know the fate of Nigrodhakappa who had recently attained Nirvâ*n*a, 10 (ii), 57–60; praises Buddha, 10 (ii), 73; saying of V. the Elder, 36, 322.

Vaṅgîsasutta, t.c., 10 (ii), 57–60.

Vânî*d*âr, son of Aîrî*k*, 5, 133.

Vâ*n*i*g*agrâma, Mahâvîra at, 22, 264.

Vanity, absence of, 8, 103, 114–16, 166, 246; destructive of a man's life, 8, 181; is dark conduct, 8, 320 sq.

Vâ*n*îya Kula of the Kau*t*ika Ga*n*a, 22, 292.

Vanôfravi*s*n, the Âspîgân, 47, 34.

Vapâhoma, *see* Animal sacrifices (*c*).

Vappa, is converted by, and receives the ordination from Buddha, 11, 155 n.; 13, 99.

Varadatta, at the head of the *S*ramaṇas, under Arish*t*anemi, 22, 278.

Varâhamihira, quotes Manu, 25, xcvii.

Varakasa, n.p., 23, 212.

Vara*n*â, t.t., 'that which wards off,' the non-released soul abides in it, 34, 153.

Vara*n*âvatî, river, its water wards off poison, 42, 26, 376.

Varaprabha, n. of a Bodhisattva, 21, 21 sq., 26 sq.; the 23rd Tathâgata, 49 (ii), 6.

Varâza, n.p., 23, 203, 205.

Vardast, an author of the Sad Dar, 24, xxxvii.

Vardhamâna, *see* Mahâvîra.

Vardhamânaka, one of the celestial regions, 22, 190.

Vardhamânamati, one of the sixteen virtuous men, 21, 4.

Vâ*r*eda*d*-gadman, Zd. Vareda*d*-*hv*arenô, one of the producers of the renovation, 18, 78 n., 79; 23, 220, 220 n.

Vareda*t*-*hv*arenah, or Vareda*d*-*hv*arenô, *see* Vâreda*d*-gadman.

Varedhakas, a tribe, conquered by Vî*s*tâspa, 23, 117, 117 n., 280.

Varena, *see* Varenya.

Varenô, demon of lust, of illicit intercourse, 5, 110; 18, 93; 37, 253, 253 n.; opposes Ar*d* the righteous, 18, 270, 270 n.

Varenya daêvas, fiendish inhabitants of Varena, V. fiends, 4, 140; 23, 59, 224, 251, 292; spell against them, 4, 140, 140 n.; the female V. fiend, 23, 29; Ahura-Mazda helps to smite them, 23, 33; flee from Mithra, 23, 136, 144, 155; Fravashis protect from the female V. fiend, 23, 197.

Vareshava, the Dânayan, smitten by Keresâsp, 18, 370; 23, 296.

Vareshna, son of Hanghaurv*a*ungh, 23, 208.
Varesmapa, son of *G*anara, 23, 213.
Varesmô-rao*k*ah, son of Frânya, 23, 204.
Varesmô-rao*k*ah, son of Perethu-afzem, 23, 219.
Var*g*âvand, a producer of the renovation, 37, 437, 437 n.
Vârkakha*nd*i, quoted by Gobhila, 30, 97.
Vârkali, a saying of his, 44, 169.
Vârkâru*n*îputra, n.p., 15, 224 n., 225.
Varmin, worshipped at the Tarpa*n*a, 30, 244.
Vârshaga*n*a, *see* Asita V.
Vârshaga*n*îputra, n. of a teacher, 15, 224 n.
Varshna, son of Hanghaurv*a*ungh, 4, 371.
Vârsh*n*a, *see* Barku V.
Vârsh*n*(y)a, n.p., Yâ*gñ*avalkya sacrificed for him, 26, 3, 3 n.
Vârshyâya*n*i, quoted by Âpastamba, 2, xxviii, 70, 88.
Var*n*i, son of Vâgereza, 23, 213.
Varu*n*a, Vedic Indian god.

(*a*) V. in mythology.
(*b*) Worship of V.
(*c*) Mitra and V.

(*a*) V. IN MYTHOLOGY.
At the head of the Âdityas, 1, 42; 26, 93; 32, 244; 42, 12; by the mind of Purusha, the water and V. were created, water yields to him faith, V. keeps his offspring within the law, 1, 212; world of V. beyond lightning, on the path of the gods, 1, 275; 38, 386, 389; 48, 747 sq.; V. and Ahura-Mazda, 4, xxx, lii; world of V. attained by a digger of pools, 7, 270; chief among aquatic beings, 8, 89, 89 n.; a form of K*ri*sh*n*a, 8, 97; in the Anugîtâ, 8, 219; emancipated being identified with V., 8, 220 sq., 345; the King of the Waters, 8, 346; 29, 232, 280; 38, 386; 42, 105, 112, 329, 349 n., 535 sq.; relation between Indra and V., 12, xvii, xvii n.; noose or fetters of V., 12, 72 sq. and n., 262 n.; 26, 132 n., 161, 181, 217, 221; 29, 169; 30, 84, 131, 163, 213; 32, 434; 34, 217 n.; 41, 57, 279 sq.; 42, 14, 88 sq., 290, 393; 44, 221; the waters, the wives of V., 12, 277 n.; established the fire and obtained sovereignty, 12, 313; is the injurer, a violent, hostile deity, 12, 340; 41, 137; when the fire burns rather brightly, it is V., 12, 340; Pra*g*âpati delivered his creatures from V.'s noose, 12, 391–8, 408, 445; 41, 47 sq.; is the nobility (Kshatriya) or ruling power, 12, 393, 401 sq.; 43, 239; punishes sin, 12, 397–9; 41, 57 n.; leader of the gods in their fight against V*ri*tra, 12, 449 sq.; will not seize him who performs the twilight devotions, 14, 249; gold-horned V., 14, 250; teaches his son Bh*ri*gu the Brahman and the Agnihotra, 15, 64–6; 34, 199; 44, xiv, 108–12, 108 n.; is the devatâ of the person in the water, 15, 145, 147; deity in the Western quarter, 15, 147; 42, 188, 193; a manifestation of the highest Brahman, 15, 303; one-half of the year (when the sun moves southward) belongs to V., 15, 316; a guardian of the world, 25, 185, 216 sq.; 35, 37; perjurer bound by V.'s fetters, 25, 269, 269 n.; 33, 92, 92 n.; a king shall punish like V., 25, 396 sq., 397 n.; the ordinances, laws (vrata) of V., 26, 76; 32, 237 sq.; 41, 57 n.; 42, 105; 46, 335; *into the hearts V. hath laid wisdom, into the homesteads fire, into the heaven hath he placed the Sun, and Soma upon the rock*, 26, 77; Soma identified with V., 26, 83 sq.; is the feathers of the arrow, the Upasads, 26, 108 n.; the Wise, the sage of heaven, 26, 122; 42, 27; 44, 251; is the year, 26, 272, 383; once V. struck King Soma in the eye, 26, 281; gave Dakshi*n*âs, 26, 347 sq.; has made a broad path for the sun, 26, 380; the parts of flowing water which flow not are holden by V., 26, 381; all distress caused by V., 26, 412 sq.; in the *S*atapatha-brâhma*n*a, 26, 472; 44, 582 sq.; Savit*ri* shaved the beard of V., 29, 56, 185, 302; 30, 217; V. Dharmapati, lord of righteousness, 29, 127; 41, 71; seven daughters of V. (serpents), 29, 131, 204, 327; V. and Aditi deliver from sin, 32, 256, 258 sq.; witnesses watched by

V. and other gods, 33, 245; Bh*ri*gu and other sons of Brahman's mind were again born at the sacrifice of V., 38, 235; Agni is the king V. whose laws are firm, 41, 51; 43, 238 sq.; 46, 38, 186, 240, 371; what is black belongs to V., 41, 58; the horse is V., connexion of horse with V., 41, 60, 405; 44, xix sq., 279 n.; standing pools of flowing water belong to V., 41, 76; the habitations of V., 41, 85; consecrated as king by the Râ*g*asûya, 41, 98, 103, 113–16; friendship between V. and the Earth, 41, 103; in the homesteads, 41, 106, 108 n.; 44, 251; of true power, 41, 109; seized creatures with vehemence, 41, 116; in the sacrifice the cord relates to V., 41, 222, 236; husbandry beneficial to V. and other gods, 41, 329; the ewe sacred to V. and Tvash*tri*, 41, 406, 411; Sun, the eye of V., 41, 408; Takman, a son of King V., 42, 3, 273, 273 n.; the Asura V. rules over the gods, 42, 11, 241; his golden chamber in the waters, 42, 12; loosens fetters, 42, 12; king among the gods, 42, 30; 46, 307; the Gandharva dug up a plant to promote V.'s virility, 42, 31, 370; plants exempt from V., 42, 42; toils of V., 42, 44; King V. knows the life-bestowing gold, 42, 63; helps to destroy the demons, 42, 65; the amulet tied by B*ri*haspati yields him truth, 42, 86; is everywhere and sees everything, 42, 88, 389; the two oceans, the loins of V., 42, 88, 391; his spies, the stars, 42, 88, 391; elects the king, 42, 113, 330 sq.; amulet instructed by V., to strengthen the king, 42, 114; among the Vasus, 42, 116; brilliancy of V. transferred on the king, 42, 116; V., Soma, Agni, 42, 135; the waters sent forth by V., 42, 146, 349 sq.; to Indra belongs the first chariot, to the gods the second, to V. the third, 42, 152; in a list of gods, 42, 160, 221; King V. pronounced the cow of a Brâhma*n*a to be poison (for the robber) prepared by the gods, 42, 172; as a teacher, 42, 216; disease, the fetter of V., 42, 290; Vasish*th*a steals food in the house of V., 42, 372; lordship bestowed on V., 43, 68; the lord of one-hoofed animals, 43, 75; is the repeller of shafts, 43, 101; the heavenly king, the universal sovereign, the representative of the earthly king, 44, xix, 63; representative of the waters, the heavenly sea, 44, xx, xxiii; his position in the Vedic pantheon, 44, xx–xxiii; called *G*umbaka, 44, xxxix, 343; Pra*g*âpati wounded by the shafts of V., 44, 36 sq., 36 n.; seizes him who is seized by evil, 44, 221; connected with winter, 44, 247; the upholder of the sacred law, 44, 251; healed the form of Indra, 44, 252; delivers from sin against V., 44, 265, 265 n.; the whirlpool in the water is either V.'s son or brother, 44, 266; a white-spotted, baldheaded man with protruding teeth is V.'s form, 44, 343; seizes him who dies in water, 44, 346; King V. Âditya, whose people are the Gandharvas, 44, 365; is the self of all the gods, 44, 506; Agni invoked to protect from harm that comes from V., the great god, 46, 138; is glorious through Agni, 46, 148; Agni alone rules over gods like V., 46, 157; the righteous Âditya who supports the human tribes, 46, 307; Agni announces man's sins to V., 46, 325; protector of the laws of the gods, 46, 367, 370; Indra, Yama, V., 49 (i), 197; city of V. in the West, Mukhyâ, Sukhâ, or Nimlo*k*anî, 49 (ii), xxii.

(*b*) WORSHIP OF V.

Prayers addressed to V., 1, 21; 2, 85, 295; 11, 180; 14, 161, 161 n., 246 sq., 250 sq.; 15, 45, 53; 26, 216 sq., 216 n.; 29, 232, 280; 41, 241; 42, 48, 50 sq., 133; hymns to V. ascribed to Vasish*th*a, 12, xvii; offerings to V., 12, 394–407, 406 sq. n.; 14, 304; 25, 91; 30, 144, 161 sq., 186, 203 sq., 208, 215 sq.; 41, 50–2, 57 sq., 71, 113, 116, 125, 136 sq.; 42, 349 n.; 43, 238 sq.; 44, 62–6, 75 n., 76, 81, 221, 221 n., 260 sq., 263 sq.; 46, 13, 38, 307, 316, 378, 418; by the Varu*n*apraghâsas the sacrificer reaches the world of V., 12, 450 sq.; barley sacred to V., 14, 297, 297 n.; 44, 346; expiatory prayers and obla-

tions to V., 25, 272, 272 n.; 26, 381–3, 412 sq.; 44, 208, 346, 506; property of a mortal sinner thrown into the water as an offering to V., lord of punishment, 25, 385, 385 n.; invoked with the Rudras, 26, 122, 122 n.; animal sacrifice for V., 26, 221, 428; expiatory bath frees from V.'s snare, 26, 381 sq.; invoked and worshipped at the wedding rite, 29, 32, 169, 281; 30, 187 sq.; the girls worship V., 29, 44; invoked for the protection of a child, 29, 54; sacrifice of sacrificial cord, &c., in water with a V.-verse, 29, 84; Bali offerings to V. and those belonging to V., 29, 85, 85 n., 161; worshipped on crossing water, 29, 127; worshipped at the consecration of ponds, 29, 135; Bali offering and prayer to V. at the house-building ceremony, 29, 214; 30, 123; 'if thou belongest to V., I buy thee for, or redeem thee from V.,' 30, 53, 269; worshipped for the thriving of horses, 30, 89; Nyagrodha tree sacred to V., 30, 122; invoked at the Upanayana, 30, 151; King V. worshipped at the Tarpana, 30, 243; invited to the Soma, 32, 408; worshipped at the ordeal by water, 33, 256, 258 sq.; the Râgasûya called a V.-sava, 41, xxv; knot sacred to V., 41, 58; offering to V. in the Sûta's house, 41, 60; the garment of initiation belongs to V., 41, 87; the horse sacrificed for V., 41, 162; 44, xx, xxiii sq.; invoked in medical charms, 42, 1, 3, 10–12, 237, 241 sq., 443; the sin of using V.'s name in vain, 42, 12, 563; prayer to V. for protection against treacherous designs, 42, 88 sq., 389–93; invoked to remove evil bodily marks from a woman, 42, 109; deity and metre, 43, 53; V. and the sacrifice of *S*una*h*s*epa, 44, xxxiv–xxxvi; invoked for universal sovereignty, 44, 63; is the king of the gods, hence invoked by the Kshatriya, 44, 251; worshipped at the A*s*vamedha, 44, 281; the eldest god who accepts the sacrifice, 46, 307; Agni invoked to cause, by sacrificing, V. to go away, 46, 307; Agni invoked to deprecate V.'s anger, 46, 307.

(*c*) Mitra and V.

M. and V. invoked, 12, 91; 29, 43, 97, 231 sq., 287; 30, 52, 56, 92; 32, 441; 42, 37, 102, 122, 153, 211; 44, 385; 46, 110, 115, 127, 237, 309; I*d*â produced by them, 12, 217 n.; meet I*d*â, 12, 218, 218 n., 224; grant rain, 12, 241; 32, 115; 42, 172, 436; principal sons of Aditi, 12, 356; 32, 242, 244, 246, 248; prayers to Mitra, Aryaman, and V., 12, 356; new moon offerings to M. and V., 12, 375, 378–81; the waxing and the waning moon, 12, 380; Vasish*th*a, their son, 14, xii, 140; 38, 235; are outbreathing and in-breathing, 26, 39, 144, 213; 41, 89, 122; 43, 270; 44, 181; that which is of M. is not of V., 26, 57; Sûrya or Sun, the eye of M. and V., 26, 83, 343; the Vasatîvarî water not to be taken for them, 26, 225; Soma libations to M. and V., 26, 266 n., 269–72, 278, 296 sq.; are intelligence and will, 26, 269 sq.; are priesthood and nobility, 26, 270 sq.; V., Mitra, Agni, 26, 285 sq.; curds offered to them, 26, 315 sq., 316 n.; 41, 105, 108 n.; 44, 268 sq.; deities of a *Ri*tu-graha, 26, 320 n.; Agni, M.-V., Indra, win in the race of the gods, 26, 327 n.; offering of a barren cow for M. and V., 26, 387–9; 42, 176; 44, 411; deities of the Maitrâvaru*n*a priest, 26, 436; I*d*â, their mother, 29, 296; M. and V. compared with Ahura and Mithra, 31, 199 n.; called v*ri*sha*n*au, 32, 146; mount their golden chariot, see Aditi and Diti, 32, 243; sons of Daksha, 32, 248; allied with Aditi, 32, 263; the Maruts protect them, 32, 273, 278; Aryamans, i. e. Aryaman, M. and V., 32, 326, 330; invoked with the Maruts, 32, 375, 386, 419, 423; the Mitrâvaru*n*a-eyed gods in the North, 41, 49; that which is hewn by the axe, churned, and cooked by fire belongs to V., that which is broken off by itself, self-produced, and cooked by steam, to Mitra, 41, 67 sq.; to V. belong plants grown in ploughed ground, to Mitra the Nâmba plants, 41, 71; anointed

with water from the river Sarasvatî, 41, 73 sq.; by his two arms the king belongs to M. and V., 41, 88, 93, 93 n., 99, 105; informed of the king's consecration, 41, 89; offerings to M. and V., 41, 120-2, 186; 43, 270, 270 n.; 44, 215 n.; 46, 95; disease shut out by their command, 42, 39 sq.; allies against enemies, 42, 91; poured love into the waters, 42, 105; call the king to the throne, 42, 113; the gods that guard the amr*i*ta, 42, 135, 364; the house enfolded by V. is uncovered by Mitra in the morning, 42, 195; surround the sun with lustre, 42, 210; the heavenly rulers, 42, 557; share of Mitra, lordship of V., 43, 68; the divine duad, M. and V., expressing the close relation between the sun and the heavens, 44, xx-xxii; from out of M. and V. the Go and Âyus (Stomas) were formed, 44, 139; worshipped at the performance of the Go and Âyus Stomas, 44, 142 sq.; Mitra is this world, V. is yonder world, 44, 268 sq.; who is righteous unto M. and V.? 44, 382; animal sacrifices to M. and V., 44, 402; V., Mitra, Aryaman kindle Agni, 46, 31; the two Mitras = Mitra and V., 46, 33, 36; (*there are*) *the two kings M. and V. with graceful hands, who watch over the beloved ambrosia in the cows*, 46, 75; Aryaman, Mitra, and V., he who walks round the earth, 46, 103; Aryaman, M., and V. fill the cloud, 46, 103; Agni makes them get refreshing drink, 46, 109; thrice every day V., Mitra, and Agni bring Tanûnapât to the sacrifice, 46, 236; M. and V. and the Maruts sing a pleasant song to Agni, 46, 268; invited to the sacrifice together with Agni, 46, 281; follow the law, when they make the Sun rise on heaven, 46, 356.

Varu*n*adatta, one of the sixteen virtuous men, 21, 4.

Varu*n*ânî, n.d., mother of Sleep, 42, 167, 485.

Varu*n*apraghâsa, t.t., the second of the four seasonal sacrifices, 44, 75, 75 n., 78. *See* Sacrifices (*j*).

Vâru*n*î, n. d., invocation to, 14, 251.

Vâru*n*y-upanishad, *see* Upanishads (*a*).

Varûthin, n. of a teacher, worshipped at the Tarpa*n*a, 30, 244.

Va*s*a A*s*vya, hymn of, 43, 112, 112 n.

Vâsabhagâma, Bhikkhu Kassapagotta of, 17, 256-61.

Vâsabha-gâmika, appointed on the jury at the council of Vesâlî, 20, 407.

Vasalasutta, t.c., 10 (ii), 20-4.

Vasatîvarî-waters, *see* Water (*b*).

Vâsava, the gods hear the well-spoken words of, 10 (ii), 64.

Vâse*tth*a, Pali for Vasish*th*a, the *R*ishi, 11, 172.

Vâse*tth*a and Bhâradvâga, two young Brâhma*n*as, instructed and converted by Buddha, 10 (ii), 108-17; 11, 168-203; addressed by Buddha, 35, 229.

Vâse*tth*as, the Mallas addressed as 11, 101 sq., 121-8.

Vâse*tth*asutta, t.c., 10 (ii), 108-17.

Vasha*t*, *see* Sacred syllables.

Vâshkalin, questions Bâhva about Brahman, 38, 157.

Vâshpa, one of the five first disciples of Buddha, 19, 172; converts *S*âriputra, 19, 193; a distinguished Arhat, 21, 2; 49 (ii), 2.

Va*s*inî, the initiated boy given in charge to, 30, 154.

Vasish*th*a, famous *R*ishi, author of Vedic hymns, esp. of the 7th Ma*nd*ala of the Rig-veda, 1, 216, 220; 29, 127; 32, 376, 380, 383, 386, 388, 437; 48, 332; married a *K*â*nd*âlî Akshamâlâ, 2, 175 n.; 25, 331, 331 n.; 49 (i), 45; asks Brahman about final emancipation, 8, 314; most Varu*n*a hymns ascribed to V., 12, xvii; the Dâkshâya*n*a sacrifice called the V.-sacrifice, 12, 376, 376 n.; mentioned in the Vâsish*th*a Dharma*s*âstra, 14, xi sq., 16, 124, 140; born without a mother, 14, 180 n.; one of the seven *R*ishis, 15, 106; reverenced by King Antideva, 19, 12; 49 (i), 10, 101; Bharata and the *R*ishi V., 19, 95; a great *R*ishi king, 19, 274; Ga*n*adhara of Arhat Pâr*s*va, 22, 274; Khumbya and V., 23, 224 n.; a sage and Pragâpati, 25, 14; Sukâlins (manes), offspring of V., 25, 112; swore an oath before King

Sudâs, 25, 273, 273 n.; 33, 98, 98 n.; formerly only priests of the V. family could be Brahmans, 26, 434 n.; 44, 212; worshipped at the Tarpa*n*a, 29, 122, 220; 30, 244; honoured as teacher, 29, 141; imprecations against V., 32, xlvi n.; quoted by Nârada, on lawful interest, 33, 66; accused of witchcraft, 33, 98; 42, l; the son of Brahman's mind, having parted from his former body in consequence of the curse of Nimi, was, on the order of Brahman, again procreated by Mitra and Varu*n*a, 38, 235; Indra makes V. his Brahman priest, 42, lx; a Brahman and Purohita, 42, lxv; V. and the Atharva-veda, 42, lxv, lxv n.; steals food in the house of Varu*n*a, 42, 372; is the breath, 43, 5; on the relation between Varu*n*a and Indra, 44, xxii; V. taught Indra the Virâ*g*, and Indra taught V. the expiation rites of a Soma-sacrifice, 44, 212; teacher of Parâ*s*ara, 48, 92; had reached intuition of the highest truth, yet entered after death on other embodiments, 48, 650 sq.; could not arrange the Vedas, 49 (i), 9.

Vâsish*th*a-Dharma-*s*âstra, or V.-Dharma-sûtra: relation between the Baudhâyana, V., and Gautama-Dharma-sûtras, 2, liii, lvii–lx; its relation to other works on Dharma, 7, xvi–xx; 14, xvii–xxv; connected with the *Ri*shi Vasish*th*a of the Rig-veda, 14, xi sq.; belongs to one of the schools of the Rig-veda, 14, xii–xv; 25, 613; its position in Vedic literature, 14, xiii, xv–xvii, xix, xxvii; its date, 14, xv, xxv–xxvii; its home in Northern India, 14, xvi, xxvii; portions of the work not genuine, 14, xxi–xxv; text and translation, 14, xxvii sq., 1–140; quotes a Mânava Dharma-sûtra, 25, xxii, xxxi–xxxiv; quoted in Manu-sm*ri*ti, 25, xxix sq., 278, 278 n.

Vâsish*th*a gotra, Tri*s*alâ of the, 22, 191, 193, 226, 230; Sthaviras of the V. gotra, 22, 286, 288, 290, 292, 294.

Vasish*th*as, descendants of Vasish*th*a, wear braided hair, 32, 424. *See also* Vâse*tth*as.

Vâsish*th*as, a school of the Sâma-veda, 14, xv n.

Vâsish*th*î = Ya*s*â, wife of the Purohita Bh*ri*gu, 45, 65 sq.

Vâsish*th*îyâ *S*âkhâ of the Mânava Ga*n*a, 22, 292.

Vasor dhârâ, t.t., 'shower of wealth' oblation, 43, 213 sq.; its mystic meaning, 43, 221 sq. *See also* Sacrifices (*i*).

Vassa, V. rules, *see* Monks, *and* Rainy season.

Vassakâra, n. of a Brâhman, prime-minister of Magadha, 11, 2–5; Sunîdha and V., the ministers of Magadha, who build Pâ*t*aliputta, 11, 18–21; 17, 101 sqq.

Vâstavya, a name of Rudra, the god of cattle, 12, 200 sq.

Vâstoshpati, n.d., 'lord of the homestead,' prayers and offerings to, 25, 91, 91 n.; 29, 85; 30, 95, 158; 41, 43 n.; 42, 640; sacrifice to V. on entering a new house, 29, 95 sq.; worshipped at house-building rites, 29, 215, 346 sq., 429; 30, 123, 205 sq.; the genius of home, 42, 135, 343, 494 sq.

Vasu, *see* Vasus.

Vasubandhu, composed a commentary on the Saddharma-pu*nd*arîka, his date, 21, xxii; refers to the Milindapa*ñ*ha, 36, xvii.

Vasudêva, king of *S*auryapura, 45, 112 sq., 115 sq.

Vâsudeva, n. of K*ri*sh*n*a, 8, 75, 91, 98, 130, 230, 235, 254, 310, 312, 393; is everything, 8, 75; appears in four forms, as V., Sa*n*karsha*n*a, Pradyumna, Aniruddha, 11, 267 n.; 34, 440 sq.; called bhagavat, the highest Lord, is the highest Brahman, and the highest cause, 34, xxiii, li, 440; 48, 23, 87, 127, 524 sq., 527, 529; from V. originated Sa*n*karsha*n*a, 34, li; a surname of Kapila, who burned the sons of Sagara, 34, 294; to be worshipped, 34, 440; the only real essence, 34, 442; dialogue of V. and Arguna on knowledge originating in a future life, 38, 328 sq.; the god with the conch, discus, and club, who fights with an irresistible strength, has

no equal, 45, 48; *when V. is not meditated on for an hour or even a moment only; that is loss, that is great calamity, that is error, that is change*, 48, 85 sq.;—Vâsudevas are never born in low families, 22, 225; the mothers of Vs. wake up after seeing seven auspicious dreams, 22, 246. *See also* God (*d*), K*r*ish*n*a, Pradyumna, *and* Vish*n*u.

Vâsuki, n. of a Nâga king, chief among serpents, 8, 89, 353 n.; 21, 5; offering to V. at the house-building, 30, 124.

Vasukra, author of a Marutvatîya hymn, is Brahman, 1, 169.

Vasundara: Sundara and V. (should be Sunda and Upasunda), 19, 125.

Vâsupûgya, n. of a Tîrthakara, 22, 280.

Vasus, a class of gods, 1, 35; 46, 42, 45; the morning-oblations belong to them, 1, 35 sqq., 50; 44, 173, 443, 480 n.; a Sâman addressed to them, 1, 36; with Agni at their head, 1, 41; 8, 88; 34, 216; seen within K*r*ish*n*a, 8, 92; alarmed at the greatness of K*r*ish*n*a, 8, 94; invited to sit on the Prastara, 12, 93; V., Rudras, Âdityas, the three classes of gods, 12, 135, 239; 26, 350, 411; 41, 241, 246, 264; 42, 135, 161; 43, 33, 75; 44, 291 n., 312 sq.; 'Vasu's means of purification,' Vasu is the sacrifice, 12, 186–8; eight V., enumerated, 15, 140; 26, 411; 44, 116; the purifying power of Vasu invoked against the sin caused by defiled food, 15, 312; rise in the East, lords of the East, 15, 338; 43, 100; Buddha mistaken for one of the eight V., 19, 72; 49 (i), 71; the manes of fathers, 25, 127; practised penance, 25, 475; Rudra together with the V., 26, 59; Agni with the V., 26, 93; 46, 157; invoked, 29, 198, 207, 344, 347; 30, 157, 159; 32, 296; 42, 55; 43, 25; 46, 198, 253; the cow, or Aditi, the daughter of the V., 29, 199, 275; 30, 174; 'if thou belongest to the V., I buy thee for the V.,' 30, 53; worshipped at the Tarpa*n*a, 30, 243; Maruts called V., 32, 334, 374, 378, 386, 412; Rudra the best Vasu, 32, 419; are non-eternal beings, 34, 202; enjoy the nectars of the sun, 34, 216; 48, 368–70; the Vasu, dwelling in the air, the wind, 41, 103, 281; eight V. created, 41, 149 sq.; the wise gods, 41, 231; fashioned the earth, 41, 233; Âdityas, V., and Aṅgiras, 42, 89; bestow goods (vasu), 42, 116; help in battle, 42, 119, 121; B*r*ihaspati with the V., 42, 135; the honey-lash (of the A*s*vins), daughter of the V., 42, 230; deities and metres, 43, 53; share of the V., lordship of the Rudras, 43, 68; where they wish to lay the Gârhapatya, 43, 118; Agni is Vasu, 43, 213; 46, 22; *but see* Agni (*d*); invited to the sacrifice together with Agni, 46, 281; have released the buffalo cow bound by the foot, 46, 354; Agni kindled by the V., 46, 372; Âdityas and V. are qualified for meditations, 48, 335–7; V. and Manus, 49 (i), 197; Indra and the V., *see* Indra (*e*).

Vasu*s*ruta Âtreya, author of Vedic hymns, 46, 372, 376, 378, 380.

Vasûyava*h* Âtreyâ*h*, authors of Vedic hymns, 46, 417, 419.

Vasvî, is the Soma-cow, 26, 59.

Vâta, Wind (god): offering to V. by the student who broke his vow, 25, 454; the friend of the waters, 32, 449; the greatness of his chariot, 32, 449; the breath of the gods, the germ of the world, 32, 449 sq.; hymns to V., 32, 449–51; the treasure of the immortal placed in his house, 32, 451; wafts medicine, 32, 451; B*r*ihaspati tied an amulet for swift V., 42, 85 sq.; the broad atmosphere guarded by V., 42, 89; V. and Parganya invoked against the serpents, 42, 153, 161; Prâ*n*a is V., 42, 219; is the Gandharva, his Apsaras the waters, 43, 232; expiatory oblation at a Soma-sacrifice to V., 44, 210; goes forward in triumph, 46, 325.

Vâtagiri, demon converted by Buddha, 19, 242.

Vatsa, underwent the ordeal of fire, 25, 274, 274 n.; *R*ishi, 41, 358. *See also* Vatsas.

Vatsa gotra, Sthaviras of the, 22, 287, 293.

Vâtsalîya (Prk. Va*kkh*ali*gg*a) Kula, of the *K*âra*n*a Ga*n*a, 22, 291; of the Kau*t*ika Ga*n*a, 22, 292.

Vatsanapât Bâbhrava, n. of a teacher, 15, 119, 187.

Vâtsapra hymn, *see* Prayers (*c*).

Vatsas, make five Avadâna cuttings, 12, 192 n.

Vâtsîma*nd*avîputra, n. of a teacher, 15, 224 n.

Vâtsîputra, n.p., 15, 224 n., 225.

Vâtsya, n. of a teacher, 12, xxxiii; 15, 118 n., 119, 186 n., 187, 227; 43, 272, 404.

Vâtsya gotra, Sthiragupta of the, 22, 295.

Va*tt*agâmani, King, Buddhist canon written down during his reign, 10 (i), xiii sq., xxv, xxxix.

Vatthugâthâs, certain verses of the Sutta-nipâta so called, 10 (ii), 56, 125–8, 184–90.

Vatthu-vi*gg*â, a quack science, 11, 19 n.

Vâvâtâ, t.t., the king's favourite wife, 44, 387.

Vavri Âtreya, author of a Vedic hymn, 46, 407.

Vâyasa, knew the kush*th*a plant, 42, 6, 681.

Vayodhas, *see* Indra (*a*).

Vayu, or Vâi, or Vâê, the Genius of Destiny, good or evil, 4, 52, 52 n., 89 n.; 24, 17, 17 n.; invoked by Zarathu*s*tra, 4, 213 sq., 213 n.; good Vaê comes to meet the departed soul, 4, 373; pitiless V. or Destiny, 4, 382 sq.; meat-offering to V., 5, 336, 336 n.; cake-offering to the good V., the spirit of air, 5, 383; 18, 62, 62 n.; stationed at the *K*inva*d* bridge, 5, 383 n.; 'the good spirit,' 18, 59 n., 64 n.; the bad V., identified with the demon of death, 18, 62, 62 n.; the long-continuing lord, 18, 78, 78 n.; the bad V. who carries off the soul, 18, 93, 96, 341, 341 n., 353, 353 n.; powerful to destroy, invoked, 23, 10, 18, 34, 334; worshipped in the Râm Ya*s*t, 23, 249–63; one part of V. belongs to the Good Spirit, one to the Evil Spirit, 23, 250, 250 n., 260, 260 n., 262 sq.; invoked by maids for a husband, 23, 258, 258 n.; glorification of his many names, 23, 258–62; works the good of Ahura-Mazda and the Amesha-Spe*n*tas, 23, 259; invoked in battle, 23, 260 sq.; Sovereign V. of the long Period, invoked, 23, 350, 350 n., 353; no one can escape from V. the bad, 24, 89, 89 n.; warning against the demon V., 31, 189, 192 sq. and n.; V. whose influence appertains to Spe*n*ta-Mainyu, worshipped, 31, 271 sq., 272 n., 277; Khûsrôî's meeting with V., 37, 223–5, 223 sq. n. *See also* Râm.

Vâyu, Air, Wind, Vedic god.

(*a*) V. in mythology.
(*b*) Worship of V.

(*a*) V. IN MYTHOLOGY.

V. who dwells in the sky, who dwells in the world, 1, 37; 15, 334; is the child of the quarters, 1, 49; 15, 221; 41, 188; is one foot of Brahman, 1, 54; V. (and Prâ*n*a) as Brahman, 1, 55–8, 55 n., 58 n.; 15, 302 sq.; 38, 19 n.; is the end of all, 1, 58; in the shape of the bull of the herd, tended by Satyakâma, explains one foot of Brahman, 1, 61; V. or he who purifies is the sacrifice, 1, 68 sq.; is the essence squeezed out from the sky, 1, 70; the Yagur-veda squeezed out from V., 1, 70; 44, 102; if Udâna is satisfied, V. is satisfied, and ether is satisfied, 1, 91; could not take up a straw put before him by Brahman, 1, 150; is the deity who lays hold of food (by the apâna or down-breathing, digestion), 1, 241; world of V. on the path of the gods, 1, 275; 38, 384–6; 48, 745 sq.; V. who hears, 2, 114; in the Anugîtâ, 8, 219; presiding deity of earth and smell, 8, 337, 340, 349; the sharp-edged V., 12, 53; rules over rain, 12, 241, 446; Agni, V., Sûrya, and earth, air, sky, 12, 325–7; 44, 27; *S*una and Sîra, or V. and Âditya, 12, 445 n.; by the *S*unâsîrîya the sacrificer reaches the world of V., 12, 451 n.; invoked as the visible Brahman, 15, 45, 53; secret union (sa*m*hitâ) through V., 15, 46; Prâ*n*a, breath, the vital airs, identified with V., 15, 80 sq., 275, 331; 38, 257; 43, 60 sq., 208, 363; 44, 345; is the deity that never sets,

15, 98; 38, 18 sq.; Udgâtri priest identified with V., 15, 122 sq.; is everything by itself, and all things together, 15, 128; conveyed the Pârikshitas to where the performers of horse-sacrifices dwell, 15, 128; is the thread by which the worlds and all creatures are strung together, 15, 132 sq.; is one of the eight Vasus, 15, 140 sq.; 44, 116; quoted as a legal authority, 25, 334; called Ûrdhvanabhas, son of the Maruts, 26, 198, 198 n.; finds out that Vritra is slain, 26, 265; leader of beasts, 26, 361 sq.; 43, 75; lord or ruler of the air, Nabhasaspati, 26, 453 n.; 29, 280; 42, 499; 43, xx, 43 sq., 44 n., 208, 382; dwells in the womb of the regions, 29, 45; 30, 199; aerial serpents belonging to V., 29, 328 sq.; the swiftest god, the swiftest of all beings, exists in the three worlds, 29, 335; 43, 61; 44, 278; 48, 330; Yagus, V., air, breath, 30, 152 sq., 231; has made a fruit fall from a tree, 30, 180; is the surveyor of food offered to the ancestors, 30, 228; the lord of aerial beings, 30, 237; comes to the offering on quick racers, on his chariot, 32, 444; yokes the two ruddy horses to the chariot, 32, 444; father of the Maruts, 32, 444, 448; V. and Prâna not to be identified, 34, lxxiv; 38, 256–9; having become breath, V. entered into the nostrils, 38, 91; is the best among the Devas, 38, 256; created, 41, 148; V. and the Rudras, 41, 149 n., 150; identified with Pragâpati, Agni, and the Sacrificer, 41, 152, 284; 43, 57 sq., 363; V. and Ugra identical, 41, 160; V. Mâtarisvan is the wind, 41, 221; frees from misfortune, 42, 51; companion of cattle, 42, 142 sq., 304; Visvakarman is V., 43, 6, 106; is all the light in the air-world, 43, 47 sq.; the support of all beings, 43, 66; the second Visvagyotis, 43, 130; V. or wind, and sky are close together, 43, 140 sq.; is of trishtubh nature, 43, 142; is the self (body) of all the gods, 43, 179; 44, 505; deity of Vikkhandas metre, 43, 331; the waters are his food, 43, 335; identified with the Yagus, 43, 336; one-third of fire, 43, 402; is one and a half god, 44, 117, 117 n.; heard, but not seen, 44, 130; light is Agni, might V., glory Âditya, 44, 173; Soma purified by V.'s purifier, 44, 225 sq.; delivers from sin, 44, 265; gods of the air headed by V., 44, 291 n.; the singer of praise, 44, 312; sacrificed as animal, 44, 319; the transformer of seeds, 44, 345; purifies the burial-ground, 44, 431; purifies by blowing, 44, 457; V. and the atmosphere are immortal, 48, 568; Agni, V., and Âditya, *see* Agni (*b*); Indra and V., *see* Indra (*e*). *See also* Wind.

(*b*) WORSHIP OF V.

V. invoked for protection, &c., 2, 114; 7, 86 n.; 15, 334; 29, 41, 44, 184, 210, 232, 280, 288, 301, 398; 30, 61, 188, 197; 32, 445; 42, 54, 128, 140; 43, 43; 44, 316; 46, 44; Agnihotra libation to V., 12, 327, 334; 44, 81, 81 n.; offerings to V., 12, 446; 26, 195, 265–9, 277 sq.; 29, 320 sq., 388; 30, 22, 51, 123; 44, 77, 77 n., 84, 209, 345, 347, 505 n.; the warp of the Dîkshita's cloth belongs to V., 26, 9; worshipped at the Tarpana, 29, 121, 149; 30, 243; student worships V. as lord of the vow, 30, 156; invited to the Soma, 32, 440, 444 sq.; Indra and V. invoked jointly, 32, 440; hymns to V., 32, 440–8; invoked as Vâta, 32, 450 sq.; an object of worship, 38, 19; animal sacrifice for V. Niyutvat, 41, 173–8, 184; V.'s layer of the fire-altar, 43, 81; he-goat killed at the building of the fire-altar for V., 44, xxxviii sq., 371 n.; worshipped at the Asvamedha, 44, 281, 300, 316; worshipped under the name of Ocean, 44, 479; offering of a white animal to V., 48, 626 sq.

Vâyubhûti, n. of a Gaina monk, 22, 286.

Vâyupurâna, to be recited at the Asvamedha, 44, 369 n.

Vazâspa, n.p., 23, 206.

Vâzista or Vâzist fire, the lightning, 4, 223; 5, 28, 28 n.; 24, 133, 133 n.; opposes the demon Apâôsh, 5, 171.

Vebhâra, mount at Râgagaha, 11, 56 sq.

Veda, Vedas.

(*a*) Vedic Literature.
(*b*) The three Vedas.
(*c*) Study and knowledge of V.
(*d*) Prerogatives of those who know or study the V.
(*e*) Sacredness and deification of the V.
(*f*) Contents and authority of the V.
(*g*) Vedic schools (*Kara*n*as*, *Sâkhâs*).

(*a*) VEDIC LITERATURE.

Colebrooke on the translation of the V., 1, xvii; list of Vedic texts, 1, 109–11, 115; 14, 266 sq.; 15, 111, 153, 184; 29, 218 sq.; 42, xxx n.; 44, 98, 98 n., 101, 101 n.; 48, 527; Veda of the Vs., or grammar, 1, 109–11, 115; fanciful interpretations of Vedic hymns and verses, 1, 163–5, 179 sq., 182, 196, 197–9, 202, 210, 213 sq., 227–9, 234, 244, 254–6, 259 sq.; the Pragâpati-Sa*m*hitâ, 1, 256; Vedic texts quoted by Âpastamba, 2, xxv–xxvii, xli sq.; Vedic texts quoted in the Gautama Dharma-sûtra, 2, li sq., lxi; definition of the term V., 2, 121, 121 n.; 29, 312; Zend-Avesta and V., Vedic religion and Zoroastrianism, 4, xxvii–xxxi, lii sq.; 31, xxix, xxxvi sq.; attitude of Bhagavadgîtâ towards the V., 8, 16–20, 25; Âkhyânas as the fifth V., 8, 145; attitude of the Sanatsugâtîya towards the V., 8, 145–7; four and three Vs., 8, 170 sq.; phraseology of Vedic hymns and of Buddhist writings, 11, 141, 245; the *Ri*shis of old, the authors of the V., 11, 172 sq.; the Sa*m*hitâs of the V., and the four classes of priests, 12, xxi sq.; 30, 320 sq.; quotations of Vedic texts in the Vâsish*th*a Dharma*s*âstra, 14, xiii, xv–xvii, xix, xxvii, 7–11, 7 n., 13, 25 sq., 30–4, 56, 61, 76, 84–8, 106, 109, 116 sq., 119, 119 n., 138; Vedic texts quoted by Baudhâyana, 14, xxxix sq., 156–8 and notes, 162, 164, 164 n., 169, 172 sq., 174, 186, 191, 199, 209 sq., 215 sq., 224, 231, 245, 249–52 and n., 257 sq., 261 sq., 274–7, 280 sq., 302, 310 sq.; the four Vs. and their Aṅgas, Itihâsa and Nigghа*n*tu, being the fifth and sixth V., 22, 221; riddles from the V., 25, 118, 118 n.; Nigamas which explain the V., 25, 132, 132 n.; Rig-veda, Yagur-veda, Sâma-veda, and Brahma-veda, 29, 41 sq.; Naigamas, followers of the V., the rules of their orders to be maintained by the king, 33, 153–5; the Brâhma*n*as concerned with the four Vs., 35, 247; the V. and Vedic religion, 42, lxii sq.; epic germs in Vedic hymns, 42, 197 sq., 688–92; devaganavidyâ (demonology), magic and the Purâ*n*a are the V., 44, 368 sq., 368 n.; should be made to grow by Itihâsa and Purâ*n*a, 48, 91; divided into *Rik*, Yagus, Sâman, and Atharvan, and difficult to fathom, 48, 528; arranged by Sârasvata, Va*s*ish*th*a, and Vyâsa, 49 (i), 9, 9 n.; 'Sûtra of the discourse of the V.,' 49 (ii), 163. *See also* Atharva-veda, Mantras, Rig-veda, Sacred Books, Sâman, Sâma-veda, Sciences, Upanishads, *and* Yagur-veda.

(*b*) THE THREE VEDAS.

Sâma-veda, Yagur-veda, and Rig-veda in the Udgîtha, 1, 8; the Devas entered into the three V., 1, 11; the three V. squeezed out from Agni, Vâyu, and Âditya, 1, 70; 30, 231; 44, 102 sq.; the three Vyâh*ri*tis are the three V. or are produced from them, 1, 177 sq.; 15, 49; 44, 102 sq.; *Rik*, Gâthâ, and Kumbyâ are metrical, Yagus in prose, and Sâman is music, 1, 230; the person of the Veda, i.e. that by which we know the three V., its essence is Brahman, 1, 259; *Rik* and Sâman, Yagus, and the Udgîtha represented as belonging to the couch of Brahman, 1, 278; study and knowledge of three V., 2, 160; 8, 20, 146, 162 sq.; 25, 74 sq. and n.; king must be instructed in the trayî vidyâ or threefold sacred science, 2, 234, 234 n.; father, mother, and teacher compared to the three V., 7, 128; 25, 71; K*ri*sh*n*a is *Rik*, Sâman, and Yagus, 8, 83; the three branches of knowledge lead to heaven, 8, 84; Brâhma*n*as who are masters of the three V., 10 (ii), 98, 110, 189; 11, 167–85; Tevigga-Suttanta, or Discussion on Knowledge of the Three V., 11, x, 157–203; *the threefold wisdom of the Brâh-*

mans, wise in their Three V., is called a waterless desert, their threefold wisdom is called a pathless jungle, their threefold wisdom is called destruction, 11, 185; the sacrifice identified with or established by the three V., 12, 24; 26, 249, 341; 30, 317 sq.; 41, 139 sq.; the Brahman and the threefold science, 12, 449 sq.; *Rik*, Sâman, and Yagus come from the highest Person, 15, 34 sq.; the three V. identified with speech, mind, breath, 15, 94; speculations on the three V., 15, 196, 198; 26, 436–40; the three V. are fixed in Prâ*n*a, 15, 275; *Rik*, Yagus, Sâman form the knowledge-endowed body of the Self, 15, 308; the threefold V. created, 25, 12; 41, 145, 196; 43, 403; term for studying the three V., 25, 74 sq. and n.; adherents of the three V. fed at *S*râddhas, 25, 102; Rig-veda sacred to gods, Yagur-veda to men, Sâma-veda to manes, 25, 148; Om and Gâyatrî, the essence of the three V., 25, 149, 149 n.; 38, 282 sq.; definition of triple V., 25, 482 sq.; song of praise is *Rik*, libation is Sâman, and a muttered formula is Yagus, 26, 294 sq.; the All-gods are everything, *Rik*, Yagus, and Sâman, 26, 360; priests perform with Yagus, recite *Rik*, chant Sâman, 26, 453; threefold knowledge handed down in Mantras and Brâhma*n*as, 29, 16; the new-born child adjured with *Rik*, Yagus, and Sâman, 29, 50; the three V., Vâkovâkya, Itihâsa, and Purâ*n*a, laid into the new-born child, 29, 51; teacher says to student at the initiation: 'I place thee in the *Rik*as, . . . in the Yagus . . . in the Sâmans . . . ,' 30, 152; Rig-veda and Sâma-veda Mantras have to be recited aloud, Yagur-veda by murmuring, 30, 318 sq.; science defined as knowledge of Rig-veda, Sâma-veda, and Yagur-veda, 33, 344; Nâgasena is taught the three V. called Sikkhâ, 35, 17 sq.; V*ri*tra gives up the three V. to Indra, 41, 138 sq.; the Traidhâtavî sacrifice, relating to the three V., 41, 138–41; the triple V. is the thousandfold progeny of Vâ*k*, 41, 140; 44, 343 n.; Pragâpati entered the waters with the threefold science, 41, 192 sq.; all the metres make up the threefold science, 41, 193; Pragâpati identified with the threefold science, the V., 41, 193; 43, xxvi, 352–4; *Rik*, Yagus, Sâman, the three kinds of divine speech, 41, 239; 43, 364–6; from the mind-ocean the gods dug out the triple science, 41, 415; *Rik*, Sâman, Yagus, are in the u*kkh*ish*t*a, 42, 226, 228 sq.; the triple science is food, 43, 220; truth is the threefold lore, 43, 258, 258 n.; the three oceans of Yagus, Sâman, and *Rik*, 43, 278; the three V. and the triad Fire-altar, Mahad uktham and Mahâvrata, 43, 282–4; the Arkya in respect of the three V., 43, 349; all things are in the threefold lore, 43, 352, 354; number of syllables of the three V., 43, 353, 353 n.; priests of the three V., 43, 373; 44, 103 sq.; *Rik*, Yagus, Sâman as the three bricks of the Fire-altar, 43, 374; *Rik*, Yagus, Sâman constitute the divine body of the Sacrificer, 44, 38; honey is the essential part of the triple science, the V., 44, 90; the unexhausted threefold science, 44, 170; light is the Rig-veda, might the Yagur-veda, glory the Sâma-veda, and what other V. there are they are everything, 44, 174. *See also* Tevigga.

(*c*) STUDY AND KNOWLEDGE OF V.

Promiscuous communication of the V. prohibited, but the V. not kept from the people, 1, xxii sq.; duty of V.-study, that is of reading the V. and learning it by heart, inculcated for every man of the three higher castes, 1, xxiii; 2, 1, 153, 160; 7, 194; 8, 146; 14, 38 sq., 44, 199, 261 sq.; 15, 51 sqq.; 25, 24, 158 sq., 170, 205, 419 sq.; 45, 62 sq.; 48, 5 sq., 255, 338; *S*ûdras and outcasts excluded from reading or hearing the V., 1, xxiii; 2, 281; 14, 95, 109; 48, 564; duties of sacrifice, study of V., and charity, 1, 35; 8, 22 sq., 81, 98 sq., 340, 359; 15, 179; 48, 695, 699; the proper age for study of the V., 1, 92, 92 n.; the Self cannot be gained by knowledge of the V., 1, 110,

110 n.; 8, 367; 15, 11, 40; 48, 527, 617; study of V. or knowledge of V., the first step towards obtaining knowledge of, or the world of, or union with Brahman, 1, 144; 8, 147, 171–4, 185, 369; 15, 300 sq.; 25, 34, 165, 507; 34, 10; 44, 99; 48, 3; rules about the study of the V., 1, 268; 2, 32–51, 97 sq., 111–13, 183–5, 259–65; 7, 123–8; 14, 63–7, 120 sq., 208–11, 245; 25, xxxix n., xlvi–xlviii, 43, 49, 60 sq., 143–9, 193 sq.; 29, 66–73, 119 sq., 191–3; 44, xv; the Gâyatrî is learnt for the sake of all the Vs., 2, 2; whatever else besides the V. a student learns from his teacher brings the same reward as the V., 2, 19; Upâkarma and Utsarga (Utsargana) ceremonies, solemn opening and closing of the Brâhmanic term, 2, 32, 32 n., 33 n., 41, 41 n., 111, 111 n., 259 sq., 259 n., 264; 7, 123, 125; 14, 63, 185 sq.; 25, 143 sq. and n., 148; 29, 112–15, 221–3, 321–3, 325, 413 sq.; 30, 77–9, 79 sq. n., 161, 241–6, 266 sq.; 42, 487 sq., 510, 553, 606; causes of interruption of the study of the V., 2, 36, 36 n., 264; 14, 121 sq., 208; 25, 110, 144–9; 29, 81, 114–18, 141 sq., 220, 244 sq., 323 sq., 357, 414 sq.; 30, xxxiv sq., 78–81, 242, 325; Svâdhyâya, or Brahmayag*ñ*a, one of the 'five great sacrifices,' the daily recitation of a portion of the V., 2, 42–9, 201, 201 sq. n., 221 sq.; 7, 193; 8, 61, 61 n.; 14, 224, 245, 256 sq.; 25, 87 sq.; 29, 19 sq., 19 n., 217–20; 30, xx, 246; 44, 95–101; the daily recitation of the V. procures as much merit as austerity, procures imperishable worlds, 2, 45; 44, 96; Vedic texts to be studied with a vow of obedience, except the Tri*h*srâva*n*a and Tri*h*sahava*k*ana texts, 2, 49, 49 n.; he who learns the V. from his son, an unworthy person, 2, 69; one who neglects the (daily) study of the V. loses caste, is not to be invited to a *S*râddha, and his food must not be eaten, 2, 69, 74, 258; 14, 46; 25, 103, 103 n., 107, 107 n.; reciting the entire *S*âkhâ of his V. purifies a man from sin, 2, 87; repeating the V. with a guest, 2, 116; renowned teacher of the V. honoured as a guest, 2, 120 sq.; 30, 279; daily recitation of the V. enjoined for the ascetic, 2, 154; 14, 46; 283, 283 n.; abandoning the V., the ascetic shall seek the Âtman, 2, 154; daily recitation of the V. enjoined for the hermit, 2, 155, 157; 7, 277; 8, 362; sacred learning more important than other good qualities, 2, 210 sq.; teaching and studying the V., the duty of Brâhma*n*as, 2, 215; 8, 182, 359; 25, 24 sq.; Snâtaka shall take pleasure in the study of the V., 2, 226; 25, 134; punishments for the *S*ûdra who listens to or recites or teaches the V., 2, 239; 33, 356; 34, 228 sq.; reciting the V. as a penance, 2, 275; 8, 119; 14, 30, 109, 116, 125 sq., 129, 311, 316 sq., 327; 25, 445 sq., 471, 477, 479, 482; one who divulges the V. to be cast off, penance for it, 2, 278; 14, 77; 25, 471, 471 n.; forgetting the V., a minor offence, penance for it, 2, 281; 7, 135, 176; 14, 4, 104; 25, 441 sq., 442 n.; penance for employing Vedic texts for unworthy people, 2, 286; sin of, and penance for, neglecting the daily recitation of the V., 2, 287; 7, 179, 253; 25, 442, 470; he who performs the three K*rikkh*ras becomes perfect in all the Vs., 2, 299, 299 sq. n.; *he who, not having studied the V., applies himself to another study, will degrade himself, and his progeny with him, to the state of a Sûdra*, 7, 119; should be taught only to worthy people, not to scorners and unworthy men, 7, 119–22; 14, 10 sq., 155 sq.; sin of teaching the V. for wages or learning it from a paid teacher, 7, 126 sq. and n., 137, 253; 25, 442; acquiring sacred knowledge, without his teacher's permission, from another constitutes theft of the V., 7, 127; 25, 51; he must not recite the V., while unclean, 7, 220; study of V. an obstacle to the attainment of the summum bonum, 8, 16 sq., 355; fruit of study of the V., 8, 81; 25, 27, 27 n.; K*r*ish*n*a cannot be seen in his divine form by the power of

V.-study, 8, 98 sq.; he who knows the Asvattha tree (symbol of life), knows the V., 8, 111, 111 sq. n.; meritoriousness of V.-study and V.-knowledge, 8, 114, 167, 376; 14, 130; 25, 47, 49, 60 sq., 131, 143, 152, 307, 385, 479, 482 sq., 491, 501, 504, 507 sq. and n.; knowledge of V. with the Âkhyânas, 8, 170 sq.; pupil goes to preceptor for Vedic learning, and performs the directions of the Vedic texts, 8, 269; question of final emancipation connected with knowledge of V., 8, 312; 34, xxvii; imparting instruction, and study (of V.), are acts of the quality of passion, 8, 324; he who understands the Kshetra*gñ*a, understands the V., 8, 390; Brâhma*n*as called 'friends of the hymns,' 10 (ii), xiii, 23; the teacher is called father because he gives instruction in the V., 14, 9; good conduct more important than study of the V., 14, 34 sq.; that V., two syllables of which are studied in the right manner, purifies, 14, 35; study of the V., a debt or sacrifice owing to the *Ri*shis, 14, 56; 25, 89; 49 (i), 100; sacred learning and austerities joined together are powerful, and destroy sin, 14, 129 sq.; touching a seller of the V. defiles, 14, 171, 183; by neglect of V.-study families are degraded, 14, 175 sq.; particular dress worn when reciting certain Vedic hymns, 14, 187; begging allowed for the sake of studying the V., 14, 240; Ana*s*natpârâya*n*a, recitation of the whole V. during a fast, 14, 307–9; the four Vs. belong to the lower knowledge, 15, 27; secret union of teacher and pupil through the recitation of the V., 15, 46; study of the V. a means of becoming a Muni, 15, 179; Brâhma*n*as seek to know the Self by the study of the V., 15, 179; 48, 699, 703; meditation on Yagus and Sâman, 15, 195; Brahmâ knows this which is hidden in Upanishads and V. as the Brahma-germ, 15, 256; ascetics who disregard the recitation of the V., 22, xxxii; study of V. grounded on desire for rewards, 25, 29; 'Connexion through the V.' with outcasts forbidden, 25, 37, 37 n., 105; Brahmasattra or teaching of the V., best occupation of Brâhma*n*as, 25, 49, 129, 129 sq. n., 419 sq.; who is entitled to instruction in the V., 25, 50 sq.; new birth through the gift of the V., 25, 57 sq., 61; knowledge of the V. more than wealth and age, 25, 58 sq.; to be recited at a *S*râddha, 25, 118; prayer for increase of V.-knowledge, 25, 123; Snâtaka during V.-recitation keeps his right arm uncovered, 25, 138; rules for the study of the Âra*n*yakas, 25, 148; 29, 141–50; gift of the V. surpasses all other gifts, 25, 165; status of men according to V.-study, 25, 178 n.; to be learnt by the king, 25, 222; the wealth of Brâhma*n*as, 25, 398; to be learnt by the three castes, to be taught by Brâhma*n*as only, 25, 401 sq. and n.; a performer of the Agnihotra must know the whole V., 25, 437; the foundation for the teaching of the Brâhma*n*a, 25, 447; the Gandharvas recite the V. to Vâ*k*, 26, 53; people make a living by reciting the V., 26, 129; teaching secret parts of the V., 29, 78; study of the V. and prayers equivalent to sacrifice, 29, 159 sq.; a prayer to avoid forgetting a lesson of the V., 29, 368; different vows for studying the V., 29, 404 sq.; 30, 69–77, 69 n.; ceremonies and sacrifices connected with the study of Vedic texts, 29, 405; 30, xxviii, 74–6, 75 sq. n., 161, 302 sq.; Tarpa*n*a at the end of the study of the whole V., 30, 246; *see also* Sacrifices (*b*); gift of the V., an instance of inalienable gift, 33, 314, 314 n.; Vedic texts have for their object that which is dependent on Nescience, 34, 8; men are entitled to the study of the V., 34, 196–8; also beings above men (gods, &c.) are qualified for the study and practice of the V., 34, 198 sq.; to the gods the V. is manifest of itself (without study), 34, 199; study of the V. demands as its antecedent the upanayana-ceremony, 34, 224; the four Vs. known to Milinda, 35, 6; Nâgasena, erudite in Vedic lore,

35, 34; story of a partridge (the Bodisat) who knew the V., 35, 286; the reading of the V. extends up to the comprehension of its purport, 38, 289; Scripture enjoins works for such only as understand the purport of the V., 38, 289; of him who has merely read the V. there is qualification for works, 38, 293; he who is unable to study his V.-lesson, should at least read a single divine word or verse, 44, 99, 101; *the study and teaching (of the V.) are a source of pleasure to him, he becomes ready-minded, and independent of others, and day by day he acquires wealth. He sleeps peacefully; he is the best physician for himself; and (peculiar) to him are restraint of the senses, delight in the one thing, growth of intelligence, fame, and the (task of) perfecting the people,* 44, 99; 'you are only the bearer of words, as it were, you do not understand their meaning, though you have learnt the V.,' says the monk to the Brâhma*n*a, 45, 52; the V. fears that a man of little reading may do it harm, 48, 91; handed on by an unbroken succession of pupils, 48, 487; 'reading' of the V., what it means, 48, 691 sq.; student of the V., *see* Brahma*k*ârin. *See also* Brahman (*b*), G*ñ*âna-kâ*nd*a, Karma-kâ*nd*a, Knowledge, *and* Teacher.

(*d*) PREROGATIVES OF THOSE WHO KNOW OR STUDY THE V.

Only a Brâhma*n*a learned in the V. is fit to initiate, 2, 2; persons who have studied certain portions of the V. or in whose family the study of the V. is hereditary sanctify the company at a *S*râddha, 2, 146, 146 n., 259; 7, 253 sq.; 14, 19; great meritoriousness of gifts made to *S*rotriyas and those who know the whole V., 2, 203, 203 n.; pardon may be given by an assemblage of persons learned in the V., 2, 245; gifts to Brâhma*n*as who have studied the V., 7, 274 sq.; veneration due to one who has studied the V., 8, 164 n.; 25, 100 sq.; a Brâhma*n*a unacquainted with the V. has no right to the prerogatives of his caste, 14, 16–18; four students of the four Vs. belong to a legal assembly, 14, 20; Brâhma*n*as versed in the V., though deformed, sanctify the company at a *S*râddha, 14, 52, 266 sq.; knowledge of the V. a chief qualification for *S*ish*t*as and members of a legal assembly, 14, 143–6; 25, 510 sq.; property which the king takes from men who died without heirs should be given to men well versed in the three Vs., 14, 179; the science of Brahman to be told to those who are versed in the V., 15, 41; a wife not to be chosen from a family in which the V. is not studied, 25, 76; families prosper by study of the V., 25, 86; only Brâhma*n*as knowing the V. shall receive alms, 25, 93; Brâhma*n*as learned in the V. to be entertained at *S*râddhas, 25, 99 sq., 102 sq., 107, 110; student of the V. allowed to beg, 25, 430; disputes of ascetics and sorcerers should be settled by persons versed in the three Vs., 33, 281; great merit of him who refrains from killing, even in self-defence, one who regularly recites the V., 33, 285; a person engaged in V.-study must not be put under restraint, 33, 288; persons acquainted with the V. shall be heads of associations, 33, 347; they say of him who has studied the V., 'he is like Agni,' 41, 146; works enjoined on him only who has learnt the V., 48, 689, 691 sq.

(*e*) SACREDNESS AND DEIFICATION OF THE V.

Om is the beginning of all the Vs., 1, xxiv, 2; 8, 353; speculations on *Rik* and Sâman, 1, 2, 7 sq., 10, 12–15; lucubrations on the four Vs., as connected with the rays of the sun, 1, 38–40; are the limbs of the Brâhmî-upanishad, 1, 153; speech and mind are the two pins that hold the wheels of the V., 1, 246; the great *Ri*shi, whose belly is the Yagus, the head the Sâman, the form the *Rik*, is to be known as being imperishable, as being Brahman, 1, 279; Vedic texts which purify from sin, 2, 275 sq. and n.; 14, 134, 311, 321, 328, 330; the Vs. are created, 7, 4; 8, 120; Vs. and Vedâṅgas in

Vishnu, 7, 10; sin of reviling the V., 7, 135; 25, 154, 441 sq., 442 n.; Lakshmî resides in the sound of the V., 7, 299; he who rises above the Divine word, the V., 8, 17, 73; a reservoir of water into which waters flow from all sides, 8, 48, 48 n.; the Vs. come from the Indestructible, 8, 54; Krishna is Om in all the Vs., 8, 74; Krishna alone to be learnt from the Vs., 8, 113 sq.; Krishna alone knows the Vs., 8, 113; those who are first in the V. are forms of the Brahman, 8, 161; 'he about whom the words of the V. were uttered, 8, 163, 163 n.; the V. cannot save him who is tainted by sin, 8, 163 sq.; 48, 592; constant talk in disparagement of gods, Brâhmanas and V., is dark conduct, 8, 320; *the Brâhmana makes the V. rich*, 14, 8; the syllable Om, the Vyâhritis, and the Sâvitrî are the five V.-offerings cleansing from sin, 14, 252; offerings and (Tarpana) libations made to the four Vs., 14, 255, 308, 320; 29, 121, 219 sq., 325; 30, 242, 244; Om, Brahman, Sun, and V. identified, 14, 278, 278 n., 316; rites securing success, connected with the four Vs., 14, 322 sq.; Yagus, *Rik*, Sâman, âdesa, and Atharvâṅgiras constitute the body of the inner Self, 15, 56; breathed forth from Brahman, 15, 111, 184; 34, xxxii, 19–22; 48, 386 sq.; all Vs. have their centre in speech, 15, 111, 184; Sâman and *Rik*, as husband and wife, 15, 220; 43, 14 sq.; God delivers the Vs. to Brahman (m.), 15, 266; all the four Vs. proceed from the Self, 15, 330; *what is taught in the V., that is true. What is said in the V., on that the wise keep their stand. Therefore let a Brâhman not read what is not of the V.*, 15, 343; greatness of the V., 25, 12, 504–7; an atheist and a scorner of the V., 25, 31, 31 n.; sacred syllables and Sâvitrî the essence of the V., 25, 44; he who cavils at the V. excluded from Srâddha meals, 25, 106; 'the eternal V.' quoted, 25, 127; the V. was revealed to the sages, 25, 477, 479; in the second order of existences caused by Goodness, 25, 495, 495 n.; the images of the *Rik* and Sâman, 26, 27; *Rik* and Sâman, the bay-steeds (of Indra), 26, 371; 'the *Rik* art thou, the Sâman I,' 29, 36, 168, 282; 30, 190; Yagus and Sâman, and Garutmat, 29, 49; Vs. with the metres, invoked in danger, 29, 232; 'the V. called son,' 30, 210; the four Vs. sacrificed at the medhâganana for the child, 30, 213; in the V. which is not the work of man no wish can be expressed, 34, 110; from the word of the V. the world, with the gods and other beings, originates, 34, 202–4; the V. is eternal, though the Rishis are the makers of sections, hymns, and so on, 34, 211–16, 317; 48, 332–4; seen by men of exalted vision (rishis), 34, 213, 223; the thousandfold progeny of Vâk, 41, 140; diseases healed by the V., 41, 141; by *Rik* and Sâman the gods were able to sustain Agni, 41, 266; *Rik*s, Sâmans, Atharvans, Yagus, as divine beings, 42, 161; *Rik*s and Yagus born from Time, 42, 225; hymn-verses and hymn-tunes as Apsaras, 43, 233; all the Vs. enter him who knows the mystery of a Brahmakârin's life, 44, 50; the *Rik*-texts are milk-offerings, the Yagus-texts ghee-offerings, the Sâman-texts Soma-offerings, the Atharvâṅgiras-texts fat-offerings, the other Vedic texts honey-offerings to the gods, 44, 96–8, 100 sq.; imperishable are the Vs., 44, 174; the Aṅgiras are the V., 44, 366; he for whom the revolving legend at the Asvamedha is recited secures for himself all the Vs., 44, 370; V. and sacrifices, being causes of sin, cannot save the sinner, 45, 140; Pragâpati creates the gods by means of the V., 48, 331 sq.; taught to Hiranyagarbha, 48, 334; the Âranyaka is churned from the Vs., 48, 528; of non-human origin, Aparântatamas their teacher, 48, 529; Sâṅkhya, Yoga, Vs., and Âranyakas, members of one another, 48, 530. *See also* Revelation, *and* Sruti.

(*f*) CONTENTS AND AUTHORITY OF THE V.

V. texts, either extant or lost, the sole or first source of the law,

2, 1, 46 sq., 93, 158, 171, 175, 237; 14, 1, 4, 143; 25, 30 sq., 508; 48, 426; slaughter of animals which is in accordance with the precepts of the V. is no slaughter at all; *because it is from the V. that law shines forth*, 7, 170; 25, 175 sq.; Vs. refer to action (ritual), not to devotion, 8, 16 sq., 48, 48 n., 156; 34, 24, 38 sqq.; 48, 148–56; Vs. relate only the effects of the three Qualities, 8, 17, 48; *Gñâna-kâ*nda and Karma-kâ*nd*a distinguished, 8, 17, 146; 34, xxix; rejected by Buddhism, 8, 25; the all-comprehending Vs. are always concerned with sacrifices, 8, 54, 54 n.; enjoin sacrifices, 8, 54, 62; 30, 323–5; the seat which those who know the V. declare to be indestructible, 8, 78; an authority for higher knowledge, for knowledge of Brahman, 8, 157, 159; 34, 23, 38, 317; Vs. proclaim the difference of Brahman from the universe, 8, 164; Brahman not to be seen in the four Vs., 8, 179 sq.; attacks on their authority, 8, 214; Vedic texts appealed to as authoritative, 8, 290, 305, 305 n., 322; to deny the authority of the V. is to destroy one's soul, 14, 62; opponents of the V. refuted, 15, 342; life of mortals, mentioned in the V., 25, 23; *S*ruti defined as V., 25, 31; the acts taught in the V., the best means of attaining supreme bliss, 25, 502 sq., 502 n.; cannot aim at conveying information about accomplished substances, 34, 21; prohibitory passages of the V., 34, 39 sq. and n.; authoritativeness of V. proved from its independence, basing on the original (eternal) connexion of the word with its sense, 34, 201, 295; Yoga practices enjoined in the V., 34, 297; the real sense of the V., that Brahman is the cause and matter of this world, 34, 361; *S*â*nd*ilya did not find highest bliss in the V., 34, 443; the Bhâgavata contains passages contradictory to the V., 34, 443; all parts of the V. are equally authoritative, and hence must all be assumed to have a meaning, 38, 156; Mantras enjoined in one V. only, are taken over into other Vs. also, 38, 274; the members of the sacrifice on which the meditations rest are taught in the three Vs., so also the meditations, 38, 282; the most essential subject in the V. is the Agnihotra, 45, 137 sq.; gives rise to the knowledge of the four chief ends of human action, 48, 6; Mantras and Arthavâdas, their purpose, 48, 327–30; about the powers of the gods we know from V. only, 48, 472; gives information as to the nature of good and evil works, 48, 487; doctrines of Kapila, &c., opposed to the V., 48, 520 sq.; only works enjoined by the V. subserve the knowledge of Brahman, 48, 522; non-acceptability of all views contrary to the V., 48, 523. *See also* Scripture, *and S*ruti.

(*g*) VEDIC SCHOOLS (*K*ARA*N*AS, *S*ÂKHÂS).

Influence of *S*âkhâs on certain Upanishads, 1, lxx; geographical distribution of Vedic schools, 2, xxxiv sq.; Gautama *K*ara*n*as of the Sâma-veda, 2, l sq.; a Parishad or a Brâhmanical school decides knotty points with regard to V.-study, 2, 44 sq. and n.; one *S*âkhâ of the V. should not invidiously be compared with others, 2, 113, 113 n.; there are Addhariya, Tittiriya, *Kh*andoka, *Kh*andava, and Brahma*k*ariya Brâhmans, 11, 171, 171 n.; Kâ*n*va and Mâdhyandina *S*âkhâs, 15, xxx; *S*vetâ*s*vataras and *K*arakas, 15, xxxi; Pippalâda-*S*âkhâ of the Atharva-veda, 15, xlii; Maitrâya*n*îya-*s*âkhâ of the Black Yagur-veda, 15, xliii sq., xlvii–l; Ga*n*a, Kula, *S*âkhâ, 22, 288 n.; Vedic schools supplanted by schools for special branches of learning, 25, xlvi–lvi; adherents of Rig-veda, Yagur-veda, and Sâma-veda who study an entire *S*âkhâ, 25, 102; *S*âkala and Bâshkala texts, 29, 220; a Brâhma*n*a of the Rauruki *S*âkhâ quoted, 30, 72; members of a Vedic school had only to digest their own Brâhma*n*a and Sa*m*hitâ, 34, x; sacrifices performed in different ways by members of different Vedic schools, 34, x; in the same *S*âkhâ also there is unity of vidyâ, 38, 214–16; although the

*S*âkhâs of the V. differ as to accents and the like, the vidyâs refer to all *S*âkhâs, 38, 272–4; Mantras and the like enjoined in one *S*âkhâ are taken over by other *S*âkhâs also, 38, 273 sq.; all *S*âkhâs teach the same doctrine, 48, 13, 28, 80, 676.

Vedagû, t.t., Buddha's definition of the term, 10 (ii), 91.

Vedanâs, t.t., sensations, pain arises from them, 10 (ii), 136 sq.

Vedâṅgas, the six, 2, 121; one who knows the Vedas and V., 2, 215; 25, 182, 182 n., 230, 334; created, 7, 4; Vedas and V. in Vish*n*u, 7, 10; teaching of the V., 7, 119; to be studied, 7, 123; one who knows the Nirukta among the members of a legal assembly, 25, xxvi, l, 510; mentioned in the Manu-sm*ri*ti, 25, xxvi, 56, 56 n., 58, 68, 73, 100, 110, 144; the V. and the special schools of science, 25, xlvi–lii; Brâhma*n*as versed in the V., 44, 66.

Vedânta, meaning and use of the word, 1, lxxxvi n.; 8, 246 n.; germs of V. doctrines, 8, 147, 159 n.; the oldest of the six systems of philosophy, 15, xxxiv; is monistic, Sâṅkhya is dualistic, 15, xxxv; the orthodox view of V. not Evolution, but Illusion, 15, xxxvii; through V. and Yoga anchorites become free in the worlds of Brahmâ, 15, 41; the highest mystery in the V. only to be taught to a son or pupil, 15, 267; doctrines of V. philosophy in Manu, 25, 3 n., 5 n.; doctrines concerning the origin of the world which are opposed to the V., 34, 289; philosophical view forming part of the V. system, 36, xxv; the V. heresy described in *G*aina books, but hardly mentioned by Buddhists, 45, xxv, xxv n.; V. or *S*ârîraka-doctrine connected with *G*aimini's doctrine, 48, 5; *S*ârîraka-*s*âstra, i.e. V., its relation to other philosophical systems, 48, 531. *See also* Philosophy.

Vedânta-mîmâ*m*sâ, or inquiry into the Brahman as being one with the embodied self, 34, 9, 9 n.

Vedânta-paribhâshâ, t.w., quoted 8, 220, 258 n., 286 n., 314 n., 333 n., 338 n., 339 n., 387 n.

Vedânta-sâra, t.w., quoted, 8, 186 n.

Vedânta-*s*âstra, or *S*ârîraka-*s*âstra (*S*ârîraka-mîmâ*m*sâ), 'Sâṅkhya system' explained as, 8, 123 n.; literature of V., 34, xi; its aim, 34, 190; 48, 7–9; by whom to be studied, 48, 255.

Vedânta-sûtras, Upanishads referred to in the, 1, lxix; posterior to the Bhagavadgîtâ, 8, 30–3; their date, 8, 31–3; called Bhikshu-sûtra? 8, 33; quoted, 8, 105 n., 188 n., 191 n.; *S*vetâ*s*vatara-upanishad referred to as 'revealed' in the V., 15, xxxi sq.; make frequent references to the views of earlier teachers, 34, xii, xix; the *G*ñâna-kâ*nd*a is systematized in the V. only, 34, xii; presuppose the Pûrva-Mîmâ*m*sâ-sûtras, 34, xiii; other names for the V., 34, xiv n., 9, 190; called Brahma-sûtras, 34, xiv n.; looked upon as an authoritative work, at a very early period, 34, xvi; numerous commentaries on them, 34, xvi; differences of Vedânta doctrine existed before their final composition, 34, xviii sqq.; conspectus of their contents, 34, xxxi–lxxxv; are throughout Mîmâ*m*sâ, 34, xlv; claim to be systematizations of the Upanishads, 34, cii; translated with *S*aṅkara's commentary, *Vols.* 34 and 38; have merely the purpose of stringing together the flowers of the Vedânta passages, 34, 17; translated with Râmânu*g*a's commentary, *Vol.* 48; their explanation by Bodhâyana, 48, 3.

Vedânta texts, meaning 'Upanishads,' 1, lxxxvi; 8, 8, 174 n.; 25, 213, 213 n., 215; K*ri*sh*n*a the author of the V. t., 8, 17 sq., 113; reward conferred by them, 25, 59, 59 n.; what the study of the V. t. presupposes, 34, xxxii, 9–15; Brahman the uniform topic of all V. t., 34, xxxii, 22–47, 190; why V. t. are to be studied, 34, 9; all the V. t. teach that the cause of the world is the intelligent Brahman, 34, 60 sq.; have a twofold purport; some of them aim at setting forth the nature of the highest Self, some at teaching the unity of the individual soul with

the highest Self, 34, 198; there is a conflict of V. t. with regard to the things created, but not with regard to the Lord as the cause of the world, 34, 263-6; do not contradict one another with regard to the mode of creation and similar topics, 34, 290; the cognitions of Brahman intimated by all the V. t. are identical, 38, 184-279; discussed in the *S*ârîraka-mîmâ*m*sâ, 48, 7; studied for the destruction of Nescience, 48, 39, 215; principle of unity the purport of all V. t., 48, 386 sq.; aim not only at knowledge, but also at the injunction of meditation, 48, 680. *See also* Scripture, *and* Upanishads.

Vedântins, speak of Mâyâ, 8, 331 n.; objections against the V., based on the relation of suffering and sufferer, 34, 376-81; doctrines of V. refuted, 45, ix, 236 sq., 343-5; aim to ascertain the nature of Brahman from Scripture, 48, 148-56; disputation between Ârdraka and a V., 45, 417 sq.

Vedapâragas, *see* Holy persons.

Vedârtha-sa*m*graha, a work of Râmânuga, 34, xxi; 48, 78; quoted, 48, 138.

Vedehiputto, metronymic of Agâta*s*atru, king of Magadha, q. v.

Vedi, *see* Altar.

Vedic Schools, *see* Veda (*g*).

Vedisâ, n. of a town, 10 (ii), 188.

Vêdvoi*s*t, a rich Karap, Zoroaster sent to, 47, xi, xxv.

Ve*g*ayanta, n. of a heavenly palace, 35, 11.

Vêh-âfrî*d*, n.p., 5, 138.

Vehicles, rules about the use of, for Bhikkhus and Bhikkhunîs, 17, 25-7; 20, 359 sq.

Vehicles (yâna), t.t.: in spite of the apparent trinity of v. there is only one vehicle, the Buddha-vehicle, which leads to omniscience, 21, xxix, 40-59, 78-82, 88-91, 128-41; the three v., to attain the summum bonum, and the one Buddha-vehicle, 21, xxxiv; the three v. imitations of the Â*s*ramas, 21, xxxiv n., xxxvi; the threefold v. only used in times of decay to designate the one Buddha-vehicle, 21, 42; the Buddha Padmaprabha will preach the law by means of the three v., 21, 66; the three v. of the disciples, of the Pratyekabuddhas, of the Bodhisattvas, only a device of Buddha's, 21, 78-82, 88-91, 134, 136 sq., 180-3, 189 sq.

Veils, *see* Hindrances.

Veins, *see* Arteries.

Velâmikânî: the wife of Bodhisatta Sudassana was either a lady of noble birth, or a V., 11, 287.

Ve*l*uvana, n.pl., 10 (ii), 85, 87.

Vema*k*itri, for Prâkrit Vema*k*itti, Pali Vepa*k*itti, Sk. Vipra*k*itti, a chief of demons, 21, 6, 6 n.

Vena, King, perished through want of humility, 25, 222; Niyoga arose in his rule, 25, 339, 339 n.

Ve*n*â, female disciple of Sambhûtavigaya, 22, 289.

Vendîdâd, contents of the, 4, viii-xii, lxx-lxxxvii; 37, 152-66, 152 sq. n.; is pre-Alexandrian, 4, lxv sq.; its fragmentary character, 4, lxx; translated, 4, 1-241; quoted, 5, 239, 239 n., 245, 250, 259, 270, 274, 310, 317, 323, 323 n., 340 sq. and n., 342, 348, 356, 360; 18, xxix sq.; 24, 331, 356; the revelation 'given against the Daêvas,' 31, 199 sq. n.; 37, 156, 402, 446; considered complete by the writers of the Persian Rivâyats, 37, 481 sq.

Vengantas, a Brahman clan, Upasena of the, 36, 270, 270 n.

Ve*n*udeva, a name of Garu*d*a, 45, 290, 290 n.

Vepa*k*itti, *see* Vema*k*itri.

Veracity, *see* Truth.

Vera*ñg*â, n.pl., Buddha takes a meal there, and the gods moisten it with the sap of life, 36, 37 sq., 38 n.

Verethraghna, n.d., who wears the glory made by Mazda, 4, 221, 221 n.; invoked and worshipped, 4, 248; 23, 6, 10, 15, 17, 32, 34, 36, 38; friendship between Mithra and V., 23, 137, 139; in the shape of a boar, with iron feet, &c., 23, 137, 235; ten incarnations in which V. appeared to Zarathu*s*tra, 23, 231-8; powers given by V. to Zarathu*s*tra, 23, 231, 238-40; the Bahrâm Ya*s*t dedicated to V., 23, 231-48; invoked in battle, 23, 242 sq., 246-8; his raven incarnation, 23, 294 sq.;

a conqueror of foes, 23, 327; V. the Ahura-given 'Blow of victory,' worshipped, 31, 205, 215, 219, 224, 309, 337, 337 n., 340, 348, 350, 385 sq., 391; 'slaying of V*ri*tra,' victory, 32, 198.
Vesâlî (Pali), Sk. Vai*s*âlî, the city of Magadha, 10 (ii), 188; Sârandada temple at V., 11, 4; Buddha at V., 11, 28–34, 40, 57, 59 sq.; 17, 108–24, 210; 19, 252–67; 20, 101 sqq., 189, 320 sq.; Buddha's followers spend the rainy season round about V., while he stays at Beluva, 11, 34 sq.; Buddha praises V. and its *K*etiyas, 11, 40; Buddha's farewell to V., 11, 64; 19, 282 sq. and n.; Dâgaba at V., 11, 134; the courtesan Ambapâlî of V., 17, 105, 171 sq.; the Li*kkh*avis of V., 17, 106–8; *see also* Li*kkh*avis; council of V., 19, xi, xiii, xv; 20, 386–414; the place of Buddha's Nirvâ*n*a, 19, 277; Buddha sets out on a journey from Râgagaha to V., 20, 98; a stronghold of *G*ainism, 22, xiii, xvi; Mahâvîra, a native of V., 22, 264; 45, 261.
Vesâlie, i.e. Vai*s*âlika, Mahâvîra called so, 22, xi.
Vesavâ*t*ika Ga*n*a, founded by Kâmarddhi, 22, 291.
Ve*s*kô, progeny, slain by Keresâsp, 37, 198, 198 n.
Vessa or Vessika, Pali for Vai*s*ya caste, 10 (ii), x. *See* Vai*s*ya.
Vessâmitta, n. of a *Ri*shi, 11, 172.
Vessantara, an earthquake caused by his unbounded generosity, 35, 170–8; why did V. give away his wife and children? 36, 114–32; etymology of the name, 36, 125 sq. n.
Vessava*n*a Kuvera, *see* Kubera.
Vetâla, a kind of ghost, kills him who does not lay him, 45, 105.
Vetara*n*î, *see* Vaitara*n*î.
Ve*th*adîpa, n.pl., a Dâgaba at, 11, 132, 135.
Vêvan, among the preparers of the renovation of the universe, 18, 78, 78 n.
Vibhu, the hall of Brahman, 1, 276, 277.
Vibhu-pramita, a name of the hall in the city of Brahman, 1, 132 n.
Vibhus: Savit*ri* accompanied by *Ri*bhus, V., and Vâgas, 44, 480.
Vibhvan, one of the *Ri*bhus, 32, 343, 345; 44, 381.
Vices, conquered by King Ambarîsha, 8, 301–3; the v. of priests, warriors, husbandmen, and artisans, 24, 105 sq.; death better than v., 25, 224; about oppression and greed, 37, 105; four heinous v., 37, 177. *See also* Morality, *and* Sin.
Victorious Ascendancy, worshipped, 31, 197, 205, 209, 215, 219, 224, 340, 385 sq., 391.
Vîdadhafshu, worshipped, 31, 349.
Vidagdha *S*âkalya, *see* Sâkalya.
Vidarbhî-kau*nd*inya, n. of a teacher, 15, 119, 187.
Vidârva, or Vidarva: the white horse, the son of V., 29, 131, 204, 327; 30, 238.
Vidas (n. of a family), make five Avadâna cuttings, 12, 192 n.
Vîda*s*t, n.p., 5, 141.
Vîda*t*-gau, n.p., 23, 219.
Videgha, *see* Mâthava.
Videha: Videgha = V., 12, 104 n., 106; Mahâvîra lived as householder in V., 22, 194, 256.
Videhadattâ, other name of Tri*s*alâ, 22, 193, 256.
Videhas, mentioned in the *S*atapatha-brâhma*n*a, 12, xlii sq. *See also* Kâ*s*î-Videhas.
Vidhart*ri*: Agni addressed as V. or Bhaga, 46, 186, 190.
Vidhât*ri*, a name of the Self, 15, 311; Vai*s*vadeva offering to V., 29, 86, 320; invoked at the house-building rite, 29, 347.
Vîdhâtu, Sraosha invoked against, 31, 304.
Vidhura: the Bodisat a wise man named V., 35, 288.
Vîdi-sravah, n.p., 23, 215.
Vîdôtu, Aêshma rushes along with, 23, 143; demon assaulting the embryo, 23, 183, 185, 187.
Vidura, has a discourse with Dh*ri*tarâsh*t*ra, 8, 136, 149 sq.; though born from a *S*ûdra mother, he possessed knowledge of Brahman, 34, 224, 228; 48, 338 sq.
Vidut, n. of a religious book, 42, xx.
Vidyâ, Sk. t.t. 'knowledge,' 34, lxvii–lxxvi, 6, 152. *See* Cognition, Knowledge, *and* Meditation.

Vidyâdharagopâla, founder of the Vidyâdharî *S*âkhâ, 22, 293.

Vidyâdharas, the palankin *K*andraprabhâ adorned with a train of couples of, 22, 197; a V. entered the mouth of a Dânava who had swallowed his wife, 35, 217; a V. committed adultery with a queen, was caught, and became invisible, 35, 217; enemies of the Dânavas, attendants of *S*iva, 35, 217, 217 n.; souls of V:, 48, 198.

Vidyâdharî *S*âkhâ of the Kau*t*ika Ga*n*a, 22, 292; founded by Vidyâdharagopâla, 22, 293.

Vidyâkara, a Brahman converted by Buddha, 49 (i), 191.

Vidyâra*n*ya, Upanishads eferred to by, 15, ix.

Vi*g*arâ ('age-less'), river in the world of Brahman, 1, 275–7; 34, lxxxi n.

Vi*g*aya, king of Dvârakâvatî, became a *G*aina monk, 45, 87, 87 n.

Vi*g*ayadevî, mother of Ma*nd*ikaputra and Mauryaputra, 22, 286 n.

Vi*g*ayaghôsha, a Brâhma*n*a, converted by the monk *G*ayaghôsha, 45, 136–41.

Vi*g*ayasutta, t.c., 10 (ii), 32 sq.

Vi*gñ*âna, t.t., 'knowledge' or 'understanding,' a name of the individual soul, 34, lvi; 48, 214, 760; is the self-consciousness springing up in the embryo, 34, 404 n.; Bauddhas maintain that only V. exists, 34, 418; 48, 502; a name of the internal organ, 38, 48, 82; 'he who dwells in V.,' 48, 214, 279; external things only inferred from V. or ideas, 48, 500;—vi*gñ*ânako*s*a, vi*gñ*ânamaya, he who consists of knowledge, the soul, 34, xxxviii, 66, 273; 38, 33; 48, 210, 213, 236, 384, 760. *See also* Understanding.

Vi*gñ*âna Bhikshu, acquainted with the Anugîtâ, 8, 197, 201–4.

Vi*gñ*ânaskandha, Buddhist t.t., group of knowledge, 34, 402, 402 n., 426 n.

Vi*gñ*ânâtman, t.t., cognitional self or soul, 34, 70, 120, 124, 174, 329.

Vi*gñ*ânavâdin, t.t., an idealist, 34, li, 401, 418 n.

Vi*gñ*âne*s*vara, quotes Medhâtithi, 25, cxxi.

Vihâras, Buddhist monasteries: Ânanda went into the V., 11, 95 sq., 95 n.; rules about cleaning V., 13, 158–60; 20, 272–84, 294–8; V. allowed to Bhikkhus, 13, 173; built by laymen for Bhikkhus, 13, 302–5; on the furniture allowed in the V., 17, 27–31; 20, 163–9, 209, 216–20; storerooms for robes to be appointed by the Sa*m*gha, 17, 201 sqq.; fastened with a bolt, 17, 234; meaning of the word V., 17, 386 sq. n.; rules about cloisters (*k*a*n*kama) and bathrooms (*g*antâghara) for the Bhikkhus, 20, 102–13, 103 n.; rules about pools and tanks for bathing, 20, 114 sq.; on the building of privies in the Ârâmas, 20, 154 sq.; on the building of V. and other dwellings for Bhikkhus, 20, 157–63, 170–9, 189–91, 208–16; to give V. to the Sa*m*gha is the best of gifts, 20, 160; pictures in V., 20, 172 sq.; rules about the apportioning of lodging-places in V., 20, 200–6; why should V. be built for the houseless monks? 36, 1–4; why do Bhikkhus trouble about superintending buildings? 36, 92–6; King Milinda has a V. built, 'the Milinda Vihâra,' 36, 374.

Vihârabhûmi, *see* Holy places.

Vi*k*aksha*n*â, the throne in the world of Brahman, 1, 276, 277.

Vi*k*ârabhûmi, *see* Holy places.

Vikar*n*a, a Kaurava, 8, 38.

Vikâ*s*a, t.t., expansion (of intelligence), 34, xxix.

Vikhanas, *see* Vaikhânasa-sûtra.

Vi*k*itravîrya, grandson of *S*a*m*tanu, 49 (i), 138 n.

Vilambâ, n. of a giantess, 21, 373.

Viligî, and Âligî, snake-deities, 42, 28.

Vilikhat, a demon harassing children, 30, 211.

Village-boundaries, contiguous in time of peace, 44, 306 sq.

Vimala, n.p., receives the upasampadâ ordination from Buddha, 13, 110 sq.

Vimala, a *R*ishi, defeated by the love-god, 19, 149.

Vimala, n. of a Tîrthakara, 22, 280.

Vimala, n. of a Bhikshu, 49 (ii), 2.

Vimala, a world, in it the daughter

of the Nâga-king Sâgara appears as a Buddha, 21, 253 sq.
Vimaladatta, n. of a king, 21, 380.
Vimaladattâ, wife of King *S*ubhavyûha, converted with all the other women of the harem, became afterwards a Bodhisattva, 21, 419–30.
Vimalagarbha, prince, converts his father *S*ubhavyûha, 21, 419–30; is reborn as Bhaisha*g*yarâ*g*a, 21, 430.
Vimalânana, the 7th Tathâgata, 49 (ii), 6.
Vimalanetra, the 48th Tathâgata, 21, 22, 27; 49 (ii), 6.
Vimalanetra, prince, converts his father *S*ubhavyûha, 21, 419–30; is reborn as Bhaisha*g*yarâ*g*asamudgata, 21, 430.
Vimalaprabha, the 9th Tathâgata, 49 (ii), 6.
Vimânas, or palaces of the gods: Mahâvîra descended from the V. Pushpottara, 22, 190, 218; the Laukântika V. are eightfold and infinite in number, 22, 195; Arish*t*anemi descended from the V. Aparâgita, 22, 276; *Ri*shabha descended from the V. called Sarvârthasiddha, 22, 281.
Vimatisamudghâtin, son of a former Buddha *K*andrasûryapradîpa, 21, 19.
Vimokkhâ, Pali t.t., stages of deliverance, 11, 213 n. *See* Deliverance, *and* Meditation (*b*).
Vînâsp, n.p., 5, 146.
Vinatâ, Garu*da*, son of, 8, 90, 90 n.
Vinaya, 'Discipline,' rules of the Buddhist Order, taught under the head of Dhamma, 10 (i), xxxiii; Oldenberg's researches into the growth of the V., 10 (i), xxxiv; oral tradition to be considered as authority for the true teaching of Buddha, when agreeing with Scripture and V., 11, 67–70; regulations concerning putting and answering questions about V., 13, 262 sq.; the rehearsal of the V. of the Five Hundred at Râgagaha, 20, 370–85; Upâli and Ânanda examined about V. regulations, 20, 374–7; discussion about the minor and lesser rules at the council of Râgagaha, 20, 377–9.
Vinaya-pi*t*aka, its early date, 10 (i), xxxii; 13, xxi sqq.; the Dhamma*k*akkappavattana-sutta in the V., Mahâ Vagga, 11, 139; its divisions, and what it is, 13, ix; the Pâtimokkha, the nucleus of the V., 13, ix–xix; 30, xxxiv; the Suttavibhaṅga contains an old commentary of the Pâtimokkha, 13, xv–xix; the Sutta-vibhaṅga built up of three portions, 13, xviii sq.; the nature and contents of the Khandakas, 13, xix sqq.; the Parivâra-pâ*th*a, a later addition to the V., 13, xxiii sq.; peculiar use of the term Suttavibhaṅga, 13, xxx sq.; translated into Chinese, 19, xi–xiii; different copies of the V. brought to China from Ceylon and from Patna, 19, xxvi sq.; life of Buddha in the V., 19, xxvi–xxviii; on the division of the V. into Bhâ*n*avâras or Portions for Recitation, 20, 415–18; kept secret from laymen, 35, 264–8, 264 n., 265 n. *See also* Tipi*t*aka.
Vinayavâda, *see* Philosophy.
Vindâ*d*-i-pê*d*âk, n.p., 5, 146 sq.
Vindhya, one of the princes of mountains, 8, 346.
Vindhyakosh*th*a, n.pl., the Muni Arâ*d*a lives on, 49 (i), 77.
Vinirbhoga, n. of an aeon, 21, 354.
Vinîtâ, n.pl., *Ri*shabha entered the state of houselessness in, 22, 283.
Viññâna, *see* Consciousness, *and* Vi*g*ñâna.
Vipa*sk*it, invoked at birth ceremonies, 30, 55.
Vipassî, a saint, afflicted with disease, 36, 10.
Vipa*s*yin, the first of the seven Tathâgatas, 21, 193.
Vîpînî*d*ak, 'the paederast,' one of the seven heinous sinners, 18, 218, 218 n.
Viprabandhu, one of the Gaupâyanas, 46, 415.
Vipra*k*itti, n. of a teacher, 15, 120, 187. *See also* Vema*k*itri.
Vipras, satiated at the Tarpa*n*a, 29, 219. *See also* Superhuman beings.
Vîptak, 'the pathic,' one of the seven heinous sinners, 18, 217 sq. and n.
Vipula, the chief of Râ*g*agaha hills, 36, 55.

Vîra, a disciple of A*s*vaghosha, wrote a treatise on 'non-individuality,' 19, xxxiii.
Vîrabhadra, a Ga*n*adhara of Pâr*s*va, 22, 274.
Vîrâf, had seven sisters who were as wives to him, 18, 397 sq.
Virafsang, son of Tâz, 5, 132.
Virâ*g*, Sk., name of a metre of ten syllables, 1, 59 n.; 26, 68; 29, 145; 41, 183, 196; 44, 65, 335, 335 n., 403 n., 408, 418, 459; 46, 55; food identified with V., 1, 59 sq.; 30, 175; 43, 12, 38, 50, 54, 87, 204; 44, 291, 408, 418; resembles the sacrifice (with ten utensils), 12, 11, 11 n.; 44, 3; an incomplete V., 12, 390; 26, 374; wife of Indra, 15, 159; connected with Manu, 25, lxiv, 14; Somasads, sons of V., 25, 111; Soma is of V. nature, 26, 68; consists of thirty syllables, 26, 112; 43, 94, 385; 44, 291, 310 n.; water, the milk of Padyâ V., 29, 97 sq., 199, 274; 30, 129, 172; V. and Svarâg, 30, 167; the âtman purushavidha identified with the V. of the latter Vedânta, 34, cvi, cxxiii sq.; Varu*n*a gained the V. metre, 41, 40 n.; Agni is the V., 41, 183, 196, 297; 43, 70, 87, 204; in a list of gods, 42, 80; the shining female heaven (dawn), 42, 211, 667; begotten by the Brahma*k*ârin (the sun), 42, 215; became Indra, the ruler, 42, 216; Prâ*n*a is V., 42, 219; Vâ*k* V., daughter of Kâma, 42, 221, 593; tigers and two-year-old kine were produced in the form of V., 43, 38 sq.; the undiminished V. is the world of Indra, 43, 94; the sacrifice is V., 44, 3, 459; identified with *S*rî, beauty and prosperity, 44, 65; the meeting of the Agnihotra cow and the calf is the V., 44, 81; Indra learnt the V. from Vasish*th*a, 44, 212; is this earth, 44, 212; Varu*n*a is V., the lord of food, 44, 222; created by Pragâpati, 44, 310; is the metre belonging to all the gods, 44, 351; consists of forty syllables, 44, 403, 403 n.; Purusha born from the V., and V. from Purusha, 44, 403 sq.
Vira*g*a, n. of the Buddha-field of the Padmaprabha, 21, 66, 68.
Vira*g*â, river in the world of Brahman, 48, 648.
Vira*g*a*h*prabha, n. of a Tathâgata, 49 (ii), 66.
Vîrâspa, son of Karesna, 23, 209.
Virâ*t*a, n. of a warrior, 8, 37, 39.
Viriyavat, *see* Dhîra.
Vîrô*d* religion, perhaps Mohammedanism, 24, 127, 127 n.
Viro*k*ana and Indra as pupils of Pragâpati, 1, 134–42.
Virtues: penance, liberality, righteousness, kindness, truthfulness form the sacrificial gifts at a sacrifice performed in thought only, 1, 51; lists of faults and v., 2, 78; 8, 242 sq.; enumeration of v. in witnesses, 7, 49; fruits of v. lost by false evidence, 7, 51; v. included in the definition of knowledge, 8, 103; truth, straightforwardness, modesty, restraint, purity, knowledge: the six impediments in the way of respect and delusion, 8, 162, 162 n.; a man who is a friend of all, who moves among all beings as if they were like himself, who is self-controlled, pure, free from vanity and egoism, is released, 8, 246; day and night destroy the fruit of man's righteousness in yonder world, 12, 344; liberality, truthfulness, and sympathy are better than any penances, 14, 328; the triad of subduing, giving, and mercy taught as Da Da Da, 15, 189 sq.; chief v. in the different ages, 25, 23 sq.;—the four v., viz. truth, justice, firmness, and liberality, 10 (ii), 31; *virtue's the base*, 35, 53, 306; how v. is stronger than vice, 36, 144–57; v. is the place in which Nirvâ*n*a is realized, 36, 203 sq.; the categories of v. taught by Buddha, 36, 214 sq.; only the v. of a virtuous man are a place of pilgrimage, 49 (i), 74; v. according to Buddha's precepts, 49 (ii), 188; *see also* Karman, Pâramitâs, Perfection, *and* Sîla;—five v. of a righteous Zoroastrian, 4, 285–7, 286 n.; every man in this world may love v., 4, 295; of liberality, truth, gratitude, wisdom, mindfulness, and contentment, 24, 26; heaven the reward of v., 31, 390; origins of v. and vice, 37, 62;

five excellences, 37, 179; things to be amassed in youth, 37, 179 sq.; merit and benefits of teaching v. to all, 37, 348–51, 354–7; virtuous deeds promoted by teaching v., 37, 372 sq., 377 sq.;—*it is virtue that moves Heaven; there is no distance to which it does not reach. Pride brings loss, and humility receives increase; this is the way of Heaven*, 3, 52; nine v. in conduct, 3, 54 sq., 221; *there is no invariable model of v.; a supreme regard to what is good gives the model of it*, 3, 102; the five v., 3, 129, 466 n.; the three v., 3, 140, 144 sq., 144 n., 260, 260 n.; love of v., one of the five sources of happiness, 3, 149; bright v. more fragrant than the millet, 3, 232; the end of punishment is to promote v., 3, 254 sq., 260, 264; the cherishing of v. secures repose, 3, 409 sq., 409 n.; outward demeanour is an indication of inward v.: admonitions to practise them both, 3, 413–17; filial piety as the root of all v., 3, 462, 465–88, 466 n.; the ten v., 27, 379 sq.; virtuous men selected to take part in sacrificial ceremonies, 27, 409 sq., 410 n.; the ancient kings paid honour to the virtuous, 28, 216; wisdom, benevolence, fortitude, three universal v., 28, 313; v. is light as a hair, but few can bear its burden, 28, 329, 335; v. is the root, wealth is the branches, 28, 420; purity and stillness, the chief v., 39, 88; v. and wisdom become weapons of contention, when used with a view to display, 39, 204. *See also* Morality.

Virûdhaka, n. of a god, 21, 4; one of the four rulers of the cardinal points, pronounces talismanic words for the benefit of preachers, 21, 373.

Virûpa, n.p., 46, 42.

Virûpâksha, n. of a god, 21, 4; worshipped at the Tarpana, 29, 121, 149.

Vis, i.e. the Vaisya caste. *See* Caste, *and* Vaisya.

Vîsadha, n.p., 23, 210.

Vîsak, n.p., 5, 135.

Visâkhâ Migâramâtâ, the mother of Migâra, a pious lay devotee, 10 (ii), 131; V. and her grandson, 13, 320; makes various presents to Buddha and the Samgha, 17, 216–25, 227 sq.; 20, 130, 208; questions Buddha with regard to the behaviour towards litigious Bhikkhus, 17, 318.

Visâla, n.d., worshipped at the Âgrahayana festival, 29, 131.

Visâlâ, n. of the palankin of the Arhat Pârsva, 22, 273.

Vîsaris, *see* Vîzaresha.

Vîsasêna, *see* Vishvaksena.

Viseshamati, one of the sixteen virtuous men, 21, 4; son of a former Buddha, 21, 19.

Viseshas, t.t., elements, 15, 313.

Vishavidyâ, Sk., science of venoms, 44, 367 n.

Vishnu, the god.

(*a*) In mythology.
(*b*) In mysticism and philosophy.
(*c*) Worship of V.

(*a*) In mythology.

Epithets and names of V., 7, xxviii sq., 9–11, 292–6; assumed the shape of a boar and raised up the earth from the water, 7, 1–5, 9, 296; 48, 95; resides in the Kshîroda or milk-ocean, 7, 6 sq.; seated on Sesha, the serpent, 7, 7 sq.; praised by the goddess of the Earth, 7, 9–11; world of V., 7, 108, 156; colloquy of V. and the goddess of Earth, 7, 291–7; Krishna is V. among the Âdityas, 8, 88, 94 sq.; Parasurâma an incarnation of V., 8, 221; the presiding deity of the feet and of motion, 8, 338; is the chief among the strong, 8, 346; is the ruler of men, demigods, gods, demons, and Nâgas, 8, 347; the three steps of V., 12, 15, 268–70; 26, 62 n., 130, 133, 155 sq.; 30, 191 sq.; 32, 52, 133 sq.; 44, 179, 399, 399 n.; 45, 86 n.; legend of the dwarf V. through whom the gods obtained the whole world, 12, 59–61, 59 sq. n.; 41, 55, 55 n.; the veshya of V., 12, 73, 73 n.; the wide-striding, 15, 45, 53; 26, 162 sq., 171, 352; 32, 363; 42, 89; called Visvabhrit, 15, 315; V. in the sun, V. is the sun, 15, 318; 44, 442 sq.; omitted in the enumeration of gods gathering round

Buddha, 21, 5 n.; the Avatâras of V., and the Buddhistical and Gaina belief in innumerable Buddhas or Tîrthakaras, 22, xxxiv; Vishnu-smriti revealed by the god V., 25, xxi; called Mârtânda, 26, 12 n.; identified with Soma, 26, 82 sq., 126, 126 n., 160 sq.; the day is Agni, the night Soma, and V. is what is between the two, 26, 108; part of the thunderbolt, 26, 108, 108 n.; props and holds fast the earth, 26, 130, 133; companion of Indra, esp. in his fight against Vritra, 26, 171 sq.; 32, 127, 133 sq.; 41, 138 sq., 396; *see also* Indra (*e*); the highest step of V., fixed like an eye in the heaven, 26, 172; lord of mountains, 29, 280; the whitish one, the lord of the beings that dwell in the quarters, 30, 237; saved the Soma, and the Maruts sat down around it, 32, 127, 133–7; connected with the Maruts, 32, 134; called vrishan, 32, 144; holds the kakra, 32, 230; V. esha or the rapid V., or Soma = rain, 32, 296, 306, 403; the terrible, the wanderer, 32, 363; Agni and V. are all the deities, Agni being the lower end, V. the upper end, 41, 44; when an embryo, was a span long, 41, 235, 255, 260, 268, 393; identical with Agni, 41, 235, 235 n., 276; 46, 186; became an eater of food, 41, 393, 395; the four Vedas sprung from V., 42, lii; in a list of gods, 42, 80, 160, 221; lord of the nadir, 42, 193, 655; has stepped out upon the earth, 42, 200; passes through three regions, 42, 251; lordship bestowed on V., 43, 68; V. Sipivishta the bald (?), 44, 9, 207, 293, 293 n.; entered the world at three places, 44, 388; V. with other gods performs sacrifice at Kurukshetra: he excels, becomes overweening, and his head is cut off and becomes the sun, 44, 441 sq.; is the most excellent of the gods, 44, 442; Svayambhû, i. e. V., sleeping on the ocean, 45, 49 n.; Venu = V.? 45, 290 n.; the wide-ruling V., 46, 186, 246, 326; Agni invoked to bring V. to the sacrifice, 46, 316; Agni announces the sins of men to V., 46, 326; the footprint of V. in the highest place, 46, 371; water is the body of V., 48, 423; Brahman, V., and Siva, 49 (i), 196 sq., 200. *See also* Ganârdana, Hari, Kesava, Krishna, *and* Vâsudeva.

(*b*) In mysticism and philosophy.

V. is the sacrifice, 7, 1–3, 9; 12, 15, 19, 27, 59–61, 85, 94, 128, 190, 214 sq., 268; 26, 12, 35, 155 sq., 160, 162, 165, 290, 352, 390, 413, 436; 41, 45, 113, 118, 235 n., 276; 44, 9, 179, 293, 300, 442 sq.; is composed of the Vedas and Vedângas, 7, 10; worship of V. (Kesava) who has become one with Brahman, and of V. absorbed in meditation, 7, 156, 156 sq. n.; is the Self of all fields, i.e. bodies, 7, 287; praise of V. as the supreme being, the Lord of all, 7, 292–7; 48, 608; pervades the three worlds, 7, 298; 48, 92 sq.; in the Anugîtâ, 8, 219–21; the emancipated sage is V., 8, 220 sq., 345; one of the ten fires at the allegorical sacrifice of the sense-organs, 8, 261; a name of the highest Self, 8, 332; 15, 311; 34, 239; 48, 87 sq., 92 sq., 266; the self-existent V. is the Lord in the primary creations, 8, 333; is the ruler and creator, the uncreated Hari, 8, 347; the great V., full of the Brahman, is the king of kings over all, 8, 347; the unthinkable, self-existent V. is identical with Brahman, 8, 354; 15, 302 sq., 322, 338; 34, xxxi n.; 48, 89 sq., 92 sq., 266, 355, 358; *the great V., who is full of the Brahman, and than whom there is no higher being in these three worlds, is the source of all the universe*, 8, 354; through V. exists the earth, 14, 134; the highest place of V., the place whence a man is not born again, the highest abode, 15, 13, 324; 34, 239, 245 sq.; 38, 205, 241, 391; 48, 87 sq., 266, 269, 272, 313, 355, 358, 363; that part of the Self which belongs to sattva is V., 15, 304; identified with the power of motion, 25, 512; he who is consecrated becomes V., 26, 29; Yagus are V., 26, 436; in the Bhagavad-gîtâ, 34, cxxvi; from out of V. the gods formed the guest-offering, 44, 138; Hiranyagarbha, Hari, Sankara,

Pradhâna, Time, and the totality of embodied souls are forms of V., 48, 93; the soul of the Brahma-egg (world), 48, 127; is the Evolved, the Supreme Person under the name of V. glorified, 48, 359; *from V. there sprang the world and in him it abides; he makes this world persist and he rules it—he is the world*, 48, 410, 461.

(*c*) WORSHIP OF V.

The sacrificer makes the V.-strides at the end of the sacrifice, 2, 118, 118 n.; 12, 268–70; 44, 120; worship of Bhagavat Vâsudeva or V., 7, xxvii–xxx, 208–11, 266, 268 sq.; worship of V. (called Vâsudeva, or Ke*s*ava) as an expiatory ceremony, 7, 155 sq.; meditation on Bhagavat Vâsudeva or V., 7, 289; meditation on Purusha V., 7, 290 sq.; oblations for Agni and V., 12, 7; 26, 88, 364 n.; the pavitras or purifying ku*s*a blades dedicated to V., 12, 19; 29, 25, 378; 30, 33; 41, 84; prayer to V., a penance or expiation, 12, 27, 27 n., 214 sq.; 26, 35, 412 sq.; 30, 30; invoked to protect the sacrifice, 12, 94, 190; 26, 290 sq.; the priest propitiates V., 12, 128; worship of V. alluded to in Upanishads, 15, l, 45, 53; invoked in a prayer at conception, 15, 221; 29, 385; 30, 51, 199; offerings to V., 26, 55, 87 sq., 106–8, 364 n., 390; 29, 327; 30, 91, 151; 44, 3 n.; the Soma-cart belongs to V., 26, 131, 133 sq., 137, 139 sq.; invoked and worshipped, 26, 159 sq., 352; 29, 27, 84, 86, 121, 127, 136, 149, 219, 280, 398; 30, 61, 244; 41, 38, 241; the sacrificial stake sacred to V., 26, 162–4, 172; Soma libations for V., 26, 295; 32, 305; morning offering to V., 29, 14; worshipped at the new moon sacrifice, 29, 17 n.; invoked at the ceremony of the seven steps, 29, 284; invoked in company with the Maruts, 32, 305, 363–5; contemplated in the sacred *S*âlagrâm, 34, 126, 178; contemplated in an image, 38, 338, 339, 345; offering to Agni and V., Indra and V., and to V., 41, 54 sq., 54 n.; the king, at the consecration, makes the three V.-steps, 41, 96; oblations to Agni, Soma, and V. at the Da*s*apeya, 41, 113 sq., 116 n., 118; the V.-strides at the building of the altar, 41, 261, 275–83, 286–90; 43, 298; deity of Dvipadâ metre, 43, 331; the Mahâvîra pot (at the Pravargya) the head of V., 44, xlviii; rice pap for V. *S*ipivish*t*a (the Bald), 44, 9; when the Agnihotra milk belongs to V., 44, 81; by performing the guest-offering they sacrifice to V., and become V., 44, 141; expiatory oblation to V., to V. *S*ipivish*t*a, V. Narandhisha, V. Âprîtapâ in case of certain mishaps at the Soma-sacrifice, 44, 207–9; worshipped at the A*s*vamedha, 44, 281, 291 n., 293; a dwarfish cow sacrificed to V. at the A*s*vamedha, 44, 300.

Vish*n*u, Ârya, of the Mâ*th*ara gotra, a Sthavira, 22, 294.

Vish*n*ukumâra, elder brother of Mahâpadma, 45, 86 n.

Vish*n*u-purâ*n*a, quoted, 48, 780 sq.

Vish*n*u-sm*ri*ti, belongs to the *K*ârâya*n*îya-kâ*th*aka *S*âkhâ of the Black Yagur-veda, and is closely connected with the Kâ*th*aka G*ri*hya-sûtra, 7, ix–xvi, xxv–xxvii; V. and Vâsish*th*a Dharma-sûtras, 7, xvi–xx; 14, xxi sq., xxv; and Baudhâyana's Dharma-sûtra, 7, xix sq.; 14, xxxiv; and Gautama Dharma-sûtra, 7, xx; and Yâg*ñ*avalkya-sm*ri*ti, 7, xx–xxii, xxxii; and Manu-sm*ri*ti, 7, xxii–xxvii, xxxii; 25, xliv, lxvi, lxix sq., lxxii; Vish*n*uitic tendencies in it, 7, xxvii; 25, lv; its more modern ingredients, 7, xxvii–xxxii; archaic forms in it, 7, xxxii; its date, 7, xxxii sq.; 25, cxxii sq.; 33, xvi sq.; editions and MSS. of the V., 7, xxxiii sq.; revealed by the god Vish*n*u, 25, xxi; based on a Kâ*th*aka Dharma-sûtra, 25, xxi, xxiii, lxvi, lxx; deficient in systematic arrangement, 25, civ n.

Vishuvat, t.t., *see* Sacrifice (*j*).

Vishvaksena (Vîsasêna), i.e. K*ri*sh*n*a, the best of warriors, 45, 290, 290 n.

Vi*s*ish*t*a*k*âritra, n. of a chief Bodhisattva, 21, 284, 364, 367, 394, 442.

Vispân-fryâ, n.p., 5, 135, 135 n.

Visparad, or Vîspêrad, studied by priests, 18, 153, 153 n.; translated, 31, 333–64, 335 n.; the V. service, 37, 170, 170 n.

Vîspa-taurvairi, other name of Eredat-fedhri, 23, 226; Saoshyant, son of V., 23, 307.

Vîspataurvashi, n. of a holy woman, 23, 225.

Vîspa-thaurvô-asti, Asta-aurvant, son of, 23, 117, 279.

Vîspêrad, *see* Visparad.

Vîsrûta, n.p., 23, 217.

Vîsrûtâra, n.p., 23, 216.

Vissakamma, *see* Visvakarman.

Vîstâspa, Vistâsp, or Kaî-Vistâsp (Pers. Gûstâsp), king, Zoroaster brought the Nasks to, 4, xxxvii; protector of Zarathustra, champion of Zoroastrianism, 4, lxiii; 18, 444, 444 n.; 23, 204 sq., 306; 24, 40, 40 n.; 31, 133, 142, 166 n., 169 sq., 173, 173 n., 250; 37, 285, 389, 430; 47, xxi–xxiii, 43; a human incarnation of Sraosha, 4, 101 n.; routed Aregat-aspa (Argâsp), 5, 40, 218; 23, 79–81, 84; 37, 412; 47, xi, 68–70, 68 n., 72 sq., 75, 126; fire established at the Rôshan mountain under King V., 5, 63 sq.; Pêshyôtanû, son of V., 5, 117, 142, 142 n.; 37, 203, 203 n.; his descendants, 5, 137; son of Lôharâsp, 5, 137; 37, 29, 29 n.; 47, xiii; was 120 years, 5, 150; converted by Zarathustra, 5, 187; 23, 78, 78 n.; 37, 181, 230, 235, 424, 435, 442; 47, xi, xv, xxv sq., xxx, 16, 50, 64–77, 123–5, 164; accepts the religion of Zoroaster and destroys the idols, 5, 193; the golden reign of King V., 5, 198, 212 sq.; 47, 16; Fravashi of V. worshipped, 5, 336, 336 n.; 23, 204 sq.; 31, 273, 278; exalted like Kaî-V., 18, 90, 90 n.; his care for the sacred fire, 18, 380; descended from Nôdar, the Naotaride, 23, 77; 37, 262; 47, 147; lord of swift horses, 23, 77, 77 n.; 37, 220; worships Drvâspa, 23, 117; his conquests, 23, 117 sq., 117 n., 279 sq., 306; 24, 57, 65; his wife Hutaosa, 23, 257; worships Ashi Vanguhi, 23, 279 sq., 282; kingly glory clave to V., 23, 306, 308; 47, 117; Zarathustra exhorts V. to adhere to the Law of Mazda, 23, 324, 330–45; Zarathustra pronounces blessings on V., 23, 324–30; 31, 15, 22; the V. Yast, 23, 324–45; shared heaven through wisdom, 24, 102; Gâmâspa and V., 31, 76, 76 n.; Kavi V. reached wisdom (Kisti), 31, 177, 185; Kavi V. offers prayers, &c., to Ahura-Mazda, 31, 190 sq.; caused the Avesta to be written, 37, xxxi; particulars about King V., 37, 23–5, 24 sq. n.; family of V., 37, 97, 97 n.; Hûmâî of the family of V., 37, 220; warriors of V., 37, 227; a priest at the renovation, 37, 262, 355; praise of V., 37, 280 sq., 297, 299; is privileged, 37, 369; suitable for sovereignty on account of Magianship, 37, 397; descendant of Gâyômard, through the Pêsdâdian and Kayânian rulers, 47, x; his soul in heaven, 47, xi; sees his future position in heaven, 47, xxiii; V. and Zoroastrian chronology, 47, xxvii; his accession, 47, xxix; his date, 47, xxxviii sq.; those of the region of King V., 47, 3; revelation brought to King V., 47, 15; Zoroaster cures the horse of V., 47, 66, 66 n.; Ashavahistô gives him Hôm to drink, 47, 70 sq.; presented with a heavenly chariot by Srîtô, 47, 77–81, 126; Iran after V., 47, 82, 93.

Vistauru, son of Naotara (Gustahm, son of Nôdar), 23, 71 sq., 206, 206 n.

Vistîrnavatî, n. of the world of the Buddha Sâlendrarâga, 21, 429.

Visuddhakâritra, n. of a chief Bodhisattva, 21, 284.

Visva, a name of Pragâpati, 15, 292, 304.

Visvadhâyas, 'all-sustaining,' mystic name of a cow milked at the sacrifice, 12, 179 n., 188, 188 n.

Visvakarman, 'all-doing,' mystic name of a cow milked at the sacrifice, 12, 179 n., 188, 188 n.

Visvakarman, n.d., Pali Vissakamma, sent by Sakka to build a mansion for Sudassana, 11, 264–7; oblations to V., 12, 408 n., 419; 30, 126; 43, 266–9, 347; 44, 76 n., 77, 207; invoked, 26, 123; 41, 264; Soma libation for V. or Indra V.,

26, 431 sq., 431 n.; worshipped at domestic rites, 29, 127, 136; invoked at the house-building rite, 29, 347; man (purusha) sacrificed for V., 41, 162; Indra and Agni and V. saw the air, 41, 188; Indra, Agni, and V. assist in laying down the third layer of the altar, 41, 188, 190; 43, 41–3, 47; is Pragâpati, 41, 378; 43, 28, 37, 233; begat living beings from Vâ*k*, 41, 407; 44, 202 sq.; sought out the earth by means of oblations, 42, 206; Rohita arranged a sacrifice for V., 42, 209; the Creator, 42, 209; 43, xiv; is Vâyu, 43, 6, 106; the *R*ishi V. is speech, 43, 12, 28; Agni is V., 43, 189 sq., 204, 266–8, 266 n.; V. Bhauvana performed the Sarvamedha, and by it overpassed all beings, 44, 421.

Vi*s*va*k*arsha*n*i, *see* Dyumna V. Âtreya.

Vi*s*vâ*k*î, an Apsaras, 43, 107; V. and the seer-king Yayâti, 49 (i), 45.

Vi*s*vâmitra Gâthina, the *R*ishi, 'was the friend of all,' 1, 170; author of Vedic hymns, the *R*ishi of the 3rd Ma*nd*ala of the Rig-veda, 1, 215; 12, xvii; 46, 222, 230, 233, 237, 241, 245, 249, 253, 257, 260, 262, 264, 289, 291, 293, 297, 300, 304; legend of V. and Indra, 1, 218 sq., 220; V. and other sages ask Brahman about final emancipation, 8, 314; *S*una*hs*epa became the son of V., 14, 88; 44, xxxv; one of the seven *R*ishis, 15, 106; seduced by the nymph Gh*r*itâ*k*î, 19, 39 sq.; 49 (i), 39; the *R*ishi V. is the ear, 25, 10; became a Brâhma*n*a, 25, 222, 222 n.; tried to create other worlds, 25, 398 n.; accepted the haunch of a dog from a *Kand*âla, 25, 425, 425 n.; worshipped at the Tarpa*n*a, 29, 122, 220; 30, 244; Madhu*kkh*andas possibly of the V. family, 46, 2; Agni kindled by the Vs., 46, 222; Agni invoked by the Vs., 46, 277; another name, or a branch of the Ku*s*ikas, 46, 292, 294.

Vi*s*vânara = Vai*s*vânara, 34, 150.

Vi*s*vantara Saushadmana and the *S*yâpar*n*as, 43, 344 sq. n.

Vi*s*varûpa, the three-headed son of Tvash*tri*, slain by Indra or Trita, 12, 47, 47 sq. n., 164–6; 41, 130; 42, 318, 522; 44, 213; n. of a teacher, 15, 119, 187.

Vi*s*vasâman, author of a Vedic hymn, 46, 413.

Vi*s*vas*rig*, a name of the Self, 15, 311.

Vi*s*vavada, title of a book, 42, xx.

Vi*s*vavârâ Âtreyî, *R*ishi of a Vedic hymn, 46, 424.

Vi*s*vavâsa, a demon harassing children, 30, 211.

Vi*s*vâvasu, *see* Gandharva.

Vi*s*vavya*k*as, 'all-embracing,' mystic name of a cow, milked at the sacrifice, 12, 188 n.

Vi*s*vâyu, 'containing all life,' mystic name of a cow milked at the sacrifice, 12, 179 n., 188, 188 n.

Vi*s*ve Devâs, 'the All-gods,' a class of deities.

(*a*) The V. D. in mythology.
(*b*) Worship of the V. D.

(*a*) THE V. D. IN MYTHOLOGY.

V. D. who dwell in heaven, who dwell in the world, 1, 37; the blowing air is united with the V. D., the V. D. with the heavenly world, 1, 255; alarmed at the greatness of K*r*ish*n*a, 8, 94; identified with the Vai*s*ya caste or the peasantry, 12, xvi–xviii; 43, 344; Vasus, Rudras or Maruts, Âdityas, and V. D., 12, 264; 41, 241, 246; are endless, 15, 126; world of the V. D., 25, 157; V. D., Sâdhyas, and great sages made substitutes for principal rules in times of distress, 25, 435; are the ear, 26, 39; B*r*ihaspati with the V. D., 26, 93; 44, 480 sq.; the air belongs to them, 26, 208; are the rays of the sun, 26, 223 sq.; 44, 194, 196; including gods, Gandharva-Apsaras, serpents, manes, 26, 359 n.; the *R*ishis of a Kâ*n*da, 30, 242; who know the great sky, appellation of the Maruts, 32, 53, 55; are non-eternal beings, because produced, 34, 202; the Vi*s*vadeva-eyed gods in the west, 41, 49; are created, 41, 150, 150 n.; 43, 33; fashioned the quarters, 41, 234 sq.; bear Agni upwards, 41, 290; are the seasons, 41, 311; have power over rain, 41, 328; the kush*th*a plant thrice begotten by them, 42, 6; have poured love into the waters, 42,

105; help in battle, 42, 119; deities and metres, 43, 53, 330; 44, 106; share of the Ribhus and lordship of the V. D., 43, 69; the lords of the Great region, 43, 102 sq.; where they wish to lay the Gârhapatya, 43, 118; are Indra and Agni, 43, 344; become the Yagus, 43, 390; from out of the V. D. the Dasarâtra was formed, 44, 140; are the most famous of the gods, 44, 278 sq.; are all the gods, 44, 392, 419; were the counsellors of King Marutta, 44, 397; perform sacrifice, 44, 441; are the vital airs, 44, 488; Indra accompanied by the V. D., 46, 154; they dwell in Agni, 46, 371.

(*b*) Worship of the V. D.

The evening libation belongs to them, 1, 36 sq.; 12, 204, 204 n., 378; 44, 444; Sâman addressed to them, 1, 37; worshipped at Srâddhas, 7, 232, 237, 251; 29, 107 n., 109; the place of Agni, Indra, and the V. D. at various sacrifices, 12, xviii sq. and n.; remnants of oblations offered to the V. D., 12, 245 sq., 260 n.; offerings and prayers to them, 12, 369, 371, 388 sq.; 25, 90, 90 n.; 26, 24, 24 n., 157, 208; 29, 83, 203, 290; 30, 91, 243; 41, 108 sq. n., 120–2; 43, 26, 85, 193, 291; 44, 75, 75 n., 81, 143, 195 sq., 208, 210, 290 n., 337 n., 382, 488; 46, 198; the threads of the Dîkshita's cloth belong to the V. D., 26, 10, 10 n.; the Âgnîdhra fire sacred to them, 26, 147 sq.; animal offerings to V. D., 26, 188, 220 sq., 388 sq., 389 n.; 41, 126; 44, 332, 392, 392 n., 402, 411; Soma libations to the V. D., 26, 288–92, 317 n., 323–5, 359–62, 410; gods of the Âgrayana, 26, 288–92; 29, 98 n., 337, 337 n.; invoked to protect the bride, 29, 33; 30, 188; invoked and worshipped for protection of the child, 29, 55; 30, 59; the Brahmakârin given in charge of the V. D., 29, 64, 79, 306; 30, 154; worshipped at the Vaisvadeva sacrifice, 29, 84, 161 sq., 290, 320, 388; 30, 22, 158, 266; invoked at the reception of guests, 29, 199; the Ashtakâ sacred to the V. D., 29, 206, 341, 341 n.; 30, 97; invoked and worshipped at the marriage, 29, 278; 30, 49; invoked at the house-building rite, 29, 347; barley corns, &c., at Pumsavana bought for the V. D., 30, 53; bricks of the fire-altar sacred to them, 43, 30–4; sacrificer sits down with the V. D., 43, 124, 202; the Soma asked to enter the dear seat of the V. D., 44, 108.

Visvesvaratîrtha, explained the Mahaitareyopanishad from a Vaishnava point of view, 1, xcv, xcviii.

Vîsya, genius, worshipped, 23, 23, 23 n.; 31, 196, 196 n., 202, 204, 209, 212, 215, 219, 223, 251, 254, 259, 278, 367, 379–81.

Vîtahavya, brought a curative plant from Asita's dwelling, 42, 31.

Vital air, *see* Breath.

Vital airs, *see* Prânas.

Vituda, the goblins, servants of, 2, 109 n.

Vitûla, a demon harassing children, 30, 219.

Vîvanghat, or Vîvanghvant, or Vîvangha, or Vîvanghâû, father of Yima, 4, lii, 10 sq., 262; 5, 133, 141 n.; 18, 110, 127; 24, 59 sq. and n.; 31, 55, 61, 232; 37, 255; 47, 9 sq., 35, 140; Tahmûraf, son of V., 4, 384; 5, 130; Narsih, son of V., 5, 118; son of Yanghad, 5, 130, 130 n.; first worshipper of Haoma, 31, 232.

Vîvareshvant, son of Ainyu, 23, 217.

Vivasvat, the father of Yama, 14, 102; 42, 57; 46, 123; the Âditya (or the sun), fashioned from Mârtânda, 26, 13; V.'s son invoked against danger, 29, 281; V. and Vîvanghvant, 31, 232 n.; Amsa and V. invoked with other gods, 42, 160; Tvashtar's daughter married to V., 42, 366; Agni became manifest to V., belongs to V., 46, 22, 391 sq.; Agni the messenger of V., 46, 45, 47, 343; Manu, son of V., 49 (i), 90.

Vîzak, daughter of Airyak, 47, 34; mother of Mânûs-khûrnâk, 47, 140.

Vîzaresha, or Vîzarêsh, or Vîzarâsh, the fiend who carries off the souls of the wicked, 4, 89 n., 218; 5, 108 sq., 108 n.; 18, 71 sq., 71 n., 346 n.; 24, 22 sq., 22 n.; a demon

of death, 18, 93; called Vîsaris, 18, 346, 346 n.

Vîzyarsti, n.p., 23, 206.

Vohu-dâta, son of Kâta, 23, 218.

Vohukhshathra, Gâtha, 31, 176–87.

Vohûman, *see* Vohu-manô.

Vohûman, King, son of Spend-dâd, grandson of Vistâsp, 5, 137 sq., 137 n., 150 sq. and n., 199; 47, xi, xxx, 83, 83 n.

Vohûman-kîhar, n.p., 5, 145.

Vohu-manô, or Vohumanah, or Vohu Manô, or Vohûmanô, or Vohûman, or Bahman, 'Good Thought,' and Philo's Logos, 4, lvi sq.; god of good thoughts, 4, 47, 47 n.; 5, 10 n.; 18, 286, 286 n., 443; 31, 5, 12; protector of cattle, how to be propitiated, 4, 47 n.; 5, 359, 372–5; 23, 88; the doorkeeper of heaven or paradise, 4, 100 n., 220, 220 n.; invoked against the demons, esp. the Drug, 4, 100 sq., 230, 241; Airyaman invoked, for V. to rejoice, 4, 144; V., Asha Vahista, Khshathra Vairya, and Spenta Ârmaiti, 4, 191, 213, 245; 31, 167; the gifts of V., 4, 210; used as a designation of the faithful one, and of 'clothes,' 4, 215–17, 215 sq. n.; Mazda reigns according as V. waxeth, 4, 276 n., 277; receives the righteous soul in heaven, 4, 374; 18, 64, 64 n.; 37, 164; first creature of Aûharmazd, 5, 9; 23, 31; 37, 303 n., 411 sq.; 47, 4; creates the light of the world and the religion of the Mazdayasnians, 5, 9, 9 n.; one of the seven Ameshaspends, 5, 10 n.; co-operator with Tîstar, 5, 26, 169; 23, 102 n.; has the white jasmine, 5, 104; smites Akem-manô (Evil Thought, Akôman), 5, 128, 179; 23, 308; 24, 161, 161 n.; invoked and worshipped, 5, 401, 404; 23, 4, 13, 35, 37, 351, 353; 31, 196, 256, 291, 295, 325, 387; 37, 296; V. in the thoughts, Srôsh in the words, Ard in the actions, 18, 18 sq., 18 n.; men ought to assist V., 18, 26; prepares the account of sin and good works, 18, 32, 66; sacred shirt, the garment of V., 18, 129, 129 n., 133, 133 n., 162; son of Aûharmazd, 18, 393, 393 n.; 31, 37, 44, 123, 126, 126 n.; 37, 273 n., 274, 393; worshipped by the Bahman Yast, 23, 21 sq., 31–4; the riches of V. shall be given to him who works in his world for Mazda, 23, 23; Sraosha with V. comes for help, 23, 30; throwing down the destroyer of V., 23, 39; connected with the Moon, 23, 88, 88 n.; V. and Âtar help Ahura against Angra-Mainyu, 23, 198; assists the Good Spirit, 23, 297; Ashô-zust, the bird of V., 24, 276, 276 n.; invoked and worshipped with Ahura and Asha, 31, 14–24, 70, 75, 174 sq.; the Kingdom gained for Mazda by V., 31, 27, 33; the vigour of V. bestowed on the righteous, 31, 39, 52; V. = Good Mind = Heaven, 31, 66, 66 n.; the path of V., 31, 89; Ahura and His Fire and Good Mind, 31, 132, 138, 285; the Realms of V., 31, 143; the mouth and tongue of V., 31, 146, 148; the sheltering leadership of V., 31, 163; the Mãthras proceed from the tongue of V., 31, 179; 37, 406; the Ameshôspentas dwell together with V., 31, 348, 352; the doctrines of the Mazdayasnian religion receive nourishment from V., 31, 354; gratification of V. by purification of polluted clothing, 37, 164; at the renovation of the universe, 37, 235; virtuous knowledge and other benefits through V., 37, 243, 246, 248 sq.; reports to Aûharmazd thrice a day, 37, 263; stipulations of V., 37, 270; the friend of Zoroaster, 37, 276, 290, 297 sq.; reign of V., 37, 280 sq.; Wrath and Envy destroyed by V., 37, 287; his destructiveness (of evil) and wisdom, 37, 287 sq., 312; protection of good creations by V., 37, 290 sq.; reward of V. for good works, 37, 306 sq.; he who loves V. preserves the religion, and increases wisdom, 37, 313 sq., 341 sq., 356, 372, 382; understanding good and evil through V., 37, 320 sq.; virtuous speaking is worship of V., 37, 323; he whose V. is Aûharmazd's progeny, 37, 333; reverence for V. is virtuous submission, 37, 335 sq., 366; growth and increase owing to V., 37, 339; development of Vohûmanic rule, 37, 346; one whose words are through

V., 37, 354, 368; the decrees of Vistâsp are through V., 37, 355; Vohûmanic attainment to the religion, 37, 362; protection from the annoying spirit through resemblance unto V., 37, 363; guards the creatures of Aûharmazd, 37, 375, 396 sq.; the words of V., 37, 380, 386; Vohûmanic peacefulness, 37, 381; in whose body V. is lodging, 37, 382; Zoroaster's meeting with V., 47, x, xv; makes the new-born Zoroaster laugh, 47, xiv, 123; V. and Ashavahistô descend with a stem of Hôm to cause the birth of Zaratûst, 47, xxix, 22–8; Srôsh and V. protect Zaratûst, 47, 39, 146; conveys Zoroaster to a conference with Aûharmazd and the archangels, 47, 41, 47–50, 57, 62, 156–8; assists Zoroaster in converting Vistâsp, 47, 67–9, 164; reliance upon V., 47, 87; enters the reason of Zoroaster at his birth, 47, 142, 151; prescribes to Zaratûst the protection of animals, 47, 160 sq., 161 n.

Vohûmanô, King, *see* Vohûman, King.

Vohunemah, or Vohûnêm, son of Avâraostri, 23, 208; 47, xxx, 165; an upholder of the religion, 47, 166.

Vohunemah, son of Katu, 23, 213.

Vohu-peresa, son of Ainyu, 23, 218.

Vohuraokah, son of Frânya, 23, 204.

Vohuraokah, son of Varakasa, 23, 212.

Vôhûrôkô-î Frahânyân, ancestor of the mothers of apostles, 47, 106, 111, 115.

Vohu-ustra, son of Ãkhnangha, 23, 217.

Vohûvastô, *see* Vohvasti.

Vohuvazdah, son of Katu, 23, 213.

Vohvasti, son of Snaoya, or Vohûvastô, son of Snôê, a priest at the renovation, 23, 203; 37, 262, 262 n.

Vohv-asti, son of Pouru-dhâkhsti, 23, 211.

Voice, and the Lord of the V., worshipped at the end of the Svâdhyâya, 29, 219.

Void, a Bodhisattva looks upon all things as, 21, 264 sq., 266 sq.; doctrine of a general v., 34, 439; 38, 14, 168. *See also* Nirvâna.

Volition, not dependent on a body, 48, 168 sq. *See also* Will.

Vologeses I, *see* Valkhash.

Vouru-baresti, worshipped, 31, 349.

Vouru-garesti, worshipped, 31, 349.

Vouru-Kasha, the sea, the gathering-place of the waters, 4, 54–6, 221, 231–4, 232 n.; 23, 172 sq.; Ardvi Sûra Anâhita flows into the sea V., 23, 54 sq., 181 sq.; 31, 317; the shores of the sea V. boiling over, 23, 63; the Glory waving in the middle of the sea V., 23, 64 sq., 298–301, 305; Aregat-aspa and Vandaremaini sacrifice by the sea V., 23, 80 sq.; Tistrya, in the shape of a horse, flies towards the sea V., 23, 94, 96, 99–101, 103 sq., 106; the Fravashis watch over the sea V., 23, 194, 196; the sacred beast in the sea V., and V., worshipped, 31, 291, 321, 346.

Vouru-nemah, n.p., 23, 220, 220 n.

Vouru-savah, n.p., 23, 220, 220 n.

Vows (Sk. Vrata): a vow by which one obtains good memory, fame, wisdom, heavenly bliss, and prosperity, 2, 147; one who desires prosperity shall perform special v. under the constellation Tishya, 2, 148–52; connected with Veda-study, 2, 216; 25, 60, 60 n., 62, 62 n.; 30, 69–77, 69 n.; special v. undertaken by the Brahmakârin, 7, 121, 121 n.; 25, 476, 476 n.; 29, 8 sq., 69 n., 76–83, 404 sq.; the good householder shall be of pure v., 8, 359 sq.; teaching the ritual for making v. and performing them, a 'low art' to be avoided by the Bhikkhu, 11, 199; how the sacrificer, by divesting himself of the v., becomes human again, 12, 273; observance of the v. before entering on sacred rites, 12, 292, 294; no impurity for those engaged in v., 14, 102; 25, 183 sq.; the v. called Siras purify from sin, 14, 128, 128 n.; the vow of silence, 14, 136; nine modes of living with special v. for householders, 14, 284–91; are a preparation for union with Brahman, 25, 34; performed under false pretences, 25, 160; women not to undertake v., 25, 196; sin of breaking v., 25, 442, 442 n.; observances for special v., 29, 187,

193, 193 n.; the universal vow taken at the Samâvartana, 29, 229; observances for the Godâna-vrata, 29, 403 sq.; *see also* Hair; one performing a vow shall not be arrested, nor put under restraint, 33, 19, 288; ordeals should not be administered to persons performing v., 33, 101; eight v. taken by Milinda before being instructed in the secret doctrine, 35, 138 sq.; special v. taken by Bhikkhus, 36, 231 sq., 234 sq.; laymen, who attain to Nirvâ*n*a, had practised the thirteen v. in a former birth, 36, 253–5, 268–71; similes showing that keeping the v. is a condition of attaining to Nirvâ*n*a, 36, 255–61; punishments of those who, being unworthy, take the v., 36, 261–4; he who, being worthy, takes the v., is like a king, 36, 265–7; list of the thirteen v. or Dhutaṅgas, 36, 268, 268 sq. n.; *see also* Bhikkhus (*b*); he who has practised the thirteen v. is endowed with thirty graces, 36, 272 sq.; the four rites or vratas, the great vrata, 43, 333 sq., 342; the daily study of the Veda, a vow, 44, 101, 101 sq. n.; Lord of the v., *see* Vratapati. *See also* Abstinence, Begging, Chastity, Fasting, Holy persons, Mahâvrata, *and* Mauna.

Vrata, vow, *see* Vow.

Vratapati, or Lord of the Vows: by offerings to Vai*s*vânara and V. one sanctifies ten ancestors, 14, 117; worshipped by the student, 30, 156.

Vrâtya: reception of a V., or mendicant Brâhma*n*a, 2, xxvii; men who have not been initiated at the proper time, called V., 7, 115; *but see* Caste (*e*), *and* Initiation; Prâ*n*a is a V., 15, 276.

V*ri*ddha, of the Gautama gotra, a Sthavira, 22, 294.

V*ri*haspati, *see* B*ri*haspati.

V*ri*sa *G*âna, author of Vedic hymns, 46, 367; story of the Purohita V., 46, 368.

V*ri*shâkapi, seer of a Vedic hymn, 14, 187.

V*ri*shala, *see* Caste (*e*).

V*ri*shan, n.p., 32, 152 sq.; 46, 32, 35.

V*ri*sha*n*a*s*va, Indra became the wife of, 26, 81, 81 n.

V*ri*shaparvan, dialogues between the daughters of U*s*anas and, 14, xli, 237, 237 sq. n.

V*ri*sh*n*i, K*ri*sh*n*a, descendant of, 8, 41, 56, 235; K*ri*sh*n*a is Vâsudeva among the descendants of V., 8, 91; Arish*t*anemi, the hero of the Vs., 45, 114; the Vs. suffered destruction, 49 (i), 116.

V*ri*shotsarga, *see* Bull.

V*ri*tra, origin of, 12, 166; one should enter the fast on the full moon thinking 'Now I will slay V.,' 12, 172; full and new moon oblations represent the slaying of V., 12, 180; is the moon, 12, 180, 182; 41, 45, 45 n.; slain by the gods, 12, 408–10, 417–20, 437, 444 sq., 449; 26, 271, 371; 41, 48; was Soma, 26, 100, 239, 265–9, 271, 314, 371; 44, 437 n.; slain by the waters, 26, 242 sq., 247; trodden to pieces by the Maruts, 32, 392; is evil or sin, 44, 11, 351; of old everything (the three Vedas) was in V., 41, 138 sq.; Agni, the killer of V., 41, 218; 46, 51, 92, 102, 187; the waters loathing V., 41, 332, 332 n.; held fast the ever-flowing waters, 42, 40; the cloud, 42, 62, 384; Bhava and *S*arva, slayers of V., 42, 158; Varu*n*a = V., 42, 370; the butter-portions to Agni and Soma relate to the slaying of V., 44, 189, 193 sq., 350 sq. and n., 356. *See also* Indra (*f*).

V*ri*ttikâra, 'author of a V*ri*tti,' referred to by *S*aṅkara, 34, xx sq.; quoted, 48, 206, 261, 302, 337. *See also* Bodhâyana.

Vulture, *see* Birds (*b*).

Vulture's Peak, *see* G*ri*dhrakû*t*a.

Vunda (or *K*unda), a Yaksha, with whom Buddha dwells, 49 (i), 170.

Vyâghrâpatya gotra, Sthaviras of the, 22, 288, 292.

Vyâh*ri*tis, the three holy words, Bhû*h*, Bhuva*h*, Sva*h*, proceeded from the threefold knowledge, 1, 35; the meanings of the V. explained, 1, 49 sq.; mistakes happening during a sacrifice are remedied by the V., 1, 68 sq. n., 70–2; are the essence of the three worlds, of the deities, and of the threefold know-

ledge, 1, 70 sq. *See also* Sacred syllables.
Vyakta, Ârya, Sthavira of the Bhâradvâga gotra, 22, 286.
Vyâna, *see* Prânas.
Vyantara gods, *see* Superhuman beings.
Vyapagatakhiladosha, the 58th Tathâgata, 49 (ii), 7.
Vyapagatakhilamalapratighosha, the 25th Tathâgata, 49 (ii), 6.
Vyarsvant, n.p., 23, 210.
Vyâsa, or Krishna Dvaipâyana, and Dhritarâshtra, 8, 3; author of Mahâbhârata, 8, 6 sq., 204, 206 sq.; author of Vedânta-sûtras, 8, 33; 48, 528; calls Krishna the first god, 8, 87; chief among sages, 8, 91; by the favour of V., Sañgaya heard the dialogue between Krishna and Arguna, 8, 130; satiated at the Tarpana, 14, 255; 30, 244; the author of numerous treatises, 19, 11; conversed with the gods face to face, 34, 222 sq.; quoted, 38, 43; 48, 406; Apântaratamas was born again as V., 38, 235; sets free the sacrificial horse, 44, xxvii; Parâsara's son, his teaching, 48, 3; arranged the Vedas, 49 (i), 9.
Vyâsâdhikaranamâlâ, t.w., 34, xxxi.
Vyâsa-smriti, date of the, 33, xvi.
Vyashti, n. of a teacher, 15, 120, 187 sq.
Vyâtana, n.p., 23, 218.
Vyavahâra, Sk. t.t., the phenomenal world, 34, xxvi.
Vyûha, Sk., Vedântic term, 34, xxiii.
Vyûharâga, a prominent Bodhisattva, 21, 394.

W

Wadd, Arabian god of heaven, 6, xii; an idol worshipped by the Arabs, 9, 303.
Wages, law about, 14, 81; 25, 253, 293; 33, 134, 139–44, 273 sq.; 37, 91; are valid gifts, 33, 129, 343; abstracting the increase of labourers' wages, a crime, 37, 44 sq. *See also* Labour, *and* Labourers.
Walîd ibn Mughâirah, an apostate and enemy of Mohammed, 9, 253 n., 295 n., 309 n.
Wa-lung, a class of sprites, 40, 19.
Wăn, Duke, an ancestor of Ȝze-kâo served under, 28, 169, 169 n.; Duke W. and Kieh Ȝze-thui, 40, 173 sq.
Wăn, the earl of Thăng, wore mourning for his uncle, 27, 152.
Wăn, the king: the Shih from the time of W. to that of Ting, 3, xvi; authorship of Yî King ascribed to King W. and his son Tan, 3, xvi sq.; 16, xiii, xv–xix, 5 sq., 10, 19–23, 26 sq., 31–5, 54, 57, 58 n., 351 n., 396 sq. n., 404 n., 423 n.; father of Wû, 3, 126, 130, 134; 28, 290; ancestor of the duke of Kâu, 3, 152 sq.; ten sons of W., 3, 164; his virtue and fame, eulogies on him, 3, 165 sq., 169 sq.; 28, 67, 339, 416; gave instructions to the young nobles, 3, 174–6; W. and Wû the model kings, 3, 192 sq., 222–5, 235 sq., 241, 244–6, 251–3, 265 sq.; 28, 167, 282, 322 sq., 352, 355, 363; W. and Wû worshipped as departed ancestors, 3, 194 sq., 328; 28, 202, 209; mild and humble, was king for fifty years, 3, 203 sq., 203 n.; the tranquillizing king, 3, 206, 208; his excellent ministers, 3, 208 sq.; punishments of his sons, the princes of Kwan, of Ȝhâi, and of Hwo, 3, 211; grandfather of Hû, 3, 212; sacrifices to and praises of King W., 3, 313–17, 325, 328, 335 sq.; W. and Wû continued the work of Thâi, 3, 342; praise of King W., dead and alive, as the founder of the Kâu dynasty, 3, 377–81, 385–8, 390–5; his birth, 3, 380 sq.; his marriage, 3, 381; King W. and the chiefs of Yü and Zui, 3, 385, 385 n.; warns Kâu-hsin, 3, 410–12; 'the Accomplished One,' 3, 427, 427 n.; worshipped in the Brilliant Hall as the correlate of God, 3, 477; first multiplied the figures from the trigrams to the sixty-four hexagrams, 16, 13 sq.; state of the country in the time of W., 16, 19 sq., 63 n.; in prison occupied with the lineal figures, 16, 21; table of his trigrams, 16, 33; treatise on the

Thwan, or King W.'s explanations of the hexagrams, 16, 213–66; involved in difficulties, 16, 241 sq., 242 n.; during the troubles of King W. and the tyrant *K*âu, the Yî flourished, 16, 403, 404 n.; ordered the compilation of 'the Royal Ordinances,' 27, 3, 18; as eldest son and heir, 27, 23, 343–5, 344 n., 362 sq.; passed over his eldest son and appointed Wû, 27, 120; one of the six great men, 27, 366; *K*âu's overthrow by W. and Wû, 27, 396; temple of the duke of Lû like that of W., 28, 36; King W. who was *Kh*ang, 28, 60; his reverence in sacrificing to the departed, 28, 212 sq.; had no cause of grief, 28, 309; the ways of W. and Wû displayed by Confucius, 28, 326; 40, 168, 172; was obedient to *K*âu-hsin, 39, 359; King W. and the old man of ȝang whose fishing was no fishing, 40, 51–3, 51 n.; was imprisoned in Yû-lî, 40, 173, 173 n.; his music of the Phi-yung, 40, 218, 218 n.

Wăn, king of *K*âo, his love of the sword-fight cured by *K*wang-ȝze, 39, 158 sq.; 40, 186–91, 186 n.

Wăn, Marquis, of *K*in, or *Kh*iû, or Î-ho, charge to him, delivered by King Phing, 3, 22, 265–7.

Wăn of Wei, Duke, praise of, 3, 436 sq.; asks ȝze-hsiâ about the effects of music, 28, 116–21, 116 n.; the Marquis W. of Wei, and Thien ȝze-fang, 39, 151 sq.; 40, 42 sq.

Wân-fû, his dying charge, 28, 358 n.

Wang, or kings of the *K*âu dynasty, 3, xxvi, xxviii.

Wang-hsiang, sprites haunting rivers, 40, 19.

Wang Î, falls in battle, 27, 185; a perfect man, 39, 172 n.; states the limits of knowledge, 39, 190–2, 190 n.; teacher of Nieh *Kh*üeh, 39, 259, 312; 40, 279.

Wang Kwo, an officer at *Kh*û, 40, 114.

Wang Thâi, a cripple, and a famous Tâoist teacher, 39, 223 sq., 223 n.

Wăn-hui, King, the method of Tâo illustrated by his cook cutting up an ox, 39, 130, 198–200.

Wăn-ming, n. of the Great Yü, 3, 46, 46 n.

Wăn-po, son of *K*ing *K*iang, 27, 176.

Wăn-po Hsüeh-ȝze, a Tâoist sage, his interviews with the people of Lû, 40, 43 sq., 43 n.

Wăn Shû, father of *K*wang Shû, 28, 252.

Wăn Tî, called Yang *K*ien, of the ruling House of Sui, and his minister Hsieh Tâo-hăng, 40, 311 n., 315, 318 sq.

Wăn-ȝze, mourning for his brother Hui-ȝze, 27, 143; mourning for General W., 27, 144; W. or *K*âo Wû, minister of ȝin, congratulated on the completion of his residence, 27, 196, 196 n.

War: slaughter of those who have laid down their arms forbidden, 2, 124; laws and regulations relating to w., 2, 228 sq.; 3, 132; 14, 98, 200; 27, 220; 37, 77 sq., 86–90, 120 sq., 126, 129; impurity for men killed in battle, 2, 250; 25, 185 sq.; appointment of Minister of W., 3, 228 sq.; address of a general to his host, 3, 268–70; ode used in declarations of w., 3, 335; the ears of prisoners and of the slain taken as trophies, 3, 339, 339 n., 392; equipment for w., 3, 344, 344 n.; sacrifice to the 'Father of W.,' 3, 392, 392 n.; 27, 220; the stars a specimen of a w.-like army, 5, 12; prayers when going to battle, 5, 391; believers exhorted to fight for God and Islâm, and promised Paradise if they fall, 6, 27 sq., 31 sq., 32 n., 37–9, 82 sq., 86, 167 sq., 170 sq.; 9, 63, 65, 124, 235, 241; martial law, 6, 84 sq.; punishments of those who make w. against God and His Apostle, 6, 102; beacon-fires lit as a proclamation of w., 6, 106, 106 n.; how to divide the spoils, 6, 167 sq., 171; 9, 274 sq.; 25, 231; 33, 341; exhortations to fight against the misbelievers and hypocrites, 6, 173 sq., 176–80, 183–6, 189, 191; 9, 229, 231 sq., 292; people who may lawfully be excused from fighting in religious w., 6, 185; 9, 235; w. music, 8, 38 sq.; 28, 120; protests against w., 8, 40–3; 19, 327–9, 331–3; 39, 32, 72–4, 112; 40, 218, 222 sq.; w. and peace, are of the quality of passion, 8, 323; if men

did not fight for religion, places of worship would be destroyed, 9, 60 sq.; Muslims are not to treat with the enemies of Islâm, but may make friends with idolators who have not fought against them, 9, 277–9; God loves those who fight in His cause, 9, 281 sq.; fighting and dying in battle, a penance, 14, 106; rules about conducting military expeditions, 16, 23–5, 71 sq., 72–4 n.; 27, 235; only defensive war is right, 16, 24, 74 n.; the king should not have recourse at once to arms, 16, 152, 249, 286 sq., 287 n.; denounced as opposed to husbandry, 18, 173, 173 sq. n.; instruments of w., 19, 326 sq. and n.; pleas for w., 19, 329–31; duties of ambassadors in respect to w., 25, 226; duties of the king with regard to w., 25, 226–8, 230–3, 240–50; kinds of fortresses, 25, 227 sq.; five classes of spies, 25, 240, 240 n.; on w. operations, 25, 395 sq.; 27, 300 sq.; a king shall seek death in battle, 25, 399, 399 n.; presents made of captives, 27, 84; about w. chariots, 27, 90 sq.; of banners in w., 27, 91 sq.; colours used for w., 27, 125 sq.; fighting in w. a sad necessity, 27, 185; instruments of w. not to be sold, 27, 238; not to be commenced in spring, 27, 256; Minister of W. called the 'Grand Peace-maintainer,' 27, 270, 270 n.; military movements must not interfere with the business of husbandry, 27, 279; preparations in autumn, 27, 284 sq.; teaching the use of the five weapons of w. by means of hunting, 27, 294; exemption from military service during mourning, 27, 341 sq.; exhibition of scenes of w. by music, 28, 92; ceremonies before the beginning of battle, 29, 233–5; a soldier at the time of battle must not be put under restraint, 33, 288; the headless corpses dance over the battlefield after a great slaughter, 36, 147; hostages and ransom, 37, 69; sacred ceremonial on the day of battle, 37, 89; Iranians assisting foreigners in battle, 37, 107; Marquis Wû of Wei wants to abolish w., 40, 94–6; poisoned arrows, 42, 25; a battle-song, 42, 98, 545. *See also* Warriors, *and* Weapons.

Waraqah, Mohammed's cousin, converted by him, 6, xv, xx, xlix.

Warriors: reward of w. fighting for a good cause, 2, 163; implements of w., 4, 173; Lakshmî resides in an arrow, and in the w. who have returned from battle, or fallen in it and proceeded to a seat in heaven, 7, 299; fighting, the natural duty of w., 8, 46 sq., 127; cattle for w., advancement of religion by force, 37, 292. *See also* Kshatriyas, *and* Soldiers.

Water.

(*a*) The element w.
(*b*) Sacredness of w.
(*c*) The Ws. deified, goddesses.

(*a*) The element w.

W. produces earth or food, 1, 94, 100; 38, 23 sq.; 43, 232; produced from fire, 1, 94, 100; 34, lii; 38, 22 sq.; 41, 85; 48, 536; white the colour of w., 1, 95, 96; its subtilest portion becomes breath, 1, 96–8; the root, the five elements of the body, 1, 100; 8, 179 n.; assumes different forms, earth, sky, &c., 1, 117; meditation on (the person in the) w. as Brahman, 1, 117, 304; 8, 283; fire creates w. (in a thunderstorm), 1, 117 sq.; in the beginning this world was w., from w. everything is produced, 1, 212; 15, 191; 41, 294, 363; 44, 12; *Brahman says to him (the departed): 'W. indeed is this my world, the whole Brahman world, and it is thine,'* 1, 279; shall not be divided between heirs, 2, 310; ws. come from the sky to the earth, and rise from the earth to the sky, 4, 232–4, 232 n.; creation of the w., 5, 10; 41, 145, 157, 192; 43, 402; seventeen species of liquid, 5, 83–5; on the nature of lakes, 5, 85–7; not to be drawn from a well at night, 5, 345 sq.; K*r*ish*n*a is the taste in w., 8, 74; one of the developments of the Brahman, 8, 156 n.; from the Brahman the ws. are produced, from the ws. the gross body, 8, 187, 187 n.; the self moving about above the w., 8, 189; causes cold, 8, 238; one of the seven 'wombs,' 8, 260; the

fourth entity, as connected with the self it is the tongue, with objects taste, its presiding deity Soma, 8, 337, 340; the flowing element of the body, 8, 343; taste is the characteristic of w., 8, 348–50, 352; is the best of all drinks, 8, 354; relation of fish and w., lotus-leaf and w., 8, 374; sound, touch, colour, and taste are the qualities of w., 8, 384; storehouse of ws. beneath the earth, 11, 130; this universe is pervaded by w., 12, 8; 44, 15; symbolically ws. indicate assembled multitudes of men, 16, 22; a symbol of the course to be followed by the sage in dealing with danger, 16, 236, 237 n.; sins caused by actions injuring the souls in w., 22, 5–7; how the *G*aina monk may use w., 22, 107 sq.; how it is mingled in the earth, 24, 36; how the flow of the w. is arranged, 24, 85 sq.; nature of fire and w., 24, 123 sq.; diverting and obstructing w.-courses, 25, 106; fire sprang from w., 25, 399, 399 n.; the essence of plants, 26, 142; there are no souls in w., 36, 85–91; qualities of w. oozing and flowing, 37, 119; about canals and fords, 37, 127–9; w. is dissolved into fire, earth is dissolved into w., 38, 26; the soul goes from one body into another, enveloped by w., 38, 103–5, 106–10, 112; the soul assumes a body of w. in the moon, 38, 127; essence of the ws. contained in the sun, 41, 7; the foundation of the universe, 41, 293; 44, 205; is unsettled, 41, 301; heaven is the w. of the atmosphere beyond and below the sun, 41, 305; there is w. not only in the channels of the vital airs, but in the whole body, 41, 337; 43, 35; lotus-leaf means w., 41, 343, 364; the earth lies spread on the ws., 41, 364; founded on the mountains, 41, 405; the eye is the abode, the ear the goal, the sky the seat, the air the home, the sea the womb, sand the sediment of the ws., 41, 416; the ants dig up w. to destroy poison, 42, 27, 511; fire in the w., 42, 54; by union with the ws. Pragâpati produces creatures, 43, 32; is food, 43, 35; 44, 275, 425, 443; springs forth from the rock, 43, 169 sq.; the food of Vâyu, 43, 335; the sun floats along the w., 43, 367 sq., 368 n.; found in the earth by digging, and in the sky (rain), 44, 15; one of the six doors to the Brahman, 44, 66 sq.; 'from the ws. I take thy blood,' 44, 133; *G*ainas believe that w. is possessed of life, 45, xix; women and w. cause loss of sanctity to a *G*aina monk, 45, 266; in old times some great sages reached perfection, though they drank cold w., 45, 268 sq.; by ablutions w.-beings are hurt, 45, 295; origin and feeding of w.-bodies, 45, 396 sq., 396 n.; eight good qualities of w., 49 (ii), 93, 93 n. *See also* Parables (*f*), *and* Rain.

(*b*) Sacredness of w.

Rinsing of the mouth with w., w. a dress for breath, 1, 74, 74 n.; 15, 204, 312; 38, 211–14; 48, 640 sq.; is a sacred object, 2, 94; 14, 36; 33, 222, 277–80; 38, 105, 108 sq.; the w.-vessels in the house shall never be empty, 2, 101, 101 n.; 8, 359; overturning the w.-vessel of a sinner who is cast off, 2, 278; sipping w. a purification, 7, 94 n., 95, 104, 198 sq.; 14, 320; a means of purifying, 7, 96–102, 105; 12, 3, 211, 213, 267; 25, 191; not to be contaminated, 7, 227; 25, 137; offering of w., 8, 85; Brahma*k*ârin must always carry w. with him, 8, 360; the devotee should bathe in and do everything with clean w., 8, 364; 'brought forward' (pra*n*îtâ*h*) for sacrifice, the Pra*n*îtâ or lustral w., 12, 7–9, 7 n., 9 n., 23 n., 265; 26, 12, 12 n.; 44, 21, 35, 119 sq., 120 n., 270, 492; is a thunderbolt, 12, 9, 65, 189 sq.; 26, 7; 44, 266, 438, 501; a means of expiation, 12, 45, 56; 14, 121, 320; 29, 248 sq.; 44, 266 sq.; means ambrosia, 12, 268; 44, 87; sprinkling w. on the fire-place = supplying the fire with food, 12, 277; libation of w. accompanying a gift, 13, 143; 17, 250 sq., 251 n.; the Brâhma*n*a must always keep w. or carry a w.-pot, 14, 44, 44 n., 49, 160–4, 163 n.,

224; is always pure, 14, 132; Ekadhanâ w. used for mixing with the Soma, 26, 102, 102 n., 232 sq., 232 n., 237 sq., 423; a means of appeasement, of soothing, a medicine, 26, 120, 144, 192 sq., 199, 374; 41, 220; 43, 169, 187; 44, 179 sq., 497 sq., 501; the Vasatîvarî w. for the Soma pressings, 26, 147, 222–6, 231, 232 n., 233, 235 sq., 247, 293 sq., 454; 41, 10, 73 n.; 44, 275, 275 n., 372, 372 n., 377; an elixir of immortality, 26, 374; 44, 425; the Svastyayana ceremony performed when going to cross w., 29, 127; leading the bride round the w.-pot, 29, 168; poured out for the manes, 29, 252 sq.; sprinkling the bride or bridal pair with w., 29, 284, 380, 383; 30, 43, 46 sq.; ceremony of putting up the w.-barrel, 29, 349 sq.; 30, 286; designated by sraddhâ, 38, 106–8; preparation of the (king's) consecration w., 41, 73–80; different kinds of w. for consecration, 41, 73 sq.; king sprinkled with consecration w., 41, 83–5, 94–6; 42, 111 sq., 378–81; ws. are the udders of the sky, 41, 284; poured out as a thunderbolt to clear himself of all evil, 41, 324; jarfuls of w., symbolical of rain, poured on the altar-ground, 41, 335–7; diseases healed with spring-w., 42, 9, 277 sq.; plants and w. foremost among remedies, 42, 41; *the ws. cure all disease*, 42, 41; preparation of holy w., 42, 628; frog, lotus-flower, and bamboo-shoot, three kinds of w., 43, 174 sq.; all objects of desire are the ws., 43, 389; thrown for exorcising, 43, 438; is a beautiful object, 44, 426; is the body of Vish*n*u, 48, 423; will not cleanse away sin, 49 (i), 74; ordeal by w., *see* Ordeals;—sacredness of w. in Zoroastrianism, 4, lxii, lxiv, lxxv–lxxvii; does not kill, 4, 49, 52, 52 n.; how Ahura-Mazda purifies the w. defiled by corpses, 4, 49, 54 sq.; sin of contamination of w., 4, 51, 121; 5, 84, 248 n., 258, 265–9, 268 n., 282 sq., 285, 310, 378; 37, 108, 149 sq.; purification of w., when defiled by the dead, 4, 67, 71–3; purifying power of w., 4, 80, 80 n., 83 sq., 93, 106–12, 126–31, 216 sq.; defiling w. by bringing a corpse into it, an abomination, 4, 82; 18, 229; the cleanser delights w., 4, 133; spell to purify w., 4, 142 sq.; killing a w.-dog brings about a drought, 4, 168; how to keep it from defilement, 4, 186; cleansing and generative power of the w., 4, 232 n.; defiled by pouring dast-shô into it, 4, 264 sq.; consecration of fire and w., 5, 224–7; the holy-w. (zôhar) not to be contaminated, 5, 257, 257 n.; holy-w. (zôhar) presented to the sacred fire, 5, 300, 341; atonement for sins against w., 5, 307; rites performed with holy-w., 18, 170 sq., 204–7, 205 n., 209, 251 sq., 283, 286; 24, 28; 37, 253 sq.; the course and benefit of the w. of Arekdvisûr, 18, 262 sq.; healing power of w., 18, 262 sq.; 31, 292; Gôpaîtôshah pours holy-w. into the sea, to kill noxious creatures, 24, 111 sq.; sin of pouring away or drinking water in the dark, 24, 292; contaminated by a menstruous woman, 24, 332; polluted by dead matter, 24, 336–9; 37, 155–7, 159; disturbed by untruth, 37, 73; consecration of w. at the beginning of battle, 37, 89; ceremonial of the w., 37, 96 sq.; sin of carrying evil to w., 37, 103; offering up of w., 37, 107; care and propitiation of w., 37, 124, 127, 195; 47, 162; sin of concealing w. on a road, 37, 146; reverencing w., 37, 231; uncleanness of well-w. at night, 37, 471; conveying holy-w. to the priest, 47, 91; squeezing Hôm into w., 47, 154;—used at sacrifices, 27, 445; striding over the well, a crime, 40, 243. *See also* Purification, *and* Sacred objects.

(*c*) THE WS. DEIFIED, GODDESSES.

Prayers and homage to the W., 2, 85, 295; 12, 21–3; 14, 250 sq.; 26, 23, 42, 231 sq., 232 n., 234 sq.; 29, 67; 30, 61, 150, 165, 230; 41, 19, 230, 230 n.; 42, 146 sq., 348; offerings to the W., 2, 107, 203; 25, 91; 26, 23; 29, 320, 388; 30, 22; adjured at the ordeal by w.: 'Thou, O W., dwellest in the interior of all creatures, like a witness,' &c.,

7, 59 sq.; Varu*n*a is the king of W., 8, 346; *see also* Varu*n*a (*a*); copulation between the w. (female) and fire (male), 12, 9 sq.; the deities that are in the w., 12, 214 n.; world of the w., 25, 157; expiatory prayer to the W., 25, 272, 272 n.; the celestial cows, 26, xvii, xx sq.; the mothers, 26, 8; the W. slew V*ri*tra, 26, 242 sq., 247; are immortal goddesses, the wives of the immortal Soma, 26, 243; Soma made over to the W. for protection, 26, 384; with Varu*n*a, invoked in danger, 29, 232; invoked to watch over mother and child, 29, 296; 30, 214; the initiated boy given in charge to the W., 30, 154; 44, 87; the supporters of the whole world, 30, 226; the great W. held the germ Hira*n*yagarbha, 32, 2, 10; the Lord of the W. invoked at the ordeal by w., 33, 114; the mothers of Agni, 41, 294; 43, xx; 46, 145, 157 sq., 219 sq., 256; 49 (i), 45; ws. are the truth, 41, 363; self-rule belongs to the ws., 41, 364; the deepest place of the heavenly w. is where the sun burns, 41, 391; the Apasyâ*h* or water-bricks of the fire-altar put on with prayers relating to the W., 41, 413–17; the healing W. invoked, 42, 12 sq., 15, 48, 471; plants the offspring of the W., 42, 42; the golden-coloured W., 42, 147, 349; the divine W., and Pragâpati, 42, 161; as divine women, 42, 181–3; Agni and the w. in the house, 42, 195 sq., 600; Agni, Sûrya, the W., and all the gods, 42, 205; divine physicians, 42, 389; Apyâ yosha*n*â, the woman of the w., 42, 409, 521; Pragâpati is the ws., for they are in the highest place, 43, 37; deity and brick of fire-altar, 43, 91; as Apsaras, the mates of Vâta (Wind), 43, 232; deity of defective metres, 43, 331; Vai*s*vânara as W., 43, 395; are the law, 44, 18; worshipped as deities at a sacrificial session, 44, 142; are all the deities, 44, 252; oath by the Inviolable W., 44, 265; W. and Plants invoked, 44, 266, 438, 501; worshipped at the A*s*vamedha, 44, 280; divine W. carry the sacrifice to the gods, 44, 321 n.; expiatory oblation to the W. which are a place of abode for all the gods, 44, 506; have furthered Agni, 46, 119; the daughters of Heaven, 46, 219 sq.; the W., the immortal goddesses, have sped forward by *Ri*ta, 46, 326; horse produced from the ws., *see* Horse; w. libations to gods, &c., at the Tarpa*n*a, *see* Sacrifices (*b*);—the Zoroastrian should worship the good W., 4, 195; sacrifice to the good W., 4, 207, 335, 337, 349; 5, 337; Zarathu*s*tra sacrifices to the good W. of the good Dâitya, 4, 210; the W. which Ahura-Mazda made, invoked and worshipped, 4, 221; 23, 6, 12, 20, 36, 38, 199, 227, 249, 251–8, 316, 344, 356 sq.; 31, 197, 204, 208 sq., 215, 219, 223 sq., 256, 270 sq., 274 sq., 296 sq., 316–24, 326, 350, 383 sq., 392; joint invocations to the W. and the light of sun, moon, and stars, 4, 230–4, 232 n.; the seed of W. in the stars, 4, 234, 234 n.; prayers to the Good W., 4, 250; 23, 8, 16, 330, 349, 356 sq.; libations brought to the W., 4, 349; Aharman's contest with the W., 5, 17, 168–73; attacked by the Evil Spirit, protected by Tî*s*tar, 5, 25–9; duties with regard to w. and plants, the counterparts of Horvada*d* and Amerôda*d*, 5, 373, 377 sq.; ceremony in honour of the w., 18, 232; the w. is female and fire male, 18, 267, 267 n., 410; 23, 6 n.; worshipped in the shape of a horse, 23, 39; the Âbân Ya*s*t in praise of the W., 23, 52–84; purified by the Sun, 23, 86; worshipped in connexion with Ti*s*trya, 23, 93; Fravashi of the W. worshipped, 23, 200; W. or rivers, the wives of Ahura, 23, 353, 353 n.; the wives of Ahura-Mazda, and mothers of life, 31, 286 sq.; Ahura-Mazda gave names to the W., 31, 287; reverenced by a traveller, 37, 120; ceremonial of the lord of females, the descendant of W., and of W., 37, 184; W. and Plants, worshipped, *see* Plants (*b*);—seas, rivers, lakes, &c., worshipped in winter, 27, 303 sq., 304 n.; sacrifice to the W. (rivers and seas), 28, 91.

Water-beings, water-bodies, *see* Water (*a*).

Water-dwellers, fish and fishermen, the people of King Matsya Sâmmada, 44, 369.

Way, *see* Path.

Weakness, *see* Humility.

Wealth, the sacrifice of, 8, 61 sq.; pride of w., 8, 114 n., 116; human w. and Brahmic w., 8, 161 sq., 161 n.; the triad piety, w., and lust, 8, 246, 325, 331; only w. acquired honestly is good, only by it a man is to be considered fortunate, 24, 41–3, 93; w. acquired by crime, the worst pleasure, 24, 49; how far worldly w. can be obtained by exertion, 24, 54; the richest of the poor, and the poorest of the rich, 24, 55 sq.; seven kinds of men who are rich, and seven who are poor, 24, 70 sq.; why worldly goods are not allotted to the worthy, 24, 75 sq.; necessary for good works and worship, 37, 319 sq.; discussion on the pursuit of w., 40, 180–5; lord of w., *see* Kubera.

Weapons, do not pierce the soul, 8, 45, 250; thunderbolt the first of w., 8, 89; celestial w., 8, 93; how to give w. to generals and frontier governors, 37, 52; famous swords, 39, 249, 249 sq. n.; 40, 84, 84 n. *See also* Arrow, Bow, *and* War.

Weather: prayer for good w., w.-prophet, 42, 160, 532 sq.; ceremony against stormy w., 42, 248, 249 sq.

Wedding, *see* Marriage.

Weeping: no tear must be shed on the food at a *S*râddha, 7, 248; 25, 117 sq.

Wei, count of, and the ruin of the Shang dynasty, 3, 121–3; invested with the dukedom of Sung, 3, 161–3; as the duke of Sung, received by the king in the ancestral temple, 3, 327; made Yen his successor, 27, 120.

Wei, duke of Kâu, Thien Khâi-*k*ih has an interview with him, 39, 150; 40, 16 sq.

Wei, king of *Kh*û, offers *K*wang-ȝze the administration of his territories, 39, 390, 390 n.

Weights and Measures: one who uses false w. and m. not to be invited to a *S*râddha, 2, 258; give full w. and m., 6, 149, 214; 9, 5, 323 sq.; law regarding w. and m., 7, 23 sq., 35; 25, 276 sq.; penance for buying or selling with false w., 7, 177; to be guarded by the king, 14, 97; standard w. and m. given out by government, 28, 31; fixed by the emperor, 28, 324; gift of false w. and m. forbidden, 36, 121; wickedness of false w. and m., 40, 243.

Wei Shăng committed suicide, when the girl with whom he had made an appointment did not come, 40, 174; was drowned, 40, 180.

Wei-tâu, the Great Bear, got the Tâo, 39, 136, 244, 244 n.

Wei-tho, sprites haunting marshes, 40, 19 sq.

Welfare, conditions of, for a country, 11, 3 sq.; for the community of Bhikkhus, 11, 6–11; goddess of w., *see* Bhûti.

Weregeld, *see* Homicide.

West, *see* Quarters.

Wheat, headpiece of sacrificial post made of, 41, 31 sq.

Wheel: King *G*anaka is capable of turning the w. whose nave is the Brahman, 8, 215, 306; the w. of time or worldly life, 8, 355–8, 355 n.;—'The turning of the *W. of the Law*,' a false rendering of Dhamma*k*akkappavattana, 11, 140 sq.; Buddhas turn the 'W. of the Law,' 19, 168–79, 168 n., 316; 21, 159–73, 184 sq.; 49 (i), 168 sq., 172 sq., 180 sq.; second turn of it and commemoration of the first turn, 21, xxix, 70; set in motion at Benares, 21, 56;—treasure of the w. of King Sudassana, 11, 141, 252–4; the w. of sovereignty, 23, 136, 201, 201 n.; the w. treasure of a king of kings, 36, 136–8; the chariot w. of the Kingdom of Righteousness, 36, 234, 273 sq.; the Brahman priest mounts a cart-w., 41, 22; cart-w., or potter's w. would creak if not steadied, 44, 126.

White horse, *see* Horse, *and* Pedu.

Whore, *see* Prostitution.

Wickedness: there is a hope for everything but w., 5, 396; a bad

mind and wicked deeds are what defile a man; and no outward observances can purify him, 10 (ii), 40–2; produced by the evil spirit and his demons, 18, 95–7, 107, 113; Buddha preaches against wicked desires, 20, 262 sqq.; the fate of the worldly and wicked, 24, 51–3; the way of a bad man, 40, 238–44. *See also* Morality.

Widows, cannot inherit, 2, 133 sq. n.; portions of the harvest to be left for the benefit of w., 3, 373, 373 n.; 28, 296; re-marriage of w., 3, 434 sq., 435 n.; 27, 152 n.; 33, xv, 329; *but see* Marriage (*c*); a w. mourns the death of her husband, 3, 441 sq.; self-immolation of w., 7, xxix sq., 81, 111, 111 n.; 25, 196 n.; 33, 368 sq., 369 n.; 42, 185, 645, 648; duties of w., 7, 111, 111 n.; 14, 89 sq., 234; 25, 196 sq.; 33, 381; son of a re-married w., is unholy, excluded from *S*râddha feasts, 12, 7; 25, 104, 108; the firm correctness of a solitary w., 16, 182, 184 n., 334 sq.; keeps ornaments, worn during husband's lifetime, 25, 372; with the son of a w. one should not associate, 27, 78; 28, 298; buried alive with the deceased husband, 27, 181–4; compassion with orphans, widowers, and w., they receive regular allowances, 27, 243 sq., 298; property of w., 33, 47 sq. and n.; 'appointment' of w., *see* Niyoga.

Wife, Wives.

(*a*) In Indian religions and popular views.
(*b*) In Indian law and custom.
(*c*) In Zoroastrianism.
(*d*) In China.
(*e*) In Islâm.

(*a*) In Indian religions and popular views.

Therefore does a man, after having found a w., consider himself a more perfect man, 1, 182; 25, 335; how the pupil should honour the teacher's w., 2, 28, 190; 7, 129–31; alms (food) given by an unfaithful w. should not be accepted, 2, 71; 14, 71; penances for husband who forsakes w., for w. who forsakes husband, and for unfaithful ws., 2, 89 sq.; 14, 31, 31 sq. n., 110 sq., 232; 25, 467; a w. compared to the vessel which contains the curds for the sacrifice, 2, 91 sq.; 14, 220 sq.; the w.'s share in sacrifice, and other religious ceremonies, 2, 126 sq., 126 n., 137, 159, 217; 7, 111 sq.; 12, 1 sq., 28, 28 n., 65, 71–6, 84 n., 256–9, 256 n., 261 sq., 262 n., 275 sq., 291, 345 n., 369 n., 396–400, 397 n., 398 n., 406 sq. and n., 415 n., 424 n.; 14, 111, 186, 193–5; 19, 89; 25, 78 sq., 97, 342–4; 26, 19 n., 61 sq., 61 n., 73 n., 86, 99 n., 130 sq., 156, 177, 190–2, 225, 233 sq., 235 n., 352 n., 365–9, 385, 385 n., 442 sq.; 29, 290 sq., 386; 30, 21, 23, 28 sq., 81, 99, 105, 196, 316 sq.; 33, 264; 41, 31–5, 154 n., 190 n., 238 sq.; 42, 179–82, 185–92, 610 sq., 614, 645; 44, 48, 240; a man should not shave during the pregnancy of his w., 2, 220 n.; period of impurity for ws. and slaves, 7, 89; when a w. is to be avoided by a Snâtaka, 7, 226; 25, 135 sq.; the leavings of funeral repasts are for husbands who have deserted ws. descended from good families, 7, 251; by giving a bed, one procures a good w. or husband, 7, 267, 273 sq.; a hermit must entrust the care of his w. to his sons, or let her accompany him into the forest, 7, 276; 25, 199, 199 n.; ws. attain to the worlds acquired by their husbands, 8, 256; dialogue between husband and w., a Brâhma*n*a instructing his w. in the doctrine of Brahman, 8, 256–310; Dhamma being lost, the castes disagreed, and the w. despised her husband, 10 (ii), 52; 'ws. for those who wanted ws.' included in the perpetual grant made by Sudassana, 11, 263 sq.; the gods do not accept the offerings of a man whose w. is of the *S*ûdra caste, who lives in subjection to his w., or who allows a paramour to his w., 14, 70; a *S*ûdra w. not to be approached during the performance of a *S*rauta sacrifice, 14, 96; faithful and good ws. reside after death with their husbands, unfaithful ones are born as jackals, 14, 112; one's own w. is pure for oneself, impure for strangers, 14, 171;

females who have been purchased cannot assist at sacrifices, 14, 207; Heaven the reward of faithful w., 14, 232; husband and w. produced by the Self, 15, 85 sq.; all blessings come from a good and beautiful w., 25, 86, 332; how a dead w. is to be burned, 25, 198; etymology of gâyâ or 'w.,' 25, 329; acquires qualities of husband, 25, 331 sq.; the husband is one with the w., 25, 335; husband receives his w. from the gods, 25, 344; *'let mutual fidelity continue until death,' this may be considered as the summary of the highest law for husband and w.*, 25, 345; the house is the w.'s resting-place, 26, 61; is one half of husband, 26, 61 n.; 41, 32; 43, 132; the Pâtnîvata cup for Agni with the ws. of the gods (with reference to the sacrificer's w.), 26, 365–9, 365 n.; Patnîsâlâ, 'the w.'s or ladies' hall,' 26, 448, 448 n.; 43, 307, 307 n.; where the w. or the fires are, there is the home, 29, 89; fasts and performs the Vaisvadeva for the husband who is on a journey, 29, 90; prayer of an illegitimate child making offerings to the Manes, 29, 104; when the domestic fire goes out, the w. shall fast, 29, 172; made to lie down on the funeral pile, but rises again, 29, 239; *his w. is (as it were) his house*, 29, 386; 30, 21; rite against a w.'s paramour, 30, 177, 295; Brâhma*n*as have the right to converse with other men's ws., 33, 219; oaths by the heads of ws., 33, 315; is considered half the body of her husband, sharing the result of his good and wicked deeds, 33, 369, 377; a w. deceased before her husband takes away his consecrated fire, 33, 377; how a w. gains over her husband, 35, 302; a w. who has no son is possessed with Nir*ri*ti, 41, 65; charm to obtain a w., 42, 95, 502 sq.; prayer for the w. at a Soma-sacrifice, 42, 179–82; symbolical import of the Patnîsa*m*yâga by which offering is made to gods and their ws., 44, 44, 44 n.; at the horse-sacrifice the king's ws. anoint the horse and walk round the dead horse and lie down near it, 44, 312 sq., 321–6, 321 sq. n., 349, 386 sq.; derisive and obscene conversation between priests and queens at the horse-sacrifice, 44, 386 sq.; sacrificer's w. excluded from Pravargya, 44, 452 n., 463, 472, 495 sq. n., 502 n., 504; *the creator was not satisfied when he had given (to man) the w. as a fetter, he added a chain round his neck in the form of children*, 45, 24 n.; Agni, the lover of maidens, the husband of ws., 46, 57, 59; men worship Agni together with their ws., 46, 82; Agni accompanied by the Divine Ws., 46, 186; Agni makes husband and w. united, 46, 371; one whose w. has died, or who cannot procure a w., is prevented from belonging to an âsrama, 48, 705; do not adorn themselves, while their lord is absent, 49 (i), 82; husband and w. retire into the forest together, 49 (i), 87 sq.; *husband and w. are both consecrated in sacrifices, and both purified by the performance of the rites of the Veda, and both destined to enjoy the same results afterwards*, 49 (i), 88; ws. of gods, *see* Goddesses.

(*b*) IN INDIAN LAW AND CUSTOM.

The w.'s share of the inheritance, 2, 135; 25, 367 n.; 33, 377 sq.; no division of property takes place between husband and w., as they are one in spiritual and worldly matters, 2, 136 sq.; bride is given to the family, not only to the husband, 2, 166; both the w. and the husband have power over their common property, 2, 170, 170 n.; a Brâhma*n*a (Snâtaka) shall not take his meals with his w., 2, 222; 7, 221; 14, 61; 25, 135; 43, 369 sq. and n.; a Sûdra shall live with his w. only, 2, 233, 233 n.; duties of a w., 2, 270; 25, 195–7, 329, 332; 33, 368 sq.; law relating to a w. whose husband has gone abroad or renounced domestic life, her duties, 2, 272; 25, 340 sq.; plurality of ws., 7, xxi, 70–3; 14, 196 sq.; 32, 129; 43, 230; 46, 74; a king must appoint eunuchs for his ws. as their guardians, 7, 16; the crime of a w. who violates the

duty which she owes to her lord, 7, 27; duties of husband and w., a title of the law, 7, 38; 25, lxx, 254, 327–45, 327 n.; abandoning one's w., a crime in the fourth degree, 7, 135; the dowry of a w. is called 'white property,' 7, 190; a husband is lord over his ws., 7, 215; the w. takes her meal when the husband has eaten, 7, 216, 216 n.; husband and w. eat after the guests and the rest of the household have eaten, 7, 216 sq.; hating his w., one of the seven cruelties, 8, 167, 167 n., 182; householder shall be always devoted to his own w., 8, 216, 358; the old man who marries a young w., 10 (ii), 19; ws. consort with other men, 12, 76; there are more ws. to one man, but only one husband to one woman, 12, 148 sq., 148 n.; husband and w., the enjoyer and the one to be enjoyed, 12, 238; the ws. of slain soldiers shall be provided for, 14, 98; king's duty towards the mother and ws. of his predecessor, 14, 100; ws. who should be abandoned, 14, 111 sq., 234; 25, 342; should never be forsaken, 14, 133; 25, 321; giving a thousand oxen equals the gift of a maiden, 14, 137; to eat in the company of one's w. a custom of the south, 14, 146; ws. to be jealously watched, for the son belongs to the begetter, 14, 229; must be guarded more carefully than wealth, 14, 233; ws., sons, daughters, slaves, male and female, given away as presents, 21, 243; an excellent w. may be taken even from a base family, 25, 73; qualifications required for w., 25, 75–8; ws. of several castes, 25, 77, 342 sq.; quarrels with a w. to be avoided, 25, 157; one's w. to be considered as one's own body, 25, 158; must obey the husband, 25, 195 sq.; to be preserved at the expense of wealth, but life to be preserved at the expense of w. and wealth, 25, 251; the king in his harem, 25, 251 sq.; fine for defaming one's w., 25, 302; may be beaten, 25, 306; husband living on w.'s adultery, 25, 317; can have no property, 25, 326; a w., though sold or repudiated, cannot re-marry, 25, 335, 335 n.; repudiation and supersession of w., 25, 335, 341 sq., 344; sale of w., 25, 335, 442; position of children according to seniority and caste of ws., 25, 350 sq. and n., 356–8, 365 n., 371, 371 n.; all ws. of one husband are mothers through the son of one w., 25, 365; should not make a hoard from the property of their families or their husbands, 25, 372, 372 n.; Vaidehakas serve in the harem, 25, 413, 413 n.; sin of subsisting on w.'s earnings or property, 25, 443, 443 n.; atonement for killing his w., 25, 448, 448 n.; two classes of ws. in Vedic times, 32, 275 sq.; ws., sons, slaves, are dependent, 33, 51; one who has forsaken his w. cannot be a witness, 33, 87; miserable condition of a w. who has been superseded by another, 33, 92, 92 n.; gift of a w., an invalid gift, 33, 128, 342; slavery analogous to the condition of a w., 33, 136 n., 138; compared with fields, 33, 169, 176 sq.; lawsuits between husband and w. forbidden, 33, 183, 183 n., 234; husband though feeble must always be worshipped by his ws., 33, 217; debts contracted by ws., 33, 329; property of the w. belongs to one person even in an undivided family, 33, 382; a brother living with a deceased brother's w., 33, 389; should receive presents from her husband and from relations, 33, 391; a w. conciliates her husband with what belongs to him, 35, 302; the queen, one of the king's 'jewels,' 41, 60; *a discarded w. is one who has no son*, 41, 65; 46, 59 n., 65; many ws. are a form of prosperity, 44, 313; Pâlâgalî, the king's fourth w., of low caste, 44, 313 n.; how ws. treat their (hen-pecked) husbands like slaves, 45, 275–8. *See also* Adultery, Marriage, *and* Woman.

(*c*) In Zoroastrianism.

Worship to be performed by the w. as well as by the husband, 5, 351; the earth distressed by ws. who are disrespectful to their husbands, 5,

377; classes of ws., 18, 185 n.; 24, 316, 316 n.; to be obedient to their husbands, 23, 345; 24, 78; a virtuous w. is a good helper of enjoyment, 24, 41; to be protected, 24, 67; the worst w., 24, 69; may conduct legal proceedings for her husband, 37, 55, 55 n.; litigation about the ownership of a w., 37, 61; quarrels between husband and w., 37, 65 sq., 66 n., 100; crime of not maintaining ws. and children under control, 37, 68; husband's inquiry into the sin of a w., 37, 77; limit of w.'s liberality, of w.'s reverence for a husband, 37, 99; duties of a w., 37, 100, 381–3; income of w. and child, 37, 113; evil-speaking to ws. of others, 37, 130; a good w. among the four things to be acquired in youth, 37, 180; merit of giving a virtuous w. to a righteous man, 37, 204; Zoroaster's desire for a good w., 47, 153 sq.

(*d*) In China.

His w. and mother take part in the feast of Duke Hsî, 3, 346, 346 n.; assists at sacrifices and rites in ancestral temple, 3, 366 sq., 366 n.; 27, 454, 457, 459; 28, 33, 212, 214, 240 sq., 247; a w.'s complaint of being forsaken or badly treated by her husband, 3, 376, 376 n., 433 sq.; the industry and reverence of a prince's w. assisting him in sacrificing, 3, 431 sq. and n.; husband and w. looking on each other with averted eyes, 16, 77; an old husband and a young w.—an old w. and a young husband—extraordinary associations, 16, 117, 118 n., 302 sq., 303 n.; auspiciousness of union with a young w., 16, 123, 124 sq. n.; duties of husband and w., 16, 126, 127 sq. n.; 28, 245, 245 n., 247 sq.; 40, 243; the duties of a good w., 16, 136–8, 138 n.; 27, 55; 28, 431–4; 40, 243; it will not be good to marry a female who is bold and strong, 16, 154, 156 n.; an economical w., 16, 178; the correct place of the w. in the family, 16, 242, 243 n.; relations between husband and w., 16, 278 sq.; 27, 27, 457 sq., 470 sq.; submission fortunate in a w., while the husband must decide what is right, 16, 307; 27, 380; mutual love of husband and w., 16, 313, 313 n.; 27, 440; entering into his palace and not seeing his w. is inauspicious, 16, 326, 390; origin of the relations of husband and w., father and son, 16, 435 sq.; position of w. in China, 27, 27, 457 sq., 470, 479; in the ruler's court one should not speak of ws. and daughters, 27, 103; titles and designations of ws., 27, 112 sq.; buried in the same grave with the husband, 27, 132, 202; does not dare to see her husband's parents without her upper robes, 27, 176; presides at the funeral rites, 27, 316; 28, 75; ladies of the harem as teachers, 27, 350 n.; husband and w. at ceremonies, 27, 410–12; faithfulness the virtue of a w., 27, 439; supplied with what was left from the ruler's meal, 28, 4, 4 n.; demeanour of ws. on festive occasions, 28, 74 sq.; as personatrix of the dead, 28, 75; look after the silkworms, 28, 239; respect to be shown to the w., 28, 266; inside the female apartments a man may sport, but should not sigh, 28, 291; virtue of w. and virtue of husband, 28, 364; Âi-thâi Tho's w. would rather be his concubine than the w. of any other man, 39, 229; bad men led by ws. or concubines to disobey their parents, 40, 242.

(*e*) In Islâm.

Pure ws. for the believers in paradise, 6, 4, 48; ws. *are a garment unto you, and ye a garment unto them*, 6, 26; maintenance for a year to be bequeathed to ws., 6, 37; arbitration between husband and w., 6, 77; punishment of refractory ws., 6, 77; impartiality and kindness towards ws., 6, 90; law concerning an imputation of unchastity to a w., 9, 73 sq.; God created ws. for men and made between them affection and pity, 9, 126, 206; special injunctions for the ws. of Mohammed, 9, 142 sq. and n., 147 sq.

Will: about free w., 24, 236 sq.; *where the w. is not diverted from its*

object, the spirit is concentrated, 40, 15; no more deadly weapon than the w., 40, 84, 84 n.; repress the impulses of the w., 40, 87; w. or testament, *see* Inheritance. *See also* Saṅkalpa, *and* Volition.

Will-o'-the-wisp, or 'little shiner,' 42, 411.

Wind: Aryan storm myths, 4, lxiv; spell against the w.-daêva, 4, 140; the powerful W., made by Mazda, 4, 213 sq.; 31, 291; Bâ*d*, the W., invoked and worshipped, 4, 213 sq.; 23, 10, 18, 166, 285, 334, 352; 31, 256, 277, 291, 346; description of the w. spirit, 5, 169; chief among those that blow, 8, 90, 90 n.; K*r*ish*n*a is the W., 8, 97; carries away perfumes, 8, 112; comes from the eternal divine being, 8, 192; heat in the body urged by a sharp w., 8, 237 sq.; the soul shaken about by the w., 8, 239; one of the ten fires at the allegorical sacrifice of the sense-organs, 8, 261; presiding deity of nose and smell, 8, 337, 349; the three constituent elements, w., bile, and phlegm, 8, 343 n.; presiding deity of skin and touch, 8, 350, 350 n.; is the source of the feeling of touch, 8, 352; purifies, 14, 171; purified by Ka, 14, 331; appeased by Keresâsp, 18, 372, 376 sq.; 37, 198, 198 n.; both angel and demon, 18, 372 n.; 24, 17 n.; Indian philosophers on the nature of w., 22, 9 n.; sins caused by actions injuring the lives in w., 22, 13 sq.; Ti*s*trya worshipped on the day of Bâ*d* (the W.), 23, 92; assists Ti*s*trya, 23, 102; the fiend-smiting W. present at the ordeal, 23, 170; victorious W. helps in battle, 23, 191; not to ease nature against the w., 25, 136 sq.; a guardian deity of the world, 25, 185, 216 sq.; king to emulate the w., 25, 396 sq.; tells the gods the thoughts of man, 26, 94; Ws., 'the noisy goddesses,' invoked to protect cattle, 29, 99, 99 n.; invoked for protection, 29, 349; the quarters, the consorts of W., 30, 213; the bounteous W. of blessed gift, 31, 256; the good and holy W., 31, 277, 326; as the wind cannot be pointed out, yet exists, so Nirvâ*n*a, 36, 106 sq.; the breath of nature, 39, 177; the bad man reproaches the w. and reviles the rain, 40, 242; Pa*ñk*avâtîya, or oblation to the five ws., 41, 48–50; invoked in a medical charm, 42, 14; breath from the w., eye from the sun, 42, 56; mind fashioned from the w., 43, 6; is everywhere, 43, 33 sq.; deity and metre, 43, 53; by means of the twenty-onefold hymn-form one frees both rain and w. for living beings, 43, 68; Vâyu is the w., 43, 142; is the arrows of the Rudras in the air, 43, 165; Vâta, the w., as a Gandharva, the waters, as the Apsaras, his mates, 43, 232; is on this side of the sun, and also in this and the other world, 43, 235 sq.; bestowing the w. (which blows in the three worlds) on the fire-altar by the 'oblations of air,' 43, 235–7; fire, sun, moon, quarters pass into the w., 43, 333; kindled by the fire, 43, 399; one of the six doors to the Brahman, 44, 66 sq.; *all beings, indeed, pass over into the w., and from out of the w. they are again produced,* 44, 84; 'from the w. I take thy breathings,' 44, 133; the w.-names (Ocean, Flood, Unassailable, Irresistible, Favourable, Ogress-ridder), and offerings to the W. under these names, 44, 478 sq.; the aerial ocean is the w., 44, 479; deities identified with the W., 44, 479–81; five kinds of w., as living beings, 45, 218, 218 n.; origin and feeding of w.-bodies, 45, 397; Agni goes along with the flame-coloured Ws., 46, 187. *See also* Breath, Maruts, Prâ*n*as, Sacred objects, Vâta, *and* Vâyu.

Wine, *see* Spirituous liquors.

Winter, *see* Seasons.

Wisdom, is beneficial, like fire, 5, 394; wise men, 10 (i), 23–6; Buddha explains the state of w., 10 (ii), 128–31; the sevenfold higher w., seven kinds of w., 11, 9, 14, 61, 63, 306; 35, 128; how a Bhikkhu may obtain higher w., 11, 233; w. and justice, 18, 11 sq.; every good achieved through w., and the best w. is the pure religion, 18, 20 sq.; created as an appliance of man, 18,

88; two kinds of w., 18, 90, 90 n., 133 sq., 134 n.; what w. and intellect are good, 18, 271 sq.; is the handy bark across the sea of birth and death, 19, 303 sq.; heavenly W., and W. acquired through the ear, 23, 4, 4 n., 12 sq., 20, 35, 37; address, all the night long, the heavenly W., 23, 339; Spirit of W., the innate w. of Aûharmazd, 24, xvi; conversation with the Spirit of W., 24, 3–113, 3 n.; the creator created and managed the world through w., 24, 5, 7 sq.; the power of w., 24, 7 sq.; homage to the Spirit of W., 24, 8; w. without goodness and skill without w. are useless, 24, 37; the wise and contented man cannot be disturbed, 24, 70; he who is perfect in w. is rich, 24, 70; who is more complete in w., 24, 76 sq.; through w. every one is satisfied, 24, 80; the most perfect wealth, 24, 89; the seat of w. in the body, 24, 89 sq.; the many advantages and uses of w., 24, 98–104; a wise poor man is more esteemed by the angels than an ignorant king, 24, 105; w. and intelligence or reasoning distinguished, 35, 50 sq., 66–9; its characteristic mark, 35, 61 sq.; where is it? 35, 120; instinctive and acquired w., 37, 20 sq.; is for Aûharmazd, 37, 317; increased by recitation of the revelation, 37, 330; of the good religion, 37, 342; discriminating through w., 37, 373 sq.; *put away your small w., and your great w. will be bright*, 40, 137; Zoroaster sees the omniscient w., 47, 158. *See also* Knowledge.

Wishes, rites for obtaining special, 26, 145, 251, 454 sq.; 30, 189, 259; 43, 138, 240 sq., 247, 265; different rules for building a house according to different w. one may have, 30, 120 sq.; the anointed king chooses a boon, 41, 108; three w. of the sacrificer fulfilled, 42, 181; in w. nothing is excessive, 43, 241, 247, 265.

Witchcraft: sorcery and curses cause impurity, or even loss of caste, 2, 92; magic rites and incantations enjoined for the king against enemies, 2, 236; Brâhmans and Buddhists credited with w. practices, 4, 8; created by Angra-Mainyu, 4, 8, 8 n.; men killed by w., 4, 77; w. and evil-doing introduced by Azi Dahâka, 4, 385; 18, 217; the sorcery of Nôktargâ, 5, 138; Bhikkhus must not practise, learn, or teach the low arts of divination, spells, w., &c., 11, 196 sq., 199; 20, 152; diseases caused by w., 17, 60; a most grievous sin, 18, 417; 24, 72; spells, w., and herbs pernicious to life revert thither whence they come, when one thinks of Avalokitesvara, 21, 414; slander more grievous than w., 24, 9; the religion of the Manicheans denounced as w., 24, 170; charms buried to do injury to enemies, 26, 135, 135 n., 137 sq.; ceremony to avert death through w., 30, 118; disputes of persons versed in w. to be settled by persons familiar with the three Vedas only, 33, 281; ordeal by poison to be administered without the application of spells, 33, 318; a vanishing root which makes men invisible, 35, 281; 36, 119; burying images of another to obtain an injurious power over him, 40, 241, 241 n.; return from w. practices without looking back, 41, 44, 53 sq.; he who knows the mystic meaning of 'year' is not overcome by magic art, 44, 14; Indra exorcized by Tvashtri with Soma-juice suitable for w., 44, 213 sq.; Raivata skilled in sacred spells, and able to counteract poison, 49 (i), 194. *See also* Amulets, Auspicious rites, Imprecations, Incantations, Magic, Magic rites, Magician, Sorcerers, Spells, *and* Witches.

Witches and wizards, believed in by the Arabs, 6, xiv; the soul's unatoned sin collected by w., 18, 54; wizards and w. vanquished by the angels, 18, 88 sq.; w. whose vesture is shooting stars, meteors, and comets, 18, 96, 96 n.; w. described, 18, 97; demons, w., and wizards, 18, 126, 384, 418–20, 424; 24, 91 sq., 103; execution of supposed w., 18, 428; the seven planets have the form of w., 24, 128, 128 n., 131, 132 n.; nail-parings become

weapons of wizards, 24, 276; Haoma invoked against demons, sorcerers, and w., 31, 236; wizards and w. to be punished, 37, 259; *K*i-hsien, a wizard and soothsayer, 39, 262 sq.; a female practiser of love-spells sacrificed at the Purusha-medha, 44, 414; Sîtô slain by w., 47, 137 sq.; wizards attempt to harm the infant Zoroaster, 47, 145.

Witnesses, law about, 2, 170 sq., 246–9; 7, 39, 44, 47–52; 14, 80, 82 sq., 202–4; 25, 263–75, 284, 284 n.; 33, xiii, 21, 23, 30, 34, 38, 58–60, 64 sq., 70, 77, 79–96, 235, 244–8, 295, 297, 299–304, 311–14, 331, 334, 339, 352; 37, 38; examining and exhorting w., 2, 248 sq.; 33, 90–6; false witnesses not to be invited to a *S*râddha, 2, 257; giving false evidence a mortal sin, causes loss of caste, 2, 281; 7, 134; 14, 218; 25, 441; false evidence permitted, if true evidence would cause death, 7, 50; penance for false w., 7, 176; 25, 448; women and slaves not accepted as w., 24, 78; one quarter of the guilt falls on a false w., 25, 255; false evidence for pious ends, 25, 272; w. concerning boundary marks, 25, 299 sq.; false w. and slayers of a Brâhma*n*a equally guilty, 33, 301; perjured w. punished as 'open thieves,' 33, 360 sq. *See also* Judicial procedure, Oath, Ordeals, *and* Woman (*a*, *g*).

Wives, *see* Wife.

Wizards, *see* Witches.

Wolf, origin of, 41, 131; 44, 215. *See also* Animals (*k*).

Woman, Women.

(*a*) Social and legal position of w. in India.
(*b*) W. in Brâhma*n*ism.
(*c*) W. in Buddhism.
(*d*) W. in *G*aina religion.
(*e*) W. in Zoroastrianism.
(*f*) W. in China.
(*g*) W. in Islâm.

See also Abortion, Adultery, Daughters, Impurity, Marriage, Mother, Niyoga, Prostitution, Sexual intercourse, Widows, *and* Wife.

(*a*) SOCIAL AND LEGAL POSITION OF W. IN INDIA.

How female relations and other w. should be saluted, 2, 53 sq., 208 sq.; 14, 67, 153 sq.; 25, 52, 54; sin of, and penances for, slaying w., 2, 79 sq., 284–6; 7, 158; 14, 107 sq., 212; 25, 444, 448; way must be made for a (pregnant) w., 2, 126, 171, 211; 7, 203; 14, 68 sq., 243; 25, 55; w. in the law of inheritance, 2, 133 sq. n., 303 n., 305 sq. n., 306, 310; 7, 68–70, 73 sq.; 14, xxvi, 89, 230 sq. and n.; 25, 348, 349 n., 352 sq. and n., 358 n., 366 n., 367 n., 370–2 and n., 377 n., 378, 378 sq. n.; 33, xv, 49, 189–96, 201 sq., 202 n., 377–81, 383; all or some w. are free from taxes, 2, 164; 14, 99; not lost to the owner by adverse possession, 2, 243; 14, 81; 25, 279, 279 sq. n.; 33, 61, 61 n.; in an action concerning w., or the procreation of offspring, the defendant must answer without delay, 2, 249; *in childhood a female must be subject to her father, in youth to her husband, when her lord is dead to her sons; a w. must never be independent*, 2, 270 n.; 7, 111; 14, 31, 231; 25, 195, 327 sq.; 33, 196 sq.; separate property of w. (strîdhana), 2, 306; 7, 69 sq.; 25, 84 sq. and n., 370–2 and n.; 33, 136 n., 183, 190, 190 sq. n., 263 sq., 383; fine for defamation of a maiden, 7, 29; 25, 294; pregnant w. exempt from fare or toll, 7, 36; 25, 325; of female slaves and cattle, the offspring shall be taken as interest, 7, 43; 33, 67; w. in the law of debts, 7, 45; 33, 45–9; a document executed by a w. makes no evidence, 7, 47; 33, 76, 307; cannot be witnesses, 7, 48; 25, 268; 33, 86, 89 sq.; certain ordeals fit, others unfit for w., 7, 54; 33, 98, 101, 113, 248 sq.; illegitimate intercourse with w., 7, 62–5, 222; w. and the intermixture of castes, 7, 66; duties of w., 7, 110 sq.; 25, lxix, 42, 194–7; 33, 368; the crime of killing a w. in her courses, or a pregnant w., or an âtreyî, equal to the murder of a Brâhma*n*a, 7, 133 sq.; sin of intercourse with w. who drink spirituous liquor, 7, 137; 25, 443 sq.; the male the ruler of females, 8, 345 sq.; adorned w. enumerated among the wealth of kings, 10 (ii), 50; 35, 267; the male represents energy, the female is without energy, 12,

402; 43, 230; 44, 219; *husbands, doubtless, are the support of w.*, 12, 441; can neither give nor receive a son except with husband's permission, 14, 75, 334; w. shall be witnesses in cases concerning w., 14, 82; 25, 266, 266 n.; 33, 82; false evidence regarding w., 14, 83; 25, 271; the son of an unmarried damsel, 14, 86 sq., 227; punishments and penances for w. who have offended, 14, 108–12; 25, 382; fine for killing a female of the Sûdra caste, 14, 118; crimes by which w. become outcasts, 14, 133; fighting with w. forbidden, 14, 200; punishments for murder of w., 14, 202; purchase and sale of w. denounced as a crime, 14, 207 sq.; laws regarding w., 14, 231–5; 25, 611 sq.; 33, xiii; the learned lady Gârgî Vâkaknavî, 15, 130 sq., 136–9; violence towards w. recommended, 15, 217; the sixty-four accomplishments of w., 22, 282, 282 n.; honour due to w., 25, lxvii, 85 sq.; deceiving w. and Sûdras, 25, 160; forming part of the booty, 25, 231; employed in the royal service, 25, 236; betray secrets, hence to be removed from a king's council, 25, 239; the king must deliberate on the behaviour of the w. in his harem, 25, 240; the king shall protect the property of unprotected w., 25, 257 sq. and n.; may exceptionally be witnesses, 25, 267; swearing falsely to w. at marriages allowed, 25, 273; stealing w., punishment for it, 25, 310, 498; 33, 227, 362 sq.; to protect w., arms may be taken up, 25, 315; all w. must be carefully guarded, 25, 327–30; 33, 367; six causes of the ruin of w., 25, 329; slayers of w. put to death, cannot be purified, 25, 382, 469; pregnant w. not punished for committing nuisance, 25, 392; how w. allure men, 26, 30 sq.; are given to vain things, 26, 53; beauty of w., 26, 113; 44, 294 sq.; neither own any self nor do they own any heritage, 26, 367; shall not be charioteers, 29, 364; a w. approaches a friend for a gift, 32, 313; a charitable w. is worth more than a miserly man, 32, 356; in the case of a w. a sentence passed may be reversed, 33, 16 sq. and n.; valid and invalid transactions of w., 33, 49 sq.; law of limitation regarding property of w., 33, 61 sq.; females (slaves) as articles of sale, 33, 150, 150 n.; purchased, 33, 175 sq., 176 n.; intercourse with unchaste w. permitted, 33, 180 sq.; lawsuits raised by w. inadmissible, 33, 234; w. are not entitled to bestow gifts, or to sell property, 33, 264; must not be put under restraint, 33, 288; for w., representatives must proffer plaint or answer, 33, 288; are easily deceived by forged documents, 33, 307; law about possession of w. and slaves, 33, 311; gifts to be bestowed on idiots, aged and infirm, w. and children, 33, 349; treatment of a w. violated against her will, 33, 366 sq.; punishment for adulterous w., 33, 367; *see also* Adultery; vices of w., 33, 368; gift of w. forbidden, 36, 121; the male lies on the right side of the female, 41, 199; 43, 81; a female injures no one, 41, 202; a perfect w. is fair-knotted, fair-braided, fair-locked, 41, 232; sisters without a brother, bereft of strength, 42, 22, 258 sq.; mentioned before men, 42, 93; unmarried girls live with mother, father, or brother, 42, 254; female head-gear, 42, 538 sq.; *people do not kill a w., but rather take (anything) from her (leaving her) alive*, 44, 62; there is no friendship with w., 44, 71 sq.; wool and thread is w.'s work, 44, 219; one who is in his prime of life dear to w., 44, 295; made to be attendant upon man, 44, 300; brotherless girls, i.e. w. of evil conduct, go to hell, 46, 335.

(*b*) W. in Brâhmanism.

Some w. to be approached, others not, no w. to be avoided at the Vâmadevya, 1, 30 n.; 38, 310; seeing a w. in a dream is prophetic of success, 1, 76; 48, 604; is the altar on which the Devas offer seed, 1, 79; 15, 208; *here the blood of the w. is a form of Agnî (fire); therefore no one should despise it. And the seed of a man is a form of Âditya (sun); therefore no one should despise it*, 1, 232; w., the Self, and child-

birth, 1, 243–5; Arthaśâstra, the knowledge which Sûdras and w. possess, a supplement of the Atharva-veda, 2, xxxii, 171, 171 n.; are not initiated, 2, 2 n.; how the Brahmakârin should behave towards w., 2, 11, 34; 14, 152–4, 157; 25, 69; must not refuse alms to Brahmakârins, 2, 12; the Brahmakârin should not gaze at, or touch w., 2, 25 sq., 188; the recitation of the Veda must be interrupted, when a student and a Sûdra w. look at each other, 2, 34; purification prescribed on touching a w., 2, 59; penances to be performed by w., 2, 84, 84 n.; an initiated person shall not eat the leavings of w., 2, 122, 122 n.; rites and customs to be learnt from w., 2, 138, 138 n., 171; 29, 182; 30, 255; shall not perform religious rites, sacrifices, vows, fasts, 2, 139, 270, 270 n.; 25, 161, 196, 437; 30, 267; newly-married or unmarried damsels, sick w., and pregnant w. must eat before the householder, and may eat even before guests, 2, 204; 7, 216; 14, 265; 25, 96, 96 n.; 29, 86; rules for the Snâtaka with regard to w., 2, 222, 224; 14, 243; 25, 137; 29, 123, 317–19, 409; 30, 85; funeral rites for female relations, 2, 253; 7, 86; 14, 28, 28 n., 177 sq.; 29, 358 sq.; a person who sacrifices for w. not to be invited to a Srâddha, 2, 257; sins whereby w. become outcasts, 2, 281, 281 n.; dying in defence of w. and children secures beatitude, 7, 67; 25, 416; impurity of w. after a miscarriage, 7, 90; 14, 182; 25, 179; impurity on the death of w., 7, 90; 25, 180; the marriage ceremony is considered as the initiation of w., 7, 90; impurity by death and childbirth, with regard to w., 7, 91 sq.; the mouth of a w. is always pure, 7, 103; 25, 192; religious rites for girls, except marriage rites, performed without sacred texts, 7, 114; 25, 42, 330, 330 n.; 29, 57, 183 sq., 298, 397; 30, 59, 62; while engaged in performing penances or rites securing success, one must avoid conversing with w., 7, 151; 14, 124, 305, 323; 25, 476; rule about sipping of water for w., 7, 199; the share of departed w. and maternal ancestors in the Srâddhas, 7, 238 sq.; Lakshmî resides in the body of a married w., and of an unmarried damsel, 7, 299; Lakshmî resides in virtuous w., 7, 300 sq.; become corrupt by neglect of family rites, 8, 41; even w. attain the supreme goal, 8, 85, 85 n., 255; 'seven females,' giving birth to the universe, 8, 287, 287 n.; association with w. belongs to the quality of passion, 8, 324; among w. who are a source of happiness, the Apsarases are chief, 8, 347; the goddess Mâheśvarî, the chief of 'those who are followed by men full of desires,' 8, 347; the altar represented as a w. embracing the man (fire), 12, 63; 26, 119 sq.; the offering-spoon is female, the dipping-spoon is male, 12, 71; w. eat apart from men, 12, 259; maidens worship Rudra Tryambaka to obtain husbands, 12, 441; rules of purification for w., and Sûdras, 14, 21, 167; what has been handled by w. must be purified, 14, 22; Indra and the w., 14, 33, 61; belong to Soma, Gandharva, and Fire, before they belong to men, 14, 133; begging from w., 14, 157; 44, 50; are pure at the time of dalliance, 14, 170; *are considered to have no business with the sacred texts*, 14, 178; 25, 330; less severe penances for w., 14, 221, 223; an ascetic must not speak with w., 14, 282; are the devatâ of the loving person, 15, 143; the creation of w., 15, 215; aged w. perform rites at the birth of a child, 19, 7; names of w., 25, 35, 76 sq.; 29, 183, 297; 30, 58, 283; are naturally wicked, 25, 69, 330; milk of w., forbidden food, 25, 171; no funeral libations for wicked w., 25, 184; mode of purification for w., 25, 193; punishment in future births of w., 25, 499; pursued by Rakshas, 26, 35; Gandharvas fond of w., 26, 53; 42, 34; auspicious or evil bodily marks of w., 29, 21, 165; 30, 42, 256 sq.; 42, 109, 260 sq.; 43, 81; happy young w. who are not widows

employed at weddings, 29, 32; perform a dance at the wedding, 29, 32; different rules as to salving for w., 29, 228; ceremonies to be performed by the w. of the house, 29, 247, 249; perform sacrifice to agricultural deities, 29, 336; a perjurer will become a w. in a future birth, 33, 92; created for the sake of propagation, 33, 169; impure is the part of w. below the navel, 41, 32; female conceives again after birth, 41, 311; are fond of kush*th*a plant, 42, 6, 680; brings forth within a year, 44, 12; 'w.'s rites' (strîkarmâ*n*i), charms pertaining to w., 42, 94–110, 275, 311, 371 sq., 479 sq., 496 sq.; w. of the waters, 42, 409, 521; Belief and Unbelief as two w., 44, 110 sq.; by the womb of w. Pragâpati bore creatures, 44, 114; four w., a maiden, and four hundred female attendants given as sacrificial gift, 44, 402; unchaste, barren, and other w. sacrificed at the Purushamedha, 44, 413, 415; different sepulchral mound for men and w., 44, 435; w., the *S*ûdra, the dog, and the crow are untruth, sin, darkness, 44, 446; the Mahâvîra pot is a w., 44, 449; Agni and Aryaman connected with w., 46, 371; *w. are Brahman, and so are men*, 48, 191; compared to a fire in which seed is offered, 48, 585;—when one who is about to study the Veda wishes to speak to a w. in her courses, he should speak to a Brâhma*n*a before and after speaking to her: this is auspicious for her offspring, 2, 34; w. in their courses are Apapâtras, 2, 61 n.; purification for touching a w. in her courses, or a w. after confinement, 2, 253; 7, 94; 14, 30, 182; 25, 183; food of a w. who has no male relatives, of a w. in her courses, of an unchaste w., of a w. in childbed, or of men who are ruled by w., must not be eaten, 2, 266 sq.; 7, 163 sq.; 14, 69; 25, 161–3; punishment of menstruous w. who touches an Aryan, 7, 34; a w. is purified by her monthly discharge, 7, 97; 14, 24, 31–3, 132 sq., 233; 25, 188; a Snâtaka must not speak to, nor approach a w. in her courses, 7, 228; 25, 135, 137; the look of a w. in her courses is contaminating at a *S*râddha, 7, 250; 25, 119; rules for w. during their courses, 14, 32 sq.; 15, 218 sq.; 25, 179; 30, 199, 199 n., 268; sin of intercourse with menstruating w., 25, 466; the Dîkshita's garment beaten by the priest, in case part of it may have been spun or woven by an unclean w., 26, 10; in the presence of a recently confined woman or one in her courses, Veda-study must be interrupted, 29, 81, 117, 141. *See also* Âtreyî.

(*c*) W. IN BUDDHISM.

Bad conduct is the taint of w., 10 (i), 61; love of man towards w., to be destroyed by the Bhikkhu, 10 (i), 69; contempt for w.'s body, 10 (ii), 160; as mourners, at funerals, 11, xli; excluded from accompanying the funeral procession, 11, xlii; so long as no w. or girls belonging to their clans are detained among the Vaggians, by force or abduction, so long they will prosper, 11, 3 sq.; *'how are we to conduct ourselves, Lord, with regard to womankind?' 'Don't see them, Ânanda.' 'But if we should see them, what are we to do?' 'Abstain from speech, Ânanda.' 'But if they should speak to us, Lord, what are we to do?' 'Keep wide awake, Ânanda,'* 11, 91; the Bhikkhu abstains from the getting of any w. or girl, of bondmen or bondwomen, 11, 191; the W.-Treasure of King Sudassana, 11, 256 sq.; the ideal of a beautiful w. and a virtuous wife, 11, 256 sq.; a Bhikkhu must not lie down, nor take a seat in secret with a w., 13, 32, 42; a Bhikkhu must not preach the Dhamma, in more than five or six words, to a w. unless another man be present, 13, 32 sq.; a Bhikkhu must not journey with a w. even as far as the next village, 13, 47; female lay disciples of Buddha, 13, 109 sq.; 17, 216–25; delusions by w., one of the dangers in which interruption of Vassa is permitted, 13, 315 sq.; the longing of pregnant w., 17, 295; attempts to delude Buddha by w., 19, 38–46,

53 sq.; 49 (i), 36–48; Buddha disgusted at the sight of the sleeping w., 19, 54–6; 49 (i), 56–9; cf. 13, 102 sq.; the wiles of w., 19, 253–6; 35, 294–7, 297 n.; not to be saluted by Bhikkhus, 20, 195; a Bhikkhu should not look into the face of the w. who gives him food, 20, 291; Buddha is very reluctant to admit w. into the Order, and declares that that religion will not last long in which w. are allowed to enter into the homeless state, 20, 320–6; are capable of Arhatship, 20, 322; 35, 297 n.; if no w. had been admitted to the Order, Buddhism would have endured for a thousand years, 20, 325; 35, 186; Ânanda caused the dead body of Buddha to be saluted by w. first, 20, 379; Ânanda blamed for exerting himself for the admission of w. into the Order, 20, 380; there is no womankind in Buddha-fields, 21, 194, 197, 377, 417; w. as preachers, 21, 213–20, 336 sq., 336 n., 346, 348; ladies hear the Saddharmapu*nd*arîka, 21, 248, 424; cannot occupy the ranks of Brahma, Indra, chief guardian of the four quarters, *K*akravartin, Bodhisattva, 21, 252; cannot reach Buddhaship, but the daughter of Sâgara changes her sex to become a Buddha, 21, 252–4; a Bodhisattva's conduct towards w., 21, 263–6; capable of perfect enlightenment, 21, 316 sq., 319–24; 49 (ii), 199; merits acquired by young ladies who hear the law preached, 21, 328–35; a preacher of the law discerns by his smell whether a pregnant w. will bear a boy or a girl, &c., 21, 344; a w. who hears the Bhaisha*g*yarâ*g*a chapter of the Saddharmapu*nd*arîka will never be reborn again as w., but as a Bodhisattva in Sukhâvatî, 21, 389 sq.; Gadgadasvara assumes the shape of a w. in order to preach the Lotus to w., 21, 401 sq.; w. who wish to have beautiful offspring adore Avalokite*s*vara, 21, 409; conditions under which the Lotus of the True Law may be entrusted to w., 21, 432 sq.; ladies studying the Abhidhamma, 35, 24 sq.; mentioned before men in the phrase 'a w. or a man,' 35, 83, 83 n.; 36, 89, 127 sq. n., 175; 49 (ii), 123, 125, 129, 139; Khuggutarâ remembered her previous births, 35, 122; reveal secrets through infirmity, 35, 141; w. whose good actions bare fruit in this life, 35, 172; influence of Buddhism on w., 35, 297 n.; a married w. sins only in secret, 36, 82; rules of conduct towards w. for Bhikkhus, 36, 98, 98 n., 100; there are men who have become w., and w. who have become men, 36, 101; a w. without a husband despised, 36, 140; the life of w. is always darkness, 49 (i), 4; w. of the seraglio viewing a royal procession, 49 (i), 28–30; saints seduced by w., 49 (i), 38 sq.; despise their female nature, 49 (ii), 19; Stryâgâra, 'Frauenzimmer,' 49 (ii), 64 n. *See also* Bhikkhunîs.

(*d*) W. IN *G*AINA RELIGION.

The world is greatly troubled by w. who are the causes of all sin, 22, 21, 48, 81; Mahâvîra renounced the female sex, 22, 80; on the conduct of *G*aina monks with regard to w., 22, 303; 45, 5, 74–6; one of the twenty-two troubles (parîsaha) to be vanquished by a *G*aina monk, 45, 9, 11; empty houses i.e. in which there are no w., 45, 12 n.; *do not desire* (*w.*), *those female demons, on whose breasts grow two lumps of flesh, who continually change their mind, who entice men, and then make a sport of them as of slaves. A houseless* (*monk*) *should not desire w., he should turn away from females*, 45, 35; nothing in the world offers so many difficulties to the monk as w., he should therefore avoid their company altogether, 45, 186, 204; w. and water cause loss of sanctity to a *G*aina monk, 45, 266; heretics, slaves of w., see no harm in intercourse with w., 45, 270; are a great temptation to monks, how they must be avoided, 45, 270–8; *one man* (*w.*) *have in their heart, another in their words, and another still in their actions. Therefore a monk should not trust w., knowing that they are full of deceit*, 45, 274; though acquainted with the Strî-

veda, men get into the power of w., 45, 274; seduced by their senses and by w., men are born again and again, 45, 318; men whom w. do not seduce value Moksha most, 45, 330. *See also* Gaina monks and nuns, *and* Gaina nuns.

(*e*) W. IN ZOROASTRIANISM.

Impurity of, and rules regarding to, w. during their menses, defilement by menstruous matter, 4, lxxviii sq., lxxxi, 65, 80, 185–9; 5, lx, 248, 251, 261, 265, 270 sq., 276–85, 304, 333, 340 sq. n.; 18, 191, 228, 447; 24, 111, 270, 296, 302–5, 332–4, 340, 353; 37, 45, 100–2, 162, 164, 187, 432, 446; 47, 168; w.'s diseases (abnormal issues) created by Angra-Mainyu, 4, 9; the earth wanting a good husbandman, is like a maiden without a husband, 4, 29; an object of contract, like cattle or fields, 4, 45 sq., 45 n.; a w. who has been delivered of a still-born child, 4, 62–5, 91 sq.; difference of rules of purification according to sex, 4, 110, 127; belong to the earth, 4, 144; law about seduction, 4, 178 sq.; atonement for intercourse with a w. during her sickness, 4, 206–8; may act as priests, as well as men, 4, 307–9, 307 n., 327; 5, 332 sq., 332 n.; 37, 95; the sacrifice of w. and children accepted, 4, 339; the fiend of menstruation (Gêh), 5, 15 sq., 15 n., 283, 283 n.; menstruation and generation, 5, 60 sq.; carrying the corpse of a pregnant w., 5, 247, 247 n., 319, 319 n.; pollution of pregnant w. punishable, 5, 272; fire to be maintained in the dwelling of a pregnant w., 5, 316 sq.; not marrying a husband a sin worthy of death, 5, 322 sq.; honourable position of Mazdayasnian w., 5, 367, 367 n.; virtuous w. protected by Spendarma*d*, 5, 373, 376 sq.; provisions made for wives and daughters of a deceased pater familias, 18, 183–90; law of inheritance and w., 18, 183–7, 195 sq.; 37, 486; fit and unfit w. for adoption, 18, 190 sq.; Fravashis of holy w., of w. who have many sons, worshipped, 23, 224–8; 31, 197, 204, 209, 215, 219, 224, 273, 279; maids pray to Vayu for a husband, 23, 258, 258 n.; the holy w., well principled and obedient to her husband, 23, 318, 321; not to be witnesses, 24, 78, 78 n.; 37, 38, 58; virtues of a w., 24, 108; ceremonies performed both by men and w., 24, 263; sacred thread-girdle to be worn by w. and men (sic), 24, 268, 270; dangers to menstruation, 24, 277; dangers to pregnant w. to be avoided, 24, 277 sq.; sin of slander regarding w., 24, 305 sq.; the only Nyâyi*s* for w. is obedience to their husbands, 24, 320 sq.; all w. must have the Dvâzdah-hômâst celebrated, as an atonement for menstruation, 24, 330 sq., 330 n.; sin and punishment of w. committing adultery, 24, 331 sq.; garments fit for menstruous w., 24, 355; Haoma grants offspring to w., and husbands to the maidens, 31, 237; good men and w., whom Ahura knows, worshipped, 31, 253, 257, 268; the w. who have many sons worshipped, 31, 336, 385; stately w. of good parentage worshipped, 31, 340; holy w. summoned to the sacrifice, 31, 342; the house-mistress, and the holy woman forward in good thoughts, words, and deeds, 31, 386; law about property of w., 37, 18, 148; conflicts between childless w. and pregnant w., 37, 41; about well-taught w., 37, 45; about the care of a pregnant w., 37, 45; stealing w. (slaves), 37, 58 sq.; condemned for wizard's spells, 37, 65; sin of bartering w. for w., 37, 66; about a w. without a guardian, 37, 71; about theft by w., 37, 76; sin of giving weapons to w., 37, 78; a w. may marry one of two men condemned to death, 37, 78; fitness of w. for judgeship, if acquainted with the law, 37, 80; relation of sexes, 37, 109–12; damsel given by an idolator to a Mazda-worshipper, 37, 148; a w. who is reverent, 37, 485; heretics buying their w. as sheep, 47, 89.

(*f*) W. IN CHINA.

One of Wû's 'ten men' (ministers) was a w., 3, 128 n.; overseers of states shall find helping connexions for (destitute) w., 3, 180; worship of female ancestors, 3, 323, 326,

326 n., 332; an unfortunate w. who has been seduced bemoans her fate, 3, 437 sq.; a lady assures her lover of her affection unto death, 3, 440; those who exercise forbearance with the ignorant, learn even from w., 16, 65, 66 n.; ignorance and retirement are proper in w., 16, 100, 101 n.; rules for w. driving in a chariot, 16, 205, 206 sq. n.; 27, 96 sq.; male and female are separate, but they seek the same object, 16, 243; 'the firm correctness of a w., in peeping out from a door,' 16, 293; their work in the preparation of silk, 27, 36; 28, 16, 16 n., 223 sq.; rules of propriety in intercourse between male and female, 27, 77 sq., 105, 454 sq., 470; 28, 298 sq.; ladies who should not be called by their names, 27, 100 sq.; tie up their hair in mourning, 27, 129; selling of concubines, 27, 145; mourning costume of w., 27, 156; w. paying visits of condolence, 27, 163; 28, 166; places of men and of w. at the funeral, 27, 175; on the roads men take to the right, w. to the left, 27, 244; their part in the ceremonies connected with the silkworm rearing, 27, 265; regulation of w.'s work, 27, 278, 278 n., 303, 435, 479; 28, 431; deer and w. sent as tribute to the ruler, 27, 433, 433 n.; the strong and the weak, 27, 440; *the w. follows (and obeys) the man:—in her youth, she follows her father and elder brother; when married, she follows her husband; when her husband is dead, she follows her son. 'Man' denotes supporter. A man by his wisdom should (be able to) lead others*, 27, 441; education of girls, 27, 477, 477 n., 479; w.'s dress, 28, 15 sq.; at festival meals w. do not remove the dishes, 28, 20; different mourning for males and females, 28, 44; the positions and functions of male and female, 28, 62; distinction between males and females, 28, 104; a man not to die in the hands of w., nor a w. in the hands of men, 28, 173; a man considers the head the most important to him, a w. the waist, 28, 389; the female overcomes the male by her stillness, 39, 32, 104; the members of the royal harem do not pare their nails nor pierce their ears, 39, 231; the male precedes, the female follows, 39, 335; to be gentle and obedient, 40, 243; the masculine is pure and moves, the feminine turbid and at rest, 40, 250.

(*g*) W. IN ISLÂM.

Female infanticide of ancient Arabs, 6, x, 132 sq., 132 n.; position of w. amongst the Arabs, 6, xi; female infanticide forbidden by Mohammed, 6, lxxv, 135, 256, 256 n.; 9, 4, 280, 322; degradation of w. in Islâm, 6, lxxv sq.; 'believing w.' included in the promise of reward in future life, 6, lxxvi, 70, 70 n., 89, 183, 261; 9, 143 sq., 194, 233; *your w. are your tilth*, 6, 33; not to be approached during menstruation, 6, 33; two w. equal to one man as witnesses, 6, 45; property of w., 6, 71–5, 77; 'the chapter of w.' in the Qur'ân, 6, 71–96; men superior to w., 6, 77; law regarding w., 6, 90; Jewish and Christian w. allowed to Muslim, 6, 98; preference of sons to daughters, 9, 5, 174; those who cast imputations on chaste w. shall be cursed in this world and the next, 9, 76; persons by whom w. may be seen unveiled, 9, 76 sq., 147 sq.; to be chaste and modest, not display their ornaments, 9, 76 sq., 148; rules for social intercourse of w. past childbearing, 9, 81; privileges granted to Mohammed in the matter of w., 9, 146; damsels in paradise, 9, 170, 180, 220, 249, 261–3, 317; female offspring despised, 9, 212; absurdity of ascribing daughters to God, while men have sons, 9, 250, 252; law relating to w. who have fled from idolators to the Muslims, 9, 279 sq.; duties of Muslim w., 9, 280.

Womb: the great Brahman is the w., in which K*r*ish*n*a casts his seed, 8, 107; earth, air, space, water, light, mind, and understanding, termed seven ws., 8, 260; performances for steadying the w., 42, 284, 467. *See also* Birth, Body (parts of), *and* Transmigration.

Wood, defiled, must not be used, 24, 353; w.-bricks of the fire-altar,

41, 155, 166; two kinds of w. (found on the ground, and cut by the axe), 41, 257. *See also* Trees.

Words, Om or a Mantra the first among, 8, 89, 209; indicate a class, a quality, an action, or a relation, 8, 103 n.; a man of many w., a Brâhma*n*a who merely reads much, 8, 171; *first, verily, are w. produced, and the mind runs after them*, 8, 262 sq.; are the characteristics of speech, 8, 348; Prâ*n*a is the beginning of all w., 8, 353; *S*aṅkara on the nature of w., 34, xxxvii, 204–11; the original (eternal) connexion of the w. with its sense, 34, 201; the world originates from the w., as is shown by perception and inference, 34, 201–11; connected with the species, not with the individual, 34, 202 sq.; whether spho*t*a is the w. or not, 34, 204–6, 209 sq.; whether the letters are the w. or not, 34, 205–10; w. and thing are different, 34, 222; denote always something to be done, 48, 148 sq., 152; how a child learns w. and meanings, 48, 150 sq.; good w., *see* Morality (*c*), *and* Thought; holy w., *see* Prayers. *See also* Speech.

Works, or Actions.

(*a*) Good, useful, holy w.
(*b*) Knowledge or devotion, and w.
(*c*) Results of w., retribution.

(*a*) Good, useful, holy w.

Throwing bridges over canals, an atonement, 4, 175, 208; good and bad w. of the deaf and dumb and helpless, 5, 293; how to proceed when doubts occur as to good or bad w., 5, 326–30; an offering to a god is named w., 8, 77; what w. should or should not be abandoned, 8, 121 sq., 127; are of threefold quality, 8, 124; some sects extol w., others tranquillity, 8, 375 sq.; Mâra tempts Buddha to exert himself for good w., 10 (ii), 69 sq.; by w. one is a Brâhma*n*a, not by birth, 10 (ii), 116 sq.; the Buddhist saint does not cling to virtue and holy w., 10 (ii), 151 sq., 153, 159–62, 200; six kinds of w., performing sacrifices, &c., 29, 114, 114 n.; the inquiry into the duty of performing religious w. carried on in the *G*aimini-sûtra, 34, 26; the possession of supernatural powers depends on the performance of religious w., 34, 293; are characterized by injunction, 34, 293, 293 n.; in the case of religious w. we entirely depend on Scripture, 34, 299; how to become a ruler as to actions, 37, 334; five classes of action, and five organs of it, 38, 81; obligatory for the three former â*s*ramas, but not for the mendicant, 38, 301 sq.; are incumbent on him also who does not desire release, 38, 312 sq.; those performing w. are not overpowered by passion and the like, 38, 315; good w. are mentioned together with evil w., and the term 'evil' is used without any distinction for both, 38, 356; all action with a personal purpose is sure to fail, 39, 72, 100–2; whatever good deed man does that is inside the Vedi, and whatever evil deed he does that is outside the Vedi, 44, 45; heretics cannot tell you anything about good and bad w., 45, 341, 343, 345 sq.; studied from Karma-Mîmâ*m*sâ, 48, 255; enjoined in *S*ruti and Sm*ri*ti, lead to Sa*m*sâra, proceed on command of Brahman, 48, 285 sq., 311; the nature of good and evil w. can only be learned from the *S*âstra, 48, 487; a man who is not pure is unfit for all religious w., 48, 592; w. enjoined by Scripture, have the power of pleasing the Supreme Person, 48, 701. *See also* Good works, *and* Sacrifices.

(*b*) Knowledge or devotion, and w.

Sacred w. are of no avail, meditation on Om alone can procure true salvation, 1, xxv; necessity of w. as a preparation for the reception of the highest knowledge, 1, ci, 312 sq., 315–19; 38, 306 sq., 313–15; 48, 18 sq., 147; performance of sacred duty depends on the obtaining of bliss, 1, 122; attention on a tutor depends on performance of sacred duty, 1, 122; good w. are only a preparation for the highest knowledge, 1, 311, 314 sqq.; through not-knowledge, i.e. good w., one overcomes death, through knowledge one obtains immortality, 1,

312 sq., 319; interrelation of w. and knowledge, 1, 314–20; 48, 9–11, 698–700, 703, 725–7; inferior to knowledge and devotion, 8, 48 sq., 52; 38, 267; w. joined with devotion and knowledge, lead to final emancipation, 8, 59–63; 38, 359, 361; 48, 9; a means of attaining devotion, 8, 67; K*ri*sh*n*a cannot be seen by means of w., 8, 98; by w. people conquer perishable worlds, by knowledge everlasting glory, 8, 179; good w. lead to misery (rebirth), while knowledge of Brahman leads to immortality, 8, 391; 15, 30–3; w. and knowledge cannot be together, 15, xxvi; he who knows the Self, does not become greater by good w., nor smaller by evil w., 15, 179; he who has reached knowledge of Brahman is not affected by the consequences of either past or future evil or good w., 15, 180; 34, lxxvii sq.; 38, 119, 237, 353–7; 48, 646–51; knowledge is independent of w., 34, lxxv; 38, 285–95, 306; knowledge and w. are the two roads for entering on the road of the gods and the road of the fathers, 38, 123–5; knowledge is subordinate to w., this view refuted, 38, 289; 48, 686–96; are enjoined for such only as understand the purport of the Veda, 38, 289; are enjoined for him who has merely read the Veda, 38, 293; destruction of the qualification for w., by knowledge, 38, 294 sq.; are the washing away of uncleanliness, but knowledge is the highest way, 38, 307; w. of permanent obligation enjoined by the Veda, such as the Agnihotra, have the same effect as knowledge, 38, 358–62; w. undertaken for the fulfilment of some special wish, do not contribute towards knowledge, 38, 360; depend on false knowledge, 38, 363; refraining from w. of any kind whatsoever cannot lead to final release, which can only be accomplished by knowledge, 38, 397–400; for one who does not possess perfect knowledge, it is impossible to refrain from all w., 38, 399; abandoned by men who know Brahman, 48, 690; knowledge arises as the result of good w., if not obstructed by other w., 48, 712 sq.; salvation by w. and salvation by faith, 49 (ii), viii sq.

(*c*) RESULTS OF W., RETRIBUTION.

Those who practise useful and pious w., go after death through smoke, &c., to the world of the fathers, &c., and the moon, 1, 80; 15, 272 sq.; 34, 27; 38, 124; a destroyer of religious merit (fruit of w.) is an 'assassin,' 7, 41; penance for selling religious merit, 7, 177; merit and rewards of w. of public utility, 7, 270 sq.; action is better than inaction, the highest good to be attained by it, 8, 52–6; not to be performed for the sake of reward, 8, 60; renunciation and pursuit of w. both instruments of happiness, 8, 63; to be regardless of the fruits of w. is true renunciation, 8, 67; abandoning all w. to attain immortality, 8, 110; godlike endowments are means for final emancipation, demoniac persons go to hell, 8, 114–17; the ascetic must avoid all w. involving expectation of fruit or destruction of life, 8, 365; those who perform w. with expectations go near Pragâpati, 8, 389; the Buddhist is untarnished by the belief in the efficacy of outward w., 11, 10, 10 n., 27; performance of w. has for its fruit transitory felicity, 34, 11; Bh*ri*gu's vision of retribution of bad w., 44, 109 sq.; Vedic idea of the evil deeds recoiling on the evildoer, 46, 170, 172; the fruit of mere w. limited and non-permanent, 48, 4, 5, 155 sq., 255; four chief ends of human w., viz. religious duty, wealth, pleasure, and final release, 48, 6; the rewards for w. prescribed by the Veda, come from the highest Person only, 48, 625–8; religious w. bring about their rewards of themselves, 48, 626; the good w., shaken off by him who goes to the world of Brahman, go to his beloved, the evil w. to his unbeloved relatives or to his enemies, 48, 646–8, 726 sq.; Sukhâvatî obtained by prayers, not by w., 49 (ii), 98, 98 n.;—*accordance with the right leads to good fortune; following what is*

opposed to it, to bad;—the shadow and the echo, 3, 47; the way of Heaven is to bless the good, and make the bad miserable, 3, 90; *good and evil do not wrongly befal men, but Heaven sends down misery or happiness according to their conduct*, 3, 101; retribution of good and evil taking place in the family, not in the individual, 16, 47 sq., 419 sq.; on accumulation of good and evil deeds, 16, 391; retribution in this life, not in after life, 39, 39; 40, 235 sq., 244, 244 n.; *there are no special doors for calamity and happiness (in men's lot); they come as men themselves call them. Their recompenses follow good and evil as the shadow follows the substance*, 40, 235;—souls met by good w. in shape of a maiden, by bad w. in shape of an old woman, 4, 219, 219 n.; 23, 315–17, 319 sq. n., 343 sq.; active merit can repel evil that is destined, 4, 267 sq.; the soul leaves the body, but his virtue never parts from a man, 4, 378 sq.; a store of good deeds is full of salvation, 4, 383; recompense and punishment for good and evil deeds, 5, lxi, 157 sq., 168, 293–5, 350 sq.; 24, 137 sq., 146, 149, 259–62, 265–7; 37, 201; 'a good work of three Srôshô-*k*aranâms,' 5, 289, 289 sq. n.; why the good suffer more than the bad in this world, 18, 23–5; rewards of the virtuous, 37, 244, 312, 370 sq.;—good w. rewarded tenfold, evil w. only by the same amount, 6, 137; good w. remove evil w., 6, 218; *wealth and children are an adornment of the life of this world; but enduring good w. are better with thy Lord, as a recompense, and better as a hope*, 9, 19, 33; recompense for good and evil w. on the last day, no soul being wronged, 9, 107, 166; he who brings a good deed shall have better; evildoers only rewarded for that which they have done, 9, 117; all w. of men recorded, 9, 163; whoso does evil, is recompensed with the like thereof, and who does right, his is the paradise, 9, 194; *every man is pledged for what he earns*, 9, 249; Siggîn register of the w. of the sinners in hell, and the book of the righteous in 'Illiyûn, 9, 324 sq. *See also* Future Life, Karman, *and* Transmigration.

World, worlds.

(*a*) Views about this w. (cosmology) and worldly existence.
(*b*) Origin, dissolution, and renovation of the w.
(*c*) Two, three, and more worlds.

(*a*) Views about this w. (cosmology) and worldly existence.

Existence of the w. limited to 12,000 years and four periods, 4, lxi, lxiv, lxvii, 213 n.; all the bodily w. shall become free from old age, death, and corruption, 4, 253; Aûharmazd kept the w. for 3,000 years in a spiritual shape, &c., 4, 264; anxiety for this w. is not to be suffered, 5, 396; this w. is the w. of actions, 8, 239 sq.; he who looks on this w. as transient and full of birth, death, and old age, is released, 8, 246 sq., 255; worldly life represented as a great tree of which the branches are egoism, &c., and the seed of which is the Brahman, 8, 313, 313 n., 370 sq.; 15, 262; the w. consisting of creatures is the truth, 8, 315; the five Prâ*n*as, speech, mind, and understanding make up the eight constituents of the w., 8, 336; worldly life with its defects and troubles, described as a wheel, 8, 355–8; oneness of the w., with the Brahman, 8, 374, 374 n.; 15, 307; 38, 9; 48, 91–3, 394, 430–67; *but see also* Brahman (*d*); blessedness of retirement from the w., 10 (i), 24–30; 22, 32 sq.; *be not a friend of the w.*, 10 (i), 47; contempt for this w., 10 (ii), 1–3, 56, 70–2, 106–8, 129, 137, 147 sq., 177 sq.; 15, 288–90; *look upon the w. as void*, 10 (ii), 208; this earth is established on water, the water on wind, the wind on space, 11, 45; 35, 106; undefined is the w., 12, 98, 107 sq., 303; the six spaces or wide expanses, 12, 136, 136 sq. n.; is imperishable, 12, 159; 44, 174; description of the ends of the w., where those go who have performed a horse-sacrifice, 15, 127 sq.; the manifest, but unreal w. represented as the vast Brahma-wheel,

15, 234, 260; the Asvattha tree as a name of the w., 15, 307; impermanence of the w., 19, xiv, 99–101, 236–8, 274 sq., 306 sq., 306 n., 309–13, 315, 370 sq.; unreality of the w., 19, 205, 264, 264 n.; 48, 127; 49 (ii), xiv–xix, 114 sq., 117–44; Buddhist theory of the w., 19, 273, 273 n.; the reality of the phenomena of the w. is only apparent, 21, xxix, 129–41; compared to an old decaying house filled with filth and horrible beings, being in a blaze, 21, 77 sq., 82–5, 88; the folly of attachment to this w., 22, 15–27; the ideal state of those who are free from attachment to this w., 22, 44 sq.; all parts of the w. enumerated, 23, 168, 171–7; changeableness of worldly things, 24, 50; sky, earth, and water arranged like an egg, 24, 84 sq.; arrangement of the w. through wisdom, 24, 100 sq.; an oblation to the W., at the funeral, 29, 242; cosmography of the Rig-veda, 32, 49–52, 55–7; the phenomenal w. consists of individual souls and the external material objects, 34, 26; trembles in the prâ*n*a, 34, 229–31; the w. is non-intelligent, impure, and has pain for its very essence, hence different from Brahman, 34, 299–305; 48, 413 sq., 417; being based on the individual soul, the w. cannot have an independent existence, 34, 322 sq.; is in all time only that which is, 34, 332; 'the cause of suffering,' 34, 376 n., 378; four great continents, 35, 130; questions about eternity of the w. not answered by Buddha, 35, 205; different philosophical views about w., gods, and soul, 36, xxiii–xxv; 49 (i), 99 sq.; list of beings and things in the w., 36, 101 sq.; the text 'the w. is a fire indeed,' does not mean that the w. really is a fire, 38, 267; the term 'w.' denotes places of enjoyment, 38, 387, 389, 390; the whole w. is under a delusion, 39, 326 sq.; Three Regions, 40, 249, 249 n.; the Fire-altar as the Universe, 43, 381–90; *as far as there are Form and Name so far, indeed, extends this* (*universe*), 44, 28; imperishable w. gained by libations to Mind and Speech, and by the daily study of the Veda, 44, 29, 96; consists of sixteen parts, 44, 302, 302 n.; the w. (loka) is made up of living beings and things without life; where only the latter are found, that is Non-world (aloka), 45, 207; the perfected souls reside on the top of the w., 45, 211 sq.; a *G*aina should maintain that the w. exists, 45, 407; the w., a manifestation of the power of Brahman, is real, Brahman the Self of the w., 48, 89–91, 94 sq., 133, 306, 399; is the body of Brahman or of Vâsudeva, 48, 95, 129, 135; the w. is of the nature of pain or limited pleasure, 48, 306, 467; the w. apart from Brahman is unreal, 48, 432, 434; evils of the w., birth, old age, death, hell, &c., 48, 477; Buddha creates in his one person a form comprehending the universe, 49 (i), 196 sq.; w. of gods, men, and evil spirits, 49 (ii), 130, 144, 149; the w. and its beings, *see* Beings; worldly l., *see* Life.

(*b*) Origin, dissolution, and renovation of the w.

Discussions and speculations on the origin of the w., 1, 16 sq.; 19, 206–12, 206 n.; 39, 185, 187; 40, 85 sq., 128 sq.; 44, 102; 'arranger of the w.,' 5, 228; springs from Brahman, 8, 244, 258; 34, xl, 15–19, 202, 305–8, 317, 320–30, 381–6, 442; 38, 16, 21; 48, 142, 285; *but see also* Brahman (*e*); origination and salvation of the w., according to Buddha, 10 (ii), 27 sq.; God the cause of the bondage, existence, and liberation of the w., ruler and guardian of the w., 15, 265; origin of all things after heaven and earth, 16, 433, 435 sq.; worldly existence has arisen from spiritual existence, 24, 153 sq.; rests on Âtman, 25, 512; the appearance of the w. is due to Mâyâ, 34, xxv, 329 sq., 345; 38, 138; upâdâna the material cause of the w., 34, xxv; a new material w. sent forth by the Lord, 34, xxvii; originates from the word, 34, 201–11; how that origination is to be understood, 34, 203; is without a beginning, 34, 212, 359–61; is evolved by names

and forms, 34, 233, 242, 357; evolution of the w. under the superintendence of a ruler, 34, 268; doctrines concerning the origin of the w. which are opposed to the Vedânta, 34, 288 sq.; the pradhâna cannot be the cause of the w., on account of the orderly arrangement of the w. being impossible on that hypothesis, and Scripture texts do not refer to it, 34, 363–7; 48, 200–8; cannot be produced without activity, and therefore cannot have a non-intelligent cause, 34, 367–9; *the Tâo produced One; One produced Two; Two produced Three; Three produced All things*, 39, 85 sq.; heaven and earth produced from the Tâo, 39, 243 sq.; the Grand Beginning of all things, and the rise of existences, 39, 315–17; evolution of things out of the chaos, 40, 4, 4 n.; Lâo-ȝze enjoying himself in thinking about the commencement of things, 40, 46–8, 47 n.; production of all things from the (two forms of the) Tâo, 40, 63, 250 sq.; origin of the w. from the Primal Ether, 40, 311 sq.; the w. is eternal, it has not been created, nor will it perish, 45, 245, 318; *G*ainas should not believe that the w. is eternal or not eternal, 45, 405; view of the w. being the effect of Nescience refuted, 48, 102–19; sprung from ag*ñ*âna of Brahman, 48, 126; existed in the shape of Darkness, 48, 400; origination of the w. according to the Sâṅkhya, 48, 424 sq.; the entire w. from Brahmâ down to a blade of grass springs from Nescience attached to Brahman, 48, 445; each god creates in his own w., Brahman creates the entire w., 48, 472; Buddhist views of the origination of the w. refuted, 48, 500–16; *see also* Cause, *and* Creation;—periodical creation, destruction, and regeneration of the w., 2, 160; 8, 107; 11, 216, 216 n.; 25, 21 sq.; 34, xxvii, 211 sq., 214; 48, 394, 419; the Universal Soul annihilates and produces by turns the w., 7, 291; those who possess highest knowledge are not born at the creation, and not afflicted with the destruction of the w., 8, 107; the wicked are born for the destruction of the w., 8, 115; the dissolution of the w. approaches at the termination of the destruction of the great elements, 8, 335; destruction (pralaya, mahâpralaya) of the w. by fire and water at the end of the Kalpa, 8, 387 sq.; 19, 184, 237, 263, 309, 309 n., 317; 21, 241; 25, 17 sq., 18 n.; 34, 212 sqq.; 38, 238; 49 (i), 143; the dreadful wicked last epoch of the w., 21, 259–61; the material w. is merged into Mâyâ at the time of reabsorption (pralaya) of the w., 34, xxvi, xciv; is the w. coeternal with Brahman, or does it issue from it and is it refunded into it at stated intervals? 34, lii; 38, 3–73; its origin, subsistence, and dissolution proceed from Brahman, 34, 15–19, 286 sq., 309–14, 328; 38, 395 sq., 416; 48, 156–61, 174, 255, 259–61, 266; the periodical renovation of the w. is no contradiction to the eternity of the Veda, 34, 211–16; the periodical dissolution and origination of the w. compared to the sleeping and waking states, 34, 212; the phenomenal w. is the same in all Kalpas, 34, 215; in the pralaya of the w. the elements are merged in Brahman only in such a way as to continue to exist in a seminal condition, 34, 242–5, 255; 38, 371; the highest Self is the one unchanging witness of the creation, subsistence, and reabsorption of the w., 34, 312; the power of distinction founded on wrong knowledge remains even after the reabsorption of the w., 34, 313; pralaya of the w. would be impossible if we adopted the atomic theory, 34, 386–9; there exists, potentially, a connexion between the Self and the buddhi even in the state of pralaya, 38, 47 sq.; dissolution of the w. means final release, 48, 178 sq.; on account of sameness of names and forms there is no difficulty in the way of the renovation of the w. after a total destruction (pralaya), 48, 333–5; the same ws. created again and

again in successive yugas and kalpas, 48, 405; the alternating states of creation and pralaya only possible if Pradhâna is guided by a Lord, 48, 486 sq.; *see also* Brahman (*e*), *and* Pradhâna;—periods of the w. in Greek philosophy and in Zoroastrianism, 4, liv sq.; renovation of the w., 5, 45, 65, 70, 86, 100, 119, 158, 164, 167; 18, 13, 13 n., 15, 21, 21 n., 25, 34, 66, 68, 72–4, 77–80, 86, 91, 110 sq., 114–18, 138, 160, 165, 225 sq., 400; 24, 52, 58, 99, 104, 119, 128, 207; 37, 11, 30, 33, 193, 235, 248, 271 sq., 274, 284, 287–9, 335, 348, 358, 363 sq., 372, 395; 47, 14 sq., 17; condition of the creation after the renovation of the w., 18, 118–20; Sôshâns, producers of the renovation of the w., 31, 275, 279; 37, 225 sq., 243 sq., 260; 47, xiii, xxxi, 114–18, 115 sq. n.; final punishment in melted metal at the renovation, 37, 260; priests at the renovation of the w., 37, 261 sq. and n.; Aûharma*z*d exhibits the creatures in the future existence to Zaratû*s*t, 37, 267; preparers and disturbers of the renovation, 37, 300 sq.; assistance for the renovation, 37, 343, 345, 355. *See also* Ages of the world, Future life, *and* Pralaya.

(*c*) TWO, THREE, AND MORE WORLDS. Meditation on the fivefold Sâman as the ws., 1, 23 sq.; three ws., (earth, sky, heaven), 1, 31–3, 70 sq.; 2, 294 sq.; 8, 330 sq., 354; 12, 98 sq.; 15, 141 sq., 196, 198; 25, 71 sq., 71 n.; 26, 436–9; 41, 22, 238, 282, 371; 43, 137 sq., 144 sq., 163, 191, 208, 235 sq.; 44, 4, 26, 37, 102 (created), 150, 155, 165, 178, 235, 247, 291, 323, 402, 494 sq., 507; ws. of the blessed obtained by members of the three first â*s*ramas, 1, 35; from the ws. brooded on by Pragâpati, the sacrifice issued forth, 1, 35; the highest w. is the same light which is within man, 1, 47; why the w. of the Fathers never becomes full, 1, 77, 82, 82 n.; 15, 205, 209; 38, 123 sq.; 48, 595; he who desires the w. of the fathers, of the mothers, of the brothers, of the sisters, of the friends, of perfumes and garlands, of food and drink, of song and music, of women—by his mere will they come to receive him, 1, 127 sq., 141; creation of the four ws., called Ambhas (water above heaven, and heaven), Marî*k*i (light, and sky), Mara (mortal, the earth), and Ap (water under the earth), 1, 237, 237 n.; creation of the guardians of the ws., 1, 238–40; seven ws. obtained by sacrifices, 7, 3, 3 n.; 15, 31; father, mother, and teacher are equal to the three ws., and by honouring the former, he gains the latter, 7, 128 sq.; if K*r*ish*n*a did not act, the ws. would be destroyed, 8, 55; all ws., even that of Brahman, are temporary, 8, 79; untainted ws., reached by those who know the highest, 8, 108, 155, 317; all the everlasting ws., 8, 230; the heavenly w. and the w. of Brahman (m.), 8, 231; sages perceive the true nature of all ws., survey all ws., 8, 231, 234, 234 n., 388; 21, 302; 25, 478; mortals attain to this w. or to the w. of the gods by their actions, 8, 233; the Siddha goes to the higher w. (Satyaloka) and thence to the still higher w., the seat of the Brahman, 8, 234, 234 n.; the ws. of stars, moon, and sun, are the seats of men who perform meritorious actions, 8, 240, 321; Brahman created all the three ws., 8, 244; the released devotee is lord of the three ws., 8, 249; temporary and final dissolutions of the ws., 8, 314 n.; he who understands the elements, qualities, and deities, attains to all the spotless ws., 8, 317; the Mahat is the creator of the three ws., 8, 334; the wheel of life moves through all the ws., 8, 356; a devoted hermit conquers the ws., 8, 362; better than lordship over all ws., is the reward of the first step in holiness, 10 (i), 48; w. or ws. of men and gods, Mâra and Brahma, 10 (ii), 200; 13, 97, 136; 17, 95, 125, 129; 20, 196; 35, 222; *there is this w., the other w., Brahman's w., together with the w. of the gods*, 10 (ii), 208; three ws., and a fourth beyond, 12, 54 sq., 58; at the

beginning the two ws. were well-nigh contiguous, so that one could touch the sky by stretching the arms upwards, 12, 107; earth, sky, ether, represented by three Agnis, 12, 306; the ten thousand ws. quaked, when Buddha founded the Kingdom of Truth, 13, 98; the different ws. gained by Veda-study, 14, 308 sq.; how to gain the three ws., of men, Fathers, and Devas, 15, 95 sq., 124; ws. of the Gandharvas, &c., woven into one another like warp and woof, 15, 130 sq.; Rudra created all ws. and will roll them up at the end of time, 15, 244; *the three ws. are but as the froth and bubble of the sea*, 19, 223; there are innumerable thousands of ws. in the point of space below, and further below the w. Ratnavi*s*uddha, 21, 229; enumeration of ws., 25, 157; Brâhma*n*as could create other ws., 25, 398; the three ws. known by means of the Veda, 25, 505; the two, or the three, ws. represented by the antelope skins at the Dîkshâ, 26, 25 sq.; ws. gained by means of the sacrificial stake, 26, 173 sq.; there are three ws., and Pragâpati over and above them, 26, 424; four ws. (earth, air, heavens, regions), gained, 29, 41 sq.; 44, 124, 127; ten thousand w. systems, 36, 116, 120; these ws. are the heavenly abodes, 41, 195; ws. are founded on the waters, and the sun is the connecting link, 41, 269, 269 n.; the two ws. are round, 41, 271; ascent of the ws. (by Vish*n*u-strides), 41, 276–8; the air-w. is the smallest of these ws., 41, 317; the ws. are strung on a thread and joined with the sun, 41, 360; the existent and the non-existent are born from these ws., 41, 366; the serpents are these ws., for they glide along with everything, 41, 369; all the ws. conquered by Time, 42, 225; *these ws. are the resting-place and the moving-place*, 43, 143; seven ws. of the gods, three ws. and four quarters, 43, 277, 314; the ws. created together, 43, 286; three ws. gained by three oblations, 44, 4; the three deities, Agni, Vâyu, and Sûrya, made to ascend the three ws., 44, 27; this and yonder w. joined together, 44, 81; the ws. of trees, of cattle, of herbs, of waters, conquered by the Agnihotra, 44, 111; the three ws. are the three gods, 44, 117; the ws. were unfirm and unsteadied, Pragâpati stablished the earth by mountains and rivers, the air by birds and sun-motes, and the sky by clouds and stars, 44, 126; these Ws. worshipped by entering upon the *Kh*andomas of the Sattra, 44, 140, 143; these ws. are possessed of light on both sides (fire and sun), 44, 149, 405; the three ws. (earth, air, heaven) are light, might, and glory respectively, 44, 173; imperishable are the ws., 44, 174; two ws. there are, the w. of the gods and the w. of the Fathers, 44, 225; he who is consecrated by the Sautrâma*n*î, enters the ws., 44, 259; Mitra is this w., Varu*n*a is yonder w.: the Sacrificer establishes himself in both ws., 44, 269; Pragâpati desired to gain both ws., that of the gods and of men, 44, 306; this terrestrial w. is the great vessel, 44, 315; there are deaths connected with all the ws., 44, 339; these ws. (earth, air, sky) and the regions are the universe, 44, 404; highest heaven, w. of the gods, w. of men, and all the ws., 44, 415; Brahma-w. and other ws., 48, 313, 429; fourteen ws. beginning with the w. of Brahmâ, 48, 328; all the ws. originated from the Self, 48, 367; numbers, or millions of ws., 49 (ii), 119, 122, 125, 134–6, 139, 142 sq.; yonder world, *see* Future life. *See also* Earth (*a*), Heaven (*d*, *g*, *h*), Hell, *and* Saha-world.

Worms, *see* Animals (*k*).

Wrath, the sage free from, 8, 50, 59, 66 sq., 114–17, 128, 151, 246, 289, 315, 325, 332, 364; is a foe in the world, a cause of transmigration, 8, 57, 154 sq., 233, 241, 284; one of the twelve things to be avoided, 8, 166, 181, 185; one of the eighteen defects of frenzy, 8, 183; is of the quality of passion, and is dark conduct, 8, 301, 320, 323; *anger is called the great obscurity*, 8, 322; W., a

demon, 31, 303 sq.; represented as a black man with yellow eyes, 44, 110–12. *See also* Anger, *and* Passion.

Writing: the book of remembrance, 3, 59, 59 n.; mentioned in the Shû, 3, 96 sq., 96 n.; written communications by kings, 3, 113; seven kinds of w., extorted from Ahriman, brought out by Tâkhmorup, 4, 384, 384 n.; 24, 59; unknown in the age of Buddha, 11, xxii; though known to the early Buddhists, was not used for literary purposes, 13, xxxii–xxxvi; to learn w., as a profession for a young man, 13, 201; the invention of w., 16, 385, 387 n.; known in the time of the Manusm*ri*ti, 25, xcix–ci; names of written characters determined by the emperor, 28, 324; the Creator has created w. as an excellent eye, as it were, 33, 58 sq., 304; the beginner is clumsy in the art of w., 35, 92; a w.-master exhibits his skill in w., 36, 247; the letter apprehended through the stroke, 48, 76 sq.

Wû, Duke, of Wei, composed odes of the Shih, 3, 295, 374; ninety-five years of age, admonishes himself, 3, 413; his temple like that of King Wû, 28, 36; Hsü Wû-kwei and the Marquis W. of Wei, 40, 91–6, 91 n.

Wû, King, his successful war against *K*âu or *K*âu-hsin, 3, 124–37; 27, 396; 28, 31; 39, 359; 40, 171, 173, 178; called Fâ, 3, 126, 132, 135; formally establishes the *K*âu dynasty, 3, 134 sq.; King W. and the count of *Kh*î, 3, 137, 139; 'the Great Plan' communicated to W., 3, 138 sq.; receives hounds from Lü, exhorted by the Grand-Guardian, 3, 149–51; his illness, and the prayer of the duke of *K*âu by which his life is preserved, 3, 151–4; his death, 3, 154, 155 n.; 'the Tranquillizing king,' his son *Kh*ăng anxious to complete the father's plans, 3, 157, 159–61; worshipped as an ancestor, 3, 194 sq., 319, 328; 28, 202, 209; sacrifices to Heaven and to the Spirits of hills and rivers, 3, 317 sq.; sacrifice by W. to his father Wăn, 3, 325; praise of W., 3, 334 sq., 393–6; 28, 282, 309 sq., 334, 414; dance in honour of W., 3, 334–6; Wăn and W. continued the work of Thâi, 3, 342; his birth, 3, 381; his victory over Shang in the wilderness of Mû, 3, 382, 382 n.; 28, 60, 60 n.; passage of the Yellow River by W., 16, 68 n.; changed the appointment of the line of Shang, 16, 254; successor to King Wăn, as eldest son and heir, 27, 23, 120, 344, 344 n.; one of the six great men, 27, 366; temple of Duke Wû like that of King W., 28, 36; music of W., 28, 121–5; 40, 218; account of his achievements, 28, 122–5; worshipped under *K*âu, 28, 202; pantomimic representation of King W.'s feats, 28, 241; ascribes his merits to his father Wăn, 28, 289 sq.; ways of Wăn and W. displayed and inculcated by Confucius, 28, 326; 40, 168, 172; secured the people's faith, 28, 354; Ȝze-hsü and W., 39, 2 n.; involved in war, 39, 324 sq., 324 n.; Thang and W. contended for the sovereignty, 39, 380; 40, 73; not a ruler according to the Right Way, 40, 163 sq.; Thang and W. set up as Sons of Heaven, yet their posterity cut off, 40, 170 sq.; W. and Wăn as model kings, *see* Wăn.

Wû-âo, n. of a Tâoist teacher, 39, 247.

Wû Hsien and his son, ministers of Thâi-wû and Ȝû-yî, 3, 207.

Wû-hsien Thiâo on the kings who ruled in accordance with Heaven, 39, 346, 346 n.

Wû-*k*âi, the Northerner, commits suicide, because the throne is offered to him by Shun, 40, 161 sq., 161 n.

Wû Kwang, a worthy, but not a True Man, 39, 239, 239 sq. n.; drowned himself, when Thang offered him his throne, 40, 141, 163.

Wû-*k*wang lost and recovered his beauty, 39, 256.

Wû-ting, reigned 59 years, 3, 23, 202; appoints Yüeh his chief minister, 3, 112–18; his early life, 3, 116 sq. and n.; Kâo Ȝung, his title after death, worshipped as an

ancestor, 3, 118 sq., 202, 204, 303, 307 sq.; 28, 468 sq.; had Kan Phan as minister, 3, 207; his success, especially in the war against *K*ing-*kh*û, 3, 311-13, 311 n. *See also* Kâo Ȝung.

Wû-yo, n. of a Tâoist sage, 40, 179, 179 n.

Wû Yün or Wû Ȝze-hsü made his escape along the *K*iang, 40, 131, 131 n.

Wû-ȝze of Sui eulogized by Wăn-ȝze, 27, 199, 199 n.

Wû Ȝze-hsü, *see* Ȝze-hsü.

Y

Yâdava, n. of K*r*ish*n*a, 8, 97.

Yâdavaprakâ*s*a, t.w., quoted, 48, 459.

Yadu, n.p., 32, 391; 46, 33, 36.

Yaêtu*s*g*a*u, son of Vyâtana, 23, 218.

Ya*g*â, the goddess of sacrifice, worshipped, 29, 334.

Ya*gh*ûTH, an idol worshipped by the Arabs, 6, xii; 9, 303.

Ya*gñ*a, Sk., Sacrifice, personified, *see* Sacrifice (*g*).

Yâ*gñ*atura, *see* *R*ishabha Y.

Ya*gñ*ava*k*as Râgastambâyana, n. of a teacher, 15, 227; 43, 349; pupil of Tura Kâvasheya, 43, 404.

Yâ*gñ*avalkya Vâgasaneya, and King Ganaka of Videha, 1, lxxiv sq.; 8, 304 n.; 12, xlii sq., 121-49; 15, 152-77, 161 n.; 44, 46, 66, 112-15; promulgator of the White Yagur-veda, contemporary of *S*vetaketu, 2, xli sq.; 15, 226; vomited the Black Yagur-veda, 2, 113 n.; his relation to the *S*atapatha-brâhma*n*a, 12, xxx-xxxv; 43, xviii; relative date of Pâ*n*ini and Y., 12, xxxv-xxxix; his teacher *S*vetaketu Âru*n*eya, 12, xli; his teacher Uddâlaka Âru*n*i, 12, xlii; 15, 213 sq., 226; 48, 280; his opinions quoted, 12, 5, 76, 76 n., 77, 77 n., 259, 271, 333, 370; 26, 2, 2 n., 11, 14, 279, 425, 442; 34, cxv; 41, 141; 44, xxxviii, 182, 393; satiated at the Tarpa*n*a, 14, 255; on husband and wife, 15, 85; teaches his wife Maitreyî the Self, 15, 108-13, 181-5; 34, 274 sqq.; 48, 387, 395; colloquy of Y. and Ârtabhâga, 15, 125-7; 34, lxxxi, cxii; 38, 373 sq.; 48, 734; discourses of Y. and Ushasta, 15, 128 sq.; 48, 655 sq., 658; conversation between Y. and Gârgî, 15, 136-9; 48, 309; Y. and *S*âkalya on the gods and the one God, 15, 139-51; 44, 115-17; cursed by a *K*araka-Adhvaryu, 26, 197; colloquy of the Gandharva and Y., 34, 219; Y. and others who knew Brahman did not take their stand on works, 38, 292; Dharma*s*âstra or code of Y., *see* Yâ*gñ*avalkya-sm*r*iti.

Yâ*gñ*avalkya-sm*r*iti, or code of Y., belongs to the White Yagur-veda, 7, x; date of the Y., 7, xx-xxii; 33, xvi sq.; Y. and Vish*n*u-sm*r*iti, 7, xx-xxii, xxxii; later than Manu-sm*r*iti, 25, liv, xcvi, xcix, ci-civ, cvii; quoted, 48, 736.

Ya*gñ*avâstu, *see* Rudra (*b*).

Yâ*gñ*ikî-upanishad, called a Khila, 15, xxvii.

Ya*gñ*opavîta, t.t., the sacrificial cord, *see* Costume.

Yâ*g*û*g*, *see* Gog.

Ya*g*ur-veda, Upanishads occur in the Sa*m*hitâ of the, 1, lxvi; Sa*m*hitâ of the White Y. more modern than that of the Black Y., 1, c; Î*s*â-upanishad part of the Sa*m*hitâ of the Y., 1, c; the liturgical Veda par excellence, 1, ci; date of the White Y., 2, xlii, xlii sq. n.; the Mânava School of the Black Y., 7, xxv-xxvii; its schools, 12, xxii, xxv-xxx, xxxix sq., xliii-xlvi; legend of the origin of Taittirîyas, 12, xxvii sq. and n.; on the Sandhi peculiar to the Maitrâya*n*îyas, 15, xlviii; meaning of 'White' Yagur-veda, 15, 226 n.; passages from the three redactions of the Y. on Manu, 25, xvi n., lx; index of the *R*ishis in the White Y., 25, lx; Kâ*th*aka and Maitrâya*n*î Sa*m*hitâ of the Black Y. give mantras of the A*s*vamedha, 44, xvi. *See also* Kâ*th*aka, Maitrâya*n*îya-sa*m*hitâ, Taittirîya-âra*n*yaka, Taittirîya-brâhma*n*a, Taittirîya-sa*m*hitâ, Taittirîya-upanishad, Vâgasaneyins, Vâgasaneyi-sa*m*hitâ, *and* Veda.

Yagus, belong to the Âdityas, 26, 383, 383 n.; by means of the Brahman or prayer, the Y., he makes what is not, 26, 392, 394; the highest Self is Y., 34, 79; power of the Brahman, the Y., in yonder world, 43, 173; are built up in building the fire-altar, 43, 282, 282 n.; mystic import of the Y., 43, 336–41; *this Y. is silent, indistinct, for the Y. is the breath*, 43, 340; the Y. are the Veda, 44, 365. *See also* Veda, *and* Yagur-veda.

Yâirya, yearly feasts, worshipped as deities, 31, 198, 205, 210 sq., 216, 220, 224, 335, 338, 368, 379.

Yakhmâyûsad, son of Fryân, one of the seven immortals, 18, 256, 256 n.

Yakkhas, *see* Yakshas.

Yakshâ, female disciple of Sambhûtavigaya, 22, 289.

Yakshadattâ, female disciple of Sambhûtavigaya, 22, 289.

Yakshas, Sk., Pali Yakkhas, a class of superhuman beings, created, 7, 4; 25, 15; Kubera or Vessavana, chief of Y., 8, 88; 35, 38; alarmed at the greatness of Krishna, 8, 94; worship of Y. and Rakshases, of the quality of Passion, 8, 118; extol the emancipated saint, 8, 345; Vishnu, or Îsvara, is the lord of men, Kinnaras, Y., &c., 8, 347; giants, malignant spirits, 10 (ii), x; dialogue between two Y. on the qualities of Buddha, 10 (ii), 25–7; dialogue between the Y. Hemavata and Buddha on salvation, 10 (ii), 27 sq.; ten hundred Y. possessed of supernatural power and of fame, take refuge in Buddha, 10 (ii), 29; two Y. threaten Buddha, 10 (ii), 45; Mâra called an evil-minded Y., 10 (ii), 72; purification of a Y., 10 (ii), 78, 167; Sîvaka the Y., 20, 181 sq.; feasts at festivals of Y., 22, 92; their manes, 25, 112; their food and drink, 25, 450; produced by Activity, 25, 494 n.; satiated at the Tarpana, 29, 219; etymology of the word, 32, 335; Maruts compared to Y., 32, 374, 377; of inferior power, 35, 176; Devadatta and the Bodisat as Y., 35, 289, 289 n.; are 'gods,' devaputtâ, 35, 289 n.; worms, beetles, &c., are the remains of dead Y., 36, 108 sq.; invoked as divine beings, 42, 161; beings living in the heavenly regions, 45, 16 sq.; the pious householder, on leaving this body, will share the world of the Y., 45, 23; worship at shrines, 45, 50 n.; a Y., presiding deity of a grove, became a follower of a Gaina monk, 45, 50 n., 51, 54 sq.; possess women, causing madness, 45, 50 n., 53; protect the monk Harikêsa-Bala, 45, 51, 53 sq.; souls of Y., 48, 198; guard the infant Buddha, 49 (i), 7; throw lotuses on Buddha's flight from his palace, 49 (i), 61; Buddha dwells in the abodes of Y., 49 (i), 170; where Buddhism is preached, there shall be no fear of gods, Nâgas, and Y., 49 (i), 188. *See also* Superhuman beings.

Yakshinî, Ârya, at the head of the nuns under Arishtanemi, 22, 278.

Yama, Vaivasvata, son of Vivasvat, King, ruler of the departed, god of Death.

(*a*) Y. in mythology.
(*b*) World (realm, abode) of Y.
(*c*) Worship of Y.

(*a*) Y. IN MYTHOLOGY.

Y. is the Self which is conscious (in dreams), 1, 305; a name of the sun, 1, 313; 15, 199; 44, 460; compare Yima, son of Vivanghant, 4, lii; the two four-eyed dogs of Y., Kerberos, and the four-eyed dog of the Parsis, 4, lxxiv sq.; 29, 297; 42, 54, 318, 404, 500; 46, 29; path of Y., 7, 81, 142; 32, 81, 88; ministers of Y., 7, 142 sq.; chief among rulers, 8, 89, 89 n.; a form of Krishna, 8, 97; dwells in the self, different from Death, 8, 153, 153 n.; in the Anugîtâ, 8, 219; at the head of the Fathers, 8, 346; 42, 161, 186; messengers of Y. or Death, roam about, 10 (i), 60; 42, 57, 59; King Y. (Gârhapatya fire) carried to the south, 12, 338, 338 n.; punishes those who offend secretly, 14, 102; 33, 230; Lord of Justice, 14, 135; 25, 217; Y.'s court, Y.'s hall, 14, 229; purified by Ka, 14, 331; colloquy between Y. and Nakiketas, 15, 2–24; 34, 247–52; 48, 270 sq.,

361 sq.; in the south, 15, 146; 41, 49 n.; 42, 186, 192; judge of the dead, 15, 299; 33, 14, 14 n.; a manifestation of Brahman, 15, 303; a guardian of the world, 25, 185, 216 sq.; 35, 37; knows the conduct of all beings, 25, 269; resides in the heart of man, 25, 270; 33, 246; a king shall behave like Y., 25, 285, 396 sq.; 33, 217 sq.; torments in hell imposed by Y., 25, 487, 487 sq. n., 489; the thought-swift, 26, 122 sq., 123 n.; receives the horse as Dakshi*n*â, 26, 348; Y. and all gods contained in the Ash*t*akâ, 29, 102; a shrieking bird addressed as 'messenger of Y.,' 29, 367; the attendants of Y. inflict punishments in hell, 33, 94; witnesses watched by Y. and other gods, 33, 245; with a staff in his hand, 34, 217 n.; men who have not offered sacrifices, fall into the power of Y., 38, 122 sq.; the evil-doers suffer punishments allotted by Y., 38, 123; 48, 593; chief ruler in the seven hells, 38, 123; the Y.-eyed gods in the south, 41, 49; rules over the settling on this earth, 41, 298; is the Kshatra (nobility), the Fathers are the clansmen, 41, 299; 44, 365; Y. is Agni, and Yamî the earth, 41, 322; the blood of the brown horse of Y., 42, 21, 422; the foot-fetter of Y., 42, 44; Y. or death, 42, 110; enemies handed over to Y., god of death, 42, 118; father of Sleep, 42, 167; as a bowman, 42, 192; the god of heaven, and death, 42, 361; the tree in which Y. drinks with the gods, 42, 416; he who is in Y.'s power (Rudra), 43, 153; dead man's head, used at building of the fire-altar, redeemed from Y., 44, xxxix; grants the deceased an abode, 44, 431; the ten rulers of the worlds headed by Y., 49 (i), 196; Indra, Y., Varu*n*a, 49 (i), 197. *See also* Death (*a*), *and* Vaivasvata.

(*b*) WORLD (REALM, ABODE) OF Y.

The son belongs to the begetter in the world of Y., 2, 131; Y. governs his kingdom in the world of the Pit*ri*s, 8, 153; torments in the house or world of Y., 8, 233; 25, 209; the disciple of Buddha will overcome the world of Y., 10 (i), 16; the kingdom of Y., gained by an Agnish*t*oma, 15, 337; rebirth in hells, brute creation, and realm of Y., 21, 77, 233, 248, 402, 415; the Dakshi*n*â makes the sacrificer a sharer in Y.'s world, 26, 348; the Fathers live in Y.'s realm, 29, 139; 44, 236 sq.; the first season has become a cow in Yama's realm, 29, 343; Sa*m*yamana, the abode of Y., 38, 122 sq.; from Y.'s realm none ever return, 38, 151; existence in yonder world of Y. (death), 42, 52; 'thou shalt go to the seat of Y.' = 'thou shalt die,' 42, 90; Y.'s house, 42, 107, 167; kingdom of Y., 42, 177, 185; no realm of Y. in Sukhâvatî, 49 (ii), 97; celestial palace of Y., 49 (ii), 177, 180.

(*c*) WORSHIP OF Y.

Offerings and prayers to Y., chief of Añgiras and Fathers, 7, 84; 11, 180; 12, 364 n.; 14, 135, 268; 25, 114; 26, 122 sq., 123 n.; 30, 226; 42, 60; 44, 460, 481; sacrifice of an ass to Y., 14, 215; Bali offerings to Y. and those belonging to Y., 25, 91; 29, 85, 85 n., 161; 30, 123; Y. of the earth, invoked for protection, 29, 280; singing the Y. song, and the Y. hymn, at a child's funeral, 29, 355; worshipped for the thriving of horses, 30, 89; Plaksha tree sacred to Y., 30, 122; initiated boy given in charge to Y., 30, 154; invoked for life and protection, 30, 206; worshipped at the Tarpa*n*a, 30, 243; invoked against the evil demons, 42, 37; a Sâman to Y. sung at the Purushamedha, 44, xliii sq.; expiatory oblations to Y., 44, 209, 337 n.; a white and a black goat sacrificed to Sûrya and Y., 44, 300; a barren woman and one who bears twins sacrificed to Y. at the Purushamedha, 44, 415; the wind worshipped as identical with Y., 44, 481.

Yama, law-book of, quoted by Vâsish*th*a, 14, xvii sq.; 20, 52, 73, 95, 102.

Yâma heaven, the third Devaloka, 49 (i), 187, 187 n.

Yamataggi, n. of a *Ri*shi, 11, 172.

Yame*l*u and Tekula, the Brâhmans

who wanted to put the word of the Buddhas into Sanskrit, 20, 149 sq.
Yamî, is the earth, 41, 322; a woman who bears twins sacrificed to Y. at the Purushamedha, 44, 415.
Yamunâ, river, *S*yâvâ*s*va Âtreya on the, 32, 313, 323; salve from the Y., 42, 62; Bharata offered horse-sacrifice on the Y., 44, 399.
Yâna, the great, attained by Buddha, 49 (i), 183.
Yang, heresiarch, *see* Yang *K*û.
Yang: all things done by the Y. influence of Heaven and Earth, 40, 63, 63 n.; its operation on life, 40, 146; penumbrae and shadow both produced by the strong Y., 40, 147; Yin and Y., *see* Yin.
Yangha*d*, son of Hôshyang, 5, 130, 130 n.
Yang Hû, Confucius mistaken for him, 39, 386 sq.
Yang Khû-fû, did not die a natural death, 27, 199.
Yang *K*ien, *see* Wăn Tî.
Yang *K*û, a great heresiarch, 39, 41 n., 261 n., 270, 270 n., 287; Y. and Mo have not hit on the proper course, 39, 329; his followers, a philosophical school, 40, 99 sq. *See also* Yang-ȝze, *and* Yang Ȝze-*k*ü.
Yang Tî, of the Sui dynasty, put Hsieh Tâo-hăng to death, 40, 311 sq. n.
Yang-ȝze and the master who had two concubines, the beautiful one being contemned and the ugly one honoured, 40, 41.
Yang Ȝze-*k*ü has an interview with Lâo-ȝze, 39, 137, 261 sq.; 40, 322 sq.; humbles himself to be taught by Lâo-ȝze, 39, 156; 40, 147 sq.; or Yang *K*û, famous philosopher, 39, 287.
Ya*ññ*a, one of the eight Brâhmans who took note of the marks on Buddha's body, 36, 44.
Yâo, Shû King begins with his reign, 3, xv; spoken of as Tî, 3, xxvii–xxix; the record of the reign of Y. in the Shû later and more legendary, though based on ancient documents, 3, 13–15; the flood under Y., and the labours of Khwăn and Yü to assuage it, 3, 16–18, 34–6; a historical personage, 3, 19; his care for the regulation of the calendar, 3, 24–8, 32–4; of the Thang dynasty, 3, 31; 'The Canon of Y.' translated, 3, 31–6; his personality and government, 3, 32; his names 'Tî Y.' and Fang-hsün, 3, 32, 32 n.; his death, 3, 41; the lord of Thâo and Thang, 3, 80, 80 n.; his instructions to the astronomers, 3, 142 n.; deserves ancestor worship, 28, 208; Y. and Hsü Yû, 39, 127, 169 sq., 169 n.; his successful government, 39, 172, 291, 359; attacked the states of Ȝhung-*k*ih and Hsü-âo, 39, 206; the ideal king, 39, 227; 40, 99; men praise Y. and condemn *K*ieh, 39, 242; 40, 64, 136; branded and disfigured Î-*r* Ȝze, 39, 255 sq.; how he punished his ministers, 39, 295, 295 n.; disturbed the world by his benevolence and righteousness, 39, 295, 295 n.; 40, 108; Hsü Yû his teacher, 39, 312; Y. and the border-warden of Hwâ, 39, 313 sq.; Y. and prince Po-*kh*ăng Ȝze-kâo, 39, 315; Y. and *K*ieh, each of them approved of his own course, and condemned the other, 39, 380; would neither own men, nor be owned by them, 40, 31; proposed to resign the throne to Hsü Yû, who would not accept it, 40, 141, 149; offered the throne to Ȝze-*k*âu *K*ih-fû, 40, 149; was not kind to his son, 40, 173, 173 n.; killed his eldest son, 40, 178; had his Tâ *K*ang music, 40, 218; with the deep-sunk eyes, a Great Man, 40, 274;—the period of Y. and Shun, 3, 24–7; 39, 386; appoints Shun his successor, 3, 38; 27, 396; 39, 359; Y. and Shun, the ideals of kings, 3, 118; 39, 225, 319; Y. and Shun established a hundred officers, 3, 227; Hwang Tî, Y., and Shun, their work for civilization, 16, 383–5; worshipped by Shun, 28, 201; the ways of Y. and Shun handed down by Confucius, 28, 326; Y. and Shun ruled with benevolence, 28, 418; dialogue between Y. and Shun, 39, 190; 40, 279; Y. and Shun lived securely, 39, 282; Y. an ideal ruler, Shun an ideal minister, 39, 331; Shun instructs Y. about the ideal king, 39, 338; Y. and Shun, the lords of Thang and Yü, 39, 370,

370 n.; Y. and Shun resigned their thrones, 39, 380; the ways of Hwang-Tî, Y., and Shun, 40, 7; Y. and Shun did not benefit the world, the greatest disorder was planted in their times, 40, 76 sq., 76 n.; having heard of Shun's virtue, Y. appoints him to a new territory, 40, 110; Y. and Shun are the subjects of men's praises, 40, 120; Y. and Shun possessed the whole kingdom, while their descendants were greatly reduced, 40, 170; Y. and Shun instituted their crowd of ministers, 40, 171; harmony prevailed when Y. and Shun were the sovereigns, 40, 183. *See also* Shun.

Yasa, the son of a se*tth*i, having become weary of worldly pleasures, leaves his palace, is taught by Buddha, and finally receives the upasampadâ ordination, 13, 102–8; his father converted by Buddha, 13, 106; his mother and wife become lay-disciples of Buddha, 13, 109 sq.; his friends, instructed by Buddha, become Arhats, 13, 110–12; a believing disciple of Buddha, 19, xiv; son of Kâka*nd*aka, appointed on the jury at the council of Vesâlî, 20, 387–400, 407.

Ya*s*â, mother of the *G*aina Kapila, 45, 32 n.; wife of the Purohita Bh*r*igu, 45, 62.

Ya*s*a*h*prabha, n. of a Tathâgata, 49 (ii), 100.

Ya*s*a*h*prabhâva, n. of a Tathâgata, 49 (ii), 100.

Ya*s*as, converted by Buddha, 19, 180–2; a Ga*n*adhara of Pâr*s*va, 22, 274; n. of a Tathâgata, 49 (ii), 100.

Ya*s*askâma, n. of a lazy Bodhisattva, afterwards reborn as Maitreya Agita, 21, 22 sq., 28.

Yâska, n. of a teacher, 15, 118 n., 119, 187; mentions grammarians, etymologists, and ritualists, 25, l; quotes Manu on the law of inheritance, 25, lxi sq., lxi n.

Yasna, studied by priests, 18, 153, 153 n.; date of Pahlavi translation of the Y., 18, 394; translated, 31, 195–332; the Y. Haptanghâiti, 31, 281–4, 290 sq., 303, 336, 340, 358 sq., 380; mentioned in the Srôsh Ya*s*t, 31, 303; the Praises of the Y. worshipped, 31, 308, 310, 328, 349, 355 sq.

Yasnô, t.t., 'Ritual,' 5, lxxiii.

Ya*s*obhadra, n. of a Sthavira, 22, 287; disciple of Sambhûta-vigaya, 22, 289; Pr. *G*asabhadda, Kula of the U*d*uvâ*t*ika Ga*n*a, 22, 291.

Ya*s*oda, converted by Buddha, 49 (i), 191.

Ya*s*odâ, wife of Mahâvîra, 22, 193, 256.

Ya*s*odeva, n. of a Bhikshu, 49 (ii), 2.

Ya*s*odharâ, or Ya*s*od*r*îh, the wife of the Bodhisattva, 19, 24 sq., 28, 64; 49 (i), 21, 24, 65, 163, 195; her grief on hearing that Buddha has become an ascetic, 19, 86–90; 49 (i), 83–9; Buddha's prophecy about the nun Y. who is to become a Bodhisattva and a future Buddha, 21, xxx, 257 sq.; the mother of Râhula, a principal nun, 21, 3.

Ya*s*od*r*îh, *see* Ya*s*odharâ.

Yaso*g*a, n. of a Bhikkhu, 17, 121.

Ya*s*ovatî, n. of *S*eshavatî, Mahâvîra's granddaughter, 22, 194, 256.

Ya*s*t, composition of the, 4, lxvii; means 'prayers, ritual, worship,' 5, lxxiii; 23, 1; commentary of the Vohûman Y., Horvada*d* Y., and Â*s*tâ*d* Y., 5, 193 sq., 193 n.; translated, *Vol.* 23; Ormazd Y., when recited, 23, 21, 26, 28 sq.; two Srôsh Ys., 23, 159–67; 31, 296–306; selection from the whole Y., 37, xxvii, 384, 384 n.; Stô*d* Y., 37, 169–71, 169 n., 172 sq. n., 487 sq.

YaTHrib, Mohammed and the inhabitants of, 6, xxx–xxxiii. *See also* Medînah.

Yati, *see* Holy persons.

Yâtudhânas, a class of demons supposed to disturb the effect of a *S*râddha, driven away at the beginning of a *S*râddha, 7, 233 sq., 250; 14, 269.

Yâtus and Pairikas, creatures of Angra-Mainyu, spells against them, *see* Pairika; Y. and Za*nd*as, sorcerers and apostles of Ahriman, 4, 204, 204 n.; the *G*ahi, who follows the Y., 4, 234; 23, 44–7; Y. and those addicted to the works of Y., either Daêvas or men, 23, 38, 38 n., 105, 262; Agni invoked against sorcerers and the allies of the Y., 46,

33; a Yâtu, a bad demon, 46, 393.
Ya'ûq, Arabian god, worshipped under the figure of a horse, 6, xii; 9, 303.
Yavanas, mentioned in the Gautama-Dharma-sûtra, 2, lx sq.; in Manusm*ri*ti, 7, xxiv; 25, cxiv–cxvii; degraded Kshatriyas, 25, 412.
Yavas and Ayavas, lords of creatures, 43, 69, 69 n., 76.
Yayâti, Agni sacrificed for, 46, 24; the son of Nahusha, 49 (i), 18; sported with the Apsaras Vi*s*vâ*k*î, 49 (i), 45.
Yazads, Yazatas, *see* Gods (*m*).
Yazad-yâr, n.p., 24, 256.
Ya*zd*akar*d*, King, 'the sinner,' 37, 257 n.
Yazdân, Phl. 'angels, sacred or celestial beings, God,' 5, lxxiii. *See* God (*c*), *and* Gods (*m*).
Yazdân-aîrikht, n.p., 5, 135.
Ya*zd*ân-pânak, sent by Mânû*sk*îhar to Zâ*d*-sparam, 18, xxv, 321–3, 322 n.
Yazdân-*s*arâ*d*, n.p., 5, 135.
Year, a stage on the soul's road after death, 1, 68, 80, 82 n.; 38, 384–6; 48, 745; three acknowledged commencements of the y., 3, 77, 77 n.; sacrifice to introduce the coming y., 3, 399; Agni (fire-altar) and Pragâpati identified with Father Y., 12, 62, 62 n., 135; 15, 95; 41, 174; 43, xv sq., xxii sq., 29 sq., 33, 49, 62–6, 70 sq., 76, 96, 120, 126 sq., 147, 163, 166 sq., 177, 184, 193, 204 sq., 207, 216, 219–22, 219 n., 240, 253 sq., 264, 271, 281, 294, 313, 320–7, 347, 349–52, 356–60, 362–4, 386, 403 n.; 44, 1, 15, 432, 432 n., 506; twelve or thirteen months in the y., 12, 321; 26, 318–22; 41, 119, 142, 260, 272, 308, 334–9, 355; 43, 159, 219, 320; 44, 147, 168, 384, 395, 435, 466, 506; the y. in three divisions, 12, 444; born from Death and Speech, 15, 76; the holy sacrifice to the Ys., and masters of holiness, 23, 5, 14, 36 sq., 49, 52; in the second order of existences caused by Goodness, 25, 495; the sacrifice is the y., 26, 108 sq.; 44, 1, 38 sq., 154, 276; close of the y., 27, 308 sq.; personified, invoked at the Ash*t*akâ, 29, 207; water oblation to the Year and its divisions at the Utsarga, 29, 325; the Âgrahâya*n*î night, the consort of the Y., and the Sa*m*vatsara, Parivatsara, Idvatsara, and Vatsara worshipped, 29, 338 sq. and n.; 30, 240; is seventeenfold, there being twelve months and five seasons in a y., 41, 174; 43, 62; 44, 37; six seasons are a y., and Agni is the y., 41, 244, 269; 43, 363; is linked to the moon by means of the seasons, 41, 269; has 720 days and nights, 41, 353; divisions of the y. deified, 42, 162; Pragâpati produces creatures by union with the y., 43, 32 sq.; Agni Vai*s*vânara is the y., 43, 33; is space, 43, 62; speed is the y., it speeds all beings, 43, 63; it burns, assails all beings, 43, 63; is the most vigorous of all things, 43, 63; is arrayed over all beings, is the womb of all beings, as an embryo enters the seasons, 43, 64; is the strength of all beings, 43, 64; designs all beings, 43, 64 sq.; is the foundation of all beings, 43, 65; is the firmament, 43, 65; the y. is the sun, 43, 65, 313; 44, 445, 467, 481; all creatures are evolved from it, 43, 66; is eighteenfold, 43, 66; the lord of the months, 43, 74; the world of heaven is the y., 43, 100; means generative power, 43, 125; the y. is everything, 43, 125, 320 sq.; 44, 5, 248, 395, 406, 507; the y. is these worlds, 43, 127; the birth of the gods is the y., 43, 144; consists of seven months, 43, 163; includes all objects of desire, 43, 313; beyond the y. lies immortality, 43, 322; is fivefold, viz. food, drink, well-being, light, and immortality, 43, 326 sq.; divisions of the y., 43, 351 sq.; is Death, the Ender, 43, 356 sq.; created, 43, 402 sq.; 44, 14; there are 360 nights and days in a year, 44, 4 sq., 168 sq.; by the y. the gods were immortal, 44, 5; the Sacrificer is the Y., the Seasons officiate for him, 44, 44 sq., 432, 432 n.; means life, 44, 119; he who knows the mystery of the birth of the Y. goes as the Y. to the gods, 44, 140, 153–5; by the *K*aturvi*ms*a day and by entering upon the

Dasarâtra they sacrifice to the Y., and they become that deity, the Y., 44, 141, 141 n., 143; the Y. is Man, the ceremonies of the sacrificial session being his limbs, 44, 144 sq., 160–70; the months are the limbs of the y., 44, 158; is a great eagle, 44, 158; means constantly existing food, 44, 222; the thirteenth month is the y. itself, 44, 247; days and nights, half-months, months, and seasons are established in the y., 44, 252; is the bull among the seasons, 44, 276; the thirteenth month is an excrescence of the y., 44, 276; by means of the seasonal sacrifice the Sacrificer gains the y., 44, 309, 309 n.; samvatsara, parivatsara, &c., years of the five ys.' cycle, 44, 415. *See also* Time.

Yen, younger brother of the count of Wei, 27, 120.

Yen, Minister of War to King Yung of Wei, 40, 118 sq.

Yen Ho, being about to undertake the office of teacher to Duke Ling's son, consults *K*ü Po-yü, 39, 132, 215–17; describes Confucius to Duke Âi of Lû as unfit to be entrusted with the government, 39, 161; 40, 207–9; warns the reckless driver Tung-yê *K*î, 40, 23, 23 n.; had attained to the Tâo, refuses a gift of silks sent by the ruler of Lû, 40, 153.

Yen Hui, or Hui, or Yen Yüan, disciple of Confucius, nearly attained the standard of perfection, 16, 392 sq., 395 n.; 40, 160; mourning rites for him, 27, 137, 139; his conversation with Ȝze-lû, 27, 185; wishes to go to Wei to reform the character and government of its ruler, 39, 132, 203–10; Confucius's sorrow at Hui's going to *Kh*î, 39, 149; 40, 7 sq.; instructed about Tâoism by Confucius, 39, 253 sq., 256 sq.; asked the music-master *K*in about Confucius, 39, 351 sq.; asks Confucius about the ferryman who handled the boat like a spirit, 40, 15 sq.; instructed by Confucius about Heaven, 40, 37–9; complains that he is unable to follow Confucius in explaining the Tâo, 40, 44–6; Confucius reports to him his conversation with Lâo-ȝze, 40, 49; questions Confucius, 40, 53, 72; is poor, but contented, 40, 158 sq.; accompanies Confucius as his charioteer, 40, 167, 200; became one with the Great Pervader, 40, 283.

Yen Kang, condoles on the death of Lâo-lung *K*î, 40, 68.

Yen *Kh*âng Ȝze-yû, disciple of Nan-kwo (or Nan-po, or Tung-kwo) Ȝze-*kh*î, 39, 176–8, 176 n.; 40, 103, 145 sq.

Yen *K*ih, hid a copy of the Hsiâo King, 3, 452.

Yen Liû, an authority on funeral rites, 27, 188.

Yen Pû-î, friend of the king of Wû, 40, 102 sq.

Yen-sze, Shăn-hsiang wailing for, 27, 133.

Yen Tî, divine ruler of summer, 27, 268, 272, 276.

Yen Ting, mourned skilfully for his father, 27, 179.

Yen Yen = Ȝze-yû, q. v.

Yen Yû, disciple of Confucius, 28, 270 sq.

Yen Yüan, *see* Yen Hui.

Yen-ȝze, and Confucius, 40, 293.

Yesh*t*iha, moments, in the world of Brahman, 1, 275, 276.

Yî, forester to Shun, helped Yü in his work against the inundation, 3, 16 sq., 44, 56–8; conversation between Shun and Yü and Y. on right government, 3, 46–8; helped Yü to bring the lord of Miâo to submission, 3, 52.

Yî, n. of a Recorder, 3, 195, 195 n.; funeral rites for his son who died prematurely, 27, 340 sq.; Ȝze-kung's interview with the music-master Y., 28, 129–31.

Yî-khâo, eldest son of King Wăn, 27, 120.

Yî King, or Book of Changes, 3, xvi–xviii; 16, 208 sq. n.; exempted from the burning of Confucian literature, 3, xvii; 16, 2; now made up of the Text and the Appendixes, the latter ascribed to Confucius, 16, xiii sq., xvii–xix, 1–3, 7 sq.; difficulties of its interpretation, 16, xiii–xvi; ascribed to King Wăn and his son Tan, 16, xiii, xv–xix, 5 sq., 404 n.; considered as a book of divination, 16, xv, 2,

4 sq., 364 n., 365–74, 368 sq. n., 371 n., 374–6 n., 380 sq., 381 sq. n., 404 sq.; translation of it, 16, xv–xix, 6 sq., 9; there was a Yî in the time of Confucius, 16, 1–3; its history from the twelfth century B.C. to the commencement of the Christian era, 16, 1–9; not the most ancient of Chinese books, 16, 6 sq., 7 n.; labours of native commentators, 16, 8 sq.; the subject-matter of the text, the lineal figures and the explanation of them, 16, 9–26; the authorship of the Appendixes, 16, 26, 28–31, 46 sq., 53–5, 360 n., 364 sq. n., 371 n.; nature and contents of the Appendixes, 16, 26–8, 31–55; information about its constituent parts given in 'The Great Appendix,' 16, 38–46, 348–407; meaning of the name, 16, 38 sq., 357 n.; mythology in it, 16, 49 sq., 429 sq.; translated, 16, 57–210; Appendix on the Thwan, or King Wăn's explanations of the entire hexagrams, 16, 213–66; the Appendixes translated, 16, 213–444; Appendix on the symbolism of the hexagrams, and of the duke of *K*âu's explanations of the several lines, 16, 267–347; studied by the superior man, 16, 351, 351 n.; its greatness celebrated, 16, 358 sq.; its fourfold use, 16, 367–70, 370 sq. n.; the progress of civilization indebted to it, 16, 382–5, 385 sq. n.; its scope and object, 16, 395 sq., 396 sq. n., 402; began to flourish in the middle period of antiquity, in the last age of Yin, 16, 397, 403, 404 n.; method of studying it, 16, 399–401, 399 sq. n., 401 sq. n.; its makers, the sages, were independent of it, 16, 404, 406 n.; how the sages devised and constructed it, 16, 405, 406 sq. n.; its origin from the manipulation of divining-stalks, 16, 422, 422 sq. n. *See also* Symbols.

Yima (Av.), or Yim (Phl.), or *G*im, son of Vîvangha*n*t, compared with Yama, son of Vivasvat, 4, lii; corresponding to Noah, 4, lviii sq.; myths of Y., the founder of civilization, 4, lxx, 10–21, 384 sq.; 24, 59 sq. n.; 37, 212–15; 47, 9 sq.; rules over the creatures for 1,000 years, and three times enlarges the earth, 4, 10–15, 264, 264 n.; 47, 9; being warned by Ahura-Mazda, that the evil winters (snowfall, deluge) are about to fall, builds a Vara (enclosure), where he keeps the best specimens of every kind of creatures, and they live there a life of happiness, 4, 10 sq., 15–21; 18, 109 sq. and n.; 24, 59 sq.; the first mortal with whom Ahura-Mazda conversed, 4, 11; Y. Khshaêta (or Y. Shê*d*, or *G*emshîd), the good shepherd, 4, 223; 23, 59 sq., 59 n., 112, 252 sq., 276, 326; was one of the faithful, 4, 261 sq.; born immortal, became mortal, 4, 262; threefold proceeding of Y. towards the South, 4, 263; towns erected on the Bakyîr in the days of Y., 5, 38, 38 n.; the three fires in the reign of Y., 5, 63; the bird Kar*s*ipt brought the religion to the enclosure of Y., 5, 70; takes a demoness as wife, 5, 87; the bird Kar*s*ipt was brought to the enclosure of Y., 5, 89; enclosure made by Y., 5, 118, 120, 142, 234, 234 n.; 18, 109 sq. and n.; 24, 59 sq., 59 n., 108–10, 108 n.; 47, 9 sq.; one of 'the Rashnû of *K*înŏ,' 5, 130, 130 n.; cut up by Spîtûr (Spityura) and Dahâk, 5, 131; 23, 297, 297 sq. n.; legend of Y. and his sister Yimak, a pair, man and woman, born from them, 5, 131; 18, 418 sq.; Dahâk smitten by Frêdûn in revenge of Y., 5, 133; 37, 177; duration of his reign, 5, 149 sq.; primaeval sovereign, 18, 13, 13 n.; 47, 121, 128; among the preparers of the renovation of the universe, 18, 77; Kingly Glory of Y., 18, 90, 90 n.; 23, 293–5; 47, 12 sq.; the fravashi of Y. kept away all trouble, 18, 104, 104 n.; his apostasy, and his pardon, 18, 127 sq. and n.; ordered the sacred thread-girdle, 18, 128, 130 sq.; 24, 268; drove death away, 18, 200 sq., 201 n.; overthrown by Azi Dahâka, 23, 60 n.; his daughters ravished by Azi Dahâka, 23, 62 n.; brings immortality down to the world, 23, 112, 276; the fravashi of Y., worshipped, 23, 221; Y. and his brother Takhma Urupa, 23, 252 n.; golden age under his reign, 23, 253, 293; 31, 232; became false, and his Glory

departed from him three times, 23, 293–5, 294 n.; created immortal, misled by Aharman, 24, 34 sq. and n.; neglected religion, 24, 102; introduced the eating of kine's flesh, 31, 55, 61, 61 n.; third ruler of the earth, 37, 27, 27 n.; Aûharmazd discloses the religion to Y., 37, 153; drove away the four vices, 37, 177; Aîrân-vêg, abode of Y., 37, 190 n.; contrasted with Dahâk, 37, 212; man and cattle gratified by Y., 37, 255; saying about Y., 37, 386; opening of the enclosure made by Y., 47, xii, 108; his accession, 47, xxix; Y. who is of mankind, 47, 23; announces the birth of Zaratûst, 47, 31; monarch of the seven regions, 47, 34 sq.; ancestor of Zoroaster, 47, 122; Zoroaster's connexion with Aûharmazd through Y. and Nêryôsang, 47, 139 sq. *See also* Vîvanghat.

Yimak, sister of Yim, becomes the wife of a demon, ape and bear sprang from them, 5, 87; 18, 418 sq.; 47, 143 n.; Yim and Y. became husband and wife, 5, 131; 18, 418 sq.

Yin, n. of a town, capital removed from Ho to, 3, 103 sq., 122 sq.

Yin, or Yin-Shang, other name of the Shang dynasty, 3, 84, 103, 108, 120, 122, 156–62, 170 sq., 176–8, 183–7, 194, 196–9, 201, 205, 208, 214, 217 sq., 233, 236, 244, 246, 248 sq., 308, 311, 411 sq.; 28, 123; 40, 164; laws of Y., 3, 168; practices and ceremonies of Y., 3, 190; 27, 138–40, 145, 168–70, 172, 191, 240, 242 sq., 341, 368, 405 sq., 438, 443 sq., 464, 467; 28, 31, 34–9, 202, 218, 229, 294, 324, 342 sq.; people of Y. used wooden coffins, 27, 125; music of Y., 28, 106. *See also* Shang.

Yin, n. of a mountain, 39, 260.

Yin, 'Grand-Master' of King Yû, 3, 351 sq.

Yin, Marquis of, charged to punish the ministers of the Board of Astronomy Hsî and Ho, 3, 81–3.

Yin, the warden of the gate, and Lieh-ʒze, 39, 150; 40, 12–14, 12 sq. n.

Yin and Yang, symbolically represented, 16, 16; mean bright and dark, and analogous qualities, not yet ether, 16, 43 sq., 44 n.; the two elements, the dual forces of nature, 27, 380 sq., 381 n., 383; 40, 99; the constituents of the primal ether, 39, 249, 297 sq. and n., 301 n.; 40, 47, 47 n.; Yang, the element of expansion, Yin the opposite element, 39, 291 sq.; their repositories, 39, 299; masters of the Tâo possess the Y. and Y., 39, 333; their harmony, 39, 349; Confucius tried in vain to find the Tâo in them, 39, 355; the dragon nourished by the Y. and Y., 39, 358; the Tâoist sage like Y. and Y., 39, 365; were harmonious and still in the chaotic condition of the world, 39, 369; the ocean has received his breath from Y. and Y., 39, 376; to be followed and honoured, 39, 381; revolve by the Tâo, 40, 61; man feels himself independent of Y. and Y., 40, 64; no robber greater than the Y. and Y., 40, 84; reflected light on each other, covered and regulated each other, 40, 128; the greatest of all elemental forces, 40, 128; when they act awry, a thunderstorm arises, 40, 132; want of harmony between them, one of the troubles of a king, 40, 195; their successive movement constitutes the course of things, 40, 257; overcome each other by turns, 40, 263 sq.; the greatest enemies of men's serenity, 40, 294.

Yin Fû King, or 'Classic of the Harmony of the Seen and the Unseen' translated and explained, 40, 255–64.

Yin Hsî, prevails on Lâo-ʒze to write his book, 40, 314.

Yin Khî, first instituted the *kâ* sacrifice, 27, 431, 431 n.

Yin Kî-fû, author of odes of the Shih, 3, 296.

Yin Wăn, and Sung Hsing, founders of a modified system of Mohism, 40, 221–3, 221 sq. n.

Yî-yang, a class of sprites, 40, 19.

Yoga (Concentration, Devotion, Meditation), faults eradicated by means of, 2, 78; he who meditates on Purusha for a year, obtains the accomplishment of Y., 7, 288, 288 n.; practice of Y. described and recommended, 8, 9, 48–50, 68–71; 14, 125; definitions of Y., 8, 9–11;

15, xxxv, 323; knowledge superior to Y., 8, 12; more important than Vedas, 8, 17; 14, 125; explained, 8, 47–9, 47 n.; action inferior to Y., 8, 48 sq., 52; in the shape of knowledge, and in the shape of action, 8, 52; in the shape of action it is best, 8, 53–5; taught by K*ri*sh*n*a to the sun, and to Arguna, 8, 58; action, Y., and knowledge, 8, 59–63; a means of attaining Brahman, 8, 64; he who is possessed of Y. attains tranquillity, 8, 65; renunciation is Y., 8, 67; obtained through self-restraint, 8, 71 sq.; leads to, practised for, final emancipation, 8, 72 sq., 81, 248–53, 332; 48, 413, 516; higher than knowledge, 8, 73, 100 sq.; who knows the emanations of K*ri*sh*n*a becomes possessed of Y., 8, 87; is the only means of seeing K*ri*sh*n*a in his divine form, 8, 99, 128; practised constantly throughout six months, 8, 255; the sacrifice of Y., 8, 279; Ha*th*a-yoga, 8, 297 n.; the only means to conquer the senses, 8, 300; wheel of Y., 8, 306 n.; a means for reaching the highest world, 8, 326, 389 sq.; a man who has achieved Y. does not need a preceptor, 8, 381 n.; eight requisites for Y., 8, 394 n.; in Bhagavadgîtâ, Sanatsugâtîya, and Anugîtâ, 8, 441 sq.; *through the practice of Y. (true) knowledge is obtained, Y. is the sum of the sacred law, all good qualities are gained through Y.; therefore let him always be absorbed in the practice of Y.*, 14, 125, 316; Y. or the highest state, the firm holding back of the senses, 15, 22; through Vedânta and Y. anchorites become free in the worlds of Brahmâ, 15, 41; God, the cause to be apprehended by Sâṅkhya and Y., 15, 264; the practising of the sixfold Y., and its result, 15, 318–26; he who restrains his organs need not practise Y., 25, 48; leads to the acquirement of extraordinary powers, 34, 223; the means of attaining the knowledge of the highest place of Vish*n*u, 34, 241, 297; highest beatitude is not to be attained by the road of Y., 34, 298; is of the nature of lower knowledge, 38, 375; the remedy of Sa*m*sâra, 48, 89; perception based on Y., 48, 162; the highest Self is intuited by persons practising Y., 48, 273; a means of knowledge, 48, 284; Y.-knowledge enables Raikva to know everything that passes in the three worlds, 48, 340; Sâṅkhya and Y., i.e. the concentrated application of knowledge and of works, 48, 528; not to be rejected absolutely, 48, 531; through the power of Y., some men were able to choose the time of their death, 48, 742; practitioner of Y., *see* Yogin. *See also* Meditation.

Yogâ*k*âras, Idealists, a school of Buddhists, 8, 213, 377 n.; 34, 401 n.; 48, 510–13. *See also* Idealists.

Yoga-sâstra, or Yoga-smr*i*ti, system of Yoga philosophy: Vish*n*u-smr*i*ti knows Y. and Sâṅkhya systems, 7, xxiv, xxviii; propounded by the Bhagavadgîtâ, 8, 23; reference to Sâṅkhya and Y. in the Bhagavadgîtâ, 8, 27; quoted in the Anugîtâ, 8, 210–12, 215, 226; Nîlaka*n*t*h*a refers to it, 8, 251 n., 252 n.; Prâ*n*âyâma and Pratyâhâra in Y., 8, 266 n.; refuted, 34, xlvii, 50, 296–9; 48, 412 sq.; teaches a Lord in addition to individual souls, 34, 15 n.; assumes a pradhâna, as the independent cause of the world, and the 'great principle,' &c., as its effects, 34, 296; in giving rules for the condition of the wandering religious mendicant, agrees with the Veda, 34, 298; Y. and Sâṅkhya-system maintain duality, do not discern the unity of the Self, 34, 298; on the Y. system the Lord acts as the ruler of the pradhâna, and of the souls, 34, 434 sq.; the five functions of the manas known from it, viz. right knowledge, error, imagination, slumber, and remembrance, 38, 90; teaches different sitting postures, 38, 350; Y. and Sâṅkhya are mere Sm*ri*ti, not of scriptural character, 38, 381; books on Y. treat of the connexion of one soul with several bodies, 38, 414; supports the Vedânta texts, 48, 412 sq.; proclaimed by Hira*n*yagarbha, 48, 413; in the Mahâbhârata, 48, 529–

31; teaches certain practices and means of mental concentration, 48, 530. *See also* Philosophy.

Yoga-sûtra, of Patañgali, Bhagavadgîtâ compared with, 8, 8–11; its date, 8, 210–12; (and its Bhâshya) quoted, 8, notes to 74, 234, 250, 252, 260, 266, 271, 274, 285 sq., 300, 319, 324, 327, 343, 373; 34, 223.

Yogavâsish*th*a, t.w., quoted, 8, 206, 240 n.

Yogin(s), or Devotees, are especially worthy to take part in a *S*râddha repast, 7, 255; four classes of Y., 8, 11, 75; K*ri*sh*n*a's devotee, dear to K*ri*sh*n*a, 8, 58, 75, 79, 86 sq., 99–102, 104, 129; sacrifices of Y., 8, 61; those who follow the Yoga path, 8, 64, 64 n.; description of a Y., 8, 66–73; the path of the Y. after death, 8, 81, 84 sq.; God (K*ri*sh*n*a) preserved by and in Y., 8, 112, 186–94; reward of the Y., 8, 243; perceive the Self, 8, 248 sq.; obtains various bodies as he pleases, and casting aside old age and death, he grieves not and exults not, 8, 249 sq.; in Bhagavadgîtâ, Sanatsugâtîya, and Anugîtâ, 8, 442; become visible in the Buddha-fields, 21, 7; their omniscience, 34, 46, 49, 50; does the term 'the internal Ruler' refer to some Y.? 34, 131; may animate several bodies at the same time, 34, 200; in the state of perfect conciliation, apprehend the highest Brahman, 38, 171 sq.; rules for Y. as to dying by day and during the northern progress of the sun, 38, 380, 381; magical perception of Y., 48, 51, 116; do not at first attain to knowledge of the Self, but meditate upon the second form of Vish*n*u, 48, 89 sq.; should meditate on the path of the gods, 48, 742 sq.

Yôi*s*ta, or Yôi*s*tô, or Yô*s*tô, or Yô*s*kŏ Fryânŏ, son of Fryân, one of the seven immortal rulers, 18, 256, 256 n.; 23, 216, 216 n.; 37, 29, 29 sq. n.; worships Anâhita, and solves the riddles of Akhtya, 23, 72 sq. and n. *See also* Gô*s*t-i Fryân.

Yo *K*ăng, mother of Ʒze-*kh*un, 27, 201.

Yo-*k*ăng Ʒze-*kh*un, sitting by the couch of the dying Ʒăng-ʒze, 27, 128; Yo-*k*ăng *Kh*un, a disciple of Ʒăng-ʒze, 28, 228 sq., 228 n.

Yonakas, the Bactrian Greeks, Milinda, king of the, 35, xviii, 2.

Yô*s*tô, *see* Yôi*s*ta.

Youth, to rise before seniors, 8, 139 sq., 203; 25, 52; *but see also* Old age; in the prime of life becomes dear to women, 44, 295.

Yû, King, reigned eleven years, 3, 22; called Nieh, 3, 265; King Y. and his cruel and negligent 'Grand-Master' Yin, 3, 351–3; ministers and officers of Y., 3, 355 sq., 356 n.; makes Sze of Pâo his queen, and banishes his eldest son, 3, 360; ceremonies at the court of Y., 3, 374; his queen complains of being degraded and forsaken, 3, 376; misgovernment of Y., 3, 428, 439 n.; corrupted the ways of *K*âu, 27, 372.

Yû, disciple of Confucius, *see* Ʒze-lû.

Yü, founder of the Hsiâ dynasty, and of the hereditary monarchy, 3, 13, 19; credibility of 'the Tribute of Y.' in the Shû, 3, 13–19; labours of Y. in coping with the inundation, and his work for agriculture and civilization, 3, 16–18, 57 sq., 60 sq., 63–76, 309, 312, 395; married in Thû-shan, 3, 17, 60, 60 n.; date of his reign, 3, 23; in spite of his refusals, appointed to be his successor by Shun, 3, 37, 48–51; 27, 396; 39, 181 n., 315, 359; 'The Books of Y.' in the Shû, translated, 3, 37–62; meaning of the names of the Great Y., 3, 46, 46 n.; 'The Counsels of the Great Y.' translated, 3, 46–52; 'The Tribute of Y.,' translated, 3, 63–76; 'The great plan' first given to Y., 3, 138, 140; son of Khwăn, 3, 140; made all about the southern hill manageable, 3, 369, 369 n.; mountain of Liang made cultivable by Y., 3, 426; helped by Yî, Y. brings the lord of Miâo to submission, 3, 51 sq.; conversation between Kâo-yâo and Y., 3, 53–6; the cautions to kings of the Great Y., 3, 79 sq.; one of the six great men, 27, 366; assessor at

the border sacrifice in *Kh*î, 27, 372; worshipped by the sovereigns of Hsiâ, 28, 202; deserves ancestor-worship, 28, 208; his great virtues, 28, 339; the spirit-like Y., 39, 181, 181 n.; attacked the ruler of Hû, 39, 206; acted according to the Tâo, 39, 210, 210 n.; how he ruled the world, 39, 359; floods in the times of Y., 39, 388; Shun when about to die, instructs Y., 40, 35 sq.; was paralysed on one side, 40, 173, 173 n.; had his Tâ Hsiâ music, 40, 218; the model of the Mohists, 40, 219 sq. *See also* Po-yü, *and* Shun.

Yü, captain of the guards to Yû, 3, 356.

Yüan, ruler of Sung, chooses a draughtsman to have a map drawn, 40, 50 sq.; Y. and the artisan Shih, 40, 101, 101 n.; Y. and the divining tortoise, 40, 136 sq.

Yüan Fung and *K*un Mâng discourse together, 39, 322–4, 322 sq. n.

Yüan Hsien, explains to 3ze-kung that he is poor but not in distress, 40, 157 sq., 157 n.

Yüan Kû, his text of the Shih King, 3, 286 sq.

Yuan Thsang, on the Council of Kanishka, 36, xvi.

Yüan *Z*ang, an old acquaintance of Confucius, 27, 199 sq., 199 n.

Yûdân-Yim, priest, father of Mânû*sk*îhar and Zâ*d*-sparam, 5, xlii, xlvi sq., lxiv, 147 sq., 155; 18, xiii, 3 sq., 3 n., 276, 279, 323, 325, 357, 359 sq., 365; son of Shahpûhar, 18, 289, 289 n.; quoted as an authority, 18, 306.

Yudhâmanyu, n. of a warrior, 8, 37.

Yudhish*th*ira, the Pâ*nd*ava, 8, 38, 394; his gambling, 25, lxxi, lxxx, 381 n.; performs the horse sacrifice, 44, xxvii.

Yüeh, the sheep-butcher, declines all honours offered by King *K*âo of *Kh*û, 40, 155–7.

Yüeh, a recluse, appointed chief minister by King Wû-ting, 3, 112–18; called Fû Yüeh, 3, 113; got the Tâo, and was raised to the stars, 39, 135 sq., 245, 245 n.

Yugas, *see* Ages of the World (*a*).

Yü Hwang Tî, worshipped by the Tâoists, 39, 43 sq.

Yü-*kh*iang, got the Tâo, 39, 245, 245 n.

Yukhtâspa, n.p., 23, 212.

Yukhtavairi, n.p., 23, 205.

Yung, King, of Wei, and his counsellors, 40, 118–20.

Yung-*kh*ăng, a primaeval sovereign, 39, 287; a saying of Y., 40, 118, 118 n.

Yung *K*ü, as a messenger of condolence on the death of Duke Khâo, 27, 193, 193 sq. n.

Yung-3ze, example of a 'Perfect Man,' 39, 127, 168, 168 n.; Y. of Sung not Great, 40, 274.

Yün *K*iang, asks Hung Mung about governing men, 39, 143, 300–3, 300 n., 302 n.; 40, 286 sq.

Yûpa, Yûpâhuti, *see* Animal sacrifices (*d*).

Yü Shû *K*ing, or 'The Classic of the Pivot of Jade,' 40, 265–8.

Yû*s*ta, son of Gâuri, 23, 215.

Yuyudhâna, n. of a warrior, 8, 37.

Yû *Z*o, mourning rites for him, 27, 165, 165 n.; about An-3ze, 27, 174; an authority on funeral rites, 27, 188.

Yü 3ü, the fisherman who caught a wonderful tortoise, 40, 136 sq.

Yû-3ze, period of mourning kept by him, 27, 130, 130 n.; on a saying of Confucius, 27, 149 sq.; asks 3ze-yû, about mourning rites, 27, 176 sq.; on grave offerings, 28, 141.

Z AND 3

Zachariah, Mary the Virgin brought up by, 6, 51; a chosen of God, 6, 125; prays for an heir, is promised a son, who is to be called John: struck dumb for three days as a sign, 9, 27 sq.; called Dhu 'l Kifl, 9, 53, 53 n., 180.

Zâ*d*-sparam, son of Yûdân-Yim, high-priest of Sîrkân, brother of Mânû*sk*îhar, 5, xxxviii, 147 sq. and n., 155, 155 n., 168 n., 434; his relation to the Bundahi*s*, 5, xxxviii, xlii sq., 148 n., 172 n., 178 n., 186 n.; his date, 5, xlii sq.; 47, xvii; the Selections of Z., 5, xlvi–l, 153–87; 18, 366 n.; 37, 401–5, 401 n.; his style,

5, 164 n., 182 n.; contents of his works, 5, 186 sq. n.; quoted, 5, 195 n., 368 n.; 37, 14 n.; epistles addressed to him by his brother Mânû*sk*îhar, 18, xiii sq., xxv sq.; his heresy regarding the purification ceremony, 18, 279, 279 n., 280 n., 284 n., 295 n., 300 n., 320 n., 321 n., 360, 364, 455; quotes the Pahlavi Yasna, 18, 394; Âtûr*p*â*d*, contemporary of Z., 24, xxvii; 37, xxxiii; on the Nasks, 37, xxxix; legendary history of Zoroaster in the Selections of Z., 47, ix, xiv–xvii, 133–70, 133 n.

Zaê*s*m, n.p., 5, 135.

Zafîyah bint 'Huyâi, wife of Mohammed, 9, 240 n.

Zâgh, n.p., 5, 146.

Z*ă*h-*k*ung Shih, n. of a teacher, 39, 137, 260.

Z*ă*h Yung *K*ing, or 'Classic of the Directory for a Day,' translated, 40, 269–72.

Zâid, converted by Mohammed, 6, xxiii, xlix; Mohammed's adopted son, 6, xxix; 9, 139 n., 144, 144 n., 233 n.; slain in battle, 6, xli.

Zâid ibn 'Amr, friend of Mohammed, 6, xv, xx, xxiii.

Zâid ibn THâbit, amanuensis of Mohammed, 6, lvii; collected and arranged the text of the Qur'ân, 6, lvii–lix.

Zâinab, divorced wife of Zâid, wife of Mohammed, 6, xxix; 9, 139 n., 144, 144 n.

Zâinîgâv: wars of Z. and Frangrasyan (Turanians and Arabs), 4, l sq.; Khrûtâsp, son of Z., 5, 131.

Zairi, *see* Zâîrî*k*.

Zâîrî*k*, = Av. Zairi*k*a or Zairi, one of the six demons of Aharman, 4, 139, 139 n., 224; 5, 10, 10 n.; 18, 96, 96 n., 319, 319 n.; maker of poison, 5, 107; attacked by Amerôda*d*, 5, 128; demon Zârî*k*ô, propitiated by walking barefoot, 37, 182, 182 n.

Zairi*k*i, n. of a holy woman, 23, 224.

Zairita, n.p., 23, 204.

Zairivairi, protector of Zarathu*s*tra, 4, lxiii; struggle between Z. and Arega*t*-aspa and other enemies, 23, 80 sq., 80 n.; brother of Vî*s*tâspa, 23, 205, 205 n.

Zairyã*k*, n.p., 23, 213.

Ȝâi Wo, and Confucius, on the constitution of man, 27, 36; 28, 220, 222 n.

Zâk, a Karap, 47, 20 n., 64 sq.

Zâli'h, sent unto Thamûd, with the sign of the she-camel, 6, 146 sq., 147 sq. n., 211 sq.; 9, 96, 103.

Zamyâ*d*, the crocus belongs to, 5, 104; invoked, 5, 404 sq. *See also* Earth (*c*).

***Z*ăn**, *see* Thâi-*z*ăn.

***Z*ăn**, duke of, his son, after fishing for a whole year, caught a huge fish, 40, 133 sq.

Za*nd*as, and Yâtus (sorcerers), 4, 204, 204 n.; 31, 313.

Ȝăng Shăn, son of Ȝăng-ȝze, 27, 128; asks Ȝăng-ȝze about mourning rites, 28, 161; famous for righteousness, 39, 269, 274, 287, 295; Ȝ. S. and Shih Ȝhiû, classed together with the robber *K*ih, 39, 292, 328; 40, 285; famous for filial piety, met with misfortune, 40, 132, 132 n.

Ȝăng Tien, at the mourning rites for Wû-ȝze, 27, 162, 162 n.

Ȝang Wăn-*k*ung, failed to stop Hsiâ Fû-*kh*î in committing an irregularity in ceremonies, 27, 403 sq. and n.; a sacrifice ordered by him, 28, 35.

Ȝăng Yüan, son of Ȝăng-ȝze, 27, 128.

Ȝăng-ȝze, the Hsiâo King, conversations between Confucius and, 3, xx, 451; supposed author of the Tâ Hsio, 3, xx; 27, 53; 28, 412 n., 413 n.; conversations of Confucius with Ȝ., 3, 465, 472, 476, 483; Ȝ. or Shăn, styled Ȝze-yü, honoured disciple of Confucius, 3, 465 n.; 39, 269, 269 n.; 'The questions of Ȝ.' put to Confucius, 27, 21 sq., 311–42; the book Nêi Ȝeh ascribed to him, 27, 27; on filial piety, 27, 37; 28, 226–9; on funeral and mourning rites, 27, 124, 126, 133–5, 141 sq., 147–54, 174 sq., 187; 28, 143, 143 n., 152, 156 sq., 161; his illness and death, 27, 128 sq.; mourning rites for him, 27, 132; in mourning for his mother, 27, 164 sq.; on *Kh*ien Âo's charity, 27, 195; Ȝ. and Ȝze-kung paying a visit of condolence, 27, 197; quoted, 27, 406, 467; 28,

413; change of feeling in him in his poverty and prosperity, 39, 156; 40, 145; though poor, is happy in the possession of the Tâo, 40, 158.
Zăn-hsiang, a sovereign who possessed the Tâo, 40, 117.
Zăn *Kh*iû, asks Confucius about what was before heaven and earth, 40, 71 sq., 293.
Za*n*tuma, worshipped, 31, 197, 204, 209, 215, 219, 223, 251, 259, 278, 373, 381 sq.
Zan Yû, sent to *K*ing by Confucius, 27, 150.
Zan-3ze, made a gift of condolence, as a substitute for Confucius, 27, 134.
Zaosha, n.p., 23, 218.
Zaotar, *see* Priests (*d, e*).
Zaothra, *see* Sacrifice (*b*).
Zaqqûm, tree in hell, *see* Hell (*c*).
Zarathu*s*tra, *see* Zoroaster.
Zarathu*s*trians, *see* Zoroastrians.
Zarathu*s*trôtema, chief of priests, 23, 149, 149 n.; worshipped, 31, 197, 204, 209, 215, 219, 224, 259, 278, 337, 384–6.
Zaratû*s*t, the prophet, *see* Zoroaster.
Zaratû*s*t, son of Âtû*r*-frôbag (Âtû*r*-farnbag), editor of the Dînka*rd*, 24, xxvii, 139 n.; his fate, 37, xxxii.
Zaratû*s*t, son of Âtû*r*pâ*d*, 37, 30 n.; 47, xxxvi sq. *See also* Avarethraba*u*.
Zaratû*s*t, n.p., Vâhrâm-shâ*d*, son of, 5, 147.
Zaratû*s*t, 'the club-footed,' n. of a priest, 18, xxvi, 329.
Zaratû*s*t-nâmak of Zâ*d*-sparam, t.c., its contents, 47, xiv–xxiv.
Zarazdâti, son of Paêshatah, 23, 213.
Zaremaya, the oil of, the food of the souls in Paradise, 23, 318, 318 n., 345.
Zarenuma*nt*, the good, created by Mazda, 31, 391.
Zargar, adopted Zoroastrianism, 24, 171, 171 n.
Zârî*k*ŏ, *see* Zaîrî*k*.
Zarîr, brother of Vi*s*tâsp, 5, 137 sq., 137 n., 146; converted, 47, 125, 125 n.
Zarmân, demon of decrepitude, 5, 110; 18, 93, 95.
Zartu*s*t Bahrâm Pa*z*dû, author of Zartu*s*t-nâmah, 47, xx.
Zartu*s*t-nâmah, the Persian, legends of Zoroaster in, 47, xx–xxiv, 66 n., 77 n.
3âu, Recorder of the Interior to Yû, 3, 356.
Zaurva, demon of old age, 4, 224.
Zavan, n.p., 23, 218.
Zbaurva*nt*, n.p., 23, 209.
3eh-yang, or Phăng Yang, wishes to be introduced to the king of *Kh*û, 39, 154; 40, 114 sq.
Zemyâd, *see* Zamyâ*d*.
Zend, language, and Sanskrit, 4, xxii–xxvi; rather Avesta language, 4, xxxi n.; the Gâthas written in a dead or dying language, 4, lxvi.
Zend-Avesta, Anquetil Duperron's translation of the, 1, xvii–xix; 4, xvii–xx; fire in the Z., 1, xxii; discovery of the Z., 4, xiii–xxvi; modes of interpretation of the Z., 4, xxvii–xxxi, lxxxvii sq.; Veda and Z., 4, xxvii–xxxi; 31, xxix, xxxvi sq.; the name Z., 4, xxxi n.; the different parts of the Z., 4, xxxi–xxxvii, lxv; the remnants of a large literature, 4, xxxii sq.; 37, xxix; history of Z. literature, 4, xxxiii–xlvii; Parthian elements in the Z., 4, xlvii–li; concordance between Z. and Pentateuch, 4, lviii sq.; age and growth of the Z., 4, lxiv–lxvii; 31, xxxiii–xxxvii, 281 sq.; 47, xi, xlvi sq.; one who knows the Gâthas, the Yasna, and the revealed Law, 4, 203; punishments for mistakes in the recitation of the Z., 4, 278 n., 279; the Erpatistân and Nîrangistân, 4, 300–68; the Staota Yêsnya, ancient productions, recollected, 4, 312 n., 313; 31, 294 n., 295; uttered in the language of birds, 5, 70 sq.; chanting Gâtha hymns and reciting a Vendîdâd, 5, 212 sq. and n.; to be recited, not to be mumbled, 5, 327; not to be mumbled when one laughs outright, 5, 330; Bakân-yastô (Bâg-yasnô) quoted, its contents, 5, 346, 346 n.; to be studied by priests, 18, 152 sq., 152 n.; liturgies from the Z. for the ceremonial, 18, 167–9, 168 n.; revealed, 18, 215 n.; quoted, 18, 292–4; 24, 6; of Zaratû*s*t, 18, 447; mutual relation of Ya*s*ts and Sîrôzahs, 23, 1–3; the Sîrôzahs translated, 23, 3–20; passages quoted in the Sad Dar, 24, xxxviii; must be properly learnt and remembered, 24, 290 sq.;

recited after a death, 24, 351, 359; must be learnt from priests, 24, 359 sq.; the Pahlavi translations of the Z., 31, xxxvii–xliii; 37, xli sq.; 47, xvii sq.; metres of the Z., 31, xliii sq.; value of its doctrines, 31, xlvi sq.; certain Gâthas and Yasnas worshipped, 31, 328–31, 361–3; as Ahura-Mazda and Zarathustra directed that it should be said, 31, 353; the Âfrînagân translated, 31, 365–75; Zoroastrian legends in the Z., 47, xix sq.; written by Gâmâsp, 47, xxx; demons shattered by revelation from the Z., 47, 64; *one is the marvel of the Avesta itself, which, according to all the best reports of the world, is a compendium of all the supremest statements of wisdom*, 47, 76; deposited in Shapîgân, 47, 82, 82 n.; prophecies in the Z., 47, 93, 93 n.; injured by apostates, 47, 99; blessed utterances of the Z., 47, 102; written with gold on oxhides, 47, 127, 127 n. *See also* Avesta, Gâthas, Nasks, Prayers (*f*), Vendîdâd, Visparad, Yasna, *and* Yast.

Ʒhâi Yung, his work for the Confucian classics, 27, 8.

Ʒhan-liâo, a Tâoist teacher, 39, 247.

Ʒhâo Shang, boasts of the gifts he received from the king of Sung and is rebuked by *K*wang-ʒze, 39, 161; 40, 207.

Ʒhui *Kh*ü, his erroneous view about government, 39, 142, 294.

Ʒiang of Lû = Âi, 27, 39; 28, 261 n. *See* Âi.

Zighri, n.p., 23, 219.

Zîyânak Zardâhim, and Mîrak the Âspiyân, 5, 131.

*Z*o, the Spirit-lord of the Northern Sea, explains the greatness of the Tâo to the earl of the Ho, 39, 148, 374–84, 374 n.

Zôb, the Tûhmâspian = Aûzôbô, 5, 150, 150 n.

Zobeir, converted by Mohammed, 6, xxiii.

Zodiac, *see* Stars.

Zohâk, *see* Dahâka.

Zôis, father of Zoroaster's mother, 47, 18, 18 n.

Zoroaster (Zarathustra, Zaratûst).

(*a*) Epithets, attributes, and character of Z.
(*b*) Life and legends of Z.
(*c*) Z. and the Avesta, Z. and his religion.
(*d*) Z. in his relation to gods (archangels) and fiends (Daêvas).
(*e*) Praise and worship of Z.

(*a*) Epithets, attributes, and character of Z.

The heavenly priest, who founded the Religion by a sacrifice, 4, 21 n.; the chief of worldly existences, 5, 88, 88 n.; 18, 92; spiritual chief of Khvanîras, 5, 115 sq., 116 n.; the greatest of apostles, 18, 13, 13 n., 92, 386; 24, 270; his greatness, 18, 21; among the preparers of the renovation of the universe, 18, 77; completely good, 18, 90; 37, 196; the master of the material world, 23, 74, 190; possessed of Kingly Glory, 23, 304 sq.; shared heaven through wisdom, 24, 102; created as the best in the world, in the middle period, 24, 345; mythical attributes of Z. in the Yasts, 31, xxii; called a feeble and pusillanimous man, 31, 5, 11, 11 n.; the ideal husbandman, 31, 38, 45, 45 n.; the first teacher, 31, 126, 126 n.; the first tiller, warrior, and priest, 31, 153; the possessor of the Mãthra, 31, 355; the living chief and master, 31, 359; his beneficence and worthiness, 37, 234–6, 241; is privileged, 37, 369; reward of Z. the smiter and developer, 37, 387; nature and character of Z., 37, 420; 47, 46 sq.; righteousness of his desires, his compassion and liberality, 47, xv, 151–4; the delight of the righteous, 47, 87; his complete virtue, 47, 126.

(*b*) Life and legends of Z.

Converted from a Magus into a magician, 4, xv; Z. and Sakyamuni, 4, liii; had forerunners, like Moses, 4, lix; the Spîtâmân, i. e. the descendant of Spitama, 4, 2, 2 n.; 5, 192 sq., 192 n.; the sons of Z., the three future apostles, his assured offspring, 4, 21 n.; 5, 118, 361; 18, 92 sq., 93 n., 170; 37, 33 sq.; 47, 106, 111, 115; a historical personage, 5, lxxii; birthplace of his father, 5, 82; his birthplace, 5, 89; genealogy and descendants of Z., 5, 140–4; 47, 34 sq., 34 n., 139 sq., 139 n.; wives of Z., 5, 142–4, 143 n.; 37, 297, 297 n.; account of his

career by Zâd-sparam, 5, 186 sq. n.; begotten in consequence of Hôm drinking, 5, 187; 18, 164, 164 n.; Hôm symbolical of his birth, 18, 170; murdered by Tûr-î-Brâdar-vakhsh, 18, 218 n.; 24, 267 sq.; 47, 126; promised to destroy Knâthaiti by means of the apostle Saoshyãs, 18, 369; his supplication for the soul of Keresâsp, 18, 372, 379–81; 37, 198 sq.; sacrifices to Anâhita and obtains the boon, that he converts Vîstâspa, 23, 78, 78 n.; worshipped Drvâspa, 23, 116; converts Hutaosa, 23, 116, 279; worshipped the Fravashis in every struggle, 23, 190; the Fravashis watch over the seed of Z., 23, 195, 195 n.; the sons and daughters of Z., 23, 204, 204 n., 224; 47, 166; sacrificed to *K*ista, 23, 265; his good narcotic (Bangha), 23, 267 sq. and n.; exhorts Vîstâspa (Kaî Gustâsp) to adhere to the Law of Mazda, and converts him, 23, 324, 330–45; 24, 170 sq.; 37, 24, 285, 424; 47, xi, xv, xxv; pronounces blessings on Vîstâspa, 23, 324–30; told not to distress father or mother or priest, 24, 302, 302 n.; who was Z.? 31, xxii–xxv; temptation of Z., 31, 26, 177, 183; marriage of Z.'s daughter, 31, 92, 187–94; prays for long life, in order to convert men, 31, 97, 104 sq.; afflicted and discouraged, 31, 131, 134 sq.; son of Pourushaspa, 31, 235; instructs Frashaostra with regard to the rites, 31, 327; his birth, 37, 12, 31, 32 n., 226 sq., 444; 47, x, xiv, xxi, xxvii, xxix sq., 16–33, 17 n., 122, 139; attaining the religion, 37, 12; legendary life of Z., 37, 31–3, 32 n.; *Vol.* 47; his vision of the past, future, and other world, after receiving omniscience, 37, 32 sq.; communication of his knowledge to the world, 37, 33; family of Z., 37, 97; four periods in the millennium of Z., 37, 181, 451 sq.; 47, 16; appointed high-priest, 37, 232; produced for the assistance of cattle, 37, 239; descendant of Aêzemnô (Ayazem), 37, 261, 261 n.; the Zôti at the renovation of the universe, 37, 261 sq. and n.; given a wife by Frashôstar, 37, 397; miracles of Z., 37, 425; the fourth chieftain, 37, 460; descent of his glory upon his mother at her birth, 47, x, xiv, 17–29, 138 sq.; his mission to the Kîgs and Karaps, 47, x sq., xiv sq., xxv, xxx, 50–7; his useful work and advice, 47, xi, 75 sq.; four brothers of Z., 47, xiv, 144, 144 n.; converts Mêdyômâh, 47, xv; legends of Z. in various Pahlavi and Pâzand texts, 47, xviii sq.; legends of Z. in the Avesta, 47, xix sq.; legendary history of Z. in the Persian Zartust-nâmah, 47, xx–xxiv; his struggles with demons and magicians, 47, xxi; dream of his mother, 47, xxi; legends of Z. and King Gustâsp, 47, xxi–xxiii, 123–5; cures the horse of Vîstâsp, 47, xxii, 66, 66 n.; denounced as a sorcerer, 47, xxii; has a vision of heaven and hell, and of a tree with seven branches, 47, xxiii sq.; cures the bull of Parshad-tôrâ, 47, xxv; sent to Vêdvôîst, 47, xxv; his spiritual body framed, 47, xxviii, xl sq., 122; his childhood and youth, attempts at his life, 47, xxx, 35–46, 122 sq., 145 sq.; his conversions, 47, xxx; his death, 47, xxx, 73, 77 n., 165; date of Z., 47, xxxviii–xlvii; predecessors of Z., 47, 15; his coming announced by Yim Frêdûn, and the primaeval ox, 47, 31–3, 136; in the protection of Vîstâsp, 47, 43; cures the bull of Parshad-gau, 47, 57 sq.; opposed by Kîgs and Karaps, 47, 63–6, 145–51; left to starve in prison, 47, 65 sq., 65 n., 75; the coming of Z., 47, 121; utters the Ahunavair immediately after his birth, 47, 142, 142 n.; why the new-born Z. laughs, 47, 142 sq.; opposed by the Karaps and Aûsikhshes, 47, 143 sq.; descended from Râgh, 47, 147; accused of folly, taken to the Karaps to be cured, 47, 148 sq.; made himself into a bridge for seven women and old people to pass over a stream, 47, 151 sq.; his desire for a good wife, 47, 153 sq.; has a vision of all mankind led by Mêdyômâh following him, 47, 154 sq.

(*c*) Z. AND THE AVESTA, Z. AND HIS RELIGION.

Λόγια τοῦ Ζωροάστρου, 4, xv;

brought the Nasks to King Vîstâsp, 4, xxxvii; the founder of Zoroastrianism, 4, lxiii, 21 n.; produced confidence in the progress of religion, 5, 64; sent to take away the defilement of water, 5, 84; the bringer of the good religion, 5, 141 sq.; has not provided about everything whatsoever, 5, 326 sq.; the upholder and reminder of Mazda-worship, 18, 14, 14 n.; 47, 3, 3 n.; commanded the wearing of the sacred thread-girdle, 18, 128, 130; revelation of Z., 18, 341; quoted, 18, 349, 349 n.; admonishes mankind to practise next-of-kin marriage, 18, 410, 412 sq.; Avesta of Z., 18, 447; his authorship questioned, 31, 21, 21 n.; is he the author of the Gâthas? 31, 107, 167–9, 187 sq.; promises not to leave the faithful, 31, 132, 140; Vîstâspa refers to Z. as a propagator of Ahura's religion, 31, 169 sq., 173, 173 n.; an exhortation by Z. to follow his faith, 31, 229 sq.; the remedies of Z. and Zarathustrôtema, 31, 347; directed how the Avesta should be said, 31, 353; questions as to the sacrifice addressed to Z., 31, 369 sq.; material chieftainships through Z., 37, 167; a supplicant for the immortal progress of the soul, 37, 275; advice to Z., as to religion, 37, 281 sq.; wealth to be kept in control of Z., 37, 342; through discrimination as to duty one is similar to Z., 37, 363; *men and women are taught as being given in discipleship to Z. by him who keeps his own males and females in the control of Z.*, 37, 368; the words of Z. are the best prayers, 37, 397; a reformer, not a founder of a new religion, 47, xxvi.

(*d*) Z. IN HIS RELATION TO GODS (ARCHANGELS) AND FIENDS (DAÊVAS).

Z. receives the revelation from Ahura-Mazda, 5, lxx–lxxii, 2, 11, 22, &c., 208, 212, 240 n.; 23, 24, 24 n.; 24, 40, 170; 37, 181, 230 sq., 442; Mithra and Z., 4, 258; Aûharmazd gives Z. a prophecy about the future of the Iranian nation and religion, 5, 1 sq.; receives omniscience from Aûharmazd, 5, 1 sq., 192, 196 sq.; 18, 92, 92 n.; asks Aûharmazd for immortality, and has a vision of a tree which is symbolical of periods in the history of Iran, 5, 1 sq., 192–201; his Fravashi exhibited to Gôsûrvan by Aûharmazd, 5, 21, 21 n.; conversations between Aûharmazd and Z., 5, 121, 192–235, 310, 314, 348, 352, 372–9, 382, 386; 18, 21, 26, 44, 289, 293, 307, 328, 381, 415–17, 419–23, 431–53, 455; 24, 4, 4 n., 261, 288, 322, 329, 331, 343, 345, 349, 360; 31, 249, 260 sq., 374 sq., 390; 37, 31, 164, 193 sq., 206, 210 sq., 210 n., 233–6, 246 sq., 260, 267–72, 367, 375 sq., 379, 384–90, 453–64, 469, 474 sq.; 47, x sq., xv, 14–16, 35, 46–50, 47 n., 54, 56, 60–2, 64, 86–93, 99–105, 123, 135, 138, 157–60, 163; Aûharmazd exhibits to Z. the punishments of hell, 5, 350; heterodoxy, contest with Aûharmazd and Z., 18, 330, 346; Aûharmazd shows him the state of the soul of Keresâsp, 18, 371–82; Anâhita grants to Ahura-Mazda the boon, that Z. should teach his religion, 23, 58; established above men by Ahura-Mazda, 23, 105; the first and best follower of Ahura, 23, 228; first worshipper of Ahura-Mazda and the Amesha-Spentas, 23, 274; waters and plants rejoiced in Z.'s birth, 23, 274; loved and praised by Ashi Vanguhi, 23, 275; sacrifices to Ashi Vanguhi, 23, 279; archangels came meeting Z., 24, 270; appointed by Ahura-Mazda to proclaim his religion, 31, 4 sq., 8–11, 40 sq.; prays to Ahura for the people, 31, 5, 12 sq.; asks Ahura-Mazda for knowledge of what may be and what may not be, 31, 37, 42 sq.; offers obedience to God, 31, 79; questioned by Sraosha, replies, 31, 95 sq., 101 sq.; Ahura-Mazda will give spiritual life to him who propitiates Z., 31, 133, 141; dialogue between Z. and Haoma, 31, 231–5; Ahura-Mazda taught Z. the rules of sacrifice, 31, 318 sq.; *these are the best of words, those which Ahura-Mazda spoke to Z.*, 31, 330; the chieftains of the ritual mentioned to Z. by

Ahura-Mazda, 31, 338 sq.; chants taught by Aûharmazd to Z., 37, 23; coming of Z., and conference with Aûharmazd, 37, 29, 31; all prosperity given to Z. and his disciples by Aûharmazd, 37, 68; his profession of the religion, and his accepting the advice of Aûharmazd, 37, 228–30; teaching of the primitive faith to Z. by Aûharmazd, 37, 261; produced by Aûharmazd, 37, 264; Aûharmazd exhibits to Z. the future existence, 37, 267; praised and gratified by Aûharmazd, 37, 267–9; assisted by Aûharmazd, 37, 291; his conference with the sacred beings, 47, ix, xxvii, xxx; meets with Vohûmanô, 47, x; his conferences with the archangels, 47, xv, xxi, xxiv, 159–62; his spiritual body with the archangels, 47, xxviii sq.; his connexion with Aûharmazd through Yim and Nêryôsang, 47, 139; appointed priest by Aûharmazd, 47, 142 sq.; conducted by Vohûmanô to a conference with Aûharmazd and the archangels, 47, 155–9; subjected to ordeals by the archangels, 47, 158 sq.; *see also* Ahura-Mazda (*c*), *and* Aûharmazd (*c*);—repels the attacks and rejects the temptations of Angra-Mainyu and his demons, 4, 208–12; 23, 274 sq.; 24, 103 sq.; 31, 235; 37, 164; 47, 33, 123 sq.; the Daêvas dismayed by the birth of Z., 4, 209, 224 sq.; 37, 165; demons eager to destroy Z. in the womb of his mother, and at his birth, 5, 317, 343; 37, 469; 47, 140 sq.; sees the archangels opposed by the archfiends, 18, 319; at his sight the fiends drew back, 23, 305; as an infant, attacked by demons, 24, 277; his first three utterances that routed the demons, 37, 227 sq.; colloquy of the demon Aresh and Z., 37, 246 sq.; confounds the demons with the Ahunavair, 47, 58–60, 62 sq.; tempted by a female fiend in the guise of Spendarmad, 47, 62 sq.

(*e*) PRAISE AND WORSHIP OF Z.

Praised in a benediction, 18, 276, 357 sq., 366; the Fravashi of Z. worshipped, 5, 337; 23, 93, 201 sq., 351; 31, 208, 212, 218, 222 sq., 227, 244, 252 sq., 255, 273, 275, 278, 324, 351, 358, 380; 37, xxxi, 9; 47, 4 sq., 16, 73; the Glory of Z. invoked, 23, 11, 19; worshipped, 23, 229, 271; 31, 255, 325, 327, 339, 355, 362, 380, 385; 47, 16; a blessing is the thought, word, and deed of the righteous Z., 31, 17; sacrifice (Haomas) offered to Z., 31, 291, 353; the words of Z. worshipped, 31, 298, 381; invoked, 31, 313; material existence, guardian spirit, and soul of Z., 37, 31; what is given to a disciple of Z. is as if it had been given to Z., 37, 196, 196 n.; glorification of Z., 37, 275 sq., 290, 294, 298, 311; whose thoughts are for Z., 37, 370; wisdom of Z., benefiters of Z., 37, 377; faith in the mission of Z., 37, 435; blessedness of Z., 37, 439.

Zoroastrianism.

(*a*) Profession and teaching of Z.
(*b*) History of Z.

(*a*) PROFESSION AND TEACHING OF Z.

Z. called Dualism, Mazdeism, Magism, or Fire-worship, 4, xiii; profession of faith of Z. (Fravarânê), 4, xlvii n., 210, 246, 249; 18, 387; 23, 22, 35, 41, 48, 53, 85, 88, 92, 119, 159, 168, 180, 231, 249, 264, 283, 286, 310, 352, 354, 358; 31, 202, 212, 247–50, 254, 344 sq., 367, 372 sq., 379, 381, 383 sq., 387, 389; 37, 229; 47, 58; a moral religion, 4, liii; summary of old Z., 4, lxii; sins (even of one who is not a Zoroastrian) atoned for by a confession of Z., 4, 33 sq., 103 sq.; the fiend-destroying Law of Zarathustra, 4, 56–8, 210, 213 sq.; 18, 107–9, 109 n., 126; 37, 410; has an atonement for every crime, 4, 266; *in every religion there are righteous men*, 4, 266; *there is only one way of Righteousness; . . . it is Religion, that destroyer of Angra-Mainyu, which tears to pieces the Daêva-worshippers, the men who live in sin*, 4, 370, 370 n.; ethics of Z., 4, 375 sq.; 24, 113, 113 n.; 37, 11; 47, 154; the true meaning of its dualism, 5, lxviii–lxx; 18, xxiv; technical terms of Z., 5, lxxii–lxxiv; the glory of the religion of the

Mazdayasnians, deified, 5, 228; its superiority to other religions, 5, 296 sq. and n.; 24, 5–7, 40 sq.; the true religion, the best of knowledge, 18, 88; 37, 412, 417; infidels, foreigners, and demon worshippers unfit to be adopted, 18, 191; rights of foreigners and infidels, 18, 196 sq.; Mazda-worship is the true faith, 18, 386; Sraosha, the incarnate Holy Word, 23, 160–7; the Holy Word is true and happy and powerful, 23, 169; its doctrine of good and evil not proceeding from the same source, 24, xxv; the unquestionable and well-betokened good religion, 24, 4; a true man is he who believes in the dogmas of Z., 24, 82 sq.; unwavering faith in Z., the first good work, 24, 257 sq.; the good religion the word of God, 24, 270; steadfastness in the religion leads to heaven, helping others to be steadfast is the best good work, 24, 321 sq.; sin of intercourse with women of a different religion, 24, 325; four principles of Z., 24, 329 sq.; to be defended by the sword, 31, 39, 50; the 'primaeval law' followed by Zoroaster, 31, 68, 72; the thrift-law, 31, 71, 78; the pantheon of Z., 31, 195–203; the Zoroastrian law, with its long descent, worshipped, 31, 199 sq., 206, 211, 217, 221, 225, 259, 272, 277, 328, 349; the religion of Zarathustra and former religions devoted to Asha and Ahura-Mazda, worshipped, 31, 255 sq.; 37, 3; the doctrines of Z. delivered by Ahura-Mazda and nourished by Vohu Manah, 31, 354; conversion to Z., 37, 114; benefits of the good religion, 37, 264; seven perfections of the religion, 37, 273–5; advancement of the religion by good works, 37, 323 sq.; a good thinker about the religion of righteousness, 37, 344; principal doctrines of Z., 47, 51, 69; the triumph of Aûharmazd, 47, 119; coming of the religion compared to the birth of a child, 47, 133 sq.; ten admonitions as to the religion, 47, 167, 167 n., 169 sq. *See also* Daêna, *and* Morality (*c*).

(*b*) History of Z.

History of Z., 4, xiii–xvi, lxiv–lxix; as known in the first centuries A.D., 4, xiv sq.; Thomas Hyde on Z., 4, xvi, xvi n.; the state religion during the Sassanian period, 4, xxxiii, xxxviii sq., xli; religious persecution, 4, xxxviii, xlvi n., xlvii; Brâhmanical, Buddhist, and Greek elements in Z., 4, li–lvii, lxv sq., lxviii sq.; Jewish elements in Z., 4, lvii–lx, lxviii sq.; Chaldaean influences on Z., 4, lix sq., lxiv; Achaemenian and earlier elements in Z., 4, lx–lxiv; Media, its centre, 4, lxii sq., lxvi sq.; Aryan elements in Z., 4, lxiii sq.; Scythian origin of Z., 4, lxiv; Z. of the Avesta, and of the Pahlavi texts, 5, ix sq.; men of the 'primitive faith,' or Z. in all ages, before and after Zoroaster, 5, lx, 242–4, 244 sq. n.; 23, 180, 180 n., 228–30; 24, 87, 87 n.; Z. and Christianity, 5, lxix sq.; 18, xxiv; Avestic and Indo-Iranian myths, 5, lxxi sq.; the good religion of the Mazdayasnians produced by Vohûman, created in Khvanîras, 5, 9, 33; elements of Z. in Islâm, 6, lxviii sq.; struggling with Mohammedanism, 18, xxvi sq.; advancement of religion through Peshyôtanû and his companions, 18, 258; Semitic elements in Z., 23, 3; accepted by Vîstâsp, 24, 65; represented as an immense tree, 24, 118 sq.; how it was revealed and spread abroad, 24, 170–2; remarkable events in the history of Z., 24, 314 n.; as represented in the Gâthas, 31, xviii–xxii; where was its original home? 31, xxvii–xxxiii; religion of Darius Mazda-worship, but not Z., 31, xxx–xxxii; its influence on Gnosticism and Judaism, 31, xlvi; aggressive and missionary in its spirit, 31, 37, 41, 41 n.; opponents of Z., 31, 122 sq., 125; migration of Z., 31, 291 n.; Zoroaster accepts the religion from Aûharmazd, 37, 230 sq., 243; progress of the religion of Aûharmazd, 37, 245, 271 sq.; three codes of Z., 37, 407 sq.; Khûsrôî son of Kavâd on Avesta and Z., 37, 415–18; lamentation over the anarchy in

religion at the end of Zoroaster's millennium, 47, xii, 94–104; difference between the primaeval religion and Z., 47, xxv–xxvii, 12 sq. n.; preceded by demon-worship, 47, xxvi, 43 sq. and n.; chronology of Z., 47, xxvii–xlvii, 134 sq., 135 n., 138, 165; arrival of the religion in the seven regions, 47, 80; proceedings of the destroyers of Z. in Iran, 47, 90–3; four systems of belief at the end of a millennium, 47, 94 sq., 94 n. *See also* Parsis.

Zoroastrians, are not fire-worshippers, 1, xxii; assimilated by Islâm to 'the People of the Book,' 4, lxix; physicians shall practise on Daêva-worshippers, before practising on Z., 4, 85 sq.; business relations with non-Z., 18, 176 sq., 182 sq.; are not to drink from the same cup as those of a different religion, until it is purified, 24, 300, 300 n.; struggle between Z. and Daêva-worshippers, 31, xxi sq.

Zôrvân, 'boundless time,' produced by Aûha*r*ma*zd*, 5, lxx.

Zôti, *see* Priests (*d*, *e*).

Zrayah, n.p., 23, 213.

Zrayangh*au*, a high-priest, 47, 83 sq.

Zuhâib ibn Sinân er Rûmî, allowed to escape to Medînah, 6, 30, 30 n.

***Z*ui**, Minister of Works to Shun, 3, 43, 43 n.

ℨû Î prophesies the ruin of the dynasty of Yin, 3, 120 sq.

ℨû *K*î, censures Kâo ℨung, 3, 119.

ℨû-*k*iâ, a model king who ruled thirty-three years, 3, 23, 202, 204.

***Z*ung**, behaved rudely in mourning, 27, 177.

ℨun-*k*î, son of *Kh*ăn Kan-hsî, 27, 183 sq.

ℨun-lû, a primaeval sovereign, 39, 287.

***Z*û Pî**, sent to Confucius by Duke Âi, 28, 167.

Zû*s*ak, n.p., 5, 134; 47, 34, 140.

***Z*û-shâu**, attending spirit of Shâo Hâo, 27, 283, 283 n., 287, 291.

ℨû-yî, king of the Thang dynasty, 3, 103 sq., 104 n.; had Wû Hsien's son as minister, 3, 207.

ℨze-fan, had got the Tâo, 40, 283.

ℨze-fû Hui-po, assistant-commissioner with ℨze-shû *K*ing-shû, 27 187.

ℨze-fû Po-ʒze, on law of inheritance, 27, 120.

ℨze-han of Sung wailing at the death of a man-at-arms, 27, 197 sq.

ℨze-hsiâ, preface to the Shih ascribed to him, 3, 296; book ascribed to him, 27, 30; mourning for his son, 27, 135 sq.; asked Confucius about revenge for bloodshed, 27, 140; mourning for his parents, 27, 142; sent to *K*ing by Confucius, 27, 150; on mourning and funeral rites, 27, 151, 155 sq., 342; pays a visit of condolence, 27, 174; on music, 28, 116–21, 116 n.; conversation between Confucius and ℨ., 28, 278–83.

ℨze-hsien, sent as a messenger of condolence to *Kh*ung-*r*, 27, 166.

ℨze-hsü, met with a dreadful death, 39, 283, 283 n.; 40, 2 sq., 2 n., 174; had his eyes gouged out, 40, 180.

ℨze-hui or Yen Yüan, his character, 28, 303, 303 n.

ℨze-hwâ ℨze counsels the Marquis *K*âo-hsî of Han, 40, 152 sq.

ℨze-*k*ang, dying, 27, 132; mourning for him, 27, 140; as a mourner, 27, 142 sq.; ℨăng-ʒze in mourning for his mother, when ℨ. died, 27, 164; on mourning rites, 27, 175, 179; disciple of Confucius, 28, 270 sq., 276; ℨ. and Mân Kâu-teh converse together on right conduct, 40, 176–80.

ℨze-kâo, on mourning rites, 27, 153; (or Kâo *Kh*âi) made a man of *Kh*ăng mourn for his brother, 27, 200 sq., 201 n.; dressing of his corpse, 28, 142 sq., 143 n.; ℨ. and Duke Âi, 28, 169; duke of Sheh, entrusted by the king of *Kh*û with a difficult mission to *Kh*î, 39, 132, 210–14. *See also* *Kh*ăng-ʒze Kâo.

ℨze-*k*âu *K*ih-fû, refused the throne offered by Yâo, 40, 149, 149 n.

ℨze-*k*âu *K*ih-po, refused the throne offered by Shun, 40, 149.

ℨze-*kh*ân, to be regarded as a mother of the people, 28, 270 sq., 271 n.; minister of *K*ăng, studied with Shăn-thû *K*iâ under Po-hwăn Wû-zăn, 39, 226–8, 226 n.

Ȝze-*kh*î, Minister of War to King Yüeh, 40, 156.
Ȝze-*kh*î. *See* Nan-kwo Ȝ.
Ȝze-*kh*in *K*ang, a Tâoist, 39, 250, 250 n.
Ȝze-*kh*un, mourning for his mother, 27, 201.
Ȝze-kung, Confucius instructs him about the jade symbol, 27, 59; 28, 463 sq.; ordered by Confucius to act as presiding mourner, 27, 134; disciple of Confucius, 27, 136–8; 28, 270 sq.; 39, 251–3, 319; 40, 7, 160 sq., 193 sq.; on mourning rites, 27, 139; 28, 153; ordered by Confucius to bury his dog, 27, 196; Ȝ. and Ȝăng-ȝze paying a visit of condolence, 27, 197; questions Yî about music, 28, 129–31; conversation of Ȝ. and Confucius on sacrifices, 28, 167, 213; grieves at his not possessing the simplicity of the Tâoist sage, 39, 319–22; defeated by Lâo-ȝze, 39, 358–60; Ȝ. and Yüan Hsien, 40, 157 sq.; accompanies Confucius on his way to the robber *K*ih, 40, 167.
Ȝze-lâi, a Tâoist, 39, 247, 249; Ȝ. and Ȝze-lî, 40, 282.
Ȝze-lâo, and the Border-warden of *Kh*ang-wû, 40, 121 sq.
Ȝze-lî, a Tâoist, 39, 247; 40, 282.
Ȝze-liû, performing the mourning rites for his mother, 27, 145; her mode of mourning, 27, 200, 200 n.
Ȝze-lû, also called Yû, made into pickle, Confucius mourns for him, 27, 123 sq., 124 n., 139; rebuked by the Master, 27, 127; extravagant in mourning, 27, 131; on mourning rites, 27, 141, 182; Ȝ. and Yen Yüan, 27, 185; disciple of Confucius, 27, 191; 39, 386; 40, 44, 160 sq., 193, 200; steward to the House of *K*î, 27, 415, 415 n.; asks Confucius about fortitude, 28, 303, 303 n.; wished to slay the ruler of Wei, Confucius's teaching of Ȝ. came to nothing, 40, 172.
Ȝze-phû, called Mieh, 27, 153.
Ȝze-pien *Kh*ing-ȝze, Sun Hsiû complains to him, 40, 24.
Ȝze-sang and Ȝze-yü, 39, 257 sq.; exhibited the highest obliviousness, a True Man, 40, 283.
Ȝze-sang Hû, a Tâoist, 39, 250 sq., 250 n.; instructs Confucius on Tâoism, 40, 34–6, 289 sq.
Ȝze-shang, did not perform mourning rites for his divorced mother, 27, 122, 122 n.
Ȝze-shih, on the expense of mourning rites, 27, 145.
Ȝze-shû *K*ing-shû, sent on a mission of condolence for Duke *Kh*ăng, 27, 187.
Ȝze-sze, or Khung *K*î, author of the *K*ung Yung, 3, xx; 27, 43; the Hsiâo King ascribed to him, 3, 465 n.; author of 'the Doctrine of the Mean,' 16, 46; the book Tâ Hsio ascribed to him, 27, 53 sq.; father of Ȝze-shang, 27, 122; on mourning and funeral rites, 27, 124, 133, 173; wailing for his sister-in-law, 27, 133; mourning on the death of his mother, 27, 151 sq., 152 n., 194; a Tâoist, 39, 247.
Ȝze-yang, premier of *K*ăng, sends a gift of grain to Lieh-ȝze, 40, 154 sq.
Ȝze-yû, or Yen Yen, disciple of Confucius, 27, 18, 24, 364, 367, 326; the book Lî Yun ascribed to him, 27, 24; asked Confucius about inheritance, 27, 120; on funeral and mourning rites, 27, 141 sq., 144, 146, 151, 153 sq., 176–8, 326; 28, 155; at the mourning rites for Hui-ȝze, 27, 143; on a saying of Confucius, 27, 149 sq.; received Duke Tâo when he came to condole at the mourning rites for Yû Zo, 27, 165; pays a visit of condolence, 27, 174; as an authority on ancestor worship, 27, 337, 337 n.; quoted, 28, 16. *See also* Yen *Kh*ăng Ȝ.
Ȝze-yü, a Tâoist, 39, 247; and his friend Ȝze-sang, 39, 257 sq.; the hunchback, 40, 282.

ADDENDA AND CORRIGENDA

Page 18, col. 1, l. 20, read '*see* (*i*)' for '*see* (i)'
" 32, " 2, l. 15 from below, read '*Âtar*' for '*Atar*'
" 121, " 1, l. 29 sq., read '*see* Holy persons. *See also* Castes' . . .
" 122, " 2, l. 5 from below, insert '26, 452, 452 n.;' before '44, 79' . . .
" 135, " 2, l. 11, after 'three)' insert 'Morality (*b*)'
" 138, " 1, l. 9, read '7, 135' for '17, 135'
" 170, " 2, l. 27, read 'befools' for 'be fools'
" 202, " 1, l. 10, read '(*n*)' for '(*n.*)'
" 202, " 1, l. 11, read '(*n*)' for '(*n.*)'
" 216, " 2, l. 23 from below, read '**Frê*d*ûn**' for '**Frêdûn**'
" 233, " 1, l. 9, read '**S̱âkhâ**' for '**Sâkha**'
" 249, " 2, l. 25, read 'Âtman' for 'Atman'
" 258, " 2, l. 16, read 'Sacrifices (*i*)' for 'Sacrifices (*k*)'
" 262, " 1, l. 7, read '**Hâliṅgava**' for '**Hâlingava**'
" 268, " 1, l. 16 from below, put *comma* instead of *semicolon* after 319 sq.
" 283, " 2, after l. 22 insert '**Hui ot Liang**, King, contemporary of *K*wang-ʒze, 40, 321'
" 285, " 2, l. 5 from below, read '**Î**' for '**I**'
" 297, " 2, l. 22, read '**Ingratitude**, penance for, 7, 177; those who have' . . .
" 305, " 1, l. 9, read 'Vî*s*tâspa' for 'Vi*s*tâspa'
" 318, " 2, l. 5 from below, add '*See* ʒze-kâo'
" 342, " 1, l. 14, read '**Lî-*kh*û**' for '**Lî*kh*û**'
" 383, " 1, l. 19 from below, after '*See also*' insert 'Bhikkhus (*b*), *G*aina monks, *G*aina religion, *G*ainas, *and*'
" 392, " 1, l. 29, add '*See also* Nô*d*ar'
" 399, " 2, l. 13, read '*see* Bhikkhus (*c*)' for '*see* Sa*m*gha'
" 400, " 1, l. 20, add '*See also* Naotara, Vî*s*tâspa, *and* Vistauru'
" 408, " 2, l. 5, read '**Pa*n*itabhûmi**' for '**Pañitabhûmi**'
" 413, " 1, l. 23 from below, read '36, 52 sq.' for '36, 52 sq.'
" 442, " 1, l. 2 from below, read '172–4, 482 sq.' for '172–4; 482 sq.'
" 515, " 1, l. 8, read 'inner' for 'sinner'
" 536, " 2, l. 9, read 'Vasatîvarî' for 'Vasativarî'
" 600, " 1, l. 19, read '**Uspãsnu**' for '**Uspâsnu**'
" 634, " 1, l. 31, after 'Abstinence' insert 'Ascetics, Brahma*k*ârin,' and after 'Fasting' insert '*G*aina monks, *G*ainas, Hair, Hermits'

The references to Volumes 2, 4, 10 are to the editions of 1897, 1895, and 1881: other editions of these volumes differ in pagination and to some extent in contents.

If the Index is used with Volume 2, edition 1879, in introduction after p. xiv deduct from one to five pages, and in text deduct after page 99 from one to three pages; if with Volume 10, edition 1898, *add* in part I in introduction eight pages, and in text after page 48 one page; in part II after page 35 *deduct* one page to eleven pages, increasing the allowance gradually through the part.